The International Legal Order: Current Needs and Possible Responses

The International Legal Order: Current Needs and Possible Responses

Essays in Honour of Djamchid Momtaz

Edited by

James Crawford
Abdul G. Koroma
Said Mahmoudi
Alain Pellet

BRILL
NIJHOFF

LEIDEN | BOSTON

Library of Congress Cataloging-in-Publication Data

Names: Mumtāz, Jamshīd, honouree. | Crawford, James, 1948– editor.
Title: The international legal order : current needs and possible responses :
   essays in honour of Djamchid Momtaz / Edited by James Crawford, Abdul G. Koroma, Said Mahmoudi,
   Alain Pellet.
Description: Leiden : Brill Nijhoff, 2017. | Includes bibliographical
   references and index.
Identifiers: LCCN 2017007114 (print) | LCCN 2017008644 (ebook) | ISBN
   9789004314368 (hardback : alk. paper) | ISBN 9789004314375 (E-book)
Subjects: LCSH: International law.
Classification: LCC KZ3410 .I59 2017 (print) | LCC KZ3410 (ebook) | DDC
   341—dc23
LC record available at https://lccn.loc.gov/2017007114

Typeface for the Latin, Greek, and Cyrillic scripts: "Brill". See and download: brill.com/brill-typeface.

ISBN 978-90-04-31436-8 (hardback)
ISBN 978-90-04-31437-5 (e-book)

Copyright 2017 by Koninklijke Brill NV, Leiden, The Netherlands.
Koninklijke Brill NV incorporates the imprints Brill, Brill Hes & De Graaf, Brill Nijhoff, Brill Rodopi
and Hotei Publishing.
All rights reserved. No part of this publication may be reproduced, translated, stored in a retrieval system,
or transmitted in any form or by any means, electronic, mechanical, photocopying, recording or otherwise,
without prior written permission from the publisher.
Authorization to photocopy items for internal or personal use is granted by Koninklijke Brill NV provided
that the appropriate fees are paid directly to The Copyright Clearance Center, 222 Rosewood Drive,
Suite 910, Danvers, MA 01923, USA. Fees are subject to change.

This book is printed on acid-free paper and produced in a sustainable manner.

Contents

Preface XI
Foreword XIV
Publications of Djamchid Momtaz XVI
Abbreviations/Abréviations XXV
List of Contributors/Liste des auteurs XXXII

PART 1
General Issues

Brèves remarques sur la contribution de l'Académie de droit international de la Haye au développement du droit international 3
  Yves Daudet

Quelques remarques sur la place du droit au sein des organisations internationales 8
  Pierre Michel Eisemann

The Iran Nuclear Deal: Some International-Law Aspects 23
  Said Mahmoudi

Scientific Knowledge and the Progressive Development of International Law: With Reference to the ILC Topic on the Protection of the Atmosphere 41
  Shinya Murase

Rethinking Iran and International Law: The *Anglo-Iranian Oil Company Case* Revisited 53
  Sundhya Pahuja and Cait Storr

Statehood, Proto States and International Law: New Challenges, Looking at the Case of ISIS 75
  Anicée Van Engeland

PART 2
Dispute Settlement

La Cour internationale de Justice et le traitement du contentieux dans la durée : Le temps retrouvé   89
Mohamed Bennouna

The Place of the International Court in International Dispute Settlement   95
James Crawford

International Lawyers and the International Court of Justice: Between Cult and Contempt   117
Jean d'Aspremont

Le règlement des différends investisseur/État (RDIE) : brève revue de doctrine avant réforme   131
Marie-Françoise Labouz

Legal Decisions and Their Implementation in International Law   149
W. Michael Reisman and Mahnoush H. Arsanjani

Peremptory Norms and the Jurisdiction of the International Court of Justice   162
Jamal Seifi

Some Comments on the *Temple* (*Interpretation*) Judgment and the Impact of Possible Mistakes on the *Temple* Saga   174
Sienho Yee

PART 3
State Responsibility and State Immunity

Alleged Support of Terrorism as a Ground for Denying State Immunity   187
Mohsen Abdollahi

Types of Injury in Inter-States Claims: Direct Injury to the State   199
Hirad Abtahi

Réflexions sur l'immunité des États en matière civile   212
    Lucius Caflisch

Responsibility of States in Cases of Human-rights or Humanitarian-law Violations   230
    Alain Pellet

PART 4
Law of the Sea

Exporting Environmental Standards to Protect Underwater Cultural Heritage in the Area   255
    Mariano J. Aznar

Migration and the Law of the Sea: Solutions and Limitations of a Fragmentary Regime   274
    Ida Caracciolo

La dimension internationale de la compétence de l'Union européenne en matière de pêche   288
    Rafael Casado Raigón

Provisional Measures in Maritime Delimitation Cases   312
    Pierre-Emmanuel Dupont and Alexia Solomou

The Contribution of the States of Central America to the Evolution of the New Law of the Sea   334
    Víctor L. Gutiérrez Castillo

Does the Freedom of the Seas Still Exist?   346
    Gerhard Hafner

Les pays sans littoral et le droit de la mer   373
    Zalmaï Haquani

Considérations actuelles sur la méthode de délimitation maritime devant la Cour internationale de Justice. De charybde en scylla ?   383
    Maurice Kamto

Compulsory Jurisdiction under the Law of the Sea Convention: Its Achievements and Limits 421
Mariko Kawano

L'Algérie et la Méditerranée 440
Ahmed Mahiou

Judicial Application of Environmental Standards under the Law of the Sea Convention 452
Bernard H. Oxman

The Future of the High Seas Fisheries Legal and Institutional Framework 460
Jean-François Pulvenis de Séligny-Maurel

Sunken Warships and Cultural Heritage 476
Natalino Ronzitti

Users of the Law of the Sea: Some Recent Developments 487
Emmanuel Roucounas

The Relationship between Two Conventions Applicable to Underwater Cultural Heritage 504
Tullio Scovazzi

The Dispute Concerning the *Enrica Lexie* Incident and the Role of International Tribunals in Provisional Measure Proceedings Instituted Pursuant to the United Nations Convention on the Law of the Sea 519
Roberto Virzo

PART 5
Human Rights

La jurisprudence de la Cour Interaméricaine des Droits de l'Homme et le *jus cogens* (2013-fevrier 2016) 535
Ricardo Abello-Galvis

The Notion of Human Rights and the Issue of Cultural Relativism 544
Ove Bring

Droit a l'éducation et diversité : le droit à une éducation inclusive et
équitable de qualité   559
   Jorge Cardona

Immunités juridictionnelles des États étrangers et droit de l'homme : quel
équilibre entre les valeurs fondamentales de l'ordre national et le droit
international coutumier ?   571
   Giuseppe Cataldi

Protecting Children in and at War: From Legally Protected Subjects to
'Others' in the Conflict   591
   Nasrin Mosaffa

A propos de quelques éclaircissements jurisprudentiels dans le ciel gris de
la lutte contre la torture   602
   Amir Hossein Ranjbarian

Les relations entre droits de l'homme et droit international humanitaire
dans la jurisprudence de la Cour européenne des droits de l'homme   614
   Linos-Alexandre Sicilianos

Brèves remarques sur la répression du génocide   625
   Joe Verhoeven

PART 6
International Humanitarian Law

Protection of the Environment in Relation to Armed Conflicts—
A Preliminary Comment on the Work of the International Law
Commission   641
   Michael Bothe

Regards sur le contenu des qualifications des principaux acteurs des
conflits armés   660
   Zakaria Daboné

Contemporary Challenges for International Humanitarian Law   677
   Knut Dörmann and Tilman Rodenhäuser

Le droit international humanitaire à l'épreuve des conflits
contemporains   700
  Yves Sandoz

L'espace humanitaire : un passage souhaitable de la pratique au
droit ?   719
  Sandra Szurek

L'évolution du droit international humanitaire au XXIème siècle :
une nécessité ?   732
  Paul Tavernier

PART 7
Use of Force

Le droit international au défi de « l'exceptionnalisme nucléaire »   751
  Abdelwahab Biad

Intervention by Invitation as a Tool of New Colonialism   766
  Farideh Shaygan

L'intervention par invitation d'un État tiers : le consentement au recours à
la force contre des combattants étrangers terroristes   783
  Yvenson St-Fleur

Preface

This volume is a tribute to the prominent Iranian scholar, Professor Djamchid Momtaz, in recognition of his outstanding achievements as an international lawyer. The essays it contains reflect his numerous contributions to international law discourse in general. They also focus on those areas that have been particularly addressed in his own studies, including international humanitarian law, the law of the sea, human rights, the use of force, and dispute settlement. The general theme of the book is the current needs of the international legal order. The majority of the contributions address these needs with a view of the future. The book is dedicated to him by his colleagues, friends and students on the occasion of his 75th birthday.

Djamchid Momtaz was born in 1942 in Izmir, Turkey, to a family of diplomats. His father and his grandfather served as Iran's ambassadors and consular agents to several countries including Russia, France, Turkey and Egypt. His grandfather was a member of the Iranian delegation to the Hague Conferences in 1899 and 1907. This influenced Djamchid Momtaz in later years to choose international law as his academic major and career.

After completing his high school education in France in 1961, he studied at the Faculty of Law and Economics of Paris, where he graduated in 1966 with a degree in public law. He then got a diploma at the Institut d'études politiques de Paris (Sciences Po) in 1968. In 1971, he received his PhD (Doctorat d'Etat) in public law from the University of Law, Economics and Social Sciences, Paris II. After some years of teaching at the University of Paris X (Nanterre), he joined the University of Tehran in 1974 where he was professor of international law until his retirement in 2010.

As a brilliant and highly appreciated teacher, Djamchid Momtaz has taught in many renowned universities around the world. He also gave a course in international humanitarian law applicable to non-international armed conflicts at the Hague Academy of International Law in 2000 and, more recently, masterfully taught the general course in public international law at the same Academy in 2014. This centred on the 'idea of ranking the international legal order'.

Exceeding a hundred in number, Momtaz's scholarly publications in French, English and Persian witness distinguished intellectual curiosity, a subtle mind and a sharp analytical ability. His broad and profound knowledge of the practice of international organizations and international courts, particularly that of the International Court of Justice, infuses his writings.

His burning interest in teaching international law and disseminating knowledge thereof has had an undeniable impact on the status of the subject in the law schools in Iran. His always positive and friendly attitude and his genuine belief in the significant role of international law in today's world have since the early 1970s created an unmistakable and unprecedented enthusiasm and popularity among generations of students. The result is the establishment in Iran of several associations and research centres specifically devoted to international law studies. A prime example is the Iranian Association for United Nations Studies—the largest NGO in the field. The Association was founded in 1999 with Momtaz as a main initiator: he was Chairman of its Board until 2013.

Djamchid Momtaz can be proud of training numerous excellent teachers of international law now working in this subject in many Iranian universities. In addition, some of his students, among them contributors to the present book, are practising in international organizations or in leading international law firms.

Over and above his academic successes, Djamchid Momtaz has through his membership of various international organs effectively contributed to the development of their work. Particular mention should be made of his work for the UN International Law Commission (ILC) between 2000 and 2006 (which he chaired with great distinction in 2005–2006), the Institut de droit international, the Group of International Advisers of the International Committee of the Red Cross (ICRC), the Curatorium of the Hague Academy of International Law, the Permanent Court of Arbitration, and the Commission for the Settlement of Disputes related to Confidentiality of the Organization for the Prohibition of Chemical Weapons (OPCW).

As a long-time advisor on international law matters to the Iranian Ministry for Foreign Affairs, Djamchid Momtaz has played an important and active role in assisting the Iranian Government to deal with many complicated legal matters. This has been an especially important and difficult task since Iran, both as a revolutionary State and a major actor in the Middle East region, has been involved in many international controversies and disputes in the past 38 years. Some examples are the *United States Diplomatic and Consular Staff in Tehran Case* (United States of America v Iran), the *Iran-Iraq War 1980–1988*, the *Aerial Incident Case* (Islamic Republic of Iran v United States of America), the *Oil Platforms Case* (Islamic Republic of Iran v United States of America), the legal regime of the Caspian Sea after the collapse of the Soviet Union, and perhaps most importantly the Iranian nuclear programme file both before the Board of Governors of the International Atomic Energy Agency and before the Security Council (2003–2015). In most of these international law issues, the wisdom, experience and knowledge of Djamchid Momtaz were of great help to the Iranian

Foreign Ministry, which had to tackle the problems professionally, sometimes under the chaotic conditions that so often characterize a post-revolutionary era.

In addition to regular provision of legal opinions and consultations to the Iranian Ministry for Foreign Affairs, Djamchid Momtaz has acted as legal counsel for Iran in the *Oil Platforms Case* (Islamic Republic of Iran v United States of America). He has also been a member of Iranian delegations to diplomatic conferences for the adoption of many international agreements such as the 1982 Law of the Sea Convention and the Rome Statute of the International Criminal Court.

This brief account shows only a part of what Momtaz has achieved during a long and successful career as an international lawyer. Let it, however, suffice to demonstrate why he is such an exceptional scholar and admirable person. It is our hope that international lawyers will continue to benefit from his excellent contributions for many more years.

The editors wish to thank Tim Crosfield, Sarah Deveau, Ylva Nohre and Vera Yllner for their invaluable editorial assistance. We are also grateful to the *Stockholm Law Faculty Trust Fund for Publications* (Stiftelsen Juridisk Fakultetslitteratur) for the financial support that has made this book possible.

James Crawford
Abdul G. Koroma
Said Mahmoudi
Alain Pellet

Foreword

Today, there seems to be worldwide acknowledgement that the international legal order is a system under stress. Breaking news and headlines remind us every day that—in this transitional era—we are not yet equipped to tackle global issues efficiently and meaningfully.

Enchained by old paradigms, structural shortcomings, political considerations and meager means, international organizations have not yet learned to address already-protracted global dilemmas. In fact, especially in security matters, they sometimes seem inclined to stifle reasonable diplomacy, or even to help manufacture crises that will further destabilize international peace and security. The lack of agreement on structural reform, which sometimes encourages informal sectoral cooperation, still impedes our ability to find and devise more inclusive, concerted and sustainable solutions.

Our outdated outlook on enforcement mechanisms is also *itself* a source of escalation and aggravation of conflicts. Reductive and zero-sum approaches still dominate the dynamics and lead major powers to pursue their political objectives through unproductive economic sanctions and the use of force, to which they tend to resort much more readily thanks to self-serving expansive legal doctrines. In fact, in recent years the stability and inviolability of our international borders has been challenged by 'lawful' states and lawless non-state actors alike.

The emergence of sophisticated and consequential new actors who do not consider themselves bound by international rules and the laws of war is also another source of concern. All the more so, as states have hitherto been unable even to reach consensus on a legal characterization of these new players. In consequence, as we sadly see in our region, these new actors are grabbing land by force, setting up capitals and proclaiming statehood in broad daylight, just as they desensitize public opinion concerning grave IHL violations, and banalize their war crimes by filming, documenting and proudly reporting heinous acts on social media as a recruitment device.

Today, seemingly extinguished calamities—such as the slave trade or public auctions of innocent women—have resurfaced from the darkest corners of history only to highlight the international community's inefficiency and helplessness in the 21st century.

Likewise, in the past few years we have witnessed that the principle of state immunity—a longstanding cornerstone of the international system—has also been unilaterally waived by powerful states through national legislation, further undermining the integrity of international public order and setting the stage for more instability in inter-state relations.

Add to the above our challenge to deal effectively with cyberwarfare, computer viruses capable of impacting physical structures, undetectable hackers capable of disrupting or disabling essential services or stealing classified data, and we realize how much work there is to be done to preserve our future generations from chaos, lawlessness, insecurity and general mayhem.

These negative developments are all at odds with the goals and ideals that we had set for ourselves as the post-WWII 'global community'. A quick look at the United Nations' founding documents, or even a glimpse at the U.N. headquarters art collection, show how far we have strayed—albeit not always intentionally—from our original dream.

Finding solutions to these increasing and seemingly uncontainable problems is not easy. But I know from experience that any solution we think of must be all-inclusive, firmly grounded in the new reality and based on the premise that in today's world, it is simply impossible to achieve any sustainable or meaningful order at the expense, and certainly with the exclusion, of others.

The good news is that throughout history, brilliant minds have sought such solutions, have had them applied, revised them when necessary, adapted them, and taught them to future generations. Professor Djamchid Momtaz, with his lifetime work on issues of global significance, is one of those brilliant minds. Indeed, Dr. Momtaz's contributions and record, whether in his advisory capacity at Iran's Foreign Ministry, as an academic, a practitioner, or as a member of the International Law Commission, are a clear example not only of how good ideas can lead younger generations to construct and lay theoretical grounds for action, but of how they can help diplomats and visionary politicians forge better policies, negotiate more sustainable accords, bridge more gaps, and reach more win-win settlements.

May this brilliant mind help us overcome our challenges for many more years to come.

Mohammad Javad Zarif
Foreign Minister of the Islamic Republic of Iran

Publications of Djamchid Momtaz

1   Books / Monoghaphs

- *Le régime juridique des fonds marins et des océans au-delà des limites de la juridiction nationale : inventaire et solutions possibles*, Thèse pour le doctorat d'Etat en droit, Université de droit, d'économie et de science sociales de Paris (Paris II), 1971.
- *Le droit international humanitaire applicable aux conflits armés non internationaux*, Receuil des cours de l'Académie de droit international, Tome 292, 2001, Martinus Nijhoff Publishers, The Hague / Boston / London, 2002.
- *Rules and Institutions of International Humanitarian Law Put to the Test of Recent Armed Conflicts*, with M.J. Matheson, Hague Academy of International Law, Martinus Nijhoff Publishers Leiden, Boston, 2010.
- *Proclamation of Tehran*, 1968, United Nations Audio-Visual Library of International Law.

2   Books Chapters

- *Les problèmes de la délimitation du plateau continental du Golfe Persique*, in Essays on International Law, 20th Anniversary, Commemorative Volume published by the Secretariat of Asian-African Legal Consultative Committee, New Delhi, 1976.
- *L'Iran et le droit international*, in Aspects de la politique étrangère de l'Iran et de la France, Université de Téhéran, Centre des hautes études internationales, Téhéran, 1976.
- *Les détroits de l'Océan Indien et les grandes puissances*, in Golfe Persique et Océan Indien; bilan et perspectives, Université de Téhéran, Centre des hautes études internationales, Téhéran, 1977.
- *L'évolution du droit de la mer de la Conférence de Genève de 1958 à celle de 1975*, in Droit de la mer, Institut des Hautes Etudes Internationales de Paris, A. Pedone, Paris, 1977.
- *The high Seas*, in Handbook on the New Law of the Sea, René-Jean Dupuy and Daniel Vignes (eds), Hague Academy of International Law, Nijhoff, 1991.
- *Les forces navales et l'impératif de sécurité dans la Convention des Nations Unies sur le droit de la mer*, in Essays on the Law of the Sea, Budislav Vukas (ed), Zagreb, 1985.

- *Le statut juridique du Golfe Persique* in Legal Regime of Enclosed and Semi-Enclosed Seas : the Particular Case of the Mediterranean, Budislav Vukas (ed), Zagreb, 1988.
- *Le statut juridique du Chatt-el-Arab*, in Actualités juridiques et politiques en Asie, Etudes à la mémoire de Tran Van Minh, Institut des Hautes Etudes Internationales de Paris, A. Pedone, Paris, 1988.
- *La Commission préparatoire de l'Autorité internationale des fonds marins et du Tribunal du droit de la mer*, in Droit de la mer 2, Institut des Hautes Etudes Internationales de Paris, A. Pedone, Paris, 1990.
- *Les obligations des investisseurs pionniers enregistrés par la Commission préparatoire, de l'Autorité internationale des fonds marins et du Tribunal international du droit de la mer*, in Essays on the New Law of the Sea, n° 2, Budislav Vukas (ed), Zagreb, 1990.
- *The inherent Right of Individual Self-Defence in The Iran-Iraq War; The Politics of Aggression*, Farhang Rajaee (Ed), University Press of Florida, 1993.
- *A Commentary on Iranian Practice in The Iran-Iraq War (1980–1988) and the Law of Naval Warfare*, Andrea de Guttry and Natalino Ronzitti (eds), Cambridge, Grotius Publications Ltd, 1993.
- *La juridiction larvée des Etats côtiers sur les stocks de poissons chevauchants et grands migrateurs situés au-delà de leurs zones économiques*, in International Legal Issues Arising under the United Nations Decade of International Law, Dr Najeeb Al Nauimi and Richard Messe (eds), Martinus Nijhoff Publishers, 1995.
- *Le régime de transfert des substances chimiques dans la Convention sur l'interdiction des armes chimiques*, in The Convention on the Prohibition and Elimination of Chemical Weapons: a Breakthrough in Multilateral Disarmament, Hague Academy of International Law, Daniel Bardonnet (ed), Martinus Nijhoff Publishers, 1995.
- *Les Nations Unies et les Commissions d'établissement des faits*, in International Law as a Language for International Relations, Proceedings of the United Nations Congress on Public International Law, New-York 13–17 March 1995, Kluwer International Law, 1996.
- *The Implementation of Security Council Resolution 598*, in Iranian Perspectives on the Iran-Iraq War, Farhang Rajaee (ed), University Press of Florida, 1997.
- *Nuclear Weapon-Free Zones in Africa and Asia*, in Essays on International Law, fortieth Anniversary, Commemorative Volume, prepared by the Secretariat of the Asian-African Legal Consultative Committee, New-Delhi, 1997.
- *The United Nations and the Protection of the Environment*, in the United Nations at Work, Martin Ira Glassner (ed), Praeger, 1998.

- *Intervention des Etats-Unis dans les affaires iraniennes et la requête de l'Iran devant le Tribunal des différends irano-américains*, in Sanctions unilatérales, mondialisation du commerce et ordre juridique international, à propos des lois Helms-Burton et d'Amato Kennedy, Habib Ghérari et Sandra Szureck (sous la direction de), CEDIN Paris X Nanterre, Cahiers internationaux, Montchrestien, 1998.
- *Le droit international des armes de destruction massive*, in International Law at the Turn of the Century: Thesaurus Acroasium, vol. XXVII, Sakkoulas Publications, Thessaloniki, 1998.
- *Les conventions "mort-nées"* in Making Better International Law. The International Law Commission at 50. Proceedings of the United Nations Colloquium on Progressive Development and Codification of International Law, United Nations, 1998.
- *Le recours à l'arme nucléaire et la protection de l'environnement : l'apport de la Cour internationale de Justice*, in International Law, the International Court of Justice and Nuclear Weapons, Laurence Boisson de Chazournes and Philippe Sands (eds), Cambridge University Press, 1999.
- *A Study of Multilateralism in Iran: The United Nations and Iran-Iraq Conflict*, in Multilateralism in Multinational Perspective. Viewpoints from different Languages and Literatures, James P. Sewell (ed), United Nations University Press, 2000.
- *La piraterie en haute mer*, in Droit international pénal, Hervé Ascensio, Emmanuel Decaux et Alain Pellet (Sous la direction de) Cedin, Paris X Nanterre, A. Pedone, Paris 1ère édition 2000, 2ème édition 2012.
- *Les infractions liées aux activités maritimes,* in Droit international pénal- Hervé Ascensio, Emmanuel Decaux et Alain Pellet, Cedin, Paris X Nanterre, A. Pedone, Paris 1ère édition 2000, 2ème édition, 2012.
- *La compatibilité des sanctions du Conseil de Sécurité avec le droit international humanitaire*, in United Nations Sanctions and International Law, Vera Gowlland (ed) Kluwer Law International, The Hague / London / Boston, 2001.
- *La libre navigation à l'épreuve des conflits armés*, in La mer et son droit, Mélanges offerts à Laurent Lucchini et Jean-Pierre Quéneudec, A. Pedone, Paris, 2003.
- *Les actions de secours au cours d'un conflit armé*, in Studi di Diritto Internazionale in Onore di Gaetano Arangio Ruiz, Editoriale Scientifica, Napoli, 2004.
- *Article 36 de la Charte des Nations Unies*, in La Charte des Nations Unies, Commentaire article par article, Jean-Pierre Cot, Alain Pellet, Mathias Forteau (Sous la direction de), 3ème édition, Economica, Paris, 2005.

- *Le régime de passage dans le détroit d'Hormuz* in Europe and the Sea, Fisheries, Navigation and Marine Environment, Rafael Casado Raigon (ed), Bruylant, Brussels, 2005.
- *Sécurité collective et droit d'ingérence humanitaire* in Les métamorphoses de la sécurité collective: droit, pratique et enjeux stratégiques, A. Pedone, Paris, 2005.
- *Conflit armé non international: Interaction des différents régimes juridiques*, in International Humanitarian Law and other Legal Regimes: Interplay in Situations of Violence, Guido Ravasi, Gian Luca Beruto (eds), Edizione Nagard, Milano, 2005.
- *The ICRC Study on Customary International Law an Assessment*, in Custom as a Source of International Law, Larry Maybee, Bennarji Chakka (eds), ICRC New-Delhi, Asian African Legal Consultative Organization, 2006.
- *Le droit international et la répression des crimes internationaux*, Bancaja Euromediterranean Courses of International Law, Vol. X, 2006.
- *De l'incompatibilité des amnisties inconditionnelles avec le droit international*, in Promoting Justice, Human Rights and Conflict Resolution Through International Law, Liber Amicorum, Lucius Caflisch, Martinus Nijhoff Publishers, 2007.
- *La Convention sur la protection du patrimoine culturel subaquatique*, in Law of the Sea, Environment Law and Settlement of Disputes, Liber Amicorum Judge Thomas A. Mensah, Martinus Nijhoff Publishers, 2007.
- *Non-Proliferation of Chemical Weapons through Export Control OPCW*, Academic Forum, Ralf Trapp (ed), Netherlands Institute of International Relations Clingendael and TNO Netherlands Organization for Applied Scientific Research, 2007.
- *Intervention d'humanité et responsabilité de protéger* in Quel droit international pour le XXIème siècle ? Actes du Colloque international (Neuchatel, 6–7 May 2006), Yves Sandoz (ed.) Bruylant Bruxelles, 2007.
- *La participation directe des personnes civiles aux hostilités* in Paix en liberté, Festschrift für Michael Bothe. Nomos-Dike Baden-Baden (Germany), 2008.
- *Le pavillon en temps de crise. Le pavillon dans l'engrenage de la lutte contre la prolifération des armes de destruction massive* Le pavillon Colloque international, Institut océanographique de Paris (2–3 March 2007), A. Pedone, Paris, 2008.
- *De la nécessité de préciser la nature et le contour de certaines règles relatives à la protection des personnes civiles contre les dangers résultant d'opérations militaires* in Studi in Onore di Umberto Leanza, Editoriale Scientifica, Napoli, 2008.

- *L'adaptation du droit humanitaire à l'épreuve des opérations militaires motivées par la responsabilité de protéger*, in La responsabilité de protéger, Colloque de Nanterre (7–9 June 2007), Société française pour le droit international, A. Pedone, Paris, 2008.
- *L'exercice de la compétence de la Cour pénale internationale à l'égard des crimes commis au Darfour* in Essays in Honour of Professor Kalliopi K. Koufa, Martinus Nijhoff Publishers, 2009.
- *La lutte contre la criminalité en mer*, in L'évolution et l'état actuel du droit international de la mer, Mélanges de droit de la mer offerts à Daniel Vignes, Bruylant, Bruxelles, 2009.
- *Attribution of Conduct to the State: State Organs and Entities Empowered to Exercise Elements of Governmental Authority in the Law of International Responsibility*, James Crawford, Alain Pellet and Simon Olleson (eds) Oxford University Press, 2010.
- *La protection de la population civile au cours des conflits armés*, in International Challenges to peace and Security in the New Millenium, Thesaurus Acroasium, Vol. XXXIII, Sakkoulas Publications, Thessaloniki, 2010.
- *Le programme nucléaire de l'Iran et le régime de non-prolifération nucléaire*, in Looking to the Future. Essays on International Law in Honor of W. Michael Reisman, Mahnoush H. Arsanjani, Jacob Katz Cogan, Robert D. Sloane, Siegfried Wiessner (eds), Martinus Nijhoff Publishers, 2011.
- *The Interaction between International Humanitarian Law and Human Rights Law and the Contribution of the I.C.J.* (in cooperation with Amin Ghanbari Amirhandeh) in The I.C.J. and the Evolution of International Law. The Enduring Impact of the Corfu Channel Case Karine Bannelier et al. (eds) Routledge, 2012.
- *Créer une zone exempte d'armes nucléaires au Moyen-Orient: une mission impossible?* in The 90th Birthday of Boutros Boutros-Ghali. Tribute of the Curatorium to its President, A Publication of The Hague Academy of International Law, Martinus Nijhoff Publishers, Leiden, Boston, 2012.
- *L'encadrement de la sécession en droit international*, in l'homme dans la société internationale, Mélanges en hommage au Professeur Paul Tavernier, Bruylant Larcier, Bruxelles, 2013.
- *Tension entre gouvernance zonale et gouvernance globale dans la prévention et la répression des actes illicites en mer*, in The Contribution of the United Nations Convention on the Law of the Sea to good Governance of the Oceans and Seas, Jose Manuel Sobrino Heredia (ed) Papers of the International Association of the Law of the Sea, Editoriale Scientifica, Napoli, Italy, 2014.

- *Les obstacles politico-culturels à la coopération interétatique dans le Golfe persique et la mer Caspienne*, in Diretto internazionale e pluralita delle culture, Giuseppe Cataldi e Valentina Grada (A cura de) Societa Italiana de Diritto Internazionale 18 Editoriale Scientifica, Napoli, Italy, 2014.
- *L'attachement de la Cour internationale de justice au consensualisme judiciaire est-il sans faille?* in Les limites du droit international, Essais en l'honneur de Joe Verhoeven, Bruylant Larcier, Bruxelles, 2014.
- *Délimitation du plateau continental du Golfe persique: une entreprise inachevée*, in Law of the Sea, from Grotius to the International Tribunal for the Law of the Sea, Liber Amicorum Judge Hugo Caminos, Brill Nijhoff, 2015.
- *L'évolution du droit international humanitaire applicable à la conduite des hostilités* in Conduct of hostilities : the Practice, the Law and the Future 37th Round Table on Current Issues of International Humanitarian Law (San Remo, 4th–6th September 2014) Edoardo Greppi (ed), 2015.
- *L'activisme judiciaire des organes de contrôle et la souveraineté des Etats : Commentaire sur Christakis* in Select Proceedings of the European Society of International Law, Fourth Volume, Regionalism and International Law, Valencia, 13th-15th September 2012, Mariano Aznar and Mary E. Footer (eds), Hart Publishing, Oxford and Portland, Oregan, 2015.
- *La conformité du blocus maritime de Gaza par Israël avec le droit international humanitaire*, in Ombres et lumières du droit international, Mélanges en l'honneur du Professeur Habib Slim, A. Pedone, Paris, 2016.
- *Garantir la nature exclusivement pacifique du programme nucléaire de l'Iran (le Plan conjoint du 24 novembre 2013)* in Nuclear Weapons : Strengthening the International Legal Regime, Ida Caracciolo, Marco Pedrazzi and Talitha Vassalli di Dachenhausen (eds), Eleven International Publishing, 2016.
- *Iran* (In collaboration with Esmaeil Baghaei Hamaneh) in Crime of Aggression, Library The Crime of Aggression: A Commentary, Clan Kreß and Stefan Barriga (eds), Cambridge University Press, 2017.

3   Articles

- *Le fond des mers et des océans : dernière frontière de l'homme*, Après-demain, n° 149, Paris, décembre 1972.
- *Vers un nouveau régime juridique des pêcheries adjacentes*, Revue Générale de Droit International public, tome 78, Paris, 1974.
- *Partager équitablement un patrimoine commun*, Journal « Le Monde », Paris, 20 juin 1974.

- *Du droit de passage dans le détroit de Tiran*, Revue égyptienne de Droit international, vol. 30, 1974.
- *Le terrorisme international*, Revue Egyptienne de Droit international, Vol. 30, 1974.
- *La question des détroits à la troisième Conférence des Nations Unies sur le droit de la mer*, Annuaire Français de Droit International, vol. XX, Paris, 1974.
- *La mer et l'égalité entre les Etats*, Revue iranienne de Relations internationales, n° 2, Téhéran, 1975.
- *Le régime de la navigation dans le canal de Suez*, Revue iranienne de Relations internationales, n° 5-6, Téhéran, 1976.
- *Les ressources biologiques de l'Océan Indien : un nouvel enjeu économique*, Revue iranienne de Relations internationales, n° 8, Téhéran, 1976.
- *Une convention pour la protection du golfe Persique contre la pollution*, Revue iranienne de Relations internationales, n° 11-12, Téhéran, 1978.
- *Le droit international dans un monde hétérogène*, Revue iranienne de Relations internationales, n° 13-14, Téhéran, 1979.
- *Le droit, la justice et les tyrans*, Journal « Le Monde », Paris, 29 novembre 1979.
- *La Commission préparatoire de l'Autorité internationale des fonds marins et du Tribunal international du droit de la mer*, Annuaire Français de Droit International, vol. XXX, 1984.
- *La délimitation du plateau continental du Golfe Persique*, Collection Espaces et Ressources maritimes, n° 3, Presses Universitaires de France, 1988.
- *La Convention sur la répression d'actes illicites contre la sécurité de la navigation maritime*, Annuaire Français de Droit International, vol. XXXIV, 1988.
- *La frontière irano-irakienne dans le Chatt-el-Arab*, Revue iranienne de Relations internationales, vol. 1, Téhéran, 1989.
- *La protection de l'environnement marin du golfe Persique et de la mer d'Oman*, Collection Espaces et Ressources maritimes, n° 4, Presses universitaires de France, 1990.
- *Le statut juridique de la mer Caspienne*, Collection Espaces et Ressources maritimes, n° 5, A. Pedone, Paris, 1991.
- *Les règles relatives à la protection de l'environnement au cours des conflits armés à l'épreuve du conflit entre l'Irak et le Koweit*, Annuaire Français de Droit International, vol. XXXVII, 1991.
- *La conservation et la gestion des stocks de poissons chevauchants et grands migrateurs*, Collection Espaces et Ressources maritimes, n° 7, A. Pedone, Paris, 1993.

- *Le statut juridique de certaines îles éparses du Golfe Persique : Abou Moussa et la Petite et Grande Tumb*, Collection Espaces et Ressources maritimes, n° 8, A. Pedone, Paris, 1994 (Traduit en arabe Shu'un al Awsat, n° 47, 1995).
- *Les interprétations discordantes des dispositions de la Convention de Montego Bay : tracé des lignes de base droites et passage des navires de guerre dans la mer territoriale*, Collection Espaces et Ressources maritimes, n° 9, A. Pedone, Paris, 1995.
- *L'Accord relatif à la conservation et à la gestion des stocks de poissons chevauchants et grands migrateurs*, Annuaire Français de Droit International, vol. XLI, 1995.
- *The Legal Regime of the Caspian Sea*, Amu Daria the Iranian Journal of Central Asian Studies, vol. I, n° 2, 1996.
- *Quel régime pour la mer Caspienne ?* Collection Espaces et Ressources maritimes, n° 10, A. Pedone, Paris, 1996.
- *Impermissibility of the Use or Threat of Use of Nuclear Weapons : A Case for an Advisory Opinion from the International Court of Justice* (In collaboration with Saeed Mirzaee and Javad Zarif), Iranian Journal of International Affairs, vol. VIII, n° 1, 1996.
- *The United Nations and the Protection of the Environment: from Stockholm to Rio de Janeiro,* in Political Geography, vol. 15, Issue 3-4, 1996.
- *La délégation par le Conseil de Sécurité de l'exécution de ses actions coercitives aux Organisations régionales*, Annuaire Français de Droit International, vol. XLIII, 1997.
- *Les règles humanitaires minimales applicables en période de troubles et de tensions internes*, Revue Internationale de la Croix-Rouge, n° 831, 1998.
- *War Crimes in Non International Armed Conflicts Under the Statute of the International Criminal Court*, Yearbook of International Humanitarian Law, T.M.C. Asser Press Vol. 2, 1999.
- *La lutte contre l'introduction clandestine de migrants par mer,* in Annuaire du droit de la mer, A. Pedone, Tome IV, Paris, 1999.
- *L'intervention d'humanité de l'OTAN au Kosovo et la règle du non recours à la force,* Revue Internationale de la Croix Rouge, n° 837 mars 2000 (Traduit en espagnol, Temas de derocho internacional, VI, Ginebra, Suiza, 2001).
- *La compétence complémentaire de la Cour pénale internationale à l'épreuve des lois d'amnistie inconditionnelle*, Die Friedens-Warte (Journal of International Peace Organization) Inhalt 78 (2003) 1 Heft 1 BWV. Berliner Wissenschafts Verlag Gmbh, 2003.
- *L'engagement des Etats à « faire respecter » le droit international humanitaire par les parties aux conflits armés*, in Collegium n° 30, College of Europe, I.C.R.C., 2004.

- *Did the Court Miss an Opportunity to Denounce the Erosion of the Principle Prohibiting the Use of Force?* Symposium *Reflections on the ICJ's Oil Platforms Decision*, Yale Journal of International Law, vol. 29, Number 29, 2004.
- *Impunité et amnistie: Analyse des concepts*, Collegium n° 32, College of Europe I.C.R.C., 2005.
- *La Convention-cadre de Téhéran sur la protection de l'environnement de la mer Caspienne*, Annuaire français de droit international Vol. LI, 2005.
- *Israel and the Fourth Geneva Convention : On the ICJ Advisory Opinion Concerning the Separation Barrier* Yearbook of International Humanitarian Law, T.M.C. Asser Press Vol. 8, 2005.
- *La protection des membres étrangers de l'équipage du navire par l'Etat du pavillon*, in Annuaire du droit de la mer, A. Pedone, Tome XI 2006.
- *La contribution de l'Organisation des Nations Unies au développement du droit international humanitaire*, Annuaire brésilien de droit international, Vol. 1, n° 8, 2010.
- *L'apport du Conseil de sécurité à la lutte contre l'impunité des pirates opérant au large des côtes de Somalie*, in Annuaire du droit de la mer, A. Pedone Tome XV, 2010.
- *L'obligation de ne pas prêter aide ou assistance au maintien d'une situation créée par la violation d'une norme impérative du droit international général*, Anuario Colombiano de Derecho Internacional (ACDI), Vol. 10, 2017.

Abbreviations/Abréviations

AALCO	Asian-African Legal Consultative Organization
ABNJ	Areas beyond national jurisdiction
ACP	Pays d'Afrique, Caraïbes et Pacifique
ADEPA	Antiterrorism and Effective Death Penalty Act
AECG	Accord Economique et Commercial Global entre l'UE et le Canada
AFDI	Annuaire français de droit international
AGNU	Assemblée générale des Nations Unies
AIEA	Agence internationale de l'énergie atomique
AJIL	American Journal of International Law
AOF	l'Afrique occidentale française
API	Protocol Additional to the Geneva Conventions of 12 August 1949, and Relating to the Protection of the Victims of International Armed Conflicts (Protocol I), of 8 June 1977
AP II	Protocol Additional to the Geneva Conventions of 12 August 1949, and relating to the Protection of Victims of Non-International Armed Conflicts (Protocol II), 8 June 1977
APICD	Agreement on the International Dolphin Conservation ProgramC/Accord relatif au programme international pour la conservation des dauphins
Area	the seabed and ocean floor and subsoil thereof, beyond the limits of national jurisdiction
ARSIWA	International Law Commission's Articles on Responsibility of States for Internationally Wrongful Acts
ASIL	American Society of International Law
Authority	International Seabed Authority
BBNJ	Biodiversity Beyond National Juridiction
BIMCO	Baltic and International Maritime Council
BIT	Bilateral Investment Treaty
CAFTA	Central America Free Trade Agreement
CAI	Conflits armés internationaux
CANI	Conflits armés non internationaux
CBD	Convention on Biological Diversity
CCBSP	Convention on the Conservation and Management of the Pollock Resources in the Central Bering Sea/Convention sur la conservation et la gestion des ressources en colin dans la partie centrale de la mer de Béring

CCMLAR	Convention on the Conservation of Antarctic Marine Living Resources/ Convention sur la conservation de la faune et de la flore marines de l'Antarctique
CCR	Regulations on Prospecting and Exploration for Cobalt-Rich Ferromanganese Crusts
CCRF	FAO Code of Conduct for Responsible Fisher
CCSBT	Commission for the Conservation of the Southern Bluefin Tuna/ Commission pour la conservation du thon rouge du Sud
CD	Conférence du désarmement
CdG	Conventions de Genève
CDI	Commission du droit international, Comisión de Derecho Internacional
CDR	Carbon Dioxide Removal
CECAF	Fishery Committee for the Eastern Central Atlantic/Comité des pêches de l'Atlantique Centre-Est
CEDH	Convention européenne des droits de l'homme
CETA	Comprehensive Economic and Trade Agreement
CHR	European Court of Human Rights
CIA	Central Intelligence Agency
CICR	Comité International de la Croix-Rouge
CIJ	Cour internationale de justice
CIRDI	Centre international pour le règlement des différends relatifs aux investissements
CJCE	Cour de justice des Communautés européennes
CJUE	Cour de justice de l'Union européenne
CLCS	Commission of the Limits of Continental Shelf
CLRTAP	Convention on Long-Range Transboundary Air Pollution
CNDUM	Convention des Nations Unies sur le droit de la mer
CNUCED	Conférence des Nations Unies sur le commerce et le développement
CNUDCI	Commission des Nations Unies pour le droit commercial international
COFI	Committee on Fisheries
CourEDH	Cour européenne des droits de l'homme
CourIDH	Cour Interaméricaine des droits de l'homme
CPC	Members and Co-operating Non-Members
CPUCH	Convention on the Protection of the Underwater Cultural Heritage
CREDHO	Centre de Recherches et d'Etudes Sur les Droits de l'Homme et le Droit Humanitaire
CSCE	Conférence pour la sécurité et la coopération en Europe
CSCM	Conférence sur la sécurité et la coopération en Méditerranée
CSFT	1999 International Convention for the Suppression of the Financing of Terrorism

CSRP	Commission sous régionale des pêches
DHI	Droit international humanitaire
DIdH	Droit international des droits de l'homme
DOAG	Documents officiels de l'Assemblée générale des Nations Unies
ECOSOC	Economic and Social Council
EDAN	Etats dotés d'armes nucléaires
EECC	Eritrea—Ethiopia Claims Commission
EEZ	Exclusive Economic Zone
EIA	Environment Impact Assessment
EJIL	European Journal of International Law
EU	European Union
EUNAFO	EU Naval Force
FAD	Fish Aggregating Device
FAO	Food and Agriculture Organization of the United Nations
FDA	Forces démocratiques alliées
FET	Fair and Equitable Treatment
Frontex	European Border and Coast Guard Agency
FSIA	Foreign Sovereign Immunity Act
GAIR	Gesellschaft für Arabisches und Islamisches Recht
GC	Grande Chambre
GCC	Gulf Cooperation Council
GFCM	General Fisheries Commission for the Mediterranean/Commission générale des pêches pour la Méditerranée
IAC	International Armed Conflict
IAEA	International Atomic Energy Agency
IATTC	Inter-American Tropical Tuna Commission/Commission interaméricaine du thon tropical
ICANN	Internet Corporation for Assigned Names and Numbers
ICC	International Criminal Court
ICCAT	International Commission for the Conservation of Atlantic Tunas/Commission internationale pour la conservation des thonidés de l'Atlantique
ICJ	International Court of Justice
ICRC	International Committee of the Red Cross
ICSID	International Centre for Settlement of Investment Disputes
ICTY	International Criminal Tribunal for the former Yugoslavia
IDI	Institut de droit international
IDMS	Internal Displacement Monitoring Centre/Centre de surveillance des déplacements internes
IGF	l'Institut géographique de France

IHFFC	International Humanitarian Fact-Finding Commission
IHL	International Humanitarian Law
IHRL	International Human Rights Law
IIAS	International Investment Agreements
ILA	International Law Association
ILC	International Law Commission
ILM	International Legal Materials
ILO	International Labour Organiztion
IMO	International Maritime Organization
INPFL	Independent National Patriotic Front of Liberia
Interpol	International Criminal Police Organization
IOC	International Oceanographic Commission
IOTC	Indian Ocean Tuna Commission/Commission des thons de l'océan Indien
IPHC	Commission internationale du flétan du Pacifique
IPPC	Intergovernmental Panel on Climate Change
ISA	International Seabed Authority
ISBA	International Seabed Authority
ISDS	Investor-State Dispute Settlement
ISIS	Islamic State of Iraq and the Levant/Islamic State of Iraq and Syria
ITLOS	International Tribunal for the Law of the Sea
IUCN	International Union for Conservation of Nature
IUU	Illegal, unregulated and unreported (fishing)
IWC	International Waling Commission/Commission internationale de la chasse à la baleine
JCPOA	Joint Comprehensive Plan of Action
JVTA	Justice for Victims of Terrorism Act
LGDJ	Librairie générale de droit et de jurisprudence
LNTS	League of Nations Treaty Series
LOSC	1982 UN Convention on the Law of the Sea
LRA	Lord's Resistance Army
LTC	Legal and Technical Commission
MARPOL	International Convention for the Prevention of Pollution from Ships
MN	Margin number
MPA	Parine Protected Areas
MSF	Médecins Sans Frontières
MSY	Maximum Sustainable Yield
NAFO	Northwest Atlantic Fisheries Organization/Organisation des pêches de l'Atlantique du Nord-Ouest
NAFTA	North American Free Trade Agreement

NAMMCO	Commission des mammifères marins de l'Atlantique Nord
NASCO	North Atlantic Salmon Conservation Organization/Organisation pour la conservation du saumon de l'Atlantique Nord
NATO	North Atlantic Treaty Organization
NEAFC	North East Atlantic Fisheris Commission/Commission des pêches de l'Atlantique du Nord-Est
NGO	Non-governmental Organizations
NIAC	Non-international Arm Conflict
NIE	National Intelligence Estimate
NPAFC	Commission des espèces anadromes du Pacifique Sud
NPFC	Commission des pêches du Pacifique Nord
NPT	Treaty on the Non-Proliferation of Nuclear Weapons
NSC	National Security Council
OCDE	Organisation de Coopération et de Développement Économiques
ODD	Objectif de Développement Durable
OJ	Official Journal
OMD	Objectif du Millénaire pour le développement
OMS	Organisation mondiale de la Santé
ONU	Organisation des Nations Unies
ORGP	organisations régionales de gestion de la pêche
OSPAR Convention	Convention for the Protection of the Marine Environment and Coastal Areas of the South East Pacific
OSRSGCAC	Office of the Special Representative of the Secretary-General for Children and Armed Conflict
OTAN	Organisation du traité de l'Atlantique Nord
PA I	Protocole additionnel aux Conventions de Genève du 12 août 1949 relatif à la protection des victimes des conflits armés internationaux
PA II	Protocole additionnel aux Conventions de Genève du 12 août 1949 relatif à la protection des victimes des conflits armés non internationaux
PCA	Permanent Court of Arbitration
PCIJ	Permanent Court of International Justice
PCP	politique commune de la pêche
PCSP	Commission permanente du Pacifique Sud
Pêche INN	pêche illicite, non déclarée et non réglementée
PIFFA	Agence des pêches du forum des îles du Pacifique
PNB	Produit national brut
PNR	Regulations on Prospecting and Exploration for Polymetallic Nodules

PSR	Regulations on Prospecting and Exploration for Polymetallic Sulphides
PSSA	Particularly Sensitive Sea Areas
PTCI	Partenariat transatlantique de commerce et d'investissement
R2P	Responsibility to Protect
RCRC	Red Cross and Red Crescent
RDC	Republique Democratique du Congo
RDIE	Mécanisme de règlement des différends entre investisseurs et États
REMO	Regional Fisheries Management Organizations
RFB	Regional Fisheries Bodies
RFMA	Regional Fisheries Management Arrangments
RFMO	Regional Fisheries Management Orgnaization
RIAA	Reports of International Arbitration Awards
RSN	Regional Fishery Body Secretariats Network
SEAFO	South East Atlantic Fisheries Organization/Organisation des pêches de l'Atlantique du Sud-Est
SFDI	Société française pour le droit international
SIA	State Immunity Act
SIOFA	Accord relatif aux pêches dans le sud de l'océan Indien
SMCA	Sunken Military Craft Act
SOFIA	State of World Fisheries and Aquaculture
SPRMFO	South Pacific Regional Fisheries Management Organisation/ Organisation régionale de gestion des pêches du Pacifique Sud
SRFC	Subregional Fisheries Commissions
SRM	Solar Radiation Management
START	Strategic Arms Reduction Talks
SWIOFC	Southwest Indian Ocean Fisheries Commission
TAC	Total Allowable Catch
TAFTA	Partenariat transatlantique de commerce et d'investissement
TFG	Transitional Federal Government/Gouvernement fédéral de transition
TFUE	Traité sur le fonctionnement de l'Union européenne
TICE	Traité d'interdiction complète des essais
TIDM	Tribunal international du droit de la mer
TNCO	Texte de négociation composite officieux
TNP	Traité sur la non-prolifération des armes nucléaires
TPIY	Tribunal pénal international pour l'ex-Yougoslavie
TRR	Tehran Research Reactor
TRW	Toxic Remnants of War Project
TTIP	Transatlantic Trade and Investment Parternership
UCH	Underwater Cultural Heritage
UE	Union européenne

ABBREVIATIONS/ABRÉVIATIONS

UMA	Union du Maghreb arabe
UN	United Nations
UNCC	United Nations Compensation Commission
UNCIO	United Nations Conference on Intrernational Organization
UNCITRAL	United Nations Commission on International Trade Law
UNCLOS	United Nations Conference on the Law of the Sea
UNCRC	United Nations Convention on the Rights of the Child
UNECE	United Nations Economic Commission for Europe
UNEP	United Nations Environment Programme
UNESCO	United Nations Educational, Scientific and Cultural Organization
UNFCCC	United Nations Convention on Climate Change
UNFSA	UN Fish Stocks Agreement
UNHCR	United Nations High Commissioner for Refugees/ le Haut Commissariat des Nations Unies aux Réfugiés
UNICEF	United Nations Children's Fund
UNIDO	United Nations Industrial Development Organization
UNSC	United Nations Security Council
UNTS	United Nations Treaty Series
UPM	Union pour la Méditerranée
USSR	Union of Soviet Socialist Republics
VCLT	Vienna Convention on the Law of Treaties
WCPFC	Commission des pêches pour le Pacifique occidental et central
WECAFC	Western Central Atlantic Fishery Commission/Commission des pêches pour l'Atlantique Centre-Ouest
WMO	World Meteorological Organizations
WTO	World Trade Organization
YBILC	Yearbook of International Law Commission
ZEAN	zones exemptes d'armes nucléaires
ZEE	zone économique exclusive

List of Contributors/Liste des auteurs

Mohsen Abdollahi
is Associate Professor of International and Environmental Law at Shahid Beheshti University (SBU) in Iran. He serves as the Head of the Environmental Law Department in the Faculty of Law of SBU, the Head of International Law Committee of Iran Expediency Discernment Council and Legal Adviser at the Presidential Office. His main areas of research interest include international responsibility, anti-terrorism law, law of immunities, environmental law and international criminal law.

Ricardo Abello-Galvis
est professeur principal de droit international public à l'Universidad del Rosario (Bogotá – Colombie), membre de la Cour Permanente d'Arbitrage – CPA (2014–2019), Agent de la Colombie auprès de la Cour Interaméricaine des droits de l'homme dans la demande d'opinion consultative, Directeur/Editeur de l'*ACDI – Anuario Colombiano de Derecho Internacional* (*ACDI – Annuaire Colombien de Droit International*), membre Associé de IHLADI – Instituto Hispano-Luso-Americano de Derecho Internacional, membre de SLADI – Société Latino-Américaine de Droit International, de l'Académie Colombienne de Jurisprudence et Ancien Président de l'Académie Colombienne de Droit International. Son travail de recherche se centre sur les sources du droit international, le droit de la mer, la jurisprudence de la Cour internationale de Justice et la Cour Interaméricaine des droits de l'homme.

Hirad Abtahi
has twenty years of experience in international criminal justice. Since 2004, he has headed the Legal and Enforcement Unit of the Presidency of the International Criminal Court. Previously, he served the Milosevic trial chamber at the United Nations International Criminal Tribunal for the former Yugoslavia, and worked for the International Commission of Jurists. Hirad Abtahi has widely lectured, including at The Hague Academy of International Law, and published, including two volumes on the Genocide Convention's travaux préparatoires. He serves on the Boards of the International Criminal Law Review and the Forum for International Criminal and Humanitarian Law. He is a member of the Société Française pour le droit international and the European Society of International Law. Holding a Diplôme d'études approfondies in international law, Hirad Abtahi has been educated in Iran, France, Canada and England.

Mahnoush H. Arsanjani

former Director of the Codification Division of the Office of Legal Affairs of the United Nations, served as Vice-President of the American Society of International Law, is a member of the Board of Editors of the *American Journal of International Law*, and a member of the Institut de droit international. She served as a member of the Expert Group established by the 2008 Ad Hoc Energy Ministers Meetings held in Jeddah and London, and as a special consultant to the International Energy Forum, Charter of the International Energy Forum 2010. She served as a member of the Bahrain Independent Commission of Inquiry, is a judge on the World Bank Administrative Tribunal and practices international law.

Mariano J. Aznar

is Professor of Public International Law at University Jaume I, Spain. Former Professor of Public International Law at the University of Valencia, and Editor-in-Chief of the Spanish Yearbook of International Law. Author of numerous publications on different aspects of international and EU law, Mariano Aznar has acted as legal expert for UNESCO and counsel-advocate of the Kingdom of Spain before ITLOS. Main areas of expertise include international protection of cultural heritage, particularly underwater cultural heritage, law of the sea, international responsibility of States and international peace and security.

Mohamed Bennouna

qui est actuellement juge à la Cour internationale de Justice, est membre de l'Institut de droit international et du Curatorium de l'Académie de droit international de La Haye. Il a exercé comme Représentant permanent du Maroc auprès des Nations Unies, Juge au Tribunal pénal international pour l'ex-Yougoslavie, Directeur général de l'Institut du monde arabe à Paris, professeur de droit international et Doyen de la Faculté de droit de Rabat. Il a été membre de la Commission du droit international des Nations Unies et de la Commission d'indemnisation des Nations Unies à Genève. Il a publié des ouvrages et de nombreux articles en droit international.

Abdelwahab Biad

est maître de conférences à l'Université de Rouen où il enseigne les Relations internationales et le Droit international. Il est membre du CUREJ où il dirige l'équipe du CREDHO. Il a été chercheur invité à l'Académie internationale de La Haye et à l'UNIDIR. Ses champs de spécialisation concernent le droit international humanitaire, le droit du désarmement et de la sécurité internationale, le droit nucléaire et les droits de l'homme.

Michael Bothe
is Professor Emeritus of Public Law at the J.W. Goethe University, Frankfurt/ Main. He was previously Professor at the Universities of Heidelberg and Hannover, Head of Research Unit, Peace Research Institute Frankfurt. He was President of the European Environmental Law Association and of the German Society of International Law as well as Chair of the International Humanitarian Fact-finding Commission. He is author of numerous books and articles on both international and constitutional law, in particular the law relating to the maintenance of peace and international humanitarian law, comparative and international environmental law and comparative federalism.

Ove Bring
is Professor Emeritus of International Law at Stockholm University and the Swedish National Defence University. Before that, he was Professor of Public International Law at Uppsala University and Legal Adviser at the Swedish Ministry for Foreign Affairs. He represented Sweden in the Sixth (Legal) Committee of the UN General Assembly (1983–1993). He has participated in human rights missions to former Yugoslavia, Vietnam, China and Tibet. During 2001–2006 he was a member of the International Humanitarian Fact-Finding Commission (IHFFC) in Geneva. Since 1999 he has been a member of the Permanent Court of Arbitration (PCA) in The Hague. He serves as President of the Swedish Branch of the International Law Association (ILA) and is a member of the Executive Council of the ILA in London.

Lucius Caflisch
professeur honoraire, Institut de hautes études internationales et du développement, Genève. Membre de l'Institut de droit international et de la Cour permanente d'Arbitrage. Jurisconsulte du Département fédéral des affaires étrangères, Berne (1991–1998) ; juge à la Cour européenne des droits de l'homme, Strasbourg (1998–2006), membre de la Commission du droit international des Nations Unies (2006–2016).

Ida Caracciolo
is Professor of International Law, vice-director of the Department of Political Sciences and President of the MA Course on International Relations and Organizations at the University of Campania "Luigi Vanvitelli". She is a barrister, member of the Permanent Court of Arbitration and Conciliator in the OSCE Court of Arbitration and Conciliation. She collaborates with the Legal Department of the Italian Ministry of Foreign Affairs. Her main areas of

expertise include the law of the sea, international criminal law and international humanitarian law.

Jorge Cardona
est professeur de droit international à l'Université de Valence (Espagne) et membre du Comité des droits de l'enfant des Nations Unies. Il a occupé plusieurs postes internationaux et il est auteur de près de 200 publications portant sur le droit international, et plus particulièrement sur le droit des traités, le droit de la responsabilité internationale, le droit des organisations internationales, le maintien de la paix et de la sécurité internationales, et les droits de l'homme (spécialement, droits des enfants et droits des personnes en situation de handicap)

Rafael Casado Raigón
est rofesseur (*Catedrático*) de droit international public et Directeur du Département des Sciences juridiques de l'Université de Cordoue (Espagne). Ancien Doyen de la Faculté de Droit de la même université et ancien Président de l'*Association internationale du droit de la mer*. Il est auteur de *Derecho internacional* (Madrid 2014) et de nombreux écrits (monographies, chapitres d'ouvrages collectifs, articles de revues ou d'annuaires) dans ce domaine : règlement des différends, droit de la mer, organisations internationales (ONU, UE), droit de la responsabilité internationale ou normes internationales et obligations découlant.

Giuseppe Cataldi
est professeur de droit international à l'Université de Naples L'Orientale, où il est chargé d'une Chaire « Jean Monnet » *ad personam* de l'Union européenne sur la « Protection des droits de l'homme en Europe », et où il est Directeur du « Centre d'excellence Jean Monnet sur les droits des migrants dans la Méditerranée ». Il est Président de l'« Association internationale du droit de la mer » (Assidmer). Membre de la Société Italienne de Droit International, de la Société Française de Droit International, membre du Sénat d'EMUNI (Université Euro-Méditerranéenne). Il est auteur et directeur de plusieurs ouvrages et articles de droit international public et du droit de l'Union européenne, concernant en particulière le droit de la mer, les droits de l'homme et les relations entre le droit interne et le droit international.

James Crawford
is a member of the International Court of Justice. Before his election to the Court in 2015, he held chairs at the Universities of Adelaide, Sydney and

Cambridge. He was a member of the Australian Law Reform Commission (1982–1989) and the International Law Commission (1992–2001) and Special Rapporteur on State Responsibility. He is a Distinguished Visiting Professor at Xi'an Jiaotong University School of Law, Xi'an, China. His books include The Creation of States in International Law (2nd edn 2006), Chance, Order, Change. The Course of International Law (2013) and State Responsibility: The General Part (2014). He is the editor of Brownlie's Principles of public International Law (8th edition, 2012; 9th edition in press). As a member of the Australian and English bars he practiced extensively before the International Court and other international courts and tribunals.

Zakaria Daboné
a obtenu son doctorat en droit à l'Université de Genève et a effectué son postdoctorat à l'Université de Michigan (Ann Arbor). Il est enseignant chercheur à l'Université Polytechnique de Bobo-Dioulasso. Son champ d'enseignement et de recherche recouvre le droit public général, le droit international public général, le droit international humanitaire, le droit international des droits de l'homme, le droit constitutionnel et la philosophie du droit. Il est depuis avril 2016 Secrétariat permanent du Comité interministériel des droits humains et du droit international humanitaire du Burkina Faso.

Jean d'Aspremont
is Professor of Public International Law at the University of Manchester where he founded the Manchester International Law Centre (MILC). He is General Editor of the Cambridge Studies in International and Comparative Law and director of the Oxford Database on International Organizations. He is a member of the Scientific Advisory Board of the European Journal of International Law. He is series editor of the Melland Schill Studies in International Law. He has acted as counsel in proceedings before the International Court of Justice. He has published widely on international law, international dispute resolution and international legal theory.

Yves Daudet
est professeur émérite de droit international public de l'Ecole de droit de la Sorbonne et président du Curatorium de l'Académie de droit international de La Haye. Auparavant, il a été professeur à l'Université d'Aix Marseille et dans plusieurs universités étrangères et a exercé des fonctions administratives, notamment celle de premier vice-président de l'Université Paris 1 Panthéon Sorbonne. Ses missions dans plus de soixante pays étrangers ont été à l'origine de nombreuses actions de coopération. Ses ouvrages et articles, portent

essentiellement sur le droit international général avec un intérêt particulier pour les sources du droit international (un cours à l'Académie de La Haye a porté sur la codification) et le système des Nations Unies sur lequel il a organisé plusieurs colloques, notamment dans le cadre des rencontres internationales d'Aix en Provence.

Knut Dörmann

has been Head of the Legal Division and Chief Legal Officer of the International Committee of the Red Cross (ICRC) since December 2007. He was Deputy Head of the Legal Division (2004–2007) and Legal Adviser at the Legal Division (1998–2004). He holds a Doctor of Laws (Dr. iur.) from the University of Bochum in Germany (2001). He has been a member of several groups of experts working on the current challenges of international humanitarian law. He has extensively presented and published on international law of peace, international humanitarian law and international criminal law. He received the 2005 Certificate of Merit of the American Society of International Law for his book Elements of War Crimes under the Rome Statute of the International Criminal Court, published by Cambridge University Press.

Pierre-Emmanuel Dupont

is a lawyer and a consultant in public international law, including the law of the sea and maritime boundary delimitation, as well as in international investment law and dispute resolution. He is currently serving as legal adviser to the UN Special Rapporteur on unilateral sanctions (unilateral coercive measures) and has worked on investor-State disputes under the ICSID Convention, the Energy Charter Treaty and bilateral investment treaties. He is a Senior Lecturer at the Free Faculty of Law, Economics and Management of Paris (FACO), where he teaches investment treaty arbitration and commercial arbitration. He is a member of the International Law Association's (ILA) Committee on nuclear weapons, non-proliferation and contemporary international law.

Pierre Michel Eisemann

est professeur émérite de l'École de droit de la Sorbonne (Université Paris 1 Panthéon-Sorbonne). Ses champs de compétence couvrent le droit international public général, le contentieux international, le droit des organisations internationales ainsi que le droit de la fonction publique internationale. Il est associé en qualité d'expert à la délégation de la France auprès de l'UNESCO depuis de longues années et il conseille par ailleurs plusieurs organisations internationales.

Victor Luis Gutiérrez Castillo

joined the University of Jaen in 2010 as a Lecturer in Public International Law. In Jaen (Spain), he leads the *International Studies Group* and the International Law Department. His research is focused on the law of the sea and human rights. Before joining Jaen, he was a Lecturer in the University of Cordoba, CEADE-Wales University and International University of Andalusia. He also served as Chief of the Department of Institutional and Academic Relations of the International Institute of Arab and Muslim World Studies (Spanish Ministry of Foreign Affairs and Cooperation) and Vice-Rector of the International University of Andalusia. He is currently a member of several international research networks, including the *Institut Économique du Droit de la Mer* in Monaco (member of the Scientific Council).

Gerhard Hafner

is retired Professor of International Law at Vienna University and Comenius University at Bratislava, legal consultant to the Austrian Federal Ministry of Europe, Integration and Foreign Affairs, member of the Institut de droit international, and former member of the International Law Commission. His works particularly deal with law of the sea, law of immunities, international criminal law, law of State succession, and treaty law.

Zalmai Haquani

professeur émérite à l'Université de Caen Normandie, a enseigné aux différents universités et établissements d'enseignement supérieur en France et à l'étranger durant presque 40 ans. Il fut l'expert prés l'Organisation des Nations Unies entre 1982 et 2002, et ambassadeur d'Afghanistan en France entre 2002 et 2006. Il est membre de l'Académie des sciences, des Arts et des Belles-lettres de Caen. Ses ouvrages et articles, ses directions de recherche et de thèse de doctorat, ses missions et expertises couvrent durant toute cette période de vastes domaines de droit international et de relations internationales, en Europe, en Afrique, en Asie et sur le continent américain.

Maurice Kamto

est Professeur de droit public à l'Université de Yaooundé II (Cameroun) et ancien doyen de la Faculté des Sciences juridiques et politiques de cette Université. Membre et ancien Président de la Commission du droit international, il fut aussi Rapporteur spécial de ladite Commission sur l'" Expulsion des étrangers". Membre de l'Institut de droit international et Rapporteur de l'Institut sur les "Migrations de masse". Membre de la Cour permanente d'arbitrage. Conseil et avocat de plusieurs États devant la Cour international de Justice. Arbitre.

Conseiller juridique des délégations du Gouvernement à diverses conférences internationales. Membre du Curatorium de l'Académie de droit international de La Haye. Principaux domaines de spécialité : droit international public ; droit constitutionnel ; droit de l'environnement. Il a publié une dizaine d'ouvrages et près d'une centaine d'articles scientifiques.

Mariko Kawano

is Professor of International Law at Waseda University, Faculty of Law, Tokyo. She was councilor at the Headquarters for Ocean Policy of the Government of Japan and is the chairperson of the Consultative Committee on Maritime Affairs, Ministry of Land and Transport and a member of the Council on Customs, Tariff, Foreign Exchange and Other Transactions, Ministry of Finance. Main areas of expertise include peaceful settlement of international disputes, law of the sea, State responsibility, and diplomatic protection of foreign investment.

Marie-Françoise Labouz

professeure émérite de droit public de l'Université de Versailles-St-Quentin-en-Yvelines, Chaire Jean Monnet ad personam. Ses domaines de recherche sont le maintien de la paix et de la sécurité internationale, la justice pénale internationale, la convention européenne des droits de l'homme et des libertés fondamentales, les relations extérieures de l'Union européenne avec le Canada et les Etats-Unis, le régime des régions polaires.

Ahmed Mahiou

ancien doyen de la Faculté de droit d'Alger, ancien directeur de l'Institut de recherches et d'études sur le monde arabe et musulman (Aix en Provence, France), ancien président de la CDI (Nations Unies), membre de l'Institut de droit international, juge ad hoc à la Cour internationale de justice. Professeur invité auprès de nombreuses universités dans le monde.

Said Mahmoudi

is Professor of International Law and former dean at the Faculty of Law of Stockholm University. He served as a diplomat at the Iranian Embassy in Stockholm before the 1979 Revolution. He is nominated by Sweden as arbitrator according to Article 2 of Annex VII to the 1982 UN Convention on the Law of the Sea. His main fields of research are law of the sea, international environmental law, EU environmental law, use of force and international organizations. He has also published several studies on the relation between Islam and international law.

Nasrin Mosaffa
is Professor of International Relations at the Faculty of Law and Political Science of the University of Tehran, where she is also the vice dean. She is currently Chairperson of the Iranian Association for United Nation Studies. She is also former Director of the Centre for Graduate International Studies (1997–2010) and first Director of the Centre for Human Rights Studies at the University of Tehran. Her main areas of expertise include international organizations, peace studies, human rights, particularly women's and children's rights, and interface of international law and politics.

Shinya Murase
is Professor Emeritus of International Law at Sophia University in Tokyo and has been Visiting Professor at the Law School of China Youth University of Political Studies in Beijing since 2014. He has served as member of the UN International Law Commission since 2009, and has been its Special Rapporteur for the topic of the Protection of the Atmosphere since 2013. He is also associate member of the Institut de droit international. His major publication is *International Law: An Integrative Perspective on Transboundary Issues,* Sophia University Press, 2011.

Bernard H. Oxman
is Richard A. Hausler Professor of Law at the University of Miami, where he teaches international law, the law of the sea, and conflict of laws, and directs the maritime law program. He participated in the Third UN Conference on the Law of the Sea as U.S. Representative and chair of the Drafting Committee's English Language Group, was appointed judge *ad hoc* of the International Court of Justice and the International Tribunal for the Law of the Sea, and served as Co-Editor in Chief of the American Journal of International Law.

Sundhya Pahuja
is Professor of Law and Director, Institute for International Law and the Humanities at Melbourne University. She has served as Director of Studies in Public International Law at The Hague Academy, Research Professor at SOAS, Visiting Chair at Birkbeck, Visiting Fellow at the London School of Economics (LSE), and Fulbright Senior Scholar at Harvard Law School. Sundhya's research centres on the history, theory and political economy of international law and institutions. Her publications include *Decolonising International Law: Development, Economic Growth and the Politics of Universality* (CUP, 2011), (American Society of International Law Prize (2012), Woodward Medal (2014)) and the anthologies, *Events: The Force of International Law* (2011, with Johns

and Joyce), and *Reading Modern Law: Critical Methodologies and Sovereign Formations* (2012, with Buchanan and Motha).

Alain Pellet
is Professor Emeritus at Université Paris Nanterre. He is the author of numerous books and articles with special emphasis on general international law and international investment law. He is a former Member (1990–2011) and Chairperson (1997–1998) of the ILC. He has been the ICANN Independent Objector for generic top level domain names (2012–2015). He has acted as counsel before the ICJ in more than 50 cases as well as before the ITLOS and several international and transnational arbitrations, international investment cases in particular. He has been nominated on the List of arbitrators under Annex VII of the United Nations Convention on the Law of the Sea (2015) and to the Panel of Arbitrators of the ICSID (2011), and has been appointed arbitrator or president in several cases.

Jean-François Pulvenis de Séligny-Maurel
is the Senior Policy Advisor of the Inter-American Tropical Tuna Commission (IATTC). Former Director, Fisheries and Aquaculture Policy and Economics Division, FAO (2002–2011), and before that was Ambassador Plenipotentiary to Guyana and CARICOM (2000–2002) and Ambassador and Director, Land and Maritime Boundaries (1988–2000)), Ministry of External Relations (Venezuela). He participated in numerous bilateral, regional and global negotiations on the law of the sea, fisheries and environmental law (e.g. UNCLOS, UNCED, UNFCCC, UNFSA, FAO CCRF and IPOAS, GPA). He chaired the negotiations leading to the adoption of the 2003 IATTC "Antigua Convention". He has lectured at the Summer Academy of the International Foundation for the Law of the Sea (Hamburg) and the Rhodes Academy of Oceans Law and Policy.

Amir Hossein Ranjbarian
est professeur associé à la Faculté de Droit et des Sciences Politiques de l'Université de Téhéran, où il enseigne le droit international humanitaire, le droit international pénal et les droits de l'homme. Il est aussi l'auteur des ouvrages concernant les matières qu'il enseigne.

W. Michael Reisman
Myres S. McDougal Professor of International Law at Yale, is a member of the Institut de droit international, Fellow of the World Academy of Art and Science, member of the Advisory Committee on International Law of the Department of State, President of the Arbitration Tribunal of the Bank for

International Settlements and member of the Board of the Foreign Policy Association. He was President of the Inter-American Commission on Human Rights, Vice-President and Honorary Vice-President of the American Society of International Law, Editor-in-Chief of the American Journal of International Law and Vice-Chairman of the Policy Sciences Center. His most recent books are *International Commercial Arbitration: Cases, Materials, and Notes on the Resolution of International Business Disputes* (with Craig, Park and Paulsson) (2015), and *Foreign Investment Disputes: Cases, Materials and Commentary* (with Bishop and Crawford) (2014).

Tilman Rodenhäuser

is legal adviser in the legal division of the International Committee of the Red Cross. He holds a PhD from the Graduate Institute of International and Development Studies in Geneva. Prior to joining the ICRC, he worked with different international and non-governmental organizations on the implementation of international humanitarian and human rights law, focussing both on State and non-State actors.

Emanuel Roucounas

is Professor Emeritus at University of Athens and a former member of the International Law Commission and the UN Committee on the Elimination of All Forms of Racial Discrimination. He has served as judge *ad hoc* of the International Court of Justice and is Chair of International Law at the Academy of Athens, a member of the Permanent Court of Arbitration, and a member and former President of the Institut de droit international.

Natalino Ronzitti

is Professor Emeritus of International Law at Luiss University, Rome, and a Member of the Institut de droit international.

Yves Sandoz

a été délégué du CICR sur différents terrains opérationnels avant de rejoindre le siège de l'Institution, dans laquelle il a été de longues années Directeur du droit international et de la doctrine. Il a ensuite contribué à la création de l'Académie de droit international humanitaire et de droits humains de Genève, dans laquelle il a enseigné le droit international humanitaire, ainsi, notamment, qu'à l'Université de Fribourg et au Collège d'Europe de Bruges. Il est l'auteur de nombreuses publications dans ce domaine.

Tullio Scovazzi

is Professor of International Law at the University of Milano-Bicocca, Milan, Italy. He occasionally participates, as legal expert, in negotiations and meetings relating to law of the sea, cultural properties, human rights.

Jamal Seifi

is a judge at the Iran-United States Claims Tribunal in The Hague. He was a Member of the Permanent Court of Arbitration (2006–2016). His main areas of expertise include arbitration, judicial dispute settlement, State responsibility and State succession. He has long practice in international arbitration as arbitrator, counsel and expert alongside work as a university professor and teaching international law and arbitration in universities in Iran (Shahid Beheshti University), the United Kingdom (University of Hull) and the Netherlands (Tilburg University). He is currently Distinguished Visiting Professor at Tilburg University, the Netherlands, which follows the completion of his annual Chair of Global Law for the year 2015 at this university. He has written and published on arbitration and international law topics continuously, including the Iran National Report in the Encyclopedia of International Arbitration.

Farideh Shaygan

is Assistant Professor of International Law at the University of Tehran Kish International Campus. Her main areas of expertise include the law of the UN Charter, peace keeping operations, human rights, and international humanitarian law.

Linos-Alexander Sicilianos

is President of Section at the European Court of Human Rights, Associate Member of the Institut de droit international, Member of the Curatorium of The Hague Academy of International Law, Professor at the Faculty of Law of the University of Athens and Member of the Permanent Court of Arbitration. He has also served as Vice-president and Rapporteur of the UN Committee on the Elimination of Racial Discrimination and Member of the Executive Board of the EU Fundamental Rights Agency. He has taught international law in several universities and academic institutions including The Hague Academy of International Law. Main areas of interest and expertise include the law of the UN Charter, state responsibility, economic sanctions, use of force and human rights law. He has published many books and articles on these subjects in English, French and Greek.

Yvenson St-Fleur
est actuellement candidat à l'École du Barreau du Haut-Canada (2016–2017). Anciennement, il a été juriste en défense auprès du Tribunal Pénal International pour le Rwanda. Son champs de spécialisation est le droit international humanitaire des conflits armés, le droit international pénal, les droits de la personne et le droit des traités.

Alexia Solomou
is currently Associate Legal Officer at the International Court of Justice and President of the Cypriot Branch of the International Law Association, which she founded in 2016. She was previously Research Associate to Professor James R. Crawford AC, SC at the University of Cambridge and before that Research and Publications Assistant to the Director of the Lauterpacht Centre for International Law. She holds an LL.M from Columbia Law School and an LL.B with French Law from University College London and the University of Paris II (Panthéon-Assas). Her main areas of expertise include the law of the sea, boundary delimitation, the use of force and international dispute resolution.

Cait Storr
is Research Fellow with the Institute of International Law and the Humanities at Melbourne Law School. A former solicitor with a background in administrative law and indigenous affairs, she researches at the intersection of law, history, politics and geography, and is currently completing her PhD thesis, entitled 'Nauru: Imperial Form, International Status and the Histories of International Law'.

Sandra Szurek
est professeur émérite de l'Université Paris Nanterre. Agrégée de droit public, elle est spécialiste de droit international public et professeur associé de l'Institut des Hautes Etudes Internationales (IHEI) de l'Université Paris II Panthéon-Assas. Ses recherches portent principalement sur le droit international général (droit des traités, de la responsabilité), le droit de la Charte des Nations Unies (maintien de la paix, action du Conseil de sécurité, responsabilité de protéger), le droit international des droits de l'homme et le droit international humanitaire. Elle est notamment codirectrice, aux Editions Pedone, de la collection *La France et le droit international*, consacrée à la pratique juridique française du droit international.

Paul Tavernier
est professeur émérite à l'Université Paris-Sud (Paris XI) et Directeur du CREDHO (Centre de recherches et d'études sur les droits de l'Homme et le

LIST OF CONTRIBUTORS/LISTE DES AUTEURS XLV

droit humanitaire). Il a enseigné le droit international et les relations internationales dans plusieurs universités (Alger, Grenoble, Rouen et Paris). Il a fondé le CREDHO à Rouen et à Paris. Ses principaux centres d'intérêt et d'expertise portent sur le droit de la Charte des Nations Unies (notamment sur les opérations de maintien de la paix et le droit de la sécurité internationale), le droit des droits de l'Homme (en particulier le droit de la Convention européenne des droits de l'Homme et la jurisprudence de la Cour de Strasbourg) et le droit international humanitaire. Il a dirigé et publié un grand nombre d'ouvrages et d'articles sur ces questions.

Anicée Van Engeland
is a Senior Lecturer at the Centre for International Security and Resilience, Cranfield University. She previously held positions at the University of Exeter, School of Oriental and African Studies (SOAS) and Cardiff University in their law schools. Prior to becoming an academic, she was a human-rights and an aid worker. She continues to advise non-governmental and international organizations. Her areas of expertise include international law and Islamic law.

Roberto Virzo
is Associate Professor of International Law at the University of Sannio (Benevento), Adjunct Professor of International Organizations at LUISS Guido Carli University (Rome) and, since 2011, a Visiting Professor of International Law of the Sea at University of Florida, Levin College of Law. He has authored *Il regolamento delle controversie nel diritto del mare: rapport tra procedimenti* (CEDAM, 2008) and co-edited *Evolutions in the Law of International Organizations* (Brill/Nijhoff, 2015). He has also published 45 articles and book chapters in, i.a., *Law and Practice of International Courts and Tribunals, Rivista di diritto internazionale, Rivista del diritto della navigazione*, the *Max Planck Encyclopedia of Public International Law* and in a number of edited volumes.

Sienho Yee
is Changjiang Xuezhe Professor of International Law and Chief Expert, Wuhan University Institute of Boundary and Ocean Studies and Institute of International Law, China; Editor-in-Chief, *Chinese Journal of International Law*; member of Institut de droit international and the Bar of the US Supreme Court and adviser in international litigation; AALCO Special Rapporteur on Customary International Law; formerly Sub-reporter on ICJ matters for the ILA Study Group on UN Reform and chair of the ILA American Branch Committee on Interstate Dispute Settlement. He served as the principal presenter on applicable law in the seminar organized in 2016 by the ICJ for its 70th anniversary and lectured on *jus cogens* and the ICJ at The Hague Academy in 2012.

PART 1

General Issues

Brèves remarques sur la contribution de l'Académie de droit international de la Haye au développement du droit international

Yves Daudet

Le professeur Djamchid Momtaz est membre du Curatorium de l'Académie de droit international de La Haye où il a donné en 2014 le prestigieux cours général qui fut unanimement apprécié et dont la publication sera d'un grand apport pour le *Recueil des cours*.

Une courte note sur « le rôle de l'Académie de droit international dans le développement du droit international » m'a donc semblé appropriée en hommage à celui qui fut aussi membre de la Commission du droit international et donc, précisément, au premier plan des opérations de développement progressif du droit international. Ce double titre de compétence justifie donc de se pencher sur le thème de la doctrine dans le développement du droit international à travers le prisme de l'Académie de La Haye.

La question de savoir comment et par quelle autorité le droit international est développé consiste à s'interroger sur le rôle des sujets de droit international et sur celui des juges et des arbitres pour ce qui est d'une possible action « directe » résultant de créations normatives par les Etats, de reconnaissance de l'existence de coutumes par la Cour internationale de Justice ou, éventuellement d'autres juges ou des arbitres ou de créations prétoriennes par exemple l'établissement de règles en matière de délimitation des espaces maritimes par la Cour au terme d'une jurisprudence longuement élaborée. Ces actions peuvent être qualifiées de « directes » pour la simple raison qu'elles viennent concrètement combler un espace vide ou incertain du droit international et, ce faisant, le développent. On a beau dire que la fonction du juge ne consiste qu'à trancher un litige par une décision qui n'a de force jugée qu'entre les parties, il est bien évident que l'existence aujourd'hui d'une jurisprudence abondante a directement développé le droit international et se trouve consolidée par la Cour elle-même qui se réfère constamment à sa propre jurisprudence ainsi réaffirmée et renforcée. La « res judicata » a finalement un effet davantage procédural en ce qu'elle interdit de revenir devant le juge que de fond car, en termes de prévisibilité et même en l'absence d'une règle de précédent, ce qui a été jugé constitue une position assez fixée pour que la Cour elle-même considère qu'elle ne pourra pas désormais facilement s'en écarter. Un effet créateur de droit s'est donc réalisé. L'adoption de textes, souvent de grandes conventions largement ratifiées ou expressions coutumières, contribuent aussi à la réduction des « lacunes du droit international » affectant autrefois un droit international qui aujourd'hui figure de moins en moins une peau de léopard et dont le développement est réalisé de manière non médiatisée par les acteurs officiels, Etats, organisations internationales, juges etc.

De ce point de vue de l'analyse, la doctrine visée à l'article 38 du statut de la Cour internationale de Justice présente une caractéristique différente qui est moins d'être, selon les termes du texte, « auxiliaire » que d'être « indirecte » et de jouer ainsi un rôle médiatisé pouvant inspirer les acteurs du développement du droit international, sans contribuer à celui-ci de manière directe. Ainsi, la Cour ne fait pas de référence expresse dans ses arrêts à tel auteur ou à telle publication doctrinale. Les juges cependant lisent la doctrine, sont ou ont été eux-mêmes la doctrine en d'autres circonstances et peuvent en tout cas s'en inspirer pour déterminer leur position qui se reflètera dans la décision rendue ou dans une opinion séparée qui précisément présente parfois, sous la plume de certains juges, un aspect doctrinal.

Les modalités d'élaboration des conventions de la Conférence de La Haye de droit international privé conduisent à une observation du même ordre : le caractère marqué de technique juridique des sujets faisant l'objet des conventions adoptées sous ses auspices conduit les Etats à désigner des spécialistes de droit international privé pour les représenter. Ils sont souvent des professeurs de cette discipline qui, sous réserve des instructions qui leur ont été données, adoptent des positions évidemment dans la ligne de leurs opinions doctrinales qu'on les reverra exprimer ensuite – ou qui les avaient préalablement exposées – dans un cours à l'Académie. Il en va de même des grandes conférences, notamment de codification et de développement du droit international, qu'elles fassent ou non suite à des travaux de la Commission du droit international, dont les délégations comprennent également souvent des universitaires. L'exemple donné par le professeur Djamchid Momtaz est emblématique à cet égard.

Toute doctrine, néanmoins n'est cependant pas bonne à prendre ! L'article 38 précise que la doctrine à considérer doit être celle des « publicistes les plus qualifiés ». Faute de l'existence, difficilement concevable, d'une procédure de « qualification » internationale, la reconnaissance de celle-ci résulte de la « notoriété » qui s'établit d'une manière assez informelle, reposant sur la « fama » et donc peu rigoureuse. A cette appréciation relativement diffuse et teintée de subjectivité s'ajoutent des éléments plus objectifs tels que l'appartenance à l'Institut de droit international, la fréquence des apparitions à la Cour internationale de Justice, la participation, à des arbitrages etc.

L'Académie de droit international de La Haye peut également être considérée comme un élément sérieux de certification de la qualification d'un auteur et un instrument significatif de développement du droit international. En effet, elle peut être perçue comme un « *creuset* » de la doctrine des publicistes les plus qualifiés que l'on trouve parmi les professeurs invités à y donner un cours. Elle peut aussi, si on se tourne vers ses auditeurs être vue comme un « *relais* » par le message qui leur est transmis et que certains d'entre eux sauront mettre en œuvre et contribuer ainsi à l'établissement d'une « société internationale de droit ».

En tant que « *creuset* » de la doctrine, l'Académie s'enorgueillit en effet d'accueillir pour donner des cours les meilleurs représentants de la doctrine du droit international public ou privé ainsi que, pour certains des directeurs de son centre de recherches, les meilleurs espoirs de celle-ci. Cela ne signifie pas que les choix ne soient pas parfois discutés et qu'à telle personnalité invitée il aurait mieux valu préférer telle autre qui ne l'a pas été. Surtout, il est bien évident que n'être pas invité à l'Académie ne signifie pas qu'on ne le mérite pas ! En effet, on ne peut exclure des oublis, il y a des empêchements, des imprévus, et aussi la contrainte d'essayer de réaliser un certain équilibre géographique qui peuvent expliquer des absences surprenantes. Un signe en tout cas ne trompe pas : la satisfaction exprimée par ceux qui reçoivent une invitation surtout lorsque, quelques années après une précédente invitation pour délivrer un enseignement, celle-ci porte sur le cours général, consécration suprême.

Le cours général n'est en effet nullement une répétition du cours de droit international général au programme de nombreuses universités, qui serait d'ailleurs compacté en un nombre d'heures plus réduit. Il est en réalité le fruit d'une pensée sur le droit international développée au fil d'années de recherches, de réflexions et d'écritures permettant aux plus brillants tenants de la doctrine d'offrir une vision distanciée et critique conduisant les auditeurs à une quête d'approfondissement de la matière ou, parfois aussi, à des remises en cause de celle-ci. D'un cours général émanent un certain nombre d'idées forces qui reflètent le plus souvent les préoccupations du moment ainsi que le montre Robert Kolb dans son ouvrage sur *Les cours généraux de droit international de l'Académie de La Haye* contenant des développements pertinents sur l'esprit et l'évolution de ceux-ci. Aux messages ainsi recueillis par ceux qui les suivent comme ceux qui les lisent une fois publiés et voient leur savoir s'enrichir, s'ajoute un effet d'inspiration possible des « faiseurs de droit » évoqués plus haut. On ne peut en effet négliger dans les opérations de développement du droit international l'impact d'environ 130 cours généraux de droit international public ou privé auxquels s'ajoutent plusieurs centaines de cours spéciaux pour constituer dans un ensemble de 380 volumes du *Recueil des cours de l'Académie de droit international,* une véritable encyclopédie du droit international exprimant la temporalité de celui-ci et aidant ainsi à son développement réfléchi au regard du contexte du moment.

Il n'est cependant pas certain que l'Académie ait su parfaitement rendre compte de l'universalité du droit international et de la diversité de la société internationale. Si la centaine de nationalités qui y est représentée par les 600 auditeurs de chaque été auxquels s'ajouteront en 2019 ceux de la session d'hiver est un indéniable succès, le même pluralisme ne se rencontre pas parmi les professeurs. Il a curieusement fallu attendre 2014 pour qu'un cours général de droit international public soit donné par un Asiatique, précisément le professeur Djamchid Momtaz, tandis que le professeur Georges Abi-Saab et le juge Bedjaoui avaient été précédemment les seuls représentants du continent africain et du monde arabe, le troisième ayant été en 2016 le juge Mohammed Bennouna, tandis que, plus longtemps avant, le juge uruguayen Eduardo Jimenez de Arechaga assurait une présence de l'Amérique latine, réaffirmée longtemps plus tard par le professeur Antonio Cançado-Trindade, élu par la suite à la Cour internationale de Justice. Le reproche d'être trop « occidentale » est parfois adressé à l'Académie, y compris par les auditeurs eux-mêmes, quelle que soit leur appréciation positive des cours généraux. Cette situation a pu se justifier par l'origine européenne du droit international combinée avec la densité du tissu universitaire en Occident. Cette justification n'est aujourd'hui plus guère fondée : le droit international du XXIème siècle, même si l'influence occidentale y perdure, est marqué par une plus grande variété d'influences et un nombre considérable d'universités ont été créées dans les divers pays du monde. Peut être ne sont-elles pas assez connues ou l'Académie n'y a-t-elle pas encore assez pénétré ?

« Creuset » de la doctrine favorisant le développement du droit international, elle est aussi un « *relais* » de celui-ci.

D'une certaine manière, on pourrait penser qu'en dispensant des cours de droit international l'Académie ne fait rien d'autre qu'une université offrant une formation à ses étudiants. Il n'en est rien. Si l'Académie est présentée ici comme un relais, c'est précisément parce qu'elle permet d'aller au-delà de la simple transmission d'un savoir. Elle se situe entre l'Université d'une part et la vie internationale d'autre part à laquelle participeront ceux de ses auditeurs qui parviendront à réaliser le rêve de tous. Cela se comprend dès l'abord : Il suffit d'observer les auditeurs à la grille d'entrée du Palais de la paix le premier jour de la session pour mesurer l'impact du symbole qui s'offre à leurs regards. La Cour sur la droite, l'Académie sur la gauche, la CPA au centre. C'est la réalité du droit international qu'ils s'apprêtent à toucher du doigt et l'impression est forte. Cela se fera d'abord et surtout par les cours que l'on vient d'évoquer, souvent donnés par de grands noms dont ils vont découvrir le visage et la façon d'être. Mais il ne faut pas négliger l'environnement dans lequel ils sont plongés. Car c'est bien d'immersion dont il faut parler pour décrire un programme qui du matin au soir est totalement consacré au droit international et concentré sur lui. Aux cours succèdent les séminaires et aux séminaires les conférences, les visites d'institutions internationales, les rendez vous inoubliables auprès de juges de la Cour, puis les accueils dans les ambassades où les acteurs de la vie diplomatique leur découvrent les aspects diversifiés de leurs fonctions. *Last but not least*, dans les intervalles de ces activités la découverte de l'autre, les échanges de doctorants avec d'autres doctorants venus d'ailleurs, la prise de conscience que les nationaux d'un pays ne sont pas nécessairement le reflet des régimes de ces mêmes pays et que la rencontre entre eux est permise là où les dirigeants se l'interdisent. Les exemples sont légion de dialogues réputés impossibles et qui pourtant se déroulent avec un évident effort pour rechercher les moyens pacifiques et le secours du droit international plutôt que de penser recourir à la force. C'est donc une démonstration de paix par le droit que les auditeurs s'administrent à eux-mêmes et il ne faut pas sous-estimer le fait que parmi ces centaines d'auditeurs, tous de bon niveau car généralement parmi les meilleurs de leurs universités nationales, motivés et désireux d'embrasser, sous un angle ou un autre, une carrière internationale, certains d'entre eux occuperont des positions importantes, voire de premier plan. Si, un jour au pouvoir, ils n'oublient ni les leçons qu'ils ont suivi à l'Académie ni les serments qu'ils ont faits à La Haye, alors en effet, l'Académie aura bien été un « relais » entre le monde du savoir et le monde de l'action l'un et l'autre marqués de l'empreinte du droit international et de la culture de la paix.

Quelques remarques sur la place du droit au sein des organisations internationales

Pierre Michel Eisemann

Contribuer à un volume de mélanges destiné à honorer un maître ou un collègue, c'est toujours l'occasion de revenir sur le passé et sur les moments qui ont vu se former la relation privilégiée entre l'auteur et le dédicataire. En l'espèce, il faut retourner, après près d'un demi siècle, sur le campus de Nanterre où l'un et l'autre avons fait nos premières armes universitaires.

Alors que je venais de m'inscrire en thèse, je postulais à un emploi d'assistant et je fus recruté par ce qui était alors la Faculté de droit et des sciences économiques de Nanterre. Ainsi, deux ans après les évènements de mai 1968 (dont les prodromes s'étaient manifestés dès le 22 mars à Nanterre) qui ont durablement ébranlé les anciennes structures universitaires françaises, je devais commencer ma carrière d'universitaire sur ce campus de l'ouest parisien en voie de construction où les nouveaux bâtiments (déjà décorés des slogans les plus divers) le disputaient aux terrains encore vagues. Près de la voie du chemin de fer, l'un des côtés du quadrilatère formant le campus était réservé aux juristes et aux économistes. Ces derniers bénéficiaient du bâtiment G qui présentait la particularité d'être pourvu d'ascenseurs accessibles aux étudiants (un privilège qui, disait-on, était dû au fait que l'emplacement aurait été originellement destiné à l'agrandissement de l'Institut d'études politiques de Paris qui, en fin de compte, n'aurait pas estimé le lieu digne de lui). Les juristes, quant à eux, étaient logés dans le bâtiment F voisin, quasi identique si ce n'est qu'il ne comportait qu'un minuscule ascenseur qui, selon une terminologie déjà bien datée à l'époque, était « réservé à MM. les professeurs ». Outre les amphithéâtres et les salles de travaux dirigés, l'endroit le plus important était certainement la salle des professeurs, une salle ouverte à tous les enseignants sans distinction de grade et où chacun possédait son casier. C'est là que les quelque soixante-dix assistants – qui ne possédaient pas de bureau individuel – se retrouvaient régulièrement. Je ne peux qu'éprouver une légère nostalgie pour cette époque où nous pouvions échanger quelle que fût notre spécialité et développer, non seulement un certain esprit de corps, mais de véritables amitiés qui perdurèrent lorsque, devenus professeurs, nombre d'entre nous se retrouvèrent sur la colline du Panthéon.

C'est sans doute dans cette salle que je rencontrais pour la première fois Djamchid. Nous étions tous deux internationalistes et donc intégrés à l'équipe d'assistants formée autour du titulaire du cours de droit international public, le professeur Hubert Thierry, dont le « chef d'état-major » était Jean Combacau, bientôt brillant major de son concours d'agrégation. Mon aîné de peu d'années, Djamchid m'avait devancé à Nanterre et il était déjà proche de la soutenance de sa thèse consacrée au régime juridique du fonds des mers et des océans au-delà des limites de la juridiction nationale. En tant qu'assistant novice, je n'ai pu qu'être impressionné par son aménité souriante et sa simplicité. Point de bizutage mais, tout au contraire, un accueil amical et fraternel de sa part facilita grandement mon intégration. Nos relations et notre amitié ne se sont jamais interrompues alors même qu'il avait quitté la France pour occuper un poste de professeur à l'Université de Téhéran. Tout au long de nos carrières respectives nous restâmes en contact, intervenant d'ailleurs chacun dans l'université de l'autre. Ce fut ainsi toujours un bonheur de pouvoir faire intervenir Djamchid devant mes étudiants qui appréciaient ses enseignements présentés de la manière la plus lumineuse et dans un français d'une rare élégance que plus d'un pouvait lui envier.

Excellent professeur, Djamchid Momtaz fut naturellement, au fil des années, directement mêlé à la vie internationale notamment en tant que membre de la Commission du droit international ou comme jurisconsulte près le ministère iranien des Affaires étrangères, ce qui lui valut de participer à de nombreuses négociations et de siéger dans plusieurs organisations internationales. C'est en référence à ces dernières activités – et en me fondant sur ma propre expérience en la matière – que je voudrais maintenant évoquer quelques aspects du rôle du droit et des juristes au sein des organisations internationales. J'aborderai cette question sous deux angles : d'abord en évoquant la fonction de conseiller juridique (prenant celui-ci comme une sorte de personnification du droit au sein de secrétariat), ensuite en me penchant sur le rapport au droit des délégués représentant les États membres.

Il faut, cependant, rappeler au préalable que le droit est rarement au centre des préoccupations des organisations intergouvernementales. Si l'Union européenne a été qualifiée de « communauté de droit », elle fait plutôt figure d'exception car la plupart des organisations sont essentiellement centrées autour de préoccupations politiques ou bien encore techniques. Dès lors, les juristes n'y jouent qu'un rôle marginal et leur nombre est souvent très limité au sein du secrétariat tout comme au sein des délégations. On ne peut que le regretter car la qualité du travail d'une organisation internationale – qu'il s'agisse de ses organes directeurs ou du secrétariat – suppose un respect scrupuleux des règles de fonctionnement de l'institution. Or, c'est loin d'être toujours le cas du fait de la faiblesse de la « culture juridique » régnant au sein de nombre de ces organisations.

1 La place du conseiller juridique au sein d'une organisation internationale

Même s'ils jouent un rôle essentiel au sein de l'organisation, la mission des conseillers juridiques est souvent assez mal connue, y compris des autres membres du secrétariat et des représentants des États membres. Ainsi, lorsque, en 1999, l'Organisation des Nations Unies publia un recueil d'articles de conseillers juridiques et de praticiens du droit international[1], très peu nombreux furent ceux qui présentèrent une véritable réflexion sur leur métier[2]. On ne dispose donc malheureusement pas de beaucoup de témoignages directs dévoilant les états d'âme de ceux qui remplissent cette fonction extrêmement délicate, plus encore que celle du jurisconsulte d'un gouvernement car ils ont en face d'eux non seulement le plus haut fonctionnaire de l'organisation mais également l'ensemble des États membres.

Dans sa préface au recueil susmentionné, le Secrétaire général de l'époque, Kofi A. Annan, écrivait, de manière assez conventionnelle, que « [l]es conseillers juridiques des États et des organisations internationales, de même que les praticiens du droit international, sont parmi ceux qui se dévouent le plus à la cause du respect du droit international »[3]. Mais qu'en est-il concrètement ?

La première des questions concerne la présence même, au sein de l'organisation concernée, d'un conseiller juridique. On pourrait penser qu'il est de l'ordre naturel des choses que toute organisation internationale soit dotée d'un tel conseiller mais ce n'est pas nécessairement le cas. Si l'on observe l'existence d'un emploi de conseiller juridique dans toutes les grandes organisations, il en est de taille plus modeste qui n'en prévoient pas. Or, si l'on peut comprendre

---

1 *Collection of Essays by Legal Advisers of States, Legal Advisers of International Organizations and Practitioners in the Field of International Law / Recueil d'articles de conseillers juridiques d'États, d'organisations internationales et de praticiens du droit international*, New York : United Nations, 1999, xii-524 p.

2 On ne trouve dans cet ouvrage que deux approches générales, respectivement proposées par F. Maupain du BIT (« Gardien du patrimoine ou inventeur juridique ? Le rôle du conseiller juridique d'une organisation international face au changement », p. 259-283) et par A. A. E. Noll de l'UIT (« The Role of the Legal Adviser of an Intergovernemental Organization », p. 285-313), tandis que I. F. I. Shihata de la Banque mondiale (« The Role of the World Bank's General Counsel », p. 315-328) et A. A. Yusuf de l'Organisation des Nations Unies pour le Développement Industriel (« The Role of the Legal Adviser in the Reform and Restructuring of an International Organization: the Case of UNIDO », p. 329-350) se limitèrent à évoquer leurs propres fonctions.

3 Ibid., p. x.

qu'une organisation technique ne comprenant que quelques agents puisse se contenter des services de consultants externes, le fait qu'une organisation de taille moyenne estime possible de se dispenser des services d'un juriste permanent révèle un singulier manque de sagesse de la part des États membres acceptant ainsi de reléguer le droit à une place par trop subalterne. Une telle situation ne peut qu'être source de dysfonctionnements – pour ne pas dire de situations contentieuses – qu'il aurait été sage et prudent d'éviter en s'attachant les services d'un conseiller juridique.

La seconde question est celle du choix du conseiller juridique et elle s'articule en deux interrogations distinctes. D'une part, il convient de s'interroger sur l'instance la plus appropriée pour procéder à la sélection : faut-il laisser toute liberté pour ce faire au plus haut fonctionnaire de l'organisation ? Le choix doit-il relever de son cabinet ? Faut-il faire intervenir un comité technique (ou politique) *ad hoc* ? Doit-on demander à celui qui quitte ses fonctions de choisir son successeur ? D'autre part, on peut se demander où il convient de rechercher celui qui aura la responsabilité d'apporter ses conseils en matière juridique : doit-on privilégier un recrutement interne (généralement accompagné d'une promotion) ? Est-il préférable de faire appel à un juriste venant d'une autre organisation internationale ? à un praticien privé externe ? à un juriste ou à un magistrat d'un État membre ? ou encore à un universitaire ? Il n'y a évidemment pas de réponse simple à de telles questions et on peut aisément concevoir la difficulté à trouver la personne idoine. Non seulement cette dernière doit posséder de solides compétences juridiques et être capable de maîtriser des domaines très variés du droit mais elle aura également à montrer son aptitude à s'adapter au cadre de travail particulier que constitue l'organisation concernée ainsi qu'à la spécificité de la fonction. S'il peut être relativement aisé de vérifier les compétences techniques d'un candidat, il l'est beaucoup moins d'évaluer son autorité et son sens de l'indépendance, sa rapidité de réaction, sa capacité à diriger une équipe... sans compter sa subtilité et son sens diplomatique ! Dès lors, si le choix revient naturellement en dernier ressort au plus haut fonctionnaire de l'organisation, il serait hautement souhaitable que la procédure de sélection du conseiller juridique fasse intervenir un certain nombre de personnes qualifiées (dont certaines devraient être extérieures à l'organisation) afin qu'elles confrontent leurs évaluations et puissent ainsi donner un avis aussi objectif que possible sur chacun des candidats.

Évoquer les qualités attendues d'un conseiller juridique conduit tout naturellement à la troisième question qui est celle de la définition du rôle de celui-ci. Le conseiller juridique est bien entendu, avant toutes choses, le jurisconsulte de l'organisation qui l'emploie et, dans ce cadre, le conseiller direct du secrétaire ou du directeur général, mais il exerce une double fonction car il est également, *volens nolens*, conduit à répondre aux sollicitations des États membres.

Lorsqu'il agit en sa première qualité, le conseiller juridique peut être écartelé entre deux rôles très différents. D'un côté, il est une sorte de « grand-prêtre » ou, pour reprendre une formule d'un ancien conseiller juridique du Bureau international du travail, le « gardien vigilant du droit et de la loi »[4]. Il lui appartient de proposer son analyse juridique, de rappeler les précédents et d'appeler sans cesse au respect de la règle de droit et des procédures établies. Ce faisant, il exerce pleinement sa fonction de conseil quitte à s'opposer à ceux qui, au sein de l'organisation, entendent s'affranchir de la légalité, soit par simple ignorance, soit de manière volontaire pour parvenir à un résultat qu'il aurait été plus difficile voire impossible d'atteindre autrement. C'est dans ce dernier cas que le conseiller juridique doit savoir montrer tout à la fois son caractère et son talent diplomatique. De fait, il n'est que rarement en position de faire prévaloir hiérarchiquement son point de vue, notamment lorsqu'il se trouve face au plus haut fonctionnaire de l'organisation. Ce dernier est, quant à lui, soumis à des influences contradictoires notamment lorsque certains de ses collaborateurs le pressent de prendre une décision – dont ils vantent l'opportunité politique ou d'autres avantages – quitte à contourner les règles juridiques. Pour faire prévaloir son point de vue, le conseiller juridique doit alors compter sur son aura personnelle – qui découle essentiellement du respect et de la confiance qu'il aura su gagner – mais aussi de ses talents de pédagogue et de son imagination technique. En effet, s'il doit parvenir à faire comprendre pour quelles raisons telle décision ou action serait contraire au droit et quelles seraient les conséquences néfastes d'une violation de ce dernier, il lui appartient, dans le même temps, de faire preuve de créativité et de proposer une voie alternative permettant de parvenir légalement au résultat recherché. Il peut cependant être confronté à des cas dans lesquels il n'y a pas d'alternative légale – par exemple, la nomination d'une personne ne répondant pas aux conditions requises par les textes réglementaires – et, face à une telle situation, l'honneur du conseiller juridique consistera à défendre le respect du droit, quitte à déplaire. Il est important que son pouvoir de conviction soit fortement établi car, ses avis demeurant le plus souvent confidentiels, il risquera de se voir reproché, par la suite, de ne pas avoir été un gardien assez vigilant du droit et de la loi (pour reprendre l'expression de Francis Maupain) alors même qu'il avait fait tout ce qui était en son pouvoir pour tenter de s'opposer à l'édiction de l'acte illégal,

---

4 Maupain, *op. cit.*, note 2, p. 259.

une situation pour le moins inconfortable dont son obligation de réserve l'empêchera de sortir.

Dans le cadre de sa fonction de jurisconsulte, le conseiller juridique est également conduit à défendre son institution vis-à-vis des tiers, qu'il s'agisse des États membres, des agents (dans le cadre du contentieux de la fonction publique internationale), des contractants ou de toutes autres personnes ou entités en relation avec l'organisation. Que cette dernière ait agi dans le respect du droit ou non, il lui appartiendra, comme à tout avocat, de défendre et de justifier l'action de l'institution qu'il représente et, dans le cadre d'une procédure contentieuse, de s'efforcer de minorer les conséquences néfastes pour l'organisation de l'acte irrégulier qu'elle aurait pu commettre. On pourrait penser que l'exercice de ce rôle de « défenseur » est quasi mécanique et qu'il n'appelle pas à une réflexion particulière du « conseil », ce dernier étant simplement appelé à utiliser ses compétences techniques et ses qualités de plaideur au secours de la défense de l'organisation. Tel n'est pourtant pas le cas car il appartient également au conseiller juridique de faire entendre sa voix quant à l'opportunité et à la nature de la réaction de l'organisation. Cette dernière agit sous le regard de ses États membres, de ses agents et de l'opinion publique en général et il peut être contreproductif de tenter de contester l'illégalité d'un acte ou la responsabilité de l'organisation contre toute évidence. L'acceptation des conséquences d'un acte illicite et des conséquences pécuniaires qu'elle implique peut se révéler plus opportune qu'une dénégation difficile à maintenir. Il en est ainsi, par exemple, dans le domaine contractuel ou bien dans celui du contentieux du personnel, où il peut s'avérer particulièrement judicieux de recommander la recherche d'un compromis amiable avec le demandeur plutôt que de s'arc-bouter sur une défense aveugle de la position de l'organisation. Il est de l'office du conseiller juridique d'évaluer la situation juridique de l'organisation au regard de chaque contentieux et d'en tirer les conclusions qui s'imposent quant à la meilleure façon de mettre un terme au litige. De fait, une organisation internationale n'est sans doute pas un sujet de droit comme les autres car toutes sont porteuses de valeurs particulièrement importantes, notamment en matière de protection internationale des droits de l'homme. Il serait ainsi particulièrement préjudiciable à l'image d'une organisation intergouvernementale qu'elle nie ou minore sa responsabilité et son obligation de réparer, ou encore qu'elle s'abrite derrière ses immunités, après qu'elle a commis un manquement au droit ou provoqué un dommage. Il appartiendra au conseiller juridique de s'efforcer de faire prévaloir la réponse la plus en adéquation avec le respect des valeurs de l'organisation, tout en sachant que de nombreux autres facteurs (comme la crainte du précédent, la volonté explicite des États membres ou bien encore la situation financière de l'organisation) pourraient conduire vers une autre attitude que celle qu'il serait amené à préconiser[5].

On pourrait avancer que ce qui vient d'être dit jusqu'à présent n'est guère original et pourrait caractériser le travail de n'importe quel juriste, qu'il soit amené à travailler pour le compte d'une organisation internationale, d'une organisation non gouvernementale, d'un État, voire même d'une entreprise privée. Il est vrai que l'on peut relever nombre de points communs tenant à la nature même de la mission du jurisconsulte mais on se permettra de penser que le cadre de son action, à savoir une organisation intergouvernementale constituée en vue de la réalisation de missions d'intérêt commun et porteuse de valeurs universelles, astreint le conseiller juridique au respect d'une éthique professionnelle particulièrement rigoureuse.

Mais, outre cette considération essentielle, on doit également faire état du fait que le conseiller juridique d'une organisation internationale se trouve structurellement placé dans une position qui le distingue de ceux qui exercent ailleurs une fonction analogue. Alors que ces derniers œuvrent généralement au service d'une seule personne (président, ministre, directeur général...), le conseiller juridique d'une organisation internationale se voit régulièrement sollicité par d'autres que le secrétaire ou directeur général.

De fait, il n'est pas rare que les représentants des États membres le sollicitent directement pour obtenir son avis sur une question liée au fonctionnement de l'organisation. De telles demandes peuvent être exprimées de manière confidentielle à tout moment, ou encore publiquement à l'occasion de réunions officielles rassemblant les États membres. Face à ces demandes la situation du conseiller juridique peut s'avérer délicate dans la mesure où celui qui l'interroge peut poursuivre des objectifs éloignés – voire opposés – de ceux du secrétariat (dont le conseiller juridique fait lui-même partie). Dans le premier cas, il lui appartient de faire preuve de toute la diplomatie requise pour éviter de fournir à son interlocuteur des arguments que celui-ci pourrait utiliser à l'encontre de la politique conduite par l'organisation sans pour autant lui présenter une analyse juridiquement incorrecte ou par trop biaisée. Le cas échéant, le conseiller juridique pourra se réfugier derrière sa mission et rappeler que son rôle n'est pas de donner des avis juridiques aux États membres pris *ut singuli* quoi qu'en pensent les délégués qui estiment souvent – mais

---

5 Pour ne donner qu'un seul exemple de ces difficultés, on mentionnera la façon – largement contestée – dont l'Organisation des Nations Unies traite de manière générale la question de sa responsabilité dans le cadre des opérations de maintien de la paix et, plus particulièrement, s'agissant de la Mission des Nations Unies pour la stabilisation en Haïti (MINUSTAH) et de l'épidémie de choléra survenue dans l'île en 2010-2011.

à tort – que les membres du secrétariat sont également à leur service. Dans le deuxième cas, les échappatoires sont plus difficiles à trouver : au cours des débats d'une réunion des États membres, l'un d'eux invite le président à demander l'avis du conseiller juridique sur un point de procédure ou un élément de fond en discussion. Ce dernier (ou son représentant) qui siège à la tribune – se livrant généralement dans le même temps à une autre tâche – est ainsi sommé d'éclairer sur le champ l'assemblée sans disposer du temps de la réflexion. Si l'on peut attendre du conseiller juridique qu'il maîtrise parfaitement les règles de procédure, il ne saurait pour autant être considéré comme une sorte d'« encyclopédie juridique » capable de fournir instantanément une réponse à toutes les questions pouvant surgir dans l'esprit des délégués. Son art consistera alors à livrer une réponse parfois partielle mais suffisante pour permettre la poursuite des débats quitte à être conduit, le cas échéant, à revenir ultérieurement sur le point en cause. Il ne faudrait cependant pas croire que l'intervention du conseiller juridique soit purement technique et relève d'une simple connaissance de la règle de droit. Lorsqu'au cours des débats surgit ce que d'aucuns présentent comme une question de droit (appelant donc au respect d'une règle préexistante), il n'est pas rare qu'elle masque une divergence de fond extrêmement délicate – non dépourvue de prolongements politiques – qui constitue l'un des enjeux du débat. Ainsi, malgré la monotonie de bien des sessions, le conseiller juridique se doit de rester constamment sur le qui-vive et de suivre le sens général des échanges afin de percevoir la dynamique de la négociation en cours et, s'il devait être sollicité, d'être en mesure de livrer une réponse juridique qui soit en phase avec cette dynamique et qui ne bloque pas la souhaitable marche vers un consensus.

Revenant sur le rôle du conseiller juridique dans l'ensemble des situations qui viennent d'être évoquées, on ajoutera que son rôle de « gardien vigilant du droit et de la loi » ne doit pas le conduire à se borner à dire le droit d'une manière par trop rigide et univoque. Tout juriste sait l'importance de l'interprétation dans sa pratique professionnelle et il serait faux de penser qu'une seule lecture de la règle de droit s'impose nécessairement. Ainsi, sera-t-il conduit le plus souvent à mettre en lumière les diverses voies légales envisageables, à faire l'inventaire des possibles et à montrer les limites à l'action, plus qu'à devoir faire prévaloir une norme absolue. Non pas juge mais simplement conseiller, le jurisconsulte se doit de présenter l'ensemble des potentialités offertes par le droit applicable. Qui plus est, dans certaines situations, le conseiller juridique devra savoir aller plus loin et montrer sa capacité à innover, non pas en contribuant à violer le droit mais tout au contraire en participant à son développement. En effet, les organisations internationales sont pour l'essentiel régies par les règles juridiques qu'elles édictent elles-mêmes et ce corpus normatif doit être constamment adapté à des besoins qui se transforment avec l'évolution du temps et la diversification des activités. Ce travail normatif appartient aux États membres mais ces derniers doivent pouvoir compter sur le concours du conseiller juridique qui élaborera les propositions sur lesquelles ils auront à se prononcer. Ainsi, à sa fonction de « gardien » du droit existant, le conseiller juridique doit ajouter celle d'« inventeur » de règles nouvelles.

Cette brève présentation montre la diversité et la complexité des tâches assignées au conseiller juridique. Pour être à la hauteur de sa mission, il doit posséder les compétences professionnelles que nous avons déjà évoquées ci-avant, mais il n'est pas moins fondamental qu'il sache faire preuve d'indépendance tant face à sa hiérarchie que face aux États membres. S'agissant de ces derniers, il est de règle générale que les fonctionnaires internationaux doivent, pour paraphraser la Charte des Nations Unies, ne solliciter et n'accepter d'instructions d'aucun gouvernement ni d'aucune autorité extérieure à l'organisation. Cette obligation fait partie des principes essentiels de la fonction publique internationale et elle ne doit pas souffrir d'exceptions. Les choses sont nettement plus délicates lorsque l'on examine la situation qui est faite au conseiller juridique au sein même du secrétariat. En effet, s'il est certainement vrai que l'indépendance constitue avant tout une vertu personnelle que l'on peut associer à l'éthique même du conseiller juridique, on ferait preuve d'un idéalisme par trop marqué en voulant ignorer que l'exercice de cette indépendance sera plus ou moins aisé en fonction des conditions de travail qui lui sont faites. Sans prétendre à l'exhaustivité, on mentionnera trois éléments qui jouent un rôle important en la matière. Le premier est constitué par la durée de l'engagement du conseiller juridique. Si les contrats à durée indéterminée tendent à disparaitre dans les organisations internationales, il convient d'éviter le recours à des contrats de durée trop brève plaçant leur titulaire en perpétuelle situation de renouvellement. Certes, le conseiller juridique ne saurait revendiquer l'inamovibilité dont bénéficient la plupart des juges nationaux mais au moins pourrait-il voir son contrat aligné sur la durée des mandats des membres des juridictions internationales. Cette garantie lui faciliterait l'exercice d'une sorte de « droit de déplaire », en d'autres termes la faculté d'aller, sur la base du droit positif, à l'encontre des attentes de ses interlocuteurs. Le deuxième élément tient à la classe de l'emploi du conseiller juridique. Si aux Nations Unies ce dernier est secrétaire général adjoint, telle n'est nullement la situation générale et il peut arriver que le conseiller juridique soit un simple « professionnel » (P-5, par exemple). Quelle que puisse être sa force de caractère, il est aisé de comprendre que moins son rang sera élevé, plus il lui sera difficile de tenir tête à des interlocuteurs mieux placés dans la hiérarchie (secrétaires généraux adjoints, sous-secrétaires généraux, directeurs, administrateurs généraux). La question de la classe est liée à celle de la place du conseiller juridique dans l'organigramme de l'organisation. Il nous paraît essentiel que celui-ci soit directement rattaché au plus haut fonctionnaire de l'organisation et qu'il soit ainsi en mesure de communiquer directement avec lui sans passer par le moindre filtre. De fait, étant donné qu'il a pour charge de dire le droit au regard de l'ensemble des activités de l'organisation, il serait pour le moins paradoxal de le placer en position de dépendance de quiconque (et notamment d'une direction) hormis, bien entendu, le secrétaire ou directeur général qui possède le pouvoir ultime de décision.

L'indépendance du conseiller juridique – qui est consubstantielle à la bonne réalisation de sa mission – ne signifie pas pour autant qu'il puisse agir en total isolement du monde qui l'entoure. À l'indépendance, il doit nécessairement ajouter l'autorité, c'est-à-dire non pas le pouvoir d'imposer mais la capacité de faire respecter son point de vue. Et cette capacité découle non seulement de ses compétences techniques mais aussi de la confiance qu'il inspire à ses interlocuteurs. On imagine mal qu'il puisse être véritablement possible de faire travailler ensemble le plus haut fonctionnaire de l'organisation et son conseiller juridique si le dernier ne bénéficie pas de la confiance du premier. Quand bien même il se serait fait le défenseur avisé du droit au sein de l'organisation, le conseil juridique ne pourrait que s'effacer faute d'avoir su conquérir ou conserver l'oreille du chef du secrétariat. On pourrait imaginer que, dans une telle situation, le conseiller juridique trouve néanmoins appui du côté des États membres, mais le conflit interne au secrétariat révèlerait un grave dysfonctionnement porteur de futures difficultés et il serait périlleux de laisser perdurer un antagonisme latent ou une perte de confiance vivace. Le problème peut également se poser de manière inverse : le conseiller juridique dispose de la confiance du plus haut fonctionnaire mais il a perdu celle des États membres qui lui reprochent, par exemple, de privilégier la défense du pouvoir sur celle du droit. Il est évident qu'une telle situation est hautement délétère car la parole du conseiller juridique sera systématiquement discréditée quand bien même ses analyses seraient juridiquement pertinentes. Certes, en règle générale, le conseiller juridique ne sera pas mis directement en danger car ce ne sont pas les États membres qui possèdent le pouvoir de révocation mais on peut douter qu'il soit approprié de laisser perdurer une telle situation. Encore faut-il ajouter que la solution à de telles situations anormales ne se trouve pas dans la simple application du statut du personnel et que le conseiller juridique se trouve avant tout soumis aux commandements de l'éthique qui doit être la sienne.

Cette évocation du rôle du conseiller juridique au sein d'une organisation internationale contribuera, on l'espère, à faire prendre conscience de la difficulté de sa mission mais aussi de son caractère fondamental tant est essentiel le respect du droit au sein de l'organisation. À ce titre, il incarne la « conscience juridique » de cette dernière (ce qui rend critiquable toute organisation fractionnant les fonctions juridiques, en faisant échapper certaines à l'autorité du conseiller juridique) mais il n'est pas seul à traiter des questions juridiques. Même si l'effectif des directions juridiques est souvent modeste, il est rare que le conseiller juridique ne soit pas entouré d'une équipe. Parmi les qualités attendues de lui, on doit donc encore ajouter celles d'un chef et d'un animateur qui doit savoir s'entourer de collaborateurs compétents et créer un cadre de travail favorisant tant leur épanouissement personnel que la réalisation de leur tâche dans le respect de l'indépendance inhérente à la fonction.

On comprendra que je m'abstienne de citer des exemples nominatifs alors même que les considérations précédentes ont tracé un portrait en creux du conseiller juridique idéal. Il faut cependant savoir que perdure, dans la plupart des organisations internationales, le souvenir de ceux qui ont exercé leurs fonctions de manière exemplaire, gagnant ainsi le respect de tous. Ces modèles, qui incarnent de manière emblématique la noblesse de la mission du conseiller juridique, ne peuvent que servir d'inspiration à leurs successeurs.

2 Les représentants des États membres et le droit

Au sein d'une organisation internationale, le conseiller juridique et son service ne sont pas les seuls à approcher les questions juridiques. Ces questions émergent régulièrement au fil de l'action que ce soit de manière incidente ou bien principale (par exemple lorsqu'il s'agit d'élaborer un instrument normatif). Les délégués sont donc conduits à prendre part à des débats appelant une certaine connaissance technique des mécanismes et des règles juridiques alors qu'ils n'ont pas nécessairement la formation idoine pour traiter de ces sujets. De même que tous les juristes ne possèdent pas nécessairement les qualités requises des diplomates, tous les diplomates ne disposent pas automatiquement des compétences attendues du juriste. Dans un monde idéal on pourrait imaginer que chaque État membre inclue un juriste dans sa délégation, mais tel est loin d'être le cas. Seul un nombre très limité d'États procèdent de la sorte (et pas nécessairement les plus riches), le plus grand nombre laissant à un membre non spécialisé de sa délégation le soin de participer aux travaux juridiques. Ayant, comme le dédicataire de ces lignes, participé à de tels travaux, je voudrais évoquer quelques « figures » de délégués afin de mettre en lumière les problèmes rencontrés dans la négociation.

Avant toutes choses, il convient de rappeler que le droit constitue une technique plutôt qu'un ensemble normatif. Il offre un langage commun à des acteurs dont les intérêts divergent. Au sein d'une négociation internationale, le juriste – pas plus que le diplomate – ne peut prétendre posséder la vérité et il ne fait qu'exprimer, dans son jargon propre, les intérêts de son mandant. Le juriste-diplomate ne saurait donc se prévaloir d'une quelconque autorité du droit pour appuyer sa position, mais il est intellectuellement outillé pour dialoguer avec ses interlocuteurs qui fondent, eux aussi, leurs prétentions sur une argumentation juridique. L'argumentation est une construction intellectuelle reposant sur l'articulation d'un certain nombre d'éléments comprenant des principes et règles communément partagés. Pour dire les choses autrement – et sans doute de façon quelque peu simplificatrice –, les désaccords tiennent généralement moins à une contestation de l'existence même de la norme qu'à celle de sa portée (son interprétation) et de son applicabilité à une situation particulière, ou encore de la nécessité de l'articuler avec une autre norme pour répondre au problème posé.

Pour être mené de manière utile, ce jeu de l'argumentation suppose que les participants en maîtrisent les éléments constitutifs. Cela fait par définition partie des compétences professionnelles du juriste, mais pas nécessairement de celles du diplomate. S'il existe des diplomates-juristes (ou des juristes-diplomates), il en est d'autres dont la formation professionnelle n'a pas comporté la moindre initiation au droit. Ce n'est pas pour autant que ces derniers soient automatiquement fermés aux questions juridiques, certains pouvant faire preuve d'un réel intérêt et d'une véritable sensibilité à ces questions. Mais il ne faut cacher le fait qu'il en est d'autres qui demeurent totalement imperméables à toute discussion de nature juridique.

Dès lors, se pose une question relevant de l'art diplomatique : comment, dans un débat impliquant des points de droit, peut-on se faire entendre d'une assemblée dont tous les membres ne sont pas des juristes accomplis ? Sans doute convient-il d'admettre que l'on ne parviendra pas à convaincre tout le monde – ce qui n'est pas propre aux confrontations juridiques – mais il ne faudra pas, pour autant, négliger les efforts pédagogiques afin d'inclure le plus grand nombre dans la discussion et de montrer que l'approche juridique défendue relève de la raison, qui plus est une raison pouvant être partagée par tous. Mieux encore, au-delà des fractures politiques, le représentant d'un État membre aura pu gagner l'estime et la confiance de ses collègues qui, dans le cours normal des choses (c'est-à-dire hors de circonstances particulièrement conflictuelles), auront alors tendance à le suivre alors même lorsqu'ils ne saisissent pas nécessairement toutes les subtilités de son argumentation. Comme pour le conseiller juridique, la confiance et l'autorité reconnue par ses pairs constituent les meilleurs atouts du négociateur, atouts qui ne seraient toutefois rien s'ils n'étaient accompagnés d'une parfaite connaissance du point à l'ordre du jour.

Revenons maintenant sur la galerie de « figures » que nous avions annoncée. Le recours au droit dans la diplomatie multilatérale n'intervient pas uniquement lorsque sont discutées des questions juridiques car elles peuvent surgir à tout moment du débat, notamment lorsque se présente une difficulté d'application du règlement intérieur. Quel est alors le comportement de chaque délégué ? Sans aucune prétention scientifique et revendiquant une perception toute subjective, je distinguerai un certain nombre de personnages rencontrés au fil des ans.

Il y a le délégué « innocent » qui se caractérise par sa totale insensibilité à l'aspect juridique des questions débattues (généralement liée à son incompétence en matière de droit). Reste que ce délégué ne s'abstiendra pas nécessairement de prendre la parole et que, au moment de prendre la décision, sa voix comptera à l'égal de celles des autres. La question est donc de savoir comment arriver à le gagner à votre propre position sachant que vos arguments ne pourront principalement reposer sur la logique juridique puisqu'elle lui demeure étrangère. Il faudra donc savoir convaincre en diversifiant les arguments quitte à devoir mettre en avant ceux qui ne vous paraissent pas nécessairement les meilleurs.

À côté du premier, il y a le délégué « hostile ». Celui-ci voit avec la plus grande méfiance l'invocation de tout argument juridique car il privilégie le résultat qu'il entend obtenir. L'essentiel pour lui est de parvenir au résultat espéré et il ne voit le juriste que comme un perturbateur susceptible de soulever des objections venant contrarier son entreprise. Pour ce type de délégué, l'objectif à atteindre prime sur le respect de la légalité et il n'aura de cesse de disqualifier celui qui se fera l'écho de préoccupations juridiques. Il appartient alors à son interlocuteur de faire comprendre à l'ensemble des participants que la prise en compte de la règle de droit n'a pas pour conséquence de paralyser l'action mais bien plutôt de la conforter.

À l'inverse, le délégué « dangereux » est un obsessionnel et un maniaque du droit. Au nom d'une interprétation rigoriste – et pas nécessairement exacte – des règles applicables, il soulèvera d'innombrables objections quitte à mettre en danger la réalisation d'un objectif auquel il peut par ailleurs, non sans paradoxe, adhérer. Oubliant la part qu'il faut parfois savoir laisser à l'ambiguïté constructive, il ne manquera jamais d'imagination pour présenter des obstacles juridiques souvent très hypothétiques, au risque d'instiller le doute dans l'esprit des autres participants. Ce faisant il manifeste un excès de juridisme qui tend à paralyser l'action.

D'une autre espèce encore est le délégué « pervers ». Ce dernier possède de réelles compétences de juriste mais il avance – tout à fait volontairement – des analyses juridiques fausses ou captieuses en vue de justifier ses propres prétentions ou de déconsidérer celles de ses adversaires. Or, si certains se rendront compte sans difficulté de la fausseté des arguments ainsi avancés, d'autres pourront se laisser convaincre sans qu'il soit toujours facile de les détromper.

Reste enfin la figure du délégué « incontrôlable » dont le comportement est sans doute l'un des plus caricaturaux. Ce délégué est fier de son expertise juridique et il s'en prévaut ostensiblement. Malheureusement, quand bien même il aurait fait des études de droit et exercé des fonctions juridiques dans une vie antérieure, ses compétences se sont évanouies et il ne possède aucune réelle connaissance des règles et mécanismes juridiques pertinents. Ses prises de position, affirmées avec l'autorité qu'il se reconnaît à lui-même, ne sont dès lors que de pures divagations qui mettent en danger l'ensemble des travaux. Quoi qu'avancent d'autres délégués et parfois même le conseiller juridique pour rectifier ses dires, il persiste dans ses erreurs car il est certain de détenir la vérité. Or, ici encore, si certains participants seront à même de prendre avec recul ses élucubrations, d'autres pourront se laisser séduire par elles sans qu'il soit aisé de les détromper compte tenu des règles de courtoisie de mise dans le dialogue diplomatique qui interdisent une trop brutale réfutation. Faute d'avoir su lui faire entendre raison, il est alors indispensable d'arriver à endiguer la parole d'un tel délégué afin qu'il ne précipite pas la négociation vers l'échec.

Les cinq « figures » qui viennent d'être présentées ne décrivent fort heureusement pas l'ensemble des délégués participant aux débats et on ne saurait omettre la sixième, celle du délégué de qualité qui sait défendre les positions de l'État qu'il représente en articulant une argumentation raisonnable fondée sur une saine lecture du droit. La plasticité de ce dernier laisse place à des positions différentes bien qu'également justifiées par des arguments juridiques et l'on ne pourra s'attendre à une miraculeuse convergence des points de vue au seul motif que les divers interlocuteurs partagent une même approche technique. Il n'empêche que le recours au même langage – celui de l'argumentation juridique – permet un véritable dialogue et facilite la recherche du compromis. Tout en ne perdant pas de vue son obligation de veiller aux intérêts nationaux – ceux-ci n'étant toutefois pas toujours directement en jeu –, le représentant d'un État se doit de prendre en considération les positions des autres participants et de négocier de bonne foi. Il ne fait pas de doute que l'appartenance à une même communauté, celle des juristes, contribue à faciliter le dialogue et ce même lorsque le débat est imprégné d'une forte connotation politique.

Ces quelques observations sont loin d'épuiser la question du rôle du droit au sein des organisations internationales. Elles se bornent à jeter quelques lueurs sur le sujet en l'évoquant au travers du rôle du conseiller juridique et de la pratique des représentants des États membres. Elles sont aussi l'occasion de rendre l'hommage qui lui est dû à Djamchid Momtaz qui, profondément attaché à son pays, sert avec talent ce dernier au sein de nombreuses institutions internationales tout en faisant bénéficier ces dernières de son excellente connaissance du droit international et de son sens de la mesure.

The Iran Nuclear Deal: Some International-Law Aspects

Said Mahmoudi

1   Introduction

On 14 July 2015, the Islamic Republic of Iran brokered a deal with five permanent members of the UN Security Council, Germany and the High Representative of the European Union for Foreign Affairs. This was done through the adoption of a document entitled the Joint Comprehensive Plan of Action (JCPOA),[1] intended to put an end to an international crisis that Iran's nuclear program has caused since 2002.

The JCPOA contains a number of novelties as regards the mechanism for controlling Iran's nuclear program, its legal status, supervision of the participants' obligations, dispute settlement provisions, and the sanctions system. The agreed arrangement in the document also constitutes a novelty in respect to developing peaceful means for dealing with an assumed risk of a State becoming a new nuclear power.

The following will address some of the novel features of the JCPOA and their possible contribution to the development of the law of disarmament. The paper also deals briefly with the possible impact of this document on the definition of the rights and obligations of the Parties to the Treaty on the Non-Proliferation of Nuclear Weapons (NPT)[2] and of the members of the International Atomic Energy Agency (IAEA).[3]

2   Background to the Problem

Developments of the Iranian nuclear file, one of the top issues on the world political agenda between 2003 and 2015, can be conveniently divided into

---

1   For the text of JCPOA and its annexes, see UN Security Council Resolution 2231, dated 20 July 2015 http://www.un.org/en/ga/search/view_doc.asp?symbol=S/RES/2231(2015).
2   For the text of the NPT, see https://www.iaea.org/publications/documents/treaties/npt.
3   For the Statute of the IAEA, see https://www.iaea.org/sites/default/files/statute.pdf.

three periods.[4] The first period covers events during 2003–2005, when Iran's secret nuclear activities had been disclosed and the country tried to settle the problem through co-operation with the IAEA and negotiations primarily with France, Germany and the UK. The second period—between 2006 and 2012—coincided with the referral of the file to the Security Council and imposition of harsh sanctions against Iran by the Council and by the European Union (EU). Finally, the third period, 2013–2015, saw intensive serious negotiations, which resulted in the adoption of the JCPOA.

Iran joined the NPT[5] in 1970. Compliance of State Parties with their obligations is supervised by the IAEA. Such supervision must be regulated by a bilateral agreement—a Full-scope Safeguards Agreement—between each Member State and the IAEA. In the case of Iran, this agreement entered into force in 1974. Within the framework of the Safeguards Agreement, each State Party and the IAEA agrees on exactly how the Agency's supervision should be regulated with respect to e.g. the method and the time for informing the latter of the State's nuclear activities. This more detailed agreement, which is called the Subsidiary Arrangements, entered into force for Iran in 1976. An Additional Protocol was adopted in 1997 to enhance the IAEA's possibilities to supervise implementation of the Treaty. Iran signed the Protocol in 2003, but has not yet ratified it. Another measure that was adopted during the 1990s to strengthen the system of supervision of implementation was the amendment of the standard form for a safeguards agreement, and adoption of a new form, the Comprehensive Safeguards Agreement. The latter and its Revised Subsidiary Arrangements, like the Additional Protocol, are considered together in international law as a new legal accord in need of ratification by each Member State to become legally binding for that State. Iran's relation to the Revised Subsidiary Arrangements is a matter of controversy, as will be seen below.

The starting point for Iran's nuclear crisis was a press conference by the National Council of Resistance of Iran, a group in political opposition to the Islamic Republic of Iran, held in Washington DC on 14 August 2002. It was claimed in this conference that Iran was secretly building a plant for enrichment of uranium at industrial level in Natanz, a small town in central Iran. Various information that reached the IAEA following this claim and the

---

4 For a detailed and insightful description of the development of the Iranian nuclear file between 2002 and 2009, see Dj. Momtaz, 'Le programme nucléaire de l'Iran et le régime de non-prolifération nucléaire', in *Looking to the Futur, Essays on International Law in Honor of Michael Reisman*, Martinus Nijhof Publishers, 2010, pp. 989–1002.

5 Today, all UN Member States, except for North Korea—which withdrew from the Treaty in 2003—India, Israel, Pakistan and South Sudan, are parties.

findings of the Agency's own inspectors confirmed that Iran, in violation of its obligations under the Full-scale Safeguards Agreement, had for years been involved in various nuclear activities including injection of UF6 gas into a limited number of centrifuges without informing the IAEA.[6]

Iran tried to handle the situation and defy the risk of moving the issue from the IAEA to the Security Council due to the possible threat to international peace. This was done both by increasing its cooperation with the Agency and engaging in direct negotiations with France, Germany and the UK. The result of these negotiations was the Tehran Declaration of 21 October 2003, according to which Iran committed itself to promptly inform the IAEA of 'all its present and previous nuclear activities'. More importantly, Iran accepted to implement the Additional Protocol even before its ratification and to suspend uranium enrichment activities as long as negotiations with the three European Powers were going on.

The additional information that Iran submitted to the IAEA showed that the country had performed a number of enrichment and reprocessing tests during the 1990s without informing the Agency. The report of Director-General ElBaradei to the Board of Governors, which is the highest decision-making organ of the IAEA, declared in November 2003 that Iran had breached its obligations under the Safeguards Agreement on several accounts. At the same time, it underlined that there was no evidence that the previously undeclared nuclear material and activities were related to a nuclear weapons program.[7]

Continued negotiations between Iran and the three European countries resulted in the adoption of the Paris Agreement in 2004.[8] Accordingly, Iran accepted to voluntarily continue and extend its suspension to include all enrichment-related and reprocessing activities, specifically the manufacture and import of gas centrifuges and their components; the assembly, installation, testing or operation of gas centrifuges; work to undertake any plutonium separation or to construct or operate any plutonium separation installation, and all tests or production at any uranium conversion installation. The three

---

6 The details of these activities and Iran's initial hasty reactions to accusations and its useless denials are recorded in several studies, including H. Rouhani, *Amniyate Melli va Diplomaciye Hastehee (National Security & Nuclear Diplomacy)* [in Persian], Center for Strategic Studies, the Expediency Discernment Council of the System, Tehran, 2011; M. ElBaradei, *The Age of Deception, Nuclear Diplomacy in Treacherous Times*, Bloomsbury Publishing, 2012; S. H. Mousavian, *The Iranian Nuclear Crisis, A Memoir*, Carnegie Endowment for International Peace, 2012.
7 GOV/2003/75, 10 November 2003, para. 52.
8 The Agreement was published as an information circular by the IAEA in document INFCIRC/637 dated 26 November 2004.

European countries in response promised firm guarantees to Iran on nuclear, technological and economic cooperation.

In August 2005, when the three European Powers submitted their concrete cooperation proposals, this was considered by Iran as total humiliation. ElBaradei describes these proposals as not only poor in content and insignificant, but also arrogant.[9] In its response to France, Germany and the UK, Iran called the proposals 'colonial', and demanded that these countries apologize to the Iranian people for this.[10]

After the disappointing European proposals, Iran restarted injecting uranium oxide into a number of its centrifuges. This led to the adoption of a resolution by the IAEA Board of Governors declaring for the first time that Iran's many failures and breaches of its obligations to comply with the Safeguards Agreement constituted 'non-compliance'.[11] According to Article XII. C of the Statute of the IAEA, the Board of Governors is obliged to report cases of 'non-compliance' if it decides that failure of a Member State to fulfill its obligations indeed amounts such. Aware of this, Director-General ElBaradei had until August 2005 tried to avoid using this term in his reports to the Board. Instead alternative terms such as 'breach' or 'violation' were used.

When Iran in January 2006 informed the IAEA of its decision to resume the enrichment activities in Natanz, the IAEA Board of Governors reacted by adopting a resolution in February the same year referring Iran's nuclear file to the Security Council.[12] Iran has insistently considered the referral inconsistent with the requirements of IAEA's Statute and thereby illegal. According to Iran, the necessary requirements for such a referral, i.e. clear and firm evidence of the nuclear activities of Iran being in violation of the NPT or the Safeguards Agreement, had not been fulfilled. Iran distinguishes between the procedural obligation of timely informing the IAEA of a certain nuclear activity on the one hand, and the substantive obligation to abstain from unauthorized activities.

Pursuant to the Security Council involvement in the Iran nuclear file, the three European States expanded to include the remaining permanent

---

9 ElBaradei, supra, note 5, pp. 144 & 199.

10 This is mentioned in the book by Iran's chief negotiator and today's President, Hassan Rouhani. See supra, note 5, pp. 593–595. According to Rouhani, the three European countries indeed wanted Iran to fully stop its enrichment activities as an objective guarantee for the peaceful nature of the nuclear program, which was neither politically nor legally acceptable to Iran as a Party to the NPT.

11 Doc. DOV/2005/77 dated 24 September 2005, para. 1. Other cases of non-compliance before Iran were Iraq (1991), Romania (1992), North Korea (1993, 1994 and 2003) and Libya (2004).

12 Resolution GOV/2006/14 dated 3 February 2006.

members of the Council, i.e. China, the Russian Federation and the US. In June 2006, this group—also called 5+1 and later E3/EU+3—proposed a new package to Iran, which was popularly referred to as the 'carrots and sticks' proposal. The purpose was to give certain well-defined privileges to Iran if the country agreed to limit its nuclear activities. If it did not, sanctions would be imposed. The new package, compared with the previous set of proposals submitted by the three European Countries in August 2005, contained more tangible privileges for Iran and was drafted in more respectful language from the perspective of the recognition of Iran's rights. While Iran was preparing its answer, the Security Council adopted Resolution 1696 on the basis of Chapter VII of the UN Charter. The suspension of all enrichment activities became in this way legally binding on Iran.[13] ElBaradei wonders if the Resolution was logical or legal. In his view, the IAEA had no evidence to prove that Iran's nuclear program was also for military purposes. He argues that whereas enrichment of uranium for peaceful purposes is fully legal under the NPT, it is simply an exaggeration to claim that a limited number of centrifuges in a small laboratory threaten international peace and security.[14]

The Security Council's second and third resolutions imposing sanctions against Iran were adopted on 23 December 2006 and 24 March 2007 respectively.[15] They both strengthened existing limitations and introduced new sanctions. In a new effort to solve the problem, Iran took the initiative to a deal with the IAEA in August 2007, according to which all the remaining questions relating to the Iranian nuclear program should be answered within three months. In December 2007, when the IAEA and Iran were still working on the remaining questions, the U.S. National Intelligence Estimate (NIE)[16] on Iran's nuclear file was published. According to this assessment, even if Iran had previously had a nuclear weapons program, it was abandoned in 2003. This was strong support for the cautious position of the IAEA.

Iran gradually answered many of the remaining questions. The important exception was the suspected military studies within the framework of the nuclear program of which Iran was accused. Information about these studies had

---

13 Doc. S/RES/1696 (2006), para. 2.
14 ElBaradei, supra, note 5, p. 200.
15 Doc. S/RES/1737 (2006) and S/RES/1747 (2007).
16 According to Council on Foreign Relations, a National Intelligence Estimate (NIE) represents the U.S. intelligence community's most authoritative and coordinated written assessment of a specific national-security issue. Today, 17 government agencies and departments participate in drafting the documents. See http://www.cfr.org/iraq/national-intelligence-estimates/p7758.

been brought to the attention of to the IAEA by the US. The origin of this information, according to the US, was a laptop that had reached the US secret services indirectly. The US could not divulge its source to the IAEA, neither could it deliver many of the documents in the laptop memory. *A fortiori*, Iran could not be allowed to have access to these documents. Iran rejected these claims as fabricated and groundless, but eventually agreed to address questions relating to the suspected military studies within the framework of its agreement with the IAEA concerning all the remaining issues.

Security Council resolutions 1803 and 1835 in 2008[17] imposed new sanctions and thereby further pressure on Iran. During the summer of 2009, Israel submitted documents to the IAEA showing that Iran at least until 2007 had continued its nuclear military studies. The authenticity of these documents was questioned by the IAEA's experts.[18]

In September 2009 news of yet another undeclared Iranian fuel enrichment plant, in Fordow, close to the city of Qom, was circulated widely. The US considered that, due to its small size, Fordow could not be used for industrial enrichment. The only function, according to the US, could be military activities. Iran argued that, given the repeated threats of force by various American and Israeli officials, Fordow underground nuclear sites were established only as a supporting enrichment facility.[19] The IAEA strongly criticized Iran for not having informed the Agency of Fordow in time, thereby acting in breach of its obligations under the Subsidiary Arrangements of the Safeguards Agreement. According to the original version of Code 3.1 in the Subsidiary Arrangements from 1976, Iran was required to inform the IAEA of any new nuclear facilities at least 180 days prior to injection of gas into centrifuges. In the Modified Code 3.1 that appears in the Revised Subsidiary Arrangements of the 1990s, no reference is made to '180 days', but all parties are required to inform the Agency *before* approving any plan of new nuclear activities or commencing such an activity.

To compensate for its past failures, Iran approved the Revised Subsidiary Arrangements and the Modified Code 3.1 through exchange of notes with the IAEA in 2003.[20] However, pursuant to adoption of the Security Council's Resolution 1747 in March 2007, Iran informed the IAEA that it would suspend application of Modified Code 3.1 and would return to the previous

---

17   Doc. S/RES/1803 (2008) dated 3 March 2008 and S/RES/1835 (2008) dated 27 September 2008.
18   ElBaradei, supra, note 5, p. 291.
19   Ibid., pp. 294–300.
20   Rouhani, supra, note 5, p. 117.

arrangements.[21] The IAEA did not accept this and answered Iran that Modified Code 3.1 would remain applicable.[22] After disclosure of the Fordow enrichment plant in September 2009, Iran argued that it had not breached any legal obligation since it had suspended Modified Code 3-.1 in 2007 and was only bound by the requirements of the original version of the Code, which permits the parties to inform the IAEA of new nuclear facilities at least 180 days before injection of gas into centrifuges. The Agency was of the view that Iran's 2003 note on acceptance of Modified Code 3.1. was final and binding,[23] and Iran could not unilaterally withdraw or suspend it.[24]

In the meantime, the IAEA informed the US and the Russian Federation in the autumn of 2009 that Iran had long been asking the Agency to help her buy 20-percent-enriched uranium as fuel for a Tehran research reactor. The previous fuel had been imported many years ago and was about to finish. The reactor produced isotopes for medical purposes. Despite the initial positive response of the US and Russia, this did not materialize. In February 2010, Iran announced that it would produce its own 20-percent-enriched uranium. Consequently, the Security Council adopted a new resolution in June 2010[25] imposing far harsher sanctions. This was followed by a resolution by the IAEA Board of Governors in 2011[26] that for the first time clearly spoke of 'possible military dimensions' of Iran's nuclear program. This concept had appeared in the reports of the Director-General since February 2008 (GOV/2008/4). However, the relevant text was formulated cautiously not to imply a clear accusation.[27]

The standstill in negotiations between Iran and the 5+1 (E3/EU+3) somehow changed in 2013. Several factors could have contributed to this: the consequences of Security Council and EU sanctions; the change of government in Iran; the increased role of Iran in the political developments in Iraq and Syria; and modification of US policy *vis-à-vis* the Iranian nuclear file. Thus, several new efforts, formal and informal contacts between Iran and the 5+1 (E3/EU+3)

---

21 GOV/2007/22, paras. 22–14.
22 www.jurist.org/forum/2010/03/qom-enrichment-facility-was-iran-php.
23 GOV/2009/74, para. 27.
24 D. Joyner, 'Qom Enrichment facility', *Jurist*, 2010, http://jurist.org/forumy/2010/03/qom-enrichment-facility-was-iran.php.
25 S/RES/1929 (2010) dated 9 June 2010.
26 GOV/2011/69 dated 18 November 2011, para. 1.
27 This was done in ElBaradei's reports by a stronger emphasis on Iran's '*alleged*' studies (GOV/2006/15 and later reports). The emphasis was shifted in the reports of his successor, Yukiya Amano, to 'possible' military dimensions. This shift was despite the fact that no new facts about Iran's military activities had come forth after the American/Israeli accusations in 2009.

during 2012 and 2013, and a round of serious negotiations, led to adoption of the Joint Plan of Action in Geneva on 24 November 2013.[28] This was an interim agreement for further negotiations on a more detailed arrangement to ensure the peaceful nature of Iran's nuclear program and to end the sanctions against Iran.[29] The result of subsequent intensive contacts and negotiations during the following twenty months was the Joint Comprehensive Plan of Action (JCPOA), finalized on 14 July 2015 (Finalization Day).

The JCPOA was endorsed through Security Council Resolution 2231 on 20 July 2015 (Endorsement Day), and was formally adopted 90 days later, i.e. 18 October 2015 (Adoption Day). The participants started implementing it on 16 January 2016 (Implementation Day). The reasons for this unprecedented arrangement were among others a considerable lack of confidence and deep mutual suspicion, the political sensitivity of the matter both at national and international levels that could at any time quash the results of the finalized negotiations, and complications of the sanctions system.[30]

3   Structure of the Deal

The JCPOA is a comprehensive document of almost 150 pages. After the Preamble and General Provisions, the 36-paragraph substantive part describes in general terms the measures to which the two sides commit themselves and the timeframe for this. These measures, whose voluntary nature was particularly important for Iran to have underscored,[31] are explained under three general headings: Nuclear, Implementation Plan, and Dispute Resolution Mechanism.

The first section entitled 'Nuclear', which spells out the outline of the JCPOA participants' various undertakings (paras. 1–17), starts by declaring Iran's commitments with respect to limitations on the enrichment program

---

28   For the text of this document, see http://eeas.europa.eu/statements/docs/2013/131124_03_en.pdf.

29   For a full account of this interim agreement, see Dj. Momtaz, 'Garantir la nature exclusivement pacifique du programme nucléaire de l'Iran (Le Plan d'Action conjoint de 24 Novembre 2013)', I. Caracciolo, M. Pedrazzi and T. Vassalli di Dachenhausen (eds), *Nuclear Weapons: Strengthening the International Legal Regime*, Eleven International Publishing, 2015, pp. 45–74.

30   A description of the undertakings of both sides during all these various stages before the JCPOA's implementation started can be found in http://jcpoatimeline.csis.org/.

31   This is also mentioned in the paragraph preceding the substantive part of the JCPOA, which reads: 'Iran and E3/EU+3 will take the following voluntary measures within the timeframe as detailed in this JCPOA and its Annexes.'

and on stockpiles of enriched uranium (subsection A), limitations relating to the heavy water plant in Arak and reprocessing (subsection B), and Iran's undertakings regarding transparency and confidence-building measures. It then clarifies the commitments of the E3/EU +3 (paras. 18–33) with respect to termination or suspension of sanctions against Iran. The substantive part ends with general provisions regarding various stages of implementation of the JCPOA (paras. 34–35) and the dispute resolution mechanism (paras. 36–37).

The details of the two sides' undertakings are expressed in five comprehensive annexes. Annex I, which elaborates Iran's commitments, consists of 82 paragraphs and regulates, inter alia, all the steps Iran must take to limit its uranium enrichment and stocks as well as centrifuge manufacturing, and to build confidence through transparency; application of the Additional Protocol and Modified Code 3.1; to provide information about its past issues of concern, and to give access to undeclared locations and activities.

Annex II, which is by far the longest and most comprehensive part of the JCPOA, details all the steps that E3/EU + 3 shall take to terminate or suspend the sanctions imposed on Iran in relation to its nuclear program. Section A, deals with the EU sanctions, Section B the US sanctions. Both have targeted all vital sectors of Iran's economy such as banking and insurance, oil and gas, shipping, gold and precious metals, and software. In addition, the sanctions apply to listed persons, entities, and bodies. The timeframe for lifting various sanctions is provided for in Annex V.

A main argument of many developing countries including Iran is that they are not receiving the technical assistance necessary for peaceful nuclear activities they are entitled to under the NPT either from the IAEA or other Member States of that organization.[32] Annex III on civil nuclear cooperation can thus be seen as an undertaking by the E3/EU+3 to assist Iran in nuclear safety, safeguards, security, and waste management; and in redesigning the reactor in Arak.

For implementation of the JCPOA, a Joint Commission is established through Annex IV. This Commission consists of representatives of all seven participating States and that of the High Representative of the European Union for Foreign Affairs and Security Policy, who acts as the Coordinator. The Commission may establish working groups. Its main functions are to review and approve, inter alia, the final design of the modernized heavy-water

---

32   In the case of Iran, a recent example is the request of that country to receive fuel for its research reactor in Tehran. As was mentioned earlier, the IAEA forwarded this request to the US and the Russian Federation. In the absence of the positive result, Iran started producing its own 20 percent enriched uranium in the 2010.

research reactor, to review and approve plans submitted by Iran to initiate R&D on uranium-metal-based TRR fuel, to receive advance information about the specific project that will be undertaken at Fordow, to review and consult, to address issues arising from the implementation of sanctions lifting, to review and decide on proposals for nuclear-related transfers to or activities with Iran, and to review, with a view to resolving, any issue that a JCPOA participant believes constitutes non-performance by another JCPOA participant of its commitments under the JCPOA.

The Joint Commission will meet quarterly and at any time upon the request of a JCPOA participant to the Coordinator. Decisions are normally made by consensus.

The last annex—Annex V—contains an implementation plan for the undertakings of the participants as specified in Annexes I and II. This plan defines various dates as regards finalization of negotiations and adoption, entry into effect and implementation of the resulting document as described above.

4 Security Council Resolution 2231

As regards the Security Council resolutions imposing sanctions on Iran, Annex V to the JCPOA foresaw the adoption of a new Security Council resolution to both endorse the JCPOA and terminate all previous relevant resolutions, subject to re-imposition in the event of significant non-performance by Iran of its JCPOA commitments.[33] By adopting Resolution 2231,[34] the Security Council first endorses the JCPOA (para. 1) and calls upon Member States to take action to support its implementation (para. 2). It then decides (para. 7) that upon the receipt of a report from the IAEA confirming that all nuclear materials in Iran remain in peaceful activities, it would terminate the provisions of all seven previous resolutions relating to Iranian nuclear activities. It also decides that the provisions of the present resolution will also terminate ten years after JCPOA Adoption Day, i.e. 18 October 2025: At that date, the Security Council 'will have concluded that its consideration of the Iranian nuclear issue, and the item 'Non-Proliferation' will be removed from the list of matters of which the Council is seized.' (para. 8)

An important part of the Resolution is devoted to the dispute-settlement mechanism of the JCPOA, in which the Security Council has an important role. In essence, this part (paras. 10–15) details the conditions for reapplication of

---

33   Annex V, Article 18.
34   S/RES/2231 (2015) dated 20 July 2015.

the provisions of all previous relevant resolutions in the event of significant non-performance of commitments of one of the JCPOA participants.[35]

The whole text of the JCPOA is appended to Resolution 2231 as Annex A. In addition, a statement has been attached to the Resolution as Annex B. In this annex, certain provisions have been put forth 'to improve transparency and create an atmosphere conductive to the full implementation of the JCPOA.' The statement contains further views and understanding of E3/EU+3 of the JCPOA and its implementation, details that for various reasons did not fit in the JCPOA itself.

5 Salient Features of the Deal

5.1 *An Inherent Right to Enrich Uranium?*

From the perspective of international law relating to peaceful uses of nuclear energy and the law of disarmament, two core issues should be commented on. One basic question is whether Parties to the NPT have a right to enrich uranium for peaceful purposes. The position of Iran and of many other non-nuclear-weapons States is that such a right exists. This position is based on these countries' interpretation of Article IV (1) of the NPT, which stipulates: 'Nothing in this Treaty shall be interpreted as affecting the inalienable right of all the Parties to the Treaty to develop research, production and use of nuclear energy for peaceful purposes without discrimination and in conformity with Articles I and II of this Treaty.' Iran argues that enrichment is a constituent part of the nuclear fuel circle.[36]

Iran's claim of an inherent right to enrich and its interpretation of Article IV have been consistently repeated by various Iranian authorities and representatives in the IAEA and the UN.[37] Other non-nuclear-weapons countries such as Argentina, Brazil, Germany and Japan have their own enrichment programs,

---

35   For discussion, see infra.

36   The nuclear fuel circle is the series of industrial processes, which involve the production of electricity from uranium in nuclear power reactors. This circle starts with the mining and milling of uranium, conversion, enrichment and fuel fabrication. For more details, see http://www.world-nuclear.org/information-library/nuclear-fuel-cycle/introduction.

37   See, e.g., Iranian President Hassan Rouhani's statement after the adoption of the initial joint plan of action in Geneva in November 2013: https://www.washingtonpost.com/world/tehran-satisfied-with-nuclear-deal/2013/11/24/2836224e-5506-11e3-bdbf-097ab2a3dc2b_story.html?hpid=z1&tid=a_inl.

obviously based on the same legal argument. The formal position of these countries is that the NPT does not prohibit enrichment.[38]

The US has had a long-standing policy of opposing a right to enrich under the NPT.[39] This view is shared by France and the UK, whereas China and the Russian Federation recognize this right for all the Parties to the NPT.[40] The NPT is silent on this matter and does not expressly confer or deny enrichment and reprocessing rights. The present position of Iran is that the JCPOA has recognized Iran's right to enrichment. The American position has not changed, and there is a difference between recognizing an inherent right to enrichment and acknowledging that a program exists.[41] Irrespective of whether the US has indeed recognized Iran's right to enrich, the very fact that Iran is actually permitted to continue a part of its enrichment activities may have consequences for the claim of the same right by other non-nuclear-weapons Parties to the NPT. The Security Council, aware of this fact, had therefore underscored in Resolution 2231 that 'all provisions contained in the JCPOA are only for the purposes of its implementation between the E3 /EU+3 and Iran and should not be considered as setting precedents for any other State or for principles of international law and the rights and obligations under the Treaty on the Non-Proliferation of Nuclear Weapons...'[42]

5.2   *Access to Nuclear Sites and Information*

The second core issue in this file was the IAEA's expanded rights of access to Iran's nuclear information and sites. The Additional Protocol provides this possibility and aims to fill the gaps in the information reported by State Parties under the Comprehensive Safeguards Agreements. The significance of the Additional Protocol lies in the fact that it enables the IAEA to obtain a much fuller picture of nuclear programs, plans, nuclear material holdings and trade. More importantly, the Additional Protocol helps to provide much greater

---

38   The principle of what is not prohibited is permitted.
39   See, e.g. the statement of Secretary of State John Kerry in November 2013: https://www.washingtonpost.com/news/post-politics/wp/2013/11/24/kerry-on-iran-we-do-not-recognize-a-right-to-enrich/. See also Elias Groll, 'Did the United States Just Grant Iran the Right to Enrich Uranium', *Foreign Policy*, 24 September 2013.
40   G. Samor, 'Nuclear Rights and Wrongs: Why One Legal Term Stalled Negotiations with Iran', *Foreign Affairs,* November 14, 2013.
41   K. Davenpart, 'Myths and Misconceptions: the Right to Enrich' in *Arms Control Now*, The Blog of the Arms Control Association, 18 September 2014, https://armscontrolnow.org/2014/09/18/myths-and-misconceptions-the-right-to-enrich/.
42   Para. 27.

assurance on the absence of undeclared nuclear material and activities in States with Comprehensive Safeguards Agreements.

The demand of E3/EU+3 during the negotiations was that Iran would ratify and apply the Additional Protocol. Iran has committed itself in the JCPOA to provisionally apply the Protocol as from Implementation Day[43] and seek to ratify the document after Transition Day, i.e. eight years after the Adoption Day of the JCPOA.[44] To that extent, Iran's commitment seems to be in line with what can reasonably be expected from a country that has obviously failed to inform the IAEA of some of its nuclear activities in time. Today, 128 Additional Protocols are in force with 127 States and EURATOM.[45] These have accepted the same rigorous inspection conditions that the JCPOA has imposed on Iran.

The requirement of enhanced access to Iran's nuclear sites is not limited in the JCPOA to the provisional application and then ratification of the Additional Protocol. What the E3/EU+3 wanted and the US insisted on was a by far more intrusive inspection regime, something that has been referred to as an 'anywhere- anytime' inspection.[46] However, the inspection arrangement in the JCPOA is really less than an 'anywhere-anytime' order, but it is far more stringent than what is stipulated in the Additional Protocol. It has been described by President Obama as 'the most intrusive inspections regime of any arms control agreement'.[47]

The details are given in Section Q (paras. 74–78) of Annex I to the JCPOA. In sum, it means that if the IAEA has concerns about undeclared nuclear materials or locations, it will request clarification. If not satisfied with Iran's answer, it will request access to such locations. Iran may propose alternative means for resolving the IAEA's concerns. If the two sides are unable to reach satisfactory arrangements to verify the absence of undeclared nuclear materials and activities within 14 days of the IAEA's original request for access, Iran, in consultation with the members of the Joint Commission, will resolve the IAEA's concerns through means agreed between those countries and the IAEA. If no agreement can be reached, the members of the Joint Commission, by consensus or by a vote of five or more of its eight members, will advise on the necessary means

---

43 The JCPOA, Article 13.
44 The JCPOA, Article 34 (iv); Annex I, Section L. para. 64; Annex V, para. 22.1.
45 https://www.iaea.org/safeguards/safeguards-legal-framework/additional-protocol.
46 http://www.politifact.com/truth-o-meter/statements/2015/jul/19/marco-rubio/rubio-iran-deal-breaks-anytime-anywhere-inspection/.
47 Ibid.

to resolve the concerns (para. 78).[48] Consultation with and any action by the members of the Joint Commission will not exceed seven days, and Iran will implement the necessary means within three additional days.

This inspection arrangement means that if the IAEA requests access for inspection of a suspected undeclared location and Iran for any reason refuses to give the access within 24 days, there is in fact a risk of punitive measures such as a new Security Council resolution and new sanctions. Although para. 78 of Annex I speaks of the Joint Commission's *advice*, the outcome of such 'advice' by a majority of five members of the Commission is not difficult to guess. Given the background of Iran's nuclear file and the fact that some accusations have arguably been politically motivated rather than being prompted by pure concern for non-compliance with the Safeguards Agreement,[49] Iran seems to have been forced to accept a solution that is unprecedented. This arrangement is limited to 15 years.[50]

5.3 The Status of the JCPOA

One issue that attracted some attention in Iran and the United States after finalization of the negotiations and publication of the JCPOA was the legal nature of the document. Some members of the Iranian Parliament (*Majles*) and of the US Congress considered that the JCPOA is an agreement in the sense of the 1969 Vienna Convention on the Law of Treaties.[51] The reason in both cases was that the document constitutionally had to be approved by the *Majles* (or Congress in the case of the US) as if it were an international treaty. The argument was put forward mainly by those who were against the deal. Both the government of Iran and that of the US expressly described the accord as a political agreement.[52]

This is a correct assessment for many reasons. The intention of the participants was to resolve an important international crisis through a political deal. The purpose was not to create new rights and obligations through a new treaty, but to ensure compliance with obligations under existing treaties. The

---

48 There is no requirement of quorum, which means that only five members can, in the absence of the other three, take a decision.

49 Former IAEA Director-General ElBaradei elaborates in several places of his book this aspect of accusations particularly by the US, France and Israel, supra, note 5.

50 The JCPOA, para. 15.

51 1155 UNTS 331.

52 For the US position, see John Kerry's testimony before the House Foreign Affairs Committee, http://www.cnsnews.com/news/article/patrick-goodenough/kerry-iran-deal-not-treaty-because-you-cant-pass-treaty-anymore.

designation of the deal as a 'plan' rather than an 'agreement' is an indication of this intention. The language used in the document further strengthens this assumption. The choice of terms such as 'commitments' instead of 'duties' or 'obligations' and 'participants' instead of 'parties' can also be seen in this light.

Another important question is the legal capacity of the participants to conclude an international agreement on this specific issue. The genesis of the dispute is Iran's non-performance of its obligations under its Safeguards Agreement with the IAEA. Iran is thus one side of the issue. Legally, the other side is in the first place the Board of Governors of the IAEA, which is the highest authority within the Agency in charge of supervision of obligations incumbent upon the Parties to the NPT, and the UN Security Council as the guardian of international security. The countries that have negotiated with Iran (E3/EU+3) and come to an agreement with that country are members of the IAEA and/or the Security Council. However, they have had no direct or indirect mandate from either of these entities to negotiate on their behalf with Iran. They have lacked the legal capacity to commit any of these organizations. Their actions can perhaps be considered as good offices to solve an important international problem. The result of these good offices, i.e. the JCPOA, is a political agreement on an arrangement to resolve the contested issue.

One more question is the legal consequences of breaches of obligations by either side. Breach of an international legal obligation entails responsibility, and such responsibility has legal consequences. In the case of the JCPOA, serious non-performance can result in the re-imposition of sanctions against Iran. At the same time Iran will withdraw from the arrangement in such a case,[53] and restart its nuclear enrichment activities. This means only a return to the situation that existed before finalization of the negotiations without any other *legal* repercussions.

5.4   *Dispute Settlement Mechanism*

Articles 36 and 37 of the JCPOA provide for a unique mechanism for the settlement of disputes relating to Iran's non-performance of its commitments towards the other participants or the other participants' failure to meet their commitments towards Iran. In a case of non-performance, the issue can be referred to the Joint Commission, which has 15 days to resolve it unless the time can be extended by consensus. If the issue is considered not resolved, any participant can refer it to Ministers for Foreign Affairs, who also have 15 days to resolve the issue. Instead of review by the Ministers or parallel with it, the issue can be referred to an Advisory Board consisting of three persons—one each

---

53   The JCPOA, para. 37.

appointed by the participants in the dispute and an independent member. This board should provide a non-binding opinion within 15 days. The Joint Commission will consider the opinion within five more days. If the issue is not yet resolved to the satisfaction of the complaining participant, and if that participant deems the issue to constitute a *significant* non-performance, it can cease performing its commitments and notify the Security Council.

Upon receipt of the notification from the complaining participant, the Security Council *shall* vote on a resolution to maintain the lifting of the sanctions. If such a resolution has not been adopted within 30 days of the notification, then the provisions of the old Security Council resolutions would be re-imposed, unless the Council decides otherwise. Inclusion of this unusual and reversed order was to ensure that if a permanent member of the Security Council as participant in the JCPOA[54] believes that Iran is not meeting its commitments, it can singlehandedly reinstate all the previous Security Council resolutions by using its veto.

To forestall any risk of Security Council not being able to act, Resolution 2231 specifies that if within 10 days of the notification no member of the Council has submitted a draft resolution to continue sanction lifting, then the President of the Security Council *shall* submit such a draft resolution and put it to the vote within 30 days of the notification.[55] Iran, with no possibility to stop such a move, has according to para. 37 of the JCPOA made it clear that it would cease performing its commitments if the sanctions were reinstated. This peculiar order gives the impression that the function of the dispute settlement mechanism here is not to resolve a dispute between two equal parties to an agreed arrangement. The real purpose seems to be to use it as the Sword of Damocles to reinstate sanctions against Iran at the will of one or more participants in the group of E3/EU+3.[56]

6 Concluding Remarks

The JCPOA is undoubtedly an outstanding diplomatic achievement both for Iran and for E3/EU+3, particularly the US. It has successfully put an end to an important international crisis. More importantly, it has shown that even in a delicate, complicated and politically difficult area such as non-proliferation of

---

54 In the first place probably the US, the UK or France.
55 Para. 11.
56 Although the mechanism is established to prevent non-performance by Iran, there is almost no way to stop a participant using it for other reasons.

nuclear weapons it is possible to peacefully settle a dispute with an unfriendly counterpart.

There is no doubt that Iran has failed to fulfill some of its obligations with respect to timely informing the IAEA of its existing or planned nuclear activities. There have also been accusations of possible prohibited military activities, although these accusations have never been confirmed by the IAEA. But the real cause of concern has been Iran's insistence on its right to enrich uranium, something that is legally not forbidden; but for various political reasons is unacceptable, particularly to the western permanent members of the Security Council. As a result of these failures and accusations, and particularly because of Iran's uncompromising attitude with respect to the right to enrich, the JCPOA has severely curtailed the rights of Iran as a Party to the NPT for a defined period of time. A rigorous mechanism for monitoring the implementation of these limitations is also in place. The timeframe of limitations and extraordinary control of Iran's nuclear activities ranges between 8 and 25 years.[57]

Imposition of these limitations and rigorous control on Iran, even for a limited time, should be compared with the IAEA's and the Security Council's responses to similar cases of non-performance of legal duties by other Parties to the NPT.[58] Such a comparison witnesses a double standard, something that ElBaradei has extensively commented on in his book.[59] It seems that it is not always non-performance as such that is decisive for shaping a reaction to a breach of obligation under the NPT and related agreements. The political considerations surrounding a State Party that is in non-compliance are probably more important in this context.

---

57   The details of each period of limitation are given in the JCPOA Preamble and General Provisions, para. xiv; JCPOA, paras. 1, 2, 3, 15 & 34; Annex I, para. 78; Annex IV, para. 4.4.

58   Some of these cases are mentioned in ElBaradei's book. See, supra, note 10. The case of the Resende nuclear plant in Brazil is illustrative. Despite repeated requests of the IAEA in 2004 to visit the enrichment facilities when they were under construction, Brazil refused to give access for inspection. Also South Korea during the same year had enriched 77 percent uranium without informing the IAEA. The Board of Governors of the IAEA only 'took note' of these cases without taking any further measures.

59   Supra, note 5, pp. 210–240. As regards North Korea, he writes it is 'staggering to compare the difference in treatment of North Korea and Iran. North Korea had walked out of the NPT and made explicit threats about developing nuclear weapons... yet the Americans were ready to join them in a direct dialogue... By contrast, Iran, which remained under safeguards and party to the NPT, was penalized for possibly having future intentions to develop nuclear weapons, and America refused to talk to them without preconditions.' Supra, p. 203.

The confidence-building measures demanded by E3/EU+3 and the ensuing restrictions on Iran's exercise of its rights under the NPT do not seem to be proportionate to the scope and type of non-performance for which Iran is formally responsible. Nevertheless, Iran has prudently accepted them in order to come out of the isolation and hardship that the sanctions have caused.

The diplomatic management of one of our time's most difficult crises is commendable. However, the achieved solution in the JCPOA may have legal implications for the development of compliance mechanisms far beyond the NPT. The balance between the substantive rights of a State Party to a multilateral agreement and its procedural obligations is the core issue in defining that development.

Scientific Knowledge and the Progressive Development of International Law: With Reference to the ILC Topic on the Protection of the Atmosphere

Shinya Murase

1   Introduction

Development of international environmental law would not have been possible without contributions by 'epistemic communities'.[1] International environmental lawmaking is one area where science has played and will continue to play a crucial role.[2] For instance, since its establishment in 1988, the Intergovernmental Panel on Climate Change (IPCC) has made significant contributions to reporting and assessing scientific findings regarding climate change. The first IPCC report was published in 1990 and served as the basis of discussion in drafting the United Nations Convention on Climate Change (UNFCCC), adopted in 1992. The second report, published in 1995, had a decisive impact on formulating the principles incorporated in the Kyoto Protocol of 1997. The IPCC fourth and fifth reports of 2007[3] and 2014[4] led to the adoption of the Paris Agreement of 2015. Thus, the link between scientific knowledge and international lawmaking has been more than vivid in the context of climate change.[5]

Likewise, the International Law Commission (ILC, or the Commission) has been faced in recent years with the problem of scientific input into its

---

1   P. Haas, 'Epistemic Communities' in M. Fitzmaurice, et al. (eds), *Research Handbook on International Environmental Law*, Edward Elgar, pp. 792–806.
2   S. Andresen & J. B. Skjaerseth, 'Science and Technology: From Agenda Setting to Implementation,' D. Bodansky, et al. (eds), *The Oxford Handbook of International Environmental Law*, Oxford University Press, 2007, pp. 182–202.
3   IPCC, *Climate Change 2014: Mitigation of Climate Change*, Cambridge University Press, 2007. The present writer served as lead author of this Report, WG-III, Chapter 13. The IPCC received Nobel Peace Prize in 2007.
4   IPCC, *Climate Change 2014: Mitigation of Climate Change*, Cambridge University Press, 2014.
5   S. Murase, 'International Lawmaking for the Future Framework on Climate Change' in S. Murase, *International Law: An Integrative Perspective on Transboundary Issues*, Sophia University Press, 2011, pp. 168–181.

activities for progressive development of international law.[6] In pursuing one of the current ILC topics, 'Protection of the Atmosphere', for which the present writer serves as Special Rapporteur, the Commission has taken steps to reach out to the relevant international organizations as well as the scientific/technical community whose advice and expertise are needed for the Commission to understand what has to be regulated. The situation is similar to the one faced by contemporary judges of international courts and tribunals who, confronted with an increasing filing of environmental disputes, require experts for proof of scientific evidence in these fact-intensive and science-heavy cases.[7]

The ILC has been at a crossroads in selecting its topics. It has been pointed out since the 1970s that the shift of topics from 'codification' to 'progressive development' has made the work of the Commission increasingly difficult. Note also that there has been another aspect of this difficulty: having exhausted most of the 'traditional' topics of international law, the Commission has had to shift to those related to 'special regimes' of international law such as human rights law, environmental law and economic law. While some consider that development of the law of special regimes should be left to experts in their respective fields rather than the ILC,[8] others consider that the topics on special regimes should also be included in the agenda of the Commission, precisely because it is expected to perform the function of safeguarding the integrity of the international law system and avoiding the tendency towards 'compartmentalization' (or fragmentation) caused by dominant 'single-issue' approaches under special regimes.[9]

---

6   While the mandate of the ILC is the codification of 'established' rules of customary international law and the progressive development of international law based on the 'emergent rules' of customary law (see the Statute of the ILC, article 15), science is naturally more relevant to the latter phase of the ILC work.

7   Most notably, see the *Pulp Mills on the River Uruguay* (Argentina v Uruguay), Judgment, *ICJ Reports 2010*, p. 14, paras. 160–168 (on the burden of proof and expert evidence), and the joint dissenting opinion of Judges Al-Khasawneh and Simma, ibid., pp. 1–6. The main focus of the *Whaling in the Antarctic* (Australia v Japan, New Zealand intervening), Judgment, *ICJ Reports 2014*, paras. 74–246, was the scope of 'scientific research' under the 1946 International Whaling Convention.

8   M. Koskenniemi, 'International Law and Hegemony: A Reconfiguration', 17 *Cambridge Review of International Affairs*, 2004, pp. 197–218; M. Koskenniemi, *The Politics of International Law*, Hart Publishing, 2011, p. 237.

9   Murase, supra, note 5, p. 10. See also S. Murase, *First Report on the Protection of the Atmosphere*, UN Doc. A/CN.4/667, 14 February 2014, paras. 17–18. The atmosphere is not yet subject to a comprehensive regime such as the law of the sea, and instead, the global 'atmospheric commons' are regulated by a 'regime complex' comprising a multitude of international

Given that the ILC is a body that primarily' comprises experts in general international law, it can, as such, contribute to establishing linkages among the special regimes. The enormous growth in the number of treaties in those specialized fields has led to 'treaty congestion' or 'treaty inflation'.[10] The multitude of conventions notwithstanding, they are faced with significant gaps as well as overlaps because there has been little or no coordination or harmonization, and therefore, no coherence among them. The need to enhance 'synergies' among the existing conventions has been emphasized repeatedly;[11] and in the opinion of the present writer, the Commission should seize upon this opportunity. In its exercise of progressive development of international law, the Commission should deal with these proposed new topics in specialized fields from the perspective of general international law. This should be done with a view to ensuring coordination among the various sub-fields (compartments) of international law. The Commission appears to be best placed to play

> instruments dealing with (a) different—and sometimes conflicting—*economic uses* of the atmosphere (*inter alia*, as a medium for aviation and radio-communications, or as a waste receptacle for pollutant substances and energy); (b) different *geographical sectors* (such as airspace over the high seas and other areas beyond national jurisdiction); (c) different *vertical zones* (troposphere, stratosphere); and (d) different *categories of risks* (to safety, health, environment, climate, security) addressed by different international agencies and global/regional institutions or programmes. (P. H. Sand, 'Towards a New International Law of the Atmosphere', *Goettingen Journal of International Law*, forthcoming in 2017).

10   See E. Brown Weiss, 'International Environmental Law: Contemporary Issues and the Emergence of a New World Order', 81 *Georgetown Law Journal*, 1993, pp. 675–710, at pp. 697–702; S. Murase, Chair, 'Compliance with International Standards: Environmental Case Studies,' *Proceedings of the 89th Annual Meeting of the American Society of International Law*, 1995, pp. 206–224; D. K. Anton, 'Treaty Congestion in Contemporary International Environmental Law', in S. Alam et al. (eds), *Routledge Handbook of International Environmental Law*, Routledge, 2013, pp. 651–665.

11   The UNEP has been emphasizing the need for synergy among multilateral environmental agreements: See, UNEP/GCSS.VII/1, Annex, 15 February 2002, entitled the 'Report of the open-ended intergovernmental group of ministers or their representatives on international environmental governance', section C 'Improved coordination among and effectiveness of multilateral environmental agreements', in particular paragraph 27. (Doc. UNEP/GCSS.VII/6 of 5 March 2002). The UNEP's Governing Council has adopted similar decisions almost every year. The latest one is: UNEP/GCSS.XI/9, 26 February 2010 entitled 'Nusa Dua Declaration', section C, paragraphs 10–12. (Doc. UNEP/GCSS.XI/11 of 3 March 2010). See also P. Roch & F. Xaver Perrez, 'International Environmental Governance: The Strive Towards a Comprehensive, Coherent, Effective and Efficient International Environmental Regime', 16 *Colorado Journal of International Environmental Law and Policy*, 2005, pp. 1–25.

that role.[12] This is the background against which the topic on the Protection of the Atmosphere has been proposed and adopted by the Commission as its active agenda.

2 Progressive Development of the Law of the Atmosphere and Atmospheric Science

Taking on a subject of a special regime of international law such as the law of the atmosphere, however, requires the Commission to have a certain level of understanding of the scientific and technical aspects of this complex problem such as the sources and effects of the damage in question. This is in order to avoid the Commission's approach being directed towards absurd or unreasonable results. It was thus considered that any concepts used in the draft guidelines should reasonably correspond to scientific findings and that minimum reference to scientific sources is inevitable in this project; though admittedly, for the ILC as a legal body, the final judgment should be made by legal dictates in a case of conflict between science and law. It has therefore been necessary for the Commission to reach out to international environmental organizations and to the scientific community.

The drafters of the Statute of ILC seem to have anticipated the need for scientific input in its work on the progressive development of international law. Thus, the Statute authorizes the Commission in article 16 (e) 'to consult with scientific institutions and individual experts'. There is also a notable precedent in this respect: Mr. Chusei Yamada, as Special Rapporteur for the topic on the law of transboundary aquifers, engaged UNESCO's experts on the hydrology of aquifers for successful completion of the draft articles on the subject in 2008. Following Yamada's footsteps, the present writer undertook to establish contacts with representatives of interested intergovernmental organizations, including the United Nations Environmental Programme (UNEP), the World Meteorological Organizations (WMO) and the United Nations Economic Commission for Europe (UNECE).

---

12   There is a tendency to consider that taking on a topic of interdisciplinary character is 'an ingredient in the decline of the Commission from its central position in the law-making process' (M. El-Baradei, T. M. Franck & R. Trachtenberg, *The International Law Commission: The Need for a New Direction*, United Nations Institute for Training and Research, 1981, p. 11). However, in the opinion of the present writer, this assumption is simply outdated.

The Commission recognized the importance of informal exchanges with the aims of increasing ILC members' familiarity with scientific concepts relevant to international law in the field and encouraging broader dialogue between expert scientific and legal bodies in the international community. Thus, two such dialogue sessions so far were held in 2015 and 2016, attended by the world's leading atmospheric scientists in pursuing the ILC topic on the Protection of the Atmosphere.

The first session in 2015 was devoted mainly to overall issues relating to atmospheric pollution and atmospheric degradation,[13] which was in line with the Special Rapporteur's Second Report.[14] Professor Øystein Hov (President, Commission of Atmospheric Sciences, WMO) noted the human consequences of air pollution, including PM 2.5, laying out the losses in life expectancy that have and potentially will be suffered around the world due to adverse effects, citing 'WHO estimates that there are seven million annual premature deaths linked to air pollution.' Professor Peringe Glennfelt (Chair of the Working Group on Effects, CLRTAP, UNECE) identified different scopes of pollutants, including local or street level, sub-regional (e.g. Los Angeles basin), regional transboundary (e.g. South East Asia Brown Cloud), inter-continental, and hemispheric and even global pollutant scales. These have notably different patterns of behavior and effects on the atmosphere and human health. Dr. Jacqueline McGlade (Chief Scientist, UNEP) outlined various opportunities and challenges in regulating air pollution, referring to the importance of data in understanding phenomena of atmospheric pollution. She stressed the need

---

13 The first session of the dialogue with scientists on the protection of the atmosphere was held on 7 May 2015 and chaired by the Special Rapporteur, Prof. Shinya Murase. Prof. Øystein Hov (President, Commission of Atmospheric Sciences, WMO) spoke on 'Scientific aspects of the atmosphere: A General Overview', Prof. Peringe Grennfelt (Chair of the Working Group on Effects, CLRTAP, UNECE) on 'Trans-continental transport of pollutants and their effects', Mr. Masa Nagai (Deputy Director, Division of Environmental Law and Conventions, UNEP) on 'Pollutants affecting the global environment through the atmosphere', Mr. Christian Blondin (Director of Cabinet and External Relations Department, WMO) on 'The role of the atmosphere in the global climate' and Ms. Jacqueline McGlade (Chief Scientist and Director, Division of Early Warning and Assessment, UNEP) on overall issues on atmospheric pollution and atmospheric degradation. Ms. Albena Karadjova (Secretary to CLRTAP, UNECE) also spoke on the economic implication of transboundary atmospheric pollution. For a summary of the meeting, see the UNEP document: C. Wharton, 'UN ILC's Dialogue with Scientists on the protection of the atmosphere', available at: http://www.unep.org/delc/Portals/119/documents/montevideo/ilc-dialogue-wharton.pdf.

14 UN Doc. A/CN.4/681, 2 March 2015.

to realize how much science genuinely is done, how much consensus there is, and yet how long it takes to actually arrive at legislation and treaty action. The members of the Commission posed a number of questions to the scientists such as the definition of the atmosphere in science, health-standard issues relating to specific pollutants, relations between scientific findings and treaty-making efforts, etc. The scientists offered detailed responses and explanations.[15]

The second dialogue session held in 2016 focused on more specific scientific aspects of geo-engineering and environmental impact assessment (EIA),[16] the issues discussed in the Third Report.[17] Professor Øystein Hov spoke on geo-engineering, an advertent alteration of the climate by managing solar radiation (SRM) or removing greenhouse gas (CDR). He pointed out that there is complexity and uncertainty on climate science, technical, ethical, legal, policy, and economic issues involving geo-engineering, and that geo-engineering could have unforeseen consequences if conducted on a large scale. He emphasized that geo-engineering should be governed by internationally accepted guidelines such as the Oxford Principles. Mr. Christian Blondin (Director of Cabinet and External Relations Department, WMO) recalled the emissions scenarios developed by the Intergovernmental Panel on Climate Change (IPCC) for its fifth Assessment Report (AR5), pointing out that, for the purpose of the AR5, only carbon dioxide removal (CDR) has been used in several mitigation scenarios to try to limit global warming to 2°C or less, a geo-engineering technique that nevertheless plays a major role in achieving this goal, while still operational at the required scale. At the same time, he suggests that geo-engineering should be used with careful consideration of its global and long-term implications.[18]

---

15   Wharton, supra, note 14.
16   The second dialogue session with scientists on the protection of the atmosphere, was held on 4 May 2016. Prof. Øystein Hov addressed 'Geoengineering—away forward?', Prof. Peringe Grennfelt considered 'Linkages between transboundary air pollution and climate change', Mr. Christian Blondin analyzed the 'Scientific aspects of the 2015 Paris Agreement', Mr. Valentin Foltescu (Head of Thematic Assessments Unit in the Division of Early Warning and Assessments, UNEP) presented 'An overview of the latest findings and estimates of the effects of air pollution', Mr. Masa Nagai discussed 'Linking science with law'. The dialogue was followed by a question-and-answer session. See Y. Fukunaga, 'Informal Meeting of the International Law Commission: Dialogue with Scientists (Second Session)', at: http://legal.un.org/ilc/sessions/68/pdfs/informal_dialogue_4may2016.pdf.
17   UN Doc. A/CN.4/692, 25 February 2016.
18   Fukunaga, supra, note 17.

Professor Peringe Glennfelt addressed linkages between transboundary air pollution and climate change, using the tropospheric ozone and its relation to methane emissions as an example. In his view, the existing regional institutions are fragmented and not sufficiently effective in dealing with transboundary air pollution, which is not merely a local problem but indeed is becoming a global one. He pointed out that the 2015 Paris Agreement is expected to contribute not only to reduced emission of greenhouse gases but also to cleaner air. Mr. Masa Nagai (Deputy Director, Division of Environmental Law and Conventions, UNEP), who discussed 'Linking science with law', recalled that planetary ecosystems are affected by human activities, while human health and well-being are affected by the ecosystems. He introduced the concept of 'planetary boundaries', which define safe operating space for the earth and humans. He then discussed 'pollution of global significance' such as global transboundary air pollution, global transport of hazardous chemicals, ocean acidification, marine debris and micro-plastic, pointing out that these are interconnected. Mr. Nagai then underlined the fact that, while many international treaties and other instruments have been adopted to address particular pollution problems, no overarching framework convention exists on global environmental concerns. By stressing horizontal linkages between various environmental problems as well as vertical linkages between global, regional, and national levels, he indicated the need to design the 'future shape of international law', Mr. Nagai stated that future international law would be defined by establishing the linkage between science and international law. Finally, he invited Commission Members to consider the future shape of international law to address pollution of global significance affecting the Earth's ecosystems. After these presentations, there was active exchange of views between the Commission members and the scientists on issues such as whether geo-engineering is good or bad, what should be the forms of cooperation among States in this field, and what would likely be the future shape of international law.[19]

The members of the Commission have found these dialogue sessions very useful, and accordingly, the third session is planned in 2017, which will help clarify, *inter alia*, the relationship between the atmosphere and the oceans from scientific perspectives, since the Special Rapporteur's Fourth Report on the Protection of the Atmosphere is scheduled to discuss the interrelationship of the law of the atmosphere with other fields of international law, in particular, the law of the sea.

---

19   Ibid.

3 ILC Draft Guidelines on the Protection of the Atmosphere

The Commission so far provisionally adopted in 2015 and 2016 eight draft guidelines and the preamble. Some of the guidelines are closely related to atmospheric science. Definition of the 'atmosphere' in draft guideline 1 and 'intentional large-scale modification of the atmosphere' (geo-engineering) in draft guideline 7 are such examples.

3.1 *Definition of the Atmosphere*

Draft guideline 1 on 'use of terms'[20] provides simply that 'for the purpose of the present draft guidelines, (a) 'Atmosphere' means the envelope of gases surrounding the Earth.' There was a view that it would not be necessary to provide for a definition of the atmosphere, because it is not defined in the relevant international instruments and because, for instance, the 'sea' is not defined in the Law of the Sea Convention. However, the Commission considered it desirable to provide a working definition for the present draft guidelines.[21] Even though the definitional guideline is vey simple, the Commission supplied rather elaborate commentaries thereto. It should be borne in mind that guidelines and their commentaries are normatively integral propositions. In its commentary on draft guideline 1 (a), paragraph (3), the Commission 'considered it necessary that its legal definition be consistent with the approach of scientists.

According to scientists, the atmosphere exists in what is called the atmospheric shell...,' followed by a lengthy scientific description of the composition of the atmosphere with citations of abundant scientific data.[22] Although the sentence of the commentary begins with the words '[a]ccording to scientists',

---

20   Draft guideline 1:
    "Use of terms: (a) 'Atmosphere' means the envelope of gases surrounding the Earth; (b) 'Atmospheric pollution' means the introduction or release by humans, directly or indirectly, into the atmosphere of substances contributing to deleterious effects extending beyond the State of origin, of such a nature as to endanger human life and health and the Earth's natural environment; (c) 'Atmospheric degradation' means the alteration by humans, directly or indirectly, of atmospheric conditions having significant deleterious effects of such a nature as to endanger human life and health and the Earth's natural environment."

21   The definition given in paragraph (a) was inspired by the definition given by a working group of the IPCC. See 5th Assessment Report, Working Group III, Annex I. IPCC, Climate Change 2014, available at: http://www.ipcc.ch/pdf/assessment-report/ar5/wg3/ipcc_wg3_ar5_annex-i.pdf.

22   Report of the International Law Commission, Sixty-seventh Session, 2015, UN Doc. A/70/10, p. 29.

in order to avoid the impression that the Commission itself is committed to the scientific findings, this is nonetheless rather unprecedented for commentaries provided by the Commission.

The definition, in draft guideline 1, paragraph (a), represents a 'physical' description of the atmosphere. There is also a 'functional' aspect, which involves the large-scale movement of air. Atmospheric movement has a dynamic and fluctuating feature. The air moves and circulates around the earth in a complicated formation called 'atmospheric circulation'. The Commission decided to refer to this functional aspect of the atmosphere in the second paragraph of the preamble.[23] Long-range transboundary movement of polluting and degrading substances is recognized as one of the major problems of the present-day atmospheric environment, with the Arctic region being identified as one of the most seriously affected by the world-wide spread of deleterious pollutants, as substantiated by scientific evidence.[24]

Another issue that was controversial in the Commission was the definition of 'atmospheric pollution' (or air pollution). My initial proposal as Special Rapporteur included the words 'introduction of substances *or energy*' into the atmosphere, which was in line with article 1 (a) of the 1979 CLRTAP and article 1, paragraph 1 (4) of the 1982 LOSC. 'Energy' is understood to include heat, light, noise and radioactivity introduced and released into the atmosphere through human activities.

However, the Commission decided not to include the term 'energy' in the text of paragraph (b) of the draft guideline. It is the understanding of the Commission reached as a compromise that, for the purposes of the draft guidelines, 'the word 'substances' includes 'energy'.'[25] This issue will be re-visited in the second reading of the draft guidelines and commentaries thereto in the future (probably in 2020), with the support of relevant scientific data.

3.2 Geo-engineering

One of the most controversial issues in the Commission's debate on the protection of the atmosphere in the 2016 ILC session was 'intentional large-scale

---

[23] The second preambular paragraph reads: 'Bearing in mind that the transport and dispersion of polluting and degrading substances occur within the atmosphere,' (Ibid., paragraph 4 of the commentary to the preamble). My original proposal as Special Rapporteur was: 'Atmosphere' means the envelope of gases surrounding the Earth, within which the transport and dispersion of degrading substances occurs.' (UN Doc. A/CN.4/681, 2 March 2015, para. 17.)

[24] See UN Doc. A/CN.4/681.

[25] Ibid., pp. 29–30, paras. 8–9.

modification of the atmosphere'[26] (or 'geo-engineering'), which refers to techniques for changing—through the deliberate manipulation of natural processes—the dynamics, composition or structure of the Earth, including its biota, lithosphere, hydrosphere and atmosphere. These activities include the methods and technologies which encompass carbon dioxide removal and solar radiation management. Activities related to the former involve the ocean, land and technical systems and seek to remove carbon dioxide from the atmosphere through natural sinks or through chemical engineering. Proposed techniques for carbon dioxide removal include: soil carbon sequestration; carbon capture and sequestration; ambient air capture; ocean fertilization; ocean alkalinity enhancement; and enhanced weathering. Afforestation has traditionally been employed to reduce carbon dioxide.[27]

Activities aimed at intentional large-scale modification of the atmosphere have a significant potential for preventing, diverting, moderating or ameliorating the adverse effects of disasters and hazards, including drought, hurricanes and tornadoes; and enhancing crop production and the availability of water. At the same time, it is also recognized that they may have long-range and unexpected effects on existing climatic patterns which are not confined by national boundaries. As noted by the World Meteorological Organization with respect to weather modification: 'The complexity of the atmospheric processes is such that a change in the weather induced artificially in one part of the world will necessarily have repercussions elsewhere.... Before undertaking an experiment on large-scale weather modification, the possible and desirable consequences must be carefully evaluated, and satisfactory international arrangements must be reached.' It is not the intention of the present draft guideline to stifle innovation and scientific advancement. Accordingly, the draft guideline does not seek either to authorize or to prohibit such activities unless there is agreement among States to take such a course of action. It simply sets out the principle that such activities, if undertaken, should be conducted with 'prudence and caution'.[28]

---

[26] Draft guideline 7 (Intentional large-scale modification of the atmosphere), provisionally adopted by the Commission, provides as follows: 'Activities aimed at intentional large-scale modification of the atmosphere should be conducted with prudence and caution, subject to any applicable rules of international law.'

[27] Report of the International Law Commission, Sixty-eighth Session, 2016, UN Doc. A/71/10, Guideline 7, commentary 3, p. 313.

[28] Ibid., commentary 7–9, p. 314.

Here again science has played an important role in formulating the draft guideline and the commentaries thereto. Thus commentary (4) to draft guideline 7 states as follows: 'According to scientific experts, solar radiation management is designed to mitigate the negative impacts of climate change by intentionally lowering the surface temperatures of the Earth. Proposed activities here include: 'albedo enhancement', a method that involves increasing the reflectiveness of clouds or the surface of the Earth, so that more of the heat of the sun is reflected back into space; stratospheric aerosols, a technique that involves the introduction of small, reflective particles into the upper atmosphere to reflect sunlight before it reaches the surface of the Earth; and space reflectors, which entail blocking a small proportion of sunlight before it reaches the Earth.'[29]

The Commission remains divided as to this draft guideline, and it will be re-visited in the second reading,[30] taking into account the development of science on the subject.

4   Conclusion

Thus, it can be seen that the ILC has been working in part in close collaboration with scientists, though it may hastily be added that most of the work of the Commission still remains that of 'lawyers', basically guided and dictated by legal reasoning and legal judgment. It is gratifying to note that the scientific experts of UNEP, WMO and UNECE have been extremely helpful to the Commission's work, and their advice and support were always a source of confidence for Commission members in pursuing the topic on the protection of the atmosphere. Scientific evidence has often served as a basis for legitimating proposed guidelines and facilitating their acceptance.

Should the ILC wish to continue its time-honored mandate and remain relevant to the need of the international community as a whole, it will inevitably be required to take on the topics of special regimes of international law, which in turn requires collaborating with scientific experts in the relevant fields.

---

29   Ibid., commentary 4, p. 313.

30   The commentary 12 to draft guideline 7 concludes as follows: 'A number of members remained un-persuaded that there was a need for a draft guideline on this matter, which essentially remains controversial, and the discussion on it was evolving, and is based on scant practice. Other members were of the view that the draft guideline could be enhanced during second reading.' (Ibid., p. 315).

As one author observes, such a relationship with specific experts is indispensable [and they] 'must be present at all stages until the very last minute of the drafting of the relevant instrument'.[31] In this sense, it appears that the ILC is moving in the right direction, and it is hoped that this relationship will continue until the very completion of the project.

---

31   C. Tomuschat, 'The International Law Commission: An Outdated Institution?' *49 German Yearbook of International Law*, 2006, p. 82.

Rethinking Iran and International Law: The *Anglo-Iranian Oil Company Case* Revisited

Sundhya Pahuja and Cait Storr

1 Introduction

> *Il n'est guère possible d'entreprendre, à notre avis, l'étude de l'attitude de l'Iran face aux règles de droit international sans avoir présenté l'histoire des dernières décennies de ce pays. Elle explique en effet largement certaines de ses positions actuelle dans le domaine qui nos retient. Deux faits largement interdépendents ont été déterminants: d'une part les atteintes répétées et sans cesse plus graves portées à la souveraineté de l'Iran et, d'autre part, sa mise à l'écart de la communauté internationale jusqu'à la création de la Société des Nations.*[1]
>
> DJAMCHID MOMTAZ, 'L'Iran et le Droit international' (1976)

It seems to have long been a commonplace in the West to describe Iran as an outlaw; irredeemably defiant of international law at worst, recalcitrant at best.[2] And yet like most commonplaces, the story is more complicated than it first appears. As Djamchid Momtaz observed in 1976, in an essay entitled

---

[1] Roughly translated, this reads: '(i)n our view, it would hardly be possible to undertake a study of the attitude of Iran toward the rules of international law, without having offered a study of the last decades in that country. It would largely explain several of Iran's contemporary positions in relation to the question at hand. Two largely interdependent facts have been determinative: on one hand the repeated and serious attacks on Iran's sovereignty, and on the other hand, the exclusion of Iran from the international community since the creation of the League of Nations'. D. Momtaz, 'L'Iran et le Droit International', in M.-R. Djalili (ed), *Aspects de la politique étrangère de l'Iran et de la France*, Université de Téhéran, Centre des Hautes Etudes Internationales, 1976, p. 199.

[2] For an article which gives a particular example with respect to nuclear weapons, of the broader tendency in the US and UK (and elsewhere) to describe Iran as an 'outlaw' regardless of the legality of its actions, see R. Dalton, 'Iran is Not in Breach of International Law', *The Guardian*, June 9, 2011, available at https://www.theguardian.com/commentisfree/2011/jun/09/iran-nuclear-power-un-threat-peace. Dalton, former British Ambassador to Iran, co-wrote the article with five other former ambassadors to Iran, including P. von Maltzahn (Germany), S. Hohwü-Christensen (Sweden), G. Metten (Belgium), F. Nicoullaud (France) & R. Toscano (Italy).

L'Iran et le Droit International, in order even to begin to understand Iran's relationship to international law, one must have regard to historical context. In this essay, we take up the invitation to think about Iran and international law in historical context by revisiting the *Anglo-Iranian Oil Company Case* of 1952 through a lens we call 'historically inflected jurisprudence'.[3]

Historically inflected jurisprudence invites us to pay attention to the way in which law and jurisprudence have been written over time.[4] It does not start with a single definition of law and work backwards to trace its histories. Instead our lens orients us toward seeing and describing practices which both authorize conduct, and which claim authority to speak the law, as well as the historical (and political-economic) contexts in which those practices take place.[5] Such an approach enables us to recover the different ways in which the role of international law in the global order has been and may be understood by different people and at different times.[6] It also enables us to see the historical struggles that lie beneath seemingly stable doctrines, rules and forms, what is required to 'stabilize' those formations in an ongoing way, and what might be at stake in that stabilization.

What we see when we re-read the *Anglo-Iranian Oil Company Case* through the lens of historically inflected jurisprudence is at least twofold. First, we see that Iran sought to conduct itself in a lawful way, whereas Britain, with the support of the United States, did not. Britain's response to the ICJ's decision—which supported Iran's position that the Court did not have jurisdiction to deal with the merits of the case—was to resort to force to 'repossess' Iranian oil, and to orchestrate a coup with the assistance of the United States to depose

---

3   *Anglo-Iranian Oil Company Case* (United Kingdom v Iran), *ICJ Reports 1952*, p. 93. On historically inflected jurisprudence, see S. Pahuja, 'Letters from Bandung: Encounters with Another Inter-National Law,' in L. Eslava, M. Fakhri & V. Nesiah (eds), *Bandung, Global History and International Law: Critical Pasts and Pending Futures*, Cambridge University Press, 2016.

4   For a recent example of how this attention might be paid, see A. Genovese & S. McVeigh, 'Nineteen Eighty Three: A Jurisographic Report on Commonwealth v Tasmania,' 24 *Griffith Law Review* 2015, pp. 68–88.

5   These are practices we might call practices of jurisdiction, using an older, wider meaning of the term than that assumed in its narrower, technical usage since the late twentieth century. See S. Dorsett & S. McVeigh, *Jurisdiction,* Routledge, 2012; S. Dorsett & I. Hunter, (eds), *Law and Politics in British Colonial Thought: Transpositions of Empire,* Palgrave Macmillan, 2010; P. Rush, 'An Altered Jurisdiction: Corporeal Traces of Law,' 6 *Griffith Law Review* 1997, pp. 144–168; S. Pahuja, 'Laws of Encounter: A Jurisdictional Account of International Law', 1 *London Review of International Law* 2013, pp. 63–98.

6   On this point, see S. Dorsett & S. McVeigh, 'Jurisprudences of Jurisdiction: Matters of Public Authority', 23 *Griffith Law Review* 2014, pp. 570–71.

the parliamentary nationalist Mohammad Mossadeq.[7] The consequences of British and American actions in Iran in the 1950s have cast long shadows, not only in Iranian political history, but also in the structuring of the international investment regime, and the militarization of resource disputes in the Middle East. Second, when we look 'slant'[8] at this seemingly rather dry procedural dispute over whether the Court had the power to issue an interim protective order in a case where its jurisdiction to hear the merits was at issue, we can see a kaleidoscope of disputed visions of what the role of the ICJ in the world might, could and should be, at a crucial moment in the Court's formation. While these competing visions of the role of the Court may have fallen out of view for those who regard international legal decisions as the best approximation of justice that can be struck in a politically volatile system, or even as simply 'good enough' for the world today, they remain present to those who have come habitually to regard those same decisions as manifestations of an enduring Eurocentric bias in international law.[9]

In this chapter, we begin by offering a story of the background to the dispute between the Iranian Government under Prime Minister Mossadeq and the Anglo-Iranian Oil Company,[10] which led the United Kingdom to commence an action in the ICJ. In Section 3, we describe the legal dispute, the form it took and the two decisions of the ICJ which flowed from it. In Section 4, we

---

7   The CIA officially admitted its role in the 1953 coup in 2013. See M. Byrne, 'CIA Admits It Was Behind Iran's Coup,' *Foreign Policy*, August 19, 2013, available at http://foreignpolicy.com/2013/08/19/cia-admits-it-was-behind-irans-coup/. The UK Government is yet to do so. For just one detailed account of this story by an eminent historian who revisited the story in 2004 and 2006, drawing on newly available documents and discussions and correspondence with four former British Officials involved with the events of 1951–53, see W. Roger Louis, 'Mussadiq, Oil and the Dilemmas of British Imperialism', chapter 28 in *Ends of British Imperialism: The Scramble for Empire, Suez and Decolonization*, Tauris, 2006. This chapter was originally published as W. Roger Louis, 'Britain and the Overthrow of the Mosaddeq Government', in M. J. Gasiorowski & M. Byrne (eds) *Mohammad Mosaddeq and the 1953 Coup in Iran*, Syracuse University Press, 2004, pp. 126–77.
8   We refer here to the poem by Emily Dickinson, 'Tell All the Truth but Tell It Slant.'
9   A third thread which is worth unravelling through this lens is the company-state relation. We omit it here for reasons of space, but will address it in a forthcoming essay explicitly situating the case in a Cold War context.
10 The Anglo-Iranian Oil Company was known as the Anglo-Persian Oil Company until 1935, when 'Persia' became 'Iran'. In 1954, after the events described here, Anglo-Iranian was renamed the British Petroleum Company. The company currently trades as BP Global. For the company's public version of the events described in this chapter, see the website of BP Global; 'Post War,' available at http://www.bp.com/en/global/corporate/about-bp/our-history/post-war.html.

describe the events that followed, and the implications of our redescription for understanding both this particular case, and to some extent, the relationship between Iran and international law in historical context, as urged by Djamchid Momtaz. We conclude with some brief reflections on what an historically inflected jurisprudential lens might offer to scholarly practice and to our understandings of international law more broadly.

2 Background to the Dispute

Beginnings are generally either arbitrary or mythic, and beginning our story with the grant of the infamous D'Arcy Concession of 1901 could go either way. In 1901, the Persian empire was a socio-political entity with a history of over two millennia, although its status in the European law of nations was unclear. European companies had been formed to exploit Persian oil deposits from the mid-nineteenth century,[11] putatively authorized by the legal device of the 'concession'.[12] The concession granted to English mining entrepreneur William Knox D'Arcy by the Persian Government of Amin al-Sultan under the auspices of Qajar ruler, Muzzafer al-Din Shah, was notable for its sheer scale: D'Arcy was granted the 'special and excusive privilege to search for and obtain, exploit, develop, render suitable for trade, carry away and sell' oil and gas 'throughout the whole extent of the Persian Empire for a term of sixty years', in exchange

---

11 R. W. Ferrier, *The History of the British Petroleum Company: Volume 1 The Developing Years 1901–1932*, Cambridge University Press, 2009, pp. 24–27. This is the authorised history of the Company and is read as such.

12 The precise nature of the 'concession' in international law remains unclear and highly contested. It usually denotes a contract between a ruler or public authority with a foreign company or State to exercise both commercial and 'public' functions in a given area, often enormous. It was a favoured colonial instrument for two centuries, and taken up by the petroleum industry in the early twentieth century. It is a term which fell out of favour in the era of decolonisation. For a statement as to the conceptual difficulties of defining the concession in international law, see *Saudi Arabia v Arabian American Oil Company* (Aramco Arbitration), 'Award', *ILR 1963*, p. 117. For an overview and account of contests over the meaning and legality of concessions, see M. Sornarajah, *The International Law on Foreign Investment*, 3rd ed., Cambridge University Press, 2010, pp. 38–41. For an account of the terminology used today to apportion rights in functional modes not dissimilar to the older concession agreement (such as production sharing agreements, joint ventures, public-private partnerships, service contracts and so on), see C. Ohler, 'Concessions', in *Max Planck Encyclopedia of Public International Law*. Oxford University Press. Last modified February, 2013, available at http://opil.ouplaw.com/view/10.1093/law:epil/9780199231690/law-9780199231690-e1512?rskey=S34v0A&result=4&prd=EPIL, accessed August 23, 2016.

for a lump sum of sterling, paid-up shares to the value of £20,000 in the company formed to exercise the concession, and royalty payments of 16% of annual profits.[13]

The granting of the D'Arcy Concession is often cited as a contributing factor in what has subsequently become known as the Iranian Constitutional Revolution of 1905, a movement which disputed the authority of the Qajar Shahs to represent Persia in agreements, and to create and grant rights such as those contained in the D'Arcy Concession.[14] The Constitutional Revolution resulted in the formation of the *Majlis*, the Iranian parliament.[15] The D'Arcy Concession, however, remained on foot. Following the Anglo-Russian Entente of 1907 in which Britain and Russia agreed, without the involvement of the Shah or the *Majlis*, to divide Iranian territory into respective spheres of influence, the Anglo-Persian Oil Company was incorporated in London in 1909 with the close involvement of the British imperial Government after the discovery of commercial quantities of oil.[16] Anglo-Persian became the first large scale oil operation in the Middle East.[17] In 1921, the Qajar dynasty was overthrown, preventing the ratification of the 1919 Anglo-Iranian Treaty that would have rendered Persia a British protectorate in international law; and Reza Khan became the first Shah of the Pahlavi dynasty in 1925.[18]

---

13   Sornarajah, supra, note 12, p. 42. Despite the phrasing of the Concession, the arrangement was understood by both parties to exclude the five northern provinces, the traditional areas of Russian influence. See also A. W. Ford, *The Anglo-Iranian Oil Dispute of 1951–1952: A Study of the Role of Law in the Relations of States*, University of California Press, 1954, p. 15.

14   N. Keddie & M. Amanat, 'Iran under the Later Qājārs, 1848–1922', in P. Avery, G. Hambly & C. Melville (eds), *The Cambridge History of Iran*, vol. 7, Cambridge University Press, 1991, pp. 202–203. See also E. Abrahamian, *Iran Between Two Revolutions*, Princeton University Press, 1982, p. 74 et seq. Other unpopular and potentially unauthorised economic policies pursued by Muzaffer al-Din Shah reportedly included granting road tolls to the Imperial Bank of Britain, and the assumption of several loans including borrowing money from French companies to buy arms, from Russia to replay previous loans, and from Britain to finance personal ('medical') travel to Europe.

15   Ferrier, supra, note 11, p. 203; for detail on the composition of the parliament, see Abrahamian, supra, note 14, pp. 86–92.

16   P. J. Beck, 'The Anglo-Persian Oil Dispute 1932–33', 9 *Journal of Contemporary History* 1974, p. 124. On the Anglo-Russian Entente of 1907, see M. Behravesh, 'The Formative Years of Anglo-Iranian Relations (1907–1953): Colonial Scramble for Iran and Its Political Legacy', 21 *Digest of Middle East Studies* 2012, pp. 388–89.

17   Ferrier, supra, note 11, p. 107.

18   Behravesh, supra, note 16, p. 391.

The relationship between the Anglo-Persian Oil Company and the British imperial Government was symbiotic from the time of its formation. In 1914, the Company secured a contract to supply fuel oil to the Royal Navy at a fixed below-market price, and the British Government acquired a majority shareholding.[19] The Company involved itself both overtly and covertly in Iranian politics, seeking to monopolize both the oil industry and Iran's foreign relations in the south, against Russian attempts to do the same in the north.[20] The extent to which the Company was involved in the ascendance of the Pahlavi dynasty remains historically contentious.[21] Yet it is clear that as domestic political movements in the first half of the twentieth century sought to build a modern Iranian State that would shift the weight of sovereignty away from the Persian Shahs and toward a democratically constituted *Majlis*, the Anglo-Persian Oil Company sought to use its position to secure political outcomes that would favour its profit margin and the interests of its majority shareholder, the British Government.[22] Supporters of the Company maintained then—as now—that those interests were consistent with the interests of the Iranian people: royalty payments from the Company's operations were the Government's main source of income, and the Company developed the industrial infrastructure of significant regions of the country.[23] Yet within Persia, critics of the Company maintained that the interests of the Iranian people and of the fledgling Iranian State were chronically subordinated to the interests of the Company, and of the British empire, in the exploitation of Persian oil.[24]

A key critic of the Company was Mohammad Mossadeq, a legal academic elected to the first *Majlis* who advocated a constitutionally grounded Iranian nationalism. Popularly held as the first Iranian to receive a doctorate in law from a European university,[25] Mossadeq had in 1914 written and self-published

---

19 R. W. Ferrier, 'The Iranian Oil Industry,' in Avery, Hambly and Melville, *Cambridge History of Iran*, 642.

20 Behravesh, supra, note 16, pp. 391–392; Abrahamian, supra, note 14, p. 110.

21 See for example Ford, supra, note 13, pp. 12–14; A. Saikal, 'Iranian Foreign Policy 1921–79', P. Avery, G. Hambly & C. Melville (eds), in *The Cambridge History of Iran*, vol. 7, Cambridge University Press, 1991, pp. 429–431; and Behravesh, supra, note 16, pp. 391–392.

22 N. Abdelrehim, 'Rethinking 'Oil Nationalism': The Case of the Anglo-Iranian Oil Company', 4 *International Journal of Signs and Semiotic Systems* 2015, pp. 34–49.

23 See for example L. Lockhart, 'The Causes of the Anglo-Persian Oil Dispute', 40 *Journal of the Royal Central Asian Society*, 1953, pp. 134–50; and BP Global, supra, note 10.

24 Keddie & Amanat, supra, note 14, p. 435; Abrahamian, supra, note 14, pp. 143–44.

25 Mossadeq studied at Sciences Po in Paris, and Neuchâtel in Switzerland. J. A. Bill & W. Roger Louis, 'Introduction,' in J. A. Bill & W. Roger Louis Tauris (eds), *Mussaddiq, Iranian Nationalism and Oil*, 1988, p. 3.

a monograph calling for the abolition of the capitulation treaties in Persia in order to strengthen Persia's territorial sovereignty.[26] In 1928, as Reza Shah pursued a program of State modernization that sought both to maintain British support for the Pahlavi regime and to placate the nationalist movement in the *Majlis* in which Mossadeq was becoming increasingly central, the Shah abolished the British capitulation treaties and made a formal request to the Company to renegotiate the terms of the D'Arcy Concession.[27] The onset of the Great Depression in Europe and the United States and resulting fall in Company profits exacerbated the key issues which the Iranians sought to address: on its own terms, the Concession was unfair, and the 16% royalty manifestly inadequate. Added to these formal iniquities, the Company was using accounting practices that limited its on-paper profit in order to reduce the sum of royalties it owed to Iran.[28]

As protracted negotiations took place between the Iranian Government and the Company over the terms of the Concession, in September 1932 the *Majlis* and Senate ratified the Government's 1930 Declaration submitting to the jurisdiction of the Permanent Court of International Justice (PCIJ). Made under Article 36, paragraph 2 of the Statute of the PCIJ on condition of reciprocity, the Declaration recognized the compulsory jurisdiction of the Court in disputes arising 'with regard to situations or facts relating directly or indirectly to the application of treaties or conventions accepted by Persia and subsequent to the ratification of this declaration'.[29] The Declaration excluded *inter alia* any 'dispute with regard to questions which, by international law, fall exclusively within the jurisdiction of Persia'.[30] In November 1932, the D'Arcy Concession

---

26 R. Mottahedeh, *The Mantle of the Prophet: Religion and Politics in Iran*, Simon and Schuster, 1985; A. Pirzadeh, *Iran Revisited: Exploring the Historical Roots of Culture, Economics, and Society*, Springer, 2016, p. 208. For an analysis of the function of capitulation treaties in the Ottoman context, see U. Özsu, 'Ottoman Empire', in A. Peters & B. Fassbender (eds), *Oxford Handbook of the History of International Law*, Oxford University Press, 2012, pp. 429–448; and generally M. Craven, 'What Happened to Unequal Treaties? The Continuities of Informal Empire', 74 *Nordic Journal of International Law* 2005, pp. 335–382.

27 Keddie & Amanat, supra, note 14, p. 435; Behravesh, supra, note 16, p. 392.

28 J. Bamberg, *The History of The British Petroleum Company, Volume 2: The Anglo-Iranian Years, 1928–1954*, Cambridge University Press, 1994, pp. 22–26. The price at which the oil was being sold to the British Government (its majority shareholder) was also very low, further reducing profits and royalties to Iran.

29 The text of the Declaration, written in French, is provided in English translation in the ICJ's judgment of 22 July 1952. *Anglo-Iranian Oil Company Case*, supra, note 3, p. 103.

30 Ibid.

was cancelled by the Iranian Government at the direction of the Shah.[31] In response, the British Cabinet authorized an appeal to the Council of the League of Nations on the basis of the right of diplomatic protection, seemingly without consultation with the Company, a decision indicative of the imbrication of company and State.[32] In February 1933, both Governments agreed to suspend all proceedings before the Council of the League, so that the Company and the Iranian Government could renegotiate the terms of the oil concession. In April 1933, a new Concession agreement with refined royalty and dispute resolution provisions was signed by the Iranian Government and ratified by the *Majlis*. In October, the Rapporteur declared to the Council of the League that 'the dispute between His Majesty's Government in the United Kingdom and the Imperial Government of Persia is now finally settled'.[33] This assessment proved premature.

In 1935, Reza Shah requested that the name 'Iran' be used in place of the exonym 'Persia' in all diplomatic relations, and shortly after the Company name was amended to Anglo-Iranian.[34] Although relations with Britain were formally restored following entry into the 1933 Concession, the Shah worked to develop international relationships with 'third powers' as both a bulwark against the imperial interests of the United Kingdom and the Soviet Union in Iranian territory, and a means of building international recognition of Iran as an independent nation.[35] Both the United States and Germany were approached. While the increasingly autocratic Shah succeeded only in establishing limited trade and diplomatic links with the US due to Soviet protest, a tactical relationship was formed with the National Socialist Government in Germany. By the late 1930s, a significant portion of Iran's foreign trade was with Germany, and on the outbreak of war, Iran declared its neutrality.[36] The Shah's attempt to manoeuvre in European *realpolitik* was thwarted when Germany invaded the Soviet Union in June 1941. In the resulting Soviet-British alliance, Iran was occupied by Soviet armed forces in the north, and British armed forces in the south, essentially along the lines drawn by the Anglo-Russian

---

31   Bamberg, supra, note 28, p. 33.
32   Ibid.
33   *Anglo-Iranian Oil Company Case*, supra, note 3, p. 111.
34   It is noteworthy that the British Government continued to refer to Iran as Persia, it seems well into the 1950's and beyond, particularly in intra-British conversations and correspondence. This was no doubt irritating and quite possibly experienced as insulting by the Iranian Government. See Ford, supra, note 13, pp. 54–55.
35   Saikal, supra, note 21, pp. 433–434.
36   Ibid., p. 434; Bamberg, supra, note 28, p. 230.

Entente of 1907, while both imperial powers officially committed themselves to 'respect the sovereignty and territorial integrity' of Iran.[37] The invasion ruptured Reza Khan's autocratic hold on political power, and in September 1941, he was forced to abdicate.[38] Reza Khan's son Muhammad Reza Pahlavi was crowned as Shah.

The new Shah was supported by conservatives in the *Majlis*, but politically rejected by the growing nationalist movement, organized from 1949 as the National Front of Iran.[39] This domestic instability was exploited by both the British and the Russians. The British sought to bolster pro-British sentiment within the conservative opposition to the nationalist movement, whilst the Russians sought to foster pro-Soviet agitation within the banned Iranian communist movement, incorporated during the war into the *Hezb-e Tudeh Iran* (Tudeh) party.[40] By the late 1940s, the various political movements in Iran had adopted incommensurable positions on the continued economic dominance of the Anglo-Iranian Oil Company. The Shah and conservative supporters under General Ali Razmara advocated for the dedication of oil revenues to agricultural and industrial development, a reflection of the rise of development discourse in the international arena. The National Front under Mossadeq campaigned for nationalization of the oil industry.[41] Political instability intensified on the election of Razmara as Prime Minister in 1950. In March 1951, Razmara was assassinated, and the *Majlis* and Senate passed the *Oil Nationalisation Acts*. The *Acts* approved the principle of nationalization of oil resources, and provided that all of the Company's rights in Iranian oil and related infrastructure would pass to a newly created National Iranian Oil Company for compensation at market rates.[42] In April 1951, Mossadeq was elected Prime Minister[43] and, in May, formally advised the Company of the Government's intention

---

37   Saikal, supra, note 21, pp. 434–436.
38   Abrahamian, supra, note 14, pp. 163–165.
39   Ibid., p. 252.
40   Saikal, supra, note 21, pp. 434–436. Abrahamian considers the social history the Tudeh movement at length; see Abrahamian, supra, note 14, pp. 281–318.
41   On the National Front, see H. Katouzian, 'Mosaddeq's Government in Iranian History: Arbitrary Rule, Democracy and the 1953 Coup', in M. J. Gasiorowski & M. Byrne (eds), *Mohammad Mosaddeq and the 1953 Coup in Iran*, Syracuse University Press, 2004, pp. 1–26, pp. 1–6.
42   Bamberg, supra, note 28, pp. 418–419; also S. Nakasian, 'The Anglo-Iranian Oil Case: A Problem in International Judicial Process', 41 *Georgetown Law Journal* 1953, pp. 467–468.
43   Hussein Ala served as Prime Minister immediately after the Assasination of Razmara, but only for 51 days as he could not garner the co-operation of parliament. Ford, supra, note 13, p. 52; Abrahamian, supra, note 14, pp. 266–67.

to implement the nationalization policy.[44] As had been the case in 1932, the United Kingdom immediately commenced international legal action on the Company's behalf, and an action was commenced in the new International Court of Justice on 26 May 1951.

3   Summary of the Case

Against the dramatic backdrop of this struggle for independence against vested interests and imperial entitlement, the primary argument of the United Kingdom was quite simple in its construction. In its Application Instituting Proceedings lodged on 26 May 1951, the United Kingdom submitted that the *Nationalisation Acts* constituted a 'unilateral annulment' of the 1933 Agreement between the Imperial Government of Persia and the Anglo-Persian Oil Company; and that Iran had failed to respond to the Company's attempts to resolve the matter both under the good faith and arbitration clauses of the 1933 Agreement, and through diplomatic means via the United Kingdom.[45] The UK's standing to bring the application in the ICJ on behalf of the Company was again asserted on the basis of the right of diplomatic protection.[46] According to the Application, Iran had 'treated a British national in a manner not in accordance with the principles of international law and [had], in consequence, committed an international wrong against the Government of the United Kingdom'.[47] The UK submitted that because Iran had in September 1932 accepted the jurisdiction of the PCIJ with respect to all situations or facts that dealt directly or indirectly with the application of treaties and conventions entered into after that date, and the Application concerned the 1933 Agreement, the matter was within the jurisdiction of the ICJ.[48]

---

44 Bamberg, supra, note 28, p. 420.
45 *Anglo-Iranian Oil Company Case*, 'Application Instituting Proceedings', 26 May 1951, ICJ Pleadings, p. 10.
46 On the doctrine of diplomatic protection, see generally United Nations General Assembly, *Report of the International Law Commission on the work of its fifty-eighth session*, UN Doc. A/61/10, August 2006. The fifty-eighth session of the ILC was opened by Momtaz, who served as member of the ILC from 2000 to 2006, and President in the fifty-seventh session in 2005. On the historical use of diplomatic protection in international investment law, see generally Chapter 2 in Sornarajah, supra, note 12, especially pp. 37–38.
47 'Application Instituting Proceedings', supra, note 45, p. 12.
48 Ibid., p. 13.

The UK also ran a series of alternative arguments. The first sought to bring within jurisdiction treaties of friendship and commerce entered into by the UK and Persia in 1857 and 1903, well prior to Iran's accession to the ICJ and therefore ostensibly outside jurisdiction. The UK listed every treaty of friendship and commerce Iran had entered into after 1932 that could be used to ascertain most favoured nation status as had been promised the UK in the 1857 and 1903 treaties. Of these, only treaties with Denmark, Switzerland and Turkey post-dated 1932.[49] The second alternative argument was that Iran's conduct constituted a breach of Article 36(3) of the new Charter of the United Nations, pursuant to which legal disputes between Member States should be referred to the ICJ; and the third was that Iran's conduct breached general principles of customary international law, although this argument was left undeveloped.[50] By way of relief, the UK sought a declaration that the dispute was one that fell under the 1933 Agreement, and an order that Iran submit to arbitration; or in the alternative, a declaration that the execution of the *Nationalisation Acts*, insofar as it breached the 1933 Agreement, was contrary to international law.[51] The UK reserved the right to request the Court to order provisional measures to protect the 'rights of the Government of the United Kingdom that their national, the Anglo-Iranian Oil Company, should enjoy the rights to which it is entitled'.[52]

The Mossadeq Government's response to the ICJ proceeding was to continue with implementation of the *Nationalisation Acts*.[53] Prime Minister Mossadeq and his Ministers asserted in writing to the Company, and in diplomatic engagements with the UK and the United States, that nationalization was a sovereign act entirely within Iran's domestic jurisdiction and a right not limited by private agreements beyond the obligation to make just compensation.[54] The head of the Iranian Mixed Parliamentary Oil Commission appointed to oversee the nationalization process made public statements assuring 'the west' of an uninterrupted oil supply under the new National Iranian Oil Company.[55]

49　Ibid., pp. 14–17.
50　Ibid., p. 17.
51　Ibid., pp. 8–19.
52　Ibid., p. 19.
53　Bamberg, supra, note 28, pp. 430–436.
54　*Anglo-Iranian Oil Company Case*, 'Other Documents Submitted to the Court', pp. 684–697, especially p. 693.
55　Ibid., pp. 688–90.

In response to the Iranian Government's actions, on 22 June 1951 the UK lodged a Request for the Indication of Interim Measures of Protection in the ICJ.[56] The request sought an order for a series of measures that would prevent Iran from implementing the nationalization process until the merits of the case could be decided upon by the Court. Brought under Article 41 of the ICJ Statute, which states that the Court has power to indicate 'any provisional measures which ought to be taken to preserve the respective rights of either party',[57] the grounds for the request were cited as 'actions involving or threatening to involve the loss of skilled personnel, interference with management or the disruption of the integrated enterprise operated by the Anglo-Iranian Oil Company' on the one hand, and 'inflammatory speeches, broadcasts and articles' on the other.[58]

A week later on 29 June 1951, Iranian Minister for Foreign Affairs Baqer Kazemi sent a letter to the ICJ containing a 'statement which the Imperial Government of Iran has prepared rejecting the petition submitted by the British Government'.[59] In stark contrast to the UK's highly technical submissions to the Court, the Kazemi letter is an elegiac appraisal of the failings of the international order and the history of British intervention in Iran. At variance with European court practice and procedure, and adopting an epistolary mode of engagement with the court,[60] the letter opens with a passage of bold rhetoric:

> ... the question is often asked by many nations, how is it that with the existence of the United Nations Organization, the Security Council and the International Court of Justice, the foundations of world peace are still shaky and insecure?... If we view this question impartially, it will become clear to us that greed and selfishness on the part of the strong to procure illicit advantages from the weak nations are to be regarded as the main causes of this instability and the insecurity which prevails at

---

56 *Anglo-Iranian Oil Company Case*, 'Request for the Indication of Interim Measures of Protection'.
57 Statute of the International Court of Justice, art 41 (adapted from Article 41 of the Statute of the Permanent Court of International Justice).
58 'Request for the Indication of Interim Measures of Protection', supra, note 56, p. 54.
59 'Other Documents Submitted to the Court', supra, note 54, p. 672.
60 For two meditations on epistolary form and court judgment, see B. Kunbor, 'Epistolary Jurisdiction of the Indian Courts and Fundamental Human Rights in Ghana's 1992 Constitution: Some Jurisprudential Lessons', 2 *Law, Social Justice and Global Development*, 2001, available at https://www2.warwick.ac.uk/fac/soc/law/elj/lgd/2001_2/kunbor/#a2; and P. Goodrich, 'Epistolary Justice: The Love Letter as Law', 9 *Yale Journal of Law and the Humanities*, 1997, available at http://digitalcommons.law.yale.edu/yjlh/vol9/iss2/1/.

the present; and for so long as fair play and justice are not governing the relations of the strong and the weak, there can be no hope of bringing about world stability and achieving a lasting peace.[61]

The letter goes on to state in narrative form the bases of Iran's argument against the UK's original Application: that Iran's acceptance of the jurisdiction of the ICJ in 1932 applied prospectively only, and excluded from the ICJ's purview any matters bearing on Iran's national sovereignty, and therefore according to Article 36 of the ICJ Statute, the case was outside jurisdiction; that its treaties of friendship with the UK predated Iran's acceptance of ICJ jurisdiction; that the 1933 Agreement between Persia and the Company was invalid; and that even if it was valid, the 1933 Agreement was between Iran and a private company, and therefore not within jurisdiction.[62] Regarding the UK's Request for Interim Measures, the letter states that

> the respite given us by the Court is so short that one could not even procure the necessary visa for passports. Hence the Iranian government owing to the short respite, curtails its arguments; but earnestly hopes that the Court will not spare a moment to declare the case beyond its jurisdiction, as otherwise it would bring disappointment to the weaker nations as far as international justice and good-will are concerned.[63]

The ICJ chose not to recognize the Kazemi letter as a submission to the Court in the nature of a preliminary objection to its jurisdiction. An *ex parte* hearing on the UK's Request for Interim Measures was held the following day on 30 June. On 5 July 1951, the ICJ issued an Order declaring that neither party should undertake any action that would prejudice the rights of the other or 'aggravate or extend the dispute'.[64] On the question of its competence to issue provisional measures, the Court stated that the matter 'could not be regarded *a priori* to fall completely outside the bounds of international jurisdiction', which 'suffice(d) to empower the Court to entertain the Request for interim measures of protection'; and that 'the indication of such measures in no way prejudges the question of the jurisdiction of the Court to deal with the merits of the case

---

61   'Other Documents Submitted to the Court', supra, note 54, pp. 672–673.
62   Ibid., pp. 674–678.
63   Ibid., p. 678.
64   *Anglo-Iranian Oil Company Case*, Order of 5 July 1951, *ICJ Reports 1951*, p. 93–94.

and leaves unaffected the right of the Respondent to submit arguments against such jurisdiction'.[65]

In keeping with its position that the ICJ had no competence to issue interim orders, the Mossadeq Government continued with implementation of the *Nationalisation Acts*. In September 1951, the UK sought to have the Security Council enforce the ICJ's Order under Article 94(2) of the UN Charter, which gives the Council the power to 'make recommendations or decide upon measures to be taken to give effect to' judgments of the ICJ in cases of non-compliance.[66] In October 1951, Prime Minister Mossadeq appeared at the United Nations to present Iran's case to the Security Council.[67] Mossadeq commenced his address by stating that the Iranian population had one of the 'lowest standards of living in the world', and that under British control the oil industry had 'contributed practically nothing to the people's well-being, or to the technical progress or industrial development of the country'.[68] He then reiterated Iran's position that the ICJ had no competence to hear the original Application, and therefore no competence to issue provisional orders.[69] The Security Council, unable to reach agreement on the question of the ICJ's jurisdiction in either the principal or the interim matter, resolved to adjourn the debate until the Court had ruled on its own competence.[70]

On 22 July 1952, the ICJ delivered its judgment on the merits, holding that the Court had no jurisdiction to deal with the original Application submitted by the UK.[71] In its reasons, the Court held that it had jurisdiction over Iran only by virtue of Iran's Declaration made under Article 36(2) of its Statute, which applied only to disputes relating to the application of treaties or conventions entered into by Iran after in September 1932 when the Declaration was ratified.[72]

---

65 Ibid., p. 93.
66 Article 94(2), Charter of the United Nations, provides as follows: '(i)f any party to a case fails to perform the obligations incumbent upon it under a judgment rendered by the Court, the other party may have recourse to the Security Council, which may, if it deems necessary, make recommendations or decide upon measures to be taken to give effect to the judgment'.
67 *Report of the Security Council to the General Assembly covering the period from 16 July 1951 to 15 July 1952*, UN Doc. A/2167, 1952, pp. 17–24.
68 Ibid., p. 20.
69 Ibid., p. 20.
70 Ibid., p. 24. Nakasian offers an analysis of the Security Council debate in Nakasian, supra, note 42, pp. 475–480.
71 *Anglo-Iranian Oil Company Case*, supra, note 3, p. 114, (nine judges to five; Alvarez, Hackworth, Read, and Levi Carneiro JJ dissenting; separate opinion by McNair J).
72 Ibid., p. 107.

Rejecting the UK's submission that the 1933 Agreement between Persia and the Company was of 'a double character', being both a concessionary contract with the Company and a treaty with the UK, the ICJ held that the Agreement was a private contract, and thus not within the jurisdiction accepted by Iran in 1932.[73] The Court also rejected the UK's argument that treaties of friendship completed with Denmark, Switzerland and Turkey subsequent to Iran's acceptance of ICJ jurisdiction were sufficient to bring Iran's earlier treaties promising the UK most favoured nation status within its jurisdiction.[74] The majority decision is silent on the matter of whether Iran's nationalization of its oil industry was a sovereign act and thus beyond the justiciability of the Court.[75]

4   Implications for Analysis of International Law

Legal accounts of the *Anglo-Iranian Oil Company Case* typically end with the Court's decision of 22 July 1952. The case has been incorporated into the jurisprudence of both procedural international law and international investment law.[76] Such decontextualized accounts are of course a familiar aspect of the traditional legal casebook.[77] Yet this 'snapshot methodology'[78] common to much legal training radically dehistoricizes legal memory of the significance of a case, and encourages us as lawyers to believe that authority—and legal forms—exist in the world as stable formations, rather than being produced through contested practices of authorization which require ongoing

---

73   Ibid., p. 112.
74   Ibid., p. 113.
75   In his Dissenting Opinion, under a subheading 'Iran's nationalization of the oil industry and the 'reserved domain' of that State', Judge Alvarez describes a shift from 'classical international law', under which a State could freely exercise sovereign rights within its 'reserved domain', and the 'new international law', in which 'the reserved domain of States has been modified and considerably reduced'. *Anglo-Iranian Oil Company Case*, supra, note 3, pp. 127–129.
76   A. Orakhelashvili, 'Anglo-Iranian Oil Company Case', in *Max Planck Encyclopedia of Public International Law*, Oxford University Press, Last modified October, 2007, available at http://opil.ouplaw.com.ezp.lib.unimelb.edu.au/view/10.1093/law:epil/9780199231690/law-9780199231690-e93?rskey=13EZWx&result=1&prd=EPIL.
77   See for example J. Crawford, *Brownlie's Principles of Public International Law*, 8th ed. Oxford University Press, 2012, pp. 630–631; Sornarajah's account of the case is a notable exception to this tendency toward dehistorication. See Sornarajah, supra, note 12, p. 36.
78   J. Faundez, *Democratization, Development and Legality: Chile, 1831–1973*, Palgrave Macmillan, 2007, p. 9.

stabilization. Such 'snapshot methodology' also creates an impression of power as extrinsic, rather than intrinsic to law and the exercise of legal authority. Separating law from the world in this particular instance bolsters misconceptions around who adhered to international law and who did not in the events surrounding the nationalization of this particular oil company, and leaves uncontested wider Eurocentric mythologies about the adherence to and departure from international law in the attempted assertions of 'economic sovereignty' by decolonizing States in the twentieth century.[79]

Britain's response to the decision of the ICJ was to resort to extralegal force, both overt and covert. Prior to the Court's decision, Britain had declared economic sanctions against Iran. The Company withdrew all British workers from the Abadan oilfields, and Iran was blocked from accessing its assets held in British banks.[80] Mossadeq entreatied other States with whom Iran had diplomatic ties to provide technical support to the new National Iranian Oil Company during the transition to national control. The United States, Sweden, Belgium, the Netherlands, Pakistan, and West Germany all refused, whilst Italy agreed. The UK continued to hold that the nationalization was unlawful and that the Company's rights and interests under the Concession remained proprietary. In July 1952 after the ICJ decision, a British RAF plane forced an Italian-chartered tanker carrying Iranian oil into the waters of the British protectorate of Aden and issued an action in detinue, claiming the Italians were in unlawful possession of British property.[81] In August 1952, US President Truman and British Prime Minister Churchill issued a joint communiqué calling for the compensation of the Company to be arbitrated. Mossadeq responded by

---

79 For an indicative account of the belief that Britain and the US were adhering to law whilst Iran was departing from it, even as the coup was being planned, see the postscript to the book by Alan Ford written in 1954, which announces 'the overthrow of Mossadegh's Government' in an 'army coup led by General Fazollah Zahedi', and ends with the conviction that 'the British and American Governments will try to extend a helping hand as quickly and tactfully as possible'. (Ford, supra, note 13, pp. 231–232).

80 Bamberg, supra, note 28, pp. 457–458.

81 The Supreme Court of Colony of Aden gave a decision in favor of the Company in *Anglo-Iranian Oil Company Ltd v Jaffrate* [1953] 1 W.L.R. 246, which dismissed the ship master's testimony that the action was invalid as the ship entered the jurisdiction under duress with the following statement: '(n)o reasonable person could think it likely that H.M. Government in the year 1952 would try to resolve a commercial dispute by what would be little short of an act of war'. See 'Anglo-Iranian Oil Co. v. Jaffrate *et al.*', 47 *American Journal of International Law* 1953, p. 326.

demanding 49 million pounds in compensation from the Company for intentional underpayment under the 1932 Concession.[82]

By February 1953, an anti-Mossadeq collaboration had formed between the United Kingdom, the United States, and the conservative movement in Iran, that together sought to strengthen the position of the Shah against the National Front.[83] By April 1953, in a joint operation of the American Central Intelligence Agency and the British Military Intelligence Agency, action was underway to further destabilize Mossadeq, accelerating the political disintegration of the structure of the Iranian Government.[84] Entering into a strategic alliance in the *Majlis* with the Tudeh party, the Mossadeq Government moved in 1953 to strip the Shah of his official powers, and forbade contact between the Shah and foreign officials.[85] In June 1953, the US State Department approved a CIA-led coup operation, dubbed Operation Ajax.[86] After a failed coup attempt and increasing socio-political volatility, on 19 August 1953 Operation Ajax succeeded. Following a nine-hour siege on Mossadeq's house that split the Iranian military, Mossadeq was arrested and charged with treason, and Muhammad Reza Shah Pahlavi was reinstated to political power in Iran with US and British support.[87] The historical consequences of foreign sponsorship of the Shah's prolonged rule in Iran are far more widely known than the story of oil nationalization under Mossadeq that precipitated that sponsorship. Twenty-five years later, the movement toward Iranian independence away from dynastic rule and foreign interference first formalized in the Constitutional Revolution of 1905 had been reframed within the Islamist discourse of the Ayatollahs.[88]

---

82 Bamberg, supra, note 28, pp. 473–476.

83 For a detailed account of this alignment against Mosaddeq, see F. Azimi, 'Unseating Mosaddeq: The Configuration and Role of Domestic Forces', in M. J. Gasiorowski & M. Byrne (eds), *Mohammad Mosaddeq and the 1953 Coup in Iran*, Syracuse University Press, 2004, pp. 27–101.

84 As Louis points out, in 1952 British diplomats were expelled from Iran, and MI6 had handed over control of its intelligence network to the CIA. (Roger Louis, supra, note 7, p. 129).

85 Abrahamian, supra, note 14, pp. 271–73.

86 In 2000, the New York Times published the CIA's internal report on Operation Ajax. Central Intelligence Agency, National Security Archive, D. N. Wilber, 'Overthrow of Premier Mossadeq of Iran: November 1952–August 1953', March 1954, available at http://nsarchive.gwu.edu/NSAEBB/NSAEBB435/, accessed August 23, 2016. For a popular history of the operation by a New York Times journalist, see S. Kinzer, *All the Shah's Men: An American Coup and the Roots of Middle East Terror*, Wiley and Sons, 2003.

87 See M. J. Gasiorowski, 'Coup d'Etat against Mosaddeq' in M. J. Gasiorowski & M. Byrne, *Mohammad Mosaddeq and the 1953 Coup in Iran*, Syracuse University Press, 2004, 256–58.

88 Abrahamian, supra, note 14, pp. 530–37.

As well as playing into a prevailing atmospherics of a law-abiding 'west' and recalcitrant Iran (if not a law-breaking 'rest'), recounting the *Anglo-Iranian Oil Company Case* without an attention to its historical context also smooths over the variety of views which were in play at the time about what an international court of justice should be and what it should do in the world, at a crucial moment in both the ICJ's formation and in the transition from an imperial to a putatively decolonizing world. Such differences inhered amongst States of all kinds,[89] but were particularly potent as 'new' States 'entered' a juridical world not of their own design, and sought to engage with it in more or less syncretic ways.[90] Indeed, what looks from the vantage point of today like a routine procedural dispute about interim measures and jurisdiction, warranting only a footnote in most texts, looks from the historical milieu of the case itself like a battle about the proper role and function of the international court in a radically changing world.[91]

For the Iran of Mosaddeq at least, the *Anglo-Iranian Oil Company Case* was the stage upon which its sovereignty would be performed, in the space between technical legal doctrine and political struggle. What was at issue was not simply a point of procedural jurisdiction, but the power to define what sovereignty would mean for decolonizing States, and the relationship of that concept to the question of international adjudication. As both the content and form of the letter from Kazemi to the Court make clear, to Iran a dispute between a private company and the Government was a matter for domestic resolution. Compensation was envisaged as a way of settling with the Company, but the right of a State to determine who had control of its most significant resources was understood as squarely within the purview of sovereign decision making. The idea that this new international law might not only support

---

[89] For and exemplary document which gives some sense of the range of views of those behind the establishment of the court, see generally the report of the Commission headed by William Malkin, *Report of the Informal Inter-Allied Committee on the Future of the Permanent Court of International Justice*, reproduced in 39 *American Journal of International Law*, 1945 pp. 1–56. See also J. Headlam-Morley, *Studies in Diplomatic History*, Alfred H. King, 1930, especially chapter 2.

[90] On the question of syncretism and international law in the context of decolonisation, see Pahuja, supra, note 3. For a survey of 'new' States and their attitude to the ICJ, see I. F. I. Shihata, 'The Attitude of New States Toward the International Court of Justice,' 19 *International Organization*, 1965, pp. 203–222.

[91] On the project of trying to reconstruct in detail a historical milieu in order to understand the concerns animating the actors at the time, particularly in the context of understanding struggles over decolonisation, see D. Scott, 'The Temporality of Generations: Dialogue, Tradition, Criticism', 45 *New Literary History* 2014, p. 157–181.

the international adjudication of such a dispute, but could potentially prevent the nationalization of natural resources from happening at all even before the Court had established its jurisdiction,[92] was a grave disappointment of hopes for the institution of a new era in which 'fair play and justice [might] govern the relations of the strong and the weak'.[93]

It is more than ironic, then, that sovereign statehood was the only legal form by which a socio-political entity could enter the world and take up a lawful place in it; and yet even as non-European States took it up, the invocation of 'sovereignty' itself was decried as being *against* the (international) law of which it is a key jurisdictional form.[94] Accounts which treat contestations over the ICJ's jurisdiction during this crucial moment as purely technical questions miss the texture of what were jurisprudential struggles over the kind of worlds being authored and authorized through international law in the wake of empire, and risk participating in the rituals of contemporary international law which imply that there is nothing outside Europe and the world of its making.[95]

---

92 Iran was of course not alone in arguing against the ICJ's jurisdiction to 'indicate provisional measures' under Article 41 of the Statute where its jurisdiction to hear the merits was in doubt. There was contemporaneous debate about whether the Court's interim decision was good law. See C. G. Fenwick, 'The Order of the International Court of Justice in the Anglo-Iranian Oil Company Case', 45 *American Journal of International Law* 1951, pp. 723–727; B. F. Brown, 'The Juridical Implications of the Anglo-Iranian Oil Company Case', 1952 *Washington University Law Quarterly* 1952, pp. 384–397; and Ford, supra, note 13, p. 90. The legal threshold for jurisdiction to indicate interim measures is still not settled; it remains unclear whether the ICJ has to satisfy itself that the primary case does not *a priori* fall outside its jurisdiction, as held in *Anglo-Iranian*, or whether it has to satisfy itself that it *prima facie* has jurisdiction to hear the primary case, as held in *Legality of Use of Force* (Yugoslavia v Belgium et al.), *ICJ Reports 1999*, p. 124 and *Armed Activities on the Territory of the Congo* (Democratic Republic of the Congo v Rwanda), New Application, *ICJ Reports 2002*, p. 219.

93 'Other Documents Submitted to the Court', supra, note 54, p. 672.

94 On sovereignty as a 'jurisdictional form' of European international law, see S. McVeigh & S. Pahuja, 'Sovereignty as Promise and Loss', in C. Barbour & G. Pavlich (eds), *After Sovereignty: On the Question of Political Beginnings*, Routledge, 2010.

95 For the seminal critique of Eurocentric diffusionism, or the idea that Europeans are 'the makers of history', and that cultural processes tend to flow out of the European sector and toward the non-European sector over the course of history, see J. M. Blaut, *The Colonizer's Model of the World: Geographical Diffusionism and Eurocentric History*, Guilford Press, 1993. For an account of international law which describes the way in which administrative arrangements and legal forms moved from 'periphery' to 'centre' rather than the

5 Conclusion

Accounts of post-war decolonization and state-making in the non-European world, at least in international legal scholarship in English, have tended to under-emphasize the significance of the Iranian experience. It may well be that the history of Iran's status in twentieth century international law has defied ready analysis precisely because the Iranian experience of 'coming into' international law raises issues which have remained unresolved into the contemporary moment.

Djamchid Momtaz sought to remind us in 1976 that it was not possible to understand Iran's attitude to international law without being alive to the history of that relationship. Specifically, Momtaz wrote, the international legal scholar needed to be attentive to the Iranian experience of 'repeated attacks on [its] sovereignty' on the one hand, and 'its exclusion from the international community, from the inception of the League of Nations onwards, on the other'.[96] It later turned out that 1976 was a moment in which Iran was poised 'between two revolutions', as Abrahamian has put it, each quite different in character.[97] And from a vantage point some forty years later, with the benefit of both hindsight and documents which have become declassified since 1976, Momtaz' essay takes on a character both prescient and poignant. Its prescience lies in its observation that as a State, Iran is both porous and shunned. Its poignancy foreshadows the turn of the promise of decolonization, and post-imperial state-making more broadly, both in Iran and elsewhere, from 'romance' to 'tragedy', to paraphrase David Scott.[98]

In the Iranian version of that now all too familiar story, the romance of an urbane and enlightened European-trained lawyer, poised to translate the post-war promise of modernization into real political and economic independence for Iran through constitutional reform and the nationalization of the oil industry, is subverted by the geo-strategic desires of empires new and old, inflamed by oil and distorted through the prism of Cold War paranoia.[99]

---

other way around, see C. Storr, 'End State: Nauru and the History of International Law', (doctoral thesis in progress).

96 Momtaz, supra, note 1, p. 199 (our translation).
97 Abrahamian, supra, note 14.
98 See D. Scott, *Conscripts of Modernity: the Tragedy of Colonial Enlightenment*, Duke University Press, 2004.
99 This patterning—from the European-educated nationalist leader with faith in the constitution and the desire to nationalise economic engines previously exploited for the benefit of the coloniser—was repeated all over the Third World. The 'lessons' learned by Britain and the United States from the putative success of the Iranian venture when assessed

The democratically elected Mossadeq dies under house arrest in 1967 after a coup orchestrated by Britain and the United States. From the British perspective, the coup was 'necessary' to reverse the nationalization of the oil industry. From the American perspective, the coup was meant to prevent the communist takeover of the Iranian Government, a belief which was almost certainly spurious as it turns out, and encouraged by Britain as a way to encourage the United States to support its own aims.[100]

Historically de-contextualized readings of the *Anglo-Iranian Oil Company Case* miss the shift from romance to tragedy which the case and its aftermath represent, and belie the way in which the case cut across matters of international ordering which were profoundly uncertain in 1951. Tensions between the 'international' jurisdiction constructed in the nineteenth century to govern the relations of imperial powers and the domestic jurisdiction of newly sovereign States formerly subject to imperial rule were becoming increasingly apparent.[101] Whereas the administrative apparatus of imperial rule was largely in retreat as the movement toward formal self-determination gathered momentum, the continued operation in decolonizing States of companies founded under imperial conditions was fiercely defended by the old imperial powers. Whilst the era of formal empire was declared to be coming to an end, the fate of the economic order constructed during that era remained an open question. As newly independent States attempted to nationalize domestic resources, arguing that nationalization was in keeping with principles of sovereign equality and self-determination, foreign companies and States alike defended foreign ownership of those resources, arguing that the proper observance of contract and property rights was in keeping with principles of peace and stability. There were deeply diverging views, too, around the character of international law, and the proper role of international institutions. Different peoples had very different ideas about what kind of institution the International Court of

---

from a short temporal horizon, were carried over into Suez and Guatemala respectively. By the end of the 1970s, it may have seemed fairly clear to many that imperial hubris and Cold War paranoia were perhaps clouding judgments in the North.

100 A. N. Rubin, *Archives of Authority: Empire, Culture and the Cold War*, Princeton University Press, 2012, p. 34; and Gasiorowski, supra, note 87, pp. 229–233. This story is the subject of a forthcoming essay we are writing on Iran, international law and the Cold War as part of the Australian Research Council-funded project, 'International Law and the Cold War', see http://www.coldwarinternationallaw.org/

101 See generally G. Simpson, *Great Powers and Outlaw States: Unequal Sovereigns in the International Legal Order*, Cambridge University Press, 2004; M. Koskenniemi, *The Gentle Civilizer of Nations: The Rise and Fall of International Law 1870–1960*, Cambridge University Press, 2002; and Dorsett & McVeigh, supra, note 6.

Justice should be, and the role it should play in ordering the world. The effect of the United Nations Charter on the interpretation of the jurisprudence of the PCIJ was unclear.[102] As States like Iran sought to participate as equals in the international community, profoundly political and historical questions about the meaning of decolonization and the proper shape and role of international institutions and international laws in the world were being reframed by former imperial powers as technical questions of jurisdiction and interpretation.[103] When read through the lens of historically inflected jurisprudence, the *Anglo-Iranian Oil Company Case* offers a significant insight into this moment of transition.

---

102 The legal status of the general obligations listed in Article 2(2)–2(6), including the obligation to settle international disputes by peaceful means, was untested, as was the meaning of Article 2(7), which placed matters 'essentially within the domestic jurisdiction of any State' beyond UN intervention. This was a key part of the debate in the Security Council over the Anglo-Iranian case. See Nakasian, supra, note 42, pp. 475–480.

103 As an iteration of an argument describing the role of technical expertise in shaping political struggles, see D. Kennedy, *A World of Struggle: How Power, Law, and Expertise Shape Global Political Economy*, Princeton University Press, 2016.

Statehood, Proto States and International Law: New Challenges, Looking at the Case of ISIS[1]

Anicée Van Engeland

Introduction

While the existence and role of ISIL (Islamic State of Iraq and the Levant)/Daesh/ISIS will be short-lived in the span of history, the movement's impact on international law could be permanent:[2] by occupying a territory and subjecting its inhabitants to their own interpretation of Islamic law, ISIS has not only raises questions regarding the nature of the international community's reaction to a transnational religious radical movement that seems have state-like features; the movement has also compelled the international community to question its approach to the concept of nation State and its role in public international law.

While some scholars have discarded the possibility of considering ISIS as a State from the onset,[3] preferring to call it a non-state actor, others have attempted to apply the Montevideo criteria to the movement, with little success. The two approaches come with their own strategies under public international law: those considering ISIS solely as a radical transnational movement approach it as a non-state armed group operating on a territory;[4] for practitioners and scholars arguing that ISIS could be a State, actions under the UN Charter are open. It is therefore fair to say that even if ISIS has not been

---

[1] This paper was presented at American Society of International Law (ASIL) Annual Conference in April 2016. The author wishes to thank Steven Feldstein, Scott Lyons, Boris Mamlyuk, and Rafael Porrata-Doria for their support.
[2] To remain neutral, I will call the movement ISIS rather than Daesh.
[3] R. Cryer, 'Syria and International Criminal Law' (paper presented at the Army Legal Services Annual Conference, Shrivenham, 2 June 2016).
[4] M. P. Scharf, 'How The War Against Isis Changed International Law', 48 *Case Western Reserve Journal International Law*, 2016 pp. 15–67; D. E. Stigall & C. L. Blakesley, 'Non-State Armed Groups And The Role Of Transnational Criminal Law During Armed Conflicts', 48 *The George Washington International Law Review*, 2015, p. 1, available at http://scholars.law.unlv.edu/cgi/viewcontent.cgi?article=1968&context=facpub, accessed June 20, 2016; K. Ambos, 'The new enemy of mankind: The Jurisdiction of the ICC over members of 'Islamic State'', Comment on European Journal of International Law (EJIL)Talk, 26 November 2015, http://www.ejiltalk.org/the-new-enemy-of-mankind-the-jurisdiction-of-the-icc-over-members-of-islamic-state/.

declared a State, the international community has met a new challenge, that of the emergence of a proto-state, as labelled by Cronin,[5] which does not meet the Montevideo criteria and yet seems to have state-like features. This chapter will consider the ISIS's possible claim to statehood, despite the fact that the majority of academics consider it to be a non-state actor. The reason for examining ISIS as a State results from the overall necessity for international law to prepare the future, may it include proto-states. I am therefore not concluding that ISIS is a State, but I am using its emergence as an opportunity to discuss the flexibility of international law and to encourage a dialogue between public international law and an alternative legal system, Islamic law.

Muslim scholars and practitioners have also questioned the nature of ISIS, scrutinizing the movement to know whether it is a State under public international law, a Caliphate under Islamic law or a religious radical movement to be classified as a non-state armed group. The stakes of labelling ISIS are not the same for the international community and for Muslim actors: the existence of the movement and its actions in the name of Islam has created a sense of unease for some Muslim believers and an outright rejection for others. Yet, strategies to comprehend the movement differ: some scholars prefer to reject ISIS as being un-Islamic.[6] They consider that the movement has of Islam only but the name. This is indirectly sustained by Roy who speaks of a radicalization of Islam,[7] rejecting the idea of a radicalized Islam supported by Kepel.[8] Others believe ISIS must be addressed as its fighters and followers claim they are Muslims. I take the stance that the very fact that ISIS claim it is Muslim and rely on Islamic teachings is sufficient to deliver a proper response to ISIS's existence and its possible claim to statehood.[9]

The heart of this paper, and its originality, is consequently a matter of labelling and its consequences: What is at stake when one qualifies the movement as a radical group to be associated with all non-state armed actors or when

---

5   A. K. Cronin, 'ISIS is not a Terrorist Group', 94 *Foreign Affairs*, 2015, pp. 87–98.
6   J. Cole, 'How 'Islamic' is the Islamic State?', *The Nation*, 24 February 2015, available at http://www.thenation.com/article/how-islamic-islamic-state/.
7   O. Roy, 'Le djihadisme est une révolte générationnelle et nihiliste', *Le Monde*, 24 November 2015, available at http://www.lemonde.fr/idees/article/2015/11/24/le-djihadisme-une-revolte-generationnelle-et-nihiliste_4815992_3232.html; T. Peace, 'Who becomes a terrorist and why?', *Washington Post*, 10 May 2016, available at https://www.washingtonpost.com/news/monkey-cage/wp/2016/05/10/who-becomes-a-terrorist-and-why/.
8   G. Kepel, *Terreur dans l'Hexagone : genèse du djihad français*, Gallimard, 2015.
9   A. Emon, 'Is ISIS Islamic? Why it Matters for the Study of Islam', Comment on *The Imminent Frame*, 27 March 2015, available at http://blogs.ssrc.org/tif/2015/03/27/is-isis-islamic-why-it-matters-for-the-study-of-islam/.

another accepts the view that ISIS could pretend to statehood? Determining the legal shape of ISIS is crucial: it will have an impact on how the threat is addressed by the international community but also by Muslim authorities, scholars and practitioners. The latter tend to consider ISIS as a non-state actor rather than as a State for fear that statehood could grant it legitimacy. International law practitioners and scholars have also been clear in the rejection of ISIS's statehood: the UN Security Council Resolution 2249 and the ensued discussion about the use of self-defence address ISIS as a non-state armed group.[10] While I agree that for the time being ISIS can be approached as a non-state armed group, I also suggest the international community and the Muslim communities need to rethink the way they approach the concept of State to be able to embrace differences: ISIS is not only a transnational religious radical group. It is also a proto-state that could crystallize and become permanent, or that could be multiplied in the future. This is why this book chapter will apprehend the issue of the nature of ISIS as a proto-State, looking firstly at how the movement positions itself with regard to statehood: while the movement does not endorse the Montevideo criteria, or international law as a whole, it still displays some signs of wishing to embrace statehood. The second part of the paper will look at ways the international community can look at the ISIS phenomenon. I argue that the Montevideo criteria are not relevant in the case of a proto-state that seeks legitimacy in a violent interpretation of Islam. In the third part, I insist on the importance of looking at the contribution made by Islamic law and Muslim views, without however reducing the ISIS threat to a Muslim issue only.

1   Analysis of ISIS's Message with Regard to Statehood

When Obama declared, in December 2015, that ISIS is not part of the Muslim civilization, he conveyed the thoughts of many Muslims, as illustrated by the 2014 'not in my name' British campaign. The general reaction amongst Muslim believers has been a rejection of the ISIS phenomenon whose violations of

---

10   D. Akande & M. Milanovic, 'The Constructive Ambiguity of the Security Council's ISIS Resolution', Comment on EJIL Talk, 21 November 2015, available at http://www.ejiltalk.org/the-constructive-ambiguity-of-the-security-councils-isis-resolution/; M. Weller, 'Permanent Imminence of Armed Attacks: Resolution 2249 (2015) and the Right to Self Defence Against Designated Terrorist Groups', Comment on EJIL Talk, 25 November 2015, available at http://www.ejiltalk.org/permanent-imminence-of-armed-attacks-resolution-2249-2015-and-the-right-to-self-defence-against-designated-terrorist-groups/.

human rights do not represent the message of the Quran. Others have embraced ISIS as offering a new discourse to understand the world.[11] Emon stresses the importance of apprehending the movement as Muslim to avoid any elitism:[12] ISIS fighters consider themselves to be Muslims and believe they are fighting in the name of Islam. They should, as a result, be considered as such. This is why examining the movement and its rhetoric is relevant: it contributes to our understanding of the group. The ISIS rhetoric with regard to statehood is rather muddled despite the 2014 declaration by al-Baghdadi that ISIS is a Caliphate and the 2015 discovery of a twenty-four pages constitution-like document. Yet, ISIS, despite calling itself an Islamic State (*ad-Dawlah al-Islāmiyah*) and adopting some state-like features, does not wish to play a part in the international community.[13]

This rejection of international law and the refusal to adhere to the international community's values sets ISIS apart: it projects itself as a movement whose entire existence is based on conflict. It only engages with the outside world through violence. Yet, it does occupy a portion of the Iraqi and Syrian territory in which it holds hostages that are its 'citizens'. ISIS even applies the concept of *dhimmi* to non-Muslims, effectively turning them into second-class citizens. The movement has also attracted a population from abroad. ISIS certainly has a form of Government, as attested by the impressive local, departmental and regional structures dealing with budget or education. These four points, all to be found in the Montevideo Convention, lead us to the question: could ISIS claims it is a State?

The twenty-four pages document found in 2015 sheds light on how ISIS understands the world through conflict. It demonstrates that the movement is organized in its approach to war; it also shows that the group also has begun erecting what could at first glance appear to be a State.[14] It has laws, social services, a constitution (the twenty-four pages manual), a banking system, a tax system, a police and an army. However, a critical analysis from a Muslim perspective reveals that, while all these roles are endorsed by the State, they are for the sole purpose of jihad. The ISIS experiment is not a classic state-building

---

11 S. Atran, *L'Etat islamique est une révolution,* Les Liens Qui Libèrent Editions, 2016; R. Liogier, *Le Mythe de l'Islamisation: Essai sur une obsession collective*, Seuil, 2012.
12 Emon, supra, note 9.
13 E. Benvenisti, 'The Paradoxes of Sovereigns as Trustees of Humanity: Concluding Remarks', 16 *Theroretical Inquiries In Law*, 2015 pp. 535–548, 536.
14 Y. Shany, A. Cohen & T. Mimran, 'ISIS: Is the Islamic State Really a State?', *Israel Democracy Institute*, 14 September 2014, available at http://en.idi.org.il/analysis/articles/isis-is-the-islamic-state-really-a-state/.

exercise but rather the emergence of a proto-state that has adopted the post-classicist definition of jihad as being a permanent state of war to be exported.[15] The entirety of the so-called State apparatus is geared towards war, from the training of children to jihad to the redistribution of wealth through provinces to sustain the war effort. As a result, ISIS does not create a nation State but a jihadi State. This is a novelty for both international law and Islamic law. It leads me to conclude that ISIS constitutes a dystopian understanding of the concept of State: it is a proto-state where a cult organizes every aspect of life. Besides, ISIS is not interested in following the rules the international community abides by, leading to the conclusion that ISIS does not seek to be a State according to the Montevideo convention.

Based on these observations, my argument is that ISIS is neither a nation State nor a caliphate, but a proto-state taking the shape of a jihadi State. I use the term jihadi in the way radical groups refer to war:[16] they understand the term of jihad as allowing a permanent aggressive war that should be exported.[17] ISIS's proclaimed caliphate is a new form of State that should urgently be addressed under international law and Islamic law. This will help providing the relevant instruments to comprehend it, but also any future proto-state that relies on radical views (religious or not). As stated before, the movement's existence might be temporary and will only constitute a small reference in the history of the world and of Islam. It remains that the movement offers an opportunity to revisit the concept of nation-state as we know it. Other proto-states similar to ISIS could emerge in the future and both legal systems, international and Islamic, are currently not able to address them as States. Approaching ISIS and any other proto-state as a non-state armed group might not be sufficient in the future. The risk is that we could witness a crystallization of ISIS or any future proto-state into a State, and that the international community would then be powerless in addressing a phenomenon it has not reflected upon. ISIS

---

15 A. Van Engeland, 'Islam as Religion of Peace: an Articulated Reply to Terrorism', in R. Barnidge Jr (ed), *The Liberal Way of War: Legal Perspectives*, Ashgate, 2013, p. 243.

16 A. Van Engeland, 'Verse 9:5 of the Quran as an Intermixed Ground for jus ad bellum and jus in bello: Adapting Islamic Classical Theory to Modern Asymmetric Conflict', 7 *GAIR*, 2015 pp. 129–150.

17 A. Van Engeland, 'Islam and the Protection of Civilians in the Conduct of Hostilities: the Asymmetrical war from the Transnational Terrorist Groups' Viewpoints and from the Muslim Modernists' Viewpoints', in C. Bassiouni & A. Guellali (eds), *Jihad And The Challenges Of International And Domestic Law*, Cambridge University Press/The Hague Academy Press, 2010, pp. 139–166.

offers the opportunity to rethink statehood differently, while considering the possible 'socialization' of a rogue state.[18]

2 The Public International Law Perspective on ISIS as a State

ISIS self-proclamation as a Caliphate raises questions under international law: was ISIS's declaration a claim to statehood? It should instead be understood in ISIS own parameters: the movement does not refer to the concept of statehood as it is not a constitutive element of its ideology. Yet, it calls itself 'Islamic State' (*ad-Dawlah al-Islāmiyah*). While it clear that calling itself a State does not make it one,[19] it is still relevant to go through the Montevideo criteria to analyze whether ISIS as a proto-jihadi State has a claim to statehood.

The usual benchmark for public international law scholars under the declaratory theory is to refer to the Montevideo criteria. While some scholars have said that ISIS should not be considered as State because it could never meet the Montevideo requirements, others have agreed that ISIS meets some of the expectations to a degree.[20] For example, it is uncertain whether ISIS has a defined territory but it still occupies one. It is clear its Government is effective, as per the description found in the twenty-page pages documents and the reports made by survivors. The issue of the permanency of the population has also been raised: ISIS has drawn in people from abroad and has trapped in the local populations, effectively ruling over a population. Its interactions with other nations are based on violence but do exist: the movement does not operate in a vacuum. So the conclusion could be that ISIS is a State in becoming or an incomplete nation State.[21]

Looking at the constitutive theory is also helpful: in the case at hand, recognition by other States has not occurred. In the past, States have recognized others as States on a purely pragmatic basis, granting rights and duties deriving

---

18 K. Waltz, *Theory of International Politics*, Reading, Mass: Addison-Wesley Pub. Co., 1979, p. 127.

19 P. Neumann, director of the International Center for the Study of Radicalization at King's College London, in D, Bifelsky, 'In New Front against Islamic State, Dictionary Become a Weapon', *New York Times*, 2 October 2014, available at http://www.nytimes.com/2014/10/03/world/europe/islamic-state-isis-muslims-term.html?_r=0.

20 Shany, supra, note 14.

21 S. M. Walt, 'ISIS as Revolutionary State: New Twist on an Old Story', 94 *Foreign Affairs*, 2015, pp. 42–51.

from this recognition.[22] This raises the question as to whether or not the international community constitutes some form of club that only accepts members based on interest. It is important to understand why the international community refuses to include ISIS as it questions the conception of the right to statehood: is ISIS not recognized as a State because it is a Muslim form of State? Or it is because the group violates all public international law values that international community is attached to? After all, statehood constitutes, as stressed by French, the very core of modern international law.[23]

My conclusion, that of a pseudo-proto-jihadi State, creates a conundrum for international law: accepting ISIS as a fellow State undermines the entire system and its post-World War II origins. Excluding it not only gives the impression that the international community is an elite club; it might also be a tactical error with heavy consequences for the future. Relying on Waltz's socialization theory of States is certainly a solid point to argue. There is an argument made for the crystallization of ISIS as a State and its socialization: scholars like Walt[24] and Katagiri[25] have noted that revolutionary States like France post 1789, Russia post 1917 and Iran post 1979 tend reject norms of statehood before embracing them to sustain themselves.[26] This rational has also been applied to non-state actors that fought for self-determination and won, adapting from leading an asymmetric conflict to managing a State.[27] There is therefore a literature on non-actors, including armed groups, transforming into States.[28] Yet, countries like North Korea reject international law and refuse to contribute to the international community, violating human rights along the way. ISIS could crystallize in a similar way, except for its constant desire to expand and attack civilians abroad, therefore never socializing because it does not have an interest in joining the international community.

The stakes when discussing ISIS's claims to statehood are multiple, ranging from compliance with international law to an intervention under Chapter VII

---

[22] A. Coleman, *Resolving Claims To Self-Determination: Is There a Role for the International Court of Justice?*, Routledge, 2013, p. 139.

[23] D. French, *Statehood and Self-Determination. Reconciling Tradition and Modernity in International Law*, Cambridge University Press, 2013, p. 1.

[24] Walt, supra, note 21.

[25] N. Katagiri, 'ISIS: Insurgent Strategies for Statehood and the Challenge for Security Studies', 26 *Small Wars and Insurgencies*, 2015 pp. 542–556, at p. 544.

[26] Walt, supra, note 21, p. 42.

[27] I. Arreguin-Toft, *How the Weak Win Wars: A Theory of Asymmetric Conflict*, Cambridge University Press, 2005; J. Lyall & I. Wilson, 'Rage Against the Machines: Explaining Outcomes in Counterinsurgency Wars', 63 International Organization, 2009, pp. 67–106.

[28] Katagiri, supra, note 25, p. 544.

of the UN Charter. Deciding that ISIS is a State would clarify the current legal situation. Yet, it is clear from the analysis above that the movement does not yet fully fulfil the Montevideo criteria, for the better or worst. ISIS is consequently still approached as an armed non-state actor. This has consequences in international law with regard to compliance and others matters such as intervention.[29] This is illustrated by the debate on the possibility to prosecute ISIS at the International Criminal Court (ICC): Syria and Iraq are not parties to the ICC, making it impossible to use the territorial jurisdiction link to prosecute ISIS.[30] While the current ICC Prosecutor, Bensouda, has established that ISIS members could be prosecuted on the personal jurisdiction's basis,[31] it seems that the leaders will never make it to court.[32] Indeed, the personal jurisdiction will only allow prosecuting individuals who are citizens of States Parties to the Rome Statute. A way forward would be to 'broaden' the jurisdictional links so that the leaderships of ISIS could be included.[33] An option could be the referral by the Security Council, as per Article 13(b) of the Rome Statute, to take the whole movement to the ICC. This example demonstrates that stakes when it comes to prosecuting a proto movement or a proto-state.

While Cronin has spoken of proto-state to describe States that would not match the Montevideo expectations, Ronen has suggested calling them quasi-states; she defines the quasi-state as one that does not bear the essential features of statehood and that does not claim to be a State. Quasi-states can even fulfil the requirements of statehood but still refuse to declare statehood to avoid taking any responsibilities. ISIS could be seen as one of these quasi-states, except that it has sinister intentions motivating its refusal to declare

---

29 L. Arimatsu & M. Schmitt, 'The Legal Basis for the War Against Isis Remains Contentious', *The Guardian*, 6 October 2014, available at https://www.theguardian.com/commentisfree/2014/oct/06/legal-basis-war-isis-syria-islamic-state.

30 K. L. Corrie, 'Could the International Criminal Court Strategically Prosecute Modern Day Slavery?', 14 *Journal of International Criminal Justice*, 2016, pp. 285–303.

31 Statement of the Prosecutor of the International Criminal Court, Fatou Bensouda, on the Alleged Crimes Committed by ISIS, International Criminal Court, 8 April 2015, available at http://www.haguejusticeportal.net/index.php?id=13249.

32 A. Skander Galand, 'The Situation Concerning the Islamic State: Carte Blanche for the ICC if the Security Council Refers?', Comment on EJILTalk, 27 May 2015, available at http://www.ejiltalk.org/the-situation-concerning-isis-carte-blanche-for-the-icc-if-the-security-council-refers/.

33 A. M. Brennan, 'Prosecuting ISIS before the International Criminal Court: Challenges and Obstacles', 19 *American Journal of International Law*, 2015, available at https://www.asil.org/insights/volume/19/issue/21/prosecuting-isil-international-criminal-court-challenges-and-obstacles.

itself as a proper State. Ronen suggests that these quasi-states need to see the law applicable to them, extending the law applicable to States to quasi-states, and arguing along the lines of attributing statehood to non-state actors that have State features. This ensures compliance with international law. This approach is interesting and would help finding a solution to the prosecution of ISIS at the International Criminal Court. Ronen's contribution challenges the current approach to ISIS as non-state armed group only and demonstrates that an in-depth analysis of the emergence of proto-states is therefore needed. The answer to ISIS's claim to statehood could well come from Islamic law, in complement to international law.

3   Addressing ISIS under International Law and Islamic Law: Dissuasion, Containment or Intervention?

Some have argued that the debate on ISIS's statehood and its possible prosecution under international law is not a tenable proposition because of the secular nature of the international community versus the religious nature of the movement.[34] While such proposition leads to a strict seclusion between international law and Islamic law, it is of interest as it puts forward the role of Islam in the case of ISIS: the movement is a self-proclaimed Caliphate that refers only to its own interpretation of Islamic law. Could it then be that Islamic law has the answer to the statehood of ISIS? Looking at how Muslims authorities, practitioners and scholars evaluates ISIS's claim to statehood via the Caliphate is an opportunity to consider the 'other' side; it provides the international community with the option to listen to alternative voices that, are more familiar with ISIS.

The declaration of ISIS as a caliphate is not surprising considering most radical movements have reached towards this ideal. The concept of Caliphate has become, through the centuries, a perfect form of Government aligned with Islam and in which Islamic law is applied. This 2014 declaration certainly contributes to the current discussion as to whether a caliphate can exists in modern times and whether it can take the shape of a nation State.[35] This could well be the case if we were to admit that ISIS has a statehood strategy[36] of

---

[34]   S. Sayapin, 'A 'Hybrid' Tribunal for ISIS?', Comment on EJILTalk, 4 May 2016, available at http://www.ejiltalk.org/a-hybrid-tribunal-for-ISIS/.

[35]   W. Hallaq, The Impossible State: Islam, politics, and Modernity's Moral Predicament, Columbia University Press, 2013.

[36]   Katagiri, supra, note 25.

any sort, let it be through a caliphate. While it would be convenient to take such declaration for granted as it will help qualifying ISIS as a proper State, I argue that the proto-state created is not a caliphate. A caliphate is a political entity with a spiritual role: it administers the life of the livings and prepares them to the after-world. Islamic law is at its very core, and no caliphate can exist without it. The model presented by ISIS today is a governance system reached through distorted views of Islam.[37] ISIS is removing the caliphate's Muslim basis and turning it into an anomaly: an example can be found in the sexual enslavement of minorities which is not authorized in any interpretation of Islam. While there are debates about slavery in Islam, enslaving minorities for sexual purposes is in full contradiction of Islamic ethics and Islamic law. Minorities are to be respected in Islam, and are expected to pay a tax to live in peace. By following this policy of sexual abuse, ISIS violates the basic Islamic humanitarian standards. This shows that ISIS is not a caliphate in the proper meaning but rather, and yet again, a dystopian version of a State.

Muslim scholars have the difficult task of unravelling the discourse of ISIS when it comes to consequences of the existence of the movement and its declaration that it is a caliphate. The letter addressed by Muslim scholars to ISIS, deconstructing its entire approach Islam is the illustration of why the statehood of the movement is actually a Muslim problem in addition to an international law one: a large group of Muslim scholars opted to confront the movement's rhetoric to undermine ISIS's legitimacy as a caliphate.[38] ISIS's interpretation of Islamic law, its claim to a caliphate and its claim to any sort of statehood were clearly rejected by this group of experts. When it comes to statehood, the Association of Muslim Scholars in Iraq declared that ISIS is not 'legally entitled to any party to take [any] measures' not being a recognized State and not having a Sultan to represent the nation (undermining ISIS's claim to a Caliphate).[39] The International Union of Muslims Scholars adds that 'All the affairs of the State and religious political practice should be based on Shura (consultation),' criticizing the current structure of the so-called Caliphate that does not have a Sultan or a Parliament. Iranian authorities consider ISIS to be a non-state armed group, paving the way for the use of Article 51 of the UN Charter in self-defence or allowing the use of jihad (in its real meaning) to defend Islam and Muslims who are oppressed and live inside ISIS occupied territories. The British-based Quilliam Foundation has also rejected the idea of ISIS reaching

---

37   Van Engeland, supra, note 17.
38   The letter can be found here: http://www.lettertobaghdadi.com/.
39   Wilson Center, 'Muslims against ISIS Part 1: Clerics and Scholars', 24 September 2014, available at https://www.wilsoncenter.org/article/muslims-against-isis-part-1-clerics-scholars.

for some sort of statehood through the Caliphate, also preferring to see the movement as a non-state armed group.[40] The Muslim Word League organized a meeting to discuss the nature of ISIS and its jihadi enterprise, stressing the use of a distorted Islam to justify its deeds. During the conference, the secretary-general of the Muslim World League, Abdullah bin Abdelmohsin al-Turki, said that 'the terrorism that we face within the Muslim Ummah and our own homelands today... is religiously motivated. It has been founded on extremism, and the misconception of some distorted Sharia concept.[41]' This view of ISIS as a child of Islam that provides a new interpretation of Islam supports my view of a proto-jihadi State. These are examples of scholars taking a stance to undermine any possible claim to statehood and refuting ISIS's claim to be a Caliphate.[42]

The work above demonstrates that public international law scholars and Muslim scholars have not only an academic but also a practical interest at working together when solving the riddle of the existence of ISIS: Muslim countries, scholars and communities have attempted to stress that ISIS is not a State but is a group that disrespects Islam and Islamic law; it would not be of interest to have ISIS pictured as a State as it would grant it a legitimacy that the majority of Muslims refuse to give it. It therefore remains to see how the international community reacts to such arguments.

Conclusion

It is crucial to determine the nature of ISIS as the group grows fast. While March and Revkin have suggested that this proto-state could be the future normal state,[43] and Waltz has said that if ISIS becomes a State, we might have to

---

[40] E. M. Saltman & C. Winter, *Islamic State: The Changing Face of Modern Jihadism*, Quilliam Foundation, November 2014, available at https://www.quilliamfoundation.org/wp/wp-content/uploads/publications/free/islamic-state-the-changing-face-of-modern-jihadism.pdf.

[41] HRH Prince Khalid Al-Faisal, 'Secretary General Speech in opening of conference Address', Muslim World League, Mecca, February 2015, available at http://en.themwl.org/secretary-general-speech-opening-conference.

[42] I am, for the sake of the discussion, associating a caliphate with a nation-state but this is open to debate as demonstrated by Hallaq's book, see supra, note 35.

[43] A. F. March & M. Revkin, 'Caliphate of Law: ISIS' Ground Rules', *Foreign Affairs*, 15 April 2015, available at https://www.foreignaffairs.com/articles/syria/2015-04-15/caliphate-law.

accept it,[44] there are other options available. This is why I have surveyed different possibilities, looking at ISIS as a proto-jihadi State, a quasi-state or a non-state armed group. The movement could be approached differently: it could be analyzed as a self-determination movement of religious inspiration. After all, ISIS does question the borders inherited from colonial agreements. The movement could also been seen as a competitor to the State, or a new form of State emerging from the ruins of a failed State or a counter-state created by an authoritarian State's collapse.[45] Cronin has also suggested that ISIS needs to be approached differently than any other non-stated armed groups:[46] the effect would be to perhaps develop a whole new approach to the way international law addresses non-state actors. ISIS is certainly affecting international humanitarian law,[47] supporting Cronin's but also supporting my argument of looking at a jihadi State differently under international law. The emergence of the ISIS phenomenon certainly questions opportunities for further developments, either of ISIS itself or of different non-state actors. It is therefore clear that we are facing what Scharf calls a 'Grotian Moment', 'a fundamental paradigm shift that will have broad implications for international law'.[48]

---

44 S. Waltz, 'What Should We do if the Islamic State Wins?', *Foreign Policy*, 10 June 2015, available at http://foreignpolicy.com/2015/06/10/what-should-we-do-if-isis-islamic-state-wins-containment/.
45 A. I. Ahram & E. Lust, 'The Decline and Fall of the Arab State', 58 *Survival*, 2016, pp. 7–34, 12, available at http://dx.doi.org/10.1080/00396338.2016.1161897.
46 Cronin, supra, note 5.
47 J. D. van der Vyver, 'The Isis Crisis And The Development Of International Humanitarian Law', 30 *Emory International Law Review*, 2016, pp. 531–563.
48 Scharf, supra, note 4.

PART 2

Dispute Settlement

∴

La Cour internationale de Justice et le traitement du contentieux dans la durée : Le temps retrouvé

Mohamed Bennouna

Le temps retrouvé évoque l'œuvre majeure de Marcel Proust « A la recherche du temps perdu » et sa partie finale. C'est la quintessence de l'art du roman, l'art de convoquer le passé et de lui redonner sens. L'art de recomposer le temps, de retrouver cette mémoire incorporée en chacun d'entre nous et de la transfigurer. Au point que l'artiste finit par considérer que « la vraie vie, la vie enfin découverte et éclaircie, la seule vie par conséquent pleinement vécue, c'est la littérature ».

Le juriste ne peut se permettre le luxe de la poésie, qui vogue au gré de la mémoire involontaire. Pourtant, il nous a été demandé à nous, juges internationaux, indépendants, de revisiter des passés lointains, des réalités révolues et de conclure, ici et maintenant, à l'état de la règle applicable dans les relations entre les Parties.

Des querelles interétatiques ont traversé des époques avec différentes pratiques, divers arrangements successifs pour finir dans le moule de certaines affaires, avec des argumentations juridiques opposées ; la Cour ayant tout de même le dernier mot par la production d'un arrêt, un texte revêtu de l'autorité de la chose jugée, comme le récit, pour paraphraser Proust, de la vraie vie.

L'affaire du *Différend maritime* (*Pérou c. Chili*) tranchée par un arrêt de la Cour, en janvier 2014, est caractéristique à cet égard puisqu'elle couvre une période d'une soixantaine d'années[1].

D'autres querelles remontent même à un passé encore plus lointain où les deux protagonistes n'avaient pas encore d'existence étatique, ce qui ne les a pas empêché de se réclamer d'un droit et de pratiques issus d'une même autorité coloniale. L'affaire récente qui a opposé le Burkina Faso au Niger, et qui s'est résolue par l'arrêt du 16 avril 2013, me permettra d'évoquer cet autre aspect du traitement du contentieux dans la durée[2].

Concernant l'affaire *Pérou c. Chili*, celle-ci a été introduite au rôle de la Cour, le 26 janvier 2008, par une requête du Pérou qui demandait la délimitation, dans sa totalité, de sa frontière maritime avec le Chili.

---

1 Affaire du *Différend maritime* (*Pérou c. Chili*), arrêt, CIJ Recueil 2014, p. 3.
2 Affaire du *Différend frontalier* (*Burkina Faso c. Niger*), arrêt, CIJ Recueil 2013, p. 44.

Ce dernier, par contre, soutenait que les espaces maritimes entre les deux Parties avaient été délimités par voie d'accord et que la déclaration de Santiago du 18 avril 1952, signée entre le Chili, l'Equateur et le Pérou, avait établi une frontière internationale sur une distance de 200 milles marins, en suivant le parallèle de latitude passant par le point de la frontière terrestre séparant les deux pays.

La Cour a été appelée ainsi à revenir sur l'évolution des relations entre le Pérou et le Chili et sur leurs engagements juridiques, en la matière, sur une longue période d'une soixantaine d'années, au cours de laquelle l'ordre international des Océans a subi un bouleversement sans précédent, qu'il s'agisse des revendications de plus en plus poussées des Etats sur le sol et le sous-sol de la mer ou sur la colonne d'eau ou qu'il s'agisse de l'apparition de nouveaux concepts comme le patrimoine commun de l'humanité qui couvre tout le sol et le sous-sol au-delà des limites des juridictions internationales ou qu'il s'agisse enfin de la tenue de la troisième conférence internationale des Nations Unies sur le droit de la mer, entre 1973 et 1982, qui portait sur tous les aspects de ce droit dans un espace couvrant près des trois quarts de la surface du globe.

La Convention, conclue à Montego Bay le 10 décembre 1982[3], a été ratifiée par. 167 Etats, y compris le Chili ; le Pérou n'en étant pas partie. Ce contexte étant donné, la Cour se devait d'analyser la déclaration de Santiago, en elle-même, les accords subséquents intervenus entre les Parties, ainsi que le comportement au cours de cette période de leurs flottes respectives, pour en déduire l'existence d'une frontière maritime qui aurait été convenue entre elles et jusqu'à quelle distance.

Si le titre de souveraineté doit s'apprécier, en fonction de l'état du droit international, au moment où il a été établi, ainsi que l'avait affirmé Max Huber en 1928 dans l'arbitrage de l'Ile de Palmas, il en est de même du tracé d'une frontière maritime. En effet, il fallait se demander quel était l'état du droit international au moment de l'adoption de la déclaration de Santiago en 1952. C'est ce qui m'avait amené, lors de la procédure orale dans cette affaire, le 7 décembre 2012 (CR 2012/32), à poser la question suivante aux Parties :

> « Considérez-vous, en tant que signataires de la déclaration de Santiago de 1952, que vous pouviez à cette date, conformément au droit international général, proclamer et délimiter une zone maritime de souveraineté et de juridiction exclusive sur la mer qui baigne les côtes de vos pays respectifs jusqu'à 200 milles marins au minimum desdites côtes ? »

---

3   Nations Unies, *Recueil des traités*, vol. 1834, p. 3.

La Cour va constater, tout d'abord, qu'il a fallu trente ans, après l'adoption de la déclaration de Santiago, pour que la notion de ZEE soit acceptée dans la pratique des Etats et consignée dans la Convention de Montego Bay de 1982.

Elle relève ensuite qu'en réponse à une question d'un Membre de la Cour, les Parties ont toutes deux reconnu que la revendication qu'elles avaient formulée, dans la déclaration de Santiago de 1952, n'était pas conforme au droit international d'alors et ne pouvait être opposée aux Etats tiers à l'époque.

La Cour a dû revisiter l'ensemble de l'évolution du droit de la mer, soit la série des déclarations unilatérales revendiquant soit le plateau continental, soit des zones de pêche ou la souveraineté, ainsi que la première et la deuxième conférence des Nations Unies sur le droit de la mer, 1958–1960, où il n'a été question que d'une mer territoriale de 6 milles marins, d'une zone de pêche jusqu'à 12 milles marins et d'un plateau continental limité.

La Cour, ne pouvant s'appuyer sur la seule déclaration de Santiago pour délimiter la frontière maritime, s'est livrée à tout un travail de reconstitution des engagements convenus entre les deux pays, de leur pratique en matière de pêche et des moyens à leur disposition dans les décennies cinquante et soixante. Elle conclut finalement que la frontière maritime suivant le parallèle ne pouvait s'étendre au-delà de 80 milles marins depuis son point de départ. Ce qu'elle considérera comme une frontière convenue entre ces deux pays. Elle va poursuivre cette longue rétrospective historique dans les décennies suivantes, soixante-dix et quatre-vingt, ce qui l'amènera à considérer que les deux Parties ont reconnu la ZEE comme espace maritime. Elle s'engagera alors dans le tracé d'une ligne de délimitation en se fondant sur les articles 73 et 84 de la Convention sur le droit de la mer considérés comme reflétant le droit coutumier. Cette délimitation se fera à partir du point terminal de la frontière convenue entre les deux Etats, en suivant le parallèle sur une distance de 80 milles marins.

Cela donnera une ligne curieuse et inédite, la ligne du temps retrouvé, avec les approximations propres à ce genre d'exercice de reconstitution d'un passé révolu.

En effet, la première ligne qui suit le parallèle n'a pas manqué de soulever des interrogations, notamment pour se demander comment est-on passé d'un accord en 1954 sur une frontière maritime spéciale pour une zone de tolérance pour les petites embarcations le long du parallèle, jusqu'à la fixation d'une frontière maritime le long de ce même parallèle jusqu'à 80 milles marins ? La seule réponse de la Cour : c'est que les activités halieutiques de l'époque s'exerçaient jusqu'à une distance de 60 milles marins, à partir des principaux ports de la région, distance qui a été poussée finalement jusqu'à 80 milles. Encore fallait-il aussi questionner le droit international de l'époque pour savoir s'il autorisait une zone de pêche exclusive allant jusque-là.

On se rend compte ainsi que c'est une approche pragmatique qui a prévalu et qui nécessitait de prendre en compte certaines traditions établies dans la région.

Malgré tout, et c'est l'essentiel, les deux Parties ont aussitôt accepté ce schéma et ont déterminé, par accord entre elles, les coordonnées des lignes tracées par la Cour. Elles ont pu clôturer une période historique incertaine quant à leurs droits respectifs en mer, alors qu'ils figurent parmi les premiers pays pour l'exploitation des ressources halieutiques. Cette situation leur permettra de coopérer désormais sur de meilleures bases.

Le sens de ce voyage dans le temps est là, même si, parfois, la pure rationalité cartésienne n'y trouve pas son compte.

Dans l'affaire du *Différend frontalier* (*Burkina Faso/Niger*), la Cour a été saisie, le 20 juillet 2010, par voie d'un compromis conclu entre ces deux pays, par lequel ils rappellent un accord frontalier existant entre eux ainsi que le bornage d'une partie de la frontière et demandent à la Cour de déterminer le tracé de la frontière dans les secteurs de celle-ci au sujet desquels ils n'ont pu s'entendre. A ce propos, ils soulignent leur attachement au principe de l'intangibilité des frontières héritées de la colonisation. C'est ainsi que les deux pays se sont mis d'accord pour considérer que le droit applicable sur lequel ils doivent se fonder pour tracer leur frontière commune est un arrêté du 31 août 1927, tel qu'il a été précisé par son erratum du 5 octobre 1927, « fixant les limites des colonies de la Haute-Volta [devenue Burkina Faso] et du Niger », et qui a été édicté par le Gouverneur général de l'Afrique occidentale française (AOF) sur la base d'un décret du Président de la République française du 26 décembre 1926. Enfin, il est possible, selon le compromis, de s'en remettre à la carte de l'Institut géographique de France (IGF) datant de 1960, en cas d'insuffisance de l'arrêté et de son erratum.

Par conséquent, la Cour s'est vue confier la tâche de mettre en œuvre un arrêté du Gouverneur général de la puissance coloniale, en l'interprétant dans son contexte de manière à tenir compte des circonstances de son adoption et de son exécution. Bien entendu, l'objectif de l'arrêté, datant du premier tiers du XXe siècle, était de tracer les limites administratives entre deux colonies relevant de la même autorité coloniale. C'est probablement ce qui explique le caractère sommaire de cet arrêté, des informations et des repères qu'il contient. On comprend qu'ils puissent s'avérer parfois insuffisants ou inadéquats, lorsque la Cour a été appelée à tracer une frontière internationale entre deux Etats indépendants. Par ailleurs, on peut se demander, à juste titre, comment la Cour – organe judiciaire principal des Nations Unies – peut-elle tracer une telle frontière en se fondant sur un texte de droit colonial datant de 1927 ?

Cette question, comme on s'en doute, n'est pas nouvelle puisque la Cour s'est occupée de bien d'autres affaires, aussi bien en Afrique qu'en Amérique latine, où le respect des frontières héritées de l'époque coloniale était en cause. De ce point de vue, l'arrêt que la Cour a rendu dans l'affaire *Burkina Faso c. Mali*, du 22 décembre 1986, est significatif à cet égard, puisqu'il concerne, là aussi, deux pays relevant de la même puissance coloniale et qu'il fait partie de l'opération de délimitation frontalière dans la même sous-région de l'Afrique de l'Ouest, de même une chambre de la Cour a rendu un autre arrêt, en 2005, dans une affaire de délimitation entre le Bénin et le Niger.

Dans l'affaire *Burkina Faso c. Mali*, la Cour avait pris la précaution de préciser la fonction qui sera celle du droit colonial dans ce contexte. Celui-ci « peut intervenir, non en tant que tel (comme s'il y avait un *continuum juris*, un relais juridique entre le droit colonial et le droit international), mais seulement comme un élément de fait, parmi d'autres, ou comme un moyen de preuve et de démonstration de ce qu'on a appelé le [legs colonial] »[4].

Pourtant dans l'affaire du *Différend frontalier* (*Burkina Faso c. Niger*) la Cour va se référer, pour le tracé, à l'interprétation donnée à l'arrêté par les fonctionnaires de l'administration coloniale (par. 79). Entre la preuve du legs colonial et l'application du droit colonial, la distinction peut paraître ténue. Par ailleurs, la Cour a tenu compte du fait que l'arrêté a été pris sur la base du décret du Président de la République française et, notamment que son objet qui « était de transférer certains cercles et cantons de la colonie de la Haute-Volta vers la colonie du Niger » (par. 90). De cette façon, la Cour en déduit, à partir de la hiérarchie entre deux sources du droit colonial, que la ligne tracée par l'arrêté devait respecter les limites des circonscriptions existantes transférées. Et, dans la suite de ce raisonnement, on relèvera que ce gouverneur général a délégué à deux lieutenants gouverneurs de chacune des deux colonies le soin de démarquer sur le terrain les circonscriptions en cause, cercles et cantons, dans le but de préparer l'arrêté. Enfin, pour suppléer les titres coloniaux, on va même jusqu'à rechercher les effectivités coloniales, soit l'exercice de l'autorité administrative dans chacune des colonies. Et, pour finir, on se rabattra sur la carte de l'IGF de 1960. C'est dire à quel point il existe tout de même dans cette jurisprudence un *continuum juris* entre droit colonial et droit international.

---

[4] Affaire du *Différend frontalier* (*Burkina Faso c. République du Mali*), arrêt, CIJ Recueil 1986, p. 568, par. 30.

On peut rétorquer que les Parties l'ont voulu ainsi et qu'ils appliqueront sans difficulté l'arrêt rendu par la Cour.

Le juge *ad hoc* Abi-Saab a souligné qu'on ne saurait trouver là une quelconque légitimation du droit colonial[5]. La question qui se pose est de savoir si, intervenant presque un siècle après le tracé colonial et dans un autre contexte, la Cour n'aurait pas dû se pencher plus qu'elle ne l'a fait sur le devenir des populations frontalières concernées. Or, comme elle le fait souvent, lorsqu'elle s'enferme dans une approche positiviste, dont elle ne maîtrise pas vraiment les coûts humains, la Cour tente d'y remédier en émettant des souhaits et des vœux. Elle souhaite en l'occurrence que « chaque Partie [...] tienne dûment compte des besoins des populations concernées [...] » et elle engage les deux Parties à poursuivre leur coopération[6].

Cependant, comme dans l'affaire *Pérou c. Chili*, la Cour a finalement géré ce contentieux dans la durée avec une grande dose de pragmatisme, ce qui est probablement la meilleure façon de rapprocher les Parties autour de la solution proposée. Avec le temps, il faut retenir l'essentiel, la consolidation du passé et la préparation de l'avenir.

---

5   Ibid., voir son opinion dissidente, p. 659.
6   Affaire du *Différend frontalier* (*Burkina Faso c. Niger*) *op. cit.*, note 2, par. 112.

The Place of the International Court in International Dispute Settlement

James Crawford AC[1]

1 Introduction

The 'judicial Power of the United States' is 'vested in one supreme Court', among other courts.[2] As Bertrand Russell once commented, the US Supreme Court is given 'the reverence which the Greeks gave to the oracles and the Middle Ages to the Pope'.[3] In international law, by contrast, we have no court that is 'supreme' in the sense of being the highest organ in a judicial hierarchy, for the simple and sufficient reason that there is no international judicial hierarchy. What we have instead, according to the Charter, is the 'principal judicial organ', the international Court of Justice, of the principal international organization, the United Nations.[4] It lacks several of the features of a supreme court. Its jurisdiction (although general *ratione materiae*) is not compulsory; its decisions are not precedents binding on other courts and tribunals; it must compete with other forums of international dispute settlement.

This competition has two aspects that I want to discuss here. The first concerns the question of choice between the Court and other interstate forums, such as those provided for in Part XV of the United Nations Convention on the Law of the Sea (LOSC). The Court has always coexisted with the older method of referring interstate disputes to *ad hoc* arbitration, but it now also competes with standing specialist tribunals, including the International Tribunal for the Law of the Sea (ITLOS). The second aspect concerns the cases the Court cannot hear because its contentious jurisdiction is limited to interstate cases by Article 34 of its Statute, even though a significant proportion of international cases these days involve as Parties entities other than States. Taken together, these two factors raise questions about the place of the Court in international

---

[1] With thanks to Rowan Nicholson for his considerable assistance with the original paper which was delivered at a conference in Berlin in 2014, prior to the author's election to the Court. The views expressed were and remain personal to the author.
[2] Constitution of the United States of America, Article III (1).
[3] B. Russell, *Power*, Routledge, 1937, reprinted 2004, p. 53.
[4] Charter of the United Nations, 892 UNTS 119, 26 June 1945, Article 92.

judicial settlement. If it is not 'supreme', we might ask what place a 'principal' judicial organ has in this array of alternatives.

Judge Rosalyn Higgins, then President of the Court, answered this question directly on the sixtieth anniversary of the Court's inaugural sitting, in 2006. She said:

> The Court is not only the principal judicial organ of the United Nations, but it also is the only international judicial body to possess general jurisdiction. Very important work is being done by the more recently established international criminal courts and tribunals, which we much admire. At the same time, and notwithstanding that the accountability of individuals for crimes is a pressing issue, the resolution of disputes between States is at the heart of the United Nations Charter system. The maintenance of international peace and security, one of the cardinal principles of the United Nations Charter, necessitates that disputes between States can be resolved without undue tensions or recourse to force, and judicial settlement by the International Court can play a signal role in this.[5]

As with international criminal tribunals, so we might say, *mutatis mutandis*, with ITLOS and *ad hoc* arbitration—and equally with other specialist forums, such as the Appellate Body of the World Trade Organization (WTO). Unlike the Court, those forums do not have general jurisdiction. But ITLOS and *ad hoc* arbitration *do* directly compete with the Court for 'the resolution of disputes between States'.

In fact, although the Court has always been at the 'heart' of the Charter system, its place has varied relative to the alternatives. Its place in the array of dispute settlement forums also depends on our perspective. I am going to look, first, at choice of forum both in interstate cases and in the broader international context; secondly, at the Court's performance in the cases that *do* come before it; and finally, at its contribution to the development of international law.

---

5   ICJ, 'Speech by HE Judge Rosalyn Higgins, President of the International Court of Justice at the solemn sitting on the occasion of the sixtieth anniversary of the inaugural sitting of the Court, 12 April 2006', available at www.icj-cij.org/court/index.php?pr=1004&pt=3&p1=1&p2=3&p3=1.

2   The Court and Choice of Forum

2.1   *Alternatives to the Court in Interstate Cases*

The Court's caseload (like that of its predecessor, the Permanent Court of International Justice) rose and fell and rose again during the 20th century. From 1947–56 it was relatively busy, but after that its caseload began to taper off, especially after its 1966 decision in *South West Africa*.[6] Its decision was that Ethiopia and Liberia lacked standing to bring a claim that South Africa had breached its League of Nations mandate by introducing apartheid in what is now Namibia.[7] This was controversial at the time and remains so. It contributed to a perception that the Court was too oriented towards the West. That was only partially remedied by the Court's subsequent 'apology' in *Barcelona Traction*:[8] its belated recognition of a category of communitarian norms with respect to which all States could have standing (norms *erga omnes*). The Court's caseload did not really recover until the 1980s, most notably after it interpreted its jurisdiction liberally in *Military and Paramilitary Activities in and against Nicaragua*, to the advantage of a small developing State claiming against the United States.[9]

At present, the Court's calendar is fairly busy. But a comparable number of general interstate disputes continue to come before other forums. In the ten years from 2003 to 2012, an average of 2.2 contentious cases per year were initiated before the Court.[10] In December 2016, there were eleven cases on its docket, but this figure can be misleading. For example, *Gabčíkovo-Nagymaros*[11] has been moribund for years.

---

[6]   See I. Sinclair, 'The Court as an institution: Its role and position in international society'. in D W Bowett et al. (eds), *The International Court of Justice: Process, Practice and Procedure*, British Institute of International and Comparative Law, 1997, pp. 21, 22–3.

[7]   *South West Africa* (Ethiopia v South Africa; Liberia v South Africa), Second phase, *ICJ Reports 1966*, p. 6.

[8]   *Barcelona Traction, Light & Power Co. Ltd* (*New Application: 1962*) (Belgium v Spain), Second phase, *ICJ Reports 1970*, p. 3.

[9]   *Military and Paramilitary Activities in and against Nicaragua* (Nicaragua v United States of America), *ICJ Reports 1986*, p. 14.

[10] Three advisory opinions were also requested during those ten years. Between 2013 and 2016, 12 new cases were started, a slight increase in rate of commencement.

[11] *Gabčíkovo-Nagymaros Project* (Hungary/Slovakia), *ICJ Reports 1997*, p. 7.

Seventy two States currently accept the compulsory jurisdiction of the Court under Optional Clause declarations.[12] Of the ten largest economies, Germany, India, Japan and the United Kingdom all have declarations in effect, although subject to various conditions.[13] The others do not. Brazil's declaration was for a fixed period and expired in 1953.[14] China indicated in 1972 that it did not recognize its predecessor Government's declaration.[15] France withdrew in 1974,[16] after Australia and New Zealand brought the *Nuclear Tests* cases against it.[17] The US withdrew in 1985,[18] after Nicaragua brought proceedings.[19] Italy and Russia have never made declarations. As the withdrawals by France and the US suggest, powerful States may believe they have more to lose than to gain by allowing other States to haul them before the Court—although France has twice accepted jurisdiction after a case was brought.[20]

Even those States that do accept the compulsory jurisdiction of the Court tend to attach reservations, often with stringent conditions that constrain their scope. Malgosia Fitzmaurice notes that given how the Statute was drafted, States *might* have followed a general practice of accepting the Court's jurisdiction unconditionally, but instead the practice of making reservations has 'weakened the whole system'.[21]

---

12 Statute of the International Court of Justice, 15 UNCIO 355, 26 June 1945, Article 36(2). The figure of 72 includes declarations accepting the compulsory jurisdiction of the Permanent Court, which are deemed to have the same effect: ibid., Article 36(5).

13 Declarations by Germany (30 April 2008), India (18 September 1974), Japan (9 July 2007) and the UK (5 July 2004). The text of Optional Clause declarations is available at United Nations Treaty Collection, chapter I.4, available at https://treaties.un.org/pages/ViewDetails.aspx?src=TREATY&mtdsg_no=I-4&chapter=1&clang=_en.

14 Declaration by Brazil (12 February 1948).

15 Communication from the People's Republic of China to the Secretary-General (5 December 1972).

16 Subsequently decided in *Nuclear Tests* (Australia v France), ICJ Reports 1974, p. 253; *Nuclear Tests* (New Zealand v France), ICJ Reports 1974, p. 457.

17 Notification from France to the Secretary-General (10 January 1974).

18 Notification from the US to the Secretary-General (7 October 1985).

19 Subsequently decided in *Military and Paramilitary Activities in and against Nicaragua*, supra, note 9.

20 *Certain Criminal Proceedings in France* (Republic of the Congo v France), Provisional measures, ICJ Reports 2003, p. 102; *Certain Questions of Mutual Assistance in Criminal Matters* (Djibouti v France), ICJ Reports 2008, p. 177.

21 M. Fitzmaurice, 'International Court of Justice, Optional Clause' (last updated April 2011) in R. Wolfrum (ed), *Max Planck Encyclopedia of Public International Law*, Oxford University Press, www.mpepil.com.

Yet there are no signs of an exodus from the Court by States generally. The only recent example of a withdrawal is Colombia: it terminated its Optional Clause declaration in 2001.[22] In 2012, after receiving what it regarded as an unfavourable decision in *Nicaragua v Colombia*,[23] it also denounced the Pact of Bogotá,[24] which gives the Court jurisdiction over disputes between States Parties.[25] There have been a few other withdrawals.[26] On the other hand, the number of States recognizing the Court's compulsory jurisdiction has grown slightly in recent years, even if this is in large part thanks to acceptances by very small States such as the Marshall Islands.[27]

As well as under the Optional Clause, the Court continues to exercise jurisdiction under treaties such as the Pact of Bogotá or by special agreement. Benedict Kingsbury points out that although newer treaties seldom include obligations to accept the Court's jurisdiction, in recent years the Court's 'route into major security-related issues has ... often been through oblique paths',[28]

---

22   Notification from Colombia to the Secretary-General (5 December 2001).
23   *Territorial and Maritime Dispute* (Nicaragua v Colombia), *ICJ Reports 2012*, p. 624.
24   'Presidente Santos confirma que Colombia denunció el Pacto de Bogotá' (Press release by the president of Colombia, 28 November 2012), available at wsp.presidencia.gov.co/Prensa/2012/Noviembre/Paginas/20121128_01.aspx.
25   American Treaty on Pacific Settlement, 30 UNTS 55, 30 April 1948, (Pact of Bogotá), Article 31.
26   In addition to Brazil, China, France and the US (already discussed above), the following States have ceased to be bound by the compulsory jurisdiction of the Court for various reasons: Bolivia, El Salvador, Guatemala, Nauru, Thailand and Turkey made Optional Clause declarations for fixed periods that have since expired; South Africa terminated its declaration on 12 April 1967; Israel terminated its declaration on 21 November 1985; and on 13 May 2008, following a complex series of events arising from assertions of succession to the Socialist Federal Republic of Yugoslavia, Serbia indicated that it did not recognize a declaration deposited on 26 April 1999 by the Federal Republic of Yugoslavia. (United Nations Treaty Collection, chapter I.4, https://treaties.un.org/pages/ViewDetails.aspx?src=TREATY&mtdsg_no=I-4&chapter=1&clang=_en) I.e., only South Africa, France, the US, Israel and Colombia have withdrawn as such.
27   The most recent Optional Clause declarations are by Ireland (15 December 2011); Timor-Leste (21 September 2012); Lithuania (26 September 2012); Marshall Islands (23 April 2013) and Romania (23 June 2015).
28   B. Kingsbury, 'International courts: Uneven judicialisation in global order' in J. Crawford & M. Koskenniemi (eds), *The Cambridge Companion to International Law*, Cambridge University Press, 2012, pp. 203, 211.

such as the Genocide Convention[29] in *Croatia v Serbia* and the Racial Discrimination Convention[30] in *Georgia v Russia*.

But the usual means of submitting disputes to the Court has become by special agreement. In 2010, for instance, the Court was seised in *Frontier Dispute (Burkina Faso/Niger)* by a special agreement (*compromis*) between two States that had not made Optional Clause declarations.[31]

Frontier Dispute is, however, typical of the disputes that seem to be considered suitable for submission to the Court: land boundary or other disputes that principally concern events from the 'past'—in that case dating back to French colonial rule in 1927. A minister from Burkina Faso said after the judgment that the two States were 'parting as good friends, very good friends'.[32] Of course, States do not always part as 'good friends' following territorial disputes: Colombia's withdrawal from the Optional Clause is a case in point. Perhaps the ongoing proceedings between Costa Rica and Nicaragua, which encompass both territorial and environmental issues, will be another, given that the record so far is not encouraging. Often, however, such disputes can be determined mildly and modestly, at least as compared with more urgent disputes about the 'present'—what I have called 'relationship disputes'.[33] About one-third of the Court's disputes involve land or maritime boundaries. Another third involve questions of State responsibility.[34] The remainder are harder to classify and concern a mix of 'past' and 'present' elements.[35]

---

29 Convention on the Prevention and Punishment of the Crime of Genocide, 78 UNTS 277, 9 December 1948; *Application of the Convention on the Prevention and Punishment of the Crime of Genocide* (Croatia v Serbia), Preliminary objections, *ICJ Reports 2008*, p. 412.

30 International Convention on the Elimination of All Forms of Racial Discrimination, 660 UNTS 195, 21 December 1965); *Application of the International Convention on the Elimination of All Forms of Racial Discrimination* (Georgia v Russia), Preliminary objections, *ICJ Reports 2011*, p. 70.

31 Special Agreement seising the International Court of Justice of the Boundary Dispute between Burkina Faso and the Republic of Niger (20 July 2010). http://www.icj-cij.org/docket/files/149/15985.pdf.

32 Jerome Bougouma, Burkina Faso Minister of Territorial Administration and Security, quoted in 'Niger–Burkina Faso border set by ICJ ruling', *BBC News*, 16 April 2013, www.bbc.co.uk/news/world-africa-22165499.

33 J. Crawford, 'The International Court of Justice, judicial administration and the rule of law', in D. W. Bowett et al. (eds), *The International Court of Justice: Process, Practice and Procedure*, British Institute of International and Comparative Law, 1997, p. 112.

34 E.g., *Application of the Interim Accord of 13 September 1995* (Former Yugoslav Republic of Macedonia v Greece), *ICJ Reports 2011*, p. 644.

35 J. Crawford, 'The International Court of Justice and the law of state responsibility', in C. J. Tams & J. Sloan (eds), *The Development of International Law by the International Court of Justice*, Oxford University Press, 2013, p. 71.

Several factors explain the reluctance of States to submit relationship disputes to the Court, including the political fact that bringing proceedings in *any* international court or tribunal can be regarded as unfriendly. But I am going to explore some of the reasons why States, when they do decide to submit such disputes, might opt against the Court.

2.1.1   Choice of Forum under LOSC

The first factor tending against the use of the Court, at least in disputes about the law of the sea, is the over-elaborate dispute resolution system under Part XV of LOSC.[36]

Historically, the Court has been popular as a forum for disputes about law of the sea. It has rendered about twice as many decisions in the area as arbitral tribunals since 1945,[37] including such important contributions to the jurisprudence as *North Sea Continental Shelf*,[38] *Libya/Malta*[39] and *Romania v Ukraine*.[40] But since LOSC came into force in 1994, the situation has changed. LOSC allows States Parties to choose from among four methods to settle disputes concerning its interpretation or application: the Court; ITLOS; an arbitral tribunal under LOSC Annex VII; and in certain cases, a 'special' arbitral tribunal under Annex VIII.[41] If two States Parties have accepted the same procedure, a dispute between them may be submitted only to that procedure, unless they otherwise agree.[42] Twenty States have selected the Court as their first or equal-first preference.[43] Yet the choice of procedure disadvantages the Court. This is for two reasons.

First, if States Parties have *not* accepted the same procedure, the default procedure is Annex VII arbitration.[44] Since only a minority of the 166 parties have made any choice of procedure, and since many of those that have chosen have chosen differently, this makes it more likely that a dispute between

---

36   1833 UNTS 3, 10 December 1982.
37   V. Lowe & A. Tzanakopoulos, 'The development of the law of the sea by the International Court of Justice' in C. J. Tams & J. Sloan (eds), *The Development of International Law by the International Court of Justice*, Oxford University Press, 2013, pp. 177, 180.
38   *North Sea Continental Shelf* (Germany/Denmark; Germany/Netherlands), ICJ Reports 1969, p. 3.
39   *Continental Shelf* (Libya/Malta), ICJ Reports 1985, p. 13.
40   *Maritime Delimitation in the Black Sea* (Romania v Ukraine), ICJ Reports 2009, p. 61.
41   LOSC, Article 287(1).
42   LOSC, Article 287(4).
43   For a list of the choices made by States Parties see United Nations Division for Ocean Affairs & the Law of the Sea: Settlement of disputes mechanism, see www.un.org/Depts/los/settlement_of_disputes/choice_procedure.htm.
44   LOSC, Article 287(5).

any given two States will go to arbitration than to the Court. In contrast, for a dispute to be submitted to the Court, the parties must either have agreed on the Court in advance or must rapidly agree in the immediate aftermath of the commencement of proceedings. In other words, if they have not already expressed a preference for the Court, they must do so while in dispute with each other. It is, naturally, difficult to agree on anything while in dispute.

Secondly, ITLOS has an additional jurisdiction to prescribe provisional measures pending the constitution of an arbitral tribunal to which a dispute is submitted.[45]

In total, since LOSC came into force, fourteen cases have gone to Annex VII arbitration. Twenty five have gone to ITLOS. These are comprised eight requests for provisional measures (seven of which went to Annex VII tribunals following the decision on provisional measures), nine prompt release cases and eight others. No cases at all have yet been referred to the International Court under Part XV of LOSC. Insofar as this imbalance is a consequence of those provisions, it is, of course, not the Court's fault. Nor does it necessarily indicate a clear preference against the Court, since States continue to submit cases relating to the law of the sea to the Court on other jurisdictional bases. For example, *Romania v Ukraine* was brought under a special agreement;[46] and there are several delimitation cases before the Court commenced under the Pact of Bogotá[47] or the Optional Clause.[48] It may be that States still see judgments by the Court on questions such as maritime delimitation as being more authoritative than the alternatives, or it may simply be that there are no alternatives.

Vaughan Lowe and Antonios Tzanakopolous suggest that the Court's place in the resolution of disputes on the law of the sea is also changing in a qualitative sense. They write that:

---

45 LOSC, Article 290(5).
46 *Maritime Delimitation in the Black Sea* (Romania v Ukraine), *ICJ Reports* 2009, p. 61.
47 Nicaragua's application, para. 9 states: 'On 27 November 2012, Colombia gave notice that it denounced as of that date the Pact of Bogotá; and in accordance with Article LVI of the Pact, that denunciation will take effect after one year, so that the Pact remains in force for Colombia until 27 November 2013'. Proceedings were instituted by Nicaragua against Colombia on 16 September 2013, see *Question of the Delimitation of the Continental Shelf between Nicaragua and Colombia beyond 200 nautical miles from the Nicaraguan Coast* (Nicaragua v Colombia), *Preliminary Objections*, judgment of 17 March 2016 (contentious case).
48 *Maritime Delimitation in the Indian Ocean* (Somalia v Kenya), Preliminary Objections, Judgement of 2 February 2017. The Court resolved a crucial question of the relationship between the Optional Clause and Part XV of LOSC.

THE PLACE OF THE ICJ IN INTERNATIONAL DISPUTE SETTLEMENT 103

[the Court's] influence has not been great, and … it is indeed diminishing as other tribunals take on some part of the task of applying the rules of the law of the sea. Only a handful of the delimitation cases are dated in the last couple of decades, and most of the 'seminal' cases are quite a bit older than that.[49]

This is to some extent not the Court's fault either: LOSC, in particular, has codified much of the law of the sea, and, as Lowe and Tzanakopolous also point out, it is natural for the Court to 'fall more and more into deciding cases rather than 'making' the law'.[50] In that sense, it is a sign of the maturity of the Court's jurisprudence that many of its cases do not raise novel points of international law.

2.1.2   Delay

But LOSC is not the only factor tending against use of the Court. A second factor is delay. For example *Bangladesh/Myanmar*, a maritime delimitation case, was litigated in two years three months, counting from the submission of the dispute to ITLOS to the date of judgment.[51] In contrast, over the last twenty years, the average time from the submission of a dispute to the Court to its conclusion has been three years eight months.[52] Counting only those disputes that went to judgment on the merits, the average time has been four years two months.[53] If even that does not sound so bad in comparison, then

---

49   Lowe & Tzanakopoulos, supra, note 37, p. 193.
50   Ibid.
51   Bangladesh initially instituted arbitral proceedings against Myanmar (along with parallel proceedings against India) under annex VII on 8 October 2009. But it was only on 13 December 2009 that, following a proposal by Myanmar and declarations by both States accepting jurisdiction, it submitted the dispute to ITLOS. ITLOS gave judgment two years three months later, on 14 March 2012 (*Dispute concerning delimitation of the maritime boundary between Bangladesh and Myanmar in the Bay of Bengal* (Bangladesh/Myanmar), ITLOS Case No. 16, Judgment of 14 March 2012.
52   I.e., the average length of time from the submission of a dispute to its conclusion for cases submitted to the Court in or after 1994 (coincidentally, the year LOSC came into effect), other than the ten cases still on the Court's docket. There were 47 such cases. The average length of time was 1325.34 days. Figures expressed in years and months come from dividing by the average length of a month, which is 30.436875 days after accounting for leap years.
53   I.e., excluding cases that concluded after an award of provisional measures, with a finding of inadmissibility or want of jurisdiction or because they were removed from the list. That leaves 21 cases. The average length of time was 1561.1 days.

it hides some severe delays in particular cases. In 1997, I was part of a study group of the British Institute of International & Comparative Law on the process, practice and procedure of the Court. The study group expressed concern that in *Qatar v Bahrain* the Court had taken three and a half years simply to adjudicate on jurisdiction and admissibility and that the date fixed for filing counter-memorials on the merits was some six and half years since the application.[54] In the end, the Court delivered judgment on the merits nine years eight months after the application.[55] More recently, *Nicaragua v Colombia* took ten years eleven months,[56] and *Diallo (Guinea v DRC)* took thirteen years six months (though that included an award of compensation to Guinea following judgment on the merits).[57]

At the other end of the scale, only a few cases submitted to the Court in the last twenty years have reached judgment on the merits in less than two years.[58] As things stand, it would be difficult for the Court to deal with a maritime delimitation case or another factually complex case as quickly as ITLOS or an *ad hoc* tribunal.

Some of the reasons for delay are not directly attributable to the Court. The Court has dealt with more incidental procedures, notably more provisional measures applications, in recent years, which require flexibility in its schedule and may disrupt the timetable for other cases. A delay may also suit the parties or be directly instigated by one or both of them. Nicaragua commenced proceedings in *Construction of a Road in Costa Rica along the San Juan River* on

---

54   Report of the Study Group Established by the British Institute of International and Comparative Law as a Contribution to the UN Decade of International Law, published with additional comments in D W Bowett et al., (eds) *The International Court of Justice: Process, Practice and Procedure*, British Institute of International and Comparative Law, 1997, pp. 27, 31–32.

55   *Maritime Delimitation and Territorial Questions* (Qatar v Bahrain), ICJ Reports 2001, p. 40 (3539 days).

56   *Territorial and Maritime Dispute*, supra, note 23 (4001 days).

57   *Ahmadou Sadio Diallo* (Guinea v Democratic Republic of the Congo), ICJ Reports 2012, p. 324 (4922 days).

58   *Arrest Warrant of 11 April 2000* (DRC v Belgium), ICJ Reports 2002, p. 3 (485 days); *Application for Revision of the Judgment of 11 September 1992 in the Case concerning the Land, Island and Maritime Frontier Dispute (El Salvador/Honduras: Nicaragua intervening)* (El Salvador v Honduras), ICJ Reports 2003, p. 392 (464 days); *Avena and Other Mexican Nationals* (Mexico v United States of America), ICJ Reports 2004, p. 12 (447 days); *Certain Questions of Mutual Assistance in Criminal Matters*, supra, note 20 (665 days); *Request for Interpretation of the Judgment of 31 March 2004 in the Case concerning Avena and Other Mexican Nationals (Mexico v US)* (Mexico v United States of America), ICJ Reports 2009, p. 3 (228 days—by far the fastest time to judgment on the merits in the last 20 years).

22 December 2011, but then indicated that it would only be in a position to file its memorial a full year later;[59] following the (questionable) joinder of the case with another brought by Costa Rica against Nicaragua, judgment in the joined cases was delivered on 16 December 2015. Such delays might occur because a State needs time to prepare its pleadings or reframe its case, because it is attempting to negotiate a political settlement, because it expects to lose the case, or because of the filing of preliminary objections—which can add years to the length of the case. This sort of delay is especially likely in cases commenced for tactical reasons, either to exert pressure during negotiations or in order to obtain provisional measures rather than judgment on the merits.[60] The 1997 study group noted that even the withdrawal of a case from the Court's list may not reduce congestion: it appeared to disrupt the Court's translation program, and it was not always possible to bring another case forward, since the translation of the documents in such a case may not be ready and the parties not prepared for a sudden acceleration.[61]

Thirdly, it is important that interstate disputes not be resolved hurriedly. There is less cause in the Court than in some overburdened domestic court systems to pressure parties into managing their disputes expeditiously, and there may be political reasons for not doing so. If a territorial dispute has been simmering since 1927, it is probably more important to resolve it justly and definitively than to get it off the docket quickly. A focus on the Court's 'productivity'—and still more a mere statistical analysis of the time it takes to resolve cases—can be misleading. The late Sir Ian Sinclair commented, speaking of the lower output of the Court per year compared with its predecessor, the Permanent Court, that:

> the raw data ... conceal more than they reveal. They do not distinguish between cases in terms of their relative complexity or simplicity. Nor do they distinguish between judgments on preliminary objections to the jurisdiction and admissibility, on the one hand, and judgments on the merits on the other hand, it being self-evident that the formulation of a judgment on the merits of a dispute will in most cases require a much greater input in the way of argument by the parties and deliberation by the judges....[62]

---

59 *Construction of a Road in Costa Rica along the San Juan River* (Nicaragua v Costa Rica), Order of 23 January 2012, *ICJ Reports 2012*, p. 7.
60 Report of the Study Group, supra, note 54, pp. 32–33.
61 Ibid., p. 33.
62 Sinclair, supra, note 6, p. 22.

But as Sir Ian nonetheless agreed, the figures 'make depressing reading'.[63] We cannot explain the Court's propensity for delay solely as a consequence of thoroughness. And that explanation is even less persuasive in relationship disputes, in which delays of up to a decade cannot be satisfactory. *Cameroon v Nigeria*, for example, was a cause of significant friction between the two States—including over implementation of the Court's judgment—and took eight and a half years.[64] As one of the more factually complex disputes dealt with by the Court in recent years, the length of time taken is problematic. But even here, some things can be said in defence of the Court—there were several interlocutory procedures (jurisdictional objections and a successful application to intervene by Equatorial Guinea), and the case was materially delayed by Cameroon's decision to place in issue the entire and very long boundary between the two States, whereas the core of the original dispute concerned sovereignty over the Bakassi Peninsula and the offshore. In the event, the Court dealt with the many individual territorial disputes thereby raised (not all of them minor) with meticulous care.

The result is that, at present, legal advisors can make no promises about how long the process will take in recommending to their Governments whether to commence proceedings in the Court, to commence them in some other forum, or to seek some other means of resolving a dispute.

2.1.3   Procedural Considerations

A clear advantage of submitting a dispute to the Court rather than to *ad hoc* arbitration is that it saves States from having to agree on the procedures and composition of the tribunal and from meeting its costs. But this is only an advantage insofar as States are satisfied with those procedures. A final factor tending against the choice of the Court as a dispute resolution forum is that they are sometimes perceived to be inadequate.

The Rules of Court have not been revised comprehensively since 1978. In the meantime, the Court's caseload has increased and it has dealt with a number of cases of great factual complexity. In *DRC v Uganda*,[65] the Democratic Republic of the Congo made allegations against Uganda concerning armed aggression, human rights, international humanitarian law and the illegal exploitation of natural resources in the context of what has been called 'Africa's world

---

63   Ibid.
64   *Land and Maritime Boundary between Cameroon and Nigeria* (Cameroon v Nigeria: Equatorial Guinea intervening), *ICJ Reports 2002*, p. 303.
65   *Armed Activities on the Territory of the Congo* (Democratic Republic of the Congo v Uganda), *ICJ Reports 2005*, p. 168.

war'—the deadliest war in recent history, involving seven African States and various rebels.[66] Making findings of fact in such cases is a demanding task for any court, let alone for one that has not often dealt with such a mass of complex and often contested evidence. But it is also a necessary task if the Court is to function as an effective method of resolving such disputes. The Court must adapt, whether that is by making decisions in consultation with the parties about the relative importance of annexes or their need for translation, making greater use of experts and of cross-examination, adjusting the timetable for pleadings, or otherwise. Commendably, in the last few years the Court has taken some meaningful steps to improve its procedures for fact-finding and other matters. I will have more to say about this shortly.

2.2 The Trend towards International Cases in which the Court is not an Alternative

The second aspect of the Court's competition with other forums concerns the considerable proportion of international cases that do not take the form of interstate disputes. Because Article 34 of the Statute limits the Court's contentious jurisdiction to interstate cases, it has no opportunity to 'compete' for these cases. These include investor–state disputes, human rights cases initiated by individuals before bodies such as the European Court of Human Rights, and cases involving international organizations.

Of particular significance are cases involving the European Union. The EU fulfils many of the functions of a State on behalf of its Member States, including in some types of international dispute. It is a member of the WTO in its own right and appears before the WTO dispute settlement body as a matter of course. It has also been a party to disputes before other international forums, including *Swordfish Stocks (Chile/EU)* before ITLOS[67] and the Annex VII arbitration initiated against it by the Kingdom of Denmark in respect of the Faroe Islands.[68] But since the EU is not deemed to be a State for the purposes of Article 34, disputes such as these are not capable of falling within the

---

66 See further C. E. Philipp, 'Congo, Democratic Republic of the' in R Wolfrum (ed), *Max Planck Encyclopedia of Public International Law*, Oxford University Press, www.mpepil.com.

67 *Case concerning the Conservation and Sustainable Exploitation of Swordfish Stocks in the South-Eastern Pacific Ocean* (Chile/EU) ITLOS Case No. 7 (removed from list 16 December 2009).

68 Prime Minister's Office (Faroe Islands), 'The Faroe Islands takes the EU to international tribunal over intended economic measures', press release, 16 August 2013, www.mfa.fo/Default.aspx?ID=13626&Action=1&NewsId=5264&PID=23631. The claim was eventually settled.

jurisdiction of the Court, even though that jurisdiction is general *ratione materiae*.

We might ask whether this must inevitably be so. Consider the Court's 1952 decision in *US Nationals in Morocco*.[69] The parties to the case were the United States and France. At the time, France exercised a protectorate over a zone of Morocco (there was also a Spanish Zone). Despite this, the Court found that Morocco had 'retained its personality as a State in international law'.[70] It had simply, by a 1912 treaty with France...

> made an arrangement of a contractual character whereby France undertook to exercise certain sovereign powers in the name and on behalf of Morocco, and, in principle, all of the international relations of Morocco. France, in the exercise of this function, is bound... by all treaty obligations to which Morocco had been subject before the Protectorate and which have not since been terminated or suspended by arrangement with the interested States.[71]

The Court went on to find that the US was entitled to exercise consular jurisdiction in the French Zone in certain cases. This followed from an act of a 1906 multilateral conference that was binding on France in its own right. But it *also* followed from an 1836 treaty between the US and Morocco.[72] In other words, France exercised—and was held responsible for exercising—certain sovereign powers of Morocco.

France, of course, was a State in its own right, whereas the EU has never held itself out to be a State. But the EU plainly approximates to a 'Government' and exercises certain sovereign powers of its Member States under what might, as in the Moroccan case, be characterized as 'an arrangement of a contractual character' comprising various treaties. By analogy with *US Nationals in Morocco*, could this 'Government' represent a member State in the International Court? Since it is extremely unlikely that the Statute (an integral part of the Charter with all that entails) could be amended in the foreseeable future, it may be that the Court will have to seek out such creative approaches if it is to compete with forums where the EU can already participate.

---

69   *Rights of Nationals of the United States of America in Morocco* (US v France), *ICJ Reports 1952*, p. 176.
70   Ibid., p. 185.
71   Ibid., p. 188.
72   Ibid., p. 212.

It may seem improbable that the Court will accept the EU as a party—though an *amicus* intervention pursuant to a change in the Rules allowing interventions by States and public international organizations may be another matter.

But the Court has no route at all into another category of disputes involving parties other than States: investor-state cases. This category includes some disputes that might historically have come before the Court in the form of diplomatic protection claims brought by States on behalf of their nationals. Yet the proliferation in recent decades of bilateral investment treaties (BITs), usually providing for arbitration directly between the host State and the investor, seem to have put such disputes firmly out of the Court's reach.

This disaggregation of disputes from the interstate level is illustrated sharply by the long-running dispute between Ecuador and Chevron. Proceedings have taken place in a number of forums, including investor-state arbitration under the UNCITRAL Rules.[73] In 2012, Ecuador also attempted to initiate an interstate arbitration against the US concerning the interpretation of a provision in the Ecuador-US BIT.[74] The US made a strong case that there was no interstate dispute. Among other things, Ecuador had made no allegation that the US had engaged in any wrongful conduct that impaired Ecuador's rights under the BIT, and so there was no concrete dispute about its interpretation. The award is confidential, but in late 2012, following receipt of the US memorial on jurisdiction, the tribunal terminated the proceedings.[75] Evidently, at least in the ICSID context, it is now for the investor to defend its own rights at the international level, and not for its State of nationality to bring a diplomatic protection or other claim on its behalf.

On the other hand, the fact that an investor-state dispute can be so thoroughly disaggregated from any potential interstate dispute might suggest that something similar is possible in other contexts. Is this another ground on which it might be argued that a dispute with the EU could be disaggregated from its individual Member States?

---

73 *Chevron Corporation and Texaco Petroleum Corporation v Ecuador*, UNCITRAL, PCA Case 2009–23 (pending). The First Partial Award was delivered on 17 September 2013.

74 *Ecuador v US*, PCA Case 2012–5 (case concluded 2012). The application, statement of defence, memorial and counter-memorial are available at PCA, www.pca-cpa.org/showpage.asp?pag_id=1455.

75 See J. R. Crook (ed), 'Contemporary practice of the United States relating to international law', 107 *American Journal of International Law*, 2013, pp. 431, 474.

3 The Court's Performance in the Cases before It

The Court's performance in individual cases is another detriment of its place in the international dispute settlement framework. Overall its performance gives reason for optimism.

It is true that some of its recent decisions have attracted criticism. A case in point is its advisory opinion in *Kosovo*.[76] But the problem in *Kosovo* was not that the Court gave the wrong answer—it was that the Court was asked the wrong question. What happened was this. In 2008, the Assembly of Kosovo declared Kosovo a sovereign State, independent of Serbia. The question was formulated by Serbia and submitted to the Court by the General Assembly: 'Is the unilateral declaration of independence by the Provisional Institutions of Self-Government of Kosovo in accordance with international law?'[77]

The main deficiency of this question was that it assumed that there are rules of international law governing when independence can be declared. In fact, the applicable international law depends on the *consequences* of such a declaration; it is written in water unless given effect by subsequent events. The question did not ask, for example, about the legality of *recognizing* Kosovo's independence or about Kosovo's actual legal status. The Court was required only to determine whether the declaration itself breached general international law or the *lex specialis* created by the Security Council resolution authorizing the UN presence in Kosovo (which was part of the applicable international legal framework). It held that the declaration did not breach general international law.[78] This was clearly the right answer to the question asked.

The question also contained, in effect, an assertion of fact that the declaration of independence was 'by' the provisional institutions of self-government. The Court disagreed: it held that the authors of the declaration were acting as representatives of the Kosovar people and hence were not subject to the constraints of a UN organ constituted under the resolution. Here the Court's decision was somewhat artificial, since the authors of the declaration were members of the Assembly of Kosovo and very much seemed to be acting in

---

76 *Accordance with International Law of the Unilateral Declaration of Independence in Respect of Kosovo*, Advisory opinion, ICJ Reports 2010, p. 403.

77 *Accordance with International Law of the Unilateral Declaration of Independence in Respect of Kosovo*, Request for advisory opinion (8 October 2008). See the essays in M. Milanović & M. Wood (eds), *The Law and Politics of the Kosovo Advisory Opinion*, Oxford University Press, 2015.

78 Supra, note 76, pp. 436–439, paras. 79–84.

that capacity. But since the Court had held that the provisional institutions were part of international law, it was compelled to draw that distinction if it was to find that the declaration did not breach the *lex specialis* created by the resolution.

If the Court's opinion was of only limited significance, then that was mainly because the question posed was itself of only limited significance to the broader political issue.

This illustrates a feature of the Court that, to a variable extent, characterizes every international court or tribunal. Like earlier advisory opinions, such as *Nuclear Weapons*[79] and *Wall*,[80] the *Kosovo* opinion gave the Court the chance to pronounce boldly on a deeply political controversy. But although the political character of a dispute does not prevent the Court from ruling on it, there are still limits on the role the Court can play in such disputes. J G Merrills notes that 'judicial tribunals have no general mandate to decide all matters of international controversy, but occupy a special place in the machinery of dispute settlement'.[81] This is true not only of cases that fall outside the Court's competence, but even of some that come within it. Even if jurisdiction and admissibility can be established in a case such as *Nicaragua*,[82] for example, the Court clearly cannot always solve the underlying political dispute between two States—let alone a problem such as the threat of nuclear weapons.

Merrills suggests that newer tribunals as ITLOS and the WTO Appellate Body have reduced the Court's 'emblematic significance' as 'a constant reminder to States of the availability of litigation as a means of peaceful settlement'.[83] But the Court has shown that it has the capacity to enter into dialogue with other institutions that influence the law. We saw this in its introduction of the notion of norms *erga omnes* in *Barcelona Traction*.[84] The Court is also aware of the challenge posed to its 'emblematic significance' by alternative forums for dispute resolution and has taken some steps to meet that challenge.

---

79 *Legality of the Threat or Use of Nuclear Weapons*, Advisory opinion, ICJ Reports 1996, p. 226.
80 *Legal Consequences of the Construction of a Wall in the Occupied Palestinian Territory*, Advisory opinion, ICJ Reports 2004, p. 136.
81 J. G. Merrills, *International Dispute Settlement*, 5th ed, Cambridge University Press, 2011, pp. 162–163.
82 *Military and Paramilitary Activities in and against Nicaragua*, supra, note 9.
83 Merrills, supra, note 81, p. 166.
84 *Barcelona Traction, Light & Power Co. Ltd*, supra, note 8.

The most obvious instance of this is *LaGrand*, in 1999.[85] For a long time, it had been unclear whether provisional measures ordered by the Court were binding. Article 41(1) of the Statute of the Court empowers the Court to 'indicate ... any provisional measures which ought to be taken to preserve the respective rights of either party'. But there are no clues to what 'indicate' means, and the following paragraph describes provisional measures as measures 'suggested' by the Court (though the French text is more imperative).[86] In contrast, it was accepted that provisional measures ordered by ITLOS *were* binding.

LaGrand was a dispute under the Vienna Convention on Consular Relations[87] concerning two German nationals sentenced to death in Arizona. The Court ordered as a provisional measure that the US 'take all measures at its disposal to ensure' that one of the two German nationals was 'not executed pending the final decision in these proceedings'.[88] The Arizona authorities proceeded to execute him.

At the merits stage, the question was whether the Court could grant Germany a remedy for the breach by the US of both the Vienna Convention and the provisional measures order. The Court took the opportunity to hold that it followed 'from the object and purpose of the Statute, as well as from the terms of Article 41 when read in their context, that the power to indicate provisional measures entails that such measures should be binding'.[89] Evidently, the Court was attempting to 'compete' with ITLOS. The result is that since *LaGrand*, provisional measures have been more often sought but less often ordered.

More recently, the Court has demonstrated an openness to procedural innovation. The hearing in *Whaling in the Antarctic*,[90] in June and July 2013, had a few features that, although taken as a matter of course in domestic law and many *ad hoc* tribunals, have previously played relatively little role in the Court: in particular, the cross-examination of witnesses, including on technically complex scientific evidence; and a greater number of questions from the bench. This change in the character of proceedings is welcome. If sustained, it might do away with a long-standing source of complaint about the Court:

---

85   *LaGrand* (Germany v United States of America), *ICJ Reports 2001*, p. 466.
86   Statute of the International Court of Justice Article 41(1)–(2). The French text uses the more imperative verb '*devoir*' instead of 'ought': '[*l*]*a Cour a le pouvoir d'indiquer ... quelles mesures conservatoires du droit de chacun doivent être prises à titre provisoire*'.
87   596 UNTS 261, 24 April 1963.
88   *LaGrand* (Germany v United States of America), Provisional measures, *ICJ Reports 1999*, p. 9, para. 29.
89   *LaGrand*, supra, note 85, paras. 101–102.
90   *Whaling in the Antarctic* (Australia v Japan: New Zealand intervening), *ICJ Reports 2014*, p. 226.

that it is too passive, partly out of an exaggerated concern to ensure that States are not embarrassed. Certainly, it indicates the Court's grasp of the challenges posed by alternative forums for dispute resolution and the ossification of its procedures.

4   The Court's Contribution to the Development of the Law

Finally, I want to say something about the Court's contribution to the development of international law. It is in this respect that the Court has retained its place at the 'heart' of international law, despite procedural limitations and despite the emergence of alternatives.

As the only standing international court of general jurisdiction, the Court has been able to develop an integrated body of jurisprudence over time. Its role in developing the law goes beyond what *ad hoc* tribunals or even specialist tribunals such as ITLOS are capable of. By definition, arbitral tribunals constituted *ad hoc* for specific disputes cannot be expected to contribute as much to the gradual development of concepts.

In a few areas, the Court has been especially influential. These include the interpretation of the Charter,[91] land and maritime boundary disputes, state and diplomatic immunities and diplomatic protection. Malcolm Shaw has written that the Court's jurisprudence 'has contributed in no small measure to the successful management of territorial and boundary disputes' and 'has helped to render the law of territory more predictable' and that the Court 'has come to be accepted as an authoritative guide' to the area.[92]

The same could be said of the area of State responsibility. One of the earliest cases of the Permanent Court, *Factory at Chorzów*, continues to be cited for the proposition 'that any breach of engagement involves an obligation to

---

91   *Conditions of Admission of a State to Membership in the United Nations (Article 4 of the Charter)*, ICJ Reports 1948, p. 57; *Reparation for Injuries Suffered in the Service of the United Nations*, ICJ Reports 1949, p. 174; *Competence of the General Assembly for the Admission of a State to the United Nations*, ICJ Reports 1950, p. 4; *Voting Procedure on Questions Relating to Reports and Petitions Concerning the Territory of South West Africa*, ICJ Reports 1955, p. 67; *Certain Expenses of the United Nations (Article 17, paragraph 2, of the Charter)*, ICJ Reports 1962, p. 151; *Legal Consequences for States of the Continued Presence of South Africa in Namibia (South West Africa) notwithstanding Security Council Resolution 276 (1970)*, ICJ Reports 1970, p. 16.

92   M. Shaw, 'The International Court of Justice and the law of territory' in C. J. Tams & J. Sloan (eds), *The Development of International Law by the International Court of Justice*, Oxford University Press, 2013, pp. 151, 176.

make reparation', and the '*Chorzów* dictum' has entered the language of international law.[93] This case was part of a strong tradition of jurisprudence in the area by the Permanent Court that the International Court inherited at its inception in 1945.[94] In *Gabčíkovo-Nagymaros*,[95] it took an activist approach that also engaged with the work of the International Law Commission (ILC) (and the case was, in turn, quoted in the commentary on the Articles on State Responsibility[96]). In particular, the Court affirmed that if a State is in an overwhelming situation of 'necessity', it may be entitled to disregard its international obligations. This was a bold decision by the Court to clarify what was then an open question. It could instead have decided the issue 'hypothetically'—by stating that the parties *agreed* that the ILC draft article on necessity[97] represented international law, without deciding whether it actually did. Having recognized the existence of the defence of necessity, the Court decisively rejected Hungary's attempt to invoke it.[98]

Yet it is not just in specific areas that the Court has been influential. It has touched virtually every area of international law. Exceptions include self-contained treaty regimes where other tribunals have exclusive jurisdiction, such as the WTO; areas that have been shaped more by State practice and multilateral treaties rather than by judicial decision-making, such as many aspects of the law of the sea; and a few other areas, such as substantive questions of international human rights law, where the Court's involvement has so far been tangential.[99]

The Court is also generally considered to be authoritative in the different areas where its decisions have influenced the behaviour of the parties before it—and this is the central point. There are some cases in which States have not deferred to a decision of the Court and the decision has become a jurisprudential dead-end. After the Permanent Court's decision in *The SS Lotus* on flag State jurisdiction over collisions on the high seas,[100] States effectively

---

93 *Chorzow Factory Case* (Germany v Poland), 1928 PCIJ, (Series A) No. 17, p. 29.
94 See Crawford, supra, note 35, p. 72.
95 *Gabčíkovo-Nagymaros Project*, supra, note 11.
96 Commentary to the ILC Articles on the Responsibility of States for Internationally Wrongful Acts Article 22, *ILC Yearbook* 2001/II(2), pp. 75–76.
97 Now ILC Articles on the Responsibility of States for Internationally Wrongful Acts Article 25, *ILC Yearbook* 2001/II(2).
98 See further Crawford, supra, note 35, p. 79–81.
99 See C. J. Tams, 'The ICJ as a 'law-formative agency': summary and synthesis', in C. J. Tams & J. Sloan (eds), *The Development of International Law by the International Court of Justice*, Oxford University Press, 2013, pp. 377, 381–384.
100 *The SS Lotus* (France v Turkey), 1927 PCIJ (Series A) No. 10, p. 27.

THE PLACE OF THE ICJ IN INTERNATIONAL DISPUTE SETTLEMENT   115

reversed the rule by treaty.[101] But this does not seem to happen often. And the Court is also not alone among international judicial bodies in facing challenges to its authority. China has 'rejected' the proceedings brought against it by the Philippines under LOSC Annex VII concerning maritime jurisdiction in the South China Sea, which went ahead to the production of a lengthy adverse award without any participation by China.[102]

D. P. O'Connell wrote in 1970 that the Court's decisions are given 'a truly astonishing deference'.[103] Overall, despite the occasional break in the pattern, that statement remains accurate. Christian Tams adds that this is generally true even of controversial decisions with strong dissents, such as *Nicaragua*,[104] which 'have matured with age and have come to be accepted notwithstanding initial criticism'.[105]

5   Conclusion

Today the Court faces a number of challenges. Most, though troubling, are not insurmountable. There are signs that the Court recognizes the need to adapt its procedures to deal more expeditiously with factually complex disputes and to compete with alternative forums for international dispute settlement. International disputes involving parties other than States do pose a more fundamental challenge to the role of the Court, though even here there may be room for creative solutions. And it is also arguable that the popularity of alternative forums reflects the expansion and diversification of international dispute settlement as much as it reflects any perception that the Court is deficient. There may simply be 'too much' international law for any one international court to handle—and that is no bad thing in itself. Finally, in several respects the Court is as important as it has ever been. Its performance in the

---

101   International Convention for the Unification of Certain Rules Relating to Penal Jurisdiction in Matters of Collision or Other Incidents of Navigation (Brussels Convention), 439 UNTS 233, 10 May 1952, Article 1. See Lowe & Tzanakopoulos, supra, note 37, p. 184.
102   'On 19 February 2013, China presented the Philippines with a diplomatic note in which it described 'the Position of China on the South China Sea issues', and rejected and returned the Philippines' Notification'. For the eventual award, see Permanent Court of Arbitration, *The South China Sea Arbitration* (The Republic of Philippines v The People's Republic of China), PCA Case 17, award of 12 July 2016, available online at http://www.pcacases.com/pcadocs/PH-CN%20-%2020160712%20-%20Award.pdf.
103   D. P. O'Connell, *International Law*, vol 1, 2nd edition, Stevens, 1970, p. 32.
104   *Military and Paramilitary Activities in and against Nicaragua*, supra, note 9.
105   Tams, supra, note 99, p. 379.

cases that it does receive is generally well-regarded, and it continues to influence the development of international law in a greater variety of areas and to a greater extent than any rival forum could. The Court does not sit atop a hierarchy of lower courts on the model of domestic legal systems, but it still has no rival as the centre of gravity of international dispute settlement.

International Lawyers and the International Court of Justice: Between Cult and Contempt

Jean d'Aspremont

The contrast in the attitudes of international lawyers towards the International Court of Justice (hereafter the Court) in contemporary scholarship and practice is remarkable. Indeed, a large cohort of international lawyers worship the Court and its judgements. For these devotees, the Court deserves a capitalized C and no other pointer as there is only one such Court. For them, scholarship's main task is often reduced to distilling and interpreting the holy scriptures produced by the Court. This attitude is what is referred to here as *the cult*.[1] In contrast, another large cohort of international lawyers lampoon the Court as a vile and expensive bureaucratic machine that exacerbates political disputes which would be better dealt with outside the Great Hall of Justice of the Peace Palace in The Hague. These lawyers dismissively refer to the Court as 'a UN body' or 'a Hague court'. They satirize the Court as a 'political' creature composed of judges 'politically' appointed to serve the 'political' agendas of their 'political' constituency of origin. For them, judgments of the Court do not warrant the attention they traditionally draw in international legal scholarship. This approach is called here *the contempt*. These two extreme attitudes can hardly be reconciled and the discipline is often torn between these fanatic aficionados and these vilifying disparagers of the Court.

Interestingly, such opposite attitudes towards the Court cannot simply be apprehended and explained along cultural and geographical divides. The cult cannot be reduced to a continental European or Latin American phenomenon while contempt cannot exclusively be traced back to northern American or Asian professional circles.[2] Nor could such a contrast be captured through

---

1   This attitude has also been called 'tribunalism'. See T. Skouteris, 'The New Tribunalism: Strategies of (De)Legitimation in the Era of International Adjudication, 17 *Finnish Yearbook of International Law*, 2006, p. 307.

2   For some general historical considerations on the role of the US in the creation of an international court, see R. Kolb, *The Elgar Companion to the International Court of Justice*, Elgar, 2014, pp. 1–15. For other expressions of support, see e.g. the support for a strong judicial organ of the United Nations expressed by the American and Canadian Bar Associations expressed in the document entitled 'Consensus of Views on the International Court of the United Nations Organizations', 22 March 1945, reproduced in 39 *American Journal of International Law, Supplement.*, 1945, p. 143. See also the joined statement of the United States and the

variations in terms of substance of expertise: veneration is not more common among generalist international lawyers and contempt is not more wide-spread among human rights lawyers and investment lawyers. The varying capacities in which one engages with international law[3] are similarly unhelpful to explain the oscillation between cult and contempt of the Court among international lawyers. What is more, international lawyers themselves do not espouse one single attitude throughout their career as they regularly seesaw between reverence and derision irrespective of the changes of capacities in which they engage with international law.[4]

It is true that the two abovementioned attitudes, namely cult and contempt, may look caricatural and extreme. Yet, it is submitted here that few international lawyers would not verse, at some point, in either cult or contempt of the Court. Indeed, it is very common for the heat swirling around each new case or request for advisory opinion to simultaneously give rise to bouts of veneration and bouts of contempt. The same holds with remote observers who also happen to transform themselves in diehard supporters or detractors of the Court. Even general legal theorists are not less aloof from cult and contempt, for they will usually either articulate their theories around judicial practice and illustrate their teachings on the basis of the judgments of the Court or completely ignore it, thereby manifesting some veneration or disdain.

Professor Djamchid Momtaz to whom these observations are dedicated is probably one of the few international lawyers who, throughout his career, has consistently articulated a remarkably well-balanced and moderate attitude towards the Court, engaging in neither cult nor contempt. Actually, one of the greatest lessons which I drew from my enriching exchanges with Professor Momtaz[5] in almost two decades as well as my reading of his refined scholarship

---

USSR on the desirability of enhancing the role of the Court. See US Department of State, Fact Sheet, International Court of Justice Initiative (23 September 1989). See also the remarks of R. B. Bilder, 'The United States and the World Court in the Post-'Cold-War' Era', 40 *Catholic University Law Review*, 1990–1991, p. 251. See also David S. Patterson, 'The United States and the Origins of the World Court', 91 *Political Science Quarterly*, 1976, p. 279. On President Eisenhower's proposal proposed to the Senate that the Connally Amendement to the optional clause of the US be dropped, see the remarks of Oscar Schachter in 80 *ASIL Proceedings* (1986), 204–217, p. 212.

3   See generally J. d'Aspremont, T. Gazzini, A. Nollkaemper, & W. Werner (eds), *International Law as a Profession*, Cambridge University Press, 2017.
4   This is for instance the case of the former judge disillusioned by the Court. This is also the case of the theorist elected member at the International Law Commission.
5   I vividly recall my first encounter with Professor Momtaz on the occasion of the International Law Seminar organized under the aegis of the International Law Commission of which he was a member at the time.

is precisely the possibility of embracing a more composed approach to the Court and its decisions. In particular, whether as a Counsel[6] or as a commentator,[7] Professor Djamchid Momtaz has always demonstrated simultaneous respect and suspicion towards the Court without never fully versing into either cult or contempt. In my experience, he has demonstrated an attitude which I would call 'respectful suspicion' and which I will discuss here. This chapter, which is meant to pay tribute to Professor Djamchid Momtaz, makes the point that international lawyers are not condemned to either venerate or denigrate the Court and can approach the latter with respectful suspicion.

In the following paragraphs, I formulate a few remarks on each of the three attitudes, i.e. cult, contempt and respectful suspicion. I start by discussing the declared and unacknowledged rationales for the cult (1) and the contempt (2) of the Court. Thereafter a few general observations are put forward with a view to shedding light on what it means to be respectfully suspicious towards the Court (3).

1   Rationales of the Cult of the Court

Veneration of the Court is ripe among international lawyers[8] and may take various forms.[9] Indeed, there are a variety of conscious and unconscious drivers that can potentially explain the cult of the Court among international lawyers. It suffices here to mention a few of them.

---

6   Case concerning Oil Platforms (Islamic Republic of Iran v United States of America), Judgment, *ICJ reports 2003*, p. 161.

7   See e.g. D. Momtaz, 'L'attachement de la Cour internationale de justice au consensualisme judiciaire est-il sans faille?', in P. d'Argent, B. Bonafe, and J. Combacau (eds), *The limits of international law: essays in honour of Joe Verhoeven*, Bruylant, 2015, pp. 487–500; D. Momtaz, 'The Interaction between International Humanitarian Law and Human Rights Law and the Contribution of the ICJ' in K. Bannelier and Th. Christakis (eds), *The ICJ and the evolution of international law: the enduring impact of the 'Corfu Channel' case*, Routledge, 2012, pp. 256–263; D. Momtaz, 'Did the Court Miss an Opportunity to Denounce the Erosion of the Principle Prohibiting the Use of Force?' 29 *Yale Journal of International Law*, 2004, pp. 307–313.

8   For some general remarks on the reverence of the Court, see generally A. M. Weisburd, *Failings of the International Court of Justice*, Oxford University Press, 2016, pp. 1–4.

9   The inclination of international lawyers to seek to salvage the Court when it is put under stress can also be construed as a form of cult. On this attitude, see the remarks by Anthony D'Amato, 80 *ASIL Proccedings*, 1986, pp. 204–217, at p. 214.

1. Although its role has 'guardian of peace'—inherited from the 19th and 20th century project of peace through law is less central[10] and is being superseded by a wide array of other functions,[11] the Court remain hailed for its contribution to peaceful relations between States.
2. The achievements in terms of dispute settlements are often accompanied by a representation of the Court speaking on behalf of some kind of 'international community' which it is meant to serve.[12]
3. Whilst the Court is not meant to play a central role in terms of law-creation according to international lawyers' mainstream discourses on sources,[13] its contribution to the determination of the content of existing rules is deemed very critical and unparalleled, even by most orthodox international lawyers.[14] In that sense, the cult of the Court is largely informed by the recognition of central responsibilities in terms

---

10 For some critical remarks, see C. Tams, 'World Courts as Guardian of Peace?', 15 *Global Cooperation Research Papers*, 2016. See also Y. Shany, 'No Longer a Weak Department of Power? Reflections on the Emergence of a New International Judiciary', 20 *European Journal of International Law*, 2009, pp. 73–91, at pp. 77–78; I. L. Claude, *States and the Global System. Politics, Law and Organization*, MacMillan Press, 1988, pp. 160–173.

11 On the variety of functions of international courts, see generally B. Kingsbury, 'International Courts, Uneven Judicialization in Global Order' in J. Crawford and M. Koskenniemi (eds), *The Cambridge Companion to International Law*, Cambridge University Press, 2012, pp. 203–228; J. Alvarez, 'What Are International Judges for? The Main Functions od International Adjudication', in C. P. Romano, K. J. Alter & Y. Shany (eds), *The Oxford Handbook of International Adjudication*, Oxford University Press, 2013, pp. 158–179.

12 See the critical remarks by A. von Bogdandy and I. Venzke, 'In Whose Name? An Investigation of International Courts' Public Authority and Its Democratic Justification', 23 *European Journal of International Law*, 2012, pp 7–41. See also A. von Bogdandy and I. Venzke, 'On the Functions of International Courts: An Appraisal in Light of Their Burgeoning Public Authority' 26 *Leiden Journal of International Law*, 2013, pp. 49–72.

13 For a recent re-statement of the doctrine of sources as is 'found' in Article 38 of the Statute of the International Court of Justice, see H. Thirlway, *The Sources of International Law*, Oxford University Press, 2014.

14 The idea that international courts contribute to the consolidation and the development of international law is an old one. As early as 1934, Hersch Lauterpacht published a series of papers on The Development of International Law by the Permanent Court of International Justice. For a recent re-examination of this question, see C. Tams and A. Tzanakopoulos, 'Barcelona Traction at 40: The ICJ as an Agent of Legal Development', 23 *Leiden Journal of International Law*, 2010, pp. 781–800.

of content-determination, and more incidentally in terms of law-ascertainment.[15]

4. The Court is the object of veneration as it helps international lawyers think of international law in institutional terms. In particular, the Court is almost all what the international lawyers have at their disposal in terms of centralization of interpretive powers.[16] The cult of the Court accordingly expresses the vesting of some central(ized) and hierarchically superior interpretive powers into the one single institution which international lawyers can draw on. From this perspective, the cult simultaneously is the materialization of the hopes that the abiding confrontation of the discipline can be played down.[17]

5. In the same vein, the Court is adored as it helps international lawyers think of international law in systemic terms. In that sense, the cult stems from the elevation of the Court by international lawyers into an architect of what they see as an international legal system, In fact, it is very common among international lawyers to resort to the practice of the Court to 'unearth' an international legal system or validate their projection of an international legal system,[18] irrespective of whether the Court is actually interested in contributing to giving international law a macro systematic character.[19]

---

15 This is especially the case with respect to customary international law for which the distinction between law-ascertainment and content-determination often collapses. On this distinction, see J. d'Aspremont, 'The Multidimensional Process of Interpretation: Content-Determination and Law-Ascertainment Distinguished' in A. Bianchi, D. Peat & M. Windsor (eds), *Interpretation in International Law*, Oxford University Press, 2015, pp. 111–129.

16 As the Court is probably the only one court that can play that role, international lawyers cling to it. In this respect, see A. D'Amato, supra, note 9, p. 214.

17 On the idea that the discipline of international law is intrinsically confrontational, see J. d'Aspremont, *Epistemic Forces in International Law*, Elgar, 2015, pp. 1–27.

18 Particular value is attached to advisory opinions in this respect. See e.g. K. Oellers-Frahn, 'Law-Making by Advisory Opinions' 12 *German Law Journal*, 2011, p. 1033, esp. pp. 1041–1042. See also R. Kolb, *La Cour Internationale de Justice*, Pedone, 2013, p. 1227.

19 This is what I have called elsewhere the 'irony' of system-design because the Court is elevated into the main architect of the international legal system whereas it is barely interested in building a macro legal system. See J. d'Aspremont, 'The International Court of Justice and the Irony of System-Design', *Journal of International Dispute Settlement*, 2016.

6. The Court is often adulated for its legitimizing of international law by resolving disputes in a principled manner[20] and the resort to more politically acceptable means to dispute resolution.[21] In that sense, the Court is seen as what makes international law a useful toolbox to settle dispute, thereby simultaneously vindicating the functional legitimacy of international law.

7. The judgements of the Court—and those of its predecessor—are often commended for their quality and attentiveness,[22] a perception that helps consolidate the cult of the Court.

8. The composition of the Court and the finding of high standards of personal integrity and competence of its members can be a feeling that contributes to the veneration of the Court.[23]

9. The reification of the Court can stem from the conviction of international lawyers that placing the Court at the center of the debates on international law constitutes a noble empirical attitude. From this perspective, relying on anything the Court says makes international legal discourses more practical or grounded in practice.[24] That dimension of the cult reinforces the belief of international lawyers that the main rules of international law can be established through empirical observation of judicial practice.

10. The cult of the Court manifests the inclination of endowing the Court with the ultimate power of validation of the key doctrines of international law. Indeed, once a key doctrine or a set of modes of legal reasoning is approved by the Court, it seems that it can no longer be put into question.[25] In that sense, the Court is approached as the guardian of international lawyers' modes of legal reasoning. This is particularly

---

20 T. Franck, *Fairness in International Law and Institutions*, Oxford University Press, 1995, p. 346.
21 R. E. Lutz II, 'Perspectives on the World Court, the United States, and International Dispute Resolution in a Changing World', 25 *The International Lawyer*, 1991, p. 682.
22 See the remarks of Kolb, supra, note 2, pp. 14–15.
23 S. Rosenne, *The World Court, What it is and How its Works*, 5th edition, Martinus Nijhoff, 1995, p. 19.
24 See D'Amato, supra, note 9, p. 215.
25 See Tams & Tzanakopoulos, supra, note 14, p. 783. See also J. d'Aspremont, 'If International Judges Say So, It Must Be True: Empiricism or Fetishism?', 4 *ESIL Reflections*, No. 9, 2015.

noticeable in relation to sources,[26] State responsibility,[27] or jus cogens,[28] to take but a few examples.

11. The cult of the Court may be the result of international law being an argumentative practice in constant need of input by actors in a position to impose their views on the modes of legal reasoning of international law. Said differently, the Court is revered because it is one of the main actors that nourish—in terms of content and legal forms—the modes of legal reasoning which are constantly deployed by international lawyers.[29]

12. The cult of the Court may be the emanation of international lawyers inclination to approach international legal controversies as 'ruling from the bench'.[30] From that perspective, scholarships boils down to evaluate any legal question from the vantage point of a virtual judge.[31] The cult of

---

[26] See Thirlway, supra, note 13, pp. 1–30. See the remarks of J. d'Aspremont, 'Book review of H. Thirlway, "The Sources of International Law"', 57 *German Yearbook of International Law*, 2014. Regarding the influence of the Court on the modes of legal reasoning pertaining to the establishment of customary law, see e.g. UN Doc. A/CN.4/682, 27 March 2015, para. 4. For a detailed study of the contribution of the International Court of Justice to the structures of legal argumentation in terms of customary international law, see C. Tams, 'Meta-Custom and the Court: A Study in Judicial Law-Making', 14 *The Law and Practice of International Courts and Tribunals*, pp. 51–79.

[27] The modes of legal reasoning on the allocation of the burden of compensation and the possibility to take countermeasures that have been codified by the International Law Commission are often seen as a 'synthesis' of what is essentially judicial practice. See e.g. J. Crawford, *State Responsibility. The General Part*, Cambridge University Press, 2013, pp. 45–93.

[28] I have discussed the practice of taking refuge in judicial validation in relation to jus cogens in greater depth elsewhere. See J. d'Aspremont, 'Jus Cogens as a Social Construct without Pedigree', *Netherlands Yearbook of International Law*, 2016, (forthcoming).

[29] See generally, J. d'Aspremont, *Formalism and the Sources of International Law*, Oxford University Press, 2011, esp. chapter 8. It should be noted that the Court does not have a monopoly when it comes to feed the modes of legal reasoning of international lawyers. On the role of other actors, see J. d'Aspremont, 'Non-State Actors and the Social Practice of International Law', in M. Noortmann, A. Reinisch & C. Ryngaert (eds), *Handbook on Non-State Actors in International Law*, Hart Publishing, 2015, pp. 11–31.

[30] P. Schlag, *Laying Down the Law*, New York University Press, 1996, p. 142. See also P. Schlag, 'Spam Jurisprudence, Air Law, and the Rank Anxiety of Nothing Happening (A Report on the State of the Art)', 97 *Georgia Law Journal*, 2009, pp. 803–835, at p. 813.

[31] According to D'Amato, international law think of the law 'as if an imaginary court were making an imaginary decision with respect to the facts that we have in mind' and 'we go through a miniadjudicative process, sensing how a hypothetical judge would rule on these facts.' See the remarks by A. D'Amato, supra, note 9, pp. 214–215.

the Court may just be the continuation of such judicialization of international legal thought.[32]

The foregoing is not meant to constitute an exhaustive list of what motivates the cult. There may be other—declared and unacknowledged—rationales behind the cult of the Court witnessed in international legal thought and practice. What is more, each of these various driving forces of the veneration of the Court may express themselves very distinctively. For these reasons, the account made above is thus necessarily simplistic. Yet, for the sake of the discussion carried out here, it is not necessary to delve into further detail. Rather, the attention should turn to the rationales of those behaviors very contemptuous of the Court. It will be seen that the forces and perceptions underpinning the cult of the Court may simultaneously vindicate its contempt.

2   Rationales of the Contempt of the Court

The Court has been the object of contempt for all kinds of reasons, some of them being even contradictory. For the sake of this chapter, it suffices to mention a few of them.[33] Some of them are expressly invoked by international lawyers whilst some others have remained unacknowledged.

1.   The Court is scorned for the inappropriateness of its interventions in highly political disputes[34] or its venturing into areas—like political and

---

32   Pierre Schlag prefers to speak about the 'juridification' of legal thought. See P. Schlag, *Laying Down the Law*, New York University Press, 1996, pp. 139 and 141–142.

33   For a recent overview, see A. Mark Weisburd, *Failings of the International Court of Justice*, Oxford University Press, 2016.

34   See e.g. H. Steinberger, 'The International Court of Justice', in *Judicial Settlement of International Disputes*, Max Planck Institute for Comparative Public Law and International Law, 1974, p. 209. This was also one of the charges of the Reagan Administration against the ICJ after its decision on jurisdiction in the Nicaragua case. See US Department of State, US Withdrawal from the Proceedings Initiated by Nicaragua in the ICJ, 85 *Department of State Bulletin*, March 1985, reprinted in 24 ILM 246, 1985. For an overview of some important cases where the argument plaid out, see A. Coleman, 'The International Court of Justice and Highly Political Matters', 4 *Melbourne Journal of International Law*, 2003, pp. 43–60. For a discussion of that argument in relation to the South West Africa cases, see M. Pomerance, 'The ICJ and South West Africa (Namibia): A Retrospective Legal/Political Assessment', 12 *Leiden Journal of International Law*, 1999, pp. 425–436. For a discussion of that argument in relation to the Wall Advisory Opinion, see N. Rostow, 'Wall of Reason:

security disputes that were never within the Court's mandate.[35] The Court is similarly derided for its disruption of domestic systems.[36]
2. The Court is accused of exacerbating international disputes rather than settling them.[37]
3. The Court is very regularly disparaged for being politically 'influenced' or 'biased'.[38] In the same vein, it is lampooned for its illusory independence.[39]

Alan Dershowitz v. The International Court of Justice' 71 *Albany Law Review*, 2008, pp. 955–988; M. Pomerance, 'The ICJ's Advisory Jurisdiction and the Crumbling Wall between the Political and the Judicial', 99 *American Journal of International Law*, 2005, pp. 26–42.

[35] A. Sofaer, 'The United States and the World Court', 80 *ASIL Proceedings*, 1986, pp. 204–217, at p. 206.

[36] C. Lane, 'U.S. Quits Pact Used in Capital Cases; Foes of Death Penalty Cite Access to Envoys', *Washington Post*, 10 March 2005, at A1. For a discussion of this argument in relation to 2005 US' withdrawal from the Optional Protocol to the Vienna Convention on Consular Relations Concerning the Compulsory Settlement of Disputes, see J. Quigley, 'The United States' Withdrawal from International Court of Justice Jurisdiction in Consular Cases: Reasons and Consequences', 19 *Duke Journal Comparative and International Law*, 2009, pp 263–306.

[37] J. Sztucki, 'International Organizations as Parties to Contentious Proceedings before the International Court of Justice?' in A. S. Muller, D. Raic, & J. M. Thuranszky (eds), *The International Court of Justice: Its Future Role after Fifty Years*, 1997, pp. 141 and 155–156.

[38] This was another of the various criticisms made by the Reagan Administration against the ICJ after its decision on jurisdiction in the Nicaragua case. See US Department of State, supra, note 34. See also D. R. Robinson, 'The Role of Politics in the Election and the Work of Judges of the International Court of Justice', 97 *ASIL Proceedings*, 2003, p. 277; Gordon, 'Observations on the Independence and Impartiality of the Members of the International Court of Justice', 2 *Connecticut Journal of International Law*, 1987, p. 397; Weiss, 'Judicial Independence and Impartiality: A preliminary Inquiry', in L. Damrosch (ed), *The International Court of Justice at a Crossroads*, 1987, p. 123. On national biases and the tendency of judges to vote in favour of their country of origin, see T. Hensley, 'National Bias and the International Court of Justice', 12 *Midwest Journal of Political Science*, 1968, p. 568. On the tendency of ad hoc judges to vote in favor of the country appointing them, see Il Ro Suh, 'Voting Behaviour of National Judges in International Courts', 63 *American Journal of International Law*, 1969, p. 224; E. A. Posner & M. F. P. de Figueiredo, 'Is the International Court of Justice Biased?', 34 *Journal of Legal Studies*, 2005, pp. 599–630 (for them, there are strong empirical evidence that judges favor the States that appoint them). For a rejection of the assumption that judges would vote along the lines of the position of their State of origin, see R. Higgins' remarks in 'Alternative Perspectives on the Independence of International Court', 99 *ASIL Proceedings*, 2005, p. 135; R. Higgins, 'Reflections from the International Court' in M. Evans (ed), *International Law*, Oxford University Press, 2006, p. 3; A. Chayes, 'Nicaragua, The United States and the World Court',

4. The Court is the object of disdain for its composition and the flawed procedure of appointment of its judges.[40]
5. The Court is denigrated for failing to deliver on the hopes placed therein, especially in terms of dispute settlement.[41] By the same token, the Court is the object of contempt for its waning credibility and utility in resolving conflicts[42] or, more generally, for its waning jurisdiction.[43]

---

85 *Columbia Law Review*, 1985, p. 1445, at pp. 1447–1448. On the idea that an accurate scholarly treatment of judicial behavior is unattainable, see T. Franck, 'Some Psychological Factors in International Third Party Decision-Making', 19 *Stanford Law Review*, 1967, p. 1217; Terris et al., *The International Judge: An Introduction to the Men and Women Who Decide the World's Cases,* Oxford University Press, 2007, at p. 209. It is noteworthy that a number of serious studies have been produced to enlarge the perspectives on the debate on the political biases in international judicial processes. For instance, on the idea that judges are more influenced by their legal training and experience rather than the national interest of their country of origin, see A. Coleman, 'The International Court of Justice and Highly Political Matters', 4 *Melbourne Journal of International Law,* 2003, pp. 29–73, at pp. 69–70. On the idea that judicial decision-making is articulated around a wide array of factors that cannot be reduced to the political bias or the interest of the country of origin of the judge, see G. Hernandez, 'Impartiality and Bias at the International Court of Justice', 1 *Cambridge Journal of International and Comparative Law,* 2012, pp. 183–207. See also D. Kennedy, 'Freedom and Constraint in Adjudication: A Critical Phenomenology', 36 *Journal of Legal Education,* 1986, p. 518; O. Spiermann, *International Legal Argument in the Permanent Court of International Justice,* Cambridge University Press, 2005, p. 27.

39 For some expressions of concerns over judicial independence, see E. Benvenisti and G. W. Downs, 'Prospects for the Increased Independence of International Courts and Tribunals', 12 *German Law Journal,* 2011, p. 1057; R. Mackenzie & P. Sands, 'International Courts and Tribunals and the Independence of the International Judge', 44 *Harvard International Law Journal*, 2003, p. 271.

40 A. Sofaer, supra, note 35, p. 207.

41 Ibid. p. 206.

42 For a discussion of that argument in relation to the Wall Advisory Opinion, see N. Rostow, 'Wall of Reason: Alan Dershowitz v. The International Court of Justice', 71 *Albany Law Review*, 2008, p. 986.

43 E. Posner, 'The Decline of the International Court of Justice' in S. Voigt, M. Albert & D. Schmidtchen (eds), *International Conflict Resolution*, Mohr Siebeck, 2006, pp. 111–142; J. Ku, *UN Reform: How about the ICJ?* Opinio Juris, 22 April 2005, http://lawofnations.blogspot.nl/2005/04/un-reform-how-about-icj.html ('All of this suggests that the ICJ... is one of those fancy-sounding international institution that doesn't really matter very much'). For some critical remarks on the disinclination of States to resort to the Court, see Claude, supra, n. 10, pp. 160–173.

6. The Court is discredited for being subject to abuses by states for political or propaganda ends.[44]
7. Court's judgments are depreciated because of the Court's handling of evidence,[45] or the evidentiary aspects of its procedure.[46]
8. The Court is, more generally, ridiculed for its procedure[47] or its procedural errors.[48]
9. The Court is the object of criticisms for its dependence on the will of the Parties to conduct the procedure and enforce its judgments.[49]
10. The Court is pilloried for its commitment to 'positivism' and its attachment to overly formal argumentative construction.[50]
11. The Court is mocked for its tepidity and lack of activism.[51]
12. The Court is stigmatized for the liberty it has taken with the doctrine of sources and its adoption of 'new rules of recognition' at convenience.[52]
13. More generally, the Court is derided for any 'failure' of international law in managing the world.

---

44 A. Sofaer, supra, note 35, p. 207.
45 W. M. Reisman, C. Skinner, *Fraudulent Evidence before Public International Tribunals. The Dirty Stories of International Law*, Cambridge University Press, 2015.
46 A. Sofaer, supra, note 35, p. 209.
47 Cassese, 'The International Court of Justice: It Is High Time to Restyle the Respected Old Lady', in A. Cassese (ed), *Realizing Utopia: The Future of International Law*, Oxford University Press, 2012, p. 239.
48 A. M. Weisburd, *Failings of the International Court of Justice*, Oxford University Press, 2016, chapter 3.
49 See J. Charney, 'Disputes Implicating the Institutional Credibility of the Court: Problems of Non-Appearance, Non-Participation and Non-Performance', in L. Damrosch (ed), *The International Court of Justice at a Crossroads*, Dobbs Ferry, N.Y. Transnational Publishers, 1987, pp. 288, 303–304.
50 According to E. Posner, it is the softening of the Court's commitment to positivism that made it offset the reputational disaster of the South West Africa cases. See Eric Posner, 'The Decline of the International Court of Justice' in S. Voigt, M. Albert and D. Schmidtchen (eds), *International conflict resolution*, Mohr Siebeck, 2006, pp. 111–142; See also McWhinney, Judicial Settlement of International Disputes, Martinus Nijhoff, 1991, pp. 16–23 and 92–93 or S. Rosenne, *The World Court: What it Is and How it Works*, (Terry Gill ed.), Martinus Nijhoff, 2003, at p. 117.
51 Cassese, supra, note 47, p. 240.
52 A. Sofaer, 'Adjudication in the International Court of Justice: Progress through Realism', 44 *Records of the Association of the Bar of the City of New York*, 1989, p. 477.

It must be acknowledged that the numerous reasons which international lawyers invoke in their bouts of contempt as well as their abovementioned inclination to turn to the Court for anything that goes wrong with international law still presupposes some recognition of the significance of the Court. The Court would not be worthy of any expression of contempt—and justification thereof—should it be completely ignored and deemed of negligible impact on international legal argumentation and the world. Be that as it may, the above overview of some of the reasons of the contempt of the Court—as the account of the rationales behind the cult of the Court examined in the previous section—is necessary cursory. Yet, the brief outline provided here suffices to move the discussion towards a third—and less common—attitude in relation to the Court which is called respectful suspicion.

3 Approaching the Court with Respectful Suspicion

The previous sections have expounded on the wide range of—declared and unacknowledged—reasons informing the veneration or scorning of the Court. It is noteworthy that the same reasons may justify either the cult or the contempt (e.g. the Court's approach to disputes in a principle manner, its composition, its intervention in intricate situations, its activism, its formalism, its composition, etc.). Of all the abovementioned reasons which can potentially justify both the cult and the contempt, those pertaining to the rightfulness or wrongfulness of the intervention of the Court in political matters warrant closer attention. As far as I am concerned, I have always looked with amusement at the debate on the question of the non-justiciability of a dispute because of its intrinsic political character.[53] It seems to me that the last decades of critical thinking have—sometimes *ad nauseum*—showed that the strict distinction between law and politics and the idea of a displacement of the

---

53   That debate is not new. See H. Lauterpacht, *The Function of the Law in the International Community*, Clarendon, 1933, p. 389; see H. Mosler, 'Political and Justiciable Legal Disputes. Revival of an Old Controversy' in B. Cheng & Brown (eds), *Contemporary Problems of International Law—Essays in Honour of Georg Schwarzenberger on His Eightieth Birthday*, Stevens, 1988, p. 216 et seq. See also the Separate Opinion of Judge Lachs appended to the Judgment of the Court in *Military and Paramilitary Activities in and against Nicaragua* (Nicaragua v United States), *ICJ Reports 1986*, p. 168. See also R. Jennings, 'The Proper Work and Purposes of the International Court of Justice' in A. S. Muller, D. Raic, & J. M. Thuranszky (eds), *The International Court of Justice: Its Future Role after Fifty Years*, Martinus Nijhoff, 1997, p. 40.

former by the latter is illusory,[54] if not unintelligible. Indeed, this idea that international law—and its institutions—allow the settlement of international dispute in a de-politicized way—a pattern of legal thought inherited from the Enlightenment project[55]—has been compellingly dismantled over the years. Moving away from this liberal paradigm is precisely what allows the espousal of a respectfully suspicious attitude towards the Court that simultaneously makes all the abovementioned arguments invoked by international lawyers for and against the Court rather inconclusive.

Indeed, respectful suspicion is an attitude that does away with the belief that law and politics are distinct and that the former displaces the latter.[56] More precisely, such attitude is suspicious[57] because it recognizes that the use of the Court, the establishment of the jurisdiction of the Court, the evidencing of the facts, the ascertainment of the law, and the application of the ascertained law to the established facts, are all part of the same political phenomenon whereby political arguments about the world are continued in legal terms and through institutional judicial frameworks. Suspicion thus means that Court's decisions are not held to be about unearthing any pre-existing truth to any objectively established situations. It also entails the recognition that interpretation of existing rules and facts is constitutive of the applicable standard and of the situation to which such standards are applied. As a result of such suspicious attitude, the Court is not evaluated for 'correctly' and 'objectively'

---

54   In the same vein, Claude, supra, note 10, pp. 164–170.

55   This is what is sometimes called liberal legalism. See F. Hoffman, 'International Legalism and International Politics', in A. Orford & F. Hoffmann (eds), *The Oxford Handbook of the Theory of International Law*, Oxford University Press, 2016, pp. 954–984, at p. 961. See more generally R. M. Unger, *Knowledge and Politics*, The Free Press, 1975, pp. 76–81; M. Koskenniemi, *From Apology to Utopia—The Structure of International Legal Argument*, Cambridge University Press, 2006, p. 71; M. Koskenniemi, 'The Politics of International Law, 1 *European Journal of International Law*, 1990, pp. 4–5; T. O'Hagan, *The End of Law?*, Blackwell, 1984, p. 183; P. W. Kahn, *The Cultural Study of Law. Reconstructing Legal Scholarship*, The University of Chicago Press, 1999, at pp. 16–18; J. N. Shklar, *Legalism—Law Morals, and Political Trials*, Harvard University Press, 1986, pp. 8–9 and 16–23.

56   On how the idea of a leap from politics to law informed the proposals that led to the creation of a permanent international court, see Kolb, supra, note 2, pp. 1–15, esp. pp. 1–2.

57   Comp with the idea of 'hermeneutic of suspicion' permeating contemporary legal thought as was contended by Duncan Kennedy. See D. Kennedy, 'The Hermeneutic of Suspicion in Contemporary American Legal Thought', 25 *Law Critique*, 2014, pp. 91–139: 'the contemporary elite jurists pursue, vis-à-vis one another, an 'hermeneutic of suspicion', meaning that they work to uncover hidden ideological moves behind the 'wrong' legal arguments of their opponents, while affirming their own right answers allegedly innocent of ideology.'

unearthing and interpreting the law and evidencing the facts. From such a suspicious perspective, the Court is judged and scrutinized for the consequences of the choices it makes in constituting the law, the facts and the relationship between them.

And yet, suspicion, as is understood here, should not be construed as a demotion of judicial processes in the Great Hall of Justice to vile politics. International law (and the Court) are not less noble because they are articulated around a continuation of political debates in legal categories. On the contrary, evaluating the Court for the consequences of its choices means taking the Court much more seriously than if naïvely reduced to an oracle of the facts and the law. Evaluating the Court on such grounds also entails a recognition of the immense and painstaking work behind judgments and opinions of the Court as well as the appreciation of the challenges brought about by the difficult environment in which the Court operates. From the perspective of respectful suspicion, the Court is a highly valuable bureaucratic body[58] that can potentially produce authoritative and persuasive positions in the eyes of those stakeholders—including international lawyers themselves—that resort to it to perpetuate their debates in legal terms.[59] Professor Djamchid Momtaz to whom these observations are dedicated is one of those who has most concretely shown that suspicion towards the Court and respect thereof are not antithetical and that neither cult nor contempt of the Court is the fate of international lawyers.

---

58   On the idea of courts as bureaucratic bodies, see I. Venzke, 'International Bureaucracies from a Political Science Perspective—Agency, Authority and International Institutional Law', 9 *German Law Journal*, 2008, p. 1401. See also see R. P. Burns, 'Is Our Legal Order Just Another Bureaucracy?', *Northwestern Public Law Research Paper* No. 16–15, 2016.

59   In the same vein, see I. Scobbie, "All right, Mr. DeMille, I'm ready for my close-up': Some Critical Reflections on Professor Cassese's 'The International Court of Justice: It Is High Time to Restyle the Respected Old Lady" 23 *European Journal of International Law*, 2012, pp. 1071–1088.

Le règlement des différends investisseur/État (RDIE) : brève revue de doctrine avant réforme

*Marie-Françoise Labouz**

C'est pour l'auteur de ces lignes un honneur et un plaisir de contribuer à l'ouvrage offert au professeur Djamchid Momtaz. Nos chemins se sont croisés à l'Université de Paris X Nanterre puis à l'Institut National des Langues et Civilisations Orientales où il accepta à ma demande d'intervenir dans le Diplôme des Hautes Etudes Internationales.

Qu'il s'agisse du volume des Investissements Directs Etrangers entre les Etats-Unis et l'Union européenne (UE) puisque les Etats-Unis sont le premier partenaire de l'UE pour les IDE et le principal investisseur ; qu'il s'agisse de la compétence exclusive de l'UE depuis le Traité de Lisbonne (article 206 du traité sur le fonctionnement de l'UE-TFUE) ou encore du nombre d'accords d'investissements dans le monde (plus de 3700), c'est assez dire le retentissement critique du règlement des différends entre l'investisseur et l'Etat (RDIE/ISDS). Ce mécanisme arbitral transnational est de longue date à la fois accablé d'honneur pour les uns et d'indignité pour les autres (I). S'ajoute aujourd'hui l'attention portée à l'évaluation des propositions européennes de réforme de l'ISDS en faveur de l'instauration d'un appel dans le cadre d'un système juridictionnel (II), d'abord à moyen terme dans le futur Accord Economique et Commercial Global entre l'UE et le Canada (AECG)/Comprehensive Economic and Trade Agreement (CETA) dont le chapitre sur l'investissement a fait l'objet de modifications lors de l'examen juridique conjoint du texte en 2016[1], puis dans le futur accord de partenariat avec les Etats-Unis (Transatlantic Trade and Investment Parternship – TTIP/TAFTA) enfin à plus long terme à l'échelle multilatérale avec l'instauration souhaitée d'une Cour Internationale des investissements.

---

* L'auteur remercie Adeline Favier, ingénieur d'étude au Centre de recherche Versailles Institutions Publiques (VIP) pour son assistance informatique de mise en page.
1 Le texte a été rendu public exclusivement à des fins d'information avant la traduction des versions officielles et le processus de ratification (Déclaration conjointe du 29 février 2016 de la Commissaire européenne au commerce et la ministre du commerce international du Canada).

1 Le RDIE/ISDS : excès d'honneur ou d'indignité ?

L'interrogation s'impose dès l'énoncé du mécanisme étudié et c'est à la mesure des commentaires critiques, négatifs ou positifs, parfois les deux, souvent diffusés en ligne. Ils émanent pour les uns des ONG et sont souvent repris par des Etats et par les Institutions de l'Union européenne. Pour les autres, ceux sont ceux des arbitres[2], des investisseurs et de leurs avocats, sans omettre le nombre considérable de commentaires académiques[3] et de longue date, les études de l'OCDE[4] et de la CNUCED[5]. L'étude du Service de recherche du Congrès des Etats-Unis a rappelé en 2015 que les siècles précédents ont connu des interventions militaires pour la défense des intérêts commerciaux américains. Dès lors, estime-t-on, la généralisation de l'ISDS dans les accords de libre-échange « represented a more peaceful, effective mechanism for addressing disputes between investors and host countries »[6], contribuant affirme-t-on, à dépolitiser les différends. Le débat est circonscrit ici autour des griefs d'opacité et de partialité de l'ISDS.

---

2   B. Stern, « The Future of International Investment Law: a Balance between the Protection of Investors and States' Capacity to Regulate », J. E. Alvarez et al. (Dir.), *The Evolving International Investment Regime : Expectations, Realities, Options*, Oxford University Press, 2011 p. 174-193.

3   Parmi les publications récentes, C. Henckels, *Proportionality and Deference in Investor-State Arbitration, Balancing Investment Protection and Regulatory Autonomy*, Cambridge University Press, 2015, 266p ; J. E. Kalicki, A. Joubin-Bret (Dir), *Reshaping the Investment-State Dispute Settlement System*, Brill, 2015 ; C. Leben (Dir.), *Droit international des investissements et de l'arbitrage transnational*, Paris, Pedone, 2015, 1141p ; « Symposium Investor-State Dispute », *Maryland Journal of International Law*, vol. 30, Issue 1 (2015), p. 3-131; Dossier sur « Les techniques conventionnelles du droit international des investissements », *Revue Générale de Droit International Public*, 2015, n° 1; Canadian Center of Policy Alternatives, *Making Sense of the CETA, an analysis of the final text of the Canada-European Union Comprehensive Economic and Trade Agreement*, 2014 ; European Center for International Political Economy, *Demystifying Investor-State Dispute Settlement (ISDS)*, ECIPE Occasional Paper n° 5 / 2014.

4   Document de travail 2006/1 « Améliorer le mécanisme de règlement des différends entre investisseurs et Etats ; vue d'ensemble », Organisation de Coopération et de Développement Economiques (OCDE), 2006, 41p; Lire aussi P. Juillard, « Le rôle joué par l'OCDE dans l'élaboration du droit des investissements », *Le pouvoir normatif de l'OCDE*, Paris, Pedone, 2013, 148p, p. 71-78, sp. P. 75 et s.

5   Etude sur les politiques d'investissement au service du développement : « Différends entre investisseurs et Etat ; prévention et modes de règlement autres que l'arbitrage », Conférence des Nations Unies sur Commerce Et le Développement, 2010, 165p.

6   International Investment Agreements (IIAS) ; Frequently Asked Questions 15 May 2015, Congressional Research Service, 7-5700, www.crs.gov.

1.1 *Le grief d'opacité*

Quant à la transparence de la procédure, satisfaisante dans l'Accord de Libre-Echange Nord – Américain, elle le serait moins dans les règles CIRDI. Dans les négociations euro-atlantiques, la confidentialité fermement exigée des Etats-Unis a d'abord conduit à filtrer de manière très restrictive les documents de négociation accessibles, de nature à empêcher les fuites recherchées par WikiLeaks—pourtant opérées en mai 2016 par Greenpeace Netherlands- au détriment peut-être du Parlement européen qui pouvait être désavantagé par rapport au Congrès américain. Mais les Etats-Unis ont pu faire remarquer que le défaut de transparence s'illustre ailleurs comme dans « the French-Egyptian case » car « we don't know much about it because the facts and briefs are not public »[7].

La Convention des Nations Unies sur la transparence dans l'arbitrage entre investisseurs et Etats[8], ouverte à la signature le 17 mars 2015 parviendra-t-elle à effacer pour les ONG le grief que constitue l'opacité de cette procédure arbitrale. La Commission européenne, en réponse à l'opinion publique et à l'hostilité de nombre d'ONG a publié le 7 janvier 2015 un ensemble de textes juridiques[9] (*legal texts negotiating with US*) soumis aux Etats membres et au Parlement européen ainsi que des « position paper..reader's guide, facts-sheets », destinés à informer le public de la nouvelle approche européenne. Toujours pour « déminer les polémiques », la Commission européenne a publié cinq mois après le mandat de négociation du traité transatlantique[10], celui du *Trade in Services Agreement*[11]. Toutefois, la pierre d'achoppement des négociations transatlantiques fait seulement alors l'objet de *factsheets*. Elle est ainsi exceptée des documents publiés au titre des *textual provisions*, alors même que la Commission européenne évoque l'entrée en vigueur le 1 avril 2014 du règlement de la CNUDCI sur la transparence dans l'arbitrage entre investisseurs et Etats. Mais l'autorisation a été demandée au Conseil par la Commission européenne dès janvier 2015 de signer la Convention des Nations Unies. Ce n'est que le 12 novembre 2015 que l'Union européenne a finalisé et publié sa proposition présentée officiellement aux Etats-Unis. Dans un communiqué de presse du même jour, la Commission européenne annonce alors la prochaine reprise

---

[7] https:www.whitehouse.gov/blog/2015/02/26/investor-state-dispute-settlement-isds-q....
[8] United Nations Convention on Transparency in Treaty-based Investor-State Arbitration, texte in A/RES/69/116 et http:uncitral.org.
[9] EU negotiating texts in TTIP, http://trade.ec.europa.eu/doclib/press/index.cfm?id=1230.
[10] La version déclassifiée du document de juin 2013 a été publiée le 9 octobre 2014 (11103/13 DCL 1).
[11] Le document déclassifié de mars 2013 a été publié le 10 mars 2015 (6891/13 ADD 1 DCL 1).

des négociations suspendues en 2014 à la suite de la consultation publique sur le RDIE dans le TTIP[12].

Le défaut global de transparence est selon les ONG destiné à taire la nature plus politique que commerciale des différends opposant les investisseurs aux Etats et par voie de conséquence, d'assurer via la justice privée – faute toutefois assurent les entreprises plaignantes, de juridictions internes dignes de ce nom, même en Europe parmi les nouveaux membres de l'Union européenne-, la discrétion et la confiance des investisseurs. Mais les modes de saisine, rétorque-t-on, excluent les ONG, celles qui dénoncent précisément « les profiteurs de l'injustice »[13]. Pourtant les attentes légitimes des investisseurs étrangers ne sont pas toujours prioritairement de maximiser leur profit mais de voir préserver par des arbitres spécialistes du commerce international et de son droit, le respect du standard du traitement juste et équitable. Cependant, ce dernier principe est loin d'être sans reproches dès lors que se pose aussi la définition de l'expropriation indirecte[14], en dépit d'un mouvement perceptible aux yeux des commentateurs des sentences, d'un certain rééquilibrage en faveur de l'Etat d'accueil.

1.2 *Le grief de partialité*

Enfin, les tribunaux d'arbitrage ne sont-ils pas faits selon nombre d'ONG « pour détrousser les Etats »[15] et les priver par peur des compensations financières mises à leur charge, voire par autocensure, de leurs politiques publiques en faveur notamment de la santé, de l'environnement ou encore de la conservation

---

12   Le 21 mars 2016, La Commission a publié d'autres documents qui ne portent pas sur le règlement des différends et le 27 avril un état général des négociations (*advanced state of consolidation* pour l'ISDS).

13   Corporate Europe Observatory, Transnational Institute, 2012.

14   Sur le traitement juste et équitable, « La sécurité pleine et entière », Y. Nouvel, Leben (Dir.), *op. cit.*, note 3, p. 288-345 ; C. Santulli « Stipulation particulière ou principe général de bonne conduite ? », *Revue Générale de Droit International Public*, n° 1, 2015 p. 69-88 ; sur l'expropriation indirecte, A. de Nanteuil, Pedone, 2014, 650 p, préface de C. Leben ; R. Mellske, « For greater certainty », *Calibrating Investment Treaties to protect foreign investment and public health*, 3 Md.J.Int'Il.82, 2015, p. 84 ; P.M Dupuy et Y. Radi, « Le droit de l'expropriation directe et indirecte », Leben (Dir.), *op. cit.*, note 3, p. 375-414. Voir aussi J. Cazala, « la protection des attentes légitimes de l'investisseur dans l'arbitrage international », *Revue internationale de droit économique*, 2009/1 (t.XXX.1) p. 5-12.

15   *Le Monde Diplomatique*, 6 / 2014 p. 14-15. Pour une étude juridique de l'impartialité des tribunaux arbitraux, S. Cassella, A.de Nanteuil (Dir.), *L'accès de l'investisseur à la justice arbitrale*, Paris, Pedone, 2015, 216p (p. 167-191).

des ressources, comme l'exprimait en 2013 une Déclaration transatlantique adoptée par une centaine d'ONG militant contre l'inclusion de l'ISDS dans le futur Accord Economique et Commercial Global entre le Canada et l'Union européenne ?[16] Des droits humains qui seraient donc insuffisamment pris en compte par des études d'impact, préalables aux négociations des partenariats euro-atlantiques, comme le soutient la Fédération Internationale des Droits de l'Homme. A l'opposé, pour le Représentant au Commerce des Etats-Unis, réfutant « in most ISDS cases, the disputing parties retain and appoint the experts. The provision provides arbitral tribunals with the power to appoint experts of their own choosing on environmental ; health, and safety matters to ensure maximal objectivity in the evaluation of claims challenging such measures »[17]. Et objecte-t-on encore pour la défense de l'ISDS, le tribunal arbitral ne peut contraindre *de jure* au retrait de ces politiques publiques nationales, comme le rappelle avec force une note de la Présidence des Etats-Unis, en réponse à un questionnaire du Sénateur Warren sur l'ISDS : « The reality is that ISDS does not and cannot require countries to change any law or regulation »[18].

Pourtant il y a des cas révélateurs des effets de la clause arbitrale et de son usage à l'encontre d'Etats d'accueil, quel que soit leur niveau de développement et le continent. Ainsi l'entreprise suédoise Vattenfall s'était plaint des politiques environnementales de l'Allemagne au CIRDI. Elle put ensuite se satisfaire en 2011 de normes plus clémentes que celles qui contrariaient son projet de centrale au charbon, avant de contester en 2012 la décision de la Chancelière de sortir à terme du nucléaire, usant à la fois du recours à l'arbitrage transnational et à la Cour Constitutionnelle de Karlsruhe[19]. Les cas de l'Australie et de l'Afrique du sud illustrent eux, le rejet de la clause ISDS dans

---

[16] Texte in http://rqic.alternatives.ca/spip.php?article119. Voir aussi l'étude « Marchander la démocratie », publiée en novembre 2014 par le Réseau Québécois sur l'intégration continentale (Corporateeurope.org).

[17] https://ustr.gov/about-us/policy-offices/press-office-office/fact-sheets/2015/march/investor-s.

[18] https://www.whitehouse.gov/blog/2015/02/26/investor-stte-dispute-settlement-isds-q.

[19] La plainte dans l'affaire *Wattenfall II* a été enregistrée au Centre International pour le Règlement des Différends relatifs aux Investissements (CIRDI) le 31 mai 2012. L'Allemagne a formulé des objections préliminaires le 10 janvier 2013. Sur l'état de la procédure en 2014 et le rapport transparence/confidentialité, N. Bernasconi-Osterwalder, M. Dietrich Brauch, *International Institute For Sustainable Development*, 2014 (www.iisd.org). Sur la saisine du Tribunal Constitutionnel, Press Release n° 13 / 2016 of 19 February 2016 (http://www.bundesverfassungsgericht.de).

les nouveaux accords d'investissement[20]. Philip Morris s'était plaint de la législation de l'Australie en lutte contre le tabagisme, réclamant un droit national stable et prévisible. L'entreprise multinationale fut d'abord déboutée devant la Haute Cour de Sydney qui rejeta son recours contre la loi australienne sur les paquets neutres de tabac. Puis l'entreprise, pratiquant le *forum shopping*, invoqua devant le tribunal arbitral ISDS sur plainte de Philip Morris Limited (Hong-Kong) contrôlant Philip Morris Australia, la violation des dispositions sur l'expropriation et le traitement juste et équitable, inscrites dans l'accord de promotion et de protection des investissements conclu en 1993 par l'Australie et Hong-Kong. Le 15 Décembre 2015, le Tribunal arbitral siégeant à Singapour a décliné à l'unanimité sa compétence. L'affaire n'ayant donc pas été tranchée sur le fond par un arbitrage ISDS, la décision attendue par l'Organe de Règlement des Différends de l'Organisation Mondiale du Commerce, sur plainte cette fois notamment de Cuba et de l'Ukraine contre l'Australie, toujours pour les prescriptions relatives à l'emballage neutre des produits du tabac, devait *a priori* retenir l'attention devant le risque d'un effet domino[21]. Plusieurs Etats pourraient en effet imiter l'Australie[22]. Le 2 juin 2015, le Groupe spécial a informé l'ORD de sa décision de suspendre ses travaux à la demande de l'Ukraine puis de l'Australie « en vue de l'obtention d'une solution mutuellement convenue ».

---

20   Sur la procédure dans l'affaire australienne, https://www.ag.gov.au/tobaccopackaging;https://www.pca-cpa.org;Investmenttreatynews.

21   Organisation Mondiale du Commerce, Affaire DS 458, Australie-Certaines mesures concernant les marques de fabrique ou de commerce, les indications géographiques et autres prescriptions en matière d'emballage neutre applicables aux produits du tabac et à leur emballage.

22   La directive sur le tabac 2014/40/UE du Parlement européen et du Conseil du 3 avril 2014 a pour date limite de transposition dans le droit des Etats membres mai 2016. Plusieurs Etats membres font alors le choix d'un emballage neutre du paquet. C'est le cas de la France dans la loi du 26 janvier 2016 de modernisation du système de santé, au grand dam des industriels du tabac dénonçant une « sur-transposition » de la directive qui concilie au contraire le droit des marques et l'objectif sanitaire en restreignant et non en supprimant l'espace des marques. Les bureaux de tabac pour leur part ont craint en France la concurrence déloyale d'autres Etats membres. La France a souligné sa ratification du protocole contre le commerce illicite du tabac issu de la convention cadre de lutte antitabac de l'Organisation Mondiale de la santé, entrée en vigueur en 2005 (Assemblée nationale, réponse à une question écrite 91033 de M. Heinrich, *Journal Officiel de la République Française*, 2016, p. 1569). Voir aussi le débat au Québec en janvier 2015, en ce sens le libre propos de D. Turp en faveur d'une révision de la législation respectant les directives de l'Organisation Mondiale de la Santé (http://www.lapresse.ca/lesoleil/actualites/sante/201501/18/01-4836326-quebec).

L'Afrique du sud pour sa part se vit reprocher par des investisseurs européens une loi anti-apartheid relative au quota d'actionnaires noirs dans les sociétés minières.

Dans ce contexte, Remy Davison[23] s'interroge sur l'intention de l'Australie de ratifier ou non l'accord de Partenariat Trans-Pacifique[24]. Il inclue certes la clause ISDS mais elle ne serait pas invocable par les investisseurs du tabac, selon la volonté expresse de l'Australie. Pour les Etats-Unis, les garanties de transparence, d'indépendance, de compensations raisonnables figurent bien dans le Partenariat Trans-Pacifique. Enfin, la *Trade Promotion Authority* 2015 (ex Fast Track)[25] sans mentionner expressément le mécanisme ISDS se réfère pour les accords d'investissements à l'élimination des plaintes peu sérieuses, voire même évoque l'idée d'un organe d'appel ou d'un mécanisme similaire « to provide coherence to interpretations of investment provisions in trade agreements », comme l'explique le service de recherche du Congrès des Etats-Unis en 2015.

Quant aux Etats européens, si certains, au premier chef la France et l'Allemagne[26] ont milité pour un aménagement de la clause ISDS dans les accords de partenariat avec les Etats nord-américains, en faveur de l'instauration d'un mécanisme d'appel, c'est sans nul doute devant l'ampleur de certaines objections des opposants de tout bord, quelle que soit la nature de ces objections,

---

23 http://theconversation.com/ratifying-the-tpp.

24 Conclu entre 12 pays, l'Accord a été signé à Auckland le 4 février 2016 (http://www.inerrnational.gc.ca/trade-agreements-accords-commerciaux). Il inclue le recours à l'ISDS mais exige des arbitres une expertise spécialisée comme l'environnement, les services financiers, le travail et la lutte contre la corruption. Le processus de ratification risque d'être long, souligne un cabinet d'avocats d'affaires international (https://www.dlapiper.com). Pour un commentaire du chapitre 9 « *Dispute Settlement Mecanism* », J. Hillman, *Peterson Institute For International Economics*, « Assessing the Trans-Pacific Partnership », volume 2 ; « Innovations in Trading Rules », 2016, p. 101-109.

25 I. F. Fergusson, R. S. Beth, Trade Promotion Authority (TPA), Frequently Asked Questions, Congressional Research Service, 12 June 2015.

26 Sur la position française, la matinée d'étude du Ministère des Affaires Etrangères et du développement international du 5 mai 2015 sur l'inclusion de l'arbitrage d'investissement dans les traités de libre-échange ; bilan et perspectives (http://convention-s.fr/agenda/matinee-detude-inclusion-de-larbitrage-dinvestissement-dans-les-accords-de-libre-échange) ; sur le débat en Allemagne, G. Felbermayr, Institut Français des Relations Internationales, Centre d'études des relations franco-allemandes, 2015 ; E. Fabry, « Le TTIP à l'épreuve des craintes légitimes de l'opinion publique allemande », synthèse du 17 décembre 2015, Institut Jacques Delors, Notre Europe.

économique, sociale, environnementale voire constitutionnelle[27]. Les Opposants à la clause ISDS comptent en grand nombre des ONG, comme l'ont montré les résultats de la consultation publique, publiée le 13 janvier 2015 par la Commission européenne (SWD 52015)3 final) tout comme dans un registre plus offensif, le Collectif Stop TAFTA en lutte ouverte contre le traité transatlantique euro-américain. Ce Collectif est l'auteur d'une pétition réunissant plus de trois millions de signatures. Elle a été remise à la Commission européenne qui avait refusé en 2014 d'enregistrer une Initiative citoyenne (article 24 TFUE) de demande d'arrêt des négociations. Mais plus surprenant de prime abord, les objections sont aussi celles d'un directeur honoraire à la Commission européenne Pierre Defraigne, auditionné par le Parlement fédéral belge le 25 mai 2015, pour qui l'ISDS participe d'un abandon de souveraineté à Corporate America.

L'Institut International pour le développement durable note que les investisseurs n'ont pas nécessairement recours à l'arbitrage dont le coût est élevé mais usent de moyens de pression non judiciaires, politico-économiques pour « décourager les Etats d'adopter certaines politiques ». Ainsi vit-on la firme Philip Morris utilisait les deux moyens de pression et fermer son usine australienne. Enfin, compte tenu du fait que les investissements étrangers directs se font plus rares, que l'arbitrage soit rendu en faveur du défendeur ou du plaignant, il est manifeste que les Etats d'accueil voient de toute façon leur marge d'action réduite. La pression d'un grand investisseur comme Philip Morris ne s'exerce pas seulement contre les Etats d'accueil dont les politiques publiques lui sont défavorables, mais aussi via un lobbying puissant, en faveur cette fois de l'inclusion par les Etats-Unis de la clause ISDS dans le Partenariat Trans-Pacifique. En Europe, une enquête diligentée par des ONG en 2015 a dénoncé l'écrasante présence des lobbys consultés par la Direction générale du Commerce de la Commission européenne (Business Europe, Transatlantic Business Council).

Pour le Congrès US, les statistiques infirment le grief de partialité car « cumulatively, in 2014, the global number of concluded ISDS cases reached 356,

---

[27] C. Lepage, ancienne ministre de l'environnement invoque le non-respect du droit à un recours juridictionnel effectif pour les citoyens (hhtp://www.huffingtonpost.fr/corinne-lepage/ttip-traite-transatlantique-tafta); en Allemagne, comme le rapporte L. Hahnlein, un ancien juge du Tribunal constitutionnel considère que le mécanisme ISDS signifie un abandon de souveraineté de l'Etat (http://stop-ttip.org/fr/bmog/la-procédure-de-reglement-des-differends-entre-investisseurs-et-Etats); aux Etats-Unis, sur Alliance for Justice (http://afj.org), des professeurs d'université et d'anciens juges signent une lettre d'opposition à l'ISDS, adressée aux « Congressional leaders », en invoquant la menace que ce mécanisme fait peser « *to Us sovereignty* ».

with 37% decided in favor of the host country ; 25% in favor of the investor, and 28% settled »[28].Cependant les Etats-Unis jusqu'en 2015 n'avaient jamais eu à payer de compensation, au contraire d'autres Etats d'accueil. Beaucoup d'entre eux ont été privés d'un développement durable, comme le fit savoir l'Equateur ou encore El Salvador poursuivi par une société minière canado-australienne Oceanogold/Pacific Rim, pour refus de permis et moratoire sur de nouveaux projets. Après la dénonciation par la Bolivie en 2007, l'Equateur en 2009 et le Vénézuela en 2012 de la Convention de Washington établissant le CIRDI/ICSID[29], le 22 avril 2013 a été adoptée à Guayaquil par les Etats latino-américains une Déclaration sur la vigilance politique face aux pressions politico-économiques des entreprises multinationales. Même pour les pays émergents à l'exception de l'Inde, la récession et l'endettement sont significatifs. Pour l'ONG Corporate Europe Observatory, le boom de cet arbitrage d'investissement repose en vérité sur deux facteurs décisifs : l'existence d'un club d'acteurs, voire interchangeables au point qu'un auteur a pu parler « d'endogamie »[30], composés de conseillers juridiques, d'avocats, d'arbitres, avec des risques élevés estime-t-on, de conflits d'intérêts et une financiarisation de l'ISDS en raison du coût de l'arbitrage, du financement par des Fonds d'investissement, de la rémunération élevée des arbitres et des avocats.

2   Vers un système juridictionnel ?

La virulence des attaques contre l'ISDS et sa défense relativement modérée depuis quelque temps, ont conduit à réactualiser au sein de l'Union européenne le débat sur la correction substantielle de ses abus dans la version révisée du chapitre sur l'investissement du futur accord avec le Canada, puis dans le cadre de la négociation du TAFTA/TTIP en novembre 2015, enfin à proposer parallèlement aux négociations en cours avec les Etats-Unis, d'ouvrir avec des pays tiers un « échange de vues » sur la création – sans doute à plus long terme – d'une juridiction internationale permanente des investissements, proposition

---

28   International Investment Agreements (IIAS), Frequently Asked questions, Congressional Research Service, op. cit., note 6.

29   Sur la dénonciation de la Convention de Washington, A. de Nanteuil, « Réflexions sur les droits de l'Etat d'accueil dans le droit international de l'investissement », *Mélanges offerts à Charles Leben, Droit international et culture juridique*, Pedone, 2015, 591p, p. 321-343, sp. 327 et s. ; J. Cazala, « La dénonciation de la Convention de Washington établissant le CIRDI », *Annuaire Français de Droit International*, 2012, p. 551-565.

30   K. Benyekhlef (http://www.karimbenyekhlef.ca/blogue/2014/08/11).

inscrite d'ailleurs dans la version révisée de l'AECG (article 8.29) et pour laquelle néanmoins se dresseront aussi d'autres obstacles. Simple correction des abus ou comme le proclame avec force la Commissaire au Commerce, Cecilia Malmström, le 7 juillet 2015 devant le Parlement européen de l'Union européenne « a new approach. A new system that sets down the right to regulate in black and white. A new system that takes us away from the private arbitration tribunals of the past. Instead we want a future in which disputes are decided in an international investment court, by judges and with a right of appeal. TTIP will be a step towards that goal, not the final result. But it is an essential step, given the role of the US as a global investor. »[31] ? A vrai dire, Florian Grisel et Thomas Schultz ont opportunément rappelé que le débat sur l'arbitrage et le règlement des différends fut soulevé lors de la Conférence de la Paix de 1907 qui vit le représentant des Etats-Unis déplorer son coût et plaider pour une Cour réellement permanente, assurant sa propre jurisprudence.[32]

2.1 *An Investment Court System?*

Les propositions formulées par la Commission européenne en mai 2013 puis en mai, janvier et novembre 2015, en partie inscrites dans la version initiale de l'accord conclu en 2014 avec le Canada sont présentées comme des améliorations nécessaires du mécanisme arbitral contesté. Elles s'inspirent alors des lignes de force dégagées de la consultation publique précitée et s'accordent avec les prises de positions de la France et de l'Allemagne, matérialisées par une Déclaration commune le 21 janvier 2015[33]. L'économie générale des propositions de la Commission européenne repose sur l'idée que l'indépendance de ce mécanisme arbitral serait d'abord assurée par l'incorporation de règles de fond dans les dispositions du futur accord avec les Etats-Unis. Un « libellé clair et exhaustif » du traitement juste et équitable et de l'expropriation indirecte, expurgée des mesures légitimes de politiques publiques, supprimerait pense-t-on, la « marge d'appréciation indésirable des arbitres » en allant de pair avec la consécration expresse du droit de légiférer de l'Etat et de l'Union européenne, assortie d'une compétence d'interprétation dévolue à ces derniers, au besoin pour rectifier d'éventuels errements. La Commission européenne concède alors que la probabilité de telles erreurs serait faible, au regard de l'introduction de règles éthiques et de sélection « à partir d'une liste préétablie », voire à l'aptitude à exercer une fonction judiciaire interne, le tout pour écarter le

---

31 Intervention de la Commissaire au commerce lors du débat plénier sur le TTIP.
32 http://www.lemonde.fr/idees/article/2015/09/18/cour-permanente-ou-tribunaux-arbitraux.
33 http://www.diplomatie.gouv.fr/fr/politique-etrangere-de-la-france/diplomatie.

risque de conflits d'intérêts et plus encore pour asseoir une jurisprudence cohérente d'application « de principes juridiques connus et prévisibles » à travers l'institution souhaitée d'un mécanisme d'appel[34], qui sera inscrite dans la version révisée de l'AECG (article 8.28).

Bien que soutenu largement par toutes les Institutions de l'Union européenne, par l'opinion publique, les entreprises, les ONG et même entrevue par les Etats-Unis, l'introduction d'un mécanisme d'appel des sentences, jusqu'ici ignoré des accords d'investissements, divise notamment sur la question de ses modalités possibles. S'agirait-il de sanctionner d'éventuelles erreurs de droit, peu fréquentes ? S'agirait-t-il de sanctionner des erreurs manifestes d'appréciation des faits et de citer l'exemple « d'un traitement factuel erroné du droit interne » ?, en sachant toutefois que le tribunal n'est pas habilité à se prononcer sur le droit de l'Union ou d'un Etat membre. *L'Investment Court System* proposé dans la négociation de l'accord avec les Etats-Unis est alors décrit par Cécilia Malmstrom le 16 septembre 2015 en ces termes : « it will be judges, not arbitrators »[35]. Une justice publique excluant donc à terme la justice privée du modèle ISDS dans l'accord euro-américain. La proposition européenne est bien celle de l'instauration d'un système judiciaire avec un tribunal de première Instance (*Investment Tribunal*) de quinze juges et une Cour d'Appel (*Appeal Tribunal*) de six membres, soit deux nationaux pour les Etats-Unis et deux nationaux pour l'Union européenne, enfin deux nationaux de pays tiers. Les juges du Tribunal de première instance et les membres de la Cour d'Appel se verraient interdire d'agir comme conseils juridiques « on any investment dispute ». *L'Appeal Tribunal* appliquerait exclusivement les dispositions de l'Accord « in accordance with international law »[36]. Quant à la version révisée de l'AECG cette fois, elle consacre depuis, la rupture avec le mécanisme de l'arbitrage *ad hoc*, même amélioré de la version initiale. Une Cour composée de quinze juges est inscrite à l'article 8.27.

La proposition européenne sur le « right to regulate » a identifié cinq garanties (pas d'expropriation sans compensation, transfert des fonds, traitement juste et équitable, respect des obligations de l'Etat d'accueil à l'égard de l'investisseur étranger, compensation exceptionnelle en cas de conflit armé)

---

34   L'investissement dans le TTIP et au-delà- La voie de la réforme, Commission européenne, Note de synthèse du 5 mai 2015, http://tade.ec.europa.eu/doclib/docs/2015/may/tradoc_153456.pdf.

35   http://ec.europa.eu/commission/2014-2019/malmstrom/blog/proposing-investment-co.

36   La version finale de la proposition européenne issue de la négociation avec les Etats-Unis a été rendue publique le 12 novembre 2015. Voir Chapter II « Investment », *Transatlantic Trade and Investment Partnership*.

dont seule la violation autoriserait l'usage de *l'Investment Court System*. La prévention des plaintes parallèles serait assurée par le choix de l'investisseur entre les solutions nationales et *l'Investment Court System* selon le principe *electa una via*. Mais pour les meilleurs commentateurs, comme Gus Van Harden « the Commission's approach does not contemplate a duty for foreign investors to use domestic courts before going to ISDS. This is a major gap in the Commission's approach »[37].

Le Parlement européen dans sa résolution du 8 Juillet 2015[38] s'est prononcé nettement en faveur du « nouveau système de règlement des litiges entre investisseurs et Etats, soumis aux principes et contrôle démocratiques, où les affaires éventuelles seront traitées dans la transparence par des juges professionnels indépendants, nommés par les pouvoirs publics, en audience publique, et qui comportera un mécanise d'appel, dispositif qui garantira la cohérence des décisions de justice et le respect de la compétence des juridictions de l'Union européenne et de ses Etats membres et qui évitera que les objectifs de politique publique soient compromis par des intérêts privés »[39]. La Commissaire au commerce[40] en a immédiatement déduit que l'ancien système « ne peut pas être reproduit dans le TTIP ». La doctrine américaine a pu émettre des doutes sur l'efficacité d'un mécanisme d'appel qui pourrait allonger les délais et les coûts de l'arbitrage. C'est également le sens de l'évaluation négative du

---

37 G. Van Harten, « A parade of reforms: The European Commission's proposal for ISDS », Osgoode Hall Law School, York University, *Legal studies research paper series*, Research Paper N° 21, vol. 11/Issue.05/2015, http://ssrn.com/abstract=2603077. Voir aussi J. Cazala, « Le traitement de l'exigence du recours préalable au juge interne dans le contentieux arbitral de l'investissement », *Journal of International arbitration-Cahiers de l'arbitrage*, n° 4, 2014.

38 Le rapporteur de la Commission du commerce international du Parlement européen, B. Lange, se fondant le 9 janvier 2015 sur les positions respectives des partenaires considérait alors l'ISDS et le recours aux juridictions nationales comme les moyens les plus appropriés de résolution des différends. Le 28 mai 2015, ce n'est qu'au prix de compromis que la Commission du commerce international s'accorda sur l'idée d'un système juridictionnel, amendé à la demande du rapporteur dans le sens de l'exclusion de l'ISDS et de la création à terme d'une Cour publique internationale des investissements. Le 10 juin 2015, le vote au Parlement européen fut reporté en raison des 116 amendements déposés, renvoyés à la Commission du commerce international.

39 PTCI (2014 / 2228(INI)). L'engagement du Parlement européen en faveur des positions de la Commission européenne contraste avec les réserves du rapport Lange du 5 février 2015 et la vigueur des discussions au sein de la Commission du commerce international avant l'obtention du consensus.

40 Déclaration du 8 juillet 2015 sur le vote au Parlement européen sur la résolution TTIP.

règlement des différends que fait Emmanuel Gaillard sur la base du projet CETA de 2014, « mécanisme d'une extrême lourdeur »[41]. Il est clair aussi que l'inexistence d'une règle de précédent explique des sentences contradictoires et que les limites apportées à l'annulation des sentences CIRDI, comme le soulignent Alain Pellet[42] ou encore Enrique Fernandez Masia[43] ont joué contre le maintien de ce mécanisme arbitral. Ne peut-on cependant penser que le vrai point d'achoppement des positions américaines et européennes réside dans la place insuffisante voire occultée des droits humains ?[44] Si la proposition européenne promeut expressément le droit de légiférer des Etats et de l'Union, ce n'est pas suffisant pour l'expert Gus Van Harden consulté par la Commission européenne en 2014 et qui, en mai 2015, considère sérieusement inadéquate et sur de très nombreux points, la proposition de la Commission européenne. Dans son évaluation de l'ISDS, G. Van Harden plaidait pour un équilibre des droits et responsabilités des investisseurs étrangers et pour une représentation des champs d'expertise en droit public et droits humains[45]. La version révisée de l'AECG se contente de poser qu'il serait souhaitable que les membres du Tribunal qui devront évidemment posséder une expertise en droit public international, soient familiers du droit international des investissements, sans mentionner expressément d'autres champs de compétence (article 27).

2.2 *A Permanent International Investment Court ?*

Quant à l'option avancée par la Commission européenne d'une future juridiction internationale des investissements, le Comité Economique et Social de l'Union considère « qu'il n'y a pas de perspective viable d'avancer si l'on mène

---

41   E. Gaillard, « L'avenir des traités de protection des investissements », C. Leben (Dir.), *Droit international des investissements et arbitrage transnational*, Paris, Pedone, 2015, p. 1036-1037.

42   A. Pellet, « Appel ou annulation des sentences CIRDI ?, retour sur un débat sans conclusion », *Mélanges offerts à Charles Leben – Droit international et culture juridique*, Pedone, Paris, 2015, p. 355-374.

43   E. Fernandez Masia, « Arbitraje Investor-Estato : de « Bella durmiente » a « Léon en la jungla » », www.reei.org, 2013.

44   B. Audit rappelle qu'un tribunal arbitral, faute d'inscription expresse d'obligations relatives aux droits de l'homme dans le traité d'investissement ne peut connaitre d'une demande portant sur une violation de ces droits, « Le droit applicable en matière d'arbitrage fondé sur un traité de protection des investissements », J. S. Bergé et al. (Dir.), *La fragmentation du droit applicable aux relations internationales, regards croisés d'internationalistes privatistes et publicistes*, Paris, Pedone, 2011, 208 p, p. 66-81, sp. 75.

45   Van Harten, *op. cit.* note 37, p. 10.

en parallèle des négociations sur le RDIE dans le cadre du partenariat transatlantique et à moyen terme sur cette juridiction internationale permanente. En cas de conclusion du partenariat transatlantique, il est fort probable que celui-ci devienne une sorte de « mètre étalon » et mine toute perspective de rallier des soutiens en faveur d'un tribunal international »[46]. Mais il est vrai que se profile désormais la perspective un peu plus rapprochée de l'entrée en vigueur cette fois de l'AECG[47]. Selon une livraison de *Investment Treaty News* intitulée *Rethinking Investment-Related Dispute Settlement*[48], outre qu'il conviendrait pour les investisseurs étrangers de privilégier les voies internes avant de recourir au mécanisme de l'ISDS (le cas de l'Inde), la proposition européenne de *l'investment Court for ISDS* doit nécessairement déboucher à terme sur la solution d'une Cour multilatérale, déjà recommandée par un Forum de la CNUDED en 2014 et 2015. Dans le cas contraire, *this effort would seem very narrow*. Toutefois sur le « global appellate body » certains commentateurs se sont demandés s'il « would be able to reconcile inconsistent decisions based on numerous investments treaties that provide different substantive and procedural rights to investors »[49].

Au terme de cette brève revue de doctrine, peut-on conclure sans nuances à une publicisation du règlement des différends Investisseur/Etat ? Les propositions européennes ont bien été examinées voire négociées entre partenaires euro-américains mais le sort des accords euro-atlantiques demeure encore incertain à l'heure où ces lignes sont écrites en 2016, même si se dessinent aux yeux des Institutions européennes, le calendrier idéal pour l'AECG de la signature puis des ratifications[50]. Certes, l'idée d'une justice publique fait son chemin. L'accent est mis sur un droit international public du règlement des différends Investisseur-Etat et pas seulement pour la négociation du TTIP

---

46 Avis du 27 mai 2015 sur « La protection des investisseurs et le règlement des différends entre investisseurs et Etats dans les accords de commerce et d'investissement de l'UE avec des pays tiers », REX/411.

47 Il faut toutefois tenir compte du fait que le mécanisme d'appel ne sera effectif qu'après un accord *ad hoc* sur son fonctionnement, que l'AECG dans sa version révisée rendue publique fait mention d'autres possibles améliorations au vu des progrès dans d'autres enceintes et qu'enfin le système multilatéral expressément évoqué par les deux partenaires à l'article 8.29 suppose qu'ils œuvrent effectivement de concert à son instauration et avec succès auprès d'autres partenaires commerciaux.

48 https://www.iisd.org/itn/20&5/05/21/rethinking-investment-related-dispute-settlement.

49 Congressional Research Service, *op. cit.* note 6, p. 23.

50 La signature en juin 2016, les ratifications en 2017 sont espérées par la Commission européenne. La Commission du commerce international du Parlement européen a fait le point le 14 mars 2016 sur les négociations mises à jour de l'AECG et sur les derniers développements du TTIP.

comme le montre la publication de l'Accord de libre-échange UE-Vietnam[51] mais comme la doctrine l'a souvent relevé, jusqu'ici les traités d'investissement ont donné lieu à des interprétations erratiques par les arbitres des principes généraux du droit[52] dont il sera difficile de se défaire comme de la *lex mercatoria*[53], arbitres ou juges sans doute. Plus encore, la perception pluraliste du droit global a conduit à la généralisation du recours à des instruments informels. Comme l'écrit Katia Fach Gomez « Arbitral awards are turning ever more frequently to instruments created and managed by the private sector-i.e. codes of conduct, economic indexes, economic indicators, financial premiums, valuation methods, audits-to resolve the complex disputes arising from international business »[54]. Surtout, pour l'Union européenne, comme le proclame la Commission européenne, le traité avec les Etats-Unis devra être équilibré, sans sacrifice des normes européennes[55]. Sur la base de sa compétence exclusive en matière d'investissements étrangers directs (article 207 TFUE), dans le cadre de sa politique commerciale commune, l'Union est en mesure de veiller à la préservation de son identité lors des négociations intra-européennes[56] comme avec les pays tiers et ce d'autant plus qu'il s'agirait d'un

---

[51] Commission européenne, Communiqué de presse du 1 février 2016 : « L'accord conclu avec le Viêt Nam comporte toutes les dispositions essentielles du nouveau système juridictionnel des investissements pour les négociations européennes sur les échanges et les investissements, proposé par la Commission européenne ».

[52] A. Stone Sweet, G. della Cananea, « Proportionality, general principles of law and Investor-State Arbitration, a response to Jose Alvarez », *Yale Law School Public Law*, Research paper n° 507, 2014, 28 p.

[53] A. Pellet, « Les transformations de la gouvernance mondiale », *Société Française pour le Droit International, L'Etat dans la mondialisation*, Paris, Pedone, 2013, 591p, p. 562-571, sp. 568.

[54] K. Fach Gomez, « Enforcing global law : international arbitration and informal regulatory instruments », *The Journal of legal pluralism and unofficial law*, vol. 47, 2015, N° 1, p. 112-139. L'Union européenne est loin de méconnaitre cet *unofficial law*, M.F Labouz, « La méthode ouverte de coordination », A. Zaradny, N. Wolff et T. Fleury Graff (Dir.), *La fin du droit ?*, Paris, Mare et Martin, 2015, 293p, p. 191-201.

[55] Committee of the Regions, Draft Opinion, « A more responsible trade and investment policy », 2016, ECON-VI/009.

[56] C. Crépet Daigremont, « Les interactions normatives dans le domaine des investissements : la remise en cause du droit international par le droit de l'Union européenne », L. Burgorgue-Larsen, E. Dubout, A. Maitrot de la Motte, S. Touzé (Dir.), *Les interactions normatives, droit de l'Union européenne et droit international*, Paris, Pedone, 2012, préface d'A. Pellet, 380 p, p. 167-179, sp. P 173 et s. Voir aussi, E. Gaillard, « L'avenir des traités de protection des investissements », C. Leben (Dir.), *op. cit.*, note 3, p. 1027-1047, sp. 1021-1033 ; S. Monetrey, « Droit international des investissements et droit de l'Union européenne », C. Leben, p. 614-638.

accord mixte[57]. La retentissante affaire *MICULA*[58] l'a illustré en 2015, sans que se concrétise, en dépit des souhaits d'une partie de la doctrine, la promotion d'un ordre économique public[59] ou encore d'un pluralisme ordonné[60] pour

---

[57] La répartition des compétences entre l'Union et ses Etats membres explique l'action conjointe de l'UE et des Etats membres, puisqu'il s'agit de partenariats qui portent sur plusieurs domaines (article 207-6 TFUE). Ainsi l'accord mixte sera signé et ratifié par l'UE et ses Etats membres selon les procédures respectives : approbation du Conseil puis du Parlement européen ; ratifications par chacun des vingt-huit Etats membres selon les modalités constitutionnelles nationales. Sur les divergences qui subsistent dans certains Etats membres de l'UE dont la France, l'avis du Conseil économique, social et environnemental sur saisine du Premier ministre français rendu le 22 mars 2016 sur le projet de partenariat transatlantique (http://www.lecese.fr). Sur l'ensemble des questions soulevées par les accords mixtes avant le Traité de Lisbonne, E. Neframi, *Les accords mixtes de la Communauté européenne : aspects communautaires et internationaux*, préface de C. Leben, Bruxelles, Bruylant, 2007, 711 p., ainsi que *L'action extérieure de l'Union européenne, fondements, moyens, principes*, Paris, LGDJ, Lextenso éditions, 2010, 208 p. (Collection Systèmes droit).

[58] CIRDI affaire n° ARB/05/20. P. Jacob, F. Latty, A. de Nanteuil, « Arbitrage transnational et droit international général » (2013), *Annuaire Français de Droit International*, 2013, p. 433-434-474. A comparer avec *Electrabel SA c. Hongrie*, n° ARB/07/19, 2012, commentaire de P. Jacob et F. Latty, *Annuaire Français de Droit International*, 2012, p. 632 et s. pour qui la sentence Electrabel « oscille entre la volonté de maintenir un regard sur les actes en cause afin de ne pas faire disparaître totalement la protection dont bénéficient les investisseurs et le souci de ne pas faire obstacle à la construction européenne en mettant les Etats membres de l'Union face à des obligations européennes et internationales contradictoires » (p. 635).

[59] Le Compte rendu de la matinée d'étude du Ministère des Affaires étrangères et du développement international, *op. cit.*, note 26, p. 16 « il faut repartir des fondamentaux : quelles sont les fonctions que doit remplir un mécanisme efficace de règlement des différends entre Etat et investisseurs ? Deux objectifs doivent être pris en compte ; il s'agit de régler rapidement, efficacement et de façon impartiale un litige casuistique, particulier, de dimension privée. Par ailleurs, il s'agit aussi de dire le droit et de produire une norme qui doit devenir un standard afin d'assurer une certaine sécurité juridique aux opérateurs lors de futurs contentieux. Cette fonction a pris une importance considérable ces dernières années. Il s'agit en réalité de construire un ordre public économique international qui articule les règles du marché avec les éléments d'intérêt public que la régulation des Etats doit faire prévaloir pour discipliner le pouvoir économique des différends acteurs ». Pour C. Kessedjian, cet ordre public transnational doit être en phase avec la globalisation de la société et donc « s'entendre de tous les acteurs, à tous niveaux, quelles que soient leurs fonctions » Dès lors écrit-elle, le droit de cette société globale doit « secréter les normes éthiques et, par la suite, juridiques qui lui seront propres », C. Kessedjian, *Le droit international collaboratif*, introduction de F. Latty, Paris, Pedone, 2016, 188 p, sp. 145.

[60] M. Delmas Marty, *Les forces imaginantes du droit (II)*, *Le pluralisme ordonné*, Paris, Seuil, 2006, p. 101 et s. Voir J. E. Vinuales, « Conflits normatifs en droit international : normes

apaiser les rapports de systèmes et résoudre les conflits de normes. Dans sa décision du 30 mars 2015[61], la Commission européenne a considéré que constitue une aide d'Etat au sens de l'article 107-1 du TFUE incompatible avec le Marché intérieur, le versement par la Roumanie de dommages et intérêts accordés par la sentence arbitrale CIRDI du 11 décembre 2013, en faveur des Frères MICULA, une « unité économique unique » selon la Commission européenne. La Roumanie devra récupérer toutes les aides incompatibles versées et celles non notifiées à la Commission européenne qui exécuteraient la sentence arbitrale de 2013, de même que toute aide versée après la date d'adoption de la décision. La Commission européenne était d'ailleurs intervenue sans succès lors de la procédure arbitrale en qualité *d'amicus curiae*. Dans ses observations, la Roumanie avait fait valoir que la Convention CIRDI lui impose d'exécuter la sentence arbitrale et que le CIRDI n'a pas établi « si c'est la Convention CIRDI ou le droit de l'Union européenne qui devrait prévaloir ». En conséquence, pour la Roumanie ne constituait pas une aide d'Etat illégale la mise à exécution de la sentence de 2013[62] et comme l'a écrit S. Menetrey, la position roumaine relevait bien d'un « étau juridique »[63].

Dans la conclusion de son essai sur la politique du droit international, Martti Koskenniemi[64] use de métaphores, celles du pont et du mur, pour cerner la différence entre les conceptions juridiques des Etats-Unis et de l'Union européenne. Mais explique-t-il, Etats-Unis et Union européenne s'incarnent tous deux dans chacune de ces métaphores ; ainsi croit-on comprendre, celle du pont (se différencier) et celle du mur (se protéger[65]). La différence ne

---

environnementales vs protection des investissements », *Société Française pour le Droit International, Le Droit international face aux enjeux environnementaux*, Paris, Pedone, 2010, 489 p, p. 407-426.

61 Décision (UE) 2015/1470 de la Commission concernant l'aide d'Etat SA.38517 (2014/C) (ex 2014/NN) mise en œuvre par la Roumanie-Sentence arbitrale dans l'affaire *Micula/Roumanie* du 11 décembre 2013, Journal officiel de l'Union européenne, 2015, 1.232/43.

62 Dans le recours en annulation de la décision de la Commission européenne enjoignant à la Roumanie de suspendre toute action susceptible de mener à l'exécution de la sentence de 2013 (affaire T-646/14), les requérants arguaient comme premier moyen d'incompétence le fait que « le droit international impose à la Roumanie d'exécuter la sentence CIRDI sans tarder [...] que les obligations de droit international de la Roumanie ont primauté sur le droit de l'Union ». Le 29 février 2016, l'affaire a été rayée du rôle.

63 Menetrey, *op. cit.*, note 56, p. 619.

64 M. Koskenniemi, *La politique du droit international*, préface de B. Stern, présentation critique d'E. Jouannet, Paris, Pedone, 2007, 423p, p. 216 et s.

65 La Cour de Justice de l'Union européenne a validé le 4/5/2016 la directive Tabac de 2014 dans l'affaire C-547/14Philip Morris Brands. Dans une affaire CIRDI Philip Morris-Uruguay, le tribunal arbitral a jugé le 2/7/2016 que les mesures de contrôle de l'Uruguay ne violaient pas le traité d'investissements Suisse-Uruguay (CSID Case n° ARB/10/7).

réside-telle pas alors pour garder la pensée de l'auteur qui participa aussi à la conférence publique du 2 mars 2015 au Parlement européen sur « Investor-State Dispute Seettlement (ISDS) in EU law and International Law », dans le fait que le « légaliste » européen, face à « l'instrumentaliste » américain, pense le pont comme un possible rassemblement avec les tiers ? La formule pourrait illustrer l'évolution proposée par l'Union européenne d'une disparition complète du RDIE/ISDS et de son remplacement à terme à l'échelle multilatérale par une Cour internationale permanente des investissements.[66]

---

66   Après la levée du veto Wallon à la signature par la Belgique du CETA, l'Accord non modifié a été signé le 30 octobre 2016 lors du XVI Sommet Euro-Canadien. Le 5 octobre avait été adoptée une Déclaration interprétative commune « to provide a clear and unambiguous statement of what Canada and the European Union and its Member States agreed in a number of CETA provisions that have been the object of public debate and concerns ». Le 28 octobre, le Conseil européen visait « une interprétation contraignante des termes de l'AECG sur certaines questions ». Pour les uns, la Déclaration est inadéquate car elle ne répond pas notamment au rejet de l'Investment Court System. Pour les autres, elle ne s'inscrit pas dans le droit des traités. Dans l'attente des nombreuses ratifications politiquement incertaines et des incertitudes juridictionnelles, en Allemagne depuis l'autorisation sous conditions de signer l'AECG donnée le 13 octobre par la Cour Constitutionnelle, voire de la Cour de Justice de l'Union européenne sur saisine annoncée par la Wallonie, l'AECG s'appliquera à titre provisoire.

Legal Decisions and Their Implementation in International Law

W. Michael Reisman and Mahnoush H. Arsanjani

John Marshall has made his decision; now let him enforce it.
PRESIDENT ANDREW JACKSON

∴

An important distinction must be drawn between the making of lawful decisions, on the one hand, and their implementation, on the other. Making a lawful decision involves the consultation of the law and policy of the relevant community and then adapting them to the facts, as authoritatively determined by the decision-maker. Implementing a lawful decision, by contrast, involves the mobilization and application of political power in order to effect the decision in lawful ways. In organized national political systems, the mere fact of the availability of implementation power in the administrative apparatus of an executive branch is usually sufficient to secure 'voluntary' compliance. Even here, however, the implementation of lawful decisions which pose significant costs to political or economic elites or other entrenched interest groups may be resisted; a failure to implement in these circumstances erodes the overall effectiveness of the political system within which the lawful decision has been taken.

The assignment of the application of the law and the implementation of those applications to separate institutions ensures that those applying the law will not be adjusting their decision to the exigencies of implementation. Without such institutional differentiation, the ultimate consequence would be that the law would merely be certifying extant power relationships and dressing them in the raiment of authority. Yet, if appliers of the law simply ignored power relationships in legal systems in which authority and power were not aligned, they would run the risk of condemning their decisions to ineffectiveness. In the international system as it currently exists, formal law and power are not aligned and the institutional arrangements for the implementation of many decisions reflect the misalignment. How then are third-party international legal decisions implemented and how are they to be implemented?

We propose, in this contribution in honor of our friend Djamchid Momtaz to explore the arrangements and challenges which four different forms of third-party international decision face when it comes to their implementation. We will first consider international commercial arbitration, then international investment arbitration, then International Court of Justice adjudication, and finally classical inter-state arbitration. Based upon our survey, we will draw certain conclusions as to the relationship between lawful decisions and their implementation in international law.

1

International commercial arbitration is a legally authorized method of commercial dispute resolution conducted within the framework of the United Nations Convention on the Recognition and Enforcement of Foreign Arbitral Awards (the New York Convention),[1] for which 154 States are parties. It is optional to the parties and subject to national and international regulation. By contrast to national arbitration, international commercial arbitration is subject to simultaneous or sequential legal regulation by a number of legal systems as well as by conventional international law and generally provides for possible judicial supervision and enforcement by more than one national legal system.[2]

On its face, international commercial arbitration does not confront the quintessential implementation problem of public international law, because arbitrators are never beyond the reach of a (usually effective) national political-legal system. Thanks to the New York Convention, at least one national court is available to compel arbitration at the front-end, to provide minimal supervision in the middle, and, most important for our discussion, to enforce awards at the back-end. Substantive international law plays a marginal role in this form of decision, for these arbitrations are most often between private parties from different jurisdictions; while they sometimes have the potential for complex choice-of-law issues, decision usually turns on contract interpretation and what one might refer to as the shared normative universe of the parties, as identified by the arbitral tribunal. Tens of thousands of these arbitrations take place each year, most are serviced by not-for-profit institutions and

---

1 330 UNTS 3.
2 See generally, M. Reisman, L. Craig, W. Park and J. Paulsson, *International Commercial Arbitration: Cases, Materials, and Notes on the Resolution of International Business Disputes*, 2nd edition, West Academic, 2015.

the vast majority of awards are complied with voluntarily; indeed, most are never reported anywhere, which, in itself, is a measure of their effectiveness.

Defenses of sovereign immunity will present themselves only when the respondent is a State or its agency or instrumentality. In many jurisdictions in which international commercial arbitration is common, national sovereign immunity regimes may distinguish between *acta jure imperii* and *acta jure gestionis*, enabling national courts to implement awards against some of the property of States, their agencies or instrumentalities. But the sovereign award debtors in some arbitrations may be, in effect, enforcement-proof.

Non-governmental organizations (NGOs) and international and national arbitration bars appraise and update the rules and procedures under which international commercial arbitration operates so, as problems arise, the process of refinement and updating is constant and smooth. (That is probably thanks, in no small measure, to the fact that States play little role in the process.) The chief recurring problem in this form of arbitration is not national judicial under-enforcement but rather national judicial over-enforcement. It relates to the scope of the supervisory role which national courts should play under the New York Convention;[3] not all judges understand the limited role which the Convention assigns them. But national judiciaries which are independent are learning. Because international commercial arbitration has many self-correcting mechanisms, it continues to adjust to the implementation requirement.

2

International investment arbitration, while using the same arbitral techniques and some of the same institutions of international commercial arbitration, is radically different. For one thing, it is always a creature of one of some 3000 bilateral investment treaties or BITs and multilateral treaties, such as NAFTA, CAFTA and the Energy Charter Treaty. All of these treaties declare a commitment to a public international program to facilitate direct foreign investment as an instrument for national development and the State Party is always the respondent. Substantively, all of these treaties incorporate *grosso modo* customary international law's protections for aliens but their most distinguishing feature is their procedural innovation: they include *ex ante* consent by the

---

3 See, generally, M. Reisman & B. Richardson, 'Tribunals and Courts: An Interpretation of the Architecture of International Commercial Arbitration', in A. J. van den Berg (ed), *Arbitration—The Next Fifty Years: 50th Anniversary Conference, Geneva 2011*, ICCA Congress Series No. 16,, Kluwer Law International, 2012, pp. 17–65.

State Parties to proceed to arbitration on the unilateral application of a national investor of the other State Party for alleged violations of the treaty. The World Bank's arbitration system and the Permanent Court of Arbitration at The Hague often service these arbitrations but enforcement, if necessary, depends ultimately on the same network of national courts operating under the New York Convention. Sooner or later, most investment awards enjoy compliance or settlement.

Investor-state arbitration, while widely used, is more controversial than its international commercial counterpart because the respondent is always a State, viewing the matter in political terms for which it demands special consideration. At the opposing table, the investor, as claimant, views it in commercial contractual terms. Critics contend that in this confrontation, international investment law is biased in favor of investors; in a sense it is, though statistics indicate that in slightly more than half of the cases, the investor loses; even when the investor prevails, it rarely secures all of its claim. When a State loses, it has domestic political consequences for the Government in power. The loss may be viewed by the political opposition as a reflection of an ineffective Government and a usurpation of national sovereignty. (Of course, like its analogue, international human rights law, that is precisely what it is supposed to do.) A more cogent criticism of international investment law focuses on its ambiguous stance with regard to the scope of State authority to enact and implement regulatory measures affecting a foreign investment without breaching the obligations it has undertaken in a BIT. This problem has emerged as an increasingly acute source of discontent with some investment tribunals' applications of a provision ensuring the investor FET or 'fair and equitable treatment'. Decisions under this rubric have frequently run counter to what the respondent State believes changing domestic regulatory challenges require. Concern about this trend has led to some murase resistance to the conclusion of an EU-US BIT which will include provision for investor-state arbitration. Efforts to restrain the scope of FET decisions by revising the language in second and third generation BITs have not been successful, given that the rule in question is one which, by its nature, requires case-by-case contextual evaluation.[4] Efforts to restrain it by criticism of arbitrators could ultimately weaken the protection of foreign investment. At the extreme, denunciations of investment treaties threaten to inevitably bring back what is euphemistically called 'diplomatic protection of nationals'.

---

4 See M. Reisman, 'Canute Confronts the Tide: States versus Tribunals and the Evolution of the Minimum Standard in Customary International Law', 30:3 *ICSID Review-Foreign Investment Law Journal*, 2015, pp. 616–634.

Inasmuch as the respondent in international investment disputes is almost always a State or its agency or instrumentality, the implementation of awards will almost always encounter the defense of sovereign immunity. But persistent and adroit award creditors have still been able to engage national courts in whichever jurisdiction the respondent has attachable property, such that the record of implementation is strong enough to sustain the expectation of the effectiveness of this form of international third-party decision.

Investment arbitration gives every indication of being able to continue to adjust to these challenges and to contribute to the flow of direct foreign investment.

3

The Statute of the International Court of Justice makes no reference to the Court playing any role in enforcement of its judgments and provides no institutional arrangements whereby the Court might play some role in this function. The absence of a provision in the Court's Statute on enforcement of its judgments is not the result of an oversight by the drafters of the Charter. To the contrary: it is the result of a deliberate decision, reached after thorough discussion of the issue and a careful weighing of the various arguments in favour and against such a possible role. The Committee of Jurists designated by the United Nations to prepare and submit to the San Francisco Conference a draft Statute for the new court, expressed the view that 'it was not the business of the Court itself to ensure the execution of its decisions, that the matter concerns rather the Security Council.'[5] It is not that the Committee of Jurists was oblivious to the importance of compliance with the decisions of the Court, but rather that it saw utility in differentiating the functions of judgment and enforcement. This view also prevailed at the San Francisco Conference. A number of

---

5 The Report of the Committee of Jurists contains the following:

"A Member of the Committee called its attention to the importance which exact execution of the decisions of the Court has for the reign of law and the maintenance of peace, and he wondered whether the Statute ought not to contain a provision concerning the proper means for assuring this effect. The importance of this suggestion was not contested, but the remark was made that it was not the business of the Court itself to ensure the execution of its decisions, that the matter concerns rather the Security Council, ...' see 14 Doc. U.N.C.I.O., 1945, p. 853."

proposals in favour of stricter rules and procedures to compel compliance with the decisions of the Court by the Security Council were rejected.[6]

Judge Guillaume, former President of the International Court of Justice, has written:

> The International Court itself can play only a limited role in this respect. Its judgements are, of course, final and binding on the parties to the case, and therefore, in the event of any dispute as to the meaning or scope of a judgment, it is for the Court, and for it alone, to construe its decision. However, while this power of interpretation is conferred upon the Court by Articles 60 and 61 of the Statute, the Statute does not empower the Court to prescribe measures that may be necessary for the implementation of its judgments. At most, Article 61, paragraph 3, provides that the Court may make compliance with the terms of a judgment a condition for the opening of proceedings in revision. Moreover, any dispute relating to compliance is regarded as separate from the dispute resolved by the decision and cannot therefore be brought before the Court without a further agreement between the parties concerned.[7]

Shabtai Rosenne emphasizes the importance of this functional differentiation in international law:

> In international law this separation of the adjudication from the post-adjudication phase is fundamental, operative both in the sphere of arbitration and in that of judicial settlement. This is reflected in the distinction between the binding force and the enforceability of the judgment or award.[8]

---

[6] Proposals by Bolivia and Cuba for a much compulsory approach to the enforcement of the judgments of the Court failed at the San Francisco Conference. Bolivia proposed that non-compliance with the judgments of the Court be considered as an act of aggression. See proposal by Bolivia for the definition of aggression which contains also 'g. Refusal to comply with a decision pronounced by a court of international justice.' 3 Doc. U.N.C.I.O., 1945, p. 579. Cuba proposed, because of the importance of the compliance with judgments of the Court, the inclusion of Article 92 of the Charter in the Statute of the Court. That proposal was also failed at the San Francisco Conference. 4 Doc. U.N.C.I.O., 1945, p. 695.

[7] G. Guillaume, 'Enforcement of Decisions of the International Court of Justice' in Jasentulivana (ed) *Perspectives on International Law*, Kluwer Law International, 1995, pp. 280–281.

[8] S. Rosenne, *The Law and Practice of International Court, 1920–2005*, Vol. I, Martinus Nijhoff Publishers, 2006, p. 199.

Judge Guillaume also sees the functional differentiation assigned by the Charter between the Court and the Security Council with regard to the judicial resolution of the disputes and their implementation. Indeed, Judge Guillaume finds this functional differentiation, reflected in procedural requirements, namely that any dispute regarding compliance with a judgment is separate from the original dispute that was the subject of the decision and requires further agreement between the parties. This functional distinction is acknowledged by other scholars as well.[9]

The United Nations Charter, of which the Statute of the Court is a part, provides in Article 94(2)

> 2. If any party to a case fails to perform the obligations incumbent upon it under a judgment rendered by the Court, the other party may have recourse to the Security Council, which may, if it deems necessary, make recommendations or decide upon measures to be taken to give effect to the judgment.

As is apparent on its face, this provision does not make the Security Council into anything approaching the sheriff, bailiff or huissier of a national system. In national systems, those roles enjoy no discretion; they simply certify and implement. By contrast the Security Council, under Article 94(2), while expanding the plenary decision power of the Council beyond Chapter VII, makes doubly clear ('may, if it deems necessary') that the exercise of that power is entirely discretionary. But if the Council elects to 'decide upon' rather than 'recommend' 'measures to be taken to give effect to the judgment', its

---

9 Karin Oellers-Farhm takes the view that:
   "The execution of decisions is not a matter of the ICJ, but for the parties to the dispute which, according to Article 94, para. 1 UN Charter, have to comply with the Court's decisions. K. Oellers-Farhm, 'Article 94', in A. Zimmermann et al. (eds), *The Statute of the International Court of Justice: A Commentary*, Oxford University Press, 2012, p. 191."
   In another comment on Article 94, A. Phillepich writes:
   "With respect to the judicial pronouncements of this Court, the distinction is maintained between their force as *res judicata*, which the Statute [of the International Court of Justice] treats in unchanged terms (Articles 59–61) and their executory effect, which is governed by the Charter. This means that the Court deals with the binding and final nature of its pronouncements and must rule itself on requests for interpretation and revision, whilst a conflict over non-execution is considered as distinct from the controversy submitted to the Court and must be solved through channels which are political and no longer judicial..."
   A. Phillepich, 'Article 94' in J. P. Cot and A. Pellet (eds), *La charte des nations unies, commentaire article par article*, Economica, Vol. II, 2005, para. 13.

decision, by operation of Charter Article 25, is binding upon all State Parties to the Charter.

There is little practice under Article 94(2). In the *Anglo-Iranian Oil Co. Case*,[10] the International Court of Justice issued interim measures of protection,[11] ordering that the Anglo Iranian Oil Company should continue to be managed under the original management pending a final decision by the Court. When Iran defied the order and expelled all the *Company's* remaining staff from Iran, the United Kingdom, on 28 September 1951, requested the Security Council to consider the matter.[12] While the United Kingdom formal request invoked Articles 34 and 35 of the Charter, in arguing for the Council's competence, the United Kingdom representative also referred to the special function of the Council under Article 94(2) of the Charter. Most of the discussions in the Council centered on whether provisional measures fell within the scope of Article 94(2). Eventually, at the request of France, the Security Council decided to adjourn the debate on the item until the Court had decided on its own jurisdiction. On 22 July 1952, the Court decided that it did not have jurisdiction.

Following the ICJ Order of Provisional measures in *United States Diplomatic and Consular Staff in Tehran*,[13] the United States requested a meeting of the Security Council to consider the measures to be taken to induce Iran to comply with its international obligations. During the debate several delegations drew attention to the Court Order, but there was no reference to Article 94(2) of the Charter.[14]

Following the Judgment of the International Court of Justice in *Military and Paramilitary Activities in and against Nicaragua*, Nicaragua addressed two letters to the Security Council stating that the United States had failed to comply with the Judgment of the Court and requesting a meeting of the Security. Nicaragua did not invoke Article 94(2) of the Charter. A draft resolution sponsored by Congo, Ghana, Madagascar, Trinidad and Tobago and the United Arab Emirates, without reference to Article 94(2) of the Charter, called for 'full compliance of the judgement of the International Court of Justice'.[15] The draft

---

10 *Anglo-Iranian Oil Co.* (United Kingdom v Iran), ICJ *Reports* 1952, p. 93.

11 Ibid., *Order of July 5th, 1951: I C J Reports 1951*, p. 89.

12 For the request of the United Kingdom, see SC, 6th Yr., Suppl. For Oct., Nov. and Dec. pp. 2–3, S/2358.

13 *United States Diplomatic and Consular Staff in Tehran* (United States v Iran), Judgment, ICJ *Reports 1980*, p. 3. For the Order of 15 December 1979 see, ICJ *Reports*, 1979, p. 21.

14 For a summary of discussions in the Security Council, see *Repertory of Practice of United Nations Organs*, 1979–1984, Vol. 6, pp. 13–14.

15 UN Doc. S/18250, 31 July 1986, operative para. 2.

resolution was vetoed by the United States. A few months later, Nicaragua again requested a meeting of the Security Council, this time, 'in accordance with the provisions of Article 94 of the Charter, to consider the non-compliance with the judgment of the International Court of Justice'.[16] The Council again failed to adopt a resolution, as a result of the United States' veto.

Following the 1992 judgment of the International Court of Justice in the *Land, Island and Maritime frontier dispute*,[17] on 22 January 2002 Honduras, invoking Article 94(2) of the Charter, requested the Security Council to intervene to ensure execution of the judgment of the Court.[18] In September of 2002, El Salvador, denying Honduras' accusation of delay in complying with the judgment, expressed no objection to the consideration of the issue by the Security Council.[19] However, in October of the same year, El Salvador filled an application with the Court for revision of the judgment. The application was rejected and the parties ultimately complied with the judgment. The Security Council made no recommendation on this request.

National Courts, under different national regimes of sovereign immunity, have been effective in the implementation of international investment awards against respondent States. Yet, national courts have not been promising institutions for the enforcement of International Court judgments.

On March 25, 2008, the US Supreme Court decided *Medellin v Texas*[20] in which a Mexican national on death row in Texas challenged his conviction on the ground that he was not afforded his right under Article 36 of the Vienna Convention on Consular Relations.[21] The appellant, Medellin, also relied on the judgment of the International Court of Justice in *Avena and other Mexican Nationals* (Mexico v United States of America),[22] which had required the United States to provide further 'review and reconsideration' of the convictions of petitioner Medellin and 51 other Mexican nationals on death row in the US. The Supreme Court acknowledged that the *Avena* judgment was a binding international obligation of the United States but it said that whatever legal effect the Supreme Court could give to the *Avena* judgment was a question of domestic

---

16   UN Doc. S/18415, 20 October 1986.
17   *Case concerning the Land, Island and Maritime Frontier Dispute* (El Salvador v Honduras; Nicaragua intervening), Judgment, *ICJ Reports 1992*, p. 350.
18   UN Doc. S/2002/108, 23 January 2002, p. 2.
19   UN Doc. S/2002/1102, 24 September 2002.
20   552 U.S.A. 491, 2008.
21   596 UNTS 261.
22   *Avena and Other Mexican Nationals* (Mexico v United States of America), Judgment, *ICJ Reports 2004*, p. 12.

law. Distinguishing between self-executing and non-self-executing treaties, the Supreme Court concluded that the Optional Protocol, the UN Charter and the ICJ Statute—are non-self-executing and cannot be given effect as federal law absent Congressional implementing legislation.[23] With regard to Article 94 of the Charter, the Supreme Court observed:

> The remainder of Article 94 confirms that the U. N. Charter does not contemplate the automatic enforceability of ICJ decisions in domestic courts.[6] Article 94(2)—the enforcement provision—provides the sole remedy for noncompliance: referral to the United Nations Security Council by an aggrieved state. 59 Stat. 1051.

The U.N. Charter's provision of an express diplomatic—that is, nonjudicial—remedy is itself evidence that ICJ judgments were not meant to be enforceable in domestic courts.[24]

In 2014, the Italian Constitutional Court was also confronted with domestic implementation of the ICJ judgment in *Jurisdictional Immunities of the State* (Germany v Italy)[25]. The ICJ, in that case, ruled against Italy for denying Germany's immunity from civil jurisdiction for claims for compensation for war crimes committed by German forces during the Second World War. Following the ICJ judgment, the Italian Parliament enacted laws in order to ensure domestic implementation of the ICJ Judgment. The Italian Constitutional Court, however, declared the law unconstitutional, holding that the customary international law of State immunity from civil jurisdiction does not apply to cases at hand which concern war crimes and crimes against humanity in breach of fundamental human rights. The Constitutional Court declared:

> ... the unconstitutionality of Article 1 of Law No. 848 of 17 August 1957 (Execution of the United Nations Charter, signed in San Francisco on 26 June 1945), so far as it concerns the execution of Article 94 of the United Nations Charter, exclusively to the extent that it obliges the Italian judge to comply with the Judgment of the ICJ of 3 February 2012, which requires that Italian courts deny their jurisdiction in case of acts of a foreign State

---

23 552 U.S.A. 491 (2008), pp. 11–13.
24 Ibid., p. 13.
25 *Jurisdictional Immunities of the State* (Germany v Italy: Greece intervening), Judgment, *ICJ Reports 2012*, p. 99.

constituting war crimes and crimes against humanity, in breach of inviolable human rights;[26]

4

A good deal of inter-state third party dispute resolution does not go to the International Court but to ad hoc and essentially non-institutional state-to-state arbitration tribunals. The United Nations Charter does not provide an analogue to Article 94(2) for decisions of ad hoc institutions. In theory, the Security Council could take up non-compliance under Chapter VII, for Article 39's 'threat to the peace' has proven to be elastic. Nor have national courts presented themselves as potential enforcers, especially as boundary cases do not concern *acta jure gestionis*.

The absence of institutional means for implementation of these inter-state decisions may actually be aggravated by the more aggressive approach to confirmation of jurisdiction by inter-state tribunals upon unilateral application. When two States agree to submit a particular dispute and specify the alternative options for the arbitrators, each State knows a priori the upside and downside limits of the outcome; each has already decided that even a downside loss is to be preferred to a perpetuation of the dispute. Here one can usually—but not always—expect quick compliance. And, in all cases in which jurisdiction is denied or the claim on the merits is denied, concern about compliance does not arise. (While some species of international decision, for example, the delimitation of a maritime boundary, may seem to be 'self-executing', two recent cases[27] may now put that assumption in doubt.) But where a State has made a general and comparatively open-ended commitment to arbitration which another State invokes, the ensuing arbitration is often an unwelcome surprise to the State that finds itself respondent. Not having negotiated beforehand the upside and downside of the prospective decision, a loss may be so politically costly for the Government that it will simply elect to ignore the award. What do arbitrators faced with this prospect do?

---

26 For the 22 October 2014 decision of the Italian Constitutional Court, see https://italys practice.info/judgment-238-2014/

27 Territorial and Maritime Disputes (Nicaragua v Colombia), Judgment, *ICJ Reports 2012*, p. 624; *The South China Sea Arbitration* (The Republic of Philippines v The People's Republic of China), Award of 12 July 2016, www.pcacases.com/web/view/7.

If there are indications that the 'international system' (which usually means strong States with an interest in seeing the dispute settled) will take the award seriously and the award can, thus, provide the cover of authority for forms of robust international action, arbitrators can proceed with the confidence that their award will be effectuated. If not, the options open to them are unappealing. One is to 'duck the case' by finding that the respondent's consent does not cover the dispute, hence there is no jurisdiction. (This is sometime coupled with a theoretical finding on the merits, as in *Case Concerning Oil Platforms*[28] and *Chagos Marine Protected Arbitration*;[29] the effect of these merit findings are then terminated by the denial of jurisdiction.) Another is to fashion a 'package deal' by crafting a decision that takes account of what are believed to be the minimum needs of the respondent in the hope that it will induce compliance. A third is to apply the law *comme il faut,* ignoring speculations about the post-adjudicative phase and passing the problem on to the political institutions of international law. All of these options have varying but unwanted implications for the legitimacy of inter-state arbitration.

5

International law's actual apparatus for the implementation of lawful decisions is more promise than fulfillment. '[O]ne of the achievements of the Charter of the United Nations,' the former Secretary-General Boutros Boutros-Ghali observed, 'was to empower the Organization to take enforcement action against those responsible for threats to the peace, breaches of the peace or acts of aggression.' Boutros-Ghali acknowledged that 'neither the Security Council nor the Secretary-General at present has the capacity to deploy, direct, command and control operations for this purpose, except perhaps on a very limited scale.'[30] And after reviewing the modalities available to the United Nations, he conceded that '[t]he United Nations does not have or claim a monopoly of

---

28 *Oil Platforms* (Islamic Republic of Iran v United States of America), Judgment, *ICJ Reports 2003*, p. 161.

29 *Chagos Marine Protected Area Arbitration* (Mauritius v United Kingdom), Award, 18 March 2015, http://www.pcacases.com/pcadocs/MU-UK%2020150318%20Award.pdf.

30 *An Agenda for Peace: Preventive Diplomacy, Peacemaking and Peace-keeping, Report of the Secretary-General*, UN Doc. A/47/277-S/24111, 17 June 1992, para. 77.

any of these instruments. All can be, and most of them have been, employed by regional organizations, by ad hoc groups of States or by individual States....'[31]

The concern about the actions of 'ad hoc groups of States or by individual States' has always been that, when ostensibly performing a disinterested international function, they will actually be pursuing their own interests rather than those of the community. This is certainly true, but then again, the whole is never greater than the sum of its parts. The same States that act on their own to implement international decisions are the States who make implementation decisions within the United Nations.

---

31 Ibid., para. 23. It is notable that like the tribunal in the *Chevron v Ecuador* case, the Iran-US Claims Tribunal had occasion to issue a number of orders for interim measures, including interim awards for stay of parallel proceedings in the Iranian courts. Upon non-compliance by Iran, the tribunal issued further interim awards, declaring the decision of the Iranian court, which was inconsistent with the interim award, 'without legal effect.' See *Watkins-Johnson Company* and *Islamic Republic of Iran*, Award No. 429–370 of 28 July 1989, in 22 Iran-U.S. Cl. Trib. Rep. 218, 220. Judge Brower, a former president of the American Society of International Law and a long-time member of the Iran-US Claims Tribunal, reflected on the dilemma of international tribunals of that sort which 'can only rely upon the States Parties' duties placed upon them by international agreement'. But Brower added that this structural problem of tribunals could be remedied by 'supporting institutions such as municipal legal systems'. C. N. Brower and J. D. Brueschke, *The Iran-United States Claims Tribunals*, Kluwer Law International, 1998, p. 241.

Peremptory Norms and the Jurisdiction of the International Court of Justice

Jamal Seifi[*]

Introduction

The relationship between peremptory norms and the jurisdiction of the International Court of Justice (ICJ) has been of particular interest especially in view of the Court's status as the 'principal judicial organ' of the United Nations (UN). One may ask what procedural and jurisdictional consequences flow from the peremptory character of the norm breached. Does the peremptory character establish jurisdiction in the absence of an applicable jurisdictional instrument? Does it influence the scope of an existing jurisdictional instrument? To what extent is the Court's position as the 'principal judicial organ' of the UN relevant for a determination made under either of the above scenarios?

I shall address these matters in light of the ICJ's jurisprudence in order to establish whether the solution to the question lies with the Court itself in its interpretive endeavours, or whether the matter needs to be resolved elsewhere, in a comprehensive way. For this purpose, I shall first briefly review two preliminary issues: (i) the advent of peremptory norms and (ii) the role of the ICJ as the principal Judicial Organ of the UN. Thereafter, I will consider the extent to which the jurisprudence of the Court concerning the consensual basis for its jurisdiction has developed to offer sufficient guidance on the aforementioned questions.

1   The Advent of Peremptory Norms in International Law

Peremptory norms reflect the interests of the international community and represent the basic elements of the international public order.[1] As such, they create obligations that are owed to the international community as a whole

---

[*]   The author gratefully acknowledges and thanks Ms. Maryam Ansari for her invaluable assistance with the research and preparation of this article. The author also acknowledges and thanks Dr. Mahdad Assadi for his assistance with research.
[1]   See generally, A. Orakhelashvili, *Peremptory Norms in International Law,* Oxford University Press, 2006, pp. 7–35.

(obligations *erga omnes*). It is now over four decades since the issuing of the celebrated dictum in the ICJ Judgment in the *Barcelona Traction* case that,

> an essential distinction should be drawn between the obligations of a State towards the international community as a whole, and those arising vis-à-vis another State in the field of diplomatic protection. By their very nature the former are the concern of all States. In view of the importance of the rights involved, all States can be held to have a legal interest in their protection; they are obligations erga omnes.[2]

Ever since that pronouncement, international legal doctrine has been struggling to ascertain the consequences, whether procedural, jurisdictional or substantive, of violations of peremptory norms, as distinct from those deriving from violations of ordinary rules. Indeed, the classification of rules of international law into distinct categories of ordinary and peremptory would be futile if distinct consequences could not be derived from their violations.

An important part of this task was addressed by the International Law Commission (ILC) during the preparation of its Draft Articles on State Responsibility. The ILC partially addressed this issue by recognizing that, while there may be a difference in emphasis, there is a substantial overlap between peremptory norms and *erga omnes* obligations.[3] The first focus on the fundamental character of the obligation, while the second focus on the legal interest of complying States.[4] These two lines of inquiry have led to two areas of development. The first is the development of the concept of serious breaches of peremptory norms and the specific consequences arising therefrom, in addition to the consequences of an ordinary wrongful act.[5] The second development is the formulation of the concept that all States are entitled to invoke responsibility for breaches of *erga omnes* obligations.[6]

The regime of serious breaches of peremptory norms of international law as formulated by the ILC is a rather underdeveloped regime of responsibility compared to the existing regime of ordinary breaches. Rather, it is effectively a supplementary system that creates an additional consequence to those of the existing regime, i.e., the obligation for all States (i) to bring any serious breach to an end by lawful means, and (ii) to not recognize as lawful a situation created

---

2 *Barcelona Traction, Light and Power Company, Limited,* (Belgium v Spain), Judgment, ICJ Reports 1970, p. 3, 32, para. 33.
3 See generally, *Yearbook of the International Law Commission (YBILC), vol. II, Part Two,* 2001.
4 Ibid., pp. 111–112.
5 ILC Draft Articles, Articles 40 and 41; Ibid., p. 112.
6 Ibid., Article 48; *YBILC, supra,* note 3, p. 112.

by that breach.[7] Other consequences of violations of peremptory norms were left for future development.[8]

On the other hand, the regime of 'invocation of responsibility by a State other than an injured State', as formulated in Article 48 of the Draft Articles, became a potential basis for the seizing of the Court by any State for violations of peremptory norms within the confines of that Article, provided that a jurisdictional basis could be established between the claimant and the respondent States in accordance with Article 36 of the Statute. This development offered a significant expansion of the conditions for *locus standi* and admissibility of claims before the Court. Indeed, by the same token interventions envisaged under Article 62 of the Statute of the Court could also be expanded to include invocation of responsibility by a State other than the injured State under Article 48 of the Draft Articles.[9] On that basis it appears that the circumstances denying the claimant States in the *South West Africa* cases[10] the legal interest to bring a claim against South Africa concerning the violation of Namibia's right to self-determination would no longer be in place. Nevertheless, it is not clear whether, despite the acceptability of such an intervention in a contentious case, the Court would be in a position to make decisions of a general nature directing all States to act in a certain way.

2   ICJ as the Principal Judicial Organ of the UN

As the principal judicial organ of the UN, the Court has an established place in the UN Charter,[11] of which its Statute is an integral part. This position makes it quite distinct from other international courts and tribunals, especially as concerns the interpretation and application of peremptory norms of international law. This is not only because the core elements of the concept of peremptory

---

7   Ibid., Article 41(1) and (2).
8   Ibid., Article 41 (3). See also, ILC Commentary to the Draft Articles, supra, note 3, pp. 115–116.
9   For the first instance of intervention on the basis of Article 62, see generally, J. Seifi, 'Nicaragua Granted Permission to Intervene in the Land, Island and Maritime Frontiers Case', 6 *International Journal of Estuarine & Coastal Law*, 1991, pp. 253–263.
10   *South West Africa Cases* (Ethiopia v South Africa; Liberia v South Africa), *Second Phase*, Judgment, ICJ Reports 1966, p. 6, 34–36, paras. 49–54. Para. 99: 'In the light of these various considerations, the Court finds that the Applicants cannot be considered to have established any legal right or interest appertaining to them in the subject-matter of the present claims, and that, accordingly, the Court must decline to give effect to them.'
11   Charter of the United Nations, 24 October 1945, 1 UNTS XVI, Articles 7, 92–96.

norms are enshrined in the principles and objectives of the UN Charter, but also because the UN, as an institution, may be described as the custodian of the international legal order. The Court's position within the organization of the UN seems to resemble an embryonic notion of a judicial branch of the international legal order, alongside an embryonic notion of a parliamentary and executive function for the General Assembly and the Security Council, respectively. Thus the Court is an integral part of a system that, by virtue of its Charter, shares the same ideals, purposes and principles. Accordingly, obligations arising from the Statute of the Court are regarded on the same level as those arising from the UN Charter within the confines of the provisions of the Statute. To that end the Court should strive to realise the purposes and principles of the UN by, if necessary, interpreting the Charter within the confines of its specific powers and responsibilities as defined by the Statute.

The Court has made good use of its position when providing advisory opinions. Notably, in *Reparations*, where the Court was faced with a new situation that had not been regulated by the Charter, it embarked upon a broad and systematic interpretation of the Charter and international law to conclude that 'the Organization must be deemed to have those powers which, though not expressly provided in the Charter, are conferred upon it by necessary implication as being essential to the performance of its duties.'[12] In subsequent advisory opinions,[13] the Court has provided a comprehensive analysis of the structure of the UN and the relationship between the General Assembly and the Security Council as enshrined in the UN Charter. It has also opined on the powers and legal consequences of decisions by these organs. The Court in particular emphasized that the responsibility conferred upon the Security Council is 'primary' but not 'exclusive' and that the General Assembly is also to be concerned with international peace and security, and can recommend measures in that field.[14] Finally, in the Advisory Opinion on *the Construction of a Wall*,[15] while indicating an immense awareness of the humanitarian aspects of the case,[16] the Court specifically noted that the peremptory character of the

---

12 *Reparations for Injuries Suffered in the Service of the United Nations*, Advisory Opinion, ICJ Reports 1949, pp. 174, 182, and generally pp. 182–184.

13 *Competence of Assembly regarding admission to the United Nations*, Advisory Opinion, ICJ Reports 1950, p. 4, 8–9; *Certain Expenses of the United Nations (Article 17, Paragraph 2, of the Charter)*, Advisory Opinion, ICJ reports 1962, p. 151.

14 *Certain Expenses*, supra, note 13, p. 163.

15 *Legal Consequences of the Construction of a Wall in the Occupied Palestinian Territory*, Advisory Opinion, ICJ Reports 2004, p. 136.

16 Ibid., paras. 99–122.

norms involved entailed legal consequences for other States, including their duty not to recognize the illegal situation brought about by violations of the peremptory norms of international law.[17]

When dealing with contentious cases, however, the Court's primary task is to decide on the dispute between the parties within the confines of its jurisdiction. The provisions of the Charter relating to the Court, and the responsibilities and powers conferred upon it by the Statute, indicate that the framework of its responsibilities is defined and distinguished, such that it acts independently from the other principal organs of the UN.[18] Ultimately, and in accordance with Article 38(1) of the Statute, the Court's function is to decide only upon disputes submitted to it in accordance with Article 36 of the Statute.

Accordingly, the mere fact of being the 'principal judicial organ' of the UN does not seem to afford a basis for the Court to entertain jurisdiction beyond the specific parameters of the Statute on the mere ground of the peremptory character of the norm in dispute.[19] Indeed, even if the Court had the power to expand the scope of its jurisdiction merely on this ground, then it would be questionable what exactly it would be able to do with such disputes. The consequences of the international legal responsibility arising from a serious breach of peremptory norms of international law are not adequately developed and are, as yet, confined to the notion of non-recognition by all other States. Further, the Court's authority to pronounce in a contentious case that all other States are under a duty of non-recognition may be undermined by the specific provision of Article 59 of the Statute, which provides that 'the decisions of the Court have no binding force except between the parties and in respect of that particular case.'

---

17   Ibid., paras. 154–160.
18   Chapter by H. Mosler, in B. Simma et al. (eds), *The Charter of the United Nations: A Commentary*, Oxford University Press, 1995, p. 978.
19   The peremptory character of the norm may, however, influence the Court's conduct of the proceedings. It has been suggested elsewhere that the Court's prioritization of consideration of the issue of self-defence and the inclusion of a related finding on the United States essential security measures in the *dispositif* of the Judgment in the *Oil Platforms Case* (Islamic Republic of Iran v United States), *ICJ reports 2003*, p. 161) was motivated by the peremptory character of the norm involved. (See generally, J. Seifi, 'Procedural and Evidentiary Innovations in the Judgment of the ICJ in the Oil Platforms Case', in J.-H. Paik et al., *Asian Approaches to International Law*, Routledge, 2013, pp. 9–24 and pp. 20–23.

3 Peremptory Norms and the Principle of Consent to Jurisdiction

One practical consequence of the recognition of peremptory norms in the jurisprudence of national and international courts and tribunals has been the growing concern over whether violations of peremptory norms can, or should, affect the consensual basis for the Court's jurisdiction. It has been noted that 'it is one thing to ask whether *jus cogens* can establish judicial jurisdiction in the absence of an applicable jurisdictional instrument; it is quite another to ask whether *jus cogens* could influence the scope of an existing jurisdictional instrument.'[20] While the Court's stance on this issue has been consistent, there are concerns that its position may be overly 'passive' which, effectively, 'deconstructs' the place that peremptory norms occupy in international law.

The principle of consent has been a key part of the debate on the expansion of the Court's jurisdiction on grounds of a breach of peremptory norms. The *East Timor Case*[21] stands out as an example of the application of the principle of consent in the most absolute terms. Applying the *Monetary Gold* principle, the Court highlighted the status of the principle of consent as one of the *fundamental principles* of its Statute.[22] The Court pronounced that the *erga omnes* character of a norm and the rule of consent to jurisdiction *were two different things*.[23]

> Whatever the nature of the obligations invoked, the Court could not rule on the lawfulness of the conduct of a State when its judgment would imply an evaluation of the lawfulness of the conduct of another State which is not a party to the case, even if the right in question is a right erga omnes.

One distinguished commentator described the Court's 'overly cautious attitude' as regrettable.[24] Although the Court rightly set *erga omnes* obligations within the traditional State-centric framework,[25] Judge Kooijmans noted that

---

20 Orakhelashvili, supra, note 1, p. 490.
21 *East Timor* (Portugal v Australia), *ICJ Reports 1995*, p. 90.
22 Ibid., para. 26 (emphasis added).
23 Ibid., para. 29 (emphasis added).
24 P. Kooijmans, 'The ICJ in the 21st Century: Judicial Restraint, Judicial Activism, or Proactive Judicial Policy', 56 *International and Comparative Law Quarterly*, 2007, pp. 741, 744.
25 G. I. Hernandez, 'A Reluctant Guardian: The International Court of Justice and the Concept of 'International Community'', 83 *British Yearbook of International Law*, 2013, pp. 13–60, at p. 46.

'since basic principles and values of the international community were at issue... a reasoned opinion on these matters by the highest legal organ of the UN would have been highly significant.'[26] Similarly, in the aftermath of the judgment, Christine Chinkin noted that 'the Court's narrow ruling and formalism promote procedural requirements above the development of substantive principle... the deference accorded to the jurisdictional position of Indonesia seems likely to inhibit progressive development of international law in ways beneficial to the wider international community.'[27]

However, despite these criticisms the Court's approach on this matter remained consistent, and the *Legality of Use of Force* case is a vivid example.[28] The Court established the qualitative distinction between pleas on the basis of breaches of substantive norms and conditions for the exercise of the Court's adjudicatory powers. Reaffirming its previous jurisprudence, it held unequivocally that, while States remain responsible for acts attributable to them which are contrary to international law, there is 'a fundamental distinction between the question of the acceptance by States of the Court's jurisdiction and the conformity of their acts with international law'.[29] Similarly, elaborating on this latter point in the *Fisheries Jurisdiction* case,[30] the Court explained that '[t]he former requires consent' while '[t]he latter question can only be reached when the Court deals with the merits, after having established its jurisdiction.'[31] There, the Court held that 'a State's lack of confidence' as to the compatibility of its actions with international law 'does not operate as an exception to the principle of consent to the jurisdiction of the Court and the freedom to enter reservations.'[32] It concluded this point by remarking that 'whether or not

---

26 Kooijmans, supra, note 24, p. 744.
27 C. Chinkin, 'The East Timor Case (Portugal v. Australia)', 45 *International and Comparative Law Quarterly*, 1996, pp. 712–725, at pp. 724–725.
28 *Legality of Use of Force* (Yugoslavia v United States of America), *Provisional Measures*, Order of 2 June 1999, ICJ *Reports 1999*, p. 916.
29 Ibid., p. 925, paras. 30–31. See also, *Fisheries Jurisdiction* (Spain v Canada), *Jurisdiction of the Court*, Judgment, ICJ *Reports 1998*, p. 432. paras. 56 and 79; *Armed Activities on the Territory of the Congo (New Application: 2002)* (Democratic Republic of Congo v Rwanda), Judgment, ICJ *Reports 2006*, p. 53, para. 127.
30 *Fisheries Jurisdiction*, supra, note 29.
31 Ibid. para. 55. See also supra, note 28, para. 30. There the Court also noted the relevance of Article 33 of the UN Charter, which leaves States free to choose their desired peaceful means of dispute settlement (supra, note 28, p. 925, para. 31).
32 *Fisheries Jurisdiction*, supra, note 29, para. 54.

States accept the jurisdiction of the Court, they remain responsible for acts attributable to them that violate the rights of other States.'[33]

In a Declaration expressing the reasons behind his disagreement with the majority's decision to reject provisional measures in *Legality of Use of Force*, Judge Shi pointed out that the Court, as the principal judicial organ of the UN, should have seized the opportunity to issue 'a general statement of appeal' for the Parties to act in compliance with their UN Charter obligations and that such an initiative was 'within the implied powers of the Court'. Had it not failed to do so, the Court could have 'contributed to the maintenance of international peace and security in so far as its judicial functions permit'.[34]

Also of relevance here is the statement by Judge Verechetin in his dissenting opinion in the *Fisheries* case, where he touches upon the restricted nature of the principle of consent and the possibility for its circumscription on the basis of requirements of international law. In examining the compatibility of a State's reservations to the Court's jurisdiction, he notes that a State is 'absolutely free' to decide upon the scope of its participation in the optional clause system. However, he notes, 'a State is not absolutely free to make any reservation or condition it pleases to its optional declaration.'[35] He observes that it is the role of the Court to assess the compatibility of such limitations to its jurisdiction in the context of the optional clause system, noting that 'Generally, reservations and conditions must not undermine the very raison d'être of the optional clause system.'[36] While this opinion contradicts, in part, the finding of the Court in the case of *Military and paramilitary activities in and against Nicaragua*,[37] it is interesting that the Judge addresses the restricted nature of

---

33 *Fisheries Jurisdiction*, supra, note 29, paras. 56 and 79.
34 Contrasting the Court's decision with its past practice in the *LaGrand* case, where the Court made use of its power to decide on provisional measure *proprio motu*, Judge Shi noted that 'in response to the similar request ... in a situation far more urgent' the Court failed to take any positive action). *Legality of Use of Force*, supra, note 28, p. 927.
35 Judge Verechetin notes that 'For example, it is uncontested that the Court cannot give effect to a condition imposing certain terms on the Court's procedure which run counter to its Statute or Rules (*Fisheries Jurisdiction*, supra, note 29, at 575). As Judge Armand-Ugon rightly argued in the *Interhandel* case, '[t]he rules of substance and procedure fixed by the Statute must be regarded as immutable: neither the Court nor the parties can break them' [*Interhandel Case* (Switzerland v United States of America) (Preliminary Objection), Judgement, ICJ Reports 1959, p. 6, Dissenting Opinion of Judge Armand-Ugon, at p. 93].
36 *Fisheries Jurisdiction*, supra, note 29, *Dissenting Opinion*, pp. 574–576, paras. 10–11.
37 *Military and Paramilitary Activities in and against Nicaragua* (Nicaragua v United States of America), *Jurisdiction and Admissibility*, Judgment, ICJ Reports 1984, p. 418, para. 59: 'Declarations of acceptance of the compulsory jurisdiction of the Court are facultative,

the principle of consent and the possibility for its circumscription on the basis of substantive provisions of international law.

The Judgment in *Armed Activities on the Territory of the Congo*,[38] addressed the attempt by the Congo to found the Court's jurisdiction on the basis of alleged violations by Rwanda of the peremptory norms of international law. Relying on a number of compromissary clauses contained in international conventions, the Congo claimed that any reservations by Rwanda to the Court's jurisdiction must be found to be invalid. The strategy behind the claim in this case seemed to be to appeal to the Court to expand its jurisdiction due to the nature of the norms breached. Although this may have been what some anticipated as the best 'opportunity' for the Court to grant peremptory norms, the consequence that their elevated status had seemingly been condoned, the Court rejected the Congo's claim by holding that the fact that a dispute relates to compliance with peremptory norms 'cannot of itself provide a basis for the jurisdiction of the Court.'[39] Hinting at the distinction between procedural and substantive rules, the Court held that Rwanda's reservation 'bears on the jurisdiction of the Court' and does not affect the substantive obligations under the conventions at issue.[40] Indeed the Court had previously held that a compromissary clause did not constitute a manifest basis for jurisdiction, in the light of a State's reservations thereto.[41] The Court dismissed the Congo's attempt to circumvent the well-established requirement for its jurisdiction by conclusively noting that no peremptory norm *presently* exists which requires a State to consent to the jurisdiction of the Court to settle a dispute.[42] This observation is quite telling. It shows that the Court fully appreciates its own limits as a court for resolution of disputes between sovereign States, who are not obliged to accept its jurisdiction.

In their Joint Separate Opinion, and in an apparent exhortation to States, a number of judges expressed their 'serious concern' over the ability of States to shield themselves from judicial scrutiny, by way of their reservations to the Court's jurisdiction, in instances of alleged breaches by them of peremptory norms of international law.

---

    unilateral engagements, that States are absolutely free to make or not to make. In making the declaration a State is equally free either to do so unconditionally and without limit of time for its duration, or to qualify it with conditions or reservations.'

38 *Armed Activities*, supra, note 29, p. 6.
39 Ibid., p. 32, para. 64.
40 Ibid., p. 32, para. 67.
41 *Legality of Use of Force*, supra, note 28, p. 924.
42 *Armed Activities*, supra, note 29, p. 33, para. 69 (emphasis added).

It is a matter for serious concern that at the beginning of the twenty-first century it is still for States to choose whether they consent to the Court adjudicating claims that they have committed genocide. It must be regarded as a very grave matter that a State should be in a position to shield from international judicial scrutiny any claim that might be made against it concerning genocide. A State so doing shows the world scant confidence that it would never, ever, commit genocide, one of the greatest crimes known.[43]

[...]

It is thus not self-evident that a reservation to Article IX could not be regarded as incompatible with the object and purpose of the Convention and we believe that this is a matter that the Court should revisit for further consideration.[44]

In the more recent *Jurisdictional Immunities* case, the Court held that peremptory norms could not be relied upon to trump other well-established rules of international law that do not benefit from the same status.[45] Although this exercise did not involve issues of the Court's jurisdiction or consent thereto, the Judgment sheds light on other consequences that peremptory norms *do not* entail. Addressing Italy's claim that upholding the jurisdictional immunity of States would conflict with peremptory norms of international law, the Court unequivocally pronounced that 'no such conflict exists' as these 'two sets of rules address different matters'.[46] The Court clarified this position by noting that 'recognizing the immunity of a foreign State in accordance with customary international law does not amount to recognizing as lawful a situation created by the breach of a *jus cogens* rule.'[47] This position was reminiscent of the Court's prior pronouncement regarding the non-existence of peremptory norms obliging a State to consent to the jurisdiction of the Court.[48]

In a heartfelt dissent, Judge Cançado Trindade notes, in part, that '[t]he finding of the particularly grave violations of human rights and of international humanitarian law provides, in my understanding, a valuable test for the removal of any bar to jurisdiction, in pursuance of the necessary realization of

---

43 *Armed Activities*, supra, note 29, Joint Separate Opinion of Judges Higgins, Kooijmans, Elaraby, Owada, and Simma, p. 71, para. 25.
44 Ibid. p. 72, para. 29.
45 *Case concerning the Jurisdictional Immunities of the State* (Germany v Italy: Greece Intervening), Judgment, *ICJ Reports* 2012, p. 140, para. 92.
46 Ibid., p. 140, para. 93.
47 Ibid.
48 Supra, note 41 and accompanying text.

justice.'[49] By referring to 'any bar to jurisdiction', Judge Cançado Trindade apparently intended to advocate that in cases of grave violations of human rights and of international humanitarian law, no jurisdictional impediment whatsoever, *inter alia* reservation to jurisdictional clause or state immunity, would apply because the realization of justice prevails over any jurisdictional barrier in the domain of *jus cogens*. However, Judge Cançado Trindade does not seem to address the question of whether the principle of consent to jurisdiction is itself a fundamental aspect of the international legal order or whether any *ad hoc* adjustment of this principle may manipulate the international legal order on an *ad hoc* basis and in an uneven manner.

Concluding Remarks

The Court is integrated into the United Nations and its Statute forms an indivisible part of the Charter. This fact by itself, as noted by Rosenne, means that 'there is a general measure of consent that the Court should exist and function.'[50] However, as he rightly points out, this preliminary consent is not the same as consent that the Court should decide a particular case. It is submitted that calls for greater judicial activism, noble as they are, overlook the fact that States do not submit to the jurisdiction of the Court as a result of signing the Statute: further expression of consent is required.[51] Indeed, while States have committed to the principle of peaceful settlement of disputes, what settlement may be pursued must be invoked by formal and legal procedures that rest on the consent of the parties. Moreover, the horizontal legal order that dominates the context of judicial settlement in international relations,[52] and the place that the Court occupies therein, simultaneously allocate adjudicatory power and constrain it by the foundational principles of consent, which is a corollary of the sovereign equality of States.[53] Other than its description as the principal judicial organ of the United Nations, the provisions of the Charter do not place emphasis on the role of the Court.[54]

---

49 *Jurisdictional Immunities*, supra, note 45, paras. 213 and 309.
50 S. Rosenne, *The Law and Practice of the International Court 1920–2005*, vol. I, 4th ed., 2006 p. 555.
51 I. Brownlie, *Principles of Public International Law*, 3rd ed., 1979, p. 718.
52 See, R. Higgins, *Problems and Process: International Law and How We Use it*, Oxford University Press, 1994.
53 Brownlie, supra, note 51, p. 289 *et seq*.
54 Ibid., p. 731.

Siding with the majority in the *Armed Activities* case, Judge Dugard notes that asking the Court 'to invoke a peremptory norm to trump a norm of general international law accepted and recognized by the international community of States as whole, and which has guided the Court for over 80 years' would be a request that went 'a bridge too far'. Judge Dugard reminds his audience, and rightly so, that it is 'only States who can amend Article 36 of the court's Statute', i.e. the conditions pertaining to the Court's jurisdiction.

While pleas and exhortations to, or by, the Court may be justified and may hasten the international community to action, the solution to this problem, as noted by Rosenne, 'can be found not so much by questioning the principles upon which the exercise of jurisdiction rests, as by reformulating, perhaps in more emphatic terms, the broader principles regarding the very existence and functioning of the Court, to which States have agreed'.[55] Indeed significant changes to the practice of the Court may realistically be brought about through a change in the policy that members of the United Nations have in respect of the jurisdiction of the Court over peremptory norms of international law. This change may be achieved through concerted and collective efforts to remove all reservations to treaties that regulate peremptory norms of international law.

---

55   Rosenne, supra, note 50, p. 556.

Some Comments on the *Temple* (*Interpretation*) Judgment and the Impact of Possible Mistakes on the *Temple* Saga*

Sienho Yee

Yet another chapter in the Temple saga between Cambodia and Thailand was concluded on 11 November 2013, when the International Court of Justice (the Court or ICJ) delivered its judgment in *Request for Interpretation of the Judgment of 15 June 1962 in the Case Concerning the Temple of Preah Vihear (Cambodia v. Thailand)* (*Cambodia v Thailand*).[1] This judgment on interpretation[2] is of great interest on many fronts, but only aspects that are significant for the law and practice of the Court are highlighted and discussed here.

The saga centers on the sovereignty over the Temple of Preah Vihear and its immediate surroundings. The temple sits on the Preah Vihear promontory in the eastern part of the Dângrêk Mountains, with Cambodia to the south and Thailand to the north. A 1904 treaty between France (protector of Cambodia) and Siam (now Thailand) specified that the frontier in question would follow the watershed line. The treaty also provided for a mixed-commission process of delimiting this line, which produced a map showing the frontier line, although the mixed commission never approved the map because the commission ceased to function several months before the map was produced. As illustrated in Figure 1 below, using the watershed line as the boundary would have given the temple, the Preah Vihear promontory, the hill of Phnom Trap, and the valley between the promontory and Phnom Trap to Thailand, while using the frontier line indicated on the map would have given these areas

---

* This essay was first published in a slightly different form as Sienho Yee, 'Notes on the International Court of Justice (Part 5): Temple of Preah Vihear (Interpretation)' (2013), 14 *Chinese Journal of International Law* (2015), pp. 655–663. The author thanks Oxford University Press for permission to reuse this paper.

1 Request for Interpretation of the Judgment of 15 June 1962 in the *Case Concerning the Temple of Preah Vihear* (Cambodia v Thailand), *ICJ Reports 2013*, p. 281.

2 On the interpretation of judgments generally, see S. Rosenne, *The Law and Practice of the International Court, 1920–2005*, volume III, 4th edition, Brill, 2006, p. 1611; A. Zimmermann & T. Thienel, 'Article 60', in A. Zimmermann, C. Tomuschat, K. Oellers-Frahm & C. J. Tams (eds), *The Statute of the International Court of Justice: A Commentary*, 2nd edition, Oxford University Press, 2012 (hereinafter ICJ Statute Commentary); K. H. Kaikobad, *Interpretation and Revision of International Boundary Decisions*, Cambridge University Press, 2007.

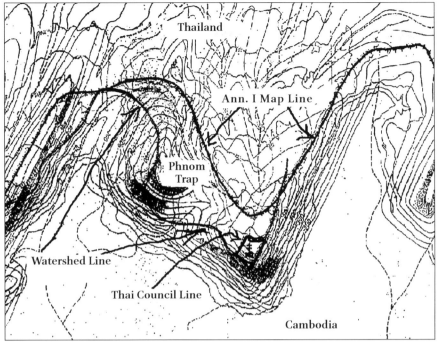

FIGURE 1   *Competing Claims of Cambodia and Thailand.*
SOURCE: FIGURE MODIFIED WITH THIS AUTHOR'S LABELLING, INSPIRED BY OTHER WRITERS BUT BASED ON CASE MATERIALS, ESPECIALLY FIGURE 13 (OVERLAY MAP PRODUCED BY CAMBODIA), IN: ANNEXES TO FURTHER WRITTEN EXPLANATIONS OF THE KINGDOM OF THAILAND, *REQUEST FOR INTERPRETATION OF THE JUDGMENT OF 15 JUNE 1962 IN THE CASE CONCERNING THE TEMPLE OF PREAH VIHEAR* (*CAMBODIA V. THAILAND*) (CAMBODIA V THAILAND) (21 JUNE 2012), 321, ANNEX 46.

to Cambodia. Without registering any objections, Thailand requested and distributed copies of the map and conducted itself in a way that suggested acceptance, although there was some evidence indicating Thai local official *effectivités*, after the alleged acceptance, in some areas that would have been allocated to Cambodia under that map line. After Cambodia's independence in 1953, Thailand occupied the temple. Negotiations could not settle their dispute, and Cambodia instituted proceedings against Thailand in 1959. The map mentioned above was reproduced by Cambodia in its pleadings and became known as the 'Annex I map'.

In its 1962 judgment, the Court held that 'the Temple of Preah Vihear is situated in territory under the sovereignty of Cambodia;' that, in consequence, 'Thailand is under an obligation to withdraw any military or police forces, or other guards or keepers, stationed by her at the Temple, or in its vicinity on

Cambodian territory;' and that 'Thailand is under an obligation to restore to Cambodia any objects of the kind specified in Cambodia's fifth Submission which may, since the date of the occupation of the Temple by Thailand in 1954, have been removed from the Temple or the Temple area by the Thai authorities.'[3] The questions on the legal status of the Annex I map and on the frontier line in the disputed region, which are of singular importance in a final settlement of the dispute between the parties, were only dealt with in the reasoning part of the judgment, as reasons or grounds for the Court's final decision.

After that judgment was delivered, Thailand withdrew its personnel from the temple and, using barbed wire, fenced up for Cambodia a small area on the promontory around the temple, following the line specified in July 1962 by the Thai Council of Ministers, now known as the 'Thai Council of Ministers' line'.[4] Thailand apparently thought that the 'vicinity' of the temple was undefined and attempted to determine unilaterally its limits using the barbed-wire fence. In November 1962, Cambodia published an aide-mémoire stating that the barbed-wired limit of the temple zone 'was in complete disagreement with the Court's decision which confirmed the frontier as it appeared on the 1907 [Annex I] map'.[5] For many decades, the parties seemed to have no problem with their border. But after Cambodia requested in 2007 the inscription of the temple site on the UNESCO World Heritage List, controversy resurfaced, and in 2011, Cambodia ultimately requested that the Court interpret its 1962 judgment and sought provisional measures which the Court indicated.[6]

Cambodia argued that the findings in the operative part of the 1962 judgment were the consequence of the Court's determination in the reasoning of that judgment, which has binding force because it stated a condition essential for the findings, that the Annex I map line constituted the relevant frontier; that the 'vicinity' in the second operative paragraph included all the land in the disputed area, encompassing the entire promontory as well as the hill of Phnom Trap as far north as the Annex I map line; and that the obligation imposed in that paragraph on Thailand to withdraw is a continuing one. Thailand essentially argued that the 1962 case was one about territorial sovereignty, not about delimitation of a frontier, and the Court decided in the 1962 judgment that the temple was situated on Cambodia territory and that Cambodia had

---

3   *Temple of Preah Vihear (Cambodia v Thailand)*, ICJ *Reports 1962*, pp. 6, 36–37.
4   ICJ *Reports 2013*, supra, note 1, p. 293, para. 22.
5   Ibid., p. 299, para. 42.
6   *Request for Interpretation of the Judgment of 15 June 1962 in the Case concerning the Temple of Preah Vihear* (Cambodia v Thailand), Provisional Measures, ICJ *Reports 2011*, p. 537.

sovereignty over only the area encircled by the Council of Ministers' line. The Annex I map line, at most, was only one of the factors on which that judgment was based.

In its November 2013 judgment, the Court affirmed that the dispute before the Court in 1962 was concerned only with sovereignty in the region of the temple and not with delimitation of the common frontier between Cambodia and Thailand.[7] It further noted that the principal dispute before it in 2013 concerned the interpretation of the second operative paragraph of the 1962 judgment, or more precisely, of the term *vicinity* therein.[8] The Court interpreted that term as covering the whole territory of the promontory of Preah Vihear and considered it unnecessary to further address the question either whether the 1962 judgment determined with binding force the frontier line between the two countries or whether the obligation imposed on Thailand by the second operative paragraph was of a continuing character.[9]

Several points in the Court's judgment are notable for their potential impact on future practice.

First, Cambodia attempted to rely on a headnote to the 1962 judgment in support of one of its arguments, suggesting that the headnote at issue demonstrated that the judgment determined the course of the frontier in the relevant area.[10] However, the Court rejected this attempt outright:

> Under Article 95, paragraph 1, of the Rules of Court (Article 74, paragraph 1, of the Rules of Court of 1946 applicable in 1962), the headnote is not one of the elements of the Judgment and it does not form part thereof. Moreover, the purpose of the headnote is only to give the reader a general indication of the points examined in a judgment; it does not constitute an authoritative summary of what the Court has actually decided. The Court does not consider that the headnote to the 1962 Judgment assists in resolving the questions of interpretation raised in the present proceedings.[11]

With unmistakable clarity, the Court's ruling should discourage any party from relying on a headnote as support for its case.

---

7   *ICJ Reports 2013*, supra, note 1, p. 292, para. 20 and p. 308, para. 76.
8   Ibid., p. 300, para. 46.
9   Ibid., p. 317, paras. 104–105.
10 Ibid., p. 307, para. 72.
11 Ibid., para. 73.

Interestingly, this scene at the Court replays the same which occurred more than 107 years ago in the United States Supreme Court in *United States v. Detroit Timber & Lumber Co.*[12] Lest any lawyer should be too busy to notice this case, a note appears to have been placed at the beginning of each slip opinion issued by the Supreme Court since a long time ago, if it is accompanied by a syllabus, at least in some versions of the opinions, although not in the bound volumes, stating in part: 'The syllabus constitutes no part of the opinion of the Court but has been prepared by the Reporter of Decisions for the convenience of the reader. See *United States v. Detroit Timber & Lumber Co.*, 200 U.S. 321, 337.'[13] On one search in the WESTLAW database of Supreme Court cases this disclaimer has appeared 2514 times as of 8 December 2016, from 23 November 1970.

Second, the Court's treatment of the subsequent conduct of the parties in the context of a request for interpretation of a judgment—conduct that took place after the delivery of the judgment to be interpreted, between 16 June 1962, and 2007–2008, in this case—is illuminating. The Court held that this type of conduct was relevant to assessing whether a dispute within the meaning of Article 60 exists, but not to interpreting the judgment:

> A judgment of the Court cannot be equated to a treaty, an instrument which derives its binding force and content from the consent of the contracting States and the interpretation of which may be affected by the subsequent conduct of those States, as provided by the principle stated in Article 31, paragraph 3 (*b*), of the 1969 Vienna Convention on the Law of Treaties.[14] A judgment of the Court derives its binding force from the Statute of the Court and the interpretation of a judgment is a matter of ascertaining what the Court decided, not what the parties subsequently believed it had decided. The meaning and scope of a judgment of the Court cannot, therefore, be affected by conduct of the parties occurring after that judgment has been given.[15]

Moreover, the Court held that, when interpreting a judgment, the Court does not examine facts that were not before it when making the initial judgment.[16]

While the Court's analysis seems reasonable, one may wonder whether subsequent conduct is always irrelevant, which should not be presumed lightly.

---

12   200 U.S. 321, 19 February 1906, p. 337.
13   Examples can be found at: http://www.supremecourt.gov/opinions/opinions.aspx.
14   1155 UNTS 331.
15   *ICJ Reports 2013*, supra, note 1, p. 307, para. 75.
16   Ibid.

To the extent that the words in the Court's judgment need to be understood in their *ordinary* meaning,[17] would not subsequent conduct play some role in reflecting that understanding? Reflecting the ordinary meaning of the terms of a judgment is different from affecting that judgment or from indicating acceptance of a meaning that may or may not exist at the time of the delivery of the judgment. One may also wonder whether subsequent conduct may have any significance beyond what the Court noted here. Perhaps this last question is not one of interpretation; nonetheless it may be of some importance.

Third, in making more precise the extent of the temple's 'vicinity', which can be considered a process of 'precisionization', the Court identified specific and concrete factors considered in the 1962 judgment and related proceedings, although it claimed that no single factor was conclusive.[18] By pointing to the stationing of Thai police outside the Thai Council of Ministers' line, the Court observed that the vicinity must be larger than the area encircled by that line because the 1962 judgment obligated the Thai police to withdraw; by pointing to several factors indicating that Phnom Trap was outside the temple area—including statements by a former Cambodian provincial governor and by Cambodia's counsel—the Court excluded Phnom Trap from the 'vicinity'.[19]

This precisionization process is laudable, but one wonders whether the Court has carried it to its best, because the Court seems to have resorted to a 'natural understanding of the concept of the 'vicinity' of the Temple', which, in its view, 'would extend to the entirety of the Preah Vihear promontory'.[20] If one were to continue with this process, perhaps other factors might be identified to further refine the size of the 'vicinity'. For example, Judge *ad hoc* Jean-Pierre Cot pointed out that the 1962 judgment contains language that suggests that the temple area is smaller than the whole promontory.[21] Perhaps more such factors with effect either way can be found and weighed. In any event,

---

17   The secret state of mind of the ICJ Judges should not be the basis for an interpretation. As Judge Lauterpacht eloquently argued in a separate opinion, 'It is for this Court, confronted as it is with an apparent gap in the opinion of the Court of 1950 with respect to a situation which calls for clarification, to fill the lacuna by all available means of interpretation. These do not include the knowledge of any particular member of the present Court as to the state of his—or his colleagues'—minds at the time when the Advisory Opinion was rendered in 1950.' *Voting Procedure on Questions Relating to Reports and Petitions Concerning the Territory of South-West Africa,* Advisory Opinion, ICJ Reports 1955, p. 67, at p. 96.
18   *ICJ Reports 2013,* supra, note 1, p. 315, para. 97.
19   Ibid., para. 98.
20   Ibid., p. 313, para. 89.
21   Ibid., p. 351, para. 11.

the process of making boundary delimitations more accurate warrants greater attention.

Fourth, the Court did 'not consider it necessary [...] to address [further] the question whether the 1962 Judgment determined with binding force the boundary line between Cambodia and Thailand.'[22] Undoubtedly narrow, the decision is correct insofar as the interpretation of the operative paragraphs can be conducted without addressing this question. Taking account of the case law holding that the interpretation of a judgment is limited to the operative part but may also address the reasoning if it is inseparable from the operative part,[23] one may infer, but the Court did not specifically state, that it considered the operative paragraphs of the 1962 judgment as not 'inseparable' from its treatment of the Annex I map line.[24] Does the judgment embody just an appreciation of the relationship between the two or a more restrained approach to interpretation of judgments that would read an operative paragraph narrowly, in effect giving greater play to the parties themselves in securing a final settlement of their disputes?

In this regard, the rigorous approach telegraphed in the joint declaration of Judges Hisashi Owada, Mohamed Bennouna, and Giorgio Gaja[25] as well as the emphasis placed by Judge Cançado Trindade[26] on 'reason and persuasion' are of interest. Whatever inferences one may make, it remains true that the Annex I map line played a central role in the reasoning of the Court in the 1962 judgment, and the Court's 2013 decision leaves the parties to their own devices as to what *res judicata* effect the Court's 1962 treatment of that line has, in reading the interpretation judgment or in other settings such as negotiations. For Judge *ad hoc* Gilbert Guillaume, 'It is true that the reasoning did not have the executory force attaching to the operative parts of judgments, but it had the authority of *res judicata*, that is to say, binding force.'[27] Or, perhaps one may find some distance between 'not [...] necessary' and 'not [...] inseparable' and wonder whether the approach applied by the Court in this case has allowed the discovery of the true meaning and scope of the earlier judgment.

---

22   Ibid., p. 317, para. 104.
23   E.g., *Request for Interpretation of the Judgment of 11 June 1998 in the Case concerning the Land and Maritime Boundary between Cameroon and Nigeria* (Cameroon v. Nigeria), Preliminary Objections (Nigeria *v* Cameroon), *ICJ Reports 1999*, pp. 35–36, paras. 10–11.
24   *ICJ Reports 2013*, supra note 2, p. 281, paras. 34, 77, 90, 104.
25   Ibid., p. 320.
26   Ibid., pp. 337–343, paras. 43–61.
27   Ibid., p. 348, para. 12.

Fifth, the sordid saga was probably the result of a series of 'likely mistakes' committed by both parties. I hope I will be pardoned for *apparent* lack of charity in criticizing others; the promotion of the rule of law is a greater value. I am using only 'likely mistakes' here, giving others the chance to pass final judgment on whether these are *indeed* mistakes. The first likely mistake was that when the mixed commission of French and Siamese members was set up to delimit the boundary, the Siamese members were apparently content with leaving it to the French members to draw the boundary line and therefore take care of Siamese national interests. Thus, the Siamese minister in Paris reported to the Minister of Foreign Affairs that 'regarding the Mixed Commission of Delimitation of the frontiers and the Siamese Commissioners' request that the French Commissioners prepare maps of various frontiers, the French Commissioners have now finished their work'.[28] Another likely mistake is that when the Annex I map came, the Siamese officialdom apparently did not fully appreciate its full significance and conducted itself in a series of acts and/or non-acts that the Court found sufficient to show acknowledgement or acquiescence.[29] The officials seemed to be acting under some mistaken understanding of the various matters surrounding the process and the map.

If the likely Siamese mistakes were made by officials in their workaday business operations, a likely Cambodian mistake was made by its earlier lawyers in the formulation—by design or oversight—of its claims back in 1959 when it instituted proceedings leading to the 1962 judgment. Cambodia formulated its claims in its application as that 'the Kingdom of Thailand is under an obligation to withdraw the detachments of armed forces it has stationed since 1954 in the ruins of the Temple of Preah Vihear' and that 'the territorial sovereignty over the Temple of Preah Vihear belongs to the Kingdom of Cambodia.'[30] The Annex I map line was pleaded during the better part of the proceedings as a basis for those claims. When the time came for final submissions at the end of the oral proceedings in 1962, Cambodia apparently had some revelations about potential problems and attempted to remedy the situation by introducing two final submissions in addition to the two stated in the application as follows:

1. To adjudge and declare that the map of the Dangrek sector (Annex 1 to the Memorial of Cambodia) was drawn up and published in the name and on behalf of the Mixed Delimitation Commission set up by the Treaty of 13 February 1904, that it sets forth the decisions taken by the said

---

28 *ICJ Reports 1962*, supra, note 3, p. 23.
29 Ibid., p. 23, et seq.
30 Ibid., p. 9.

Commission and that, by reason of that fact and also of the subsequent agreements and conduct of the Parties, it presents a treaty character;

2. To adjudge and declare that the frontier line between Cambodia and Thailand, in the disputed region in the neighborhood of the Temple of Preah Vihear, is that which is marked on the map of the Commission of Delimitation between Indo-China and Siam (Annex I to the Memorial of Cambodia); [...][31]

Thailand objected that these were put forward too late and that they were not presented in the application.[32] The Court refused to address these in the *dispositif*, but referred to them only in the reasoning. The Cambodian attempt and the Court's refusal to accept it would seem to give us sufficient ground to consider the first formulation a 'likely' mistake. In any event, the Court said at the beginning of the 1962 Judgment:

> The subject of the dispute submitted to the Court is confined to a difference of view about sovereignty over the region of the Temple of Preah Vihear. To decide this question of territorial sovereignty, the Court must have regard to the frontier line between the two States in this sector. Maps haven been submitted to it and various considerations have been advanced in this connection. The Court will have regard to each of these only to such extent as it may find in them reasons for the decision it has to give in order to settle the sole dispute submitted to it, the subject of which has just been stated.[33]

Towards the end of that judgment, the Court recapped:

> Referring finally to the Submissions presented at the end of the oral proceedings, the Court, for the reasons indicated at the beginning of the present Judgment, finds that Cambodia's first and second Submissions, calling for pronouncements on the legal status of the Annex I map and on the frontier line in the disputed region, can be entertained only to the extent that they give expression to grounds, and not as claims to be dealt with in the operative provisions of the Judgment.[34]

---

31 Ibid., p. 11.
32 Ibid.
33 Ibid., p. 14.
34 Ibid., p. 36.

Then the Court came to the operative paragraph that has given rise to much controversy and this very judgment of interpretation, which does not even address the legal status of this now famous line.

The current state of affairs serves as proof that a case may be won or lost at the stage of claim formulation[35] or that the initial formulation of claims can be of pivotal importance, a point that should be on the minds of decision-makers and practitioners aiming to win a case. In boundary matters, which, the Court recognizes, are of 'grave importance',[36] this point takes on greater poignancy.

The likely mistakes in workaday business on the part of the Siamese officials should also give us some lessons. It would seem that technical expertise (whether cartographic or legal) was not given sufficient attention, respect or play in the running of that business. While Siam secured good language for the treaties in issue, it did not select sufficiently capable or responsible technical experts to participate in the delimitation of the boundary, only to be stuck with the fate of having to savor the taste of letting one's opponents' experts draw the boundary line for oneself. Upon receipt of the materials from Paris the Siamese officials did not seem sufficiently well versed in the technical significance of them or of receiving them and therefore seemed to be conducting themselves under a mistaken understanding of such significance. Nor did the arrival of the bundle of maps coming from Paris seem to give the officials any cue that they should seek good legal advice. Apparently the saying that 'in the midst of counsellors there is safety' did not register in their minds. Or perhaps the perceived need to save money prevailed then, only to yield to the rude awakening decades later that expertise must be respected either in the workaday running of business or in future litigation, with potential unpleasant consequences sometimes leading to showdown in the battlefield of the future, where the parties in this case did indeed meet briefly. In any event, it is heart-breaking to see such matters to be the source of such a big storm in the relations between the two neighboring countries with friendly relations. One wonders whether better and more genuine respect for expertise including cartographic or legal expertise could have prevented this from happening.

Finally, after so many rounds of court battles, the dispute regarding the other parts of the contested area is now back in the hands of the parties themselves, who will have to settle it through bilateral negotiations or other peaceful

---

35   For a detailed treatment of claim formulation, see S. Yee, 'Article 40', in Zimmermann, et al. (eds), ICJ Statute Commentary, supra, note 2, p. 922.

36   *Territorial and Maritime Dispute between Nicaragua and Honduras in the Caribbean Sea* (Nicaragua v Honduras), *ICJ Reports 2007*, p. 735, para. 253.

means. Thus, this state of affairs shows that judicial settlement of disputes has its limits, for whatever reasons.[37] Ultimately, States themselves are the masters of their fates and they have the charge of settling their disputes peacefully and managing their relations to their mutual benefit.

---

[37] For an example showing that arbitration also has its limitations in dispute settlement, see J. Barboza, 'The Beagle Channel Dispute: Reflections of the Agent of Argentina', 13 *Chinese Journal of International Law*, 2014, p. 147. But adjudication does settle the long running dispute between Peru and Chile about their maritime boundary, despite misgivings. See M. T. Infante Caffi, 'Peru v. Chile: The International Court of Justice Decides on the Status of the Maritime Boundary', 13 *Chinese Journal of International Law*, 2014, pp. 741, 761.

PART 3

State Responsibility and State Immunity

∴

Alleged Support of Terrorism as a Ground for Denying State Immunity*

Mohsen Abdollahi

1   Introduction

In 1996, the US Congress amended the Foreign Sovereign Immunity Act (FSIA) and lifted the immunity of States sponsoring terrorism. Sixteen years later, the Canadian Parliament introduced similar amendments in the Canadian State Immunity Act (SIA). Both Acts deny the immunity of States designated by the administration branch as sponsors of terrorism because they have committed or supported terrorism materially. On the basis of this legislation, the US federal courts have issued more than 100 default judgments against States allegedly sponsoring terrorism such as Iran, Cuba, Syria and Libya and have ruled huge amounts of compensatory and punitive damages.

This short article seeks to answer the question of whether support of terrorism can be a ground for denying State immunity as a right under customary international law and whether such legislation contributes to the creation of a new 'terrorism exception' or breaches the immunity of targeted States.

To this end, in Part II the concept and history of State immunity is briefly addressed. Part III deals with the status of terrorism in 'territorial tort exceptions' to State immunity, and in Part IV the possible consistency of the 1996 FSIA with international law is examined. Finally, in Part V the 2012 SIA amendment is discussed. It will be argued that there is nothing in the law on combating international terrorism that can justify the denial of immunity of States that actually commit terrorist acts or are alleged to have committed or materially supported such acts.

2   The Rule of State Immunity: From Absolute to Restrictive Doctrine

The rule of State immunity deals with the protection of a sovereign State from any legal action, whether jurisdictional proceedings or executive

---

* To Professor *Djamhid Momtaz* for his endless support. I would like to thank Professor *Said Mahmoudi* and also my colleagues *Fatemeh Keyhanlou* and *Mirshahbiz Shafe* for their support and useful feedback.

measures, by another State.[1] While State immunity derives historically from Head of State immunity, its nature is different from that immunity and other personal and institutional immunities in international law.[2] Like Head of State immunity, State immunity has progressively developed through domestic case-law and more recently through national legislation. Two major international instruments relate to State immunity. The European Convention on State Immunity[3] (the Council of Europe Convention) is a regional instrument whereas the United Nations Convention on the Jurisdictional Immunities of States and Their Property (the UN Convention)[4] as a global treaty is based on draft articles prepared by the International Law Commission (ILC).[5] It is deemed to be the codification of the customary rules on the subject.[6] Less doubt has been raised about the customary nature of State immunity[7] and it has recently been considered by the International Court of Justice (ICJ) as a 'rule... [which] occupies an important place in international law and international relations. It derives from the principle of sovereign equality of States, which, as Article 2, paragraph 1, of the Charter of the United Nations makes clear, is one of the fundamental principles of the international legal order.'[8]

Originally, absolute immunity was the dominant perception. However, after World War II, due to increasing governmental engagements in commercial

---

1 Traditionally, jurisdictional immunity is regarded distinct from immunity against enforcement measures. See H. Fox & P. Webb, *The Law of State Immunity*, Oxford University Press, 2013; A. Reinisch, "European Court Practice Concerning State Immunity from Enforcement Measures", 17 *European Journal of International Law*, 2006, p. 803.
2 J. Bröhmer, 'Diplomatic Immunity, Head of State Immunity, State Immunity: Misconceptions of a Notorious Human Rights Violator', 12 *Leiden Journal of International Law* 1999, pp. 361–371.
3 *European Treaty Series* 74 (1972).
4 UN Doc. A/RES/59/38, 2 December 2004.
5 Draft articles on Jurisdictional Immunities of States and Their Property, *Yearbook of the International Law Commission* (YBILC) II, Part 2, 1991.
6 One commentator, referring to the few signatures and adoptions of the UN Convention, argues that 'These numbers fall far short of what is typically considered reliable evidence that a treaty reflects customary international law binding on nonparties to the treaty.' L. Fisler Damrosch, 'Changing the international law of sovereign immunity through national decisions', 44 *Vanderbilt Journal of Transnational Law*, 2011, p. 1190.
7 J. Finke, 'Sovereign Immunity: Rule, Comity or Something Else?', 21 *European Journal of International Law*, 2010, pp. 853–881; *Immunity v Accountability: Considering the Relationship between State Immunity and Accountability for Torture and other Serious International Crimes*, Redress Trust, 2005, p. 15, accessed February 10, 2016, at http://www.redress.org/downloads/publications/Immunity_v_Accountability.pdf.
8 *Jurisdictional Immunities of the State* (Germany v Italy: Greece intervening), Judgment, *ICJ Reports 2012*, p. 123, at 57.

activities, this doctrine became less practical. The new doctrine differentiates between *acta jure imperii* and *acta jure gestionis* of States and restricts the immunity to former activities. According to the doctrine of restrictive immunity, a foreign State is regarded as immune from the jurisdiction of another State except for acts falling in one of the generally recognized exceptions to the rule of State immunity. Commercial acts, torts, counterclaims, employment contracts and the consent of foreign State are among these exceptions. A recently established list of such exceptions can be found in the UN Convention.[9]

Generally speaking, terrorism has not explicitly been recognized as an exception to the principle of State immunity. Whether any of the established exceptions to immunity can be interpreted to cover terrorism is a question that will be answered later.

3   Terrorism as a Territorial Tort Exception

In general, territorial tort exception implies that a foreign State cannot invoke immunity for its tortious acts or omissions that lead to personal injury or death, or damage to or loss of property, in the territory of the forum State. This exception exists in the Council of Europe Convention and the UN Convention[10] and in national State immunity Acts,[11] except for Pakistan's State Immunity Ordinance of 1981.

Historically, the US Foreign State Immunity Act (FSIA) from 1976 is regarded as the leading legislation in this area. The legislative history of the 'territorial tort exception' in the FSIA shows that this exception was originally developed to cover insurable risks such as accidental death or physical injuries to persons or damage to tangible property involved in traffic accidents.[12] However, the exception has been gradually extended to cover 'intentional physical harm *such as assault and battery, malicious damage to property, arson or even* homicide,

---

9   See Articles 7–17.
10 The Council of Europe Convention Article 11 and the UN Convention Article 12.
11 US FSIA 1976, Section 1605 (a)(5); UK State Immunity Act 1978, Section 5; South Africa Foreign States Immunities Act 1981, Section 6; Canada State Immunity Act 1985, Section 6; Australia Foreign States Immunities Act 1985, Section 13; Singapore State Immunity Act 1985, Section 7; Argentina Law No. 24.488, 1995, Article 2(e); Israel Foreign State Immunity Law 2008, Section 5; Japan, Act on the Civil Jurisdiction of Japan with respect to a Foreign State, 2009, Article 10.
12 H.R.Rep.No.94–1487, 94th Cong., 2d Sess. 7 (1976), reprinted in: *Letelier v Chile*, 488 F. Supp. 665, US District Court for the District of Columbia, 11 March 1980, p. 671, accessed 15 February 2016, at http://law.justia.com/cases/federal/district-courts/FSupp/488/665/1400196/.

including political assassination.' (emphasis added)[13] This development is the result of textual ambiguity. In the *Jurisdictional Immunities* case, the ICJ noted that, none of the mentioned instruments expressly distinguishes between *acta jure gestionis* and *acta jure imperii*.[14] According to the ILC commentary on the proposed text of what became Article 12 of the UN Convention, 'the *locus delicti commissi* offers a substantial territorial connection regardless of the motivation of the act or omission, whether intentional or even malicious, or whether accidental, negligent, inadvertent, reckless or careless, and indeed irrespective of the nature of the activities.'[15] Members of the International Law Association (ILA) commented on the same commentary, saying that 'it is irrelevant whether that act or omission has the nature *de jure imperii* or *de jure gestionis*.'[16]

Worthy of note is that the ILC and the ILA both explicitly referred to the precedent established by a US Court in *Letelier v Chile*.[17] The case concerned the assassination of Orlando Letelier, the former diplomat and foreign minister of Chile together with Ronni Moffitt, his American aide, in 1976. They were allegedly assassinated by the Chilean Secret Police. Chile, while denying any involvement in the events, asserted that the Court had no subject-matter jurisdiction and Chile was entitled to immunity under the FSIA, which did not cover political assassinations because of their public, governmental character.[18] Chile's argument was rejected by the Court and Judge Green held that 'Nowhere is there an indication that the tortious acts to which the Act makes reference are to only be those formerly classified as 'private' …'[19]

The final decision of the court in the *Letelier* case remained unexecuted because Chile did not recognize its legitimacy[20] and the dispute was eventually settled by an international agreement between Chile and the US.[21]

---

13 *YBILC*, supra, note 5, p. 45, para. 4.
14 Supra, note 8, p. 127.
15 *YBILC*, supra, note 5, p. 45.
16 *Draft declaration of international law principles on compensation for victims of war*, ILC Rio de Janeiro Conference, 2008, commentary on Article PS-1 (Non-Immunity from Jurisdiction), accessed 1 March 2016, at http://www.ila-hq.org/download.cfm/docid/0128BA4F-C0A3-43C0-ADAD76A989965AFF.
17 *Letelier v Chile*, 488 F. Supp. 665, US District Court for the District of Columbia, 11 March 1980, p. 671, accessed 15 February 2016, at http://law.justia.com/cases/federal/district-courts/FSupp/488/665/1400196/.
18 Ibid., p. 671.
19 Ibid.
20 Letter of Octavio Errazuriz, ambassador of Chile, 84 *American Journal of International Law*, 1990, pp. 233–234.
21 Agreement between the US and Chile with regard to the dispute concerning responsibility for the deaths of Letelier and Moffit, 31 *International Legal Material*, 1992, p. 3; P. De Sena &

Notwithstanding US courts' subsequent jurisprudence, the *Letelier* precedent was followed by the Supreme Court of Canada after two decades.[22] It shows that the customary nature of the 'tort exception' to State immunity applicable to *acta jure imperii* cannot easily be contended. In this regard, in the *Jurisdictional Immunities* case, Germany criticized the ILC contention about the customary nature of Article 12 of the UN Convention on State immunities based on the *Letelier* decision.[23] Studies show that no State, other than the US and Canada, has denied the distinction between *jure gestionis* and *jure imperii* as regards the territorial tort exception. Thus, the positions taken in the ILC by for example China[24] and the US[25] regarding Article 12 of the UN Convention is very telling.

The customary nature of 'public territorial tort exception' is still controversial. If it is established, one may contend that terrorist actions in the forum State can be regarded as an exception to State immunity under 'the territorial tort exception'. Regrettably, the ICJ did not consider it necessary 'to resolve the question whether there is in customary international law a 'tort exception' to State immunity applicable to *acta jure imperii* in general'. However, as the practice of national courts shows, the *Letelier* precedent is an isolated one, denying the immunity of a foreign State for an alleged terrorist act in the forum State by referring to the 'territorial tort exception'. No other State, even those that have been victims of numerous fatal terrorist activities,[26] has denied the immunity of a foreign State in similar situations. This silence is meaningful.

    F. De Vittor, 'State Immunity and Human Rights: The Italian Supreme Court Decision on the Ferrini Case', 16 *European Journal of International Law*, 2005, p. 92, footnote 11.

22   *Schreiber v Federal Republic of Germany and the Attorney General of Canada*, 3 S.C.R. 269, 2002 SCC 62, Canada Supreme Court, 12 September 2002, paras. 33–36, accessed 13 March 2016, at https://scc-csc.lexum.com/scc-csc/scc-csc/en/item/2003/index.do.

23   Supra, note 8, p. 127, at 64.

24   'The Article [12] had gone even further than the restrictive doctrine, for it made no distinction between sovereign acts and private law acts' (UN Doc. A/C.6/45/SR.25, 19 November 1990, p. 2), quoted in the ICJ judgement, supra, note 8.

25   Article 12 'must be interpreted and applied consistently with the time-honoured distinction between acts *jure imperii* and acts *jure gestionis*" since to extend jurisdiction without regard to that distinction "would be contrary to the existing principles of international law' (UN doc. A/C.6/59/SR.13, p. 10, para. 63), quoted in the ICJ judgment, supra, note 8).

26   For instance, none of the States allegedly suspected of ordering assassinations were sued by forum States: Chapour Bakhtiar in his home in Paris, France (1991); Sadegh Sharafkandi in the Mykonos Greek restaurant in Berlin, Germany (1992); Alexander Litvinenko by polonium-210 in the UK (2006). In all these cases criminal trials were held against the suspected individuals. The same goes for the AMIA bombing in Buenos Aires, Argentina (1994).

4   The US 1996 FSIA Amendment: Lifting Immunity of State-sponsored Terrorism

Increasing terrorist attacks towards the end of the past century, and in particular the 1988 Pan Am Flight explosion over Lockerbie, Scotland, forced the US congress to amend its code and strengthen its anti-terrorism efforts. The FSIA was an obstacle to compensating victims of terrorism and the decision of the US District Court, under this Act, in favour of the immunity of Libya,[27] led to its reform by adopting the Antiterrorism and Effective Death Penalty Act (ADEPA)[28] 1996.[29]

The ADEPA provides that a foreign State is not immune from US District Court jurisdiction in any case, 'in which money damages are sought against a foreign state for personal injury or death that was caused by an act of torture, extrajudicial killing, aircraft sabotage, hostage taking, or the provision of material support or resources for such an act.'[30] Accordingly, a US court may only adjudicate a case if the following conditions are met: i) the foreign State should be listed by the Secretary of State as a 'State sponsor of terrorism under Federal legislation'; ii) the claimant or the victim was a national of the US[31] when the terrorist act occurred; (iii) 'in a case in which the act occurred in the foreign State against which the claim has been brought, the claimant has afforded the foreign State a reasonable opportunity to arbitrate the claim.'[32]

Providing compensation for the victims of terrorist acts and making foreign States more reluctant to sponsor acts of terror against US citizens have been

---

27   *Smith and Hudson v Libya et al.*, 886 F. Supp. 306,. United States District Court, E.D. New York, 17 May 1995, p. 315, accessed 19 March 2016 at http://uniset.ca/other/cs5/886FSupp306.html (stating that: 'Libya's alleged terrorist actions do not fall within the enumerated exceptions to the Foreign Sovereign Immunities Act and therefore Libya must be accorded sovereign immunity from suit.').

28   Public Law, No. 104–132, 110 Stat. 1214 (1996).

29   M. Reisman & M.Hakimi, '2001 Hugo Black Lecture: Illusion and Reality in the Compensation Of Victims Of International Terrorism', 54 *Alabama Law Review*, 2003, p. 566.

30   28 U.S.C. § 1605(a)(7) 1996.

31   This part of the act was amended in 2008 and extended to members of the US armed forces and otherwise employees of the US Government, individuals performing contract awarded by the Government.

32   See generally I. Arnowitz Drescher 'Seeking justice for America's Forgotten Victims: Reforming the Foreign Sovereign Immunities Act Terrorism Exception', 15 *Legislation and Public Policy*, 2012, pp. 791–834.

the two primary purposes of adopting this Act.[33] Apart from a recent Canadian amendment to its State Immunity Act that will be addressed in the next chapter, the US FSIA 'terrorism exception' to State immunity has no other counterpart among the laws enacted by other States.

Although aware of the inconsistency between FSIA and customary rules of State immunity, Congress deliberately provided a number of caveats and excluded any kind of automaticity.[34] Such caveats cannot preclude the wrongfulness of the Statute. Indeed, the inconsistency of the amendment with international law has also been notified to Congress by the State Department.[35] The legality of the amendment may therefore be questioned due to the customary nature of State immunity.

Judge Lamberth defended the amendment in the *Flatow* case by referring to the doctrine of 'universal jurisdiction' as the legal basis for the consistency of the new exception with international law.[36] The argument was that immunity of a foreign State could no longer be invoked in cases of international crimes where universal jurisdiction applies. The same reasoning was used by Italy against Germany before the ICJ in the case of *Ferrini*.[37] The Court commented on this argument given the 'gravity of the violations' and held that 'apart from the decisions of the Italian courts which are the subject of the present proceedings, there is almost no State practice which might be considered to support the proposition that a State is deprived of its entitlement to immunity in [the case of serious violations of human rights and IHL] ... In addition, there is a substantial body of State practice from other countries which demonstrates that customary international law does not treat a State's entitlement to immunity as dependent upon the gravity of the act of which it is accused

---

33   J. Kim, 'Making State Sponsors of Terrorism Pay: A Separation of Powers Discourse under the Foreign Sovereign Immunities Act', 22 *Berkeley Journal of International Law*, 2004, pp. 516–517.

34   C. Tomuschat, 'The International Law of State Immunity and Its Development by National Institutions', 44 *Vanderbilt Journal of Transnational Law*, 2011, p. 1126.

35   See Foreign Terrorism and US Courts: Hearings before the Subcommittee on Courts and Administrative Practice of the Senate Committee on the Judiciary, 103d Cong. 14 (1994) (statement of Jamison S. Borek, Deputy Legal Advisor to the United States State Department), cited in: L. McKay, 'A new take on antiterrorism: Smith *v*. Socialist People's Libyan Arab Jamahiriya', 13 *American University International Law Review*, 1997, p. 463.

36   *Flatow v Iran et al.*, 999 F.Supp. 1, US District Court, District of Columbia, March 11, 1998, titles 2, 4, at 15, 17.

37   Ferrini v Republica Federale di Germania, no. 5044/04, Corte di Cassazione, 11 March 2004, 128 *International Law Reports*, 2007, paras. 11–12.

or the peremptory nature of the rule which it is alleged to have violated.'[38] The analogy between Head of State immunity and State immunity was denied by the Court as well.[39] Worthy of note is that universal jurisdiction has emerged in the context of criminal proceedings and cannot be extended to civil proceedings without widespread repetition of State practice.

The role of the FSIA amendment and its subsequent case law in forming a new customary exception to the rule of State immunity has been considered by three different bodies. First, the ILC Working Group in 1999 considered the practice of States in some areas of State immunity, but it could not authenticate enough changes in the existing practice of States to amend the ILC Draft Articles on State Immunities.[40] This issue was subsequently considered by a Working Group established by the Sixth Committee as 'it did not seem to be ripe enough for the Working Group to engage in a codification exercise over it.'[41]

Two years later, the matter was raised before the European Court of Human Rights (ECHR). The Court considered the FSIA alongside with the *Pinochet judgment* in the *Al-Adsani case* and concluded that sufficient practice to demonstrate a shift in customary the international law of immunity could not be established. The court argued that 'the very need for the FSIA amendment at all served to demonstrate that as a general rule of international law State immunity can be claimed even in respect of violations of *jus cogens* norms such as officially-sanctioned torture.'[42]

Finally, the ICJ, in the *Jurisdictional Immunities* Case, considered the 1996 amendment to the FSIA as an isolated law that 'has no counterpart in the legislation of other States.'[43] Shortly after this judgment and quite in attentive to it, the Canadian Parliament passed a similar exception to its Act of State immunity. This exception will be addressed in the next chapter.

In response to those who criticized the ICJ for not sufficiently dealing with the legitimacy of the US amendments to the FSIA,[44] McMenamin argued that

---

38   Supra, note 8, paras. 83–84.
39   Ibid., para. 87.
40   *YBILC*, supra, note 5, pp. 171–172.
41   UN doc. A/C.6/54/L.12, 12 November 1999, p. 7, para. 13.
42   *Al-Adsani v The United Kingdom* (App 35763/97[2001]), para. 64.
43   Supra, note 5, para. 88, See also M. McMenamin, 'State immunity before the international court of justice: jurisdictional immunities of the state (Germany v. Italy)', 44 *Victoria University of Wellington Law review*, 2013, p. 200.
44   The Court, most recently, has been called upon by the Iranian Government to adjudge and declare the illegitimacy of FSIA amendments by which US Courts 'have awarded total damages of over US$ 56 billion' against Iran and Iranian State-owned companies, including Bank Markazi, and their property, that are entitled immunity under customary

the Court was correct to attach little weight to the relevance of the US and even the Canadian legislation because these Acts were political in nature since the only States that could be sued were those that the US and the Canadian executive authorities identify as sponsors of terrorism.[45] In other words, contrary to the practice of Greece and Italy, this legislation is limited to States recognized as sponsors of terrorism, based on the nationality of the victims or claimants.[46] It provides exceptions to State immunity in only a few cases of serious violations of human rights. Therefore, one may truly call this legislation *lexs pecialis*[47] which cannot be extended to the international community in general[48] or change the international law of sovereign immunity.[49]

5 Canada's State Immunity Act: Terrorism Exception and the Law on Combating International Terrorism

The Canadian State Immunity Act (SIA)[50] includes civil claims against foreign States. Until very recently this Act, like all its counterparts, afforded immunity principally to foreign States except in generally recognized exceptions to State immunity in customary international law. Sixteen years after the US FSIA, Canada decided to add the terrorism exception to its own State Immunity Act.[51] The new amendment was adopted because when cases were brought in Canadian courts for compensating alleged acts of torture outside Canadian

---

international law. See case concerning *Certain Iranian Assets* (Islamic Republic of Iran v United States of America), Application, 14 June 2016, Paras. 7, 33 (b) & (d), accessed Oct. 13, 2016, at http://www.icj-cij.org/docket/files/164/19038.pdf.

45 McMenamin, supra, note 43, p. 208. Most recently, the US Congress, despite Obama's administrative veto, passed the Justice Against Sponsors of Terrorism Act (JASTA), (Public Law No: 114–222, 28 September 2016). This act amends the FSIA and confers an independent jurisdiction on federal courts in cases relating to acts of international terrorism in the US. Specifically, it authorizes federal court jurisdiction over a civil claim against a foreign state for physical injury to a person or property or death that occurs *inside* the United States as a result of an act of international terrorism (Sec. 3).
46 De Sena & De Vittor, supra, note 21, p. 103.
47 Ibid., 92.
48 *C.f.* Tomuschat, supra, note 34, p. 1137.
49 For opposite view see Damrosch, supra, note 6, pp. 1185–1199.
50 R.S.C., 1985, c. S-18.
51 J. G. Robert, 'International law—state immunity: Canada amends its state immunity act to allow victims of terrorism to sue in Canadian courts', Lette & Associés, Publications, November 2012, accessed 29 March 2016, at http://www.lette.ca/docs/default-source/articles/state-immunity.pdf?sfvrsn=0.

territory they failed. Examples are *Zahra (Ziba) Kazemi v Iran*,[52] *Houshang Bouzari v Iran*[53] and *Arar v Syria*.[54] The reasoning of the courts was similar in all mentioned cases: 's. 6 [of the SIA] appears to deal with acts causing injury in Canada, and the language does not lend itself to one approach for injury caused by torture outside the country...[Then] This action is barred by s. 3(1) of the State Immunity Act. As this Court has no jurisdiction over the IR Iran, the action is dismissed'.[55]

In response to these judgments, the first proposed amending bills were introduced to the Parliament in 2005. However, it took more than seven years for the final Bill C-10 of Justice for Victims of Terrorism Act (JVTA) to be adopted. Sect. 4(1) of the Bill titled *cause of action*, provides that: 'Any person that has suffered loss or damage in or outside Canada on or after January 1, 1985 as a result of an act or omission that is, or if it had been committed in Canada would be, punishable under Part II of the *Criminal Code*,[56] may, in any court of competent jurisdiction, bring an action to recover an amount equal to the loss or damage...' Canadian courts may hear the lawsuit 'only if the action has a real and substantial connection to Canada or the plaintiff is a Canadian citizen or a permanent resident.' Clauses 3 to 9 of Bill C-10 amended the SIA and led to the addition of a new exception to sect. 6 of this Act titled '*Support of terrorism*'. According to this new exception: 'A foreign State that is set out on the list referred to in subsection (2) is not immune from the jurisdiction of a court in proceedings against it for its support of terrorism on or after January 1, 1985.'[57]

The legislative history of the Bill reveals that the first proposed drafts were intended 'to allow States to be sued civilly when their agents commit torture, genocide, war crimes and crimes against humanity.'[58] However, the adopted Bill was eventually limited to the crime of terrorism under Part II.1 of the Canadian *Criminal Code*. It seems that the Canadian Parliament, being aware of the ICJ ruling on absolute immunity of States even for serious violation of *jus cogens*, deliberately chose a different path of legislating. The preamble to

---

52   *Kazemi Estate v Islamic Republic of Iran*, 2011 QCCS 196, Superior Court of Québec, 25 January 2011.
53   *Houshang Bouzari et al. v Iran*, [2002] O.J. No. 1624, Ontario Superior Court of Justice, 1 May 2002.
54   *Arar v Syria* [2005] O.J. No. 752 (Sup. Ct.).
55   Supra, note 53, paras. 41, 90; Supra, note 54, para. 28; Supra, note 52, paras. 213–214.
56   This part relates to the crime of terrorism.
57   SIA, 6.1(1) as amended 2012.
58   Library of Parliament, 'Legislative summary of Bill C-10: Justice for Victims of Terrorism Act', publication NO, 41-1-C10-E, Ottawa, Canada, 2012, p. 7, accessed 10 April 2016, at http://www.lop.parl.gc.ca/Content/LOP/LegislativeSummaries/41/1/c10-e.pdf.

the JVTA shows that the Parliament had relied on Security Council Resolution 1373 (2001) and the 1999 International Convention for the Suppression of the Financing of Terrorism (CSFT) rather than on the universal jurisdiction of the FSIA amendment, or the Italian courts' *jus cogens* arguments. The question is how these instruments provide a legitimate legal basis for the 2012 amendment.

Security Council resolution 1373, which was adopted after the 9/11 terrorist attacks, set a series of obligations for all States to suppress international terrorism *including* 'prevent and suppress the financing of terrorist acts'.[59] However, nothing in this resolution justifies waiving the immunity of one State by another even if the former has supported or is alleged to support terrorism.

This interpretation is not seen in the reports of States to the Committee of Anti-Terrorism either. Indeed, a State cannot enforce its obligation under the Charter of the UN through unlawful means. According to article 25 of the UN Charter, UN Member States 'agree to accept and carry out the decisions of the Security Council in accordance with the present Charter.' Under Art. 2 (1) of the Charter 'the organization is based on the principle of the sovereign equality of all its Members.' The Preamble of the 1373 resolution '*Recognize(s)* the need for States to complement international cooperation by taking additional measures to prevent and suppress, in their territories through *all lawful means*, the financing and preparation of any acts of terrorism'.

One may invoke para. 2(e) of the Resolution, which obliges all States to 'ensure that any person who participates in the financing, planning, preparation or perpetration of terrorist acts or in supporting terrorist acts is brought to justice and to ensure that ... such terrorist acts are established as serious criminal offences in domestic laws and regulations ...'

This argument is unconvincing for two reasons. First, the last part of the same paragraph reveals the emphasis of the Resolution on the criminal responsibility of individuals, and secondly, the criminal responsibility of States has not been recognized in international law yet.[60]

The reliance of the Canadian Parliament on the 1999 CSFT is also controversial. Nothing in this convention authorizes a Member State to waive the immunity of another Member State that has financed or is alleged to finance terrorism. On the contrary, Article 20 of the Convention obliges State Parties to 'carry out their obligations under this Convention in a manner consistent with the principles of sovereign equality ... of other States.'[61] Moreover, according

---

59 Para. 1 (a).
60 G. Gilbert, 'The Criminal Responsibility of States', 39 *International and Comparative Law Quarterly*, 1990, p. 351.
61 Also see article 21.

to Article 34 of the 1969 Vienna Convention on the law of treaties 'A treaty does not create either obligations or rights for a third State without its consent.' As such, Canada cannot rely on the CSFT against non-Member States.

6   Concluding Remarks

Although terrorism may be deemed an exception to the rule of State immunity in the frame of a 'territorial tort clause', States practice does not support such a proposition. Few States believe in a 'tort exception' to State immunity applicable to *acta jure imperii*: some expressly contest and others are silent. In this situation, a claim to benefit of the customary nature of such exception would be questionable.

The 'State-sponsored terrorism exception', which first was adopted by the US Congress in 1996, added a new exception to the international customary rules on States' immunity. While the Act called upon other States to adopt legislation similar to the FSIA's terrorism provisions,[62] it was only the Canadian Parliament that sixteen years later passed almost similar legislation. No other State has welcomed this approach. Yet States targeted by this exception have not only questioned the legality of the US/ Canadian legislation, but also refused to appear before their courts. All claims have been questionably awarded *in absentia*. Therefore, it can be said that the practice of States does not support terrorism as a new exception to the customary rules of State immunity. As the ICJ holds in the *North Sea Continental Shelf Case*, a rule of customary international law can be recognized where State practice is 'settled' among those States 'whose interests are specifically affected'[63] by the purported customary international law.[64]

---

62 D. M. Strauss, 'Reaching out to the international community: Civil lawsuits as the common ground in the battle against terrorism', 19 *Duke Journal of Comparative and International Law*, 2009 p. 355.

63 *North Sea Continental Shelf* (Germany v Netherlands), Judgment, ICJ Reports 1969, pp. 43–44.

64 McMenamin, supra, note 43, p. 208.

Types of Injury in Inter-States Claims: Direct Injury to the State

Hirad Abtahi[1]

1 Introduction

In the context of State responsibility, significant focus has been placed on the legal consequences of a breach of an international obligation by a State.[2] Thus, prior studies have generally addressed the forms of reparations rather than the typology of injuries in inter-States claims mechanisms. This study explores the latter by focusing on direct injuries to States, including to territory and government apparatus.[3]

State responsibility refers to the legal consequences of a breach of an international obligation by a State. The close link between that breach and its immediate legal consequence in the form of reparations was recognized by the Permanent Court of International Justice (PCIJ) in the *Chorzow Factory* case.[4] Article 36(2) common to the Statutes of the PCIJ and the International Court of Justice (ICJ), provides both courts with jurisdiction upon States' declarations, *inter alia*, in all legal disputes concerning:

(c) The existence of any fact which, if established, would constitute a breach of an international obligation; [and]
(d) The nature or extent of the reparation to be made for the breach of an international obligation.

---

1 The views expressed in this article are those of the author and not necessarily those of the International Criminal Court. The author expresses his gratitude to Peter Bozzo, Amy Foan and Kate Pitcher for their excellent research assistance.
2 See, for example, F. V. García-Amador, L. B. Sohn & R. R. Baxter, *Recent Codification of the Law of State Responsibility for Injuries to Aliens*, 1974; M. M. Whiteman, *Damages in International Law*, Vol. I, 1937; Special Rapporteurs G. Arangio-Ruiz & J. Crawford, International Law Commission, Reports on State Responsibility (1988–2001), at http://legal.un.org/ilc/guide/9_6.shtml#srapprep (last visited 28 January 2016).
3 For indirect injury to the State through its nationals, See H. Abtahi, 'Types of Injury in Inter-State Reparation Claims: A Guide for the International Criminal Court', 30 *Canadian Journal of Law and Society*, 2015, pp. 259–276.
4 *Chorzow Factory Case* (Germany v Poland), 1928 PCIJ, (Series A) No. 17, p. 29.

Article 31 of the International Law Commission's Articles on Responsibility of States for Internationally Wrongful Acts (ARSIWA) would later address the types of injury caused to the State and their related reparations:[5]

1. The responsible State is under an obligation to make full reparation for the injury caused by the internationally wrongful act.
2. Injury includes any damage, whether material or moral, caused by the internationally wrongful act of a State.

Article 31(2) is the subject of this study which seeks to shed light on the evolution of the concept of 'injury' in inter-States claims mechanisms. According to Article 42 of the ARSIWA, an injured State is entitled:

> to invoke the responsibility of another State if the obligation breached is owed to:
> (*a*) that State individually; or
> (*b*) a group of States including that State, or the international community as a whole,
> and the breach of the obligation:
> (i) specially affects that State; or
> (ii) is of such a character as radically to change the position of all the other States to which the obligation is owed with respect to the further performance of the obligation.[6]

In inter-States responsibility mechanisms,[7] one can distinguish the types of injuries in accordance with Statehood indicia, as provided by Article 1 of the Monte Video Convention: a) a permanent population; (b) a defined territory; (c) Government; and (d) capacity to enter into relations with the other states.'[8] The fourth indicia aside, one may distinguish between an injury caused to the State 'directly', through its territory and/or Government (indicia b and c), and

---

5 International Law Commission, Draft articles on Responsibility of States for Internationally Wrongful Acts, with commentaries, 2001, 53rd session (the 2001 ILC Draft Articles), Article 31 and, for the forms of reparation, Article 34.
6 Ibid., Article 42, p. 117.
7 For the purpose of this study, inter-States mechanisms will include all but regional human rights courts.
8 Convention on Rights and Duties of States (Monte Video Convention) 165 LNTS 19, 26 December 1933, Article 1.

an injury caused to the State 'indirectly' through its nationals (indicia a).[9] In other words,

> [t]he wrongful act or omission ... may consist of a direct injury to the public property of the [claimant] state, to its public officials, or to the state's honor or dignity, or of an indirect injury to the state through an injury to its national.[10]

This study proposes a typology of injuries, which may be both material (2) and moral (3), in inter-States claims mechanisms. As will be seen, inter-States claims mechanisms have long recognized that States can sustain a variety of injuries, including through harm caused to a State's nationals, or damage to its environment, or cultural property.

2   Material Injury

Material injury concerns both the State's territorial sovereignty (2.1) and property (2.2).

2.1   *Territorial Sovereignty*

Violations of territorial sovereignty are a classic type of injury caused to a State and can be seen in the following two early examples from the 1930s. In the *Legal Status of Eastern Greenland* (Denmark v Norway), after Norway's declaration of occupation of territories in Eastern Greenland over which Denmark claimed sovereignty, the latter brought a case before the PCIJ.[11] The PCIJ held that Norway's declaration of occupation and its related steps constituted a violation of Denmark's territorial sovereignty and accordingly were unlawful and invalid.[12] Contemporaneously, the *Case of the Free Zones of Upper Savoy and the District of Gex* concerned a free customs zone in French territory to which Switzerland had been a beneficiary since the 19th century. Following World War I, the Treaty of Versailles declared that the arrangements concerning the free zones (including the District of Gex) were no longer consistent with the new situation, and that France and Switzerland had to agree on the

---

9   García-Amador et al., supra, note 2, p. 91, paras. 29–30.
10 M. M. Whiteman, *Damages in International Law*, Vol. I, 1937, pp. 80–81. See UN Doc. A/CN.4/96, 20 Jan. 1956, pp. 195–97, paras. 117–122.
11 *Legal Status of Eastern Greenland* (Denmark v Norway), 1933 PCIJ, (ser. A/B) No. 53, p. 23.
12 Ibid., p. 75.

status of these territories.[13] Having failed to reach any agreement, France unilaterally established its customs line on the political border. Switzerland objected to this and, when brought before the Court, the PCIJ ultimately decided in favour of Switzerland, requiring that France withdraw its customs line.[14]

Another example is the *Case Concerning the Temple of Preah Vihear*, which concerned an ancient sanctuary on a promontory of the mountain ranges that constituted the boundary between Cambodia and Thailand.[15] The ICJ found that the Temple was located in Cambodian territory and, consequently, Thailand was under an obligation to withdraw its armed forces or other guards stationed at and around the Temple on Cambodian territory.[16] Furthermore, the *Case Concerning United States Diplomatic and Consular Staff in Tehran* provides a different example of a sovereignty dispute involving diplomatic and consular premises. The case arose from the takeover of the United States (US) Embassy in Tehran as well as its consulates in Tabriz and Shiraz.[17] The ICJ held that the Iranian officials had an obligation to end the 'flagrant infringements of the inviolability of the *premises,* archives and diplomatic and consular staff of the United States Embassy' [emphasis added],[18] and ordered Iran to hand over control of all premises and property that belonged to the US.[19]

2.2 *Property*

A State may sustain injury through its property, which has been understood to encompass not only general public property, but also, and most interestingly, cultural property and the natural environment.

2.2.1 General Public Property

In the context of the Eritrea-Ethiopia armed conflict, the Eritrea-Ethiopia Claims Commission (EECC) decided that State property at risk of injury might include government administration buildings, such as schools, clinics,

---

13 *Case of the Free Zones of the Upper Savoy and the District of Gex* (France v Switzerland), 1932 PCIJ (ser. A/B) No. 46, pp. 118, 127–28 & 141.
14 Ibid., pp. 97, 164 & 172.
15 *Case Concerning the Temple of Preah Vihear* (Cambodia v Thailand), Merits, Judgment, *ICJ Reports 1962*, pp. 14–15.
16 Ibid., pp. 36–37.
17 *Case Concerning United States Diplomatic and Consular Staff in Tehran* (United States of America v Tehran), Judgment, *ICJ Reports 1980*, paras. 14–19.
18 Ibid., para. 69.
19 Ibid., para. 95. The case was instituted by the United States by means of a unilateral Application under Article 40 of the Statute of the Court and Article 38 of the Rules of Court. Ibid. paras. 1–2.

veterinary clinics, water supply systems and agricultural training centers.[20] Specifically, the EECC awarded Ethiopia US$315,000 as compensation for damage caused to 'public buildings and infrastructure', including 'health institutions and educational institutions'.[21] As for Eritrea, it received over US$13 million for damage to buildings, including schools, Ministry of Agriculture facilities, hospitals and health stations.[22]

Of interest is Eritrea's claim of US$400 million for consequential injuries caused by Ethiopia's destruction of civilian infrastructure, including schools, telecommunications facilities and health centers. Eritrea alleged four specific types of consequential injuries: (1) nationals were unable to obtain an education; (2) nationals suffered economic harm as a result of damage to telecommunications infrastructure; (3) nationals endured general 'adverse economic conditions'; and (4) nationals were denied access to medical care.[23] Noting that 'international law does not recognize a separate category of compensable 'consequential damages'', the EECC nevertheless analyzed Eritrea's claims.[24] The EECC held that Eritrea's allegations about 'adverse economic conditions' were inadmissible, and it dismissed the claims about education and telecommunications on the basis of insufficient proof.[25] However, the EECC awarded Eritrea US$1.5 million to compensate for its nationals' lack of access to medical care.[26] As these damages emerged from destruction of infrastructure, they are best viewed as injuries relating to general public property.

---

20   Final Award: Ethiopia's Damages Claims (Ethiopia v. Eritrea), 26 RIAA 631 (Eritrea-Ethiopia Claims Commission) (17 Aug. 2009), paras. 162–79 & 357–79. See also Final Award: Eritrea's Damages Claims (Ethiopia v. Eritrea), 26 RIAA 505 (Eritrea-Ethiopia Claims Commission) (17 Aug. 2009), paras. 49, 81, 105–09, 140–93 (noting that the EECC held Ethiopia liable for the destruction of police stations and courthouses in several towns, and awarding compensation for injuries that were adequately proven).

21   Final Award: Ethiopia's Damages Claims (Ethiopia v. Eritrea), 26 RIAA 631 (Eritrea-Ethiopia Claims Commission) (17 Aug. 2009), paras. 174 & 179.

22   Final Award: Eritrea's Damages Claims (Ethiopia v. Eritrea), 26 RIAA 505 (Eritrea-Ethiopia Claims Commission) (17 Aug. 2009), paras. 77, 81, 99, 108, 110, 125, 136 & 139. Eritrea's largest claim for building damages related to a cotton factory, where Eritrea had spent, inter alia, over US$4 million on machinery and supplies, which was burnt during the conflict. The EECC granted Eritrea US$12.6 million to compensate for damage caused to the factory. 26 RIAA 505, paras. 150–56.

23   Ibid., paras. 195–96.

24   Ibid., para. 203.

25   Ibid., paras. 202–07.

26   Ibid., paras. 208–16.

Loss of tourism has also been invoked as a form of material damage. For example, Ethiopia argued that its war with Eritrea resulted in the loss of $104 million in tourism revenues.[27] The EECC did not specify whether Ethiopia sought damages for loss suffered directly by the State or loss suffered by nationals and businesses that would have benefitted from increased tourism.[28] The EECC eventually dismissed the claim for lack of evidence.[29] Thus, injuries for loss of tourism might be linked to general public property where this term includes tourism related economic benefits.

Property damage to a State may also arise out of the destruction of its vessels. This can be seen in the claim against the US following the *Aerial Incident of 3 July 1988*. This consisted of the US shooting down the State owned Iran Air in the Persian Gulf during the Iran-Iraq war, resulting in the death of all 290 passengers and crew. Iran sought reparation for 'the injuries suffered by [Iran] and the bereaved families [...], including additional financial losses which Iran Air and the bereaved families [...] suffered for the disruption of their activities.'[30] Similarly, property damage to a State may also involve the sinking of its ships. The Bahamas paid $5.4 million to Cuba after sinking the latter's patrol boat; the vast majority of the payment ($5 million) constituted reparation for the loss of the vessel.[31]

Attacks on diplomatic premises constitute another form of harm to general public property. Courts assessing damages for such attacks account for 'pecuniary losses' in addition 'to the outrage against [the State's] mission'.[32] In 1966, China sought reparations following anti-Chinese protests and attacks against the Chinese embassy and its consulates across Indonesia, resulting in damage to premises, furniture and the seizing of archives and the Chinese flag—although it is not clear if this was provided.[33] In one case, Indonesia

---

27 26 RIAA 631, supra, note 21, paras. 273, 458.

28 Ibid., paras. 458–61.

29 Ibid., para. 461.

30 *Aerial Incident of 3 July 1988* (Islamic Republic of Iran v United States of America), Application Instituting Proceedings filed in the Registry of the Court, ICJ General List No. 89 (17 May 1989), pp. 8–11.

31 'Bahamas et Cuba: Versement par le gouvernement cubain au gouvernement des Bahamas de l'indemnité dûe pour l'incident maritime du 10 mai 1980', 85 *Revue Générale de Droit International Public*, 1981, p. 540.

32 García-Amador et al., supra, note 2, p. 95, para. 46. See P. A. Bissonnette, *La satisfaction comme mode de réparation en droit international*, 1952, Impr. Granchamp, pp. 59–61, for examples of cases involving material damage to consular premises.

33 'Chronique', 70 *Revue Générale de Droit International Public*, 1966, pp. 1013–115. A Chinese diplomat was also injured by stones thrown at him.

compensated the United Kingdom for damage to a British embassy resulting from mob violence. In another, Pakistan issued funds to the US after a crowd sacked the US Embassy in Islamabad in 1979.[34] Elsewhere, following the 1979 occupation of US Embassy and consulates, the ICJ ordered Iran to provide redress for, *inter alia*, the takeover of premises, property, archives, and documents, which had to be returned.[35] Thus, the same acts and omissions may amount to an injury as a result of both the violation of sovereignty but also the seizure of property (see 2.1 above).

2.2.2   Cultural Property

Cultural property has also been the subject matter of claims for reparations by States. For the present purposes, cultural property is to be understood in its broadest meaning, regardless of its formal listing in accordance with any international instrument, such as the UNESCO 1972 Convention Concerning the Protection of the World Cultural and Natural Heritage.[36] In the *Case Concerning the Temple of Preah Vihear*, the ICJ held that Cambodia's claim for the restitution of objects removed by Thailand from the temple since its occupation in 1954 was in fact 'implicit in, and consequential on, the claim of sovereignty itself.'[37] This said, the ICJ still held that Thailand was under an obligation to return the property including sculptures, stelae, fragments of monuments, sandstone models and ancient pottery which may have been removed from in and around the Temple.[38]

Similarly, the EECC has decided that State property at risk of injury might include government administration buildings in the form of religious institutions, such as churches, monasteries, mosques and parochial schools.[39] In one

---

34   Exchange of Notes Between the Government of the United Kingdom of Great Britain and Northern Ireland and the Government of the Republic of Indonesia concerning the losses incurred by the Government of the United Kingdom and by British nationals as a result of the disturbances in Indonesia in September 1963, Treaty Series No. 34, 1967, p. 81; 85 *Revue Générale de Droit International Public* (1981), p. 880. See also ILC Draft Articles, supra, note 5, p. 101, para. 12, n. 530 (discussing both cases).

35   *Case Concerning United States Diplomatic and Consular Staff in Tehran* (United States of America v Tehran), Judgment, *ICJ Reports 1980*, paras. 14–19, 57 & 95.

36   Convention concerning the Protection of the World Cultural and Natural Heritage, 16 November 1972, at http://whc.unesco.org/en/conventiontext (last visited on 24 December 2015).

37   *Case Concerning the Temple of Preah Vihear* (Cambodia v Thailand), Merits, Judgment, *ICJ Reports 1962*, pp. 36–37.

38   Ibid., pp. 10–11 & 36–37.

39   26 RIAA 631, supra, note 21, paras. 180–98.

particular case, the EECC awarded Eritrea US$50,000 for damage to the Stela of Matara, an ancient monument in the Senafe Sub-Zoba which was deliberately damaged by an explosion during Ethiopia's occupation.[40] Eritrea also received compensation for damage caused to a cemetery and various religious buildings, while Ethiopia gained reparations for the looting of churches and the shelling of religious institutions.[41] The EECC noted that damage to organizations dedicated to religion 'is a particularly severe consequence of armed conflict that tears at the fabric of the affected communities and deprives them of safe places of worship.'[42]

2.2.3 Natural Environment

Reparations have also been awarded in relation to the natural environment. In the 1930s' *Trail Smelter* case, the Tribunal awarded reparations to the US for damages caused to land by Sulphur dioxide emissions from a smelter across the border in Canada.[43] This included damage to the cleared land used for crops, damage to the crops and the reduction of the crop yield arising from the injuries.[44] Decades later, following the crash of the Soviet *Cosmos 954* satellite in Canada in 1978, the USSR agreed to pay Canada for the injury caused to its territory, land and environment by radioactive debris.[45]

Additionally, the practice of the United Nations Compensation Commission (UNCC) provides examples of natural environmental based injuries during armed activities.[46] In the *Well Blowout Control Claim*,[47] the Kuwait Oil

---

40   Ibid., paras. 217–23.
41   26 RIAA 505, supra, note 22, paras. 105–09 & 224–26; 26 RIAA 631 supra, note 21, paras. 174, 273, 380–86.
42   26 RIAA 631 supra, note 21, para. 381.
43   *Trail Smelter Case* (United States v Canada), 3 RIAA 1905 (Trail Smelter Arbitral Tribunal) (16 Apr. 1938), pp. 1922 & 1924–33. The Trail Smelter Tribunal operated under the 15 April 1935 Ottawa USA-Canada Convention. Under Article II of the Convention, the US and Canada were each to select one member of and a scientist to assist the tribunal, and to select jointly a Chairman. Trail Smelter Case (United States v Canada), 3 RIAA 1905 (Trail Smelter Arbitral Tribunal) (16 Apr. 1938), pp. 1911.
44   Ibid., p. 1925.
45   Canada: Claim Against the Union of Soviet Socialist Republics for Damage Caused by Soviet Cosmos 954, Annex A: Statement of Claim, 23 Jan. 1979, 18 ILM 899, pp. 902–08; Canada-Union of Soviet Socialist Republics: Protocol on Settlement of Canada's Claim for Damages Caused by 'Cosmos 954', 2 Apr. 1981, 20 ILM 689, p. 689.
46   UN Doc. S/RES/687, 3 Apr. 1991, para. 16.
47   See Report and Recommendations Made by the Panel of Commissioners Appointed to Review the Well Blowout Control Claim (the 'WBC Claim'), UN Doc. S/AC.26/1996/5/

Company was granted reparations in relation to the injury caused to the Kuwaiti oil fields by Iraq following the well-head fires. Part of the injury to the Kuwait Oil Company involved 'losses or expenses resulting from...[the a]batement and prevention of environmental damage, including expenses directly relating to fighting oil fires and stemming the flow of oil in coastal and international waters.'[48]

3 Moral Injury

The term 'moral injury' usually signifies a 'failure to respect the honor and dignity of the State'.[49] Because they involve harm to the State's honor, moral injuries are often less tangible than material injuries. A State may suffer moral injury as a result of an act aimed directly at either the State or its officials (3.1); or the State's nationals (3.2).

3.1 *Moral Injury Suffered by the State as a Result of Injury Caused to It Directly*

This type of injury can take the form of insults to the Head of State and State symbols (3.1.1) and diplomatic and consular personnel and premises (3.1.2).[50]

3.1.1 Insults to the Head of State and State Symbols

The late 19th century provides an early example in which a crowd hissed at the Spanish King during his visit to Paris and, consequently, the French President

---

Annex, 15 Nov. 1996, paras. 66–86. The report was approved by the Governing Council in its Decision 40 of 17 December 1996. See UN Doc. S/AC.26/Dec.40, 18 Dec. 1996.

48 UN Doc. S/AC.26/1996/5/Annex, 15 Nov. 1996, paras. 66–86 & 233.

49 In French: «méconnaissance de la valeur et de la dignité de l'Etat en tant que personne du droit des gens», see 'La responsabilité internationale des états...', 13 *Revue Générale de Droit International Public* (1906), pp. 13–14. This has been reaffirmed overtime, including in the *Rainbow Warrior* case, where the arbitral tribunal found that France's violation of its treaty obligations had caused non-material injury 'of a moral, political and legal nature' which was the result of 'affront to the dignity and prestige not only of New Zealand as such, but of its highest public authorities.' See *Case concerning the difference between New Zealand and France concerning the interpretation or application of two agreements, concluded on 9 July 1986 between the two States and which related to the problems arising from the Rainbow Warrior Affair* (New Zealand v France), 20 RIAA 215 (France-New Zealand Arbitration Tribunal) (30 April 1990), paras. 107–10.

50 See generally García-Amador et al., supra, note 2, pp. 94–95, paras. 45–47.

issued an apology to the King.[51] However, the insult need not come from non-State actors necessarily. In 1974, the US Treasury Secretary indicated that his comments on the Shah of Iran being 'a nut' were taken out of context.[52] Unconvinced, US Secretary of State and National Security Adviser Henry Kissinger asked him 'just exactly how do you call the 'King of Kings' a 'nut' out of context?' and, in response to Iran's letter of protest to President Nixon, Kissinger asked the Iranian Ambassador to 'convey to His Imperial Majesty our affection, regard, and mortification.'[53]

Manifestations of moral injury may also take the form of insults to the flag and emblems of a State, or insulting words or demonstrations against the State. These acts are symbolic in character as there is often no or negligible material injury arising from them.[54] In the mid-19th century *Petit Vaisseau* case, Brazil agreed to provide reparations after Brazilian customs officials had lowered the flag of an Italian ship upon its seizure.[55] Another example is when a crowd tore down the French flag from the French embassy in Berlin in 1920. Germany not only apologized and solemnly restored the flag, but it also offered a large reward for the capture of the individual who had torn down the flag, and subsequently punished him.[56] In another case in 1949, the US issued a declaration of regret to Cuba after US sailors climbed on the statue of José Marti, Cuba's war for independence hero.[57]

---

51 J. B. Moore, *A Digest of International Law as Embodied in Diplomatic Discussions, Treaties and Other International Agreements, International Awards, the Decisions of Municipal Courts, and the Writings of Jurists, and Especially in Documents, Published and Unpublished, Issued by Presidents and Secretaries of State of the United States, the Opinions of the Attorneys-General, and the Decisions of Courts, Federal and State*, Vol. VI, 1906, p. 864.

52 *Simon to Skirt 'nut' Meeting*, Chicago Tribune, July 16, 1974, cited by A. S. Cooper, *The Oil Kings, How the U.S., Iran, And Saudi Arabia Changed the Balance of Power in The Middle East*, 2011, p. 446.

53 A. S. Cooper, *The Oil Kings, How the U.S., Iran, And Saudi Arabia Changed the Balance of Power in The Middle East*, Simon & Schuster, 2011, pp. 176–177.

54 García-Amador et al., supra, note 2, p. 95, para. 47.

55 UN Doc. A/CN.4/425, 9 June 1989, 22 June 1989, para. 1010.

56 C. Eagleton, *The Responsibility of States in International Law*, 1928, pp. 186–87.

57 Yearbook of the International Law Commission, UN Doc. A/CN.4/SER.A/1993/Add.1 (Part 2), p. 79, citing P. A. Bissonnette, La satisfaction comme mode de reparation en droit international (thesis, University of Geneva) (Annemasse, Imprimerie Grandchamp, 1952), pp. 67–68.

3.1.2 Diplomatic and Consular Premises and Personnel

Whether generated by armed forces or by civilians, moral injuries may also involve diplomatic and consular premises or personnel. In 1908, Britain asked Persia to offer apologies as a result of its troops surrounding its embassy which was hosting political refugees.[58] In the 1920s, Hungary presented its apologies to Yugoslavia for the hostile demonstrations of a crowd outside the Budapest Yugoslav legation.[59] In the 1989 *Operation Nifty Package*, US forces successfully obtained Manuel Noriega's surrender from the Holy See's Panama Apostolic Nunciature where the former Panamanian leader had sought refuge. To do so, among other actions, the US forces beamed very loud psychedelic, heavy metal and punk rock music for ten days toward the Nunciature.[60] Interestingly, the Vatican does not seem to have officially asked for reparations.

While the aforementioned examples show no apparent case of trespassing upon the diplomatic premises, attack on diplomatic or consular personnel, they may also amount to a moral injury to the State. This can be seen in the early 1920s where Bulgaria agreed to meet Yugoslavia's demands for satisfaction following an attack on a military *attaché* accredited to the Yugoslavia embassy at Sofia.[61]

3.2 *Moral Injury Suffered by the State as a Result of Injury Caused to its Nationals*

As held by the PCIJ in the 1920s' *Mavrommatis* case, when the State asserts 'its own rights' while taking diplomatic steps or initiating judicial action against another State, it is in reality affirming 'its right to ensure, in the person of its subjects, respect for the rules of international law.'[62] Therefore, any injury caused to the person or property of a State's national simultaneously constitutes an injury to that State itself.[63]

---

58   C. Eagleton, 'The Responsibility of the State for the Protection of Foreign Officials', 19 *American Journal of International Law*, 1925, p. 297.
59   P. Fauchille, *Traité de Droit International Public*, Vol. I, Part I, Rousseau & Cie, 1923, p. 528.
60   *Panama's General Manuel Noriega and his fall from grace*, http://www.bbc.com/news/world-latin-america-15853540 (last visited on 24 December 2015).
61   Eagleton, supra, note 58, p. 299.
62   *The Mavrommatis Palestine Concessions* (Greece v United Kingdom), 1924 PCIJ (ser. A) No. 2, p. 12.
63   García-Amador et al., supra, note 2, p. 93, para. 41. See also Dickson Car Wheel Company (U.S.A.) v United Mexican States, 4 RIAA 669, (Mexico/U.S.A. General Claims Commission) July 1931, p. 678, where a Mexico/U.S.A. General Claims Commission held: 'The injury inflicted upon an individual, a national of the claimant State, which implies a violation of the obligations imposed by international law upon each member of the

However, in inter-States practice, this type of injury has not often been alleged, taken into consideration or resulted in reparations.[64] One early such case is *Jean Maninat*, where a French national was arrested in 1898, severely wounded and kept in close confinement for four days by Venezuelan armed forces before he was released following the intervention of Caracas.[65] One month later, he died as a result of the wounds inflicted.[66] The greater portion of the damages assessed by the France-Venezuela Claims Commission was due to France for the indignity it suffered as a result of the death of its national and the lack of punishment for those responsible for the acts.[67]

In the Eritrea-Ethiopia case, the EECC addressed Ethiopia's claim that 'moral injuries were suffered by hundreds of thousands of Ethiopians and by the State itself.'[68] Ethiopia argued that the EECC should take into account damage to the State's 'national interests and international standing in assessing the moral injury inflicted upon its nationals.'[69] The EECC did not consider moral injury in and of itself to constitute a distinct category of injury for the purposes of determining compensation. However, it stated that it would consider some of the factors involved in assessing moral injury—such as 'the gravity of a particular type of violation'—in awarding compensation for material harms.[70]

4   Conclusion

As demonstrated by the examples provided above, inter-States mechanisms have long recognized that States can directly suffer both material and moral injuries. In relation to the former, the typology has gone beyond the classical territorial sovereignty concept to include, as early as the 1930s and 1950s, cultural property and the natural environment—areas that one might have thought mattered less in earlier times. These inter-States mechanisms have similarly revealed their forward thinking with regards to moral injury. They have of course recognized moral injuries sustained by the State as a result of an injury caused

---

Community of Nations, constitutes an act internationally unlawful, because it signifies an offense against the State to which the individual is united by the bond of nationality.'
64   García-Amador et al., supra, note 2, p. 94, para. 43.
65   *Heirs of Jean Maninat Case* (France v Venezuela), 10 RIAA 55 (France-Venezuela Mixed Claims Commission), 31 July 1905, pp. 55 & 75.
66   Ibid., pp. 80–81.
67   Ibid., pp. 81–82.
68   26 RIAA 631, supra, note 21, para. 54.
69   Ibid., paras. 54–55.
70   Ibid., para. 65.

to it directly, including through insults and attacks against its Head, diplomatic or consular staff and premises. However, and more importantly, even in the 19th century, those mechanisms accepted that an injury caused to the person and property of a State's nationals may also amount to an injury indirectly suffered by that State itself.

By constantly rethinking its own foundations over decades, an initially Westphalian system has progressively paved the way for the materialization of less State-centric issues of crucial importance in the 21st century. This is evident both during armed activities and in times of peace as individuals now have standing through international humanitarian law and, more acutely, international criminal law. Likewise, these historical examples have also contributed to the development of the international legal protection of cultural property and the natural environment. Accordingly, this paper has sought to classify and focus upon the past practice of inter-States mechanisms in relation to direct injuries to States to demonstrate some of the historical legal roots of current issues and to highlight its ongoing relevance.

Réflexions sur l'immunité des États en matière civile

Lucius Caflisch

Le 21 novembre 2001, la Cour européenne des droits de l'homme (ci-après: Cour, Cour EDH ou Cour de Strasbourg) a failli prononcer un jugement qui aurait fait date dans l'histoire longue et mouvementée du précepte de l'immunité des Etats. Si cet arrêt avait été rendu dans le sens qu'on avait voulu initialement lui donner, il aurait peut-être recueilli l'approbation de l'Ami et Collègue auquel le présent volume est destiné. Il s'agit de l'arrêt *Al-Adsani* c. *Royaume-Uni*[1]. Il ne manquait qu'une seule voix pour parvenir à ce résultat, l'arrêt ayant finalement été adopté à la majorité étroite de neuf voix contre huit. La présente contribution vise à revenir sur cette affaire, à en rappeler les suites et à formuler quelques observations sur la Résolution adoptée par l'Institut de droit international le 30 août 2015 et relative à « La compétence universelle civile en matière de réparation pour crimes internationaux »[2].

1 L'affaire Al-Adsani c. Royaume-Uni

Soumis à la Grande Chambre de la Cour EDH, ce cas trouve son origine dans une requête présentée par M. Al-Adsani, double national britannique et koweïtien résidant au Royaume-Uni. Pilote de son métier, le requérant avait suivi un appel à l'aide de sa première patrie et participé à la Première Guerre du Golfe du côté des Alliés. Au cours de sa présence de l'Etat, des informations compromettantes pour la Maison régnante du Koweit tombèrent entre ses mains. Informés de ce fait, des agents de cet Etat s'emparèrent de lui, l'arrêtèrent et le torturaient. Par la suite, le requérant recouvra toutefois sa liberté à et regagna le Royaume-Uni.

Une fois rentré, M. Al-Adsani assigna l'Etat du Koweït devant les tribunaux civils britanniques afin d'obtenir une indemnité pour le préjudice souffert. Invoquant la règle de l'immunité de juridiction des Etats étrangers, ces tribunaux refusèrent toutefois de d'examiner l'affaire, ce qui incita le demandeur à

---

[1] Arrêt du 21 novembre 2001, *Al-Adsani c. Royaume-Uni* [GC], No. 35763/97.
[2] *Annuaire de l'Institut de droit international*, vol. 76, Editions A. Pedone, 2015 (session de Tallinn) (ci-après : *Annuaire* 2015), p. 263.

saisir la Cour de Strasbourg[3]. Devant celle-ci, il allégua que le Royaume-Uni avait enfreint l'article 6.1 de la Convention européenne des droits de l'homme (ci-après: CEDH, la Convention)[4] en lui refusant l'accès aux tribunaux britanniques, accès qui aurait dû permettre au requérant de se plaindre d'une entorse à l'article 3 de la Convention qui prohibe la torture de même que les peines et traitements inhumains ou dégradants[5].

Dans son arrêt, la Grande Chambre de la Cour constate que l'accès aux juridictions internes garanti à l'article 6.1 de la CEDH est régi par le droit national de chaque Etat partie. Ce dernier peut apporter certaines restrictions à l'exercice de ce droit; autrement dit, les Etats parties à la Convention jouissent d'une certaine marge d'appréciation en la matière. Il faut toutefois veiller, précise la Grande Chambre, à ce que ces restrictions visent un but légitime et qu'il y ait un degré de proportionnalité raisonnable entre le but poursuivi par la restriction et les moyens utilisés pour atteindre ce but (§ 53).

Passant au cas d'espèce, la Grande Chambre estime que la règle de l'immunité des Etats a pour but légitime d'assurer le respect des règles du droit des gens concernant la souveraineté de l'Etat (§ 54). Puis, se référant à l'article 31.3.c de la Convention de Vienne du 23 mai 1969 relative au droit des traités[6], elle explique que la CEDH, et notamment son article 6.1, doit être interprétée compte tenu des « principes pertinents » du droit international et de façon à concilier ses dispositions avec les autres règles de ce droit (§ 56).

---

3 L'affaire fut d'abord portée devant une chambre de la Troisième Section de la Cour qui, se fondant sur l'article 30 de la Convention européenne des droits de l'homme du 4 novembre 1950, Série des traités européens, n° 5 (ci-après: CEDH), s'en dessaisit en faveur de la Grande Chambre de la Cour.

4 L'article 6.1 a la teneur suivante: « Toute personne a droit à ce que sa cause soit entendue équitablement, publiquement et dans un délai raisonnable, par un tribunal indépendant et impartial, établi par la loi, qui décidera, soit des contestations sur ses droits et obligations de caractère civil, soit du bien-fondé de toute accusation en matière pénale dirigée contre elle. Le jugement doit être rendu publiquement, mais l'accès de la salle d'audience peut être interdit à la presse et au public pendant la totalité ou une partie du procès dans l'intérêt de la moralité, de l'ordre public ou de la sécurité nationale dans une société démocratique, lorsque les intérêts des mineurs ou la protection de la vie privée des parties au procès l'exigent, ou dans la mesure jugée strictement nécessaire par le tribunal, lorsque dans des circonstances spéciales la publicité serait de nature à porter atteinte aux intérêts de la justice ».

5 Voir le texte de l'article 3: « Nul ne peut être soumis à la torture ni à des peines ou traitements inhumains ou dégradants ». Nations Unies, *Recueil des traités,* vol. 1465, p. 85.

6 Nations Unies, *Recueil des traités,* vol. 1155, p. 331. Selon la disposition en cause, il sera tenu compte, en même temps que du contexte, « [d]e toute règle pertinente de droit international applicable dans les relations entre les parties ».

La Cour examine ensuite l'argument du requérant suivant lequel l'immunité de juridiction des Etats doit trouver sa limite là où elle aura une incidence sur les actions civiles en réparation consécutives à des actes de torture. Selon le requérant, il en va ainsi parce que, contrairement aux règles sur l'immunité des Etats, l'interdiction de la torture prononcée à l'article 3 de la CEDH est de caractère péremptoire (*jus cogens*) et, de ce fait, doit l'emporter sur les règles dispositives du droit international, telles que celles relatives à l'immunité des Etats[7]. La Grande Chambre souligne l'importance de l'interdiction de la torture prononcée à l'article 3 – qui est impérative – ; mais elle ajoute, et c'est ici que les choses prennent un tournant discutable, que les décisions dans les affaires *Pinochet* (*n° 3*)[8] et *Furundzija*[9] portaient sur la responsabilité *pénale* résultant d'actes accomplis par des individus pour le compte d'un Etat et non sur des conséquences *civiles* d' actes de torture (§ 61). A l'appui de cette thèse, la Chambre se prévaut de l'attitude du Comité spécial sur les immunités juridictionnelles des Etats et de leurs biens de la Commission du droit international[10], attitude qui a consisté à accorder la priorité à l'immunité dans la plupart des cas (§ 62). Elle explique ensuite que le « Foreign Sovereign Immunity Act » (amendé) des Etats-Unis et la décision en l'affaire *Pinochet* n'ont pas suffi pour accréditer la thèse selon laquelle les Etats seraient privés d'immunité en tant que défendeurs dans le cadre de procès *civils* consécutifs à des actes de torture. De plus, pour ce qui est de la législation américaine amendée, l'exception à l'immunité qui s'applique en cas de violations graves des droits de l'homme n'est accepté que si le Secrétaire d'Etat confirme que l'Etat étranger concerné cautionne le terrorisme et que le plaignant est ressortissant des Etats-Unis[11]. En outre, la nécessité même où l'on s'est trouvé d'amender la loi américaine « semble confirmer la persistance de la règle générale » en la matière (§ 63 à 64).

---

7   Sur le *jus cogens*, voir tout dernièrement D. D. Tladi, « Premier Rapport sur le *jus cogens* », Nations Unies, Assemblée générale, document A/CN.4/693 du 8 mars 2016.

8   *International Law Reports*, vol. 119, p. 135.

9   *Ministère public* c. *Furundzija*, affaire IT-95-17/1-T (1998), *International Legal Materials*, American Society of International Law, vol. 38, 1999, p. 317.

10 Voir les Rapports du Comité spécial sur les immunités juridictionnelles des Etats et de leurs biens, des 11 février 2002, 27 février 2003 et 5 mars 2004, documents des Nations Unies A/AC.262/L.2, Annexe, et A/AC.262/L.4, Add. 1, ainsi que Nations Unies, Assemblée générale, Documents officiels, 59ᵉ session, Supplément n° 22 (A/59/22), Annexe I. 1985.

11 *International Legal Materials*, American Society of International Law, vol. 25, 1986, p. 715. L'« Anti-Terrorism and Effective Death Penalty Act » de 1996 (110 Stat. 1214) limite l'immunité des Etats étrangers lorsqu'il s'agit de demandes en réparation de préjudices causés par des actes de torture, des exécutions extrajudiciaires et certains autres actes, mais ces limites font elles-mêmes l'objet des exceptions indiquées dans le texte.

Pour terminer, la Chambre revient sur l'affaire *Pinochet* pour préciser que celle-ci concernait l'aspect *pénal* de la responsabilité *ratione materiae* d'un ancien chef d'Etat et non l'immunité d'un Etat sur le plan *civil*.

Ce raisonnement amène la Grande Chambre à constater que l'attitude des juridictions britanniques ne constituait pas une restriction injustifiée du droit d'accès aux tribunaux protégé par l'article 6.1 de la CEDH, même si ce droit, comme dans le présent cas, était revendiqué dans le cadre d'une violation du *jus cogens* contenu à l'article 3 de la Convention.

Ce résultat, approuvé par une majorité de neuf juges contre huit[12], a poussé six juges à rédiger une opinion dissidente commune[13]. Cette opinion commence par citer un arrêt rendu en 1983 déjà par le Tribunal fédéral suisse[14], qui avait qualifié de *jus cogens* l'interdiction de la torture, ce qui signifiait, selon les juges dissidents, que l'interdiction, étant impérative, devait l'emporter sur les règles dispositives du droit international, y compris celles relatives à l'immunité. Cela signifiait que les règles en question cessaient d'être applicables, l'Etat du Koweït ne pouvant plus désormais s'abriter derrière le voile de l'immunité et les tribunaux britanniques n'ayant plus la possibilité de reconnaître cette immunité.

L'opinion dissidente commune critique la distinction faite entre poursuites pénales et actions civiles, distinction qui avait permis à la majorité d'affirmer que, sur le *plan pénal*, l'interdiction de la torture figurant à l'article 3 de la CEDH et susceptible d'être mise en œuvre à l'aide de l'article 6.1 de cette Convention était absolue et l'emportait sur l'immunité, mais que cette dernière persistait sur le plan *civil*. L'opinion dissidente commune mentionne deux raisons pour repousser cette distinction. Premièrement, celle-ci a été ignorée par la pratique internationale. En second lieu, elle va à l'encontre du but même visé par des règles impératives du droit international telles que l'interdiction de la torture : ces règles doivent prévaloir sur l'immunité de juridiction des Etats, *quelle que soit la nature* – pénale ou civile – *de la procédure*. On voit mal, en effet, pourquoi l'Etat étranger serait assujetti à la juridiction des tribunaux locaux pour des actes de caractère pénal mais soustrait à cette juridiction lorsqu'il s'agit de demandes d'indemnisation – civiles – liées à de tels actes. De plus,

---

12   Judges Palm, Jörundsson, Jungwiert, Bratza, Zupančič, Pellonpää, Tsatsa-Nikolovska, Levits et Kovler.

13   Juges Rozakis et Caflisch, auxquels se rallient les juges Wildhaber, Costa, Cabral Barreto et Vajić. A cette opinion dissidente, on ajoutera celles de MM. Ferrari Bravo et Loucaides.

14   *Sener c. Département fédéral de justice et police,* arrêt du 22 mars 1983, Arrêts du Tribunal fédéral 109 Ib 64 (72), « Pratique suisse 1983 », n° 1.1, *Annuaire suisse de droit international,* vol. XL, 1984, p. 118.

si l'on a vu de nombreuses actions civiles contre des Etats étrangers soumises aux tribunaux locaux, il n'y a guère eu de procédures *pénales* cela s'explique essentiellement par la nature même de l'Etat, dont la responsabilité sur le plan international n'a pas de caractère spécifiquement pénal. Opérer la distinction proposée par la majorité de la Grande Chambre revenait, en pratique, à priver de sens et d'effet la responsabilité internationale de l'Etat pour des actes de torture. Les six juges dissidents concluent donc à la violation de l'article 6.1 de la CEDH par le Royaume-Uni. Le regretté juge Ferrari Bravo, qui dit partager les vues de la minorité, ajoute que la majorité, prisonnière d'un formalisme excessif, a galvaudé l'occasion de prononcer une condamnation nette et forte de la torture et a ainsi manqué de courage. On ne saurait dire mieux, sauf peut-être en ajoutant que derrière les explications données par la majorité on sent une volonté délibérée de freiner la tendance contemporaine à réduire l'immunité de juridiction des Etats étrangers à un minimum.

L'affaire qui vient d'être décrite offrait à la Cour de Strasbourg une occasion rêvée d'ouvrir aux victimes d'actes de torture l'accès aux tribunaux étatiques pour obtenir au moins la réparation du préjudice causé par ces actes, la voie pénale restant pratiquement fermée. Comme l'a noté le juge Ferrari Bravo, la Cour EDH a manqué de courage; elle a aussi manqué de sagacité; et son argumentation paraît peu solide.

2 La Confirmation : Jones et autres c. Royaume-Uni

L'affaire *Jones et autres* c. *Royaume-Uni*, décidée dans un arrêt du 14 janvier 2014 par la Quatrième Chambre de la Cour EDH[15], se rapporte à une situation factuelle semblable à celle de l'affaire *Al-Adsani*. Il s'est agi, dans le cas *Jones*, d'un ressortissant britannique blessé en 2001 à Riad (Arabie saoudite) par l'explosion d'une bombe. A sa sortie d'hôpital, le requérant fut pris en charge par des agents saoudiens, placé en détention pendant 67 jours, entendu par un officier saoudien et torturé. En 2002, il assigna l'Etat saoudien et l'officier en question devant les tribunaux britanniques. Ces derniers faisaient valoir que l'Etat et l'officier en cause étaient couverts par l'immunité. Invoquant l'arrêt *Al-Adsani*, la Quatrième Chambre conclut qu'on ne pouvait établir l'existence, en droit international, d'un principe selon lequel les Etats ne jouiraient d'aucune immunité à propos de réclamations civiles consécutives à des actes de torture.

---

15 Arrêt du 14 janvier 2014, *Jones et autres c. Royaume Uni*, n°s 34356/06 et 40528/06, rendu à six voix contre une, celle de la juge Kalaydjeva, qui fait écho à l'opinion dissidente du juge Ferrari Bravo dans l'affaire *Al-Adsani*.

A l'appui de cette conclusion, la Chambre cita l'arrêt d'une autre chambre de la même Cour dans l'affaire *Kalogeropoulou et autres* c. *Grèce et Allemagne*[16]. Ce litige portait sur le refus du Ministre grec de la Justice de permettre aux requérants, victimes de crimes contre l'humanité commis par l'Allemagne en 1944, de faire saisir des biens allemands situés en Grèce. Cependant, ajouta la Chambre, la jurisprudence de la Cour EDH dans *Al-Adsani* n'était pas immuable et on ne pouvait exclure que le droit international évolue dans le sens suggéré par les requérants.

3 La jurisprudence de la Cour internationale de Justice : l'affaire des Immunites juridictionnelles des Etats

3.1 *L'arrêt de la Cour*

Le cas des *Indemnités juridictionnelles des Etats*[17], opposant l'Allemagne à l'Italie, est lié à l'affaire *Kalogeropoulou*. Il a été soumis à la Cour internationale de Justice (ci-après: CIJ) par l'Allemagne, qui se plaignait du refus des tribunaux italiens de lui accorder l'immunité de juridiction lorsqu'ils avaient procédé à hypothéquer des biens appartenant à l'Etat allemand situés en Italie pour satisfaire les revendications civiles de citoyens italiens qui avaient été déportés en Allemagne au cours de la Seconde Guerre mondiale et forcés à travailler dans l'industrie de production d'armes. L'Allemagne se plaignait aussi du fait que l'Italie avait déclaré exécutoires sur son territoire des jugements de tribunaux grecs rendus dans des circonstances similaires, ce qui revenait également à violer l'immunité de l'Etat allemand – reproche qui explique l'intervention grecque dans cette affaire[18].

Dans ses grandes lignes, l'arrêt de la Cour, qui accueille les conclusions de l'Allemagne, confirme la jurisprudence *Al-Adsani*. Dans son arrêt, la CIJ commence par constater (§ 54 à 57) que la souveraineté de l'Etat est protégée par une règle coutumière solidement ancrée dans la pratique des Etats, comme l'a relevé, en 1980, la Commission du droit international (CDI)[19] et comme l'a confirmé la Convention des Nations Unies du 2 décembre 2004 sur l'immunité

---

16 Arrêt du 12 décembre 2002, *Kalogeropoulou et autres* c *Grèce et Allemagne*, n° 5902/00, Première Section.

17 Affaire des *Immunités juridictionnelles de l'Etat (Allemagne c. Italie ; Grèce (intervenant))*, arrêt du 3 février 2012, *CIJ Rec. 2012*, p. 99.

18 Sur cette intervention, voir l'ordonnance du 4 juillet 2011, *CIJ Rec. 2011*, p. 494.

19 Voir le commentaire 26 à l'article 6, cité au § 56 de l'arrêt de la Cour, *Annuaire de la Commission de droit international*, 1980, vol. II/2, p. 144.

juridictionnelle des Etats et de leurs biens[20]. L'Allemagne avait prétendu que le droit applicable à ce cas était celui en vigueur à l'époque allant de 1943 à 1945, alors que l'Italie avait estimé que c'était au droit applicable lors des procédures devant les tribunaux italiens qu'il fallait se référer. Sur ce premier point, la Cour décide de retenir la thèse italienne (§ 58).

Les parties étaient en désaccord sur deux autres questions : 1) Quelle était la portée du principe de l'immunité des Etats étrangers: incluait-il les activités des forces armées (et d'autres organismes de l'Etat coopérant avec celles-ci) ? L'Allemagne prétendait que si; l'Italie était d'un avis contraire. 2) Le refus de l'immunité était-il justifié, comme le prétendait l'Italie et comme l'Allemagne le contestait, eu égard à la nature des réclamations adressées aux tribunaux italiens et aux circonstances entourant leur formulation ?

Le premier point est celui de l'applicabilité du principe de l'immunité aux actes commis par les forces armées d'un Etat étranger. Examinant ce point sous l'angle de la Convention européenne du 16 mars 1972 sur l'immunité des Etats[21] et sous celui de la Convention précitée de 2004, la Cour pense que le contenu ni de l'un ni de l'autre instrument ne permet d'affirmer que le principe est inapplicable aux situations de conflit armé. Pour ce qui est de la pratique des Etats telle qu'elle ressort des législations nationales, la CIJ admet que, d'une manière générale, l'Etat étranger ne peut se prévaloir de son immunité quand il s'agit d'actes délictueux causant la mort ou des lésions corporelles, ou d'un préjudice matériel infligé sur le territoire de l'Etat du for; mais elle garde le silence sur les activités des forces armées étrangères. Cela étant, et vu la jurisprudence de la Cour EDH en la matière, la CIJ parvient à la conclusion que le droit international coutumier continue à couvrir d'immunité les actes des forces armées étrangères et que l'« exception territoriale » (« tort exception »)[22] n'est pas applicable dans ce contexte (§ 62 à 79).

Le second point litigieux est l'argument de l'Italie suivant lequel le refus de l'immunité par les tribunaux italiens est justifié par les circonstances particulières entourant les revendications adressées aux tribunaux internationaux et

---

20   Résolution 59 / 38 du 2 décembre 2004.
21   *Recueil systématique du droit fédéral suisse* (RS) 0.273.1.
22   Voir l'article 12 de la Convention de 2004, qui prévoit ceci : « A moins que les Etats concernés n'en conviennent autrement, un Etat ne peut invoquer l'immunité de juridiction devant un tribunal d'un autre Etat, compétent en l'espèce, dans une procédure se rapportant à une action en réparation pécuniaire en cas de décès ou d'atteinte à l'intégrité physique d'une personne, ou en cas de dommage ou de perte d'un bien corporel, dus à un acte ou à une omission prétendument attribuables à l'Etat, si cet acte ou cette omission se sont produits, en totalité ou en partie, sur le territoire de cet autre Etat et si l'auteur de l'acte ou de l'omission était présent sur ce territoire au moment de l'acte ou de l'omission ».

par les circonstances dans lesquelles elles avaient été présentés, à savoir: a) la gravité des violations commises; b) la relation entre *jus cogens* et règle de l'immunité; et c) le fait que l'attitude des tribunaux italiens découle du refus de l'Allemagne de dédommager les individus concernés (§ 80).

Selon l'Italie, une règle du droit international refuse l'immunité, ou du moins la limite, quand l'Etat qui s'en prévaut s'est rendu coupable de violations graves du droit des conflits armés. Cela étant, on se demande si une telle règle existe effectivement. La CIJ répond par la négative, en soulignant que sa réponse vaut pour l'immunité de l'Etat comme tel ; le point de savoir si elle est également valable pour les procédures pénales contre des fonctionnaires de l'Etat concerné ne nécessite pas de réponse pour régler le présent cas (§ 81 à 91).

Quant au conflit entre *jus cogens* et immunité des Etats que l'Italie invoque pour établir que l'Allemagne ne peut se prévaloir de l'immunité, la Cour estime qu'il n'existe pas, les deux catégories de règles se rapportant à des domaines différents. Les règles sur l'immunité sont de nature procédurale et visent la question de la compétence des tribunaux locaux; elles ne portent pas sur la question de savoir si la conduite de l'Etat étranger a été licite ou non. Le caractère illicite des actes commis de 1943 à 1945 est admis par tous, mais le débat sur le point de savoir si les tribunaux italiens pouvaient juger de ces actes n'a rien à voir avec l'argument suivant lequel le *jus cogens* l'emporterait sur le droit à l'immunité. Selon la Cour de La Haye, les tribunaux italiens sont seuls à avoir accepté cet argument (§ 92 à 97).

L'argument du « dernier ressort » consiste à affirmer que les tribunaux italiens pouvaient refuser l'immunité à l'Etat allemand parce que toutes les autres tentatives d'obtenir satisfaction avaient échoué. Cet argument est lui aussi rejeté par la Cour, qui n'a pas pu identifier de règle coutumière faisant dépendre l'immunité des Etats de l'existence de voies alternatives effectives; de plus, la CIJ relève que la mise en œuvre d'une telle condition pourrait présenter des difficultés, notamment dans des situations comme la présente, où les revendications des victimes ont fait l'objet de longues discussions entre les Gouvernements concernés (§ 98 à 104).

L'Italie fait également valoir que les trois volets de son second argument doivent être examinés conjointement en raison de l'effet cumulé des violations commises, qui ont déterminé l'attitude de ses tribunaux. La Cour note qu'aucun de ces éléments ne peut être retenu. De plus, si l'on tentait de balancer ces éléments et les intérêts qui fondent l'immunité, une telle approche serait contraire à la nature même de l'immunité (§ 105 à 106).

Tous ces arguments permettent de conclure, selon la CIJ, que l'attitude des tribunaux italiens a été contraire au droit international (§ 107 à 108). Il reste à examiner les mesures d'exécution relatives à l'immeuble situé en Italie et appartenant à l'Etat allemand. Aux termes de l'article 19 de la Convention précitée de 2004 et dans la mesure où cette disposition reflète le droit coutumier, l'immeuble ne pouvait faire l'objet de telles mesures que s'il était affecté à des utilisations non-gouvernementales par l'Etat étranger, si le Gouvernement propriétaire avait consenti aux mesures en cause ou s'il l'avait réservé à la satisfaction de réclamations qui lui seraient adressées. Puisque l'immeuble ainsi grevé par l'Italie devait servir à des fins culturelles, la mesure prise constitue une violation, par l'Italie, de son obligation de respecter l'immunité de l'Allemagne (§ 109 à 120). La Cour arrive à une conclusion similaire pour la décision d'accorder l'*exequatur* aux arrêts des tribunaux grecs (§ 121 à 133).

Ainsi la Cour décide: 1) par douze voix contre trois, que l'Italie a manqué à son obligation de respecter l'immunité de l'Etat allemand; 2) par quatorze voix contre une, que l'Italie a également enfreint cette obligation en prenant des mesures d'exécution forcée visant une villa située en Italie et appartenant à l'Allemagne; 3) par quatorze voix contre une, que l'Italie a violé cette immunité en déclarant exécutoires des décisions judiciaires grecques fondées sur des violations du droit international humanitaire commises par le *Reich* allemand en Grèce; 4) par la même majorité, que l'Italie doit veiller à ce que les décisions incriminées soient rapportées (§ 139).

3.2   *Les opinions dissidentes*

Une première opinion dissidente, dense et fouillée, est celle du juge Cançado Trindade[23] qui fustige la « myopie de la perspective strictement étatique » (§ 161 à 171), la « perspective interétatique viciée face à l'impératif de justice » (§ 172 à 176) et le maintien de la perspective strictement interétatique (§ 177 à 198), pour s'intéresser ensuite à certains massacres intervenus au cours de la Seconde Guerre mondiale, à la déportation de citoyens italiens et à leur affectation aux travaux forcés au sein d'usines d'armement (§ 192 à 198). Le juge Cançado Trindade fait état de la priorité du droit d'accès à la justice des individus (§ 199 à 210), de l'évolution de ce droit vers le statut de *jus cogens* (§ 214 à 226), de la primauté qui revient à la « *recta ratio* », y compris les garanties procédurales qui l'entourent (§ 227 à 239), et du droit de l'individu à la réparation du préjudice subi dans les cas de violations graves des droits de l'homme ou du droit international humanitaire (§ 240 à 281). Dans ce contexte, il examine 1) la réparation par l'Etat du préjudice souffert par les victimes (§ 257 à 259); 2) la détermination des catégories de victimes dans la présente espèce (§ 258 à 260); 3) le cadre juridique offert par la fondation allemande « Remembrance, Responsibility and Future » (2000), dont les victimes dans la présente affaire

---

23   *CIJ Recueil 2012*, p. 179.

n'ont pas pu bénéficier (§ 261 à 267); et 4) les conclusions des parties (§ 268 à 281). Il estime qu'il est impératif d'accorder réparation aux victimes de violations graves des droits de l'homme ou du droit international humanitaire (§ 282 à 287).

Le juge Cançado Trindade souscrit ainsi à la thèse selon laquelle l'immunité de juridiction de l'Etat étranger ne peut prévaloir face aux demandes de victimes qui ont subi, de la part de cet Etat, des violations graves des droits de l'homme ou du droit international humanitaire.

Dans son opinion dissidente[24] le juge Yusuf critique la Cour pour avoir affirmé (§ 100 de son arrêt) que « le fait que l'immunité puisse faire obstacle à l'exercice de la compétence judiciaire dans une affaire donnée est sans incidence sur l'application des règles matérielles du droit international ». Selon lui, la question qui peut être posée à cet égard

> est celle de savoir si, dans l'hypothèse où l'immunité serait accordée dans une affaire de cette nature, l'Etat défendeur serait tenu d'offrir aux victimes des violations qu'il a reconnues une voie de recours. Il s'agit là d'une question importante à laquelle une réponse aurait dû être apportée en cours d'instance ou dans l'arrêt.

De plus, l'auteur de cette opinion doute « qu'une mise en cause de la responsabilité n'offrant ni voie de recours ni système de réparation serait vraiment utile aux victimes » (§ 53).

Selon le juge Yusuf, la question qui se pose dans la présente affaire n'est pas celle de savoir s'il faut déroger à la règle de l'immunité chaque fois que des droits de l'homme ou le droit international humanitaire sont en cause. Ce qui importe, selon lui, c'est le point de savoir si, dans des circonstances exceptionnelles, quand l'immunité risque de priver les victimes de crimes internationaux de tout remède, elle peut être écartée par les juridictions nationales. « Autrement dit », poursuit le juge Yusuf,

> lorsque la réparation n'a pas été prévue par le biais d'un mécanisme spécifique, l'immunité devrait-elle [pouvoir] être utilisée comme un rempart contre l'obligation d'accorder réparation aux victimes ? (§ 56)

Dans de tels cas, estime-t-il (§ 59), c'est-à-dire dans les circonstances de la présente affaire, où les violations ont été reconnues par l'Etat défendeur et aucun mécanisme spécifique d'indemnisation n'est intervenu, une décision des

---

24 Ibid., p. 291.

instances nationales de se déclarer compétentes n'est pas de nature à perturber les relations interétatiques harmonieuses mais, au contraire, contribue au respect des droits de l'homme et du droit humanitaire.

L'opinion dissidente du juge Yusuf repose sur une base relativement étroite. Elle assigne aux tribunaux internes un rôle important dans la formulation des règles relatives à l'immunité. Elle affirme le droit de ces tribunaux à faire abstraction de l'immunité dans des cas extrêmes afin de prévenir des dénis de justice et de favoriser ainsi le respect des droits de l'homme et du droit international humanitaire.

Reste l'opinion dissidente du juge ad hoc Gaja,[25] qui aborde l'affaire sous l'angle de l'« exception territoriale » ('tort exception') inscrite à l'article 11 de la Convention européenne précitée de 1972 et à l'article 12 de la Convention de 2004 sur les immunités juridictionnelles des Etats[26]. Ayant examiné la pratique des Etats, l'auteur de cette opinion conclut que l'on ne peut clairement établir que les activités militaires sont exclues du domaine déterminé par l'article 12 de la Convention de 2004, c'est-à-dire comprises dans le champ de l'immunité, de sorte que les tribunaux nationaux peuvent adopter des attitudes différentes « sans nécessairement s'écarter des prescriptions du droit international général » (§ 9). Le juge Gaja se demande du reste pourquoi on hésiterait à exclure les activités militaires de l'exception formulée par l'article 12 : pourquoi, en effet, créer un régime de faveur pour des activités hostiles à l'Etat territorial (§ 9) ? Ce qui milite contre un tel régime, c'est aussi la nature de l'obligation prétendument violée (§ 10). Il est vrai que ce n'est pas tant le caractère de *jus cogens* de la règle enfreinte qui est en cause mais le droit d'accès à la réparation, qui n'est pas forcément de *jus cogens*. Mais, puisqu'on se trouve dans une « zone d'incertitude », il est concevable que, même si les activités militaires menées par un Etat sur le territoire d'un autre sont en principe soustraites à l'exception territoriale – c'est-à-dire protégées par l'immunité –, il n'en irait pas de même dans les cas portant sur des massacres de civils ou des actes de torture commis sur le territoire de l'Etat où se trouvent les victimes. Il serait en revanche plus difficile de justifier une entorse à l'immunité de l'Etat étranger pour des actes accomplis à n'importe quel endroit (§ 11).

Le juge Gaja arrive ainsi à la conclusion que, vu les enseignements tirés de la pratique, la nature de la violation ne suffit pas à justifier l'exercice de sa compétence par un tribunal dès que celui-ci est confronté à des comportements contraires à des règles impératives du droit international et quel que ce soit leur lieu. A l'inverse, on ne saurait admettre que la nature des actes perpétrés

---

25   Ibid., p. 309.
26   Voir supra, notes 20 et 21.

n'a aucune incidence sur la définition du champ d'application de l'exception territoriale (§ 11). La Cour aurait dû examiner de façon plus approfondie et à la lumière des faits de chaque espèce les décisions des juridictions italiennes, ce qui aurait conduit à la conclusion, pour au moins certaines d'entre elles, que l'exercice de leur juridiction par ces entités ne pouvait être contraire à une obligation de droit international général (§ 12).

Cette dernière opinion dissidente est fondée sur l'exception territoriale et sur le sens qui peut lui être attribué par les juridictions nationales dans telle ou telle situation.

La conclusion générale qui découle des trois opinions dissidentes est qu'il y a plus d'une manière d'expliquer l'attitude des tribunaux italiens sans y voir des violations du droit international lorsque certaines conditions sont réunies, notamment quand il n'y a plus d'autre moyen pour venir en aide aux victimes de violations graves des droits de l'homme ou du droit international humanitaire. Dans ces conditions, l'accès à la justice semble indispensable; c'est le refus d'un tel accès qui est injustifiable.

3.3   *Les critiques doctrinales*

La CIJ a également été critiqué par la doctrine, en particulier par A. Carrillo-Salcedo, ancien juge de la Cour EDH, qui regrette que la Cour de La Haye ait manqué l'occasion de s'associer à l'idée selon laquelle

> l'immunité devrait être rejetée en cas de mort ou de dommages corporels résultant d'actes qu'un Etat aurait commis au mépris des normes impératives en matière de droits de l'homme ou de la conduite des conflits armés[27].

Ce disant, l'auteur attire l'attention sur une résolution adoptée le 10 septembre 2009 par l'Institut de droit international et intitulée « L'immunité de juridiction de l'Etat et de ses agents en cas de crimes internationaux »[28]. Dans ce texte, l'Institut a soutenu que les immunités sont octroyées aux Etats dans le but de sauvegarder leur égalité souveraine, mais qu'elles « ne devraient pas faire obstacle à la réparation adéquate à laquelle ont droit les victimes de crimes internationaux ».

---

27   J.-A. Carrillo-Salcedo, « Les immunités de juridiction des Etats devant la Cour internationale de justice: permanence et regrettable primauté de la souveraineté dans l'arrêt du 3 février 2012 », Académie de droit international de La Haye (Dir.), *Le 90ᵉ anniversaire de Boutros Boutros-Ghali*, Leyde, Nijhoff, 2012, p. 53-57 (56).

28   Article II.2, *Annuaire de l'Institut de droit international*, vol. 73, 2009, p. 228.

La Cour, poursuit Carrillo-Salcedo, n'a pas davantage accepté l'argument italien suivant lequel les règles de *jus cogens* prévalent toujours sur les règles dispositives du droit international, y compris celles relatives à l'immunité des Etats. Selon la CIJ, les deux types de règles appartiennent à des espèces différentes: les règles sur l'immunité, qui ont un caractère procédural et se limitent à indiquer quand les tribunaux d'un Etat sont habilités à exercer leur juridiction à l'égard d'un autre Etat; et celles relatives à la licéité du comportement de ce dernier. Les premières n'ont, selon la Cour, aucune incidence sur les secondes. C'est là, selon Carrillo-Salcedo, une conclusion regrettable car les violations graves du *jus cogens* devraient entraîner une restriction de l'immunité. Et l'auteur de conclure que

> [l]a Cour est donc restée dans une conception traditionnelle du droit international, droit destiné à régir les relations de coexistence et de coopération entre des Etats souverains, sans tirer les conséquences qui dérivent du processus d'humanisation et l'ordre international et de l'existence de règles impératives en droit international contemporain[29].

Cette critique paraît justifiée.

Il reste maintenant à examiner les observations d'Andreas Bucher, auteur d'un rapport intitulé « La compétence universelle civile en matière de réparation pour crimes internationaux », rapport adressé à l'Institut de droit international en 2015[30] qui a conduit à l'adoption, au cours de la même année, d'une résolution par l'Institut lors de sa session de Tallinn.

4   Le Rapport Bucher et les suites

Le Projet de résolution initial soumis par A. Bucher, Rapporteur, à la Première Commission de l'Institut contenait six articles[31]. *L'article premier* disposait que les victimes de crimes internationaux ayant porté atteinte à leur dignité humaine[32] avaient droit à une réparation appropriée et effective et, dans ce but, devaient disposer d'un accès effectif à la justice. Selon *l'article 2*, un Etat devait accepter la compétence civile universelle de ses tribunaux pour traiter les demandes en réparation, à condition qu'aucun autre Etat n'ait des « intérêts

---

29   Carrillo-Salcedo, *op. cit.* (note 27), p. 57.
30   *Annuaire* 2015, p. 1.
31   Ibid., p. 133.
32   Dont la torture, voir l'article 3 de la CEDH reproduit à la note 5.

prépondérants » pour en connaître, ou, dans l'hypothèse d'un ou de plusieurs autres Etats ayant de tels intérêts, qu'aucun de ces Etats n'offre des moyens de recours « raisonnablement disponibles », c'est-à-dire des moyens permettant d'examiner les demandes des victimes et prévoyant une procédure équitable pour obtenir une réparation appropriée et effective[33]. Un tribunal étatique pouvait toutefois décliner sa compétence ou surseoir à statuer lorsque les demandes des victimes avaient déjà été soumises à une instance internationale, telle la Cour pénale internationale, à une autorité internationale d'indemnisation ou aux tribunaux d'un autre Etat ayant des « intérêts prépondérants » et offrant un moyen de recours « raisonnablement disponible ».

Aux termes de *l'article 3*, les Etats étaient invités à lever autant que possible les obstacles juridiques et financiers rencontrés par les victimes, tandis que *l'article 4* les encourageait à établir des procédures permettant à des collectivités de victimes de crimes internationaux de présenter des demandes communes (« class actions »). Dans la perspective de la présente contribution, une disposition particulièrement importante était *l'article 5* du Projet, ainsi libellé: « L'immunité de l'Etat ne doit pas rendre sans effet l'obligation de l'Etat de réparer le préjudice causé aux victimes de crimes internationaux ». On notera le caractère impératif des termes employés (« l'Etat ne *doit* pas »). *L'article 6*, enfin, recommandait que, lors de l'élaboration d'instruments relatifs à l'exécution des jugements en matière commerciale, en particulier par la Conférence de droit international privé de La Haye, le droit d'accès à la justice des victimes de crimes internationaux soit pris en compte.

On ne saurait essayer de décrire la totalité des arguments avancés par le Rapporteur à l'appui de son Projet. On se limitera donc à ceux qui pouvaient avoir une incidence sur la matière traitée à l'article 5 du Projet et qui résultent d'une analyse détaillée de l'arrêt de la CIJ relatif à l'affaire des *Immunités juridictionnelles*[34].

Le Rapporteur de la Première Commission de l'Institut commence par indiquer que le juge saisi par une victime des agissements d'un Etat étranger doit déterminer si l'on se trouve dans le domaine du *jus gestionis* ou dans celui du *jus imperii*, ce dont la CIJ semble peu sûre puisqu'elle indique qu'elle

> doit néanmoins rechercher si le droit international coutumier a évolué au point d'interdire à un Etat de se prévaloir de son immunité en cas de violations graves des droits de l'homme ou du droit des conflits armés (§ 83).

---

33   Voir l'article 6.1 reproduit à la note 4.
34   Voir le Rapport de A. Bucher, « La compétence universelle civile en matière de réparation pour crimes internationaux », *Annuaire* 2015, p. 109-127, par. 213-245.

Mais le résultat de cet examen sera entièrement négatif (§ 91 de l'arrêt), malgré la formule contraire figurant à l'article 8 de la Déclaration universelle des droits de l'homme[35]. Cela tiendrait au fait, selon la Cour, que la jurisprudence considérée – essentiellement européenne – est négative et que les exceptions à l'immunité alléguées par l'Italie ne figurent pas dans la Convention précitée de 2004. En revanche, la CIJ omet de mentionner le fait que l'immunité ne peut pas être invoquée devant des juridictions pénales. Or, note Bucher, il est contradictoire de constater une volonté des Etats de faire punir les crimes internationaux par les tribunaux pénaux internationaux et d'affirmer en même temps que cette volonté ne révèle aucune intention des Etats d'en faire de même pour leurs tribunaux nationaux. Les développements qui permettraient aux victimes de crimes internationaux d'accéder à la justice ne peuvent donc s'appuyer ni sur une pratique des Etats ni sur une *opinio juris*. Ainsi serait démentie l'affirmation, faite par le Tribunal pénal international pour l'Ex-Yougoslavie dans l'affaire *Furundzija*, que les dispositions du Statut de ce Tribunal sont « indisputably declaratory of customary international law »[36].

La jurisprudence, dit la CIJ, a toujours écarté l'idée d'une primauté du *jus cogens* par rapport aux règles relatives à l'immunité de l'Etat. Mais tel n'est pas le cas de la jurisprudence citée par le Rapporteur Bucher[37], ni de celle de la Cour constitutionnelle italienne qui a déclaré inconstitutionnelle une loi italienne enjoignant aux tribunaux italiens de respecter l'arrêt de la CIJ[38].

Dans son arrêt relatif aux *Immunités juridictionnelles*, la Cour de La Haye distingue l'immunité de l'Etat de son éventuelle responsabilité, ce qui signifierait que « l'immunité de juridiction permet d'échapper non seulement à un jugement défavorable mais aussi au procès lui-même », et aussi entre l'obligation de réparer et les « moyens par lesquels il doit lui être donné effet »[39]; l'immunité ne porterait que sur ces moyens et non sur l'obligation au fond. Ainsi l'immunité de l'Etat peut aboutir au non-respect de l'obligation de réparer, sans toutefois mettre en doute l'existence de cette dernière. Or, comme le note Bucher, s'il n'est pas donné effet à cette obligation, cela doit signifier que

---

35 Déclaration adoptée par l'Assemblée générale des Nations Unies dans sa Résolution du 10 décembre 1948, A/RES/217A (III). Texte dans: Conseil de l'Europe (Dir.), *Droits de l'homme en droit international*, 3ᵉ éd., Strasbourg, 2007, p. 11.

36 Voir *Ministère public* c. *Furundzija, op. cit.*, note 9, p. 347.

37 Voir le Rapport de A. Bucher, « La compétence universelle civile en matière de réparation pour crimes internationaux », Annuaire 2015, p. 114-115, par. 223-224.

38 Voir l'arrêt n° 238 du 22 octobre 2014, *Rivista di diritto internazionale*, vol. XCVIII, 2015, p. 237.

39 Affaire des *Immunités juridictionnelles de l'Etat (Allemagne c. Italie ; Grèce : intervenant)*, arrêt du 3 février 2012, § 82 et 94.

l'obligation n'est pas encourue. L'arrêt relatif au *Mandat d'arrêt (République démocratique du Congo c. Belgique)* du 14 février 2002[40] affirme pourtant que l'immunité de juridiction accordée à un ministre des affaires étrangères en exercice n'entraîne pas son impunité pour les crimes qu'il a pu commettre (§ 60), car l'immunité peut s'effacer dans certaines hypothèses : lorsque le ministre est traduit devant les juridictions de son propre pays, que son immunité a été levée, qu'il a cessé ses fonctions ou qu'il fait l'objet de poursuites devant un tribunal pénal international. Mais aucune de ces hypothèses n'est réalisée dans la présente espèce. Si, dans l'affaire du *Mandat d'arrêt*, plusieurs possibilités restaient donc ouvertes, toutes les portes demeuraient closes pour les autorités et victimes italiennes dans la présente affaire. La Cour n'a pas fait état de cette différence dans son arrêt sur les *Immunités juridictionnelles*, sauf à relever que les victimes ne disposaient d'aucune voie judiciaire et ne pouvaient qu'espérer de nouvelles négociations.

Au lieu d'ainsi éconduire les victimes, la CIJ aurait dû, selon Bucher, chercher à identifier une voie pouvant être utilisée par elles. En l'état actuel des choses, l'obligation de réparer était impossible à mettre en œuvre, d'où la conclusion qu'en fait il n'y en avait pas[41]. Une telle obligation n'est effective que si les victimes disposent d'un moyen judiciaire pour obtenir réparation; l'accès à la justice doit être protégé par le droit international tout autant que l'immunité de l'Etat. Il n'y a pas, selon Bucher, d'ordre hiérarchique et, en particulier, de primauté de l'immunité par rapport au droit des victimes. L'immunité peut l'emporter là où il y a des voies alternatives. La Cour, dit Bucher, aurait dû prêter plus d'attention à l'argument italien selon lequel l'immunité ne pouvait être concédée que là où existait un moyen effectif d'agir autre que de saisir les tribunaux italiens (argument du « dernier recours »). Le droit de l'immunité n'est pas, d'ailleurs, insensible à l'argument que l'immunité ne peut être accordée que s'il existe une voie alternative sur le plan interne ou international. Cette idée est celle admise dans le cas des organisations intergouvernementales qui doivent pouvoir offrir une voie de recours effective sur le plan interne de l'organisation si elles veulent bénéficier de l'immunité[42].

L'argument du « dernier recours » fait implicitement intervenir l'idée de proportionnalité, ajoute le Rapporteur Bucher : l'idée de l'immunité devient moins insupportable si la justice peut être cherchée ailleurs que devant les

---

40   *CIJ Rec. 2002*, p. 3.
41   Ibid., § 104.
42   On citera, à ce propos, deux affaires bien connues: *Beer et Regan* c. *Allemagne*, arrêt du 18 février 1999, Cour EDH, n° 26083/94, [GC] ; *Waite et Kennedy* c. *Allemagne*, arrêt du 18 février 1999, Cour EDH, n° 2893 / 95, [GC].

juridictions d'un Etat étranger. S'agissant de l'exigence de proportionnalité, appliquée par la Cour EDH lorsque la question de l'immunité se pose, la situation s'apprécie à la lumière de ce critère, notamment lorsque des violations graves des droits de l'homme sont en cause. Selon la Cour, la proportionnalité est un élément inhérent à l'article 6.1 de la CEDH, de sorte que l'immunité n'est pas écartée si cette proportionnalité existe. Elle estime qu'il serait difficile de faire autrement; et ce point de vue est d'autant plus fondé, selon elle, que des négociations ont déjà eu lieu entre les deux Etats sans produire de règlement. Et il serait douteux, ajoute la CIJ, que des tribunaux civils puissent correctement évaluer les chances de succès de négociations.

Enfin, à supposer qu'un règlement négocié forfaitaire soit déjà intervenu, il serait difficile aux organes judiciaires de connaître la part versée à chaque réclamant et celle pour laquelle il resterait habilité à actionner l'Etat débiteur[43]. De plus, si un accord a déjà été conclu, c'est l'exercice de la protection diplomatique qui a conduit à l'acceptation d'une prestation forfaitaire et une clause de renonciation, de sorte que les victimes n'ont plus de prétentions à faire valoir.

Les accords de paix et d'indemnisation ou de réconciliation comportent normalement des clauses de renonciation à des revendications ultérieures présentées par l'Etat ou ses ressortissants[44]. De telles revendications peuvent provoquer une menace de procédures civiles, ce qui pourrait inciter l'Etat concerné à établir des fondations en vue d'indemniser les victimes, ce que l'Allemagne a fait en 2000, avec le soutien de l'industrie allemande, pour des individus ayant ouvert des procédures aux Etats-Unis dès 1998. L'immunité des Etats n'a pas fait et ne devrait pas faire obstacle à de telles indemnisations.

Pour terminer, le Rapporteur suggère d'assurer l'accès à la justice tout en préservant l'immunité[45]. On rappellera, à ce propos, que l'indemnisation ne doit pas nécessairement être complète; mais elle doit être appropriée[46]. Elle peut émaner de tribunaux pénaux civils ou d'arbitrage, mais également d'organes mis sur pied spécialement à cette fin, tels que des commissions d'indemnisation, ou trouver son origine dans un accord contenant une renonciation globale à toute revendication future. On pourrait voir dans l'immunité juridictionnelle de l'Etat un principe consacré du droit international, mais également un précepte dont l'application devient incertaine s'il n'y a pas d'autre issue pour les victimes. Dans l'affaire des *Immunités juridictionnelles*,

---

43   Ibid., § 102.
44   Ibid., § 104.
45   Ibid., § 105.
46   Le Rapport Bucher cite l'affaire *Diallo (Guinée c. République démocratique du Congo)*, arrêt du 19 juin 2012, *CIJ Rec. 2012*, p. 324, § 25 et 33.

la Cour a omis, selon Bucher, d'examiner le problème sous tous ses angles. Le fait que les juridictions pénales internationales habilitées à se prononcer sur les conséquences civiles des violations commises[47] n'ont pas à tenir compte de l'immunité est un signe que la communauté internationale « tend à faire prévaloir la protection de la dignité humaine des victimes davantage que le respect de l'égalité souveraine des Etats »[48].

5 Conclusion

Les arguments développés par les juges dissidents autant que par le Rapporteur de la Première Commission de l'Institut de droit international montrent qu'il y avait plus d'une manière de justifier l'attitude des tribunaux italiens dans l'affaire des *Immunités juridictionnelles* et qu'il y a une limite à ne pas franchir lorsqu'il s'agit d'accorder l'immunité de juridiction à un Etat étranger: quand on se trouve en présence de demandes d'indemnisation formulées devant des tribunaux nationaux par des individus victimes de crimes internationaux, c'est-à-dire de violations graves des droits de l'homme ou du droit international humanitaire. Le principe de l'immunité de juridiction de l'Etat responsable doit s'effacer, du moins lorsque les actes en question ont été commis sur le territoire de l'Etat dont relèvent ces tribunaux et qu'il s'agit d'une démarche de « dernier recours ».

L'article 5 proposé par A. Bucher aurait pleinement satisfait à cet objectif, contrairement à ce qui a été le cas d'un texte précédent, adopté par l'Institut de droit international en 2009, l'article 11.2 de la Résolution sur l'« Immunité de juridiction de l'Etat et de ses agents », qui se limite à prévoir que dans de tels cas l'immunité de juridiction « ne *devrait* pas » rendre sans effet l'obligation de l'Etat de réparer le préjudice causé aux victimes[49]. Malheureusement la majorité des membres de l'Institut de droit international n'a pas pu se résoudre à remplacer ce conditionnel par une formulation contraignante. C'est dommage.

---

47 Voir à ce sujet l'article 75 du Statut de Rome de la Cour pénale internationale, du 17 juillet 1988 (RS 0.312.1).
48 Voir le Rapport de A. Bucher, « La compétence universelle civile en matière de réparation pour crimes internationaux », *Annuaire* 2015, p. 127, par. 244.
49 Voir ci-dessus, p. 223.

Responsibility of States in Cases of Human-rights or Humanitarian-law Violations

*Alain Pellet**

The topic of this paper has been dwelled upon again and again.[1] However, I deem it interesting to review this literature briefly in a book honouring Djamchid Momtaz. Professor Momtaz is known as one of the world's very best specialists in international humanitarian law and nothing concerning

---

* With my thanks to Benjamin Samson and Jean-Rémi de Maistre, PhD candidates, Université Paris Nanterre for their assistance in preparing this paper.

1 See e.g. I. Boerefijn, 'Establishing State Responsibility for Breaching Human Rights Treaty Obligations: Avenues under UN Human Rights Treaties', 56 *Netherlands International Law Review*, 2009, pp. 170–171; L. A. Castellanos-Jankiewicz & E. Wyler, 'State Responsibility and International Crimes', in W. A. Schabas & N. Bernaz (eds), *Routledge Handbook of International Criminal Law*, Routledge, 2010, pp. 385–405; D. M. Chirwa, 'State Responsibility for Human Rights', in M. A. Baderin & M. Ssenyonjo (eds), *International Human Rights Law: Six Decades after the UDHR and Beyond*, Ashgate, 2010, pp. 397–410; D. Fleck, 'Individual and State Responsibility for Violations of the Ius in Bello: An Imperfect Balance', in W. H. von Heinegg & V. Epping (eds), *International Humanitarian Law Facing New Challenges*, Springer, 2007, pp. 171–206; A. R. Jay, 'The European Convention on Human Rights and the Black Hole of State Responsibility', 47 *International Law and Politics*, 2014, pp. 207–244; M. Longobardo, 'State Responsibility for International Humanitarian Law Violations by Private Actors in Occupied Territories and the Exploitation of Natural Resources', 63 *Netherlands International Law Review*, 2016, pp. 252–274; B. Simma, 'Human Rights and State Responsibility', in A. Reinisch & U. Kriebaum (ed), *The Law of International Relations: Liber amicorum Hanspeter Neuhold*, Eleven International Publishing, 2007, pp. 359–381; C. Tomuschat, 'Specificities of Human Rights Law and International Humanitarian Law Regarding State Responsibility', in R. Kolb & G. Gaggioli, *Research Handbook on Human Rights and Humanitarian Law*, Elgar, 2013, pp. 198–222; A. A. Cançado Trindade, 'Complementarity between State Responsibility and Individual Responsibility for Grave Violations of Human Rights: the Crime of State revisited', in M. Ragazzi, *International Responsibility Today*, Brill Nijhoff, 2005, pp. 253–269; and A. Zimmerman & M. Teichman, 'State Responsibility for International Crimes', in H. van der Wilt & A. Nollkaemper (eds), *System Criminality in International Law*, Cambridge University Press, 2009, pp. 298–313. This topic is at the cross-road of subjects on which I have written extensively; see e.g. A. Pellet, 'Vive le crime! Remarques sur les degrés de l'illicite en droit international', in ILC, A. Pellet (ed), *International Law at the Dawn of the Twenty-First Century—Views from the I.L.C.*, UN, 1997, pp. 287–315; A. Pellet, 'The New Draft Articles of the International Law Commission on the Responsibility of States for International Wrongful Acts: A Requiem for States' Crimes?', 32 *Netherlands Yearbook of International Law*, 2001, pp. 55–79; A. Pellet, 'Can a State Commit a Crime? Definitely, Yes!', 10 *European Journal of*

international responsibility is unknown to him.[2] In doing so, I have been struck by the frequent 'human rightist' approach taken by the authors in question;[3] they seem to consider that special treatment has been, or should be, reserved for human-rights violations. This is not so and this approach evinces ignorance of the developments in the law of State responsibility in cases of breach of obligations arising from peremptory norms of international law. It therefore seems of interest to focus on these developments and to show that, although perfectible, the new rules of State responsibility are indeed applicable to responsibility of States in cases of serious violations of human rights or humanitarian law

The global background to the question of the responsibility of States in cases of serious breaches of obligations arising from peremptory norms—including human-rights or humanitarian-law violations and of obligations to prevent and to punish, consists of two layers:

- the law of international responsibility of States with the development of a special regime for aggravated violations;
- the development of international criminal law (and international criminal justice), which raises the issue of the combination of State responsibility with that of individual perpetrators.

International Law 1999, pp. 425–434; A. Pellet, 'Responsabilité de l'État et responsabilité pénale individuelle en droit international', *Série de Conférences du Bureau du Procureur*, Cour pénale internationale, La Haye, 30 May 2006, available at https://www.icc-cpi.int/NR/rdonlyres/71E341A4-C87D-4192-8732-BA18A8B3517E/0/ICCOTP060530Pellet_Fr.pdf, and A. Pellet, 'Chapitre 48. La responsabilité de l'État pour la commission d'une infraction internationale', in H. Ascensio, E. Decaux & A. Pellet (eds), *Droit international pénal*, Pedone, 2012, pp. 607–630.

2 Among D. Momtaz' writings of relevance for the present topic, see e.g.: 'Le droit international humanitaire applicable aux conflits armés non internationaux', 292 *Recueil des cours*, 2002, pp. 1–145; M. J. Matheson & D. Momtaz (eds), *Rules and Institutions of International Humanitarian Law Put to the Test of Recent Armed Conflicts*, Brill Nijhoff, 2010, p. 1032; D. Momtaz, 'L'exercice de la compétence de la Cour pénale internationale à l'égard des crimes commis au Darfour', in A. Constantinides & N. Zaikos (eds), *The diversity of international law : essays in honour of Professor Kalliopi K. Koufa*, Brill Nijhoff, 2009, pp. 597–606; D. Momtaz, 'Attribution of Conduct to the State: State Organs and Entities Empowered to Exercise Elements of Governmental Authority', in J. Crawford, A. Pellet & S. Olleson (eds), *The Law of International Responsibility*, Oxford University Press, 2010, pp. 237–246; 'La controverse sur le statut de la Palestine', in R. Wolfrum, M. Seršić & T. M. Šošić, *Contemporary Developments in International Law: Essays in Honour of Budislav Vukas*, Brill Nijhoff, 2015, pp. 102–115.

3 See: A. Pellet, 'Human Rightism' and International Law', 10 *Italian Yearbook of International Law*, 2000, pp. 3–16.

1 An Aggravated Regime of State Responsibility

1.1 Re-thinking the Law of State Responsibility

There can be no doubt that, as expressed with remarkable concision in Article 1 of the Articles on Responsibility of States for internationally wrongful acts adopted by the International Law Commission of the United Nations (ILC) and annexed to General Assembly Resolution 56/83 of 12 December 2001: '[e]very internationally wrongful act of a State entails the international responsibility of that State.' However, an internationally wrongful act is not necessarily an 'offence' in the criminal meaning of that term.

It is however true that there has been, in some respects, a 'criminalization' of the law of international responsibility which has resulted in its 'objectification'. Traditionally, the responsibility of States under international law was defined as being similar to 'civil responsibility'.[4] while, as now codified in the ILC Articles finally adopted in 2001, it is 'neither civil or criminal' but[5] simply 'international responsibility'.

The most sensational expression of the new way of thinking lies in the absence of damage as a pre-condition for entailing States' international responsibility. Not that damage lacks a role in the new law of international responsibility, but it enters into play only at the reparation stage.[6] As for triggering responsibility only two elements are necessary:

---

4   D. Anzilotti, *La responsabilité internationale des États à raison des dommages soufferts par des étrangers*, Pedone, 1906, reprinted in *Scritti di diritto internazionale publico*, Padoue, CEDAM, 1956, vol. II-1, pp. 161–162, and in *Cours de droit international*, Éds. Panthéon-Assas, 1999 (reprinted), pp. 466–468; C. Eagleton, *The Responsibility of States in International Law*, New York University Press, 1928, p. 182; K. Strupp, 'Das Völkerrechtliche Delikt', *Handbuch des Völkerrechts*, Kohlhammer, 1920, tome III, Part. 1, pp. 217 *et seq.*; C. de Visscher, 'La responsabilité des États', *Bibliotheca Visseriana*, Brill, 1924, tome II, pp. 115–116; E. Jiménez de Aréchaga, 'International Responsibility', in M. Sørensen (ed), *Manual of Public International Law*, Palgrave Macmillan, 1968, pp. 564–572; D. P. O'Connell, *International Law*, Stevens, 1965, vol. II, p. 1019–1020; see also J. Combacau & S. Sur, *Droit international public*, Montchrestien-Lextenso, 10th edition, 2012, pp. 517–531.

5   J. Crawford, First Report on State Responsibility, UN Doc. A/CN.4/490 and Add. 1–7, *ILC Yearbook* 1998, vol. II, Part 1, p. 13, para. 54; see also R. Ago, Third Report on State Responsibility, UN Doc. A/CN.4/246 and Add.1–3, *ILC Yearbook* 1971, Vol. II, Part. 1, p. 209, para. 38.

6   See Article 34, ILC, *Draft articles on Responsibility of States for Internationally Wrongful Acts*, annexed to UN Doc. A/RES/56/83, 12 December 2001.

Article 2. *Elements of an internationally wrongful act of a State*
There is an internationally wrongful act of a State when conduct consisting of an action or omission:
  (*a*) is attributable to the State under international law; and
  (*b*) constitutes a breach of an international obligation of the State.

This evolution, which is tremendously important and is now accepted by a clear majority of States and scholars is largely due to Roberto Ago's brilliant intuition.[7]

I suggest that there is no exaggeration in saying that this has changed our very conception of international law itself: it now appears as a common good of the international society of States, in some respects of the international community of States and, maybe, of the community of mankind or of the whole humanity. Law must be respected *per se*, in itself, not only because a violation has caused an injury to another State.

This calls for at least two more remarks:

- *First*, this is effectively the way the mechanism of responsibility works in domestic law: you have to comply with the law. If you don't, you are subject to penal prosecution; if, in addition, you have caused an injury you must make reparation for it. If you jump the lights you will be fined whether or not you have hurt a pedestrian.
- *Second*, this new approach is a sign of the existence of a community of values which did not exist in the past or, at least, was not perceived as existing. In the Westphalian society of states, responsibility was a bilateral, purely inter-personal, concern. Inasmuch as it is possible today to speak of a 'community' of states *volens nolens* having common interests and even sharing common values, then, very logically, all States have an interest in the respect of legal rules reflecting such interests and values.

This 'objective' conception of responsibility reflects the relative progress of international solidarity. In a society where sovereignties were juxtaposed and where the very concept of international 'community' had no existence, responsibility could easily be defined on a purely inter-subjective basis, that is to say exclusively by the effects it produced in the relations between States directly concerned. This is no longer possible when one accepts that law is no

---

7 R. Ago, 'Le délit international', 68 *Recueil des Cours*, 1939, pp. 415–554. See also R. Ago, Second Report on State responsibility, UN Doc. A/CN.4/233, *ILC Yearbook 1970*, Vol. II, pp. 177–197; and Third Report, supra, note 5, pp. 199–274.

longer exclusively the guarantor of the independence of States, but also the reflection and the guarantee of their interdependence and of their common interests, of which the 'international community' is the imperfect custodian. Therefore, the consequences of establishing the responsibility of the State cease to be unique (obligation to make reparation) and include more generally (and more in keeping with reality) all the responses to the internationally wrongful act recognized in international law. This includes the right of States to take counter-measures, on behalf of the injured State or of the beneficiary of the breached obligations, under certain conditions.[8] As Djamchid Momtaz excellently notes : '*En cas de violation d'une obligation du droit international humanitaire, obligation* erga omnes *par excellence, tous les Etats ont un intérêt à agir et sont évidemment habilités à prendre des mesures pour que la violation de ce droit cesse, même s'ils ne peuvent se prévaloir d'un préjudice direct et subjectif.*'[9]

On the other hand, it is logical and, indeed, inevitable, to distinguish two categories of internationally wrongful acts: those concerning only relations between States which do not question the very foundations upon which the weak integration of the international community is based; and those which, on the contrary, threaten the fundamental interests of the international community as a whole.

1.2 *From Common Values to Peremptory Norms*

It must also be recognized that these common values are limited, at world level at least. While the community of values within the State is well established and covers a large part of 'living together', the sense of solidarity is much more limited internationally;[10] and even should necessity create commonality *vide* global warming or more generally, the preservation of the environment, the corresponding legal rules are, for the most part, still in their infancy. And the diversity of ideologies and historical and cultural backgrounds of some 200 States forming the international society make difficult the crystallization of most rules and principles concerning national and international governance or the protection of human rights.

With this in mind, at least some of these principles have reached the stage of peremptory norms of general international law (or *jus cogens*) defined in

---

8   See below pp. 18–19.

9   D. Momtaz, 'Les défis des conflits armés asymétriques et identitaires au droit international humanitaire', in M. J. Matheson & D. Momtaz (eds), *Rules and Institutions of International Humanitarian Law Put to the Test of Recent Armed Conflicts*, Brill Nijhoff, 2010, p. 92.

10 There can be special solidarities, based on common values, at regional levels; this is clearly the case in Europe and in Latin America.

Article 53 of the 1969 Vienna Convention on the Law of Treaties[11] as norms 'accepted and recognized by the international community of States as a whole as [norms] from which no derogation is permitted and which can be modified only by [...] subsequent norm[s] of general international law having the same character'. Despite frequent attempts by human-rights activists, including some scholars,[12] to use this concept as a tool for enhancing progress in the protection of human rights or humanitarian law even if the test is rather vague, it is pointless to consider all or a great many human-rights principles as belonging to *jus cogens*. Law has nothing to gain by galloping before reality: it will always be brought back to realism as shown by the misfortune of the 'new international economic order': for having confused its wishes with hard law, the Third World sold the shop for sixpence.[13] Law can take stock of and consolidate values, it is not the role of lawyers to confuse their own values and aspirations with existing legal rules.

Most of the limited number of peremptory norms listed as part of positive international law exist in the field of human rights. Given the enormous disparities in the conceptions of human rights and, more widely, of the relationship between the sovereign State and the individual around the world, this might look astonishing. This situation is mainly the consequence of post-World-War-II trauma, or more exactly of the repulsion universally felt *vis-à-vis* Nazi abominations. The speech attributed to Goebbels following the petition addressed by Franz Bernheim to the League of Nations[14] would certainly no more be in

---

11   1155 UNTS 331.

12   See Pellet, supra, note 3.

13   See A. Pellet, 'Le bon droit et l'ivraie – Plaidoyer pour l'ivraie (Remarques sur quelques problèmes de méthode en droit international)', in *Mélanges Charles Chaumont*, Pedone, 1984, pp. 470 and 480–482, also published in A. Pellet, *Le droit international entre souveraineté et communauté*, Collection Doctrines, Pedone, 2014, pp. 189 and 198–200.

14   'Gentlemen, each is lord in his manor. We are a sovereign State. All this individual said is not your business. We do what we deem appropriate with our socialists, our pacifists and our Jews and we have no control to endure neither from humanity nor from the LoN.' In reality, this text is apocryphal; but the episode is nevertheless very symbolic and edifying (see e.g.: G. Burgess, 'The Human Rights Dilemma in Anti-Nazi Protest: The Bernheim Petition, Minorities Protection, and the 1933 Sessions of the League of Nations', CERC *Working Papers Series*, no. 2/2002, p. 56; or J. H. Burgers, 'The Road to San Francisco: The Revival of the Human Rights Idea in the Twentieth Century', 14 *Human Rights Quarterly*, 1992, pp. 455–459. The real text of the Goebbels' speech, which was read to journalists (and not before the Assembly of the LoN) was published in German in J. Goebbels, *Signale der neuen Zeit* (*Messages from the new era*), Zentralverlag der NSDAP, 1934 (J. H. Burgers, ibid., p. 457, note 2). For a pious legendary version, see: M. Agi, *De l'idée d'universalité comme fondatrice du concept des droits de l'homme d'après la vie et l'œuvre de René Cassin*,

keeping with contemporary international law: *basic* human rights—not all human rights—have become the common concern of mankind and, as such, they are protected by peremptory norms of general international law.

Given that not all rules protecting human rights are peremptory—and, therefore, not all violations are 'crimes' within the meaning defined above—it remains that peremptory norms are essentially norms protecting human rights. The list is not easy to establish,[15] not least because *jus cogens* norms are not rigidly fixed.[16] However, as far as fundamental human rights are concerned,[17] a minimal list would certainly include the prohibition of the use of force in contravention of the UN Charter, the right of peoples to self-determination, the prohibition of slavery, human trafficking, racial discrimination,[18] torture and genocide, and crimes against humanity; together with 'a great many rules of humanitarian law applicable in armed conflict'.[19]

The same goes for the list of breaches giving rise to the increased responsibilities of States: they concern mainly the protection of fundamental human rights. Thus Article 19, paragraph 3, of the ILC draft of 1996 on State responsibility gave the following examples of 'State crimes':

> 3. Subject to paragraph 2, and on the basis of the rules of international law in force, an international crime may result, *inter alia,* from:

Alp'azur, 1980, p. 354; or M. Bettati, *Le droit d'ingérence – Mutation de l'ordre international*, Odile Jacob, 1996, p. 18; See also R. Cassin, 'Les droits de l'homme', 140 *Recueil des cours*, 1974, p. 324.

15 For a recent firm clarification according to which the right of access to a court is not *jus cogens*, see *Al-Dulimi and Montana Management Inc. v Switzerland* (App. 5809/08[2016]), para. 136.

16 See Article 53, para. 1, of the Vienna Convention on the Law of Treaties, adopted the 23 May 1969, entry into force the 27 January 1980, 1155 UNTS 331: peremptory norms '... can be modified [...] by [...] subsequent norm[s] of general international law having the same character.'

17 The most widely generally accepted peremptory norms outside human rights and humanitarian law include the prohibition of the use of force in contravention of the UN Charter (for a recent reaffirmation, *Sargsyan v Azerbaijan* (App. 40167/06 [2015]), para. 21 and, probably, the basic diplomatic immunities (see *Diplomatic and Consular Staff in Tehran* (United States of America v Iran), Judgment, ICJ Reports 1979, p. 20, para. 41).

18 For a recent reaffirmation see *Granier y Otros (Radio Caracas Televisión) v Venezuela*, Inter-American Court of Human Rights, Judgment, 20 June 2015, para. 215.

19 See *Legality of the Threat or Use of Nuclear Weapons*, Advisory Opinion, ICJ Reports 1996, p. 257, para. 69; see also: *Legal Consequences of the Construction of a Wall in the Occupied Palestinian Territory*, Advisory Opinion, ICJ Reports 2004, p. 199, para. 157.

(a) A serious breach of an international obligation of essential importance for the maintenance of international peace and security, such as that prohibiting aggression;
(b) A serious breach of an international obligation of essential importance for safeguarding the right of self-determination of peoples, such as that prohibiting the establishment or maintenance by force of colonial domination;
(c) A serious breach on a widespread scale of an international obligation of essential importance for safeguarding the human being, such as those prohibiting slavery, genocide and apartheid;
(d) A serious breach of an international obligation of essential importance for the safeguarding and preservation of the human environment, such as those prohibiting massive pollution of the atmosphere or of the seas.[20]

This list is marked by the context in which it was established and an indisputable sense of demagogy;[21] however, there is no doubt that the 'crimes' listed *sub litt.* (c) are the best examples of uncontroversial 'serious breaches'.[22]

In the (Bosnian) *Genocide* case, the ICJ questioned the interrelationship between the prohibition of genocide on the one hand, and the duty to prevent and punish genocide[23] and it described the main components of these two last duties.

Concerning the duty to prevent, the Court considered that

> it is clear that the obligation in question is one of conduct and not one of result, in the sense that a State cannot be under an obligation to succeed, whatever the circumstances, in preventing the commission of genocide: the obligation of States parties is rather to employ all means reasonably available to them, so as to prevent genocide so far as possible. (...) In this area the notion of 'due diligence', which calls for an assessment *in concreto*, is of critical importance. Various parameters operate

---

20   Report of the International Law Commission on the work of its twenty-eighth session, *ILC Yearbook 1976*, Vol. II, Part. 2, p. 75.
21   See Pellet, 'Vive le crime!...', supra, note 1, pp. 299–301.
22   For confirmation, see: Report of the ILC on the work of its 53th session, *ILC Yearbook 2001*, Vol. II, Part. 2, pp. 112–113, paras. 4 and 5 of the commentary of Article 40.
23   *Application of the Convention on the Prevention and Punishment of the Crime of Genocide* (Bosnia and Herzegovina v Serbia and Montenegro), Judgment, *ICJ Reports 2007*, p. 43, see in particular pp. 199–201, para. 379–383, and pp. 219–229, para. 425–450.

when assessing whether a State has duly discharged the obligation concerned. The first, which varies greatly from one State to another, is clearly the capacity to influence effectively the action of persons likely to commit, or already committing, genocide. (...) On the other hand, it is irrelevant whether the State whose responsibility is in issue claims, or even proves, that even if it had employed all means reasonably at its disposal, they would not have sufficed to prevent the commission of genocide. As well as being generally difficult to prove, this is irrelevant to the breach of the obligation of conduct in question...[24]

Although the Court warned that it did not 'purport to find whether, apart from the texts applicable to specific fields, there is a general obligation on States to prevent the commission by other persons or entities of acts contrary to certain norms of general international law.',[25] it can be asserted that these guidelines generally apply to all peremptory norms protecting fundamental human rights—which all imply for all States a duty to prevent.

Less can be inferred from the *Genocide* case concerning the obligation to punish the authors of a genocide, since in its 2007 judgment, the Court, very controversially, concluded that, the genocide in Srebrenica not having been carried out in Serbia's territory, Serbia could not be 'charged with not having tried before its own courts those accused of having participated in the Srebrenica genocide...'[26] However, despite the disastrous ICJ Judgment in *Yerodia*,[27] the general philosophy should be the same: since the rules prohibiting breaches of fundamental human rights reflect common values of the whole community of States, all components of this community should be under an obligation to punish the authors of such breaches[28]—at least when they have a title to do so.[29]

---

24 Ibid., p. 221, para. 430. For further clarifications concerning the obligation to prevent, see *Application of the Convention on the Prevention and Punishment of the Crime of Genocide* (Croatia v Serbia), Judgment of 3 February 2015, *ICJ Reports*, notably p. 44, para. 95, p. 46, para. 98 or p. 61, para. 153.

25 *ICJ Reports 2007*, supra, note 23, p. 220, para. 429.

26 Ibid., p. 226, para. 442.

27 Where the Court denies the existence of an 'exception to the rule according immunity from criminal jurisdiction and inviolability to incumbent Ministers for Foreign Affairs, where they are suspected of having committed war crimes or crimes against humanity' (*Arrest Warrant of 11 April 2000* (Democratic Republic of the Congo v Belgium), Judgment, *ICJ Reports 2002*, p. 28, para. 54).

28 See Momtaz, 'L'exercice de la competence...' supra, note 2, p. 601.

29 For reasons which would be too long to be exposed in the present paper, the author is strongly opposed to an 'absolute' universal jurisdiction when the State exercising

1.3   From Peremptory Norms to International 'Crimes' of States

Very logically, *jus cogens* consisting as it does of norms belonging to a particular category, produces specific legal effects which are added to those normally resulting from an internationally wrongful act—and this was very probably in Ago's mind when he suggested his new approach to the responsibility of States.[30] This resulted in a differentiation between two categories of internationally wrongful acts in Article 19 of the ILC first-reading draft articles adopted in 1996:[31] crimes and delicts.[32] While Ago and the ILC had initially not linked this concept of an international crime of a State to that of *jus cogens* for rather obscure reasons,[33] the ILC directly linked both concepts in its final draft in which Articles 40 and 41 relate to 'the international responsibility that is entailed by a serious breach by a State of an obligation *arising under a peremptory norm of general international law*'.

It can of course be argued that the 2001 Articles do not expressly refer to 'international crimes' of States. However,[34] the word has simply been replaced by its definition; but I deem it absolutely clear that the concept itself has not changed: those two articles take note of the existence of two different forms of State international responsibility and (very shyly) initiate a progressive development and codification of the consequences of particular serious breaches of international law.

Although it could have been seen as a step backward, the omission of the word 'crime' to name the most serious violations of international law—those stemming from peremptory norms—must be welcome: it flushes the concept out of its penal connotation while, fortunately, maintaining the difference

---

jurisdiction cannot prevail itself of a territorial or national (or, maybe, a treaty) link entitling it to punish.

30   See Ago, Second Report, supra, note 7, pp. 183–185.

31   Draft article 19 was first adopted in 1976 (see Report of the International Law Commission on the work of its twenty-eighth session, *ILC Yearbook 1976*, Vol. II, Part. 2, pp. 95–122, para. 78 and Pellet, 'The New Draft Articles . . .', supra, note 1, p. 57).

32   Article 19, paras. 2 and 4: '2. An internationally wrongful act which results from the breach by a State of an international obligation so essential for the protection of fundamental interests of the international community that its breach is recognized as a crime by that community as a whole, constitutes an international crime' and '4. Any internationally wrongful act which is not an international crime in accordance with paragraph 2, constitutes an international delict.'

33   See Report of the ILC, supra, note 31, pp. 119–120, para. 62 of the commentary of Article 19; R. Ago, Fifth report on State Responsibility, UN Doc. A/CN.4/291 and Add.1 and 2, *ILC Yearbook 1976*, Vol. II, Part. 1, p. 53, para. 150.

34   Pellet, 'The New Draft Articles . . .', supra, note 1, pp. 55–79, see in particular at pp. 58–67.

between 'ordinary' breaches of international law on the one hand and 'serious breaches of obligations arising under a peremptory norm' on the other.

2 International 'Crimes' of States and Criminal Responsibility of Individuals under International Law

However, this means neither that States cannot commit 'crimes' in the penal sense of the word, nor that the notion of 'serious breaches of obligations arising under peremptory norms of international law' has no relationship with this notion.

2.1 *A Criminal Responsibility of States?*

The first point is a delicate and controversial one. In 1998, in his first Report to the ILC as Special Rapporteur on the responsibility of States Professor Crawford, while not denying that there existed an international criminal responsibility of States, alleged that it had nothing to do with the topic under review.[35] He was both right and wrong.

Crawford was right in that the 'serious breaches' as dealt with in the draft were certainly not necessarily 'criminal' and in that it was clearly outside the scope of the project to prescribe sanctions imposed on the authors of infractions, let alone to organize proceedings for inflicting such penal sanctions. He was also right in that it can certainly not be excluded that there are precedents of State behaviours which have resulted in 'criminal-like' repression as were the sanctions imposed on Germany and its allies following the two World Wars or the measures decided by the Security Council under Chapter VII of the UN Charter. However, I would think that these precedents relate to other chapters of public international law, namely the law of war or that of the Charter—which is clearly distinct from the law of international responsibility.[36] As a consequence, the ILC was right to exclude from its Articles any penal connotations—not only by abandoning the penal terminology implied by the words 'crime' and 'delict', but also by not envisaging any repressive sanctions

---

35 See Crawford, First report, supra, note. 5, pp. 18–19, para. 70; or p. 23, paras. 91–93.
36 On the distinction and the relationship between both fields, see M. Forteau, *Droit de la sécurité collective et droit de la responsabilité internationale de l'État*, Pedone, 2006, p. vi-699, in particular p. 631.

(including aggravated interests, as was done in the 1996 first draft)[37] with the apparent exception of counter-measures, to which I will come later.[38]

But the Special Rapporteur was wrong to suggest completely abandoning the distinction between two different kinds of breach: it is obvious that the violation of a provision of a trade treaty on the reduction of custom duties is different in kind—not only in degree—from the breach of the rule prohibiting genocide.

Wisely, the Commission did not follow Crawford here and, in conformity with the suggestions he finally made in his fourth and last Report,[39] included in its final draft a short Chapter—not to say a rump Chapter—dealing with 'serious breaches by a State of an obligation arising under a peremptory norm of general international law'. The good thing in this decision is that it preserves the idea that the breaches of some legal norms, reflecting universally recognized fundamental values, call for stronger reactions than those of 'ordinary rules'. The unfortunate aspect is that the reactions in question, as described in Article 41 of the ILC Articles are reduced to a minimum.

According to that provision:

1. States shall cooperate to bring to an end through lawful means any serious breach within the meaning of article 40.
2. No State shall recognize as lawful a situation created by a serious breach within the meaning of article 40, nor render aid or assistance in maintaining that situation.

These consequences are less insignificant than sometimes alleged.[40] But they are of limited interest for our inquiry: they have clearly no implication in criminal matters.

More relevant is paragraph 3 of Article 41, which provides:

3. This article is without prejudice to the other consequences referred to in this Part and to such further consequences that a breach to which this chapter applies may entail under international law.

---

37   See Article 45(2)(c), *ILC Yearbook 1996*, Vol. II, Part. 2, p. 63.
38   See Section 2.3.
39   See *ILC Yearbook 2001*, Vol. II, Part. 1, pp. 12–13, para. 47.
40   See Pellet, 'The New Draft Articles...', supra, note 1, pp. 69–70; A. Pellet, 'Les articles de la C.D.I. sur la responsabilité de l'État pour fait internationalement suite – et fin?', 48 *Annuaire Français de Droit International*, 2002, pp. 17–18; or Pellet, 'Chapitre 48. La responsabilité de l'État...', supra, note 1, pp. 617–619.

Among the non-expressed consequences of a 'serious breach', one is crucial: the 'transparency' of the State.[41]

2.2 Penal Consequences of Serious Breaches of Obligations Arising under a Peremptory Norm of General International Law

Even though State responsibility, at least as dealt with in the 2001 ILC Articles, is not of criminal nature, it may result in criminal consequences when leaders of a State responsible for an internationally wrongful act are sued in a criminal court, either national or international. This is a serious departure from the fundamental principle guaranteeing immunity of leaders—including Heads of State—which can only be explained by the piercing of the State veil, which alone makes it possible to reach the individual beyond the institution. This is possible only if that State's breach of international law constitutes a serious breach of an obligation arising from a norm of *jus cogens*. The transparency of the State is one of the necessary consequences. It is true that the unfortunate *Yerodia* judgment rendered by the ICJ in 2002 cast doubts that this principle is now part of positive law;[42] it is nonetheless applied in the Statutes of all international criminal courts and tribunals, from the Nuremberg Tribunal to the ICC, although States take precautions to limit their jurisdiction.[43]

However, the ICJ maintained in another Judgment that 'under customary international law as it presently stands, a State is not deprived of immunity by reason of the fact that it is accused of serious violations of international human rights law or the international law of armed conflict.'[44]

In any case, the punishment of officials who commit these crimes 'does not *per se* release the State itself from its own international responsibility for such acts.'[45] In this respect, Article 25 of the Rome Statute provides that '[n]o provision in this Statute relating to individual criminal responsibility shall affect the responsibility of States under international law.'[46] In return, Article 58 of the ILC Articles on State responsibility specifies that '[t]hese articles are

---

41   See e.g. R. Maison, 'The 'Transparency' of the State' in Crawford, Pellet & Olleson (eds), supra, note 2, pp. 717–724.

42   *Arrest Warrant of 11 April 2000*, supra, note 27, p. 3, in particular p. 24, para. 58.

43   See Momtaz, 'L'exercice de la compétence de la Cour pénale internationale…', supra, note 2, p. 600.

44   *Jurisdictional Immunities of the State* (Germany v Italy, Greece intervening), Judgment, ICJ Reports 2012, p. 139, para. 91.

45   Report of the ILC, supra, note 31, p. 104, para. 21 of the commentary of Article 19.

46   See also, Article III (3) (b) the Resolution adopted in 2009 by the Institut de droit international on the Immunity from Jurisdiction of the State and of Persons Who Act on Behalf of the State in case of International Crimes, 73 *III Yearbook 2009*, p. 228.

without prejudice to any question of the individual responsibility under international law of any person acting on behalf of a State.' As explained in the commentary on this Article:

> Where crimes against international law are committed by State officials, it will often be the case that the State itself is responsible for the acts in question or for failure to prevent or punish them. In certain cases, in particular aggression, the State will by definition be involved. Even so, the question of individual responsibility is in principle distinct from the question of State responsibility.[47]

Furthermore, in its 1996 Judgment on the Preliminary Objections filed by Serbia in the *Genocide* case, the ICJ has recognized that 'Article IX [of the 1948 Genocide Convention][48] does not exclude any form of State responsibility',[49] even though it was fully aware that the International Criminal Tribunal for the Former Yugoslavia (ICTY) had criminal jurisdiction over individuals, regardless of their official functions.

2.3   Reacting to 'Serious Breaches'
Now, contrasting with the tremendous progress of international criminal law,[50] the implementation of the special legal regime applying to serious breaches is most uncertain—for mainly two reasons:

---

47   Report of the ILC, supra, note 21, p. 142, para. 3 of the commentary of Article 58.
48   78 UNTS 277.
49   *Application of the Convention on the Prevention and Punishment of the Crime of Genocide* (Bosnia and Herzegovina v Serbia and Montenegro), Preliminary Objections, Judgment, 11 July 1996, *ICJ Reports 1996*, p. 616, para. 32. See also *Application of the Convention on the Prevention and Punishment of the Crime of Genocide*, (Bosnia and Herzegovina v Serbia and Montenegro), Judgement, 26 February 2007, supra, note 22, p. 119–120, paras. 181–182; or *Armed Activities on the Territory of the Congo (New Application: 2002)* (Democratic Republic of the Congo v Rwanda), Jurisdiction and Admissibility, 3 February 2006, Joint Separate Opinion of Judges Higgins, Kooijmans, Elaraby, Owada and Simma, *ICJ Reports 2006*, p. 72, para. 28.
50   In writing this, I am mindful of the impatience shown by many specialists towards the insufficiency of international criminal justice and the criticisms addressed to the ICC—which I largely share. Nevertheless, in spite of the recent denunciation of the Statute by several African States and Russia's withdrawal of its signature, one cannot ignore the impressive progresses in international criminal law achieved since the early 1990s.

- *first*, the absence of compulsory jurisdiction to make findings with binding effect as to the existence of the breaches; and
- *second*, the absence of any mechanism of forced implementation under international law.

Both obstacles are linked to weaknesses inherent in international law and, beyond, in the international society of States, which can be described only very imperfectly as a 'community'. However, they are not absolute.

There do exist international courts which may have their words on the responsibility of States for 'serious breaches' but their intervention can only be uncertain and sometimes indirect.

The ICJ (or, as the case may be, *ad hoc* arbitral tribunals) can decide on the responsibility of States,[51] including of course on responsibility for serious breaches; and it has done so (not always very convincingly) in several cases.[52] The Court's jurisdiction is limited by the consensual principle; however, this inconvenience is less significant in such cases than in other cases before the Court. In effect, another consequence specific to serious violations, which is already an integral part of positive law, is the possibility of an *actio popularis* (with the understanding that it does not establish the jurisdiction of a court or tribunal not based on an existing consent of the States involved).[53] However, any State which can invoke a jurisdictional link has an interest sufficient to enable it to request the court or tribunal to grant it the benefit of the right stemming from the violation of the essential interests of the international community as a whole.

---

51 It is with boundary cases one of the two main fields in the World Court activities.

52 See e.g. *Corfu Channel case*, (United Kingdom of Great Britain and Northern Ireland v Albania), Judgment, *ICJ Reports 1949*, p. 4; *Military and Paramilitary Activities in and against Nicaragua* (Nicaragua v United States of America), Judgment, *ICJ Reports 1986*, p. 14; *Armed Activities on the Territory of the Congo* (Democratic Republic of the Congo v Uganda), Judgment, *ICJ Reports 2005*, p. 168; *Application of the Convention on the Prevention and Punishment of the Crime of Genocide*, (Bosnia and Herzegovina v. Serbia and Montenegro), 26 February 2007, supra, note 23, p. 43; *Jurisdictional Immunities of the State*, supra, note 44, p. 99; and *Questions relating to the Obligation to Prosecute or Extradite* (Belgium v Senegal), Judgment, *ICJ Reports 2012*, p. 422; *Application of the Convention on the Prevention and Punishment of the Crime of Genocide* (Croatia v Serbia), 3 February 2015, supra, note 24, p. 5.

53 *Armed Activities on the Territory of the Congo (New Application: 2002)*, supra, note 48, pp. 31–32, paras. 64 and pp. 51–52, para. 125. See also *Jurisdictional Immunities of the State*, supra, note 44, p. 141, para. 95; or ECHR, Grand Chamber, 21 November 2001, *Al-Adsani v United Kingdom*, Rep. 2001-XI, p. 101, para. 61.

In some respects, the *Hissène Habré* case is a step on this promising path. In its judgment of 20 July 2012, the ICJ concluded that it had no jurisdiction to decide on Belgium's submissions relating to breaches of customary law obligations;[54] but the Court accepted that it ought to assess the Belgian submission's bearing upon the violation of the Convention against Torture[55] and that, even if Belgium had endured no special harm as a consequence of Senegal's behaviour,

> [t]he common interest in compliance with the relevant obligations under the Convention against Torture implies the entitlement of each State party to the Convention to make a claim concerning the cessation of an alleged breach by another State party. If a special interest were required for that purpose, in many cases no State would be in the position to make such a claim. It follows that any State party to the Convention may invoke the responsibility of another State party with a view to ascertaining the alleged failure to comply with its obligations *erga omnes partes*, such as those under Article 6, paragraph 2, and Article 7, paragraph 1, of the Convention, and to bring that failure to an end.[56]

Obviously, human-rights courts and international criminal tribunals can also have their say in matters involving State responsibility for 'serious breaches'. This is very directly the case for regional courts of human rights when they decide on the most serious allegations of breaches of the human-rights conventions that instituted them. This is the case, for example, when a State is convicted by the European Court of Human Rights of torture[57] or racial discrimination.[58]

Things might seem less obvious as far as international criminal courts and tribunals are concerned. However, it must be recalled that, as recognized in Article 7 of the Draft Code of Crimes against the Peace and Security of Mankind adopted by the ILC in 1996:

---

54   *Questions relating to the obligation...*, supra, note 52, p. 445, para. 55.
55   Convention against Torture and Other Cruel, Inhuman or Degrading Treatment or Punishment, 1465 UNTS 85.
56   Ibid., p. 450, para. 69.
57   See e.g. *Selmouni v France,* (App 25803/94 [1999]); *Al-Adsani v United-Kingdom,* (App 35763/97 [2001]); *Chitayev v Russia,* (App 59334/00 [2007]); *Al-Nashiri v Poland,* (App 28761/11 [2014]).
58   *Cyprus v Turkey,* (App 25781/94 [2001]); See also *Juridical Condition and Rights of the Undocumented Migrants,* Inter-American Court of Human Rights, Advisory Opinion, 17 September 2003, Series A, no. 18, para. 101.

The official position of an individual who commits a crime against the peace and security of mankind, even if he acted as head of State or Government, does not relieve him of criminal responsibility or mitigate punishment.[59]

Therefore, when an international criminal tribunal decides on the guilt of an official, it indirectly decides on the responsibility of the State itself.[60] As the ICTY noted in the in *Tadić* case, when it recognized the penal responsibility of the accused, 'The continued indirect involvement of the Government of the Federal Republic of Yugoslavia (Serbia and Montenegro) in the armed conflict in the Republic of Bosnia and Herzegovina... gives rise to issues of State responsibility...'[61]

As noted by Professor R. Maison, this logic could even be inverted since it can be sustained that '*la sanction pénale de l'individu trouve sa source dans la réaction au crime d'État.*'[62] If this is the case, '[*l*]*e crime d'État fait donc naître deux formes de responsabilité internationale – la responsabilité de l'État, présentant une nature collective, la responsabilité pénale de ses agents – qui sont étroitement imbriquées. Ainsi, la responsabilité individuelle peut être considérée comme une forme de réparation de l'illicite étatique.*'[63] However tightly linked, the responsibilities remain distinct.

---

59   Article 7 of the Draft Code of Crimes against the Peace and Security of Mankind, *ILC Yearbook 1996*, Vol. II, Part. 2, p. 26; see also Article 27 of the Rome Statute of the International Criminal Court, UN Doc. A/CONF.183/9, 17 July 1998, or Article III of the 2009 Resolution of the IDI, supra, note 46. For an uncertain statement of the Rule see: Regina v Bow Street Metropolitan Stipendiary Magistrate and Others, ex parte Pinochet Ugarte (No. 3), [2000] A.C. 147, House of Lords, Judgment, 24 March 2000; Cass. Crim, 13 March 2001, *S.O.S. Attentats et as. (Khadafi), Bull.* p. 218; or *A. v Attorney General and Others*, no BB.2011.140, TPF 2012, Swiss Federal Criminal Court, 25 July 2012, p. 97, paras. 5.4.3–5.5.

60   This idea is the core thesis presented in R. Maison, *La responsabilité individuelle pour crime d'État en droit international public*, Bruylant/Ed. de l'Université de Bruxelles, 2004, p. xiv–547.

61   Prosecutor v Tadić, Case No. IT-94-I-IT, Trial Chamber II, Judgment, International Criminal Tribunal for the former Yugoslavia, 7 May 1997, para. 606.

62   'The criminal punishment of the individual is rooted in the reaction to State crime.' (Maison, supra, note 59, p. 433).

63   'Two forms of international responsibility stem from a State crime—the responsibility of the State, with a collective nature, the criminal liability of its agents—which are closely intertwined. Thus, individual responsibility can be seen as a form of reparation for the wrongful act of the State', Ibid., p. 511.

From the differentiation between the crime of the individual and the responsibility of the State which he or she represented stem several important consequences:

- International criminal courts and tribunals apply rules of criminal law embodied in their Statutes. The ICJ is called upon to settle interstate disputes in accordance with international law as summarily set out in Article 38 of its Statute;
- Applicable standards of evidence differ:[64] even though the facts are identical, their legal characterization may be different depending on the responsibility at stake: the international responsibility of the State or the criminal responsibility of its leaders. Thus, in the *Genocide* case, the Court said that it attaches

    > the utmost importance to the factual and legal findings made by the ICTY in ruling on the criminal liability of the accused before it and, in the present case, the Court takes fullest account of the ICTY's trial and appellate judgments dealing with the events underlying the dispute. The situation is not the same for positions adopted by the ICTY on issues of general international law which do not lie within the specific purview of its jurisdiction and, moreover, the resolution of which is not always necessary for deciding the criminal cases before it.[65]

- Rules on criminal conviction of an individual—who may only be convicted in the absence of any 'reasonable doubt'—are distinct and more demanding than those relating to the attribution to a State of an internationally wrongful act.

Therefore, in a particular case, the ICC, or, in the Bosnian case, the ICTY, may condemn an individual for any reason other than his or her participation in genocide, but the offense or offenses for which he or she was condemned may appear as elements of a genocide instigated and organized by a State; in other words, crimes against humanity and war crimes committed by persons

---

64 D. Groome, 'Adjudicating Genocide: Is the International Court of Justice Capable of Judging State Criminal Responsibility?', 31 *Fordham International Law Journal*, 2007, pp. 945–976.

65 *Application of the Convention on the Prevention and Punishment of the Crime of Genocide*, (Bosnia and Herzegovina v Serbia and Montenegro), 26 February 2007, supra, note 23, p. 209, para. 403.

convicted by the ICTY or the ICC or accused before this Tribunal or this Court can constitute elements of genocide even though, considered in isolation, they do not justify a charge or conviction for such offence.

The near-absence of any mechanism of forced implementation under international law is another congenital weakness of international law. However, here again, it is in some respects less pronounced when 'serious breaches' are at stake than for other violations of international law. There are two reasons for this.

First, concerning 'ordinary breaches', the traditional mechanism for giving effect to the principles and rules applying to international responsibility were (and remain) 'counter-measures'—that is, an international variant of the law of retaliation. According to Article 49 (1) of the ILC Articles, '[a]n injured State may only take countermeasures against a State which is responsible for an internationally wrongful act in order to induce that State to comply with its obligations' concerning reparation and the other consequences of an internationally wrongful act. Moreover, besides being submitted to various conditions,[66] counter-measures must not affect any obligation arising from peremptory norms of general international law.[67] Thus defined, counter-measures are illustrative of the traditional approach of State responsibility: they are purely 'inter-subjective' and quasi-exclusively aimed at obtaining reparation. However, in this respect too, the ILC Articles offer promising prospects by 'communy-tizing' the invocation of the responsibility of the State and the reactions called by 'serious breaches':

(i) under some conditions, Article 42 recognizes that '[a] State is entitled as an injured State to invoke the responsibility of another State if the obligation breached is owed to (..) (b) a group of States including that State, or the international community as a whole';

(ii) according to Article 48, paragraph 1:
Any State other than an injured State is entitled to invoke the responsibility of another State (...) if:
(a) the obligation breached is owed to a group of States including that State, and is established for the protection of a collective interest of the group; or
(b) the obligation breached is owed to the international community as a whole.
and

---

66 Including proportionality (Article 51) and, in principle, reversibility (Article 49(2)).
67 This is the meaning of the uselessly complicated Article 50 of the ILC Articles.

(iii) most importantly, Article 54 states that the rules on counter-measures in the ILC Articles do not prejudice the right of any State, entitled under Article 48, paragraph 1, to invoke the responsibility of another State, to take lawful measures against that State to ensure cessation of the breach and reparation in the interest of the injured State or of the beneficiaries of the obligation breached.

There can be no doubt that there is a marked discrepancy between the very idea of these 'measures'—usually called 'sanctions'—on the one hand and the traditional international legal system characterized by its fundamental decentralization and the absence of any authority over juxtaposed sovereign States. The simple fact that sanctions can be imposed by international institutions and, in some cases, by individual States or regional organizations acting in the name of the international community, shows that this long-established analysis of international law is no longer tenable—even though it still accurately describes essential aspects of it, as shown by the survival of counter-measures as a valid means to react to internationally wrongful acts. The existence of sanctions bears witness to the slow establishment of the concept of community within the international legal order, in line with institutions like *jus cogens* or international crimes.[68] These rules end the exclusive *tête-à-tête* between the injured State and the wrongdoer and introduce into the game a third actor: the international community of States.[69] Breaches of rules whose respect is of interest for all States can give rise to action by all of them. There are, admittedly, important limits, the main one being the prohibition of the use of military force.

For their part, 'measures' that can be decided by the Security Council under Chapter VII of the Charter are not subject to such limitations—at least, the Council is not barred from utilizing armed force as provided for in Article 42. Indeed, not more than the Charter as a whole, Chapter VII has been conceived as providing means for reacting to international wrongful acts, including serious breaches of obligations arising from peremptory norms of international law. However, the UN system has progressively evolved so that coercive measures may be used to sanction serious violations of peremptory norms of

---

[68] On the break-up marked by Article 54 of the ILC Articles from the traditional approach of State responsibility, see e.g.: A. Pellet & A. Miron, 'Sanctions', in R. Wolfrum et al. (eds), *The Max Planck Encyclopaedia of Public International Law*, vol. IX, Oxford University Press, 2012, pp. 11–12.

[69] Or defensibly the international community *tout court*—but this a vast and complicated issue.

international law other than the prohibition of the use of force. In so doing, the Security Council '*met les ressources du droit de la sécurité collective à la disposition du droit de la responsabilité*'.[70]

Through the enlargement of the concept of 'threat to the peace', a link has progressively been created between humanitarian disasters (and the risks they involve) and Chapter VII of the Charter. If it is true that not all violations of international law necessarily threaten international peace and security, the most serious breaches of the most essential obligations of international law always constitute a violation of the fundamental interests of the international community and, as long as peace cannot be reduced to the mere absence of war, massive violations of human rights or humanitarian law, even if they occur in one State, are 'international concerns' because, potentially at least, they threaten international peace and security—and can also turn into truly international armed conflicts. Examples are the tragedies of Bosnia and Herzegovina, Rwanda or Darfur, or the civil war in Libya or Syria. In this perspective, there is nothing incongruous in the characterization by the Security Council of situations of massive violations of human rights and of the law of armed conflict as 'threats to peace' that could trigger the application of Chapter VII of the Charter.[71]

3   Conclusion

By way of conclusion:

(i)   Contemporary general international law includes useful tools to deal with human-rights violations, and obligations to prevent and to punish serious violations of human rights and international crimes;

(ii) These violations do not offer a 'legal profile' different from that of other serious breaches of obligations arising under peremptory norms of general international law (*jus cogens*);

---

70   'puts the resources of the law of collective security at the disposal of law of responsibility' (Forteau, supra, note 36, p. 631).

71   See in particular J. M. Sorel, 'L'élargissement de la notion de menace contre la paix', in SFDI, colloque de Rennes, *Le chapitre VII de la Charte des Nations Unies*, Pedone, 1995, pp. 3–57 ; or M. Zambelli, *La constatation des situations de l'article 39 de la Charte des Nations Unies par le Conseil de sécurité – Le champ d'application des pouvoirs prévus au chapitre VII de la Charte des Nations Unies*, Helbin & Lichtenhaum, 2002, pp. 267–285.

(iii) While it cannot be excluded that, in exceptional circumstances, States entail some kind of criminal responsibility, the legal regime of these 'serious breaches' does not involve criminal aspects;
(iv) However, they call for reactions from the international community of States as a whole (*actio popularis*) before international courts and tribunals or at diplomatic level; 'sanctions' not involving the use of force; measures taken by the Security Council; and
(v) These 'community' reactions do not exclude the criminal responsibility of the individuals who are the direct authors of the breaches even when they have acted in their capacity as State officials.

PART 4

Law of the Sea

Exporting Environmental Standards to Protect Underwater Cultural Heritage in the Area

*Mariano J. Aznar**

1   Introduction

When our friend Djamchid Momtaz analyzed the 2001 UNESCO Convention for the protection of underwater cultural heritage,[1] he first reviewed the general regime offered for the protection of that heritage by the 1982 UN Law of the Sea Convention.[2] In assessing its Article 149 ('Archaeological and historical objects'), he regretted that

> [c]ette disposition de la Convention manque malheureusement de précision et sa mise en œuvre est laissée à la discrétion des Etats. Elle omet par ailleurs de reconnaître une quelconque responsabilité à l'Autorité internationale du fond des mers pourtant chargée par la Convention des Nations Unies sur le droit de la mer d'organiser et de contrôler les activités menées dans cette partie du fond des mers.[3]

Article 149 LOSC states that '[a]ll objects of an archaeological and historical nature found in the Area shall be preserved or disposed of for the benefit of mankind as a whole, particular regard being paid to the preferential rights of the State or country of origin, or the State of cultural origin, or the State

---

*   The author would like to thank Tullio Scovazzi, Gwénaëlle Le Gurun and Ángel Rodrigo for their invaluable comments on an earlier draft of this article. The views expressed, however, are solely those of the author, as are any errors. This article was prepared with funding from Research Grant DER2013-48826-R, awarded by the Spanish Secretary of State for Research, Development and Innovation. All websites were last accessed on 15 July 2016.

1   Adopted 2 November 2001, entered into force 2 January 2009, 2562 UNTS 1 (UNESCO Convention hereinafter).

2   United Nations Convention on the Law of the Sea, adopted and opened for signature 10 December 1982, entered into force 16 November 1994, 1833 UNTS 397 (LOSC hereinafter).

3   D. Momtaz, 'La convention sur la protection du patrimoine culturel subaquatique', in T. M. Ndiaye and R. Wolfrum (eds), Law of the Sea, Environmental Law and Settlement of Disputes: Liber Amicorum Judge Thomas A. Mensah, Martinus Nijhoff, 2007, pp. 443–461, at p. 444 (footnotes omitted).

of historical and archaeological origin.'[4] It thus establishes a generic duty to preserve underwater cultural heritage (UCH) in the Area, in line with the general obligation for all marine zones established by Article 303(1) LOSC, which provides that 'States have the duty to protect objects of an archaeological and historical nature found at sea and shall cooperate for this purpose.'

The mandate drafted in Article 149 contains so many caveats—how to interpret and apply, for example, the concepts of '*disposal* for the benefit of mankind as a whole', 'preferential rights' or States of 'cultural, historical or archaeological origin'—that the legal regime it creates fails to provide clear answers on how to protect the UCH located in the Area.[5] As Momtaz warned, the International Seabed Authority (ISA or the Authority) has not been given any responsibility for that protection. Yet nor does the UNESCO Convention give the Authority much room in this matter: its Secretary-General must merely be notified by States Parties to the Convention of any discovery or activity directed at UCH located in the Area;[6] but the ISA does not participate in the protection system foreseen for the Area in Article 12 of the UNESCO Convention.[7] In any case, the ISA does not seem to be well equipped either normatively or institutionally to perform such tasks, at least explicitly. As we will see, the ISA regulations include a basic reference to human remains and to historical or archaeological objects and sites only in general terms and more for information purposes (see below, section 2).

However, following the general mandate to protect and preserve the marine environment in the Area, a mandate endorsed in general principles and in the LOSC, the ISA has produced a more complete array of (hard and soft) rules

---

4 'Area' is defined in Article 1 LOSC as 'the seabed and ocean floor and subsoil thereof, beyond the limits of national jurisdiction'. On the drafting of Article 149, see A. Strati, *The Protection of the Underwater Cultural Heritage: An Emerging Objective of the Contemporary Law of the Sea,* Kluwer, 1995, pp. 297–300.

5 Sarah Dromgoole has called it 'an empty shell'. S. Dromgoole, *Underwater Cultural Heritage and International Law,* Cambridge University Press, 2013, p. 261.

6 Article 11(2) UNESCO Convention. Article 1(6) defines 'activities directed at underwater cultural heritage' as 'activities having underwater cultural heritage as their primary object and which may, directly or indirectly, physically disturb or otherwise damage underwater cultural heritage'. Article 1(7) defines 'activities incidentally affecting underwater cultural heritage' as 'activities which, despite not having underwater cultural heritage as their primary object or one of their objects, may physically disturb or otherwise damage underwater cultural heritage'. Therefore, any mining, commercial or research activities in the Area not initially targeting UCH are not covered by the duty to report in advance.

7 This Article establishes a cooperative system based on notifications, shared information and consultations among the 'interested States'. See below, section 4.1.

protecting the environment in the Area (below, section 3).[8] The question is whether these rules or the principles on which they are founded might also apply to the historical or archaeological objects and sites located in the Area (below, section 4).[9] The remarks concluding this analysis will discuss possible improvements to the current system (below, section 5).

This contribution will thus try to link three areas of research to which Djamchid Momtaz has devoted time and interest: the law of the sea, international environmental law, and cultural heritage law. It will discuss how exploration, prospection and mining activities in the Area, understood as activities that may incidentally affect the UCH located in that Area, might be managed not only keeping in mind existing environmental standards in international law but also—by analogy and through deduction/induction of applicable principles—the archaeological variable into such activities. To this end, it will offer an analysis that moves from general (LOSC) rules to specific (UNESCO Convention) rules. This is because the answer eventually lies not in the latter, which mainly address activities *directed* at UCH in the Area,[10] but rather in general international law, including the law of the sea and international environmental law. This contribution will discuss, as a hypothesis, whether these two overlapping regimes could fill any existing gaps in the protection provided for UCH in the Area, some originated by the still-limited ratification of the UNESCO Convention,[11] by applying the ample, general regime established under the LOSC by the ISA Mining Code.

---

8   All ISA documents are available at <https://www.isa.org.jm>. A recent appraisal of the Authority's work can be found in M. Lodge, 'The International Seabed Authority and the Exploration and Exploitation of the Deep Seabed', *Revue belge du droit international*, 2014/1, pp. 129–136.

9   At the very outset, it should be noted that protection of UCH, if any, has historically been addressed by impact reports within the context of the general protection of the marine environment, and sometimes as a simple sub-chapter thereof. One of the ideas underlying this paper is that UCH deserves a specific, distinct methodological approach, notwithstanding its close relationship with the marine environment. This can be achieved through an independent procedure or its integration with other aspects and interests.

10 See supra, note 6.

11 As at July 2016, the UNESCO Convention was in force for the following 55 States: Albania, Algeria, Antigua and Barbuda, Argentina, Bahrain, Barbados, Belgium, Benin, Bosnia and Herzegovina, Bulgaria, Cambodia, Croatia, Cuba, Democratic Republic of the Congo, Ecuador, France, Gabon, Ghana, Grenada, Guatemala, Guinea-Bissau, Guyana, Haiti, Honduras, Hungary, Iran, Italy, Jamaica, Jordan, Lebanon, Libya, Lithuania, Madagascar, Mexico, Montenegro, Morocco, Namibia, Nigeria, Palestine, Panama, Paraguay, Portugal, Romania, Saint Kitts and Nevis, Saint Lucia, Saint Vincent and the Grenadines, Saudi

2 Protection of the Underwater Cultural Heritage through ISA Decisions

The ISA has adopted several instruments that together constitute what the Authority calls the 'Mining Code'. To date, the ISA has issued three different Regulations: the Regulations on Prospecting and Exploration for Polymetallic Nodules in the Area (as revised),[12] the Regulations on Prospecting and Exploration for Polymetallic Sulphides[13] and the Regulations on Prospecting and Exploration for Cobalt-Rich Ferromanganese Crusts.[14] The Mining Code is supplemented by recommendations by the ISA Legal and Technical Commission (LTC) for the guidance of contractors. In particular, these include the Recommendations for the guidance of contractors for assessing the possible environmental effects of exploration for polymetallic nodules in the Area.[15]

The ISA is also developing regulations for exploiting mineral resources in the Area. Following a Council decision,[16] on 23 March 2015 along with a discussion paper on the financial terms of exploitation contracts, the Authority issued a special consultation document.[17] This was followed on 15 July 2015 by the 'Draft Framework, High level Issues and Action Plan (Version II)',[18] which is expected to initiate a process for a 'zero draft' of the regulations for exploitation in the Area, to be submitted to the ISA Council in July 2016.

Finally, the Authority also concluded in 2000 a memorandum of understanding with the International Oceanographic Commission (IOC) of UNESCO, which—alas!—fails to mention, even tangentially, the protection of UCH. This was mainly due to the lack of IOC archaeological competence.[19]

Arabia, Slovakia, Slovenia, South Africa, Spain, Togo, Trinidad and Tobago, Tunisia and Ukraine.

12 ISBA/19/C/17, 13 July 2000 (revised 22 July 2013) (PNR hereinafter).
13 ISBA/16/A/12/Rev.1, 7 May 2010 (PSR hereinafter).
14 ISBA/18/A/11, 27 July 2012 (CCR hereinafter).
15 ISBA/7/LTC/1/Rev.1, 13 February 2002.
16 ISBA/20/C/31, 23 July 2014, para. 3.
17 ISA, *Report to Members of the Authority and all stakeholders*, available at https://www.isa .org.jm/files/documents/EN/Survey/Report-2015.pdf.
18 Reviewed and revised for stakeholder responses to the *Report* cited in previous note. Available at https://www.isa.org.jm/files/documents/EN/OffDocs/Rev_RegFramework_ ActionPlan_14072015.pdf.
19 Available at https://www.isa.org.jm/sites/default/files/documents/EN/Regs/ISA-IOC-MOU.pdf. It likewise does not mention Article 149 LOSC, as the Memorandum refers mainly to 'marine scientific research' and to cooperation 'in the field of ocean services, particularly in the collection of environmental data and information'. On the possible

2.1   An Overly Generic Regime...

All the Regulations adopted include the same scheme for dealing with UCH: a proviso regarding prospecting and another proviso applicable to exploration and regarding the protection and preservation of the marine environment, all with similar if not identical wording. First, entitled 'Objects of an archaeological or historical nature', Regulation 8 of all the texts states:

> A prospector shall immediately notify the Secretary-General in writing of any finding in the Area of an object of actual or potential archaeological or historical nature and its location. The Secretary-General shall transmit such information to the Director General of the United Nations Educational, Scientific and Cultural Organization.

Secondly, entitled 'Human remains and objects and sites of an archaeological or historical nature', Regulations 35 PNR and 37 PSR/CCR state:

> The contractor shall immediately notify the Secretary-General in writing of any finding in the exploration area of any human remains of an archaeological or historical nature, or any object or site of a similar nature and its location, including the preservation and protection measures taken. The Secretary-General shall [20] transmit such information to the Director-General of the United Nations Educational, Scientific and Cultural Organization and any other competent international organization. Following the finding of any such human remains, object or site in the exploration area, and in order to avoid disturbing such human remains, object or site, no further prospecting or exploration shall take place, within a reasonable radius, until such time as the Council decides otherwise after taking account of the views of the Director-General of the United Nations Educational, Scientific and Cultural Organization or any other competent international organization.[21]

The regime thus created imposes (1) a duty on the prospector/contractor to notify the Authority's Secretary-General, (2) a duty on the Secretary-General

---

inclusion of UCH research within marine scientific research, see S. Dromgoole, 'Revisiting the relationship between marine scientific research and the underwater cultural heritage', 25 *The International Journal of Marine and Coastal Law,* 2010, pp. 33–61.

20   Only the CCR includes the term 'immediately' here.
21   This duty is included *expressis verbis* as a standard clause in exploration contracts under Section 7 of Annex 4 of all Regulations.

to transmit this information to the Director General of UNESCO and to any other competent international organizations, and (3) a duty to suspend any prospection or exploration until the ISA Council adopts a decision after taking account of the views of the UNESCO and these other organizations. The duties apply to finding in the Area of any human remains, object or site of an archaeological or historical nature, and their purpose is to prevent the disturbance of such remains, objects or sites and of the surrounding zone within a reasonable radius.

There are some caveats in this process: there is no system for monitoring the findings of the prospector/contractor; the process for identifying other 'competent international organizations' is not clear; the preservation of human remains seems to be required only when they are of an archaeological or historical nature; and there is no clear pattern regarding how to determine the radius of the surrounding area to be temporarily protected. But perhaps the main problem lies in the contrast in the assessments of both archaeological views, those expressed by UNESCO and other competent organizations and those of the prospector/contractor. In a case of conflict, there is no provision specifying which should prevail. This brings us to a dilemma detected early in the doctrine: the regulations had 'to find a balance between the interests of the development of resources and those of environmental protection and they [had] to decide how preventive the regulations should be while scientific uncertainty remains as to the effects of deep sea-bed mining'.[22]

This conflict can also be viewed from the other side: what if any of the measures foreseen in the cooperative process directed at an archaeological site in the Area is decided under Article 12 of the UNESCO Convention and the site is located in an exploration zone already attributed by the ISA to stakeholders with (or without) the nationality of a UNESCO Convention State Party? Article 3 of the latter provides that '[n]othing in this Convention shall prejudice the rights, jurisdiction and duties of States under international law, including the United Nations Convention on the Law of the Sea. This Convention shall be interpreted and applied in the context of and in a manner consistent with international law, including the United Nations Convention on the Law of the Sea.'[23] Does this mean that the archaeological activities must irremediably be

---

22 A. Nollkaemper, 'Deep sea-bed mining and the protection of the marine environment', 15 *Marine Policy*, 1991, pp. 55–66, at p. 56.

23 Article 311(2) LOSC recalls that '[t]his Convention [LOSC] shall not alter the rights and obligations of States Parties which arise from other agreements compatible with this Convention and which do not affect the enjoyment by other States Parties of their rights or the performance of their obligations under this Convention.'

subordinated to the mining activities? Is it conceivable that in such cases of the application of successive treaties—the LOSC and the UNESCO Convention—the former applies only to the extent that its provisions are compatible with those of the latter as between States Parties to both conventions? What place is to be given to the rule *lex specialis derogat generali* notwithstanding the overarching role recognised to the LOSC as the 'Constitution of the Oceans'?

2.2 ... Neglected in Practice?

When discussing the responsibilities of States sponsoring activities in the Area in accordance with Part XI LOSC and its 1994 Implementation Agreement, and notwithstanding the efforts made by UNESCO,[24] in its Advisory Opinion of 1 February 2011, the Seabed Disputes Chamber of the International Tribunal of the Law of the Sea (ITLOS or the Tribunal) did not mention, even tangentially, any obligation or duty of States regarding the general protection of UCH in the Area as provided for under Articles 149 and 303 LOSC.[25] The Chamber envisaged only an environmental responsibility on the part of sponsoring States, basically, 'due diligence', but said not a word on the diligence likewise imposed with regard to UCH found in the Area. It is true that the scope of the question submitted to the Chamber limited its possible answer since the 'activities directed at underwater cultural heritage' are not envisaged among those that may entail the responsibility of States sponsoring activities in the Area. But a reference would have been very welcome.

The general absence of references to UCH has also characterized contractors and ISA practice to date. As we have seen, Section 7 of the Standard clauses for exploration contracts obliges contractors to notify the Secretary-General of any finding in the exploration area of any human remains of an archaeological or historical nature, or any object or site of a similar nature and its

---

24 The Intergovernmental Oceanographic Commission of the UNESCO appeared before the Tribunal in the oral proceedings and, among other issues, its representative expressly cited Articles 149 and 303 LOSC, as well as the 2001 UNESCO Convention, and reminded the Tribunal that '[t]he oceans are filled with the traces of human existence. This includes some millions of shipwrecks, prehistoric dwellings, ruins and artefacts. Many of them are located in the Area and are of immense importance for the comprehension of the development of humanity. Unfortunately, many cases arise, where such submerged archaeological sites are damaged or destroyed by negatively-impacting activities. These range from pipeline laying, drilling, mineral extraction, trawling and dredging to international treasure hunt.' ITLOS/PV.2010/4/Rev.1, 16 September 2010, p. 12 (all ITLOS documents are available electronically at http://www.itlos.org).

25 *Responsibilities and obligations of States with respect to activities in the Area, Advisory Opinion*, 1 February 2011, *ITLOS Reports 2011*, p. 10, at pp. 74–75, para. 242.

location, including preservation and protection measures taken; and to stop further prospecting or exploration until such time as the ISA Council, having received the opinion of the UNESCO Director General, decides otherwise. But as far as this author knows, there has been no discussion between the ISA and contractors on how mining activities in the Area might affect UCH, in general or particular terms. Indeed, none of the proposed activities seems to be concerned with the duties generally imposed. For example, the 'Environmental Management Plan for the Clarion-Clipperton Zone', submitted on 13 July 2011[26] and approved by the ISA Council on 26 July 2012,[27] makes no mention of UCH, even though it refers to a zone of the Pacific Ocean that was historically subject to transit which may have originated numerous underwater remains of cultural or archaeological nature.

However, the 'Regulatory Framework for Deep Sea Mineral Exploitation in the Area' currently under discussion at the ISA[28] does include within its priority actions that of addressing human remains and objects and sites of an archaeological or historical nature as part of the 'Social impact assessment' (SIA) process. Specifically, '[t]he SIA and action plan should address any specific matters relating to the cultural heritage in the exploitation area(s).'[29] A more precise approach to these aspects is therefore expected in forthcoming ISA decisions.

3 Outlining Applicable General Environmental Obligations

Protection of the marine environment from activities in the Area is governed by the LOSC, the 1994 Agreement Relating to the Implementation of Part XI of the LOSC[30] and the rules, regulations and procedures adopted by the ISA. Some general, customary principles and some soft-law rules likewise apply.[31]

---

26 ISBA/17/LTC/7, 13 July 2011.
27 ISBA/18/C/22, 26 July 2012. See M. Lodge et al., 'Seabed Mining: International Seabed Authority environmental management plan for the Clarion-Clipperton Zone. A partnership approach' 49 *Marine Policy,* 2014, pp. 66–72.
28 See supra, notes 17 and 18.
29 Supra, note 17, p. 33; supra, note 18 pp. 37, 58.
30 Adopted 28 July 1994, 1836 UNTS 42 (1994 Agreement hereinafter). Under Article 2(1), '[t]he provisions of this Agreement and Part XI shall be interpreted and applied together as a single instrument. In the event of any inconsistency between this Agreement and Part XI, the provisions of this Agreement shall prevail.'
31 See, among others, T. Scovazzi, 'Mining, Protecting the Environment, Scientific Research and Bioprospecting: Some Considerations on the Role of the International Sea-bed Authority', 19 *The International Journal of Marine and Coastal Law,* 2004, pp. 383–410;

The basic protection regime for the Area established under the LOSC begins with Article 192—'States have the obligation to protect and preserve the marine environment'—and continues in Part XII and, particularly, in Article 209. The evolution of the international law of the sea and international environmental law, and consequently that of general international law, have introduced new rules and principles. It has already been said that '[t]he system is based on the application of the precautionary approach and is evolutionary in nature.'[32] This flexibility enables its continuous adaptation to new challenges, mostly when activities in the area are not only increasing quantitatively but are changing qualitatively.[33] These activities may inevitably and negatively affect the seafloor, its substrate and deep sediments, home to both a relatively unknown biodiversity and, often, the embedded remains of cultural or archaeological artefacts. Under Article 147(1) LOSC, '[a]ctivities in the Area shall be carried out with reasonable regard for other activities in the marine environment.'

Under Article 209 LOSC, the ISA is obliged to adopt and adapt the necessary rules, regulations and procedures to prevent, reduce and control pollution of the marine environment caused by activities in the Area.[34] These rules—which oblige the ISA itself, the sponsoring States and the contractors—are based on the *precautionary approach* as reflected in Principle 15 of the Rio Declaration,[35]

M. Lodge, 'Protecting the marine environment of the deep seabed', in R. Rayfuse (ed), *Research Handbook on International Marine Environmental Law,* Elgar, 2015, pp. 151–169. See further in the same book R. Churchill, 'The LOSC regime for the protection of the marine environment—fit for the twenty-first century?', pp. 3–30.

[32] Lodge, supra, note 31, p. 152. See further S. Marr, *The Precautionary Principle in the Law of the Sea: Modern Decision Making in International Law,* Martinus Nijhoff, 2003. As at March 2015, the Authority had approved a total of 26 contracts for exploration covering areas of the seabed in the Pacific, Indian and Atlantic oceans in excess of 1.2 million km² (Lodge, supra, note 8, p. 133).

[33] For a recent appraisal, see 'Chapter 23. Offshore Mining Industries', in L. Inniss & A. Simcock (coordinators), *The First Global Integrated Marine Assessment,* United Nations, 2016, available at http://www.un.org/Depts/los/global_reporting/WOA_RPROC/Chapter_23.pdf.

[34] See further Articles 145 and 162(2)(o)(ii) LOSC and Article 17(1)(ix) and (xii) of Annex III LOSC. The 1994 Agreement emphasizes the duties of the Authority with respect to the marine environment in the drafting of regulations and the approval of any plan of work in the Area: see the 1994 Agreement, Annex, Section 1, paragraphs 5(g) and 7, respectively. See also Regulation 31(1) PNR/CCR and Regulation 33(1) PSR. These regulations 'may be supplemented by further rules, regulations and procedures, in particular on the protection and preservation of the marine environment' (Regulation 1(5) PNR/PSR/CCR).

[35] 'In order to protect the environment, the precautionary approach shall be widely applied by States according to their capabilities. Where there are threats of serious or irreversible

which—as ITLOS observed—perhaps has not yet crystallized as a customary principle of environmental international law[36] but is included as a contractual obligation in all ISA regulations.[37] It is a precautionary approach that must be supplemented with an obligation to apply 'best environmental practices', today understood—as ITLOS also reminded—as 'enshrined in the sponsoring States' obligation of due diligence'.[38] The latter comprises, as a by-product, the obligation to conduct a prior environmental impact assessment as required by both Article 206 LOSC and by customary law.[39]

Precaution, in general terms, thus applies *before* and *during* any activity planned or to be performed in the Area:[40] an impact assessment report must be submitted prior to the activity, and best environmental practices must be followed throughout its duration. Technical advances notwithstanding, environmental uncertainty still exists, making it impossible to issue any conclusive risk assessment of the effects of large-scale commercial seabed mining. The precautionary approach tries to cope with this uncertainty through (1) knowledge of the baseline conditions in potential mining areas, the natural variability

---

damage, lack of full scientific certainty shall not be used as a reason for postponing cost-effective measures to prevent environmental degradation.' UN Doc. A/CONF.151/26 (Vol. 1), 12 August 1992.

36   Supra, note 25, p. 47, para. 135. For a recent review, see J. Corti Varela, 'El principio de precaución en la jurisprudencia internacional', 69 *Revista Española de Derecho Internacional*, 2017, pp. 219–243.

37   Regulation 31(2) PNR/CCR and Regulation 33(2) PSR.

38   Supra, note 25, p. 48, para. 136.

39   *Pulp Mills on the River Uruguay* (Argentina v Uruguay), Judgment, *ICJ Reports 2010*, p. 83, para. 204; for ITLOS see supra, note 25, p. 50, para. 145. See G. Le Gurun, 'EIA and the International Seabed Authority', in K. Bastmeier & T. Koivurova (eds), *Theory and Practice of Transboundary Environmental Impact Assessment*, Martinus Nijhoff, 2008, pp. 221–263.

40   For the implementation of these broad principles, the system enables the LTC to issue technical or administrative recommendations for the guidance of contractors and to assist them in the implementation of the rules, regulations and procedures (Article 165(2)(e) LOSC). Contractors with the Authority are required to observe any such recommendations as far as reasonably practicable (Reg. 31(3), 32(1), 39 (1) PNR/CCR and 33(3), 34(1), 41(1) PSR). The LTC has already issued four recommendations: *Recommendations for the guidance of contractors on the content, format and structure of annual reports* (ISBA/21/LTC/15), *Recommendations for the guidance of contractors for the reporting of actual and direct exploration expenditure* (ISBA/21/LTC/11), *Recommendations for the guidance of contractors for the assessment of the possible environmental impacts arising from exploration for marine minerals in the Area* (ISBA/19/LTC/8), and *Recommendations for the guidance of contractors and sponsoring States relating to training programmes under plans of work for exploration* (ISBA/19/LTC/14).

of these baseline conditions and their relationship with impacts related to mining, keeping a standardised database provided by contractors and updated by the Authority with independent scientific inputs and recommendations from the LTC; (2) the preparation and submission of the environmental impact assessment, following the recommendation issued by the LTC;[41] and (3) the incorporation of a monitoring system and assurance of compliance during and after the mining activities.

4   Applying Environmental Standards to UCH

As we will see below, the regime provided for under the UNESCO Convention to deal with UCH in the Area is limited.[42] It governs mainly the activities directed at UCH, i.e. those with underwater cultural heritage as their primary object and which may, directly or indirectly, physically disturb or otherwise damage UCH (Article 1(6)). Mining activities in the Area, however, basically fall under the concept of activities that *incidentally* affect UCH, i.e. activities that, despite not having UCH as their primary object or one of their objects, may physically disturb or otherwise damage UCH (Article 1(7)). Could environmental principles, regulations and recommendations provided for under the LOSC, the ISA Mining Code and other rules of general international law be 'exported' to protect UCH during these indirect activities?

4.1   *The UNESCO Convention in the Area*

Articles 11 and 12 of the UNESCO Convention govern the management of UCH in the Area. Article 11 establishes a reporting and notification system: nationals or vessels of a State Party are required by such State to report any discovery or activity directed at UCH to it.[43] That state must then notify the Director-General of UNESCO of these reports (who, in turn, must make any such information

---

41 Following a workshop held in Fiji, a template was drafted for this environmental impact assessment. It includes several references to UCH. See *Environmental Management Needs for Exploration and Exploitation of Deep Sea Minerals*, ISA Technical Study: No. 10, 2011, available electronically at <http://www.isa.org.jm/files/documents/EN/Pubs/TS10/TS10-Final.pdf>.

42 Not to mention the intrinsic limit *ratione personæ*: the UNESCO Convention only obliges its current 55 States Parties (see supra, note 11).

43 The regime refers mainly to private operators. Article 13 provides that State vessels and aircraft, undertaking their normal mode of operations, and not engaged in activities directed at UCH, shall not be obliged to report discoveries of UCH under the UNESCO Convention. States parties shall ensure, however, by the adoption of appropriate measures

available to all States Parties), as well as the Secretary-General of the ISA. Any State Party with a verifiable link to the UCH concerned may declare its interest in being consulted on how to ensure the effective protection thereof to the Director-General and thus become an 'interested State'.[44]

Under Article 12 of the Convention, all interested States Parties are to be invited by the Director-General of UNESCO to hold consultations on how best to protect the heritage and to appoint from among themselves a 'Coordinating State', with the Secretary-General of the ISA also being invited to these consultations. This Coordinating State, always acting for the benefit of humanity as a whole and on behalf of all States Parties, shall normally implement measures of protection that have been agreed by the consulting States[45] and shall normally issue all necessary authorisations for these agreed measures.[46] The Coordinating State may also conduct any necessary preliminary research on the UCH, shall issue all necessary authorisations therefor, and shall promptly inform the Director-General of the results; the Director-General, in turn, shall make such information available to other States Parties.

Interestingly, the system so described, although mainly focused on activities *directed* at UCH, and therefore excluding mining exploration or prospection,[47] also mentions the simple discovery of such heritage, as do the ISA Regulations. The latter require the contractor immediately to notify the ISA Secretary-

---

not impairing the operations or operational capabilities of their State vessels and aircraft, that they comply, as far as is reasonable and practicable, with the Convention.

44   Under Article 11(4) of the UNESCO Convention, for assessing that verifiable link, particular regard is paid to the preferential rights of States of cultural, historical or archaeological origin. Jie Huang, 'Chasing provenance: Legal dilemmas for protecting states with a verifiable link to underwater cultural heritage', 84 *Ocean & Coastal Management*, 2013, pp. 220–225.

45   Under Article 12(7), '[n]o State Party shall undertake or authorize activities directed at State vessels and aircraft in the Area without the consent of the flag State.' With regard to the legal status of such vessels and aircraft, see M. J. Aznar, 'Treasure hunters, sunken State vessels and the 2001 UNESCO Convention on the Protection of Underwater Cultural Heritage', 25 *The International Journal of Marine and Coastal Law*, 2010, pp. 209–236. See further the Resolution on 'The Legal Regime of Wrecks of Warships and Other State-owned Ships in International Law', adopted by the Institut de droit international on 29 August 2015, Tallinn Session, available at http://www.justitiaetpace.org/idiE/resolutionsE/2015_Tallinn_09_en.pdf.

46   'Normally' because the consulting States, which include the Coordinating State, may agree that another State Party shall implement these measures or issue these authorizations.

47   Such as other activities that may incidentally affect UCH, like the laying of submarine cables. On the latter, see E. Pérez-Álvaro, 'Unconsidered Threats to Underwater Cultural Heritage: Laying Submarine Cables', 14 *Rosetta*, 2013, pp. 54–70, available at http://www.rosetta.bham.ac.uk/issue14/perezalvaro.pdf.

General—who will transmit such information to the UNESCO Director-General and any other competent international organisation—of any finding in the Area 'of an object of actual or potential archaeological or historical nature and its location';[48] and 'of any finding in the exploration area of any human remains of an archaeological or historical nature, or any object or site of a similar nature and its location, including the preservation and protection measures taken'.[49] If the contractor is a national of any UNESCO Convention State party, the latter should stop its prospection or exploration activities and initiate the consultation system provided for under the Convention. If not, and so as not to disturb the human remains, object or site in question, no further prospecting or exploration shall take place, within a reasonable radius, until such time as the ISA Council decides otherwise after taking account of the views of the UNESCO Director-General or any other competent international organisation. Ostensibly, if the UNESCO Convention applies, the views of the Director-General are supposed to be the result of the consultations held by the latter, the interested States under Article 11(4) of the Convention, and the ISA Secretary-General. If not, the ISA Council shall only decide on the views received from the UNESCO Director-General[50] or from any other competent organisation.

4.2   Completing the System with the Environmental Model

This system of mere notification and, in case of application of the UNESCO Convention, consultation seems incomplete or, at least, insufficient for the effective protection and management of the UCH located in the Area. As we have seen, it should apply, essentially, to activities *directed* at UCH but not necessarily to activities affecting UCH only incidentally, such as mining.

However, the regime established for environmental protection under the LOSC by the ISA offers other ways to better protect and manage that heritage. Among the possible measures, attention should be called to the following four:

---

48   Regulation 8 PNR/PSR/CCR.
49   Regulation 35 PNR and Regulation 37 PSR/CCR.
50   Although a Scientific and Technical Advisory Body (STAB) was created under Article 23 of the UNESCO Convention to assist only the Meeting of States parties, its Statutes generically include among its functions that of giving guidance 'in questions directly related to Rules in the framework of the practical application of the State cooperation mechanism contained in the Convention (Articles 8 to 13)' (Article 1(a)(iii)). Nothing would thus prevent the UNESCO Director-General, who is represented in the STAB by the UNESCO Secretariat (Article 6(a)), from receiving such guidance from the STAB on how to address the finding in the Area of an archaeological object by a contractor. See the STAB Statutes at http://www.unesco.org/new/fileadmin/MULTIMEDIA/HQ/CLT/pdf/StatutesAdvisoryBody_Final_EN.pdf.

- The possible application of a similar monitoring system to that foreseen for the marine environment,[51] whereby prospectors would cooperate with the Authority on the establishment and implementation of programmes for monitoring and evaluating the potential impact of mining activities (including prospection and exploration) upon the UCH located in the Area. One unresolved point of this system that deserves a thoughtful analysis is the open-access nature of the data collected[52] with regard to unlawful activities against UCH, including looting.[53]
- The possible establishment of 'preservation reference zones' to protect not only the marine environment but UCH as well. Under ISA regulations, these zones are defined as 'areas in which no mining shall occur to ensure representative and stable biota of the seabed in order to assess any changes in the biodiversity of the marine environment'.[54] This would entail introducing the archaeological variable into that concept. These zones would follow the monitoring and evaluation programmes discussed above and, if required by the ISA Council, might also be established to protect UCH through assessment of changes in the ocean floor and its environment.[55]
- Another possible export from environmental standards to protect UCH could be the use of emergency orders, including those for the suspension or adjustment of operations, as may be reasonably necessary to prevent,

---

51 As provided for in Regulation 5(2) PNR/PSR/CCR and Regulations 31(6) PNR/CCR and 33(6) PSR. See further, Regulations 32 PNR/CCR and 34 PSR.

52 Regulation 7(1) PNR/PSR/CCR.

53 In this sense, under the ISA Council's Recommendations for the guidance of contractors for the assessment of the possible environmental impacts arising from exploration for marine minerals in the Area, '[c]ontractors shall permit the Authority to send its inspectors on board vessels and installations used by the contractor to carry out exploration activities in the Area to, among other things, monitor the effects of such activities on the marine environment' (ISBA/19/LTC/8, 1 March 2013, para. 12).

54 Regulations 31(6) PNR/CCR and 33(6) PSR. For example, the Plan for the Clarion-Clipperton Zone (see Lodge, above, note 27) includes the designation of an area of about 1.6 million km² as being of particular environmental interest.

55 The concept of preserved zones has been developed in various fora (IMO, UNDP, MedPlan) and well analysed by the doctrine, including how they apply to UCH. See for example A. Blanco-Bazán, 'The IMO guidelines on Particular Sensitive Sea Areas', 20 *Marine Policy,* 1996, pp. 343–349; or T. Scovazzi, 'Marine Protected Areas in Waters beyond National Jurisdiction', in M. C. Ribeiro (coordinator), *30 Years after the Signature of the United Nations Convention on the Law of the Sea,* Coimbra Editora, 2014, pp. 209–238.

contain and minimise serious harm or threat of serious harm to the UCH arising as a result of activities in the Area.[56]
- Finally, and inextricably linked to the previous idea, the archaeological variable could be included in the general idea of 'serious harm to the marine environment', understanding the latter as 'any effect from activities in the Area on the marine environment which represents a significant adverse change in the marine environment determined according to the rules, regulations and procedures adopted by the Authority on the basis of internationally recognized standards and practices'.[57] The concept is perfectly adapted to UCH: as already noted, Article 12(3) of the UNESCO Convention provides that States Parties may take all practicable measures in conformity with the Convention to prevent any immediate danger to UCH, whether arising from human activity or any other cause including looting.[58]

Along with these proposals, note that the surrounding principle inspiring them—the precautionary approach—also applies to UCH. It actually underlies the principle of *in situ* protection as the first option embodied in Article 2(5) of the UNESCO Convention and its Annexed Rule 1.[59] As explained

---

[56]   Regulations 33(6) PNR/CCR and 35(6) PSR. The ISA Council may adopt these orders, taking into account the recommendations of the LTC, the report of the Secretary-General, any information provided by the contractor and any other relevant information.

[57]   Regulation 1(3)(f) PNR/PSR/CCR.

[58]   During the drafting of the Operational Guidelines of the UNESCO Convention, immediate danger was provisionally defined as the existence of conditions that can reasonably be expected to cause damage, destruction or looting to specific UCH within a short period and which can be eliminated with safeguards. However, this definition was not ultimately included in the Guidelines (text on file with the author, who served in the Spanish Delegation in the Working Group that drafted these Guidelines, adopted by Resolution 6/MSP 4 and 8/MSP 5 of the Conference of States Parties to the Convention, UNESCO Doc. CLT/HER/CHP/OG 1/REV, August 2015, available at http://unesdoc.unesco.org/images/0023/002341/234177E.pdf).

[59]   Under Article 2(5), '[t]he preservation *in situ* of underwater cultural heritage shall be considered as the first option before allowing or engaging in any activities directed at this heritage'. Under Rule 1, '[t]he protection of underwater cultural heritage through in situ preservation shall be considered as the first option. Accordingly, activities directed at underwater cultural heritage shall be authorized in a manner consistent with the protection of that heritage, and subject to that requirement may be authorized for the purpose of making a significant contribution to protection or knowledge or enhancement of underwater cultural heritage'. And under Rule 3 '[a]ctivities directed at underwater cultural heritage shall not adversely affect the underwater cultural heritage more than is necessary for the objectives of the project'. See generally M. R. Manders, 'Unit 9: *In situ*

in the Convention's Operational Guidelines, '[b]efore deciding on preservation measures or activities, an assessment should be made of: (a) the significance of the concerned site; (b) the significance of the expected result of an intervention; (c) the means available; and (d) the entirety of the heritage known in the region.' And '[a]ctivities directed at underwater cultural heritage must use non-destructive techniques and survey methods in preference to the recovery of objects. If excavation or recovery is necessary for the purpose of scientific studies or for the ultimate protection of the underwater cultural heritage, the methods and techniques used must be as non-destructive as possible and contribute to the preservation of the remains.'[60] This sounds like the by-products of the precautionary approach: the need to submit an archaeological impact assessment report and the best archaeological practices to be followed during activity in the Area.[61] Under Rule 14, the preliminary work shall include 'an assessment that evaluates the significance and vulnerability of the underwater cultural heritage and the surrounding natural environment to damage by the proposed project, and the potential to obtain data that would meet the project objectives'.[62] The rest of the best practices are clearly found in the Annex to the UNESCO Convention, which summarizes the internationally accepted archaeological protocols to be followed when dealing with UCH.[63]

Protection', in *Training Manual for the UNESCO Foundation Course on the Protection and Management of Underwater Cultural Heritage in Asia and the Pacific*, UNESCO, 2012, available electronically at http://unesdoc.unesco.org/images/0021/002172/217234e.pdf.

60 UNESCO Convention Operational Guidelines, supra, note 58, paras. 38 and 40.
61 This has already been foreseen by some industrial States with a strong interest in protecting UCH. In the United Kingdom, for example, the UK Offshore Energy Strategic Environmental Assessment (March 2016) explicitly mentions cultural heritage as one of the 'potentially affected receptors'. See the Report available at https://www.gov.uk/government/uploads/system/uploads/attachment_data/file/504827/OESEA3_Environmental_Report_Final.pdf. Note that, although the UK has decided not to ratify the UNESCO Convention (for now), the British Government accepts its main principles and has adopted the Rules of its Annex as 'best practices for archaeology' (*Hansard Written Answers*, 24 January 2005, Col. 46W). For another 'reluctant State' with regard to the UNESCO Convention- the United States- see the 2003 version of 'Principles and Guidelines for Social Impact Assessment', available at http://www.nmfs.noaa.gov/sfa/reg_svcs/social%20guid&pri.pdf.
62 Under Rule 15, '[t]he assessment shall also include background studies of available historical and archaeological evidence, the archaeological and environmental characteristics of the site, and the consequences of any potential intrusion for the long-term stability of the underwater cultural heritage affected by the activities'.
63 Additionally, in Resolution MSP 4/5 of 2015, the Fifth Session of the Meeting of States Parties to the UNESCO Convention invited these States to provide examples of best

Underwater archaeology is also governed by the principle of minimum impact on the marine environment. The definition of UCH in the UNESCO Convention logically includes the natural context of any cultural, historical or archaeological object,[64] and any archaeological activity must include an environmental policy.[65] The path from underwater archaeology to environmental protection has already been thus firmly traced; now a return route from the environment to archaeology can be expected. Both questions are inextricably linked:[66] most historical wrecks, for example, have become artificial reefs deserving not only archaeological but also environmental protection.[67] Mining activities in the Area should therefore include a comprehensive canvas of rules protecting the fragile cultural and historical heritage located in the Area.

5   Some Concluding Remarks

As in almost every period of sessions, the UN General Assembly once again recently urged 'all States to cooperate, directly or through competent

---

practices related to UCH. The responses will allow the STAB to draw up an inventory of best practices for use by all States parties.

64   Article 1(1)(a) UNESCO Convention.

65   Under Rule 29 of the Annex, '[a]n environmental policy shall be prepared that is adequate to ensure that the seabed and marine life are not unduly disturbed'. The Convention's Operative Guidelines include the idea that 'any activity directed at underwater cultural heritage must balance the environmental impact or damage to be created, if any' (supra, note 58, para. 41).

66   But without confusing their legal nature: when analysing the concept of 'natural resources' located on the continental shelf, and particularly those to which Article 77(1) LOSC refers, the International Law Commission early affirmed on that '[i]t is clearly understood that the rights of the coastal State do not cover objects such as wrecked ships and their cargoes (including bullion) lying in the seabed or covered by sand in the subsoil' (*Yearbook of the International Law Commission*, vol. II, 1956, p. 289).

67   In the US, for example, the 1953 Submerged Lands Act (67 Stat. 29, 43 U.S.C. Sec. 1301–1315) helped an Admiralty Court protect an historical vessel sunk in Floridian waters, arguing that 'the remains of abandoned, two-hundred-year old shipwrecks, which have lain undisturbed for centuries under an undetermined amount of sand, reasonably can be characterized as natural resources for purposes of the federal Act.' *Subaqueous Exploration and Archaeology, Ltd. And Atlantic Ship Historical Society, Inc., v. The Unidentified, Wrecked and Abandoned Vessel et al.*, 577 F. Sup. 597, 613 (D. Md. 1983), aff' d, 765 F.2d 139 (4th Cir. 1985). See M. J. Aznar, 'Regarding « Les épaves de navires en haute mer et le droit international. Le cas du Mont-Louis » by Guido Starkle (1984/1985-1). 'Sensitive' wrecks: protecting them and protecting from them', *Revue belge de droit international*, 2015, pp. 74–88.

international bodies, in taking measures to protect and preserve objects of an archaeological and historical nature found at sea, in conformity with [LOSC]'.[68] Article 149 LOSC obliges States Parties to protect UCH located in the Area, as does the UNESCO Convention for its States Parties. However, the specific systems provided for by each text still have some gaps and possible inconsistencies that might be solved through a complementary and imaginative reading of their protective standards.

The present contribution to this well-deserved tribute to our friend Djamchid Momtaz has sought to advocate complementary and imaginative reading, connecting the protection of UCH in the Area with the general protection of the marine environment envisaged under the LOSC and in the ISA Mining Code. This Code has already established a notification system for when UCH is discovered during prospection and exploration activities, but it does not clearly deal with the consequences of such a discovery. The UNESCO Convention establishes a consultation process, but logically only for its States Parties. It would be desirable to find a solution under the LOSC and the ISA Mining Code, should conflicting views emerge in the Authority's Council after receiving the views of the UNESCO Director-General or any other competent organization on how to manage the discovery of UCH in a mining zone of the Area.

On the other hand, the LOSC and the ISA Mining Code include an effective enforcement mechanism that the UNESCO Convention lacks. Article 153 LOSC states that the ISA 'shall exercise such control over activities in the Area as is necessary for the purpose of securing compliance' (para. 4), including the adoption at any time of any measures provided for under Part XI LOSC to ensure compliance with its provisions (para. 5). This also implies 'the right to inspect all installations in the Area used in connection with activities in the Area'.[69] The consequences of non-compliance, with the guidance provided by the ITLOS in its Advisory Opinion of 2011, still need to be developed, just as they do in cases affecting not only the marine environment, but also UCH.[70]

Perhaps part of the solution could be found in the adoption of three complementary measures:

(1) The conclusion of a new memorandum of understanding between the ISA and UNESCO, similar to that concluded between the Intergovernmental

---

68 UN Doc. A/RES/70/235, 23 December 2015, para. 8. For human remains and maritime graveyards, see its para. 314.

69 The contractors are obliged to allow access to these inspections and to assist and cooperate with them under Regulations, Annex 4, Section 14 PNR/PSR/CCR.

70 See Lodge, supra note 31, p. 162.

Oceanographic Commission of UNESCO and the Authority, but dealing with the protection of UCH in the Area and with the expertise of both the LTC at the ISA and the STAB at UNESCO.

(2) The drafting by the ISA Council, with the support of the LTC, of a particular recommendation dealing with the protection of UCH in the Area. As ITLOS implicitly recalled in its Advisory Opinion, recommendations cannot be neglected due to their apparently non-compulsory nature, because they are useful to specify the contents of environmental impact assessments and, consequently, compliance with the due-diligence principle.[71]

(3) The final drafting of the Exploitation Regulations currently under discussion at the ISA, including the incorporation of the archaeological variable into the 'Social impact assessment' as currently foreseen in the process, which includes new consultations among the stakeholders and the ISA and is expected to be completed by mid-2016. This is of the utmost importance since the exploitation stage will be drawing near by the time the exploration programmes reach their final stages.

As solemnly expressed in Article 136 LOSC, the natural resources in the Area are the common heritage of mankind. UCH is an integral part of the cultural heritage of humanity, says the Preamble of the UNESCO Convention. The two concepts—common heritage of mankind and cultural heritage of humanity—are closely related.[72] However, they are not normatively or institutionally equipped with analogous tools; and perhaps they should not be. But some connections can be traced and, indeed, established between them with the ultimate goal of creating the best protection system for both dwindling resources. The well-shaped system for environmental protection in the Area (albeit still under construction) could export some of its mechanisms for the protection of UCH, and the archaeological variable could be more clearly incorporated into the Mining Code drafted by the ISA under the LOSC.

---

71 Ibid., p. 163. See also Y. Tanaka, 'Obligations and Liability of Sponsoring States Concerning Activities in the Area: Reflections on the ITLOS Advisory Opinion of 1 February 2011', 60 *Netherlands International Law Review*, 2013, pp. 205–230, at p. 213.

72 T. Šošić, 'The common heritage of mankind and the protection of the underwater cultural heritage', in B. Vukas and T. M. Šošić (eds), *International Law: New Actors, New Concepts—Continuing Dilemmas; Liber Amicorum Božidar Bakotić*, Brill, 2010, pp. 319–350. See further A. Strati, 'Deep Seabed Cultural Property and the Common Heritage of Mankind', 40 *International and Comparative Law Quarterly*, 1991, pp. 859–894.

Migration and the Law of the Sea: Solutions and Limitations of a Fragmentary Regime

Ida Caracciolo

1   Introduction

The reports and the statistics released by the International Organisation for Migration (IOM)[1] assert that international migrants—namely those people moving from their country of birth to another—numbered 244 million 2015. This large flux of migrants today constitutes a major worldwide, social, political and legal challenge. International law is under stress due to these migratory movements by land, air, and sea, mainly because the typical distinction between refugees and others in need of protection and irregular migrants is outmoded and because very often migratory movements are exploited by criminal organizations involved in human smuggling. The fragility of interstate cooperation in this field constitutes another significant weakness.

In this scenario maritime migration appears singular, not because it is recent; the phenomenon indeed goes back to the 'boat people' leaving Vietnam in 1975–1979 and 1988–1990; and it involved Albania, Cuba and Haiti later on in the 1990s.[2] Maritime migration stands out because it poses specific, also juridical, issues due to the particularity of the regimes for maritime spaces and to the discipline of navigational safety.

The 1982 UN Convention on the Law of the Sea[3] (LOSC) expressly puts migrants, irregular or not, under the sovereignty, control or jurisdiction of the coastal State when they are in its territorial sea, contiguous zone or artificial islands, installations and structures in its exclusive economic zone, while it is totally silent as far as the high seas are concerned.

LOSC specifically mentions—using similar phrases—migratory movements at sea in Articles 19 (2) (g), 21 (1) (h), 33 (1) (a) (b), 42 (2) (d), and 60 (2). The

---

[1]   See IOM, 'Global Migration Trends Factsheet 2015', available at http://iomgmdac.org/global-trends-factsheet/.

[2]   Nowadays there are migratory movements through the Gulf of Aden, towards Australia, and from Asia and Africa towards Europe, see UNHCR, 'Refugees and Asylum-Seekers in Distress at Sea—How Best to Respond?', Background Paper for the Expert Meeting in Djibouti, 8–10 November 2011, available at http://www.unhcr.org/4ec1436c9.pdf.

[3]   1833 UNTS 3.

first provision, which applies to innocent passage in territorial sea as does the second one, establishes that the navigation of foreign ships in territorial sea is prejudicial to the peace, good order and security of the coastal State if it entails the embarking or disembarking of persons contrary to the immigration laws and regulations of that coastal State. Consequently, Article 21(1) (h) allows the coastal State to adopt those innocent-passage laws and regulations regarding the prevention of infringement of its immigration regime. Article 42 (2) (d) has the same contents as Article 21(1) (h) but concerns passage in transit through international straits.

Thus the above-mentioned rules—even if indirectly—confer jurisdiction on the coastal State regarding immigration in its territorial sea.[4] Article 33, 1(a) (b) expands this jurisdiction to its contiguous zone and Article 60 (2) to artificial islands, installations and structures in its exclusive economic zone.

As against this, Part VII of LOSC is silent on migration. It contains no exception to the flag State's exclusive jurisdiction on vessels involved in transporting irregular migrants or asylum seekers or others in need of protection, nor does it impose on States Parties any kind of cooperation concerning migration by sea.

Actually, the same goes for terrorism, and the illicit traffic of weapons by sea. But LOSC was negotiated in years when these phenomena were circumscribed and irrelevant. Thus on one hand it codifies ancient and well-known unlawful conduct at sea such as piracy (Articles 100–107) and the transport of slaves (Article 99) and on the other it focuses on potential new attempts on the security of States such as the illicit traffic in drugs (Article 108) and unauthorised broadcasting (Article 109).

This being the case, the present article first addresses the issue of the legal basis for intervention against boats transporting migrants on the high seas. In this context it will analyse the duty to rescue people in distress at sea and its limits in connection with migrants in distress enshrined in LOSC, the International Convention for the Safety of Life at Sea of 1974 (SOLAS)[5] and the International Convention on Maritime Search and Rescue of 1979 (the SAR Convention).[6]

The article then deals with the problem of jurisdiction against migrant smuggling within the normative framework provided by Part VII of LOSC

---

[4] S. N. Nandan & S. Rosenne (eds), *United Nations Convention on the Law of the Sea 1982. A Commentary*, vol. I, Martinus Nijhoff Publishers, 1993, p. 201.

[5] 1 November 1974, 1184 UNTS 2, available at http://www.imo.org/en/Publications/Documents/Newsletters%20and%20Mailers/Mailers/IF110E.PDF.

[6] 27 April 1979, 405 UNTS 97, available at http://www.admiraltylawguide.com/conven/searchrescue1979.html.

and the 2000 UN Protocol against the Smuggling of Migrants by Land, and Air, Supplementing the United Nations Convention against Transnational Organised Crime (the Palermo Protocol).[7]

Finally, the effectiveness of the *ad hoc* mechanisms put in place to combat the smuggling of migrants from the Libyan coasts will be scrutinized, as will the approach thereto of the UN Security Council to overcome the existing limits to the exercise of jurisdiction at sea against migrant-smugglers.

2 A First Fragment: the Responsibility to Assist Persons in Distress at Sea Regardless of their Status

The possibility of intervention by intercepting a boat involved in the transport of migrants (including asylum seekers and others in need of protection) is provided first in Article 98 of LOSC, which codifies the customary duty of guaranteeing the safety of life at sea. This in turn stems from ages-old seafaring traditions.

Article 98 contains a twofold obligation: a State Party has the duty both to require the masters of ships flying its flag to render 'assistance to any person found at sea in danger of being lost' and to proceed 'with all possible speed to the rescue of persons in distress' as well as to 'promote the establishment, operation and maintenance of an adequate and effective search and rescue service regarding safety on and over the sea'.

Concerning the first obligation, note that masters are obliged to assist and rescue *any* person in distress at sea; thus no discrimination can be applied in relation to the status of those to be rescued and neither is the status of irregular migrant or of asylum seeker or similar relevant in any way.

Further, the rescue must be as rapid as possible and it can be conducted anywhere at sea, not only on the high seas, but also in the exclusive economic zones and contiguous zones. This is due to the absence in Article 98, 1 of any reference to a specific maritime space. The territorial sea is included in so far as Article 18 (2) of LOSC admits an exception to the fact that innocent passage in territorial sea must be continuous and expeditious precisely for the case when stopping or anchoring is necessary 'for the purpose of rendering assistance to persons, ships or aircraft in danger or distress'.

The only limitations to such a widely defined duty result from the opposite and balanced interest of ensuring the safety of the rescue vessel: assistance

---

7 UN Doc. A/RES/55/25, Annex III, 2001, available at https://www.unodc.org/documents/southeastasiaandpacific/2011/04/som-indonesia/convention_smug_eng.pdf.

can therefore be rendered only without serious danger to the ship, the crew or the passengers and rescue and if such a conduct is reasonable given the specific conditions of the event. Thus the master maintains a margin of discretion about the decision to intervene or not having regard to the safety of navigation.[8] Note that SOLAS Chapter V, Regulation 10(a) requires masters to record any reason for failing to render assistance. This provision enables a certain check on the decision-making and on the compliance with the relevant international law of the sea.

Therefore, the duty to render assistance is fully applicable when the people in distress are migrants aboard unseaworthy craft. And despite being partly inconsistent with the economic standards of commercial shipping, and involving large-scale and dangerous rescue operations, the duty is largely accepted by ship owners. Suffice it to underline that in 2015 around 1,000 merchant ships were involved in migrant rescue operations in the Mediterranean, and assisted in the rescue of more than 50,000 people.[9] The shipping industry however maintains that the European Union and the international community should 'provide refugees and migrants with alternative means of finding safety, without risking their lives by crossing the Mediterranean in unseaworthy boats'.[10]

The second obligation echoes SOLAS Chapter V, Regulation 7 and has a *de jure condendo* nature even if at the time of the adoption of LOSC a detailed discipline on effective and adequate search and rescue services at sea had already been provided for by the SAR Convention.[11]

The object of the SAR Convention is to favour the establishment of a worldwide system of national centres, each responsible for promoting efficient search and rescue (SAR) services and for co-ordinating SAR operations within a specific maritime area (Chapter 1.3.5).

This is obviously a systematic and permanent obligation accepted by States Parties, to be implemented individually or in cooperation with neighbouring

---

8   Nandan & Rosenne, supra, note 4, vol. III, pp. 172–173.

9   International Chamber of Shipping, 'Large Scale Rescue Operations at Sea. Guidance on Ensuring the Safety and Security of Seafarers and Rescued People', available at http://www.ics-shipping.org/docs/default-source/resources/safety-security-and-operations/large-scale-rescue-at-sea.pdf?sfvrsn=28.

10 See the position taken by the International Transport Workers' Federation (ITF) in March 2015, available at http://www.itfglobal.org/de/news-events/press-releases/2015/april/joint-ecsa,-etf,-ics,-itf-press-release-thousands-of-lives-will-be-lost-in-the-mediterranean-unless-eu-governments-take-urgent-action,-say-shipowner-groups-and-seafarer-unions/.

11 Also SOLAS requires States Parties to settle mechanisms of distress communication and co-ordination in their area of responsibility and for the rescue of persons in distress at sea around its coasts.

States (Chapter 2.1.1). To that end States Parties establish sufficient search and rescue regions (SRR) in each sea area by agreement among themselves (Chapter 2.1.4). SRR must be contiguous and should not overlap (Chapter 2.1.3).

The definition of SAR services is wide since it includes all connected operations, from locating persons in distress and retrieving them to providing for their initial medical or other needs, and delivering them to a place of safety through the use of public and private resources (Chapters 1.3.1–1.3.3). The rescue unit can be considered as a place of safety but only provisionally, while an assisting ship, that is a ship intervening to help but without trained personnel on board, cannot be deemed a place of safety.[12] Therefore, SAR operations necessarily end only when the rescued people are disembarked in a place of safety on the mainland.

Finally, assistance is provided regardless of the nationality or status of persons in distress or the circumstances in which these persons are found (Chapter 2.1.10).

From the SAR Convention it clearly emerges that the establishment of an SRR is subject to the capacity of a State Party to ensure adequate search and rescue services. SRRs are areas of responsibility for that State and not of sovereignty or jurisdiction. Therefore, the random duty of saving life at sea when all conditions listed in Article 98, 1 LOSC are met becomes obligatory within every SRR which shall offer its services in an organized and regular manner.

Even though the SAR Convention sets rather high and precise standards of adequacy for the services of search and rescue, they have nevertheless been defined bearing in mind ordinary assistance towards seaworthy ships that have had a collision or another maritime incident or are in danger because of external or accidental events.

The situation is completely different for craft transporting migrants which can barely float and which are totally unsafe because of the lack of any technical requirement provided for by international treaties and national laws on the safety of navigation. Then several critical points derive from this factual dyscrasia.[13]

The first point concerns the definition of distress. In the case of migratory movements at sea in boats unseaworthy for navigation, a distress signal can reach the search and rescue centres before the lives of the transported people become endangered. In other words the distress situation can only and directly be connected to the fact that the craft used is in no fit condition for

---

12   IMO Resolution MSC 167(68), 20 May 2004, 'Guidelines on the Treatment of Persons Rescued at Sea', Articles 3 (1) (8) and 3 (1) (9).
13   U. Leanza & F. Caffio, 'Il SAR mediterraneo', 148 *Rivista Marittima*, 2015, pp. 11–17.

a sea voyage. The wording used by the SAR Convention to define distress as 'a situation wherein there is a reasonable certainty that a vessel or a person is threatened by grave and imminent danger and requires immediate assistance' is sufficiently broad to include the case of unsafe boats overcrowded by migrants.[14]

The second critical point relates to the disembarkation of rescued persons to a place of safety. An amendment to the SAR Convention adopted in 2004[15] assigns to the State responsible for the SRR where the survivors were recovered the 'primary responsibility' to coordinate and cooperate so that the assisting ship delivers and disembarks the survivors to a place of safety (Chapter 3.1.9).

This is clearly an obligation of result and not of conduct: the concerned State does not fulfil it merely through its due diligence efforts in coordinating and cooperating in finding a place of safety. On the contrary the scope of the obligation is accomplished only when survivors are disembarked in a place of safety. Since States Parties to the SAR Convention have accepted to establish adequate search and rescue services, their duties must entail any necessary operation contributing to the search and rescue within their SRR. Delivery of survivors to a place of safety is included—as set out in Chapter 1.3.2 of the SAR Convention—because it concludes SAR operations. Further the appropriateness of these services is achieved when a place or places of safety is/are provided by the State within its SRR. Arrangements in cooperation with other search and rescue centres to identify the most appropriate place for disembarking persons found in distress (Chapter 3.1.6.4) are consistent with the above and offer a residual means to reach a suitable standard for guaranteeing the safety of life at sea.[16]

Finally, when groups of migrants found in distress at sea include asylum seekers or others in need of protection, a place of safety cannot just be a place where their lives are safe and where their basic human needs can be met, but also where they are free from any risk of persecution. Thus the evaluation on disembarkation should take into account the need not only to deliver the

---

14   S. Trevisanut, 'Is there a Right to be Rescued at Sea? A Constructive View', *Question of International Law*, 23 June 2014, available at http://www.qil-qdi.org/is-there-a-right-to-be-rescued-at-sea-a-constructive-view/.
15   IMO Resolution MSC.155(78), 20 May 2004.
16   Trevisanut, supra, note 14; E. Papastavridis, 'Rescuing 'Boat People' In the Mediterranean Sea: The Responsibility of States under the Law of the Sea', *EJIL: Talk!*, 31 May 2011, available at http://www.ejiltalk.org/rescuing-boat-people-in-the-mediterranean-sea-the-responsibility-of-states-under-the-law-of-the-sea/.

survivors as quickly as possible to a place of safety but also to protect their human rights.

The third critical point refers to the concepts of adequateness and effectiveness of SAR services. Since LOSC, the SAR Convention and the relevant IMO recommendations give no explicit definition or any parameters, nor offer interpretative suggestions, the only criterion to bear in mind seems to be that of the coherence between the extent of the SRR and the average intervention capability of its search and rescue units. Indeed, every SRR should be commensurate with all the resources deployed for search and rescue by the concerned State to offer a quick response to any distress signal and rapid assistance to the ship in distress.

Thus due diligence in SAR operations should be evaluated with reference to this criterion, while the cooperation and coordination between the responsible centres in different SRRs favours interoperability between the centres when the request for assistance is sent to the competent search and rescue authorities of a State from people in danger at sea within the SRR of another State. In both cases, inertia implies an infringement of the SAR Convention and more generally of the duty to render assistance under Article 98 (2) of LOSC.

Lastly, during SAR operations human rights must be protected according to the domestic law of the flag State or the international treaties binding it following the principle of the exclusive jurisdiction of the flag State (Article 92 LOSC). Nevertheless, these operations do not have the aim of protecting human rights. Neither LOSC nor the SAR Convention recognize any humanitarian function in the above-mentioned operations but only the practical function of protecting human life in distress because of maritime navigation.

3   A Second Fragment: the Exercise of Jurisdiction over Boats Transporting Migrants on the High Seas

The duty to assist migrants in distress includes no jurisdiction over the boats transporting them, the people on board or the SRR. LOSC and the SAR Convention are clear here and offer no legal basis for inferring such a jurisdiction. Thus once the rescue is completed, the relevant State has fulfilled its obligations.

But, as is well known, the majority of sea journeys by migrants, especially from Africa to Europe, are nowadays controlled by organized criminal networks which offer services to migrants at great cost, including transport and document fraud. The rescue operations must therefore also be supplemented by enforcement operations aimed at seizing the craft in order to avoid their re-use for other journeys, at identifying and arresting the smugglers of migrants, or at gathering information on these criminal groups. All these activities may finally lead to the exercise of criminal jurisdiction against the alleged smugglers.

The facts that the LOSC provides for no exception to the principle of the exclusive jurisdiction of the flag State with reference to the smuggling of migrants and that no explicit exceptions are set by the SAR Convention (or SOLAS) cannot lead to the conclusion that the jurisdiction concerns only the flag State, with the risk of impunity for the smugglers. Indeed, Part VII of LOSC permits third States under certain conditions to exercise some enforcement activities. The Palermo Protocol supplements the provisions contained in the Convention of 1982.

Enforcement activities are certainly allowed when the flag State gives its consent explicitly or *per facta concludentia* but also in cases of hot pursuit under Article 111 of LOSC. The latter is submitted to several conditions that can be easily met when irregular migration by sea is being facilitated by criminal groups. The coastal State must have good reason to believe that the ship pursued has violated its laws and regulations (including those on immigration); the hot pursuit may be commenced only when the foreign ship is in maritime spaces under the sovereignty, control or sovereign rights of the coastal State; it must be preceded by an order of arrest with visual or acoustic signals, at an adequate distance to be received by the pursued ship; it must be continuous and uninterrupted; and it must cease when the pursued ship enters the territorial sea of another State.

Also the constructive presence contemplated in Article 111 (4) may be envisaged in the smuggling of migrants. In some cases, the smugglers tow very small and unsafe craft using a 'mother ship', up to a certain point at sea where they make the migrants continue their dangerous journey all alone while they themselves remain aboard the 'mother ship'.

Some scholars suggest that a coastal State can exercise enforcement jurisdiction over a foreign flag vessel that remains seaward of coastal State waters also when the unseaworthy minor craft transporting the migrants are still on the high seas if they are clearly directed towards the coast of the intervening State and their route and destination are somehow proved.[17] This tenet is appealing but does not seem to conform with Article 111 (4) which expressly refers

---

17   U. Leanza & F. Graziani, 'Poteri di *enforcement* e di *jurisdiction* in materia di traffico di migranti via mare: aspetti operativi nell'attività di contrasto', 2 *Rivista di diritto della navigazione*, 2014, pp. 669–719, at p. 689.

to the spatial position of the 'contact vessel' in the territorial sea, the contiguous zone, the exclusive economic zone or the continental shelf.

Very often the boats used for the migrants' sea journeys are without nationality and thus the right of visit can be applied according to Article 110 of LOSC. This right can be exercised by a warship or another ship in State service if it has 'reasonable ground for suspecting' that 'the ship is without nationality.' Both conditions can be easily met in cases of irregular migration at sea. Nowadays abandoned boats of any kind are used to transport migrants. But this provision does not allow the warship to do anything but ascertain the ship's right to fly its flag through check of its papers or further examinations on board the ship, to be carried out with all possible consideration.

If under LOSC the third State is allowed very limited interference with the boats involved in the migrant smuggling and even more limited chances to exercise its criminal jurisdiction against the smugglers the Palermo Protocol, on the contrary, confers more powers.

Indeed, Article 8 of this protocol, specifically dedicated to the activities that States are entitled to exercise in their fight against migrant smuggling on the high seas, allows *inter alia* a State to go beyond the right to visit when it suspects that a vessel without nationality is engaged in smuggling migrants by sea. Precisely the State Party, once the absence of any flag is verified, may 'board and search the vessel' to obtain evidence confirming its suspicions and thereafter 'take appropriate measures in accordance with relevant domestic and international law' (Article 8 (7).

If *prima facie* the language seems rather broad, allowing the boarding State too much discretion in the choice of action, a more attentive analysis leads to a different conclusion. This provision entrenches the jurisdiction of the intervening State vis-à-vis the vessel without flag in the legal framework of relevant international law and especially of domestic law. Notably, the grounds for exercising criminal jurisdiction, as well as the possibility, the means and the extension of investigations can only be fixed by domestic law.

Article 8 does not modify the aforementioned LOSC provisions but rather fills their *lacunae* in connection with the fight against human smuggling. The rule fully complies with the principle of the flag State's exclusive jurisdiction. Thus if the vessel engaged in the smuggling of migrants flies a foreign flag, the interested State can only request authorization from the flag State to take appropriate measures (Article 8 (2). The wording used permits only specific authorization, according to circumstances, and this differs from what is provided for in other maritime treaties.[18] A major flexibility in consent, e.g. tacit

---

18 Among the others, the *Agreement on the Conservation and Management of Straddling Fish Stocks and Highly Migratory Species*, UN Doc. A/CONF.164/37, 8 September 1995,

consent after the expiration of a certain period of time, should have been contemplated in order to achieve a more rapid and fluid reaction against the smuggling of migrants.

Note that only warships or other ships on government service can carry out these activities. Thus if a merchant ship goes to the rescue of a craft carrying migrants in distress at sea it can only guarantee the safety of their lives.

4 Efforts to Fill the Lacunae: Specific Responses in Compliance with the LOSC Regime

On this basis the chances of guaranteeing the safety of life at sea and success in the fight against smugglers in the face of large-scale migrations by sea are very poor. It is no coincidence that specific multilateral operations have been mounted in the Mediterranean, which is crossed by a great number of migrants and stricken by numerous lethal shipwrecks.

The first operation, launched in 2013, was Italian only: Operation *Mare Nostrum* tackling the humanitarian emergency in the Sicilian Channel. It was aimed at identifying boats at risk of capsizing, rescuing migrants and disembarking them in Italy as well as bringing the migrant-smugglers to justice. The mission was conducted in full compliance with relevant LOSC provisions and the search and rescue system for people in distress at sea under the SAR Convention.[19]

One year later Operation *Mare Nostrum* had been supported by the Joint Operation *Triton*, conducted by the European Agency for the Management of Operational Cooperation at the External Borders of the Member States of the European Union (FRONTEX) which ultimately replaced it. The legal framework of *Triton* comes from EU Regulation No. 656/2014 of the European Parliament and the Council of 15 May 2014, establishing rules for the surveillance of external sea borders in the context of operational cooperation coordinated by FRONTEX.[20]

---

available at https://documents-dds-ny.un.org/doc/UNDOC/GEN/N95/274/67/PDF/N9527467.pdf?OpenElement. See also, Protocol of 2005 to the Convention for the Suppression of Unlawful Acts against the Safety of Maritime Navigation, IMO Doc. LEG/CONF.15/21, 1 November 2005, available at https://www.unodc.org/tldb/en/2005_Protocol2Convention_Maritime%20Navigation.html.

19 Ministero Della Difesa, 'Mare Nostrum Operation', http://www.marina.difesa.it/EN/operations/Pagine/MareNostrum.aspx.

20 *Official Journal of the European Union*, L189, 27 June 2014, p. 93.

This regulation has included new rules in the main mission of FRONTEX related to the patrolling of sea borders of Member States, in order to guarantee its compliance with the principle of *non-refoulement*, the protection of human rights and the duty—when necessary—of assisting ships in distress and disembarking rescued people in a place of safety according to the SAR Convention. Indeed this obligation is directly assumed by Member States participating in an operation since the safety of life at sea falls outside EU powers (Article 9 of the Regulation).[21]

Suffice it to underline that the Regulation explicitly refers to Article 8 of the Protocol against the Smuggling of Migrants, concerning the measures that the participating units can implement and the procedures they must follow if they have reasonable grounds to believe that a ship is engaged in migrant smuggling (Article 7).

Triton patrols the Italian sea borders and therefore its operational area covers the territorial waters of Italy as well as parts of the search and rescue (SAR) zones of Italy and Malta up to 30 nautical miles from the coasts thereof.

Triton is also completely respectful of all relevant principles contained in LOSC, particularly those stemming from the regime of freedom of the high seas; and once again no exception to these principles is envisaged.

More recently, in 2015, Operation EUNAVFOR MED, later renamed *Sophia*, was undertaken by the European Union. This Operation has its legal basis in two decisions taken by the European Council as part of the Common Foreign and Security Policy.[22] Thus the fight against migrant-smugglers has been considered as a matter of common European external security and not an EU external action in the fields of police and judicial cooperation in criminal matters.

The Operation's mission is 'to identify, capture and dispose of vessels and assets used or suspected of being used by smugglers or traffickers' (Article 1) while its mandate includes three sequential phases (Article 2) and a final redeployment phase.

The first phase (now terminated) was aimed at detecting and monitoring the modus operandi of migration networks. In the second phase (currently

---

21   Case C-355/10, Parliament v. Council, European Court of Justice (Grand Chamber), 5 September 2012.

22   'Council Decision (CFSP) 2015/778 of 18 May 2015 on a European Union Military Operation in the Southern Central Mediterranean (EUNAVFOR MED)', *Official Journal of the European Union*, L122, 19 May 2015, p. 31; 'Council Decision (CFSP) 2015/972 of 22 June 2015 Launching the European Union Military Operation in the Southern Central Mediterranean (EUNAVFOR MED)', *Official Journal of the European Union*, L157, 23 June 2015, p. 51.

in the field) the units involved can board, search, seize and divert on the high seas vessels suspected of being used for human smuggling, under the conditions provided for by applicable international law (such as LOSC and the Palermo Protocol). At a later stage, if authorised by the UN Security Council or with the consent of the Libyan Government, the Operation could be carried on also within Libyan territorial sea. The third phase will be centred on the seizure and, if necessary, the destruction of boats and structures ashore suspected of being used for smuggling migrants on the basis of the consent of the coastal State concerned or following adoption of an *ad hoc* UN Security Council resolution.

Although *Sophia* is a military operation with a well-determined objective, namely human smuggling, it appears to abide by the relevant principles of the international law of the sea: freedom of navigation and the principle of exclusive flag jurisdiction.

At the same time it does not neglect the obligation to assist persons in distress at sea and to deliver survivors to a place of safety, complying with human-rights law, refugee law and the principle of *non-refoulement* of asylum seekers (Recital 6). At this point the debate whether the decision is aimed at protecting the EU border or at saving the life of migrants seems fruitless and purely political.

Further, it is worth underlining that Operation *Sophia* has resorted to the 'ordinary' means of exercising jurisdiction on the high seas. These, however, are evidently insufficient to confront massive migration movements at sea. Thus *Sophia* faces, as do the other missions mentioned above, problems concerning the limitations on interventions on the high seas and the applicable grounds for criminal jurisdiction.

5   Further Efforts to Fill the Lacunae: the UN Security Council Approach beyond the LOSC Regime

To this end, more effective means have been given to Operation *Triton* by UN Security Council Resolution 2240 (2015) of 9 October 2015, already invoked by Decision 2015/778.

Some points of the Resolution are worthy of note. The first is the concern that growing human smuggling from Libya is exacerbating the situation in Libya because of the risk of supporting other forms of organised crime and terrorist networks there. This concern has led to activation of the primary responsibility of the UN Security Council for the maintenance of international peace and security under the UN Charter and to the adoption of Resolution

2240 under Chapter VII. Reference to this Chapter might give a legal basis for the use of force against migrant smugglers.

Thus as in the past for drug trafficking from Afghanistan[23] and more recently for piracy off the Somali coasts[24] and for the illicit trafficking of cultural objects by DAESH,[25] organised criminal activity resulting in human smuggling is considered by the Security Council as an indirect risk to international peace and security because it favours international and regional instability, or serious internal crises.

The second point of interest lies in the exercise of jurisdiction on the high seas. The Security Council not only requires Member States, with the consent of the flag State on the high seas off the coasts of Libya, to inspect vessels that they reasonably believe are engaged in migrant smuggling as well as unflagged vessels, but also—and this is important—to inspect any vessel off these coasts even without the consent of the flag State (Paragraph 7).

This exception to flag-State-exclusive jurisdiction is very cautiously tailored temporally and spatially: the authorisation is limited to one year from the date of adoption of the Resolution and it applies only on the high seas off the Libyan coasts, a definite—even if not precise—maritime area. Further, the Resolution expects a high precautionary standard by Member States. They can exercise these exceptional inspective powers not only following the usual reasonable grounds that the ships are being used for human smuggling but also if they have made 'good faith efforts to obtain the consent' of the vessel's flag State. Within the same period the exception applies also to the seizure of inspected vessels with due consideration to the interests of any third party who has acted in good faith (Paragraph 8).

But the caution of the UN Security Council leads one to reiterate that the exception does not affect the rights or obligations of Member States under international law, and under LOSC 'including the general principle of exclusive jurisdiction of a flag State over its vessels on the high seas'.

Finally, we must underline the good balance in the Resolution between the different interests and goals involved: the intention to disrupt migrant smuggling by organised crime, prevention of the loss of life at sea, respect for

---

23   E.g. UN Doc. S/RES/1817, 11 June 2008, available at http://www.un.org/en/ga/search/view_doc.asp?symbol=S/RES/1817(2008).

24   E.g. UN Doc. S/RES/733, 23 January1992, available at http://www.un.org/en/ga/search/view_doc.asp?symbol=S/RES/733(1992).

25   UN Doc. S/RES/1483, available at http://www.un.org/en/ga/search/view_doc.asp?symbol=S/RES/1483(2003); UN Doc. S/RES/2199, 12 February 2015, available at http://www.un.org/en/ga/search/view_doc.asp?symbol=S/RES/2199%20(2015).

migrants' rights and dignity and their right to seek protection under human-rights law and refugee law. From this perspective, the Resolution is better drafted than the aforementioned European decision.

Given that the regime of maritime spaces under LOSC is founded upon the sensitive equilibrium between sovereignty and freedom of the seas and that a similar equilibrium exists between rights, duties and responsibilities of coastal and flag States on the high seas, any change in this balance is awkward because of the opposing interests of different States. To this end the difficulties in negotiating Article 8 of the Palermo Protocol and the small achievements reached are self-explanatory.

In such a scenario, Resolution 2240 is an interesting outcome. The UN Security Council confirms again that organised criminal activities can—within certain situations of political crisis—together threaten international peace and security. But also on this basis it justifies the suspension—even if limited—of a fundamental pillar of the regime of the high seas, namely the principle of flag-State-exclusive jurisdiction. Thus Resolution 2240 introduces a sort of *extra ordinem* 'territorial control' on the high seas off the Libyan coasts because of the exceptional emergency situation brought about by increasing smuggling of migrants with a major risk to their lives at sea.

La dimension internationale de la compétence de l'Union européenne en matière de pêche

Rafael Casado Raigón

1   **La compétence de l'Union à conclure des traités en matière de pêche**

L'Union européenne (UE) dispose d'une compétence exclusive dans le domaine de « la conservation des ressources biologiques de la mer dans le cadre de la politique commune de la pêche » (PCP)[1]. Conformément à la nouvelle réglementation de base de la PCP, entrée en vigueur le 1er janvier 2014[2], cette politique couvre les *activités* qui sont menées sur le territoire des États membres, dans les eaux de l'Union (indépendamment de la nationalité du navire), par des navires de pêche de l'Union en dehors des eaux de l'Union et par des ressortissants des États membres (sans préjudice, dans ce dernier cas, de la responsabilité principale de l'État du pavillon).

Dans ce domaine comme dans d'autres, l'UE a la compétence pour conclure des traités avec un État tiers ou avec d'autres sujets de droit international[3]. Selon la jurisprudence de la Cour de justice de l'UE, lorsque l'Union légifère sur une matière déterminée, la compétence *extérieure* de l'Union s'étend automatiquement à cette matière, en particulier sa compétence pour conclure des accords internationaux[4]. Ces traités sont partie intégrante de l'ordre juridique communautaire et lient non seulement l'Union mais aussi les Etats membres[5].

Dans le cadre de ses compétences exclusives, l'UE conclut des traités avec des Etats tiers et avec des organisations internationales. C'est le cas, par exemple, des accords bilatéraux en matière de pêche. Mais l'UE est également partie à des traités multilatéraux auxquels participent en même temps tous ou

---

1   Article 3.1 du Traité sur le fonctionnement de l'Union européenne (TFUE).
2   Règlement (UE) n°1380/2013 du Parlement européen et du Conseil du 11 décembre 2013 relatif à la politique commune de la pêche. *Journal officiel de l'Union européenne* L 354, 2013.
3   Voir l'article 3.2 et les articles 216 et s. du TFUE.
4   CJCE, arrêt du 31 mars 1971, Commission c. Conseil, aff. 22-70. Voir T. Treves, « La Comunità Europea, l'Unione Europea e il Diritto del mare: recenti sviluppi », dans Angela del Vecchio, *La política marittima comunitaria*, Quaderni del Dipartimento di Scienze Giuridiche, Università Luiss Guido Carli, Roma, 2009, p. 188.
5   En vertu de l'article 216.2 du TFUE, les « accords conclus par l'Union lient les institutions de l'Union et les États membres ».

certains de ses Etats membres. C'est le cas, par exemple, de la Convention des Nations Unies sur le droit de la mer[6] (CNUDM) ou de l'Accord de 1995 sur les stocks chevauchants et les grands migrateurs[7]. Ces accords mixtes, qui règlent des domaines dans lesquels la compétence appartient tant à l'UE qu'à ses Etats membres (compétence partagée) et/ou, à la fois, des domaines de la compétence exclusive de l'UE et des domaines non attribués à celle-ci (et par conséquent appartenant aux Etats membres), posent un problème constant dans la pratique, pas toujours bien résolu, et qui touche non seulement les relations de l'Union avec ses Etats membres mais aussi leurs relations avec des Etats tiers et d'autres organisations internationales.

2 La répartition des compétences dans les traités conclus par l'Union européenne

Dans la déclaration de compétences prévue à l'article 5.1 de l'annexe IX de la CNUDM et contenue dans l'instrument de confirmation formelle de la Communauté européenne (aujourd'hui UE), cette organisation internationale indique que ses États membres lui ont transféré la compétence en ce qui concerne la conservation et la gestion des ressources de la pêche maritime. « Il lui appartient à ce titre, dans ce domaine, d'arrêter les règles et réglementations pertinentes (qui sont appliquées par les États membres) et de contracter, dans les limites de sa compétence, des engagements extérieurs avec les États tiers ou les organisations internationales compétentes. Cette compétence s'applique aux eaux relevant de la juridiction nationale en matière de pêche et à la haute mer ». Toutefois, l'UE reconnait dans sa déclaration que « les mesures relatives à l'exercice de la juridiction sur les navires, l'octroi du pavillon, l'enregistrement des navires et l'application des sanctions pénales et administratives relèvent de la compétence des États membres dans le respect du droit communautaire »[8]. Dans des termes similaires s'exprime la déclaration relative à

---

6 Nations Unies, *Recueil des traités*, vol. 1834, p. 3.

7 Accord aux fins de l'application des dispositions de la Convention des Nations Unies sur le droit de la mer du 10 décembre 1982 relatives à la conservation et à la gestion des stocks de poissons dont les déplacements s'effectuent tant à l'intérieur qu'au-delà de zones économiques exclusives (stocks chevauchants) et des stocks de poissons grands migrateurs, 4 août 1995, Nations Unies, *Recueil des traités*, vol. 2167, p. 3.

8 La déclaration ajoute que le « droit communautaire prévoit également des sanctions administratives ». *Journal officiel des Communautés européennes* L 179, 1998.

la compétence de la Communauté européenne pour l'ensemble des matières régies par l'Accord de 1995[9].

Le monde complexe de la distribution des compétences entre l'UE et ses Etats membres rend difficile l'actualisation des déclarations citées, mais, en vertu de l'article 5.4 de l'annexe IX de la Convention, l'UE a contracté l'obligation de notifier *promptement* au dépositaire toute modification de la répartition des compétences spécifiée dans la déclaration contenue dans son instrument de confirmation formelle, y compris les nouveaux transferts de compétence. Autrement, on peut courir le risque d'une attribution de compétences à ceux qui ne les possèdent plus, car, selon le paragraphe 3 du même article, les Etats membres de l'UE sont présumés avoir compétence en ce qui concerne toutes les matières traitées par la Convention pour lesquelles ils n'ont pas expressément indiqué, par une déclaration, communication ou notification, qu'ils transféraient compétence à l'organisation.

Ce problème ne devrait théoriquement pas se poser à propos des traités multilatéraux auxquels l'UE participe seule, comme c'est le cas de l'Accord de 1993 visant à favoriser le respect par les navires de pêche en haute mer des mesures internationales de conservation et de gestion[10] ou de l'Accord de 2009 relatif aux mesures du ressort de l'État du port visant à prévenir, contrecarrer et éliminer la pêche illicite, non déclarée et non réglementée[11], mais, même dans ces cas, la dialectique constante qui, à ce sujet, existe et oppose la Commission, institution à caractère supranational, et le Conseil, institution à caractère intergouvernemental, est toujours présente, comme en témoigne le recours en annulation présenté par la Commission devant la Cour de justice contre la décision du Conseil attribuant aux États membres le droit de vote au sein de la FAO pour adopter l'Accord de 1993 cité ci-dessus. En acceptant la thèse de la Commission, il est très significatif que la Cour se soit appuyée sur le fait que ledit Accord concernait *pour l'essentiel* un sujet qui relevait de la compétence exclusive de la Communauté[12].

---

9   *Journal officiel des Communautés européennes* L 189, 1998.
10 Décision du Conseil du 25 juin 1996. *Journal officiel des Communautés européennes* L 177, 1996.
11 Décision du Conseil du 20 juin 2011. *Journal officiel de l'Union européenne* L 191, 2011. Voir (p. 18) la déclaration relative à la compétence de l'UE.
12 CJCE, arrêt du 19 mars 1996, *Commission c. Conseil*, affaire C-25/94.

3 L'Union européenne et l'affaire N° 21 du Tribunal international du droit de la mer (TIDM)

Récemment, la justice communautaire a été appelée à se prononcer pour la première fois sur la capacité de la Commission européenne à présenter des allégations dans le cadre d'une affaire soumise à un tribunal international sans l'autorisation préalable du Conseil[13]. Par sa requête, le Conseil de l'Union demandait l'annulation de la décision de la Commission européenne de présenter « l'exposé écrit de la Commission européenne au nom de l'Union européenne » au TIDM dans l'affaire n° 21 relative à la demande d'avis consultatif soumise par la Commission sous régionale des pêches (CSRP). En rejetant le recours, la Cour de justice (grande chambre), dans son arrêt du 6 octobre 2015, a signalé, parmi d'autres, que l'objet de cet exposé a été non pas de définir une politique en matière de pêche illicite, non déclarée et non réglementée (pêche INN), ce qui au sens de l'article 16.1 du Traité de l'Union Européenne correspond au Conseil, « mais de présenter au TIDM, sur la base d'une analyse des dispositions internationales et de la réglementation de l'Union pertinentes en cette matière, un ensemble d'observations juridiques visant à permettre à cette juridiction de rendre, le cas échéant, un avis consultatif en connaissance de cause sur les questions qui lui avaient été posées »[14].

Dans l'affaire devant le TIDM[15], où sept États membres de l'UE ont également présenté des exposés écrits en tant que parties à la CNUDM, l'une des questions qui ont été posées par la CSRP faisait référence, selon la définition de sa portée faite par le Tribunal[16], à la responsabilité de l'Union européenne en cas de violation de la législation en matière de pêche d'un Etat membre

---

13   Voir G. A. Oanta, « Tres sentencias claves para la delimitación del contorno jurídico de las competencias convencionales de la Unión Europea en el ámbito pesquero », dans *Revista de Derecho Comunitario Europeo*, n° 53, 2016, p. 201-231.

14   CJUE, arrêt du 6 octobre 2015, *Conseil c. Commission*, affaire C-73/14, par. 71 de l'arrêt.

15   TIDM. Demande d'avis consultatif soumise par la Commission sous-régionale des pêches (CSRP) (Demande d'avis consultatif soumise au Tribunal). Rôle des affaires n° 21. Avis consultatif du 2 avril 2015.

16   Selon l'avis consultatif (par. 157-159), la troisième question posée au Tribunal (« Lorsqu'une licence de pêche est accordée à un navire dans le cadre d'un Accord international avec l'Etat du pavillon ou avec une structure internationale, cet Etat ou cette organisation peut-il être tenu responsable des violations de la législation en matière de pêche de l'Etat côtier par ce navire ? ») ne concerne pas les organisations internationales en général, « mais seulement celles qui sont visées aux articles 305, paragraphe 1 f), et 306 de la Convention et à l'annexe IX de la Convention, auxquelles leurs Etats membres, qui sont parties à la Convention, ont transféré compétence dans les matières régies par celle-ci ; en l'espèce,

de la CSRP par des navires avec des licences de pêche délivrées dans le cadre d'un accord entre cet Etat et l'organisation internationale citée (UE). En réponse à cette question, le TIDM a considéré que, « dans le cas où une organisation internationale, dans l'exercice de sa compétence exclusive en matière de pêche, conclut un accord d'accès aux pêcheries avec un Etat membre de la CSRP, prévoyant l'accès de navires battant pavillon de ses Etats membres pour pêcher dans la zone économique exclusive de cet Etat, les obligations de l'Etat du pavillon deviennent les obligations de l'organisation internationale. L'organisation internationale, en tant que seule partie contractante à l'accord [...], doit veiller à ce que les navires battant pavillon de ses Etats membres respectent les lois et règlements de l'Etat membre de la CSRP en matière de pêche et ne se livrent pas à des activités de pêche INN à l'intérieur de la zone économique exclusive de cet Etat »[17]. De l'avis du Tribunal, « si l'organisation internationale manque à son obligation de *diligence due*[18], les Etats membres de la CSRP peuvent la tenir pour responsable de la violation de leurs lois et règlements »[19].

L'avis consultatif du 2 avril 2015 évoque en même temps que la responsabilité d'une organisation internationale engagée par un fait internationalement illicite est liée à sa compétence[20]. Cela est clairement énoncé à l'article 6.1 de l'annexe IX de la CNUDM. Or, en application de l'article 6.2 du même annexe, tout Etat partie à la Convention peut demander à cette organisation « ou à ses Etats membres parties à la Convention d'indiquer à qui incombe la responsabilité dans un cas particulier. L'organisation et les Etats membres concernés doivent communiquer ce renseignement. S'ils ne le font pas dans un délai raisonnable ou s'ils communiquent des renseignements contradictoires, l'organisation internationale et les Etats membres concernés sont tenus pour conjointement et solidairement responsables »[21].

On a signalé que l'avis consultatif du TIDM devrait amener un changement dans la pratique conventionnelle de l'UE dans le sens d'inclure dans ses accords de pêche une *clause de compétences*[22], ce qui donnerait une plus grande sécurité juridique tant pour l'UE que pour les Etats tiers. Dans ce sens, la Commission

---

la pêche ». A ce jour, la seule organisation dans ce cas partie à la Convention est l'Union européenne.

17   Ibid., par. 172.
18   Voir la première question posée au Tribunal (par. 85-140 de l'avis consultatif).
19   Ibid., par. 173.
20   Ibid., par. 168.
21   Ibid., par. 174.
22   Oanta, *op. cit.*, note 13, p. 225.

européenne, dans sa proposition de Règlement du Parlement Européen et du Conseil relatif à la gestion durable des flottes de pêche externes, abrogeant le règlement (CE) n° 1006 / 2008 du Conseil, a considéré qu'il « est important d'organiser à la fois les activités des navires de pêche de l'Union en dehors des eaux de l'Union et le régime de gouvernance qui s'y rapporte, de manière à ce que les obligations internationales de l'Union puissent être assumées de manière efficiente et efficace *et que les situations dans lesquelles l'Union pourrait se voir reprocher des actes illégaux sur le plan international puissent être évitées* »[23].

Ceci veut dire que, bien que nous soyons théoriquement dans le domaine d'une compétence exclusive de l'UE, comme c'est le cas des accords de pêche avec des pays tiers, ladite compétence est moins exclusive que ce que l'on pourrait penser. Même, l'obligation de *diligence due* affecte principalement aux Etats du pavillon ; en particulier, « pour s'acquitter de son obligation d'exercer effectivement sa juridiction et son contrôle dans le domaine administratif, l'Etat du pavillon est tenu, en vertu de l'article 94 de la Convention, d'adopter les mesures administratives nécessaires pour veiller à ce que les navires de pêche battant son pavillon ne se livrent pas à des activités [...] qui entravent l'exercice de sa responsabilité au titre de l'article 192 de la Convention aux fins de protection et de préservation du milieu marin et de conservation des ressources biologiques marines qui en sont partie intégrante »[24].

4 Pêche en haute mer : la participation de l'Union européenne aux organisations internationales de pêche

Il est clair que, en ce qui concerne la pêche en haute mer, l'UE est également un important acteur de l'actuel DI dans la matière, comme en témoigne sa participation aux plus importantes organisations internationales de conservation et de gestion des ressources halieutiques. En effet, l'UE, représentée par la Commission, joue actuellement un rôle actif dans six organisations chargées spécifiquement de la pêche au thon et dans onze autres organisations régionales de gestion de la pêche (ORGP)[25].

Si la Convention de 1982 attribue un rôle important à la coopération institutionnalisée, l'Accord de 1995 sur les stocks chevauchants et les grands migrateurs et les autres instruments normatifs plus récents placent à juste titre la

---

23 COM(2015) 636 final, Bruxelles, le 10 décembre 2015 (considérant n° 5). C'est nous qui soulignons.
24 Par. 219.3 de l'avis consultatif du TIDM.
25 http://ec.europa.eu/fisheries/cfp/international/rfmo/index_fr.htm.

coopération canalisée à travers les ORGP au centre de gravité de la conservation et de l'administration des ressources halieutiques de la haute mer[26]. Les ORGP dont les zones (géographiques) de compétence ne s'étendent pas au-delà des eaux sous juridiction nationale, comme c'est le cas de la Commission sous régionale des pêches citée ci-dessus, ont également une véritable importance pour la conservation des ressources biologiques marines aussi bien dans les eaux visées qu'au-delà de celles-ci, mais ces ORGP sont uniquement ouvertes aux États de la région.

Les six ORGP gérant les espèces hautement migratoires (principalement le thon) dans lesquelles l'UE est partie sont les suivantes : la Commission internationale pour la conservation des thonidés de l'Atlantique (ICCAT), la Commission des thons de l'océan Indien (IOTC), la Commission des pêches pour le Pacifique occidental et central (WCPFC), la Commission interaméricaine du thon tropical (IATTC), l'Accord relatif au programme international pour la conservation des dauphins (APICD, organisme lié à la IATTC) et la Commission pour la conservation du thon rouge du Sud (CCSBT). L'UE participe au même temps à neuf ORGP gérant les stocks de poissons par zone géographique : la Commission des pêches de l'Atlantique du Nord-Est (NEAFC), l'Organisation des pêches de l'Atlantique du Nord-Ouest (NAFO), l'Organisation pour la conservation du saumon de l'Atlantique Nord (NASCO), l'Organisation des pêches de l'Atlantique du Sud-Est (SEAFO), l'Accord relatif aux pêches dans le sud de l'océan Indien (SIOFA), l'Organisation régionale de gestion des pêches du Pacifique Sud (SPRFMO), la Convention sur la conservation de la faune et la flore marine de l'Antarctiques (CCMLAR)[27] la Commission générale des pêches pour la Méditerranée (GFCM) et la Convention sur la conservation et la gestion des ressources en colin dans la partie centrale de la mer de Béring (CCBSP). Finalement, l'UE participe à deux ayant un rôle purement consultatif : la Commission des pêches pour l'Atlantique Centre-Ouest (WECAFC) et le Comité des pêches de l'Atlantique Centre-Est (CECAF).

En raison de la compétence exclusive de l'UE en matière de pêche, la plupart de ces organisations ne comptent pas avec la participation simultanée de ses Etats membres[28]. Dans certaines, comme c'est le cas, parmi d'autres, de l'ICCAT ou de la NAFO, les Etats membres qui étaient parties au préalable

---

26 R. Casado Raigón, « La pêche en haute mer », dans Daniel Vignes, Giuseppe Cataldi et Rafael Casado Raigón, *Le droit international de la pêche maritime*, Bruylant, Bruxelles 2000, p. 181 ss.

27 https://www.ccamlr.org/fr/organisation/texte-de-la-convention-camlr.

28 Voir A. de Gregorio Merino, « Notas en torno a los acuerdos internacionales de pesca de la Comunidad », dans *Noticias de la Unión Europea*, n° 287, 2008, p. 57 ss.

se sont retirés suite à l'accès de l'UE ; après cet accès, les Etats parties qui sont devenus membres de l'UE ont également dû se retirer de l'ORGP en question[29].

Mais il y a un nombre réduit de ORGP dans lesquelles participent à la fois certains des Etat membres et l'UE. C'est le cas de la CCAMLR, la GFCM, la WECAFC et le CECAF. Ces deux derniers (constitués dans le cadre de l'article VI de la Constitution de la FAO) ont, comme nous l'avons signalé, un rôle purement consultatif. La CCAMLR forme partie intégrante du système du Traité sur l'Antarctique, duquel l'UE n'est pas contractante, bien que l'article XXIX de la Convention CCAMLR stipule que « est ouverte à l'adhésion d'organisations d'intégration économique régionale constituées par des États souverains dont un ou plusieurs sont des États membres de la Commission et auxquelles les États membres de l'organisation ont transféré des compétences totales ou partielles dans les domaines auxquels s'applique la présente Convention ». En ce qui concerne la GFCM (constituée dans le cadre de l'article XIV FAO), enfin, la Décision du Conseil du 16 juin 1998 relative à l'adhésion de la Communauté européenne contient une déclaration unique sur l'exercice des compétences et du droit de vote.[30].

Il y a d'autres ORGP dans lesquelles ne participe pas l'Union européenne. Quelques-unes de ces organisations comptent, nonobstant, avec la participation de certains de ses Etats membres. C'est le cas de la Commission internationale de la chasse à la baleine (IWC), qui n'est précisément pas une organisation ni régionale ni consacrée à la chasse à la baleine et qui envisage seulement l'adhésion d'Etats. C'est également le cas du Conseil international pour l'exploration de la mer (ICES), qui a des fonctions essentiellement de recherche et qui envisage seulement la participation d'Etats[31].

Parmi les ORGP dans lesquelles ne participent ni l'UE ni ses Etats membres et où la haute mer est comprise dans leurs zones de réglementation (eaux visées), nous pourrions souligner celles qui, statutairement, sont uniquement ouvertes aux Etats de la région géographique, telles que l'Agence des pêches du forum des îles du Pacifique (PIFFA), la Commission internationale du flétan du Pacifique (IPHC), dont les Etats-Unis et le Canada sont membres, ou la

---

29   Toutefois, la France et le Royaume-Uni continuent d'être membres à certaines ORGP au nom de leurs territoires d'outre-mer : ICCAT, IOTC, WCPFC (France), IATTC (France), NAFO (France), SIOFA (France) et NASCO (France, observateur). Dans d'autres, le Danemark est partie par rapport aux Îles Féroé et au Groenland : NEAFC, NAFO et SPRFMO (Îles Féroé).
30   *Journal officiel des Communautés européennes* L 190 du 4 juillet 1998, Décision 98/416/CE.
31   Voir E. M. Vázquez Gómez, *Las organizaciones internacionales de ordenación pesquera. La cooperación para la conservación y la gestión de los recursos vivos de la alta mar*, Consejería de Agricultura y Pesca de la Junta de Andalucía, Sevilla, 2002, p. 140 ss.

Commission permanente du Pacifique Sud (PCSP), dont le Chili, la Colombie, l'Équateur et le Pérou sont membres. Ces deux dernières, simplement, ne prévoient pas l'entrée de nouveaux Etats. Cette entrée est en revanche envisagée dans d'autres organisations mais elles la subordonnent au préalable accord unanime, comme c'est le cas de la Commission des espèces anadromes du Pacifique Sud (NPAFC), de la Commission des mammifères marins de l'Atlantique Nord (NAMMCO), composée du Groenland, des Îles Féroé, de l'Islande et de la Norvège, et la plus récente Commission des pêches du Pacifique Nord (NPFC), comprenant le Canada, la Chine, le Japon, la République de Corée, la Fédération de Russie et Taipei chinois. L'instrument constitutif de cette dernière, en vigueur depuis juillet 2015, prévoit que, par consensus, les parties contractantes peuvent inviter à l'adhésion des organisations d'intégration économique dont les navires de pêche souhaitent développer des activités de pêche dans la zone de règlementation.

5 Les organisations internationales de pêcherie dans le cadre de l'actuelle politique commune de la pêche

L'Union européenne, étant consciente de l'importance qu'ont pour elle ses relations extérieures dans le domaine de la pêche (plus d'un quart du total des captures de l'UE vient de la haute mer ou de ZEE de pays tiers), le Règlement 1380 / 2013 innove en ce qui concerne le précédent Règlement pilier de la PCP (2371 / 2002) en introduisant des dispositions spécifiques (Partie VI) sur la politique extérieure (articles 28-33). L'un des principaux objectifs de la réforme de la PCP traduite dans ce Règlement a été celui de défendre et étendre au plan international les principes d'une pêche durable et responsable[32], c'est-à-dire, les mêmes objectifs et principes de cette politique de l'UE.

Comme l'a signalé la Commission européenne en 2011, près de 85 % des stocks halieutiques mondiaux pour lesquels des informations sont disponibles sont soit entièrement exploités, soit surexploités ; par conséquent l'UE devrait s'efforcer de remédier à cette situation en prenant rapidement des initiatives courageuses. Selon la Commission, du fait de ses flottes et de ses investissements, des accords bilatéraux qu'elle a conclu avec les pays tiers et de sa participation aux principales ORGP, l'UE est l'un des très rares acteurs de premier plan à maintenir une présence forte dans l'ensemble des mers et des océans de

---

32 Voir l'article 28 du Règlement 1380/2013.

la planète³³. Ce fait, celui de la présence de navires communautaires dans le monde entier, devrait octroyer à l'UE de la légitimité et de l'influence dans les ORGP qui aujourd'hui adoptent des décisions sur la pêche en haute mer.

Les ORGP sont considérées jusqu'à présent comme les meilleurs instruments de gouvernance des pêches, notamment pour ce qui est des stocks chevauchants et des stocks de poissons grands migrateurs des ZEE et de la haute mer. Cela étant dit, l'UE doit jouer un rôle plus important dans les ORGP afin de les renforcer³⁴. De même, il est très important pour l'UE que ses représentants continuent à promouvoir des pêcheries responsables et la meilleure gouvernance des mers à l'échelle mondiale dans des instances internationales telles que l'Assemblée générale de l'ONU et la FAO³⁵. Pour ces raisons, l'article 29 du Règlement 1380 / 2013, consacré aux *activités de l'Union au sein des organisations internationales de pêche*, établit (paragraphe 1) que l'Union « apporte activement sa contribution et son soutien aux activités des organisations internationales traitant de la pêche, y compris les ORGP ».

En ce qui concerne ces dernières (les ORGP), l'une des constantes préoccupations de l'UE a été que leurs décisions reposent sur les meilleurs avis scientifiques disponibles afin de faire en sorte que les ressources halieutiques soient gérées, en particulier, conformément à l'un des grands principes du DI de la pêche maritime, celui de l'approche de précaution en matière de gestion de pêches. Dans ce sens, pour le Règlement 1380 / 2013 l'UE « s'efforce de lancer le processus visant à améliorer *l'efficacité* des ORGP afin de leur permettre de mieux conserver et gérer les ressources vivantes de la mer relevant de leur compétence »³⁶. A cette effet, l'UE encourage et soutient, dans toutes les enceintes internationales, les actions nécessaires à l'éradication de la pêche INN³⁷ et les mesures appropriées, y compris des sanctions effectives et dissuasives appliquées d'une manière transparente et non discriminatoire, afin de

---

33   Communication de la Commission au Parlement Européen, au Conseil, au Comité Économique et Social Européen et au Comité des Régions relative à la dimension extérieure de la politique commune de la pêche. COM(2011) 424 final, Bruxelles, le 13 juillet 2011, p. 3.

34   Communication de la Commission au Parlement Européen, au Conseil, au Comité Économique et Social Européen et au Comité des Régions. La réforme de la politique commune de la pêche. COM(2011) 417 final, Bruxelles, le 13 juillet 2011, p. 9.

35   Voir Commission des Communautés européennes, *Livre Vert. Réforme de la politique commune de la pêche*. COM(2009) 163 final, Bruxelles, le 22 avril 2009, p. 25.

36   Règlement 1380/2013, article 29.2. C'est moi qui souligne.

37   Ibid., articles 28.2 e) et 30.

veiller au strict respect des mesures de conservation et gestion adoptées par les ORGP[38].

Or, dans le cadre de l'approche de précaution et en ce qui concerne tant les eaux sous juridiction nationale que les eaux de la haute mer, l'Union européenne doit contribuer « à la durabilité d'activités de pêche économiquement viables et favorisant l'emploi dans l'Union »[39]. Précisément, l'un des objectifs de la PCP qui doit être particulièrement pris en compte dans les positions de l'Union dans les ORGP[40] est celui de créer les conditions pour que le secteur de la pêche et de la transformation et les activités à terre liées à la pêche soient économiquement viables et compétitives[41].

Par ailleurs, en raison des impacts négatifs que cela peut avoir pour une exploitation durable des ressources halieutiques, le Règlement 1380 a été sensible à la question du processus d'adoption des décisions développé dans les ORGP. Dans ce sens, l'Accord de 1995 invite à convenir de procédures de prise de décisions, basées sur la transparence, qui facilitent l'adoption opportune et efficace des mesures de conservation et de gestion[42]. Sur cette base, l'article 29.3 du Règlement communautaire établit que l'Union « soutient activement la mise en place de mécanismes appropriés et transparents d'attribution des possibilités de pêche ».

La Commission européenne a donné comme exemple à suivre dans la réforme des processus décisionnels au sein des ORGP la procédure de vote adoptée récemment dans le cadre de la Convention sur la conservation et la gestion des ressources halieutiques en haute mer dans le Pacifique Sud (instituant la SPRFMO), qualifiée par elle de progressive et efficace[43]. Mais, plus qu'une

---

38   Ibid., articles 28.2 f) et 30.
39   Ibid., article 28.2 c).
40   Ibid., article 29.2.
41   Ibid., article 2.5 c).
42   Casado Raigón, « La pêche en haute mer », *op. cit.*, note 26, p. 190-191.
43   COM(2011) 424 final, p. 11. Elle mérite d'être synthétisée. En vertu de cette procédure de vote (voir articles 16 et 17 et l'annexe II de ladite Convention), les décisions de la Commission de la SPRFMO, en règle générale, sont prises par *consensus*. Si le président considère que tous les efforts entrepris pour la recherche du consensus restent vains, les décisions sur les questions de fond sont prises à la majorité des trois quarts des membres de la Commission exprimant un vote affirmatif ou négatif. La décision devient contraignante pour tous les membres de la Commission 90 jours après la date de la notification par le secrétaire exécutif. Nonobstant, tout membre de la Commission peut présenter au secrétaire exécutif une objection à une décision dans un délai de 60 jours à compter de la date de la notification, mais il doit en même temps préciser en détail les raisons de son objection et adopter des mesures de remplacement dont l'effet est équivalent à la

procédure de prise de décisions peu appropriée et transparente, ce qui en réalité a un impact très négatif sur l'exploitation durable des ressources halieutiques c'est l'existence d'ORGP fermées, c'est-à-dire, d'organisations qui n'admettent pas l'adhésion de nouveaux membres ou qui la subordonnent à l'accord unanime, un accord dans lequel les intérêts politiques et les contre-prestations de toutes sortes peuvent jouer de fait un rôle très important.

L'Union européenne s'est engagée, dans le cadre de la CNUDM comme dans celui de l'Accord de 1995, à participer aux travaux des diverses ORGP, « pour autant qu'elle ait un intérêt réel dans les pêcheries gérées par ces organisations »[44]. En raison de la présence, non seulement actuelle mais aussi future ou possible, de navires communautaires dans le monde entier, les ORGP dans lesquelles l'UE devrait avoir un intérêt réel ne se limitent pas à celles dans lesquelles elle participe aujourd'hui. Pour cette raison et pour d'autres, l'UE devrait aller plus loin dans la dénonciation à ce sujet dans les différents forums internationaux où sa voix est entendue.

Comme je l'ai souligné ailleurs[45], cette question de la participation dans les ORGP est réellement fondamentale puisque, sans elle, il n'est pas vraiment possible de faire appliquer l'obligation de coopérer à la conservation et à la gestion des ressources biologiques en haute mer prévue, particulièrement, à l'article 118 de la CNUDM. Dans ce sens, l'article 8.3 de l'Accord de 1995 établit que

> décision à laquelle il s'est opposé. Les seules raisons admissibles pour une objection sont les suivantes : la décision opère une discrimination de façon injustifiée dans la forme ou en fait contre le membre de la Commission, ou est incompatible avec les dispositions de la convention SPRFMO ou d'autres dispositions du droit international applicable figurant dans la Convention de 1982 ou l'Accord de 1995. Lorsqu'une une objection est présentée, un groupe de révision est mis en place dans les 30 jours suivant la fin de la période d'objection. Le groupe de révision est composé de membres choisis parmi des experts dont la compétence dans les aspects juridiques, scientifiques ou techniques de la pêche est établie et généralement reconnue et qui ont la meilleure réputation d'équité et d'intégrité. En particulier, si le groupe de révision constate que la décision contre laquelle l'objection a été présentée n'opère pas de discrimination et n'est pas incompatible avec les instruments conventionnels cités, le membre ou les membres de la Commission ayant soulevé une objection mettent en œuvre la décision dans les 45 jours ou engagent une procédure de règlement des différends en vertu de la convention SPRFMO. Mais, si le groupe de révision constate en même temps que les mesures de remplacement ont un effet équivalent à la décision et doivent être acceptées comme telles par la Commission, ces mesures de remplacement sont contraignantes pour le ou les membres de la Commission ayant soulevé une objection en remplacement de la décision en attendant la confirmation de leur acceptation par la Commission lors de sa prochaine réunion.

44 COM(2011) 424 final, p. 9.
45 Casado Raigón, « La pêche en haute mer », *op. cit.*, note 26, p. 184 ss.

les États qui ont un intérêt réel dans les pêcheries concernées peuvent devenir membres de l'organisation ou *participants*. À ce sujet, les « dispositions régissant l'admission à l'organisation [...] n'empêchent par ces États d'en devenir membres ou participants ; elles ne sont pas non plus appliquées d'une manière discriminatoire à l'encontre de tout État ou groupe d'États ayant un intérêt réel dans les pêcheries concernées ». Sous réserve de certaines critiques que mérite l'Accord de 1995[46], j'insiste sur le fait que la nature ouverte des ORGP devrait être considérée comme une caractéristique inhérente de celles-ci[47]. Si, comme l'établit l'Accord, la pêche dans la zone visée reste conditionnée à l'appartenance ou à la soumission volontaire à l'organisation, celle qui, de fait ou de droit, n'admet pas des Etats (ou des parties) différentes des originaires, rejette sans justification un droit fondamental que le droit international général reconnait : le droit qu'ont tous les Etats à ce que leurs ressortissants pêchent en haute mer.

Pour le reste, je veux commenter une proposition faite par la Commission européenne afin de renforcer la base financière des ORGP[48]. Selon la Commission, dans le but d'encourager également les flottes à utiliser les ressources de la mer de manière responsable, il convient que l'UE plaide en faveur de l'adoption du concept selon lequel les opérateurs dont les navires battent le pavillon d'un membre d'une ORGP versent à cette organisation des redevances pour pouvoir accéder aux pêcheries de haute mer. Cette proposition me paraît judicieuse et, si elle est bien conçue, ne contredit pas les dispositions pertinentes de la CNUDM. Les ressources halieutiques de la haute mer, et de la mer en général, sont limitées et doivent être partagées. Tout opérateur habilité pour la pêche dans les eaux visées par une ORGP obtient un bénéfice et il est logique que, en contrepartie, il verse une redevance à cette organisation pour qu'elle puisse se prévaloir, par exemple, des meilleurs avis scientifiques et, de cette manière, mieux contribuer à l'exploitation durable des ressources. À l'heure actuelle, les ORGP sont les meilleurs instruments pour la gouvernance des pêches en haute mer. Logiquement, cette redevance doit être décidée ou déterminée équitablement, en tenant compte notamment de la situation des pays en développement.

---

46   Voir R. Casado Raigón, « El Acuerdo de Nueva York sobre especies transzonales y altamente migratorias », dans *Cuadernos de Derecho Pesquero*, n°2, 2003, p. 49 ss.

47   E. M. Vázquez Gómez, « Las organizaciones regionales de ordenación pesquera y la reforma de la política pesquera común », dans *Noticias de la Unión Europea*, n° 326, 2012, p. 86.

48   COM(2011) 424 final, p. 11.

6 La pêche dans les eaux relevant de la juridiction des Etats tiers : catégories d'accords conclus par l'Union européenne

L'objectif de la PCP d'étendre au plan international les principes d'une pêche durable et responsable est également applicable aux activités menées par des navires de pêche de l'Union (et par des ressortissants des Etats membres) dans les eaux sous juridiction des Etats tiers. Comme l'établit le Règlement 1380 / 2013, l'Union « veille à ce que les activités de pêche de l'Union *en dehors des eaux de l'Union*[49] reposent sur les mêmes principes et normes que le droit de l'Union applicable dans le domaine de la PCP, tout en favorisant des conditions de concurrence équitables pour les opérateurs de l'Union par rapport aux autres opérateurs de pays tiers ».

En tant que traités aujourd'hui en vigueur[50], nous pouvons seulement nous référer à deux types d'accords de pêche conclus par l'UE avec des Etats tiers[51] : les dits « accords nordiques », pour la gestion conjointe des stocks partagés en mer du Nord et dans l'Atlantique du Nord-Est, conclus avec la Norvège, l'Islande et les Îles Féroé, et les « accords de partenariat dans le domaine de la pêche durable », conclus par l'UE avec treize Etats de l'Afrique et avec le Groenland et les Îles Cook, qui visent à permettre aux navires communautaires de pêcher les ressources excédentaires au sein de la ZEE du pays concerné.

Les *accords nordiques* sont basés sur un système d'échange de possibilités de pêche entre la flotte communautaire et celle des trois pays cités (accords de réciprocité). Par leur valeur économique, le plus important de ces accords est celui conclu avec la Norvège, une des principales puissances mondiales dans le secteur de la pêche. La soumission à une politique commune de la pêche a été une des plus puissantes raisons de la non-adhésion de la Norvège aux Communautés européennes, peut-être pour ne pas avoir à partager les abondantes ressources de sa ZEE avec certains Etats *pêcheurs* (lire l'Espagne ou le Portugal).

---

49   L'italique m'appartient parce que dans la version officielle en espagnol de l'article 28.2 d) de ce Règlement on fait référence à « las actividades [...] en aguas de terceros países » et pas aux « activités [...] en dehors des eaux de l'Union ». Dans le même sens que la française, les versions anglaise, italienne ou portugaise.

50   Sur les différents types d'accords de pêche conclus par l'UE (CE, CEE) depuis le début de son activité conventionnelle en la matière, voir J. M. Sobrino Heredia, « Los acuerdos internacionales de pesca, instrumentos indispensables de la política pesquera común de la Unión Europea », dans *Noticias de la Unión Europea*, nº 326, 2012, p. 51 ss, et M. Hernández García, *La política convencional pesquera de la Comunidad Europea con terceros Estados*, Tirant lo Blanch, Valencia, 2007, p. 197 ss.

51   http://ec.europa.eu/fisheries/cfp/international/agreements/index_fr.htm.

Les activités de pêche de l'UE en mer du Nord et dans l'Atlantique du Nord-Est sont étroitement liées à celles de ses voisins dans ces régions[52]. Les poissons n'entendent pas de frontières maritimes et non plus d'eaux sous juridiction étatique ; par conséquent, de nombreux stocks de poissons peuvent se trouver dans les ZEE de deux États ou plus, c'est pourquoi il est nécessaire que les parties coordonnent leurs activités, d'autant plus que les différentes flottes ne s'intéressent pas nécessairement aux mêmes stocks.

L'article 33 du Règlement 1380 / 2013 fait référence à ces stocks partagés. Pour cette disposition, lorsque des stocks présentent un intérêt commun sont aussi exploités par des pays tiers, l'Union doit *dialoguer* avec ces pays tiers afin d'obtenir que ces stocks soient gérés d'une manière durable, en particulier conforme à l'approche de précaution[53]. Dans ce but et également avec la finalité de garantir la stabilité des opérations de pêche des flottes de l'UE, « l'Union s'efforce, conformément à la CNUDM, *d'établir* avec des pays tiers des *accords bilatéraux ou multilatéraux* visant une gestion commune des stocks et prévoyant notamment, s'il y a lieu, l'établissement d'un accès aux eaux et aux ressources et les conditions de cet accès, l'harmonisation des mesures de conservation et l'échange de possibilités de pêche »[54]. De cette manière, le Règlement communautaire renvoie en particulier à l'article 63.2 de la CNUDM, selon lequel lorsqu'un « même stock de poissons ou des stocks d'espèces associées se trouvent dans les zones économiques exclusives de plusieurs Etats côtiers, ces Etats s'efforcent, directement ou par l'intermédiaire des organisations sous-régionales ou régionales appropriées, de s'entendre sur les mesures nécessaires pour coordonner et assurer la conservation et le développement de ces stocks ». Sur cette base, par conséquent, l'UE établit avec des pays tiers des accords bilatéraux et multilatéraux visant une gestion commune des stocks. De fait, certains stocks partagés sont gérés dans le cadre de la Convention sur les pêcheries de l'Atlantique Nord-Est instituant la NEAFC, de laquelle sont parties contractantes le Danemark (Îles Féroé et Groenland), l'Islande, la Norvège, la Fédération de Russie et l'Union européenne.

7 Les accord de partenariat dans le cadre de l'actuelle politique commune de la pêche

Aujourd'hui sont en vigueur quinze *accords de partenariat dans le domaine de la pêche durable*, dont dix ont été conclus avec des pays côtiers de l'Atlantique

---

52   Ibid.
53   Règlement 1380/2013, article 33 par. 1.
54   Ibid., par. 2.

et treize avec des pays de l'Afrique. Tous ces pays, à l'exception du Groenland (situé entre les océans Arctique et Atlantique), peuvent être qualifiés de pays en développement. Onze de ces accords ont pour objectif le thon : les *accords sur le thon*, qui permettent aux navires européens de suivre les stocks de thon dans leur migration (le Cabo Verde, les Comores, les Îles Cook, le Côte d'Ivoire, le Gabon, le Libéria, le Madagascar, Maurice, Sao Tomé-et-Principe, le Sénégal et les Seychelles). Le reste, quatre, sont des *accords mixtes*, qui donnent l'accès à une large variété de stocks de poissons au sein de la ZEE du pays partenaire. Ces derniers accords, conclus avec le Groenland, la Guinée-Bissau, la Mauritanie et le Maroc, sont précisément ceux qui prévoient une plus grande contribution financière de la part de l'UE, contribution qui représente un pourcentage très élevé des recettes publiques de certains d'entre eux (Mauritanie et Guinée-Bissau).

Sauf dans les cas du Groenland, dont l'accord présente des profils distincts de ceux des autres[55], et du Maroc, ces accords ont été conclus avec des Etats appartenant au groupe ACP (Etats d'Afrique, des Caraïbes et du Pacifique). L'Accord de partenariat entre les membres du groupe des États d'Afrique, des Caraïbes et du Pacifique, d'une part, et la Communauté européenne et ses États membres, d'autre part, signé à Cotonou le 23 juin 2000[56], prévoit expressément la conclusion d'accords de pêche dans le cadre de la coopération économique et commerciale, laquelle « vise à promouvoir l'intégration progressive et harmonieuse des États ACP dans l'économie mondiale, dans le respect de leurs choix politiques et de leurs priorités de développement, encourageant ainsi leur développement durable et contribuant à l'éradication de la pauvreté dans les pays ACP »[57]. Selon son article 53.1, les « parties déclarent qu'elles sont disposées à négocier des accords de pêche visant à garantir que les activités de pêche dans les États ACP se déroulent dans des conditions de durabilité et selon des modalités mutuellement satisfaisantes ».

Le Règlement 1380 / 2013 définit l'*accord de partenariat* comme « un accord international conclu avec un État tiers visant à permettre d'accéder aux eaux et aux ressources de cet État pour exploiter de manière durable une part du surplus des ressources biologiques de la mer en échange d'une compensation financière de l'Union, laquelle peut comprendre un soutien sectoriel »[58]. Il s'agit d'un nouveau type d'accord qui a été conçu depuis la réforme de la PCP de

---

55 Voir l'Accord de partenariat dans le secteur de la pêche entre la Communauté européenne, d'une part, et le gouvernement du Danemark et le gouvernement autonome de Groenland, d'autre part. *Journal officiel des Communautés européennes* L 172, 2007.
56 *Journal officiel des Communautés européennes* L 317, 2000.
57 Accord de Cotonou, article 34.1.
58 Règlement 1380/2013, article 4.37.

2002, réforme qui a permis de passer des accords traditionnels, principalement fondés sur le *principe* du « payez, pêchez, partez » (*pay, fish and go*), à une approche plus globale et plus coopérative[59]. En vertu du Règlement 1380, ces accords doivent établir un cadre de gouvernance juridique, environnementale, économique et social pour les activités de pêche pouvant comporter la mise en place et le soutien des instituts scientifiques et de recherche nécessaires, des capacités de suivi, de contrôle et de surveillance[60] et d'autres éléments permettant de renforcer les capacités d'élaboration d'une politique de la pêche durable par le pays tiers[61]. Donc, on doit tout mettre en œuvre pour garantir que ces accords soient dans l'intérêt mutuel de l'Union et des pays tiers concernés et qu'ils contribuent à maintenir l'activité des flottes de l'Union[62].

Un élément essentiel des accords de partenariat, tels qu'ils sont définis par le Règlement 1380, est celui de la compensation financière de la part de l'Union. Cette compensation financière est composée de deux éléments : d'une part, les paiements relatifs à l'accès des navires communautaires aux pêcheries ; d'autre part, les paiements effectués au titre de l'aide financière pour l'appui à la politique sectorielle de la pêche dans le pays tiers. L'un et l'autre sont des éléments dissociés[63].

Les termes et les conditions des deux éléments sont normalement définis dans les protocoles et les annexes des accords de partenariat. Le premier élément est composé à la fois de deux volets[64] : d'un côté, la part des coûts d'accès aux ressources que l'UE octroie au pays tiers ; d'un autre côté, la part des coûts d'accès aux ressources incombant aux propriétaires des navires communautaires. Ces redevances dues par les armateurs doivent être justes, non

---

59 COM(2009) 163 final, p. 25. Voir C. Teijo García, « Una aproximación a la práctica convencional de los acuerdos de asociación pesquera suscritos por la Comunidad Europea », dans Jorge Pueyo Losa et Julio Jorge Urbina (coordinadores), *La cooperación internacional en la ordenación de los mares y océanos*, Iustel, Madrid, 2009, p. 263 ss.

60 Comme il a été indiqué, le manque de moyens d'une bonne partie des États côtiers pour contrôler la pêche dans leurs ZEE est très significatif, en particulier dans le cas des États avec lesquels l'UE a conclu des accords relatifs au thon, étant donné que l'activité extractive est menée loin de la côte et presque toujours hors de portée de la (faible) surveillance maritime et aérienne de l'État, problème qui met en cause le caractère durable de ces accords (Teijo García, *op. cit.*, note 59, p. 282-283).

61 Règlement 1380/2013, article 31.1.

62 Ibid., par. 2.

63 Règlement 1380/2013, article 32.2.

64 Voir, par exemple, l'article 3 du Protocole entre l'UE et le Maroc fixant les possibilités de pêche et la contrepartie financière prévues par l'Accord de partenariat dans le secteur de la pêche. *Journal officiel de l'Union européenne* L328, 2013.

discriminatoires et proportionnelles aux avantages offerts par les conditions d'accès[65]. Le deuxième élément, le soutien financier *sectoriel*, a pour objectif la promotion d'une pêche responsable et d'une exploitation durable des ressources halieutiques dans les eaux du pays tiers[66]. Ce soutien financier est subordonné « à l'obtention de résultats spécifiques et complète les projets et programmes de développement mis en place dans le pays tiers concerné et s'accorde avec ceux-ci »[67].

Il importe de souligner, par ailleurs, l'engagement qu'acquiert l'Union en vertu du Règlement 1380 par rapport au volume de captures. Selon son article 31.4, les « navires de pêche de l'Union pêchent uniquement le reliquat du volume admissible des captures visé à l'article 62, paragraphes 2 et 3, de la CNUDM et établi de façon claire et transparente sur la base des meilleurs avis scientifiques disponibles ». Mais, en dépit de l'effort que fait l'UE pour que ces pays puissent disposer d'instituts scientifiques et de recherche, jusqu'à présent ils n'ont pas la capacité ou l'organisation technique et administrative suffisante (à l'exception du Groenland) pour la détermination du TAC (*total allowable catch*), c'est pourquoi le Règlement ajoute que celui-ci sera également établi sur la base « des informations pertinentes échangées entre l'Union et le pays tiers concernant l'effort de pêche total exercé sur les stocks concernés par l'ensemble des flottes »[68]. En fait, les possibilités de pêche prévues dans les accords en vigueur ne se traduisent pas en général par un TAC et par la fixation de quotas de capture mais par un *effort de pêche* (« pour un navire de pêche, le produit de sa capacité et de son activité; pour un groupe de navires de pêche, la somme de l'effort de pêche de l'ensemble des navires du groupe »[69]).

---

65 Règlement 1380/2013, article 32.1 a).

66 C'est-à-dire, l'établissement d'un cadre de gouvernance, « incluant la mise en place et le maintien des instituts scientifiques et de recherche nécessaires, de promouvoir les processus de consultation des groupes d'intérêt et de prévoir les capacités de suivi, de contrôle et de surveillance, ainsi que les autres éléments relatifs au renforcement des capacités d'élaboration d'une politique de pêche durable par le pays tiers » (article 32.1 b) du Règlement 1380/2013).

67 Ibid.

68 « En ce qui concerne les stocks chevauchants ou les stocks de poissons grands migrateurs, il y a lieu de prendre dûment en compte, pour la détermination des ressources accessibles, les évaluations scientifiques réalisées au niveau régional ainsi que les mesures de conservation et de gestion adoptées par les ORGP compétentes » (article 31.4 *in fine* du Règlement 1380 / 2013).

69 Règlement 1380 / 2013, article 4.1.21.

8 La clause d'exclusivité et celle relative au respect des droits de l'homme dans les accords de partenariat

Finalement, les accords de partenariat, en vertu du Règlement 1380 / 2013, doivent comporter une série de clauses : la clause relative au respect des droits de l'homme, celle qui interdit d'accorder aux autres flottes présentes dans les eaux du pays tiers des conditions plus favorables que celles accordées aux acteurs économiques de l'Union[70] et la clause (appelée) d'exclusivité. La première doit être nécessairement comprise ; la deuxième et la troisième « dans la mesure du possible ».

En vertu de la clause d'exclusivité, lorsqu'un accord de partenariat dans le domaine de la pêche durable est en vigueur, les navires de pêche de l'Union n'exercent leurs activités dans les eaux du pays tiers concerné que s'ils sont en possession d'une autorisation de pêche délivrée conformément à cet accord[71]. Avec cette clause, de mise en œuvre relativement récente dans la politique de la pêche de l'UE et qui aujourd'hui s'étend à la totalité des accords en vigueur, l'Union vise à assurer une pêche responsable et durable à travers des accords de pêche conclus avec des États tiers, en évitant ainsi que les navires communautaires puissent se soustraire au respect des règles de la PCP par la voie des accords privés, accords qui, en pratique, génèrent la surpêche dans des eaux dans lesquelles la durabilité de leurs populations n'est pas assurée[72].

Cette clause est comprise, par exemple, dans l'article 6 de l'Accord de partenariat dans le secteur de la pêche entre la Communauté européenne et le Royaume du Maroc[73]. En vertu de cette disposition, les « navires communautaires ne peuvent exercer des activités de pêche dans les zones de pêche marocaines que s'ils détiennent une licence de pêche délivrée dans le cadre du présent accord [...]. Pour des catégories de pêches non prévues par le protocole [fixant les possibilités de pêche et la contrepartie financière prévues par l'accord de pêche], des licences peuvent être octroyées à des navires communautaires par les autorités marocaines. Toutefois, et dans le cadre de l'esprit

---

70 Selon l'article 53.2 de l'Accord de Cotonou, cité plus haut, lors de la conclusion ou de la mise en œuvre des accords de pêche, « les États ACP n'agiront pas de manière discriminatoire à l'encontre de la Communauté ni entre les États membres, sans préjudice d'arrangements particuliers entre des États en développement appartenant à la même zone géographique, y compris d'arrangements de pêche réciproques; la Communauté s'abstiendra quant à elle d'agir de manière discriminatoire à l'encontre des États ACP ».
71 Règlement 1380 / 2013, article 31, par. 5 et 6 b).
72 Dans ce sens, Oanta, *op. cit.*, note 13, p. 228-229.
73 Approuvé au nom de la Communauté par le Règlement (CE) n° 764/2006 du Conseil, du 22 mai 2006.

de partenariat instauré par le présent accord, l'octroi de ces licences reste tributaire d'un avis favorable de la Commission européenne ». Récemment, la Cour de justice de l'Union européenne (CJUE) a eu l'occasion de se prononcer à l'égard de cette clause. De l'avis de la Cour (arrêt du 9 octobre 2014), l'accord de partenariat entre la CE et le Maroc, notamment son article 6, « doit être interprété en ce sens qu'il exclut toute possibilité pour les navires communautaires d'exercer des activités de pêche dans les zones de pêche marocaines sur le fondement d'une licence délivrée par les autorités marocaines sans l'intervention des autorités compétentes de l'Union européenne »[74].

L'objectif que poursuit la clause d'exclusivité figurant dans ces accords, visant à assurer l'exploitation, la gestion et la conservation durables des ressources biologiques de la mer et de l'environnement marin, se voit renforcé dans le Règlement 1380 avec d'autres dispositions relatives au contrôle des activités de pêche des navires qui opèrent hors du cadre d'accords de partenariat. En particulier, par rapport à tout navire opérant hors des eaux de l'Union, les « Etats membres veillent à ce que les navires [...] battant leur pavillon [...] soient en mesure de fournir une documentation détaillée et précise de toutes leurs activités de pêche et de transformation »[75].

Enfin, en ce qui concerne la clause relative au respect des principes démocratiques et des droits de l'homme que l'UE « veille à inclure dans les accords de partenariat dans le domaine de la pêche », le Règlement 1380[76], dans la ligne de l'Accord de Cotonou, la considère comme un *élément essentiel de ces accords*. Pour cet Accord, le respect des droits de l'homme, des principes démocratiques et de l'État de droit, sur lesquels se fonde le partenariat ACP-UE, font partie intégrante du développement durable et inspirent les politiques internes et internationales des parties et constituent les éléments essentiels dudit accord[77]. L'inclusion de cette clause dans les accords de partenariat, sans aucun doute, mérite toute notre admiration et représente un grand défi pour l'UE, qui nous espérons l'appliquera comme il convient, étant donné que la Commission a reconnu que les accords de partenariat se sont révélés difficiles à mettre en œuvre dans de nombreux pays en raison de troubles politiques[78]. En vertu de celle-ci, il ne sera pas possible de conclure un accord (ou qu'il reste en vigueur) avec un Etat soumis à une dictature, mais, le sera-t-il possible avec un régime *démocratique* particulier ?

---

74 CJUE, arrêt du 9 octobre 2014, affaire C-505/13, par. 35. Voir également par. 33.
75 Règlement 1380/2013, article 31, par. 7 et 8.
76 Règlement 1380/2013, article 31, par. 6.
77 Article 9 de l'Accord de Cotonou.
78 COM(2009) 163 final, p. 25.

L'Assemblée générale des Nations Unies a reconnu « la richesse et la diversité de la communauté des démocraties du monde entier qui sont issues de toutes les croyances et traditions sociales, culturelles et religieuses », en estimant que, « si toutes les démocraties ont des points communs, il n'existe pas un modèle unique de démocratie à caractère universel »[79]. Dans ce sens, l'Accord de Cotonou a ajouté que, sur « la base des principes universellement reconnus, chaque pays développe sa culture démocratique ». En fonction de cela, il semble malheureusement que l'UE peut interpréter avec flexibilité l'*élément essentiel de ces accords*.

Comme on le sait, la norme impérative du droit international général est une norme à laquelle aucune dérogation n'est permise. Le 14 mars 2014, le Front Polisario a introduit un recours en annulation devant le Tribunal de l'Union européenne contre la décision du Conseil de l'UE relative à la conclusion du protocole entre l'UE et le Maroc fixant les possibilités de pêche et la contrepartie financière prévues par l'Accord de partenariat dans le secteur de la pêche cité plus haut[80]. Dans cette affaire (en cours), le Front Polisario invoque, entre autres moyens, que la décision attaquée est contraire à l'article 2 dudit accord d'association (selon lequel par zone de pêche marocaine on entend les eaux relevant de la souveraineté ou de la juridiction du Royaume du Maroc), dans la mesure où elle violerait le droit à l'autodétermination.

En ce qui concerne le principe de la souveraineté permanente sur les ressources naturelles, dans l'arrêt du 10 décembre 2015 rendu dans une affaire également introduite par le Front Polisario (demande d'annulation) contre la décision 2012/497/UE du Conseil concernant la conclusion de l'accord sous forme d'échange de lettres entre l'UE et le Maroc relatif aux mesures de libéralisation réciproques en matière de produits agricoles, de produits agricoles transformés, de poissons et de produits de la pêche, ce même Tribunal a signalé que « compte tenu notamment du fait que la souveraineté du Royaume du Maroc sur le Sahara occidental n'est reconnue ni par l'Union et ses États membres ni, plus généralement, par l'ONU, ainsi que de l'absence de tout mandat international susceptible de justifier la présence marocaine sur ce territoire, le Conseil, dans le cadre de l'examen de tous les éléments pertinents du

---

[79] A/RES/55/96, 4 décembre 2000. Résolution sur la « promotion et consolidation de la démocratie ». Voir à ce sujet R. Casado Raigón, « Ética y Derecho internacional. Consideraciones acerca de los Derechos Humanos en el orden internacional », dans Rafael Casado Raigón et Ignacio Gallego Domínguez, *Personalidad y capacidad jurídicas*, Servicio de Publicaciones de la Universidad de Córdoba, Tome I, p. 319 ss.

[80] Tribunal de l'Union européenne, requête du 14 mars 2014, *Front Polisario c. Conseil*, affaire T-180/14.

cas d'espèce en vue de l'exercice de son large pouvoir d'appréciation concernant la conclusion, ou non, d'un accord avec le Royaume du Maroc susceptible de s'appliquer également au Sahara occidental, devait s'assurer lui-même qu'il n'existait pas d'indices d'une exploitation des ressources naturelles du territoire du Sahara occidental sous contrôle marocain susceptible de se faire au détriment de ses habitants et de porter atteinte à leurs droits fondamentaux. Il ne saurait se limiter à considérer qu'il incombe au Royaume du Maroc d'assurer qu'aucune exploitation de cette nature n'a lieu »[81].

9 Conclusions

L'Union européenne est un acteur important dans l'actuel droit international de la pêche maritime. Ainsi en témoigne sa participation dans les plus importants traités en droit de la mer, de la pêche maritime ou de l'environnement marin[82] ou dans les plus importants forums et organisations internationales en la matière, telles que les ORGP, tout cela uni au vaste réseau d'accords bilatéraux qu'elle a conclu avec des Etats tiers. Par conséquent, les dispositions que le nouveau Règlement de base de la politique commune de la pêche de l'UE consacre à sa politique extérieure doivent être considérées comme absolument pertinentes.

Tous ces traités posent des problèmes de répartition des compétences entre l'UE et ses États membres, tant les mixtes que même ceux dans lesquels l'UE participe seule, c'est-à-dire, sans que le fassent simultanément ses États membres. C'est le cas, par exemple, de l'Accord de 1993 visant à favoriser le respect par les navires de pêche en haute mer des mesures internationales de conservation et de gestion, au sujet duquel la Cour de justice de l'Union européenne a dû reconnaître qu'il concerne une matière qui relève *pour l'essentiel* de la compétence exclusive de l'UE. Ce problème touche les relations intracommunautaires, mais aussi les relations avec les États tiers et avec d'autres organisations internationales, qui ont le droit de savoir quel est l'interlocuteur légitimé.

---

81   Tribunal de l'Union européenne, arrêt du 10 décembre 2015, *Front Polisario c. Conseil*, affaire T-512/12. Par. 241 de l'arrêt. Cet arrêt a été l'objet d'un pourvoi formé le 19 février 2016 par le Conseil (Affaire C-104/16 P).

82   Comme l'a réaffirmé le TIDM, « la conservation des ressources biologiques de la mer constitue un élément essentiel de la protection et de la préservation du milieu marin » (TIDM *Recueil* 1999, p. 295, par. 70).

Depuis les déclarations de l'UE de 1998 à l'occasion de la CNUDM et de l'Accord de 1995, ont eu lieu dans le droit de l'Union européenne certaines transformations importantes. Il suffit de citer l'entrée en vigueur du Traité de Lisbonne ou, plus spécifiquement, de deux des règlements successifs (ceux de 2002 et 2013) qui ont gouverné la PCP. En l'absence jusqu'à présent d'une mise à jour de ces déclarations, l'UE doit se demander si elle n'a pas manqué à son obligation de notifier *promptement* à travers le dépositaire des traités les modifications ou changements qui ont eu lieu sur la répartition des compétences avec ses États membres.

Il s'agit d'une question importante car, comme l'a rappelé le TIDM, la responsabilité d'une organisation internationale engagée par un fait internationalement illicite est liée à sa compétence. Il est à cet égard paradoxal ou contradictoire que la Commission européenne soit très jalouse de ses compétences auprès des États membres et en même temps qu'elle veuille éviter sa responsabilité internationale, qu'elle tente d'attribuer à ces derniers. Le non-respect des obligations de *diligence due* évoquées par le TIDM dans son avis consultatif, qui sont des obligations de comportement, affecte autant l'UE que ses États membres, c'est pourquoi la proposition d'inclure une clause de compétences dans les accords bilatéraux de pêche semble raisonnable. La rédaction de ces clauses ne serait pas exempte de discussions entre la Commission et les États membres.

Les ORGP se révèlent être les meilleurs instruments pour la conservation et la gestion des ressources biologiques de la haute mer (et également de la ZEE, au moins en ce qui concerne les stocks chevauchants et grands migrateurs). Dans ces organisations, la contribution que fait l'Union, et celle qu'elle peut faire à l'avenir, est très précieuse. J'ai l'impression que, face à des États *écologistes*, ou écologistes dans leur intérêt propre, l'UE est l'entité qui pose ses propositions de manière la plus altruiste. À cet égard, il est très fondé que l'Union souhaite étendre au plan international les principes de la PCP. Or, en vertu notamment du règlement 1380 / 2013, l'UE a pour mandat tant de contribuer à la durabilité des activités de pêche que de favoriser l'emploi dans l'Union.

Ce mandat touche aussi logiquement les relations bilatérales pour la pêche de navires de l'Union dans les eaux de pays tiers. Les accords de partenariat, clairement fondés sur le *do ut des*, sont d'intérêt mutuel pour les parties concernées. Pêche et emploi en échange d'une compensation financière, laquelle doit également être en partie couverte par les armateurs. Bien qu'elle soit destinée à d'autres fins, la redevance proposée pour la pêche dans les eaux visées par une ORGP me semble également pertinente. En tout cas, la partie de l'aide financière qui doit être consacré au développement du secteur de la pêche et des capacités de l'État côtier (en développement dans la grande majorité des cas) est absolument nécessaire à la fois pour des raisons d'exploitation durable des ressources comme, disons, pour des raisons juridiques, c'est-à-dire, pour que puissent être correctement appliquées (ou, simplement, appliquées) les dispositions pertinentes de la CNUDM. Il ne s'agit donc de simples contrats synallagmatiques qui ont été modelés pour les rendre compatibles avec le développement des États côtiers partenaires. Il y a encore autre chose : un engagement avec l'exploitation durable et avec la lutte contre la pêche INN, comme en témoigne la clause d'exclusivité en réponse à des contrats privés des propres nationaux des États membres de l'UE.

Il convient de souligner la transparence de ces accords de partenariat, beaucoup plus développés et conformes aux principes du nouveau droit international de la pêche maritime que ceux conclus par certains États tiers, c'est pourquoi il est souhaitable pour des raisons diverses (entre autres, celle de l'emploi dans l'Union) que la flotte de pêche communautaire ne se retire pas des actuelles zones de pêche[83] et que, en outre, l'Union cherche des nouvelles zones, en évitant ainsi des activités de pêche illégales ou non durables.

Enfin, je tiens à souligner qu'il est légitime de poursuivre l'amélioration de l'emploi dans l'Union et la recherche de nouvelles possibilités de pêche, mais certainement pas au détriment des principes fondamentaux du droit international, comme celui de la souveraineté permanente des peuples sur leurs richesses et leurs ressources naturelles, ou de financer de fait des dirigeants corrompus de certains pays où le respect des droits de l'homme est en cause. Je dois dire qu'assurer la coexistence pacifique et la coopération entre les États pour créer les conditions nécessaires de paix dans un ordre international plus juste ne justifie pas l'affirmation selon laquelle il existe différentes catégories de démocraties dans le monde. Les droits de l'homme, les principes démocratiques et l'Etat de droit n'ont, ni n'admettent pas, différentes acceptions.

---

83   Dans ce sens, Teijo García, *op. cit.*, note 59, p. 290.

Provisional Measures in Maritime Delimitation Cases

Pierre-Emmanuel Dupont and Alexia Solomou

1 Introduction

The present chapter focuses on provisional measures in the context of the settlement of maritime delimitation disputes, through the evaluation of the case-law of the three international courts and tribunals that have competence in law of the sea issues, i.e. the International Court of Justice (hereinafter the 'ICJ'), the International Tribunal for the Law of the Sea (hereinafter the 'ITLOS'), and United Nations Convention on the Law of the Sea[1] (hereinafter 'LOSC') Annex VII arbitral tribunals. This chapter is a tribute to Professor Momtaz. In addition to his outstanding contribution to a number of fields of international law, Professor Momtaz is a renowned law of the sea expert, having served as a member of the Iranian delegation at the Third United Nations Conference on the Law of the Sea ('UNCLOS III').[2] He has also written a significant number of publications on law of the sea,[3] and maritime delimitation issues.[4] Furthermore, Professor Momtaz had first-hand experience of international litigation, having appeared as counsel before the ICJ in the *Oil Platforms* case.[5]

---

1 1833 UNTS 3.
2 Professor Momtaz spoke on a number of occasions on behalf of Iran during the negotiation of UNCLOS III, see e.g. 54th meeting of the Second Committee, UN Doc. A/CONF.62/C.2/SR.54, 17 April 1978, para. 8; 53rd meeting of the First Committee, UN Doc. A/CONF.62/C.1/SR.53, 7 April 1981, paras. 9–10, 50; 182nd Plenary meeting, UN Doc. A/CONF.62/SR.182, 30 April 1982, para. 133.
3 See e.g. D. Momtaz, 'Le régime de passage dans le Détroit d'Hormuz', in R. Casado Raigón (ed), *L'Europe et la mer*, Bruylant, 2005, pp. 167–174 ; The title of Djamchid Momtaz's thesis at Paris II University was *Le Régime juridique du fond des mers et des océans au-delà des limites de la juridiction nationale : Inventaire et solutions possibles* (1971).
4 See e.g. D. Momtaz, 'Le statut juridique de certaines îles éparses du Golfe Persique: Abou Moussa et la Petite et Grande Tumb', 8 *Collection espaces et ressources maritimes*, 1994; D. Momtaz, 'La délimitation du plateau continental du Golfe Persique: une entreprise inachevée', in L. del Castillo (ed), *Law of the Sea, from Grotius to the International Tribunal for the Law of the Sea: Liber Amicorum Judge Hugo Caminos*, Brill/Nijhoff, 2015, pp. 685–697.
5 See e.g. Professor Momtaz' pleading, Public sitting held on Monday 17 February 2003, at 3 p.m., at the Peace Palace, President Shi presiding, in the case concerning Oil Platforms (Islamic Republic of Iran v. United States of America), Verbatim Record, p. 43.

This chapter will first outline the legal provisions governing each of these tribunals regarding provisional measures. It will then survey the relevant case-law, before turning to the analysis of the requirements for the indication of provisional measures, in so far as they relate to maritime delimitation cases, taking each in turn: *prima facie* jurisdiction, urgency, irreparable prejudice, and the rights sought to be protected. It will also briefly explore the interaction between provisional measures and the obligations of restraint found in LOSC. This chapter will conclude with some observations on the specific characteristics of provisional measures orders in maritime delimitation cases, such as their purpose and parameters, including sovereign rights of exploration and exploitation, rights to acquire information concerning the natural resources of the continental shelf and the protection of the marine environment.

2   Legal Framework

2.1   *The International Court of Justice*

The ICJ, under Article 41 of its Statute, has the power 'to indicate, if it considers that circumstances so require, any provisional measures which ought to be taken to preserve the respective rights of either party.'[6] While the ICJ may order provisional measures *proprio motu*, it has never done so without a prior request by a party to a dispute. Furthermore, pending the final decision of the Court on either the preliminary objections or the merits of the case, 'notice of the measures suggested shall forthwith be given to the parties and to the Security Council.'[7] According to Article 73 of the Rules of the ICJ, a written request for 'the indication of provisional measures may be made by a party at any time during the course of the proceedings in the case in connection with which the request is made.'[8] Requests for provisional measures at the ICJ must specify the reasons for such a request, the possible consequences if they are not granted and the exact measures requested.[9] Requests for the indication of

---

6   Article 41(1) of the Statute of the International Court of Justice, available at: http://www.icj-cij.org/documents/?p1=4&p2=2.

7   Ibid., Article 41(2). See also Article 77 of the Rules of Court, which provides that: 'Any measures indicated by the Court under Articles 73 and 75 of these Rules, and any decision taken by the Court under Article 76, paragraph 1, of these rules shall forthwith be communicated to the Secretary-General of the United Nations for transmission to the Security Council in pursuance of Article 41, paragraph 2, of the Statute.'

8   Article 73(1) of the Rules of the International Court of Justice (1978), adopted on 14 April 1978 and entered into force on 1 July 1978, printed in *Acts and Documents No. 6*, ICJ, available at: http://www.icj-cij.org/documents/index.php?p1=4&p2=3&p3=0.

9   Ibid., Article 73(2).

provisional measures have priority over all other cases.[10] Even if the Court is not in session at the time of the request for the indication of provisional measures, it shall be convened so that it delivers a decision 'as a matter of urgency'.[11] The ICJ is not limited to the way the applicant State formulated its request for provisional measures: it may indicate such measures in whole or in part and it may even indicate measures other than those requested.[12] The rejection of a request for provisional measures by the ICJ does not constitute an obstacle for filing a fresh request in the same case, based on new facts.[13]

2.2 ITLOS

ITLOS may be requested to order provisional measures in two different settings: first, according to Article 290(1) of LOSC, where a dispute on the merits has been submitted to it, and secondly under Article 290(5), when such a dispute has been submitted to an arbitral tribunal pursuant to Part XV of LOSC, pending the constitution of the tribunal.[14]

Most of the rules on provisional measures set forth in the ITLOS Rules are closely modelled on those found in the ICJ Statute,[15] with some notable departures. First, regarding the object of the measures, under Article 290 of LOSC the parties can request provisional measures not only to preserve the respective rights of the parties to the dispute but also on the ground of the prevention of serious harm to the marine environment,[16] an innovation owed to UNCLOS III President Amerasinghe.[17] It may however be doubted that this still constitutes a significant divergence between ITLOS and the ICJ, as it may be assumed that the approach of the ICJ to the prevention of harm to the environment mirrors that of ITLOS and LOSC, especially in light of its finding in the Advisory

---

10 Ibid., Article 74(1).
11 Ibid., Article 74(2).
12 Ibid., Article 75(2).
13 Ibid., Article 75(3).
14 See P. Gautier, 'Interim Measures of Protection before the International Tribunal for the Law of the Sea' in M. H. Nordquist & J. N. Moore (eds), *Current Marine Environmental Issues and the International Tribunal for the Law of the Sea*, Kluwer Law International, 2001, pp. 243–253, at pp. 246–247.
15 See Section 2.1 above.
16 See e.g. T. A. Mensah, 'Provisional Measures in the International Tribunal for the Law of the Sea (ITLOS)', 62 *Zeitschrift für ausländisches öffentliches Recht und Völkerrecht*, 2002, pp. 43–54, at pp. 45–46.
17 See UNCLOS III, Informal single negotiating text (part IV), UN Doc. A/CONF.62/WP.9, 21 July 1975, Art. 12; Hamilton Shirley Amerasinghe served as President of the Third United Nations Conference on the Law of the Sea (1973–1980).

Opinion on the *Legality of the Threat or Use of Nuclear Weapons*, that '[t]he existence of the general obligation of States to ensure that activities within their jurisdiction and control respect the environment of other States or of areas beyond national control is now part of the corpus of international law relating to the environment.'[18]

Second, ITLOS may not act *proprio motu* in prescribing provisional measures, contrary to the ICJ.[19] Another departure lies in Article 290(6) according to which the parties to the dispute 'shall comply promptly with any provisional measures', which reinforces the use of the word 'prescribe' in Article 290(1) ('[...] the court or tribunal may prescribe any provisional measures which it considers appropriate under the circumstances [...]'). While during UNCLOS III, it was still uncertain whether the ICJ provisional measures were binding, the ICJ had the power to 'indicate' provisional measures under Article 41 of its Statute and the use of the word 'prescribe' was intended by the drafters of LOSC to underline the compulsory character –in principle– of provisional measures granted by tribunals constituted under LOSC.[20] The obligation to report to the Tribunal on the implementation of the measures is coherent with the mandatory character of measures prescribed by the Tribunal.[21] Nevertheless, recent

---

18 *Legality of the Threat or Use of Nuclear Weapons*, Advisory Opinion, *ICJ Reports 1996*, p. 226, at pp. 241–242, para. 29; In its Order on provisional measures in the *Ghana v Côte d'Ivoire* case, the Special Chamber of ITLOS referred explicitly to this dictum of the ICJ (at para. 71) and emphasized (at para. 72) previous findings of ITLOS as to the duty of States to 'act with prudence and caution to prevent serious harm to the marine environment' (referring i.a. to *M/V 'Louisa'* (Saint Vincent and the Grenadines v Kingdom of Spain), Case No. 18, Provisional Measures, Order of 23 December 2010, ITLOS Reports 2008–2010, p. 58, at p. 70, para. 77).

19 On discussions of this point at UNCLOS III, see M. Nordquist, S. Rosenne & L. B. Sohn (eds), *United Nations Convention on the Law of the Sea 1982: A Commentary*, Vol. V, Martinus Nijhoff, 1989, at p. 57.

20 Provisional measures are said mandatory 'in principle' to the extent that ITLOS remains at liberty to merely 'recommend' certain measures, thus refraining to 'prescribe' these and thus from making them mandatory. See the instances quoted by Gautier, supra, note 13, pp. 244–245.

21 Article 95(1) of the Rules of the Tribunal (ITLOS/8, 28 October 1997) mandates the parties to report on steps taken to comply with the measures prescribed: 'Each party shall inform the Tribunal as soon as possible as to its compliance with any provisional measures the Tribunal has prescribed. In particular, each party shall submit an initial report upon the steps it has taken or proposes to take in order to ensure prompt compliance with the measures prescribed.' By contrast, Article 78 of the Rules of the ICJ (supra, note 7) provides that the Court 'may request information from the parties' on implementation of any provisional measures it has indicated.

cases granting provisional measures show that the record of compliance by States with the latter remains quite low; be it before ITLOS or the ICJ.[22]

2.3 *Annex VII Arbitration*

Annex VII of LOSC does not contain any specific provision regarding the indication of provisional measures. Nevertheless, Article 5 of Annex VII provides that: 'Unless the parties to the dispute otherwise agree, the arbitral tribunal shall determine its own procedure, assuring to each party a full opportunity to be heard and to present its case.' Arbitral panels at the initial procedural meeting of each case tend to adopt their rules of procedure pursuant to Article 5 of Annex VII of LOSC, which usually include rules on provisional measures.

All, but one, of the cases brought Annex VII of LOSC have been arbitrated under the auspices of the Permanent Court of Arbitration (hereinafter the 'PCA').[23] The most recent example of a provisional measures order by an Annex VII arbitral tribunal is the *'Enrica Lexie'* incident.[24] On 19 January 2016, taking account of the discussion at the first procedural meeting, the Arbitral Tribunal, pursuant to Article 5 of Annex VII, of LOSC, adopted its Rules of Procedure.[25] Article 11 of those rules made provision for the indication of provisional measures.

Specifically, a party may submit 'a request for the prescription of provisional measures under Article 290, paragraph 1, of the Convention at any time during the course of the proceedings. The request shall be in writing and specify the measures requested, the reasons therefor and the possible consequences, if it is not granted, for the preservation of the respective rights of the Parties.'[26] The Arbitral Tribunal may prescribe measures 'different in whole or in part from those requested and indicate the Party or the Parties which are to take or to comply with each measure'.[27]

---

22 Among recent cases where the ICJ found that a party did not comply with provisional measures, see e.g. *Armed Activities on the Territory of the Congo* (Democratic Republic of the Congo v Uganda), *ICJ Reports 2005*, p. 168, para. 345.

23 For a list of all the cases that have been arbitrated under the auspices of the PCA, see: https://pca-cpa.org/en/services/arbitration-services/unclos/.

24 *The 'Enrica Lexie' incident* (Italy v India), PCA Case No. 2015–28, Order for the request for the prescription of provisional measures, 29 April 2016.

25 Ibid., Rules of Procedure, available at: http://pcacases.com/web/sendAttach/1558.

26 Ibid., Article 11(1).

27 Ibid., Article 11(3).

3   Practice of Provisional Measures in Maritime Delimitation Cases

3.1   *Introduction*

This section will present an evaluation of the provisional measures orders handed down by the ICJ (section 3.2), ITLOS (section 3.3), and LOSC Annex VII arbitral tribunals (section 3.4). Although a series of provisional measures have been ordered by these three international courts and tribunals on law of the sea matters, only a handful concern maritime delimitation cases.[28]

3.2   *ICJ Provisional Measures*

3.2.1   The *Aegean Sea Continental Shelf* Case

The *Aegean Sea Continental Shelf* (Greece v Turkey) is one of the earliest maritime delimitation cases where provisional measures were requested.[29] In that case, Greece instituted proceedings against Turkey for the delimitation of the continental shelf appertaining to Greece and Turkey in the Aegean Sea and concerning the respective legal rights of those states to explore and exploit the continental shelf of the Aegean.[30]

Greece requested the Court to indicate the following provisional measures: that both States first, 'refrain from all exploration activity or any scientific research, with respect to the continental shelf areas within which Turkey has granted such licenses or permits or adjacent to the Islands, or otherwise in dispute in the present case', secondly, that both States 'refrain from taking further military measures or actions which may endanger their peaceful relations'.[31] The ICJ found that the circumstances as they then presented themselves were not such as to require the exercise of its power under Article 41 of the Statute to indicate provisional measures.[32]

The ICJ found that the alleged breach by Turkey of the exclusivity of the right claimed by Greece to acquire information concerning the natural resources of areas of continental shelf, if it were established, was one that might

---

28   Two of the most recent law of the sea cases where provisional measures were granted do not involve maritime delimitation on the merits: *The 'Arctic Sunrise' case*, (Kingdom of The Netherlands v Russian Federation), Case No. 22, Request for the Prescription of Provisional Measures, Order of 22 November 2013; *The 'Enrica Lexie' Incident* (Italy v India), Case No. 24, Request for the Prescription of Provisional Measures, Order 24 August 2015; *'Enrica Lexie'*, supra, note 23.

29   *The Aegean Sea Continental Shelf Case* (Greece v Turkey), Interim Protection, Order of 11 September 1976, *ICJ Reports 1976*, p. 3.

30   Ibid., pp. 3–4.

31   Ibid., pp. 4–5, para. 2.

32   Ibid., p. 14, *dispositif* (by 12 votes to 1).

be capable of reparation by appropriate means.[33] As such, the ICJ was not able to find in the alleged breach of Greece's rights such a risk of irreparable prejudice to rights in issue.[34]

Furthermore, the ICJ found it not necessary to order provisional measures in the *Aegean Sea* case 'for the sole purpose of preventing the aggravation or extension of a dispute',[35] because the Security Council had also been seised by the same dispute and a few days before the handing down of that order it adopted Resolution 395 (25 August 1976). By that resolution, the Security Council urged Greece and Turkey 'to do everything in their power to reduce the present tensions in the area so that the negotiating process may be facilitated' and called on both States 'to respect each other's international rights and obligations and to avoid any incident which might lead to the aggravation of the situation'. The ICJ considered that it was not necessary to order provisional measures because both parties had been urged to fulfill their obligations under the UN Charter, and particularly to peacefully settle their dispute, by the Security Council.

3.2.2   *Land and Maritime Boundary between Cameroon and Nigeria* Case
Another case of provisional measures decided by the ICJ is the *Land and Maritime Boundary between Cameroon and Nigeria*.[36] This case revolved around the question of sovereignty over the Bakassi Peninsula.[37] In its application, Cameroon asked *inter alia* the ICJ to delimit the course of the maritime boundary between the two States beyond the line fixed in 1975.[38] The request for provisional measures was filed by Cameroon pursuant to the eruption of hostilities in the Bakassi Peninsula since 3 February 1996.[39] In so far as the maritime aspects of that case were concerned, Cameroon alleged that Nigeria employed substantial naval forces with the intention of continuing the conquest of the Bakassi Peninsula.[40]

The ICJ indicated five different sets of measures, two of which are broad enough to be considered relevant to maritime delimitation. The ICJ ordered

---

33   Ibid., p 11, para. 33.
34   Ibid., p. 11, para. 33.
35   Ibid., para. 42.
36   *Land and Maritime Boundary between Cameroon and Nigeria* (Cameroon v. Nigeria, Equatorial Guinea intervening), Provisional Measures, *ICJ Reports 1996*, p. 13.
37   Ibid., p. 14, para. 2.
38   Ibid., p. 14, para. 4.
39   Ibid., p. 17, para. 17.
40   Ibid., p. 18, para. 18.

that: (a) both 'Parties should ensure that no action of any kind, particularly no action by their armed forces, is taken which might prejudice the rights of the other in respect of whatever judgment the Court may render in the case, or which might aggravate or extend the dispute before it',[41] (b) both 'Parties should take all necessary steps to conserve evidence relevant to the present case within the disputed area.'[42] First, the ICJ was satisfied that the provisions invoked by the Applicant, namely the declarations made by the Parties in accordance with Article 36(2) of the Statute, constituted a *prima facie* basis upon which its jurisdiction in that case was founded.[43] Second, the ICJ was satisfied that its order would preserve the respective rights of the Parties because military incidents had caused military and civilian fatalities and caused major material damage, affecting the sovereign rights over the territory in question.[44] Third, the Court was satisfied that the events giving rise to the request, and particularly the killing of persons, had caused irreparable damage to the rights of the Parties over the Bakassi Peninsula.[45]

3.3 *ITLOS Provisional Measures*

A recent maritime delimitation case where provisional measures have been granted by ITLOS is *Ghana/Côte d'Ivoire*.[46] The order of 25 April 2015 granting provisional measures has attracted much commentary,[47] as the freezing (at least partial in that case) of the disputed area could have significant economic consequences for the parties—and could of course appeal to some future litigants, while deterring others from submitting to judicial or arbitral settlement of maritime disputes. Côte d'Ivoire sought the suspension by Ghana of all ongoing oil exploration and exploitation operations in the disputed area. It alleged that such activities infringed its rights relating to the seabed, its subsoil, and their resources. It also cited harm resulting from the acquisition by Ghana of information relating to the resources in the disputed area, and stressed that

---

41 Ibid., p. 24, para. 49 (*dispositif*).
42 Ibid., p. 25, para. 49 (*dispositif*).
43 Ibid., p. 21, para. 31.
44 Ibid., p. 22, paras. 38–40.
45 Ibid., p. 23, para. 42.
46 *Dispute concerning delimitation of the maritime boundary between Ghana and Côte d'Ivoire in the Atlantic Ocean* (Ghana/Côte d'Ivoire), Case No. 23, Provisional Measures, Order of 25 April 2015.
47 See e.g. N. Cappellazzo, 'Mixing Oil and Water: The Role of Natural Resource Wealth in the Resolution of the Maritime Boundary Dispute Between Ghana and Côte D'ivoire', 39 *Boston College International & Comparative Law Review*, 2016, available at http://lawdigitalcommons.bc.edu/iclr/vol39/iss3/2.

the coastal State was entitled to 'exclusive control' over such information, as an 'indispensable corollary' of the coastal State's exclusive rights over its resources.[48] The disclosure of this information was alleged to cause a shift in the 'economic balance of power between the State and the [oil] companies', thus entailing irreversible damage.[49] Côte d'Ivoire also invoked the serious harm being caused to the marine environment by Ghana's activities, referring *inter alia* to satellite imagery as evidence of endemic pollution linked to the oil exploitation in the disputed area.[50]

Ghana for its part denied that its exploration activities had adverse environmental impacts,[51] and sought to establish that a moratorium on its oil activities would have grave socio-economic consequences for the country.[52] It also insisted that the conditions set in Article 290 of LOSC were not met in that case, in particular the requirements of urgency, imminence and irreparability.[53] Most notably, Ghana sought to explain that provisional measures shall not be granted first of all because the 'disputed area' claimed by Côte d'Ivoire was in fact the result of 'a newly claimed maritime boundary that is based on a bisector approach and the abandonment of a long-agreed boundary line that was based on equidistance'.[54] Ghana submitted a number of maps produced by Côte d'Ivoire, as well as pieces of domestic legislation such as the granting of licenses, and stated that Côte d'Ivoire, which had not objected previously to the conduct of exploration and exploitation activities in the (now disputed) zone, had thus created legitimate expectations for Ghana, which had relied on Côte d'Ivoire's maps, laws, statements and consistent conduct.[55]

In dealing with the request, the Special Chamber was compelled to take into consideration a 'provisional' 'disputed area', as defined basically by the applicant—Côte d'Ivoire. This is so even if, as was recognized by the parties, 'determining a provisional equidistance line is a matter of the merits.'[56] The Special Chamber therefore dismissed Ghana's argument related to the fact that

---

48   *Ghana/Côte d'Ivoire*, supra, note 45, Request of Côte d'Ivoire for the prescription of provisional measures, 27 February 2015, para. 33.
49   Ibid., paras. 34, 35.
50   Ibid., para. 47.
51   *Ghana/Côte d'Ivoire*, supra, note 45, Written Statement of Ghana, 23 March 2015, paras. 112 ff.
52   Ibid., paras. 48 ff.
53   See ibid., paras. 85–111.
54   Ibid., paras. 3, 17–37.
55   Ibid., paras. 38–47.
56   As stated notably by Côte d'Ivoire, see supra, note 47, para. 8.

the 'disputed area' would be newly claimed by Côte d'Ivoire, in departure from an historical established equidistance-based boundary, finding that:

> by instituting arbitral proceedings under Annex VII to the Convention against Côte d'Ivoire, Ghana itself recognized the existence of a dispute concerning the maritime boundary between the two States and the existence of opposing claims of the Parties to the disputed area.[57]

In order to define the limits of this provisional disputed area, the Special Chamber asked Côte d'Ivoire to provide information on the geographical coordinates of the zone concerned by the request, and Ghana in turn to provide coordinates of the line it 'considers to be long recognized by both States as their maritime boundary'.[58] While complying with such requests, the parties made clear that these coordinates were given for the purposes of the proceedings for the prescription of provisional measures, i.e. without prejudice to the parties' claims at the merits stage.

Finding that *prima facie* it had jurisdiction over the dispute,[59] the Special Chamber then engaged in the determination of whether there was 'a real and imminent risk that irreparable prejudice may be caused to the rights of the parties in dispute'.[60] It also stressed the requirement of urgency[61] and made clear that 'the decision whether there exists imminent risk of irreparable prejudice can only be taken on a case by case basis in light of all relevant factors.'[62]

The Special Chamber then articulated—for the first time in ITLOS' jurisprudence—the 'plausibility' test.[63] It stated it needed to 'satisfy itself that the rights which Côte d'Ivoire claims on the merits and seeks to protect are at least

---

57   *Ghana/Côte d'Ivoire* supra, note 45, para. 59.
58   Ibid., para. 29.
59   Ibid., para. 38.
60   Ibid., para. 41.
61   Ibid., para. 42 : '[...] urgency is required in order to exercise the power to prescribe provisional measures, that is to say the need to avert a real and imminent risk that irreparable prejudice may be caused to rights at issue before the final decision is delivered.' The Special Chamber relied on *Construction of a Road in Costa Rica along the San Juan River* (Nicaragua v. Costa Rica), and *Certain Activities Carried Out by Nicaragua in the Border Area (Costa Rica v. Nicaragua)*, (Joined proceedings), Provisional Measures, Order of 13 December 2013, *ICJ Reports 2013*, p. 398, at p. 405, para. 25.
62   *Ghana/Côte d'Ivoire,* supra, note 45, para. 43.
63   See Y. Tanaka, 'Unilateral Exploration and Exploitation of Natural Resources in Disputed Areas: A Note on the Ghana/Côte d'Ivoire Order of 25 April 2015 before the Special Chamber of ITLOS' 46 *Ocean Development and International Law*, 2015, pp. 315–330.

plausible'[64]—and it actually found that 'Côte d'Ivoire has presented enough material to show that the rights it seeks to protect in the disputed area *are plausible*.'[65]

As to the various rights invoked by Côte d'Ivoire for protection by provisional measures, the Special Chamber first made clear that it was free to indicate measures different—in full or in part—from those requested.[66] It found that in order to preserve the rights of Côte d'Ivoire, no new drilling either by Ghana or under its control should take place in the disputed area pending the decision on the merits. However, it was unable to accept that the suspension of activities conducted by Ghana in the disputed zone should extend to activities 'in respect of which drilling has already taken place', to the extent that such full-scope suspension 'would entail the risk of considerable financial loss to Ghana and its concessionaires'.[67] The risk of harm to the marine environment was, on the other hand, found to be insufficiently documented by Côte d'Ivoire, but was nevertheless taken into account by the Special Chamber, precisely to support its decision that suspension of activities should be limited to 'new drilling'. The Special Chamber indeed stressed that complete suspension of activities would itself pose 'a serious danger to the marine environment resulting, in particular, from the deterioration of equipment'.[68]

Overall, the Special Chamber may be found to have adopted a cautious and balanced approach *vis-à-vis* Côte d'Ivoire's request, both in its application of the criteria for granting the measures and in its adjustment of the parameters of the measures it actually decided.

3.4 *Annex VII Arbitral Tribunals Provisional Measures*

In the *Guyana v Suriname* case,[69] there was no actual request for provisional measures. Guyana was reported to have considered requesting such measures, pending the constitution of the Annex VII arbitral tribunal, but it did not actually formulate a request.[70] The Tribunal, however, had an occasion to make

---

64 *Ghana/Côte d'Ivoire*, supra, note 45, para. 58.
65 Ibid., para. 62 (emphasis added).
66 Ibid., para. 97.
67 Ibid., paras. 99, 100.
68 Ibid., paras. 99, 101.
69 *Arbitration between Guyana and Suriname*, 47 ILM 166 (2008); (2007) XXX RIAA 1.
70 The Report of the UN Secretary-General on 'Oceans and the law of the sea' (A/59/62), 4 March 2004, para. 39, mistakenly stated that Guyana had formulated such request, 'that Suriname refrain from any threat or use of armed force in the maritime zone under dispute, from any conduct in the nature of reprisals against Guyana or its nationals, from any conduct that would impede the resumption of exploration in that zone, and from any

an important *dictum* of relevance to the issue of provisional measures in the Award, where it underlined that there was some conceptual relationship between and provisional measures and the obligation imposed by Articles 74(3) and 83(3) of LOSC 'to make every effort [...] not to jeopardize or hamper the reaching of the final agreement'. It stressed in that respect that '[t]he distinction adopted by this Tribunal [between activities of the kind that lead to a permanent physical change, such as exploitation of oil and gas reserves, and those that do not, such as seismic exploration] is consistent with the jurisprudence of international courts and tribunals on interim measures.'[71] The Tribunal also referred to the ICJ's decision on provisional measures in the *Aegean Sea* case.[72]

4 Requirements for the Indication of Provisional Measures in Maritime Delimitation Cases

4.1 *Prima Facie Jurisdiction*

When making a provisional measures order, a court or tribunal must have *prima facie* jurisdiction both *ratione personae* and *ratione materiae*.[73] The ICJ, for example, has held that it ought not to indicate provisional measures unless the provisions invoked appear, *prima facie*, to afford a basis on which jurisdiction may be founded.[74] Article 290(1) of LOSC reflects this requirement as it provides that the dispute submitted must be considered by a court or tribunal to be one where it has *prima facie* jurisdiction.

In light of this criterion, the State applying for provisional measures has to provide sufficient information establishing the *prima facie* jurisdiction of the tribunal and the necessity for indication of provisional measures. This is clearly established in Article 89 of the Rules of ITLOS. The Statute or the Rules of the ICJ do not contain a similar provision, but states, whenever requesting, provisional measures generally do provide relevant information establishing

---

conduct that would impede the exploitation of oil deposits, subject to equitable provisional arrangements of a practical nature'.

71 *Arbitration between Guyana and Suriname,* supra, note 68, para. 468. For a detailed analysis of this *dictum* see Section 5 below.
72 Ibid.
73 *Land and Maritime Boundary between Cameroon and Nigeria*, supra, note 35, p, 21, para. 30.
74 *Military and Paramilitary Activities in and against Nicaragua* (Nicaragua v United States of America), Provisional Measures, ICJ Reports 1984, p. 179; *LaGrand Case*, (Germany v United States of America) Provisional Measures, ICJ Reports 1999, p. 13, para. 13.

the *prima facie* jurisdiction of the Court, irrespective of its order or final judgment on the merits.

The threshold that has to be met at the provisional measures phase is lower than that States have to satisfy at the jurisdiction phase of a given case, where international courts and tribunals engage in a detailed examination of the legal basis for jurisdiction, particularly if preliminary objections are raised, because the instrument(s) invoked by the parties conferring jurisdiction must only appear, *prima facie,* to afford a possible basis on which the jurisdiction might be founded.[75] The ICJ stated in the *Military and Paramilitary Activities in and Against Nicaragua* case that it gives jurisdiction over the merits 'fullest consideration compatible with the requirement of urgency'.[76] In fact, it is possible for a tribunal to grant provisional measures in the first place, but at a later stage to find that it has no jurisdiction in a given case.[77]

For example, in the *Aegean Sea* case, whereas the Parties had diverging views as to the applicability of the General Act for the Pacific Settlement of International Disputes 1928 –Greece basing itself on Article 33 thereof—the ICJ found it not necessary to reach a final conclusion on the questions raised 'concerning the application of the 1928 Act as between Greece and Turkey' and it proceeded to examine the request for indication of interim measures only in the context of Article 41 of its Statute.[78] Furthermore, in the *Land and Maritime Boundary between Cameroon and Nigeria* case, the ICJ was satisfied that it had *prima facie* jurisdiction on the basis of the declarations made by the Parties in accordance with Article 36(2) of the Statute of the ICJ.[79] In the *Ghana/Ivory Coast* case, the Special Chamber of ITLOS, affirmed that it had *prima facie* it had jurisdiction over the dispute by noting that both parties were parties to LOSC,[80] having particular regard to Article 288(1),[81] and underlining

---

75   *Fisheries jurisdiction* (United Kingdom v Iceland) and (Federal Republic of Germany v Iceland), Provisional Measures, *ICJ Reports 1972*, pp. 12, 16, para. 17 and pp. 30, 34, para. 18.

76   *Nicaragua Case,* supra, note 73, p. 179, para. 25.

77   For example, the ICJ granted provisional measures in *Application of the International Convention on the Elimination of all Forms of Racial Discrimination* (Georgia v Russian Federation), Provisional Measures, *ICJ Reports 2008*, p. 353, but subsequently did not find jurisdiction in *Application of the International Convention on the Elimination of All Forms of Racial Discrimination* (Georgia v Russian Federation), Preliminary Objections, Judgment, *ICJ Reports 2011*, p. 70.

78   *Aegean Sea Case,* supra, note 28, p. 8, para. 21.

79   *Land and Maritime Boundary between Cameroon and Nigeria,* supra, note 35, p. 21, para. 31.

80   *Ghana/Côte d'Ivoire,* supra, note 45, p. 9, para. 35.

81   Ibid., p. 10, para. 36, quoting Article 2881(1): '[a] court or tribunal referred to in article 287 shall have jurisdiction over any dispute concerning the interpretation or application of this Convention which is submitted to it in accordance with [Part XV].'

both parties had accepted that *prima facie* the Special Chamber had jurisdiction over the dispute by submitting a Special Agreement.[82] While provisional measures were not granted in the *Aegean Sea* case, while they were in the *Land and Maritime Boundary* case and the *Ghana/ Ivory Coast*, the common thread between these cases is that the provisional affirmation of jurisdiction is a precondition of the examination whether the circumstances contributing to the necessity of provisional measures.[83]

4.2 Urgency

While the ICJ has to convene and deliver a decision 'as a matter of urgency',[84] the criterion of urgency for the indication of provisional measures is not explicitly stipulated in its Statute. However, it was clearly formulated in the case concerning the *Passage through the Great Belt*.[85] The ICJ unanimously found that the circumstances of that case, as they presented themselves to the Court at the time the provisional measures were requested, were not such as to require the exercise of its power under Article 41 of the ICJ Statute,[86] as it considered that the urgency criterion had not been met.[87] Urgency as a requirement was recently reiterated by the ICJ in the *Construction of a Road* and the *Certain Activities* cases, and it was interpreted as the need to avert a real and imminent risk that irreparable prejudice may be caused to rights at issue before the final decision is delivered.[88] This legal test was relied upon by the Special Chamber of ITLOS in the *Ghana/Côte d'Ivoire* provisional measures order.[89] Urgency also underlies the procedural rules of the ICJ and ITLOS.[90]

Urgency takes a different incarnation when it comes to Article 290(5) of LOSC. Pending the constitution of an Annex VII arbitral tribunal, any tribunal agreed upon by the parties or ITLOS, if the parties fail to agree within two

---

82 *Ghana/Côte d'Ivoire*, supra, note 45, p. 10, para. 37.
83 *Aegean Sea Case,* supra, note 28, Separate Opinion of Judge Mosler, *ICJ Reports 1976*, pp. 24–25.
84 Article 74(2), Rules of the ICJ, supra, note 7.
85 *Passage through the Great Belt* (Finland v Denmark), Provisional Measures, Order of 29 July 1991, *ICJ Reports 1991*, p. 12, available at: http://www.icj-cij.org/docket/files/86/6969.pdf, para. 23.
86 Ibid, para. 38 (*dispositif*).
87 Ibid, paras. 24–27 (*ratio* on urgency).
88 *Costa Rica and Nicaragua Border Area Case,* supra, note 60, p. 405, para. 25; See also *Case Concerning Pulp Mills on the River Uruguay* (Argentina v Uruguay), Provisional Measures, Order of 13 July 2006, *ICJ Reports 2006,* p. 129 para. 62 and p. 132, para. 73.
89 *Ghana/Côte d'Ivoire*, supra, note 45, p. 10, para. 42.
90 Articles 74(2) and 54(2), Rules of the ICJ, supra, note 7; Article 11(2) ITLOS Resolution on the International Judicial Practice of the Tribunal (ITLOS/10).

weeks from the date of the request, may indicate provisional measures. Apart from being required to find that it has *prima facie* jurisdiction, the tribunal must also find 'that the urgency of the situation so requires'. ITLOS will find that the urgency criterion is not met if the measures requested could be taken by the arbitral tribunal when it is constituted.[91] There is an emerging line of case-law where ITLOS has granted provisional measures pending the constitution of an arbitral tribunal, albeit regarding issues not concerning maritime delimitation.[92] In some cases, after the arbitral panel is composed, a second set of provisional measures is ordered by that tribunal.[93] Urgency is not only embedded in the applicable rules governing provisional measures by ITLOS and Annex VII arbitral tribunals, it is also substantively applied by such tribunals.

In terms of practical application of the urgency requirement in maritime delimitation cases, the most illuminating example is that of the *Ghana/Côte d'Ivoire* case. The first step in the assessment of ITLOS in finding an imminent risk of irreparable prejudice was to take into account all relevant factors.[94] On the facts of the case such factors included: that the provisional measures requested aimed to preserve three categories of exclusive sovereign rights arising under LOSC,[95] namely rights relating to a 'triangular disputed area', such as the right to explore and exploit the resources of Côte d'Ivoire's seabed and subsoil, the right to exclusive access to confidential information about its natural resources aiming to explore the continental shelf and to exploit its natural resources, and the right to select the oil companies for exploration and exploitation operations.[96] The Special Chamber underlined that for the purposes of granting provisional measures, it held that it need not definitively determine whether the rights sought to be protected existed, rather it was sufficient to be satisfied that such rights were 'at least plausible',[97] which was indeed the case,

---

91   *Southern Bluefin Tuna Cases* (New Zealand v Japan; Australia v Japan), ITLOS Cases No. 3 and 4, Provisional Measures, Order of 27 August 1999, para. 63; *Case Concerning Land Reclamation by Singapore in and around the Straits of Johor* (Malaysia v Singapore), ITLOS Case No. 12, Provisional Measures, Order of 8 October 2003, paras. 68 and 69.

92   *The 'Enrica Lexie' Incident*, ITLOS Case No. 24, supra, note 27, para. 30.

93   *The 'Enrica Lexie' Incident*, PCA Case No. 2015–28, supra, note 23, para. 132.

94   *Ghana/Côte d'Ivoire*, supra, note 45, p. 11, para. 43.

95   Ibid., para. 44.

96   Ibid., paras. 45–48.

97   Ibid., p. 13, paras. 57–58, citing *Certain Activities Carried Out by Nicaragua in the Border Area* (supra, note 60), p. 360, para. 27.

the Chamber found there was an imminent risk of irreparable damage to such rights.[98]

4.3 Prevention of Irreparable Prejudice or Harm

In the *Fisheries Jurisdiction Cases* the ICJ held that provisional measures are meant to protect the parties against irreparable prejudice to the rights in dispute.[99] Wolfrum argues that this legal criterion was developed to justify the preservation of rights in accordance with Article 41 of the ICJ Statute.[100] The ICJ has time and again held that it will not order provisional measures in the absence of 'irreparable prejudice' to rights that are the subject matter of the dispute.[101]

While the notion of 'irreparable prejudice' is obvious in cases where, the physical integrity of human beings is at stake, such as in the *Land and Maritime Dispute between Cameroon and Nigeria* discussed above, it is not equally the case where maritime delimitation is concerned. For example, in the *Aegean Sea* case, the 'exclusivity of the rights... to acquire information concerning the natural resources of the continental shelf' was the subject of the requested provisional measures.[102] The ICJ found that it was capable of reparation.[103]

While the legal test for the ICJ is that of irreparable prejudice to the rights at issue, Article 290(1) of LOSC provides that a 'court or tribunal may prescribe any provisional measures which it considers appropriate... to prevent serious harm to the marine environment, pending the final decision'. Three observations are in order. First, the threshold of serious harm seems lower than that of irreparable prejudice. Second, the serious harm ought to be to the marine environment, and not to the rights of the parties at issue. Third, this provision is in line with Article 192 of LOSC aiming to protect the marine environment.[104]

Practically speaking, this specific provision of Article 290(1) of LOSC was invoked by the Côte d'Ivoire, in the case discussed above, which requested

---

98 *Ghana/Côte d'Ivoire*, supra, note 45, p. 14, paras. 62–63, citing *Certain Activities Carried Out by Nicaragua in the Border Area* (Costa Rica v Nicaragua), Provisional Measures, Order of 8 March 2011, *ICJ Reports 2011*, p. 18, para. 54, and p. 20, para. 96.

99 *Fisheries Jurisdiction Cases*, supra, note 74, paras. 21–22.

100 R. Wolfrum, 'Interim (Provisional) Measures of Protection', in Wolfrum (ed), *Max Planck Encyclopedia of Public International Law*, Oxford University Press, 2015, para. 14.

101 *Land and Maritime Boundary between Cameroon and Nigeria*, supra, note 35, p, 21, para. 31; *Case concerning Armed Activities on the Territory of the Congo,* supra, note 21, paras. 39, 43; *Avena and Other Mexican Nationals Case* (Mexico v United States of America), Provisional measures, Order of 5 February 2003, *ICJ Reports 2003*, p. 89, para. 49 and p. 91, para. 55.

102 *Aegean Sea Case,* supra, note 28, p. 11, para. 33.

103 Ibid.

104 Article 192 of LOSC was considered by ITLOS in: *M/V 'Louisa',* supra, note 17, p. 70, para. 76.

provisional measures to prevent serious harm to the marine environment.[105] While he Special Chamber found that the Côte d'Ivoire did not adduce sufficient evidence to support its allegation that there was an imminent risk of serious harm to the marine environment, it stressed that parties should 'act with prudence and caution to prevent' such harm,[106] and that they have a 'duty to cooperate' to achieve that purpose,[107] and it subsequently ordered Ghana to 'carry out strict and continuous monitoring of all activities' undertaken by itself or 'with its authorization with a view to ensuring the prevention of serious harm to the marine environment'.[108]

Article 290(1) does not mean that ITLOS and Annex VII tribunals do not apply an analogous criterion to that applied by the ICJ in provisional measures cases, other than cases presenting serious harm to the marine environment. The general legal test applicable is that the tribunal must be satisfied that there is 'a real and imminent risk that irreparable prejudice may be caused to the rights of the parties in dispute'.[109] This was the case, for example, in the *Ghana/Côte d'Ivoire* case, where the Special Chamber of ITLOS considered that the exploration and exploitation activities, as planned by Ghana, may 'cause irreparable prejudice to the sovereign and exclusive rights invoked by Côte d'Ivoire in the continental shelf and superjacent waters of the disputed area, before a decision on the merits is given ... and that the risk of such prejudice is imminent.'[110] In reaching this conclusion, the Special Chamber considered whether the damage of the rights in issue was a pure financial loss that could be eventually addressed by an award of damages,[111] which was not the case

---

105   *Ghana/Côte d'Ivoire*, supra, note 45, p. 14, para. 64.
106   Ibid., p. 15, para. 72, quoting *M/V 'Louisa'*, supra, note 17, p. 70, para. 77; see also *Southern Bluefin Tuna*, supra, note 90, p. 296, para. 77; *Responsibilities and obligations of States with respect to activities in the Area*, ITLOS Case No. 17, Advisory Opinion, 1 February 2011, *ITLOS Reports 2011*, p. 10, at p. 46, para. 132.
107   *Ghana/Côte d'Ivoire*, supra, note 45, p. 16, para. 73, quoting *MOX Plant* (Ireland v. United Kingdom), ITLOS Case No. 10, Provisional Measures, Order of 3 December 2001, *ITLOS Reports 2001*, p. 95, at p. 110, para. 82; see also *Land Reclamation in and around the Straits of Johor*, supra, note 90, p. 25, para. 92; *Request for an Advisory Opinion submitted by the Sub-Regional Fisheries Commission*, ITLOS Case No. 21, Advisory Opinion of 2 April 2015, para. 140.
108   *Ghana/Côte d'Ivoire*, supra, note 45, p. 22, *dispositif*, para. 1(c).
109   *M/V 'Louisa'*, supra, note 17, p. 69, para. 72.
110   *Ghana/Côte d'Ivoire*, supra, note 45, p. 21, para. 96.
111   Ibid., p. 18, paras. 86–87.

because the activities complained of could result in 'significant and permanent modification of the physical character of the area in dispute'.[112]

4.4 The Rights Sought to Be Protected

The party applying for provisional measures needs to establish that the rights it seeks to protect meet certain requirements. First, the rights concerned must correspond to those claimed on the merits.[113] It is on this ground that the ICJ dismissed the request of Guinea-Bissau in its order on provisional measures in the *Case Concerning the Arbitral Award of 31 July 1989*, the Court found that the application of Guinea-Bissau:

> asks the Court to pass upon the existence and validity of the [1989] award but does not ask the Court to pass upon the respective rights of the Parties in the maritime areas in question; it finds that accordingly the alleged rights sought to be made the subject of provisional measures are not the subject of the proceedings before the Court on the merits of the case [...].[114]

Second, the rights concerned must be considered plausible. This requirement has been affirmed by the ICJ, first, in the case of *Obligation to Prosecute or Extradite* in 2009, then was reiterated in the case of *Certain Activities carried out by Nicaragua in the Border Area* in 2011.[115] In substance, the Court now subjects the granting of provisional measures to a test that 'the rights asserted by a party are *at least plausible*'.[116] This precondition for the granting of provisional measures now seems to have been adopted by ITLOS. While it was not yet present in the incidental proceedings on provisional measures in *Southern Bluefin Tuna Cases*, nor in the *'Arctic Sunrise' case*, for instance, it was recently articulated, in the *Ghana/Côte d'Ivoire* case, where the Special Chamber of ITLOS said it needed to 'satisfy itself that the rights which Côte d'Ivoire claims on the

---

112 Ibid, p. 18, para. 89.
113 See e.g. *Aegean Sea Case*, supra, note 28, p. 9, para. 2.
114 *Arbitral Award of 31 July 1989* (Guinea-Bissau v Senegal), Provisional Measures, Order of 2 March 1990, *ICJ Reports 1990*, p. 64, para. 26.
115 *Obligation to Prosecute or Extradite* (Belgium v Senegal), Provisional Measures, *ICJ Reports* 2009, p. 151, paras. 56–57; *Certain Activities carried out by Nicaragua in the Border Area* (Costa Rica v Nicaragua), Provisional Measures, Order of 8 March 2011, *ICJ Reports 2011*, p. 18, para. 53.
116 See G. I. Hernández, *The International Court of Justice and the Judicial Function*, Oxford University Press, 2014, p. 58.

merits and seeks to protect are at least plausible'[117]—and in the circumstances of this case it found that the rights claimed by Côte d'Ivoire (which were rights of sovereignty over the territorial sea and its subsoil, sovereign rights of exploration and exploitation of the natural resources of the continental shelf, and related rights) were indeed plausible: 'the Special Chamber finds that Côte d'Ivoire has presented enough material to show that the rights it seeks to protect in the disputed area *are plausible.*'[118] The rise of this 'plausibility test' as an additional precondition for the granting of provisional measures is seen by some as expressing the willingness of ICJ, and now ITLOS, to send a strong signal to States, that it is not prepared to entertain requests for provisional measures lightly, and that it will refrain from granting these unless the State requesting the measures has at least a plausible case on the merits.[119] Both the ICJ and ITLOS, faced with prospects of an increasing number of requests for provisional measures, are probably seeking to strike a delicate balance in that regard.

Third, it is well established in both ICJ and ITLOS jurisprudence that, for provisional measures to be granted there must exist a link between the rights claimed by the applicant and the provisional measures it seeks.[120] The Special Chamber of ITLOS in *Ghana v Côte d'Ivoire* recently reaffirmed this requirement.[121] The underlying rationale is that, insofar as the power to order provisional measures aims at (and is limited to) the preservation of the respective rights of the parties pending the decision on the merits, provisional measures can only concern the rights 'which may subsequently be adjudged by the Court to belong either to the Applicant or to the Respondent'.[122]

---

117   *Ghana/Côte d'Ivoire*, supra, note 45, para. 58.
118   Ibid., para. 62.
119   See e.g. J. J. Quintana, *Litigation at the International Court of Justice: Practice and Procedure*, Brill/Nijhoff, 2015, p. 668.
120   See e.g. *Arbitral Award of 31 July 1989*, supra, note 113, p. 64, para. 25; *Certain Activities Carried Out by Nicaragua in the Border Area*, supra, note 114, p. 18, para. 54.
121   *Ghana/Côte d'Ivoire*, supra, note 45, para. 63.
122   See *Application of the Convention on the Prevention and Punishment of the Crime of Genocide* (Bosnia and Herzegovina v Yugoslavia (Serbia and Montenegro)), Provisional Measures, Order of 8 April 1993, *ICJ Reports 1993*, p. 19, para. 34; *Land and Maritime Boundary between Cameroon and Nigeria*, supra, note 35, p. 22, para. 35; *Application of the International Convention on the Elimination of All Forms of Racial Discrimination*, supra, note 76, pp. 388–389, para. 118; *Questions relating to the Obligation to Prosecute or Extradite*, supra, note 114, p. 139, para. 56.

5 The Interaction between Provisional Measures and the Obligations of Restraint in Articles 74(3) and 83(3) of LOSC

There is some relationship between provisional measures that can be granted with respect to disputed maritime areas, and the obligations of restraint (especially 'not to jeopardize or hamper the reaching of the final agreement') set out in Articles 74(3) and 83(3) of LOSC as regards undelimited maritime areas.[123] Such interaction has been noticed by some commentators.[124] The similarity may operate with respect to several requirements for the granting of provisional measures, commonly applied by courts and tribunals when deciding on provisional measures. For example, the requirement of 'irreparable prejudice' to the parties' rights has been used by the Annex VII Arbitral Tribunal in the *Guyana v Suriname* case. The Tribunal, while noting that the regime of provisional measures is 'far more circumscribed than that surrounding activities in disputed waters generally', found inspiration in cases where provisional measures were requested with respect to disputed areas, and observed that:

> Activities that would meet the standard required for the indication of interim measures, in other words, activities that would justify the use of an exceptional power due to their potential to cause irreparable prejudice, would easily meet the lower threshold of hampering or jeopardising the reaching of a final agreement. The criteria used by international courts and tribunals in assessing a request for interim measures, notably the risk of physical damage to the seabed or subsoil, therefore appropriately

---

[123] Article 74(3) of LOSC, concerned with the delimitation of EEZ boundaries between States with opposite or adjacent coasts, provides:
"Pending agreement as provided for in paragraph 1, the States concerned, in a spirit of understanding and co-operation, shall make every effort to enter into provisional arrangements of a practical nature and, during this transitional period, not to jeopardize or hamper the reaching of the final agreement. Such arrangements shall be without prejudice to the final delimitation."
The same obligations are set out in respect of the delimitation of continental shelf boundaries by Article 83(3) of LOSC.

[124] R. Lagoni, 'Interim Measures Pending Maritime Delimitation Agreements', 78 *American Journal of International Law*, 1984, pp. 345–368, at pp. 365–366; S. P. Kim, *Maritime Delimitation and Interim Arrangements in North East Asia*, Martinus Nijhoff, 2004, pp. 57–58; *Report on the Obligations of States under Articles 74(3) and 83(3) of LOSC in respect of Undelimited Maritime Areas*, Brittish Institute of International and Comparative Law, 2016, pp. 35–39.

guide this Tribunal's analysis of an alleged violation of a party's obligations under Articles 74(3) and 83(3) of the Convention.[125]

This trend has been analyzed as suggesting that 'not only is the content of the Articles 74(3) and 83(3) obligations informed by the requirements for the granting of provisional measures as developed by the ICJ, but also that the practice of LOSC dispute settlement bodies regarding these paragraph (3) obligations could contribute to the development of the requirements for the granting of provisional measures'.[126] It remains however unclear whether the requirement of 'plausibility' of the rights claimed could also be applied to the obligation of restraint under Articles 74(3) and 83(3).[127]

6   Conclusion

In conclusion, the present chapter has demonstrated the specific characteristics of provisional measures orders in maritime delimitation cases. Such measures aim to preserve the sovereign rights of States in the disputed area, including rights of exploration and exploitation, and rights to acquire information concerning the natural resources of the continental shelf and the protection of the marine environment, until the determination of each case on the merits. Another specific feature of provisional measures in maritime delimitation cases, such as the *Ghana/ Côte d'Ivoire*, case, is the aim of preventing serious harm to the marine environment. In contrast to the general legal test of irreparability of harm, a State need not adduce evidence of actual harm to the marine environment; rather it is sufficient to demonstrate a risk of serious harm, with an aim of preventing such risk from potentially materializing. Furthermore, provisional measures in situations where offshore concessions are at stake are strategically important, because they could potentially 'stifle the parties' ability to pursue economic development in a disputed area

---

125   *Arbitration between Guyana and Surinam,* supra, note 68, para. 469.
126   British Institute of International and Comparative Law, *Report on the Obligations of States under Articles 74(3) and 83(3) of LOSC in respect of Undelimited Maritime Areas* (London: BIICL, 2016) 36, para. 121. For a contrary view, see the same BIICL *Report*, Annex III, Summary Report of Expert Roundtable held on 22 January 2016, para. 6 (Professor Churchill).
127   This 'import' of the 'plausibility' criterion was suggested in the *Report on the Obligations of States under Articles 74(3) and 83(3) of LOSC in respect of Undelimited Maritime Areas,* supra, note 125, pp. 38–39, paras. 129–133.

during a boundary dispute as the resolution of such disputes may be time-consuming, as the arbitral tribunal underlined in *Guyana v. Suriname*.[128] At the same time, as demonstrated by the provisional measures order in *Ghana/Côte d'Ivoire*, pure economic loss can be satisfied by compensation at the merits phase and as such it cannot meet the threshold of the irreparability of harm criterion, whereas permanent physical damage of the area in dispute would meet the relevant threshold.

---

128   *Arbitration between Guyana and Suriname* supra, note 68, para. 470.

The Contribution of the States of Central America to the Evolution of the New Law of the Sea

Víctor L. Gutiérrez Castillo

Introduction

Generally speaking, Latin America has made a generous contribution to the evolution and ensuing codification of the Law of the Sea. Since President Truman's famous initiative on September 28, 1945 until the Third United Nations Conference on the Law of the Sea in 1973, the countries of this region filed many claims to their sovereignty and jurisdiction over the seas off their coastlines, drawn by either the need to protect the resources of their maritime space or an interest to extend the breadth of their territorial waters. These initiatives gave rise to precedents, until then unheard-of, which would be the object of discussion in subsequent Conferences on the Law of the Sea. In this context, Central America played a leading role on account of their particularly significant input on the definition of new maritime spaces.

There is no end of examples illustrating these facts, so unjustly disregarded by legal doctrines; hence our interest in acknowledging their valuable contribution. The closeness in time and common concerns of their claims, as well as the statements made by these governments and their active participation in international conferences, were essential to the formation and development of a 'new law of the sea' in the succeeding years. Along these lines and taking into account the object of this study, we will discuss all forms of State practice on the basis of both the unilateral decisions made by Central American nations as subjects of international law and their participation in multilateral effort related to the Law of the Sea, to wit, conferences, meetings, and joint statements about this legislation.

1   Unilateral Acts by Central American States and the Definition of New Maritime Spaces

The interest of Latin American States in the oceans appeared late in life. It is in the late 1940s when this concern increased, and mainly for two reasons. On one hand, because of the entry into effect of a new legal figure—continental shelf—initially supported by Mexico and, eventually, by the rest of the region; on the other hand, because some Latin American governments (especially Chile, Peru and Ecuador) quickly became aware of the need to protect the marine resources contiguous to their coasts in light of the intense fishing activity developed by other States, in particular Norway, Great Britain and the United States.[1]

This is the reason that the concept of continental shelf and the interest of the States to reserve competences for the exploitation of living and non-living resources in maritime spaces near their shores gave rise to a number of unilateral declarations across the region. In this connection, Central America was not the exception, to the point that it became an active venue of state claims and statements that included economic considerations in the *Mare Liberum vs. Mare Clausum* debate. Latin American ingenuity was no doubt what made it possible to break with the classic approach of the debate about maritime control, traditionally linked to the concept of sovereignty. With these new claims and statements, the Latin American governments took the said debate to a higher level by bringing to the fore a horizon never before explored: the economy. Indeed, since the concept of maritime space in the 1960s and 1970s was not clearly defined, the claimed rights were neither unequivocal nor uniform. Therefore, it is safe to say that Latin America was the breeding ground for maritime spaces over which coastal States have exclusive rights to exploit living and non-living natural resources and the driving force behind the consolidation of the concepts of continental shelf and exclusive economic zone (EEZ).[2]

Now, the study of these unilateral declarations cannot be addressed without making reference to its first antecedent, namely President Truman's Proclamation 2627 of September 28, 1945, 'Policy of the United States With Respect to the Natural Resources of the Subsoil and Sea Bed of the Continental Shelf', stating literally that, 'having concern for the urgency of conserving and prudently utilizing its natural resources, the Government of the United States regards the natural resources of the subsoil and sea bed of the continental shelf beneath the high seas but contiguous to the coasts of the United States as appertaining to the United States, subject to its jurisdiction and control.'[3]

---

1 J. A. Vargas, *Contribuciones de América Latina al derecho del mar*, Universidad Nacional Autónoma de México, 1981, pp. 18–19.
2 Ibid., pp. 6 and 18–19.
3 H. S. Truman, 'Proclamation 2667—Policy of the United States With Respect to the Natural Resources of the Subsoil and Sea Bed of the Continental Shelf', September 28, 1945, Available online by G. Peters and J. T. Woolley, *The American Presidency Project*, Accessed May 30, 2016, at http://www.presidency.ucsb.edu/ws/?pid=12332.

Likewise, the second statement, Proclamation No. 2668, 'Policy of the United States with Respect to Coastal Fisheries in Certain Areas of the High Seas', stated: 'In view of the pressing need for conservation and protection of fishery resources, the Government of the United States regards it as proper to establish conservation zones in those areas of the high seas contiguous to the coasts of the United States wherein fishing activities have been or in the future may be developed and maintained on a substantial scale'.[4]

With this statement, one of the powers that won World War II established a legal precedent by declaring to the rest of the planet its interest in the exploitation and control of living and non-living resources of its surrounding seas. Since Truman's initiative was issued, the States of this region first started to claim to various rights over natural resources contained in the soil and subsoil of their continental shelves. Despite the fact that the United States was the first country to use the term *continental shelf*, the concept was developed and structured as a result of actions and statements of its regional neighbors.[5]

1.1 Panama's Jurisdictional Demands in the Constitution of 1946

One of the first actions in the region following Truman's Proclamations was undertaken by the government of Panama, which unquestionably played a very active role in the evolution of the Law of the Sea. In fact, as early as in 1946, Panama claimed to full jurisdiction over its territorial waters, airspace and continental shelf in Article 209 of the Constitution, which stated that '1) The territorial sea and the waters of lakes and rivers our maritime space, lacustrine and fluvial waters, beaches and their shores, navigable rivers; the shores and banks of the same and of navigable rivers; and ports and estuaries. All such property is for the free and common benefit, subject to regulations established the Law... 4) The air space and submarine continental shelf corresponding to the national territory.'[6] Thus Panama reasserted its rights over territorial waters without making any specific mention of their breadth, taking up again the concept of continental shelf coined a year earlier by President Truman in

---

4 H. S. Truman, 'Proclamation 2668—Policy of the United States with Respect to Coastal Fisheries in Certain Areas of the High Seas', September 28, 1945. Available online by Gerhard Peters and John T. Woolley, *The American Presidency Project*, Accessed May 30, 2016, at http://www.presidency.ucsb.edu/ws/?pid=58816.
5 Vargas, supra, note 1.
6 Constitution of Panama 1946, The English version published by Pan American Union, Washington D.C. Legal Division Depatment of International Law, 1957, available at https://catalog.hathitrust.org/Record/001156837.

what is likely to have been the first reaction to the US initiative by a Central American country.

Panama also made significant progress by regulating the use of living marine resources with the publication of Decree 449 of December 17, 1946 to control fishing in its jurisdictional waters by forcing foreign ships to request permits and pay taxes.[7] Accordingly, Panama can be said to be the first country in the region to regulate living resources, of itself a significant contribution to the evolution of the new Law of the Sea.

1.2 Guatemala's Regulation of Oil Resources and Claims to Maritime Space

On November 9, 1947 the Republic of Guatemala adopted an Oil Act intended to regulate the granting of rights to exploit its continental shelf.[8] This legislation would be modified by Decree 649 of August 30, 1949, basically a fresh claim to oil reserves in its territory.[9] At a later date, on July 7, 1955, the Guatemalan Government abolished this Act and replaced it (by Decree 345) with the Oil Code, which stated in Article 1 that 'all oil fields or natural reserves of oil located within the land or maritime boundaries of the Republic or extending up to the limits of its continental shelf belong to our Nation, and our dominion over them is inalienable and imprescriptible.'[10] This is how Guatemala became the first Central American country to establish rules designed to protect national oil fields, certainly a major advance regarding the conservation of non-living resources.

By means of unilateral instruments, Guatemala also implemented guidelines for its maritime space, dividing it into 'territorial and coastal waters' with the *Act on Fish Farming and Fisheries*, issued through Decree 1235 of January 18, 1932.[11] Similarly, Guatemala's *Regulatory Legislation for the Harbor*

---

7   *Decreto por el cual se Reglamenta la pesca del tiburón por naves extranjeras en las aguas jurisdiccionales de la República*. Official Gazette of the Republic of Panama (*Gaceta Oficial*) on 24 December 1946.

8   For more information, see J. L. Lovo Castelar, *Prolegómenos del Derecho del Mar*, 1st edition, San Salvador: Corte Suprema de Justicia, Sección de Publicaciones, 2007, p. 58.

9   For more information, see F. V. García Amador, *América Latina y el derecho del mar*, Editorial Universitaria de la Universidad de Chile, 1976, p. 71.

10 The text may be consulted on *Petroleum Code of the Republic of Guatemala*. Decree No. 345 of July 7, 1955, Library of University of Texas, 1955.

11 This decree-law was used to regulate fishing and fish farming in Guatemala for almost 70 years, but the rules were very general and contained a considerable number of legal gaps. One of the most significant characteristics of this decree-law was the lack of regulations in regard to sustainable development and with respect for the environment. There

Administration and Police of June 10, 1934 set a 12-nautical-mile territorial limit and classified its territorial waters as *fresh waters* (rivers, streams, canals, lakes and pools) and *coastal waters* (salt waters of estuaries, bays and seas), definitely a groundbreaking legislation for that time. While this Act was expected to regulate fisheries and not the jurisdiction over those waters, it was an important step toward the definition of maritime boundaries. This classification was further reinforced in the Constitution of 1956 with claims to large marine extensions, including continental shelf, soil, subsoil and territorial waters. Furthermore, this normative extended national jurisdiction over the natural resources existing within the said boundaries.[12]

1.3 Nicaragua's Claims to its Continental Shelf

Much like many other countries in the region, Nicaragua took up again the continental shelf issue at an early stage. Article 2 of the Nicaraguan Constitution of 1948 set forth that the country's territory comprised territorial waters, continental shelf, airspace and outer space.[13] Not only did Nicaragua take up again the concept of continental shelf, it also pointed out—through legislation passed in 1949—that the said shelf would comprise the underwater landmass up to a depth of 200 meters. This view would be accepted in subsequent international meetings on the Law of the Sea.

Later on, and pursuant to Article 5 of its Constitution of 1950, Nicaragua filed claims not only to spaces provided for in the old Constitution of 1948 (continental shelf, territorial waters and outer space) but also new ones until then uncovered by its legislation: subsoil and sea bed. Eight years later, national Executive Order No. 372 enacted the *Special Act on Oil Prospecting and Oil Fields*, which would divide Nicaragua's territory into four zones, including one formed by 'areas of the continental shelf of both oceans'.[14]

---

are few sections in regard to this particular matter, for example there is a section. See B. Siomara Cifuentes Velasco, *The Guatemalan fishery and aquaculture general law versus international laws related to fishery and aquaculture,* Division for Ocean Affairs and the Law of the Sea office of the Legal Affairs, United Nations, 2009, pp. 17–18.

12   Constitution of 1956 published by Pan American Union, Washington D.C., Legal Division of Department of International Law 1956.

13   The Spanish version: 'El fundamento del territorio nacional es el *uti possidetis juris* de 1821. Está comprendido el territorio entre los océanos Atlántico y Pacífico y las repúblicas de Honduras y Costa Rica, y abarca también las islas adyacentes, el mar territorial, las plataformas continentales y el espacio aéreo y estratosférico. Los tratados y la ley fijarán los límites que no estén aún determinados.'

14   Lovo Castelar, supra, note 8.

Nicaragua would also make significant contributions to the regulation of living resources by enacting in 1958 the *General Act on the Exploitation of Natural Resources* (Executive Order No.316 of March 12, 1958) and establishing in 1965 a National Fishery by Executive Order N1-L.[15] It should be underscored that the said Fishery referred to a 200 n.m. space extending from the coastlines, which confirms that, while not explicitly, the Central American States started to claim to increasingly large maritime spaces contiguous to their shorelines.

1.4 Costa Rica: Protection of and Control Over 200 n.m.

Not in its Constitution, but by Decree, Costa Rica became the first country in Central America and the third in Latin America to lay explicit claims to territorial waters extending up to 200 nautical miles. Indeed, through Decree-Law No. 116 of July 27, 1948, the Founding Board of the Second Republic of Costa Rica proclaimed national sovereignty over the waters, underwater landmass, and the continental and insular shelves near its mainland and islands.[16] Moreover, the country declared the State's protection and control over all the maritime space within a perimeter formed by the coastline and a mathematical parallel stretching across 200 n.m. from Costa Rican mainland.[17] By stating those 200 n.m., this Decree salvaged two major factors: freedom of passage and the legitimate right of other States to the principle of reciprocity.[18]

Now, we can infer from the aforesaid Decree-Law that the thesis of State protection and control over 200 n.m. did not survive for a long time: this legislation would be modified in November 1949 by another regulation—Decree-Law No. 803—that replaced the concept of 'national sovereignty' with that of 'rights and interests of Costa Rica' and also deleted the word 'control'. It was far and away a consequential change in the country's intentions, as the new Decree involved the abandonment of claims to national jurisdiction over 200 n.m. Three days later, this situation was further clarified with Article 6 of the Constitution of November 7, 1949, about the State's full and exclusive

---

15 J. F. Sáenz Carbonell, *Historia Diplomática de Costa Rica (1948–1970)*, 1st edition, Universidad Nacional de Costa Rica, 2013, p. 3.
16 H. J. Buchholz, *Law of the Sea Zones in the Pacific Ocean*, Institute of Asian Affairs, 1987; A. Székely, *Latin America and the development of the Law of the Sea:* regional documents and national legislation, Ocaeana Publications, 1976–1980. For more information, see E. K. Martens, 'Evolution for Coastal State Jurisdiction: A conflict between Developed and Developing Nations', 5 *Ecology Law Quaterly*, 1976, pp. 533–541.
17 García Amador, supra, note 9, p. 72.
18 Sáenz Carbonell, supra, note 15.

sovereignty over its airspace, territorial waters and continental shelf, in keeping with current international law principles and treaties.[19]

As to living resources in waters contiguous to its coastlines, the Government of Costa Rica also took security measures. Suffice it to mention the publication in 1948 of the *Act on Marine Fishing and Hunting* (Executive Order No. 10 of March 25, 1969) demanding foreign ships to request a permit from the Ministry of Agriculture and Industry to engage in such activities. Moreover, this Order regulated the fishing of Pacific thread herring within its jurisdictional waters, especially in the Gulf of Nicoya. Now, none of the aforesaid provisions made reference to the extent of such jurisdictional waters.[20] For this reason, and given that the issue of breadth of territorial waters remained unclear in its Constitution of 1949 for years to come, Costa Rica had recourse to the thesis of 200 n.m. of patrimonial sea, pursuant to Decree No. 2.204-RE of February 10, 1972.[21]

1.5 *Claims by Honduras and El Salvador*

Since March 28, 1936, Honduras incorporated the definition of its boundaries into the Constitution through the regulation in Article 4 of some maritime spaces that included a 12- n.m. territorial limit.[22] Even if in 1936 the concept of territorial sea was still vague about its extension, it was already accepted by the international community, and Honduras decided to include it in its legislation at a rather early date. By an Executive Order in March 7, 1950, Honduras claimed to new spaces that included underwater landmass and the continental and insular shelves in both oceans. It should be note that this Order allowed the Honduran Government to claim not only to spaces, but also to full control over any resources that may exist in the shelf and the surrounding waters. A subsequent Executive Order in January 1951 extended the State's protection

---

19   The Spanish versión: (article 6) 'El Estado ejerce la soberanía completa y exclusiva en el espacio aéreo de su territorio y en sus aguas territoriales y plataforma continental, de acuerdo con los principios de Derecho internacional y los tratados vigentes.' The text may be consulted on A. J. Peaslee, *Constitutions of Nations. The Americas in two parts*, Volume IV, 3rd edition, Martinus Nijhoff, 1970, p. 328; J. E. Romero Pérez, 'Un aspecto del derecho del mar: la plataforma continental y sus correlatos', paper presented at II Jornadas italo-latinoamericanas, San José, Costa Rica, September 1977.

20   P. Trujillo, A. M. Cisneros-Montemayor, S. Harper, K. Zylich & Dirk Zeller, 'Reconstruction of Costa Rica's marine fisheries catches, 1950–2010', The University of British Columbia, Fisheries Center, 31 *Working Paper Series, 2015.*

21   The text may be consulted on Romero Pérez, supra, note 19.

22   The Constitution of Honduras may be consulted on Gobierno de Honduras, *Constitución de Honduras de 1936*, Biblioteca Virtual Miguel de Cervantes, 2014.

and surveillance activity in the Atlantic Ocean to 200 n.m., liberating the legitimate rights of third States and the rights of passage.[23] Honduras eventually incorporated into its Constitution of 1957 spaces such as the continental shelf, only 12 years after President Truman's first reference to this term.

As to El Salvador, it should be mentioned that it was the first country in the world to lay constitutional claim to a 200 n.m. limit of territorial waters. Article 7 of its Constitution of 1950 stated, verbatim, that 'the territory of the Republic within its boundaries is irreducible and comprises the surrounding seas up to a distance of two hundred n.m. counted from the lowest level of the tide…'[24] This was a major claim, since it was the first accurate and highest ranking statement about territorial issues. Besides, it was the first time that a Constitution incorporated the notion of a territorial sea extending 200 n.m. from a State's coastline. However, this territorial sea was sui generis inasmuch as it could be freely used for navigation purposes.

Article 8 of the Constitution of 1962 reasserted that El Salvador's territory comprised 'the adjacent sea up to a distance of 200 n.m.'.[25] This claim was not modified in the last Constitution of 1983. In fact, there have been no changes so far, and El Salvador has not yet ratified UNCLOS and remains one of the few countries in the world that is still claiming to an extremely large maritime space, over which it has jurisdiction and control, at least in theory.

El Salvador also developed legal instruments in matters of fishing and regulation of possible oil concessions. Issued through Executive Order No. 1961, the Act of Marine Fishing and Hunting of 1955[26] would govern the exploitation of living resources and reconfirm the territorialist nature of its Constitution of 1950. This Order classified three types of fishing: coastal fishing up to 12 n.m.; deep-sea fishing up to 200 n.m., and commercial fishing beyond 200 n.m. Only the former (coastal fishing) was explicitly reserved by law as patrimonial for the Salvadorians.

At a later date, in 1970, the 200 n.m. territorial claim was further clarified on the basis that commercial deep-sea fishing 'is carried out beyond the 200 n.m.

---

23   F. Orrego Vicuña, *Los fondos marinos y oceánicos*, 1st edition, Editorial Andrés Bello, 1976, p. 78.
24   The Spanish version: 'El territorio de la República dentro de sus actuales límites, es irreductible; comprende el mar adyacente hasta la distancia de doscientas millas marianas contadas desde la línea de la más baja marea, y abarca el espacio aéreo, el subsuelo y el zócalo continental correspondiente…' See Gobierno de El Salvador, *Constitución Política de la República de El Salvador de 1950*, Biblioteca Virtual Miguel de Cervantes, 2014.
25   San Salvador, Asamblea Legislativa, Constitución Política de El Salvador de 1962, Decreto No. 6.
26   Official Gazette of El Salvador (*Diario Oficial*) on 7 November 1955.

limit, that is, in extraterritorial waters or on the high seas', which confirms the boundaries of the country's territorial waters (200 n.m.). With Decree No. 86 of September 1974, the Salvadoran Government approved—much later than other Central American nations—the Rules Governing Oil Concessions in Territorial Waters.[27] In addition to regulating these concessions, the said Order kept claiming to a 200 n.m. territorial limit.

2   The States of Central America: Meetings and Joint Statements on the Law of the Sea

The Declaration of Panama of 1939 is perhaps the first antecedent related to this issue. No other region in the world had laid such far-reaching claims to maritime spaces in a similar Declaration. Authors like Faidutti point out that this statement 'established a marine jurisdiction for the benefit of American States that went far beyond any limit claimed until then by the great maritime powers'.[28] This Declaration stemmed from the First Consultative Meeting of Foreign Ministers of the American Republics, whose agenda was crowned with a specific topic: the position to be adopted by American countries regarding the European war.[29] World War II was just starting in Europe, and measures were needed to preserve the security of American States. This Declaration was the region's reaction to the existing situation.

Besides adopting a position of non-involvement in the armed conflict, the Central American foreign ministers made known their intention of keeping at a reasonable distance from their coastlines any possible hostile or military action against or by the powers at war. Therefore, ensuring the security of their coastlines entailed the establishment of a 'security zone' around them. On average, this zone stretched out to 250 n.m., with a breadth ranging between 300 and 1200 n.m.

It is worth mentioning that the Republic of Guatemala formulated a corollary to the said Declaration, very similar to the proviso put forward by Argentina: there would be no recognition of any European colony or possession in the

---

27   Official Gazette of El Salvador (*Diario Oficial*) on 13 September de 1974.
28   J. C. Faidutti, 'Derecho internacional del mar', available at http://www.uees.edu.ec/servicios/biblioteca/publicaciones/pdf/70.pdf, accessed May 30, 2016.
29   La Estrella de Panamá, 'La Declaración de Panamá y su vigencia', 13 de octubre de 2009, available at http://laestrella.com.pa/opinion/columnistas/declaracion-panama-vigencia/23753033, Accessed 7 April 2015.

region. At the time, Guatemala and the United Kingdom were engaged in a dispute over Belize.

As far as the legal fallout of the new concept of 'security zone' was concerned, it should be mentioned that nowhere does it say in this Declaration, nor should it be inferred from its letter, that any part of the specified zone was submitted to the sovereignty of our coastal States. The defense of our coast is the sole purpose of the agreement.[30] There is no direct relationship then between the Declaration of Panama and the territorialist theses subsequently developed by Latin American States. We must bear in mind that this Declaration came into being under special circumstances caused by the threat of war, not as a response to the need to protect the region's offshore economic resources. All subsequent claims by the States of Central America to the 200 n.m. limit could only be ascribed to reasons of economic interest in living and non-living resources, as it became evident with the passing of time.

Now, even if the Declaration of Panama cannot be considered as a decisive contribution to the evolution of the new Law of the Sea, neither can we overlook its importance at a time like that, if we keep in mind that the Declaration laid claim to a sort of sui generis jurisdiction. Two reasons support such a conclusion: one, the collective character of its drafting, and two, the extremely vast boundaries claimed for the 'security zone'. We should also take into account the fact that, years later, this joint initiative had a great influence on the decisions made by the Inter-American Juridical Committee (former body of the Pan American Union, currently a body of the Organization of American States), and bear in mind that only two years after the Declaration of Panama, the aforesaid Committee recommended a distance of 12 n.m. as a necessary extension of the national maritime space under a State's sovereignty. Such were the reasons of this new belt of territorial water.

A second collective initiative to be considered took place in August, 1955 at the First Meeting of Central American Foreign Ministers, held in Antigua Guatemala, in which the Organization of Central American States was established and the 'Declaration of Principles of Central American Coexistence' was signed. By then all States of Central America had already made several unilateral statements, either on constitutional grounds or by issuing decrees either incumbent upon the continental shelf as a security zone or related only to the exploitation of its resources. The Central American nations gathered in Antigua confirmed their purpose of defending their cultural patrimony,

---

[30] H. Llanos Mansilla, *La creación del nuevo derecho del mar: el aporte de Chile,* 1st ed Editorial Jurídica de Chile, 1991, p. 90.

including the continental shelf and the territorial and epicontinental waters, expecting that their utilization would redound to the integral improvement of their peoples.[31]

The Specialized Inter-American Conference on 'Conservation of Natural Resources: Continental Shelf and Marine Waters' of 1956 also proved to be particularly important. The ensuing Declaration undoubtedly set a significant precedent for the development of the new Law of the Sea, since it was intended to study in detail 'the judicial and economic rules that govern the submerged landmass of the continental shelf, the sea waters and the natural resources contained therein'.[32] The fact that a topic as booming then as the continental shelf was the object of discussion was undeniably a substantial contribution to the development and evolution of such a space. On the participant States' recommendation, criteria were proposed to establish the shelf's depth up to a distance of 200 meters and to measure the State's ability to exploit its natural resources. However, even if the attending States failed to settle important issues related to the waters covering the shelf, they agreed on criteria that prevailed until the Third United Nations Conference on the Law of the Sea.

Finally, we must recall one of the most important instruments born from that period: the Declaration of Montevideo of 1970.[33] Three Central American nations participated: El Salvador, Panama and Nicaragua, in addition to six other countries from South America. This was certainly the most consequential Declaration of its time, inasmuch as it made direct reference to the topic of State sovereignty over a wide maritime space, ratified up to a distance of 200 n.m. Like other claims over such a wide maritime space, this Declaration specifically recognized freedom of passage within those limits and became a landmark in the legislative evolution of the signatory States for years to come, to the point that they had direct bearing on the legal codes of some modern-day States: El Salvador and Peru are still claiming a 200 n.m. limit.

---

31   Orrego Vicuña, supra, note 23, p. 96.
32   Pan American Union, Inter-American Specialized Conference on 'Conservation of Natural Resources: The Continental Shelf and Marine Water', Ciudad Trujillo, March 15–28, 1956, Final Act. See also, 'Problems relating to the Economic and Legal Regime of the High Seas—Inter-American Specialized Conference on Conservation of Natural Resources: Continental Shelf and Maritime Waters', 34 *Department of State Bulletin*, 1956, p. 84.
33   Full Text in 64 *American Journal of International Law*, 1970, pp. 1021–1023.

3 Conclusions

This article has been an attempt to reflect Central America's contribution to the enactment of the new Law of the Sea and, specifically, to the consolidation and development of the new maritime spaces recognized by international law: continental shelf and EEZ or presential sea. Accordingly, this contribution is intended to highlight how unilateral actions and joint statements of Central American States made it possible to structure and improve the content of President Truman's Proclamations and why these nations pioneered the promotion of important theses about maritime spaces, as well as about the management and exploitation of the living and non-living resources contained therein. Countless examples confirm these assertions: El Salvador was the first country in the world to declare constitutional sovereignty over 200 n.m.; by 1947 Guatemala was already protecting its coastal resources; Decree 449 turned Panama into one of the first nations in the world to regulate fishing rights in its jurisdictional waters, thus forcing foreign ships to get permits. These decisions (unilateral actions and joint declarations) may have seemed daring for that period of history, but they were undoubtedly critical for debate at the Third United Nations Conference on the Law of the Sea.

Does the Freedom of the Seas Still Exist?

Gerhard Hafner[1]

1 Introduction

It is a great pleasure to contribute to this book in honor of Professor Djamchid Momtaz whom I have known and with whom I have long cooperated, starting with our work on the third Law of the Sea Conference. Many common discussions have followed in various fora, in particular in the United Nations, in the most differing fields of international negotiation. Although the spectrum of Professor Momtaz' scholarly work now addresses almost all fields of international law, I would like to return to the origin of our cooperation, the law of the sea.

2 The Freedom of the Seas

Instead of giving an introduction to the present problems relating to the freedoms of the high seas, I briefly recall the historical correlation between the intensity of exploitation and the freedom of the seas, insofar as the exploitation of living resources is concerned. According to Grotius the freedom of the seas resulted from the practical inexhaustibility of the oceans assumed in his time.[2] This point is made even more explicitly by later writers, for example

---

1 My particular thanks go to Mr. Gregor Novak for his valuable assistance in the preparation of this contribution.
2 Grotius quotes Vasquius for the proposition that 'it is generally agreed that, if a great many persons hunt or fish upon some wooded tract of land or in some stream, that wood or stream will probably be emptied of wild animals or fish, an objection which is not applicable to the sea.' Yet Grotius slightly qualifies this idea by accepting the theoretical possibility that the supply of fish could be exhausted: 'Yet again, even if it were possible to prohibit some particular act of this kind, such as fishing (for it may be maintained that the supply of fish is, in a sense, exhaustible), it would in any case be impossible to prohibit navigation, through which the sea loses nothing.' (see R. Feenstra (ed), *Hugo Grotius Mare Liberum 1609–2009: Original Latin Text and English Translation*, Brill, 2009, pp. 93 and 121). See for an interpretation of Grotius' position, R. Gail Rayfuse, *Non-Flag State Enforcement in High Seas Fisheries*, Martinus Nijhoff, 2004, p. 19. See also R. J. Baird, 'Legal Factors Contributing to the Development of IUU Fishing,' in R. Baird (ed), *Aspects of Illegal, Unreported and Unregulated Fishing in the Southern Ocean* Springer, 2006, pp. 37–39.

Vattel.[3] In contrast, writers like Welwood[4] and especially Selden[5] challenged this freedom in view of the exhaustibility of maritime resources and the increased exploitation by Dutch fishermen, but those writers' views found no general recognition in a time of liberalism, where this freedom came to full growth. This freedom, however, applied to the high seas, and thus maritime areas where the competition for exploitation was not yet very intensive.[6] But already at that time, this freedom did not apply in areas where fisheries were involved in stark competition and exhaustibility was already sensed; the best example from this time was the competition between Dutch and English fisheries in the first half of the seventeenth century due to the introduction of new fishery techniques.[7] This intensive exploitation and competition resulted

---

3   Noting that '[i]t is manifest that the use of the open sea, which consists in navigation and fishing, is innocent and inexhaustible; that is to say—he who navigates or fishes in the open sea does no injury to any one, and the sea, in these two respects, is sufficient for all mankind.' E. Vattel & E. D. Ingraham (eds), *The Law of Nations, Or, Principles of the Law of Nature Applied to the Conduct and Affairs of Nations and Sovereigns*, T. & J. W. Johnson, 1854, p. 125.

4   Noting that '[t]he premise that the products of the sea and inexhaustible was [...] [for the first time] specifically denied by William Welwood.' D. M. Johnston, *The International Law of Fisheries: A Framework for Policy-Oriented Inquiries*, Martinus Nijhoff, 1987, pp. 166–167.

5   Selden notes in Chapter XXII of *Mare Clausum* that '[l]astly [...] the vast abundance of the sea, and its inexhaustible abundance, is of very little weight here. [...] [T]he plentie of such seas is lessened every hour, no otherwise than that of Mines of Metal, Quarries of Stone, or of Gardens, when their Treasures and Fruits are taken away.' (J. Selden, *Mare clausum: the right and dominion of the sea in two books*, London, 1663, p. 141). See also R. Prakash Anand, *Origin and Development of the Law of the Sea: History of International Law Revisited*, Brill, 1983, pp. 106–107.

6   R. Feenstra, 'Epilogue', in supra, note 2, p. xxviii (noting that '[s]ince Hugo Grotius' Mare liberum the leading idea has been that the open sea is free by nature, that it cannot be taken in possession through occupation and that it can never be under the sovereignty of any State. Nevertheless, during the twentieth century, in particular after the Second World War, rights over the continental shelves exacted by coastal States and the establishment of economic zones up to 200 miles wide have set in motion a continuous limitation process of the freedom of the seas.').

7   See on the history of fisheries across the world, e.g., D. Sahrhage & J. Lundbeck, *A History of Fishing*, Springer, 2012; M. Barnard, D. J. Starkey & P. Holm, *Oceans Past: Management Insights from the History of Marine Animal Populations*, Earthscan, 2012; R. Hilborn, *Overfishing: What Everyone Needs to Know*, Oxford University Press, 2012; L. Sicking & D. Abreu-Ferreira, *Beyond the Catch: Fisheries of the North Atlantic, the North Sea and the Baltic, 900–1850*, Brill, 2009. One author, Poulson, points to the massive increase in catch levels from the 18th to the 21st century by references to North Sea herring fishing, noting that '[e]ven with the very high catch level of 150,000 tonnes in the 1790s, herring catches in the period under review are still a far cry from the North Sea herring TAC of more than 500,000 tonnes in the early 21st century.'

in the reservation of the right of fisheries for the coastal States in areas where formerly freedom of exploitation had existed. Access by fishermen of other States to the fish stocks within this area became progressively restricted and came to depend on the will of the relevant coastal State.[8]

3   From Unregulated Freedoms to Rights

The growing scarcity of resources due to their increased exploitation and the growing demand for resources in the periods following spilled over beyond the reserved areas so that further expansionist demands led to the creation of the exclusive economic zone (EEZ) and the present continental shelf regime. It was felt that the regime of unregulated freedom was unable to ensure an allocation and distribution of maritime resources that could be deemed just and fair.

A similar tendency emerged with regard to the international seabed and ocean floor where, rather than a regime of freedom of the seas, the common heritage concept was presented with the clear intention of precluding a 'colonial rush' to its exploitation, from which only the more powerful and technologically advanced States were expected to benefit.[9]

While the original concept of the freedoms of the sea did not entail strict regulations for the exercise of these freedoms, the tendency towards a regulated freedom in particular regarding fisheries already became manifest in the UNCLOS I with the *Convention on Fishing and Conservation of the Living Resources of the High Seas*. This, however, is only of reduced significance since merely 39 States are parties to it.[10]

Since the UNCLOS I, numerous international treaties have been adopted, which aimed at regulating the maritime use, in particular fisheries. The *United*

(B. Poulsen, *Dutch Herring: An Environmental History, C. 1600–1860*, Amsterdam University Press, 2008, p. 80; See also T. W. Fulton, *The Sovereignty of the Sea*, W. Blackwood and Sons, 1911, pp. 139.

[8] See, e.g., Y. Tanaka, *The International Law of the Sea*, Cambridge University Press, 2012, p. 19.

[9] United Nations Division for Ocean Affairs and the Law of the Sea, *The Law of the Sea: Legislative History of Articles 133 to 150 and 311(6) of the United Nations Convention on the Law of the Sea. Concept of the Common Heritage of Mankind*, UN, 1996.

[10] D. R. Rothwell et al., *The Oxford Handbook of the Law of the Sea*, Oxford University Press, 2015, p. 161 (describing it as 'largely a dead letter'); see generally W. W. Bishop, 'The 1958 Geneva Convention on Fishing and Conservation of the Living Resources of the High Seas', 62 *Columbia Law Review*, 1962, pp. 1206–1229.

Nations Convention on the Law of the Sea (LOSC) substantially reduced free competition relating to maritime economic activities by reserving large areas of the oceans to the respective coastal States in the form of EEZs. In this Convention, the central provision regarding the regime of the high seas, Article 87 LOSC, produces a further limitation regarding fisheries insofar as this activity is made subject to the conditions in Articles 116 to 120 LOSC, where an additional modification occurs since Article 116 replaces the term 'freedom' by 'rights', signifying a certain allocation of the usage in this area to States. Moreover, States are obliged to assume certain obligations regarding this activity; in particular, they have to take necessary legislative measures with respect to their nationals, regarding limitations on allowable catches, and cooperation with other States in the conservation and management of living resources. Subsequent to the entry into force of the LOSC, the exploitation of living resources became subjected to stricter control and further restrictions as a result of *inter alia* the *United Nations Agreement for the Implementation of the Provisions of the United Nations Convention on the Law of the Sea of 10 December 1982 relating to the Conservation and Management of Straddling Fish Stocks and Highly Migratory Fish Stocks* (UN Fish Stocks Agreement),[11] and the *Agreement to Promote Compliance with International Conservation and Management Measures by Fishing Vessels on the High Seas* of 24 November 1993 of the Food and Agriculture Organization of the United Nations (FAO Compliance Agreement).[12]

4   New Attempts to Subject Marine Activities to Stricter Control

4.1   *The Establishment of Marine Protected Areas*

Further, for the sake of preventing a depletion of fish stocks, restrictions followed from the establishment of Regional Fisheries Management Organizations (RFMO) and from universally applicable treaties regarding the exploitation of certain maritime species.[13]

---

11   M.-A. E. Palma, M. Tsamenyi, & W. R. Edeson, *Promoting Sustainable Fisheries: The International Legal and Policy Framework to Combat Illegal, Unreported and Unregulated Fishing*, Brill, 2010, pp. 61–63; Jean-Pierre Lévy & G. G. Schram, *United Nations Conference on Straddling Fish Stocks and Highly Migratory Fish Stocks: Selected Documents*, Martinus Nijhoff, 1996.

12   Palma et al., supra, note 11, pp. 60–61.

13   See generally Tanaka, supra, note 8; see also P. Pintassilgo et al., 'Stability and Success of Regional Fisheries Management Organizations,' 46 *Environmental and Resource Economics*, 2010 pp. 377–402, p. 396 (concluding that 'if the international fishing community does prove to be incapable of suppressing unregulated fishing, the outlook for the

Within the framework of these institutional arrangements regarding maritime exploitation, which apply also to areas of the high seas or, in more recent terminology, areas beyond national jurisdiction (ABNJs),[14] new institutions emerged, which made certain maritime spots subject to very strict regulations, sometimes immunizing them against any exploitation: the marine protected areas (MPA). These have been established for ecological, biological, scientific, cultural, educational, or recreational reasons. Although varied definitions of MPAS are used or have been proposed,[15] one widely-cited definition is that put forward by the *Convention on Biological Diversity* (CBD) *Ad Hoc Technical Expert Group on Marine and Coastal Protected Areas*:

> (...) any defined area within or adjacent to the marine environment, together with its overlying waters and associated flora, fauna, and historical and cultural features, which has been reserved by legislation or other effective means, including custom, with the effect that its marine and/or coastal biodiversity enjoys a higher level of protection than its surroundings.[16]

These areas that figure under different designations and are endowed with different objectives, have their basis in universal as well as regional treaties:

---

emerging RFMO regime is bleak. Our findings are in line with a recently released report by an international panel of experts on RFMOs, which states that 'the success of international [fisheries] cooperation depends largely on the ability to deter free riding'[.]'); S. Cullis-Suzuki & D. Pauly, 'Failing the High Seas: A Global Evaluation of Regional Fisheries Management Organizations,' 34 *Marine Policy*, 2010, pp. 1036–42 (noting that '[t]he management of historic coastal fisheries is widely seen as having failed throughout the world, with strong impacts on coastal ecosystems [...]. The high seas, on the other hand, are still relatively pristine, and thus offer a momentary opportunity for RFMOs, if they reform themselves soon, to help turn around some very worrying trends. However, this can only happen if RFMOs actually act as stewards of the high seas, and become accountable for their actions.').

14 Areas beyond national jurisdiction (ABNJ) encompass the High Seas and the Area.
15 See, e.g., Food and Agriculture Organization of the United Nations, *Report and Documentation of the Expert Workshop on Marine Protected Areas and Fisheries Management: Review of Issues and Considerations, Rome, 12–14 June 2006*, FAO, 2007, pp. 302–304; D. Diz Pereira Pinto, *Fisheries Management in Areas Beyond National Jurisdiction: The Impact of Ecosystem Based Law-Making*, Martinus Nijhoff, 2012, pp. 159–161; R. Rayfuse, *Research Handbook on International Marine Environmental Law*, Edward Elgar, 2015, p. 275.
16 CBD Subsidiary Body on Scientific, Technical, and Technological Advice, 'Report of the Ad Hoc Technical Expert Group on Marine and Coastal Protected Areas: Marine and Coastal Biodiversity: Review, Further Elaboration and Refinement of the Programme of Work', UN Doc. UNEP/CBD/SBSTTA/8/INF/7, 13 February 2003, p. 11.

Among the universal treaties is the *Convention for the Regulation of Whaling* (Washington, 1946), according to which the International Whaling Commission (IWC) is entitled to adopt regulations with respect to the conservation and use of whale resources, defining, *inter alia*, 'open and closed waters, including the designation of sanctuary areas' (Article V, para. 1).[17] Sanctuaries where commercial whaling is prohibited were established by the IWC in the Indian Ocean (1979) and the Southern Ocean (1994). In these extremely large maritime ABNJ whaling for commercial purposes is prohibited.

The *International Convention for the Prevention of Pollution from Ships* (MARPOL)[18] provides for the establishment of special areas where particularly strict standards are applied to discharges from ships, the Particularly Sensitive Sea Areas (PSSAs). Special-areas provisions are contained in Annexes I (Regulations for the Prevention of Pollution by Oil), II (Regulations for the Control of Pollution by Noxious Substances in Bulk) and V (Regulations for the Prevention of Pollution by Garbage from Ships).

As to regional treaties, several provide for the establishment of MPAs in national maritime zones as well as in the ABNJs of certain regional seas. Examples are the *Barcelona Convention* and its *Protocol on Biodiversity and Specially Protected Areas relating to the Mediterranean Sea*,[19] the *Convention for the Conservation and Sustainable Use of the Wider Caribbean Region* and its *Protocol for Specially Protected Areas and Wildlife*,[20] the *Convention for the Protection of the Marine Environment and Coastal Areas of the South East Pacific*,[21] the OSPAR

---

17   International Convention for the Regulation of Whaling, signed 2 December 1946, entered into force 10 November 1948, 161 UNTS 72; see also *Whaling in the Antarctic* (Australia v Japan) Judgment, I.C.J. Reports 2014, p. 226, 266.

18   See International Maritime Organization, *MARPOL: Articles, Protocols, Annexes, Unified Interpretations of the International Convention for the Prevention of Pollution from Ships, 1973, as Modified by the Protocol of 1978 Relating Thereto*, International Maritime Organization, 2006.

19   Convention for the Protection of the Mediterranean Sea against Pollution, concluded 16 February 1976, 1102 UNTS 27 (original Barcelona Convention). United Nations Environment Programme 'Convention for the Protection of the Marine Environment and the Coastal Region of the Mediterranean', 10 June 1995, (amended Barcelona Convention).

20   Convention for the Protection and Development of the Marine Environment of the Wider Caribbean Region, 24 March 1983, 22 ILM 227; Protocol Concerning Specially Protected Areas and Wildlife in the Wider Caribbean Region, 18 January 1990.

21   Convention for the Protection of the Marine Environment and Coastal Area of the South-East Pacific, 12 November 1981. In I. Rummel-Bulska & S. Osafo (eds), *Selected Multilateral Treaties in the Field of the Environment*, Vol. 2, Grotius, 1991, p. 130.

Convention and its Annex V 'On the protection and conservation of the ecosystems and biological diversity of the Maritime Area',[22] the *Antarctic Treaty System* and its *Protocol on Environmental Protection*[23] *and the Convention for the Conservation of Antarctic Marine Living Resources* (CCAMLR).[24]

Irrespective of the recognized weaknesses of RFMOs, these various regulatory activities substantially reduce the freedom of exploitation even in ABNJs.

4.2 *Protection of Biodiversity*

A further resource seen to be endangered by intensified exploitation activities[25] is biological diversity as reflected in the Preamble of the Convention on Biological Diversity (CBD).[26] This confirms that 'biological diversity is being significantly reduced by certain human activities'.

It calls for the establishment of protected areas defined as 'a geographically defined area which is designated or regulated and managed to achieve specific conservation objectives'. Such areas include sites on land as well on sea. However, its application to ABNJs is quite restricted since its Article 4 (Jurisdictional Scope) defines the scope of application as follows:

> 'Subject to the rights of other States, and except as otherwise expressly provided in this Convention, the provisions of this Convention apply, in relation to each Contracting Party:
> (a) In the case of components of biological diversity, in areas within the limits of its national jurisdiction; and
> (b) In the case of processes and activities, regardless of where their effects occur, carried out under its jurisdiction or control, within the area of its national jurisdiction or beyond the limits of national jurisdiction.'

---

22 Convention for the Protection of the Marine Environment of the North-East Atlantic, 22 September 1992, 32 ILM 1069.
23 Antarctic Treaty, 1 December 1959, 402 UNTS 71; Protocol on Environmental Protection to the Antarctic Treaty, 4 October 1991, 30 ILM 1455.
24 Convention on the Conservation of Antarctic Marine Living Resources, 20 May 1980, 1329 UNTS 47.
25 See also D. J. McCauley et al., 'Marine Defaunation: Animal Loss in the Global Ocean', 347 *Science*, 2015.
26 Convention on Biological Diversity, 5 June 1992, 1760 UNTS 79.

As far as MPAs are considered only to constitute 'components of biological diversity', their establishment is restricted to national maritime spaces; only on the condition that they constitute processes and activities can they be created in ABNJs by States provided that they apply to activities performed by vessels flying their flag or by their nationals.

The creation of MPAs in ABNJs was prompted in particular by Rio + 20[27] where the States committed themselves to address, on an urgent basis, the conservation and sustainable use of the marine-biological diversity of ABNJs. One measure here was decision on the development of an international instrument under the LOSC.[28] Several resolutions of the UN General Assembly (GA) reaffirmed this commitment. Resolution A/69/292 decided to develop an international legally-binding instrument under the LOSC on the conservation and sustainable use of the marine-biological diversity of ABNJs and to that end to establish a preparatory committee to make substantive recommendations to the GA on the elements of a draft text of an international legally-binding instrument under the Convention that should address the conservation and sustainable use of the marine-biological diversity of ABNJs, in particular, *inter alia*, measures such as area-based management tools, including MPAs, environmental impact assessments (EIAS), capacity-building and the transfer of marine technology. These MPAs should not only entail management of fisheries, but also an equitable sharing of the benefits as defined in the CBD and elaborated in Article 5 of the *2010 Nagoya Protocol on Access to Genetic Resources and the Fair and Equitable Sharing of Benefits Arising from their Utilization to the CBD*.[29] This management of the exploitation of living resources and the equitable sharing of the benefits that, according to the Chair's overview of the first session of the Preparatory Committee, figured among the issues addressed in the

---

27   'The future we want', UN Doc. A/RES/66/288, 27 July 2012.

28   A. Leandro, 'Sustainable Development as Guideline for Oceans and Seas Governance', in M. Fitzmaurice, S. Maljean-Dubois & S. Negri (eds), *Environmental Protection and Sustainable Development from Rio to Rio+20: Protection de L'environnement et Développement Durable de Rio À Rio+20*, Martinus Nijhoff, 2014, pp. 135–136; House of Commons (UK) Environmental Audit Committee, *Outcomes of the UN Rio+20 Earth Summit: Second Report of Session 2013–14, Vol. 1: Report, Together with Formal Minutes, Oral and Written Evidence*, UK Stationery Office, 2013.

29   Article 5 of the 2010 Nagoya Protocol reads as follows: 'In accordance with Article 15, paragraphs 3 and 7 of the Convention, benefits arising from the utilization of genetic resources as well as subsequent applications and commercialization shall be shared in a fair and equitable way with the Party providing such resources that is the country of origin of such resources or a Party that has acquired the genetic resources in accordance with the Convention. Such sharing shall be upon mutually agreed terms.'

first meeting of the Preparatory Committee, do not coincide with the basic understanding of the freedom of the seas where these activities were decided at the total discretion of individuals or States who were not obliged to share the benefits with others.

Accordingly, those treaties and institutions, but also this new movement, entail a restriction of the former freedoms of maritime exploitation, in particular fisheries. From this perspective, one can easily speak of the end of the freedoms of the seas, at least regarding fisheries, so that the justification for listing fisheries among the freedoms of the sea in Article 87 LOSC seems to be dwindling away.

However, these restrictions apply only with regard to the States that have accepted the relevant regulation. Thus this development does not necessarily entail the end of the freedom of the seas since outside the self-commitments a residual freedom could still exist. Accordingly, the real litmus test regarding the further existence of the freedom of the seas is the possible effect on third States.[30]

5   The Effect of the Regulations on Third States

Since the regulations mentioned above are based on international treaties, their effect on third States is governed by the rules reflected in the *Vienna Convention on the Law of Treaties* (VCLT), in particular Articles 34,[31] 35,[32] 36,[33]

---

[30]   See for one recent perspective on this problem A. Serdy, *The New Entrants Problem in International Fisheries Law,* Cambridge University Press, 2016.

[31]   Article 34 VCLT (*General rule regarding third States*) reads as follows: 'A treaty does not create either obligations or rights for a third State without its consent.'

[32]   Article 35 VCLT (*Treaties providing for obligations for third States*) reads as follows: 'An obligation arises for a third State from a provision of a treaty if the parties to the treaty intend the provision to be the means of establishing the obligation and the third State expressly accepts that obligation in writing.'

[33]   Article 36 VCLT (*Treaties providing for rights for third States*) reads as follows: '1. A right arises for a third State from a provision of a treaty if the parties to the treaty intend the provision to accord that right either to the third State, or to a group of States to which it belongs, or to all States, and the third State assents thereto. Its assent shall be presumed so long as the contrary is not indicated, unless the treaty otherwise provides. 2. A State exercising a right in accordance with paragraph 1 shall comply with the conditions for its exercise provided for in the treaty or established in conformity with the treaty.'

37[34] and 38.[35] Since those regulations on MPAs impose duties on third States rather than accord them rights, Articles 34 and 35 are of particular relevance, providing that third States cannot become subject to obligations resulting from treaties in which they do not participate unless they give their written consent.

5.1   The Effect of the Envisaged MPAs on Third States

The following will discuss the effect on third States of the envisaged establishment of MPAs on the basis of an agreement implementing the LOSC. The State community is very well aware of this problem since the question of the effect on third States of rules within the framework of the law of the sea is not new:[36] it is characteristic of this field of international law, in particular relating to ABNJs, due to the lack of a uniform and centralized regime corresponding to national legislation and the intermingling and competing competences of different States plus rules of different origins, universal as well as regional, facing a multitude of States acting—mostly through the vessels flying their flag—in this area.

The existing international legal regimes applicable to this area have already sought a solution to this problem. Thus, for instance, the International Commission for the Conservation of Atlantic Tunas (ICCAT) introduced rules that request Member States *inter alia* to deny access to their ports for vessels alleged to be engaged in illegal, unreported and unregulated (IUU) fishing, or to prohibit trade in fish caught by them.[37] Such measures against third States

---

34   Article 37 VCLT (*Revocation or modification of obligations or rights of third States*) reads as follows: '1. When an obligation has arisen for a third State in conformity with Article 35, the obligation may be revoked or modified only with the consent of the parties to the treaty and of the third State, unless it is established that they had otherwise agreed. 2. When a right has arisen for a third State in conformity with Article 36, the right may not be revoked or modified by the parties if it is established that the right was intended not to be revocable or subject to modification without the consent of the third State.'

35   Article 38 VCLT (*Rules in a treaty becoming binding on third States through international custom*) reads as follows: 'Nothing in Articles 34 to 37 precludes a rule set forth in a treaty from becoming binding upon a third State as a customary rule of international law, recognized as such.'

36   See L. T. Lee, 'The Law of the Sea Convention and Third States', 77 *American Journal of International Law*, 1983, p. 541.

37   ICCAT Recommendation 2011–18, Recommendation by ICCAT Further Amending Recommendation 09–10 Establishing a List of Vessels Presumed to Have Carried out Illegal, Unreported, and Unregulated Fishing Activities in the ICCAT Convention Area, Point 9.

are said to be lawful on the basis of Articles 117[38] and 118 LOSC[39] and the requirement of cooperation they impose. Similarly, the EU has adopted a regulation addressing the issue of IUU fishing by third States.[40] It provides that 'the Community should be entitled to identify those non-cooperating States, on the basis of transparent, clear and objective criteria relying on international standards, and, after giving them adequate time to respond to a prior notification, adopt non-discriminatory, legitimate and proportionate measures with respect to those States, including trade measures'.[41] The list of IUUs is relatively long and also encompasses fishing activities[42] 'carried out in the area of

---

38 Article 117 LOSC (*Duty of States to adopt with respect to their nationals measures for the conservation of the living resources of the high seas*) reads as follows: 'All States have the duty to take, or to cooperate with other States in taking, such measures for their respective nationals as may be necessary for the conservation of the living resources of the high seas.'

39 Article 118 of the LOSC (*Cooperation of States in the conservation and management of living resources*) reads as follows: 'States shall cooperate with each other in the conservation and management of living resources in the areas of the high seas. States whose nationals exploit identical living resources, or different living resources in the same area, shall enter into negotiations with a view to taking the measures necessary for the conservation of the living resources concerned. They shall, as appropriate, cooperate to establish subregional or regional fisheries organizations to this end.'

40 Council Regulation (EC) No. 1005/2008 of 29 September 2008 establishing a Community system to prevent, deter and eliminate illegal, unreported and unregulated fishing, amending Regulations (EEC) No. 2847/93, (EC) No. 1936/2001 and (EC) No. 601/2004 and repealing Regulations (EC) No. 1093/94 and (EC) No. 1447/1999, (L 286 *Official Journal of the European Union*, 29 October 2008, p. 1).

41 Ibid., Preambular para. 31; see in particular Articles 11 and 18.

42 Ibid., Article 3 (1) reads as follows: '1. A fishing vessel shall be presumed to be engaged in IUU fishing if it is shown that, contrary to the conservation and management measures applicable in the fishing area concerned, it has:
   (a) fished without a valid licence, authorisation or permit issued by the flag State or the relevant coastal State; or.
   (b) not fulfilled its obligations to record and report catch or catch-related data, including data to be transmitted by satellite vessel monitoring system, or prior notices under Article 6; or.
   (c) fished in a closed area, during a closed season, without or after attainment of a quota or beyond a closed depth; or.
   (d) engaged in directed fishing for a stock which is subject to a moratorium or for which fishing is prohibited; or.
   (e) used prohibited or non-compliant fishing gear; or.
   (f) falsified or concealed its markings, identity or registration; or.
   (g) concealed, tampered with or disposed of evidence relating to an investigation; or.

a regional fisheries management organization in a manner inconsistent with or in contravention of the conservation and management measures of that organization and ... flagged to a State not party to that organization, or not cooperating with that organization as established by that organization'. However, given the detrimental effects to be suffered, third States not party to an RFMO are compelled to observe its rules, the effect of these measures on third States is not inconsistent with the *pacta tertiis nec nocent nec prosunt* rule since the port State exercises full control and sovereignty over the ports and is competent to regulate the landing.[43]

This problem of third States has also been addressed by the UN Fish Stocks Agreement.[44] But third States that are not parties to this agreement are only encouraged to become parties while States Parties are obliged 'to take measures consistent with this Agreement and international law to deter the activities of vessels flying the flag of non-parties which undermine the effective implementation of this Agreement' (Article 33). This particular provision seemingly refers back to the inspection measures permitted under this Agreement,[45] which

---

(h) obstructed the work of officials in the exercise of their duties in inspecting for compliance with the applicable conservation and management measures; or the work of observers in the exercise of their duties of observing compliance with the applicable Community rules; or.

(i) taken on board, transshipped or landed undersized fish in contravention of the legislation in force; or.

(j) transshipped or participated in joint fishing operations with, supported or resupplied other fishing vessels identified as having engaged in IUU fishing under this Regulation, in particular those included in the Community IUU vessel list or in the IUU vessel list of a regional fisheries management organization; or.

(k) carried out fishing activities in the area of a regional fisheries management organization in a manner inconsistent with or in contravention of the conservation and management measures of that organization and is flagged to a State not party to that organization, or not cooperating with that organization as established by that organization; or.

(l) no nationality and is therefore a stateless vessel, in accordance with international law.'

43   See for an alternative argument, but mainly focused on the new-entrants problem, Serdy, supra, note 30, pp. 2–6.

44   Agreement for the Implementation of the Provisions of the United Nations Convention on the Law of the Sea of 10 December 1982 relating to the Conservation and Management of Straddling Fish Stocks and Highly Migratory Fish Stocks, 4 August 1995, 2167 UNTS 3.

45   In particular Article 21 of the UN Fish Stocks Agreement, which provides for inspection rights.

encountered vivid protest from a group of States.[46] The caveat regarding the conformity with international law excludes measures against non-parties, which are not in conformity with the *pacta tertiis nec nocent nec prosunt* principle.[47] Nevertheless, it cannot be excluded that such an effect on third States, though not resulting from the treaty itself, nevertheless is generated by rules outside the treaty. These may be either customary international law or another convention to which the States concerned are parties, such as the LOSC.[48] So, for instance, the effect on and the opposability to third States of such agreements can derive in particular from acquiescence by the third States. Here the effect results not from the treaty itself, but from rules outside the treaty. The effect of this toleration can be explained by reference to Article 45 of the Articles on the Responsibility of States for internationally unlawful acts, according to which acquiescence could entail the loss of the right to invoke responsibility.[49]

However, further problems could arise from the fact that international trade is a matter of the WTO, and cases relating to trade in living maritime resources allegedly caught in breach of environmental standards have already been brought before the WTO dispute settlement bodies.[50]

46   Note verbale dated 22 May 2006 from the Permanent Missions of Argentina, Chile, Colombia, Cuba, Ecuador, El Salvador, Guatemala, Mexico and Peru to the United Nations addressed to the Secretariat, UN Doc. A/CONF.210/2006/12. In Point 6 of the Annex these States emphasize: 'The topics of boarding and inspection addressed in Articles 21 and 22 of the Agreement should be evaluated and reviewed, with a view to considering alternative systems of surveillance and monitoring that would make boarding and inspection unnecessary.'; See also Report of the Review Conference on the Agreement for the Implementation of the Provisions of the United Nations Convention on the Law of the Sea of 10 December 1982 relating to the Conservation and Management of Straddling Fish Stocks and Highly Migratory Fish Stocks, UN Doc. A/CONF.210/2006/15, para. 34.

47   See B. Vukas, 'Treaties, Third Party Effect', in R. Wolfrum (ed), *Max Planck Encyclopedia of Public International Law*, Oxford University Press, 2011.

48   C. Laly-Chevalier, 'Article 35', in O. Corten & P. Klein (eds), *The Vienna Conventions on the Law of Treaties*, Oxford University Press, 2011, p. 909.

49   Article 45 of the ILC Articles on State Responsibility (Loss of the right to invoke responsibility) read as follows: 'The responsibility of a State may not be invoked if: (a) The injured State has validly waived the claim; (b) The injured State is to be considered as having, by reason of its conduct, validly acquiesced in the lapse of the claim.'

50   K. Selvig, 'Expensive Freedom: Establishing Marine Protected Areas on the Open Ocean Requires an End to the Freedom of the Seas', 22 *Minnesota Journal of International Law*, 2013 (Online edition) p. 6; See in particular the US-Shrimp and US-Tuna cases (*United States—Import Prohibition of Certain Shrimp and Shrimp Products*, Report of the Appellate Body, 12 October 1998, WT/DS58/AB/R; *United States—Measures Concerning the*

With regard to the planned MPAs in the framework of the protection of marine biodiversity, the resolution of the General Assembly (GA) on the 'Development of an international legally binding instrument under the United Nations Convention on the Law of the Sea on the conservation and sustainable use of marine biological diversity of areas beyond national jurisdiction' of 6 July 2015 establishing a preparatory committee tasked to outline the main elements of an agreement including the creation of MPAs[51] explicitly refers to this problem by noting that it:

> [a]*lso recognizes* that neither participation in the negotiations nor their outcome may affect the legal status of non-parties to the Convention or any other related agreements with regard to those instruments, or the legal status of parties to the Convention or any other related agreements with regard to those instruments[.][52]

Obviously, the GA was well aware of the problem of the effect of the future agreement, in particular the establishment of MPAs, on third States, whether or not they are party to the LOSC.

5.1.1 The Effect on Third States under Customary International Law

With regard to the legal effect on States that are party neither to the LOSC nor to any other treaty regulating maritime exploitation, but only subject to customary international law, this effect is based on the fundamental rule, namely that a treaty does not create either obligations or rights for a third State without its consent as codified in Article 34 VCLT. As far as obligations are concerned the effect is defined by Article 35 VCLT—both articles reflecting existing customary international law. Article 35 reads:

Importation, Marketing and Sale of Tuna and Tuna Products, Report of the Appellate Body, 16 May 2012, WT/DS381/AB/R).

51 UN Doc. A/RES/69/292, 19 June 2015, Point 2 ('*Also decides* that negotiations shall address the topics identified in the package agreed in 2011, namely the conservation and sustainable use of marine biological diversity of areas beyond national jurisdiction, in particular, together and as a whole, marine genetic resources, including questions on the sharing of benefits, measures such as area-based management tools, including marine protected areas, environmental impact assessments and capacity-building and the transfer of marine technology').

52 Ibid., Point 4.

> An obligation arises for a third State from a provision of a treaty if the parties to the treaty intend the provision to be the means of establishing the obligation and the third State expressly accepts that obligation in writing.

Accordingly, one has to assume that such a State would not be obliged to respect the establishment of MPAs merely by such an Agreement.

5.1.2 Do Such Rules Have an Erga Omnes Effect?

Nevertheless, it could be asked whether customary international law already endows the rules of the organization of MPAs with a legal character obliging third States to accept such obligations. One candidate for such rules are *erga omnes* obligations, which have an obligatory effect for all States. The Institut de droit international (IDI) defined such obligations as obligations under general international law which a State owes to the international community, in view of its common values and its concern for compliance, so that a breach of that obligation enables all States to take action.[53] In the Preamble to its Resolution, the IDI declared that 'certain obligations bind all subjects of international law for the purposes of maintaining the fundamental values of the international community'.

The ICJ recognized such obligations in the *Barcelona Traction* case, noting that

> an essential distinction should be drawn between the obligations of a State towards the international community as a whole, and those arising vis-à-vis another State in the field of diplomatic protection. By their very nature the former are the concern of all States. In view of the importance of the rights involved, all States can be held to have a legal interest in their protection; they are obligations *erga omnes*. Such obligations derive, for example, in contemporary international law, from the outlawing of acts of aggression, and of genocide, as also from the principles and rules concerning the basic rights of the human person, including protection from slavery and racial discrimination.[54]

---

53 Institute of International Law, Resolution 'Obligations and rights erga omnes in international law', Rapporteur M. Giorgio Gaja, 2005.
54 *Barcelona Traction, Light and Power Company Limited (New Application)* (Belgium v Spain), Judgment, *ICJ Reports 1970*, p. 3, paras. 33–34.

In this sense as manifested in the IDI Resolution or the *dictum* of the ICJ, the obligations derived from the MPAs could have been understood as obligations with an effect on all States.

Although it is generally accepted, and confirmed in the 2005 IDI Resolution, that obligations *erga omnes* can also result from treaties,[55] the question nonetheless arises as to whether establishment of MPAs as a means to protect the marine environment is a matter of interest to all States. Undoubtedly, the duty to protect the marine environment is a general duty arguably having an *erga omnes* effect so that all States are bound by it. It also shows the features necessary for this qualification: the indivisibility, the non-bilateralizable nature and the non-reciprocal character of the duty.[56] The IDI Resolution enumerated in its preamble the obligation of environmental protection among such rules ():

> Considering that a wide consensus exists to the effect that the prohibition of acts of aggression, the prohibition of genocide, obligations concerning the protection of basic human rights, obligations relating to self-determination and obligations relating to the environment of common spaces are examples of obligations reflecting those fundamental values[.]

Accordingly, protection of the marine environment figures among these rules, entailing an *erga omnes* effect so that all States are to be considered as bound by it, even if they are not parties to the LOSC. This conclusion can be confirmed by reference to the first-reading text of the Draft Articles on State Responsibility by the ILC.[57] Its Article 19 still declared that 'a serious breach of an international obligation of essential importance for the safeguarding and preservation of the human environment such as those prohibiting massive pollution of the atmosphere or of the seas' constitutes an international crime of a State.[58] The commentary referred in particular to 'recent developments in international law on the subject of the safeguarding and preservation of the human environment'.[59]

---

55 See Article 1(b) of the IDI's 2005 resolution, supra, note 53.
56 See O. Lopes Pegna, 'Counter-Claims and Obligations *Erga Omnes* before the International Court of Justice,' 9 *European Journal of International Law*, 1998, pp. 724–736, p. 732.
57 See generally United Nations International Law Commission, *The International Law Commission's Draft Articles on State Responsibility: Part 1, Articles 1–35,* Martinus Nijhoff, 1991.
58 Yearbook of the International Law Commission 1976, Volume II, p. 75.
59 Ibid., p. 121, para. 71.

However, one must distinguish between the general obligation to prevent massive pollution of the marine environment, which threatens the survival of humanity, and specific obligations resulting from an MPA. Both have to be treated separately since MPAs are not the only means for protecting the marine environment; otherwise a few states could preclude the entire exploitation of the maritime spaces with a reference to their *erga omnes* effect. Although the resolutions of the GA calling for the establishment of MPAs in ABNJs are adopted without a vote, they would only become effective through a treaty. Accordingly, the *erga omnes* effect of the duty to protect the marine environment does not accord the same effect to specific and geographically strictly confined obligations. Therefore, the assertion that the obligations emanating from a MPA amount to *erga omnes* obligations can be excluded.

5.2 *MPAs as Status Agreements*

One further argument in this context could be the reference to the qualification of the agreements establishing the MPAs as status agreements, status treaties or objective regimes insofar as these agreements place certain geographically confined areas under a special regime. Status agreements can be described as treaties

> which cause general effects and contain obligations *erga omnes* regarding States not parties to them.... From this point of view such treaties are an exception to the general rule on the law of treaties contained in the principle *pacta tertiis neque nocent neque prosunt*.[60]

According to Carlos Fernández de Casadevante Romani, objective regimes

> ... are characterized, first, by the fact that the intention of the parties is to create, in the general interest, obligations and rights relating to a particular region, State, territory, locality, river, waterway, or to a particular area of the sea, seabed, or airspace. Secondly, they must include, among their parties, any State with territorial competence regarding the subject-matter of the treaty, or having consented to the provision in question. Thirdly, they are characterized by the fact that States not parties to the treaty do not have territorial competence over the subject-matter of the treaty.

---

60 C. F. de Casadevante Romani, 'Objective Regime', in R. Wolfrum (ed), *Max Planck Encyclopedia of Public International Law* (2010), para. 1.

Finally, parties to the treaty need to decide that the regime created by the treaty should be respected by third States.[61]

Accordingly, the treaties establishing MPAs can already be excluded from these regimes insofar as the States creating such MPAs in ABNJs do not possess the territorial competence required for this purpose.[62]

Although such treaties cannot be identified as status treaties, they, nevertheless, come close to treaties that also affect third States, as do 'treaties demarcating maritime or terrestrial boundaries, treaties organizing a neutrality or demilitarization regime, treaties relative to the status of international waterways conferred on certain rivers or international channels, and treaties concerning human rights or the environment'. According to Caroline Laly-Chevalier, 'the effects of those treaties are indirectly felt beyond the circle of contracting parties', similarly, but not identically, to 'objective' situations that are deemed to be binding on States not parties to the treaties establishing them'[63] The objective of MPAs undoubtedly qualifies the treaties establishing them as such concerning the environment. As the International Court of Justice stated,

> the environment is not an abstraction but represents the living space, the quality of life and the very health of human beings, including generations unborn. The existence of the general obligation of States to ensure that activities within their jurisdiction and control respect the environment of other States or of areas beyond national control is now part of the corpus of international law relating to the environment.[64]

McNair stressed one additional requirement, namely, that 'a group of great Powers, or a large number of States both great and small, assume a power to create by a multipartite treaty some new international régime or status, which soon acquires a degree of acceptance and durability extending beyond the limits of the actual contracting parties, and giving it an objective existence. This power is used when some public interest is involved, and its exercise

---

61   Ibid., para. 2.
62   In this sense in particular N. Klein, *Maritime Security and the Law of the Sea*, Oxford University Press, 2012, p. 112.
63   Laly-Chevalier, supra, note 48, p. 907.
64   *Legality of the threat or use of nuclear weapons*, Advisory opinion, ICJ reports 1996, p. 242.

often occurs in the course of the peace settlement at the end of a great war'.[65] From this consideration as well as from the ICJ's Advisory Opinion concerning *Reparations for Injuries Sustained in the Service of the United Nations*, according to which 'fifty States, representing the vast majority of the members of the international community... had the power... to bring into being an entity possessing objective international personality',[66] it can be inferred that the participation of a large number of States, including States that are particularly concerned or potentially affected by the relevant treaty, is required for generating a legal effect on third States. Accordingly, the treaty must also be open to all States.

Only under such circumstances could it be argued that already under customary international law such MPAs, irrespective of whether they are qualified as the exercise of the freedom of the high seas, are lawful and, accordingly, to be respected by all States. The States participating in the creation of MPAs can take steps to protect their MPAs, but they cannot force third States to comply actively with the rules thereof. This legal situation does not entitle States establishing MPAs to take intrusive measures against vessels of third States such as searches, inspections or visits.

5.3 *Does the LOSC Require the Respect of MPAs?*

Although the governance of the high seas relating to the exploitation of living resources and the protection of the marine environment results in particular from three universal instruments, the LOSC, the MARPOL and the CBD, the LOSC undoubtedly enjoys priority as the constitution of the oceans.[67]

Since the vast majority of States are parties[68] to this Convention it is to be discussed whether third States have to abide by the obligations under the MPAs consequential upon the LOSC. Where MPAs are placed in the water column of ABNJs it is first of all the regime of the high seas that serves as legal basis; less significant will be the Area regime since the MPAs will aim at protecting the

---

65 D. J Bederman, 'Third Party Rights and Obligations in Treaties', in D. B. Hollis (ed), *The Oxford Guide to Treaties*, Oxford University Press, 2012, p. 336.

66 *Reparation for Injuries Suffered in the Service of the United Nations*, Advisory Opinion, *ICJ Reports 1949*, p. 185.

67 See the statement by T. T. B. Koh on the LOSC as 'A Constitution for the Oceans', reprinted in M. H. Nordquist, *United Nations Convention on the Law of the Sea 1982: A Commentary. Volume I,* Martinus Nijhoff, 1985, pp. 11–16.

68 Presently there are 168 parties to the LOSC (see Chronological lists of ratifications of, accessions and successions to the Convention and the related Agreements as of 23 September 2016); http://www.un.org/Depts/los/reference_files/chronological_lists_of_ratifications.htm.

biodiversity that is connected rather with the water column than with the seabed and subsoil.

5.4 The 'Due Regard' Clause

Article 87 LOSC provides[69] that all States can enjoy the freedom of the seas; however, subject to certain limitations. The traditional limitation is first of all the duty to pay due regard to interests of other States in their exercise of this freedom.

This due-regard clause in paragraph 2 of Article 87 LOSC has its antecedent in Article 2 of the *Convention on the High Seas*[70] with the only difference that in this convention 'reasonable' instead of 'due' regard has to be paid to the interests of the other States. The interpretation of 'due regard' escapes a clear meaning. According to the Virginia Commentary it 'requires all States, in exercising their high seas freedoms, to be aware of and consider the interests of other States in using the high seas, and to refrain from activities that interfere with the exercise by other States of the freedom of the high seas.'[71] In connection with the establishment of an MPA, a similar clause, namely that regarding the EEZ, was also examined by the Arbitral Tribunal in the matter of the *Chagos Marine Protected Area Arbitration*. Mauritius contended that the envisaged creation of an MPA within the EEZ of the Chagos Archipelago would not be in conformity with Article 56 (2) LOSC, which requires that

---

69 Article 87 of the LOSC (*Freedom of the high seas*) reads as follows:

'1. The high seas are open to all States, whether coastal or land-locked. Freedom of the high seas is exercised under the conditions laid down by this Convention and by other rules of international law. It comprises, inter alia, both for coastal and land-locked States:

(a) freedom of navigation;
(b) freedom of overflight;
(c) freedom to lay submarine cables and pipelines, subject to Part VI;
(d) freedom to construct artificial islands and other installations permitted under international law, subject to Part VI;
(e) freedom of fishing, subject to the conditions laid down in section 2;
(f) freedom of scientific research, subject to Parts VI and XIII.

2. These freedoms shall be exercised by all States with due regard to the interests of other States in their exercise of the freedom of the high seas, and also with due regard to the rights under this Convention with respect to activities in the Area.'

70 M. H. Nordquist, S. Rosenne, & S. N. Nandan, *United Nations Convention on the Law of the Sea, 1982: A Commentary. Volume III*, Martinus Nijhoff, 1995, p. 86.

71 Ibid.

> In exercising its rights and performing its duties under this Convention in the exclusive economic zone, the coastal State shall have *due regard* to the rights and duties of other States and shall act in a manner compatible with the provisions of this Convention. (emphasis added)

Mauritius argued that this formulation obliged the United Kingdom 'to respect the rights of Mauritius' and to 'to refrain from acts that interfere with [Mauritius' rights]'.[72] Referring also to Article 2 of the High Seas Convention of 1958, and the commentary provided by the ILC, it submitted that in the light of this clause States were 'bound to refrain from any acts that might adversely affect the use of the high seas by nationals of other States.'[73] Accordingly, '[b]y prohibiting Mauritius from exercising [its rights], the UK has breached Article 56(2). To put it in the terms of that provision, the UK has failed to have due regard for the rights of Mauritius'.[74]

In contrast, in the United Kingdom's view, the clause 'to have due regard... stops well short of an obligation to give effect to such rights' and extends only to 'taking account' of or 'giving consideration' to Mauritian rights.[75] According to the Tribunal,

> the extent of the regard required by the Convention will depend upon the nature of the rights held by Mauritius, their importance, the extent of the anticipated impairment, the nature and importance of the activities contemplated by the United Kingdom, and the availability of alternative approaches. In the majority of cases, this assessment will necessarily involve at least some consultation with the rights-holding State.[76]

To transpose this conclusion to the general problem of MPAs in the high seas requires first a clarification of whether instituting MPAs amounts to an exercise of the freedoms of the sea. This activity does not figure among the freedoms in Article 87; however, this list is not exhaustive as can be derived from the use of the expression 'inter alia' so that any other activity in this area can be qualified as an exercise of freedoms. Contrary to Article 2 of the High Seas Convention 1958, these not mentioned freedoms need not be recognized by the principles of international law, so that a preceding recognition in international law is not

---

72 *Chagos Marine Protected Area Arbitration* (Mauritius v United Kingdom), PCA case 2011–3, Award of 18 March 2015, para. 471.
73 Ibid.
74 Ibid.
75 Ibid., para. 472.
76 Ibid., para. 519.

required.[77] Accordingly, any activity can amount to the exercise of a freedom unless it is connected with the arrogation of sovereignty over parts of the high seas or is otherwise prohibited. Since the establishment of MPAs does not amount to the exercise of sovereignty there is no problem of identifying this activity as the exercise of a freedom of the seas.

Accordingly, the conclusion drawn by the tribunal signifies that the lawfulness of the establishment of MPAs depends on a certain balance of the rights of third States against the regime of the MPAs, and the existence of certain alternatives. At least, some sort of notoriety must be established so that other States have the possibility to obtain information about it and to react. Particular regard must be paid to the existence of exploitation activities of other States in this area.

In a wider context, already Article 87 LOSC makes the freedom of fisheries subject to the conditions laid down in Articles 118 and 199 LOSC so that this freedom is conditioned by the rules relating to the conservation and management of living resources in the high seas. The duty of co-operation with other States in the conservation and management of living resources as stipulated in Article 118 LOSC, to which Article 87 LOSC refers, restricts the unfettered freedom of high-seas fisheries. Article 118 LOSC (Cooperation of States in the conservation and management of living resources) reads as follows:

> States shall cooperate with each other in the conservation and management of living resources in the areas of the high seas. States whose nationals exploit identical living resources, or different living resources in the same area, shall enter into negotiations with a view to taking the measures necessary for the conservation of the living resources concerned. They shall, as appropriate, cooperate to establish subregional or regional fisheries organizations to this end.

According to Article 119 LOSC any measures designed to maintain or restore populations of harvested species at levels which can produce the maximum sustainable yield (MSY) must not discriminate in form or in fact against the fishermen of any State. Since agreements establishing MPAs should be open to all States,[78] this condition of non-discrimination seems to be fulfilled. However, whereas Article 118 LOSC calls for participation in MPAs that are designed to conserve and manage living resources, one may wonder whether such an MPA

---

77   R.-J. Dupuy & D. Vignes, *Traité du nouveau droit de la mer*, Economica, 1985, p. 346.
78   Para. 3 of Article 119 LOSC (*Conservation of the living resources of the high seas*) reads as follows: 'States concerned shall ensure that conservation measures and their implementation do not discriminate in form or in fact against the fishermen of any State.

would fall under the measures of Article 119 LOSC as it is not designed to ensure the MSY, but to protect biodiversity or genetic resources—something that could necessitate a total ban on fishing.

Nevertheless, apart from the call for participation, these two articles offer no possibility to force third States to respect and abide by MPAs in which they do not participate.

6   The MPAs under the Regime of the Marine Environment

It is further to be asked whether and how far high seas fisheries have to respect activities aiming at protecting the marine environment. The primary objective of the envisaged MPAs is the protection of marine biodiversity[79] and, in a larger understanding, the marine environment. In Article 2 CBD, 'biological diversity' is defined as 'the variability among living organisms from all sources including, *inter alia,* terrestrial, marine and other aquatic ecosystems and the ecological complexes of which they are part: this includes diversity within species, between species and of ecosystems'.[80] Applied to the maritime area such MPAs affect in particular the freedom of fisheries. In the *Chagos Marine Protected Area Arbitration,* Mauritius positioned the issue of the MPAs in the field of the LOSC articles on the protection of the marine environment in order to claim that the UK had acted unlawfully. It claimed that the MPA was 'a measure... intended to protect the environment' and therefore should 'be considered by reference to the requirements of Part XII' of the Convention.[81] In this context, it invoked Article 194 LOSC which in its view required the UK to 'try hard to do or achieve harmonization of policies regarding pollution prevention'.[82]

---

79   According to the Chair's compilation of issues, one of the overall objectives raised during the first session of the Preparatory Committee was to '[c]onserve and sustainably use marine biological diversity of areas beyond national jurisdiction' (Annex I to the 'Chair's overview of the first session of the Preparatory Committee', Preparatory Committee established by General Assembly resolution 69/292: Development of an international legally-binding instrument under the United Nations Convention on the Law of the Sea on the conservation and sustainable use of marine biological diversity of areas beyond national jurisdiction, 2016.

80   Convention on Biological Diversity, 5 June 1992, 1760 UNTS 79.

81   *Chagos Marine Protected Area Arbitration,* supra, note 72, para. 482.

82   Ibid., para. 483.

Article 194 LOSC is relatively specific[83] as compared to the general obligation under Article 192 LOSC: the former obliges States to take measures necessary to prevent, reduce and control pollution of the marine environment from any source. However, these measures have to be taken in conformity with the

---

83 Article 194 LOSC (*Measures to prevent, reduce and control pollution of the marine environment*) reads as follows:
   "1. States shall take, individually or jointly as appropriate, all measures consistent with this Convention that are necessary to prevent, reduce and control pollution of the marine environment from any source, using for this purpose the best practicable means at their disposal and in accordance with their capabilities, and they shall endeavour to harmonize their policies in this connection.
   2. States shall take all measures necessary to ensure that activities under their jurisdiction or control are so conducted as not to cause damage by pollution to other States and their environment, and that pollution arising from incidents or activities under their jurisdiction or control does not spread beyond the areas where they exercise sovereign rights in accordance with this Convention.
   3. The measures taken pursuant to this Part shall deal with all sources of pollution of the marine environment. These measures shall include, inter alia, those designed to minimize to the fullest possible extent:
       (a) the release of toxic, harmful or noxious substances, especially those which are persistent, from land-based sources, from or through the atmosphere or by dumping;
       (b) pollution from vessels, in particular measures for preventing accidents and dealing with emergencies, ensuring the safety of operations at sea, preventing intentional and unintentional discharges, and regulating the design, construction, equipment, operation and manning of vessels;
       (c) pollution from installations and devices used in exploration or exploitation of the natural resources of the seabed and subsoil, in particular measures for preventing accidents and dealing with emergencies, ensuring the safety of operations at sea, and regulating the design, construction, equipment, operation and manning of such installations or devices;
       (d) pollution from other installations and devices operating in the marine environment, in particular measures for preventing accidents and dealing with emergencies, ensuring the safety of operations at sea, and regulating the design, construction, equipment, operation and manning of such installations or devices.
   4. In taking measures to prevent, reduce or control pollution of the marine environment, States shall refrain from unjustifiable interference with activities carried out by other States in the exercise of their rights and in pursuance of their duties in conformity with this Convention.
   5. The measures taken in accordance with this Part shall include those necessary to protect and preserve rare or fragile ecosystems as well as the habitat of depleted, threatened or endangered species and other forms of marine life."

LOSC and must not cause unjustifiable interference with activities carried out by other States in the exercise of their rights and in pursuance of their duties in conformity with the LOSC. In line with Mauritius' view, this obligation requires an assessment of whether the interference with the other States' rights is 'justifiable'.[84] Similarly to the argumentation of Mauritius, one can easily argue that any MPA on the high seas obviously interferes with the fishing rights of other States and could be seen as unjustifiable. The Tribunal did not derive from Article 194 (1) LOSC a strict obligation of result as this provision establishes only a duty to endeavor. However, its paragraph 4 expresses a clear obligation not to interfere unjustifiably with lawful activities of other States. The Tribunal compared this obligation with the due-regard clause of Article 56 LOSC (also contained in Article 87 regarding the high seas). It concluded that '[l]ike these provisions, Article 194(4) requires a balancing act between competing rights, based upon an evaluation of the extent of the interference, the availability of alternatives, and the importance of the rights and policies at issue.'[85] However, the tribunal also identified a difference insofar as Article 194(4) LOSC 'facially applies only to the 'activities carried out by other States' pursuant to their rights, rather than to the rights themselves.'[86] In the Tribunal's view, States, when taking the measures addressed in this provision, have to respect only existing lawful activities, but not prospective ones.[87] Accordingly, States establishing MPAs are bound only to enter into negotiations or consultations with other States as far as these States perform exploitation activities that could be affected by the MPAs in order to seek their assent to the MPAs. But even under this circumstance the Tribunal did not exclude the possibility that such MPAs could be established provided that the need were explained and 'less restrictive alternatives' could be explored.[88]

In view of this Award, it has to be concluded that the creation of MPAs in the high seas requires that the treaties by which they are to be founded are open to all States, are made known to all States and that States that already perform exploitation activities in the respective geographical area, and will be affected by this installation, are consulted with the objective to obtain their explicit or implicit assent.

---

84   *Chagos Marine Protected Area Arbitration*, supra, note 72, para. 485.
85   Ibid., paras. 539–540.
86   Ibid.
87   Ibid.
88   Ibid., para. 541.

7 Conclusions

Accordingly, it is necessary to distinguish between participation in the regime of an MPA, which requires written consent as provided in Article 35 VCLT in order to be binding, and the toleration by a third State of the measures under this regime against its vessels as expressed in an attitude of the other States reflecting the renunciation of any objection to such MPAs. Nevertheless, other States must refrain from activities that could totally undermine the achievements of such MPAs. Although these States are formally not bound by such MPAs, they are bound not to hinder States working in such MPAs in the achievement of the latter's objective as a consequence of the generally applicable principle of good faith.[89] Only if the establishment of MPAs infringes the fishing activities of other States, must these States be allowed to continue their activities or, at least, the proponents of the MPA must try to reach agreement with them.

Any treaty that serves as the basis of such MPAs must provide not only an accession clause but also impose an obligation on the States Parties to enter into consultations with third States if the latters' activities are affected by the MPAs. Although according to this argumentation the rights of third States are still respected, these States no longer enjoy unfettered freedom, but are protected in particular only insofar as they already perform relevant activities.

Accordingly, one may wonder whether and how far a freedom of fisheries still exists on the high seas. Fishing this maritime area is becoming a highly regulated activity where a freedom understood as the discretionary power to undertake such activities free of any local and performance restrictions (except those resulting from general international law such as the non-use of force) no longer exists. Not only have States committed themselves to abandoning such freedom, but these regulations also have effects on third States, restricting the latters' discretionary power in the performance of these activities.

It may further be asked how this legal change has occurred. In this respect reference could be made to the emergence of a new legal regime without the freedom of fisheries generated not by *opinio iuris* but by *opinio necessitatis* as referred to in the separate and dissenting opinions, respectively, of Judges Wellington Koo and Chagla in the *Right of Passage over Indian Territory* case.[90]

---

89   Laly-Chevalier, supra, note 48, p. 910.
90   *Case concerning Right of Passage over Indian Territory* (Portugal v India), Separate Opinion of Judge V. K. Wellington Koo, ICJ Reports 1960, p. 54, at pp. 60–63; *Case concerning Right of Passage over Indian Territory* (Portugal v India), Dissenting Opinion of Judge Chagla, ICJ Reports 1960, 116, at p. 121.

Both judges referred to necessity, Wellington Koo confirming it as the basis of a right,[91] Chagla denying the existence of necessity required for the creation of a right in that particular case.[92] Although necessity as a stimulus or mover for the creation of customary international law has otherwise hardly been recognized, Verdross nevertheless referred to it and spoke of the necessity to convert certain rules into general customary international law.[93] The present situation of the exploitation of living resources on the high seas, where most species are threatened by depletion, induces the application of this consideration also to the high seas. Thus it becomes arguable that the freedom of the high seas regarding fisheries has been abandoned as a consequence of the necessity to replace it by a highly-regulated regime ensuring the sustainability of the further exploitation of high-seas living resources for the benefit of mankind. Accordingly, Article 116 LOSC is quite right to replace the term 'freedom' by 'rights'.

---

91   *Case concerning Right of Passage over Indian Territory,* Separate Opinion of Judge V. K. Wellington Koo, supra, note 90, p. 60, para. 11 ('What appears even more significant is the fact, as cited above, that the British authorities expressed their preference for the continuance of this practice of non-interference with such passages, obviously in recognition of the necessity for them as well as out of consideration for their own convenience on the reciprocal basis.').

92   *Case concerning Right of Passage over Indian Territory,* Dissenting Opinion of Judge Chagla, supra, note 90, p. 121. ('It may be that Portugal realized the necessity of maintaining a liaison with her enclaves. But Portugal's necessity does not constitute the conviction of necessity required for a local custom to which effect can be given. There must be an equally clear realization on the other side of an obligation to respect this necessity. And we seek in vain to find any such realization in the whole of the record, from 1818 till 1954, when both the enclaves were lost to Portugal.').

93   A. Verdross, *Die Quellen des universellen Völkerrechts,* 1973, pp. 115, 119; see also G. Hafner, *Die seerechtliche Verteilung von Nutzungsrechten,* Springer, 1987, p. 146.

Les pays sans littoral et le droit de la mer

Zalmaï Haquani

Mes relations amicales et académiques avec le Professeur Djamchid Momtaz remontent à plusieurs décennies : en 1977, il a bien voulu publier, alors qu'il ne me connaissait pas, mon article sur la Conférence des Nations Unies sur le commerce et le développement (CNUCED) en français et en persan dans la *Revue de Relations internationales* qu'il dirigeait à Téhéran. Depuis lors, nous avons pu développer et fortifier nos relations de travail et notre profonde amitié à Paris, Caen et Téhéran au fur et à mesure de nos voyages et séjours respectifs comme professeur invité ou conférencier, ou encore comme visiteur privé en famille. Ainsi j'ai pu apprécier ses capacités scientifiques, ses fines analyses juridiques, sa haute pédagogie, sa très grande personnalité et sa fidélité dans ses convictions et dans son amitié. C'est la raison pour laquelle je suis honoré de contribuer modestement à ces *Etudes* qui lui sont offertes.

Depuis presque 60 ans les pays sans littoral maritime sa battent aux Nations Unies pour la défense de leur droit d'accès à la mer, en dépit des progrès qui ont été fait dans ce sens : reconnaissance du droit de transit, droit d'utiliser la mer comme moyen de communication, droit au pavillon, droit d'accès limité aux ressources économiques de la mer… En même temps, toutes leurs revendications n'ont pas abouti ni avec la Convention des Nations Unies sur la haute mer de 1958[1], ni avec celle de 1982 qui les écarte en grande partie de l'utilisation des ressources économiques des zones économiques exclusives de leurs voisins riverain de la mer ; et il est fort possible qu'ils aient du mal à faire valoir toutes leurs prétentions dans les négociations actuelles lancées par les Etats membres des de l'ONU, en mars dernier, en vue de faire aboutir un nouveau projet de convention sur la haute mer – BBNJ (*Biodiversity Beyond National Juridiction*) – c'est à dire un nouvel *instrument international juridique contraignant sur la conservation et l'utilisation durable de la diversité biologique*[2].

Aujourd'hui, comme hier, les difficultés et impasses à surmonter concernent surtout les pays sans littoral en développement[3] par rapport aux pays sans

---

1 Nations Unies, *Recueil des traités*, vol. 450, p. 11.
2 Cf. « La haute mer, un no man's land en quête de lois », *Le Monde*, 29 mars 2016, p. 7.
3 Très dispersés à travers le monde, il y en a 15 en Afrique, 12 en Asie dont sept en Asie centrale, deux en Amérique latine, et deux en Europe centrale et orientale. Certains de ces pays font partie aussi des PMA (pays les moins avancés).

littoral développés[4], lesquel sont parvenus depuis longtemps à la conclusion d'accords bilatéraux ou régionaux avec leurs partenaires riverains de la mer.

Ces préoccupations étaient déjà présentes au Comité du fond des mers, organe politique préparatoire de la Convention sur le droit de la mer de 1982. Lors des précédentes Conférences des Nations Unies sur le droit de la mer, ces Etats se sont opposés aux prétentions maximalistes de certains pays sur eaux territoriales et ont condamné la pratique de ceux qui, par voie unilatérale ou en application de conventions particulières, avaient décidé de soumettre à leur souveraineté « des zones maritimes s'étendant jusqu'à une distance de 200 milles marins, y compris le sol et le sous-sol correspondants ». De même, ils ont refusé de considérer le plateau continental comme limitrophe de la marge continentale constituée par la totalité de l'extension sous-marine des terres jusqu'au bord de la plaine abyssale, limitant ainsi les espaces océaniques relevant du patrimoine commun de l'humanité.

Contraints et forcés, les pays dépourvus de littoral maritime et les autres Etats géographiquement désavantagés se sont finalement ralliés à la tendance générale présente dans la Convention de 1982 sur la zone internationale et sur les zones sous la juridiction nationale des Etats côtiers.

Notre propos ici se limite au problème de la *participation des Etats sans littoral à l'exploitation des ressources de la zone économique exclusive,* conformément à la Convention sur le droit de la mer de 1982.

Cette question est étroitement liée à leur droit d'accès à la mer en général, reconnu au plan international mais dont le contenu évolue continuellement – souvent à leur détriment – au fur et à mesure du développement des nouvelles perspectives du milieu marin : sous son aspect traditionnel ou sous sa forme actuelle ou à venir.

Le droit d'accès a la surface des mers

Pour les Etats sans littoral, le droit d'accès à la mer signifie le droit d'utiliser les océans dans les mêmes conditions que les Etats riverains, et le droit de traverser le territoire d'un ou de plusieurs pays en vue d'atteindre la mer. Ils entendent ainsi exercer pleinement non seulement leur droit au commerce maritime mais aussi leur droit au commerce de transit.

Sous cet angle, le droit au libre accès à la mer des pays dépourvus de littoral a été reconnu dans des traités bilatéraux, mais aussi dans plusieurs instruments multilatéraux importants, tels que la Convention et le Statut de Barcelone du

---

4 Tels l'Autriche, le Luxembourg et la Suisse.

20 avril 1921 sur la liberté de transit[5], la Convention de Genève de 1958 sur la haute mer[6] et la Convention de New-York du 8 juillet 1965 relative au commerce de transit des Etats sans littoral[7].

La Convention et le Statut de Barcelone ont facilité le transit en général et permis à certains pays sans littoral d'avoir des voies d'accès à la mer. Cependant, ces accords ne portent pas sur tous les moyens de transport et de communication, laissant de côté en particulier les transports par route et pipe-line dont l'importance n'a cessé de croître depuis 1921. En outre, le nombre des parties contractantes à la Convention et au Statut de Barcelone, toujours en vigueur, est resté relativement limité et peu de pays non européens y ont adhéré.

A la veille de la première Conférence des Nations Unies sur le droit de la mer, l'Assemblée générale avait reconnu dans sa résolution 1028 (XI) du 20 février 1957 la nécessité pour les pays sans littoral jouir « de facilités de transit adéquates si l'on veut favoriser le commerce international [...] ». La convention de 1958 confirme que la haute mer est ouverte à toutes les nations et stipule expressément que « pour jouir des libertés de la mer à l'égard des Etats riverains de la mer, les Etats dépourvus de littoral devraient accéder librement à la mer »[8].

Plus tard, en 1964, la Conférence des Nations Unies sur le commerce et le développement (CNUCED) a adopté un certain nombre de principes garantissant de façon plus adéquate la liberté de transit des pays sans littoral.

A la suite de cette Conférence fut adoptée, en juillet 1965, la Convention de New York en tant qu'un nouveau pas vers la solution des problèmes concrets auxquels se heurtent quotidiennement les Etats sans littoral. C'est en application de cette convention notamment que ces pays doivent bénéficier d'une série de mesures et avantages spéciaux sur le plan international : les uns leur sont accordés en tant que pays sans littoral ; les autres leur sont consacrés en tant que pays en développement. L'ensemble de ces mesures et avantages sont destinés à faciliter leur commerce de transit, mais aussi leur accès au fond des mers et des océans.

Le droit d'accès au fond des mers

Le droit d'accès à la mer a pris une nouvelle dimension à partir du moment où l'Assemblée générale des Nations Unies a demandé que l'exploration du fond

---

5 *Recueil des Traités* de la Société des Nations, vol. 7, p. 11.
6 Ibid.
7 Ibid.
8 Voir les articles 2 et 3 de la Convention sur la haute mer 1958.

des mers et l'exploitation de ses ressources « se fassent dans l'intérêt de l'humanité tout entière, indépendamment de la situation géographique des Etats, qu'il s'agisse de pays côtiers ou de pays sans littoral, et compte tenu particulièrement des intérêts et des besoins des pays en voie de développement ».

Dans cette perspective, l'action des pays sans littoral, au sein de la troisième Conférence sur le droit de la mer, devait s'orienter vers un double objectif : la réaffirmation, dans la nouvelle convention, de leur droit d'accès à la mer et son réaménagement en fonction des nouvelles données techniques et économiques, d'une part, et la reconnaissance de leur droit de participer, au même titre que les autres nations, à l'exploitation des ressources du fond des mers et des océans, d'autre part.

En ce qui concerne leur « droit d'accès à la mer et depuis la mer », les Etats sans littoral ont exigé, comme par le passé, qu'il ne soit pas subordonné à la réciprocité en raison de leur situation géographique défavorable et de leurs besoins spécifiques en matière de transit, ce qui n'avait pas été accepté par les pays de transit lors de l'élaboration de la Convention de New York de 1965.

En ce qui concerne leur droit à l'exploitation des ressources sous-marines, les pays sans littoral, comme d'autres pays géographiquement désavantagés qui ont, eux aussi, des difficultés analogues ou semblables, entendaient bien l'exercer aussi bien dans la zone internationale que dans les zones économiques relevant de la juridiction nationale des Etats.

Dans la Convention adoptée en 1982[9], il n'y a pas eu de difficulté majeure à ce que les pays sans littoral ou géographiquement désavantagés participent, presque sur un pied d'égalité – à bien des égards théoriquement – au régime international, y compris au mécanisme institutionnel (autorité internationale et son entreprise), ainsi qu'au partage équitable des avantages tirés de la zone internationale[10].

En revanche, le désaccord traduit dans le droit positif figure sur la participation de ces pays à l'exploitation des ressources de la zone économique exclusive[11].

---

9   Convention des Nations Unies sur le droit de la mer, Montego Bay, 10 décembre 1982, Nations Unies, *Recueil des traités*, vol. 1834, p. 3.

10 Partie XI de la Convention des Nations Unies sur le droit de la mer de 1982.

11 Ce problème a occupé une large place dans les discussions et négociations de la Conférence sur le droit de la mer, et constitue un point de blocage pour faire aboutir ces travaux.

Au plan des revendications, la participation des pays sans littoral apparaissait comme un *droit compensatoire et égalitaire* ; mais dans la Convention en vigueur depuis 1994, il s'agit tout simplement d'un *droit résiduel et différentiel*[12].

1 La participation des pays sans littoral, droit compensatoire et égalitaire

C'est surtout au sein des groupes de négociation de la deuxième commission de l'actuelle Conférence sur le droit de la mer que furent abordés les problèmes particuliers des Etats enclavés : le groupe de négociation II qui a participé dès 1975 à l'élaboration des dispositions correspondantes du texte unique de négociation ; le « groupe des Vingt et un » qui a travaillé à la rédaction du texte de négociation composite en 1977 ; et le groupe de négociation IV composé de trente-neuf Etats et constitué en avril 1978.

Sur le fond, les pays sans littoral devaient faire face à certaines difficultés aussi bien pour justifier leurs revendications dans la zone économique que pour en défendre le contenu précis.

1.1 *Le fondement des revendications des pays sans littoral*

Ce n'est certainement pas la règle de la liberté des mers battue en brèche par les pays en développement eux-mêmes qui pourrait justifier les prétentions des pays sans littoral sur la zone économique, encore que les Etats sans littoral l'invoquent toujours pour défendre leur droit d'accès à la mer en général ou pour soutenir, comme les grandes puissances maritimes, le maintien des eaux de cette zone dans la haute mer. C'est plutôt le principe de l'équité qui est avancé comme principal fondement de leurs revendications.

D'une façon générale, l'équité signifie « l'application des principes de la justice à un cas déterminé, compte tenu de tous les éléments de l'espèce et abstraction faite des exigences purement techniques du droit positif »[13]. En droit international de la mer, en cours d'élaboration, le recours à l'équité peut constituer comme un moyen d'atténuer ou de compléter l'application des nouvelles règles de droit sur l'établissement des zones économiques, au profit des Etats côtiers. Aussi, les droits que les pays sans littoral ou géographiquement désavantagés revendiquent dans ces zones peuvent-ils apparaître comme une sorte de compensation de leur manque à gagner résultant de l'extension de la

---

12   Les articles 69 et suivants de la Convention des Nations Unies sur le droit de la mer de 1982.
13   Ch. Rousseau, Droit international public, tome 1 Sirey Paris 1971 p. 398.

juridiction nationale des pays riverains. D'autre part, les Etats à plateau continental étendu trouvent également des formules pour justifier leurs prétentions sur de larges zones maritimes, leur sol et leur sous-sol, en faisant valoir que le plateau continental est une continuation géologique de la terre ferme submergée sous les eaux côtières et que leur souveraineté et leur juridiction doivent donc s'y étendre comme il s'agissait de leur propre territoire.

Les pays sans littoral et ceux qui sont géographiquement désavantagés invoquaient avec raison ces arguments pour réclamer les mêmes droits que les Etats côtiers, car ils perdent par les fleuves, les ruisseaux et les torrents de précieux éléments biologiques et inorganiques qui aboutissent finalement à la mer et appauvrissent leurs terres. Il n'est moins vrai que les pays sans littoral font également partie des continents et sont, dans beaucoup de cas, le point d'où le territoire continental commence sa déclivité progressive jusqu'à la mer ».

Les Etats côtiers invoquent eux aussi le principe de l'équité, mais ils en tirent des conséquences tout à fait différentes. Selon ces pays, les Etats tiers doivent démontrer, pour avoir accès à la zone économique, qu'ils ont subi un préjudice. Or, celui-ci est inexistant pour les Etats enclavés qui n'ont jamais pu exploiter directement les ressources de la mer et qui ne peuvent donc valablement prétendre à un véritable droit d'accès aux ressources de la zone. Les Etats côtiers se déclarent néanmoins prêts à discuter sur le contenu de certaines revendications formulées par ces pays.

1.2 *Le contenu des revendications des pays sans littoral*

Les revendications des pays sans littoral sur les ressources de la zone économique apparaissent surtout à travers les différents projets qu'ils ont présentés à la Conférence, tels la Déclaration de Kampala élaborée par la Conférence des Etats en voie de développement sans littoral et autres Etats géographiquement désavantagés[14].

La position initiale des pays sans littoral ou géographiquement désavantagés devait profondément évoluer, aussi bien sur la notion de zone économique que sur la nature et l'étendue des droits revendiqués, au fur et à mesure de l'avancement des travaux de la Conférence et face à l'intransigeance des Etats côtiers qui en résultait.

---

14   Le projet d'articles sur la participation de ces Etats à l'exploration et à l'exploitation des ressources biologiques et minérales de la zone située au-delà de la mer territoriale, et le projet d'articles sur la zone économique régionale présenté par la Bolivie et le Paraguay, soumis au Comité des Fonds des mers, à la veille de la Conférence sur le droit de la mer.

Au départ, ils considéraient que la notion de zone économique « n'est ni la seule possible ni la seule équitable », la formule équitable étant celle qui consisterait à accorder aux Etats côtiers une mer territoriale de 12 milles au-delà de laquelle tout l'espace maritime serait placé sous le contrôle et la juridiction de l'Autorité internationale des fonds marins.

Les propositions des Etats sans littoral ne pouvaient évidemment que se heurter au refus catégorique des Etats côtiers. Aussi, les projets présentés collectivement par les pays sans littoral étaient-ils très prudents sur ce point puisqu'ils ne prenaient position ni sur la nature ni sur la largeur de la zone économique. En revanche, ils mettaient bien l'accent sur la nécessité d'une participation égalitaire de ces pays à l'exploitation des ressources de celle-ci.

Le projet d'articles déposé par ces mêmes pays précisait dans ses articles 2 et 3 que les Etats sans littoral et autres Etats géographiquement désavantagés ont le droit de participer à l'exploration et à l'exploitation des ressources biologiques et minérales de la zone économique des Etats côtiers sur un pied d'égalité et sans discrimination.

Mais là encore les pays sans littoral ou géographiquement désavantagés ne pouvaient que céder aux pressions exercées par les Etats côtiers et abandonner leurs revendications sur les ressources minérales. Quant aux ressources biologiques de la zone, elles ne profitent aux pays sans littoral, aux termes de la Convention, qu'à titre résiduel et différentiel.

2   La participation des pays sans littoral, droit résiduel et différentiel

L'attitude des Etats côtiers s'est révélée particulièrement intransigeante face aux revendications initialement formulées par les pays sans littoral ou géographiquement désavantagés. Certains d'entre eux, comme le Pérou, qui faisait partie du « groupe territorialiste », n'entendaient reconnaître à leurs voisins enclavés que la liberté d'accès à la mer et aux ressources du « patrimoine commun de l'humanité ». D'autres, tels le Mexique ou le Pakistan, ne voulaient leur accorder que « certains droits» sur les ressources biologiques. Seuls les Etats africains étaient plus conciliants : les pays sans littoral et autres pays désavantagés ont le droit de bénéficier des ressources biologiques des zones économiques voisines.

La solution envisagée par le texte de la Convention marque un recul par rapport aux prétentions des Etats sans littoral ou géographiquement désavantagés, ne leur reconnaissant qu'un droit résiduel et différentiel. Les perspectives actuelles et futures ne leur semblent pas non plus très favorables.

2.1 La solution préconisée par la Convention de 1982

Outre leur droit de jouir des libertés traditionnelles du milieu marin, les Etats sans littoral ont, en vertu du texte de la Convention[15], « le droit de participer sur une base équitable à l'exploitation des ressources biologiques des zones économiques exclusives des Etats côtiers voisins ». Bien que qualifiée de véritable droit, cette participation n'offre aux pays sans littoral que des possibilités extrêmement limitées : il ne s'agit en réalité que d'un droit résiduel dans son contenu et d'un droit différentiel dans son application.

Il s'agit d'un *droit résiduel* dans la mesure où il ne porte que sur une partie des ressources biologiques déterminée par l'Etat côtier lui-même. En effet, les dispositions de l'article 69, de même que celles de l'article 70 concernant d'autres pays géographiquement désavantagés, sont subordonnées à celles des articles 61 et 62, lesquelles permettent à l'Etat côtier de déterminer les prises autorisées et sa propre capacité de récolte de ressources biologiques. Si celui-ci « n'a pas la capacité de récolter la totalité des prises autorisées », il accorde alors à d'autres Etats, y compris à ceux qui sont dépourvus de littoral, l'accès à l'excédent des prises autorisées, conformément aux arrangements internationaux et à ses propres règlements internes.

Par le biais de cette emprise, l'Etat côtier peut, à tout moment, réduire ou enlever toute possibilité de participation des pays sans littoral, en diminuant les prises autorisées en général ou en augmentant exagérément sa propre capacité de récolte de ressources halieutiques.

Il s'agit également d'un *droit différentiel* en ce sens que sa portée varie en fonction de la situation géographique et économique des pays concernés.

Dans le cas des pays sans littoral, c'est surtout le facteur géographique régional qui est déterminant puisque les pays sans littoral de la même région d'accès aux surplus des ressources halieutiques de leurs voisins côtiers. Autrement dit, les pays sans littoral développés ne sont autorisés à exercer leurs droits qu'à l'intérieur de leurs propres zones, et non dans la zone économique exclusive extérieure à leur région.

Comme en matière d'accès à la mer, les conditions et modalités de cette participation sont déterminées par les Etats intéressés par voie d'accords bilatéraux, sous régionaux ou régionaux.

Il s'agit donc d'un droit d'accès restrictif loin des positions proclamées solidaires du groupe des « 77 » aux Nations Unies, ce qui rend aussi incertaines

---

15 Au texte de la Convention des Nations Unies sur le droit de la mer s'ajoute l'Accord relatif à l'application de sa partie XI, relative à la Zone internationale, conclu le 28 juillet 1994 et entré en vigueur le 28 juillet 1996. Nations Unies, *Recueil des traités*, vol. 1836, p. 3.

les nouvelles négociations projetées par celles-ci pour la préservation et les nouvelles perspectives du milieu marin.

2.2 Les nouvelles perspectives pour la préservation du milieu marin

Jusqu'à présent, en dépit de certains progrès accomplis, les pays sans littoral n'ont pas obtenu ce qu'ils revendiquaient depuis fort longtemps : leur accès aux ressources de la zone économique exclusive reste limité ; ce qu'ils devraient avoir du partage du patrimoine commun de l'humanité est aussi hypothétique, seuls les Etats avancés étant en réalité les gros bénéficiaires[16] ; enfin, tout passage de transit à travers le territoire de leurs voisins, nécessite – même s'il s'agit d'un droit spécial exempt de la clause de la nation la plus favorisée – la conclusion d'accords bilatéraux ou régionaux[17].

Il est fort probable qu'une fois de plus les pays sans littoral en développement soient à terme marginalisés dans le projet d'accord envisagé depuis le mois de mars dernier par les Nations Unies[18], sur la préservation de la haute mer et de ses ressources : régime juridique d'accès et partage des ressources génétiques marines, leur mise à profit selon les sciences et technologies actuelles et furfures, leur impact sur le milieu marin et son environnement, création de zones marines protégées[19]. C'est aussi une suite logique de la Conférence de Paris sur le Climat en 2015, Cop. 21[20].

Pour l'heure, les pays sans littoral, confrontés aux difficultés de commerce et de transit, ajoutées au contexte politique bilatéral et régional défavorable, sont très actifs aux Nations Unies et à l'OMC. Le *Programme d'action d'Almaty* présenté en 2003 par le Groupe des pays sans littoral insiste sur les « partenariats conçus pour répondre aux besoins particuliers des pays en développement sans littoral et créer un nouveau cadre mondial pour la coopération en matière de transport en transit entre les pays en développement sans littoral et les pays de transit « avec cinq priorités bien définies : problèmes fondamentaux liés

---

16   Par exemple les articles 148 et 254 de la Convention qui concernent indirectement ou directement les pays sans littoral et géographiquement désavantagés.
17   Des obstacles et difficultés majeurs en matière de transit sont dressés continuellement depuis des décennies, sans le respect des conventions en vigueur, par certains Etats côtiers au détriment de leurs voisins sans littoral (comme par exemple dans les relations entre le Pakistan et l'Afghanistan). Voir Z. Nézam, « la solution des problèmes de transit pour l'Afghanistan », *8h du matin* (quotidien en dari), du 4 avril 2016.
18   L'Organisation devra mener d'ici 2017 quatre pourparlers préliminaires, avant que l'Assemblée générale décide l'ouverture de négociations officielles dans le cadre d'une conférence des Nations Unies ouverte à cet effet.
19   Voir « La haute mer, un no man's land en quête de lois », *op. cit.*, note 2.
20   Voir « Le Climat, l'urgence », *Le Monde*, hors série, 2015, p. 98.

aux politiques de transit, développement et entretien des infrastructures, facilitations du commerce, mesures d'appui et application et évaluation. Sur cette base, la deuxième Conférence des Nations Unies sur les pays en développement sans littoral, réunie à Vienne en novembre 2014, a adopté le Programme d'action de Vienne en leur faveur pour la décennie 2014-2024[21]. A Vienne l'ONU a lancé un nouvel appel pour mettre fin à l'isolement des pays en développement sans littoral.

Le projet actuel de nouvelles négociations onusiennes sur la haute mer peut être prometteur pour ces pays après 60 ans de batailles sans fin pour la défense de leurs droits inaliénables reconnus internationalement. Cependant, les négociations seront aussi longues que difficiles comme celles des trois conférences des Nations Unies en la matière. Des problèmes nouveaux touchant le milieu marin s'aggravent et nécessitent des solutions urgentes inexistantes ou dépassées dans la Convention actuelle sur le droit de la mer, laquelle n'est par ailleurs appliquée que partiellement[22]. C'est la raison pour laquelle la nouvelle Conférence devra voir le jour aussi rapidement que possible, et les Etats participants devront tenir compte pour une fois des intérêts de l'humanité dans son ensemble et des hommes et peuples de plus en plus pauvres, qui ne peuvent attendre leur salut que d'une résolution planétaire, loin des seules préoccupations égoïstes de certains.

C'est là que résident à la fois l'espoir et l'espérance des pays sans littoral maritime.

---

21   Conférence précédée par la participation de ces pays à la treizième Conférence des Nations Unies sur le commerce et le développement en 2011, et par la réunion d'Almaty en 2012 sous l'égide de l'Organisation Mondiale du Commerce.

22   Sur l'ensemble des questions relatives au droit de la mer, on peut consulter utilement J.-P. Pancracio, *Droit de la mer*, Paris, Dalloz, 2010, 520 p.

Considérations actuelles sur la méthode de délimitation maritime devant la Cour internationale de Justice. De charybde en scylla ?

Maurice Kamto

Ceci n'est pas un discours de la méthode ; c'est, plus modestement, un discours sur la méthode : celle de la Cour internationale de Justice en matière de délimitation maritime. Nul n'ignore l'importante contribution du dédicataire de la présente contribution au droit de la mer : à son élaboration au cours des négociations sans précédent de la IIIe Conférence des Nations Unies sur le droit de la mer comme à son éclairage doctrinal sur divers aspects de cette matière. Jeter un regard sur la question complexe de la méthode de délimitation maritime devant la Cour internationale de Justice pour lui rendre un hommage mérité, ne m'a pas paru incongru.

La tâche de la Cour en la matière n'est pas facile, car la délimitation consiste en l'application d'une méthode ou d'une combinaison de méthodes techniques prévues dans un texte juridique particulier ou en droit international en général, en vue de la détermination des espaces maritimes respectifs de deux ou plusieurs Etats. Elle mêle considérations juridiques et données géographiques et factuelles.

La Cour a été vivement critiquée dans la passé sur sa méthode, ou plutôt sur son manque de méthode en matière de délimitation maritime. Cette critique semble avoir influencé significativement l'évolution de sa jurisprudence en la matière. Au fil de sa riche jurisprudence, elle a changé de cap tout en revendiquant la continuité. D'aucuns diront qu'elle a affiné sa méthode. Tout montre aujourd'hui qu'elle en a changé. L'exercice de composition a progressivement cédé la place à une construction géométrique structurée en phases. La Cour croit désormais avoir trouvé, enfin, une méthode satisfaisante de délimitation maritime. Elle semble s'y tenir d'autant plus fermement qu'elle est suivie en la matière par d'autres juridictions internationales. Pour autant, la méthode qui prévaut aujourd'hui devant elle est-elle vraiment en accord avec la lettre et l'esprit du droit de la délimitation maritime telle qu'il se dégage de sa jurisprudence de la seconde moitié du XXe siècle, consacrée par la Convention des Nations Unies sur le Droit de la Mer[1] (CNUDM) ?

---

1 Nations Unies, *Recueil des traités*, vol. 1834, p. 3.

La présente réflexion se propose de montrer que la méthode de délimitation mise en œuvre par la Cour pendant près d'une quinzaine d'années après 1969 – qui manquait peut-être la rigidité technique rassurante pour l'esprit mais permettait de rechercher et sans doute d'obtenir des solutions équitables pour les parties au litige – a été abandonnée au profit d'une méthode postulée rigoureuse et objective, mais qui dans nombre des cas n'a pas permis d'atteindre un résultat juste, parce qu'équitable.

La quête tâtonnante d'une méthode de délimitation par la Cour (I) l'a conduit à établir une démarche par étapes dont le point de départ – et parfois d'arrivée – semble, en toutes circonstances, l'équidistance (médiane). En vérité, on a perdu de vue qu'en la matière il existe une pluralité de méthodes (II), celle basée sur l'équidistance n'étant ni la plus pertinente pour tous les cas, ni prioritaire par rapport aux autres méthodes de délimitation maritime.

1 La quête tâtonnante d'une méthode de délimitation par la Cour

En se basant sur l'arrêt emblématique rendu par la Cour le 20 février 1969 en les affaires du *Plateau continental de la mer du Nord*[2], la Cour en est venue à établir une méthode dite de l'« équidistance-circonstances spéciales » ou méthode en deux phases (A).

Progressivement, cette méthode a donné un rôle central à l'équidistance, au point de perdre en chemin l'objectif du résultat équitable que le droit contemporain de la mer assigne à toute opération de délimitation maritime. La Cour s'est efforcée de l'affiner au cours des années récentes, la portant de deux à trois étapes, dans une démarche qui laisse penser qu'elle tient désormais *sa* méthode de délimitation (B).

1.1 L'« équidistance-circonstances spéciales » ou la méthode en deux phases

Le droit contemporain de la délimitation maritime s'est construit par étapes. Aux termes de l'article 12 (1) de la Convention du 29 avril 1958 sur la mer territoriale et la zone contigüe[3], la délimitation maritime entre deux Etats dont les côtes se font face ou sont limitrophes suit, sauf accord contraire entre ces Etats,

---

[2] Affaire du *Plateau continental de la mer du Nord* (*République fédérale d'Allemagne/Danemark ; République fédérale d'Allemagne/Pays-Bas*), arrêt, CIJ Recueil 1969, p. 3.

[3] Nations Unies, *Recueil des traités*, vol. 516, p. 205.

> la ligne médiane dont tous les points sont équidistants des points les plus proches des lignes de base à partir desquelles est mesurée la largeur de la mer territoriale de chacun des deux Etats. Les dispositions du présent paragraphe ne s'appliquent cependant pas dans le cas où, à raison de titres historiques ou d'autres circonstances spéciales, il est nécessaire de délimiter la mer territoriale des deux Etats autrement qu'il n'est prévu dans ces dispositions.

Cette méthode dite de l'« équidistance-circonstance spéciales » est restée inchangée depuis lors : elle a survécu lors de la IIIe Conférence des Nations Unies sur le droit de la mer et a été maintenue dans la jurisprudence de la Cour à ce jour.

Il en va différemment de la méthode de délimitation du plateau continental. Dans la Convention de Genève du 29 avril 1958 sur le plateau continental[4], la règle en la matière était l'équidistance stricte. Les deux premiers paragraphes de l'article 6 de cette Convention disposaient en ce sens que:

> 1. Dans le cas où un même plateau continental est adjacent aux territoires de deux ou plusieurs Etats dont les côtes se font face, la délimitation du plateau continental entre ces Etats est déterminée par accord entre ces Etats. A défaut d'accord, et à moins que des circonstances spéciales ne justifient une autre délimitation, celle-ci est constituée par la ligne médiane dont tous les points sont équidistants des points les plus proches des lignes de base à partir desquelles est mesurée la largeur de la mer territoriale de chacun de ces Etats.
>
> 2. Dans le cas où même le plateau continental est adjacent aux territoires de deux Etats limitrophes, la délimitation du plateau continental est déterminée par accord entre ces Etats. A défaut d'accord, et à moins que des circonstances spéciales ne justifient une autre délimitation, celle-ci s'opère par application du principe de l'équidistance des points les plus proches des lignes de base à partir desquelles est mesurée la largeur de la mer territoriale de chacun de ces Etats.

Puis est arrivé l'arrêt de 1969 en les affaires du *Plateau continental de la mer du Nord* qui a marqué d'une pierre blanche l'évolution en la matière : il met l'accent sur la méthode de l'équidistance-circonstances spéciales et introduit, comme on le verra dans la seconde partie de la présente contribution, l'idée majeure selon laquelle la délimitation doit aboutir à un résultat équitable. Si la

---

4 Nations Unies, *Recueil des traités*, vol. 499, p. 313.

Cour a souligné les avantages de la méthode de l'équidistance dans les cas où son application permet d'aboutir à une solution équitable, en revanche elle a jugé qu'aucune règle de droit international coutumier n'imposait l'équidistance comme méthode de délimitation du plateau continental ente des Etats limitrophes[5]. Il s'agit d'un tournant dans le droit de la délimitation maritime. Cette approche, suivie par le Tribunal arbitral constitué en l'affaire du *Plateau continental (Royaume-Uni/France)* sera codifiée dans la Convention des Nations Unies sur le droit de la mer et donnera lieu à une riche jurisprudence, tant devant la Cour que devant les juridictions arbitrales.

Ainsi, dans l'arrêt rendu le 24 février 1982 en l'affaire du *Plateau continental (Tunisie/Libye)*[6], la Cour « croit devoir formuler quelques observations au sujet de l'équidistance ». Restant résolument dans le sillage de l'arrêt rendu dans les affaires du *Plateau continental de la mer du Nord*, elle rappelle que dans ces affaires qui concernaient aussi des Etats limitrophes, « la Cour a jugé qu'aucune règle obligatoire de droit coutumier n'imposait l'équidistance comme méthode de délimitation du plateau continental (*CIJ Recueil 1969*, p. 46, par. 83, p. 53, par. 101) »[7]. Puis, elle observe que si, postérieurement à cet l'arrêt de 1969, la pratique des Etats, telle qu'elle se dégage des traités de délimitation du plateau continental, « atteste que la méthode d'équidistance a été employée dans un certain nombre de cas », elle montre aussi, cependant, « que les Etats peuvent l'écarter et qu'ils ont fait appel à d'autres critères de délimitation chaque fois que cela leur a paru préférable pour aboutir à un accord. Une solution peut consister à combiner une ligne d'équidistance dans certaines parties de la zone avec une ligne différente dans d'autres parties, en fonction des circonstances pertinentes »[8]. Elle ajoute dans le même paragraphe de son arrêt que de la pratique illustrée par les traités, ainsi que de l'historique de l'article 83 du projet de Convention sur le droit de la mer, il y a lieu de « conclure que l'équidistance est applicable si elle conduit à une solution équitable ; sinon il y a lieu d'avoir recours à d'autres méthodes ». Il convient de rappeler que dans l'espèce en question, les deux Parties avaient rejeté l'équidistance : la Tunisie, qui avait d'abord défendu une délimitation fondée sur cette méthode, avait soutenu dans son mémoire que son application « serait inéquitable pour elle », et la Libye avait formellement conclu qu'en l'espèce considérée, « la méthode de l'équidistance aboutirait à une délimitation inéquitable »[9].

---

5 Ibid., p. 46, par. 83; p. 53, par. 101.
6 Affaire du *Plateau continental (Tunisie/Libye)*, arrêt, CIJ Recueil 1982, p. 18.
7 Ibid., p. 79, par. 109.
8 Ibid.
9 Ibid., p. 79, par. 110.

Dans l'affaire du *Plateau continental (Tunisie/Libye)*, la Cour n'a décrit la méthode en deux étapes, « équidistance-circonstances spéciales », que pour l'écarter, en relativisant, comme dans son arrêt de 1969[10], le caractère normatif de la méthode de l'équidistance en raison du rôle que joue la notion de « circonstances spéciales » par rapport à cette méthode. En effet, la Cour n'a pas estimé qu'en l'espèce

> il lui incomb[ait] d'examiner en premier lieu les effets que pourrait avoir une délimitation selon la méthode de l'équidistance, et de ne rejeter celle-ci au bénéfice d'une autre méthode que si les résultats d'une ligne d'équidistance lui paraissaient inéquitables. Pour pouvoir conclure en faveur d'une délimitation reposant sur une ligne d'équidistance, il lui faudrait partir de considérations tirées d'une évaluation et d'une pondération de toutes les circonstances pertinentes, l'équidistance n'étant pas à ses yeux un principe juridique obligatoire ni une méthode qui serait en quelle que sorte privilégiée par rapport à d'autres [11].

Au contraire, la Cour s'est estimée tenue de statuer en l'espèce sur la base des principes équitables qui font « partie intégrante du droit international », et qu'il ne faudrait pas confondre avec le règlement d'un litige *ex aequo et bono*. L'expression *« principes équitables »*, ne saurait, dit la Cour, « être interprétée dans l'abstrait; elle renvoie aux principes et règles permettant d'aboutir à un résultat équitable ». Les principes en question doivent donc être choisis « en fonction de leur adéquation avec un résultat équitable »[12], sachant que « [c]e qui est raisonnable et équitable dans un cas donné dépend forcément des circonstances, et à coup sûr il est virtuellement impossible, dans une délimitation, d'aboutir à une solution équitable en méconnaissant les circonstances propres à la région »[13].

La Cour eut l'occasion de réaffirmer sa position à ce sujet, avec une particulière netteté dans l'affaire de la *Délimitation du plateau continental dans la région du Golfe du Maine (Canada/Etats-Unis d'Amérique)*. Répondant à l'argument du Canada qui, s'appuyant sur un « prétendu principe juridique » qualifié tantôt d'« adjacence », tantôt de « proximité », tantôt et surtout de « distance », et par lequel la Partie en question en était arrivée à affirmer la reconnaissance par le droit international d'une règle d'attribution de certaines

---

10   *CIJ Recueil 1969*, p. 41-42, par. 72.
11   *CIJ Recueil 1982*, p. 79 par. 110.
12   Ibid., p. 59, par. 71.
13   Ibid., p. 60, par. 72; voir aussi *CIJ Recueil 1969*, p. 46-47 et 48-49, par. 85 et 88.

zones marines ou sous-marines litigieuses à l'une ou l'autre Partie, la Chambre de la Cour observa qu'il n'y avait là finalement « qu'un nouvel effort de faire apparaître l'idée, non pas de la « distance », mais de l'« équidistance », comme étant sanctionnée par le droit international coutumier lui-même [...]. C'est une tentative de plus pour faire de l'équidistance une véritable règle de droit que le droit international coutumier aurait exprimée, tout en la tempérant par la prise en compte des circonstances spéciales, donc autre chose que ce qu'elle est en réalité, à savoir une méthode pratique aux fins de la délimitation »[14]. La Cour ne nie pas que l'application de cette méthode ait pu rendre service dans bien des situations concrètes, « qu'elle soit une méthode pratique » dont une Convention comme celle de 1958 a prévu et rendu obligatoire l'utilisation dans certaines conditions. Et de poursuivre :

> Il n'empêche qu'une telle notion, telle que la jurisprudence internationale l'a mise en évidence, n'est pas pour autant devenue une règle de droit international général, une norme découlant logiquement d'un principe juridiquement obligatoire du droit international coutumier et que ce dernier ne l'a d'ailleurs pas non plus adoptée au simple titre d'une méthode prioritaire ou préférable. La Chambre ne saurait mieux exprimer sa pensée à ce sujet qu'en rappelant le commentaire fait par la Cour, toujours dans son arrêt du 20 février 1969, à propose de la thèse analogue avancée par le Danemark [...] (*CIJ Recueil 1969, p. 33, par. 49*)[15].

Au terme de ses analyses, la Chambre de la Cour affirme:

> Les conclusions auxquelles la Chambre est parvenue l'ont amenée à constater que ce n'est pas dans le droit international coutumier qu'il faut rechercher d'éventuelles règles prescrivant spécifiquement l'application de tel ou tel critère équitable ou l'utilisation de telle ou telle méthode pratique aux fins d'une délimitation comme celle qui est requise dans le cas d'espèce. Le droit international coutumier, on l'a vu, se borne en général à l'application de critères équitables et l'utilisation de méthodes pratiques propre à traduire concrètement ces critères.

Ce passage de l'arrêt pourrait être interprété dans les deux sens : d'une part, pour dire qu'aucune méthode de délimitation n'étant prescrite par le droit

---

14 Affaire de la *Délimitation du plateau continental dans la région du Golfe du Maine (Canada/ Etats-Unis d'Amérique)*, arrêt, *CIJ Recueil 1984*, p. 246, par. 104 et 106.
15 Ibid., p. 297, par. 107.

international coutumier, l'arrêt n'écarte pas, par principe, la méthode d'équidistance qui, dès lors, pourrait s'appliquer comme n'importe quelle autre méthode pratique de délimitation ; d'autre part, que dès lors, cette méthode ne saurait s'imposer dans tous les cas, et n'est certainement pas une méthode privilégiée ou prioritaire. Mais l'arrêt de la Chambre a levé toute équivoque à ce sujet. Certes, reconnaît-elle, certaines méthodes sont tout au plus, « d'application plus facile » (c'est le cas de la méthode de l'équidistance) et « à cause de leur fonctionnement quasi mécanique, elles risquent moins de laisser subsister des doutes et d'entraîner des contestations. Cela explique, dans une certaine mesure, que l'on ait eu plus souvent recours à elles, ou que dans nombre de cas on l'ait prise en considération. Mais, en toute hypothèse, il n'y a pas de méthode qui porte en soi la marque d'une plus grande justice ni d'une plus grande utilité pratique »[16]. La rigoureuse technicité dont on a souvent paré la méthode de l'équidistance ne serait qu'un leurre de légitimation de cette méthode.

C'est dans l'arrêt rendu le 3 juin 1985 en l'affaire du *Plateau continental (Libye/Malte)* que la méthode en deux étapes, contenue implicitement dans la méthode de l'équidistance-circonstances spéciales, est déclinée expressément. La Cour, après avoir indiqué qu'en l'espèce « l'effet équitable d'une ligne d'équidistance dépend de la précaution que l'on aura prise d'éliminer l'effet exagéré de certains îlots, rochers ou légers saillants des côtes pour reprendre les termes utilisés par la Cour dans [...] son arrêt de 1969 », a établi une telle ligne médiane provisoire, puis s'est attelée à rechercher « si d'autres considérations, y compris le facteur de proportionnalité, doivent l'amener à ajuster cette ligne »[17]. Elle explique sa méthode ainsi qu'il suit:

> En retenant ainsi, dans la première étape de l'opération de délimitation, la ligne médiane comme ligne provisoire, la Cour ne peut ignorer que la méthode de l'équidistance n'a jamais été considérée comme applicable telle qu'elle en toutes circonstances, fût-ce entre côtes se faisant face[18].

La Cour rappelle à cet égard aussi bien les dispositions de l'article 6 de la Convention sur le plateau continental que celles de l'article 83 par. 1 de la

---

16 Ibid., p. 315, par. 162 ; voir aussi affaire de la *Délimitation de la frontière maritime (Guinée/ Guinée Bissau)* Sentence du 14 février 1985, par. 89, *Recueil des sentences arbitrales*, vol. XIX, p. 149-196.

17 Affaire du *Plateau continental (Jamahiriya Arabe Libyenne / Malte)*, arrêt, CIJ Recueil 1985, p. 48, par. 64.

18 Ibid., p. 48, par. 65.

Convention de Montego Bay, ainsi que la pratique des Etats telle que l'expriment les accords de délimitation, et conclut :

> Il n'est donc pas douteux que, pour aboutir à une résultat équitable, lorsque la ligne d'équidistance représente à première vue la méthode appropriée, toutes les circonstances pertinentes doivent être examinées car, dans l'appréciation de l'équité, elles peuvent être d'un poids tel que leur prise en compte se justifie et impose un ajustement de la ligne d'équidistance[19].

L'arrêt rendu le 14 juin 1993 en l'affaire de la *Délimitation maritime dans la région située entre le Groenland et Jan Mayen (Danemark c. Norvège)*[20] se situe dans le droit fil de cette conception correctrice de l'équité inspirée par la règle de l'équidistance-circonstances spéciales. On l'a souvent considérée comme étant le point de départ de la méthode en deux étapes. Sans doute à tort, comme on vient de le voir avec l'affaire *Libye/Malte*.

En effet, dans l'affaire *Jan Mayen*, la Cour trace dans un premier temps une ligne médiane provisoire, puis examine dans un second temps si les circonstances spéciales/pertinentes de l'espèce lui permettent d'ajuster ou de déplacer la ligne provisoire. Elle est arrivée

> à la conclusion que la médiane tracé à titre provisoire, employée comme point de départ pour la délimitation du plateau continental et des zones de pêche, doit être ajustée ou déplacée de manière à attribuer au Danemark une plus grande partie des espaces maritimes. En ce qui concerne le plateau continental, rien n'exige que la ligne soit déplacée vers l'est de façon égale sur toute sa longueur ; en effet si d'autres considérations militaient en faveur d'une autre forme d'ajustement, la Cour, en adoptant cette solution, resterait dans la limite du pouvoir discrétionnaire que lui confère la nécessité de parvenir à un résultat équitable[21].

Dans l'affaire de la *Délimitation maritime et questions territoriales entre Qatar c. Bahreïn*, la Cour a fait application du droit international coutumier à la délimitation de la frontière maritime entre les Parties, ni Bahreïn ni Qatar n'étant Parties aux Conventions de Genève sur le droit de la mer du 29 avril 1958, et

---

19   Ibid.
20   CIJ *Recueil 1993*, p. 38.
21   Affaire de la *Délimitation maritime dans la région située entre le Groenland et Jan Mayen (Danemark c. Norvège)*, arrêt, CIJ *Recueil 1993*, p. 79, par. 90.

Bahreïn ayant ratifié la Convention des Nations Unies sur le droit de la mer du 10 décembre 1982, mais Qatar l'ayant seulement signée. Aux termes de la formule bahreïnite, adoptée en décembre 1990, les Parties avaient prié la Cour « de tracer une limite maritime unique entre leurs zones maritimes respectives, comprenant les fonds marins, le sous-sol et les eaux surjacentes ».

Comme l'a relevé la Chambre constituée par la Cour dans l'affaire du *Golfe du Maine*, la détermination d'une ligne unique pour les différents objets de la délimitation « ne saurait être effectuée que par l'application d'un critère ou d'une combinaison de critères qui ne favorise pas l'un de ces objets au détriment de l'autre et soit en même temps susceptible de convenir également à une division de chacun d'eux »[22]. Selon la Cour, la délimitation des mers territoriales ne soulève pas de problèmes de ce genre car les droits de l'Etat côtier dans la zone concernée ne sont pas fonctionnels mais territoriaux et impliquent souveraineté sur le fond de la mer, les eaux surjacentes et l'espace aérien surjacent. Pour s'acquitter de cet aspect de sa tâche en pareil cas, la Cour doit « appliquer d'abord et avant tout les principes et règles du droit international coutumier qui ont trait à la délimitation de la mer territoriale, sans oublier que sa tâche ultime consiste à tracer une limite maritime unique qui soit valable aussi à d'autres fins »[23].

La Cour rappelle qu'il est souvent fait référence à l'article 15 de la CNUDM de 1982, qui reprend pratiquement à l'identique le paragraphe 1 de l'article 12 de la Convention de 1958 sur la mer territoriale et la zone contiguë, comme à la règle « équidistance/circonstances spéciales ». Selon elle :

> La méthode la plus logique et la plus largement pratiquée consiste à tracer d'abord à titre provisoire une ligne d'équidistance et à examiner ensuite si cette ligne doit être ajustée pour tenir compte de l'existence de circonstances spéciales. Une fois qu'elle aura délimité sur cette base les mers territoriales des Parties, la Cour déterminera quels sont les règles et principes du droit coutumier à appliquer pour la délimitation de leurs plateaux continentaux et de leurs zones économiques exclusives ou de leurs zones de pêche. La Cour décidera alors si la méthode à retenir pour opérer cette délimitation est similaire à celle qui vient d'être décrite ou si elle est différente[24].

---

22   Affaire de la *Délimitation du plateau continental dans la région du Golfe du Maine, op. cit.*, note 14, p. 327, par. 194.
23   Affaire de la *Délimitation maritime et questions territoriales (Qatar c. Bahreïn)*, fond, arrêt, CIJ Recueil 2001, p. 93, par. 174.
24   Ibid., p. 94, par. 176.

Comme on le voit, et bien qu'il lui fut demandé de tracer une ligne unique, la Cour distingue clairement entre la méthode de délimitation de la mer territoriale et celle applicable à la délimitation du plateau continental, de la ZEE et de la zone de pêche, distinction importante que l'on ne retrouve pas nécessairement dans d'autres affaires, quand est en jeu la délimitation aussi bien de la mer territoriale que du plateau continental. Au terme de l'application de cette méthode de délimitation en deux étapes, et après avoir examiné s'il existe des motifs « qui pourraient rendre nécessaire un ajustement de la ligne d'équidistance afin de parvenir à une solution équitable », la Cour a adopté une ligne d'équidistance ajustée pour délimiter la mer territoriale ; et dans la zone du plateau continental elle a estimé que « [d]ans les circonstances de l'espèce, des considérations d'équité exigent de ne pas donner d'effet à Fasht al Jarim, formation maritime située dans la mer territoriale de Bahreïn, aux fins de la détermination de la ligne de délimitation dans le secteur nord. Elle a décidé par conséquent que la limite maritime unique dans ce secteur sera constituée en premier lieu par une ligne qui, [...] rejoindra la ligne d'équidistance ajustée pour tenir compte de l'absence d'effet reconnu à Fasht al Jarim », et de là, elle « suivra ensuite cette ligne d'équidistance ajustée jusqu'à ce qu'elle rencontre la ligne de délimitation des zones maritimes respectives de l'Iran d'une part et de Bahreïn et de Qatar de l'autre »[25].

Dans l'affaire de la *Frontière terrestre et maritime entre le Cameroun et la Nigeria*, la Cour a continué à citer toute sa jurisprudence antérieure en matière de délimitation, comme si elle avait maintenu une continuité jurisprudentielle. Or, il n'en est rien : elle a appliqué l'équidistance pure, non ajustée ni corrigée, encore moins déplacée ; la Cour décide en effet que « la ligne d'équidistance aboutit à un résultat équitable aux fins de la délimitation du secteur dans lequel la Cour a compétence pour se prononcer »[26]. Or, dans les circonstances de l'espèce, la concavité des côtes et la présence de l'île de Bioko appartenant à la Guinée équatoriale, en particulier, étaient de nature à produire un « effet d'amputation » du prolongement naturel des côtes camerounaises vers le large, dans la mesure où la projection de la ligne d'équidistance se rabat rapidement vers les côtes de l'île en question[27].

---

25   Ibid., p. 115, par. 249.
26   Affaire de la *Frontière terrestre et maritime entre le Cameroun et la Nigeria (Cameroun c. Nigéria ; Guinée Equatoriale (intervenant))*, arrêt, CIJ Recueil 2002, p. 448, par. 306.
27   Voir sur ce point le résumé des arguments du Cameroun et l'abondante jurisprudence tant de la Cour qu'arbitrale citée pour les étayer, dans l'arrêt du 10 octobre 2002, Ibid., p. 431-434, par. 269-275.

Il ne semble cependant pas que la méthode en deux étapes ait donné pleine satisfaction à la Cour. En effet, elle a continué à affiner cette méthode dans laquelle l'équidistance (médiane) joue un rôle crucial en tant que point de départ invariable de la délimitation. La nouvelle méthode de la Cour n'est plus en deux étapes, mais en trois.

1.2 *Eureka ! : la méthode en trois phases*

La nouvelle méthode de délimitation maritime devant la Cour n'a pas échappé aux commentateurs de sa jurisprudence et aux conseils qui plaident devant elle. Mais, on ne s'est pas penché sur les origines de cette évolution. Alors que l'on minimise souvent l'influence de la doctrine contemporaine sur la jurisprudence internationale, on doit l'évolution jurisprudentielle observée en matière de délimitation maritime à une influence doctrinale indéniable (1). A travers sa méthode actuelle en trois étapes, la Cour a voulu donner le change à une critique doctrinale, en campant une approche de la délimitation qui lui paraît s'imposer, parce qu'elle est technique et rigoureuse, voire scientifique (2).

1.2.1 L'influence d'une doctrine sur l'évolution de la méthode de délimitation de la Cour

Dans un ouvrage[28] qui a fait date, et qui faisait suite à ses plaidoiries dans l'affaire de la *Délimitation du plateau continental dans la région du Golfe du Maine (Canada/ Etats-Unis)*[29], le professeur Prosper Weil posait le diagnostic de la jurisprudence de la Cour en matière de délimitation maritime ainsi qu'il suit :

> Ayant choisi la voie glorieuse mais difficile de la balance entre la norme générale d'application automatique et la norme équitable d'application modulée, ayant refusé également tout *diktat* de la technique, la jurisprudence n'a pu échapper à une certaine dissonance entre les développements proprement juridiques, donc généraux par nature, de ses décisions et la solution concrète apportée au problème spécifique de chaque affaire. Entre la première partie d'un arrêt, qui énonce les principes et règles de droit international applicables, et la seconde, où se trouve exposée, généralement de façon brève, la délimitation décidée dans le cas

---

[28] P. Weil, *Perspectives du droit de la délimitation maritime*, Paris, Pedone, 1988 ; traduit en anglais sous le titre *The Law of Maritime Delimitation – Reflexions*, Cambridge, Grotius Publications Limited, 1989.

[29] Arrêt du 12 octobre 1984, *op. cit.*, note 14.

concret, le lien logique n'apparaît pas toujours avec évidence, et l'on se défend mal parfois d'une impression de non *sequitur*[30].

Ce « hiatus, regrettable », était sans doute le signe de l'« indétermination » du droit de la délimitation maritime relevé par les juges Ruda, Bedjaoui et Jiménez de Aréchaga dans leur opinion conjointe en l'affaire du *Plateau continental (Libye/Malte)*. Les trois juges y déclaraient que l'on attend de la Cour qu'elle s'en tienne au droit, qu'elle ne saurait renoncer à une solution de partage égal qu'imposent des circonstances spéciales sans renoncer au droit ; mais ils opposaient aussi l'« écrasante responsabilité » du juge en matière de délimitation à ses « modestes moyens pour l'assumer », lui qui « ne sait comment échapper à la frustrante tyrannie d'un certain subjectivisme prétorien », alors même que la marge d'indétermination qui cause celui-ci trouve sa source dans un droit encore neuf, pétri d'équité, c'est-à-dire d'une notion certes juridique et éminente, mais inévitablement mesurable à « l'aune humaine ». Les plus belles dissertations juridiques sur l'équité ne parviendront pas à éliminer une part peut-être irréductible de ce subjectivisme prétorien »[31].

Ce constat dressé de l'intérieur même de la Cour a amené M. Weil à faire le point sur certains aspects clés du droit de la délimitation maritime, « dans l'espoir de discerner dans le brouillard de l'avenir les voies sur lesquelles l'évolution est susceptible de s'engager »[32]. En fait de voie d'avenir, il entonna un hymne à l'équidistance. Selon lui, la « cassure » du régime unique de délimitation de la mer territoriale et du plateau continental ainsi que du « rôle de l'équidistance dans l'opération de délimitation maritime » eut lieu dans l'arrêt de 1969 en les affaires du *Plateau continental de la mer du Nord*, lorsque la Cour « a cru devoir [...] donner le signal de la réparation »[33]. Car, « si la Cour ne voit pas d'objection à ce que la règle équidistance-circonstances spéciales régisse la délimitation de la mer territoriale, elle s'oppose à ce que la règle devienne la norme de droit coutumier gouvernant la délimitation de plateau continental »[34]. Comme le relève encore l'auteur, la « rupture prononcée en 1969 sera confirmée par la jurisprudence ultérieure, et les explications invoquées resteront inchangées : la distinction entre délimitation de courte distance et délimitation de longue distance, d'un côté ; la différence entre la

---

30 Ibid., p. 19.
31 Affaire du *Plateau continental (Jamahiriya Arabe Libyenne/Malte)*, opinion conjointe à l'arrêt du 3 juin 1985, CIJ *Recueil 1985*, p. 90, par. 37.
32 Weil, *op. cit.*, note 28, p. 20-21.
33 Ibid., p. 151.
34 Ibid. (voir les arguments de la Cour dans CIJ *Recueil 1969, par. 59*).

juridiction strictement polyvalente de la mer territoriale et la juridiction strictement fonctionnelle du plateau continental, de l'autre »[35]. Une des raisons de la critique de la méthode fondée sur les principes équitables était, comme le releva la Cour dans l'arrêt rendu le 24 février 1982 en l'affaire du *Tunisie/Libye*, que « les principes et règles énoncés et les facteurs indiqués par la Cour en 1969 peuvent donner des résultats très différents selon la manière dont ces principes et ces règles sont interprétés et appliqués et selon le poids relatif attribué à chaque facteur pour arrêter un mode de délimitation »[36].

Après les critiques ainsi articulées, M. Weil annonçait, non seulement « que la faille sera comblée un jour prochain et que le droit de la délimitation maritime, commun à l'origine à la mer territoriale et au plateau continental et dont le bloc a été désintégré par l'évolution ultérieure, retrouvera son unité » ; mais aussi que les « signes avant-coureurs de cette réunification se manifestent d'ores et déjà, de façon encore discrète certes, mais trop nombreux pour que l'on n'y prête pas attention »[37]. Il trouvait ces signes avant-coureurs dans les sentences arbitrales rendues dans l'affaire du *Canal de Beagle* et dans la Délimitation maritime entre la *Guinée/Guinée Bissau*.

Traçant la voie pour « une remise en ordre », P. Weil prescrit une méthode sous une forme digne d'un commandement biblique : « La ligne de départ sera toujours une ligne d'équidistance ; la ligne d'arrivée ne le sera pas forcément »[38]. Voici comment il résume la méthode qu'il préconise et qui a depuis lors été adoptée par la Cour :

> On essaie d'abord la méthode de l'équidistance, non pas seulement parce qu'elle est d'une application facile et objective et qu'elle peut être regardée *prima facie* comme équitable puisqu'elle divise à peu près également les zones de chevauchement des projections des deux côtes, mais surtout parce qu'elle reflète les conceptions juridiques qui sont à la base du titre des Etats sur les espaces marins et qu'elle traduit la conception moderne (*sic*)[39] de la délimitation maritime. Cela fait, on confronte la ligne d'équidistance aux circonstances pertinentes de l'espèce de manière à s'assurer

---

35   Ibid. p. 152 (voir à ce sujet, CIJ *Recueil 1982*, p. 82, par. 115 ; CIJ *Recueil 1984*, p. 302, par. 120 ; p. 314, par. 160 et p. 314-315, par. 161).

36   Affaire du *Plateau continental (Tunisie/Libye), op. cit.*, note 6, p. 44, par. 38.

37   Ibid., p. 153.

38   Ibid., p. 216.

39   On ne voit pas ce qui ferait la modernité d'une telle conception sachant que l'équidistance était déjà contenue dans les Conventions de 1958 avant d'être abandonnée un moment par la jurisprudence postérieure.

> que dans le cas concret elle ne conduit pas à un résultat inéquitable ou déraisonnable; selon le cas, on conservera la ligne comme frontière définitive, ou bien on l'aménagera[40].

Selon lui:

> Grâce à cette structure, l'opération de délimitation tient la balance entre la rigueur du droit et la flexibilité de l'équité, entre le général et le particulier. En ancrant la délimitation dans la précision invariable du *titre*, elle lui confère la généralité qui lui évite l'écueil du subjectivisme. En lui assurant une suffisante individualisation, elle évite l'écueil de l'automatisme aveugle et satisfait aux exigences de l'équité[41].

Séduisant plaidoyer qui suscite cependant d'importantes interrogations. Quel est le titre dans lequel on ancrerait dès le départ l'opération de délimitation ? Il me semble que si la délimitation n'a pas été faite par voie d'accord entre les Etats concernés, et que le juge est saisi de la question, le titre ne peut être que jurisprudentiel ; ce sera en l'occurrence la décision de délimitation rendue par le juge. Si cette manière de comprendre les choses est correcte, alors l'équidistance ne peut constituer un titre susceptible, éventuellement, d'être « aménagé » à la faveur de la prise en compte des circonstances pertinentes. L'équidistance n'est qu'un élément, un outil utilisable aux fins de la délimitation et non pas un titre juridique ; car si tel était le cas, il ne pourrait être « aménagé », il s'imposerait *ne varietur*.

L'argument de M. Weil selon lequel l'équidistance serait « équitable » *prima facie* et constituerait le point de départ inéluctable de la délimitation maritime manque donc de base juridique hors l'hypothèse d'une délimitation par voie d'accord. Il traduit une préférence méthodologique et non pas une règle de droit de la délimitation maritime établie par la CNUDM ou par une pratique généralement acceptée comme étant le droit. Habillé de l'apparence de technicité, de rigueur et d'objectivité, cet argument est cependant séduisant et a séduit la Cour : il a eu une influence indéniable sur sa jurisprudence subséquente et, au-delà, sur la jurisprudence du Tribunal international du droit de la mer (TIDM) et celle des instance arbitrales en matière de délimitation maritime.

En effet, la Cour a appliqué la méthode en deux puis en trois étapes, basée sur l'équidistance-circonstances spéciales donnant lieu à une tracé suivant une ligne d'équidistance « ajustée » – ou théoriquement « corrigée » ou

---

40   Weil, *op. cit.*, note 28, p. 300-301.
41   Ibid., p. 301 (nos italiques).

« déplacée » -, dans tous ses arrêts en matière de délimitation maritime rendus entre la parution de l'ouvrage de M. Weil en 1988 et à ce jour, à l'exception notable de son arrêt rendu en 2007, sur lequel on reviendra.

Pour sa part, le TIDM a suivi cette méthode dans son arrêt rendu le 14 mars 2012 dans la toute première affaire de délimitation[42] dont il a été saisi, en s'appuyant du reste sur la jurisprudence de la Cour dont les Parties ont usé abondamment. Le Tribunal a commencé par la construction d'une « ligne d'équidistance provisoire à partir de points de base situés sur les côtes des Parties »[43]. Puis, bien que les Parties fussent en désaccord sur la question de circonstances pertinentes, il a examiné les facteurs susceptibles d'être considérés comme tels en l'espèce, en l'occurrence la concavité des côtes avec risque d'effet d'amputation, la présence d'une île (île de Saint Martin), le système détritique du Bengale, et s'est considéré fondé au final « à procéder à un ajustement de la ligne d'équidistance provisoire en traçant une ligne géodésique suivant un azimut déterminé »[44]. Et de préciser aussitôt qu'à son avis, « aucun ajustement plausible de la ligne d'équidistance provisoire ne pourrait s'écarter sensiblement d'une ligne géodésique suivant un azimut initial de 215 », car « [m]odifier plus largement l'angle de cet azimut aurait pour effet d'amputer les projections côtières de l'une ou l'autre des Parties. Un déplacement de l'azimut vers le nord-ouest engendrerait une ligne qui ne remédierait pas suffisamment à l'effet d'amputation produit par la ligne d'équidistance provisoire sur la projection, vers le sud, de la côte du Bangladesh vers le large, tandis qu'un déplacement dans le sens opposé produirait un effet d'amputation sur la projection de la côte du Myanmar vers le large »[45].

S'agissant de la jurisprudence arbitrale, on signalera, pour s'en tenir à un cas récent, la sentence arbitrale rendue le 11 avril 2006 par le tribunal constitué dans le cadre de l'affaire *Barbade/Trinité-et-Tobago*[46].

---

42   *Différend relatif à la délimitation de la frontière maritime entre le Bangladesh et le Myanmar dans le Golfe du Bengale* (*Bangladesh/Myanmar*), Role des affaires N° 16, TIDM, 2012.
43   Ibid., p. 88, par. 271.
44   Ibid., p. 105, par. 324.
45   Ibid.
46   A ce sujet, le tribunal s'est exprimé en ces termes : « The determination of the line of delimitation thus normally follows a two-step approach. First, a provisional line of equidistance is posited as a hypothesis and a practical starting point. While a convenient starting point, equidistance alone will in many circumstances not ensure an equitable result in the light of the peculiarities of each specific case. The second step accordingly requires the examination of this provisional line in the light of relevant circumstances, which are case specific, so as to determine whether it is necessary to adjust the provisional equidistance line in order to achieve an equitable result (*Cameroon v. Nigeria, op. cit.*,

Les variations dans la jurisprudence de la Cour en la matière de délimitation montrent que l'on n'est pas sur une terre ferme. La méthode en trois phases constitue sans doute une nouvelle étape importante dans l'évolution de la jurisprudence de la Cour en la matière, mais on ne saurait dire encore si elle constitue un point d'aboutissement ultime.

1.2.2 La méthode actuelle de délimitation maritime devant la Cour : une méthode en trois phases

La méthode de délimitation appliquée actuellement par la Cour est constituée des trois étapes suivantes : équidistance, ajustement ou correction, test de dis-proportionnalité. Les deux premières étapes reprennent simplement la méthode antérieure d'équidistance-circonstances spéciales, que la jurisprudence de la Cour a traduit par la suite par équidistance « ajustée », « corrigée » ou non. Avec cette méthode en trois étapes, la Cour donne le sentiment d'être parvenue, enfin, à une méthode scientifique, techniquement rigoureuse (a).

Le test de « disproportionnalité » instauré par la Cour comme troisième étape n'est cependant pas sans susciter des interrogations sur son degré de rigueur (b).

1.2.2.1 *Le sentiment de tenir une méthode technique, rigoureuse et objective*

En matière de délimitation maritime, la Cour ne construit plus des tracés à partir d'un raisonnement embrassant toute la réalité factuelle et la complexité de la situation, qu'elle soit géographique ou autre. Elle ne fait plus que de la géométrie, mais de la géométrie souvent simplifiée à l'extrême, pourrait-on dire. En étant un brin caricatural, on dira qu'on a l'impression que devant tout cas de délimitation maritime, la Cour s'arme d'un décimètre et d'un crayon, et cherche invariablement l'équidistance. Elle a fait une trouvaille dont elle ne veut plus se détacher : désormais c'est le règne de l'équidistance (médiane), toute seule ou moyennant un ajustement, généralement le plus limité possible. La Cour semble s'être mise un corset technique là où le droit lui donne, par le principe du « résultat équitable », la latitude de construire des solutions répondant au sentiment de justice et aux attentes des parties.

---

p. 303; Weil, *op. cit.*, p. 223 (1988)). This approach is usually referred to as the « equidistance/relevant circumstances » principle (*Qatar v. Bahrein, op. cit.*, p. 40 ; *Cameroun v. Nigeria, op. cit.*, p. 303). Certainty is thus combined with the need for an equitable result » (Sentence arbitrale du 11 avril 2006, par. 242 ; voir le texte de cette sentence sur : http://legal.un.org/riaa/cases/vol_XXVII/147-251.pdf).

La méthode en trois étapes est apparue clairement pour la première fois dans l'affaire de la *Délimitation maritime dans la mer Noire (Roumanie c. Ukraine)* : la Cour a d'abord construit une ligne d'équidistance provisoire à partir des points de base situés sur les côtes des deux Parties[47] ; ensuite, elle a examiné les circonstances pertinentes, c'est-à-dire s'il existe des facteurs appelant un ajustement ou un déplacement de cette ligne afin de parvenir à un « résultat équitable »[48] ; enfin, elle a procédé à la vérification de l'absence de disproportion marquée entre les longueurs respectives des côtes et les espaces répartis par la ligne d'équidistance provisoire[49] :

> « Enfin, *dit-elle*, la Cour s'assurera, dans une troisième étape, que la ligne (une ligne d'équidistance provisoire ayant ou non été ajustée en fonction des circonstances pertinentes) ne donne pas lieu, en l'état, à un résultat inéquitable du fait d'une disproportion marquée entre le rapport des longueurs respectives des côtes et le rapport des zones maritimes pertinentes attribuées à chaque Etat par ladite ligne [...] ». La vérification finale du caractère équitable du résultat obtenu doit permettre de s'assurer qu'aucune disproportion marquée entre les zones maritimes ne ressort de la comparaison avec le rapport des longueurs des côtes. Cela ne signifie toutefois pas que les zones ainsi attribuées à chaque Etat doivent être proportionnelles aux longueurs des côtes : ainsi que la Cour l'a indiqué, « c'est [...] le partage de la région qui résulte de la délimitation et non l'inverse » (*Délimitation maritime dans la région située entre le Groenland et Jan Mayen (Danemark c. Norvège)*, arrêt, CIJ Recueil 1993, p. 67, par. 64) ». (*Délimitation maritime en mer Noire (Roumanie c. Ukraine)*, arrêt, CIJ Recueil 2009, p. 103, par. 122.)

Cette ligne d'équidistance provisoire a été considérée au final comme permettant de parvenir à un résultat équitable, la Cour ayant jugé que ni les circonstances pertinentes invoquées par les Parties, ni la disproportion entre les longueurs des côtes, ni la conduite des Parties et les concessions pétrolières, ni les considérations des Parties tenant à la sécurité ne lui permettaient d'ajuster cette ligne provisoire[50].

---

47 Affaire de la *Délimitation maritime en mer Noire (Roumanie c. Ukraine)*, arrêt du 3 février 2009, *CIJ Recueil 2009*, p. 111, par. 153 et s.
48 Ibid., p. 112, par. 155 et s.
49 Ibid., p. 129, par. 210 et s.
50 Ibid., p. 130, par. 216.

Cette nouvelle méthode, qui ne diffère de la méthode en deux étapes qu'en ce qu'elle y ajoute désormais l'étape du test de disproportionalité, a été revendiquée et assumée plus explicitement par la Cour dans son arrêt du 19 novembre 2012, sur le fond, en l'affaire du *Différend territorial et maritime (Nicaragua c. Colombie)*. La Cour a rappelé qu'elle ferait application de sa méthode en trois étapes, en renvoyant sur ce point à ses arrêts de 1985 et 2009 rendus respectivement dans l'affaire du *Plateau continental (Libye/Malte)*[51] et dans l'affaire de la *Délimitation maritime en mer Noire (Roumanie c. Ukraine)*[52]. Or, si dans l'arrêt du 3 février 2009, elle indique que les différentes étapes dégagées dans *Libye/Malte* « ont été précisées au cours des dernières décennies »[53], dans cet arrêt *Libye/Malte*, la Cour expose, comme on l'a vu, plutôt une méthode en deux étapes consistant à « effectuer d'abord une délimitation provisoire selon un critère et une méthode visiblement appelés à jouer dans la production du résultat final un rôle important, puis à confronter cette solution provisoire aux exigences découlant d'autres critères pouvant imposer la correction de ce premier résultat » ; et elle procédait alors en application des « principes équitables » dégagés auparavant. C'est dans l'arrêt du 19 novembre 2012 en l'affaire *Nicaragua c. Colombie* qu'elle a non seulement affirmé expressément, pour la première fois, qu'elle applique désormais une méthode en trois étapes, mais également procédé à l'explicitation de cette méthode :

> 191. Dans un premier temps, il s'agit pour la Cour d'établir une ligne de délimitation provisoire entre les territoires respectifs des Parties (y compris leurs territoires insulaires). Elle a recours pour ce faire à des méthodes à la fois objectives sur le plan géométrique et adaptées à la géographie de la zone. Cette tâche consiste à construire une ligne d'équidistance, lorsque les côtes pertinentes sont adjacentes, ou une ligne médiane entre les deux côtes, lorsque celles-ci se font face, à moins que, dans un cas comme dans l'autre, des raisons impérieuses ne le permettent pas (voir *Différend territorial et maritime entre le Nicaragua et le Honduras dans la mer des Caraïbes (Nicaragua c. Honduras)*, arrêt, CIJ Recueil 2007 (II), p. 745, par. 281). L'emploi des termes « ligne médiane » et « ligne d'équidistance » est sans incidence en droit puisque la méthode de délimitation consiste dans chaque cas à tracer une ligne dont chaque point se trouve à égale distance des points les plus proches des deux côtes pertinentes (*Délimitation maritime en mer Noire (Roumanie c. Ukraine)*, arrêt, CIJ Recueil 2009, p. 101,

---

51   Affaire du *Plateau continental (Jamahiriya Arabe Libyenne/Malte)*, *op. cit.*, note 17, p. 46, par. 60.
52   Affaire de la *Délimitation maritime en mer Noire*, *op. cit.*, note 47, p. 101 par. 115-116.
53   *Ibid.*, p. 101 par. 115-116.

par. 116). La ligne est tracée à partir des points les plus pertinents des côtes des deux Etats concernés (ibid., p. 101, par. 116-117).

192. A la deuxième étape, il s'agit pour la Cour de déterminer s'il existe des circonstances pertinentes qui pourraient appeler un ajustement ou un déplacement de la ligne d'équidistance (ou médiane) provisoire afin d'aboutir à un résultat équitable. Si elle conclut à l'existence de telles circonstances, elle établit une frontière différente, généralement en ajustant ou en déplaçant la ligne d'équidistance (ou médiane), de manière à tenir compte de ces circonstances (*Plateau continental* (*Jamahiriya arabe libyenne/Malte*), arrêt, CIJ Recueil 1985, p. 47, par. 63 ; *Délimitation maritime en mer Noire* (*Roumanie c. Ukraine*), arrêt, CIJ Recueil 2009, p. 102-103, par. 119-121). Lorsque les circonstances pertinentes l'exigent, la Cour peut également recourir à d'autres techniques, comme l'enclavement d'îles isolées, de manière à aboutir à un résultat équitable.

193. La troisième et dernière étape consiste pour la Cour à vérifier si la ligne, telle qu'ajustée ou déplacée, a pour effet de créer une disproportion marquée entre les espaces maritimes attribués à chacune des Parties dans la zone pertinente, par rapport à la longueur de leurs côtes pertinentes respectives[54].

De 1985 dans l'affaire *Libye/Malte* à nos jours, la Cour ne s'est départie de la ligne d'équidistance ou de la ligne médiane ajustée ou déplacée que dans un seul cas : l'affaire du *Différend territorial et maritime entre le Nicaragua et le Honduras dans la mer des Caraïbes* (*Nicaragua c. Honduras*)[55], où elle a estimé que « des raisons impérieuses propres au cas d'espèce ne (lui) permett(ai) ent pas » d'appliquer l'équidistance ajustée[56]. Elle le dit, ou le « rappelle » pour écarter l'argument du Nicaragua qui, dans l'espèce en question, alléguait que « la situation géographique est telle que la Cour aurait tort de recourir à la méthode qu'elle utilise habituellement [...] », à savoir une ligne d'équidistance (ou médiane) provisoire, éventuellement ajustée ou déplacée, avant de vérifier si elle abouti à un résultat équitable[57].

La Cour déclare, comme pour se défendre par avance, que « cette méthode en trois étapes ne doit pas être appliquée de façon mécanique » et rappelle qu'elle

---

[54] Affaire du *Différend territorial maritime* (*Nicaragua c. Colombie*), arrêt du 19 novembre 2012, CIJ Recueil 2012, p. 695, par. 191, p. 696, 192 et 193.

[55] Affaire du *Différend territorial et maritime entre le Nicaragua et le Honduras dans la mer des Caraïbes* (*Nicaragua c. Honduras*), arrêt, CIJ Recueil 2007 (II), p. 745, par. 281.

[56] Ibid., p. 101, par. 116.

[57] Affaire du *Différend territorial maritime* (*Nicaragua c. Colombie*), op. cit., note 54, p. 683, par. 185.

a reconnu dans l'arrêt de 2007 précité, rendu en l'affaire *Nicaragua c. Honduras*, « qu'il ne serait peut-être pas toujours opportun de commencer par l'établissement d'une ligne d'équidistance (ou médiane) provisoire »[58]. Cependant, non seulement elle estime que dans la présente espèce, l'établissement d'une ligne provisoire n'est pas impossible »[59], mais, de manière plus préoccupante, elle « ne croit pas devoir renoncer à sa méthode habituelle en raison de la sentence rendue dans l'affaire du *Plateau continental entre le Royaume-Uni et la France* » et qu'avait invoqué le Nicaragua au soutien de son argumentation ; cette sentence, dit la Cour, « remonte à 1977, c'est-à-dire, longtemps avant que ne soit mise au point la méthode qu'elle applique de nos jours dans les affaires de délimitations maritimes »[60]. Inutile de rappeler qu'entre 1977 et 1985 (*Libye/Malte*), il y a huit ans et non pas une éternité. Mais, de façon plus perturbante, la Cour, qui donne l'impression de tenir en ses trois étapes une méthode de délimitation rationnelle, voire scientifique, peine à convaincre dès que l'on quitte la première étape, et plus sérieusement encore lorsqu'il s'agit de vérifier si la ligne, ajustée ou déplacée, ou non, a pour effet de créer une disproportion marquée entre les espaces maritimes attribués à chacune des parties dans la zone pertinente, par rapport à la longueur de leurs côtes respectives[61].

1.2.2.2 *Le test de « disproportionnalité » et les limites de la rationalité méthodologique*

Le test de « disproportionnalité » est une innovation dans la jurisprudence de la Cour. Certes, dans l'arrêt de 1969, l'un des facteurs jugés pertinents par la Cour avait été l'exigence d'un « rapport raisonnable » entre l'étendue des zones de plateau continental relevant de l'Etat riverain et la longueur des côtes de son littoral mesuré suivant la direction générale de celui-ci[62], suggérant de la sorte la prise en compte de l'idée de proportionnalité dans la mise en œuvre des principes équitables. Mais, on peut penser que la Cour s'est inspirée plus directement de la décision du Tribunal arbitral en l'affaire de la *Délimitation du plateau continental entre la France et la Grande-Bretagne,* dans laquelle le Tribunal avait affirmé que « c'est la disproportion plutôt qu'un principe général de proportionnalité qui constitue le critère pertinent »[63]. Il y a lieu de se

---

58   Ibid., p. 696, par. 194.
59   Ibid., p. 696-697, par. 194.
60   Ibid., p. 697-698, par. 198.
61   Ibid., p. 696, par. 193.
62   Affaire du *Plateau continental de la mer du Nord, op. cit.*, note 2, p. 53-54, par. 101.
63   Affaire de la *Délimitation du plateau continental entre la République française et le Royaume-Unis de Grande-Bretagne et d'Irlande du Nord*, décision du 30 juin 1977, par. 101.

demander si la Cour n'a pas préféré la notion de « disproportionnalité » pour éviter celle d'« équité » qui est pourtant le terme contenu dans les dispositions pertinentes de la CNUDM et sa propre jurisprudence antérieure. Car, la Cour ne dit pas qu'elle procède au test de proportionnalité en vue de vérifier si son opération de délimitation conduit, à l'issue des deux premières étapes, à un « résultat équitable », comme dans sa jurisprudence pré-*Libye/Malte*.

La manière dont est mené le test de « disprorportionnalité » laisse apparaître un certain tâtonnement de la Cour. Certes, dans l'affaire du *Différend territorial et maritime (Nicaragua c. Colombie)*, la Cour s'est appuyée sur une exploitation intense tant de la jurisprudence du TIDM que de celle des instances arbitrales, au bout de laquelle il est difficile de dire ce qui détermine le choix des critères du test. Comme elle le déclare elle-même, l'application de la ligne ajustée dans cette affaire « a pour effet de partager la zone pertinente dans un rapport d'environ 1 à 3,44 en faveur du Nicaragua. Or, le rapport entre les côtes pertinentes est d'environ 1 à 8,2. La question est donc de savoir si, dans les circonstances propres à la présente affaire, cette disproportion est telle qu'elle aboutirait à un résultat inéquitable »[64]. La Cour rappelle que dans l'affaire *Libye/Malte* le rapport entre les côtes pertinentes était d'environ 1 à 8, soit presque identique à celui de la présente affaire, mais que « le rapport entre les parts respectivement attribuées à la Libye et à Malte n'était pas du tout de l'ordre de 1 à 8, même si la part attribuée à Malte était considérablement moindre qu'elle ne l'aurait été si la frontière avait suivi le tracé de la ligne médiane provisoire »[65] ; que pareillement, dans l'affaire de la *Délimitation maritime dans la région située entre le Groenland et Jan Mayen (Danemark c. Norvege)*, « le rapport entre les côtes pertinentes était d'environ 1 à 9 en faveur du Danemark [...] et cette disparité a amené la Cour à déplacer la ligne médiane provisoire. Là encore, la Cour n'a pas analysé le rapport précis entre les parts de la zone pertinente (dénommée, dans cette décision, « zone de chevauchement des titres potentiels ») respectivement attribuées aux Parties selon la ligne ainsi établie, mais il ressort de la description de la frontière donnée dans l'arrêt et de son tracé sur les cartes y annexées que le rapport était de l'ordre de 1 à 2,7. Or, la Cour a estimé qu'il ne s'agissait pas là d'une disproportion marquée »[66]. Elle conclut alors « que, compte tenu de l'ensemble des circonstances entourant la présente affaire, le résultat obtenu par application de la ligne adoptée à titre provisoire

---

64   Affaire du *Différend territorial maritime (Nicaragua c. Colombie)*, *op. cit.*, note 54, p. 716, par. 243.
65   Ibid., p. 717, par. 245.
66   Ibid., p. 717, par. 246.

à la section précédente du présent arrêt n'entraîne pas de disproportion donnant lieu à un résultat inéquitable »[67].

Il s'agit d'un véritable tour de force, car, en dépit d'un examen minutieux par la Cour de sa propre jurisprudence et de celle d'autres juridictions internationales[68] en matière de délimitation maritime, au final il paraît bien difficile de dire le rapport de proportionnalité qui, selon la Cour, ne permet pas à un ajustement de la ligne d'équidistance provisoire d'entraîner une disproportion donnant lieu à un résultat inéquitable. Comme la Cour le reconnaît elle-même, « [c]e qui constitue une telle disproportion varie selon la situation propre à chaque affaire [...] »[69]. On a reproché à la méthode basée sur les principes équitables son subjectivisme. Et la Cour a abandonné le test visant à vérifier si une délimitation aboutit à un « résultat équitable », ou encore si la méthode appliquée permet d'obtenir une « solution équitable » au profit d'expressions négatives telles que les « test de disproportionnalité » (et non pas de proportionnalité !) et de « résultat inéquitable » (et non par de résultat équitable), alors que ce sont ces expressions positives qui sont bien établies en droit positif de la délimitation maritime. Cela est révélateur d'un changement d'approche plus profond que ne le laisse croire la jurisprudence de la Cour, qui continue de citer au fil de ses arrêts sa jurisprudence antérieure comme s'il y avait une inexorable continuité jurisprudentielle. A la vérité, la nouvelle approche conduit à la légitimation de la méthode de l'équidistance, ajustée ou non, le test final visant à montrer qu'elle permet toujours d'atteindre un résultat acceptable parce non disproportionné et donc non inéquitable.

Ce changement d'approche tourne subrepticement le dos au droit positif de la délimitation maritime que la Cour a contribué à façonner par le passé et qui est consigné dans la CNUDM. Il faut bien voir pourtant qu'il existe d'autres méthodes de délimitation dont l'équité du résultat a été vérifiée et que la Cour n'ignore pas. Mais, il ne suffit pas qu'elle ne l'ignore pas, ou qu'il lui arrive exceptionnellement d'en appliquer une.

2   L'existence d'une pluralité des méthodes de délimitation maritime

Le droit contemporain de la mer et de la délimitation maritime repose pour l'essentiel sur la Convention des Nations Unies sur le droit de la mer issue de la IIIe Conférence éponyme. L'examen des travaux préparatoires de la

---

67   Ibid., p. 717, par. 247.
68   Ibid., p. 715, par. 239 et s.
69   Ibid., p. 715, par. 240.

Convention montre que de nombreux Etats n'étaient pas favorables à l'établissement de l'équidistance comme méthode de délimitation, même de la mer territoriale pour certains, et du plateau continental pour la très grande majorité des délégations à la Conférence. Il sied donc de revisiter les travaux de cette Conférence (A) pour éclairer le droit actuel de la délimitation maritime. Il en ressort que l'idée selon laquelle il existe une pluralité de méthodes de délimitation (B) fut clairement affirmée par plusieurs délégations, et que cette idée fut consacrée au final dans les dispositions relatives à la délimitation du plateau continental, écartant de la sorte la prévalence de l'équidistance.

2.1 La délimitation maritime à la IIIe Conférence des Nations Unies sur le droit de la mer

Le résultat des négociations de la IIIe Conférence des Nations Unies sur le droit de la mer, tel que reflété dans la Convention de Montego Bay de 1982, distingue la méthode de délimitation de la mer territoriale de celle du plateau continental. La jurisprudence de la Cour a développé la doctrine de la ligne unique de délimitation de toutes les zones maritimes (mer territoriale-ZEE-plateau continental), aboutissant ainsi à une application par glissement ou translation de l'équidistance ou équidistance-circonstances spéciales dans la mer territoriale au plateau continental. Il convient de rappeler les conditions de l'adoption des articles 15 et 83 de la CNUDM applicables respectivement à l'une (1) et à l'autre (2).

2.1.1 Délimitation de la mer territoriale

L'article 15 de la CNUDM dispose:

> Lorsque les côtes de deux Etats sont adjacentes ou se font face, ni l'un ni l'autre de ces Etats n'est en droit, sauf accord contraire entre eux, d'étendre sa mer territoriale au-delà de la ligne médiane dont tous les points sont équidistants des points les plus proches des lignes de base à partir desquelles est mesurée la largeur de la mer territoriale de chacun des deux Etats. Cette disposition ne s'applique cependant pas dans le cas où, en raison de l'existence de titres historiques ou d'autres circonstances spéciales, il est nécessaire de délimiter autrement la mer territoriale des deux Etats.

Cet article reprend fidèlement les dispositions de l'article 12 par. 1 de la Convention de 1958.

Rappelons que la méthode proposée par la CDI dans son projet d'articles de 1956 fut adoptée pratiquement à l'identique comme article 6 paragraphes 1 et 2 de la Convention de Genève de 1958 sur le plateau continental. Comme on sait, les deux paragraphes traitant respectivement de la délimitation entre les Etats dont les côtes se font face, et entre les Etats dont les côtes sont adjacentes, disposaient qu'à moins qu'un autre tracé de la frontière ne soit justifié par des « circonstances spéciales », la frontière est déterminée, suivant le cas, soit par la ligne médiane, soit par l'équidistance. La non consécration d'une méthode basée sur une stricte application de la ligne médiane ou de l'équidistance faisait suite aux interventions de certaines Etats qui, à l'instar de la Grande Bretagne, firent remarquer que « pour des raison d'équité et compte tenu de la configuration d'une côte particulière », il pourrait exister des circonstance spéciales rendant difficile l'acceptation d'une vrai ligne médiane comme ligne de délimitation[70].

A la IIIe Conférence, plusieurs propositions insistèrent sur la nécessité de la délimitation par voie d'accord. Diverses variantes furent proposées à cet égard dès la réunion du Comité des fonds marins en 1973[71]. A la deuxième réunion de la Conférence, en 1974, la plupart des propositions étaient partagées entre celles qui mettaient l'accent sur l'utilisation de la ligne médiane telle que reflétée dans la Convention de 1958, et celles qui étaient plutôt favorables à une méthode basée sur l'accord en tenant compte des circonstances, cependant que les Etats-Unis et la Grande-Bretagne[72] ainsi que quatre pays socialistes est-européens préféraient la reproduction intégrale des dispositions de l'article 12 de la Convention de 1958 sur la mer territoriale. Toutefois, une proposition révisée de la Turquie[73] et des propositions nouvelles des Pays-Bas[74] et de la Roumanie[75] insistèrent sur ce que la délimitation devrait se faire par voie d'accord « conformément aux principes équitables », tenant compte des circonstances spéciales (Turquie), des circonstances pertinentes (Pays-Bas), ou « toutes les circonstances affectant l'espace maritime concerné et tous les facteurs géographiques, géologiques et autres pertinents » (Roumanie). Les propositions des Pays-Bas et de la Roumanie fournissaient un régime unique de

---

70   Première Commission, 60e session, 1958, par. 36, UNCLOS, I, III, Official Records 189.

71   Voir la liste de ces variantes annexées au rapport du Comité : Item 2.3.1 article 2 Variante A, reproduit dans IV Comité des fonds marins, 1973, p. 5, 7; Item 2.3.2 article 1 Variante P, para. 2; article 3 Variante A, paras. 1 et 2, et Variante B, et « article final », reproduit dans IV Comité des fonds marins, 1973, p. 14, 18-19.

72   A/CONF. 62/C.2/L.3 (1974), Chapitre II, Deuxième Partie, Note, III Official Records 183 (Royaume-Uni).

73   A/CONF. 62/C.2/L.9 (1974), paragraphes 1 et 2, III Official Records 188 (Turquie).

74   A/CONF. 62/C.2/L.14 (1974), paragraphes 1 et 2, III Official Records 190 (Pays-Bas).

75   A/CONF. 62/C.2/L.18 (1974), article 1, article 2, paragraphes 1 et 2, III Official Records 195, 196 (Roumanie).

délimitation de tous les espaces maritimes[76]. Une proposition d'un groupe de 24 Etats[77] relevait la nécessité d'examiner plus avant les dispositions relatives à la délimitation contenue dans les deux Conventions de 1958. Pour sa part, un groupe de quatorze Etats africains[78] suggéra que la délimitation entre les Etats dont les côtes se font face ou sont adjacentes soit faite, en cas de la présence des îles, par voie d'accord entre lesdits Etats, « conformément au principe d'équité, la ligne médiane ou l'équidistance n'étant pas la seule méthode de délimitation ».

A la troisième session de la Conférence en 1975, fut créé un groupe consultatif informel sur la délimitation et le Pérou fit une proposition informelle dans les termes de l'article 12 de la Convention de 1958, insistant sur l'utilisation de la médiane et de la ligne d'équidistance dans la délimitation de la mer territoriale. A la quatrième session, fut introduit dans le Texte de négociation, un projet d'article 14 qui deviendra l'article 15 dans le Texte de négociation composite officieux (TNCO). Bien qu'à la neuvième session plusieurs Etats suggèrent l'alignement de cet article 15 sur les articles 74 et 83[79], la teneur de l'article 15 ne changera plus jusqu'à l'adoption de la Convention de Montego Bay.

En somme, comme le releva un juriste ayant prit part aux négociations de la IIIe Conférence sur le droit de la mer, hormis l'opposition entre la Grèce et la Turquie qui s'affrontèrent avec des propositions opposées[80] le problème de la délimitation de la mer territoriale ne fut que modérément débattu à cette IIIe Conférence. Mais, même si la CNUDM se borne sur ce point à reprendre le droit antérieur à la IIIe Conférence, il convient néanmoins de rappeler que ce droit antérieur n'a jamais instituer l'équidistance comme méthode ou principe unique en matière de délimitation de la mer territoriale. A vrai dire,

---

76 *United Nations Convention on the Law of the Sea 1982, A Commentary*, vol. VI, Center for Ocean Law and Policy University of Virginia School of Law, Dordrecht/Boston/London, Martinus Niholf Publisher, 2002, p. 138.

77 A/CONF. 62/C.2/L. 33 (1974), Note explicative, III Off Rec. 212 (Autriche, Belgique, Bolivie, Botswana, Burundi, Biélorussie, Finlande, Haute-Volta, Hongrie, Laos, Lesotho, Luxembourg, Mali, Mongolie, Ouganda, Paraguay, Pays-Bas, République fédérale d'Allemagne, Singapour, Suède, Swaziland, Tchécoslovaquie, Zambie).

78 A/CONF. 62/C.2/L.62 Rev. 1 (1974), article 3, III Off Rec. 232, 233 (Algérie, Côte d'Ivoire, Dahomey, Guinée, Haute-Volta, Libéria, Madagascar, Mali, Maroc, Mauritanie, Sierra Leone, Soudan, Tunisie, et Zambie).

79 A/CONF. 62/C.2/WP. 10/Rev. 2 (INCT Rev. 2 1980 mimeo) article 15; A/CONF. 62/C.2/WP. 10/Rev. 3 (INCT Rev. 3 1980 mimeo) article 15.

80 Propositions turques du 15 juillet 1974 ; grecque du 25 juillet 1974 et turque du 18 mars 1976 (réf. Caflisch, p. 78 note 25).

elle n'établit pas non plus une règle unique portant la méthode de l'équidistance-circonstance spéciale, mais deux règles distinctes.

Première règle : lorsque les côtes de deux Etats sont adjacentes ou se font face, s'applique l'équidistance, sauf accord contraire entre les Etats concernés : « le tracé doit suivre la ligne médiane dont tous les points sont équidistants des points les plus proches des lignes de base à partir desquelles est mesurée la largeur de la mer territoriale de chacun des deux Etats ».

Seconde règle : l'équidistance « ne s'applique cependant pas dans le cas où, en raison de l'existence de titres historiques ou d'autres circonstances spéciales, il est nécessaire de délimiter autrement la mer territoriale des deux Etats ». Autrement dit, dans cette seconde configuration, l'on *doit* appliquer d'autres méthodes de délimitation. On peut penser que l'objectif implicite de cette règle, qui écarte clairement l'équidistance (ou médiane) dans cette seconde hypothèse, est de dégager une autre méthode de délimitation qui permettrait d'aboutir à un résultat équitable, en tout cas acceptable pour les deux Etats concernés.

Bien évidemment, lorsque la délimitation se fait par voie d'accord, les Etats sont libres d'adopter toute méthode ou tout tracé qui leur conviennent, comme ce fut le cas, par exemple, pour la délimitation maritime au-delà de la mer territoriale entre le Cameroun et le Nigeria dans le cadre de l'Accord de Maroua de 1975 entre les deux Etats[81].

2.1.2 Délimitation du plateau continental

Comme pour la mer territoriale, il convient de rappeler les dispositions de la CNUDM relatives à la délimitation du plateau continental. L'article 83 de la Convention intitulé « Délimitation du plateau continental entre Etats dont les côtes sont adjacentes ou se font face » dispose en son paragraphe 1 :

> La délimitation du plateau continental entre Etats dont les côtes sont adjacentes ou se font face est effectuée par voie d'accord conformément au droit international tel qu'il est visé à l'article 38 du Statut de la cour internationale de justice, *afin d'aboutir à une solution équitable*[82].

---

81 Affaire de la *Frontière terrestre et maritime entre le Cameroun et le Nigeria (Cameroun c. Nigeria ; Guinée équatoriale intervenant)*, fond, arrêt, CIJ Recueil 2002, p. 425-431, par. 247-268.

82 Nos italiques.

Cette disposition est l'aboutissement de longues négociations lors de la IIIe Conférence des Nations Unies sur le droit de la mer, dont il échet de rappeler les principaux moments.

Comme on le sait, l'arrêt rendu en 1969 par la CIJ dans les affaires du *Plateau continental de la mer du Nord* a profondément influencé les négociations relatives à la délimitation du plateau continental à la IIIe Conférence sur les droits de la mer[83]. La Cour a déclaré sans ambiguïté dans son arrêt en question que la règle de l'équidistance-circonstance spéciale en matière de délimitation maritime n'est pas une règle de droit international coutumier :

> La Cour conclut que la Convention de Genève n'a ni consacré, ni cristallisé une règle de droit coutumier préexistante ou en voie de formation selon laquelle la délimitation du plateau continental entre Etats limitrophes devrait s'opérer, sauf si les Parties en décident autrement, sur la base d'un principe d'équidistance-circonstances spéciales. Une règle a bien été établie par l'article 6 de la Convention mais uniquement en tant que règle conventionnelle. Il reste à voir si elle a acquis depuis lors un fondement plus large, car comme règle conventionnelle elle n'est pas opposable à la République fédérale [d'Allemagne] comme la Cour l'a déjà constaté[84].

La Cour explique cette conclusion au paragraphe 85 de l'arrêt. Vu l'importance de ce *dictum*, il y a lieu de le rappeler *in extenso* :

> Il ressort de l'histoire du développement du régime juridique du plateau continental [...] que la raison essentielle pour laquelle la méthode de l'équidistance ne peut être tenue pour une règle de droit est que, si elle devait être appliquée obligatoirement en toutes situations, cette méthode ne correspondrait pas à certaines notions juridiques de base qui, comme on l'a rappelé aux paragraphes 48 et 55, reflètent l'*opinio juris* en matière de délimitation ; ces principes sont que la délimitation doit être l'objet d'un accord entre les Etats intéressés et que cet accord doit se réaliser selon des principes équitables. Il s'agit là, sur la base de préceptes très généraux de justice et de bonne foi, de véritables règles de droit en matière de délimitation des plateaux continentaux limitrophes, c'est-à-dire des règles obligatoires pour les Etats pour toute délimitation ; en d'autres termes, il ne s'agit pas d'appliquer l'équité simplement comme

---

83   Voir *United Nations Convention on the Law of the Sea 1982, A Commentary, op. cit.*, note 76, p. 954.

84   Affaire du *Plateau continental de la mer du Nord, op. cit.*, note 2, p. 41, par. 6.

> une représentation de la justice abstraite, mais d'appliquer une règle de droit prescrivant le recours à des principes équitables conformément aux idées qui ont toujours inspiré le régime juridique du plateau continental en la matière [...][85].

Comme on peut le voir, la Cour s'exprime dans un style énonciatif ou dispositif qu'elle n'use que rarement. Elle n'a pas dit le droit seulement pour les espèces dont elle était saisie dans ces affaires, elle a fixé le droit positif de la délimitation des plateaux continentaux, avec une telle fermeté que l'on ne pourrait pas le balayer d'un revers de plume. On a parfois fait comme si la Cour ignorait en 1969 – et sans doute même avant – les avantages indéniables de l'équidistance. Or, il n'en est rien. C'est en toute connaissance du développement du droit et de la pratique en la matière qu'elle écarte ce principe comme règle de référence en matière de délimitation. En effet, elle affirme que « malgré les avantages reconnus, la méthode d'équidistance aboutit dans certaines conditions géographiques assez fréquentes à une incontestable iniquité »[86]. Et la Cour de préciser:

> L'équité n'implique pas nécessairement l'égalité. Il n'est jamais question de re faire la nature entièrement et l'équité ne commande pas qu'un Etat sans accès à la mer se voit attribuer une zone de plateau continental, pas plus qu'il ne s'agit d'égaliser la situation d'un Etat dont les côtes sont étendues à celles d'un Etat dont les côtes sont réduites. L'égalité se mesure dans un même plan et ce n'est pas à de telles inégalités naturelles que l'équité pourrait porter remède[87].

Face à l'argument selon lequel toutes les méthodes peuvent « éventuellement aboutir à une relative injustice »[88], la Cour relève qu'un tel argument « renforce d'ailleurs l'opinion selon laquelle on doit rechercher non pas une méthode unique de limitation mais un but unique. »

Or, pour la Cour:

> Délimiter étant une opération de détermination des zones relevant respectivement de compétences différentes, c'est une vérité première de dire que cette détermination doit être équitable; le problème est surtout

---

85 Ibid., p. 46-47.
86 Ibid., p. 49, par. 89.
87 Ibid., p. 49-50, par. 91.
88 Ibid., p. 50, par. 92.

de définir les moyens par lesquels la délimitation peut être fixée de manière à être reconnue comme équitable[89].

Sur la toile de fond de cette jurisprudence inaugurale, deux positions s'affrontèrent au cours des négociations à la IIIe Conférence sur le droit de la mer. En dépit de l'arrêt de 1969, certains Etats ont continué à soutenir que la délimitation du plateau continental devrait se faire par application de la ligne médiane ou de l'équidistance couplée avec les circonstances spéciales. Au contraire, dans le sillage de cette jurisprudence, d'autres Etats ont soutenu que la délimitation devait mettre l'accent sur l'affirmation des principes équitables. Les propositions reflétant ces deux positions furent faites dès la session de 1973 du Comité des fonds marins. A la deuxième session de la Conférence en 1974, plusieurs nouvelles propositions furent faites avec des différences sur le point de savoir dans quelle mesure le principe d'équidistance, les principes équitables, les circonstances spéciales et le droit international devraient être pris en compte. Une proposition de la Turquie – remplaçant sa proposition au Comité des fonds marins – centrée sur la délimitation faite conformément aux principes équitables et consacrant en définitive la primauté de ces principes dans la méthode de délimitation du plateau continental, fut clairement affirmée lors des négociations de la Convention de Montego Bay[90].

Ainsi, en retenant la méthode de l'équidistance-circonstances pertinentes avec primauté évidente à l'équidistance, la Cour valide une position qui n'avait pas pu s'imposer lors des négociations de la CNUDM, en particulier s'agissant de la délimitation du plateau continental[91]. Certes, elle s'ouvre quelquefois à d'autres méthodes. Mais cela est si rare qu'il s'agit de l'exception qui confirme la règle. C'est bien à tort, car le choix d'une méthode ne doit pas être prédéterminé ; c'est chaque cas qui dicte la méthode pertinente au regard de la fin ultime de toute délimitation qui est le résultat équitable.

2.2 *L'ouverture judicieuse à d'autres méthodes et approches de délimitation*

Des alternatives à la méthode de l'équidistance, ajustée ou non, existent et sont consacrées par le droit de la délimitation maritime (1). La Cour n'est évidemment pas ignorante de cela puisqu'elle a eu à appliquer une méthode différente de celle

---

[89] Ibid., p. 50, par. 92.
[90] Voir, *United Nations Convention on the Law of the Sea 1982 A Commentary, op. cit.*, note 76, p. 953 et s.
[91] Sur les tentatives pour faire triompher cette position, voir *United Nations Convention on the Law of the Sea 1982 A Commentary*, ibid., p. 965.

partant de l'équidistance, fut-ce à titre exceptionnelle. On ne peut manquer de relever son souci d'améliore sa méthode ; il y a lieu de mettre à ce compte la récente nomination par la Cour des experts dans une affaire de délimitation avant la détermination de la méthode qu'elle appliquera dans l'espèce en question (2).

2.2.1 Des alternatives à l'équidistance/équidistance-circonstances spéciales

Il ressort de l'examen du droit positif de la mer, deux constats à propos de la délimitation maritime : d'une part, l'objectif de toute délimitation maritime est – ou doit être – la recherche d'une solution équitable (a) ; d'autre part, l'équidistance n'est pas une méthode objective dans tous les cas, ni une méthode prioritaire (b).

2.2.1.1 *L'objectif de toute délimitation maritime est la recherche d'une solution équitable*

Alors que l'article 15 de la CNUDM prescrit, comme on l'a vu, le recours à la méthode d'équidistance – laquelle ne s'applique pas en cas d'accord contraire entre les États concernés ou en raison de l'existence de titres historiques ou d'autres circonstances spéciales ou pertinentes – les articles 74 sur la ZEE et 83 sur le plateau continental, aux dispositions parfaitement symétriques, sont dépourvus de tout caractère normatif. Ils se contentent de déterminer le but à atteindre. Comme la Cour le dira dans son arrêt du 3 juin 1985 en l'affaire du *Plateau continental (Jamahiriya arabe libyenne/Malte)*, « [l]a Convention fixe le but à atteindre, mais elle est muette sur la méthode à suivre pour y parvenir. Elle se borne à énoncer une norme et laisse aux États et au juge le soin de lui donner un contenu précis »[92]. Le but à atteindre est une solution équitable, qui tient compte notamment des caractéristiques géographiques des côtes pertinentes. C'est bien ce que la Cour a établi dès son arrêt de 1969. Elle le réaffirme dans son arrêt du 14 juin 1993 en l'affaire de la *Délimitation maritime dans la région située entre le Groenland et Jan Mayen (Danemark c. Norvège)* en indiquant que « [l]e but, dans toute situation, quelle qu'elle soit, doit être d'aboutir à un « résultat équitable » »[93]. La sentence arbitrale rendue en l'affaire de la *Délimitation du plateau continental entre le Royaume-Uni de Grande-Bretagne et la République française* contient un *dictum* similaire[94]. Comme l'a dit un commentateur de cet arrêt « [l]e droit n'est pas à lui-même son propre but,

---

[92] Affaire du *Plateau continental (Jamahiriya Arabe Libyenne/Malte)*, op. cit., note 17, p. 30, par. 28.

[93] Affaire de la *Délimitation maritime dans la région située entre le Groenland et Jan Mayen*, op. cit., note 21, p. 62, par. 54.

[94] *Recueil des Sentences Arbitrales*, vol. XVIII, p. 188, par. 97.

mais est destiné à accomplir la justice, à parvenir à des résultats équitables »[95]. La jurisprudence internationale en matière de délimitation maritime restera pendant près de deux décennies dans cette logique finaliste de la délimitation.

L'objectif de la délimitation étant ainsi déterminé, il n'est pas impératif de baser la délimitation sur une ligne provisoire d'équidistance quitte à vérifier ensuite si elle est particulièrement préjudiciable pour un État, afin de l'ajuster voire de la corriger, ou de l'écarter purement et simplement au profit d'une autre ligne tracée en application d'une autre méthode. La Cour peut choisir d'emblée cette autre méthode ou même une combinaison de méthodes de délimitation. Une telle démarche trouverait appui dans la jurisprudence de la Cour, notamment dans un autre *dictum* contenu dans l'arrêt rendu en l'affaire de la *Délimitation du plateau continental dans la région du Golfe du Maine (Canada/Etats-Unis)* selon lequel :

> [l]a pratique, d'ailleurs, bien qu'encore peu abondante à cause de la nouveauté relative de la matière, est là pour démontrer que chaque cas concret est finalement différent des autres, qu'il est un *unicum,* et que les critères les plus appropriés et la méthode ou la combinaison de méthodes la plus apte à assurer un résultat conforme aux indications données par le droit, ne peuvent le plus souvent être déterminés que par rapport au cas d'espèce et aux caractéristiques spécifiques qu'il présente[96].

2.2.1.2 *L'équidistance n'est ni une méthode obligatoire ni une méthode prioritaire*

Les différentes méthodes de délimitation doivent poursuivre la finalité de la solution équitable ; car, faut-il le rappeler, il existe plusieurs autres méthodes de délimitation en dehors de l'équidistance-circonstances spéciales. Par exemple, la perpendiculaire à la direction générale de la côte, l'adoption de parallèles de latitude ou des méridiens de longitude, la méthode de la bissectrice, la méthode de couloir qui permet à l'État côtier de jouir de l'ensemble des zones maritimes que génère sa côte, ou encore la méthode d'enclavement des îles, en cas de délimitation dans une zone comportant des îles. Il est à noter qu'il n'existe pas, juridiquement, de hiérarchie entre les différentes méthodes de délimitation. Par ailleurs, rien n'empêche aux États ou au juge international

---

95   F. Monconduit, « Affaires du Plateau continental de la Mer du Nord : République fédérale d'Allemagne c. Danemark et République fédérale d'Allemagne c. Pays-Bas, arrêt du 20 février 1969 », *Annuaire français de droit international*, vol. 15, 1969, p. 238.

96   Affaire de la *Délimitation du plateau continental dans la région du Golfe du Maine, op. cit.*, note 14, p. 290, par. 81.

de recourir à une combinaison de ces méthodes dans le cadre d'une délimitation maritime.

Bien que la méthode d'équidistance (circonstances-spéciales) semble aujourd'hui la plus utilisée, l'on ne doit pas perdre de vue qu'en référence à cette méthode, la CIJ avait déclaré : dans l'arrêt de 1969, dans un *dictum* resté célèbre, qu'

> il est probablement exact qu'aucune autre méthode de délimitation ne combine au même degré les avantages de la commodité pratique et de la certitude dans l'application. Toutefois cela ne suffit pas à transformer une méthode en règle de droit et à rendre obligatoire l'acceptation de ses résultats chaque fois que les parties ne se sont pas mises d'accord sur d'autres dispositions ou que l'existence de circonstances spéciales ne peut être établie. Juridiquement, si une telle règle existe, sa valeur en droit doit tenir à autre chose qu'à ces avantages, si importants soient-ils. La réciproque n'est pas moins vraie : que l'application de la méthode de l'équidistance soit obligatoire ou non, ses avantages pratiques resteront les mêmes[97].

Dans le même sens, la Cour a relevé dans l'affaire *Tunisie/Libye* que « [l]es Parties reconnaissent qu'il n'existe pas en droit international de méthode de délimitation unique et obligatoire et que l'on peut appliquer plusieurs méthodes dans une même délimitation »[98].

Il apparaît ainsi que lorsque le juge international recourt à la méthode de l'équidistance, il mobilise une méthode, sans cependant obéir à une règle de droit ; il peut donc, le cas échéant, écarter la ligne d'équidistance provisoire, et utiliser toute autre méthode qui, à ses yeux, serait la plus à même d'aboutir à une solution équitable. La Cour s'est à nouveau exprimée en ce sens dans l'arrêt qu'elle a rendu le 8 octobre 2007 en l'affaire du *Différend territorial et maritime entre le Nicaragua et le Honduras dans la mer des Caraïbes (Nicaragua c. Honduras)*. Selon la Cour « la méthode de l'équidistance n'a pas automatiquement la priorité sur les autres méthodes de délimitation et, dans certaines circonstances, des facteurs peuvent rendre son application inappropriée »[99]. Dans cette espèce, elle a écarté purement et simplement la méthode de l'équidistance-circonstances pertinentes et a recouru à la méthode de la bissectrice,

---

97   Affaire du *Plateau continental de la mer du Nord, op. cit.*, note 2, par. 23.
98   Affaire du *Plateau continental (Tunisie/Libye), op. cit.*, note 36, p. 79, par. 111.
99   Affaire *du Différend territorial et maritime entre le Nicaragua et le Honduras dans la mer des Caraïbes, op. cit.*, note 55, p. 741, par. 272.

considérant que les circonstances de l'espèce ne se prêtaient pas à la mise en œuvre de la première.

Mais deux ans plus tard seulement, la même Cour a déclaré, dans son arrêt rendu à l'unanimité de ses membres le 3 février 2009 en l'affaire de la *Délimitation maritime en mer Noire (Roumanie c. Ukraine)*, que « [l]orsqu'il s'agit de procéder à une délimitation entre côtes adjacentes, une ligne d'équidistance est tracée, à moins que des raisons impérieuses propres au cas d'espèce ne le permettent pas »[100]. La Cour a insisté sur le caractère impérieux des raisons pouvant l'amener à écarter la méthode de l'équidistance-circonstances pertinentes et a renvoyé pour justifier cette position au paragraphe 281 de l'arrêt *Nicaragua/Honduras* ci-dessus cité. De la sorte, elle a confirmé que l'équidistance était à ses yeux *la* méthode, celle qui a la primauté sur les autres, auxquelles elle ne peut recourir qu'exceptionnellement, pour des « raisons impérieuses ». Une telle position contredit sa jurisprudence antérieure qui affirme, comme on l'a vu, qu'aucune méthode n'est obligatoire ou prioritaire !

Théoriquement, un nombre indéterminé de circonstances pertinentes sont susceptibles d'être prises en considération aux fins d'une délimitation équitable. Néanmoins, il ressort tant de la pratique des Etats que de la jurisprudence que ce sont les caractéristiques géographiques de la côte pertinente qui jouent un rôle crucial dans la détermination des facteurs à prendre en considération aux fins de la délimitation. Il s'agit, en général, de la configuration générale de la côte, de la longueur relative des côtes des États en cause et de l'influence de la présence des îles. Les autres considérations – économiques, politiques ou historiques – ne sont souvent invoquées que pour étayer les considérations géographiques.

Ces considérations géographiques constituent des données brutes à prendre comme telles par le juge. Dans l'arrêt rendu en 1984 en l'affaire de la *Délimitation de la frontière maritime dans la région du golfe du Maine golfe du Maine*, la Chambre de la Cour a indiqué que « les faits géographiques ne sont pas le produit d'une activité humaine passible d'un jugement positif ou négatif, mais le résultat de phénomènes naturels et ne peuvent donc qu'être constatés tels qu'ils sont »[101]. Dans l'affaire de la *Frontière terrestre et maritime entre le Cameroun et le Nigéria (Cameroun c. Nigéria ; Guinée équatoriale (intervenant))*, la Cour a résumé sa philosophie en la matière en ces termes : « La configuration géographique des espaces maritimes que la Cour est appelée à délimiter est une donnée. Elle ne constitue pas un élément que la Cour pourrait modifier,

---

100   Affaire *Roumanie c. Ukraine, op. cit.*, note 47, p. 101, par. 116 (non souligné dans l'original).
101   Affaire de la *Délimitation de la frontière maritime dans la région du golfe du Maine, op. cit.*, note 14, p. 271, par. 31.

mais un fait sur la base duquel elle doit opérer la délimitation ». Comme la Cour a eu l'occasion de le dire dans les affaires du *Plateau continental de lu mer du Nord*, « [l]'équité n'implique pas nécessairement l'égalité », et lors d'un exercice de délimitation « [i]l n'est jamais question de refaire la nature entièrement »[102]. Si certaines particularités géographiques des espaces maritimes à délimiter peuvent être prises en compte par la Cour, c'est uniquement au titre de circonstances pertinentes aux fins, le cas échéant, d'ajuster ou de déplacer la ligne provisoire de délimitation. Ici encore, comme la Cour l'a décidé dans les affaires du *Plateau continental de la mer du Nord*, toutes les particularités géographiques ne doivent pas être nécessairement prises en compte par la Cour pour ajuster ou déplacer la ligne de délimitation provisoire : « [il ne s'agit donc pas de refaire totalement la géographie dans n'importe quelle situation de fait mais, en présence d'une situation géographique de quasi-égalité entre plusieurs États, de remédier à une particularité non essentielle d'où pourrait résulter une injustifiable différence de traitement » (CIJ *Recueil 1969*, p. 50, par. 91) »[103].

Le choix de la méthode pertinente dans un cas donné est tributaire d'une bonne appréciation des caractéristiques géographiques des côtes des Etats considérés dans la zone à délimiter. Un moyen sûr pour la Cour de prendre l'exacte mesure de la configuration géographique des espaces maritimes en question est de s'appuyer sur l'avis des experts (géographes, topographes, cartographes etc.) avant de se déterminer sur une méthode. C'est ce que la Cour a fait récemment dans l'affaire *Délimitation maritime dans la mer des Caraïbes et l'océan Pacifique* (*Costa Rica c. Nicaragua*) dont elle a été saisie en 2014.

2.2.2 Le recours à l'éclairage des experts avant le choix d'une méthode, une démarche susceptible d'aider à l'atteinte d'un résultat équitable

Suite à l'instance introduite par la Costa Rica contre le Nicaragua, par requête déposée au Greffe de la Cour le 25 février 2014, au sujet d'un différend relatif à la délimitation maritime dans la mer des Caraïbes et l'océan Pacifique, la Cour a informé les Parties que, conformément aux articles 48 et 50 de son Statut, elle envisageait « de faire procéder à une expertise dans le cadre de laquelle un ou plusieurs experts seraient chargés de rassembler, en se rendant sur place, l'ensemble des éléments factuels relatifs à l'état de la côte entre le point situé sur la rive droite du fleuve San Juan à son embouchure et le point de la côte le plus proche de Punta de Castilla, tels que ces deux points peuvent être identifiés

---

102 Affaire du *Plateau continental de la mer du Nord, op. cit.*, note 2, p. 49, par. 91.
103 Affaire de la *Frontière maritime* (*Cameroun c. Nigéria*), *op. cit.*, note 26, p. 444-445, par. 295.

à l'heure actuelle »[104]. La Cour a fixé en même temps la date d'expiration du délai dans lequel les Parties pourraient exposer leur position concernant cette éventuelle expertise, notamment leurs vues sur l'objet de celle-ci, le nombre et le mode de désignation des experts et les formalités à observer, sachant que chaque Partie avait le droit de faire des observations sur la réponse de la Partie adverse dans le délai fixé par la Cour.

Le Costa Rica s'est félicité de cette perspective de désignation des experts et a fait diverses suggestions, notamment que la Cour désigne un comité d'experts composé de trois géographes indépendants et que les Parties aient la possibilité de formuler des observations sur l'identité desdits experts, l'inclusion d'un certain nombre de questions dans le mandat des experts, la possibilité pour les Parties de formuler des observations écrites sur le rapport des experts avant l'ouverture de la procédure orale et la communication par écrit de tout commentaire qu'une Partie entendrait formuler sur les observations de l'autre avant la tenue des audiences[105].

Quant au Nicaragua, il a indiqué « qu'il n'estimait pas nécessaire de faire procéder à une visite d'experts sur les lieux, soutenant que, l'emplacement du point de départ de la frontière terrestre sur la côte caraïbe ayant été fixé par divers instruments, la localisation du point de départ de la frontière maritime entre les Parties constituait une tâche purement technique et juridique qui ne nécessitait pas de visite sur les lieux ». Il a toutefois ajouté que « si, ayant examiné sa position, la Cour estimait devoir faire procéder à une visite d'experts sur place, il serait disposé à formuler en temps voulu ses vues concernant les modalités de nomination du ou des experts et leur mandat et à apporter à ceux-ci toute l'assistance possible »[106].

Pour la Cour, « certains éléments factuels relatifs à l'état de la côte pourraient se révéler pertinents aux fins de régler le différend qui lui a été soumis, lequel est notamment relatif à la délimitation de la frontière maritime entre les Parties dans la mer des Caraïbes, et que, à cet égard, elle gagnerait à bénéficier d'une expertise ». Ayant entendu les Parties, et disposant de toutes les informations nécessaires aux fins de sa décision, elle était dès lors en mesure de préciser l'objet d'une telle expertise, de fixer le nombre et le mode de désignation des experts, et d'indiquer les formalités à observer. Sa décision de faire procéder à une expertise ne préjuge cependant en rien la question de la détermination du point de départ ou du tracé de la frontière maritime litigieuse, ni

---

104 Affaire de la *Délimitation maritime dans la mer des Caraïbes et l'océan Pacifique (Costa Rica c. Nicaragua)*, ordonnance du 31 mai 2016, CIJ Recueil 2016, par. 4.
105 Ibid., par. 5.
106 Ibid., par. 6.

aucune autre question relative au différend soumis à la Cour, et laisse intact le droit des Parties de faire valoir leurs moyens de preuve et arguments en ces matières, conformément au Règlement de la Cour.

Sur la base de ces considérations, la Cour a décidé de recourir à une expertise « confiée à deux experts indépendants, désignés par ordonnance du président de la Cour une fois entendues les Parties ». Ces experts, dont chacun devra faire la déclaration dont le texte est contenu dans l'ordonnance de la Cour[107], « se rendront sur place », et « donneront leur avis à la Cour en ce qui concerne l'état de la côte entre les points invoqués respectivement par le Costa Rica et le Nicaragua dans leurs écritures, comme étant le point de départ de la frontière maritime dans la mer des Caraïbes » ; en particulier, ils devront fournir les coordonnées géographiques de certains points et répondre à un certain nombre de questions techniques indiqués dans l'ordonnance de la Cour[108]. Il s'agit d'une décision inédite, que la Cour a mise en œuvre par son ordonnance du 16 juin 2016 portant désignation des deux experts, dont un de nationalité française et un autre de nationalité espagnole[109].

La désignation des experts n'est évidemment pas une méthode de délimitation, mais une démarche de la Cour susceptible de l'aider à atteindre une solution équitable dans la délimitation maritime. Le rapport des experts, qui auront bénéficié de l'assistance requise des Parties aux fins des opérations d'expertise, lui sera probablement utile dans le choix de la méthode ; et si elle maintient sa méthode en trois phases avec pour point de départ l'équidistance, on peut penser que les éléments fourni par les experts pourront lui permettre de mieux appréhender les circonstances pertinentes à prendre à compte aux fins de la délimitation. On peut d'autant plus le penser que la Cour mais aussi les Parties pourront bénéficier de l'éclairage des experts même dans la phase orale de la procédure, au cours de laquelle les experts répondront aux

---

107 Le texte de cette déclaration est le suivant : la déclaration suivante : « Je déclare solennellement, en tout honneur et en toute conscience, que je m'acquitterai de mes fonctions d'expert en tout honneur et dévouement, en pleine et parfaite impartialité et en toute conscience, et que je m'abstiendrai de divulguer ou d'utiliser en dehors de la Cour les documents ou renseignements de caractère confidentiel dont je pourrais prendre connaissance dans l'accomplissement de ma mission. ».

108 Voir le dispositif de l'ordonnance du 31 mai 2016, *op. cit.*, note 104, par. 10.

109 Ont ainsi été désignés experts : E. Fouache, de nationalité française, professeur de géographie, vice-chancelier de l'Université de Paris-Sorbonne Abou Dhabi (Emirats arabes unis), membre sénior de l'Institut universitaire de France et président de l'association internationale des géomorphologues ; F. Gutiérrez, de nationalité espagnole, professeur de géologie et de géomorphologie à l'Université de Zaragoza (Espagne), ancien membre du comité exécutif de l'association internationale des géomorphologues. (*CIJ Recueil 2016*).

questions des agents, conseils et avocats des Parties, et le cas échéant à celles de la Cour elle-même[110].

Conclusion

La méthode de délimitation en trois étapes dégagée par la Cour paraît rationnelle ; elle est en tout cas rassurante pour ceux qui croient que la délimitation maritime, même par une juridiction internationale, peut donner lieu à une mathématique juridique ou à de la géométrie judiciaire, où la perfection des tracés est la preuve d'une justice bien rendue. On peut avoir des doutes face à une telle conception du droit de la délimitation maritime. En effet, si l'on peut s'accorder sur ce qu'est géométriquement une ligne d'équidistance, l'équité de la ligne d'arrivée n'offre pas moins d'incertitude que le choix de toute autre méthode. Le contrôle de l'équité du résultat est un exercice complexe, dont on ne peut garantir la certitude technique. Le recours à la fois aux principes équitables et aux circonstances pertinentes dépend largement de l'appréciation de chaque cas particulier par le juge. L'identification des circonstances pertinentes est une tâche juridictionnelle et non une détermination normative : ces circonstances ne sont pas énoncées par une règle de droit, et même si c'était le cas, leur pondération, c'est-à-dire la manière de les prendre en considération, en l'occurrence le poids accordé à chacune d'elles, dépendrait toujours du juge.

Il n'existe pas de méthode absolue en matière de délimitation maritime ; et s'il en existait une, celle qui met l'équidistance ou la médiane en son centre ne serait assurément pas la meilleure. Comme l'a dit cette Court il y a bien longtemps, chaque cas de délimitation maritime est un *unicum*, tant les situations géographiques et les circonstances pertinentes sont rarement identiques. La CNUDM donne à la Cour une boussole dans ses articles 15, 74 et 83 : le tracé de la ligne de limitation doit « aboutir à une solution équitable ». Rarement l'équidistance ou la médiane permettent de parvenir à un tel résultat dès que la situation géographique et les autres circonstances à prendre en compte présentent une complexité.

Les parties à un litige porté devant la Cour n'attendent pas de celle-ci qu'elle fasse ce qu'elles-mêmes peuvent faire, mais que la Cour fasse ce qu'elles n'ont pas pu ou su faire. Certes, là où la solution du litige est contenue soit dans l'équidistance ou la médiane, soit dans la position de l'une des parties, la Cour ne peut pas faire de la distorsion juridique pour inventer une solution : elle ne peut décider d'elle-même, nous le savons, de statuer *ex aequo et bono*, ni de

---

110 Ordonnance du 31 mai 2016, *op. cit.*, note 104, par. 10.

choisir une équité *contra legem*. Donc, s'il se trouve que la solution est inévitablement l'équidistance, comme il peut arriver dans certains cas, la Cour doit s'y tenir. Mais, là où il en va différemment, comme cela a été le cas dans plus d'une affaire portée devant cette Cour depuis *Libye/Malte*, les parties attendent de la Cour qu'elle déploie son art de juger.

En tournant le dos à sa jurisprudence antérieure à cette affaire *Libye/Malte*, la Cour espérait peut-être échapper à la critique selon laquelle elle créait le droit, parce que ses décisions manquaient de base juridique, entraînant de la sorte une incertitude chez les justiciables. Mais, ce faisant, elle s'est éloignée des acquis de sa jurisprudence depuis les affaires du *Plateau continental de la mer du Nord*. Elle s'est surtout écartée de la lettre et plus encore de l'esprit de la Convention de Montego Bay et des négociations de la IIIe Conférence des Nations Unies qui l'a produite et qui étaient animées par l'esprit de répartition équitable des espaces maritimes communs à plusieurs Etats et non pas par la solution du « *winner take all* ». La Cour semble ne plus soumettre ses décisions en la matière au test du « résultat équitable » ou de la « solution équitable », mais seulement au test de « disproportionnalité » ; ce n'est pas exactement la même chose.

Cela dit, il est heureux que la Cour, dont le pragmatisme judiciaire a toujours contribué à la qualité de ses décisions soit attentive aux vues extérieures exprimées sur ses décisions à ce sujet. Le recours à des experts pour l'aider à comprendre la géographie côtière avant de choisir ou d'appliquer une méthode doit être saluée. Même s'il est probable qu'un tel recours ne sera pas systématique, le principe en est, comme on l'a vu, désormais établi. Le plus important est que ce précédent existe. Il n'y a aucune raison pour que la Cour n'y recourt pas à nouveau si elle en éprouvait le besoin. Cela ne peut qu'améliorer et conforter la méthode qu'elle appliquera dans les cas où la zone à délimiter présente une complexité géographique, en particulier, dans les golfe à la concavité prononcée et où les côtes de plus de deux Etats se font face, ou lorsqu'il y a une présence insulaire. On peut donc espérer que la même subtile évolution ramènera la Cour sur une voie plus en accord avec la lettre et l'esprit du droit contemporain de la délimitation maritime tel qu'il est sorti des négociations de la IIIe Conférence des Nations Unies sur le droit de la mer, et a été suivi pendant un certain temps par sa propre jurisprudence.

Compulsory Jurisdiction under the Law of the Sea Convention: Its Achievements and Limits

Mariko Kawano

Introduction

It has been more than 30 years since the adoption of the United Nations Convention on the Law of the Sea (LOSC). The compulsory jurisdiction of international courts and tribunals under Section 2 of Part XV has been considered one of the most significant achievements of the international community to enhance compulsory jurisdictions. Over time, the number of cases referred to the compulsory procedure under this section has gradually increased. Through those precedents, the significance of LOSC's compulsory jurisdiction has been confirmed and, at the same time, the elements that restrict its scope and effect have also been revealed. This article examines the achievements and limits of the compulsory jurisdiction established by LOSC.

1   Choice of Procedures in Accordance with Article 287

Article 287 provides for the optional choice of international courts and tribunals. While State Parties of LOSC are entitled to declare their choice or preference among the courts and tribunals provided thereby, they are deemed to have accepted at least the jurisdiction of an arbitral tribunal under Annex VII of LOSC, even if no choice or preference is declared. Accordingly, the court or tribunal is endowed with compulsory jurisdiction when the conditions provided in Part XV are satisfied.

In the *M/V Louisa* case, the Parties disagreed on the scope of the declaration pursuant to Article 287. Although both Parties had chosen the International Tribunal for the Law of the Sea (ITLOS), in their declarations Saint Vincent and the Grenadines declared that they chose ITLOS as the means of settlement of disputes concerning the arrest or detention of their vessels. The Parties took different views with regard to the scope of the ITLOS jurisdiction as a result of the limitations made by Saint Vincent and the Grenadines's declaration. While Spain argued that the ITLOS jurisdiction would be limited to disputes falling under any provision of the Convention that expressly contains the terms arrest or detention of vessels, Saint Vincent and the Grenadines took the view that they accepted the ITLOS jurisdiction as the means of settling disputes concerning the arrest or detention of their vessels.[1]

ITLOS noted that LOSC did not preclude a declaration limited to a particular category of disputes and considered that this system was similar to that of ICJ under Article 36, paragraph 2, of its Statute.[2] It took the view that where State Parties had made declarations of differing scope under Article 287, its jurisdiction existed only to the extent that the substance of the declarations of the two Parties to a dispute coincided, and that it had jurisdiction only insofar as the dispute was covered by the more limited declaration.[3] Taking the view that Saint Vincent and the Grenadines' declaration was meant to cover all claims connected with the arrest or detention of its vessels, ITLOS did not admit the narrow interpretation by Spain. Accordingly, it concluded that the declaration of Saint Vincent and the Grenadines covered the arrest or detention of their vessels and all matters connected therewith.[4]

In the *Barbados/Trinidad and Tobago* Arbitration, the Arbitral Tribunal pointed out that the unilateral reference of a dispute to a compulsory dispute settlement procedure, in accordance with Article 286 was indeed similar to that in accordance with Article 36, paragraph 2, of the Statute of the ICJ.[5] It is interesting to note that ITLOS further admitted the similarity of these two institutions even with regard to the scope of the declarations made by State Parties. It seems that Part XV establishes the enhanced compulsory jurisdiction of international courts and tribunals, in the sense that the enhancement is realized only with regard to the compulsory jurisdiction of the arbitral tribunal under Annex VII. As far as the compulsory jurisdictions of judicial institutions (i.e., ICJ and ITLOS) are concerned, the will of State Parties under LOSC prevails, and their compulsory jurisdiction depends upon the consent of the Parties to a dispute.

---

1 M/V *"Louisa"* Case, (Saint Vincent and the Grenadines v Kingdom of Spain), Case No 18, Judgment, of 28 May 2013, paras. 77–78.
2 Ibid., paras. 79–80.
3 Ibid., paras. 81–82.
4 Ibid., paras. 83–84.
5 Arbitration between Barbados and Trinidad and Tobago, relating to the delimitation of the exclusive economic zone and the continental shelf between them, decision of 11 April 2006, 27 RIAA 2007, p. 208, paras. 208–209.

2 Requirements for Resorting to the Compulsory Jurisdiction under LOSC (Article 286)

The requirements for resorting to compulsory jurisdiction under Section 2 of LOSC are basically provided in its Article 286. First, there must be the existence of a dispute concerning the interpretation or application of LOSC; secondly, the condition must be one wherein no settlement has been reached by recourse to Section 1; and thirdly, it is subject to Section 3.

2.1 The Existence of a Dispute Concerning the Interpretation or Application of LOSC

The first requirement under Article 286 is repeated in Article 288, paragraph 1.

2.1.1 Dispute Concerning Specific Provisions

When a dispute settlement system provided by a treaty is invoked, it is the established principle that the Applicant should establish that the claim of one party is positively opposed by the other with regard to specific provision(s) of the convention that contains the compromissory clause invoked. This principle is applied in cases unilaterally referred in accordance with Section 2 of LOSC and is argued in the context of the existence of the dispute concerning the interpretation or application of LOSC.

In the *M/V Louisa* case, ITLOS examined the contents of the provisions invoked by the Applicant to establish the existence of a dispute concerning the interpretation and application of specific provisions. In that case, the Parties agreed that the origin of the case lay in the detention of the M/V Louisa. Saint Vincent and the Grenadines invoked several provisions as bases for their arguments. They referred to Articles 73, 87, 226, 227, and 303 from the Written Pleadings through to the final submissions. They referred to Articles 245 and 304 only in their Written Pleadings. ITLOS found that none of these provisions covered the rules and obligations relevant to the claims in this case.[6]

From this precedent, it can be pointed out that ITLOS took the view that an Applicant is required to establish a sufficiently relevant relationship between the facts and claims, on the one hand, and substantive rules in the provisions invoked, on the other.

---

6   *M/V Louisa*, supra, note 1, paras. 95–125.

2.1.2 Mixed Disputes and Disputes Concerning the Interpretation and Application of LOSC

The international courts and tribunals have repeatedly confirmed the principle that land dominates the sea through the projection of the coasts or the coastal fronts and that the land is the legal source of the power which a State may exercise over territorial extensions to seaward.[7] This principle reflects the close relationship between a territorial sovereignty and jurisdiction over maritime areas. In many cases where the Parties have a dispute concerning the maritime delimitation or the legality or compatibility of conduct allegedly undertaken in accordance with the provisions of LOSC, they also have a dispute concerning territorial sovereignty. Such disputes are called mixed disputes.[8]

In some cases of mixed disputes, the issues concerning the territorial sovereignty aspect can be separated from that of the maritime dispute. In other cases, the maritime dispute cannot be settled without settlement of the territorial dispute. The question is whether such a mixed dispute may fall within the scope of the interpretation or application of LOSC in accordance with Articles 286 and 288, paragraph 1, because LOSC contains no rules concerning territorial sovereignty.

This question was examined for the first time in the *Chagos Marine Protected Area* Arbitration. In that case, Mauritius made four submissions on the merits. In its first and second submissions, Mauritius disputed the right of the United Kingdom as a 'coastal State' to declare a marine protected area or other maritime zone[9] and its right as a 'coastal State' in relation to the area concerned.[10] In its fourth submission, Mauritius discussed the compatibility with LOSC of the marine protected area set by the United Kingdom.[11] Regarding the first submission, the Arbitral Tribunal found it properly characterized as relating to land sovereignty. According to the Tribunal, where the 'real issue in the case' and the 'object of the claim' did not relate to the interpretation or application of LOSC, an incidental connection between the dispute and some matter regulated by LOSC was insufficient to bring the dispute, as a whole, within the

---

7　*Maritime Delimitation in the Black Sea* (Romania v Ukraine), Judgment, *ICJ Reports 2009*, p. 89, para. 77.

8　Regarding the arguments about the jurisdiction of the tribunals under UNCLOS over 'mixed disputes', see I. Buga, 'Territorial Sovereignty Issues in Maritime Disputes: A Jurisdictional Dilemma for Law of the Sea Tribun *The International Journal of Marine and Coastal Law*', 27, 2012, pp. 59–95.

9　*Chagos Marine Protected Area Arbitration* (Mauritius v United Kingdom), Award of 18 March 2015, para. 163.

10　Ibid., para. 207.

11　Ibid., para. 231.

ambit of Article 288, paragraph 1. Thus, it concluded that it lacked jurisdiction to address the first submission.[12] The Tribunal also concluded that it lacked jurisdiction to address the second submission because the underlying dispute regarding sovereignty was also predominant here.[13] Note that the Tribunal stated that it did 'not categorically exclude that in some instances a minor issue of territorial sovereignty could indeed be ancillary to a dispute concerning the interpretation or application of the Convention.'[14]

In the Award on Jurisdiction and Admissibility in the *Philippines* v *China* Arbitration, the Arbitral Tribunal admitted the limits on the claims to be submitted to it. It also confirmed the findings of the Arbitral Tribunal in the *Chagos Marine Protected Area* Arbitration that the dispute concerning sovereignty could not be considered to concern the interpretation or application of LOSC. However, the Tribunal took the view that none of the Philippines' submissions required an implicit determination of sovereignty and that the Philippines had successfully narrowed the issues in dispute.[15] With regard to the nature of the dispute before it, the Tribunal also pointed out that the dispute concerning the existence of an entitlement to maritime zones was distinct from one concerning delimitation of those zones in an area where the entitlements of the parties overlap; and that the Philippines had not challenged the existence and extent of the maritime entitlements claimed by China in the South China Sea.[16] Then the Tribunal examined the nature of the Philippines' submissions and concluded that Submissions No. 1 through 7 concerned various aspect of the Parties' dispute over the sources and extent of maritime entitlements in the South China Sea while Submissions No. 8 through 14 concerned a series of disputes regarding Chinese activities in the South China Sea.[17]

2.2 *'No Settlement has been Reached by Recourse to Section 1'* (*Articles 281, 282, and 283*)

The Applicant must justify the requirements under Articles 281, 282, and 283 in order to satisfy the second condition, that 'no settlement has been reached by recourse to Section 1.'

---

12 Ibid., paras. 209–220.
13 Ibid., para. 228–230.
14 Ibid., para. 221.
15 *The South China Sea Arbitration* (The Republic of Philippines v The People's Republic of China), Award on Jurisdiction and Admissibility, 29 October 2015, paras. 153–154.
16 Ibid., paras. 155–157.
17 Ibid., paras. 158–178.

2.2.1 Exclusion of Compulsory Jurisdiction (Article 281)

The requirement under Article 281 was decisive in deciding to deny the jurisdiction of the Arbitral Tribunal in the *Southern Bluefin Tuna* cases. The Tribunal found that Article 16, the compromissory clause, of the Convention on the Conservation of Southern Bluefin Tuna providing for the settlement by the agreement of the Parties implied their intention to exclude the compulsory dispute-settlement procedure. Therefore, the Tribunal concluded that it lacked jurisdiction to entertain this case in accordance with Article 281, paragraph 1. Moreover, the Tribunal pointed out that 'a significant number of international agreements with maritime elements, entered into after the adoption of LOSC, exclude with varying degrees of explicitness unilateral reference of a dispute to compulsory adjudicative or arbitral procedures.'[18]

It may be suggested that the award in the *Southern Bluefin Tuna* cases reflected the realistic approach of the Arbitral Tribunal, emphasizing the need to respect the freedom of sovereign States to choose peaceful means for settling international disputes. However, from the viewpoint of emphasizing the basic purpose of the enhancement of compulsory jurisdiction by Section 2 of Part XV and its significance, this conclusion would affect the effectiveness of the compulsory jurisdiction.

In the *South China Sea* Arbitration, China argued that the 2002 Declaration of Conduct of Parties in the South China Sea, adopted by the foreign ministers of ASEAN and the People's Republic of China, hereafter referred to as the DOC, and other bilateral documents, expressed the Parties' intention to exclude the compulsory procedure under Section 2. Regarding the DOC, the Tribunal first found that it was not legally binding, in terms of Article 281.[19] In addition to this finding, the Tribunal added two points: first, that Article 281 only requires Parties to abide by any time limit set out in their agreement, and the DOC does not contain such a time limit.[20] Secondly, the Tribunal, took the view that the exclusion under this provision should be recorded in express terms.[21]

China also referred to other bilateral statements made by the Philippines and China before and after the DOC, indicating that the Parties had preferred other peaceful means and intended to exclude compulsory dispute settlement under Section 2. The Arbitral Tribunal did not agree with this argument.[22] It also

---

18   *Southern Bluefin Tuna* (Australia v Japan; New Zealand v Japan), Award on Jurisdiction and Admissibility, 4 August 2000, 23 RIAA 2004, p. 45, para. 63.
19   *The South China Sea Arbitration*, supra, note 15, paras. 212–218.
20   Ibid., paras. 219–220.
21   Ibid., paras. 221–228. The Tribunal explicitly opposed to the view of the Arbitral Award in *Southern Bluefin Tuna*, (para. 223).
22   Ibid, paras. 241–251.

examined the possibility of excluding compulsory jurisdiction using the Treaty of Amity and Cooperation in Southeast Asia (the Treaty of Amity), and the Convention on Biological Diversity (CBD). It admitted that they were legally binding on the Parties. However, it also concluded that the Treaty of Amity did not prescribe a particular form of dispute settlement. It also considered that while the CBD and LOSC established parallel environmental regimes that overlapped in a discrete area, they also created distinct jurisdiction. Therefore, a dispute concerning one convention does not necessarily mean that it concerns the other conventions.[23]

In examining the requirement under Article 281, the Arbitral Tribunal disagreed with the finding of the Arbitral Award in the *Southern Bluefin Tuna* cases and stated that 'Article 281 requires some clear statement of exclusion of further procedures' and that '[t]his is supported by the text and context of Article 281 and by the structure and overall purpose of the Convention.'[24]

With regard to the contradictory decisions of the Arbitral Tribunals in the cases of *Southern Bluefin Tuna* and the *South China Sea* Arbitration, it is necessary to note the difference of the two situations. In the former, the basis for the Tribunal's decision was a legally binding instrument which provided for specific rules in relation to the general rules of LOSC. Moreover, Japan submitted a list of numerous examples of conventions and treaties in which compulsory jurisdiction under LOSC is explicitly or implicitly excluded. By contrast, in the latter case, DOC lacked a legally binding effect and other conventions invoked were not very specific to the subject-matters of the dispute before the Tribunal. Not only the binding nature of the instrument but also the specificity of the convention in relation to the subject-matter of the dispute may be relevant to the decision of the existence of the requirement under Article 281. It seems that it will be necessary to wait for a further accumulation of cases in order to argue the interpretation of Article 281.

2.2.2 Obligations under General, Regional or Bilateral Agreements (Article 282)

In accordance with Article 282, when it is established that the disputing Parties are under an obligation stemming from another procedure pursuant to general, regional or bilateral agreements to submit their dispute to the procedure that entails a binding decision, that procedure shall apply in lieu of the compulsory procedure under Section 2 of Part XV of the LOSC. This provision also

---

23 For examination of the Treaty of Amity, ibid., paras. 265–269 and for the CBD, ibid., paras. 281–289.

24 Ibid., para. 223.

reflects a respect for the freedom of the Parties to enter into an agreement regarding the choice of international courts and tribunals.

In no precedent has the application of this provision been argued. In the *South China Sea* Arbitration, although China submitted no argument in accordance with Article 282 in its Position Paper, the Arbitral Tribunal invited further argument from the Philippines on the effect of the Treaty of Amity in reference to Article 282 of LOSC. It also requested the Philippines to submit arguments on the effect of the compromissory clause, Article 27 of the CBD, because the Philippines argued in its Memorial that China had violated its obligations under the CBD.[25]

With regard to the effect of the Treaty of Amity, the Tribunal found that all the provisions concerning the settlement of disputes provided for the mechanism on the basis of the agreement of the disputing Parties, and that there was no agreement on binding dispute resolution. It further stated that the Parties had agreed that none of its provisions precluded recourse to the modes of peaceful settlement in accordance with Article 33, paragraph 1, of the UN Charter. As far as the CBD's compromissory clause was concerned, the Tribunal examined the three conditions to be satisfied under Article 282.[26] It found that none of them was satisfied in this case. By examining the effects of the Treaty of Amity and CBD, the Tribunal concluded that these instruments did not satisfy the conditions provided in Article 282.[27]

2.2.3   The Exchange of Views (Article 283)

The requirement for the exchange of views under Article 283 is important for protecting the alleged Respondent against excessive unexpected referral of the dispute to compulsory jurisdiction in accordance with Section 2 of Part XV. Under the mechanism for compulsory jurisdiction, proceedings can be instituted solely by the decision of one of the disputing Parties. Although the Applicant is required to specify the subject(s) of the dispute and the bases for the jurisdiction, the formulation of such issues is totally independent of the Applicant's decision. Therefore, the alleged Respondent may consider a

---

25   Ibid., paras. 304 and 311–313.
26   The Tribunal stated that Article 27 of the CBD must have satisfied the following three conditions: '(a) Article 27 of the CBD constitutes an agreement for the settlement of 'a dispute concerning the interpretation or application of the [LOSC] Convention'; (b) that 'there is an agreement to submit such disputes to a compulsory procedure, in the sense that the dispute is capable of being unilaterally initiated, 'at the request of any party to the dispute'; and (c) that 'the agreed compulsory procedure 'entails a binding decision'.', ibid., para. 318.
27   Ibid., paras. 319–320.

unilateral referral of the alleged dispute by the Applicant to be completely unexpected and may believe that other, more appropriate procedures are available.

In the *Barbados/Trinidad and Tobago* Arbitration, the dispute was over maritime delimitation, to which Articles 74 and 83 were to be applied. Examining the requirement under paragraph 2 of these provisions, the Tribunal considered that there was a dispute concerning the interpretation or application of these provisions that could not have been settled by negotiation between the Parties within a reasonable period.[28] The Tribunal then discussed the relationship between paragraphs 1 and 2 of Articles 74 and 83 and Article 283, paragraph 1. It took the view that, when disputing Parties cannot, within a reasonable time, reach an agreement through their negotiations, in accordance with paragraph 1 of Articles 74 and 83, further exchange of views under Article 283, paragraph 1, is not required. It stated, '[t]he required exchange of views is also inherent in the (failed) negotiations.'[29]

When a dispute concerning maritime delimitation is referred to the compulsory dispute settlement procedure, the Parties have normally pursued the negotiations for some time and at least one of them believes the negotiations to be deadlocked. The finding of the Arbitral Tribunal in the *Barbados/Trinidad and Tobago* Arbitration took into account the reality of the dispute concerning maritime delimitation. In cases other than disputes concerning maritime delimitation, the requirement of an exchange of views may play a more important role.

In the *Chagos Marine Protected Area* Arbitration, the United Kingdom raised an objection regarding the requirement under Article 283.[30] The Arbitral Tribunal first stated that Article 283 required the Parties to exchange views regarding the means for resolving their dispute and decided that the obligation could not be understood as one requiring the negotiation of the substance of the dispute. The Tribunal noted that the Parties indicated the appropriateness of the bilateral negotiations to settle the dispute in addition to the substantive matters in their letters of December 2009 and considered that this was sufficient to satisfy the requirement under Article 283. It stated, '[i]t is not necessary for the Parties to comprehensively canvas the means for the peaceful settlement of disputes set out in either the UN Charter or the Convention, nor was Mauritius 'obliged to continue with an exchange of views when it concludes that the possibilities of reaching agreement have been exhausted.' It also pointed out that Article 283 required neither that the exchange of views

---

28   *Barbados/Trinidad and Tobago*, supra, note 5, p. 204, paras. 193–197.
29   Ibid., pp. 206–207, paras. 201–207.
30   *Chagos Marine Protected Area*, supra, note 9, paras. 364–366.

include the possibility of compulsory settlement nor that one party caution the other regarding the possibility of litigation or set out the specific claims that it might choose to advance.[31]

In the *Arctic Sunrise* Arbitration, the Arbitral Tribunal admitted that communication between the Parties regarding the settlement of the dispute was brief and one-sided because the Netherlands sent a letter addressed to the Ambassador of the Russian Federation to the Netherlands and a *Note Verbale* only one day before the commencement of arbitration; and there was no reply from Russia. However, it also noted that this was sufficient because of the urgency resulting from the circumstances of the case. It took the view that it was reasonable for the Netherlands to conclude that 'the possibilities to settle the dispute by negotiation or otherwise ha[d] been exhausted.'[32]

The *South China Sea* Arbitration also examined the requirement under Article 283. The Arbitral Tribunal first noted the difficulty in separating the communications on procedural and substantive matters in the negotiations between the disputing Parties.[33] It also confirmed that the requirement under 283 was limited to the exchange of views on the means for the settlement of the dispute.[34] The Tribunal examined the communications between the Philippines and China since 1995 and concluded that this requirement had been satisfied.[35] The Tribunal turned to the objection raised by China's Position Paper that 'the two countries have never engaged in negotiations with regard to the subject-matter of the arbitration,' which should have been separated from the exchange of views on the means to settle the dispute.

From these precedents, it can be concluded that the requirement of an exchange of views on the procedures to settle the dispute was interpreted rather flexibly to facilitate referral of disputes to an international court or tribunal.

3   Limitations and Exceptions in Accordance with Section 3 of Part XV

The third requirement under Article 286 is reflected in the expression 'subject to Section 3'. This requirement means that the subject of a dispute before an international court or tribunal does not fall within the scope of the limitations

---

31   Ibid., paras. 381–386.

32   *The Arctic Sunrise case* (Kingdom of the Netherlands v Russian Federation), Case No 22, Award of 14 August 2015, paras. 152–156.

33   *The South China Sea Arbitration*, supra, note 15, para. 332.

34   Ibid., para. 333.

35   Ibid., paras. 334–343.

and exceptions provided by Articles 297 and 298. Compulsory jurisdiction under Section 2 of Part xv can be restricted by the limitation or exclusion provided in Section 3. In the *Southern Bluefin Tuna* cases, the Arbitral Tribunal pointed out that Part xv did not establish a really comprehensive compulsory jurisdiction for international courts and tribunals because of the wide range of limitations and exceptions provided in this section.[36]

In recent precedents, the Respondents have invoked Articles 297 and 298 in their arguments on the objections concerning jurisdiction.

Returning to the *Chagos Marine Protected Area* Arbitration, the Arbitral Tribunal discussed the issues relating to Article 297 when examining its jurisdiction over Mauritius' fourth submission. The applicability of Article 297 (1)(c) or (3)(a) was discussed for this purpose.[37] Mauritius characterized the subject of the fourth submission concerning the marine protected area (MPA) as that of a measure 'for the protection and preservation of the marine environment,' which is provided in Article 297 (3)(a). The United Kingdom, in turn, argued that the subject of the fourth submission was an exercise of 'its sovereign rights with respect to the living resources of the exclusive economic zone,' which is excluded from the compulsory jurisdiction under Section 2 of Part xv, in accordance with Article 297 (1)(c).[38]

In its examination of the character of the dispute between the Parties, the Arbitral Tribunal did not accept the argument of the United Kingdom that the marine protected area was solely concerned with a measure relating to fisheries. The Tribunal found that 'the dispute between the Parties in relation to the compatibility of the MPA with the Convention relates more broadly to the preservation of the marine environment and to the legal regime applicable to the Archipelago and its surrounding waters when it is eventually returned to Mauritius' and thus the fourth submission could 'not be excluded entirely by the exception from jurisdiction set out Article 297 (3)(a).'[39] In the argument on the application of Article 297 (1)(c), the Tribunal first found that 'Article 297 (1) reaffirms, but does not limit, the Tribunal's jurisdiction pursuant to Article 288 (1).'[40] It concluded that 'the Parties' dispute in respect of the MPA related to the preservation of the marine environment and that Mauritius had alleged a

---

36   *Southern Bluefin Tuna*, supra, note 18, pp. 44–45, paras. 61–62.
37   *Chagos Marine Protected Area*, supra, note 9, paras. 232–323.
38   Ibid., paras. 233–284.
39   Ibid., paras. 286–304.
40   Ibid., para. 308.

violation of international rules and standards in this area,' to which 'Article 297 (1)(c) expressly reaffirms the application of compulsory settlement.'[41]

In the Arbitral Award of 29 October 2015 in the *South China Sea* Arbitration, the Arbitral Tribunal examined the possible application of Articles 297 and 298. Regarding Article 297, the Tribunal concluded that it was not barred from the consideration of issues concerning the status of a shoal or reefs (Submissions No. 3 and 7 of the Philippines) and concerning the interference by China with the traditional fishing activities of Philippine nationals at Scarborough Shoal (Submissions No. 9 and 10 of the Philippines).[42] Regarding the dispute concerning the protection and preservation of the marine environment (Submission No. 11 of the Philippines), the Tribunal stated that Articles 297 and 298 have no application in the territorial sea and that the alleged harmful activities in the EEZ fall within the scope of its jurisdiction in accordance with Article 297 (1)(c).[43]

With regard to Article 298, China, in 2006, made a declaration in accordance with this provision excluding all categories of disputes provided thereby. The Arbitral Tribunal had to examine the effects of this declaration on the case before it.[44] The Tribunal reserved consideration of its jurisdiction to rule on Philippines' Submissions No. 1, 2, 5, 8, 9, 12, 14 and 15, to the merits phase. Except for Submission No. 15,[45] the Tribunal considered the submissions related to the 'historic bays or titles' or the overlapping entitlements to the maritime zones provided by Article 298 (1)(a)(i),[46] or to military activities and law-enforcement activities provided by Article 298 (1)(b).[47] It concluded that those submissions were not exclusively preliminary and thus reserved consideration of

---

41 Ibid., para. 319. It is very interesting to note that in relation to this conclusion, the Tribunal pointed out that while the control of pollution was an important aspect of the protection and preservation of the marine environment, it was by no means the only one, (Ibid., para. 320).

42 *The South China Sea Arbitration*, supra, note 15, paras. 358–360, 400, 404, and 406–407.

43 Ibid., para. 408.

44 Ibid., para. 366.

45 With regard to Submission No. 15, the Tribunal ordered the Philippines to clarify its content and narrow its scope, ibid., para. 413.

46 The Arbitral Tribunal considered as follows: Submissions No. 1 and No. 2 by the Philippines contained the question relating to 'historic bays or titles', ibid., paras. 398 and 399; Submissions No. 5, 8 and 9 by the Philippines involved the issue of maritime delimitation, ibid., paras. 402, 405 and 406.

47 The Arbitral Tribunal considered that Submission No. 12 by the Philippines related to the question of whether the activities undertaken by China on Mischief Reef were military in nature, ibid., para. 409, and that Submission No. 14 by the Philippines depended on the status of the Second Thomas Shoal, which was a matter on the merits and China's activities in and around the Second Thomas Shoal were military in nature, ibid., para. 411.

its jurisdiction on those submissions to the merits phase. The purpose was to avoid taking up issues involving decisions on the issues excluded by China's Declaration.

In its Arbitral Award of 12 July 2016, the Arbitral Tribunal finally decided the issues of its jurisdiction in accordance with Article 298. In its consideration of Submissions Nos. 1 and 2, the Tribunal examined China's claim in the name of 'historic rights', referring to the 'historic bays and titles' under Article 298 (1)(a)(i). It found that 'China claims rights to the living and non-living resources within the so-called 'nine-dash line', but (apart from the territorial sea generated by any islands) does not consider that those waters form part of its territorial sea or internal waters.'[48] The Tribunal then examined the drafting process of the terms 'historic titles' in this provision and stated that they were a 'reference to claims of sovereignty over maritime areas derived from historical circumstances.'[49] Accordingly, it concluded that the 'historic rights' claimed by China were broader and less specific than the 'historic titles' and that it had jurisdiction to consider Submissions 1 and 2 by the Philippines regarding the compatibility of the 'historic rights' and the 'nine-dash line' claimed by China with the LOSC.[50]

With regard to the exclusion of the dispute 'concerning sea boundary delimitations' under Article 298 (1)(a)(i), the findings of the Arbitral Tribunal that some of the maritime features concerned were low-tide elevations and that the fact of there being no island that was capable of generating an entitlement to exclusive economic zone or continental shelf played a decisive role.[51] As a result of these findings, the Tribunal found that there was no possibility of overlap of maritime entitlements.[52] Accordingly, it concluded that it had jurisdiction to consider Submissions No. 5, 8, and 9.[53]

---

48 *The South China Sea Arbitration* (The Republic of Philippines v The People's Republic of China), Award of 16 July 2016, para. 214.
49 Ibid., para. 226.
50 Ibid., paras. 228–229.
51 The Arbitral Tribunal found that Hughes Reef, Gaven Reef (South), Subi Reef, Mischief Reef and Second Thomas Shoal were low-tide elevations, (ibid., para. 383), and that Scarborough Shoal, Cuarteron Reef, Fiery Cross Reef, Johnson Reef, McKennan Reef and Gaven Reef (North) were 'rocks' in accordance with Article 121, paragraph 3, of the LOSC, (ibid., paras. 643–645).
52 With regard to Submission No. 5, (ibid., paras. 646), Submission No. 8, (ibid., paras. 692–695), Submission No. 9, (ibid., para. 734), Submission No. 12, (ibid., para. 1025), and Submission No. 14, (Ibid., para. 1153).
53 Submission No. 5, (ibid., paras. 627–633), Submission No. 8, (ibid., paras. 691–695), and Submission No. 9, (ibid., paras. 733–734).

As far as the exclusion of the dispute concerning 'military activities' in accordance with Article 298 (1)(b) was concerned, the Tribunal first examined the nature of the activities taken up by the Philippines in Submission 11 as amended, Submission 12, and Submission No. 14 (d) as amended. Here the Philippines argued China's failure to protect and preserve the marine environment. The Tribunal noted that China had repeated that the land reclamation and other activities were intended to fulfil civilian purposes and for this reason concluded that it had jurisdiction to consider these submissions.[54]

With regard to this exclusion, the findings of the Tribunal regarding Submissions No. 14 (a) to (c) should be particularly noted. In Submission 14 as amended after the Arbitral Award of 29 October 2015, the Philippines raised elements concerning the aggravation or extension of the dispute through China's activities after the initiation of the proceedings. While Submission No. 14 (d) was closely related to Submissions No. 11 and 12, Submissions No. 14 (a) to (c) concerned China's interaction with the Armed Forces of the Philippines at Second Thomas Shoal. Accordingly, applicability of Article 298 (1)(b), was important to establish the jurisdiction of the Arbitral Tribunal.

The Tribunal first noted that '[w]here a State Party has initiated compulsory dispute settlement under the Convention in respect of a dispute that does not concern military activities, Article 298 (1)(b), would not come into play if the other Party were later to begin employing its military in relation to the dispute in the course of proceedings' and that '[w]here the aggravation of the dispute is alleged ... as a substantive claim, the Tribunal finds it necessary to consider whether the claim of aggravation remains dependent on an underlying dispute, or whether it itself constitutes a distinct dispute to which the military activities exception would be applicable.'[55] The Tribunal further stated that 'China's actions in and around Second Thomas Shoal and its interaction with the Philippine military forces stationed there constitute a distinct matter, irrespective of their effect in potentially aggravating other disputes before the Tribunal' and found it necessary to evaluate 'whether this dispute concerns military activities for the purposes of Article 298 (1)(b)'.[56] The Tribunal noted that there was 'a quintessentially military situation, involving the military forces of one side and a combination of military and paramilitary forces on the other, arrayed in opposition to one another' and that those facts fell within

---

54 Submission No. 11 as amended and Submission No. 12 (b), (ibid., paras. 934–938) and Submission No. 12, (Ibid., paras. 1027–1028), and Submission No. 14 (d), (ibid., paras. 1164–1165).
55 Ibid., paras. 1158–1159.
56 Ibid., para. 1160.

the exclusion of 'military activities'. Accordingly, the Tribunal concluded that it lacked 'jurisdiction to consider the Philippines' Submissions No. 14 (a) to (c)'.[57]

It seems that the standards and criteria for the decision of the military nature of the activities concerned are not very coherent. Regarding the nature of the land reclamation and other activities, the Tribunal decided it by considering their purpose explained by China. By contrast, it decided that of the activities of Chinese vessels in and around the Second Thomas shoal by examining their objective nature. It is true that the purpose or objective nature of the land reclamation and other activities was very difficult and that the nature of activities should be determined by taking account of the circumstances of respective activity. However, it may be questioned whether it is not necessary or more appropriate to ensure certain standards or criteria in order to ensure the predictability of the exception of the compulsory jurisdiction.

The freedom of exclusion by making a declaration under Article 298 was argued in the *Arctic Sunrise* Arbitration. In this case, Russia refused to appear before the Arbitral Tribunal.[58] The Tribunal first stated that, as the Parties had chosen different procedures in their respective declarations, the dispute was referred to the Arbitral Tribunal in accordance with Annex VII.[59] When Russia ratified LOSC, it made a declaration in accordance with Article 298 to exclude the compulsory jurisdiction under Section 2 with respect to certain categories which included 'the dispute concerning law-enforcement activities in regard to the exercise of sovereign rights or jurisdiction.'[60] According to Russia, the dispute referred by the Netherlands concerned law-enforcement activities and thus was excluded from compulsory jurisdiction. The Tribunal took the view that Russia's declaration 'can only apply to an exception that is permitted under Article 298' and that 'Russia's Declaration cannot create an exclusion that is wider in scope than what is permitted by Article 298 (1)(b).' The Tribunal stated that Russia could exclude only the dispute concerning law-enforcement activities in regard to the exercise of sovereign rights or jurisdiction that is validly excluded from the jurisdiction of a court or tribunal pursuant to paragraphs 2 and 3 of Article read with Article 298 (1)(b). It concluded that Russia's

---

57 Ibid., paras. 1161–1162.
58 The Arbitral Tribunal decided to bifurcate the procedure and to discuss the arguments in Russia's *Note Verbal* as preliminary objections, Procedural Order No. 4 (Bifurcation), 21 November 2014.
59 *The Arctic Sunrise case* (Kingdom of the Netherlands v Russian Federation), Case No 22, Award on Jurisdiction of 26 November 2014, para. 64.
60 Ibid., para. 65.

actions in the case before it did not fall within any of the categories provided in those paragraphs.[61]

The arbitral tribunals in the three precedents decided the scope of their jurisdiction by interpreting the limitations and exceptions in accordance with the explicit terms of Articles 297 and 298, noting that the subject of a dispute before the tribunal is very important in the examination of the interpretation and application of those provisions. Although State Parties are entitled to make a declaration to exclude compulsory jurisdiction under Section 2 under Article 298, that right can be exercised only within the scope provided by LOSC. It should be reiterated that the fundamental purpose of Section 2 of Part XV of LOSC is the enhancement of compulsory jurisdiction of international courts and tribunals: the possible right of State Parties to opt *out* of the system of compulsory jurisdiction should not be interpreted flexibly.

4   Strategic Use of Article 300

As final points to be argued, the role of Article 300 should be examined. In the *Southern Bluefin Tuna* cases, the Arbitral Tribunal found that it lacked jurisdiction to entertain the case. At the same time, it stated: 'The Tribunal does not exclude the possibility that there might be instances in which the conduct of a State Party to LOSC and to a fisheries treaty implementing it would be so egregious, and risk consequences of such gravity, that a Tribunal might find that the obligations of LOSC provide a basis for jurisdiction, having particular regard to the provisions of Article 300.'[62] This statement may allow the Applicant to request an international court or tribunal to mitigate the strict application of the requirements for the compulsory jurisdiction in a dispute concerning grave or serious violation of the substantive rules of LOSC and highlight the potential influence of the gravity or seriousness of the violation of substantive rules on the procedural requirements.

When an Applicant finds problems in the establishment of jurisdiction of an international court or tribunal, it may consider submitting the arguments by invoking Article 300. In that case, note that this provision cannot be invoked on its own. In the *M/V Louisa* case, the ITLOS confirmed that 'Article 300 cannot be invoked on its own' and that '[i]t becomes relevant only when 'the rights, jurisdiction and freedoms recognized' in the Convention are exercised

---

61   Ibid., paras. 66–78.
62   *Southern Bluefin Tuna*, supra, note 18, p. 46, para. 64.

in an abusive manner.'[63] In the *Chagos Marine Protected Area* Arbitration, the Arbitral Tribunal also confirmed that 'a claim pursuant to Article 300 is necessarily linked to the alleged violation of another provision of the Convention.'[64]

Arguments submitted on the basis of Article 300, must be raised at an early stage of the proceedings. In the *M/V Louisa* case, Saint Vincent and the Grenadines began arguments regarding this provision after closure of the written pleadings. The ITLOS considered that reliance on this provision generated a new claim in comparison to the claims presented in the Application, and there were no special circumstances to allow the submission of new claims. Accordingly, the ITLOS concluded that the arguments regarding the violation of Article 300 could not be admitted.[65] The Applicant may perhaps be required to invoke Article 300 in a strategic way.

Problems of abusive recourse to compulsory jurisdiction may also be considered. In unilaterally referred cases, the alleged Respondent may argue that the Applicant is abusing the compulsory procedure under Section 2 of Part XV and that there is no basis for referring that dispute under LOSC. Note that State Parties to LOSC are under the conventional obligation to respond to the compulsory procedure provided in Section 2 of Part XV and, moreover, that the sincere willingness of the Applicant to settle a dispute by recourse to the compulsory jurisdiction should be faithfully respected. However, compulsory procedure may be abused. Therefore, in order to protect the alleged Respondent against the abusive referral of a dispute to compulsory jurisdiction and to ensure the trust and confidence of State Parties in the system of compulsory jurisdiction under LOSC, a certain mechanism is required. Article 294, paragraph 1, provides that 'a court or tribunal provided for in Article 287 to which an application is made in respect of a dispute referred to in Article 297 shall determine at the request of a party, or may determine *proprio motu*, whether the claim constitutes an abuse of legal process or whether *prima facie* it is well founded. If the court or tribunal determines that the claim constitutes an abuse of legal process or is *prima facie* unfounded, it shall take no further action in the case.'

There has been no precedent to date in which this provision has been invoked; Article 300 has been referred to instead. In the *Barbados/Trinidad and Tobago* Arbitration, the Arbitral Tribunal stated that 'the unilateral invocation of the arbitration procedure cannot by itself be regarded as an abuse of right contrary to Article 300 of LOSC, or an abuse of right contrary to general

---

63   *M/V Louisa*, supra, note 1, para. 137.
64   *Chagos Marine Protected Area*, supra, note 9, para. 303.
65   *M/V Louisa*, supra, note 1, paras. 141–147.

international law' and 'Article 286 confers a unilateral right, and its exercise unilaterally and without discussion or agreement with the other Party is a straightforward exercise of the right conferred by the treaty, in the manner there envisaged.'[66]

In the *South China Sea* Arbitration, the Arbitral Tribunal referred to its finding in the *Barbados/Trinidad and Tobago* Arbitration and did not agree with China's argument that the Philippines had abused the procedure.[67] In its Award of 12 July 2016, the Tribunal referred to an obligation of good faith under Article 300 in the examination of Submission No. 14 of the Philippines concerning the aggravation or extension of the dispute after the initiation of the proceedings. It concluded that 'actions by either Party to aggravate or extend the dispute would be incompatible with the recognition and performance in good faith' of the obligations to settle the dispute by peaceful means in accordance with Article 279 and to recognize the finality of the award and to ensure compliance under Article 296. It also added that the duty to 'abstain from any measure capable of exercising a prejudicial effect in regard to the execution of the decision to be given and, in general not allow any step of any kind to be taken which might aggravate or extend the dispute' constitutes a principle of international law that is applicable to States engaged in dispute settlement as such.'[68]

Arguments regarding the applicability of Article 300 seem to reflect the basic purpose of the establishment by Section 2 of Part XV of the enhanced compulsory jurisdiction of international courts and tribunals, which is to facilitate settlement of disputes concerning the interpretation or application of LOSC between the Parties by recourse to judicial or arbitral procedures. Under that system, the unilateral referral of a dispute by one disputing Party is the legitimate right of a State Party and the alleged Respondent is obliged to respect and facilitate that procedure and not to aggravate or extend the dispute pending the final judgment or award.

Concluding Remarks

It can be concluded that there were reasons for the Arbitral Tribunal in the *Southern Bluefin Tuna* Arbitration to point out the incomprehensive nature of the compulsory jurisdiction of international courts and tribunals provided by

---

66   *Barbados/Trinidad and Tobago*, supra, note 5, pp. 207–208, para. 208.
67   *The South China Sea*, supra, note 14, para. 126.
68   Ibid., paras. 1172–1173.

Part XV of LOSC. However, at the same time, there are cases in which LOSC constituted the sole basis for the unilateral referral of a dispute to judicial or arbitral procedures. Moreover, international courts and tribunals have interpreted the requirements for the unilateral reference of a dispute in a reasonably flexible way. It seems that they basically respect the intention of the drafters of LOSC to enhance compulsory jurisdiction and the significance of the settlement of a dispute by judicial or arbitral procedures that are deemed to afford the judgment or award a legally binding effect. It may also be suggested that the willingness of the Applicant to settle a dispute by recourse to compulsory jurisdiction has also been respected by an international court or tribunal.

LOSC contains provisions regarding substantive rules covering the whole range of the law of the sea, and the system for compulsory jurisdiction is also very complicated. Several possible rules may be applied to disputed issues, and the applicability of the provisions in Part XV may also differ in response to the substantive provisions invoked. Therefore, it should be fully noted that formulation of the subject of a dispute plays a pivotal role both in the context of the arguments of the jurisdiction and admissibility and the arguments on the merits. It is necessary that the Applicant should in its Application strategically use the right to formulate the subject of a dispute. At the same time, the alleged Respondent may sensibly and strategically consider possible preliminary objections and arguments on the merits. Although the decision of an international court or tribunal has no binding force except between the parties and in respect of that particular dispute, findings of international courts and tribunals in the precedents may play a significant role as guidance for the interpretation of controversial provisions, both to the Applicant and the alleged Respondent.

L'Algérie et la Méditerranée

Ahmed Mahiou

L'Algérie est l'un des principaux riverains de la mer Méditerranée pour des raisons à la fois géographiques, économiques, politiques et stratégiques. En effet, elle occupe une place centrale en Méditerranée occidentale avec une façade maritime d'environ 1200 kms, en face de l'Europe son principal partenaire sur le plan économique, notamment pour y exporter la majeure partie de son pétrole et de son gaz et importer l'essentiel de ses biens d'équipement et de consommation. De ce fait les relations entre l'Algérie et l'Europe sont anciennes, surtout que l'Algérie sous domination française a été intégrée à la Communauté économique européenne (CEE) et, après l'indépendance, des accords d'association, dont le dernier en date est celui conclu le 22 avril 2002, ont défini leurs relations bilatérales qui s'insèrent également dans le cadre des relations euro-méditerranéennes découlant, d'abord, de la Déclaration de Barcelone du 28 novembre 1995, puis du nouvel accord signé à Paris le 13 juillet 2008 qui a lancé l'Union pour la Méditerranée (UPM).

Par ailleurs, l'Algérie est insérée dans d'autres relations régionales liées à la Ligue des Etats arabes, l'Union du Maghreb arabe, les différents accords concernant la Méditerranée qu'il s'agisse de sa protection ou d'autres accords subséquents concernant la coopération dans cette région.

Il s'agit donc, dans la présente contribution, de mieux comprendre le rôle de l'Algérie dans les relations méditerranéennes, en essayant de mettre en relief les aspects les plus importants[1]. Il convient, d'abord, de rappeler un certain nombre de données et d'informations concernant l'Algérie de manière à mieux situer la place du pays pour, ensuite, voir s'il y a une politique méditerranéenne de l'Algérie, tant dans ses relations avec l'Europe que dans le cadre plus général des relations internationales.

---

[1] Quelques études ont été consacrées aux problèmes évoqués dans la présente contribution politique : A. Baghzouz, « L'Algérie face à l'Europe : Quelle place dans le dispositif de coopération en Méditerranée », *Maghreb-Machrek*, n° 200, 2009, p. 45 ; « La politique méditerranéenne de l'Algérie à l'épreuve des mutations géopolitiques régionales : changement ou continuité ? », ibid., n° 221, 2015, p. 23 ; L. Martinez, « La position de l'Algérie devant l'intégration méditerranéenne », *Annuaire IEMed de la Méditerranée*, 2010, p. 193 ; A. Mahiou, « L'Algérie et les Organisations internationales », *Annuaire français de droit international*, 1982, p. 127 ; « L'Algérie et le partenariat régional », *Les limites du droit international – Essais en l'honneur de Joe Verhoeven / The limits of international law – Essays in honour of Joe Verhoeven*, Bruxelles, Bruylant, 2015, p. 309.

1   Place de l'Algérie en Méditerranée

Il s'agit de quelques données et plus précisément de quelques chiffres commentés pour donner une idée de ce que l'Algérie représente dans cet espace régional.

Avec une superficie de 2,4 million de km² soit environ un peu plus de 4,5 fois la France et 8 fois l'Italie, c'est le pays le plus vaste de l'ensemble méditerranéen (et même d'Afrique depuis la scission du Soudan). Toutefois, il faut relativiser l'intérêt d'une telle étendue du territoire par le fait qu'il y a 80% de désert, ce qui pose notamment le problème de l'agriculture et de la dépendance alimentaire, comme on le verra plus loin.

Avec une population d'environ 40 millions, l'Algérie a quadruplé sa population entre l'indépendance et 2016. Après un ralentissement qui a laissé croire que la croissance de la population serait entrée dans une phase de transition démographique, elle est de nouveau repartie à la hausse, ce qui pose de nouveaux problèmes surtout que la population est jeune (plus de la moitié de la population a moins de vingt ans) et constitue une sérieuse préoccupation pour l'éduquer et surtout lui trouver du travail afin d'éviter l'explosion sociale et l'émigration clandestine.

Le PNB global est d'environ 100 milliards de dollars, loin des pays développés méditerranéens (France 2200, Italie 1750, Espagne 1000), mais en étant le deuxième pays après la Turquie (400) au sein des autres pays de la Méditerranée. Le PNB par habitant et par an est de 4000 de dollars, ce qui situe l'Algérie dans une place moyenne, certes loin derrière les pays européens (France 35.800, Italie 30.000, Espagne 25.000), mais dans le premier groupe des pays du sud et de l'est de la Méditerranée (Libye, 5500, Turquie, 4700, Tunisie, 3750, Maroc, 2720, Egypte, 1500). Environ 6 millions d'Algériens vivent sous le seuil de pauvreté (moins de 2 dollars par jour).

Les principales ressources sont les hydrocarbures (pétrole et gaz avec une production de 150 millions de tonnes dont la moitié en gaz) dont l'exportation rapporte annuellement entre 40 et 50 milliards de dollars, en fonction de l'évolution du prix du baril de pétrole. Evidemment, cela donne une grande aisance financière au pays qui dispose présentement d'environ 130 milliards de dollars de réserves de change. L'importance de ces revenus des hydrocarbures ne doit pas cacher le grand déséquilibre que cela représente pour l'économie : les recettes provenant des hydrocarbures constituent 97% des exportations, alors qu'elles vont s'épuiser dans les décennies futures (une vingtaine d'années pour le pétrole et une cinquantaine d'années pour le gaz) ; les autres recettes représentent moins de 3%.

Une telle dépendance à l'égard d'une ressource non renouvelable est très grave pour l'avenir du pays. Le tourisme qui pourrait être un secteur intéressant en raison des potentialités du pays est bloqué parce que, d'une part, l'Algérie a accumulé un retard considérable en investissements dans ce domaine et, d'autre part, l'insécurité décourage pour le moment la venue des touristes. L'Algérie était un important producteur et exportateur de vin avant l'indépendance (15 millions d'hectolitres), mais suite à la fermeture des marchés européens (surtout français) et à l'arrachage des vignes (passage de plus de 350.000 hectares à moins de 50.000), au cours des années 1970 elle a chuté à moins de 500.000 d'hectolitres aujourd'hui. Les investissements directs étrangers restent modestes (1,5 à 2 milliards) par comparaison à l'Egypte (11 à 12 milliards en période normale) ou même au Maroc (2,5 à 3 milliards) et, en outre, ils se concentrent surtout dans les hydrocarbures.

Malgré sa grande étendue relevée précédemment (près de 2,4 millions km^2 ou 240 millions d'hectares), l'insuffisance ou le manque d'eau font que l'Algérie dispose de moins de 10 millions d'hectares cultivables (soit à peine 5% de sa superficie) dont 1,5 million de bonnes terres aptes à une production intensive (soit 1,5% de sa superficie) situées sur le littoral et dangereusement menacées par l'urbanisation au nord et la désertification au sud. A titre de comparaison, la France dispose de plus de la moitié de sa superficie en terres cultivables (soit 30 millions sur 55 millions d'hectares) et l'Italie dispose de 40 % (soit 12 millions d'hectares). A cela s'ajoute une productivité faible, ce qui explique sa grande dépendance sur le plan alimentaire puisqu'elle importe l'essentiel de ce qu'elle consomme, notamment les céréales[2], le lait, le sucre et le maïs (la facture annuelle des importations alimentaires se chiffre en milliards de dollars). Pour compenser le manque d'eau et alimenter les besoins des grandes villes, d'importants investissements sont engagés dans la désalinisation de l'eau de mer et des projets sont prévus pour utiliser l'énorme nappe souterraine du Sahara (à l'exemple de la Libye) dont on sait qu'elle ne se renouvelle pas.

Puissance militaire moyenne à l'échelle internationale, avec une armée d'environ 280.000 hommes, elle est la seconde d'Afrique (derrière l'Egypte, 400.000 hommes et devant celle du Maroc, 200.000)[3]. La Russie lui vend la majeure partie de son armement ; notons cependant que, depuis le rapprochement avec

---

2   En fonction de la pluviométrie la récolte de céréales varie du simple au double (de 20 millions à 40 millions de quintaux) et en période sèche le montant des importations de céréales dépasse 2 milliards de dollars.

3   L'évaluation concerne les effectifs de l'armée (150.000) et de la gendarmerie (130.000). Au plan de l'armement, l'Algérie dispose d'environ 1100 chars et 2000 blindés, 500 avions dont 240 de combat et une centaine d'hélicoptères, une centaine de missiles de petite ou moyenne portée, une soixantaine de navires de guerre dont 1 porte-hélicoptères, 4 sous-marins, 4 frégates, 9 corvettes et 40 patrouilleurs.

l'OTAN, des achats d'équipements ont été conclus avec la France (hélicoptères de combat), l'Allemagne (frégates) et les USA (armes de combat nocturne). Le budget militaire global est d'environ 13 milliards de dollars pour l'année 2015.

Sans constituer un carrefour stratégique, l'Algérie est au cœur de l'axe Europe/Afrique par sa position centrale et sa superficie, ce qui fait que c'est le seul pays de l'ensemble méditerranéen à avoir un voisinage géographique avec 10 autres pays (7 en Afrique si on ajoute le Sahara occidental et 3 en Europe). Cette proximité est un élément important pour l'action diplomatique, la politique de sécurité du pays et les échanges économiques, notamment avec l'Europe dont elle fournit 25 % de la consommation européenne d'hydrocarbures (occupant le 2ème rang après la Russie) et d'où elle importe la majeure partie de ses biens d'équipement et de consommation.

Ayant ainsi brossé un bref tableau du pays, il convient à présent de voir quelle est sa politique méditerranéenne.

2   La politique méditerranéenne de l'Algérie

Au lendemain de son indépendance, l'Algérie n'avait pas développé de politique méditerranéenne, mis à part le souhait que la Méditerranée revienne aux Méditerranéens et que les flottes de guerre des non-riverains (Etats-Unis et Union soviétique) se retirent de cette zone. Un certain nombre de raisons expliquent son attitude.

D'abord, elle s'est mobilisée, au départ, pour deux autres espaces régionaux (le monde arabe et le monde africain) qu'elle considérait alors comme prioritaires et, en outre, elle s'est engagée dans une action internationale plus large, celle des pays en développement, en s'inscrivant dans les revendications tiers-mondistes dont elle devient l'un des porte-paroles, en militant au sein du groupe des pays non-alignés devenu un acteur important sur la scène internationale.

Ensuite, pendant cette période, les relations méditerranéennes étaient plutôt perçues comme un réseau de relations bilatérales où la définition des nouvelles relations avec la France était la première préoccupation. Les relations algéro-françaises sont aussi étroites que compliquées et parfois conflictuelles ; il faut sans cesse les réajuster, trouver des compromis entre le souhait de l'Algérie de maîtriser son développement économique par des nationalisations portant atteinte aux intérêts français et le souci de ménager la coopération entre les deux pays. Il y a eu donc une succession de crises et de réconciliations qui a fait dire que les relations algéro-françaises ne peuvent jamais être banales et qu'elles auront toujours un aspect quelque peu passionnel lié à leur histoire commune compliquée. Aussi, même lorsque tout semble aller vers la normalisation, une tension ou une crise n'est pas loin, comme en témoigne notamment la persistante querelle sur la mémoire et l'histoire dans la mesure où l'occupation coloniale et la guerre d'indépendance donnent lieu facilement à des divergences et polémiques[4]. Du côté algérien, on reproche à la France d'avoir encore une attitude néocoloniale et une attitude frileuse en matière économique en ne s'engageant pas suffisamment en matière d'investissements directs, de ne pas faciliter la vie à l'importante communauté algérienne (la première à l'étranger, entre 2 et 2,5 millions de personnes en incluant les binationaux estimé à environ 1000.000)[5], de restreindre les échanges humains avec une politique restrictive de visas. Du côté français, on reproche à l'Algérie de brider la langue française, de bouder la francophonie et de perdre la langue française alors qu'elle était le deuxième pays francophone après la France, de décourager les investisseurs avec la multiplication des obstacles juridiques et pratiques aux initiatives économiques, de ne pas contrôler suffisamment ses frontières pour contenir les mouvements migratoires clandestins.

Par ailleurs, l'Algérie estimait que la coopération en Méditerranée était bloquée par le problème israélo-arabe et plus précisément la question palestinienne ; elle craignait qu'un projet méditerranéen global soit un moyen d'imposer aux Etats arabes la présence d'Israël dans le débat diplomatique et la coopération dans la région. L'Algérie n'exclut pas pour autant toute forme de coopération et elle se rallie notamment au projet d'une coopération en Méditerranée occidentale ; c'est ainsi qu'elle participe au Dialogue 5 + 5 dont le lancement date de la Déclaration de Rome du 10 octobre 1990 (Algérie, Libye, Maroc, Mauritanie, Tunisie, Espagne, France, Italie Malte et Portugal). Après quelques hésitations, l'Algérie a décidé de s'engager activement dans ce dialogue, en participant notamment au Sommet de Tunis (5-6 décembre 2003) et en accueillant plusieurs conférences ministérielles. Elle estime que ce dialogue constitue une bonne politique de voisinage et qu'il peut contribuer à une meilleure approche de la politique méditerranéenne de l'Union européenne, laquelle suscite les réticences ou les critiques de l'Algérie.

---

4 En période de tension entre les deux Etats, l'Algérie rappelle les exactions commises tout au long de l'occupation coloniale et plus particulièrement pendant la guerre de libération nationale entre 1954 et 1962 (cf. A. Mahiou, « A propos des crimes coloniaux : le cas de la guerre d'Algérie », *Mélanges en l'honneur du Doyen Journès*, à paraître).

5 La communauté française en Algérie, qui avait été pendant longtemps la plus importante avec plusieurs dizaines de milliers de personnes, s'est considérablement réduite pour compter environ 27 000 personnes dont la majorité (20 000) est constituée de binationaux.

Comme indiqué précédemment, l'Algérie souhaite que la Méditerranée revienne aux Méditerranéens, en militant notamment pour le départ des flottes des puissances étrangères à cette zone, selon la position exprimée en janvier 1970 dans une déclaration du chef d'Etat[6]. Lors de la 3ème conférence des Nations Unies sur le droit de la mer, elle a défendu la notion de mer semi-fermée applicable à certains espaces maritimes en vue de mieux protéger les intérêts de riverains et de restreindre les activités militaires des non riverains. C'est avec ce même souci qu'elle a tenté de réunir une conférence sur la Méditerranée en juillet 1972, mais la tentative a tourné court, faute d'accord sur la liste des participants. La liste ne pouvait pas inclure tous les riverains, car Israël n'était alors reconnu par aucun Etat arabe ; elle ne pouvait pas se limiter aux non-alignés car cela restreignait trop le nombre de participants ; elle aurait pu concerner ceux qui ne font pas partie d'un bloc militaire, ce qui est un critère plus pertinent, mais cela excluait les pays de l'Europe du sud, membres de l'OTAN. Finalement, en 1982, l'Algérie réunit une conférence des partis progressistes méditerranéens au cours de laquelle elle fit adopter un texte appelant au démantèlement des bases étrangères dans les pays riverains et au retrait des flottes extérieures à la région, mais cette conférence n'a pas eu de suite.

L'Algérie a toujours eu en vue ses intérêts de riverain d'une mer semi-fermée en veillant, pendant la conférence sur le droit de la mer, à la référence aux principes équitables et aux circonstances spéciales en matière de gestion et délimitation des espaces maritimes. Son principal souci était de faire en sorte qu'elle ne soit pas trop désavantagée en cas d'opérations de délimitation des zones économiques en Méditerranée, avec la présence d'îles dont les principales sont les Baléares qui sont à environ 300 kms de la côte algérienne. On sait que l'étroitesse de la Méditerranée fait qu'il n'y a pas de haute mer et que toute délimitation des espaces aura pour mission de fixer les limites des zones économiques exclusives et des eaux territoriales, ce qui suppose des accords entre les riverains. Pour le moment, un seul accord de délimitation a été conclu par l'Algérie avec la Tunisie[7] et l'Algérie aura à discuter avec quatre autres riverains (Maroc, Espagne, France et Italie) pour délimiter ses espaces maritimes.

Pour avoir une idée de l'impact de l'Algérie en Méditerranée, il est utile de rappeler quelques données : une façade maritime de 1280 km de côtes ;

---

6 Le Chef de l'Etat algérien a déclaré: « Nous sommes pour le départ des flottes de tous les pays qui ne font pas partie de la Méditerranée. Ce dont nous avons besoin, c'est d'une coopération réelle entre les riverains de la Méditerranée, « lac de paix » » (cité par N. Grimaud, « La politique algérienne en Méditerranée », *Awraq, Estudios sobre el mundo árabe e islámico contemporáneo*, Vol. X, (1989), p. 196).

7 L'accord date du 11 juillet 2011 et il a été ratifié par le Parlement algérien le 9 janvier 2013.

un commerce international s'effectuant à 95% par voie maritime[8]; 11 ports de commerce dont trois destinés à l'exportation des hydrocarbures ; une flottille de pêche et une flottille de petits navires de plaisance estimée à quelques milliers ; une flotte marchande de 34 navires dont 15 navires citernes pour le transport de produits pétroliers, de gaz liquéfiés et de produits chimiques qui couvre moins de 10% des besoins du pays ; trois navires de voyageurs pour assurer la moitié des besoins de transport qui se fait uniquement avec l'Europe (France, Espagne et Italie)[9].

Enfin, sur le plan environnemental, après avoir ratifié la Convention de Barcelone pour la protection de la mer Méditerranée du 16 février 1976[10] et la Convention de Montego-Bay du 10 décembre 1982 sur le droit de la mer[11], l'Algérie se dit toujours très préoccupée par la pollution marine ; toutefois, elle n'a pas pris toutes les mesures nécessaires découlant de ses engagements pour supprimer ou limiter les rejets polluants en mer (eaux usées, déchets industriels, dégazages, pesticides, etc.).

3   L'Algérie et l'Europe

Avant d'exposer les relations entre l'Algérie et la CEE, qui sont aussi anciennes qu'importantes, il faut noter que l'Algérie s'est beaucoup intéressée à l'Europe au sens large et plus précisément au processus de la Conférence pour la sécurité et la coopération en Europe (CSCE)[12]. Dès le lancement de cette conférence, elle a indiqué que les problèmes de sécurité débattus débordaient sur la Méditerranée et que, par conséquent, tous les riverains avaient un point de vue à faire valoir. L'Algérie entraîne dans son sillage les autres pays du Maghreb ainsi que l'Egypte et la Syrie pour indiquer l'intérêt de la rive sud à propos de ces problèmes. Toutefois, l'idée d'une Conférence sur la sécurité et la coopération en

---

8 Chaque année environ 10 000 navires, dont 1300 navires citernes, touchent les ports algériens. Par ailleurs, l'exportation d'hydrocarbures par voie maritime est de 90 millions de tonnes par an.

9 Il faut noter qu'il n'y a pas de cabotage national et c'est seulement en 2015 que l'Algérie a acquis deux petits bateaux (220 personnes) de transport de voyageurs, avec l'inauguration d'une première ligne entre Alger et Bejaia.

10 https://planbleu.org/sites/default/files/upload/files/Barcelona_convention_and_protocols_2007_fr(2).pdf.

11 Nations Unies, *Recueil des traités,* vol. 1834, p. 3.

12 La Conférence est lancée en 1973 et l'Acte d'Helsinki a été signé en 1975.

Méditerranée (CSCM) ne sera avancée qu'en 1990 à l'initiative de l'Espagne et l'Italie ; elle s'est traduite simplement par une conférence interparlementaire en juin 1992 et on en est resté là, car la question palestinienne et la politique d'Israël constituent encore des obstacles difficiles à surmonter. Elle va donc privilégier les relations avec l'Europe dans sa structure évolutive allant de la Communauté économique européenne (CEE), devenue Union européenne (UE), au processus de Barcelone et à l'Union pour la Méditerranée.

3.1   L'Algérie et la CEE

Notons pour commencer quelques particularités de l'Algérie dans ses relations avec la Communauté européenne par rapport aux autres pays de la Méditerranée, puisque nous avons déjà indiqué qu'elle en a fait partie, en tant que départements français, de 1957 à 1962. En effet, le Traité de Rome qui la rattache à l'Europe est signé en 1957, année où paradoxalement la lutte de libération pour se séparer de la France – et donc de l'Europe – s'est intensifiée. A la suite de son indépendance, alors que l'on aurait pu s'attendre à une remise en cause de ces liens qualifiés de coloniaux ou néocoloniaux, l'Algérie n'a pas opté pour une telle rupture parce que son économie était trop étroitement liée à celle de la rive nord de la Méditerranée (en particulier la France), tant pour ses importations que pour ses exportations. Aussi, a-t-elle continué à faire partie du « territoire communautaire » pour l'application de certains règlements communautaires et à bénéficier de manière tacite des avantages acquis par son ancienne appartenance alors qu'elle n'avait pas encore conclu d'accord d'association. Il y a eu ainsi une situation juridique ambiguë qui va durer plusieurs années, en tout cas jusqu'à l'accord d'association du 26 avril 1976[13]. La situation s'est alors normalisée avec le statut d'associé qui obéit à peu près au même schéma pour tous les pays qui ont conclu ce type d'accord avec la CEE, notamment ceux conclus avec les voisins maghrébins. L'accord de 1976 a été remplacé par celui du 22 avril 2002. Il convient de noter que le nouvel accord a été plus long à conclure si on le compare au accords conclus par les autres partenaires méditerranéens. Cela s'explique en partie par la situation interne de l'Algérie préoccupée pendant la décennie 1990 par la violence du terrorisme islamiste, mais surtout par les divergences en matière de démocratie et

---

13   Cf. P. Tavernier, « Aspects juridiques des relations économiques entre la CEE et l'Algérie », *Revue trimestrielle de droit* européen, 1972, p. 1 et A. Mahiou, « Note sur les rapports Algérie/CEE. Ambiguïtés et paradoxes », J. Touscoz (Dir.), *La Communauté européenne élargie et la Méditerranée – quelle coopération ?*, Paris, PUF, 1982.

droits de l'homme, de circulation des personnes ainsi que sur certains aspects économiques comme l'énergie, les produits agricoles ou le financement des investissements.

Ces points de divergence se sont manifestés d'ailleurs lors de la conférence de Barcelone en 1995. L'Algérie était l'un des pays de la rive sud qui était le plus critique sur le processus de Barcelone et ses trois volets. Elle a exprimé les réticences suivantes :

- le volet politique (démocratie et droits de l'homme) entraînait une immixtion exagérée dans les affaires intérieures des Etats ;
- le volet économique était insuffisant car l'UE ne s'engageait pas de façon importante comme elle l'a fait pour les pays de l'est européen et elle mettait en relief le fait que l'UE retirait chaque année de ses échanges avec l'ensemble des pays méditerranéens un bénéfice supérieur à l'ensemble de l'aide qu'elle leur accordait sur 5 ans;
- le volet humain était contestable car non seulement l'UE limite la circulation des personnes, mais en outre elle demande aux pays du sud de faire la police en matière de migration clandestine.

Bien que l'Algérie ait souscrit à certaines obligations qui l'engagent dans certains de ces domaines avec l'accord d'association, elle pense que ces points restent encore ouverts au débat dans le cadre de l'Union pour la Méditerranée (UPM) et elle a donc saisi cette occasion pour exprimer ses réticences et manifester des hésitations pour participer au sommet de Paris de 2008.

3.2 L'Algérie et l'UPM

L'UPM a été fondée lors du sommet de Paris du 13 juillet 2008 qui a réuni 43 Etats, riverains de la Méditerranée ou membres de l'UE, sous la co-présidence franco-égyptienne. On sait que l'UPM ne correspond pas exactement au projet initial du président Sarkozy qui voulait le limiter aux riverains de la Méditerranée ; il a été modifié à la suite des objections des autres membres de l'UE, notamment de l'Allemagne pour inclure l'ensemble des membres de l'UE. L'appellation elle-même a changé pour adjoindre à l'UPM le Processus de Barcelone et montrer ainsi que la nouvelle institution est la continuation de l'ancienne.

Bien que le contenu de la nouvelle institution reste encore à définir, elle repose pour le moment sur un certain nombre de projets autour desquels vont se retrouver les Etats intéressés : la dépollution de la Méditerranée, les autoroutes maritimes et terrestres, la protection civile pour répondre aux catastrophes naturelles, une université euro-méditerranéenne, l'énergie solaire. Si l'Algérie juge intéressant les projets retenus, elle demande des clarifications sur les points suivants :

- le financement des projets puisque l'Europe n'a pris aucun engagement en s'en remettant à la politique de chaque Etat et en espérant l'arrivée des pétrodollars, notamment ceux des pays du Golfe ;
- le rôle de l'UPM dans le processus de paix au Moyen Orient en souhaitant que l'Europe ne se limite pas seulement à inclure Israël dans cette Union et qu'elle fasse pression pour trouver une solution à la question palestinienne. On sait que le sommet de Paris a offert l'occasion aux présidents syrien et libanais d'annoncer la normalisation de leurs relations diplomatiques, mais les présidents israélien et palestinien n'ont annoncé aucune initiative nouvelle dans le processus de paix entamé depuis longtemps ;
- l'aspect institutionnel qui reste encore flou, comme l'organigramme, le siège et la désignation du Secrétaire général de l'Union. L'Algérie attache une certaine importance à cet aspect et a manifesté des réticences en laissant entendre qu'elle a été oubliée par l'initiateur du projet. En effet, l'initiateur du projet (le président Sarkozy) a privilégié l'Egypte pour la co-présidence de l'UPM et il a laissé entendre que le siège de l'Organisation pourrait être à Tunis et que le Secrétaire général pourrait être un marocain. Lors de la réunion ministérielle de Marseille, en novembre 2008, un consensus s'est dégagé pour que le siège de l'UPM soit à Barcelone donc dans un pays du Nord, que le secrétariat général revienne à un pays du Sud, mais avec l'assistance de cinq adjoints : trois européens et deux du Sud, dont un pour Israël et un autre pour la Palestine et, enfin que la Ligue arabe soit membre à part entière de l'UPM. Cependant, l'Algérie a émis des réserves sur ce consensus, notamment sur la création des cinq adjoints pour non-conformité à ce qui a été décidé au sommet de Paris.

Quoi qu'il en soit, l'Algérie sait qu'elle est non seulement étroitement liée à l'Europe, mais qu'elle en est largement dépendante pour ses échanges extérieurs alors qu'inversement la dépendance européenne à l'égard de l'Algérie est minime (1% de ses échanges). Même dans le domaine sensible des hydrocarbures, et plus précisément pour le gaz, les importations européennes (40 à 50 milliards de m^3) ne représentent pour le moment que moins de 10% du total, la Russie étant le premier fournisseur (plus de 160 milliards m^3). Actuellement l'Algérie discute avec l'Union européenne pour une révision de l'Accord d'association, car elle s'estime perdante dans ce partenariat déséquilibré ; en effet, l'ouverture de son marché et la suppression ou la diminution des droits de douane ont entraîné d'importantes baisses des recettes.

4 L'Algérie dans les relations internationales

Les pays du Maghreb et plus particulièrement ceux du Maghreb central (Algérie, Maroc et Tunisie) partagent beaucoup de choses en commun : longue histoire commune, même population, mêmes langues (arabe et berbère), même occupation coloniale qui a laissé un héritage juridique et administratif commun et l'influence de la langue française. Tous les éléments sont là comme facteurs d'unité de la région et pourtant, l'unité du Maghreb est en panne. La première difficulté apparue concerne les frontières qui n'ont pas été fixées pour les régions sahariennes, ce qui a entraîné des revendications au lendemain de l'indépendance de l'Algérie, notamment de la part du Maroc qui réclamait le rattachement d'une portion assez importante du territoire algérien ; cela a même entraîné une brève guerre des sables en 1963 et des tensions jusqu'à la conclusion d'un accord frontalier dans les années 1970. La seconde difficulté est celle du voisinage politique, à l'époque où le régime socialiste algérien inquiétait ses voisins. La troisième est le conflit de leadership entre l'Algérie et le Maroc qui s'est polarisé sur l'affaire du Sahara occidental qui a bloqué le processus d'union entamé en 1989. L'accord de Marrakech qui crée l'Union du Maghreb arabe (UMA) ne s'est appliqué que quelques années, car le désaccord algéro-marocain sur le Sahara occidental a resurgi en 1996 et le processus d'union est gelé depuis cette date, ce qui préoccupe l'Europe désireuse d'encourager l'intégration dans cette région pour disposer d'un marché unifié plus grand.

Les relations avec l'Afrique sont basées sur la solidarité anticoloniale, l'aide aux mouvements de libération, l'aide économique bilatérale ou multilatérale. L'Algérie soutient toute initiative allant dans le sens de l'unité du continent et elle a même engagé une action symbolique mais concrète en lançant la route de l'unité africaine dans les années 1970 qu'elle souhaite maintenant transformer en autoroute vers l'Afrique de l'Ouest et en soutenant l'ambitieux projet d'un gazoduc transsaharien permettant de raccorder l'Afrique de l'Ouest à la côte méditerranéenne en vue d'alimenter l'Europe. Elle entretient un réseau diplomatique dense en Afrique pour influer sur la politique extérieure des membres de l'Organisation de l'unité africaine devenue Union africaine[14].

---

14   De manière générale, sur le plan diplomatique l'Algérie a toujours été très présente ; elle dispose d'un réseau de représentations assez dense sur le plan bilatéral et multilatéral, avec une présence active au sein de Nations Unies, du mouvement des non-alignés, de l'Union africaine, de l'OPEP et de la Ligue arabe. Pendant les décennies 1970-80, elle a joué un rôle de premier plan pour la promotion d'un nouvel ordre économique international ; ayant souvent servi de porte-parole des pays du Tiers monde, elle est régulièrement invitée aux réunions où l'on débat des problèmes de développement, notamment au G8.

Le non-alignement demeure toujours un axe majeur de la politique internationale de l'Algérie, ce qui explique son embarras dès qu'il s'agit de se retrouver impliquée dans une alliance avec d'autres Etats. Cela est encore plus particulièrement évident dans ses relations avec une alliance militaire comme l'OTAN, qui joue un rôle en Méditerranée et avec laquelle elle a mis beaucoup de temps avant de prendre langue. Deux raisons majeures justifient cette position : d'une part, l'OTAN a soutenu la France lorsqu'elle combattait la lutte de libération ; d'autre part, l'Algérie était l'un des leaders du non-alignement dont la politique consiste à se tenir à l'écart de la confrontation entre l'est et l'ouest. Aussi, n'a-t-elle commencé à établir des contacts qu'au lendemain de l'effondrement du bloc communiste, d'abord fort timidement, puis de manière plus engagée à partir du moment où l'Algérie a été gravement affectée par le terrorisme islamiste. Depuis les années 2000, elle participe à des réunions civiles et militaires avec l'OTAN et parfois à des exercices militaires conjoints en Méditerranée comme le faisaient déjà ses deux voisins maghrébins (Maroc et Tunisie) ; en revanche elle reste très ferme sur deux principes en matière de coopération militaire : elle s'oppose à tout déploiement de forces étrangères ou implantation de base militaire sur son territoire et elle refuse tout engagement de ses forces armées en dehors du territoire national. Notons cependant l'exception importante résultant des Accords d'Evian, au moment de l'indépendance du pays en 1962, permettant à la France d'utiliser la base navale de Mers-el-Kébir (Oran) pendant une période de 15 ans et la base d'essais nucléaires de Reggane (Sahara) pendant 5 ans ; toutefois la France s'est retirée des deux bases en 1967. Notons également le soutien apporté aux pays arabes dans leurs confrontations avec Israël, notamment en 1967 et en 1973, en liaison avec la question palestinienne et la mise en œuvre de l'accord de défense de la Ligue des Etats arabes. Notons enfin la récente collaboration, lors de l'intervention de la France au Mali, pour autoriser le survol du territoire algérien par des avions militaires français.

Telle est donc la stratégie adoptée par l'Algérie dans sa politique méditerranéenne où elle s'efforce de rester fidèle à certains principes de base, tout en en essayant de s'adapter aux nouvelles donnes régionales dont deux sont préoccupantes : le développement du terrorisme islamique qui essaime maintenant dans le monde arabe et les flux de l'émigration clandestine qui tiennent en échec, pour le moment, les actions nationales et européennes pour endiguer ces deux phénomènes.

De ce fait, elle apparaît parfois comme un rival de l'Egypte qui prétend aussi au même rôle en tant que leader du monde arabe. Par ailleurs, elle bénéficie d'un personnel diplomatique suffisamment expérimenté pour que certains d'entre eux soient sollicités par l'ONU, l'Union africaine et la Ligue arabe pour différentes crises en Afrique, en Asie et dans le monde arabe.

Judicial Application of Environmental Standards under the Law of the Sea Convention

Bernard H. Oxman

What do judges do? And not do? What is their role in the system of governance? What are the constraints on that role?

These are abiding constitutive questions in the administration of a political order. They go to the heart of the structure of that order. They arise in many different ways. And they generate a rich tapestry of responses in different contexts at different times.

The international system traditionally accorded at most a very limited role to judges. That is now changing. Two developments that have propelled the change may be singled out. One is the expansion in the substantive reach of international law. The other is the expansion in the acceptance of adjudication and arbitration by States.

Multilateral treaties have played a key role in both developments. The United Nations Convention on the Law of the Sea[1] is a good example. To be sure, the system of governance at sea has been a principal object of international law from its inception. But we now have a comprehensive constitutive treaty that is globally ratified and respected, that addresses a wide variety of issues, and that brings within its orbit an impressive and expanding array of more specialized instruments.

Nowhere is the change in the substantive reach of the law of the sea more evident than in the Law of the Sea Convention's provisions on the protection and preservation of the marine environment. Nowhere is the change in the acceptance of adjudication and arbitration by States more evident than in the Convention's compromissory clauses regarding disputes concerning its interpretation and application. And nowhere is the combination of the two developments more evident than in the Convention's prohibition on reservations.[2]

---

1   1833 UNTS 3.
2   By way of contrast, the instruments adopted at the first conference on the law of the sea in 1958 divided the topic into four separate conventions and an optional protocol on dispute settlement, allowed reservations, contained only a few provisions of limited scope on pollution of the marine environment, and made limited headway in addressing emerging problems of conservation of living resources.

The system of governance set forth in the Convention is itself based on the prevailing international system of governance. That system relies principally on States acting individually and cooperatively. Much of the Convention is devoted to allocation of general powers of governance to flag States, coastal States, and port States. That includes elaborate constraints on those powers, including duties to exercise those powers to protect and preserve the marine environment.

Some of those duties are performed by participating in international regulatory institutions and giving effect to the rules that are adopted through such mechanisms. But the State remains central to the process. It is instructive that in its first advisory opinion,[3] the Seabed Disputes Chamber of the International Tribunal for the Law of the Sea (ITLOS) focused on the governance duties of individual States with respect to the mining operations that they sponsor in the international seabed Area. It is also instructive that in the full Tribunal's first advisory opinion,[4] which addressed areas where fishing is regulated by coastal States, the Tribunal emphasized the duties of the flag State to take measures to ensure that its fishing vessels respect the regulatory constraints imposed by the coastal States.

It can be useful to think of the relationship between an international tribunal and a State in an environmental case as analogous in some ways to the relationship in municipal law between an administrative tribunal and the state organ entrusted with the relevant administrative functions. In this regard, it is interesting to note that the Convention draws on well-known principles of municipal administrative law in spelling out the relationship between the Seabed Disputes Chamber of ITLOS and the International Seabed Authority. Article 189 provides:

> The Seabed Disputes Chamber shall have no jurisdiction with regard to the exercise by the Authority of its discretionary powers in accordance with this Part; in no case shall it substitute its discretion for that of the Authority.... [T]he Seabed Disputes Chamber shall not pronounce itself on the question of whether any rules, regulations and procedures of the Authority are in conformity with this Convention, nor declare invalid any

---

3 *Responsibilities and Obligations of States Sponsoring Persons and Entities with Respect to Activities in the Area* (Request for Advisory Opinion Submitted to the Seabed Disputes Chamber), Case No. 17, Advisory Opinion of 1 February 2011.

4 *Request for an Advisory Opinion Submitted by the Sub-Regional Fisheries Commission* (SRFC) (Request for Advisory Opinion submitted to the Tribunal), Case No. 21, Advisory Opinion of 4 April 2015.

such rules, regulations and procedures. Its jurisdiction in this regard shall be confined to deciding claims that the application of any rules, regulations and procedures of the Authority in individual cases would be in conflict with the contractual obligations of the parties to the dispute or their obligations under this Convention, claims concerning excess of jurisdiction or misuse of power, and to claims for damages to be paid or other remedy to be given to the party concerned for the failure of the other party to comply with its contractual obligations or its obligations under this Convention.

Needless to say, the foregoing provision addresses only the relationship with the Seabed Authority, and the Convention contains other rules expressly limiting the jurisdiction of courts and tribunals in other types of cases. But that said, the underlying question of the role of the judge within the relevant governance structure cannot be so easily escaped. The existence of jurisdiction is the start of that inquiry, not the end. The question is whether and if so how to exercise jurisdiction within the governance structure. It is instructive to consider the extensive treatment of that question by ITLOS after it determined that it had jurisdiction in its judgment in the *Bay of Bengal* case.[5]

The Convention, like other legal instruments, uses a variety of techniques that circumscribe the role of the judge. The most obvious is an express jurisdictional limitation. The most extensive is detailed drafting of substantive provisions. The importance of the first technique may well be greater in situations where the text of a substantive provision is relatively less determinate.

While there is a high level of detail in many of the environmental provisions of the Convention, Part XII opens with a general statement of environmental duty in Article 192: 'States have the obligation to protect and preserve the marine environment.' Almost as general are paragraphs 2 and 5 of Article 194:

> 2. States shall take all measures necessary to ensure that activities under their jurisdiction or control are so conducted as not to cause damage by pollution to other States and their environment, and that pollution arising from incidents or activities under their jurisdiction or control does not spread beyond the areas where they exercise sovereign rights in accordance with this Convention.

---

[5] *Dispute Concerning Delimitation of the Maritime Boundary between Bangladesh and Myanmar in the Bay of Bengal* (Bangladesh/Myanmar), Case No 16, Judgment of 14 March 2012.

5. The measures taken in accordance with this Part shall include those necessary to protect and preserve rare or fragile ecosystems as well as the habitat of depleted, threatened or endangered species and other forms of marine life.

The first question is whether the jurisdictional clauses of the Convention limit the power of judges to apply the environmental provisions quoted above. In this regard, both the text of the Convention and its negotiating history make clear that coastal States wished to limit the possibilities of judicial interference with their regulatory decisions regarding the exploration and exploitation of living and nonliving resources of the exclusive economic zone (EEZ) and the continental shelf. Article 286, the first article of section 2 of Part XV establishing compulsory jurisdiction under the Convention, opens with the words, 'Subject to section 3.'[6] The title of section 3 is 'Limitations and Exceptions to Applicability of Section 2.' The title of the first article of section 3, Article 297, is 'Limitations on applicability of Section 2.' Even before examining the text of the first paragraph of Article 297, a reader[7] is likely to conclude that it contains something to which Article 286 is subject, namely a limitation on compulsory jurisdiction under section 2. The reader then proceeds to examine the first paragraph of Article 297:

1. Disputes concerning the interpretation or application of this Convention with regard to the exercise by a coastal State of its sovereign rights or jurisdiction provided for in this Convention shall be subject to the procedures provided for in section 2 in the following cases:
   (a) when it is alleged that a coastal State has acted in contravention of the provisions of this Convention in regard to the freedoms and rights of navigation, overflight or the laying of submarine cables and pipelines, or in regard to other internationally lawful uses of the sea specified in article 58;
   (b) when it is alleged that a State in exercising the aforementioned freedoms, rights or uses has acted in contravention of this Convention or of laws or regulations adopted by the coastal State

---

6   Article 286 reads in full, 'Subject to section 3, any dispute concerning the interpretation or application of this Convention shall, where no settlement has been reached by recourse to section 1, be submitted at the request of any party to the dispute to the court or tribunal having jurisdiction under this section.'
7   The reader might be a member of parliament whose role in treaty approval protects democratic accountability.

> in conformity with this Convention and other rules of international law not incompatible with this Convention; or
>
> (c) when it is alleged that a coastal State has acted in contravention of specified international rules and standards for the protection and preservation of the marine environment which are applicable to the coastal State and which have been established by this Convention or through a competent international organization or diplomatic conference in accordance with this Convention.

At first glance at the least, this confirms what the reader thought. Why enumerate three circumstances where there is jurisdiction if, absent that enumeration, there would be jurisdiction anyway? Why would Article 286 be 'subject to' this provision if it were not a limitation? The apparent function of enumerating the three circumstances where there is jurisdiction is to limit other challenges to the exercise of coastal State sovereign rights or jurisdiction.

The reader then proceeds to paragraph 2 of Article 297, which specifically excludes jurisdiction regarding most, but perhaps not all, disputes regarding marine scientific research in the EEZ and on the continental shelf, and paragraph 3, which specifically excludes jurisdiction regarding fishing in the EEZ. If paragraph 1 is an exclusive list, then why do we need paragraphs 2 and 3? If paragraph 2 leaves the door open to some jurisdiction in the EEZ and continental shelf, and paragraph 3 makes no express reference to sedentary species of the continental shelf, how do we square them with paragraph 1? The obvious answer, one would think, is to read all the limitations in Article 297 together so that they do not contradict one another. That in turn is an obvious reason for the absence of the word 'only' from the chapeau of paragraph 1. The result is that paragraph 1 limits jurisdiction to the three enumerated situations in that paragraph except as otherwise provided in the specific cases addressed by paragraphs 2 and 3.

Under this reading, paragraph 1(c) certainly does not exclude, but does expressly limit, the justiciability of environmental provisions that apply to the exercise of the sovereign rights of the coastal State with respect to the continental shelf, in particular its nonliving resources. A tribunal's jurisdiction is limited to specific international rules or standards[8] established by the

---

8   The Arabic text reads 'القواعد والمعايير الدولية المحددة,' the Chinese text '特定国际规则和标准,' the French text 'règles ou normes internationales déterminées,' the Russian text 'конкретные международные нормы и стандарты,' and the Spanish text 'reglas y estándares internacionales específicos.' The word 'specified' in the English text should be interpreted in a manner that is in harmony with other authentic texts.

Convention or through a competent international organization or diplomatic conference in accordance with the Convention. This mirrors the substantive obligation of the coastal State under Article 208 to adopt laws and regulations with respect to continental shelf activities subject to its jurisdiction that are 'no less effective than international rules, standards and recommended practices and procedures', presumably those established by 'competent international organizations or diplomatic conference'.

Not so, says the 2015 arbitral award in the *Chagos Marine Protected Area* case.[9]

According to the award, the enumerated list in paragraph 1 is not exclusive. The word 'only' was intentionally eliminated. The effect of paragraph 1(c) of Article 297 is not to limit, but quite possibly to expand, the scope of jurisdiction over the environmental obligations of the coastal State to include those arising under other instruments.

It remains to be seen how that interpretation fares in the future. But even if it proves persuasive, that does not end the inquiry. What is a tribunal to do when confronted with an allegation that a general rather than a specific provision is violated, such as Article 192?

The contours of a plausible answer are suggested in paragraphs 941 and 956 of the July 12, 2016 award in the *South China Sea Arbitration*.[10] The former paragraph states that 'the content of [Article 192] is informed by the other provisions of Part XII and other applicable rules of international law.' The latter continues, 'CITES [the Convention on International Trade in Endangered Species][11] is the subject of nearly universal adherence, including by the Philippines and China, and in the Tribunal's view forms part of the general corpus of international law that informs the content of Article 192 and 194(5) of the Convention.' Accordingly, 'Article 192 includes a due diligence obligation to prevent the harvesting of species that are recognized internationally as being at risk of extinction and requiring international protection.'

This analysis bears a striking similarity to the analysis in paragraphs 1082 and 1083 of the award that a violation by the flag State of the widely ratified Convention on the International Regulations for Preventing of Collisions at

---

9   *Chagos Marine Protected Area Arbitration* (Mauritius v United Kingdom), Award, 18 March 2015, http://www.pcacases.com/pcadocs/MU-UK%2020150318%20Award.pdf.

10 The *South China Sea Arbitration* (the Philippines v China), Award, 12 July 2016, www.pcacases.com/web/view/7.

11 12 ILM 1085 (1973); for the latest amended version of the Convention, see https://cites.org/eng/disc/text.php.

Sea, 1972,[12] constitutes a violation of the flag State's duty under Article 94(5) to conform to generally accepted international regulations, procedures and practices with respect to the prevention of collisions. Part XII applies similar duties to flag States and coastal States to adopt and enforce measures to control pollution that are no less effective than generally accepted international standards. Interpreting and applying Article 192 in a similar fashion with respect to environmental duties on matters other than pollution would be consistent with the system used by the Convention for identifying the specific standards to which States must conform when regulating activities at sea that are subject to their jurisdiction. It would at the same time help to provide means for circumscribing the role of the judge in interpreting and applying the general language of Article 192 and some other provisions. The specific obligations would not be invented from whole cloth, as it were, but arise from widely accepted specific standards that, in most cases, are likely to have been accepted in form or in fact by the State whose conduct is at issue. Moreover, this constraint would be applicable not only to the environmental obligations of coastal States but those of flag States as well.

This approach does not, however, function only as a constraint. It also enables judicial application of generally accepted standards that emerge from instruments that are not, as such, subject to compulsory jurisdiction. That is also the effect of the numerous express incorporations by reference of generally accepted international standards by the Convention in a large number of other contexts. Still the absence of express language might perhaps suggest particular care in applying the same approach to inform the content of general provisions such as Article 192.

One might ask whether the nature of the forum makes a difference in this context. In most circumstances, albeit not all, compulsory jurisdiction under the Law of the Sea Convention is vested in an arbitral tribunal established under Annex VII, absent parallel declarations or other instruments conferring jurisdiction on the International Court of Justice or ITLOS. That in turn can raise a further question of whether the arbitrators in any given case have been selected by agreement of the parties or, absent that, by the ITLOS president. The number of cases addressing environmental issues on the merits under the Law of the Sea Convention is small, and any general conclusions regarding the nature of the forum would be speculative. In any event, even if certain tendencies regarding the answers to the questions would be different, the question of the role of the judge addressed herein applies equally to arbitrators.

---

12   1050 UNTS 16.

The approach to the same question might be different if the issue is the role of the judge vis-à-vis that of an international institution. As noted above, the Convention itself addresses the question explicitly with respect to the Seabed Disputes Chamber and the International Seabed Authority. The International Court of Justice has more than once addressed its relationship to other U.N. organs,[13] but the Court, as well as arbitral tribunals, have to date shied away from analyzing their relationship to the Commission on the Limits of the Continental Shelf in the same detail as has ITLOS. It may be that ITLOS, a Tribunal that, like the Commission, was itself created by the Convention, with members elected by the parties to the Convention, would feel more comfortable addressing the issue.

One might also inquire about the extent to which similar issues arise in the context of provisional measures. Such measures are not interim decisions on the merits. The question of how to conceive of the judicial role in the context of the interpretation and application of general environmental obligations is not posed as such. To the extent that the function of provisional measures is conservatory, one would expect judges and arbitrators to look for authoritative articulations of the *status quo* or the *status quo ante* that might be helpful in shaping measures to preserve the respective rights of the parties and protect the environment pending a final decision on the merits. To be sure, here as elsewhere, questions of the judicial role are always pertinent. But there the similarity ends.

The foregoing analysis has deliberately avoided familiar classifications, such as the common question of whether an issue is legal. Such classifications are often deployed to address the issue of whether a matter can be or should be adjudicated at all. That threshold question, if answered in the negative, of course subsumes the question of the judicial role. But if answered in the positive, it does not. The question of the appropriate judicial role persists as one of whether, and if so how, to address certain issues in a case, including those that arise under a text that articulates a general obligation.

---

13   One example is the relation of the Court to the Security Council, which is addressed in the *Case concerning Questions of Interpretation and Application of the 1971 Montreal Convention Arising from the Aerial Incident at Lockerbie* (Libyan Arab Jamahiriya v United States of America), Preliminary Objections, ICJ Reports 1998, p. 9.

The Future of the High Seas Fisheries Legal and Institutional Framework

*Jean-François Pulvenis de Séligny-Maurel**

Fishing, along with hunting and gathering, is one of the most ancient means of exploitation by humankind of the living resources of the environment. Nowadays, while hunting and gathering are practiced only on a limited scale (for recreational purposes or, in the most traditional societies, for subsistence), large-scale fishing constitutes an important worldwide source of food, employment and income, producing considerable amount of fish and fish products for which demand grows continuously. The relationship between fishers and the stocks that they exploit, unaltered since the dawn of times, remains essentially that of a top predator and its prey[1] and, fishing at its core continues to be the extraction of wild living organisms from the environment,[2] leaving it up to nature to replenish the exploited stocks.

---

* The views expressed are personal to the author and do not reflect a formal position of the institutions with which he has been associated.
1 'We need to understand the fisher putting him/her back into the ecosystem as a top predator.' (P. Hart et al., 'Sustainable exploitation with minimal conflict: is it possible?', in P. Hart & M. Johnson (eds), *Who Owns the Sea?*, University of Hull, 2014, p. 17).
2 Relatively recently, a legal definition of 'fishing' has been introduced in several international instruments, prompted by practical needs related to the adoption of regulations and measures and their implementation, in spite of the fact that they include some ancillary activities leading to or following the catch of the fish (eventually referred to in some instances as 'fishing related activities'). See, for instance the *Port State Measures Agreement*, FAO, 2009, 'Agreement on Port State Measures to Prevent, Deter and Eliminate Illegal, Unreported and Unregulated Fishing' which did not yet enter into force, states in its Article 1 on 'Use of Terms':
　　"(c) 'fishing' means searching for, attracting, locating, catching, taking or harvesting fish or any activity which can reasonably be expected to result in the attracting, locating, catching, taking or harvesting of fish;
　　(d) 'fishing related activities' means any operation in support of, or in preparation for, fishing, including the landing, packaging, processing, transshipping or transporting of fish that have not been previously landed at a port, as well as the provisioning of personnel, fuel, gear and other supplies at sea;"
Another example, borrowed from a regional instrument, the *Antigua Convention*, 2003,'Convention for the Strengthening of the Inter-American Tropical Tuna Commission Established by the 1949 Convention Between the United States of America and the Republic Of Costa Rica' which governs the Inter-American Tropical Tuna Commission and entered into force in 2010, reads as follows:

However, at the same time, developments in science and technology have put in the hands of fishers tools and means far beyond those traditionally available in hunters-gatherers societies. As a result, fishing capacity and efficiency increased considerably and new situations in terms of space and resources appropriation emerged, which were unknown and unforeseen when the 1982 UN Convention on the Law the Sea (LOSC) was negotiated and adopted.[3] The unprecedented pressure on the fish resources caused some of the stocks to collapse,[4] and brought others to the brink of collapse.[5] It also led marine

---

"2. 'Fishing' means:
   (a) the actual or attempted searching for, catching, or harvesting of the fish stocks covered by this Convention;
   (b) engaging in any activity which can reasonably be expected to result in the locating, catching, harvesting of these stocks;
   (c) placing, searching for or recovering any fish-aggregating device or associated equipment, including radio beacons; (d) any operation at sea in support of, or in preparation for, any activity described in sub-paragraphs (a), (b) and (c) of this paragraph, except for any operation in emergencies involving the health and safety of crew members or the safety of a vessel;
   (e) the use of any other vehicle, air- or sea-borne, in relation to any activity described in this definition except for emergencies involving the health or safety of crew members or the safety of a vessel;"

[3] E.g. the use of the so-called fish aggregating devices (FADs) with satellite transmitters and echo sounders and sonar equipment that make it possible to know in advance the volume and species of aggregated fish which can be caught, as well as its precise location (see i.a. A. C. Morgan, *Fish Aggregating Devices (FADs) and Tuna—Impacts and Management Options*, Ocean Science Division, Pew Environment Group, 2011, pp. 2 and 3). Another example is that of fishing vessels or supported vessels permanently or semi-permanently anchored over a seamount, and acting as FAD in addition to ensure to the owners of these vessels a kind of exclusive possession of the resource (e.g. in the Indian Ocean, during the period 2004–2010, in the Spanish purse-seine fleet, 'seven of the sixteen ships recorded at the moment have been any time anchored on a seamount. Two of them were permanently anchored on 'Coco de Mer'...'. M. L. Ramos et al., *Analysis of activity data obtained from supply vessels' logbooks implemented by the Spanish fleet and associated in Indian Ocean*, Indian Ocean Tuna Commission, doc. IOTC-2010-WPTT-22, p. 2).

[4] The example of the Newfoundland cod fishery collapse is well known. There are others such as the case of the Bering Sea Pollock: 'Pollock stocks in the Central Bering Sea high seas area have never recovered from overfishing in the late 1980s and early 1990s. A moratorium on commercial Pollock fishing has continued since 1993 but, 20 years later, there is still no relief in sight.' (Food and Agriculture Organization of the United Nations (FAO), *The State of World Fisheries and Aquaculture—2014*, (SOFIA 2014), p. 180).

[5] See *SOFIA 2014*, p. 7: 'The proportion of assessed marine fish stocks fished within biologically sustainable levels declined from 90 percent in 1974 to 71.2 percent in 2011, when 28.8 percent of fish stocks were estimated as fished at a biologically unsustainable level and, therefore,

fisheries to reach a plateau, with production stabilizing (or stagnating from a more pessimistic point of view) at around 80 million tons per year.[6]

Aquaculture, which may be seen as the equivalent in aquatic spaces of livestock farming and animal husbandry on land, has been growing fast but has not reached yet a level of production at which, as an alternate source of fish and fish products, it might ease significantly the pressure on wild stocks. In addition, marine aquaculture is still dependent upon these stocks, for feed or for restocking fish farms (e.g. sea ranching of Bluefin tuna).

Overfishing threatens not only targeted stocks, it is also a threat to associated species as well as to the marine ecosystems and environment, along with other threats such as climate change and pollution from land based sources. For that reason, the process of progressive inter-twinning between the international law of the environment and the international law of the sea is particularly relevant to fisheries, with the development of a number of new concepts, principles, rules, and approaches.[7] These were included in the various international legal instruments applicable to fisheries that were negotiated after the adoption of LOSC and constitute a robust, comprehensive, complex, and still growing framework of soft law and hard law.[8]

An essential element of this evolution has been the increasing awareness of the need to address pending issues and challenges in a more holistic and integrated manner. The concept of 'ecosystem'—mentioned once in LOSC[9]—played an important role in that process, along with that of 'biodiversity'. In the

---

overfished. Of the stocks assessed in 2011, fully fished stocks accounted for 61.3 percent and underfished stocks 9.9 percent.'

6   See *SOFIA 2014*, 4, Table 1: 2007: 80.7; 2008: 79.9; 2009:79.6; 2010: 77.8; 2011:82.6; 2012: 79.7.

7   On this phenomenon of 'greening' of the law of the sea and the development of international legal instruments relevant to fisheries, See J-F. Pulvenis de Séligny, 'The marine living resources and the evolving law of the sea', 1 *Aegean Review of the Law of the Sea and Maritime Law*, 2010, pp. 66 et seq.

8   Two of these instruments focused specifically on high seas fisheries, the 1993 *Agreement to Promote Compliance with International Conservation and Management Measures by Fishing Vessels on the High Seas* ('*Compliance Agreement*') and the 2009 FAO *International Guidelines for the Management of Deep-Sea Fisheries in the High Seas*.

9   LOSC, Article 194, Measures to prevent, reduce and control pollution of the marine environment, paragraph 5 states that 'The measures taken in accordance with this Part shall include those necessary to protect and preserve rare or fragile ecosystems as well as the habitat of depleted, threatened or an injured species and other forms of marine life.' This provision however can be said to be the seed or anchor of the subsequent evolution of the legal regime in this respect. Although not related to the provisions applicable to fisheries, this text may be seen as foreshadowing the future evolution leading to the adoption of the concept of an ecosystem approach to fisheries management. See below.

field of fisheries, these concepts were introduced in two of the most important instruments following LOSC and in the wake of the 1992 Rio Declaration and Agenda 21:[10] the 1995 FAO Code of Conduct for Responsible Fisheries (CCRF)[11] and the 1995 UN Fish Stocks Agreement (UNFSA).[12] The adoption of the CCRF and the UNFSA coincides with that of the 'Jakarta Mandate on Marine and Coastal Biological Diversity', which the second Conference of the Parties of the CBD qualified as 'the new global consensus on the importance of marine and coastal biological diversity'.[13] This evolution meant an important shift in the approach to fisheries management, since it highlighted the need to avoid considering fish stocks in isolation from their living environment and without

---

10   It is important to recall that Agenda 21, Chapter 17, contains extensive provisions on fisheries, particularly in its section C ('Sustainable use and conservation of marine living resources of the high seas') and D ('Sustainable use and conservation of marine living resources under national jurisdiction'). Provisions on fisheries are found also in the *Johannesburg Plan of Implementation* adopted by the 2002 World Summit on Sustainable Development and in '*The Future We Want*' adopted by the 2012 Rio +20 Summit.

11   CCRF, Article 6.6 '6.6 Selective and environmentally safe fishing gear and practices should be further developed and applied, to the extent practicable, in order to maintain biodiversity and to conserve the population structure and aquatic ecosystems and protect fish quality. (...)'; Article 7.2.2.:' 7.2.2 Such measures should provide *inter alia* that: (...) d) biodiversity of aquatic habitats and ecosystems is conserved and endangered species are protected;'; Article 8.4.8: 'Research on the environmental and social impacts of fishing gear and, in particular, on the impact of such gear on biodiversity and coastal fishing communities should be promoted.'; Article 12.10: 'States should carry out studies on the selectivity of fishing gear, the environmental impact of fishing gear (...) with a view to minimizing non-utilized catches as well as safeguarding the biodiversity of ecosystems and the aquatic habitat.'

12   UNFSA, UN Doc. A/CONF.164/37, 8 September 1995, Preamble: 'Conscious of the need to avoid adverse impacts on the marine environment, preserve biodiversity, maintain the integrity of marine ecosystems and minimize the risk of long-term or irreversible effects of fishing operations,' and Article 5, General principles: 'In order to conserve and manage straddling fish stocks and highly migratory fish stocks, coastal States and States fishing on the high seas shall, in giving effect to their duty to cooperate in accordance with the Convention: (...) (g) protect biodiversity in the marine environment.'

13   Jakarta Ministerial Statement on the Implementation of the Convention on Biological Diversity, UNEP/CBD/COP/2/19, 30 November 1995, Appendix. For a comprehensive review of the Convention on Biological Diversity and the Jakarta Mandate as well as related instruments, see A. C. de Fontaubert, D. R. Downes & T. S. Agardy, 'Biodiversity in the Seas: Implementing the Convention on Biological Diversity in Marine and Coastal Habitats', 10 *Georgetown International Environmental Law Review*, 1998, pp. 753–854.

taking into account their links with marine biodiversity in general.[14] Collective awareness in this respect evolved gradually until reaching its current level, as illustrated by the succession of resolutions on fisheries that were adopted by the United Nations General Assembly (UNGA).[15]

This trend towards a more holistic and less fragmented approach regarding the marine living resources might have meant also, to some degree at least, the weakening of the geographically and ecologically artificial boundaries between maritime areas under different legal regimes. Issues of governance would be addressed at the level of the seas and oceans as a whole, or at least under the angle of ecologically meaningful provinces. There are some examples of such a shift,[16] but in voicing its concerns, the international community has generally respected the differentiation between maritime areas established in LOSC and has focused on these areas separately and specifically. This is particularly the case of the high seas with regard to the situation of their living resources and ecosystems, which has received in recent years an increasingly high level of attention, probably not commensurate with their objective importance. It is well known that most of fish catches are not made in the high seas but in waters under national jurisdiction, since, to the exception of oceanic seamounts,[17] the

---

14   See A. T. Charles, *Sustainable Fishery Systems*, Blackwell Science Ltd., 2001, p. 22: '(...) the fish are not isolated within their respective fisheries, but rather live together with other fished and unfished species, in complex ecosystems. These ecosystems, in turn, involve not only living creatures, but also the physical and chemical fetches future as pictures features affecting life in the ecosystem.'

15   Two series of resolutions on fisheries were adopted successively by the United Nations General Assembly; first those on large-scale pelagic driftnet fishing (from 1998 to 2002) and, second, those on sustainable fisheries (from 2003 to date). Reference to ecosystems appears only in 2000, in Resolution 55/8 (UN Doc. A/RES/55/8, 30 October 2000), rather timidly (with a reference in its paragraph 21 to the 'importance of protecting the ecosystem'). It was expanded in Resolution 57/42 in 2002 (UN Doc. A/RES/57/42), in the wake of the adoption of the Reykjavik Declaration on Responsible Fisheries in the Marine Ecosystem. A reference to biodiversity in relation to fisheries appears for the first time in 2003 (UN Doc. A/RES/58/14, 24 November 2003) ('46. Requests the Secretary-General (...) in his next report concerning fisheries to include a section outlining current risks to the marine biodiversity of vulnerable marine ecosystems...').

16   A recent example may be found in the focus on the 'deep ocean' as such, meaning the ocean 'more than 200 m below the sea surface' as referred to in K. J. Mengerink et al. 'A Call for Deep-Ocean Stewardship', in 334 *Science*, 2014, pp. 696–698.

17   'The primary and most important fishing grounds in the World are found on and along continental shelves within less than 200 nautical miles of the shores'; 'Indeed, over half of the World's marine landings are associated with ca 7.5% of the oceans, concentrated on the continental shelves', in C. Nellemann, S. Hain, & J. Alder (eds), *In Dead*

richest and more biodiverse ecosystems are nearer the coasts, over the continental shelves. A kind of culmination of that process is the call made by the United Nations General Assembly, in June 2015, to 'develop an internationally legally binding instrument under the United Nations Convention on the Law the Sea on the conservation and sustainable use of marine biological diversity of areas beyond national jurisdiction' (ABNJs).[18] Because of the diversity of positions at this early stage, it is difficult to foresee the effects of these negotiations may on the legal regime and institutional framework of fisheries in the high seas. However, the significance of this development cannot be underestimated, the more so when it occurs at the same time as the publication of radical proposals, such as prohibiting fishing in the high seas.[19]

1   The Legal Regime of High Sea Fisheries under Scrutiny: Which Future?

During the second half of the 20th century, the international law of the sea has undergone a deep and swift mutation in response to changes in political, societal, economic, and technological circumstances. Overall, however, this mutation did not mean moving away from the traditional zonal and geometric approach that derived from the historical dichotomy between territorial sea and high seas. None of these two areas was discarded, although they are now spatially separate from one another, mainly as a consequence of the establishment of an area of an hybrid nature, the exclusive economic zone (EEZ), which, although under national jurisdiction, retains some characteristics of the high seas, regarding freedom of navigation and communication. In addition to this

---

Water—Merging of climate change with pollution, over-harvest, and infestations in the world's fishing grounds, United Nations Environment Programme, GRID-Arendal, 2008, pp. 7 and 19.

18   UN Doc. A/RES/69/290, paragraph 1.
19   See, for instance, C. White & C.Costello, 'Close the High Seas to Fishing?', 12 *PLOS Biology*, March 2014. Such bans are not unprecedented, although never on such a scale; for instance, the 'global moratorium on all large-scale pelagic drift-net fishing (...) on the high seas of the world's oceans and seas, including enclosed seas and semi-enclosed seas' established through UN Doc. A/RES/46/215, 20 December 1991. Another example, more recent, is the prohibition in 2005 by the General Fisheries Commission for the Mediterranean (GFCM) of all bottom-trawling in waters deeper than 1000m, in the Mediterranean and in the Black Sea.

legal 'decomposition',[20] the high seas greatly shrank, in terms of their surface area. They also were reduced to the column of waters, since they lost all their seabed and subsoil, which belong either to the international seabed area, common heritage of mankind, or to the extended continental shelf, pursuant to provisions of Parts XI and VI of LOSC. The negotiators of the Convention did not seriously consider getting rid of this last remnant of the Grotian *mare liberum* and replacing it with a radically new institution (such as the unified ocean regime beyond 200 miles proposed by Ambassador Pardo of Malta).[21] They did not challenge either the existence of the traditional 'freedoms' including that of fishing, which were reaffirmed in LOSC, as they had been in Article 2 of the 1958 Geneva Convention on the High Seas.[22]

This retention of the institution and its associated terminology did produce a persistent confusion in some quarters, convinced that freedom equated 'open access' and that, consequently, the marine living resources of the high seas were condemned to suffer the evils of the so-called 'tragedy of the commons'.[23] According to such views, it would be necessary to fill the void perpetuated by the negotiators of LOSC with regard to the governance of the high seas living resources and develop a new legal framework that might ensure the sustainable management of high seas fisheries. In fact, as already described above, there is no such void. On the contrary, a comprehensive and complex body of law has been progressively built up at the global and regional level, on the sound and solid basis of the provisions of Part VII of LOSC, which may be less detailed and developed than those in other parts, but are no less effective. The numerous and severe problems of governance that must still be faced stem

---

20   See D. Momtaz, 'The High Seas', in R.-J. Dupuy & D. Vignes (eds), *A Handbook on the New Law of the Sea*, vol. I, Martinus Nijhoff, 1991, p. 383.

21   On further similar proposals to extend to the high seas altogether a public trust regime presently limited to the area under the jurisdiction of the International Sea-Bed Authority, see P. H. Sand, 'Public Trusteeship for the Oceans' in T. M. Ndiaye & R. Wolfrum (eds), *Law of the Sea, Environmental Law and Settlement of Disputes*, Brill, 2007, pp. 536 et seq. On the other hand, some years ago, the eventuality of further creeping jurisdiction by the coastal State (with concepts such as 'mar epicontinental' and 'mar presencial') could not to be completely discarded. To date, these scenarios may be considered as highly improbable.

22   450 UNTS 11.

23   This expression which is commonly used nowadays comes from the title of a well-known article by Garrett Harding, published in Science in 1968. His analysis in that article was however, as he himself recognized later, affected by a 'conceptual error' that consisted in 'equating 'commons' with 'open access'...', as stressed by B. J. McCay in the foreword to S. M. Garcia, J. Rice & A. Charles (eds), *Governance of Marine Fisheries and Biodiversity Conservation—Interaction and Co-Evolution*, John Wiley & Sons, 2014.

mainly not from a lack of law but rather from failures in compliance. This has been recognized by the international community, for a number of years, when it stated that the main challenge is not a lack of rules, legal instruments or expressed commitments[24] but their inadequate implementation as well as the absence of a strong enough political will.[25] Moreover, this situation is not specific nor restricted to the high seas and there are very similar challenges concerning governance of marine living resources in areas under sovereignty or national jurisdiction, particularly in the case of developing coastal States and territories.

The cornerstone of the legal regime codified in LOSC is that there is no 'free'—in the general sense of the word—access to the high seas to fish its resources. The same principle permeates all the subsequent instruments adopted in the wake of the Convention.[26]

---

24   In March 2005 a FAO ministerial meeting on fisheries adopted the *Rome Declaration on Illegal, Unreported and Unregulated Fishing*, which sought a new approach characterized by the wish of the ministers '*to move from words to action for full implementation of various international instruments on sustainable fisheries adopted or enacted in the past decades*'. This expression was embedded in the name of a conference on the governance of the high seas that took place a few weeks later (*Conference on the Governance of High Seas Fisheries and the United Nations Fish Agreement—Moving from Words to Action*, St. John's, Canada, from 1–5 May 2005).

25   An example of a lack of such will is that of the *Port State Measures Agreement*, supra, note 2, which is of a vital importance in the fight against IUU fishing but has entered into force only recently (5 June 2016). The instruments inspired by that agreement and adopted at the regional level contain sometimes provisions that may be seen as not fully consistent with the letter and spirit of the Agreement and seriously curtailing the efficiency of such measures. For instance, within the General Fisheries Commission for the Mediterranean (GFCM), the 'Regional scheme on port state measures to combat illegal, unreported and unregulated fishing activities in the GFCM area', which was adopted in 2008, specifies in its paragraph 3 that it 'only applies to vessels which are within the GFCM Area'. A similar approach may be found in 'Resolution 10/11 on Port State Measures to Prevent, Deter and Eliminate Illegal, Unreported and Unregulated Fishing', which was adopted by the Indian Ocean Tuna Commission (IOTC) in 2010, which stipulates in its paragraph 20 that the Resolution '(…) shall be applied *to CPCs' ports within the IOTC area of competence*', adding that 'The CPCs situated outside the IOTC area of competence *shall endeavour* to apply this Resolution.' [CPCs means members and cooperating non-members].

26   This is recognized even by some of the advocates of the most radical decisions concerning the governance of high seas fisheries, for instance the adoption of a precautionary closure on the high seas to fishing; see e.g. C. M. Brooks et al. 'Challenging the 'Right to Fish' in a Fast-Changing Ocean', 33 *Stanford Environmental Law Journal -Stanford Journal of Law, Science & Policy*, 2014, p. 292: 'On the high seas, the concept of 'freedom of the seas',

The concept of 'freedom' used in its Part VII must be understood as essentially meaning equality between the fishers of all nations regarding their right to fish without any kind of discrimination.[27] This principle, which embodies an imperative of social justice, has a great legal and political importance, for which reason it has been reaffirmed in several legal instruments adopted subsequently, in particular to emphasize that the weaker components of the international community should be guaranteed to benefit from that right.[28] It has been highlighted repeatedly that the special situation and needs of developing coastal States and territories, and especially small islands developing States, must be kept in mind whenever conservation and management measures are developed and adopted, particularly for the sake of sharing in an equitable manner existing or new constraints regarding a sustainable access to the resources.[29]

The provisions of Part VII of LOSC on fisheries in the high seas, clearly not a high priority for its negotiators, are few and short. These five articles are probably the most general and less detailed of the whole Convention, when compared to the extent and magnitude of the matters that they regulate, even if the applicability of several articles of Part V to stocks that are also found in the high seas is taken into account.[30] Brevity however does not mean superficiality: these provisions define clearly and strongly the two all-encompassing

---

is sometimes interpreted as an unfettered right to fish. However, nothing could be further from the truth under LOSC and modern international law.'

[27] LOSC, Article 116 (*Right to fish on the high seas*): 'All States have the right for their nationals to engage in fishing on the high seas...'; Article 119, (*Conservation of the living resources of the high seas*): '3. States concerned shall ensure that conservation measures and their implementation do not discriminate in form or in fact against the fishermen of any State.'

[28] In this respect, most significant are the provisions of Article 5 of the FAO Code of Conduct for Responsible Fisheries on the 'special requirements of developing countries', which contemplates measures to be taken to enhance the ability of these countries 'to develop their own fisheries *as well as to participate in high seas fisheries, including access to such fisheries.*'

[29] This kind of situation can be observed particularly in relation with the question of 'new entrants' as regulated in a number of instruments, in particular the agreements establishing regional fisheries management organizations. For instance, pursuant to the 2003 *Antigua Convention*, one of the functions of the Inter-American Tropical Tuna Commission is, in relation to fully fished or overfished stocks, to '(...) determine, on the basis of criteria that the Commission may adopt or apply, the extent to which the fishing interests of new members of the Commission might be accommodated, taking into account relevant international standards and practices' (Article VII, par. 1 e).

[30] Highly migratory species (Article 64); marine mammals (Article 65); anadromous stocks (Article 66); catadromous species (Article 67).

obligations that constitute the solid ground upon which any further development of the rules of law applicable to the conservation and management of high seas fisheries resources may take place.

First, the duty to take measures for ensuring the conservation of the living resources of the high seas, not only targeted species but also those species associated with them,[31] in terms that remarkably herald concepts that would be developed later as described above.[32] Second, the duty to cooperate for the conservation and management of these resources, including through the establishment of subregional or regional fisheries organizations,[33] as expressly stated in the Convention not only in Article 118 but also in several articles in Part V: one would like to see this as an implicit affirmation of establishing an international institutional framework rather than a multiplicity of parallel *ad hoc* arrangements.[34]

Significantly, since the adoption of LOSC, the further development of the applicable body of law has not challenged the validity, legitimacy, or adequacy of the provisions of the Convention. In the field of fisheries, the subsequent

---

31   LOSC, Article 117 and 119.

32   In addition to those applicable to targeted resources, such as the concept of sustainability and sustainable exploitation, introduced in the 1992 Rio Declaration and Agenda 21, others reflect the growing awareness of the interaction and mutual dependency relationship between the fisheries stocks and their respective ecosystems, as stressed above, which coalesced into the concept of ecosystem approach to fisheries in the 2002 Reykjavik Declaration, in turn part of a broader marine ecosystem-based management. See R. D. Long et al., 'Key principles of marine ecosystem-based management', 57 *Marine Policy*, 2015, pp. 53–60.

33   LOSC, Article 118.

34   From a terminological point of view, regional fisheries bodies (RFBS) have only the mandate and competence of providing advice and recommendations to their members; their area of competence is for that reason generally circumscribed to the areas under the national jurisdiction of these members; regional fisheries management organizations (RFMOS) may also provide advice and recommendations to their members but usually can also adopt binding decisions and measures for the conservation and management of the species covered by their constitutive instrument (e.g. tuna and tuna like species in the case of the five tuna RFMOS). Regional fisheries management arrangements (RFMAS) are the same than RFMOS, but without a permanent secretariat or administration (e.g. SIOFA in the Indian Ocean). In a same geographical region, therefore, there may exist a self-complementing network of bodies which cover between them the entire range of species and all spaces under different legal regimes: for instance, in the Indian Ocean three bodies complement each other: a RFB, the SWIOFC, for the areas under national jurisdiction, a tuna RFMO, the IOTC, and a RFMA, SIOFA, for all species in the high seas other than tunas.

growth of a body of soft and hard law referred to above[35] took place either within LOSC (e.g. the 1985 UN Fish Stocks Agreement) or without, always in full consistency with the Convention and with the express recognition of its authority as reflecting existing international law.[36] There is not substantial indication that this trend should not be expected to continue, in spite of shifts in circumstances and priorities and the rise of new challenges and actors. Significant in this respect is the position taken in September 2015 by the *United Nations Summit for the adoption of the post-2015 development agenda*. In the document that the Summit adopted, entitled 'Transforming our world: the 2030 Agenda for Sustainable Development', the following provisions may be found in the section corresponding to Goal 14 'Conserve and sustainably use the oceans, seas and marine resources for sustainable development': '14.c Enhance the conservation and sustainable use of oceans and their resources by implementing international law as reflected in LOSC, which provides the legal framework for the conservation and sustainable use of oceans and their resources, as recalled in paragraph 158 of The Future We Want.'

It is noteworthy that this reaffirmation of the central role of the Convention was agreed only a few weeks after the adoption by the General Assembly, on 19 June 2015, of its resolution 69/292 'Development of an international legally binding instrument under the United Nations Convention on the Law of the Sea on the conservation and sustainable use of marine biological diversity of areas beyond national jurisdiction', as mentioned above. Not only the resolution stresses that the negotiation will take place within the framework of LOSC, but it also stipulates in its paragraph 3 that the process 'should not undermine existing relevant legal instruments and frameworks and relevant global, regional and sectoral bodies'. This language is important because it shows the desire of preventing or minimizing the risk of overlap between incompatible, competing or conflicting legal regimes, without hampering efforts to develop the rule of law where gaps exist undeniably (e.g. the situation of marine genetic resources), or the diversification and strengthening of 'measures'

---

35 See J-F. Pulvenis, 'FAO, Ocean Governance, and the Law of the Sea', in H. N. Scheiber, J-H. Paik (eds), *Regions, Institutions, and Law of the Sea: Studies in Ocean Governance*, Nijhoff, 2013, pp. 111–128.

36 E.g. Article 3.1 of the 1995 FAO Code of Conduct for Responsible Fisheries: '3.1 The Code is to be interpreted and applied in conformity with the relevant rules of international law, as reflected in the United Nations Convention on the Law of the Sea, 1982. Nothing in this Code prejudices the rights, jurisdiction and duties of States under international law as reflected in the Convention.'

and 'tools'.[37] In such a process, characterized by the welcome absence of a legal *tabula rasa*, two elements should be kept in mind when addressing globally or regionally the question of governance of high seas fisheries: first, in the case of an approach promoting the development of multi-sectoral ocean ecosystems management arrangements and schemes, the importance of the contribution of fisheries to food security and the interests of coastal communities and countries, especially developing ones. Second, because of the absence of a supranational authority, it is essential to ensure a full and open participation of all sovereign stakeholders, not only for the sake of legitimacy of the measures to be adopted but also for their efficient implementation thanks to a higher degree of commitment and ownership. Needless to say, a successful outcome depends to a high degree upon the international institutional framework within which this process takes place.

2 The International Institutional Framework for the Governance of High Seas Fisheries: Which Future?

Like the legal regime of high seas fisheries, the international institutional framework has been submitted to harsh criticism. Its inefficiencies and shortcomings would be not only the result of the persistence of gaps in the spatial coverage by competent institutions or constraints in the way these institutions operate (for instance, their decision-making procedures) but also, and maybe mainly, of a kind of inherent flaw in the system. For those sharing these views, the various fisheries bodies, and first and foremost the regional fisheries management organizations (RFMOs), would be hobbled by an inbuilt fragmented and 'siloed' approach and suffer also from a systematic bias rendering them intrinsically unable to give to the marine ecosystems and biodiversity the level of attention and priority that they deserve. According to the supporters of these

---

37 '2. Also decides that negotiations shall address the topics identified in the package agreed in 2011, namely the conservation and sustainable use of marine biological diversity of areas beyond national jurisdiction, in particular, together and as a whole, *marine genetic resources*, including questions on the sharing of benefits, *measures such as area-based management tools*, including *marine protected areas*, environmental impact assessments and capacity-building and the transfer of marine technology;'. On marine protected areas and fisheries, see FAO, 'Fisheries management, 4. Marine protected areas and fisheries', 4 *FAO Technical Guidelines for Responsible Fisheries*, Suppl. 4, 2011. As highlighted in that document, 'Closures (spatial-temporal-gear or spatial-temporal-fishing types) are one of the oldest forms of fisheries management.' (p. 28). As it happens, such closures may be considered as a kind of MPA.

arguments, RFMOs should be viewed with at least some degree of suspicion[38] and a preferred approach instead would be the unified and centralized establishment of a global arrangement or institution, which would be responsible for all matters related to governance of the seas and oceans.[39] A variety of solutions have been proposed, ranging for instance from the establishment of a global 'ocean trusteeship/stewardship'[40] to that of a 'global high seas enforcement agency to provide integrated and co-ordinated monitoring, control, surveillance, and enforcement for the full range of oceans security threats'.[41]

It must be argued that this kind of approach is neither necessary nor desirable. For good reason, it was not the path that the negotiators of LOSC chose to follow, with the exception of the Part XI International Seabed Authority—whose mandate and area of competence are anyway limited to the international seabed area and its mineral resources. Moreover, trying to replace or supplement the existing institutional framework with a new structure at the global level or at the level of each ocean and sea, would be costly, uncertain, and, at the very least, would run the risk of duplicating and undermining the operation of the current institutions. That is why this is a highly unlikely course of action.

A more realistic and appropriate solution is to consider as a positive factor and an opportunity the complexity of the current institutional framework, which has been established progressively over the years through the concerted will of sovereign entities, as well as the specialized nature of its components. There is no denying the urgent need to address and correct its shortcomings and inefficiencies and make sure that it undergoes a process of performance review of its various components.

---

38 'And the regional fishing bodies, currently dominated by fishing interests, should be opened up to scientists and charities. As it is, the sharks are in charge of the fish farm.' in 'New management is needed for the planet's most important common resource', *The Economist*, February 22, 2014. Needless to say, in fact, most if not all fisheries bodies have scientific advisory committees or organs, in order to ensure the participation of scientists, and most of them if not all have internal arrangements to organize the participation of non-governmental organizations (NGOs), both environmental NGOs and those that represent the fisheries sector.

39 This is not to be confused with proposals such as raising the hierarchical status of the current UN Division for Ocean Affairs and the Law of the Sea, which would not mean the establishment of a new international organization or the creation of a new administrative organ within the existing structure.

40 See Sand, supra, note 21, pp. 521–544.

41 See K. M. Gjerde et al., 'Ocean in peril: Reforming the management of global ocean living resources in areas beyond national jurisdiction', 74 *Marine Pollution Bulletin*, 2013, pp. 540–551.

A first challenge is to ensure that there is no gap in the spatial and thematic coverage of the seas and oceans, including the high seas, by a network of competent international organizations. This implies eventually the creation of new specialized regional institutions in addition to those already existing, as needed.

Currently, at the global level, there is no such institutional gap. All issues and matters related to the seas and oceans, including high seas fisheries, are reviewed by the United Nations General Assembly, which adopts each year two comprehensive resolutions on fisheries and on oceans and the law of the sea.[42] At that level also, many of the UN specialized agencies (e.g. IMO, ILO, UNESCO, WTO) and secretariats of UN conventions (e.g. UNFCC and CBD) do work relevant to fisheries in general and high seas fisheries in particular. The central and pre-eminent role of FAO must be recognized: its Committee on Fisheries (COFI) is the only global intergovernmental forum that is exclusively dedicated to all issues related to fisheries and aquaculture and that has the power to formulate collective commitments at the global level, which may become eventually enshrined in new international instruments, if it is deemed necessary.

At the regional and subregional levels, a similarly pre-eminent role is played by the subregional or regional fisheries organizations. Not only they provide a stable and permanent framework for the interaction of all governmental and non-governmental stakeholders, but, in contrast to the latter, they may adopt decisions and measures that are legally binding. It is therefore not surprising to note, as we already did above, that LOSC expressly refers to these bodies as the privileged vehicle for the implementation of the duty of States to cooperate for the conservation of the living resources of the high seas, including those stocks found both in the high seas and in the areas under national jurisdiction.

Once again, it would be futile to speculate at this point on the concrete impact on the current institutional framework of future changes in circumstances and, in particular as a consequence in the medium or long term of the negotiations undertaken within the ABNJ process referred to above. It may be safely assumed however that it is most unlikely that fisheries bodies, especially RFMOs, would be deprived of their raison d'être or replaced by arrangements of a different nature and scope. For its part, the United Nations General

---

42   The most recent resolutions are UN Doc. A/RES/70/75, 8 December 2015, and UN Doc. A/RES/70/235 23 December 2015. It is also significant to note that the work of the General Assembly is prepared and assisted through an ad hoc informal mechanism (the United Nations Open-ended Informal Consultative Process on Oceans and the Law of the Sea) that was established instead of a new institution as proposed by some during the discussions that took place at the time in the Committee for Sustainable Development.

Assembly, highlighted reiteratedly in its successive resolutions on fisheries the importance and relevance of these bodies. It has also taken great care in drafting its Resolution 69/292 on the development of a new international legally binding instrument, as mentioned previously, to specify that this process 'should not undermine existing relevant legal instruments and frameworks and relevant global, regional and sectoral bodies.'

It is hoped rather that the process will lead to the strengthening of the existing framework. In addition to a full spatial and thematic coverage and the improvement of the individual performance of the various bodies (e.g. with regard to decision making, enforcement of adopted conservation and management measures, settlement of disputes and effective participation by members), the most important challenge will continue to be to ensure an appropriate level of coordination between these bodies. First, between RFMOs themselves, those with a similar mandate—e.g. tuna RFMOs—or those with mandates that are complementary—e.g. the three RFBS and RFMOs in the Indian Ocean;[43] second, between RFMOs and subregional and regional bodies competent to deal with issues and activities other than fisheries, such as marine scientific research or the conservation and protection of the marine environment.[44] Coordination and cooperation should also be extended to non-governmental organizations (NGOs) with a special interest in the field of

---

43   This process can involve either the members of the bodies themselves (for instance as in the so-called Kobe process which involves the five tuna RFMOs) or their secretariats (for instance, with the assistance of FAO, the Regional Fishery Body Secretariats Network (RSN)).

44   An interesting example that might serve as a model (even taking into account that it mostly corresponds to a semi enclosed sea) is that of the Caribbean Sea with three regional organizations, one for oceanography and scientific research, IOCARIBE (of the Intergovernmental Oceanographic Commission of UNESCO); one for the marine environment, the Caribbean Environmental Program (CEP) (of UNEP), and one for fisheries, WECAFC (of FAO). Another example would be the Western Indian Ocean, with the interaction between three complementary fisheries bodies, the South West Indian Ocean Fisheries Commission (SWIOFC), covering the areas under national jurisdiction; the Indian Ocean Tuna Commission (IOTC); and the South Indian Ocean Fisheries Agreement (SIOFA) for high seas fisheries other than for tuna and tuna like species. Concerning the relationship between a fisheries body and an intergovernmental organization for the marine environment covering a high seas, the best example would probably be that of NEAFC and OSPAR (see i.a. D. Owen, 'Principles and Objectives of the Legal Regime Governing the Areas beyond National Jurisdiction—Commentary on Tullio Treves', in A. G. Oude Elferink & E. J. Molenaar (eds), *The International Regime of Areas beyond National Jurisdiction: Current and Future Developments*, Martinus Nijhof, 2010, pp. 30 et seq.

fisheries—both the so-called 'environmental NGOs' and those representing the fisheries sector—and to NGOs focusing on non-fisheries issues but whose activities are relevant to the conservation and management of marine living resources.

Second, efforts should be made to ensure that commitments that have been adopted at the global level are effectively followed by action at the regional, subregional, and local levels, and, conversely, that regional and subregional concerns and experiences are appropriately taken into account in the global debate.

In such a scenario, whatever changes may be introduced in the rules, principles or standards governing the conservation and sustainable use of marine living resources and the biological diversity in the ABNJs, would not have on RFMOs a much different impact than those that these organizations have already faced repeatedly in the past. Then, they evolved and adapted in response to the emergence of new concepts such as 'sustainable' fisheries, 'responsible' fishing, or 'ecosystem-based approach to fisheries management'. It is possible that these new developments, so far as they can be predicted, will lead to a broadening of the mandate of RFMOs, without going as far as transforming them into regional oceanic management organizations with additional competences and responsibilities resolutely beyond the field of fisheries and conservation and management of marine living resources.

Sunken Warships and Cultural Heritage

Natalino Ronzitti

1 Introduction

Confrère Djamchid Momtaz was President of the Programme Committee of the Institut de droit international (IDI) for several years. I was given the task of rapporteur dealing with sunken warships (9th Commission) in Santiago, Chile during Professor Momtaz' Presidency. This essay, which draws on the work I did for the IDI as Rapporteur, is a tribute to him for his 75th birthday.

Sunken war vessels have attracted the attention of several people. First, treasure hunters seek them because often vessels have on board valuable cargo such as bullion or other gold artefacts and coins. Progress in marine exploration over the past 30 years has permitted the recovery of wrecks and their cargo in very deep waters. The second category of persons interested in the recovery and conservation of sunken vessels is marine archaeologists who are concerned about the commercial exploitation of the wrecks that are testimony of ancient civilisations. The third category is represented by international lawyers, who have tried to regulate an issue previously almost unregulated. The literature is now flourishing and more writing is to be expected with the centenary of World War I, a conflict that saw wide recourse to submarine warfare and the sinking of a huge number of ships. The final factor prompting interest in sunken vessels is the IDI Resolution adopted at the Tallinn session (22–29 August 2015) and the set of articles on 'The Legal Regime of Wrecks of Warships and Other State-owned Ships in International Law'. The principle aim of the Resolution is the preservation and protection of cultural heritage as stated in the Preamble.

Not every relic constitutes cultural heritage. This is intuitive. The notion of cultural heritage (*rectius* archaeological and historical objects) is referred to in Articles 149 and 303 of the United Nations Convention on the Law of the Sea (LOSC)[1] without giving any definition. The 2001 UNESCO Convention on the Protection of Underwater Cultural Heritage,[2] however, gives—as we shall see—a definition of cultural heritage indicating which vessels fall under it.

---

1 1833 UNTS 3.
2 http://unesdoc.unesco.org/images/0012/001246/124687e.pdf#page=56.

2 Immunity/Property of Sunken Warships

LOSC dictates a set of provisions on the status of warships. The most relevant, for our discourse, are those connected with the immunity of warships, as set forth in Article 32. Also relevant is the UN Convention on Jurisdictional Immunities of States and their Property,[3] not yet in force but containing a number of provisions declaratory of customary international law. One such is Article 16 (2), which outlines the immunity of warships from foreign jurisdiction. The problem is that these provisions refer to warships in exercise and do not encompass vessels that have lost their buoyancy. Sunken warships are thus not regulated either by LOSC or by the Convention on Jurisdictional Immunities. Some provisions can be found in the 2007 Nairobi International Convention on the Removal of Wrecks.[4] This Convention excludes from its field of application 'any warship or other ship owned and operated by a State and used, for the time being, only on Government non-commercial service' (Article 4, para. 2), even though the flag State may decide otherwise. One can presume that the exclusion of wrecked warships is due to the presumption that such wrecks still enjoy sovereign immunity. More than a decade ago Derek Bowett introduced the subject of wrecks, including the wrecks of warships, before the International Law Commission (ILC). He noted that it was a topic unregulated and worthy of being codified.[5] However the subject was not immediately taken up by the Commission. It was first included in the 'long-term programme' of the work of the ILC in 2001 and again quoted as part of the long-term programme in 2011.[6]

Both the practice of States and the jurisprudence of domestic tribunals are in favour of sovereign immunity for sunken warships. A discussion of State practice and relevant domestic jurisprudence was given in my preliminary report on 'The Legal Regime of Wrecks of Warships and Other State-International Law' for the IDI (Rhodes Session), in the Addendum prepared for the IDI Tokyo Session and in the final document submitted to the Tallinn Session. Here the case of *Nuestra Señora de las Mercedes* is worth mentioning, a Spanish vessel recovered by the Odyssey Marine Exploration and the object of litigation

---

3 UN Doc A/RES/59/508.
4 https://www.gov.uk/government/uploads/system/uploads/attachment_data/file/228988/8243.pdf.
5 See UN doc. A/CN.4/454, 9 November 1993, p. 211. See also UN Doc. A/51/10, 9 May–26 July 1996, pp. 139–140, Addendum 2.
6 The topic is referred to as 'Ownership and protection of wrecks beyond the limits of national maritime jurisdiction', see UN Doc. A/66/10, April–August 2011, para. 369.

by Spain before the US Supreme Court. On 29 February 2012, the US Supreme Court rejected a motion from Odyssey directed at nullifying the injunction by the US Court of Appeals for the Eleventh Circuit to return the treasure recovered from the *Nuestra Señora de las Mercedes* to Spain.[7] The Court ordered the restitution to Spain of the treasure recovered by Odyssey consisting of 594,000 coins and other artefacts. In particular, the Court held that the *Mercedes* was a warship and that the wreck of a warship is entitled to sovereign immunity.

Immunity and the ownership of the wreck are interlinked[8] and immunity lasts as long as the flag State keeps the ownership of the wreck. Practice shows that title is claimed by the owner, unless the sunken ship has been abandoned. Abandonment is usually a unilateral act by the owner, either expressly stated or implied. The mere passage of time does not usually deprive the owner of its title and there exists legislation, such as that enacted by the US, which clearly affirms that the mere passage of time does not extinguish the title, unless an act of abandonment is adopted. The US Sunken Military Craft Act (SMCA) of 2005[9] states that rights and title to US sunken warships shall not be extinguished except by an express act of the United States and that the passage of time has no influence on US property rights. The SMCA abolishes the law of finds and salvage in respect of US sunken military vessels, wherever located, and in respect of foreign military vessels located in United States territorial waters or contiguous zone. Any operation on the wreck requires the consent of the flag State. Ownership may be transferred by treaty or by an act of a private nature. In this connection Article 5 of the Tallinn Resolution affirms that 'sunken State ships remain the property of the flag State, unless the flag State has clearly stated that it has abandoned the wreck or relinquished or transferred title to it.' Obviously if the title to property is transferred, sovereign immunity terminates, unless the title was transferred when the warship was still

---

7   Supreme Court of the United States, *Odyssey Marine Exploration, Inc., petitioner v. The Unidentified Shipwrecked Vessel, et al.*, February 29 2012, No. 11–1067.

8   Sarah Dromgoole, 'The Legal Regime of Wrecks of Warships and Other State-owned Ships in International Law. The IDI Resolution 2015', 25 *The Italian Yearbook of International Law*, 2015), pp. 190–191. Contra J. Symonides & M. Symonides, 'Droits de l'Etat du pavillon sur les épaves des navires de guerre et des autres navires d'Etat utilisés à des fins non commerciales', 28 *Revista europea de la navegación marítima y aeronautica*, 2012, pp. 1–17. They agree that the practice shows that the wreck remains the property of the flag State: immunity is no longer enjoyed since the rationale for keeping immunity is lacking. A warship enjoys immunity as an organ of the flag State, while a sunken warship may not be considered as a State organ.

9   The SMCA (2005) is reprinted and commented on by D. J. Bederman, 'Congress Enacts Increased Protection for Sunken Military Craft', 100 *American Journal of International Law*, 2006, pp. 649–663.

a floating vessel and the new owner wants to maintain its military nature. This may happen for instance upon capture in naval warfare. Warships and their cargo fall under the ownership of the captor State immediately after the capture without the necessity of prize adjudication. The ship should be captured in order to become the property of the captor State. The title is not transferred and the warship remains the property of the flag State if it is sunk during a military engagement without being captured.[10] Quid in the case of State succession? Warships are moveable property and their succession is regulated by the law in force for that kind of property. State succession to moveable property is dealt with by the 1983 UN Convention on State Succession on the Matter of Property, Archives and State Debts.[11] However, the Convention is hardly considered as declaratory of customary international law and has been ratified by few States. The easiest examples are the ones on incorporation, since the incorporating State succeeds to all rights and duties of the incorporated State. In the case of dissolution of the successor State, one possibility is to attribute the property of the sunken warship to the coastal State in whose territorial waters or continental shelf the wreck lies. In the case of transfer of territory, the interpreter has to check whether the transfer agreement also encompasses part of the moveable property, including a number of ships. One could also envisage moveable property connected with the activity of the territory transferred, for instance sunken vessels which were employed for coast-guarding. The most difficult issues to solve are those relating to new States and to the break-up of the predecessor State when dealing with warships sunk before the critical date of State succession. Even in this case the territorial principle may be followed and thus the property may be attributed to the State in whose territorial waters or continental shelf the wreck lies. It is unclear how to regulate the case of a wreck lying on the sea-bed outside national jurisdiction.

It is also open to question whether the transfer of property means also the transfer of the sovereign immunity which belonged to the predecessor State. In other words, if immunity is a predicate of ownership, does the transfer of property also encompass transfer of sovereign immunity? It is unlikely, as immunity is linked not only to property but also to functions carried out by the

---

10 In this connection the leading case is that of the *Admiral Nakhimov*, a Russian ship which sank in the Strait of Korea after capture by the Japanese navy during the Japanese-Russian war of 1904–1905. The ship became the property of Japan immediately upon capture, without the necessity of prize adjudication.

11 UN Doc A/CONF.117/14. C.N.358.2008.TREATIES-1.

vessel, even though—as pointed out by Sarah Dromgoole—the question is not clarified by the Tallinn Resolution.[12]

3 Sunken Warships as Cultural Heritage

As already noted, not every sunken warship constitutes cultural heritage. The passage of time is a necessary ingredient for labelling a wreck cultural heritage or, adducing LOSC, as an object having an archaeological and historical nature. The main problem lies with the definition of cultural heritage.

LOSC deals with submerged antiquities in two provisions: Articles 303 and 149. They regulate objects of archaeological and historical nature found at sea and do not specifically address sunken warships. These may fall under the abovementioned provisions in so far as they are of archaeological and historical interest, but otherwise they cannot be deemed to be governed by law of the sea provisions dealing with submerged antiquities. LOSC does not establish a date for classifying those objects which are of archaeological or historical interest. Scholars have proposed several solutions. For instance, Oxman proposes the fall of Constantinople (1453) or the discovery of the Americas (1492) as time-limit by which an object should be considered as falling under the two provisions,[13] while Caflisch prefers a more recent time-limit, for instance a hundred years.[14]

A cut-off date has been established by the UNESCO Convention. It applies to a number of objects, including vessels, provided that they have been under water for at least 100 years. As for warships, they fall under the scope of the Convention as long as they have been submerged for 100 years, and are thus subject to a special regime different from that of other wrecks or submerged antiquities. The 100-year term approximately corresponds to changes in the materials used in building modern ships. The term is a rolling date, since it is not fixed at the time of adoption of the Convention or its entry into force, but matures with the passage of time. The artistic value of the wreck or its cargo does not matter for classifying the sunken ship as cultural heritage.

---

12   Dromgoole, supra, note 8, pp. 191–192.
13   B H. Oxman, 'The Third United Nations Conference on the Law of the Sea: The Ninth Session', 75 *American Journal of International Law*, 1981, p. 241.
14   L. Caflisch, 'Submarine Antiquities and the International Law of the Sea', 13 *Netherlands Yearbook of International Law*, 1982, pp. 8–9.

The Tallin Resolution also adopts the term of 100 years. Article 2 (1), merging LOSC terminology with the letter of the UNESCO Convention, states that 'a wreck of an archaeological and historical nature is part of natural heritage when it has been submerged for at least 100 years', bearing in mind that the Resolution deals only with wrecks of sunken State ships (i.e., according to Article 1, para. 2 of the Resolution, 'a warship and naval auxiliary or other ship owned by a State and used at the time of sinking solely for governmental non-commercial purposes').

Obviously the flag State may establish that younger wrecks are worth protecting as cultural heritage. It has the power to do so since the wreck enjoys sovereign immunity, but if the wreck lies under the territorial sea or on the continental shelf of another State, this must be done in cooperation with that State.

4   The UNESCO Convention

The Convention on the Protection of the Underwater Cultural Heritage, adopted under the auspices of UNESCO in 2001, seeks to dictate a regime for underwater cultural heritage which, according to the majority of commentators, is a step forward in comparison with the provisions on submerged cultural objects in LOSC. The UNESCO Convention declares that underwater cultural heritage shall be preserved for the benefit of humanity and to this end the preservation *in situ* shall be considered as the first option before its recovery and disposition on land. In effect the marine environment constitutes a preservational factor, whilst human activity often has a negative impact. Moreover, no commercial exploitation is permitted and salvage and finds are severely curtailed and permitted only in accordance with the principles laid down in the Convention. The UNESCO Convention does not deal with ownership. While private shipping follows the ordinary regime, special rules are dictated for sunken warships. Their content has proved to be very controversial since the major maritime powers wanted to reaffirm their traditional policy of subjecting the wrecks of sunken warships to the exclusive jurisdiction of the flag State.[15]

The Convention does not allow reservations, except as to its geographical scope (Article 30), and this prohibition does not encourage its ratification by

---

15   A-Juan Zhao, 'The relationship among the Three Multilateral Regimes concerning the Underwater Cultural Heritage', in J. A. R. Nafziger & T. Scovazzi (eds), *Le patrimoine culturel de l'Humanité*, Académie de droit international de La Haye, 2008, p. 634.

the great maritime powers.[16] At the time of its adoption, they voted against or abstained since the articles on warships and State vessels proved to be unsatisfactory. This was for instance the position taken by France, the UK and the United States. The Russian Federation stated that the Convention undermined the principle of inviolability of sunken warships. The Netherlands and the United States (at time not member of UNESCO) pointed out that the Convention was not to be considered as reflecting customary international law. Other States, such as Colombia and Greece found the provisions on the rights of the coastal State too weak and considered the duty to inform the flag State a kind of infringement of its territorial sovereignty.[17] Recently, France reversed its policy and on 7 February 2013 ratified the Convention.

The compromise reached is unclear, as often happens when negotiators are obliged to have recourse to 'constructive ambiguity' in order to lay down acceptable rules. The regime envisaged for sunken warships varies according to the sea areas where the wrecks lie. If a vessel is discovered in its territorial sea or archipelagic waters, the coastal State, with a view to cooperating on the best methods of protecting the vessel, *should* inform the flag State of the discovery. The coastal State should also inform other States with a cultural, historical or archaeological link (Article 7). As far as the EEZ and the continental shelf are concerned, any activity concerning warships requires the agreement of the flag State and the collaboration of the coordinating State, which is almost always the coastal State on whose continental shelf the vessels are located (Article 10, para. 7). For warships in the Area, the consent of the flag State is required (Article 12, para. 7). The UNESCO Convention does not deal with sunken warships in internal waters. They therefore fall under the general regime in Article 7, para. 1, which gives the coastal State the exclusive right to regulate and authorise activities directed at underwater cultural heritage. Nor is there a special provision for warships in the contiguous zone. However, the regime of the continental shelf applies, for Article 10 is retained by Article 8 regulating the underwater cultural heritage in the contiguous zone. Thus the UNESCO Convention recognises only a tenuous interest of the flag State in foreign territorial waters, since it should only be informed about the discovery. Moreover, the coastal State has only a hortatory obligation as proved by the

---

16   A State may declare that the Convention does not apply to 'specific parts' of its territory, internal waters, archipelagic waters or territorial sea, but it is encouraged to withdraw the reservation as soon as possible (Article 29).

17   The proceedings on the explanation of the vote are reported by R. Garabello & T. Scovazzi, *The Protection of the Underwater Cultural Heritage, Before and After the 2001 UNESCO Convention*, Brill, 2003, pp. 241–253.

conditional tense employed. This, according to the UNESCO Convention, conforms with the exercise of sovereignty of the coastal State and with the general practice among States, as stated in the opening sentence of Article 7, para. 3. Further, the rights of the flag State increase where the wreck is located off the territorial waters. Those rights are greater in the case of vessels on the continental shelf, since any activity on them is permitted only with the agreement of the flag State and the cooperation of the coastal State. As for the Area, the flag State enjoys full rights, since any activity directed at the wreck requires its consent. Thus, it has been said that the main concern for maritime powers is the treatment of sunken warships in territorial waters, since in this case the coastal State has only a tenuous obligation ('should') to inform the flag State.[18]

5 LOSC

The United Nations Convention on the Law of the Sea (LOSC) deals with submerged antiquities in two provisions: Articles 303 and 149. They regulate objects of archaeological and historical nature found at sea and, as already noted, do not specifically address sunken warships. The latter may fall under the abovementioned provisions in so far as they are of archaeological and historical interest, otherwise they cannot be deemed to be governed by law-of-the sea provisions dealing with submerged antiquities.

While Article 149 excludes the application of salvage law and the law of finds since the objects of archaeological and historical nature found in the Area should be preserved in the interest of humanity, Article 303 does not affect the rights of identifiable owners and the rules on the recovery of sunken items and the other norms of maritime law, including salvage law and the law of finds. The Mining Code adopted by the Seabed authority to govern activities in the Area sets out an obligation that the prospector or the contractor should observe. These have to notify the Secretary-General in writing of any find in the Area of an archaeological or historical nature. The Secretary-General will transmit the information to the UNESCO Director-General.[19] A standard clause

---

18   O. Varmer, 'United States of America', in S. Dromgoole (ed), *The Protection of Underwater Cultural Heritage: National Perspectives in Light of the Unesco Convention 2001*, 2nd ed. Martinus Nijhoff, 2006, pp. 381–382.

19   ISBA/6/A/16, 20 July 2000, Decision of the Assembly of the International Seabed Authority relating to the regulation on prospecting and exploration for the polymetallic nodules in the Area, Annex, Articles 8 and 34.

of this kind should be included in any contract for exploration stipulated between the Seabed Authority and the contractor.[20]

A gap does exist in the regulation of those ships which sank between the outer limit of the contiguous zone and the outer limit of the continental shelf, and it is to be thought that the freedom of the high seas applies, with the consequence that they may be freely recovered, unless the flag State is entitled to claim its jurisdiction.

6   The IDI Resolution

As the above considerations show, a main problem of the wreck-of-warships regime lies in the relations between the immunity of jurisdiction enjoyed by the wreck and the rights of the coastal State if the wreck lies in foreign territorial waters. On this point the Resolution dictates a number of provisions (Articles 7–10) taking stock both of the principles enshrined in the UNESCO Convention and the pertinent articles of LOSC. The regulation of activities over wrecks lying in internal, territorial and archipelagic waters of a foreign State belongs to the coastal State, which should however take into account the immunity from jurisdiction enjoyed by the flag State. In the contiguous zone LOSC Article 303 applies, with the consequence that the coastal State may regulate the removal of warships sunken in this area.

On the contrary on the ZEE and on the continental shelf, jurisdiction over the wreck belongs to the flag State, which should defer to the sovereign rights of the coastal State, for instance for exploitation of fisheries or of natural resources of the continental shelf. If the wreck constitutes an obstacle to the exercise of such rights, the coastal State may remove it, whenever the flag State takes no action after having been duly notified. As far as the Area is concerned, the wreck remains under the exclusive jurisdiction of the flag State. The provision, however, is without prejudice to LOSC Article 149.

While the UNESCO Convention severely curtails salvage, almost abolishing it, the IDI Resolution continues to permit the salvage of sunken vessels, subjecting it to the applicable rules of international law, the provisions of the Resolutions and appropriate archaeological practice (Article 13). This provision should be read in conjunction with Article 2 (4), which lays down principles aimed at avoiding commercial exploitation or pillage of sunken warships constituting cultural heritage. In effect opinions on salvage vary. Whilst for some experts private enterprises may help to preserve historical objects and

---

20   Ibid., Annex 4, Standard clauses for exploration contract, Article 7.

entrepreneurs have the necessary resources for carrying out marine exploration, other experts consider the salvage industry disrespectful of cultural heritage and motivated only by profit. On this point the Resolution follows a middle ground trying to combine the principle of free enterprise with that of maintenance of cultural heritage.

Regarding the preservation of cultural heritage, the Resolution prefers preservation *in situ* and, if this is not possible, sunken warships should be recovered in accordance with appropriate archaeological practice and properly displayed. In any case, States are duty bound to take the necessary measures to ensure the protection of wrecks that are part of cultural heritage.

The Resolution also addresses the cargo on board sunken warships: a question of primary importance, since it is often speculated that a wreck contains fabulous gold treasure. Cargo and wreck are dealt with as a unit, following the *Mercedes* jurisprudence. This means that cargo enjoys immunity from jurisdiction wherever the wreck is located and without distinguishing whether it belongs to the flag State or to other States. The sinking has no effect on the property rights to the cargo on board, including private property rights, as can be inferred from Article 1 (2) on the definition of sunken State ships. Moreover, the cargo may not be disturbed or removed without the consent of the flag State.

7   Conclusion

The present writer considers that international law is oriented toward recognising the sovereign immunity of sunken warships as proved by domestic case-law and State practice. The notion of immunity and that of property coincide, as usually a warship is under the sovereign immunity of the flag State that is also its owner. One can also say that immunity is a predicate of ownership, bearing in mind that transfer of ownership does not automatically carry over the immunity.

Ownership and sovereign immunity do not conflict, in themselves, with the notion of cultural heritage. The law may impose a duty to preserve assets of historical or cultural origin to the State that has title to and/or exercises jurisdiction over sunken warships and their cargo. The phenomenon is well known under domestic law. It may happen that a physical person is owner of a historical mansion or of a famous artefact, but that the law subjects its ownership to a number of obligations aimed at its preservation.

The other point is the conflicting interests between the flag State, as titular of immunity, and the coastal State as the holder of territorial sovereignty in its internal/ territorial waters or of sovereign rights and jurisdiction in its EEZ or on its continental shelf. The only possible way out is an appeal to cooperation between the flag State and the coastal State in order to solve these competing interests, namely when the sunken vessel falls under the notion of cultural heritage.

The IDI Resolution undoubtedly represents clarification of a subject still controversial. It encompasses both sunken warships that constitute cultural heritage and sunken warships that do not. Is it possible to go further and to forecast a codification on the status of sunken warships? As we have seen, the UNESCO Convention is the only instrument dealing with sunken warships, provided that they fall under the notion of cultural heritage. The original reticence towards the Convention is slowly declining and as at 30 April 2016, the Convention had more than 55 State parties, including France that initially expressed its reservation because of the regulation of sunken warships. On 19 May 2016 the Dutch government announced its intention to ratify the 2001 Convention. If the time is not yet ripe for codification, the ILC might still resume its work on 'Ownership and protection of wrecks beyond the limits of national maritime jurisdiction' and finalise draft articles on the subject. Even though the draft is not encapsulated in a treaty, experience shows that ILC Draft Articles and Commentaries constitute an authoritative statement on the status of international law on the subject.

Users of the Law of the Sea: Some Recent Developments

Emmanuel Roucounas

1   Introduction

In international law the concept of 'subject' has been enlarged (with equally controversial legal significance) with new notions such as 'actors', 'non-state actors' and 'participants'. Each has merits, but they all express specific situations which, however, we believe, do not represent the entire image of the addressees (legal and physical persons with rights and obligations) of international law. Undoubtedly the States and, to a lesser degree, the international organizations, as well as the 'mystery' of the individual are on the agenda of scholarship. In an effort to encapsulate the whole operational spectrum of international law I suggested introducing, alongside the notions of 'subjects', 'non-state actors', and 'participants', that of *'users'* of international law.[1]

Regarding the users of the law of the sea, the 1982 United Nations Convention on the Law of the Sea (LOSC) refers more than 500 times to the State (the State Party, the coastal State, the flag State, the port State, the landlocked State and developing State, the geographically disadvantaged State, etc.), whereas it makes some ten references to the ship, the master, the ship-owner, and only one to the crew. The *millions of other users of the oceans are governed by regulations of a legal poly-system*, composed not only of 'the law of the sea', but also of international maritime law and domestic law. Hence, it seems appropriate to enlarge the spectrum of the addressees of the law of the sea by introducing the term 'users'[2] when examining developments since the adoption of LOSC. The developments confirm the customary character of most provisions of LOSC and certainly enhance the legal order of the oceans.

The present essay begins with the perennial 'user' or misuser of the law, i.e. the pirate, who in the textbooks has been a *subject par excellence* of

---

[1] See E. Roucounas, 'The Users of International Law', in M. Arsanjani, J. Cogan et al. (eds), *Looking to the Future, Essays on International Law in Honor of W. Michael Reisman*, Martinus Nijhoff, 2011, pp. 217–234.

[2] E. Roucounas, 'Effectiveness of International Law for the Users of the Sea', in *Cursos Euromediterráneos Bancaja de Derecho Internacional*, Vol. VIII–IX, Tirant lo Blanch, 2004/2005, pp. 854–992.

international law, albeit in anomalous circumstances.[3] It then examines the development of the tragic phenomenon of migration by sea, the involvement of the European Union in several activities regarding the law of the sea, the exploration of natural resources by parties and non-parties to LOSC, and finally the question of claims to historic rights in maritime areas under the new regime of dispute settlement.

This essay is dedicated to Professor Djamchid Momtaz, a scholar with a distinguished career in the service of the rule of law, the humanitarian aspects of international law, and peace and security in the oceans, with whom I cherish a long friendship in the United Nations and in particular within the Institut de droit international.

2   Piracy

Since the turn of the century the international law of the sea has seen the rise or the resurrection of an old *user* or misuser of the oceans—the pirate.[4] The extraordinary growth in piracy, first in Southeast Asia but more prominently since 2008 off the coast of Somalia, has attracted media coverage and an international response.[5] Notwithstanding successes in East Africa, the response of the international community has not succeeded in extinguishing the phenomenon: piracy still persists and piratical attacks on ships have moved back to South East Asia.[6]

As early as in 2007 the International Maritime Organization (IMO) called for international action.[7] The hijacking in April 2008 of the French yacht *Le Ponant*, mobilized the Security Council to adopt Resolution 1816 of 2 June

---

3 For James Crawford the pirate is not a subject of international law. Crawford sees piracy rather as a jurisdictional rule allowing States to exercise international jurisdiction than as a rule conferring legal personality onto pirates. See J. Crawford, 'The System of International Responsibility', in J. Crawford (ed), *The Law of International Responsibility*, Oxford University Press, pp. 17–18.

4 See D. Momtaz, 'La lutte contre la criminalité en mer', in R. C. Raigón & G. Cataldi (eds), *L'évolution et l'état actuel du droit international de la mer, Mélanges de droit de la mer offerts à Daniel Vignes* Bruylant, pp. 629–644.

5 See R. Geiss & A. Petrig, *Piracy and Armed Robbery at Sea. The Legal Framework for Counter-Piracy Operations in Somalia and the Gulf of Aden*, Oxford University Press, 2011.

6 See live piracy report at https://www.icc-ccs.org/piracy-reporting-centre/live-piracy-map. Accessed on 2 September 2016.

7 See IMO Doc A 25/Res.1002, 6 December 2007, para. 6.

2008.[8] Further, in an effort to protect commercial shipping, several States plus NATO[9] and the European Union[10] started sending naval units to patrol the Gulf of Aden. In addition, since January 2009 and pursuant to Security Council Resolution 1851 (2008) a Contact Group on Piracy off the Coast of Somalia has been established. This voluntary ad hoc international organ meets at the UN headquarters to coordinate 'political, military, and other efforts to bring an end to piracy off the coast of Somalia and to ensure that pirates are brought to justice'.[11]

By 30 November 2009, less than 18 months after Resolution 1816, the Security Council referred in the preamble of Resolution 1897 to the efforts of the following: the EU [Naval Force] Operation Atalanta, The NATO operations Allied Protector and Ocean Shield, the Combined Maritime Forces' Combined Task Force 151. It also mentioned other States acting in a national capacity in cooperation with the TFG and each other and in concert, to suppress piracy and to protect vulnerable ships transiting off the coast of Somalia.[12]

In the meantime, the international community has adopted initiatives to effectively address the thorny question of *jurisdiction* over pirates, since States had been markedly reticent to prosecute the arrested pirates.[13] As an

---

8   See i.a. D. Guilfoyle, 'Piracy off Somalia: UN Security Council Resolution 1816 and IMO Regional Counter-Piracy Efforts', 57 *International & Comparative Law Quarterly*, 2008, p. 690; T. Treves, 'Piracy, Law of the Sea, and Use of Force: Developments off the Coast of Somalia', 20 *European Journal of International Law*, 2009, p. 404.

9   See NATO Operation Shield at http://www.mc.nato.int/ops/Pages/OOS.aspx. Accessed on 2 September 2016.

10 The first maritime operation of the European Union (EU) was launched (EUNAVFOR Operation Atalanta) on 10 November 2008 pursuant to the Council Joint Action 2008/851. On the legal basis of the Operation and its everyday activities see at http://eunavfor.eu/, accessed on 2 September 2016. See also E. Papastavridis, 'EUNAVOR Operation Atalanta off Somalia: the EU in Unchartered Legal Waters?', 64 *International & Comparative Law Quarterly*, 2015, p. 533.

11 45 countries and seven international organizations (the African Union, the League of Arab States, the European Union, INTERPOL, International Maritime Organization, NATO, and UN Secretariat) now participate in the Contact Group, along with two major maritime industry groups, BIMCO and INTERTANKO, who take part as Observers' (see www.state.gov/t/pm/ppa/piracy/contactgroup/index.htm. Accessed on 2 September 2016).

12 UN Doc. S/RES/1897, 30 November 2009, Preamble.

13 See i.a. E. Kontorovich, 'A Guantanamo on the Sea: The Difficulty of Prosecuting Pirates and Terrorists', 98 *California Law Review*, 2010, p. 243; Ademun-Okede, 'Jurisdiction over Foreign Pirates in Domestic Courts and Third States under International Law', 17 *Journal of International Maritime Law*, 2011, pp. 121, 124–126. See also the various symposium

alternative, the US[14] and the UK[15] and the European Union[16] concluded memoranda of understanding with countries in the region: Kenya, the Seychelles, Tanzania and Mauritius. These memoranda provide for the transferring of suspects and bringing them to justice.

The piracy crisis has also brought to the fore another user of the seas, the *private armed guards* whose actions have proved controversial. The IMO Maritime Safety Committee at its eighty-ninth session (2011) adopted Interim Recommendations for Flag States Regarding the Use of Privately Contracted Armed Security Personnel on Board Ships in the High Risk Area.[17] Hence the

---

contributions to: 'Testing the Waters: Assessing International Responses to Somali Piracy', 10 *International Criminal Law Journal*, 2012.

14 See Memorandum of Understanding between the United States of America and the Republic of the Seychelles concerning the conditions of transfer of suspected pirates and armed robbers and seized property in the western Indian Ocean, the Gulf of Aden, and the Red Sea, signed at Victoria, July 14 2010. There had also been a US-Kenya Agreement on transferring pirates for trial (January 2009), see relevant practice at: www.reuters.com/article/worldNews/idUSTRE52480N20090305, accessed on 2 September 2016.

15 Reportedly, the UK has signed relevant agreements with Kenya, the Seychelles, Tanzania, and more recently with Mauritius. See e.g. E. Kontorovich, International Legal Responses to Piracy off the Coast of Somalia', 13 ASIL Insights (February 6, 2009); available online at https://www.asil.org/insights/volume/13/issue/2/international-legal-responses-piracy-coast-somalia; and 'Signing of Piracy Agreement with Mauritius' 8 June 2012, available online at www.number10.gov.uk/news/piracy-agreement-mauritius/

16 See Exchange of Letters between the EU and the Government of Kenya on the conditions and modalities for the transfer of persons suspected of acts of piracy (6 March 2009); Exchange of Letters between the European Union and the Republic of Seychelles on the Conditions and Modalities for the Transfer of Suspected Pirates and Armed Robbers (2 December 2009); Agreement between the European Union and the Republic of Mauritius on the Conditions and Modalities for the Transfer of Suspected Pirates and Associated Seized Property from the European-led Naval Force to the Republic of Mauritius and on the Conditions of Suspected Pirates after Transfer (14 July 2011) and Agreement between the European Union and the United Republic of Tanzania on the conditions of transfer of suspected pirates and associated seized property from the European Union-led Naval Force to the United Republic of Tanzania (11 April 2014). The text of the agreements with Kenya, the Seychelles and Mauritius and all relevant information are available online at http://www.eeas.europa.eu/csdp/missions-and-operations/eu-navfor-somalia/background-material/index_en.htm, accessed on 18 August 2016. For the agreement with Tanzania see http://eur-lex.europa.eu/legal-content/EN/TXT/PDF/?uri=CELEX:22014A0411(01)&from=EN, accessed on 18 August 2016.

17 See MSC 1/Circ.1406, 23 May 2011. On the role of the IMO in the fight against criminal acts at sea see R. Goy, 'L'émergence des actes criminels maritimes à l'OMI', in R. Raigón & G. Cataldi (eds), *Mélanges de droit de la mer offerts à Daniel Vignes*, Bruylant, 2009, 395–418.

IMO responded to ship owners' calls for guidance regarding the legal status of private armed guards, who, in an increasing number of cases, are employed to secure shipboard security when transiting the Gulf of Aden and the West Indian Ocean. The 'Revised Interim Guidance to Ship-owners, Ship Operators, and Shipmasters on the Use of Privately Contracted Armed Security Personnel on board Ships in the High Risk Area' noted that: 'Flag State jurisdiction and thus any laws and regulations imposed by the flag State concerning the use of Private Maritime Security Companies and Privately Contracted Armed Security Personnel apply to their ships.'[18] Further, note that port and coastal States' laws may also apply to such ships.

In practice, the use of private armed guards has proved successful and has significantly contributed to the decrease of pirate attacks off the coast of Somalia; however, many questions remain, in particular the use of force by these armed guards, the potential liability or responsibility of the flag State for violations of international law, and the absence of accountability of these personnel and their parent companies.[19]

3   Migration by Sea

Thousands of people are fleeing from their country of origin, especially from Syria, Afghanistan, Eritrea and Iraq, by undertaking very perilous sea journeys, putting their lives into serious danger. They flee by whatever means, including overcrowded and unseaworthy vessels. According to the UN Office of the High

---

18   See MSC.1/Circ.1405/Rev.2, 25 May 2012, available online at www.imo.org/OurWork/Security/SecDocs/Documents/Piracy/MSC.1-Circ.1405-Rev2.pdf. See also 'Revised Interim Recommendations for Flag States Regarding the Use of Privately Contracted Armed Security Personnel on Board Ships in the High Risk Area', MSC.1/Circ.1406/Rev.2, 25 May 2012; and 'Revised Interim Recommendations for Port and Coastal States Regarding the Use of Privately Contracted Armed Security', MSC.1/Circ.1408/Rev.1, 25 May 2012. For example, Greece enacted legislation concerning the use of Private Armed Guards by Greek-flagged vessels, see Law No 4058/63 A', 22 March 2012.

19   Some of these issues are discussed in C. Spearin, 'Private Military and Security Companies v International Naval Endeavours v Somali Pirates', 10 *Journal of International Criminal Justice*, 2012, pp. 823–837, A. Petrig, 'The Use of Force and Firearms by Private Maritime Security Companies against Suspected Vessels', 62 *International & Comparative Law Quarterly*, 2013, pp. 667–701, E. Williams, 'Private Armed Guards in the Fight Against Piracy' in E. Papastavridis & K. Trapp (eds), *La Criminalité en Mer/Crimes at Sea*, Hague Academy of International Law, Martinus Nijhoff, 2014, p. 339.

Commissioner for Refugees (UNHCR) in the first half of 2016, 2951 people lost their lives or were missing in the Mediterranean Sea.[20] In 2015, almost 4000 people perished in these waters.[21] All these tragic incidents mark the urgency of addressing the problem of migration by sea.

The challenges in the Mediterranean are mirrored in other regions as well. For example, according to a UNHCR Report of 17 October 2014 on the situation in Yemen, 'there has been a sharp increase this year [2014] in the number of migrants and asylum-seekers losing their lives in attempts to get to Yemen, mainly from the Horn of Africa, with more deaths at sea in 2014 than in the last three years combined [...] They bring the yearly tally for 2014 to 215, exceeding the combined total for 2011, 2012 and 2013 of 179.'[22] Equally serious is the problem in the Asia-Pacific region. The situation tends to rival in scale the 'boat crisis' in Indochina in the 1970s and 1980s, and maritime migration movements remain extremely serious.[23]

States and the international community have not remained idle; yet the response is more tailored towards averting the 'threat' posed by maritime migration to 'territorial integrity' than towards other equally important issues. Amongst the 'non-arrival' policies employed to this end,[24] a primary role is attributed to interception, witness the relevant practice of Australia[25]

---

20 See online at http://data.unhcr.org/mediterranean/regional.php, accessed on 21 July 2016.
21 See online at http://missingmigrants.iom.int/sites/default/files/Mediterranean_Update_29_January_2016_0.pdf, accessed on 21 July 2016.
22 See UNHCR, '2014 becomes the deadliest year at sea off Yemen', News Stories, 17 October 2014, available at http://www.unhcr.org/544103b06.html.
23 Reportedly, in 2012 Australia received 17,202 asylum seekers by boat, its highest annual number. See J. Phillips & H. Spinks, 'Boat arrivals in Australia since 1976', Research Paper, Australian Parliamentary Library, updated 23 July 2013, p. 22, as cited in J. Mc Adam, 'Australia and Asylum Seekers', 25 *International Journal of Refugee Law*, 2013, pp. 435, 445.
24 The usual measures employed to tackle this problem, besides interception, are: pre-inspection, visa requirements, carrier sanctions, 'safe third country' concepts, security zones, and international zones. See G. Goodwin-Gill & J. McAdam, *The Refugee in International Law* 3rd ed. Oxford University Press, 2007, p. 374.
25 In September 2013, the newly-elected Conservative government in Australia committed itself to a policy of pushing back boats carrying 'unauthorized maritime arrivals. See on the recent Australian policy see M. Crock, 'Shadow Plays, Shifting Sands and International Refugee Law: Convergences in the Asia-Pacific', 63 *International and Comparative Law Quarterly*, 2014, pp. 247–280.

and various European States, individually[26] or under EU coordination (FRONTEX).[27]

In the aftermath of the shocking death of more than 700 people in mid-April 2015 in the Mediterranean, the EU increased the resources and the operational area of the existing FRONTEX-coordinated operations in the region[28] and launched EUNAVFOR MED later renamed *Operation Sophia*. The latter is an EU naval operation designed primarily to fight migrant-smuggling in the central Mediterranean and only incidentally to save lives at sea.[29] To these initiatives has been added the deployment, since March 2016, of the standing naval forces of NATO in the Aegean Sea, tasked to curb the smuggling of migrants and refugees to Greece.[30]

More recently, the EU has decided to establish a new border Agency, the EU Border and Coast Guard Agency (EBGA) which will replace FRONTEX. According to the EU plans, 'in urgent situations that put the functioning of the Schengen area at risk and when deficiencies have not been remedied, the Agency will be able to step in to ensure that action is taken on the ground even where there is no request for assistance from the Member State concerned

---

26 European states, such as Italy or Spain, have periodically engaged in interception at sea. Most famous have been the 'push-back' operations conducted by Italy in cooperation with Libya in the central Mediterranean. See *i.a.* M.-G. Giuffré, 'State responsibility Beyond Borders: What Legal Basis for Italy's Push-backs to Libya?' 24 *International Journal of Refugee Law*, 2012, pp. 692–734.

27 FRONTEX was established in 2004 to help EU Member States implement community legislation on the surveillance of EU borders, including maritime borders, and to coordinate their operations. See Council Regulation (EC) No 2007/2004 of 26 October 2004 establishing a European Agency for the Management of Operational Cooperation at the External Borders of the Member States of the European Union as amended by Regulation (EU) No 1168/2011 of the European Parliament and of the Council of 25 October 2011, *Official Journal of the European Union*, L 304, of 22 November 2011 (hereinafter: 2011 Regulation). For further information see http://frontex.europa.eu/, accessed on 2 September 2016. On the surveillance operations of FRONTEX see E. Papastavridis, 'Fortress Europe and FRONTEX: Within or Without International Law?' 79 *Nordic Journal of International Law*, 2010, p. 75.

28 See Conclusions of the Special Meeting of the EU Council of 23 April 2015 online at http://www.consilium.europa.eu/en/meetings/european-council/2015/04/23/ and also http://frontex.europa.eu/news/frontex-expands-its-joint-operation-triton-udpbHP.

29 For further information, see <https://eeas.europa.eu/csdp-missions-operations/eunavformed_en. Accessed on 2 September 2016.

30 See Statement by the Secretary General on NATO's support to assist with the refugee and migrant crisis, 25 February 2016, available at http://www.nato.int/cps/en/natohq/opinions_128372.htm.

or where that Member State considers that there is no need for additional intervention.'[31]

It is clear that maritime migrants are becoming compelling *users of the seas*, in the sense that they use maritime routes to flee persecution and threats to life and reach the shores of their 'Promised Land'; but also in the sense that they mobilize international law-making in this regard. As mentioned above, numerous States and international organizations are now involved in the management of the phenomenon of maritime migration. More importantly, the increase in seaborne migration is calling for the application of new rules of international law in the specific environment and their adjustment to the maritime context. Reference is mainly made to international human rights law and international refugee law. Note the judgments of human rights bodies, more prominently of the European Court of Human Rights (ECHR) in cases where States have been accused of violating human-rights law at sea, in particular the prohibition of *refoulement*.[32]

For example, in the *Hirsi v Italy case*[33] the application before the ECHR was filed in 2009 by 11 Somalis and 13 Eritreans, who were among the first group of about 200 migrants interdicted by Italian authorities and summarily returned to Libya pursuant to Italy's push-back practice.[34] The applicants alleged violations of numerous provisions of the Convention, including Article 4 of Protocol 4 additional to the European Convention (prohibiting collective expulsion of aliens), as well as Article 3 (torture/*non-refoulement*), and Article 13 (effective remedies) of the European Convention. As to Article 3 of the Convention, the Grand Chamber of the ECHR noted that 'the numerous reports by international bodies and non-governmental organizations painted a disturbing picture of the treatment meted out to clandestine immigrants in Libya at the material

---

31   See European Commission, 'Securing Europe's External Borders', available online at http://ec.europa.eu/dgs/home-affairs/what-we-do/policies/securing-eu-borders/fact-sheets/docs/a_european_border_and_coast_guard_en.pdf.

32   On the principle of *non-refoulement* see E. Lauterpacht & D. Bethlehem, 'The Scope and Content of the Principle of *Non-refoulement*: Opinion' in E. Feller, et al. (eds), *Refugee Protection in International Law*, Cambridge University Press, 2003, p. 87; C. Wooters, *International Legal Standards for the Protection from Refoulement*, Intersentia, 2009.

33   See *Hirsi Jama a.o. v Italy*, (App. 27765/09 [2012]). For commentary see I. Papanikolopulu, '*Hirsi Jamaa v. Italy*. Comment', 107 *American Journal of International Law*, 2013, p. 417.

34   According to the Italian authorities, from 6 May to 6 November 2009, nine operations were carried out, returning in total 834 persons to Libya. See further information online at http://migrantsatsea.wordpress.com/2010/03/18/unhcr-files-ecthr-third-party-intervention-in-hirsi-v-italy/.

time'[35] and showed that clandestine migrants such as the applicants were disembarked in Libya following their interception by Italy on the high seas, and exposed to those risks.[36] The Chamber concluded that 'in the present case substantial grounds have been shown for believing that there was a real risk that the applicants would be subjected to treatment in Libya contrary to Article 3 [of the European Convention]'[37] and that 'by transferring the applicants to Libya, the Italian authorities, in full knowledge of the facts, exposed them to treatment proscribed by the Convention.'[38]

4 The European Union and the Oceans

The European Union (EU) is *a non-state user* increasingly expanding in many directions in situations provided for by the law of maritime affairs. Article 305(1)(f) of LOSC provides that the Convention is open for signature to international organizations, in accordance with Annex IX. Provisions in Annex IX are fairly detailed and tailor-made for the EU. When joining LOSC, the EU made the required declaration of competence.[39] The declaration contains a description of the different competences involved, namely exclusive Union competence (e.g. conservation and management of fishing resources and customs) and matters that fall within the shared competence of the Union and its Member States (e.g., maritime transport, safety of shipping, and prevention of pollution). The EU declaration of competence states also that 'the scope and exercise of such Community competence are, by their nature, subject to continuous development' and the declaration will be completed or amended if necessary. No such formal amendment has been made or requested so far.

Nevertheless, the EU actively participates in the interpretation and application of the Convention as well as on other law-of-the-sea-related issues.[40] This occurs in many ways. First, since 2011 the EU has had observer status in the UN General Assembly and thus can participate on enhanced terms in official UN meetings on the law of the sea. In practice, given that most General

---

35 See *Hirsi Jamaa v. Italy*, supra, note 33, para. 123.
36 Ibid., para. 126.
37 Ibid., para. 136.
38 Ibid., para. 137.
39 See Council Decision 98/392, *Official Journal of the European Union*, L 179, of 23 June 1998, p. 129 (EC).
40 See here E. Paasivirta, 'The European Union and the United Nations Convention on the Law of the Sea', 38 *Fordham Journal of International Law*, 2014–2015, p. 1045.

Assembly resolutions are prepared in informal consultations, the EU can and does take very active part in the consultations despite its observer status.[41] For certain subsidiary organs, notably the Open-ended Informal Consultative Process on Oceans and the Law of the Sea (ICP) established in 1999, participation is open and covers *inter alia* 'all parties to the Convention' which, in the EU case, attempts to bridge the traditional division between UN members and mere observers. That the General Assembly has reaffirmed the EU's role in the development of the law of the sea is seen, for instance, in relation to work on the conservation and sustainable use of marine biological diversity beyond areas of national jurisdiction,[42] in which the EU is a pioneer.

The EU has also been involved in international adjudication regarding the law of the sea. In the *Swordfish Case (Chile v European Community)*,[43] Chile initiated in 2000 arbitration proceedings against the EU. Pursuant to LOSC Annex VII a Special Chamber of *the International Tribunal of the Law of the Sea* (ITLOS) was established to deal with the dispute. Chile invoked its unilaterally enacted conservation measures regarding highly migratory fish, and challenged the EC's thesis on the freedoms of the high seas in an area adjacent to Chile's exclusive economic zone. While the dispute was pending, the parties pursued bilateral negotiations and after nine years a final compromise was reached.

More recently, the EU has been a party to another LOSC arbitration involving the interplay between LOSC and the WTO. The dispute originated in one between the Faroe Islands (which are territories of Denmark, but remain outside the EU) and the EU over the sharing of fishing quotas for Atlanto-Scandian herring.[44]

---

41 See E. Paasivirta & D. Porter, 'EU Coordination at the UN General Assembly and ECOSOC: A View from Brussels, A View from New York', in J. Wouters, et al. (eds), *The United Nations and the European Union*, Asser Press, 2006, p. 35.

42 In its Resolution 69/292 of 19 June 2015, the General Assembly decided to develop an international legally binding instrument under LOSC on the conservation and sustainable use of marine biological diversity of areas beyond national jurisdiction, see further information at http://www.un.org/depts/los/biodiversity/prepcom.htm?, accessed on 2 September 2016.

43 See *Conservation and Sustainable Exploitation of Swordfish Stocks in the South- Eastern Pacific Ocean* (Chile v European Community), ITLOS Case No 7.

44 See *Atlanto-Scandian Herring* (Denmark in respect of Faroe Islands v EU), PCA Case 2013-30.

Reference should also be made to the ITLOS *Advisory Opinion* on a request by the Sub-Regional Fisheries Commission ('SRFC').[45] The SRFC, a West-African fisheries organization comprising seven Member States, introduced a request for an ITLOS Advisory Opinion on four questions related to flag-State liability for illegal, unreported and unregulated (IUU) fishing activities conducted within the EEZ of States other than the flag State. The Tribunal was also requested to address a question concerning liability in a situation where a fishing license is issued to a vessel within the framework of an international agreement with an international organization in order to know where the flag State or the international organization should be held liable for violation of the fisheries legislation of the coastal State by the vessel in question. This third question was clearly addressed to the EU.

ITLOS held that 'in cases where an international organization, in the exercise of its exclusive competence in fisheries matters, concludes a fisheries access agreement with an SRFC Member State, which provides for access by vessels flying the flag of its Member States to fish in the exclusive economic zone of that State, the obligations of the flag State become the obligations of the international organization. The international organization, as the only contracting party to the fisheries access agreement with the SRFC Member State, must therefore ensure that vessels flying the flag of a Member State comply with the fisheries laws and regulations of the SRFC Member State and do not conduct IUU fishing activities within the exclusive economic zone of that State.'[46] In contemplating the interaction between theory and jurisprudence we note that it took almost thirty years for the theory of 'responsibility of the flag State', advanced by Judge Nagendra Singh in his course at The Hague Academy,[47] to find expression in the 2015 *Opinion* of ITLOS.[48]

Finally, the EU has been active lately in the fight against transnational organized crime at sea. As already mentioned, in 2008 EUNAVFOR Operation Atlanta, the first EU naval operation was established to join NATO and other individual States in the counter-piracy campaign off the coast of Somalia. This initiative was followed in June 2015 by the launch of EUNAVFOR Operation

---

45   See *Request for an Advisory Opinion Submitted by the Sub-Regional Fisheries Commission*, ITLOS Case No 21, Advisory Opinion of 2 April 2015, available online at https://www.itlos.org/en/cases/list-of-cases/case-no-21/.
46   Ibid., para. 173.
47   N. Singh, 'Maritime Flag and State Responsibility', in J. Makarczyk (ed), *Essays in International Law in Honor of Judge Manfred Lachs*, Nijhoff, 1984, pp. 657–669; Cf. Roucounas, supra, note 2, p. 878.
48   ITLOS Case No 21, supra, note 45.

Sophia, set up to combat the smuggling of migrants from the Libyan coasts to Europe.[49] Operation Sophia's mandate was expanded in order to fight also trafficking in small arms to Libya pursuant to UN Security Council Resolution 2292/2016.[50]

5 Exploitation of Natural Resources by Parties and Non-Parties to LOSC 1982

That States are *the principal users* of the seas is unquestioned. The recent addition is the tendency of States to expand their sovereign rights in areas beyond the traditional 200 nautical miles of their EEZ/Continental Shelf. This creeping jurisdiction of coastal States for the purpose of exploring and exploiting natural resources manifests itself twofold: first, in the increasing number of submissions to the *Commission of the Limits of Continental Shelf* (CLCS) for extended continental shelf rights and in the international adjudication granting such rights (the Bay of Bengal cases between Myanmar and Bangladesh in 2012 and between Bangladesh and India in 2014). Secondly, the change is shown in claims such as those of China in the South China Sea for extended historical rights, dealt with by the Arbitral Tribunal Award of 12 July 2016 in the South China Sea case between the Philippines and China.[51]

With respect to extended rights, Article 76(8) LOSC provides that information on the limits of the continental shelf beyond 200 nautical miles must be submitted by a coastal State to the CLCS.[52] The CLCS then makes recommendations to that State on the establishment of the outer limits of its continental shelf.

---

49 See Council Decision (CFSP) 2015/778 of 18 May 2015 on a European Union military operation in the Southern Central Mediterranean (EUNAVFOR MED), *Official Journal of the European Union*, L122, p. 31 and http://eeas.europa.eu/csdp/missions-and-operations/eunavfor-med/pdf/factsheet_eunavfor_med_en.pdf. See also E. Papastavridis, '*EUNAVFOR Operation Sophia* and the International Law of the Sea', 2 *Maritime Security and Safety Law Journal*, 2016, pp. 57–72.

50 See UN Doc. S/RES/2292, 14 June 2016, paras. 3–5.

51 See *The South China Sea Arbitration* (Republic of Philippines v the People's Republic of China), PCA Case No 2013-19, Award of 12 July 2016, available online at http://www.pcacases.com/pcadocs/PH-CN%20-%2020160712%20-%20Award.pdf.

52 See also A. Oude Elferink, 'Article 76 of the LOSC on the Definition of the Continental Shelf: Questions concerning its Interpretation from a Legal Perspective', 21 *International Journal of Marine and Coastal Law*, 2006, p. 269.

Note that the limits of the continental shelf beyond 200 nautical miles can be established only by a coastal State. The coastal State retains ultimate control of setting the outer limits of the continental shelf, but this power is circumscribed by the requirements of Article 76(8). However, these limits only become 'final and binding' when they are established by the coastal State 'on the basis of' the Recommendations made by the CLCS'. The limits of the continental shelf established by a coastal State on the basis of the Recommendations are final and binding.[53] In this regard, the term 'on the basis of' is ambiguous. It allows a coastal State an element of flexibility, but cannot mean that a coastal State merely 'takes into account' Recommendations made by the CLCS but rejects some or all aspects of these.[54] To date, there have been 77 submissions by coastal States with full or partial information on the outer limits of the continental shelf beyond 200 nautical miles: the Commission has adopted 25.[55]

In cases of disagreement by the coastal State with the Recommendations of the Commission, that State may, within a reasonable time make a revised or new submission to the Commission pursuant to Article 8 of Annex II. This has already happened for example in the Arctic Sea: the Russian Federation was the first State to make a submission to the CSLS with respect to its Arctic continental shelf. The Commission decided in 2002 that the information the Federation provided was insufficient, and recommended that it make a revised submission to the Commission with regard to the Central Arctic Ocean.

With reference to the Arctic,[56] it is interesting that except for the Russian Federation, all the Arctic States consider that their respective Arctic continental shelves extend beyond 200 nautical miles. However, Norway is the only State that has been able, so far, to define the outer limits of its continental

---

53   See also the ITLOS comments in the *Dispute Concerning Delimitation of the Maritime Boundary Between Bangladesh and Myanmar in the Bay of Bengal* (Bangladesh/Myanmar), ITLOS Case No 16, Judgment of 14 March 2012, para. 407.

54   See Second Report of the ILA Committee on Legal Issues of the Outer Continental Shelf, Report of the Seventy-Second Conference, 2006, pp. 215, 231–233; see also L. D. M. Nelson, 'The Settlement of Disputes Arising from Conflicting Outer Continental Shelf Claims' 24 *International Journal of Marine and Coastal Law*, 2009, p. 419.

55   See the relevant information on Commission's website. http://www.un.org/depts/los/clcs_new/commission_submissions.htm, accessed on 1 August 2016.

56   See generally on the Arctic and the law of the sea, H. Tuerk, 'The Arctic and the Modern Law of the Sea' in J. M. Van Dyke et al. (eds), *Governing Ocean Resources: New Challenges and Emerging Regimes: A Tribute to Judge Choon-Ho Park*, Brill/Martinus Nijhoff, 2013, p. 115; and V. Golitsyn, 'The Legal Regime of the Arctic' in D. Attard et al. (eds), *The IMLI Manual on International Maritime Law: Volume I: The Law of the Sea*, Oxford University Press, 2014, p. 462.

shelf in that area. Denmark made its submission on 15 December 2014 with regard to Greenland. It is uncertain whether the United States will become a Party to LOSC and therefore be able to establish the outer limits of its continental shelf on the basis of Commission recommendations. Consequently, there is much uncertainty regarding the outer limits of the continental shelf in the Arctic Ocean.

Closely linked to the position of the US in the Arctic Sea is the question of whether *States non-Parties* to LOSC may claim a continental shelf beyond 200 nautical miles under customary international law. It seems difficult to find 'extensive and virtually uniform' State practice and *opinio juris* on this issue. International justice will have an opportunity to consider the customary nature of the extended continental shelf in the context of the delimitation case between Nicaragua and Colombia pending before the ICJ at the time of writing.[57]

Although the delimitation of outer limits and boundary delimitation are separate concepts, the issues are closely linked and most submissions to the CLCS involve one or more boundary relationships. Article 76(10) expressly provides that the provisions of Article 76 are 'without prejudice to the question of delimitation of the continental shelf between States with opposite or adjacent coasts'. Article 9 of Annex II of LOSC provides that '[t]he actions of the [CLCS] shall not prejudice matters relating to the delimitation of boundaries between States with opposite or adjacent coasts.' These provisions ensure that the CLCS is not to function in determining, or to influence, negotiations on the continental shelf boundary between States with overlapping claims beyond 200 nautical miles or where there is a dispute with another State over that limit. Rather than involving third States in the consideration of a submission, the CLCS has to insulate itself from such matters.[58]

In the *Bangladesh/Myanmar* case, where both States had made such submissions to the CLCS, the Commission decided to defer consideration of them since a dispute existed between Bangladesh and Myanmar as to their claims to the continental shelf, and this dispute had not been resolved when Myanmar's

---

57   See ICJ, *Question of the Delimitation of the Continental Shelf between Nicaragua and Colombia beyond 200 Nautical Miles from the Nicaraguan Coast* (Nicaragua v Colombia) Preliminary Objections, Judgment of 17 March 2016 (contentious case).

58   See also B. Kwiatkowska, 'Submissions to the UN Commission on the Limits of the Continental Shelf: The Practice of Developing States in Cases of Disputed and Unresolved Maritime Boundary Delimitations or Other Land or Maritime Disputes, Part One' 28 *International Journal of Marine and Coastal Law*, 2013, p. 219.

submission was presented. The 2012 decision of the *International Tribunal for the Law of the Sea* (ITLOS) in the *Bangladesh/Myanmar* case is significant because it was the first time that an international tribunal had accepted jurisdiction to delimit (but not to delineate) the continental shelf boundary between two States beyond 200 nautical miles.[59]

6 Historic Rights and Dispute Settlement

Extended claims of coastal States in maritime areas that otherwise belong to the high seas or to the Area are exemplified by the Chinese claims of 'historic rights' in the South China Sea. The *Arbitral Tribunal* established under LOSC Annex VII delivered on *12 July 2016* an *Award* in the dispute between the Philippines and China regarding the South China Sea.

China claimed historic rights within the maritime areas surrounded by the so-called nine-dash-line, arguably since the end of the Second World War[60] and most definitely and publicly since the formal *Notes Verbales* of 2009 by China in reaction to the submissions of Malaysia and Vietnam to the CSLS.[61] According to the Tribunal, China's repeated invocation of rights 'formed in the long historical course' and its linkage of this concept with the 'nine-dash line' indicated that China understood that it was entitled to extend, in some form, beyond the maritime zones expressly described in the UN Convention.[62] The Tribunal held that nothing in the Convention expressly provides for or permits a State to maintain historic rights over the living and non-living resources of the continental shelf, the high seas, or the Area.[63] Consequently, according to the Tribunal, the entry into force of the Convention had the effect of superseding any claim by China to historic rights to the living and non-living resources within the 'nine-dash line' beyond the limits of China's maritime zones as provided for by the Convention. China had at the outset contested

---

59 See ITLOS Case No 16, supra, note 53, paras. 390–392.
60 See K. Zou, 'South China Sea' in D. Rothwell et al. (eds), *Oxford Handbook of the Law of the Sea* Oxford University Press, 2015, pp. 626, 634.
61 See Notes Verbales CML/17/2009 and CML/18/2009 from the Permanent Mission of the People's Republic of China to the UN Secretary-General, 7 May 2009, available online at http://www.un.org/Depts/los/clcs_new/submissions_files/submission_mysvnm_33_2009 .htm and at http://www.un.org/Depts/los/clcs_new/submissions_files/submission_vnm_ 37_2009.htm.
62 See *The South China Sea Arbitration*, supra, note 51, para. 207.
63 Ibid., para. 239.

the jurisdiction of the Tribunal on grounds first, that the subject-matter of the dispute pertained to issues of sovereignty, and not to the interpretation and application of LOSC, and secondly that the dispute fell within the scope of the exception of Article 298 concerning delimitation and historic titles.[64]

7 Enterprises Operating in the International Seabed (Area)

Users of the law of the sea are also the *private contractors* engaged in mining operations in the international seabed (the Area).[65] It was not until forty years ago that the potential of seabed mining was fully appreciated when the existence of reserves of polymetallic nodules with considerable contents of nickel, copper, cobalt, and manganese was acknowledged.[66] Deep seabed mining was considered to be a potential source of wealth.[67] Such developments conditioned the need for the establishment of a regime governing the legal status of seabed mineral resources beyond the limits of national jurisdiction. Establishing this legal framework was the 'decisive motive' for convening the Third Conference on the Law of the Sea, which culminated in the conclusion of the 1982 United Nations Convention on the Law of the Sea. Following extensive negotiations, States agreed to grant mining corporations access to seabed mineral resources and allow exploration for polymetallic nodules on the basis of a contract that corporations would enter into with the International Seabed Authority (ISA),[68] an international organization entrusted with the control of 'activities' in the 'Area', i.e. 'the seabed and ocean floor and subsoil thereof, beyond the lim-

---

64 See Ministry of Foreign Affairs of the People's Republic of China, 'Position Paper of the Government of the People's Republic of China on the Matter of Jurisdiction in the South China Sea Arbitration Initiated by the Republic of the Philippines', 7 December 2014, available at www.fmprc.gov.cn/mfa_eng/zxxx_662805/t1217147.shtml.

65 See S. Nandan, 'Administering the Mineral Resources of the Deep Sea Bed', in D. Freestone et al. (eds), *The Law of the Sea: Progress and Prospects*, Oxford University Press, 2006, pp. 75–92.

66 J.-P. Lévy, 'The International Sea-Bed Area', in R.-J. Dupuy & D. Vignes (eds), *A Handbook on the New Law of the Sea*, Martinus Nijhoff, 2001, pp. 588–589.

67 S. Oda, 'International Law of the Resources of the Sea', 127 *Recueil des Cours de l'Académie de Droit International*, 1969, p. 458.

68 For an overview of the negotiations leading to the establishment of the ISA and the commencement of its function see M. Wood, 'International Seabed Authority: The First Four Years', 3 *Max Planck United Nations Yearbook of International Law*, 1999, pp. 173–241.

its of national jurisdiction'. ISA is the guardian of the 'Common Heritage of Mankind', a fundamental principle of the 'constitution of the oceans'.[69]

According to Article 53 (2) of LOSC, activities in the Area shall be carried out ... (b) in association with the Authority by States Parties, or State enterprises or natural or juridical persons which possess the nationality of States Parties or are effectively controlled by them or their nationals, when sponsored by such States, or any group of the foregoing which meets the requirements provided in this Part and in Annex III. This Article should be read in conjunction with Article 153 (3) LOSC, which dictates that activities in the Area, undertaken by any of the entities mentioned in the above quoted provision, are to be carried out on the basis of a contract between the ISA and the entity in question.

Thus private contractors become significant users of the law-of-the sea regime established by LOSC and the 1994 Implementation Agreement.[70] However, since the entry into force of the Convention and its Implementation Agreement there have been few contracts in force. According to ISA, it has entered into 15-year contracts for exploration for polymetallic nodules, polymetallic sulphides and cobalt-rich ferromanganese crusts in the deep seabed with *twenty-four contractors*.[71] The legal regime concerning these contractors and their obligations under both international and national law is of interest.[72]

---

69   See United Nations, *The Law of the Sea: Concept of the Common Heritage of Mankind. Legislative History of Articles 131–150 and 311(6) of the United Nations Convention on the Law of the Sea*, United Nations, 1996.

70   The Agreement Relating to the Implementation of Part XI of the United Nations Convention on the Law of the Sea of 10 December 1982, adopted 28 July 1994, entered into force 28 July 1996, 1836 UNTS 3. See also E. D. Brown, 'The 1994 Agreement on the Implementation of Part XI of the UN Convention on the Law of the Sea: Breakthrough to Universality?' 19 *Marine Policy*, 1995, pp. 5–20.

71   'Sixteen of these contracts are for exploration for polymetallic nodules in the Clarion-Clipperton Fracture Zone (15) and Central Indian Ocean Basin (1). There are five contracts for exploration for polymetallic sulphides in the South West Indian Ridge, Central Indian Ridge and the Mid-Atlantic Ridge and four contracts for exploration for cobalt-rich crusts in the Western Pacific Ocean', see https://www.isa.org.jm/deep-seabed-minerals-contractors, accessed on 12 August 2016.

72   See in this regard, M. Karavias, *Corporate Obligations under International Law*, Oxford University Press, 2013, pp. 118–126.

The Relationship between Two Conventions Applicable to Underwater Cultural Heritage*

Tullio Scovazzi

1   A Heritage in Need of Protection

The greatest museum of human civilization lies on the seabed. It has been estimated that, until the 19th century, almost 5% of all seagoing ships were lost every year because of storms, incidents of navigation, naval battles or other events. Today the advanced technological means available to explore the seabed at increasing depths not only allow access to a heritage that records history of humankind, but also entail the actual risk of its looting and dispersal. The protection of underwater cultural heritage becomes a serious concern.

Two treaties of world scope apply to underwater cultural heritage, namely the United Nations Convention on the Law of the Sea (Montego Bay, 1982—LOSC)[1] and the Convention on the Protection of the Underwater Cultural Heritage (Paris, 2001—CPUCH).[2] The former, which is an instrument of codification of the whole international law of the sea, includes only two provisions (out of 320) on 'archaeological and historical objects found at sea' (Arts. 149

---

*   I am glad that this paper is included in the collection of essays in honour of Professor Djamchid Momtaz, who was one of the leading participants in the negotiations for CPUCH and is the author of an important study on this subject (see note 2).

1   1833 UNTS 3. See A. Strati, *The Protection of the Underwater Cultural Heritage: An Emerging Objective of the Contemporary Law of the Sea*, Brill, 1995.

2   2562 UNTS 1. See G. Carducci, 'New Developments in the Law of the Sea: The UNESCO Convention on the Protection of Underwater Cultural Heritage', 96 *American Journal of International Law*, 2002, p. 419; P. J. O'Keefe, *Shipwrecked Heritage: A Commentary on the UNESCO Convention on Underwater Cultural Heritage*, Institute of Art and Law, 2002; R. Garabello & T. Scovazzi (eds), *The Protection of the Underwater Cultural Heritage—Before and after the 2001 UNESCO Convention*, Brill, 2003: S. Dromgoole (ed), *The Protection of the Underwater Cultural Heritage—National Perspectives in Light of the UNESCO Convention 2001*, Martinus Nijhoff, 2006; D. Momtaz, 'La Convention sur la protection du patrimoine culturel subaquatique', in T. M. Ndiaye & R. Wolfrum (eds), *Law of the Sea, Environmental Law and Settlement of Disputes—Liber Amicorum Judge Thomas A. Mensah*, Brill, 2007, p. 443; S. Dromgoole, *Underwater Cultural Heritage and International Law*, Cambridge University Press, 2013.

and 303). The latter is an instrument specifically devoted to the subject of underwater cultural heritage.

This paper will present some considerations on the relationship between the two treaties.

2   Where LOSC and CPUCH are in Conformity

If the CPUCH provisions were only the specification of more general rules embodied in LOSC, no question of conflict between the two instruments would arise. In fact, the two treaties do present aspects of conformity, as the instances hereunder show.

2.1   *The Obligation to Protect Underwater Cultural Heritage*
A) LOSC sets forth a general obligation to protect underwater cultural heritage. Under Article 303 (1),

> States have the duty to protect objects of an archaeological and historical nature found at sea and shall co-operate for this purpose.

Despite its broad content, some legal consequences can be drawn from this provision. A State that knowingly destroys or allows the destruction of objects belonging to underwater cultural heritage, as well as a State that persistently disregards any request by other States to negotiate with a view to protecting underwater cultural heritage, can be held responsible for the breach of an international obligation.

B) As stated in Article 2 (1), the whole CPUCH 'aims to ensure and strengthen the protection of underwater cultural heritage'.

2.2   *The Rights of the Coastal State within the Territorial Sea*
A) It is implied in LOSC that the sovereignty that the coastal State is entitled to exercise in the territorial sea and in internal maritime waters includes sovereign rights over the underwater cultural heritage located within these spaces.

B) CPUCH explicitly provides that

> States Parties, in the exercise of their sovereignty, have the exclusive right to regulate and authorize activities directed at underwater cultural heritage in their internal waters, archipelagic waters and territorial sea (Article 7 (1).

Moreover, CPUCH gives some weight to the interest of flag States in the protection of sunken vessels and aircraft owned by them:

> Within their archipelagic waters and territorial sea, in the exercise of their sovereignty and in recognition of general practice among States, States Parties, with a view to cooperating on the best methods of protecting State vessels and aircraft, should inform the flag State Party to this Convention and, if applicable, other States with a verifiable link, especially a cultural, historical or archaeological link, with respect to the discovery of such identifiable State vessels and aircraft (Article 7 (3)).

The hortatory character of this provision ('should') and the limited scope of an invitation to provide information prevent any conflict between CPUCH and LOSC implied regime.

3 Where CPUCH Goes Further than LOSC

For other aspects, CPUCH builds on some ideas that can be found in LOSC, but gives them a broader meaning and scope of application.

3.1 *The Benefit of Humanity*
A) Article 149 LOSC, which is included in Part XI of LOSC, relating to 'the seabed and ocean floor and subsoil thereof, beyond the limits of national jurisdiction' ('the Area'), provides as follows:

> All objects of an archaeological and historical nature found in the Area shall be preserved or disposed of for the benefit of mankind as a whole, particular regard being paid to the preferential rights of the State or country of origin, or the State of cultural origin, or the State of historical and archaeological origin.

Article 149 LOSC appears complicated in its wording[3] and devoid of details that could ensure its practical application. However, it embodies two ideas. The first is that States are bound to use underwater archaeological and historical objects for the 'benefit of mankind as a whole'. Private interests, such as the

---

3 What is the difference between 'the State or country of origin', 'the State of cultural origin' and 'the State of historical and archaeological origin'? Why is the word 'country' used only in one of the three expressions?

search for and the disposal of the objects for trade and personal gain, are given little weight, if any.

B) Also CPUCH provides in general that States Parties are bound to 'preserve underwater cultural heritage for the benefit of humanity' (Article 2 (3). However, in this case, the obligation applies to all such heritage, without being limited to what is found in the Area.

Moreover, CPUCH draws from the rule a consequence that, although it could be considered as implied in the rule, was not explicitly stated in LOSC:

> Underwater cultural heritage shall not be commercially exploited (Article 2 (7).

In particular,

> the commercial exploitation of underwater cultural heritage for trade or speculation or its irretrievable dispersal is fundamentally incompatible with the protection and proper management of underwater cultural heritage. Underwater cultural heritage shall not be traded, sold, bought or bartered as commercial goods (Rule 2 of the Annex).[4]

LOSC does not go as far as stating that the benefit of mankind means the prohibition of trade in objects belonging to underwater cultural heritage.

3.2 *The Preferential Rights of Certain States*

A) The second idea embodied in Article 149 LOSC is that some categories of States, which have a link with the objects, are given preferential rights. However, Article 149 does not elaborate on the content of these rights or the manner in which they should be harmonized with the 'benefit of mankind as a whole'.

B) Also CPUCH, for most of the heritage—that is the heritage located in the exclusive economic zone and in the Area[5]—grants preferential rights to those States Parties which have 'a verifiable link, especially a cultural, historical

---

[4] Rule 2 of the Annex adds that 'this cannot be interpreted as preventing the provision of professional archaeological services or necessary services incidental thereto whose nature and purpose are in full conformity with this Convention and are subject to the authorization of the competent authorities.' The rules of the Annex form an integral part of CPUCH (Article 33).

[5] The position of States having a verifiable link is recalled also in Article 7 (3), CPUCH. See section 2.2 above). applicable in the territorial sea and archipelagic waters.

or archaeological link, to the underwater cultural heritage concerned'[6] (see Article 9 (5), and Article 11 (4). The State holder of such a link is entitled to participate in consultations on 'how best to protect the underwater cultural heritage' in question (see Article 10 (3)(*a*), and Article 12 (2).

CPUCH gives a more precise content to the preferential rights of States having a link with the heritage. It also extends the scope of application of such rights to cover also marine zones different from the Area.

4   Where LOSC and CPUCH Are in Conflict

For other aspects, the regimes set forth by the two treaties appear in conflict.[7]

4.1   *The Rights of the Coastal State within the Contiguous Zone*

A) Article 303 (2) LOSC provides as follows as regards the objects of an archaeological and historical nature found within the contiguous zone, whose breadth cannot extend beyond the 24 n.m. from the baselines of the territorial sea:

> In order to control traffic in such objects, the coastal State may, in applying Article 33 [= the contiguous zone], presume that their removal from the sea-bed in the zone referred to in that article without its approval would result in an infringement within its territory or territorial sea of the laws and regulations referred to in that article [= customs, fiscal, immigration or sanitary laws and regulations].

This provision grants some rights to the coastal State. But it is difficult to seize the content of such rights. If literally understood, Article 303 (2), suggests that the removal of archaeological and historical objects from the contiguous zone can determine a violation of the domestic legislation of the coastal State on matters which have little or nothing to do with cultural heritage, such as smuggling, public health and immigration. Under LOSC logic, it is only because of the competences which a State can already exercise in dealing with cigarette smugglers, clandestine immigrants and infectious patients that a coastal State can claim additional competences for the protection of underwater cultural

---

6   No attempt was made to define the concept of 'verifiable link'.

7   It seems that there is no conflict between Article 32 LOSC (Immunities of warships and other Government ships operated for non-commercial purposes) and CPUCH provisions on State vessels and aircraft, as the former applies to ships and the latter apply to wrecks which have been underwater for at least 100 years (see Article 1(1), CPUCH).

heritage. The wisdom of such a logic, which implies that underwater cultural heritage does not deserve to be protected *per se*, is not convincing, to say the least.

Other problems arise from the wording of the provision. While coastal States are empowered to prevent and sanction the 'removal' of the objects from the sea-bed, they seem defenseless if the objects, instead of being removed, are simply destroyed in the very place where they have been found (for instance, by a company holding a license for oil exploitation). Again, it is difficult to subscribe to such a result.

Such a convoluted provision was included in LOSC because, for reasons of principle, the major maritime powers were against a provision that granted more rights to coastal States and could be seen as further eroding the principle of freedom of the sea.[8] Rather than envisaging a substantive regime to deal with the concern of protecting the underwater cultural heritage, the major maritime powers preferred legalistic intricacies that had a completely different purpose.[9] But this can only cast serious doubt on whether LOSC sets forth a credible regime, as far as the underwater cultural heritage is concerned.

B) Article 8 CPUCH clearly states that the coastal State has the right to regulate and authorize the activities directed at underwater cultural heritage taking place within its contiguous zone:

> Without prejudice to and in addition to Articles 9 and 10, and in accordance with Article 303, paragraph 2, of the United Nations Convention on the Law of the Sea, States Parties may regulate and authorize activities directed at underwater cultural heritage within their contiguous zone....

---

8 'For reasons of principle whose importance transcended any interests in marine archaeology as such, the maritime powers were unwilling to yield to any further erosions in the freedoms of the seas, particularly regarding coastal State jurisdiction over non-resource uses beyond the territorial sea. The inclusion of paragraph 2 of Article 303 in the general provisions of the Convention rather than the texts dealing with jurisdiction, and the indirect drafting style employing cross-references and presumptions, were intended to emphasize both the procedural and substantive points that the regimes of the coastal State jurisdiction (...) were not being reopened or changed' (B. H. Oxman, 'Marine Archaeology and the International Law of the Sea', 12 *Columbia Journal of Law and the Arts*, 1988, p. 363).

9 'To create a new 'archaeological' zone, or expressly to expand the competence of the coastal State to include regulation of diving for archaeological objects in the contiguous zone, would amount to converting the contiguous zone from an area where the coastal State has limited enforcement competence to one where it has legislative competence'. (B. H. Oxman, 'The Third United Nations Conference on the Law of the Sea: The Ninth Session (1980)', 75 *American Journal of International Law*, 1981, p. 240).

Is this really 'in accordance with' Article 303 (2) LOSC, as Article 8 CPUCH says? What is sure is that Article 8 CPUCH states in a more understandable way what only with many difficulties could be seen as implied in the convoluted wording of Article 303 (2) LOSC. But if the conclusion were that, within the contiguous zone, CPUCH grants the coastal State more rights than LOSC does, the reason would be that CPUCH drafters were more concerned with the protection of underwater cultural rather than with the aim of preserving the abstract principle of freedom of the seas.

4.2   The Rights of the Coastal State within the Exclusive Economic Zone

A) LOSC does not establish any regime relating to underwater cultural heritage found in the space located between the 24-mile contiguous zone and the 200-mile exclusive economic zone. The rights of the coastal State within the exclusive economic zone are limited to the exploration and exploitation of the relevant 'natural resources', as stated in Article 56 (1), and cannot be extended to man-made objects, such as those belonging to underwater cultural heritage.[10] The legal vacuum in LOSC threatens the protection of cultural heritage, as it brings into the picture the principle of freedom of the seas that could easily lead to a first-come-first-served approach. Availing himself of this principle, anyone on board a ship could explore the exclusive economic zone adjacent to any coastal State, bring archaeological and historical objects to the surface, become their owner under a domestic legislation (in most cases, the flag State legislation) and sell them on the market. If this were the case, there would be no guarantee that the objects are disposed of for public benefit rather than for personal commercial gain. Nor could a State which has a link with the objects prevent the pillage of its historical heritage.

The danger of freedom of fishing for underwater cultural heritage under LOSC regime is aggravated by Article 303 (3), which subjects the whole Article 303 to a very particular set of rules:

> Nothing in this article affects the rights of identifiable owners, the law of salvage and other rules of admiralty, or laws and practices with respect to cultural exchanges.

LOSC does not clarify the meaning of the expression 'law of salvage and other rules of admiralty'. In many countries, the notion of salvage is referred to the

---

10 It seems too artificial to assume that archaeological and historical objects which are found embedded in the sand or encrusted with sedentary living organisms can be likened to natural resources.

attempts to save a ship or its cargo from imminent marine peril. It is not intended to apply to sunken ships that, far from being in peril, have been definitively lost for hundreds or thousands of years. Contrarily, in a minority of common law countries, and in particular in the United States,[11] the notion of salvage law has been enlarged by court decisions to cover also an activity, the so-called treasure salvage, that has very little to do with ships in peril. Moreover, American courts apply admiralty law in an extra-territorial manner, to grant salvors and finders rights over wrecks and properties found at sea, wherever they are located.

For example, the United States Court of Appeals for the Fourth Circuit, in the decision of 24 March 1999 on the case *R.M.S. Titanic, Inc. v. Haver*,[12] stated that the law of salvage and finds, which is part of admiralty law, is a 'venerable law of the sea'. It is said to have arisen from the custom among 'seafaring men' and to have 'been preserved from ancient Rhodes (900 BCE), Rome (Justinian's Corpus Juris Civilis, 533 CE), City of Trani (Italy, 1063), England (the Law of Oleron, 1189), the Hansa Towns or Hanseatic League (1597), and France (1681), all articulating similar principles'. Coming to the practical result of such a display of legal erudition, the law of finds means that 'a person who discovers a shipwreck in navigable waters that has been long lost and abandoned and who reduces the property to actual or constructive possession becomes the property's owner', if the original owner is not known. In its turn, the law of salvage, which applies where the original owner is known, gives the salvor a lien (or right *in rem*) over the property. Yet the expression 'the law of salvage and other rules of admiralty' simply means the application of a first-come-first-served or freedom-of-fishing approach, which can only serve the interest of private commercial gain and could be seen as a legal invitation to the looting of underwater cultural heritage.[13]

It is not clear how a 'venerable' body of rules, which developed in times when nobody cared about underwater cultural heritage, could provide any sensible tool for dealing with the protection of such heritage today. However, the body of 'the law of salvage and other rules of admiralty' is typical of a few common law systems, but remains a complete stranger to the legislation of

---

11 See T. J. Schoenbaum, *Admiralty and Maritime Law*, 4th edition, vol. II, West, 2004, p. 176.

12 *International Legal Materials*, 1999, p. 807.

13 See T. Scovazzi, 'The Application of 'Salvage Law and Other Rules of Admiralty' to the Underwater Cultural Heritage: Some Relevant Cases', in Garabello & Scovazzi (eds), supra, note 2, p. 19; M. J. Aznar Gómez, 'Treasure Hunters, Sunken State Vessels and the 2001 UNESCO Convention on the Protection of Underwater Cultural Heritage', 25 *International Journal of Marine and Coastal Law*, 2010, p. 209.

many other countries. Because of the lack of corresponding concepts, the very words 'salvage' and 'admiralty' cannot be properly translated into languages different from English. In the French and Spanish official text of the LOSC they are rendered with expressions—'droit de récupérer des épaves et (...) autres règles du droit maritime'; 'las normas sobre salvamento u otras normas del derecho marítimo'—which give the provision a broader and quite different meaning.

This worsens the already sad picture of Article 303 (3), at least if read in LOSC English version.[14] The provision gives to 'salvage law and other rules of admiralty' an overarching status. If there is a conflict between the general objective of protecting underwater cultural heritage (Article 303(1)), on the one hand, and the provisions of salvage law and other rules of admiralty, on the other, the latter prevail.[15] Does LOSC, while apparently protecting underwater cultural heritage, lead to a regime under which this heritage is used solely for commercial purposes? While there is room for proposing less disastrous interpretations of Article 303 (3),[16] this doubt is far from trivial, especially for those countries where national legislation is based on the duty of the State to preserve cultural heritage for purposes of public interest, such as research and exhibition. Again, the credibility of LOSC for achieving the objective of protecting underwater cultural heritage is put in question.

B) While most States participating in the negotiations for CPUCH concurred in rejecting the application of the law of salvage and the law of finds to underwater cultural heritage, a minority of States were not prepared to accept an absolute ban. To achieve a reasonable compromise, Article 4 CPUCH ('Relationship to law of salvage and law of finds') provides as follows:

> Any activity relating to underwater cultural heritage to which this Convention applies shall not be subject to the law of salvage or law of finds, unless it:

---

14   It is not likely that the application of Article 33 (*Interpretation of treaties authenticated in two or more languages*) of the Vienna Convention on the Law of Treaties will lead to the adoption of the English meaning of Article 303 (3), LOSC.

15   The effects of Article 303 (3), on Article 303 (2) (Section 4.1.A above) are also notable. The coastal State would be prevented from sanctioning the removal of the objects from its archaeological contiguous zone, as admiralty law grants to the finder or the salvor the right to remove the objects.

16   According to Strati, supra, note 1, p. 225, 'the reservation of salvage and admiralty law by Article 303(3) should be confined to cases in which archaeological and historical objects are not involved, i.e., objects which are less than 100 years old and are eligible for salvage.'

(a) is authorized by the competent authorities, and
(b) is in full conformity with this Convention, and
(c) ensures that any recovery of the underwater cultural heritage achieves its maximum protection.

Article 4 CPUCH, which is to be understood in connection with the already mentioned prohibition of commercial exploitation of underwater cultural heritage,[17] is in total conflict with Article 303 (3) LOSC, at least in its English version. Although the law of salvage and law of finds are not entirely excluded, the CPUCH regime has the practical effect of preventing the undesirable effects of such rules. Freedom of fishing for archaeological and historical objects is certainly banned.

Most States participating in the negotiations for CPUCH were ready to extend the jurisdiction of the coastal State to underwater cultural heritage found on the continental shelf or in the exclusive economic zone. However, a minority of States assumed, as they did during the negotiations for the LOSC, that the extension of the jurisdiction of coastal States would have altered the balance embodied in LOSC between the rights and obligations of the coastal State and those of other States. Finally, to reach a compromise, in CPUCH a procedural mechanism was envisaged which involves the participation of the States linked to the heritage. It is based on a three-step procedure (reporting, consultations, urgent measures).

As regards the first step (reporting), CPUCH bans secret activities or discoveries. States Parties must require their nationals or vessels flying their flag to report activities or discoveries to them.[18] If the activity or discovery is located in the exclusive economic zone or on the continental shelf of another State Party, CPUCH envisages two alternative solutions:

(i) States Parties shall require the national or the master of the vessel to report such discovery or activity to them and to that other State Party;

---

17 Section 3.1.A above.
18 For obvious reasons, information is limited to the competent authorities of States Parties: 'Information shared between States Parties, or between UNESCO and States Parties, regarding the discovery or location of underwater cultural heritage shall, to the extent compatible with their national legislation, be kept confidential and reserved to competent authorities of States Parties as long as the disclosure of such information might endanger or otherwise put at risk the preservation of such underwater cultural heritage' (Article 19 (3)).

(ii) alternatively, a State Party shall require the national or master of the vessel to report such discovery or activity to it and shall ensure the rapid and effective transmission of such report to all other States Parties. (Article 9 (1)(b)).[19]

States Parties are also required to notify the Director-General of UNESCO of the relevant information, who must promptly make the information available to all States Parties.

As regards the second step (consultations), the coastal State[20] is bound to consult all States Parties that have declared their interest in being consulted on how to ensure the effective protection of the underwater cultural heritage in question (Article 10 (3)(a), and Article 9 (5). This declaration must be based on the already mentioned 'verifiable link'.[21]

The coastal State[22] is entitled to coordinate the consultations, unless it expressly declares that it does not wish to do so, in which case the States Parties that have declared an interest in being consulted are called to appoint another coordinating State. The coordinating State must implement the measures of protection that have been agreed by the consulting States and may conduct any necessary preliminary research on the underwater cultural heritage.

As regards the third step (urgent measures), Article 10 (4), provides as follows:

> Without prejudice to the right of all States Parties to protect underwater cultural heritage by way of all practicable measures taken in accordance with international law to prevent immediate danger to the underwater cultural heritage, including looting, the Coordinating State may take all practicable measures, and/or issue any necessary authorizations in conformity with this Convention and, if necessary prior to consultations, to prevent any immediate danger to the underwater cultural heritage, whether arising from human activities or any other cause, including

---

19   On depositing its instrument of ratification, acceptance, approval or accession, a State Party shall declare the manner in which reports will be transmitted (Article 9 (2)).
20   Here and elsewhere, CPUCH does not use the words 'coastal State', to avoid the impression of creeping jurisdiction. It prefers the more complex expression 'State Party in whose exclusive economic zone or on whose continental shelf' the activity or the discovery is located.
21   Section 3.1. B above.
22   See supra, note 20.

looting. In taking such measures assistance may be requested from other States Parties.

The right of the coordinating State to adopt urgent measures is an important aspect of CPUCH regime. It would have been illusory to subordinate this right to the final outcome of consultations that are normally expected to last for some time. It would also have been illusory to grant this right to the flag State, considering the risk of activities carried out by vessels flying the flag of non-parties or a flag of convenience. By definition, in case of urgency, immediate measures must be taken without losing time involved in procedural requirements. CPUCH clearly states that in coordinating consultations, taking measures, conducting preliminary research and issuing authorizations, the coordinating State acts 'on behalf of the States Parties as a whole and not in its own interest' (Article10 (6)). Any such action cannot in itself constitute a basis for the assertion of any preferential or jurisdictional rights not provided for in international law, including LOSC.

By its three-step procedural mechanism, CPUCH fills the legal vacuum left open by LOSC and prevents the application of a freedom-of-fishing regime for the underwater cultural heritage. Unlike LOSC, there is no doubt that CPUCH regime, however complex it might seem, is aimed at protecting the underwater cultural heritage and preventing its dispersal for commercial speculation.[23]

5 Is Reconciliation Possible?

5.1 *Conflicting Treaties under International Law of Treaties*
The considerations developed above show that there are a number of more or less evident aspects of conflict between LOSC and CPUCH. Those States that are parties to both treaties[24] are called to determine what provisions apply.

---

[23] According to the scolar to whom this collection of essays is dedicated : 'il faut admettre que, dans un domaine comme celui de la protection du patrimoine subaquatique dans la zone économique exclusive et sur le plateau continental, où la Convention des Nations Unies sur le droit de la mer est silencieuse et le droit international inadapté, la question de la compatibilité de la Convention devrait être abordée avec une certaine flexibilité. (...) Le régime de protection du patrimoine culturel subaquatique dans la zone économique exclusive et sur le plateau continental mis en place par la Convention a le grand mérite de mettre un terme au régime de liberté tel qu'il résultait du droit international, lequel ne pouvait qu'encourager et protéger les pilleurs de trésors': Momtaz, supra, note 2, p. 456.

[24] As of February 2017, there are 165 States and one international organization parties to LOSC and 55 States to CPUCH.

Where successive treaties relating to the same subject-matter are applicable, Article 30 of the Convention on the Law of Treaties (Vienna, 1969) provides for the following regime:

1. (…) the rights and obligations of States parties to successive treaties relating to the same subject-matter shall be determined in accordance with the following paragraphs.
2. When a treaty specifies that it is subject to, or that it is not to be considered as incompatible with, an earlier or later treaty, the provisions of that other treaty prevail.
3. When all the parties to the earlier treaty are parties also to the later treaty but the earlier treaty is not terminated or suspended in operation under Article 59, the earlier treaty applies only to the extent that its provisions are compatible with those of the later treaty.
4. When the parties to the later treaty do not include all the parties to the earlier one:
   a) as between States Parties to both treaties the same rule applies as in paragraph 3;
   b) as between a State Party to both treaties and a State Party to only one of the treaties, the treaty to which both States are parties governs their mutual rights and obligations.

Accordingly, the questions to be addressed seem the following:

a) whether a provision of the earlier treaty and a provision of the later one relate to the same subject-matter;
b) if so, whether one of the two treaties specifies that it is subject to the other;
c) if this is not the case, whether and to what extent the relevant provisions in the two treaties are incompatible, considering that, whenever possible, the provisions should be interpreted according to a meaning that leads to their reconciliation.[25]
d) finally, if reconciliation between the provisions of the two treaties is not possible, it must be determined which one is the later treaty:[26]

---

25 Under Article 31 (3)(*c*), of the Vienna Convention on the Law of Treaties, in the interpretation of a treaty provision account shall also be taken of 'any relevant rules of international law applicable in the relations between the parties'.
26 Are the concepts of 'earlier' and 'later' to be determined according to the dates of adoption of the two treaties or to the dates of their entries into force on the international level

here the provisions governing the mutual rights and obligations of the parties are to be found.

5.2   *The Special Case of LOSC and CPUCH*

In the case of LOSC and CPUCH, it is evident that Arts. 149 and 303 LOSC, on one hand, and the whole CPUCH, on the other, relate to the same subject-matter and that, consequently, the two regimes overlap.

Coming to the question whether one of the two treaties specifies that it is subject to the other, Article 3 CPUCH provides as follows:

> Nothing in this Convention shall prejudice the rights, jurisdiction and duties of States under international law, including the United Nations Convention on the Law of the Sea. This Convention shall be interpreted and applied in the context of and in a manner consistent with international law, including the United Nations Convention on the Law of the Sea.[27]

This provision, which gives priority to LOSC, is however balanced by Article 303 (4) LOSC:

> This article is without prejudice to other international agreements and rules of international law regarding the protection of objects of an archaeological and historical nature.

There is no reason why this provision should be referred only to agreements concluded before the adoption of LOSC and not also to subsequent agreements, such as CPUCH itself.

The rather paradoxical situation of two treaties, each of them providing that it is subject to the other, is difficult to handle. An attempt to get out of the deadlock could be to assume that Article 3 CPUCH leaves unaffected all the many LOSC provisions different from the two specifically related to underwater cultural heritage, namely Article 149 and 303. The latter are superseded,

---

or to the dates on which the treaties have become binding in the relationship between the parties concerned? The answer is far from being clear.

27   According to R. Garabello, 'The Negotiating History of the Convention on the Protection of the Underwater Cultural Heritage', in Garabello & Scovazzi (eds), supra, note 2, p. 117, 'Article 3 does hide what is probably the most controversial issue underpinning all the Convention, that is to say its relationship with the LOSC. (...) The problem was a ghost present as early as the very beginning of the negotiations (maybe even before).'

insofar as they are in conflict with CPUCH provisions, by the more specific and later CPUCH regime. This would be consistent with the general principle of law according to which the special rules prevail over the general rules (*lex specialis derogat legi generali*).

5.3   The Contradictions within LOSC

The contradictions within LOSC itself should also be emphasized. The LOSC regime on underwater cultural heritage is fragmentary, being composed of only two provisions included in different parts of the convention.[28] The two provisions are in conceptual contradiction with one another, as one (Article 149) aims at the benefit of mankind and the other (Article 303) at the benefit of finders and salvors.

Within Article 303, where para. 2 is hardly understandable, para. 3 contradicts and thwarts para. 1, since the application of the law of salvage and other rules of admiralty cannot lead to the protection of the underwater cultural heritage, but only to its commercial exploitation. Additional elements of contradiction are due to the presence of two non-prejudice clauses in the same provision. If there were a conflict between para. 3 and para. 4—for instance if a treaty concluded under para. 4 banned the application of admiralty law to underwater cultural heritage—would this treaty by compatible with Article 303? There is no logical answer to the question.

The fact that the subject of underwater cultural heritage was taken into consideration only in the last period of a negotiation that lasted for about ten years (from 1973 to 1982) cannot be a justification for the unsatisfactory LOSC regime. When the question of protection of underwater cultural heritage was finally addressed, LOSC drafters had other concerns in mind, in particular the preservation of the balances that other LOSC provisions had established. This is the main message coming from LOSC.

CPUCH may be seen as a reasonable defense against the contradictory and probably counterproductive regime of LOSC. If the looting of the heritage is the result of LOSC regime, it is LOSC that is wrong on this matter, irrespective of all the balances that it wishes to preserve.

---

28   Article 149 is included in Part XI (The Area) and Article 303 in Part XVI (General provisions).

The Dispute Concerning the *Enrica Lexie* Incident and the Role of International Tribunals in Provisional Measure Proceedings Instituted Pursuant to the United Nations Convention on the Law of the Sea

Roberto Virzo

1 Introduction

This article deals with the *'Enrica Lexie' Incident* (*Italy* v *India*) by taking as its starting point the two orders on provisional measures issued in the case, respectively, on 24 August 2015 and 29 April 2016. The first order was rendered by the International Tribunal for the Law of the Sea (ITLOS) pending the constitution of the Arbitral Tribunal under Annex VII to the United Nations Convention on the Law of the Sea (LOSC),[1] to which the dispute has been submitted; the second, by the Annex VII Arbitral Tribunal.[2]

The aforesaid orders raise a variety of issues, only some of which will be discussed here. More specifically, two main issues will be addressed: (i) the function of provisional measures according to two different paragraphs of Article 290 LOSC (§ 3); and (ii) the tendency to interpret LOSC provisions in coordination with other norms of international law, particularly those that concern human rights (§ 4). In examining these issues, an attempt will be made to shed light on the role of international tribunals in facilitating the resolution of international disputes for which provisional measure proceedings have been initiated, especially when said tribunals issue orders that impose obligations of cooperation on the parties involved—a topic we will return to in the short concluding remarks.

---

[1] See 1833 UNTS 3. The Convention was signed at Montego Bay on 10 December 1982 and entered into force internationally on 16 November 1994; it was ratified by Italy on 12 February 1995 and by India on 29 June 1995.

[2] See *The 'Enrica Lexie' Incident* (Italy v India), ITLOS Case No 24, Order of 24 August 2015, available at www.itlos.org; *The 'Enrica Lexie' Incident* (Italy v India), PCA Case No 2015–28, Order of 29 April 2016, available at https://pcacases.com/web/sendAttach/1707, accessed on 3 August 2016.

2   The *Enrica Lexie* Incident

Before going any further, it seems worthwhile to recall briefly the facts and subject-matter of the dispute between Italy and India concerning the *Enrica Lexie* incident.[3]

Over the last twenty years, many States and some organs of international organizations, including the United Nations Security Council, have adopted measures, of varying forms, to counter maritime piracy.[4] One of these measures is Italian Law No. 130 of 2 August 2011,[5] which, among other things, provides for 'the deployment of Vessel Protection Detachments ('VPDS') from the Italian Navy on board vessels flying the Italian flag to ensure the security of such vessels travelling in international waters that are at high risk of piracy'.[6] Now, while the costs of the presence of Italian military units on board an Italian-flagged merchant vessel are to be borne by the shipowner,[7] the rules of

---

3   In the literature, see V. Eboli & J. P. Pierini, 'Coastal State Jurisdiction Over Vessel Protection Detachments and Immunity Issues: The *Enrica Lexie* Case', 51 *Revue de droit militaire et de droit de la guerre*, 2012, pp. 117–148; I. Caracciolo & F. Graziani, *Il caso dell'Enrica Lexie alla luce del diritto internazionale*, Editoriale Scientifica, 2013; N. Ronzitti, 'The *Enrica Lexie* Incident: Law of the Sea and Immunity of States Officials Issues', 22 *The Italian Yearbook of International Law*, 2012, pp. 3–22; M. Gandhy, 'The *Enrica Lexie* Incident: Seeing Beyond the Grey Areas of International Law', 53 *Indian Journal of International Law*, 2013, pp. 1–26; N. Ronzitti, 'La difesa contro i pirati e l'imbarco di personale armato sui mercantili: il caso della *Enrica Lexie* e la controversia Italia-India', 96 *Rivista di diritto internazionale*, 2013, pp. 1073–115; B. Conforti, 'In tema di giurisdizione penale per fatti commessi in acque internazionali', in *Scritti in onore di Giuseppe Tesauro*, Editoriale Scientifica, 2014, pp. 2619–2629; A. Del Vecchio, 'Il ricorso all'arbitrato obbligatorio UNCLOS nella vicenda dell'*Enrica Lexie*', 50 *Rivista di diritto internazionale privato e processuale*, 2014, pp. 259–284; T. Russo, 'Maritime Police and Functional Immunity in the Recent Italian-Indian Case', in J. M. Sobrino Heredia (ed), *La contribution de la Convention des Nations Unies sur le droit de la mer à la bonne gouvernance des mers et des océans*, Editoriale Scientifica, 2014, pp. 629–642; A. Del Vecchio, 'The Fight Against Piracy and the Enrica Lexie Incident', in L. del Castillo (ed), *Law of the Sea, from Grotius to the International Tribunal for the Law of the Sea: Liber Amicorum Judge Hugo Caminos*, Brill/Nijhoff, 2015, pp. 397–422.
4   On this subject see, among many others, D. Momtaz, 'La piraterie', in H. Ascensio, E. Decaux & A. Pellet (eds), *Droit international pénal*, Pedone, 2012, pp. 365–370.
5   Originally published in Italian in 152 *Gazzetta Ufficiale della Repubblica Italiana*, 2011, as Decree-Law No. 107 of 12 July 2011, 23–31. The English version used here is that contained in Annex 2 to Italy's Notification of dispute to India of 26 June 2015, available at https://pcacases.com/web/view/117, accessed on 3 August 2016.
6   See PCA, supra, note 2, Italy's Notification of Dispute to India of 16 June 2015, para. 4.
7   Article 5(3) of Italian Law No. 130/2011 provides that: 'Shipowners who benefit from the protection referred to in paragraph 1 shall repay the costs thereof, including the expenses for the personnel referred to in paragraph 2 and operating expenses' to the Ministry of Defence.

engagement are the responsibility of the Italian Ministry of Defense. Moreover, the military personnel embarked on the vessel are not under the command of the ship's master but, rather, under the command of the head of the VPD, who is responsible for the use of weapons on board the ship.[8]

By virtue of Law No. 130/2011, on 6 February 2012 six Italian Navy marines, including Chief Master Sergeant Massimiliano Latorre and Sergeant Salvatore Girone, were deployed from the port of Galle (Sri Lanka) on board the Italian-flagged oil tanker *MV Enrica Lexie*.

On 15 February 2012, an unidentified vessel suddenly approached the *Enrica Lexie*, approximately 20.5 nautical miles off the coastline of the Indian State of Kerala, within the Indian contiguous zone, which overlaps with India's exclusive economic zone.

According to Italy's account of the facts of the incident, the Italian marines mistook the vessel—which in fact was an Indian fishing vessel, the *St. Antony*—for a pirate ship that was trying to attack the *Enrica Lexie*: 'The craft continued to head towards the *Enrica Lexie* despite sustained visual and auditory warnings from the *Enrica Lexie* and the firing of warning shots into the water. (...) Sergeant Girone, looking at the craft through binoculars, saw what appeared to be people carrying rifles, as well as instruments for boarding ships. Eventually, after apparent attempts to approach the *Enrica Lexie*, the craft turned away and headed towards the open sea.'[9] Soon afterwards, the Indian authorities, informed that two fishermen embarked on the *St. Antony* had been killed and—in Italy's view—'acting by ruse and coercion',[10] managed to divert the *Enrica Lexie*, which was continuing its route towards Djibouti, to the Indian port of Kochi, where they detained the ship, seized the weapons of the Italian marines, and arrested Chief Master Sergeant Massimiliano Latorre and Sergeant Salvatore Girone.

According to India's account of the events, '[o]n 15 February 2012 at about 4.30 p.m. Indian Standard Time, an Indian fishing boat, the *St. Anthony*, engaged in fishing activities in India's Exclusive Economic Zone (...), faced a

---

8   In this sense, see Ronzitti, 'La difesa contro i pirati', supra, note 3, pp. 1079 and 1098.
9   Italy's Notification, supra, note 6, paras. 7–8.
10 According to Italy, '[t]he Maritime Rescue Co-ordination Centre of India ('MRCC') contacted the *Enrica Lexie* by telephone, claimed that it had caught two suspected pirate boats in connection with a 'pirate incident/firing incident' and (on that false pretext) instructed the *Enrica Lexie* to sail to Kocki to identify suspected pirates. In a subsequent email sent to the Master, the MRCC referred to this conversation and again asked the *Enrica Lexie* to head for Kochi, without explaining that the *Enrica Lexie* itself was the suspect vessel. The Indian authorities also used coercion to ensure that the *Enrica Lexie* stopped, changed course, sailed to Kochi anchorage and remained there.' Italy's Notification, ibid., paras. 11–12.

volley of bullets fired from sophisticated automatic firearms from two uniformed persons on board of an oil tanker ship, which was about 200 meters from the boat operating in clear weather. Two fishermen on St. Anthony were fatally hit by the bullets fired from the *Enrica Lexie*, and the lives of nine other fishermen on the boat were endangered due to the firing. (…) In addition to the casualties, the incident caused serious damage to the boat endangering the safe navigation of the fishing vessel.'[11] Informed of the death of the two fishermen, the Indian authorities—in India's view, without any ruse or coercion[12]—diverted the *Enrica Lexie* to Kochi port, where, as noted above, they proceeded to detain the ship and impose measures restricting the personal liberty of the two Italian marines.

Leaving aside the differences between the two accounts of the incident, the dispute between Italy and India raises a number of complex issues of international law. These include in particular: (i) the exercise of criminal jurisdiction over the two marines (Italy has claimed jurisdiction mainly on the basis of Article 97 LOSC,[13] whereas India, contesting the applicability of that article to the case, has relied on the 'passive personality' principle);[14] (ii) the interpretation and application of many LOSC provisions;[15] and (iii) the functional immunity of the two marines.

---

11   See PCA, supra, note 2, Written observations of the Republic of India on the Request of the Italian Republic for the prescription of provisional measures under Article 290, Paragraph 1, of the United Nations Convention on the Law of the Sea, 26 February 2016.

12   Ibid., paras. 2.11–2.16.

13   '1. In the event of a collision or any other incident of navigation concerning a ship on the high seas, involving the penal or disciplinary responsibility of the master or of any other person in the service of the ship, no penal or disciplinary proceedings may be instituted against such person except before the judicial or administrative authorities either of the flag State or of the State of which such person is a national. 2. In disciplinary matters, the State which has issued a master's certificate or license shall alone be competent, after due legal process, to pronounce the withdrawal of such certificates, even if the holder is not a national of the State which issued them. 3. No arrest or detention of the ship, even as a measure of investigation, shall be ordered by any authorities other than those of the flag State.'

14   On this point, see I. Klabbers, *International Law*, Cambridge University Press, 2013, p. 93, where he notes that, while '[t]he principle holds that a State can prosecute anyone who harms its nationals, no matter where this occurs', that principle is, however, 'highly controversial'.

15   'According to Italy, the dispute concerns India's breaches of its obligations under Articles 2, paragraph 3, 27, 33, 56, 58, 87, 89, 92, 94, 97, 100 and 300 of the Convention.' See PCA, supra, note 2, para. 50.

Indeed, the dispute has been intensified by the simultaneous exercise of jurisdiction by the two States. Italy started exercising its military criminal jurisdiction, albeit not vigorously, on 17 February 2012 and its ordinary criminal jurisdiction on 15 March 2012, whereas India started exercising its criminal jurisdiction on 19 February 2012, when its authorities ordered the arrest of the two Italian marines. Italy immediately challenged the exercise of Indian criminal jurisdiction: on the one hand, it unsuccessfully brought a number of proceedings before Indian courts (in September 2014, however, Sergeant Latorre, due to health problems, was granted a relaxation of the conditions of bail by the Indian Supreme Court, to allow him to return to Italy for an initial period of four months, which was later extended); on the other, it initiated bilateral consultations with the Government of New Delhi.

After over three years of unsuccessful negotiations, in April 2015 Italy decided to unilaterally submit the dispute to arbitration pursuant to Part XV, section 2, LOSC. As is very well known, under Article 286 LOSC any dispute concerning the interpretation or application of the Montego Bay Convention may, where no settlement has been reached through diplomatic means, be submitted at the request of any party to the dispute to one of the courts or tribunals referred to in Article 287—i.e., the International Tribunal for the Law of the Sea, the International Court of Justice, an arbitral tribunal constituted in accordance with Annex VII, or a special arbitral tribunal constituted in accordance with Annex VIII. Under paragraphs 1–5 of Article 287 LOSC, States are free to choose to which court(s) or tribunal(s) they want to submit a dispute. More specifically, paragraph 1 provides that, when signing, ratifying or acceding to the Convention or at any time thereafter, a State Party may choose one or more of the aforesaid courts or tribunals by means of a written declaration. Paragraph 3 establishes that if no written declaration has been made, the State Party will be deemed to have accepted arbitration in accordance with Annex VII. Under paragraph 4, if the parties to a dispute have accepted the same procedure for the settlement of the dispute, the latter may be submitted only to that procedure. Finally, paragraph 5 stipulates that if the parties have not accepted the same procedure, the dispute may be submitted only to arbitration in accordance with Annex VII.[16]

Since Italy declared its intention to accept the jurisdiction of the International Court of Justice and of the International Tribunal for the Law of the Sea, whereas India did not make—and has not made—any explicit choice

---

16 However, paragraphs 4 and 5 of Article 287 LOSC envisage the possibility for the parties to agree on a different procedure, court or tribunal.

of procedure, the only option for the claimant State was to request that an arbitral tribunal be constituted in accordance with Annex VII.

3 The Function of the Provisional Measures Ordered by the International Tribunal for the Law of the Sea and by the Annex VII Arbitral Tribunal

It is not our concern here to discuss the substantive legal issues involved in the dispute—besides, at the time of writing (August 2016), the arguments of the parties do not seem to be adequately grounded, probably because so far both parties have focused mainly on two provisional measure proceedings, which have now ended.

With regard to the first of these proceedings, pending the constitution of the Annex VII Arbitral Tribunal, Italy filed with the ITLOS a request for the prescription of provisional measures under Article 290(5) LOSC,[17] requesting the Hamburg Tribunal to order India to refrain from exercising any form of jurisdiction over the *Enrica Lexie* incident and lift the restrictions imposed on the personal liberty of the two Italian marines. However, in its order of 24 August 2015, the ITLOS confined itself to prescribing that both Italy and India were to suspend all court proceedings before their respective domestic courts and refrain from initiating new ones.[18]

Italy subsequently submitted to the Annex VII Arbitral Tribunal, which in the meantime had been constituted, a request for the prescription of provisional measures under Article 290(1) LOSC, requesting the Tribunal to order India to take such measures as were necessary to relax Sergeant Girone's bail

---

[17] 'Pending the constitution of an arbitral tribunal to which the dispute is being submitted under this section, any court or tribunal agreed by the parties or, failing such agreement within two weeks from the date of the request for provisional measures, the International Tribunal for the Law of the Sea (...), may prescribe, modify or revoke provisional measures in accordance with this article if it considers that *prima facie* the tribunal which is to be constituted would have jurisdiction and that the urgency of the situation so requires. Once constituted, the tribunal to which the dispute has been submitted may modify, revoke or affirm those provisional measures, acting in conformity with paragraphs 1 to 4.'

[18] On this order, see: A. Cannone, 'L'ordinanza del Tribunale internazionale del diritto del mare sulla vicenda della *Enrica Lexie*', 98 *Rivista di diritto internazionale*, 2015, pp. 1144–1154; N. Aloupi, 'Chronique', 120 *Revue générale de droit international public*, 2016, pp. 145–148; L. Schiano di Pepe, 'International Tribunal for the Law of the Sea, Case 24, The *Enrica Lexie* Incident (Italy v. India), Provisional Measures', 1 *Asia-Pacific Journal of Ocean Law and Policy*, 2016, pp. 146–149.

conditions and enable him to return to Italy for the entire duration of the arbitration proceedings. In its order of 26 April 2016, the Arbitral Tribunal essentially granted Italy's request; in the operative part of the order, however, it not only imposed on the parties an obligation to cooperate in order to ensure that Sergeant Girone remained under the authority of the Supreme Court of India while back in Italy, but confirmed Italy's obligation to return Sergeant Girone to India in case, at the end of the proceedings, the Arbitral Tribunal found that the respondent State had jurisdiction over him in respect of the *Enrica Lexie* incident.

As briefly noted at the beginning of this article, it is worth considering what purpose the two tribunals wanted the provisional measures they prescribed to serve.

To this end, let us begin with the ITLOS and examine point 1 of the operative part of the order, which reads: 'Italy and India shall both suspend all court proceedings and shall refrain from initiating new ones which may aggravate or extend the dispute submitted to the Annex VII arbitral tribunal or might jeopardize the carrying out of any decision which the tribunal may render.'

Thus, besides being aimed at preserving the respective rights of the parties to the dispute (a function expressly provided for in paragraph 1 of Article 290 LOSC—to which paragraph 5 of that article refers—and mentioned in the grounds of the order[19]), the provisional measures prescribed by the Hamburg Tribunal served two additional purposes. In the Tribunal's view, they were meant to avoid the aggravation or extension of the dispute, as well as to ensure that the execution of the decision(s) eventually rendered by the Arbitral Tribunal that was to be constituted would not be prejudiced, or even made impossible, due to a changed legal situation resulting from the continuation or initiation of court proceedings.

This is not peculiar to the order of 24 August 2015: quite the opposite, in fact, since the atypical purpose of preventing the aggravation of the dispute—'atypical' because not provided for by LOSC or the ITLOS Rules—can be said to be a constant feature of the Hamburg Tribunal's case law on provisional measures. It must be emphasized, however, that, due to the nature of the measures ordered by the Tribunal (which, as noted above, were different from those requested by the applicant party and prescribed under Article 89(5) of the ITLOS Rules), the two functions attributed to provisional measures in the *Enrica Lexie* case are of particular significance.

Let us examine each of them more closely, starting with the function of avoiding a situation where the Annex VII Arbitral Tribunal—which the

---

19   ITLOS, supra, note 2, paras. 125–26.

ITLOS, in accordance with Article 290(5) LOSC, regarded as having *prima facie* jurisdiction—[20] makes a decision on jurisdiction in the case after one or both parties have claimed or started to exercise jurisdiction. First of all, this function is connected with the purpose of preserving the respective rights of the parties. In other words, the main intention of the ITLOS was to remove the risk that, given the usual length of arbitration proceedings, the decisions of the Hague Tribunal will come too late for the parties to the dispute. The aforesaid purpose includes not only an award on the merits concerning whether Italy or India has the right to exercise jurisdiction under LOSC, but also any other order or decision that the Arbitral Tribunal may render. And indeed, as noted above, Italy, without requesting a modification of the measures ordered by the ITLOS, which continue to be binding on the parties, requested further provisional measures to the Arbitral Tribunal, obtaining a relaxation of the restrictions imposed on Sergeant Girone by the Indian judicial authorities.

With regard to the purpose of avoiding the aggravation or extension of the dispute, it has been noted above that, even though not expressly provided for by LOSC or the ITLOS Rules, it is a function that the Hamburg Tribunal usually attributes to provisional measures. Since its order of 11 March 1998 in the case of the *M/V 'Saiga' (No. 2) (Saint Vincent and the Grenadines v Guinea)*,[21] the ITLOS has always deemed it appropriate to use this specific purpose as one of the grounds for granting and ordering provisional measures.[22]

This is a different approach from that taken by the International Court of Justice (ICJ) in its case law concerning interim measures of protection. While the ICJ orders provisional measures aimed at preventing the aggravation or

---

20 The ITLOS was of the view that a dispute appeared to exist between Italy and India concerning the interpretation and application of LOSC: see ITLOS, supra, note 2, paras. 53–54; The Arbitral Tribunal reached the same conclusion: see PCA, supra, note 2, para. 55.

21 *The M/V Saiga*, (Saint Vincent and the Grenadines v Guinea), ITLOS Case No 2, Order of 11 March 1998, para. 44 of the grounds for the order and point 2 of the operative part, available at www.itlos.org, accessed on 3 August 2016.

22 *Southern Bluefin Tuna*, (New Zealand v Japan; Australia v Japan), ITLOS Cases Nos 3 and 4, Order of 27 August 1999, para. 90; *MOX Plant*, (Ireland v United Kingdom), ITLOS Case No 10, Order of 3 December 2001, para. 85; *Land Reclamation by Singapore in and around the Straits of Johor*, (Malaysia v Singapore), ITLOS Case No 11, Order of 8 October 2003; *Ara Libertad*, (Argentina v Ghana), ITLOS Case No 20, Order of 15 December 2012, para. 101; *Arctic Sunrise*, (Netherlands v Russian Federation), ITLOS Case No 22, Order of 22 November 2013, para. 98; *Delimitation of Maritime Boundary between Ghana and Côte d'Ivoire* (Ghana/Côte d'Ivoire), ITLOS Case No 23, Order of 22 April 2015, para. 103. available at www.itlos.org, accessed on 3 August 2016.

THE DISPUTE CONCERNING THE *ENRICA LEXIE* INCIDENT   527

extension of the dispute only when it considers that the circumstances of the case so require,[23] the ITLOS constantly reiterates this additional purpose.

After all, the ITLOS is fully aware that its principal mission is to contribute to the resolution of the international disputes submitted to it,[24] including in the context of provisional measure proceedings under Article 290 LOSC (and it makes little difference whether the Tribunal is seized of the substance of the dispute or has jurisdiction pending the constitution of an arbitral tribunal). Therefore, the ITLOS tries to identify the most appropriate remedies for preventing, among other things, the aggravation of the dispute and, where necessary, imposes on the parties an obligation to cooperate with each other.

Cooperation obligations have been imposed also in the *Enrica Lexie* case, not by the ITLOS, but by the Arbitral Tribunal. In its order of 29 April 2016, in addition to prescribing said obligations in letter (*a*) of the operative part, the Tribunal gave (at least) one[25] specific indication as to how to fulfil them, ordering that Italy and India cooperate in proceedings before the Supreme Court of India to 'achieve a relaxation of the bail conditions of Sergeant Girone'.

Now, the obligation to cooperate imposed by the order of 29 April 2016 certainly has the goal of preventing the aggravation of the dispute—or rather, that is the main goal towards which the obligation is directed, since cooperation facilitates the opening or resumption of negotiations during the course of the proceedings and may thus lead, if said negotiations are successful, to the settlement of the dispute. But there is more: this obligation is also connected with the purpose set out in Article 290(1) LOSC,[26] namely, the preservation of the

---

23 See, for instance, ICJ, *Request for Interpretation of the Judgment of 15 June 1962 in the Case Concerning the Temple of Preah Vihear* (Cambodia v Thailand), Provisional Measures, *ICJ Reports 2011*, pp. 551–552, 555, paras. 59 and 69 B4.

24 See *Dispute Concerning Delimitation of the Marine Boundary between Bangladesh and Myanmar in the Bay of Bengal* (Bangladesh/Myanmar), ITLOS Case No 16, Judgment of 14 March 2012, para. 391, available at www.itlos.org, accessed on 3 August 2016.

25 As can be inferred from the expression 'including in' contained in letter (*a*) of the operative part.

26 It should be kept in mind that, in the present case, the Arbitral Tribunal was called upon to grant provisional measures under Article 290(1) LOSC. In this regard, India argued that Italy had in fact submitted the same request for provisional measures as the one submitted to, and rejected by, ITLOS. The Arbitral Tribunal, however, dismissed this argument. After recalling the different functions of paragraphs 1 and 5 of Article 290 LOSC, it explained that '[b]efore ITLOS, Italy has made the far-reaching request 'that restrictions on the liberty, security and movement of the Marines be immediately lifted to enable Sergeant Girone to travel and remain in Italy...' By contrast, before the present Arbitral Tribunal, Italy now requests that India 'take such measures as are necessary to relax the

respective rights of the parties. Indeed, the order of 29 April 2016 insists on this aspect, with the Arbitral Tribunal raising a number of related points, lest the provisional measure, despite being imposed on both parties, be perceived as favoring the interests of the claimant State over those of the respondent State.

The first point emphasized in the order is Italy's undertaking to return Sergeant Girone to the Indian authorities should the Tribunal find that India has exclusive jurisdiction over him in respect of the *Enrica Lexie* incident. The Arbitral Tribunal, which checked the acceptability of this undertaking with the respondent State,[27] mentions Italy's obligation to guarantee the return of Girone several times in the grounds of the order[28] and finally 'confirms' it in letter (*b*) of the operative part.

Another point stressed by the Tribunal is the protection of the prerogatives of the Supreme Court of India. Almost as if in dialogue with the Court, the Arbitral Tribunal requested that Sergeant Girone's bail conditions be relaxed, but at the same time specified that this provisional measure would not alter the jurisdiction of the Court. Indeed, '[s]uch jurisdiction would continue if the Supreme Court, in light of the order of the Arbitral Tribunal, authorizes Sergeant Girone to spend time in Italy as part of his bail until the Arbitral Tribunal delivers a decision on the merits of the case.'[29]

A final point concerns the nature of Italy's second request for provisional measures: being, as noted above, a request submitted pursuant to Article 290(1), it does not aim to—and cannot—modify the measures ordered by the ITLOS. Since said measures are unaffected, all national court proceedings continue to be suspended. Therefore, according to the Arbitral Tribunal, there would be 'no legal interest in Sergeant Girone's physical presence in India' and, ultimately, 'no material change' for India.[30]

---

bail conditions on Sergeant Girone in order to enable him to return to Italy...' The requested measures are intended to change the physically location of Sergeant Girone's bail without prejudice the authority of India's courts.' (para. 75).

27 After the conclusion of the first day of the hearing, the Arbitral Tribunal put some questions to the parties (see paras. 32–47 of the Order, PCA, supra, note 2). The fifth question was, 'In light of Italy's request, what commitments on the part of Italy would be acceptable to India?' To which the Agent for India responded, '(...) India needs to be assured that in case the Tribunal finds that India has jurisdiction, the presence of Sergente Girone would be ensured. Towards that end, India would deem it necessary that the Tribunal itself fix these guarantees.'
28 See PCA, supra, note 2, paras. 95, 108, 126–131.
29 See ibid., para. 105.
30 See ibid., para. 107.

4 The Reference to 'Considerations of Humanity' in the Orders Issued by the Two Tribunals

Last but not least, the provisional measure ordered by the Arbitral Tribunal takes into account the so-called 'considerations of humanity'.

This is probably the most innovative aspect of the order of 29 April 2016. Here, for the first time we find a reference to considerations of humanity in the operative part of a decision rendered by one of the courts or tribunals having jurisdiction under Part XV of LOSC. In this regard, it should be recalled that, since its judgment in *Saiga No. 2*, the ITLOS has repeatedly held—including in the *Enrica Lexie* case—that 'considerations of humanity must apply to the Law of the Sea as they do in other areas of international law.'[31] Furthermore, it reiterated in *Louisa* that the State Parties to LOSC 'are required to fulfil their obligations under international law, in particular human rights law.'[32] And an important reference to compliance with international norms on human rights can be found in the grounds of the judgment rendered by the Annex VII Arbitral tribunal in the *Arctic Sunrise* case.[33]

In its order of 29 April 2016, however, the Arbitral Tribunal—unlike the ITLOS—goes beyond mere reference to human rights.

In its provisional measures order in the *Enrica Lexie* case, the ITLOS confined itself to: (i) reaffirm its view that considerations of humanity must apply on the law of the sea as they do in other areas of international law; and (ii) acknowledge the grief and suffering of the families of the victims of the incident and the consequences that the lengthy restriction on liberty entail for the two Italian marines.[34]

---

31 See *The M/V Saiga*, supra, note 21, Judgment of 1 July 1999, para. 155; *'Juno Trader'* (Saint Vincent and Grenadines v Guinea Bissau), ITLOS Case No 13, Judgment of 18 December 2004, para. 77; ITLOS, supra, note 2, paras. 133–135. https://www.itlos.org. Accessed 3 August 2016.

32 *M/V Louisa* (Saint Vincent and Grenadines v Spain), ITLOS Case No 18, Judgment of 28 May 2013, para. 155. With regard to the 'due process of law', see ITLOS, *'Juno Trader'*, supra, note 30, Judgment, 28 May 2013, paras. 38–39; and *Tomimaru* (Japan v Russian Federation), ITLOS Case No 15, Judgment of 6 August 2007, para. 76, available at www.itlos.org, accessed on 3 August 2016.

33 *Arctic Sunrise* (Netherlands v Russian Federation), PCA Case No 2014-02, Award on the Merits, 14 August 2015, para. 198, available at https://pccases.com/web/view/21, accessed 3 August 2016.

34 ITLOS, supra, note 2, paras. 133–135.

By contrast, the Arbitral Tribunal—in the grounds[35] as well as, and above all, in the operative part of the order—attributed an additional function to the first provisional measure ordered: namely, to 'give effect to the concept of considerations of humanity'.

The Arbitral Tribunal seems aware of the risk that the provisional measure prescribed by the ITLOS, being still in effect, may result in a violation of human rights by India. Indeed, the provisional measure ordered by the ITLOS (i.e., the suspension of all proceedings before national courts, and the priority to be given to the settlement of the inter-state dispute concerning jurisdiction over the incident) implies that the measures restricting the liberty of the two Italian marines could be contrary to international human rights obligations, due to the time required to conclude the arbitration proceedings and any criminal proceedings that may be subsequently instituted in one of the two States, as well as to the time already elapsed since the adoption of said restrictive measures by the Indian courts. Judge Jesus expressed similar concerns in his Separate Opinion to the ITLOS order of 24 August 2015: '[t]he detention or restriction on the movement of persons who wait excessively long to be charged with criminal offenses is, per se, a punishment without a trial. In such situations, every day that a person is under detention or subject to restrictions on movement is one day too many to be deprived of his or her liberty'; as a consequence, he was of the view that the Tribunal should have taken into account 'the effects on the health of the marines and their family as a result of a detention that has continued (...) for three and a half years.'[36]

Therefore, with its provisional measure, the Arbitral Tribunal 'gave effect' to the recommendation made by the ITLOS with regard to considerations of humanity and ruled that the cooperation between the parties to ensure a relaxation of the restrictive measures imposed on Sergeant Girone answers this need. In particular, the Tribunal, while deeming it unnecessary, at least in provisional measure proceedings, to engage with the question of alleged breaches of international due process norms,[37] recalled that 'social isolation has been recognized as a relevant factor in considering the relaxation of bail conditions' and emphasized the impact of the 'distance between family members' on said conditions.[38]

Having clarified the rationale behind the references to considerations of humanity made by the Arbitral Tribunal in the *Enrica Lexie* case, as well as by

---

35   See PCA supra, note 2, para. 104.
36   ITLOS, supra, note 2, Separate Opinion of Judge Jesus, paras. 10–11.
37   See PCA, supra, note 2, paras. 117–119.
38   See ibid., para. 104.

the ITLOS and the Arbitral Tribunal in the *Arctic Sunrise* case, we should now try to determine their legal basis.

These references seem to stem from a systematic and coordinated interpretation of treaty law and customary international law. 'Systematic' in that LOSC contains provisions concerning both the protection of life at sea[39] and that of other important human rights.[40] 'Coordinated' because Article 293 LOSC stipulates that a court or tribunal having jurisdiction under the Convention may apply other rules of international law that are not incompatible with the Convention.[41] In this regard, it is worth noting that States Parties, too, must rely on a coordinated interpretation, and this by virtue of the compatibility clause contained in Article 311(2) LOSC, which reads: 'This Convention shall not alter the rights and obligations of States Parties which arise from other agreements compatible with this Convention and which do not affect the enjoyment by other States of their rights or the performance of their obligations under this Convention.'

5 Concluding Remarks

As we have seen, in the orders issued in the *Enrica Lexie* case, both the ITLOS and the Arbitral Tribunal tried to promote the resumption of negotiations between Italy and India by imposing on them a negative obligation not to aggravate the dispute and a positive obligation to cooperate with each other.

The two Tribunals were probably encouraged by the outcome of a number of previous cases. In *Land Reclamation by Singapore in and around the Strait of Johor* (Malaysia v Singapore)[42] and *Ara Libertad* (Argentina v

---

39 See Articles 18(2) and 98 LOSC.

40 See Article 73(3) LOSC: 'Coastal States penalties for violations of fisheries laws and regulations in the exclusive economic zone may not include imprisonment, in the absence of agreements to the contrary by the States concerned, or any other form of corporal punishment.'

41 As confirmed in the literature—see, among others, T. Treves, 'Human Rights and the Law of the Sea', 28 *Berkeley Journal of International Law*, 2010, p. 6, as well as in *Arctic Sunrise*, supra, note 32, para. 198.

42 In its order of 8 October 2003, supra, note 22, the ITLOS, pending the constitution of an arbitral tribunal, ordered that the parties should cooperate with each other. The Tribunal specified that said cooperation was to be implemented not only through 'traditional' consultations, but mainly through the creation of an ad-hoc bilateral Committee of experts tasked with preparing a non-binding report pending the arbitration proceedings. Singapore and Malaysia accepted the recommendations made by the Committee in its report of 5 November 2004 and, based on said recommendations, reached an

Ghana),[43] for example, the execution of the provisional measures ordered by the ITLOS and related negotiations, carried out pending the arbitration proceedings, led to the two disputes being resolved through agreements, rather than adjudicated in court.

The parties to the dispute concerning the *Enrica Lexie* incident, too, could be persuaded to enter into negotiations pending the arbitration proceedings, and see the advantages of reaching an agreed settlement. If new negotiations are launched, it is desirable that they be aimed at reaching a comprehensive agreement which, for instance, defines detailed rules for implementing the repeated request of international organizations for bilateral cooperation against maritime piracy[44] and, more in general, criminal activities at sea that threaten the safety of navigation and the security of coastal States.[45]

---

agreement and thus settled their dispute on 26 April 2005. In addition, the parties requested that the Arbitral Tribunal adopted in its 2005 decision the dispute settlement terms set out in the agreement. See Arbitral Tribunal Constituted Under Annex VII LOSC, *Land Reclamation by Singapore in and around the Strait of Johor* (Malaysia v Singapore) in *Reports of International Arbitral Awards*, XXVII, 2008, 13. A copy of the Agreement of 26 April 2005 can be found in Annex 1 to the arbitration decision.

43 The dispute was due to the fact that the Argentinian warship *Ara Libertad* had been detained in the port of Tema by the Ghanaian authorities. Pending the constitution of an arbitral tribunal in accordance with Annex VII, the ITLOS, in its order of 15 December 2012, supra, note 22, after requesting that both parties refrain from adopting measures that could 'aggravate or extend the dispute' (para. 101), ordered Ghana to 'forthwith and unconditionally release the frigate *Ara Libertad*', and 'ensure that the frigate *Ara Libertad*, its Commander and crew are able to leave the port of Tema'. Following this order, the Supreme Court of Ghana rendered a judgment that led to the end of the detention of the *Ara Libertad*, as well as to the conclusion of an agreement between Ghana and Argentina through which the parties settled their dispute, requesting the Arbitral tribunal to issue a 'termination order'. The Supreme Court's judgment of 20 June 2013, the Settlement Agreement of 27 September 2013 and the termination order of 11 November 2013 are available online at https://pcacases.com/web/view/65. (Accessed 3 August 2016).

44 On the importance of international cooperation in this field, see ITLOS, supra, note 2, para. 24, (Declaration of Judge ad hoc Francioni).

45 As noted by D. Momtaz, 'La lutte contre la criminalité en mer', in R. Casado Raigón & G. Cataldi (eds), *L'évolution et l'état actuel du droit international de la mer. Mélanges de droit de la mer offerts à Daniel Vignes*, Bruylant, 2009, p. 644: 'Les Etats (...) continuent de miser principalement sur la responsabilité de l'Etat du pavillon pour la lutte contre les infractions en haute mer et dans les zones économiques exclusives et sur l'Etat côtier pour celles commises dans les zones maritimes relevant de la souveraineté des Etats. Les multiples réunions organisés au niveau régional sur la sécurité en mer montrent en effet que les Etats, tout en encourageant la coopération, restent toujours réticents quand il s'agit de renoncer à leur prérogatives.'

PART 5

Human Rights

La jurisprudence de la Cour Interaméricaine des Droits de l'Homme et le *jus cogens* (2013-fevrier 2016)[1]

Ricardo Abello-Galvis

La jurisprudence de la Cour Interaméricaine des droits de l'homme (CourIDH) est d'une incroyable richesse dans le domaine de la protection des droits de l'homme dans les États membres de la Convention Américaine relative aux Droits de l'Homme[2] – Pacte de San José-. Cependant, certains concepts ont beaucoup évolués et les critiques ne se sont pas fait attendre. Un de ces concepts est celui de *jus cogens* ; celui-ci génère encore des grandes discussions et, surtout, des différences dans la doctrine. Le but de la Cour lorsqu'elle développe le *jus cogens* est d'améliorer la protection effective des droits de l'homme dans une région qui, historiquement, est fortement frappée par ce genre de violations. Dans cet article nous voulons présenter les multiples décisions dans lesquelles la Cour fait référence au caractère de *jus cogens* de certaines normes du Pacte de San José, entre le début de l'année 2013 et février 2016[3].

L'étude que nous faisons depuis plusieurs années cherche à suivre l'évolution du concept de *jus cogens* pour déterminer s'il s'agit simplement de l'applicabilité du droit positif de l'article 53 et du 64 de la Convention de Vienne sur le droit des traités[4], ou s'il s'agit plutôt d'un développement progressif du droit international en suivant une position dans laquelle l'évolution du droit international des droits de l'homme a marqué un changement d'un droit interétatique (horizontal) à un droit supra étatique (vertical) où il y a des normes qui

---

[1] Cet article fait partie du projet de recherche « ¿Es viable un *Ius cogens* regional ? El alcance de la jurisprudencia de la Corte Interamericana de Derechos Humanos » dans le cadre de la ligne « Tribunaux Internationaux » du Groupe de recherche en Droit International de la Faculté de Droit de l'Universidad del Rosario (Bogotá – Colombie).

[2] http://www.apt.ch/content/files/cd1/Compilation%20des%20textes/5.1/5.1.1_Convention%20Americaine.pdf.

[3] Le présent article fait suite à deux publications sur le sujet et en est la continuation : R. Abello-Galvis, « La Jerarquía normativa en la Corte Interamericana de Derechos Humanos : Evolución jurisprudencial del *ius cogens* 1993-2012 », *Revista del Instituto Brasileiro do Direitos Humanos*, Ano 12, Vol. 12, n°12, 2012, p. 357-375 ; R. Abello-Galvis, « Introducción al estudio de las normas de *Ius Cogens* en el seno de la Comisión de Derecho Internacional – CDI », Universidad Javeriana Revista *Vniversitas*, 2011, p. 75-104.

[4] Nations Unies, *Recueil des traités*, vol. 1155, p. 331.

protègent les individus, même au-delà du volontarisme étatique que Mireille Delmas-Marty appelle un droit universel supra étatique[5].

Il n'y a aucun doute que la Cour Interaméricaine est le tribunal international qui s'est le plus prononcé sur le *jus cogens* dans ces décisions. Elle est aussi le tribunal qui identifie le plus grand nombre de droits à avoir un caractère impératif ou de *jus cogens*, alors que les autres tribunaux internationaux ont été plutôt réticents à faire ce lien.

C'est en 1993, dans l'affaire *Alobotoe*, que la Cour a pour la première fois fait référence à une norme qui ait le caractère de *jus cogens*. Dans cette décision elle a déclaré la nullité d'un « traité » de 1762, en affirmant que :

> The Court does not deem it necessary to investigate whether or not that agreement is an international treaty. Suffice it to say that even if that were the case, the treaty would today be null and void because it contradicts the norms of *jus cogens superveniens*. In point of fact, under that treaty the Saramakas undertake to, among other things, capture any slaves that have deserted, take them prisoner and return them to the Governor of Suriname, who will pay from 10 to 50 florins per slave, depending on the distance of the place where they were apprehended. Another article empowers the Saramakas to sell to the Dutch any other prisoners they might take, as slaves. No treaty of that nature may be invoked before an international human rights tribunal[6].

Après cet intéressant début, la Cour ne s'est plus prononcée pendant plusieurs années. Ce sont les juges qui, dans leurs opinions, ont fait référence au *jus cogens*, mais sans une structure ou un ordre clair qui établissent les conditions ou les éléments requis pour déterminer leur existence. Il a fallu dix ans à la Cour pour utiliser de nouveau le *jus cogens* dans une décision[7].

---

5 Voir M. Delmas-Marty, *Les forces imaginantes du droit, Le Relatif et l'Universel*, Paris, Éditions du Seuil, 2004, p. 53 ; C. Maia, « Le *jus cogens* dans la jurisprudence de la Cour Interaméricaine des Droits de l'Homme », *Le particularisme Interaméricain des droits de l'homme*, L. Hennebel et H. Tigroudja (eds), Paris, Editions Pedone, 2009, p. 292 ; A. A. Cançado Trindade, *International Law for Humankind, towards a New* Jus Gentium, La Haye, Martinus Nijhoff Publishers, 2010, p. 317. Voir A. A. Cançado Trindade, « International Law for Humankind, towards a New *Jus Gentium* », *Recueil des Cours de l'Académie de droit international de la Haye*, Vols. 316-317, La Haye, Martinus Nijhoff Publishers, 2006, p. 353 ; et F. Quispe Remón, « *Ius Cogens* en el Sistema Interamericano : su relación con el debido proceso », *Revista de Derecho, Universidad del Norte*, n°34, 2010, p. 60.

6 CourIDH, arrêt du 10 septembre 1993, *Aloebotoe c. Surinam*, par. 57.

7 CourIDH, arrêt du 27 novembre 2003, *Maritza Urrutia c. Guatemala*, par. 92.

LA JURISPRUDENCE DE LA COUR INTERAMÉRICAINE

Ci-après, nous ferons la révision des décisions dans lesquelles la Cour s'est prononcée sur les normes de *jus cogens*, en les organisant selon les articles du Pacte de San José auxquels elle se réfère. Ainsi, entre 2013 et février 2016, nous avons trouvé des références à trois de ces articles : 1- la torture, 2- la disparition forcée et 3- l'égalité et non-discrimination.

1   Torture

La première fois que la Cour s'est occupée du *jus cogens* en ce qui concerne la torture fut dans l'affaire *Barrios Altos c. Pérou*. Préférant utiliser le mot « indérogeable », elle n'y a cependant pas fait de référence claire et directe ; ce sont les juges qui, dans leurs opinions, s'y sont référés[8]. C'est dans l'affaire *Maritza Urrutia*[9], en 2003, qu'elle a instauré le lien direct du délit de torture avec le *jus cogens*.

Depuis 2013, la ligne jurisprudentielle continue dans le même sens. La décision dans laquelle elle s'est référée à ce délit cette année-là fut dans l'affaire *Mendoza et autres c. Argentine*, réitérant qu'il y a une prohibition absolue de torturer, que ce soit de la torture physique ou psychologique[10]. En 2015, dans l'affaire *Ruano Torres* la Cour a repris mot pour mot ce même argument, en signalant explicitement qu'il y avait violation d'une norme de *jus cogens*[11].

Ainsi, bien que la Cour considère, de façon claire, que la torture fait partie du *jus cogens*, il est curieux que dans l'affaire *Quispialaya Vilcoma*[12] elle a conservé toute l'argumentation relative à ces délits, mais sans faire référence au *jus cogens* dans sa décision. C'est étrange surtout si on tient compte que cette décision fut prise un mois après celle de *Ruano Torres*[13].

Dans l'affaire *Espinoza González*[14] la Cour est allée un peu plus loin que dans les décisions précédentes. En effet, étant donné les circonstances des faits, elle s'est référée au droit international humanitaire. En suivant sa propre jurisprudence elle a, une fois de plus, affirmé que la torture n'est justifiée dans aucune

---

8   CourIDH, arrêt du 14 mars 2001, *Barrios Altos c. Pérou*, par. 41.
9   CourIDH, arrêt du 27 novembre 2003, *Maritza Urrutia c. Guatemala*, par. 92.
10 CourIDH, arrêt du 14 mai 2013, *Mendoza et autres c. Argentine*, par. 199.
11 CourIDH, arrêt du 5 octobre 2015, *Ruano Torres et autres c. El Salvador*, par. 120. Voir aussi : L. Hennebel et H. Tigroudja, *Traité de droit international des Droits de l'homme*, Paris, Editions A. Pedone, 2016, p. 857, 858 et 861.
12 CourIDH, arrêt du 23 novembre 2015, *Quspialaya Vilcapoma c. Pérou*.
13 CourIDH, arrêt du 5 octobre 2015, *Ruano Torres et autres c. El Salvador*, par. 120.
14 CourIDH, arrêt du 20 novembre 2014, *Espinoza González c. Pérou*.

circonstance, même pas en cas de guerres ou menaces de terrorisme par exemple[15]. Dans le cas d'espèce, elle a rappelé sa position dans l'affaire du *Centre pénitencier Castro Castro*[16] en disant que la violence sexuelle à l'encontre des femmes est considérée comme torture et, en conséquence, fait partie du domaine du *jus cogens*.

En ce qui concerne le *non refoulement*, la Cour s'est prononcée sur deux affaires dans la période 2013-15. Dans l'affaire *Famille Pacheco Tineo*[17], elle n'a fait aucune référence à un éventuel caractère de *jus cogens* ; ce n'est que dans l'Avis Consultatif N°21 que la Cour a établi que le principe de *non refoulement* est une des obligations internationales :

> [...] associated with the prohibition of torture is the principle of non-return or non-refoulement. This principle seeks, above all, to ensure the effectiveness of the prohibition of torture in any circumstance and with regard to any person, without any discrimination. Since it is an obligation derived from the prohibition of torture, the principle of non-refoulement in this area is absolute and also becomes a peremptory norm of customary international law; in other words, of *ius cogens*[18].

Il est clair que la Cour a suivi ce qui a été dit par le Rapporteur des Nations Unies Theo van Boven[19], qui cite à son tour le Comité des droits de l'homme, qui affirmait en 1966 que les États parties « ne doivent pas exposer des individus à un risque de torture ou de peines ou traitements cruels, inhumains ou dégradants en les renvoyant dans un autre pays en vertu d'une mesure d'extradition,

---

15   CourIDH, arrêt du 7 septembre de 2004, *Tibi c. Equateur*, par. 143. CourIDH, arrêt du 18 novembre 2004, *De la Cruz Flores c. Pérou*, par. 125. CourIDH, arrêt du 25 novembre 2004, *Lori Berenson Mejia c. Pérou*, par. 100. CourIDH, arrêt du 25 novembre 2005, *García Asto y Ramírez Rojas c. Pérou*, par. 222. CourIDH, arrêt du 6 avril 2006, *Baldeón García c. Pérou*, par. 117. CourIDH, arrêt du 25 novembre 2006, *Pénitencier Miguel Castro Castro c. Pérou*, par. 271. CourIDH, arrêt du 11 mai 2007, *Buenos Alves c. Argentine*, par. 76. CourIDH, arrêt du 22 septembre 2006, *Goiburú et autres c. Paraguay*, par. 93. CourIDH, arrêt du 4 juillet 2007, *Zambrano Vélez et autres c. Equateur*, par. 96. CourIDH, arrêt du 24 novembre 2009, *Affaire de la Massacre de las Dos Erres c. Guatemala*, par. 140.

16   CourIDH, arrêt du 25 novembre 2006, *Pénitencier Miguel Castro Castro c. Pérou*, par. 271.

17   CourIDH, arrêt du 25 novembre 2013, *Famille Pacheco Tineo c. État plurinational de Bolivie*.

18   CourIDH, Avis Consultatif N° 21, *Droits et garantie de filles et garçons dans le contexte de la migration et / ou en besoin de protection international* ; Avis du 19 août 2014, par. 225.

19   Commission des Droits de l'Homme ; Droits Civils et Politiques et, notamment, questions de la torture et de la détention, Rapport soumis par le nouveau rapporteur spécial sur la torture, M. Theo van Boven, E/Cn.4/2002/137, 26 février 2002, par. 14.

d'expulsion et de refoulement »[20]. Même si dans ces deux documents il n'y a aucune référence au *jus cogens*, en raison du lien entre le refoulement d'une personne et le risque de torture, la Cour Interaméricaine a considéré qu'il y a un lien automatique et en conséquence elle a inclus ce principe dans son *corpus juris* de normes impératives.

D'un autre côté, la Cour a aussi analysé l'obligation des États de remplir leur devoir impératif de réaliser les enquêtes dues quand il s'agit d'un délit de torture[21]. En ce sens, elle suit sa propre jurisprudence, établie dans les affaires *Pénitencier Castro Castro*[22] et *Vélez Loor*[23]. En effet, dans *J. c Pérou* la Cour affirme :

> the Court clarifies that the Inter-American Convention against Torture establishes two situations that give rise to the State's obligation to investigate: on the one hand, when a complaint is filed and, on the other, when there is a well-founded reason to believe that an act of torture has been committed within the sphere of the State's jurisdiction. In these situation, the decision to open and conduct an investigation is not a discretionary power of the State, but constitutes a peremptory State obligation derived from international law and cannot be ignored or conditioned by domestic legal provisions or decisions of any kind[24].

Dans ces affaires, la Cour ne fait pas référence au mot *jus cogens*, elle reste dans l'impérativité des obligations d'enquête ; cependant il est clair que ce que la Cour veut instaurer c'est justement le lien qui prévoit que les normes qu'elle considère comme étant de *jus cogens* ont une obligation corrélative qui est celle de réaliser les enquêtes respectives.

Ici, comme dans d'autres affaires déjà citées, au moment où un droit semble bien établi par la Cour, elle nous présente une décision dans laquelle elle change sa rédaction. Cette fois-ci, elle l'a fait dans l'affaire *García Lucero*, en changeant l'« impérativité » habituelle par « l'indérogeabilité », tout en gardant la même idée garantiste face à une norme hiérarchiquement supérieure comme le *jus cogens*. En conséquence, pour l'analyse de cette obligation des États, il faut

---

20   Comité des droits de l'homme ; Observation générale N°20 sur l'article 7 du Pacte international relatif aux droits civils et politiques (1966).
21   Voir aussi : Hennebel et Tigroudja, *Traité de droit international des Droits de l'homme*, op. cit., note 11, p. 1296.
22   CourIDH, arrêt du 25 novembre 2006, *Pénitencier Miguel Castro Castro c. Pérou*, par. 347.
23   CourIDH, arrêt du 23 novembre 2010, *Vélez Loor c. Panamá*, par. 240.
24   CourIDH, arrêt du 27 novembre 2013, *J. c. Pérou*, par. 347.

considérer que « l'impérativité » et « l'indérogeabilité » sont synonymes et que ces deux mots sont à la fois une caractéristique qui fait que ces droits font partie du *corpus juris* du *jus cogens* établi par la Cour Interaméricaine dans sa jurisprudence[25].

Finalement, dans l'affaire *Omar Humberto Maldonado Vargas*, les représentants des victimes ont demandé à la Cour de dire qu'il devrait y avoir une cessation d'effets des preuves obtenues sous la torture[26], ce à quoi la Cour n'a pas donné de réponse.

2   Disparition forcée

De 2013 à 2015 la Cour s'est prononcée sur trois affaires de disparition forcée, mais aucune ne propose de réelles nouveautés, après qu'il lui ait fallu dix ans entre l'affaire *Blake* de 1996 et l'affaire *Goiburú* de 2006[27] pour inclure pour la première fois le mot *jus cogens* dans une décision de disparition forcée[28]. Dans deux des trois nouvelles affaires, *Osorio Rivera*[29] et *Rochac Hernández*[30], la Cour a repris sa jurisprudence constante depuis 2006. Dans *Osorio Rivera* elle réaffirme donc l'idée que :

> The Court has verified the international agreement as regards the analysis of enforced disappearance, which constitutes a gross violation of human rights, given the particular significance of the violations that it entails and the nature of the rights harmed, so that it involves a blatant rejection of the essential principles that underlie the inter-American system, and its prohibition has achieved the status of *jus cogens*[31].

---

25   CourIDH, arrêt du 29 novembre 2006, *La Cantuta c. Pérou*, par. 96, par. 157 et par. 160. CourIDH, arrêt du 24 février 2011, *Caso Gelman c. Uruguay*, par. 183.

26   CourIDH, arrêt du 2 septembre 2015, *Omar Humberto Maldonado Vargas c. Chili*, par. 115.

27   Voir R. Abello-Galvis, « La Jerarquía normativa en la Corte Interamericana de Derechos Humanos : Evolución jurisprudencial del *ius cogens* 1993-2012 », *Revista del Instituto Brasileiro do Direitos Humanos*, Ano 12, Vol. 12, n°12, 2012, p. 363-364.

28   CourIDH, arrêt du 22 septembre 2006, *Goiburú et autres c. Paraguay*, par. 93 et 128. Dans le même sens voir aussi L. Burgorgue-Larsen et A. Ubeda de Torres, « La "guerra" en la jurisprudencia de la Corte Interamericana de Derechos Humanos », *Anuario Colombiano de Derecho Internacional (ACDI)*, Vol. 3 Especial, 2010, p. 129.

29   CourIDH, arrêt du 26 novembre 2013, *Osorio Rivera et famille c. Pérou*, par. 112.

30   CourIDH, arrêt du 14 octobre 2014, *Rochac Hernández et autres c. El Salvador*, par. 92.

31   CourIDH, arrêt du 26 novembre 2013, *Osorio Rivera et famille c. Pérou*, par. 112.

Ici, comme pour la torture, la Cour affirme, dans l'affaire *Rochac*, que ce genre de délits doit être soumis à une enquête, et que la réaliser est une obligation impérative de l'Etat[32]. De façon semblable aux affaires de torture, les États ont donc aussi l'obligation impérative de commencer les enquêtes nécessaires pour que ce genre des délits ne reste pas dans l'impunité. La Cour fait donc référence à une « impérativité » sans utiliser le mot *jus cogens*. Ce que la Cour veut cependant faire, c'est visiblement mettre sur le même pied le délit principal – disparition forcée – et l'obligation d'enquêter. Cette possibilité est considérée par certains comme un « *giant steep* » dans la mesure où cela permettra d'éviter l'absence de sanctions aux plus graves violations de droits de l'homme[33].

Finalement, il est curieux aussi que ce soit dans l'affaire de la *Communauté paysanne de Santa Barbara* que la Cour ne dise pas que les délits de disparition forcée commis contre cette communauté défavorisée ont un caractère de *jus cogens*[34]. Et c'est encore plus étrange si, parmi les victimes, il y a des mineurs d'âge, comme dans l'affaire *Rochac Hernández*[35]. Ici encore, le fait de faire référence explicite ou pas au *jus cogens*, ne change en rien le résultat des sanctions, ni des mécanismes de réparation.

3   Egalité et non-discrimination

De 2013 au mois de février 2016, la Cour Interaméricaine a eu l'occasion de se prononcer six fois dans des affaires où le principe d'égalité et non-discrimination était le sujet à trancher. En termes généraux, la Cour a suivi sa jurisprudence bien établie depuis l'Avis Consultatif N°18 dans lequel elle a dit que « At the current stage of the development of international law, the fundamental principle of equality and non-discrimination has entered the domain of *jus cogens* » et que « That the fundamental principle of equality and non-discrimination, which is of a peremptory nature, entails obligations *erga omnes* of protection that bind all States and generate effects with regard to third parties, including individuals »[36].

---

32   CourIDH, arrêt du 14 octobre 2014, *Rochac Hernández et autres c. El Salvador*, par. 184.
33   L. Burgorgue-Larsen et A. Úbeda de Torres, *The Inter-American Court of Human Rights*, Oxford University Press, Oxford, 2011, p. 300.
34   CourIDH, arrêt du 1 septembre 2015, *Communauté paysanne de Santa Barbara*.
35   CourIDH, arrêt du 14 octobre 2014, *Rochac Hernández et autres c. El Salvador*, par. 184.
36   CourIDH, Avis Consultatif N°18, *Condition juridique et droits des migrants sans papiers* ; Avis du 17 septembre 2003, par. 173-4 et par. 173-5. Voir aussi Hennebel et Tigroudja, *Traité de droit international des Droits de l'homme, op. cit.*, note 11, p. 755.

Dans cinq des six affaires de la période analysée, la Cour utilise la même phrase pour dire avec toute clarté que « At the actual stage of the evolution of international law, the fundamental principle of equality and nondiscrimination has entered the realm of *jus cogens* »[37]. La sixième, par contre, ne fait pas de référence directe au *jus cogens*, elle fait un lien du point de vue des normes de droit interne pour octroyer la nationalité et dans ce sens elle établit que ces normes ne peuvent pas placer en position de discrimination des groupes de personnes qui veulent exercer le droit de demander une nationalité, c'est-à-dire que les conditions doivent être les mêmes pour tous ceux qui la demandent[38].

Conclusions

Au vu de l'évolution du *jus cogens* à la Cour Interaméricaine entre 2013 et février 2016, la Cour n'a pas eu à créer de nouveaux arguments, elle a plutôt continué à consolider la jurisprudence existante sur les divers sujets sur lesquels elle a dû se prononcer. Elle n'a pas cherché à inclure des nouveaux droits dans le domaine des normes impératives.

Comme aspects que nous pouvons critiquer, d'un point de vue général, à propos des décisions de la Cour c'est qu'il n'y a pas de différence de fond dans le fait que la cour fasse, ou pas, une référence directe et claire au concept de *jus cogens*. Le résultat des sanctions et/ou des réparations, sont toutes semblables dans la mesure où elles gardent les mêmes paramètres ; en aucun cas, sauf dans l'affaire *Aloebotoe*, la Cour n'a utilisé la vraie conséquence de l'existence d'une contradiction entre une norme et le *jus cogens*, c'est-à-dire déclarer sa nullité[39]. La Cour Interaméricaine a utilisé ce concept plutôt comme une circonstance d'aggravation punitive, sans qu'il n'y ait une plus forte sanction envers les États condamnés pour ce genre de violations des droits de l'homme.

---

37   CourIDH, arrêt du 19 mai 2014, *Veliz Franco et autres c. Guatemala*, par. 205. CourIDH, arrêt du 29 mai 2014, *Norín Catriman et autres c. Chili*, par. 197. CourIDH, arrêt du 22 juin 2015, *Granier et autres (Radio Caracas Télévision) c. Venezuela*, par. 215. CourIDH, arrêt du 19 novembre 2015, *Velásquez Paiz et autres c. Guatemala*, par. 173 et CourIDH, arrêt du 26 février 2016, *Duque c. Colombie*, par. 91.

38   CourIDH, arrêt du 28 août 2014, *Personnes dominicaines et haïtiennes expulsées c. République Dominicaine*, par. 357.

39   CourIDH, arrêt du 10 septembre 1993, *Aloebotoe c. Surinam*, par. 57.

La Cour a établi un lien direct entre certaines normes principales avec un caractère de *jus cogens* (torture / Disparition forcée) et la norme corrélative de procédure comme obligation impérative de l'État (enquêter). Nous considérons que ce lien ne correspond pas à ce que le Droit international général a conçu comme étant une norme de *jus cogens*. En effet, l'obligation d'investigations ne devrait pas dépendre de la gravité du délit principal. Ceci dit, ce que la Cour recherche est justement que l'obligation existe toujours puisque, comme l'a dit le professeur Momtaz, elle « […] pourra empêcher que le temps n'efface les conséquences de l'illégalité et que l'effectivité ne triomphe aux dépens des normes impératives du droit international général »[40].

---

40   D. Momtaz, « L'obligation de ne pas prêter aide ou assistance au maintien d'une situation créée par la violation d'une norme impérative du droit international général », *Anuario Colombiano de Derecho Internacional* (ACDI), vol. 10, 2017, pp. 218. Doi: dx.doi.org/10.12804/revistas.urosario.edu.co/acdi/a.5298.

The Notion of Human Rights and the Issue of Cultural Relativism

Ove Bring

The 1948 United Nations Declaration of Human Rights[1] was labelled 'Universal'. The ambition of later UN Conventions in the field has been universalism. However, behind the formula of 'Asian values' and the national interpretative attitudes of certain Arab and African countries lies the notion that the concept of human rights is basically a Western construct. The concept of cultural relativism, or particularism, is obviously a challenge to the ambition of universalism. But irrespective of when the modern human-rights movement is considered to have emerged (an issue which is under debate), elements of human-rights thought appeared in Oriental civilizations long before a more holistic approach was developed through the Western Enlightenment. As to rights manifestations in history, there is no clear division between the East and the West, or the North and the South. This paper lists a number of non-Western contributions to human- rights thought and concludes with a comment on Samuel Moyn's perception of human-rights history.

1 Human Rights and Sovereignty

The arrival of human rights on the international legal scene, through the UN Charter of 1945 and the Universal Declaration of 1948, constituted a dramatic break with the postulates of traditional international law. The issue penetrated the shield that so far had protected the sovereignty of States. International law had given each State the appearance of a solid structure, perceived by other States as a box, the inner mechanisms of which could not be challenged. Today, the human-rights argument is forcing States to explain how they protect certain values, how they treat their nationals and foreigners, protect minorities, administer justice, receive refugees, run prisons, and so on.

Traditionally, in international law, individuals could be protected only as members of a group, as citizens of a certain State, or as members of a religious or national minority. Now, through successive developments after 1945, they are to be protected as single human beings.

---

1 UN Doc. A/RES/III/217 A, 10 December 1948.

Protection very seldom means intervention from the outside, although this, in cases of very serious violations, is a possibility under the UN Charter. Protection means, rather, 'intervention light' (or interference), in the sense that other States, or international bodies, can address and criticize practices that are seen as human-rights violations. Otherwise, military or subversive intervention in domestic affairs is prohibited under international law.

Human rights are matters of what also could be called transnational law, since someone's nationality is irrelevant when that someone claims his or her rights. This is why the traditional approach of State-based jurisdictional exclusivity has given way to a realization that the rights of human beings are a matter of international concern. This international dimension is the standard argument against the claim that human-rights *criticism* should not be allowed as it is an intervention in domestic affairs. Human rights are a matter of international concern, not only a matter of domestic affairs. And criticism does not amount to intervention.

The Universal Declaration was planned to set the standards for further legal development. The Declaration itself was not of a legal nature when adopted in 1948 (UN Declarations are as a rule only political statements), but over time its principles have matured into binding customary law. As intended, it has served as a platform for treaty-making. In 1965 the two landmark Conventions were adopted: the International Covenant on Civil and Political Rights[2] and the Covenant on Economic, Social and Cultural Rights.[3] Among the many conventions negotiated since then are the 1984 Convention against Torture and Cruel, Inhuman or Degrading Treatment or Punishment[4] and the 1989 Convention on the Rights of the Child.[5]

2   The Nature of Human Rights

Not surprisingly, when lawyers speak of human rights they mean that they really are *rights in a legal sense*. According to the American professor Wesley N. Hohfeld's strict rights theory, first presented in 1913, the rights of one should correspond to duties of another.[6] At least, rights that constitute claims should

---

[2] 999 UNTS 171.
[3] 993 UNTS 3.
[4] 1465 UNTS 85.
[5] 1577 UNTS 3.
[6] W. N. Hohfeld, 'Fundamental Legal Conceptions as Applied in Judicial Reasoning', 23 *Yale Law Journal*, 1913, p. 16.

correspond to duties. Civil and Political Rights, like the freedoms of expression, religion and assembly and the right to respect for private and family life, all produce a negative obligation of the State. States *shall not* subject people to torture or to inhuman or degrading treatment. States *shall not* prevent the right of a fair trial or deprive persons of their liberty without support in law. States *shall not* interfere with the right to freedom of movement. And so on. These rights are claimed and States shall simply not interfere with their free exercise. The Hohfeld criterion for a claim right is thus fulfilled. These negative legal obligations of Governments are in most cases expected to be secured by legislation.

Economic and social rights, on the other hand, are rights in which positive, affirmative action by the Government is required. States are expected to *do* something. Economic and social rights are viewed as welfare claims upon Governments which may or may not be realized, depending upon availability of resources. Here the Hohfeld criterion does not seem to be fulfilled. Nevertheless, international lawyers consider economic and social rights to be on the same level and as binding as civil and political rights.

The concept of human rights operates as a binding legal relationship on two levels. On the international level States through treaties undertake to transfer the agreed human-rights obligations to the domestic scene; and on the national level States are duty bound to respect the obligations vis-à-vis their citizens and other individuals within their jurisdiction. States must implement human rights domestically in one way or another, even though they may have 'a margin of appreciation' in doing so. They are expected to enact needed legislation and to use their legal system to protect individuals from ill treatment not only by the State itself but also by other individuals.

Thus international law tries to influence States to conform to certain behaviour on the national level. It is striking that international human-rights obligations are, in some ways, fundamentally different from other international obligations. States that ratify human-rights treaties are primarily committed to respect the norms in relation *not to one another*, but in relation to persons within their jurisdiction. But if this does not work in practice, there are few binding mechanisms that can achieve compliance. One is to be found on a regional level through the Court of Human Rights in Strasbourg, established by the 1950 Convention for the Protection of Human Rights and Fundamental Freedoms (better known as the European Convention on Human Rights).

Expressing a common view, Thomas Hobbes wrote in *Leviathan* in 1651 that 'Covenants without swords are but words.'[7] In the international community

---

7 *Leviathan*, chapter 17. However, when Hobbes discussed 'the performance of covenants', he did not refer to international agreements but to the situation in domestic society. In fact, the

enforcement is a rare quantity. Under the framework of the Covenant on Civil and Political Rights, a specific Human Rights Committee has since 1967 had the power to adjudicate violations brought before it; but it has no power to enforce its decisions. In addition, this control system is established through an Optional Protocol, meaning that States can avoid being bound by it. To say that human rights are legally binding is not to say that there is an Authority (with a capital A) with the power to hold sovereign States to the law. Sovereignty may be somewhat eroded, but it is still protective of Governments. On the other hand, international obligations always reduce national sovereignty to a certain extent. There is still a certain tension between general international law protecting States and international human-rights law protecting individuals, since the goal of the human rights idea seems geared towards redefining sovereignty. But for the time being, the UN mechanisms for compliance have to rely on independent reporting and the 'naming and shaming' of Governments.

Human rights today represent the modern interpretation and expansion of the traditional concept of the *rule of law*, or with a German expression, the *Rechtsstaat*. In 2015, we celebrated the 800 Anniversary of Magna Carta, concluded on the meadow at Runnymede on the Thames, on 15 June, 1215. At that time the king of England recognized that his power had to be restricted and that the rights of barons and clergy had to be guaranteed.[8] This was the starting point for a 'rule-of-law' development in England, in other parts of Europe and later in the United States. Over time, it was recognized that not only the rights of barons and clergy were to be protected, but also those of the common man. The principle of equality before the law emerged and was soon generally recognized.

Today 'rule of law' means constitutional power-sharing, legal predictability, and human rights, including democracy. Quite another thing is the concept of 'rule *by* law', which is maintained by countries like China and Vietnam for example, where the regulation as such is seen as enough and the law in question could be completely void of individual or democratic rights. Legal predictability may be achieved thus, but not the characteristics of a *Rechtsstaat*.

---

correct quote is: 'Covenants, without the sword, are but words, and of no strength to secure a man at all.' See George H. Sabine, *A History of Political Theory*, 3rd edition, George H. Harrap, 1963, reprinted 1971, p. 468.

8   See for example N. Vincent, *Magna Carta, A Very Short Introduction*, Oxford University Press, 2012.

3 The Legacy of, and the Relationship to, Natural Law

The historical basis of the rights doctrine is to be found in ancient Greek and Hellenistic stoicism and its concept of *natural law*. The natural-law discourse was later developed by Hugo Grotius and after him by John Locke and the French philosophers of the Enlightenment. Grotius worked with a somewhat unclear distinction between natural law (descending from a higher reason) and divine law (descending from God).[9] Locke argued that human reason implied natural rights of individuals. Certain rights were seen as self-evidently pertaining to individuals as human beings; obvious examples were the rights to life, liberty and property, implying freedom from arbitrary rule.[10] The rights discourse was used to affirm that all individuals, solely by virtue of being human, have natural rights that no society or State should deny them. Since having natural rights was linked to being a human being, it was not surprising that the phraseology of *natural rights* would later be changed to *human rights*. Over time the content of the rights concept was also changed—to include less divinity and more reason.

The modernized natural-law approach of the Enlightenment enabled recourse to superior norms which restrained arbitrary governmental power; but this reliance on natural law fell out of use in the 1800s since it was not based on hard facts or empirical conclusions. Nevertheless, natural-law thinking proved to be of immense importance after World War II, as a supplement to state-centred positivism—which had served to legitimize Nazi legislation leading to suppression and the Holocaust.

The preamble of the Universal Declaration is influenced by natural-law thought in its recognition of 'the inherent dignity and ... equal and inalienable rights of all members of the human family ... [as] the foundation of freedom, justice and peace in the world.' And Article 1 of the Declaration states, in the same natural-law-oriented manner, that 'All human beings are born free and

---

9   M. Koskenniemi notes that for Grotius 'it is reason which emerges as the all-powerful authority: natural law would exist even on the assumption—*per imposssibile*—that there were no God.' *From Apology to Utopia, The Structure of International Legal Argument*, Lakimiesliiton Kustannus, 1989, p. 74.

10 Locke argued that 'no one ought to harm another in his life, health, liberty and possessions' and that 'all men may be restrained from invading others' rights'. These rights are also valid in relation to governmental power: 'And hence it is evident that absolute monarchy ... is indeed inconsistent with civil society.' *Two Treatises of Civil Government, Book II* (1690), quoted by Clarence Morris (ed) in *The Great Legal Philosophers*, University of Pennsylvania Press, 1959, pp. 137, 138 and 148.

equal in dignity of rights. They are endowed with reason and conscience and should act towards one another in a spirit of brotherhood.'

The Universal Declaration in part represented a return to the Hellenistic and Grotian heritage of natural law, a return intended to give individuals the civil courage to stand up for their rights when the State suppressed them or ordered them to do wrong; courage to stand against perverted positivism.

Martti Koskenniemi has in his famous dissertation addressed the conflict between natural law and positivism in terms of Utopia and Apology. Utopia indicated a higher reason of idealism coming from above; and Apology an earth-bound political realism. Against that background Koskenniemi pointed to the interplay or clash between descending and ascending norms, between legal arguments descending from an objective, normative 'truth' of international morality; and legal arguments ascending from a subjective State practice of consent and self-interest. In his view this has created credibility problems for the international legal project. The structure of international legal argumentation is said to allow for manipulation and positions of non-predictability.[11]

In my view, this interplay between higher norms and realistic State acceptance has been a fruitful element in what has been called the human rights revolution, the process that started in 1945 and 1948. Natural-law input was a useful start for a process that later relied on treaty positivism.

4   Universality and Particularism

The progressive human rights development after 1948 may today have come to a halt—due to cultural relativism among States and the emergence of non-state actors such as Al-Quaida, ISIS and Boko Haram, actors that neglect or deny human rights completely. But I will not deal with this extreme threat to the values of the international community here. Instead I focus on the relativistic approach to human rights, the view of some States that the cultural and geographical context defines what human rights norms need to be taken into account in a certain region.[12]

The concept of *cultural relativism*, or particularism, is a challenge to the UN ambition of universalism. The landmark Declaration of 1948 was labelled

---

11   Koskenniemi, supra, note 9, pp. 40–50.
12   See for example the texts on Cultural relativism in M. Dixon & R. McCorquodale (eds), *Cases and Materials on International Law*, Oxford University Press, 2003, pp. 184–188 and the chapter on Universality in S. Marks & A. Clapham, *International Human Rights Lexicon*, Oxford University Press, 2005.

'Universal'. The two Covenants of 1966, with numerous States parties from all over the world, have likewise a universal ambition. So have later human-rights treaties, even if they create binding law only among the contracting parties. Many of these treaty-based norms could well develop into general customary law over time, even if the number of treaty ratifications does not signal complete universality.

If human rights are *universal* they apply to all countries and to the benefit of all peoples. However, if certain human rights are qualified by regional or cultural norms when applied in that region or culture, if they are thus 'relativized', the demand for universal application is challenged. Such a rejection of universality is today a reality in the practice of certain States. For example, the debate on *Asian values* includes the argument that the West cannot press onto others its own perception of human rights. The gist of this position is that human rights as understood in the West are founded on individualism and individual freedoms, while the normative tradition of Asia is based on the primacy of community and social discipline. It could be summarized as on the one hand 'freedom and liberty', on the other 'order and discipline'. In Singapore and Kuala Lumpur and other places, it has been argued that the Western demand for individual liberty and State non-interference has to yield to Asian community values. It is also argued that in Asia economic development is more important than the civil and political rights emphasized in the West. The general proposition is that rights are culture-specific. The same argument is repeated in Islamic thought and by political elites in some African countries.

The Indian economist Amartya Sen has joined the debate on Asian values and maintained that there is *no* clear division between the East and the West in an historical perspective. He has referred to early Indian human-rights-oriented thought and has mentioned political figures like Kautilya, Ashoka and Akbar.[13] I return to these shortly.

In my own book on the history of human rights (2011),[14] I wanted to challenge the idea that human rights are exclusively Western constructs, with no universal validity. I now consider some individuals who have played an important role in history in this context. I list examples which underline the non-Western contributions to the idea of human rights.

Eleanor Roosevelt was keenly aware of the importance of anchoring the UN Declaration in trans-cultural thought. In her Human Rights Commission,

---

13   A. Sen, 'Human Rights and Asian Values', The Carnegie Council Morgenthau Lecture of 1997, published in *The New Republic*, 14 and 21 July 1997.

14   O. Bring, *De mänskliga rättigheternas väg—genom historien och litteraturen*, Atlantis, 2011.

she worked with people from different regions and she relied on answers to a questionnaire sent out to experts all over the world.[15]

Charles Malik (Lebanon), a professor of philosophy, was Rapporteur of the 1947 Commission. Although of Christian faith and educated at a German university, he saw himself as a representative of the Arabic world.

Peng Chun Chan (China), a philosopher and a diplomat, was Vice Chairman of the Commission. He underlined the need to include Confucian values in the Declaration.

Thanks to Hansa Mehta (India) the Commission included the formula of 'equal rights of men and *women*' in the Preamble of the Declaration. She is basically remembered for that contribution, but her participation in the Commission was also important from the perspective of cultural representation. Note that in 1947 Mahatma Gandhi had been asked for his views on Indian traditions and he contributed a memo on the relationship between rights and duties. Ghandi in a sense influenced the formulations in the Declaration that everyone also has 'duties to the community' and that 'respect for the rights and freedoms of others' is essential (Article 29).

The Chilean member of the Commission, Hernan Santa Cruz, pressed for the inclusion of economic and social rights, a novelty at the time, and in this he had the support of Omar Loutfi of Egypt. Both had the support Eleanor Roosevelt, who had received a mandate from President Truman to go beyond the traditional rights doctrine in order to muster support from non-Western countries.

5 Human-rights-oriented Thought before the Western Enlightenment

I now turn to different examples of human-rights-oriented thought in earlier civilizations.

According to a number of international-law textbooks, an early example of a practice on the protection of prisoners of war (POWs) is attributed to ancient Egypt during the second millennium BC, probably around 1450–1430 BC. At that time, Queen Hatschepsut conducted a progressive and peace-oriented policy in relation to Egypt's neighbours. Otherwise, the Egyptians were not known for anything other than cruelty to their prisoners, although the opposite perception was conveyed by Giuseppe Verdi in his opera *Aida*, where the

---

15   See M. A. Glendon, *A World Made New, Eleanor Roosevelt and the Universal Declaration of Human Rights*, Random House, 2001.

Ethiopian prisoners of war seemed to enjoy excellent treatment. It is believed that this was in fact the situation during Hatschepsut's reign, but we do not know for sure.

Pharaoh Ramses II of Egypt concluded a peace treaty with the Hatti kingdom in 1270 BC (the first documented treaty in international relations). Both parties recognized the rights of asylum-seekers and refugees to cross borders and receive protection.

Cyrus the Great of Persia (d. 530 BC) has gone down in history as father of the first declaration of rights and guarantees offered to his people. His kingdom stretched from the high hills of India in the East to the lowlands of Egypt in the West. For its time, it was universal coverage. To secure control of his vast country, he saw the usefulness of legal security for his citizens. He granted minority rights, freedom of religion, protection of life, protection of property, and repatriation of refugees. The Babylonian captivity of Jews was discontinued and every Jew was free to return to the homeland. The general principles were registered in what we can call the first Universal Declaration of Human Rights of 538 BC, the text of which is inscribed on a cylinder exhibited at the British Museum. The Declaration was valid as a policy during the rest of Cyrus' dynasty, for over two centuries.[16] It is a pleasure to include this reference to ancient Persian culture in a contribution honouring Djamchid Momtaz.

Confucius (d. 479 BC), the great philosopher of China, was to influence the drafting of the UN Universal Declaration. Confucius was probably the first thinker to ask for the assurance of economic and social rights by a Government. In his view, the Emperor had a duty to serve his people and produce welfare.[17] P. C. Chang, of Eleanor Roosevelt's Commission, said in a speech before ECOSOC in 1946 that implementation of the Confucian idea of economic and social justice would imply the following:

> Provisions are made for the aged, employment is provided for the able-bodied and education is afforded to the young. Widows and widowers,

---

16   See H. Abtahi, 'Reflections on the Ambiguous Universality of Human Rights: Cyrus the Great's Proclamation as a Challenge to the Athenian Democracy's Perceived Monopoly on Human Rights', in H. Abtahi & G. Boas (eds), *The Dynamics of International Criminal Justice, Essays in Honour of Sir Richard May*, Martinus Nijhoff, 2006.

17   Confucius' commented the following on welfare to the people: 'For where there is even distribution there is no such thing as poverty, where there is harmony there is no such thing as underpopulation and where there is stability there is no such thing as overturning.' M. R. Ishay (ed), *The Human Rights Reader: Major Political Essays, Speeches, and Documents from Ancient Times to the Present*, 2nd edition, Routledge, 2007, p. 45.

orphans and the childless, the deformed and the diseased, are all cared for.'[18]

Although Confucius accepted the Chinese hierarchical system of obedience, he supported freedom of dialogue and information as part of good governance. When he was asked by one of his followers 'how to serve a Prince?' he answered: 'Tell him the truth even if it offends him.'[19] Freedom of speech was not far away.

Confucius was probably the first thinker to formalize the Golden Rule: 'What you don't want others to do to you, you shall not do to them.' The negative formulation was more concrete (and more human-rights-oriented) than the later positive approach of the Christian Bible: 'Do to others as you would have them do to you.'

In ancient India, the Hindu Code of Manu was elaborated and compiled between 500 and 100 BC. It conveys the message that in warfare there are certain situations where human life should be spared. An honourable warrior is supposed not to strike an enemy who is helpless, be he asleep, naked, carrying no arms, or in flight. These prescriptions on the right to life may not have worked in practice, yet 'they characterize Indian spirituality.'[20]

This Indian spirituality was reconfirmed in the Sanskrit epos of *Mahabharata* (composed between 200 and 300 AD), where it was again stated that 'no sleeping enemy should be attacked.'[21]

Herodotus (d. 420 BC) belongs to Greek antiquity, but he was born in Asia Minor and like many other Greeks could not confidently be labelled a Westerner. He was the first to object to the Greek habit of labelling non-Greeks 'barbarians'. Peoples had different customs and religions but they were all human beings and should be recognized as equals.

Herodotus may have influenced Alexander the Great (d. 323 BC). Although a Westerner, Alexander's ideas went 'beyond borders'. As a successful conqueror he denied the concept of 'the other'. He refused to see former enemies as

---

18   Quotation by M. Glendon, supra, note 15, p. 185.
19   S. Leys, *The Analects of Confucius*, W. W. Norton, 1997, p. 70, quoted by Amartya Sen in his Morgenthau Memorial Lecture 1997 at the Carnegie Council. The title of the lecture was 'Human Rights and Asian Values'.
20   A. Nussbaum, *A Concise History of the Law of Nations*, 2nd edition, Macmillan, 1954, p. 4. For a translation of the relevant Sanskrit text, see W. Doniger & B. K. Smith, *The Laws of Manu*, Penguin Classics, 1991, p. 137.
21   L. C. Green, 'The Law of War in Historical Perspective', 72 *International Law Studies* (Naval War College), 1988, p. 41.

'barbarians'. He wanted his generals to marry the local daughters of important families in order to develop friendly relations in occupied territories. He wanted territorial control and in the process spread the idea of equality among human beings.

This idea became a cornerstone in the philosophy of Stoicism. The Stoic philosopher Zenon of Kition (Cyprus) advocated around 300 BC the equality of human beings in a cosmopolitan world. All individuals enjoyed citizenship and equality in the universal order of Cosmopolis. Zenon lectured in Athens, but was part of an emerging Hellenistic culture with its centre in Alexandria.

Alexandria became an intellectual melting pot around 290 BC. Stoicism reigned and later spread to Rome. Roman law is of interest as to the development of legal formulas, but contributed little to the issue of individual rights. Let us therefore not dwell on Rome but return to the Oriental/non-Western world in our search for additional human-rights examples.

King Ashoka (India) embarked upon a humanitarian policy of reform after 260 BC. Within the framework of Buddhism, he advocated human compassion. He pronounced a principle of security for the inhabitants of his huge kingdom. His decrees included non-use of force by State organs, the right to life, freedom of religion and freedom from violation and dishonour.[22]

Ashoka was probably influenced by an earlier Government adviser in India by the name of Kautilya. According to Amartya Sen, both argued in favour of individual rights, but Kautilya based his views on the disciplinary effect of *social institutions*, while Ashoka based his views on an optimistic focus on *human behaviour* and its progressive development.[23] Francis Fukuyama has (in his *The Origins of Political Order*, 2011) made the point that ancient India was a society based on legal rules and responsibility of local rulers. Had the governmental system been stronger, a modest rule-of-law development might have been possible.

I now enter the Islamic world after the death of Mohammed.

The Arabian conquest of Andalusia started in 712 AD and this part of Spain was soon characterized by peaceful societal coexistence between Muslims, Jews and Christians. Freedom of religion was a fact, even if the non-Muslims had to pay a certain tax. This Muslim principle of tolerance was also practised after the Ottoman conquest of Constantinople in 1453.

---

22   Ashoka's Rock Edict XII on freedom of religion is quoted in M. Ishay (ed), supra, note 17, p. 29.
23   A. Sen, *The Idea of Justice,* Penguin edition, 2010, pp. 69 and 75–77.

Sultan Mehmet II (of the Ottoman Empire) issued in 1463 AD a Declaration of Rights for conquered Bosnia. He granted protection of minorities, freedom of religion and legal safety for everyone.

Another Muslim ruler, Akbar, Moghul emperor of India, introduced human-rights-oriented reforms in his empire after 1563 AD. His first edict terminated the practice of slavery for prisoners of war. Thereafter every citizen and group was granted freedom of faith and non-discrimination. With regard to freedom of religion Akbar had this to say in one of his edicts:

> No man should be interfered with on account of religion, and anyone [is] to be allowed to convert to any religion he pleased.
>
> If a Hindu, when a child or otherwise, has been made a Muslim against his will, he is to be allowed, if he pleases, to revert to the religion of his fathers.[24]

Dialogue between Hindus and Muslims was encouraged. Dialogue and freedom of information stimulated discussion on needed reform and were seen by Akbar as important for good governance.

In modern times a number of Muslim traditions have been criticized from a human-rights point of view, but it has also been pointed out that Muslim culture has contributed to a practice of non-racial discrimination.

6 Concluding Remarks on the Historical Survey

A representative of current Asian values is Aung San Suu Kyi of Burma/Myanmar. She is a champion of human rights and democracy, but as a politician she compromises on the issue of the Rohingya minority group. That compromise may be necessary for the time being, but she is a 'universalist' by inclination. The divide between Asian and Western values is not evident in this case.

My point with the brief historical exposé above (a fuller one is found in my book referred to in note 9) is that the divide between the West and the rest is unnecessary and should be bridged over. The debate on cultural relativism could usefully include the history of human rights in the non-Western world. Whenever the relativistic (non-universal) argument pops up to deny fundamental human rights, counter arguments could be put forward. The argument

---

24 V. A. Smith, *Akbar: The Great Mogul*, Clarendon, 1917, p. 257, quoted by Amartya Sen in his 1997 Morgenthau Memorial Lecture on 'Human Rights and Asian Values'.

that human rights discourse is not only of Western origin, but also has roots in North Africa and Asia, should be put forward, both in diplomatic and academic circles. Non-Western civilizations should be given the credit for being the first to address different rights issues in a progressive way. Even if none of these early projects resulted in any holistic or sustainable system of human rights, even if they are isolated examples, history shows that human-rights thought is something natural, common and recurrent for all peoples and all regions of the world.

International law is sometimes said to be subject to a process of fragmentation. If so, the result could be less universality and more regionalism. The European Convention on Human Rights recognizes universality and in addition stands for a regional implementation which is more ambitious than anything done in other regions. This is an example of positive fragmentation. The problem with cultural relativism is that it leads to negative fragmentation. With regard to developing countries, a certain understanding and respect for regional and cultural traditions is necessary. Such transcultural understanding could contribute to a practice of smooth co-existence and cooperation. But when it comes to *fundamental* human-rights principles, deviation and denial, and thus negative fragmentation, should be opposed. Such relativism may be in the interest of certain Governments and political elites, but it will never be in the interest of the ordinary man or woman. State actors, NGOs, the academic community and civil society at large all need to take part in the current debate and shape a progressive *opinio juris*. International law in this field, as well as in many others, needs to be strengthened and not weakened.

7 A Final Remark on Samuel Moyn's Alternative Approach to Human Rights History

Samuel Moyn, professor of History at Columbia University, differs from Michael Ignatieff, Lynn Hunt, Micheline Ishay and others on the role of human rights in history. Moyn, in his *The Last Utopia* (2010), argues that there is a need for an alternative history of human rights.[25] In his view no tangible and

---

25   S. Moyn, *The Last Utopia, Human Rights in History*, The Belknap Press of Harvard University Press, 2010, paperback edition 2012, pp. 5–7. See also Moyn's *Human Rights and the Uses of History*, Verso, 2014. In *Last Utopia*, Moyn argues that 'natural rights doctrines were the children of the absolutist and expansionist state of early modern European history, not attempts to step outside and beyond the state' (p. 21). That is evidently not true for naturalists like Grotius, Pufendorf and others, who invoked natural law to 'transcend'

consistent developments in the field of human rights occurred before NGOs activated the issue in the early 1970s. At that time, the agenda of human rights emerged 'seemingly from nowhere' (p. 3). The importance of the 1948 Universal Declaration is downgraded by Moyn, since it is said to be an isolated event and had no effect on State practice. The contributions of Enlightenment thinkers, in his view, were offset by bloody revolution. And the contributions of ancient cultures were isolated manifestations in the huge stream of historical events and turning-points. Scholars who seek for the roots of human rights in ancient history are seen as naïve idealists who use history to create their ideological heroes and confirm the 'inevitable rise' of the concept of human rights.

However, from the perspective of the history of political ideas, all human-rights-related practices and manifestations are relevant, irrespective of whether they amount to examples of legal and consistent implementation. The different utterances may or may not point in a certain direction, or they may—and this is important in our discussion—indicate a certain propensity for repetition.

Moyn denies the link between the past and the present, because the rights that existed in earlier history were part of the relationship between the sovereign State and its citizens. These earlier rights 'were from the beginning part of the authority of the State, not invoked to transcend it' (p. 7). Moyn pictures the modern human-rights idea as something completely different, as a Utopian move 'beyond sovereignty and state altogether', a move to an almost supranational level of 'world government.'

However, human rights have always depended on State consent and national implementation. Consequently, since human rights have always been sovereignty-based, but nowadays with added international-law pressure, the ideological divide that Moyn constructed between the past and the present collapses.

In other words, the asserted difference between 1789 and the 1970s is a false distinction. International lawyers do not see human rights as transcending the State, going beyond sovereignty or being supranational in their implementation. The human rights concept is still (as in 1789) focused on the State's behaviour towards its citizens—with the added dimension of multilateral agreements protecting all individuals (not only citizens) within the State's

---

the authority of States and princes. In general, Moyn argues that civil rights, in the French revolutionary tradition, were linked to 'citizenship boundaries', forgetting that the French revolutionaries wanted to export their principles 'beyond borders', in the conviction that these principles, including civil rights, had the potential of being accepted in the rest of Europe.

jurisdiction. Sovereign States have used their sovereignty to limit that same sovereignty in order to advance human-rights protection. States have agreed, in multilateral negotiations, to afford rights to the individual at the domestic level. In the past, certain powerful rulers *unilaterally* used their sovereignty to limit it and afford rights to their citizens. The difference is one of method, multilateral or unilateral, not of principle.

Moyn's perception that the ultimate human-rights regime signifies supra-nationality is misinformed. International law, including human-rights law, is a phenomenon *between* States, not above them (although the decision-making power of the UN Security Council and the European Union will produce exceptions). International human-rights law has successively reached a more ambitious level, but it is still *inter*-national, not supranational.

Moyn's deconstructive criticism of the traditional perception of human-rights history is 'misconstructed'. It is not naïve to search for the roots of human rights since you don't expect all roots to give rise to forests. Plants can flourish for a while and then succumb. If similar plants turn up later, and again and again, it is a phenomenon worth noting. And we are all allowed to draw certain conclusions from it. For example, that history is relevant in modern human-rights discourse.

Droit a l'éducation et diversité : le droit à une éducation inclusive et équitable de qualité

Jorge Cardona[1]

1   Introduction

Je voudrais commencer ces lignes en remerciant les organisateurs de cette collection d'études en hommage au Professeur Djamchid Momtaz, pour m'avoir aimablement invité à participer et pouvoir rendre, de cette manière, mon particulier hommage à un ami que je respecte profondément personnellement et professionnellement.

L'œuvre scientifique de Djamchid Momtaz est très vaste. Mais un des sujets qu'il aime spécialement sont les droits de l'homme et, dans ce domaine, le respect pour la diversité humaine. Pour cette raison j'ai décidé de réfléchir sur un sujet très sensible pour moi et pour mon ami, celui de l'éducation inclusive des enfants « différents ».

Mais, avant d'entrer dans le vif du sujet, je souhaiterais faire deux observations :

Premièrement : quand je parle d'enfants « différents » je me réfère à des enfants qui sont de nationalités différentes, de groupes sociaux économiques différents, de cultures différentes, d'orientations sexuelles différentes, de capacités physiques, sensorielles ou intellectuelles différentes de la majorité, etc. C'est-à-dire, je voudrais centrer l'attention sur l'éducation inclusive de tous les enfants « différents ».

Ma deuxième observation liminaire est le point de départ de cette réflexion, résumé dans une phrase que je suis sûr Djamchid Momtaz partage avec moi : *changer le monde signifie changer l'éducation.*

Mais avant de changer l'éducation pour changer le monde nous devons nous mettre d'accord sur le monde que nous voulons. Souhaitons-nous un monde dans lequel le plus important est la richesse, l'intelligence, ou la beauté, et dans lequel celui qui est « différent », qui n'a pas de richesse, qui n'a pas de grandes capacités intellectuelles, qui n'a pas beauté doit être séparé, classé dans une seconde catégorie de citoyens ? Ou est-ce que nous souhaitons un monde dans lequel toutes les différences et les diversités sont non seulement tolérées, mais aussi respectées, valorisées, accueillies et célébrées, considérées plus comme

---

[1] Ce texte exprime l'avis de l'auteur et pas nécessairement l'avis de l'organe des Nations Unies.

une chance d'apprendre que comme un problème ? C'est là la question fondamentale à laquelle nous devons répondre pour changer l'éducation.

Etant donné que ce second souhait correspond au monde auquel Djamchid Momtaz et moi-même nous aspirons, je parlerai de changements en matière d'éducation dont l'objectif est bien de changer le monde dans ce sens.

C'est dans ce même sens qu'au *Sommet sur le développement durable*, le 25 septembre 2015, les Etats membres des Nations Unies ont adopté un nouveau Programme de développement durable, qui comprend un ensemble de 17 objectifs mondiaux pour mettre fin à la pauvreté, lutter contre les inégalités et l'injustice. Le quatrième de ces objectifs a pour titre : « assurer une éducation inclusive et équitable de qualité et promouvoir des possibilités d'apprentissage tout au long de la vie pour tous ». Comme j'essayerai de montrer dans ce travail, l'« éducation inclusive et équitable de qualité » c'est le nouveau nom du droit à l'éducation et, en conséquence il n'est pas seulement un objectif désirable, mais un droit qui doit être garanti. Et cette perspective du droit à l'éducation est en rapport directe avec le respect de la diversité et la différence.

Mais, de la même manière que le traitement de la différence au sein du système éducatif influe sur la société, le regard que porte la société sur la différence a une incidence claire sur le système éducatif. C'est pour cela que pour bien comprendre la situation actuelle, je ferai un exposé historique des diverses approches à la diversité.

2 De l'exclusion à l'éducation spéciale

Traditionnellement, la « différence » était jadis vue comme un stigmate, un châtiment divin, ou un danger pour la société, au point d'accepter, par exemple, l'infanticide d'enfants albinos ou en situation de handicap (malheureusement encore en cours aujourd'hui dans certains États), l'esclavage des personnes de différente couleur ou l'expulsion du territoire de certaines ethnies. La personne « différente » n'était pas considérée comme un citoyen et n'avait donc pas de droits. En conséquence, l'enfant « différent » n'avait pas non plus droit à l'éducation. Il était (et, dans beaucoup de pays il l'est encore) exclu de l'accès à l'éducation.

Tout le monde connaît des expériences d'exclusion de l'éducation à cause de la capacité, de la couleur de la peau, du groupe social, etc.

Cette situation est fort heureusement dépassée dans de nombreux pays. La reconnaissance de ce que toutes les personnes ont les mêmes droits va changer la situation à partir du XXème siècle. C'est alors qu'apparait la dénommée *conception individuelle de la différence*. Conformément à ce modèle, on considère que les enfants « différents » ont droit à l'éducation, mais puisque ce sont des enfants « spéciaux », ils doivent avoir une éducation « spéciale ». Les politiques inspirées de cette conception encouragent une éducation séparée qui aboutit à la création, au moins, de deux systèmes d'enseignement distincts : l'un à l'intention des enfants « différents », souvent dispensé dans les « écoles spéciales », et l'autre à l'intention des enfants « normaux », en écoles « ordinaires ». Dans certains Etats, ce sont mêmes trois, quatre ou cinq systèmes d'enseignement qui coexistent en fonction des diverses « différences » des enfants[2].

Cette ségrégation, car il s'agit bien de ségrégation, se base sur l'idée que les enfants « différents » ne peuvent pas être éduqués dans le même environnement que les autres et qu'ils constituent une charge pour le système d'enseignement régulier ou ordinaire où les particularités de chaque enfant ne sont pas souvent prises en compte. Pour cette raison, cette ségrégation n'est pas considérée comme une discrimination mais comme l'unique forme possible de scolarisation.

Naturellement, les itinéraires académiques spéciaux (pour les filles ; pour les enfants de couleur ; pour les enfants aveugles ; pour les enfants avec capacité intellectuelle réduite ; etc.) sont normalement plus courts et leurs programmes plus réduits, empêchant évidemment l'insertion a posteriori dans les niveaux d'éducation supérieurs. En outre, le système d'éducation spéciale entraine l'isolement des élèves « différents », et contribue donc à les marginaliser davantage dans la société. Le système d'éducation spécialisée officialise une ségrégation des personnes ; ségrégation qui difficilement pourra se rompre ensuite et qui se maintiendra généralement tout au long de la vie.

3 De l'éducation spéciale à l'intégration

Comme moyen de dépasser les difficultés et échecs de l'éducation spécialisée, est apparue l'idée de l'éducation intégrée[3].

---

2   Des écoles pour de garçons et pour de filles ; des écoles pour enfants blancs et pour enfants noirs ; des écoles pour des enfants avec capacités intellectuelles considérées normaux et les autres ; des écoles pour des enfants avec vision et des écoles pour les aveugles ; etc.

3   Ainsi, lors de la Conférence Mondiale sur les actions et les stratégies pour l'éducation, la prévention et l'intégration de 1981 fut approuvée la dénommée Déclaration Sundberg (en mémoire de Nils-Ivar Sundberg, chargé du programme de l'UNESCO pour l'éducation spéciale, 1968-1981) qui recommandait que les programmes en matière d'éducation soient formulés en vue d'intégrer toutes les personnes dans l'environnement ordinaire de travail et de vie. Se

Il s'agissait d'introduire les enfants « différents » dans les écoles ordinaires et d'agir sur l'enfant pour chercher à réduire les différences avec l'enfant « normal », afin de tenter de normaliser l'enfant « différent » et ainsi lui permettre de suivre des études ordinaires « dans toute la mesure du possible ».

Mais dans la plupart des cas, cette intégration s'est faite et se fait toujours sans les moyens nécessaires, si bien qu'à la fin, elle aggrave la situation initiale.

C'est le cas, par exemple, des écoles où il n'y a pas de toilettes pour les filles ; qui ont des barrières physiques pour l'accès, qui n'ont pas adapté les programmes à la diversité ; etc.

Ceci a été très bien décrit par le Rapporteur spécial des Nations Unies sur les droits à l'éducation qui a signalé dans son rapport sur le droit à l'éducation des enfants handicapés :

> On a constaté en effet que les tentatives de simple intégration dans les écoles ordinaires, sans mesures structurelles d'accompagnement (tels qu'organisations, programmes d'études et stratégies d'enseignement et d'apprentissage) ne correspondent pas et continueront pour diverses raisons à ne pas correspondre aux droits des personnes handicapées. En fait, l'« intégration » peut tout simplement aboutir à l'exclusion au sein de l'enseignement général plutôt que dans une école spéciale[4].

Si nous prenons l'exemple des enfants ayant un handicap intellectuel, l'« intégration » se trouve relativement aisée dans les premiers niveaux éducatifs, où la différence d'âge mental d'un enfant avec handicap intellectuel et d'un enfant sans handicap n'est pas très importante. Naturellement, à mesure que ces enfants accèdent à des niveaux éducatifs plus élevés, cette différence se remarque de plus en plus et chaque fois « la mesure du possible » est réduite. L'enfant finalement finit de nouveau dans l'éducation spécialisée ou marginalisé et exclu à l'intérieur même du système ordinaire.

---

posait alors la question d'un nouveau modèle d'éducation : l'éducation intégrée. Dont un des reflets sera *le Programme d'action mondial concernant les personnes handicapées* approuvé par l'Assemblée générale des Nations Unies en 1982 et qui prévoit : « Les Etats membres devraient adopter des politiques reconnaissant le droit des personnes handicapées à l'égalité en matière d'enseignement. Dans toute la mesure du possible, l'enseignement des personnes handicapées devrait se faire dans le cadre du système général d'enseignement. »

4 Rapport de V. Muñoz, Rapporteur spécial sur le droit à l'éducation, *Le droit à l'éducation des personnes handicapées*, Doc. A/HRC/4/29, 19 février 2007, par. 12.

Les causes d'une telle situation ne sont autres que la conception même de la « différence » qui porte le modèle individuel : si la « normalisation » de l'enfant n'est pas atteinte, il faudra l'exclure de l'enseignement ordinaire.

Un des exemples que j'aime le plus présenter pour comprendre l'absurdité de cette conception c'est le conte « Le pays des Aveugles » de H. G. Wells[5]. Ce conte relate l'histoire d'un explorateur qui s'introduisit au plus profond des Andes équatoriennes. Il atteignit le sommet d'une grande montagne où, à notre connaissance, jamais personne n'avait pu aller. Là, il trouva des grottes qui le menèrent, après plusieurs aventures et mésaventures, à la découverte d'un peuple qui vivait à l'intérieur de cette montagne et qui n'avait jamais eu de contact avec l'extérieur.

Tous les membres de ce peuple présentaient deux caractéristiques : ils étaient tous d'une grande beauté et étaient tous aveugles. Mais ils ne savaient pas qu'ils étaient aveugles. Personne ne savait qu'il existait des gens qui pouvaient voir. Leur société, leurs infrastructures, leur mode de vie avaient été construits pour eux et il n'était pas nécessaire de voir pour pouvoir se déplacer et vivre « normalement ».

L'explorateur arriva épuisé dans cette peuplade et perdit la conscience. Le chef de la peuplade l'accueillit chez lui et sa fille prit grand soin de lui. Comme toujours dans les contes, l'explorateur et la fille du chef finissent par tomber amoureux et décident de se marier.

Or, cette décision posa rapidement problème. La fille du chef pouvait-elle épouser un étranger, différent des autres et qui disait qu'il « voyait » des choses et décrivait des choses qu'il appelait couleurs et lumières ? Pour répondre à cette question, le Conseil de la peuplade se réunit et discuta toute une nuit. À l'aube, le chef de la tribu sortit du Conseil et se dirigea vers les jeunes amoureux :

> Félicitations, dit le chef à l'explorateur, le Conseil a décidé que tu peux épouser ma fille. Mais avant, il est nécessaire que tu deviennes comme nous, que tu te « normalises ». Pour cela nous devons t'enlever ces yeux si différents qui peuvent voir.

L'absurdité de la conclusion de cette histoire nous montre une constante dans toutes les sociétés : ce qui est différent fait peur. Ou bien on le rejette, ou bien on essaye d'éliminer la différence.

---

5 H. G. Wells, *Le Pays des Aveugles et autres récits d'anticipation* (*The Country of the Blind and OtherTtales of Anticipation*), traduction de H. D. Davray et B. Kozakiewicz, Préface de Y. Yvinec ; Ed. Roman (poche), 2000.

4 De l'intégration vers l'éducation inclusive

Cette situation commença à changer grâce aux mouvements sociaux qui débutèrent à partir des années soixante-dix du siècle passé à travers les défenseurs de l'idée que la différence n'est pas une mauvaise chose mais tout au contraire une richesse à mettre en valeur et à apprécier. Ce sont les mouvements de défense des droits civils qui se manifesteront en mouvements féministes, antiracistes, anti-xénophobes et pour l'égalité des droits de la personne en situation de handicap.

C'est un changement de paradigme du modèle individuel vers le modèle social ou également appelé modèle des droits de l'homme[6].

Conformément à ce modèle, il n'est pas juste question d'agir seulement sur la personne différente pour qu'elle puisse exercer ses droits, mais il faut aussi agir pour éliminer les diverses barrières qui font obstacle à leur pleine et effective participation à la société sur la base de l'égalité avec les autres.

D'accord avec ce nouveau paradigme, l'enfant n'a pas seulement droit à l'éducation mais le droit à une « éducation inclusive ».

L'éducation inclusive fait référence à la nécessité de créer des environnements éducatifs propres à intégrer efficacement dans le système général des élèves qui ont traditionnellement été exclus de ce dernier. Au lieu de traiter de la manière d'intégrer ces élèves dans l'éducation ordinaire, l'éducation inclusive suppose une approche dédiée à transformer les systèmes éducatifs et les environnements liés à l'apprentissage pour qu'ils puissent offrir une réponse adéquate à la diversité des élèves.

Entre l'« intégration » et l'« inclusion » il y a un changement très important. L'intégration pourrait être définie comme l'adaptation des enfants « différents » à l'école, en les intégrant dans les classes avec un critère d'assimilation, uniformité et perte des différences[7].

---

6 Un exemple clair de ce changement de modèle est la définition de handicap de la Convention relative aux droits des personnes handicapées de 2006, Nations Unies, *Recueil des traités*, vol. 2515, p. 3. Conformément à cette Convention (Article 1), on entend par personne handicapée toute personne présentant des incapacités physiques, mentales, intellectuelles ou sensorielles durables dont l'interaction avec diverses barrières peut faire obstacle à leur pleine et effective participation à la société sur la base de l'égalité avec les autres. En d'autres termes, devant un escalier, une personne en fauteuil roulant sera en situation de handicap car elle ne pourra pas avancer seule. Devant ce même escalier, si une rampe d'accès est aménagée, cette personne pourra se déplacer comme tout le monde : elle ne sera alors plus en situation de handicap.

7 Alors que, comme nous l'avons dit, la pratique de l'intégration porte un risque sur l'attention accordée de manière plus générale à la diversité et contribue à créer des phénomènes de ségrégation.

Selon la perspective de l'inclusion, c'est l'école qui doit s'adapter à la diversité des élèves. Les différences et diversités doivent non seulement être tolérées, mais aussi respectées, valorisées, accueillies et célébrées, considérées plus comme une chance d'apprendre et d'apprendre différemment que comme un problème.

Cette conception de l'éducation inclusive sera globalement consacrée dans la *Déclaration de Salamanque* et dans le cadre d'action pour l'éducation et les besoins spéciaux de 1994, dans laquelle on demande aux Etats d'« adopter, en tant que loi ou politique, le principe de l'éducation inclusive »[8].

L'éducation inclusive a ensuite été consacrée comme un véritable droit dans l'article 24 de la Convention relative aux droits des personnes handicapées[9].

La Convention relative aux droits de l'enfant[10] prévoit de sa part le droit à l'éducation de tous les enfants sans discrimination.

En interprétant cet article dans la pratique, le Comité des Droits de l'Enfant a, inlassablement, rappelé aux Etats qu'ils ont l'obligation de donner une éducation « inclusive » à tous les enfants[11]. De cette manière, conformément à

---

8   *Déclaration de Salamanque sur les principes, les politiques et les pratiques en matière d'éducation et de besoins éducatifs spéciaux*, UNESCO Conférence mondiale sur les besoins éducatifs spéciaux : accès et qualité ; Salamanque, Espagne, 7-10 juin 1994.

9   Selon lequel :
   1   Les États Parties reconnaissent le droit des personnes handicapées à l'éducation. En vue d'assurer l'exercice de ce droit sans discrimination et sur la base de l'égalité des chances, les États Parties font en sorte que le système éducatif pourvoie à l'insertion scolaire à tous les niveaux [...].
   2   Aux fins de l'exercice de ce droit, les États Parties veillent à ce que :
      a. Les personnes handicapées ne soient pas exclues, sur le fondement de leur handicap, du système d'enseignement général et à ce que les enfants handicapés ne soient pas exclus, sur le fondement de leur handicap, de l'enseignement primaire gratuit et obligatoire ou de l'enseignement secondaire;
      b. Les personnes handicapées puissent, sur la base de l'égalité avec les autres, avoir accès, dans les communautés où elles vivent, à un enseignement primaire inclusif, de qualité et gratuit, et à l'enseignement secondaire;
      c. Il soit procédé à des aménagements raisonnables en fonction des besoins de chacun;
      d. Les personnes handicapées bénéficient, au sein du système d'enseignement général, de l'accompagnement nécessaire pour faciliter leur éducation effective;
      e. Des mesures d'accompagnement individualisées efficaces soient prises dans des environnements qui optimisent le progrès scolaire et la socialisation, conformément à l'objectif de pleine intégration.

10 Nations Unies, *Recueil des traités*, vol. 1577, p. 3.

11 Nous pouvons nous référer presque à toutes les Observations finales à tous les Etats faites par le Comité. La référence à l'éducation inclusive est une constante en toutes les recommandations aux Etats.

la position constante du Comité, il faut souligner que l'éducation inclusive ne doit pas être simplement perçue comme l'intégration des enfants « différents » dans le système scolaire ordinaire, mais bien comme l'adaptation du système scolaire et la mise à disposition des enseignants et programmes, conformes aux besoins spéciaux de chacun des enfants.

On dépasse donc la notion d'intégration (l'enfant « différent » doit s'intégrer dans un environnement scolaire ordinaire) pour promouvoir l'inclusion (l'environnement scolaire doit s'adapter pour permettre de recevoir tous les enfants quelles que soient leurs différences). L'inclusion des enfants « différents » est, en conséquence, un droit (et non un privilège !) de tous les enfants, et pas seulement des enfants « différents ».

C'est dans ce sens que nous devons interpréter l'Objectif de Développement Durable (ODD) numéro 4 qui a pour titre : « assurer une éducation inclusive et équitable de qualité ». Cet objectif surmonte l'ancien objectif du Millénaire pour le développement (OMD) numéro 2 qui avait pour titre : « assurer l'éducation primaire pour tous », où les concepts d'« inclusion » ou d'« équité » sont absents.

5   Les barrières pour l'inclusion

Mais... n'allons pas nous leurrer. Ceci, nous le savons bien, reste dans de nombreux pays du domaine de la théorie et nous avons encore besoin de beaucoup de changements dans la pratique. Or ces changements se heurtent à des barrières qui empêchent l'exercice de ce droit à l'éducation inclusive.

Ces barrières sont de divers ordres :

a)   Physiques
b)   Juridiques
c)   Economiques et surtout,
d)   Culturelles

Les barrières physiques sont les plus faciles à surmonter. Mais il faut faire cet effort. Il est nécessaire d'adapter physiquement l'école pour que tout enfant, quel que soit son sexe, sa capacité physique, sa « différence », puisse y accéder.

En second lieu, ce sont les barrières juridiques qui doivent être éliminées. On ne peut accepter par exemple une législation qui établisse des moyens de nier le droit à une éducation inclusive. Est contraire au droit à l'éducation toute législation qui prévoit notamment comme règle générale la ségrégation des enfants « différents », quelle que soit la différence, dans des écoles spécialisées.

De la même manière, les dispositions qui, en acceptant l'intégration dans une école ordinaire, font dépendre celle-ci des ressources existantes dans le pays, sans toutefois imposer cette condition pour l'éducation des autres enfants, constituent également des barrières juridiques à l'exercice du droit à l'éducation inclusive. Ainsi, par exemple, il est très fréquent de trouver des législations qui prévoient la possibilité qu'une école nie son droit d'admission à un élève ayant des besoins éducatifs particuliers quand l'école « ne dispose pas des ressources nécessaires » pour s'occuper de l'étudiant. Cette clause, communément acceptée dans beaucoup d'États, n'existe pas pour l'admission des autres enfants et répond à la vision individuelle : s'il n'y a aucun moyen de réduire la différence de l'enfant ayant des besoins éducatifs particuliers par rapport aux autres enfants, s'il n'existe pas de moyens pour « normaliser » l'enfant « différent », alors l'école peut refuser son admission.

Ce raisonnement est évidemment contraire au droit à une éducation inclusive. Tous les enfants sont différents, soit en raison de leur capacité physique, de leur couleur, origine sociale ou ethnique, ou de leur niveau intellectuel. Et l'école doit s'adapter à ces différences. Elle doit valoriser ces différences et travailler avec toutes, pour que tous les enfants différents soient égaux dans l'exercice de leur droit à l'éducation.

Naturellement, il y a aussi des barrières économiques : l'éducation inclusive a besoin de plus de moyens économiques et peut même paraître coûteuse si on se borne à n'envisager les choses qu'à court terme, car sur le long terme, le coût que représente un enfant auquel on n'a pas voulu donner les moyens de devenir autonome est bien supérieur au coût que représente un véritable système d'éducation inclusive. Dans ce sens, l'éducation inclusive n'est pas chère.

Mais de toutes les barrières existantes, les plus difficiles à surmonter sont, sans aucun doute, celles que j'appelle barrières « culturelles ». Il s'agit des barrières que nous, humains, nous posons avec notre mentalité ancrée dans des conceptions passées ou dans une commodité difficile à dépasser.

Ainsi nous trouvons des barrières chez les professeurs des écoles, dans la mentalité des parents des autres enfants, et aussi, dans la mentalité des propres parents d'enfant « différents ».

On doit reconnaître que beaucoup de professeurs sont réticents au changement. Il est nécessaire de changer la mentalité de beaucoup de professeurs et de faire comprendre à tous les professeurs le besoin d'une éducation inclusive. Il faut aussi insister sur la nécessité de mettre en œuvre des réformes éducatives dans la formation professorale de base et des enseignants en service, dans le but de doter les instituteurs des compétences nécessaires pour pouvoir affronter les défis de l'éducation inclusive et rapprocher son travail des nécessités et attentes des étudiants.

Comme nous l'avons signalé précédemment, dans les années quatre-vingt, une des principales préoccupations se centra sur la manière de réussir effectivement l'intégration des élèves aux nécessités éducatives spéciales dans les écoles ordinaires. Comme on pouvait s'y attendre, l'intégration fut plus rapide et acceptée en termes de fourniture et d'accès aux conditions d'infrastructure physique et d'équipements qu'en ce qui concerne les changements de modèles scolaires, des programmes et des méthodologies d'enseignement. De ce fait, les pourcentages d'abandon scolaire augmentèrent parmi les étudiants aux besoins éducatifs spéciaux quand ils étaient intégrés dans des écoles ordinaires qui n'avaient pas adopté toute la série de changements institutionnels, de programmes et pédagogies nécessaires à l'éducation inclusive.

Il est primordial de doter les professeurs de nouvelles compétences méthodologiques et de changer la conception des programmes des étudiants.

Mais les barrières culturelles ne se trouvent pas seulement chez les professeurs. Elles se trouvent aussi chez les parents ; tant chez les parents des autres enfants inscrits dans l'école que chez les propres parents des enfants en situation de handicap.

L'aspiration à une école d'élite, dans laquelle on s'attend à obtenir les meilleurs résultats académiques, fait que quelques parents s'opposent à ce que dans la classe de leurs enfants soient inclus des étudiants avec des besoins éducatifs spéciaux qui pourraient retarder le rythme d'apprentissage de la classe entière. L'influence délétère de cette idée se reflète sur les évaluations nationales et internationales de l'éducation (comme les fameux rapports PISA). Il en résulte que les écoles ordinaires rejettent les éléments qui n'obtiennent pas de bons résultats, qu'elles ne veulent pas accepter des élèves en situation de handicap et qu'elles ont tendance à expulser les élèves qu'elles jugent difficiles. Comme si le plus important était les résultats académiques !

Mais si les parents des autres élèves peuvent amener à des barrières culturelles, ces mêmes barrières nous les trouvons aussi chez les parents des enfants « différents ».

L'instinct protecteur des parents amène, dans beaucoup de cas, à limiter les droits de leurs enfants. Si ces derniers se mettent en relation avec tous les enfants, quand un de nos enfants a un handicap ou une autre circonstance qui le fait « différent », habituellement l'instinct protecteur s'intensifie, car on considère cet enfant comme le plus faible. Et dans trop de cas, cet instinct protecteur amène beaucoup de parents à « isoler » leurs enfants pour les protéger de tout risque, du moins le croient-ils. Ce faisant, ils deviennent eux-mêmes ceux qui nient à leurs enfants le droit à une éducation inclusive.

Il s'agit de situations compliquées, où les parents revendiquent leur droit de pouvoir choisir l'éducation qu'ils préfèrent pour leurs enfants et oublient que l'éducation de leurs enfants n'est pas leur droit à eux, mais le droit de leurs enfants, et que le critère qui doit primer est l'intérêt supérieur de l'enfant et non d'autres intérêts (comme la peur qu'il leur arrive quelque chose, ou qu'ils soient discriminés, etc.) ce qui, bien que ce soit compréhensible, n'est absolument pas acceptable.

L'intérêt supérieur de l'enfant doit être déterminant, puisque les décisions doivent être basées sur l'évaluation individualisée des besoins de chaque enfant[12].

Naturellement, cette évaluation et la détermination de l'intérêt supérieur de l'enfant peut amener, dans des cas exceptionnels, à considérer qu'une attention très spécialisée doit être donnée à un enfant déterminé, un enfant qui a besoin d'un soutien très spécialisé. En revanche, cela doit rester limité à des situations très exceptionnelles.

6   Conclusion

Sans aucun doute, si nous obtenons une éducation inclusive, nous arriverons à créer une société inclusive (de la même manière que l'inclusion sociale contextualise, soutient et légitime l'éducation inclusive). Pour cela, l'inclusion ne se limite pas seulement à l'éducation, mais elle est transversale à la vie de tous les citoyens et citoyennes. Les politiques publiques d'éducation inclusive doivent se faire en même temps que d'autres politiques sociales (culture, santé …) avec une perspective multisectorielle et une stratégie partagée de développement et de bien-être de la société.

Ceux pour qui cela est clair sont les enfants eux-mêmes. En 2007, les points de vue des élèves ayant des besoins éducatifs particuliers ont été présentés dans la Déclaration de Lisbonne sur « Ce que pensent les jeunes de l'éducation inclusive »[13]. Cette Déclaration avance un certain nombre de propositions avec lesquelles sont d'accord les jeunes ayant des besoins éducatifs particuliers issus de 29 pays et fréquentant des établissements d'enseignement secondaire, professionnel et supérieur. Dans la Déclaration, les jeunes précisent que : « Nous voyons beaucoup d'avantages à l'éducation inclusive […] nous avons besoin d'avoir des amis et d'échanger avec eux, qu'ils aient ou non des besoins particuliers […]. L'éducation inclusive est mutuellement bénéfique à tous ».

---

12   Voir *Observation générale n° 14 (2013) sur le droit de l'enfant à ce que son intérêt supérieur soit une considération primordiale*, article 3, par. 1, CRC/C/GC/14, 2013.

13   https://www.european-agency.org/publications/flyers/lisbon-declaration-young-peoples-views-on-inclusive-education/declaration_fr.pdf.

Mais la principale raison pour appliquer et garantir une éducation inclusive et équitable de qualité c'est qu'il s'agit d'un droit fondamental de tous (pas seulement des enfants avec nécessités éducatives spéciales) étant donné que tous les enfants sont différents et toutes les différences et les diversités doivent être respectées, valorisées, accueillies et célébrées, puisque nous tous avons le droit d'être différents.

Immunités juridictionnelles des États étrangers et droit de l'homme : quel équilibre entre les valeurs fondamentales de l'ordre national et le droit international coutumier ?

Giuseppe Cataldi

1   Introduction

Les règles internationales sur l'immunité ont été d'abord développées par la jurisprudence nationale. Les décisions des tribunaux nationaux sont par conséquent la principale source de la pratique de l'Etat dont il faut tenir compte lors de l'établissement de la portée d'une règle particulière en matière d'immunité en vertu du droit international coutumier. Le droit de l'immunité diplomatique et consulaire est codifié dans la Convention de Vienne de 1961 sur les relations diplomatiques[1] et dans la Convention de Vienne de 1963 sur les relations consulaires.[2] Le droit de l'immunité de l'Etat est codifié dans la Convention européenne conclue à Bâle le 16 mai 1972, ainsi que par la Convention des Nations Unies sur les immunités juridictionnelles des États et de leurs biens de 2004,[3] pas encore en vigueur.

Les règles sur l'immunité sont généralement considérées comme l'exemple par excellence du rôle central joué par les tribunaux nationaux dans l'application et le développement du droit international[4]. Dans le cas des *immunités juridictionnelles de l'Etat* (*Allemagne c. Italie : Grèce intervenant*), la Cour internationale de Justice (CIJ) a souligné qu'une enquête sur la pratique des cours nationales était indispensable pour l'identification de la portée de la règle de l'immunité de l'État[5].

---

[1] Nations Unies, *Recueil des traités*, vol. 500, p. 95.
[2] Nations Unies, *Recueil des traités*, vol. 596, p. 261.
[3] Nations Unies, Assemblée générale, résolution A/59/38.
[4] Voir A. Nollkaemper, *National Courts and the International Rule of Law*, Oxford University Press, 2011, p. 10.
[5] Voir affaire des *immunités juridictionnelles de l'Etat* (*Allemagne c. Italie ; Grèce* (*intervenant*)), arrêt, *CIJ Recueil 2012*, p. 99 par. 55. La CIJ a affirmé : « Dans le cas d'espèce, une pratique étatique particulièrement importante se dégage de la jurisprudence des tribunaux internes qui ont été amenés à se prononcer sur l'immunité d'un Etat étranger, des lois adoptées par ceux des Etats qui ont légiféré en la matière, de l'invocation de l'immunité par certains Etats

Bien qu'il y ait un consensus maintenant largement répandu sur les contours des règles internationales, les interprétations des différentes règles sur l'immunité ont cependant varié entre les juridictions nationales, souvent même à l'intérieur du même Etat. Une explication de cette interprétation contradictoire des exigences du droit international dans les décisions internes en matière d'immunité est l'impact sur les juges nationaux des conceptions relatives au droit interne. En outre, les règles relatives à l'immunité ont souvent été codifiées dans la législation nationale, principalement dans les pays de *common law*, séparant ainsi ces codifications de l'évolution dans le droit international. Il faut aussi ajouter que dans les pays de *common law* une règle coutumière n'est considérée applicable par les tribunaux qu'en l'absence d'une norme nationale qui puisse régler la question spécifique, et aussi longtemps que cette coutume n'est pas incompatible avec le droit interne[6].

Une autre explication souligne le manque d'expérience et de connaissance du droit international qui caractérise parfois les décisions domestiques nationales en matière d'immunité. Il n'est pas rare que des règles du droit international soient confuses lorsqu'elles sont appliquées par les juges nationaux. Il est par conséquent à la fois difficile et inutile d'identifier des « *leading cases* » dans le domaine du droit de l'immunité, et une grande prudence est nécessaire pour tirer des conclusions de tout seul cas. Chaque décision doit être abordée dans une veine critique.

2   l'immunité de l'Etat : la théorie de la « antinomie impossible »

La tension entre l'immunité juridictionnelle de l'Etat et le droit des individus d'avoir leur cause entendue en cour par un juge est évidente, et l'argument du

---

devant des tribunaux étrangers, ainsi que des déclarations faites par les Etats à l'occasion de l'examen approfondi de cette question par la Commission du droit international puis de l'adoption de la convention des Nations Unies. Dans ce contexte, l'opinio juris est reflétée notamment par l'affirmation, de la part des Etats qui invoquent l'immunité de juridiction devant les tribunaux d'autres Etats, qu'ils sont, en vertu du droit international, fondés à en bénéficier ; par la reconnaissance, de la part des Etats qui accordent cette immunité, qu'il s'agit d'une obligation que leur impose le droit international ; et, inversement, par l'affirmation par des Etats, dans d'autres affaires, de leur droit d'exercer leur juridiction à l'égard d'Etats étrangers ».

6 Sur le point on renvoie à G. Cataldi, « On the Enforcement of Customary Rules on Human Rights by National Judges », *Italian Yearbook of International Law*, Brill, 2001, p. 101 ss. La Constitution de 1996 de l'Afrique du Sud affirme : « *Customary International law is Law of the Republic unless it is inconsistent with the Constitution or an act of Parliament* ».

droit d'accès à un tribunal contre les règles sur l'immunité est encore régulièrement invoqué devant les tribunaux[7]. Au cours des dernières années, un type particulier d'argument fondé sur les droits de l'homme contre l'application des règles de l'immunité a été porté devant les tribunaux. Il a été avancé que les Etats qui violent les normes de *jus cogens*, ou des fonctionnaires de l'État qui commettent des crimes internationaux, ne peuvent invoquer avec succès l'immunité comme défense dans les procédures devant les tribunaux nationaux étrangers.

Lorsqu'on cherche à conceptualiser la relation entre les droits de l'homme et l'immunité de l'État, il est inévitable de rappeler une théorie très influente[8]. Cette théorie remet sérieusement en question la pertinence du *jus cogens* dans le règlement des cas impliquant une exception d'immunité présentée par les Etats accusés de graves violations des droits de l'homme et / ou du droit humanitaire, dès qu'elle définit l'immunité des Etats comme une règle de procédure « *going to the jurisdiction of a national court* » et donc qui ne concerne pas le « *substantial law* »[9].

Il résulte de cette position que la relation entre les droits de l'homme et l'immunité de l'État ne peut être formulée en termes d'un conflit à résoudre en faveur des interdictions de fond posées par les droits de l'homme en tant que pourvues d'un statut présumé hiérarchiquement supérieur vis-à-vis des règles coutumières sur l'immunité de l'Etat. L'obligation procédurale d'accorder l'immunité et les interdictions de fond contenues dans les normes de *jus cogens* relatives aux droits de l'homme n'entrent tout simplement pas en conflit les unes avec les autres. Concevoir ces deux branches du droit comme donnant lieu à un véritable conflit de normes serait une tâche impossible et erronée.

Il est intéressant de noter que les implications de cette « théorie de l'antinomie impossible » vont au-delà du rejet du *jus cogens* en tant que technique

---

7 Déjà il y a deux cents ans, lorsque la Cour suprême des États-Unis a jugé l'affaire *Schooner Exchange*, l'avocat des propriétaires originaires du navire affirma : « *Your own citizens plundered. Your national rights violated. Your courts deaf to the complaints of the injured. Your government not redressing their wrongs, but giving a sanction to their spoliators* », *The Schooner Exchange v M'Faddon* 11 US 116 (1812).

8 H. Fox, *The Law of State Immunity*, Oxford University Press, 2nd edition, 2008, p. 151-152.

9 Selon cette auteur : « State immunity is a procedural rule going to the jurisdiction of a national court. It does not go to substantive law; it does not contradict a prohibition contained in a jus cogens norm but merely diverts any breach of it to a different method of settlement. Arguably, then, there is no substantive content in the procedural plea of State immunity upon which a jus cogens mandate can bite... Assuming a State has recognized the jus cogens nature of the norm, does that nature give rise to an obligation on the State to provide procedures to secure its implementation? ».

de solution des conflits pour les cas impliquant l'immunité de l'Etat pour les violations des droits de l'homme. De toute évidence, cette théorie s'applique également à toute obligation relative aux droits de l'homme qui, quel que soit son statut, peut être classée comme une règle de fond. De plus, sa logique est parfaitement apte à être appliquée à la règle de l'immunité concernant les organisations internationales.

Mais l'implication la plus importante de la théorie est encore que, dans aucun cas, le *jus cogens* ne serait un outil approprié pour le règlement des différends dans ce domaine. Lorsqu'un tribunal se dessaisit en raison des immunités internationales, seul le droit de l'homme relatif à la procédure d'accès à la justice serait affecté, quelle que soit la gravité de la violation sous-jacente imputée. Ainsi, bien qu'il résulte de l'approche de cette théorie qu'un conflit entre deux obligations procédurales est en effet en jeu dans tous les cas d'immunité, le *jus cogens* ne pouvait pas être le moyen d'en sortir, car il ne serait pas en mesure d'englober le droit d'accès à la justice.

Comme nous allons le voir, ceci est la théorie adoptée dans la décision *Jones* par les tribunaux du Royaume-Uni, confirmée par la Cour européenne des droits de l'homme, ainsi que par la Cour internationale de Justice dans la décision *Allemagne* c. *Italie*.

À notre avis, l'obligation générale pour les Etats d'« assurer » ou de « garantir » à tous les individus relevant de leur juridiction les droits de l'homme reconnus par le droit international englobe l'obligation positive de garantir la protection effective de ces droits au moyen, entre autres, de remèdes accessibles et appropriés. La jurisprudence de la Cour de Strasbourg en reconnaissant la nécessité indispensable de respecter et de protéger les droits fondamentaux dans leur dimension procédurale est révélatrice à cet égard. En outre, l'idée même que les violations de fond du *jus cogens* ne seraient jamais impliquées dans ces cas est peu convaincante, même du point de vue du droit coutumier, comme nous allons essayer de montrer.

3 La pratique judiciaire relative à l'immunité de l'Etat pour des violations graves des droits de l'homme

Lorsqu'il s'agit de traiter les demandes relatives à l'immunité formulées par les Etats accusés de graves violations des droits de l'homme perpétrées en dehors de l'État du for, la grande majorité des tribunaux a jusqu'ici rejeté l'argument selon lequel le *jus cogens* l'emporte sur la règle coutumière relative à l'immunité de l'État. Au départ, il est nécessaire de noter que ces tribunaux n'ont jamais rejeté explicitement l'effet prépondérant *in abstracto* du *jus cogens*. Ils ont plutôt mis en évidence l'absence de la pratique et de l'*opinio juris* attestant de l'émergence d'une norme coutumière permettant le refus de l'immunité de l'État en raison de violations du *jus cogens*.

Les exemples les plus remarquables proviennent de l'arrêt *Al-Adsani* de la Cour européenne des droits de l'homme et des décisions *Bouzari* par les tribunaux canadiens, les deux concernent des réclamations portant sur des indemnités pour la torture subie dans des États autres que l'État du for (Koweït et Iran, respectivement). Dans *Al-Adsani*, la Cour de Strasbourg affirma dans un passage célèbre :

> Nonobstant le caractère particulier que le droit international reconnaît à la prohibition de la torture, la Cour n'aperçoit dans les instruments internationaux, les décisions judiciaires ou les autres documents en sa possession aucun élément solide lui permettant de conclure qu'en droit international un Etat ne jouit plus de l'immunité d'une action civile devant les cours et tribunaux d'un autre Etat devant lesquels sont formulées des allégations de torture (par. 61)...(...). En conséquence, même si elle note que l'importance primordiale de la prohibition de la torture est de plus en plus reconnue, la Cour ne juge pas établi qu'il soit déjà admis en droit international que les Etats ne peuvent prétendre à l'immunité en cas d'actions civiles en dommages-intérêts pour des actes de torture qui auraient été perpétrés en dehors de l'Etat du for (par. 66)[10].

---

10   En 2001 la Cour européenne des droits de l'homme a abordé la question dans trois affaires : *Al-Adsani* c. *Royaume-Uni*, *McElhinney* c. *Irlande* et *Fogarty* c. *Royaume-Uni*. Les requérants dans les trois cas ont fait valoir que le refus des juridictions nationales de connaître leurs revendications en raison de la règle de l'immunité des Etats avait violé leur droit d'accès à un tribunal en vertu de l'article 6 de la Convention européenne des Droits de l'Homme (CEDH) http://www.echr.coe.int/documents/convention_fra.pdf. Dans *Al-Adsani* c. *Royaume-Uni* (arrêt du 21 novembre 2001, n°35763/97), par une faible majorité, la Cour de Strasbourg a déclaré que les décisions prises par les tribunaux du Royaume-Uni reconnaissant l'immunité de l'Etat étranger de la juridiction civile en dépit de la preuve d'actes de torture contre le demandeur n'étaient pas en violation de l'article 6 de la Convention. La Cour d'appel (Civil Division) du Royaume-Uni, dans son arrêt dans l'affaire *Al-Adsani* c. *Gouvernement du Koweït et autres*, le 12 mars 1996, avait déclaré que la loi anglaise sur l'immunité (Loi sur l'immunité souveraine) est un code « *comprehensive* » non soumis à des « *overriding considerations* ». La Cour de Strasbourg a estimé que la Convention « ne saurait s'interpréter dans le vide » et que « La Convention doit autant que faire se peut s'interpréter de manière à se concilier avec les autres règles de droit international, dont elle fait partie intégrante, y compris celles relatives à l'octroi de l'immunité aux Etats » (par. 55). Par conséquent « On ne peut dès lors de façon générale considérer comme une restriction disproportionnée au droit d'accès à un

Quelques mois plus tard, dans la décision *Bouzari*, la *Ontario Superior Court of Justice* affirma de façon semblable :

> An examination of the decisions of national courts and international tribunals, as well as state legislation ..., indicates that there is no principle of customary international law which provides an exception from state immunity where an act of torture has been committed outside the forum, even for acts contrary to jus cogens.

Cette approche et les décisions qui en découlent ont ensuite été appliquées par la Chambre des Lords britannique dans l'affaire *Jones*, dans laquelle les décisions *Al-Adsani* et *Bouzari* ont été largement citées et ont reçu beaucoup de poids. Dans ces situations, le besoin perçu par les tribunaux d'identifier une norme coutumière sanctionnant l'effet prépondérant du *jus cogens* est évident. Ce qui n'est pas clair est le contenu d'une telle norme. Autrement dit, on ne sait pas si les tribunaux sont à la recherche de preuves de l'effet prépondérant de la (indéniablement impérative) interdiction de la torture, ou plutôt de l'état péremptoire (et de l'effet de primauté) d'une obligation procédurale accessoire que puisse permettre un remède civil aux victimes de torture. Bien que le point reste incertain, je voudrais ici simplement rappeler que, à mon avis, cette distinction entre les effets de fond et de procédure du *jus cogens* se traduit par un formalisme juridique peut-être séduisant, mais qui est, cependant, incompatible avec la structure et les achèvements du droit international des droits de l'homme.

4 L'évolution de la jurisprudence de la Cour suprême italienne

Il y a, toutefois, la jurisprudence *Ferrini* de la Cour de cassation italienne qui fournit les aperçus les plus importants pour la méthodologie à appliquer dans

---

tribunal tel que le consacre l'article 6 par. 1 des mesures prises par une Haute Partie contractante qui reflètent des règles de droit international généralement reconnues en matière d'immunité des Etats. De même que le droit d'accès à un tribunal est inhérent à la garantie d'un procès équitable accordée par cet article, de même certaines restrictions à l'accès doivent être tenues pour lui être inhérentes ; on en trouve un exemple dans les limitations généralement admises par la communauté des nations comme relevant de la doctrine de l'immunité des Etats. » (par. 56). Étant donné que la Cour a conclu que, en vertu du droit international, l'immunité de l'État continue de s'appliquer aux violations du *jus cogens*, l'argument de l'accès aux tribunaux a échoué.

les cas impliquant des allégations de l'immunité de l'État pour des violations graves des droits de l'homme. Cette jurisprudence est visiblement caractérisée par un éloignement de la dépendance du *jus cogens* en tant que règle de conflit vers une interprétation articulée et systématique de l'ordre juridique international. Alors que dans le bien connu arrêt *Ferrini* de 2004, la Cour suprême a présenté une pléthore d'arguments à l'appui de sa décision de refuser l'immunité à l'Allemagne pour les crimes contre l'humanité commis pendant la seconde guerre mondiale, il est juste de reconnaître que l'argument essentiel était celui de la primauté du *jus cogens*, qui a été jugé en gré de mettre de côté la règle coutumière sur l'immunité de l'Etat. Après avoir rappelé qu'on ne peut jamais déroger aux normes interdisant le travail forcé et l'expulsion forcée et que diverses autres conséquences sont liées à la commission de crimes internationaux, tels que la compétence universelle, le tribunal a déclaré :

> La reconnaissance de l'immunité de juridiction pour les États qui sont responsables de ces violations est en contraste flagrant avec le cadre normatif décrit ci-dessus, étant donné que cette reconnaissance entrave plutôt que protège ces valeurs, dont la protection est plutôt à considérer comme essentielle pour [...] toute la communauté internationale [...]. Il n'y a aucun doute que cette antinomie doit être résolue en donnant la priorité aux normes de rang supérieur [...]. Cela donc exclut la possibilité que, dans ces situations, l'État puisse profiter de l'immunité de la juridiction[11].

Cette jurisprudence italienne a été perfectionnée par le cas *Milde* de 2009 impliquant une action civile avancée par les victimes (ou leurs proches) des atrocités nazies dans les procédures pénales en cour contre un ancien officier du Troisième Reich. La Cour suprême a confirmé les décisions des juridictions inférieures à l'effet que l'Allemagne porte la responsabilité conjointe et solidaire pour compenser le préjudice subi par les victimes du crime contre l'humanité en jeu (massacre et atrocités associées infligées à une population civile). Le tribunal a développé l'approche interprétative esquissée dans le cas *Ferrini* et ses décisions de suivi de 2008. Ainsi, les « arguments précis et fiables de nature logique et systématique » ont démontré que

---

11 Le texte italien de la décision est publié dans la *Rivista di Diritto internazionale*, 2004, p. 539 ss. Voir M. Iovane, « The Ferrini Judgment of the Italian Supreme Court: Opening up Domestic Courts to claim of reparation for victims of serious violations of Fundamental Human Rights », *Italian Yearbook of International law*, Brill, 2004, p. 165 ss.

> La règle coutumière sur l'immunité juridictionnelle des Etats étrangers était [...] tenue de ne pas fonctionner chaque fois qu'elle entre en compétition avec le principe de droit international coutumier légitimant l'exercice des voies de recours pour obtenir l'indemnisation des dommages causés par les crimes internationaux découlant des violations graves des droits inviolables de l'homme.

Confrontée avec le problème de la jurisprudence contraire des autres États et de la Cour européenne des droits de l'homme, la Cour italienne a souligné que la décision de l'affaire

> Ne pouvait pas être fondée sur une approche purement quantitative, à savoir selon le nombre de décisions favorables à une position ou à l'autre. Bien que la pratique judiciaire des tribunaux nationaux soit importante pour discerner l'existence du droit coutumier international positif, le rôle de l'interprète ne consiste pas à un simple calcul arithmétique des éléments de la pratique. D'autres éléments ont également à être pris en compte, tels que la nature particulière qualitative des règles coutumières existantes, leurs interrelations réciproques et leur position hiérarchique dans l'ordre juridique international[12].

Cette approche minimise le rôle du *jus cogens* en tant que principe hiérarchique remplaçant automatiquement toute norme incompatible. En revanche, le fait qu'un État étranger est accusé de violations du *jus cogens* peut représenter un élément essentiel dans l'exercice d'interprétation systématique entrepris par les tribunaux, à savoir une *considération qualitative* qui fait fortement pencher la balance en faveur de la négation de l'immunité des États.

5 De la décision de la Cour internationale de Justice du 3 février 2012 sur les *Immunités Juridictionnelles de l'Etat* (*Allemagne c. Italie*) à la décision de 2014 de la Cour constitutionnelle italienne. Est-ce que celle-ci adopte une solution « dualiste » ? Indifférence de la question

La jurisprudence italienne *Ferrini* et *Milde* a été contestée par l'Allemagne devant la Cour internationale de Justice (CIJ). La Cour de cassation italienne

---

12   Voir cette décision dans *Italian Yearbook of International Law*, Brill, 2008, p. 325 ss., avec le commentaire de M. Iovane. Voir aussi R. Pavoni, « A Decade of Italian Case Law on the Immunity of Foreign States: Lights and Shadows », ibid., 2009, p. 73 ss.

avait en effet décidé le 28 mai 2008 dans 12 décisions identiques que la nécessité d'appliquer des règles de *jus cogens* sur les droits de l'homme (violées par l'Allemagne) l'emportait sur le droit coutumier sur l'immunité.

Dans sa décision du 3 février 2012 sur les immunités juridictionnelles de l'Etat (*Allemagne* c. *Italie*), la CIJ a statué contre l'Italie pour avoir nié l'immunité de la juridiction civile à l'Allemagne en lien avec les demandes d'indemnisation pour les crimes de guerre commis par les forces allemandes pendant la seconde guerre mondiale. De l'avis de la CIJ:

> La pratique étatique qui ressort des décisions judiciaires atteste qu'un Etat continue de jouir, dans le cadre d'instances civiles, de l'immunité à raison d'actes jure imperii lorsque sont en cause des actes ayant entraîné la mort, un préjudice corporel ou un préjudice matériel commis par ses forces armées et autres organes dans le cadre d'un conflit armé, même lorsque les actes en question ont eu lieu sur le territoire de l'Etat du for. Cette pratique est assortie de l'opinio juris, ainsi que l'attestent les positions de divers Etats et la jurisprudence d'un certain nombre de juridictions nationales, qui ont clairement indiqué qu'elles considéraient que le droit international coutumier exigeait de reconnaître l'immunité. L'absence presque totale de toute jurisprudence contraire est également significative, tout comme le fait qu'aucun Etat n'a jamais déclaré – que ce soit dans le cadre des travaux de la Commission du droit international sur l'immunité de l'Etat, de l'adoption de la Convention des Nations Unies ou dans tout autre contexte dont la Cour pourrait avoir connaissance – que le droit international coutumier ne prescrirait pas l'immunité dans ce type d'affaires (par. 77).

À la lumière de ce qui précède, la CIJ estime que le droit international coutumier continue à exiger que soit accordée à l'Etat l'immunité dans les procédures pour les délits qui auraient été commis sur le territoire d'un autre État par ses forces armées et par d'autres organes de l'Etat dans le cadre de la conduite d'un conflit armé (par. 91).

La CIJ conclut en effet que :

> Même en admettant que les actions intentées devant les juridictions italiennes mettaient en cause des violations de règles de jus cogens, l'application du droit international coutumier relatif à l'immunité des Etats ne s'en trouvait pas affectée (par. 97).

Le 22 octobre 2014, la Cour constitutionnelle italienne (« la Cour ») a rendu un arrêt concernant la légitimité constitutionnelle de certaines normes italiennes, qui ont été adoptées par l'Italie afin de donner application à la décision de la CIJ[13].

Selon la Cour, il n'y avait pas besoin de décider si le droit international coutumier concernant l'immunité de l'État pour les crimes de guerre et crimes contre l'humanité était incompatible avec le droit constitutionnel interne. La raison invoquée était qu'une telle règle, selon la construction qui lui est donné par la CIJ ne pouvait pas entrer dans l'ordre juridique italien. La raison en est que son conflit avec les principes de base de cet ordre rend impossible toute réception nationale par l'article 10 de la Constitution italienne, qui transpose le droit international coutumier automatiquement dans le droit domestique interne.

Cette solution adoptée en référence à la relation entre le système italien et le système international sera sûrement accusée d'être typiquement « dualiste »[14]. Les différends entre les « monistes » et les « dualistes », en fait, reviennent périodiquement à la mode, même si leur saison semble plutôt être liée à une époque où l'évaluation correcte et la structure des relations entre le droit interne et le droit international étaient débattues en termes purement théoriques. Aujourd'hui, il ne semble pas que le choix entre l'un ou l'autre système est directement lié, dans la pratique, à un examen plus attentif de la valeur du droit international dans le système national, et donc nous ne voyons pas l'utilité d'insister sur la nécessité de classer un système comme appartenant à l'une ou à l'autre « faction »[15]. D'autre part, cette décision est en bonne compagnie, puisque même la décision de la Cour de justice de l'Union européenne dans l'affaire *Kadi* a également été critiquée pour son « dualisme » lorsqu'elle a empêché une résolution du Conseil de sécurité des Nations Unies, qui établissait des limitations aux droits individuels pour des raisons liées à la prévention du

---

13   Pour des commentaires à cette décision voir B. Conforti, « La Cour constitutionnelle italienne et les droits de l'homme méconnus sur le plan international », *Revue générale de droit international public*, Edition A. Pedone, 2015, p. 353 ss. ; et au « Focus » dans *Italian Yearbook of International Law*, Brill, 2014, p. 1 ss. : « Judgment no. 238/2014 of the Italian Constitutional Court on the Constitutional Legality of State Immunity for International Crimes », avec les articles de F. Francioni, R. Pisillo Mazzeschi, M. Bothe, G. Cataldi, P. Palchetti.

14   Pour un premier exemple dans cette direction voir R. Kolb, « The relationship between the international and the municipal legal order: reflections on the decision no. 238/2014 of the Italian Constitutional Court », *Questions of International law, Zoom out II*, 2014, p. 5 ss.

15   Pour des informations plus détaillées sur le débat entre monistes et dualistes voir G. Cataldi, « Rapporti tra norme internazionali e norme interne », *Digesto delle discipline pubblicistiche*, vol. XII, Torino, 1997, p. 391 ss. et les auteurs *ivi* cit.

terrorisme transnational, de prendre effet dans le système juridique de l'Union européenne. La raison était que la résolution n'avait pas envisagé la possibilité de recours devant un juge par les individus soumis à ces limitations, un droit inaliénable selon les principes fondamentaux du système judiciaire de l'UE.[16] Cette jurisprudence est en conflit avec les décisions déjà mentionnées rendues par les tribunaux d'autres États, et même par la Cour européenne des droits de l'homme. Ceux-ci, à mon avis, méritent une grande préoccupation. La raison en est que l'application de la législation nationale est jugée nécessaire, en dépit d'un conflit – déterminé et confirmé – avec le droit coutumier et aux normes de *jus cogens*, car ces normes n'ont pas été spécifiquement transposées en droit interne et que, comme ce fut le cas avec la décision de la CIJ dans le cas *Allemagne c. Italie*, la règle de l'immunité est considérée comme de nature exclusivement procédurale[17].

Ce que nous devons nous demander, en dehors de toute discussion stérile sur la nature « moniste » ou « dualiste » de telle ou telle autre décision, est de savoir si dans un système démocratique, un tribunal, même se dissociant de la volonté des autres pouvoirs de l'Etat, peut ou ne peut pas ignorer une obligation internationale en raison d'un conflit affirmé avec les principes fondamentaux du système interne sans encourir une responsabilité internationale de l'Etat. Selon une opinion répandue, l'acceptation d'une telle perspective conduirait à plusieurs conséquences négatives qui peuvent être essentiellement résumées comme suit : a) d'abord, le danger de légitimer les tendances relativistes. Tout

---

16   Cour de justice des Communautés européennes, décision du 3 Septembre 2008, *Yassin Abdullah Kadi e Al Barakaat International Foundation c. Conseil et Commission européenne, affaire* C-402/05. Dans son arrêt, la Cour de justice prend en considération l'acte domestique interne (un règlement) sans examiner la légitimité de la résolution du Conseil de sécurité. En ce qui concerne l'accusation de « dualisme » de la décision, et la comparaison entre les valeurs constitutionnelles de l'Union et la nécessité de respecter le droit international, voir les considérations intéressantes de Kokott and Sobotta, « The Kadi Case – Constitutional Core Values and International law – Finding the Balance? », *European Journal of International Law*, 2012, p. 1015 ss. Deux décisions importantes de la Cour européenne des droits de l'homme vont dans le même sens en affirmant la violation de l'article 6 de la Convention (droit à un procès équitable) en raison de l'absence de recours au sein du système des Nations Unies à la disposition des particuliers pour le cas des sanctions prises par le Conseil de sécurité. Il s'agit de la décision du 12 septembre 2012 *Nada c. Suisse* et de la décision rendue le 26 novembre 2013 dans le cas *Al Dulimi c. Suisse* (confirmée par la Grande Chambre dan son arrêt du 22 juin 2016).

17   Voir Fox, *op. cit.,* note 8; H. Fox, « International Law and Restraints on the exercise of Jurisdiction by National Courts of States », *International Law*, M. D. Evans (par les soins de.), Oxford, 2014, p. 331 ss.

autre système *like-minded* ou un groupe d'Etats pourrait donner sa propre interprétation « à la carte » du droit coutumier. Combien de fois, par exemple, la communauté internationale a contesté les affirmations des États fondamentalistes islamiques concernant le conditionnement nécessaire de l'application nationale du droit international au respect des règles imposées par la *Sharia* ? ; b) Le danger de porter atteinte au « principe de la voix unique » (« *one voice Principle* ») de l'Etat, ce qui veut dire la promotion d'un affaiblissement de la position internationale de l'Etat en vertu des différentes évaluations effectuées par ses différents pouvoirs d'une question relevant de l'échelle internationale ; c) le risque de contre-mesures, ou de réactions de l'État lésé. Examinons les trois hypothèses séparément.

6 Nécessité d'un examen « substantiel » de la légitimité des décisions internationales par les juridictions nationales. La contribution de ces tribunaux à la *Rule of Law* de la communauté internationale dans le cas d'une convergence entre les valeurs nationales fondamentales et les valeurs reconnues au niveau international

Comme justement relevé[18], dans le système international, contrairement aux systèmes nationaux démocratiques, un examen formel de la légalité ne suffit pas, attendu que la présomption de légitimité ne peut pas fonctionner, étant donné le degré encore modeste de l'évolution de ce système. Il en résulte que les juges nationaux ne peuvent pas limiter leur compétence à un simple examen formel de la légalité des décisions internationales. Cela explique pourquoi les tribunaux nationaux effectuent un examen approfondi de chaque décision des tribunaux internationaux destinée à avoir un effet dans le système national, afin de vérifier si elle est conforme aux valeurs fondamentales de l'État qui sont exprimées en prévalence dans la Constitution de l'Etat.

---

18   N. Petersen, « Determining the Domestic Effect of International Law through the Prism of Legitimacy », ZAÖRV, 2012, p. 223 ss. Un examen seulement formel, et pour cette raison, à notre humble avis, à critiquer, est également à la base de ces décisions de la Cour européenne des droits de l'homme laquelle, chargée d'examiner le respect par les organisations internationales des principes d'une procédure régulière selon l'article 6 de la Convention, se limite à vérifier l'existence d'une norme dans les Statuts qui prévoit l'autonomie des organes juridictionnels de l'organisation, sans vérifier l'efficacité réelle d'une telle autonomie. Voir la décision du 18 février 1999, *Waite and Kennedy* c. *Allemagne* ([GC], n°26083/94).

Cet examen diffère en fonction du système. Par exemple, aux États-Unis d'Amérique, la Cour suprême a été explicite en affirmant que l'examen doit être réalisé en premier lieu, et surtout, par le législateur fédéral, comme manifestement affirmé dans l'affaire *Avena* relative à l'exécution d'une décision de la CIJ[19]. En Allemagne, d'autre part, la Cour constitutionnelle fédérale (*Bundesverfassungsgericht*, ci-après BVG), en affirmant que le système de « protection équivalente » devait être appliqué en ce qui concerne les décisions de la Cour de justice de l'Union européenne, sans nécessiter un examen de légitimité, a également expliqué que ce système ne concerne pas les autres cas, à l'égard desquels elle se réserve le droit de révision constitutionnelle complète. Cela vaut par exemple pour les décisions de la Cour européenne des droits de l'homme, qui sont censées être rendues avec une valeur contraignante, mais pas avec un caractère inconditionnel[20]. La même conclusion vaut aussi pour les décisions de la CIJ. Le BVG a déclaré en fait (en ce qui concerne l'article 36 de la Convention de Vienne sur les relations consulaires) que les normes des traités doivent être interprétées dans le sens voulu par la jurisprudence internationale et cela en se référant également aux décisions concernant les différends auxquels l'Allemagne n'est pas partie. Cependant, dans ce cas aussi, il souligne que cette obligation est conditionnée, attendu que les garanties conventionnelles doivent être équilibrées avec tous les principes constitutionnels applicables et concurrents, tels que l'efficacité procédurale. Il est donc envisagé que les juges nationaux peuvent ne pas tenir compte des décisions des

---

19 Cour suprême des États-Unis, *Sanchez-Llamas* c. *Oregon* et *Bustillo* c. *Johnson*, décision du 28 juin 2006, 548 U.S_2006, par laquelle la Cour suprême déclare que les décisions de la CIJ « ont droit uniquement à une « respectueuse considération » en raison d'une interprétation d'un accord international par un tribunal international. [...] ». La Cour suprême a rendu une décision similaire, le 25 mars 2008, dans le cas *Medelin* c. *Texas,* 552 US 2008, *International Legal Materials*, 2008, p. 287 ss. La non-application par les États-Unis de la décision de la CIJ dans l'affaire *Avena* (*Mexique* c. *États-Unis d'Amérique*) du 31 mars 2004, a ensuite été contestée par le Mexique. La CIJ, constatant la violation par les États-Unis, n'a cependant pas donné suite à la demande du Mexique d'ordonner aux tribunaux nationaux américains la mise en œuvre de la décision internationale (CIJ, arrêt du 19 janvier 2009, demande en interprétation de l'arrêt du 31 mars 2004 en l'affaire *Avena et autres ressortissants mexicains* (*Mexique* c. *États-Unis d'Amérique*).

20 La question à l'étude est traitée dans la décision du 14 octobre 2004 (2 BvR 1481-1404), sur la relation entre le système juridique allemand et la Convention. En ce qui concerne cette décision, voir M. Hartwig, « Much Ado About Human Rights: The Federal Constitutional Court Confronts the European Court of Human Rights », *German Law Journal*, 2005, p. 869 ss.

tribunaux internationaux en cas de principes constitutionnels concurrents.[21]. Dans ce cas, par conséquent, l'examen est sans aucun doute important, et non simplement procédural, et réalisé *ex post* par le juge plutôt que par le législateur, comme cela est le cas aux États-Unis.

Lorsque les principes fondamentaux du système juridique national garantis par l'examen des juridictions nationales suprêmes correspondent aussi aux « valeurs communes » de la Communauté internationale, ces tribunaux agissent également au service du système juridique international. Fondamentalement, dans ce cas, les juridictions nationales protègent le droit international.... de lui-même ! En termes de légitimité internationale, telle est la différence entre la protection des valeurs généralement non partagées (comme dans l'exemple déjà fourni en ce qui concerne la protection des principes religieux nationaux de nature « fondamentaliste ») et l'hypothèse à l'étude, dans laquelle la Cour constitutionnelle a adhéré à une valeur de la communauté internationale, et qui est le droit d'accès à un juge pour faire valoir le droit à l'indemnisation pour les dommages résultant de l'accomplissement de crimes de guerre constatés[22]. Du point de vue de la reconstruction théorique, le *dédoublement fonctionnel* de George Scelle[23], une théorie bien connue par les internationalistes, s'applique dans ce cas. Selon cette théorie, les tribunaux agissent également, dans le cadre du système juridique national, en tant qu'agents du système juridique international, en appliquant la *rule of law* de la Communauté internationale.

Pour les mêmes raisons, nous pensons que cette décision diffère également d'une autre de la Cour constitutionnelle italienne (n ° 264/2012), dans laquelle la théorie des contre-limites n'a pas été utilisée pour soutenir la primauté des droits fondamentaux de la personne, mais des exigences budgétaires de l'Etat, en proposant une reconstruction des droits fondamentaux « conditionnée »

---

21 Voir la décision du BVG, 19 septembre 2006, *Neue Juristische Wochenschrift*, 2007, p. 499 ss., qui vise trois affaires jointes (2 BvR 2115/01, 2 BvR 2132/01, 2 BvR 348/03).

22 La question est traitée en détail dans le volume de A. Nollkaemper, *National Courts and the International Rule of Law*, Oxford, 2011. À la page 84 l'auteur affirme que « [i]n all cases International Law should accept the power of national courts not to give effect to an international obligation that is incompatible with the international rule of law itself ».

23 G. Scelle, *Précis de droit des gens. Principes et systématique. Première partie*, Paris : Sirey, 1932, p. 43 ss. ; *Deuxième partie*, Paris : Sirey, 1934, p. 10 s. Pour une évaluation plus récente de la théorie, voir A. Cassese, « Remarks on Scelle's Theory of « Role Splitting » (dédoublement fonctionnel) in International Law », *European Journal of International Law*, Vol. 1 n° 01, 1990, p. 210 ss.

par la disponibilité des ressources, une proposition certainement ouverte à la critique[24].

Le facteur décisif est cependant le lien entre les valeurs nationales et les valeurs fondamentales internationalement reconnues ; si cette « connexion » existe, le jugement est également légitime du point de vue du droit international. Lorsqu'elles ont le droit de fonctionner de façon autonome, les juridictions nationales contribuent ainsi au développement et à la pleine affirmation de la « valeur juridique » du système international. Parfois, ce rôle est même défini comme une obligation précise, comme dans les décisions de la BVG allemande déjà mentionnées. Dans tous les cas, sur la question de la protection des droits fondamentaux, les tribunaux nationaux ont démontré qu'ils exercent un rôle central. Le meilleur exemple est donné précisément par la norme coutumière sur l'immunité juridictionnelle des Etats étrangers, qui, une fois absolue, est devenu relative en conséquence de la jurisprudence des tribunaux italiens et belges au début du siècle dernier[25]. Plus récemment, et encore avec référence aux résolutions du Conseil de sécurité concernant la lutte contre le terrorisme transnational, la procédure de *delisting* des terroristes présumés qui se sont avérés ne pas être tels à la lumière des contrôles effectués par les organismes des Nations Unies est la conséquence de la pression exercée par les juridictions nationales[26]. Par conséquent, loin d'être une décision « non conventionnelle » concernant le respect de la légalité internationale, la décision de la Cour constitutionnelle italienne adhère à la jurisprudence nationale sur l'interprétation et le développement correct du droit international.

7   Violation du « principe de la voix unique » de l'Etat ?

Le « principe de la voix unique » est le principe selon lequel, à la lumière de la position délicate du gouvernement dans la conduite des relations internationales, les juges nationaux ne devraient jamais totalement « diverger » des

---

24   Pour certaines critiques intéressantes sur le rôle principal attribué à l'économie et la subordination conséquente des droits fondamentaux, voir S. Rodotà, *Solidarietà. Un'utopia necessaria*, Editori Laterza, Roma-Bari, 2014.

25   Sur la question, voir B. Conforti, *Diritto Internazionale,* Napoli, Editoriale Scientifica, 2014, p. 266 ss.

26   Voir encore les observations de Nollkaemper, *op. cit.*, note 4, p. 302 ss., qui souligne les modifications apportées par le Conseil de sécurité des Nations Unies, en particulier avec la résolution 1904 (2009), au système de « listes noires » de terroristes présumés, suite aux décisions des juges nationaux (*bottom-up effect*) sur la nécessité de développer un système de révision à la demande des parties concernées.

positions exprimées par ledit gouvernement. Il est évident, aussi en vertu de l'émanation d'une disposition spécifique de droit relative à l'application de la décision de la CIJ, que, dans notre cas, il y a eu une fragmentation de la position italienne sur l'évolution de la relation entre l'immunité juridictionnelle des États et la protection des droits fondamentaux. Selon les récentes conclusions du Rapporteur spécial concernant les travaux de la Commission du droit international sur le droit coutumier, il en résulte que la pratique de l'Etat italien « compte pour peu », en particulier parce qu'elle n'est pas unitaire, à des fins d'identification du droit coutumier sur l'immunité de l'Etat étranger de la juridiction[27]. Ayant à l'esprit ce qui a déjà été dit en ce qui concerne le rôle des juridictions nationales dans la contribution à la formation et à la transformation du droit coutumier, nous croyons que ce principe n'est pas autre chose que l'une des théories élaborées dans les systèmes juridiques nationaux pour échapper au principe de la séparation des pouvoirs de l'Etat, ou à tout le moins pour l'atténuer. En substance, il s'agit d'une menace créée artificiellement pour l'indépendance des juges, destinée à neutraliser l'autonomie du pouvoir judiciaire en ce qui concerne les questions qui, en raison de leur nature « externe », sont considérés (à tort) hors de la portée de l'examen du juge, parce que strictement « politique ». La même chose peut être dite pour les théories, parfois formulées par les juges eux-mêmes, tels que l'*Act of State*, la « question politique », la réserve au pouvoir exécutif de l'interprétation des traités, l'obligation de ne pas soumettre à un examen judiciaire les actes « d'administration de haut niveau »[28]. Nous croyons qu'une décision telle que celle en cours d'examen est plutôt une sorte de « valeur ajoutée » aux fins de l'identification du droit coutumier, en particulier parce que le tribunal rend la décision en pleine conscience de se distancier de toute question de *policy* et avec l'intention de résoudre le problème uniquement en termes purement juridiques. En fin

---

27 Voir A/CN.4/672 du 22 mai 2014, Assemblée générale des Nations Unies, Commission du droit international, 66e session, Deuxième rapport sur l'identification du droit international coutumier par Michael Wood, Rapporteur spécial, Projet de Conclusion 8. 2 : « Lorsque les organes de l'Etat ne parlent pas d'une seule voix, moins de poids doit être donné à leur pratique ».

28 Pour ces théories, voir B. Conforti, « Cours Général de Droit International Public », *Recueil des cours de l'Académie de droit international de La Haye*, Brill, 1988, V, p. 30 ss. ; Nollkaemper, *op. cit.*, p. 51 ss. L'absence de compétence à l'égard des décisions de « haut niveau administratif » de l'Etat a été confirmée par la Cour de cassation italienne dans la décision du l8 février 2002 dans l'affaire *Markovic*, relative à la responsabilité du bombardement de l'OTAN sur Belgrade de l'avril 1999 (Voir *Italian Yearbook of International Law*, 2002, p. 292 ss., avec un commentaire de G. Bruno). La Cour européenne des droits de l'homme a également statué sur cette question.

de compte, à chacun ses compétences, et les considérations de politique internationale devraient toujours être exclues de la gamme « technique » de l'action d'un tribunal.

8 Les réactions possibles à cette décisions par l'Etat étranger en cause. Conclusions

Le dernier aspect à examiner concerne la gamme des réactions possibles à cette décision par l'État concerné, qui est l'Allemagne. Il faut d'abord déterminer quelles règles internationales sont considérées comme ayant été violées par l'Italie. Cependant, il faut dire aussi que nous pouvons parler d'une violation effective de la décision de la CIJ de 2012 seulement comme conséquence d'une décision rendue par un tribunal qui refuse l'immunité à l'Allemagne dans un cas concret, attendu que la décision de la Cour constitutionnelle concernant l'impossibilité de mettre en œuvre la décision internationale dans le système national ne suffit pas à cette fin. D'une grande importance est le principe codifié à l'article 27 de la Convention de Vienne sur le droit des traités,[29] concernant l'interdiction de justifier la non-exécution d'un traité en conséquence d'un empêchement de droit interne[30]. Deuxièmement, il est incontestable que, selon le droit international, la mise en œuvre d'une décision de la CIJ est obligatoire pour l'État auquel elle s'adresse. Le consentement de l'État à la compétence de la CIJ implique également le consentement à la mise en œuvre de ses décisions. Cela ressort clairement de la lettre même de l'article 94.1 de la Charte des Nations Unies, qui dit que : « Chaque Membre des Nations Unies s'engage à se conformer à la décision de la Cour internationale de Justice dans tout litige auquel il est partie ». Il s'agit donc d'une obligation internationale de l'État, et sans doute d'une obligation de nature conventionnelle, comme confirmé par le Statut de la CIJ, en particulier par l'article 59, qui affirme que : « La décision de la Cour n'est obligatoire que pour les parties en litige et dans le cas qui a été décidé », et par l'article 60, sur le principe de la chose jugée, qui affirme que : « L'arrêt est définitif et sans recours ». Il s'agit cependant aussi d'une obligation coutumière, en application de la règle *pacta sunt servanda* et du principe général de « bonne foi ». A tout ça, il faut ajouter que la compétence de la CIJ dans le différend entre l'Allemagne et l'Italie a été fondée sur l'article 1 de la Convention du Conseil de l'Europe du 29 Avril 1957 relative au

---

29 Nations Unies, *Recueil des traités*, vol. 1155, p. 331.
30 L'article 27 affirme : « Une partie ne peut invoquer les dispositions de son droit interne comme justifiant la non-exécution d'un traité. Cette règle est sans préjudice de l'article 46 ».

règlement pacifique des différends, une règle qui peut donc également être considérée comme violée.

Commençons par le principe de l'impossibilité d'utiliser le droit interne pour éviter de se conformer à une obligation internationale. Un tel principe peut être applicable même dans le cas de l'affirmation, par la Cour suprême d'un système national, de la nécessité de mettre en œuvre les principes fondamentaux de l'ordre interne pour protéger les droits de l'individu reconnus comme tels par le système juridique international ? La réponse, à notre avis, est sans aucun doute négative, sur la base des considérations déjà fournies concernant la « double fonction » revêtue dans ce cas par la Cour constitutionnelle. Comme nous l'avons déjà précisé, cette possibilité ne peut être admise que dans le cas d'une coïncidence parfaite entre valeurs domestiques nationales et internationales. A ces considérations, nous ajoutons que les précédents, y compris ceux de la pratique italienne, ne montrent pas de réactions particulières et importantes[31]. Une autre raison d'exclusion de l'illégalité pourrait être la circonstance, déjà soulignée, que la violation du droit à un juge, résultant d'une décision d'un organisme international, a été considérée intolérable soit par la Cour de Luxembourg dans l'affaire *Kadi*, soit par la Cour de Strasbourg dans les cas *Al-Dulimi* et *Nada*, deux juridictions supranationales lesquelles, par un recours des parties intéressées, pourraient avoir (au moins en théorie) censuré le travail des autorités italiennes dans le cas de mise en œuvre de la décision de la CIJ.

Quelles mesures l'État allemand pourrait entreprendre pour contraindre l'Italie à appliquer la décision ? Le recours à des « contre-mesures » apparaît improbable, dès lors que les deux Etats sont liés par l'obligation spéciale représentée par leur appartenance à l'Union européenne[32]. L'Allemagne pourrait demander à la CIJ une nouvelle décision visant à affirmer la non-conformité

---

31 Nous devrions garder à l'esprit, par exemple, la décision de la Cour constitutionnelle italienne du 27 juin 1996, n°223. La Cour n'a pas hésité dans ce cas à déclarer contraire au principe constitutionnel fondamental interdisant la peine capitale (article 27, par. 4, Constitution) la loi qui a introduit dans l'ordre italien le traité d'extradition de 1983 avec les États-Unis, dans la section qui envisage la possibilité d'extrader un individu condamné à mort aussi longtemps que l'Etat requérant ait n'a pas fourni de « garanties suffisantes » que la peine ne serait pas appliquée. Il ne semble pas que cette décision ait suscité des réactions particulières de la part des États-Unis, même si elle signifie essentiellement la non-exécution d'un traité bilatéral qui était en vigueur. Voir G. Cataldi, *Italian Yearbook of International Law*, 1999, p. 174 ss.

32 L'adoption de contre-mesures est interdite, dans les relations entre les Etats membres, par le droit de l'Union européenne pour ce qui concerne les obligations résultant du droit de l'Union en particulier.

italienne[33]. Mais il ne semble pas qu'une telle initiative serait efficace à la lumière des précédents, en particulier, le différend déjà mentionné entre les États-Unis et le Mexique dans l'affaire *Avena*, même si ce cas particulier, dans la perspective de la prise en compte des droits de l'homme, était diamétralement opposé à l'affaire en l'examen, dès lors que la CIJ avait demandé aux États-Unis de remédier, dans le système national, à une violation d'un droit inaliénable de l'individu et, sur le recours du Mexique, avait alors qualifié le refus des États-Unis comme une nouvelle violation, sans toutefois que cette deuxième décision produisisse des effets pratiques. Il convient en effet souligner que la CIJ a habilement évité d'entrer trop dans le système national des États-Unis, nonobstant les demandes du Mexique.

Nous devons aussi considérer que, compte tenu de l'absence de toute pratique importante en la matière, cette possibilité est considérée par beaucoup une sorte de « cas d'école », défini comme « *une branche morte de l'arbre des Nations Unies* »[34].

L'instrument final abstraitement concevable que l'Allemagne pourrait utiliser serait de renvoyer l'affaire au Comité des Ministres du Conseil de l'Europe, en application de l'article 39, par. 2, de la Convention européenne sur le règlement pacifique des différends[35]. Toutefois, cette possibilité semble également improbable, en particulier à cause de la conséquence absurde résultant d'une mobilisation du Comité des Ministres du Conseil de l'Europe (l'institution établie pour garantir la mise en œuvre de la Convention européenne des droits de l'homme dans les Etats contractants) contre un Etat membre dont la

---

[33] Pour cette possibilité voir B. I. Bonafé, « Et si l'Allemagne saisissait à nouveau la Cour international de Justice ? », *Ordine internazionale e diritti umani*, 2014, p. 1049 ss.

[34] L. Condorelli, « L'autorité de la décision des juridictions internationales permanentes », *La Juridiction Internationale Permanente, Colloque de Lyon de la SFDI*, Paris, 1987, p. 297. Pour une interprétation plus optimiste de cet article voir M. I. Papa, *I rapporti tra la Corte internazionale di Giustizia e il Consiglio di Sicurezza*, Padova, CEDAM, 2006, p. 103 ss. (en particulier p. 135). Dans l'affaire des *Activités militaires et paramilitaires au Nicaragua et contre le Nicaragua* (CIJ, arrêt du 27 juin 1986, Nicaragua c. États-Unis), le Nicaragua a tenté d'utiliser l'article 94,2, mais la décision du Conseil de sécurité a été empêchée par le veto des États-Unis.

[35] L'article 39 dit : « 1. Chacune des Hautes Parties contractantes se conformera à l'arrêt de la Cour internationale de Justice ou à la sentence du tribunal arbitral dans tout litige auquel elle est partie. 2. Si une partie à un litige ne satisfait pas aux obligations qui lui incombent en vertu d'un arrêt rendu par la Cour internationale de Justice ou d'une sentence rendue par le tribunal arbitral, l'autre partie peut recourir au Comité des Ministres du Conseil de l'Europe et celui-ci, s'il le juge nécessaire, peut, par un vote à la majorité des deux tiers des représentants ayant le droit de siéger au Comité, faire des recommandations en vue d'assurer l'exécution de l'arrêt ou de la sentence. ».

Cour constitutionnelle a cherchée à ... garantir les droits fondamentaux de la personne.

La vérité est que le système législatif allemand lui-même est à considérer comme le plus proche des évaluations de la Cour constitutionnelle italienne en ce qui concerne la relation entre l'obligation de mettre en œuvre une décision internationale et la protection des droits garantis par la Constitution. Cette considération à la fin rend assez faible toute réaction ou protestation par cet Etat. Cela à la lumière de la décision du 19 septembre 2006 déjà mentionnée du BVG, concernant la violation de l'article 36 de la Convention de Vienne sur les relations consulaires, et en tenant compte également de l'évolution qui a eu lieu dans les relations entre le système juridique allemand et le système juridique de l'Union européenne. Seulement en se limitant à la « nouvelle phase » de cette évolution, mettant de côté toute la jurisprudence « Solange », dans le cas bien connu *Lissabon Urteil* du 30 juin 2009, le BVG a été clair en affirmant la nécessité du respect du « *noyau substantiel et intangible de l'identité constitutionnelle de la Loi Fondamentale allemande* »[36].

En conclusion, la décision dont on a parlé a été rendue en pleine application des principes sur la séparation des pouvoirs de l'État. Il s'agit, à notre avis, d'un insigne d'honneur pour l'Italie et pour les droits de l'homme, qui, on l'espère, peut contribuer à l'évolution de la règle coutumière sur l'immunité des Etats étrangers de la juridiction civile dans un sens qui soit respectueux des droits fondamentaux de l'individu. Toute question concernant la mise en œuvre de la décision de la CIJ dans le système italien, à partir de la loi n° 5/2013 relative aux différentes décisions nationales qui ont été émises au fil du temps, témoigne, même dans ses différentes solutions, de l'attention accordée à la question, et donc de l'existence d'une attitude positive quant à la nécessité de mettre en œuvre des jugements internationaux dans l'ordre interne, solution qui n'est certainement pas niée par la nécessité affirmée d'appliquer les principes fondamentaux du système juridique interne. Pour renforcer notre affirmation, nous rappelons que le 25 novembre 2014 le gouvernement italien a communiqué l'acceptation de la clause facultative sur la compétence de la CIJ, conformément à l'article 36, par. 2, du Statut de la CIJ.

Si la décision de la Cour constitutionnelle italienne a créé un précédent, cela pourrait ouvrir de nouveaux « fronts » de demandes d'indemnisation pour les crimes de guerre, peut-être même contre l'Italie. Encore une fois, nous croyons que ces préoccupations ne devraient pas entrer dans l'appréciation du juge.

---

36 Voir J. Ziller, « Solange III, ovvero la *Europarechtsfreundlichkeit* del *Bundesverfassungsgericht*. A proposito della sentenza della Corte Costituzionale Federale Tedesca sulla ratifica del Trattato di Lisbona », *Rivista Italiana di Diritto Pubblico Comunitario*, 2009, pp. 973 ss.

Protecting Children in and at War: From Legally Protected Subjects to 'Others' in the Conflict*

Nasrin Mosaffa

1 Introduction

Today's world is encountering an increasing number of conflicts, each challenging the basic tenets of international order and the fundamentals of international legal instruments. One common characteristic of all these conflicts is the central role of children, in and at war, or often 'at both ends of the gun' with an estimation of one billion children living in conflict zones.[1] In 2016, so far fifteen situations before the United Nations Security Council (UNSC) have been concerned with grave breaches of laws relating to children.[2] These situations are in addition to the already existing cases before the highest world body in charge of maintaining international peace and security. These have resulted in fourteen resolutions,[3] the establishment of a working group,[4]

---

* To Djamchid Momtaz, who alongside Yolande Momtaz, has never failed to embrace people with his generosity and treat them as 'ours' and not exclude them as 'others.'
1 UNICEF, *Machel Study 10-Year Strategic Review: Children And Conflict In A Changing World*, 2009.
2 These situations concern Afghanistan, Central African Region (LRA-affected areas), Central African Republic, Colombia, Democratic Republic of Congo, Iraq, Mali, Myanmar (Burma), Nigeria, the Philippines, Somalia, South Sudan, Sudan, Syrian Arab Republic, and Yemen.
3 As of 30 June 2016: UN Docs. S/RES/1261, 25 August 1999, S/RES/1314, 11 August 2000, S/RES/1379, 20 Nov 2001, S/RES/1460, 30 January 2003, S/RES/1539, 22 April 2004, S/RES/161, 25 July 2005, S/RES/1698, 31 July 2006, S/RES/1882, 4 August 2009, S/RES/1888, 30 September 2009, S/RES/1998, 12 July 2011, S/RES/2068, 19 September 2012, S/RES/2143, 7 March 2014 and S/RES/2225, 18 June 2015.
4 The Security Council Working Group on Children and Armed Conflict, comprised of representatives of all 15 members of the UNSC, was formed pursuant to the Security Council resolution 1616 (S/RES/1616, 29 July 2005) to review reports on violations against children affected by armed conflict committed by parties listed in the annexes to the Secretary-General's report on children and armed conflict. For more details on the mandate of the Working Group, see UN Doc. S/RES/1616, 29 July 2005,) and for more on conduct and activities of the Working Group, see https://www.un.org/sc/suborg/en/subsidiary/wgcaac.

and the submission of several reports by the UN Secretary-General or his[5] representatives.[6]

In this context, and twenty years after the establishment of the Office of the Special Representative of the Secretary-General for Children and Armed Conflict (OSRSGCAC), the present article offers a political-legal analysis of existing challenges in the international legal order as regards protection of children in and at war.

This paper argues that despite a growing corpus of international law and increasing global awareness to protect children during armed conflicts, significant work remains to ensure overarching protection. The evidence of existing shortcomings is the latest Annual Report of the Secretary-General on Children and Armed Conflict, which expresses shock about 'the scale of the grave violations' of law committed against children.[7] This failure is due to differences in how international law perceives (and protects) children as vulnerable (or sometimes the most vulnerable of the vulnerable groups), and how warring parties view children as a symbolic agent. Thus, children remain a separate group in and at war, and are regarded as a party in the conflict. Violating their rights is a shortcut to gaining strategic or tactical advantages. This signifies the broader shift in the nature and character of war.

This article first reviews the existing legal framework for the protection of children during armed conflicts. This includes an outline of fundamental beliefs and motives that led to drafting and implementing the existing legal regime and, specifically, a discussion on the idea of the vulnerability of children. This view is contrasted in the second section with a social interpretation of the concept of childhood. This contains various understandings of children's roles in society and a different grasp of their role during armed conflict, which runs counter to the depiction of children as silent victims.

The prevalence and centrality of children in armed conflict are the result of broad shifts in the nature and character of conflict and war. This is discussed in

---

5 A digression to this article but a (self-satisfactory and) needed note: it was my hope that by the time of the publication of this article, United Nations could welcome its first female Secretary-General. Regrettably, this did not happen even this time.

6 The Office of the Special Representative of the Secretary-General for Children and Armed Conflict (OSRSGCAC) was recommended in of Graça Machel's groundbreaking report on *the impact of armed conflict on children* (1996), which appeared after UN General Assembly Resolution 51/77 (UN Doc A/RES/51/77, 20 February 1997. For a detailed timeline on the mandate of OSRSGCAC, see The Office of the Special Representative of the Secretary-General for Children and Armed Conflict, 'Timeline.' Accessed June 2, 2016. https://childrenandarmed conflict.un.org/mandate/timeline/.

7 UN Doc. A/70/836-S/2016/360, 20 April 2016.

the second section of the paper. The conclusion shows the need for a paradigm shift in understanding the role of children in armed conflicts, and how warring parties regard children not as a protected group, but as a party to the conflict, at whose expense victory could be achieved through subjecting them to killing, traumatizing, exploiting, deporting or other grave and despicable harms.

2   Childhood, Vulnerability and Rights: The Evolving Framework of Protection

The widespread famine facing European children in 1946 in the aftermath of the Second World War (1939–1945) created an impetus for the United Nations to act for the protection of children. This led to the formation of the United Nations Children's Emergency Fund (UNICEF). But it is worth recalling that the history of international legislation on children is older than the United Nations. For example, in 1923, the Geneva Declaration of the Rights of the Child was adopted by the International Save the Children Union, and was subsequently endorsed by the League of Nations in 1924 as the World Child Welfare Charter.[8] In 1959, the Declaration of the Rights of the Child set out that 'the child shall in all circumstances be among the first to receive protection and relief.'[9] The Declaration paved the way for drafting a comprehensive document, which was adopted in 1989 as the Convention on the Rights of the Child (UNCRC),[10] to ensure the survival, growth, and protection of children.[11]

The UNCRC gives priority to social values, societal environment, and cultural traditions[12] in recognizing every human being below the age of eighteen years as a child unless under the law applicable to the child, majority age, is attained earlier.[13] The Convention signifies a quasi-universal acknowledgment of childhood, yet implies that childhood, at its core, is socially defined. The recognition of the fact that the definition of childhood is socially influenced

---

8   Geneva Declaration of the Rights of the Child, Adopted 26 September, 1924, League of Nations.
9   *Declaration of the Rights of the Child*, UN Doc. A/RES/14/1386, 20 November 1959, Principle 8.
10 United Nations Convention on the Rights of the Child, UN Doc. A/RES/44/25 of 20 November 1989 (entered into force 2 September 1990).
11 Ibid., Preamble.
12 See T. Schapiro, 'What is a Child?', 109 *Ethics*, 1999, p. 716; J. Hart & B. Tyrer, 'Research with Children Living in Situations of Armed Conflict: Concepts, Ethics and Methods', *Refugees Studies Centre Working Paper No. 30*, 2006.
13 UNCRC Article 1.

is important for assessing inconsistent treatment across the world,[14] in war or in peace.[15]

However, the common view of childhood is driven by the idea of vulnerability,[16] that the child is 'entitled to special care and assistance'[17] due to 'his physical and mental immaturity'.[18] According to the same view, given a child's inability to protect himself/herself and being exposed to greater indigenous or exogenous harms, an elaborate framework should be developed to protect children. Since the adoption of the UNCRC, a comprehensive body of law and institutions has striven to do so.

2.1 Existing Body of Law

Despite drastic changes in global realities since their inception, International Human Rights Law (IHRL)[19] and International Humanitarian Law (IHL)[20] still attempt to provide general and focused protection of children in and at war. Although the traditional distinction was to regard IHRL as peace-time-oriented

---

14　The global inconsistency is exemplified by differing standards of the western liberal order, and other cultures.

15　Section three details how differing social constructions of childhood (its status and rights) lead to elevating the child to an agent in a conflict (not just a witness) that is victimized or (perceivably and conceptually) empowered through conflict.

16　For more, see B. Turner, *Vulnerability and Human Rights*, Penn State University Press, 2006.

17　The 1949 Universal Declaration of Human Rights, Article 25.

18　See preamble of the 1959 Declaration of the Rights of the Child, G.A. res. 1386 (XIV), 14 U.N. GAOR Supp. (No. 16) at 19, UN Doc. A/4354.

19　UNCRC, Annex; UN Doc. A/RES/54/263, 16 March 2001, Annex I–II; International Labour Organization (ILO), Convention No. 182 Concerning The Prohibition and Immediate Action for the Elimination of the Worst Forms of Child Labour, 2133 UNTS 161, 17 June 1999; Convention on the Elimination of All Forms of Discrimination against Women, UN Doc. A/RES/34/180.

20　Geneva Convention (I) for the Amelioration of the Condition of the Wounded and Sick in Armed Forces in the Field, 75 UNTS 31, 12 August 1949; Geneva Convention (II) for the Amelioration of the Condition of Wounded, Sick and Shipwrecked Members of Armed Forces at Sea, 75 UNTS 85, 12 August 1949; Geneva Convention (III) Relative to the Treatment of Prisoners of War, 75 UNTS 135, 12 August 1949; Geneva Convention (IV) Relative to the Protection of Civilian Persons in Time of War, 75 UNTS 287, 12 August 1949; Protocol (I) Additional to the Geneva Conventions of 12 August 1949, and Relating to the Protection of Victims of International Armed Conflicts, 1125 UNTS 3, 8 June 1977, Article 77 & 78; Protocol (II) Additional to the Geneva Conventions of 12 August 1949, and Relating to the Protection of Victims of Non-International Armed Conflicts, 1125 UNTS 609, 8 June 1977, Article 4, reprinted in 16 ILM 1442 (1977).

and IHL as the law applicable during armed conflict, the close relation of the two is now established,[21] but needs further clarification.[22] The context of armed conflict turns the eye primarily to civil and political rights (and the right to life in the case of IHL).[23] However, economic, social and cultural rights would also be applicable.[24]

The existing interpretation of IHL and IHRL criminalizes killing, maiming, torturing and raping children, the recruitment of child soldiers, attacking schools and hospitals, and denying humanitarian access.[25] The engine behind enforcement of these laws against the involvement of children in situations of armed conflict is the United Nations Security Council, and it could be argued that the force behind change in protecting children in or at war is the UNSC. In a series of resolutions to enhance the protection of children and end the impunity of perpetrators of violations of the relevant international law, the Council requested the Secretary-General to record such violations in his Report on Children and Armed Conflict.[26]

These six grave violations are also recognized in various international criminal jurisdictions.[27] Within the existing framework of IHL, some regional

---

21   See Geneva Conventions Additional Protocol (I), Articles 72, 75, and 76.
22   H. J. Heintze, 'On the Relationship Between Human Rights Law Protection and International Humanitarian Law', 86 *International Review of the Red Cross*, 2004, pp. 789–814; L. Luball, 'Challenges in Applying Human Rights Law to Armed Conflict', 87 *International Review of the Red Cross*, 2005, pp. 737–54.
23   See C. Droege, 'Elective Affinities? Human Rights and Humanitarian Law', 90 *International Review of the Red Cross*, 2008, pp. 501–48; E. Riedel, 'International Law Shaping Constitutional Law, Realization of Economic, Social and Cultural Rights', in E. Riedel (ed) *Constitutionalism—Old Concepts, New Worlds, German Contributions to the VIth World Congress of the International Association of Constitutional Law*, Berliner Wissenschaftsverlag, 2005, pp. 105–21.
24   A very illuminating and detailed review of Economic, Social, and Cultural Rights in Armed Conflict is provided in E. Riedel, 'Economic, Social, and Cultural Rights in Armed Conflict', in A. Clapham & P. Gaeta (eds), *The Oxford Handbook of International Law in Armed Conflict*, Oxford University Press, 2014, pp. 657–678.
25   Known as six grave violations against children.
26   See UN Doc. S/RES/1882, 4 August 2009; UN Doc. S/RES/1888, 30 September 2009; UN Doc. S/RES/1998, 12 July 2011; UN Doc. S/RES/2225, 18 June 2015.
27   Rome Statute of the International Criminal Court, 2187 UNTS 90, 17 July 1998, Article 6(e), 7(c), 8(b)(xxvi), 8(e)(vii); Statute of the Special Court for Sierra Leone, UN Doc. S/RES/1315, 14 August 2000, Article 4(c), 5(a); Statute of the International Tribunal for Rwanda, UN Doc. S/RES/995, 8 November 1994, Article 2.2(e); Statute of the International Tribunal for the Former Yugoslavia, UN Doc. S/RES/827, 25 May 1993, Article 4.2(e).

arrangements have also pursued regional protection.[28] A growing body of case law is also a glowing beacon of hope to end impunity and further existing protections, but not a very shining one yet. The Special Court for Sierra Leone (SCSL)[29] and the International Criminal Court (ICC)[30] have dealt with cases that were directly concerned with a specific crime against children (use of child soldiers). Generic international crimes (i.e. killing and rape) have also been dealt with in cases[31] before the International Criminal Tribunals for the Former Yugoslavia and for Rwanda. It is worth recalling that in its first decided case the ICC convicted Thomas Lubanga Dyilo as a war criminal, which reaffirmed hope in the functioning of the ICC but also showed challenges in establishing the relevance of existing laws regarding the nature of conflicts and grave violations of laws relating to children. Nevertheless, the Dyilo case proved to be a 'ruling of precedential value in respect of the issues of both child soldiering and general sentencing.'[32]

3 Back in the Conflict: Different Interpretations of Childhood

Formulation and implementation of the much-needed legal protection regime for children (specifically during armed conflict) is based on perceiving children as vulnerable. This is particularly the case when warring parties (given their culture and traditions as regards the status of the child) do not regard

---

28 See N. Mosaffa, 'Does the Covenant on the Rights of the Child in Islam Provide Adequate Protection for Children Affected by Armed Conflicts?' 8 *Muslim World Journal of Human Rights*, 2011.

29 Prosecutor v Taylor, Case No. SCSL-03-01-T, 30 May 2012; Prosecutor v Brima, Kamara and Kanu, Case No SCSL-2004-16-A, 22 Feb 2008.

30 Prosecutor v Dyilo, Decision on Sentence, ICC-01/04-01/06-2901, 10 July 2012.

31 Prosecutor v Kunarac, Case No. IT-96-23-T & IT-96-23/1-T, Trial Judgment, International Crimiminal Tribunal for the former Yugoslavia, 22 February 2001; Prosecutor v Furundzija, Case No. IT-95-17/1-T, Judgment, International Criminal Tribunal for the former Yugoslavia, 10 December 1998; Prosecutor v Akayesu, Case No. ICTR-96-4-T, Judgment, International Criminal Tribunal for Rwanda 2 Sept. 1998; Prosecutor v Musema, Case No. ICTR-96-13-T, Judgment and Sentence, International Criminal Tribunal for Rwanda, 27 Jan. 2000. See also C. Aptel, 'International Criminal Justice and Child Protection', in S. Parmar, M. J. Roseman, S. Siegrist & T. Sowa (eds), *Children and Transitional Justice: Truth-Telling, Accountability and Reconciliation*, UNICEF, 2010, pp. 67–114.

32 M. E. Kurth, 'The Lubanga Case of the International Criminal Court: A Critical Analysis of the Trial Chamber's Findings on Issues of Active Use, Age, and Gravity', 5 *Goettingen Journal of International Law*, 2013 pp. 431–453.

children as vulnerable or in need of protection but a group to be entrusted with military assignments and 'grow' through actual participation in combat; or to be targeted and victimized because they symbolize 'the Other'—the enemy that gives meaning to war. In other words, children subjected to gross violations are often regarded as a threat because they are pictured as the long arm of their adults (or tribes, clans, State, family, etc.). Killing them would be a triumph for one side in the conflict. Simply put, in this sense, children are not vulnerable humans but powerful threats. Violating their rights, exploiting or killing them is tantamount to winning a battle or war. Before detailing this further, an explanation of the concept of 'the Other' is necessary.

3.1 Studying 'the Other'

International-relations studies of international law have been historically influenced by a traditional dichotomy between realism and liberalism.[33] Nevertheless, the rise of critical approaches to international relations has challenged traditional thinking and led to changing assumptions about international law. These approaches highlight that children may actually 'possess agency within the conflict' and have the capacity, albeit limited, to influence the trajectories of conflicts: this focuses attention on the importance of children's perspectives and experience.[34]

Specifically constructivism—where ideas have a fundamental role[35]—studies identity on the basis that 'people act towards objects, including other actors, on the basis of the meaning that the objects have for them.' This approach emphasizes that childhood is not understood simply on the basis of biological traits (i.e. the universal understanding) but is very much dependent on how childhood identity is interpreted in different societies and also on how childhood is represented. Therefore, childhood is not a universally agreed concept but a subjective understanding based on knowing Self and the Other;[36] 'what

---

[33] For a tour de force of the nexus between IL and IR, and lenses for analyzing it, see D. Armstrong, T. Farrell & H. Lambert. *International Law and International Relations*. Cambridge University Press, 2012, Kindle Edition. Specifically, see chapter 3.

[34] K. Lee-Koo, 'Children and IR: Creating Space for Children.' K. Huynh, B. D'Costa, & K. Lee-Koo (eds) In *Children and Global Conflict*, edited by Cambridge University Press, 2015, pp. 65–88.

[35] A. Wendt, *Social Theory of International Politics*, Cambridge University Press, 1999, pp. 92–138.

[36] T. Flockhart, 'Visions and Decisions: A New Security Order', in T. Flockhart et al. (eds), *From Vision to Reality, Implementing the New European Security Order*, Westview Press, 1998.

actors collectively know' is based on identities and social facts,[37] and interpreting the social reality[38] of a particular problematization.[39]

In the context of this article a Self (i.e. a warlord, a rebel group, a State) prescribes how one apprehends and understands reality (childhood), since it 'impl[ies] a particular set of interests or preferences in respect of the choice of action'[40] which determines agents and interests. In tribal clashes, for example, one tribe is defined and given meaning by its rivalry or history with another tribe. Thus, a child from that particular tribe could be considered as an 'Other' that represents the greater relation between tribes. In this understanding, child is not vulnerable but capable of agency role and status. This strand provides a refreshing focus on political, legal and ethical norms as explanatory variables in global politics, a driving force and result of international law.[41] The ideational approach in analyzing legalese owes its rise to the changing nature of politics and warfare.

3.2 *New Wars*

The increasing attention to children in armed conflict as witnesses, victims and especially participants[42] was noticed when after the end of the Cold War in 1989, a 'child soldier crisis'[43] emerged as an epidemic across every continent. Historically, though, the nexus between war and the definition of childhood is much older. For example, the United States Civil War is deemed as a 'war of boy soldiers' that started with children in support roles but gradually developed to their 'graduating' and growing into combat roles. The same can be said about Napoleon's conscription of many children and teenagers in 'the war orphans of the Guard' in 1814.

---

37 I. B. Neumann, *Uses of the Other: 'The East' in European Identity Formation.* University of Minnesota Press, 1999.

38 P. L. Berger & T. Luckmann, *The Social Construction Of Reality*, Doubleday, 1966.

39 D. Campbell, *Writing Security: United States Policy and the Politics of Identity*, University of Minnesota Press, 1998; V. Kubalkova, 'Foreign Policy, International Politics, and Constructivism', in V. Kubálková (ed) *Foreign Policy in a Constructed World*, M. E. Sharpe, 2001.

40 T. Hopf, 'The Promise of Constructivism in International Relations Theory', 23 *International Security*, 1998, p. 171.

41 For more, see M. Finnimore & K. Sikkink, 'International Norm Dynamics and Political Change', 4 *International Organisation*, 1998, pp. 887–917.

42 See H Friman, 'The International Criminal Court and Participation of Victims: A Third Party to the Proceedings?' 22 *Leiden Journal of International Law* (2009) 485.

43 D. M. Rosen, *Armies of the young: child soldiers in war and terrorism*, Rutgers University Press, 2005.

However, the current environment of war is better contextualized by grasping the difference between old wars and new wars. Mary Kaldor's seminal work on new wars[44] describes new wars with features such as organized crime and large-scale violations of human rights, which not only blatantly disregard any notion of children's vulnerability or need of protection, but are also 'anomic and chaotic',[45] unbound by any rules.

The important feature of new wars is that they are driven by identity politics and inspired by objectives such as revenge, and alienating specific identity (whether religious, ethnic or political). The ideational aspect coupled with the breakdown of social norms and values, amplifies the role of children as agents and victims of armed conflict.[46] Due to the nature of the rule-less conduct of non-State actors, and their identity-driven goals, children are identified as targets, threats or potential victims.

Whereas wars throughout history have had the objective of conquering territory, new wars are to disrupt order, change borders and unmake the system. This objective would legitimize expanding warfare into children's playgrounds, hospitals, schools, and refugee camps. The landscape of new conflicts now includes spaces designated for or previously exclusive to children and their lives. The widespread targeting of children as a strategy is not because of their vulnerability but because of their value and how they are perceived. Such 'unconventional tactics' not only 'minimize the difference between an adult and a child soldier'[47] but also pose challenges to principles of distinction and broader IHL.[48]

While imposing an environment of fear is an outcome of such disproportionate or non-distinctive attacks, children as the agent of 'the Other' are often the target of attack to wipe out future generations. In such instances, there is a broader gender relation at play too.[49] Boys are targeted to diminish

---

44　M. Kaldor, *New and Old Wars, Organized Violence in a Global Era*, Polity Press, 2013.
45　Rosen, supra, p. 10.
46　See Machel, supra, note 6, which acknowledges the changing role of children in armed conflict due to the anarchic nature of these wars.
47　S. Gates, 'Why do children fight? Motivations and the mode of recruitment', in A. Ozerdem, & S. Podder (eds), *Child soldiers: From recruitment to reintegration*, Palgrave Macmillan, 2011, p. 32.
48　See A. Cassese, 'Current Challenges to International Humanitarian Law' and N. Melzer, 'The Principle of Distinction Between Civilians and Combatants', in A. Clapham & P. Gaeta (eds), *The Oxford Handbook of International Law in Armed Conflict*, Oxford University Press, 2014.
49　See C. Chinkin, 'Gender and Armed Conflict', in A. Clapham & P. Gaeta (eds), *The Oxford Handbook of International Law in Armed Conflict*, Oxford University Press, 2014.

future armies, forces and resistance.[50] To reproduce gender relations, and signifying a broader process of 'Other' in girls vis-à-vis boys, girls are often degraded and personified as 'voiceless victims often devoid of agency, moral conscience and economic potential.'[51]

Bosnia is a revealing case of how children as part of 'the Other', despite being victims, were also instruments and a powerful tool in intensifying the conflict. Ethnic divisions inflamed the Bosnian conflict with ensuing ethnic cleansing and atrocities. The pivotal feature was how children were conveyors of the generational hatred of adults. Children were not regarded as vulnerable minors that needed to be protected but represented the Other ethnicity that should be wiped out. Such an attitude and perception was also illustrated in Liberia but in a reverse manner, when 'parents volunteered their children to the Independent National Patriotic Front of Liberia (INPFL) out of a desire to revenge tribal disputes, or in defense of their tribe'.[52]

A crucial factor of new wars and their impact on children is that acts of revenge, hatred, struggle and the conflict itself become normal for children when they represent a continuation of historical trends, and when the conflict does not take place in a specific battle front but encroaches on civilian spaces. Conflict may become 'the normal everyday background to their lives.'[53] The normalization of the conflict and the routine alienation of children throughout conflicts also weaken the social structure and this further marginalizes children. Alongside disrupted family relationships, children as a party to the conflict may take up the task of protecting themselves and form a group of their own. They define themselves against those who have ruined their lives, and tortured, abducted or killed their parents. The child would be on the lookout for an affiliation akin to family, that could be found in battle groups with senior commanders considered as 'surrogate fathers.'[54]

These facts signify the complexity of the protection of the child during armed conflicts and the necessity of not falling into a one-sided analysis of vulnerability. Analyzing representational and identity-based factors of armed conflicts is critical for furthering an understanding of children's experience throughout the conflict and for promoting their protection.

---

50   H. Brocklehurst, *Who's Afraid of Children?*, Routledge, 2006, p. 39.
51   M. Denov, *Child Soldiers: Sierra Leone's Revolutionary United Front*, Cambridge University Press, 2010.
52   I. Cohn & G. Goodwin-Gill, *Child Soldiers: The role of children in armed conflicts*, Clarendon Press, 1994, p. 42.
53   R. Brett, *Young soldiers: why they choose to fight*, Lynne Rienner Publishers, 2004.
54   Gates, supra, note 46.

4 Conclusion

The legal framework of protection of children during armed conflicts is still an evolving edifice. The existing mechanisms for protection are based on an approach that regards children as vulnerable victims. Such an approach disregards the differing nature and features of each conflict, its impact on children, and the unique experience of each and every child. The vulnerability of children prescribes their exclusion from the conflict and their need for protection. However, the critical and identity-based approach highlights the fact that children are indeed part of the conflict and protection should be extended further by taking note of their embedded character within conflicts.

In furthering this protection, there is a need for critical engagement in rapidly changing environments and objectives of conflict with the aim of achieving a comprehensive analysis. The question of children in and at war should be central to an interdisciplinary effort to understand various identities and relationships of children throughout the conflict with their own society, confronting groups and the environment of war. Such an attempt would bring children and their experience to the forefront of protection rather than pushing them back. Current global trends of war, exemplified by the tragic course of conflicts in Syria and Yemen, actively engage children. International law needs to re-engage with the issue by recognizing children's agency as well as their emancipation.

A propos de quelques éclaircissements jurisprudentiels dans le ciel gris de la lutte contre la torture

Amir Hossein Ranjbarian

« De l'injustice d'aujourd'hui je crée la justice de demain ». Antoine de Saint-Exupéry, *Citadelle*
GALLIMARD, 2000, P. 48.

∴

La guerre n'est pas le seul fléau contre lequel il faut préserver les présentes et futures générations. Il faut aussi lutter pour le respect des droits de l'homme et pour éliminer l'injustice et la tyrannie. La Charte des Nations Unies, dont le préambule et les articles1, 13 et 55, est le principal symbole d'avoir une conscience humaine et universelle de cette priorité absolue. Par une « grande innovation », la Charte tout en imposant désormais les *obligations internationales* à tous les Etats pour respecter les droits de l'Homme, fait ainsi figurer leur respect parmi les objectifs de la coopération internationale[1]. On sait que les droits à respecter n'y sont définis que d'une manière générale. En effet, les négociations sur la Chatre n'ont pas abouti à l'inclusion des droits de l'homme – comme l'ancien Secrétaire général de l'ONU l'a souhaité- en tant que partie intégrante de celle-ci[2]. Ce sont les développements ultérieurs qui montrent comment et par quelles mesures les droits humains devront être réalisés au niveau international ou régional. La *protection internationale* des droits de l'homme se poursuit donc par la voie consensuelle et à un rythme de pas à pas d'une manière continue depuis 1945. En bref, le droit international, ne peut guère offrir, à l'encontre du droit interne, que le recours à la méthode conventionnelle[3].

---

1   M. Virally, « Panorama du droit international contemporain », Recueil des Cours de l'Académie de droit international de la Haye, vol. 183, 1983, p. 123-127.
2   *La Charte des Nations Unies, Constitution mondiale?* R. Chemain et A. Pellet (Dir.), Edition Pédone, 2006, p. 10. Selon M. de Cuellar, il devrait décider que la Déclaration universelle des droits de l'homme, soit inscrite dans la Chatre de façon à renforcer son caractère obligatoire.
3   C. Rousseau, « Droits de l'homme et droit des gens », *René Cassin Amicorum Discipulorumque Liber*, vol. IV, Paris, Pédone, 1972, p. 315.

Parmi les résultats les plus considérables des efforts internationaux pour définir les moyens de garantir les droits fondamentaux, la Convention contre la torture et autres peines ou traitements cruels, inhumains ou dégradants[4] adoptée par l'Assemblée générale de l'ONU en 1984, ci-après la Convention, a une importance particulière. A côté de textes de base, c'est-à-dire la Déclaration universelle et les deux Pactes de 1966, la Convention se trouve parmi des instruments qui confirment et complètent la notion des droits de l'homme à l'échelle mondiale[5]. En interdisant la torture et en parvenant à définir cette pratique qui généraient des souffrances innombrables depuis des siècles, la Convention est *per se* un acquis non négligeable. La valeur particulière d'une Convention spécifiquement consacrée à la torture, ne se borne pas à l'interdiction d'y recourir; une interdiction partagé les autres traités internationaux comme les quatre Conventions de Genève et leurs Protocoles additionnels, réaffirmée par le Statut de la CPI, ou même par des instruments régionaux relatifs aux droits de l'homme. Elle contient également des dispositions importantes pour assurer l'application par les Etats membres qui doivent prendre les différentes mesures nécessaires. Sous cet angle, on peut dire que la Convention présente des concepts à découvrir et à éclaircir. C'est justement les commentaires judiciaires qui sont allés dans ce sens pour rendre plus claire ce qui se cache sous les mots et dire en détail ce qui incombe aux Etats pour s'acquitter de leurs obligations.

Sans vouloir nous étendre longuement sur un ensemble riche de la jurisprudence internationale concernant la torture, nous nous limiterons dans cette brève étude, à y référer sur deux aspects particuliers. Le premier qui affirme la responsabilité pénale pour la torture ne se limite pas à une seule personne qui inflige directement la douleur sur les victimes; mais couvre aussi toute personne qui y participe ou toute autre qui peut être considérée comme le complice. Le deuxième concerne une interprétation qui permet aux Etats de poursuivre les auteurs de la torture à l'étranger même en dehors de lien de nationalité avec l'accusé ou la victime.

1   Qui sont les tortionnaires ?

L'objet de la Convention est la lutte efficace contre la torture en imposant des obligations concrètes. Parmi ces obligations, celle visée par l'article 4 1) qui envisage la criminalisation de tous les actes de torture en droit pénal interne,

---

4   Nations Unies, *Recueil des traités*, vol. 1465, p. 85.
5   N. Valticos, « La notion des droits de l'homme en droit international », *Mélanges Michel Virally*, Paris, Pédone, 1991, p. 485.

est une norme essentielle pour atteindre les buts de la Convention et protéger les victimes[6]. Plus important encore cet article stipule que les Etats doivent criminaliser la tentative de pratiquer la torture ou de tout acte commis par n'importe quelle personne qui constitue une complicité ou une participation à l'acte de torture et punir toutes ces infractions par des peines appropriées. Les *travaux préparatoires* montrent que les notions de participation et de complicité ont été l'objet de plusieurs propositions et de discussions. En effet, il y avait des doutes si ces notions pouvaient couvrir toutes les personnes qui s'associent accessoirement à la torture[7].

Il est exacte que le Comité contre la torture affirme expressément que l'article 4 oblige à criminaliser tous les actes de torture y compris la participation ou la complicité, mais la relation entre certaines expressions comme le consentement des autorités officielles, citées dans l'article 1 de la Convention, avec la complicité ou la participation n'est pas claire[8]. Indépendamment de la valeur juridique des observations du Comité sur l'insuffisance de législation interne d'un Etat membre, il semble que les critiques du Comité ne vont pas au-delà d'une observation générale qui s'arrête plutôt à rappeler la non-conformité des lois de certains Etats membres avec l'obligation de l'article 4 ou à recommander quelques amendements dans les lois pénales pour mieux la respecter[9]. On trouve d'ailleurs la même imprécise interprétation dans les écrits relatifs à la responsabilité née d'instigation ou de consentement des personnes autre que l'auteur principal, y compris celles qui agissent après la commission de torture[10].

Il ne fait pas de doute que l'intérêt présenté par ces interprétations est incontestable ; car elles aident à guider comment relier les notions citées dans les articles différents de la Convention. Toutefois il faudra établir les critères bien précis pour la responsabilité des individus prenant part à la torture. Il semble que les considérations plus profondes et plus convaincantes nous sont fournies à cet égard par la jurisprudence internationale.

---

6   M. Novak and E. Mcarthur (eds), *The United Nations Convention Against Torture A Commentary*, Oxford University Press, 2008, p. 229.

7   Ibid., p. 232-233.

8   Ibid., p. 236.

9   Les commentateurs de la Convention s'appuient sur la pratique du Comité dans les cas où celui-ci fait discerner l'inconsistance de la législation des Etats membres avec l'obligation de l'article 4 1), sans, selon nous, pouvoir mettre en lumière les éléments essentiels qui devraient en être ressortis concernant la responsabilité pénale prévue par cet article. Ibid. p. 236-37.

10 A titre d'exemple; N. Rodley and M. Pollard, « Criminalisation of Torture: State obligations under the United Convention against Torture... », *European Human Rights Law Review*, n°2, 2006, pp. 120 et ss.

Quelques mois avant le célèbre arrêt de la Chambre d'appel du TPIY dans l'affaire *Tadic* en 15 juillet 1999 qui consacre la doctrine de « l'entreprise criminelle commune » s'agissant des crimes internationaux[11], la Chambre de première instance du même Tribunal dans une affaire dont le principal chef d'accusation était la torture, a expressément statué sur la responsabilité pénale de participant et de complice à l'acte de torture[12]. Après avoir parfaitement analysé les conséquences juridiques de l'interdiction absolue de la torture en droit international et la valeur de *jus cognes* reconnue à cette interdiction[13], la Chambre se penche sur la responsabilité individuelle née de la complicité.

La Chambre d'abord examine les éléments de cette responsabilité, tant pour *l'actus reus* que pour la *mens rea*, en droit international coutumier y compris la jurisprudence internationale et les instruments internationaux comme le Statut de Rome, afin de déterminer le degré requis pour être qualifié de complicité (*aiding and abetting*) au sens de l'article 7 1) de son Statut relatif à la responsabilité individuelle.

En ce qui concerne l'élément matériel, la Chambre est d'avis qu'il n'est pas nécessaire que l'aide apportée par le complice soit indispensable pour commettre l'acte de torture. Donc dans certain cas, l'assistance sous la forme d'un soutien moral et des encouragements donnés aux auteurs d'un acte de torture seront punissables même en l'absence de tout acte concret de la part du complice, s'ils ont aidé à la perpétration de torture. Cette approche se justifie surtout lorsque l'assistance ou toute facilitation se fait dans un système visant à commettre les crimes dans lequel chaque personne, tout en connaissant la

---

11   Cf. TPIY, *Le Procureur C/ Dusko Tadic*, affaire n°IT-94-1-A, 15 juillet 1999.
12   Il est à noter que dans le même dossier Tadic, les juges d'une autre Chambre de première instance avaient interprété le concept de responsabilité pénale dans l'article 7 du Statut du Tribunal. Ainsi pour établir, parmi autres, le fondement coutumier de la responsabilité individuelle pour avoir assisté, aidé et encouragé, ou participé à un acte criminel- à la différence de la perpétration directe- la Chambre cite *par exemple*, l'article 4 1) de la Convention contre la torture qui utilise la phrase « complicité ou participation à l'acte de torture ». Voir TPIY, *Le Procureur C/ Dusko Tadic*, affaire n°IT-94-1-A, 7 mai 1997, par. 666. Toutefois, la Chambre se borne à traiter la question de culpabilité, soit à titre d'auteur principal ou à titre de complice ou de toute autre manière en tant que participant d'une manière générale ; ce qui signifie que les observations de la Chambre englobent tous les actes prohibés dans le Statut sans s'attacher spécifiquement à la torture qui relève de la compétence du Tribunal à plusieurs titres. Par. 670-692.
13   TPIY, *Le Procureur C/ Anto Furundzija*, affaire n°IT-95-17/1-T, 10 décembre 1998, par. 134-157.

nature du système, joue un rôle par sa conduite, et ainsi favorise ou aide et encourage pratiquement à la perpétration des crimes[14].

Concernant l'élément moral, la Chambre estime que le simple fait de *savoir* que les actes de complice aident l'auteur à commettre le crime suffira pour constituer la *mens rea*. Le point de vue retenu par la Chambre sur la question de l'élément moral se résume en dire qu'il n'est en rien indispensable qu'un complice remplisse toutes les conditions de l'élément moral attendues d'un auteur; ni n'est aucunement nécessaire qu'il partage la volonté et l'objectif criminels de l'auteur. Il suffira seulement que le complice sache que ses actes aident l'auteur à commettre le crime[15].

La chambre soulève ensuite la question de la différence entre la perpétration de l'acte de torture et de la complicité dans les cas où des accusations de torture se posent. Tout en justement considérant une réalité non négligeable; à savoir le fait qu'aujourd'hui les actes de torture «font souvent intervenir un grand nombre de personnes »[16], la Chambre souligne l'importance de déterminer la fonction des chacune des personnes s'engageant à la torture qu'ils soient l'auteur ou coauteur d'actes de torture ou le complice ; précisément pour que tout ce qui s'implique à cette affreuse pratique soit jugé et puni. La Chambre arrive ainsi à une remarquable et réaliste analyse de sa thèse. Basée sur une constatation conforme à ce qui se passe en réalité dans de nombreux Etats, la Chambre essaye d'éclairer un point très important qui ne paraît pas avoir été noté précédemment. Reprenons ce passage – les paragraphes 253 et 254 – ici par son importance particulière :

> Ces thèses juridiques, qui reposent sur une interprétation logique des règles du droit coutumier sur la torture, sont confortées par une interprétation téléologique de ces règles. L'évolution que l'on constate de nos jours dans de nombreux États pratiquant la torture en témoigne : il y a une tendance à « morceler » et à « diluer » le fardeau moral et psychologique induit par la pratique de la torture en assignant à différents individus un rôle fragmentaire (et parfois relativement mineur) dans le processus : l'un ordonne la torture, l'autre organise tout le processus administratif, un autre encore pose des questions tandis que le détenu est torturé, un quatrième fournit ou prépare les instruments de torture, un autre inflige

---

14   Ibid., par. 190-233. Pour reprendre les termes de la Chambre dans sa conclusion sur l'effet de l'aide sur la perpétration du crime ; en droit international, *l'actus reus* de la complicité requiert une aide matérielle, des encouragements ou un soutien moral ayant un effet sur la perpétration du crime. Ibid., par. 234-235.
15   Ibid., par. 236- 249.
16   Ibid., par. 250.

des souffrances physiques ou mentales aiguës, un autre encore fournit une assistance médicale pour éviter que le détenu ne succombe à ses blessures ou ne conserve des traces des souffrances qu'il a éprouvées, un autre traite les informations recueillies sous la torture, tandis qu'un autre se procure les informations obtenues contre l'assurance que le tortionnaire ne sera pas poursuivi. S'il ne prenait pas en compte cette évolution, le droit international s'avèrerait incapable de combattre cette pratique odieuse. Les règles d'interprétation mettant en lumière l'objet et le but des normes internationales amènent à la conclusion que le droit international rend pareillement responsables pénalement comme auteurs ou coauteurs toutes les personnes susmentionnées [...].

Bien que le TPIY agisse naturellement dans le cadre de sa compétence se limitant aux crimes de guerre ou crimes contre l'humanité, son raisonnement est valable dans les cas où la torture est commise sans avoir de lien avec ces crimes en tant qu'un crime en soi.

Quelle conclusion faut-il en tirer? A notre avis, l'éclaircissement fait par cet arrêt, apporte sûrement les éléments de réponse pour toute question telle que l'insuffisance d'une législation sur l'article 4 1) de la Convention ou l'inconsistance de celle-ci avec le but prévu par la Convention. Le silence des lois ou une législation qui abandonne tout co-auteur, participant ou complice sans lequel un acte de torture ne peut pas surgir et qui doit être jugé comme véritable tortionnaire, peut être considéré contraire au but de la Convention. Dire que laisser profiter toute personne impliqué dans la torture de l'impunité, équivaut à dire qu'il s'agit d'une violation flagrante des *obligations internationales*.

On s'aperçoit donc que cet arrêt marque un progrès net et sensible. Car ces considérations sur la portée des notions relatives à la lutte contre la torture, ne laissent pas une marge d'appréciation pouvant entraîner l'impunité des différentes responsables de la torture.

Avant de se tourner vers une autre importante constatation de l'arrêt *Furundzija* concernant l'obligation d'exercer la compétence pénale visée par le droit international à l'égard de tortionnaires[17], notons brièvement qu'en apparence cette partie de l'arrêt n'a pas suffisamment attiré l'attention de ceux qui

---

17   Au point de vue qui nous occupe ici, l'une des conséquences de la valeur de jus cogens reconnue à l'interdiction absolue de la torture, illustre dans le pouvoir des Etats pour poursuivre les individus accusés de torture. Selon la Chambre, il serait contradictoire, d'une part, de restreindre, en interdisant la torture, le pouvoir absolu qu'ont normalement les États de conclure des traités et, d'autre part, d'empêcher les États de poursuivre et de punir ceux qui la pratiquent à l'étranger. La compétence universelle en matière de torture découle du caractère par essence universel du crime. Ibid., par. 156.

examinaient l'œuvre effectuée par des TPI à l'époque[18]. En revanche, cette partie a été pertinemment récompensée en étant sélectionnée et classée parmi les grands arrêts de droit international pénal[19].

2 Une interprétation inédite de l'article 5 de la Convention par la CIJ : Une compétence réellement universelle

En droit international on parle beaucoup de la nécessité d'envisager une compétence pénale pour les tribunaux nationaux sans la fonder sur les critères normaux pour établir la compétence comme compétence territoriale ou personnelle. La *raison d'être* de ce genre de compétence, nommément compétence universelle paraît claire : en tenant compte des obstacles et des difficultés de juger les auteurs présumés dans les pays où l'infraction a été commise et en considérant l'absence des juridictions internationales compétentes, il faut éviter qu'ils échappent à toute poursuite et à tout châtiment[20]. Cela n'est possible que par l'intervention des *juridictions internes* de n'importe quel pays[21].

La Convention contre la torture se trouve parmi les conventions internationales qui prévoient l'obligation d'établir la compétence pénale pour les infractions visées. Après avoir stipulé dans l'alinéa 1 de l'article 5 de la Convention, le devoir de chaque Etat d'établir sa compétence à l'égard des actes de torture commis sur son territoire ou lorsque l'auteur ou la victime en sont ressortissant,

---

18 Tandis que les études relatives à cet arrêt, examinent minutieusement les constatations de la Chambre sur le statut de *jus cogen*s de l'interdiction absolue de la torture, les observations sur l'apport de la Chambre concernant la responsabilité pour la complicité semblent brèves et rapides. Voir par exemple: *Revue Générale de Droit International Public*, tome 103, 1999-2, p. 491-492; *Annuaire Français de Droit International*, 1998, p. 371-373 et 408.

19 A. Cassese, D. Scalia, V. Thalmann, *Les grands arrêts de droit international pénal*, Paris, Dalloz, 2010, p. 307-318. N'est-il pas regrettable qu'il n'y ait aucune trace de l'argumentation de l'arrêt à apparaître dans le *Commentary* de l'article 4 de la Convention, paru dix ans après la date de l'arrêt?

20 L'objectif de cette compétence -définie comme aptitude de tribunaux de tout Etat à juger des faits commis à l'étranger, quels que soient le lieu de l'infraction et la nationalité de l'auteur ou de la victime- est « d'assurer une répression sans faille pour certaines infractions particulièrement graves ». Voir *Dictionnaire de droit international public*, J. Salmon (Dir.), Bruxelles, Bruylant/AUF, 2001, p. 212.

21 La question de compétence universelle constitue certainement l'une des questions les plus controversées en droit international. En effet la portée et les conditions de l'exercer faisaient l'objet des vives discussions soit par la doctrine ou dans la pratique. Beaucoup a été écrit sur cette question et on évite ici d'en donner même une courte bibliographie.

l'alinéa 2 du même article précise que tout Etat doit prendre également les mesures nécessaires afin d'établir sa compétence dans le cas où l'auteur présumé se trouve sur son territoire, s'il ne veut pas l'extrader vers les autres Etats visés à l'alinéa 1. Pour que le contenu exact de ce devoir soit bien éclairé, il fallait attendre le résultat d'un processus litigieux entre deux Etats membres de la Convention en 2012.

Avant de passer à l'importance de l'apport de la CIJ en l'affaire « *Questions concernant l'obligation de poursuivre ou d'extrader* » (Belgique c. Sénégal), il faut remarquer certains points. Tout d'abord, depuis des problèmes survenus entre différents Etats en raison de l'exercice de compétence universelle, également en tenant compte la décision de la CIJ en 2002 dans l'affaire *Mandat d'arrêt* (République Démocratique du Congo c. Belgique), il y avait une tendance régressive dont le résultat n'était que de limiter la mise en œuvre de la compétence universelle. En effet, des considérations politiques conduisaient certains Etats plus avancés en ce domaine à reculer en ne l'appliquant que les présumés accusés soient sur leurs territoires ou bien qu'il y ait des victimes de leurs nationalité. L'Espagne et la Belgique en sont des exemples. En outre, au moment où la Belgique allait déposer sa requête pour demander à la CIJ de dire que le Sénégal est obligé de poursuivre pénalement M. Habré pour des faits de torture et de crimes contre l'humanité, et à défaut de le poursuivre est obligé de l'extrader vers la Belgique pour qu'il réponde de ses crimes devant la justice belge; les commentateurs de la Convention estimaient toujours que demander l'extradition d'un suspect nécessite la relation de nationalité des victimes avec cet Etat. Autrement dit, pour qu'un Etat ait le droit de demander l'extradition, il faut que la victime de torture soit son ressortissant. Cette condition établit la même compétence qui est connue sous le nom de compétence personnelle passive[22]. Si l'on ajoute enfin que dans cette même affaire, l'hypothèse de telle condition pour demander l'extradition de la part de l'Etat demandeur n'est pas à exclure[23], on voit bien que l'argumentation de la CIJ relative à un droit d'agir pour n'importe quel Etat membre de la Convention est dotée des grands

---

22 *The United Nations Convention Against Torture A Commentary, op. cit.*, note 6, p. 291-292.
23 Dans sa requête, en ce qui concerne *les faits*, la Belgique précise que: «Entre le 30 novembre 2000 et le 11 décembre 2001, un ressortissant belge d'origine tchadienne et des ressortissants tchadiens déposent, successivement, des plaintes avec constitution de partie civile auprès de la justice belge contre l'ancien président du Tchad, M. H. Habré, pour des crimes de droit international humanitaire. La compétence actuelle des juridictions belges *étant fondée sur la plainte déposée par un ressortissant belge d'origine tchadienne, la justice belge entend exercer la compétence personnelle passive* ». Voir: Acte introductif d'instance, 16 février 2009, par. 3. C'est nous qui soulignons.

avantages pour éclairer la base juridique de l'action des Etats pour la poursuite des tortionnaires.

Au cours de la procédure, le Sénégal soutenait que la Cour n'a pas de compétence pour examiner la question. Il contestait également *la recevabilité* des demandes de la Belgique relatives à des manquements allégués, par le Sénégal, à des obligations que lui impose la Convention. Selon l'Etat défendeur, la Belgique n'a pas *qualité* pour invoquer la responsabilité internationale du Sénégal en raison du manquement à l'obligation de soumettre le cas de Habré à ses instances compétentes pour l'exercice de l'action pénale, à moins qu'il ne l'extrade. Car, aucune des victimes supposées des actes attribuables à Habré n'avait la *nationalité belge* au moment où ceux-ci ont été commis[24]. Devant cette contestation, la Cour confirme le fait qu'aucune des victimes supposées n'avait la nationalité belge durant la période de la présidence de Habré. Toutefois cela ne signifie pas que la demande est irrecevable. La Cour tout en gardant en vue la base de compétence de la justice belge présentée dans la requête, d'une part, et en considérant la prétention de la Belgique, au cours de l'audience, qu'elle est dans une «situation particulière», en ce qu'elle s'est prévalue du droit que lui confère l'article 5 de demander l'extradition, d'autre part, observe également une autre réclamation de l'Etat demandeur. En effet, la Belgique prétend qu'en vertu de la Convention, tout Etat partie, quelle que soit la nationalité des victimes, est fondé à revendiquer l'exécution de l'obligation en question, et peut donc invoquer la responsabilité résultant d'une inexécution[25].

Pour résoudre cette controverse et déterminer la *qualité d'agir* de la Belgique, la Cour ne prend que le *seul fait d'être partie à la Convention* et écarte l'existence d'un intérêt particulier qui distingue la Belgique des autres parties à cet instrument. Pour la Cour, *il suffit* d'être partie à un instrument aussi important que la Convention contre la torture, pour qu'un Etat soit investi de *droit* à demander à un autre Etat partie de mettre fin à des manquements aux *obligations*; nul n'est donc besoin d'attribuer un droit spécifique par la particularité d'une affaire.

Pour expliquer son point de vue, la Cour en relevant l'objet et le but de la Convention: «d'accroître l'efficacité de la lutte contre la torture [...] dans le monde entier», et puis en mettant en relief les valeurs particulières partagées entre les Etats parties, précise qu'ils ont un intérêt commun à veiller à ce que les tortionnaires ne bénéficient pas de l'impunité. La Cour ajoute que les obligations d'un Etat partie pour l'exercice de l'action pénale s'appliquent

---

[24] CIJ, *Questions concernant l'obligation de poursuivre ou d'extrader (Belgique c. Sénégal)*, arrêt, *CIJ Recueil 2012*, p. 422 par. 64.

[25] Ibid., par. 65.

du fait de la présence de l'auteur présumé sur son territoire, quelle que soit la nationalité de l'intéressé ou celle des victimes, et quel que soit le lieu où les infractions alléguées ont été commises. La Cour souligne ensuite que *tous* les autres Etats parties ont un *intérêt commun* à ce que l'Etat sur le territoire duquel se trouve l'auteur présumé respecte ces obligations. Cet intérêt commun s'est éclairci par un remarquable jugement de la Cour : cela implique que de telles obligations s'imposent à tout Etat partie à la Convention à l'égard de tous les autres Etats parties. Selon la Cour, dans le cas présent, l'ensemble des Etats parties a «un intérêt juridique» que les obligations qualifiées d'«obligations *erga omnes partes*», bien exploitées dans le dossier *Barcelona Traction*, soient respectées[26]. En conséquence, «tout Etat partie à la Convention contre la torture peut invoquer la responsabilité d'un autre Etat partie dans le but de faire constater le manquement allégué de celui-ci à des obligations *erga omnes partes*», et en la présente espèce la Belgique a qualité pour invoquer la responsabilité du Sénégal[27].

Comme certains auteurs l'ont noté, c'est pour la première fois que la CIJ statue sur les effets juridiques des obligations *erga omnes* pour les Etats tiers[28]. Rappelons que cela s'est fait dans le cadre d'une convention imposant de nombreuses *obligations internationales* qui doivent consolider la lutte contre la torture. C'est dans ce cadre que l'obligation «*aut dedere aut judicare*» a une valeur spéciale afin de favoriser la poursuite des accusés, comme la CIJ l'a bien éclairé. La portée de l'arrêt va certes beaucoup plus loin et s'étend assurément aux autres conventions relatives à la protection des droits de l'homme qui contiennent cette obligation[29]; il faut cependant noter que ce qu'il découle du raisonnement de la Cour dans cette affaire vise principalement et directement cette obligation dans le cadre d'une convention réunissant de nombreux Etats pour mener une action commune contre la torture et il la ferait valoir plus efficace par l'action de tout Etat face à tout autre Etat.

Il faut fortement souhaiter que cette approche puisse désormais entraîner l'activité d'un nombre plus considérable des Etats «to act to ensure

---

26 Ibid., par. 68.
27 Ibid., par. 69-70.
28 A. Mads and T. Weatherall, « ICJ: Questions relating to the obligation to extradite or prosecute (Belgium v. Senegal) Judgment of 20 July 2012 », *International and Comparative Law Quarterly*, vol. 62, 2013, p. 761.
29 T. Buatte, «The Time of Human Justice & the Time of Human Beings: Belgium v. Senegal & Temporal Restraints on the Duty to Prosecute», *George Washington International Law Review*, vol. 45, 2013, p. 380-381.

accountability worldwide for acts of torture »[30]. Le processus de traduire en justice l'exprésident tchadien en Sénégal, aboutissant le 30 mai 2016 à déclarer Hissène Habré coupable de tortures et de crimes contre l'humanité et le condamner à la prison à vie, n'est pas uniquement exemplaire ou même un « procès historique »[31], mais démontre aussi combien une tentative *internationale* d'un Etat auprès d'un autre Etat peut être fructueuse et une réussite. Une hirondelle ne fait pas le printemps. Il faut encore beaucoup d'autres procédures similaires. Le cas de Habré aura la valeur de modèle afin que d'autres tortionnaires soient jugés ailleurs.

Conclusion

Il est indéniable que la mobilisation judiciaire a progressivement renforcé la protection des individus contre la torture. Reste à savoir si les Etats seront prêt à poursuivre suffisamment la jurisprudence internationale et deviendront plus actifs pour s'attaquer aux problèmes de l'impunité des tortionnaires. On a l'habitude de les voir agir plutôt sous une perspective réaliste, ce qui peut affaiblir l'effectivité du système protégeant les victimes. La réflexion sur la persistance de la torture dans le monde entier, peut laisser croire qu'un manque de volonté empêche que la pratique s'adapte et réponde conformément aux exigences bien éclairées par les juges internationaux.

Restant valable, malgré le fait que la torture est couramment pratiquée dans de nombreux Etats, l'interdiction absolue de torture ne sert pas seulement à réfuter une prétention erronément formulée sur les effets d'une pratique contraire à une règle[32]; elle justifie avant tout la continuité d'un combat indispensable pour faire régner la justice. En plus des actions internes, réduire radicalement les cas de torture nécessite également un changement fondamental sur le plan de coopération internationale. C'est pourquoi l'Assemblée générale de l'ONU se voit obligée de demander régulièrement aux Etats de prendre des mesures efficaces pour prévenir et combattre *tous les actes* de torture en

---

30   C. Galway Buys, « Belgium v. Senegal: The International Court of Justice Affirms the Obligation to Prosecute or Extradite Hissène Habré Under the Convention Against Torture », ASIL, *Insights*, 2012, vol.16, Issue 29, www.asil.org.

31   http://www.lemonde.fr/afrique/article/2016/05/30/procès-habré-l'ex-president-tchadien-reconnu-coupable.

32   E. David, *Principes de droit de conflits armés*, Bruxelles, 5ème édition, Bruylant, 2012, p. 385.

insistant sur le fait que *tous les actes* de torture doivent être érigés dans le droit interne en infractions; et de s'acquitter de l'*obligation* de *poursuivre ou d'extrader* les auteurs présumés d'*actes* de torture, quel que soit l'endroit où ces actes ont été commis..., sachant qu'il faut lutter contre l'impunité[33].

---

33 A titre d'exemple voir parmi les plus récentes : A/RES/70/146, le 17 décembre 2015, par. 5 et 19. Voir aussi le rappel fait dans une résolution adoptée sur la situation des droits de l'homme en Syrie, A/RES/70/234, le 23 décembre 2015, par. 7.

Les relations entre droits de l'homme et droit international humanitaire dans la jurisprudence de la Cour européenne des droits de l'homme

Linos-Alexandre Sicilianos[1]

1 Remarques préliminaire

Connaître le Professeur Djamchid Momtaz et coopérer avec lui au sein du Curatorium de l'Académie de droit international de La Haye ou dans le cadre de l'Institut de droit international, a constitué et constitue toujours pour moi un véritable privilège. L'élégance et la finesse de ses analyses juridiques, l'ampleur et la diversité des thèmes qu'il a pu aborder dans ses écrits, ainsi que sa longue expérience de praticien font de lui l'un des maîtres incontestables du droit international contemporain. Parmi les nombreux sujets qui l'ont occupé, le droit international humanitaire (DIH) et la protection internationale des droits de l'homme relèvent de ses domaines de prédilection. C'est la raison pour laquelle j'ai choisi de consacrer cette brève contribution à la relation entre ces deux corpus normatifs.

S'il est vrai que le sujet dans sa globalité a fait couler beaucoup d'encre[2], l'articulation des droits de l'homme et du DIH dans la jurisprudence de la Cour

---

[1] Les opinions exprimées dans cet article sont personnelles à l'auteur et n'engagent pas la Cour européenne des droits de l'homme.

[2] Cf. notamment R. Kolb, « The Relationship between International Humanitarian Law and Human Rights Law: A Brief History of the 1948 Universal Declaration of Human Rights and the 1949 Geneva Conventions », *International Review of the Red Cross*, 1998, p. 409-419 ; E. Decaux, « Les organisations internationales et les conflits armés : l'application de la protection internationale des droits de l'homme », dans M. Benchikh (Dir.), *Les Organisations internationales et les conflits armés*, Paris, L'Harmattan, 2001, p. 131-157 ; H.-P. Gasser, « International Humanitarian Law and Human Rights Law in Non-International Armed Conflict: Joint Venture or Mutual Exclusion? », *German Yearbook of International Law*, 2002, p. 149-162 ; C. Droege, « The Interplay between International Humanitarian Law and International Human Rights Law in Situations of Armed Conflict », *Israel Law Review*, 2007/2, p. 310-355 ; S. Perrakis, « Le droit international humanitaire et ses relations avec les droits de l'homme. Quelques considérations », dans P. Tavernier, J.-M. Henckaerts (Dir.), *Droit international humanitaire coutumier : enjeux et défis contemporains*, Bruxelles, Bruylant, 2008, p. 115-137 ; G. Gaggioli, *L'influence mutuelle entre les droits de l'homme et le droit international humanitaire à la lumière du droit à la vie*, Paris, Pedone, 2013.

européenne des droits de l'homme (CourEDH) a relativement peu attiré l'attention. Pourtant, il s'agit là d'un thème récurrent, tant il est vrai que la Haute juridiction strasbourgeoise a eu à connaître plusieurs affaires qui s'intègrent dans le contexte d'un conflit armé international ou non-international. Il suffit de rappeler notamment les affaires dites « kurdes » ou « tchétchènes » ; les arrêts relatifs au conflit chypriote[3] ; ceux qui concernent la situation en Transnistrie ou le conflit yougoslave ; les affaires relatives aux opérations militaires en Irak ; les arrêts *Sargsyan c. Azerbaïdjan*[4] et *Chiragov et autres c. Arménie*[5], ayant trait au droit de propriété des réfugiés et des personnes déplacées suite au conflit entre les États défendeurs ; sans compter les requêtes pendantes : *Géorgie c. Russie (II)*[6] ou celles concernant différents aspects du conflit entre l'Ukraine et la Fédération de Russie (requêtes interétatiques et individuelles)[7].

Vouloir analyser toutes les affaires en question dépasserait de loin les limites de cette brève contribution. Sans prétendre à l'exhaustivité, on essaiera de tracer les grandes lignes d'une évolution qui va d'une approche réticente de la Cour face au DIH, à une ouverture à cette branche juridique, d'abord timide, de plus en plus affirmée par la suite. L'arrêt *Hassan c. Royaume-Uni*[8], adopté en 2014, a marqué un tournant dans cette évolution. La position de la Cour internationale de justice (CIJ) sur l'articulation entre le DIH et les droits de l'homme a constitué le point de départ de la Grande Chambre dans cette affaire.

2   La réticence face au DIH

Pendant des décennies et jusqu'à récemment la CourEDH s'est montrée sinon négative, du moins très réticente face à l'application du DIH. Cette attitude n'a pas manqué de soulever certaines critiques en doctrine, critiques qui ne sont pas forcément justifiées. Il ne faudrait pas oublier, en effet, que, contrairement à la CIJ, la Cour européenne est une juridiction spécialisée. Les limites de sa compétence *ratione materiae* sont définies par l'article 19 de la Convention européenne des droits de l'homme (CEDH). Cette disposition stipule en substance que la Cour est compétente pour appliquer la Convention et

---

3   Voir notamment CourEDH, *Chypre c. Turquie*, Grande Chambre (GC), arrêt du 10 mai 2001; arrêt du 12 mai 2014 (satisfaction équitable).
4   CourEDH, *Sargsyan c. Azerbaïdjan*, GC, arrêt du 16 juin 2015.
5   CourEDH, *Chiragov et autres c. Arménie*, GC, arrêt du 16 juin 2015.
6   CourEDH, *Géorgie c. Russie (II)*, n° 38263/08.
7   Voir communiqué de presse, CEDH 296 (2015) 1er octobre 2015.
8   CourEDH, *Hassan c. Royaume-Uni*, GC, arrêt du 16 septembre 2014.

ses Protocoles, toute la Convention, rien que la Convention. Cette vision stricte de la compétence de la Cour a été rappelée récemment par les juges dissidents dans l'affaire *Hassan*. Pour ces quatre collègues (les juges Spano, Nicolaou, Bianku et Kalaydjieva), la Cour ne dispose « d'aucun instrument légitime, en tant que tribunal, de remédier » à un éventuel conflit normatif entre le DIH et la Convention, comme en l'espèce. La Cour « doit donc donner priorité à la Convention, son rôle se bornant en vertu de l'article 19 à « assurer le respect des engagements résultant pour les Hautes Parties contractantes de la [...] Convention et de ses Protocoles »[9].

Les principales, sinon les seules exceptions à ce schéma sont fournies par les dispositions de la Convention et des Protocoles, qui se réfèrent explicitement à d'autres normes, d'origine nationale ou internationale. Parmi ces rares dispositions, on relèvera notamment la clause de dérogation en cas d'état d'urgence (article 15 de la Convention), stipulant particulièrement que :

> En cas de guerre ou en cas d'autre danger public menaçant la vie de la nation, toute Haute Partie contractante peut prendre des mesures dérogeant aux obligations prévues par la présente Convention, dans la stricte mesure où la situation l'exige et à la condition que ces mesures ne soient pas en contradiction avec les autres obligations découlant du droit international.

Il est évident que, compte tenu du contexte de cette clause (guerre, état d'urgence), la référence au droit international concerne avant tout le droit des conflits armés et plus particulièrement le DIH.

Pendant des décennies et encore aujourd'hui la Cour considère que l'application éventuelle du DIH passe par la clause de dérogation. Si l'État défendeur n'a pas invoqué l'article 15 de la Convention, la Cour applique en principe les dispositions de celle-ci, sans accepter aucune dérogation qui pourrait découler, le cas échéant, d'une application parallèle du DIH.

Cette position a été affirmée on ne peut plus clairement dans certaines affaires « tchétchènes » où la Cour a constaté que la Russie n'avait pas invoqué la clause de dérogation et que, par conséquent, la perte de vies humaines devait être appréciée « à l'aune d'un contexte juridique normal »[10]. Autrement dit, la Cour a fait quasiment abstraction du contexte militaire, pour envisager la mort

---

9   CourEDH, *Hassan c. Royaume-Uni, op. cit.*, note 8, opinion en partie dissidente du juge Spano, à laquelle se rallient les juges Nicolaou, Bianku et Kalaydjieva, par. 19.
10 CourEDH, *Isayeva c. Russie*, arrêt du 24 février 2005, par. 191 ; *Gubiyev c. Russie*, arrêt du 19 juillet 2011, par. 79 ; *Damayev c. Russie*, arrêt du 29 mai 2012, par. 71.

des victimes selon le droit normalement applicable en temps de paix. Cette approche pourrait paraître étonnante. Elle ne l'est pas, si l'on tient compte du fait que les deux parties avaient fondé leur argumentation exclusivement sur la Convention, le DIH ayant été complètement ignoré.

Il est par ailleurs significatif que même lorsque l'État défendeur invoque l'article 15 de la Convention dans le contexte d'un état d'urgence portant sur une partie de son territoire, la Cour évite soigneusement de se référer au droit des conflits armés non-internationaux. Il en va ainsi notamment des affaires dites « kurdes ». C'est ainsi, par exemple, que dans l'affaire *Aksoy c. Turquie* la Cour a constaté que la détention au secret du requérant était contraire à l'article 5 de la Convention, malgré l'invocation de la clause de dérogation par l'État défendeur[11]. Toute l'analyse de la Cour était axée exclusivement sur la Convention.

3   L'ouverture timide au DIH

Parallèlement à cette attitude réservée, on observe, toutefois, une ouverture certes timide, mais néanmoins importante face au DIH dans des affaires relatives à des conflits armés internationaux. Ainsi qu'il a été rappelé par la Cour dans l'affaire *Loizidou*, la Convention ne saurait s'interpréter et s'appliquer dans le vide, mais à la lumière des règles d'interprétation énoncées dans la Convention de Vienne sur le droit des traités[12]. Or l'article 31 par. 3 c) de ladite Convention précise qu'entre en ligne de compte « toute règle pertinente de droit international applicable aux relations entre les parties ». Il a néanmoins fallu attendre une autre affaire importante relative au conflit chypriote pour que la Cour s'attarde véritablement sur le DIH.

En effet, dans l'affaire *Varnava*, la Grande chambre de la Cour a estimé que :

> L'article 2 doit être interprété dans la mesure du possible à la lumière des principes du droit international, notamment des règles du droit international humanitaire, qui jouent un rôle indispensable et universellement reconnu dans l'atténuation de la sauvagerie et de l'inhumanité des conflits armés (*Loizidou*, précité, par. 43). La Grande Chambre souscrit donc au raisonnement de la chambre selon lequel dans une zone de conflit international les Etats contractants doivent protéger la vie de ceux qui ne sont pas ou plus engagés dans les hostilités, ce qui requiert notamment de

---

11   CourEDH, *Aksoy c. Turquie*, arrêt du 18 décembre 1996, par. 67 ss.
12   CourEDH, *Loizidou c. Turquie*, arrêt du 18 décembre 1996, fond, par. 43.

fournir une assistance médicale aux blessés. Quant à ceux qui meurent au combat ou succombent à leurs blessures, l'obligation de rendre des comptes implique que leurs corps soient correctement inhumés et que les autorités collectent et communiquent des informations sur l'identité et le sort des intéressés ou autorisent des organes tels que le CICR à le faire[13].

Voici donc des références assez claires au DIH dans une affaire concernant la question des personnes disparues suite à l'intervention turque à Chypre, en 1974. En l'occurrence, le droit humanitaire est invoqué pour corroborer l'interprétation de la Convention. Les obligations au titre du droit humanitaire sont convergentes avec celles de la CEDH.

Il en va de même dans une série d'autres affaires relatives à l'obligation d'enquêter sur les allégations de violations du droit à la vie en situation de conflit armé et d'occupation. C'est ainsi, par exemple, que dans l'affaire *Al-Skeini et autres c. Royaume-Uni*, la Grande chambre a invoqué les dispositions pertinentes des quatre Conventions de Genève qui font obligation à chaque Partie contractante d'ouvrir une enquête et des poursuites, notamment en cas d'homicide intentionnel de personnes protégées. Et la Cour d'affirmer que l'obligation d'enquête – c'est-à-dire l'obligation procédurale découlant de l'article 2 de la CEDH, relatif au droit à la vie – continue à s'appliquer même si les conditions de sécurité sont difficiles, y compris dans un contexte de conflit armé. Cela dit, ajoute la Cour, ladite obligation d'enquête « doit être appliquée de manière réaliste, pour tenir compte des problèmes particuliers auxquels les enquêteurs avaient à faire face »[14]. Autrement dit, la Cour tempère quelque peu les exigences strictes de la Convention européenne pour tenir compte des difficultés liées au conflit armé.

Ces quelques exemples suffisent pour illustrer l'ouverture timide de la Cour au DIH, notamment dans des situations où les obligations découlant de la CEDH et du droit humanitaire vont dans le même sens.

4   L'examen incident du DIH

Un troisième cas de figure est celui que l'on pourrait qualifier d'examen incident du droit humanitaire. Dans une telle situation le DIH n'est pas invoqué pour corroborer telle ou telle interprétation d'un droit découlant de la

---

13   CourEDH, *Varnava et autres c. Turquie*, GC, arrêt du 18 septembre 2009, par. 185.
14   CourEDH, *Al-Skeini et autres c. Royaume-Uni*, GC, arrêt du 7 juillet 2011, par. 168.

Convention européenne en tant que tel. La Cour de Strasbourg se réfère au droit humanitaire pour ainsi dire en amont, dans le contexte du principe *nullum crimen sine lege*. En l'occurrence, il s'agit de savoir si la règle pertinente du droit des conflits armés avait acquis un caractère coutumier à l'époque des faits, ce qui est décisif pour pouvoir se prononcer sur le respect ou non du principe « pas de peine sans loi », énoncé dans l'article 7 de la CEDH. Autrement dit, l'interprétation du droit des conflits armés constitue une condition préalable à l'application de la Convention au cas d'espèce.

L'exemple par excellence de cette situation est l'affaire *Kononov c. Lettonie*[15]. Les faits de l'affaire remontaient à la Seconde Guerre mondiale. La Cour suprême lettone avait reconnu le requérant coupable de crimes de guerre, infraction réprimée par le code pénal letton, qui renvoyait aux « conventions juridiques pertinentes » (notamment à la quatrième Convention de Genève de 1949) pour une définition précise des crimes de guerre. Autrement dit, la condamnation du requérant par les juridictions lettones pour crimes de guerre était fondée principalement sur le droit international auquel se référait le droit national. La question était donc de savoir si au moment des faits, c'est-à-dire en 1944, la notion de crimes de guerre faisait partie du droit international coutumier avec suffisamment de clarté pour satisfaire aux exigences du principe *nullum crimen*. Pour répondre à cette question, la Cour de Strasbourg s'est livrée à une longue analyse de l'évolution du droit des conflits armés depuis le Code Lieber de 1863 jusqu'aux Principes de Nuremberg. Et la Cour de conclure au terme de cette rétrospective que, « à l'époque où ils ont été commis, les actes du requérant étaient constitutifs d'infractions définies avec suffisamment d'accessibilité et de prévisibilité par les lois et les coutumes de la guerre »[16]. Les exigences du principe *nullum crimen* étant satisfaites, la Cour n'a pas constaté de violation de l'article 7 de la Convention.

Dans un ordre d'idées voisin se situe également l'affaire *Vasiliauskas c. Lituanie*, à propos de laquelle le requérant alléguait que sa condamnation pour génocide s'analysait en une violation de l'article 7 de la CEDH, estimant notamment que les juridictions internes avaient adopté une interprétation large de ce crime, qui ne trouvait pas d'appui en droit international. Selon la Cour, bien que le crime de génocide, en tant que tel, ait été clairement défini par le droit international avant même l'adoption de la Convention sur le génocide de 1948[17] (signée par l'Union soviétique en 1949) et bien que la définition de ce crime ait

---

15   CourEDH, *Kononov c. Lettonie*, GC, arrêt du 17 mai 2010.
16   Ibid. par. 244.
17   Convention pour la prévention et la répression du crime de génocide, A/Rés. 260 (III) A, 9 décembre 1948, Nations Unies, *Recueil des traités*, vol. 78, p. 277.

donc été accessible au requérant, celui-ci ne pouvait pas prévoir l'éventualité de sa condamnation au regard du droit international applicable au moment des faits litigieux, à savoir le meurtre commis en 1953 à l'encontre de partisans lituaniens entrés en résistance contre le régime soviétique après la Seconde Guerre mondiale. En effet, la Cour observe que la définition de génocide donnée par le droit international conventionnel n'englobe pas les « groupes politiques » et elle constate, eu égard aux divergences de vues sur cette question, que ce crime n'est pas clairement défini par le droit international coutumier. Dans l'affaire du requérant, la Cour n'est pas convaincue de la conformité de l'interprétation du crime de génocide donnée par les juridictions lituaniennes avec la notion de génocide telle qu'elle était comprise en 1953. Sur ce point, bien que les juridictions lituaniennes aient procédé à une substitution de motifs sur la question de la condamnation du requérant en qualifiant les partisans lituaniens de « représentants de la nation lituanienne », c'est-à-dire d'un groupe national protégé par la Convention sur le génocide, elles n'ont pas précisé ce qu'elles entendaient par « représentants » et n'ont pas donné d'explications historiques ou factuelles sur la manière dont les partisans lituaniens représentaient la nation lituanienne à l'époque pertinente[18].

5   La prise en compte du DIH

Un quatrième cas de figure consiste à examiner les règles du DIH invoquées par les parties au litige pour arriver à la conclusion qu'elles ne sont pas vraiment pertinentes en l'espèce. En d'autres termes, la Cour n'ignore pas le droit humanitaire, elle en tient compte, mais elle ne fonde pas la solution du litige sur le droit humanitaire.

Un exemple typique de cette situation est fourni par l'arrêt *Sargsyan c. Azerbaïdjan* du 16 juin 2015. Selon le gouvernement défendeur, le refus opposé par ce dernier de laisser les civils accéder au village de Golestan, situé en territoire azerbaïdjanais, était fondé sur le droit humanitaire. La Cour a passé en revue les règles du DIH relatives au déplacement des populations, aux transferts forcés, aux déportations, au droit des personnes déplacées de regagner leur foyer ou leur lieu de résidence habituel, etc. Cependant, la Cour est arrivée à la conclusion que dans les circonstances de l'espèce le droit humanitaire n'apportait pas « de réponse concluante » à la question cruciale de l'affaire, c'est-à-dire à la question de savoir si le gouvernement avait des raisons valables de refuser au requérant (d'origine arménienne) la possibilité

---

18   CourEDH, *Vasiliauskas c. Lituanie*, GC, arrêt du 20 octobre 2015, notamment par. 165 ss.

d'accéder à Golestan[19]. Cela dit, la Cour a invoqué également les « Principes (adoptés au sein des Nations Unies) concernant la restitution des logements et des biens dans le cas des réfugiés et des personnes déplacées », plus connus sous la dénomination de « principes de Pinheiro »[20]. Autrement dit, le droit humanitaire est pris en compte, la Cour s'y réfère dans la première et dans la seconde partie de son arrêt. Cependant, celui-ci est fondé pour l'essentiel sur un raisonnement relatif au droit de propriété, tel que protégé par l'article 1er du Protocole n° 1 à la CEDH.

6 L'application directe du DIH

La dernière hypothèse, de loin la plus intéressante, concerne les cas où le droit humanitaire et la Convention créent des obligations qui ne sont pas forcément compatibles. L'arrêt de la Grande Chambre dans l'affaire *Hassan c. Royaume-Uni*, adopté en 2014[21], mérite un examen plus attentif à cet endroit, puisqu'il marque, sinon un revirement, du moins une évolution notable de la jurisprudence de la Cour.

Il s'agissait, en l'occurrence, de l'arrestation et de la détention du frère du requérant par les forces britanniques en Irak en avril 2003. L'arrestation et la détention en question avaient été décidées en vertu des pouvoirs conférés au Royaume-Uni par les troisième et quatrième Conventions de Genève[22]. Cependant, ainsi qu'il a été observé par la Cour, une telle détention ne correspond à aucune des catégories énumérées aux alinéas a) à f) de l'article 5 par. 1 de la Convention. Or l'énumération en question est limitative, exhaustive et non pas simplement indicative. Autrement dit, une détention qui ne correspond à aucune de ces catégories est, en principe, contraire à l'article 5 de la Convention. Bref, l'arrestation et la détention litigieuses étaient permises sur la base du droit humanitaire, ce qui n'était pas le cas en vertu de la Convention.

---

19   CourEDH, *Sargsyan c. Azerbaïdjan*, op. cit., note 4, par. 232.
20   Sous-Commission de la promotion et de la protection des droits de l'homme, « Principes concernant la restitution des logements et des biens dans le cas des réfugiés et des personnes déplacées », Rapporteur Paulo Sérgio Pinheiro, NU doc. E/CN.4/Sub.2/2005/17, 28 juin 2005, Annexe.
21   CourEDH, *Hassan c. Royaume-Uni*, op. cit., note 8.
22   Convention (III) de Genève relative au traitement des prisonniers de guerre, 12 août 1949 ; Convention (IV) de Genève relative à la protection des personnes civiles en temps de guerre, 12 août 1949.

Dans son arrêt sur l'affaire *Hassan*, la Grande Chambre a cité la position de la CIJ sur l'articulation entre le DIH et les droits de l'homme. On sait, en effet, que la Cour de La Haye a estimé que la protection offerte par les conventions régissant les droits de l'homme ne cesse pas en cas de conflit armé, sous réserve des clauses dérogatoires[23]. Pour ce qui est des rapports entre le DIH et les droits de l'homme, la CIJ a distingué trois situations : « certains droits peuvent relever exclusivement du droit international humanitaire ; d'autres peuvent relever exclusivement des droits de l'homme ; d'autres enfin peuvent relever à la fois de ces deux branches du droit international »[24].

C'est précisément dans cet esprit que se situe l'arrêt *Hassan*. Face à une situation qui relevait à la fois du DIH et des droits de l'homme, la Cour européenne a adopté une approche tendant à harmoniser les obligations découlant de ces deux branches. La Cour a exclu, tout d'abord, la possibilité d'appliquer la clause dérogatoire de l'article 15 de la Convention. Elle a constaté, en effet, qu'il n'existait aucune pratique d'invocation de ladite clause dans les cas d'opérations militaires en dehors du territoire national, ni dans le contexte d'un conflit armé international, comme en l'occurrence[25].

Là réside précisément la nouveauté de l'arrêt. En effet, contrairement à l'approche traditionnelle, la Cour juge bien fondée la position du gouvernement suivant laquelle l'absence de dérogation formelle en vertu de l'article 15 ne l'empêche pas de tenir compte du contexte et des règles du DIH pour interpréter et appliquer l'article 5 de la Convention. Tout en se disant consciente que l'internement litigieux ne cadre pas avec les garanties de la CEDH, la Cour est prête à interpréter l'article 5 en tenant compte du droit humanitaire. Pour ce faire, la Cour insiste sur la quintessence du droit à la liberté et à la sûreté, à savoir la protection de l'individu contre l'arbitraire. Or, à partir du moment où la détention du requérant était conforme au DIH, elle était « régulière » au sens de l'article 5 de la Convention. Autrement dit, le but fondamental de cette disposition – l'interdiction de l'arbitraire – était réalisé[26].

---

23   *Licéité de la menace ou de l'emploi d'armes nucléaires*, avis consultatif, 8 juillet 1996, CIJ Rec. 1996, p. 240, par. 25.

24   *Conséquences juridiques de l'édification d'un mur dans le territoire palestinien occupé*, avis consultatif, 9 juillet 2004, CIJ Rec. 2004, p. 136, par. 106 ; *Affaire des activités armées sur le territoire du Congo (République démocratique du Congo c. Ouganda)*, arrêt du 19 décembre 2005, CIJ Rec. 2005, p. 168, par. 216. Il est significatif que, alors que dans les avis consultatifs précités la Cour se réfère au droit international humanitaire en tant que *lex specialis* (ibid.), dans l'arrêt de 2005 elle omet cette référence.

25   CourEDH, *Hassan c. Royaume-Uni*, op. cit., note 8, par. 101.

26   Ibid., notamment par. 105.

Pour ce qui est des garanties procédurales, la Cour considère que dans le cas d'une détention intervenant lors d'un conflit armé international, les paragraphes 2-4 de l'article 5 de la CEDH doivent être interprétés à la lumière des règles pertinentes du droit humanitaire[27]. On sait que les articles 43 et 78 de la quatrième Convention de Genève stipulent que les internements « seront l'objet d'une révision périodique, si possible semestrielle, par les soins d'un organisme compétent ». La CourEDH observe que s'il peut ne pas être réalisable, au cours d'un conflit armé international, de faire examiner la régularité d'une détention par un « tribunal » indépendant au sens de l'article 5 par. 4 de la CEDH, il faut néanmoins, pour que l'État contractant puisse être réputé avoir satisfait à ses obligations découlant de cette disposition dans ce contexte, que l'« organe compétent » offre, en matière d'impartialité et d'équité de la procédure, « des garanties suffisantes pour protéger contre l'arbitraire ». Par ailleurs, la première révision doit intervenir peu après l'incarcération et être ultérieurement suivie de « révisions fréquentes », de manière à garantir qu'un détenu qui ne relèverait d'aucune des catégories d'internement possibles en droit international humanitaire soit libéré sans retard injustifié. Or, Tarek Hassan a été jugé libérable et il a été physiquement libéré par les autorités britanniques quelques jours après son arrestation. Dans ces conditions, la Cour a estimé que les exigences du droit humanitaire et, partant, celles de la Convention avaient été satisfaites[28].

On notera que – tout comme la CIJ dans l'*Affaire des activités armées sur le territoire du Congo*[29] – la Cour évite de se référer au DIH en tant que *lex specialis*, les ambiguïtés de ce terme n'échappant à personne[30]. Elle préfère procéder à une application simultanée de la Convention et du droit humanitaire. Elle s'assure que l'objectif primordial de l'article 5 de la Convention est atteint. Elle exige également que l'État défendeur invoque explicitement le DIH. En même temps, la Cour fait preuve de pragmatisme en acceptant de baisser quelque peu le standard de protection prévu par la Convention pour tenir compte de la situation qui prévaut dans le contexte d'un conflit armé international.

L'affaire *Géorgie c. Russie No. 2*, actuellement pendante devant la Grande Chambre de la CourEDH, risque de soulever une problématique analogue.

---

27   Ibid., par. 106.
28   Ibid., par. 107.
29   Cf. *Affaire des activités armées sur le territoire du Congo* (*République démocratique du Congo c. Ouganda*), *op. cit*, note 24.
30   Cf. à ce sujet l'analyse approfondie de Gaggioli, *op. cit.*, note 2, pp. 42 ss. et *passim*.

7 Remarques finales

Ainsi qu'il apparaît à travers les développements précédents, la position de la CourEDH sur l'articulation entre le DIH et la CEDH, sans avoir radicalement changé, a néanmoins évolué. D'abord très réticente, la Cour opère désormais une ouverture timide à l'égard du droit humanitaire applicable aux conflits armés internationaux, notamment pour corroborer l'interprétation des dispositions de la Convention. Elle examine incidemment l'évolution du droit des conflits armés dans le contexte de l'application du principe *nullum crimen sine lege*. Elle prend en compte le droit humanitaire, sans pour autant fonder la solution du litige sur cette branche du droit. Enfin et surtout, la Cour accepte d'appliquer parallèlement le DIH et la CEDH dans une situation de conflit armé international et d'occupation, en s'inspirant de la position de la CIJ en la matière. Cette nouvelle approche constitue une évolution notable de la jurisprudence de la Cour et pourrait avoir des répercussions importantes dans l'avenir.

Brèves remarques sur la répression du génocide

Joe Verhoeven

Chacun sait que le terme « génocide » est dû à la plume d'un juriste polonais, Raphaël Lemkin, qui était procureur à Varsovie et qui s'intéressa, dans les années 1930, à la rédaction d'une « loi » internationale appelée à sanctionner les responsables de la destruction de groupes ethniques, nationaux ou religieux. Ce qui, loin d'être simplement une manière de passe-temps intellectuel, témoignait de la coexistence souvent de plus en plus difficile – notamment en Pologne – de communautés humaines dont la culture, la langue et les préoccupations propres à chacune d'elles, étaient souvent très différentes, sinon parfois contradictoires. Ce n'est pas que la chose était totalement nouvelle ; bien au contraire, de telles pratiques étaient, en tous les cas jadis, relativement fréquentes, sinon habituelles, dans des populations dont les composantes étaient loin souvent d'être parfaitement homogènes. Il y a là d'ailleurs une des conséquences de la recomposition qui suivit la 1ère guerre dite mondiale dont l'Allemagne, l'Autriche-Hongrie et la Turquie furent les principaux vaincus, dans le moment même où de nouveaux Etats s'installaient dans les espaces désertés par les anciens souverains. Il n'y a pas à s'étonner dès lors que les traités qui rétablirent la paix et réorganisèrent la « famille des nations » en Europe, le premier d'entre eux étant le traité de Versailles, ont eu pour conséquence d'en dessiner une nouvelle carte politique bien différente de celle l'Europe du 19ème siècle.

Que Lemkin s'y soit particulièrement intéressé se comprend aisément, sachant qu'il était de confession juive dans un pays immédiatement voisin d'une Allemagne devenue hitlérienne, dont les autorités ne faisaient pas mystère, Führer en tête, de leur volonté d'éradiquer la « juiverie » internationale. Ce qui l'incita à se réfugier promptement aux Etats-Unis.

C'est pour prévenir toute confusion avec d'autres pratiques condamnables et en souligner clairement l'originalité – tout sinistre qu'elle soit – que Lemkin forgea à cette fin un mot nouveau : le « génocide », dont il explicita les caractéristiques dans son ouvrage intitulé « Axis Rule in Occupied Europe » qui fut publié, dès 1944, par le Carnegie Endowment for Peace. Ce qui fut rapidement reconnu non point simplement comme une pratique contestable parmi bien d'autres, mais comme un « crime » dont les caractéristiques essentielles sont explicitées[1],

---

1 R. Lemkin, « Le crime de génocide », *Revue de droit international de sciences diplomatique et politiques* (RDISDP), 1946, p. 213 ; R. Lemkin, « Genocide as a Crime in International Law », *American Journal of International Law*, vol. 41, 1947, p. 147 ss.

même si définir le génocide n'est pas tellement simple, beaucoup s'en faut, par-delà des évidences[2].

On peut certainement avoir des hésitations sur la pertinence des mots qui ont été utilisés pour mettre en lumière, sinon expliciter au sens propre du terme, les caractéristiques d'un crime nouveau. Il n'empêche que l'appellation n'est plus – si elle le fut jamais – contestée, du moins à partir du moment où une convention pour la prévention et la répression du crime de génocide fut solennellement adoptée au palais de Chaillot à Paris, le 9 décembre 1948[3]. Et nul n'ignore par ailleurs qu'un Projet de code des crimes contre la paix et la sécurité de l'humanité – qui vise notamment le génocide – fut adopté, près de vingt ans plus tard (1996), par la Commission du droit international, indépendamment des crimes contre l'humanité. On eût peut-être préféré que le cheminement dans le dédale des infractions particulièrement graves soit moins compliqué, du moins en apparence. L'important n'en demeure pas moins que ces crimes ont pu être dûment incriminés et sanctionnés... et leurs auteurs punis.

Encore faut-il bien entendu que la réalité de pratiques génocidaires soit dûment établie – c'est-à-dire prouvée –, ce qui, sans surprise, est habituellement contesté par les autorités auxquelles il est reproché de les avoir organisées ou laissé l'être. Et c'est sans surprise aussi que l'on constate qu'il faut du temps pour que celles-ci acceptent de reconnaître leur responsabilité en la matière, en dépit de l'opprobre qui s'y attache... lorsqu'ils ne s'y refusent pas obstinément.

Ainsi en va-t-il par exemple du massacre des Arméniens en 1915, qui est sans nul doute le premier génocide de l'histoire moderne, que néanmoins les autorités turques se refusent toujours obstinément à ne pas reconnaître,... voire des Ukrainiens en 1932 que les autorités soviétiques persistent également à nier, même s'il est vrai que la réalité d'un génocide est en ce cas moins évidente, en dépit d'une famine qui a causé la mort de centaines de milliers de personnes dans le grenier à blé de la Russie, que ses autorités ont laissé se développer... quand elles ne l'avaient pas, du moins indirectement, organisée.

Cela dit, il est clair que les appréciations sont toujours délicates en l'occurrence, particulièrement dans les contextes politiques, inévitablement très sensibles, où la question du génocide est – à tort ou à raison – soulevée... que d'aucuns préféreront d'ailleurs ne pas évoquer tant que les autorités publiques

---

2 Voir not. I. W. Charny, « Toward a Generic Definition », *in Genocide: Conceptual and Historic Dimensions*, George J. Andreopoulos, 1994, p. 64 ss.
3 Nations Unies, *Recueil des traités*, vol. 78, p. 277.

ne sont pas en mesure d'assumer pleinement leurs responsabilités en dépit de la dureté des temps, ou s'y refusent. L'on peut certes sur les appréciations à formuler dans des contextes particulièrement sensibles, dont il n'est pas simple de mesurer correctement et la nature et l'importance. On conviendra sans doute qu'il est par exemple difficile de suivre l'actuel président de la Turquie – Mr. Erdogan – lorsqu'il accusa, en 2011, la France de génocide en Algérie ou le Président de la République algérienne et populaire – Mr Bouteflika – lorsque ce dernier accusa semblablement la France d'un tel crime, au motif apparemment que toute colonisation serait nécessairement constitutive de génocide... sans avoir autrement vérifié la réalité de pratiques génocidaires. Ce qui n'est pas très convaincant, quelles que soient les critiques qui peuvent justement être formulées à propos de toute colonisation.

Quoi qu'il en soit, on ne peut que se garder en la matière de toute conclusion hâtive... singulièrement lorsque sont en cause des situations dont les spécificités ne s'accommodent pas (souvent) de conclusions qui méconnaîtraient les particularités propres à des groupes humains dont l'histoire est ou peut avoir été cahoteuse et tourmentée. On dira que, sous la forme où elle est aujourd'hui rapportée, cette histoire est dans l'ensemble très récente. Ce n'est pas contestable si on lui fournit comme point de départ les premières condamnations « modernes » du génocide. C'est assurément plus simple. On ne peut toutefois oublier que nombreux sont les massacres qui ont précédé, ci ou là, le génocide au sens moderne du terme.

Les contextes n'étaient pas assurément les mêmes... mais l'horreur ou l'indignité des massacres ne le cédaient sans doute en rien. La destruction systématique de Babylone par Alexandre – pourtant dit « le Grand » et nourri de la sagesse des plus brillants philosophes de la Grèce antique – ou, celle de la Bibliothèque de Persépolis par son père ne sont pas si éloignées qu'on aimerait le croire des destructions de certains hommes de guerres d'aujourd'hui... On dira sans doute que l'intention n'était pas la même. Ce serait néanmoins une faute, et point seulement une erreur, de blanchir tardivement une histoire faite de noirceurs en tous genres depuis de nombreux siècles... sinon sans doute de millénaires.

D'aucuns diront peut-être que le génocide n'a pas d'histoire avant la « modernité », c'est-à-dire, en simplifiant quelque peu, avant qu'un Führer dont on eût préféré qu'il fût réellement fou ne donnât libre cours à des pratiques monstrueuses. Ce ne serait assurément pas une consolation, et encore moins un remède. On le comprend aisément. L'important reste toutefois et il faut s'en féliciter, que le génocide soit aujourd'hui juridiquement incriminé comme tel, au titre de l'un des crimes les plus monstrueux qui soit, même si les palmarès dans l'horreur n'ont d'évidence aucun sens.

Il se comprendrait difficilement que le génocide puisse apparaître et se développer au sein d'une société dont les membres sont en « paix » les uns avec les autres, même si des tensions d'ordre divers, le cas échéant vives, y surviennent inévitablement. Il est clair que cela puisse fragiliser le tissu social et la vie en commun, au risque de devoir constater que les failles s'y installent et s'y creusent, au détriment de l'intérêt dit commun,... qui n'est pas toujours celui de tous.

On eût pu espérer que les deux principaux génocides qu'a connus le 20ème siècle – celui des Arméniens en 1915 et celui des Juifs à l'occasion de la Seconde Guerre mondiale – suffirait à décourager à jamais une population de laisser s'entretuer ses membres au point d'en menacer l'existence même. On sait qu'il n'en a rien été, les horreurs semblant parfois appelées à se multiplier plutôt qu'à se dissoudre. Ce n'est pas que la Convention pour la prévention et la répression du crime de génocide (1948) soit demeurée lettre morte. Tout au contraire, on ne peut que souligner les efforts entrepris pour en assurer l'application effective. Force est néanmoins de constater que cette manière de lèpre est loin d'avoir été universellement endiguée. Il faut le répéter : cela ne signifie d'aucune manière que sont demeurés vains les efforts ou que n'ont connu aucun succès les outils mis en œuvre pour (r)établir la concorde entre les membres d'une « nationalité » – comme on le disait naguère dans un langage plus « privatiste » que « publiciste » – que rongent des pratiques génocidaires.

Il y a certainement plus d'une explication à ces échecs. Ce n'est cependant pas à un juriste qu'il revient d'en expliciter avec autorité les causes. C'est à d'autres disciplines que le droit et à d'autres actions que (purement) juridiques qu'il convient assurément de faire appel pour retrouver le ciment social qui permettra de résorber des fractures suicidaires.

Il est évident qu'il faille faire usage à cet effet de médications et autres thérapies appropriées, s'il en est. Ce devrait être le premier devoir et la première responsabilité du politique. Cela ne relève cependant que marginalement du savoir juridique. Malheureusement, il ne suffit pas à cet effet de règles, de policiers et de juges...

Qu'il me soit néanmoins permis de ne pas poursuivre dans cette voie, tout importantes que soient les questions qui s'y enchaînent en pareille perspective. Il faut le répéter : sur ce terrain, cela excède les compétences – même grandes – et les expériences – sans doute plus réduites – des hommes de droit.

Les questions sont multiples. Je me contenterai e n'en évoquer que deux – qui ne sont pas sans importance – pour honorer le grand juriste à l'intention duquel ces quelques commentaires ont été écrits. Non sans savoir qu'il est difficile de demeurer sur un terrain strictement juridique lorsque sont en cause des pratiques abominables. Chacun sait d'ailleurs qu'il a fallu un temps certain avant que le droit ne se saisisse du génocide pour le condamner sans restriction, après l'avoir incriminé spécifiquement. En tous les cas, il est clair que des pratiques dites aujourd'hui génocidaires existaient bien avant que Lemkin leur ait donné une appellation propre, dans des contextes toutefois passablement différents de ceux qui ont caractérisé le 20ème siècle... durant lequel la perversité de l'intention semble devenue bien plus monstrueuse. Même si les appréciations divergeront sans nul doute.

Cela dit, les questions soulevées par ces évolutions sont multiples, et toutes sont importantes. Qu'il me soit néanmoins permis de n'en traiter brièvement que deux, pour honorer le grand juriste à l'intention duquel ces quelques commentaires ont été écrits. Non sans taire qu'il est difficile de demeurer strictement sur un terrain juridique lorsque sont évoquées des pratiques abominables, dont il faut se réjouir qu'ont été ou seront justement punis ceux qui doivent en assumer la responsabilité.

La première question est relative à ce que l'on appellerait la dimension « quantitative » du génocide, même si l'appellation est quelque peu sinistre, et la seconde à la compétence dite universelle, qui est celle qui permet(trait) à tout Etat d'en juger les responsables alors même que l'Etat « punissant » n'a été ni directement ni indirectement impliqué dans la conception et la réalisation du génocide.

Les deux questions sont formellement étrangères l'une à l'autre. Il est clair qu'elles ne se répondent pas directement, comme il en va dans les vers bien connus du poète. Il n'empêche qu'elles ne sauraient être totalement dissociées. Cela dit, nul n'ignore plus que le texte fondateur demeure en l'occurrence la Convention pour la prévention et la répression du crime de génocide, adoptée le 9 décembre 1948 par l'Assemblée générale des Nations Unies, siégeant *extra muros* à Paris. Même s'il en existait antérieurement une manière de brouillon.

En 1948, il y avait là un corpus nouveau, qui fait honneur à ce qu'on appelle aujourd'hui – sans doute un peu hâtivement – la communauté internationale, de l'existence de laquelle il faut se féliciter. Même si certains esprits chagrins ne manqueront pas de souligner – non sans raison à maints égards – qu'elle manque encore sérieusement et de chair et de sang. Cela n'empêche que cette Convention est aujourd'hui très largement ratifiée, en matière telle que ses dispositions substantielles devraient sans nul doute être tenues pour applicables même aux Etats qui n'y sont pas parties... sans entrer plus avant dans le détail technique qui pourrait justifier cette affirmation. Le fait est qu'il y a là un corpus nouveau, aujourd'hui incontesté, qui va se développant compte tenu de l'importance croissante que revêtent des problématiques nouvelles.

Ces innovations législatives (ou jurisprudentielles) ne sont pas toujours sans déconcerter. Néanmoins, il reste qu'elles ont l'immense mérite de cimenter en quelque sorte des constructions juridico-politiques appelées à combler les failles du droit international et à en renforcer la cohérence. Ce qui est loin d'ailleurs de ne concerner que la sanction du génocide.

1 Sur l'aspect « quantitatif »

Selon l'article II de la Convention de New York du 9 décembre 1948, le génocide requiert une « intention de détruire, « en tout ou en partie », l'un des divers « groupes » visés par ses dispositions, à savoir « national, ethnique, racial ou religieux comme tel ».

Qu'il soit fait explicitement mention d'un « tout » ou d'une « partie » met clairement en lumière que ce qui est en cause à ce stade est un élément purement « quantitatif » – si sinistre en soi puisse-t-il être –, à savoir un certain nombre de membres relevant de l'un des groupes visés à l'article II. Y sont également précisés ce qu'il faut bien appeler les moyens pris en considération à cet effet meurtre, etc. ; voir les cinq alinéas a) à e). Ce qui est d'ailleurs quelque peu étrange... dans la mesure où cela pourrait laisser entendre que la destruction est licite si elle est réalisée par d'autres voies... Sauf à considérer qu'il n'y a pas d'autres « acte(s) », pour reprendre les termes de l'article II, qui puissent jamais être utilisés à des fins génocidaires... Ce qui serait surprenant. Point n'est besoin toutefois de s'attarder à ce propos.

D'aucuns estimeront peut-être qu'il eût été préférable de se contenter de « l'intention de détruire, en tout ou en partie, un groupe (...) comme tel », sans plus. Mais cela n'a pas grande importance. Sachant qu'il convient en tous les cas d'espérer que l'énumération des actes de destruction précités, fût-elle « retenue », perde à l'avenir toute pertinence. Quoi qu'il en soit, on ne voit pas bien néanmoins qu'il ne puisse jamais exister un seuil quantitatif en dessous duquel le génocide doive être en quelque sorte considéré comme « mécaniquement » exclu. Même si le groupe ne comporte qu'un nombre limité de membres, sinon dans l'absolu du moins par rapport à un autre groupe... Il est vrai que la question ne se posait pas dans les trois génocides le plus souvent mentionnés aujourd'hui : celui des Juifs dans Allemagne nazie principalement, le génocide organisé dans l'ex-Yougoslavie, et celui des Tutsis au Burundi. Mais elle pourrait assurément devoir être posée dans des contextes différents.

Dans l'affaire relative à la Convention pour la prévention et la répression du génocide (Bosnie-Herzégovine c. Serbie-et-Monténégro, 26 février 2007)[4],

---

[4] *Application de la convention pour la prévention et la répression du crime de génocide*, exceptions préliminaires, *arrêt, CIJ Recueil 1996*, p. 595.

la Cour internationale de Justice précisa que « l'intention qui caractérise le génocide doit être de détruire au moins une partie substantielle du groupe en question (§ 193 et 198) », ce qui est « corroboré par la jurisprudence constante du Tribunal international pour l'ex-Yougoslavie et du Tribunal pénal international pour le Rwanda » (ibid.). Non sans préciser et que cette « partie doit être suffisamment importante pour que sa disparition ait des effets sur le groupe entier « (ibid.), « même si l'intention ne doit pas être nécessairement l'anéantissement complet du groupe dans le monde entier » (§ 199). Ce qui semble à première vue très élémentaire,... sans taire l'ambiguïté d'un critère purement quantitatif en l'absence d'un seuil clair qui puisse être universellement pertinent, le cas échéant par référence à des pourcentages plutôt qu'à des chiffres absolus. Nul doute que ces calculs soient pour le moins sinistres, mais on voit mal que l'on puisse totalement s'en dispenser... même si la punition pourrait être identique, qu'il y ait génocide ou massacre de « droit commun ».

Cette approche quantitative répond assurément à une certaine logique, on ne saurait le nier. A la limite, elle inciterait à tenir pour massacre génocidaire celui qui concerne 50% au moins des membres du groupe concerné, voire davantage, et massacre simplement criminel en dessous de ce taux. L'intérêt de la distinction serait en ce dernier cas que les dispositions spécifiques au génocide ne sont pas applicables, même si la punition peut être identique. Ce qui, non sans raison, laissera sans doute l'honnête homme quelque peu perplexe... et devrait peut-être inciter à rechercher sur un terrain autre que le « quantitatif », ce qui pourrait caractériser – hors les sanctions répressives – la « vraie » spécificité du génocide.

Si l'on y regarde de plus près, la conclusion laisse pour le moins songeur. C'est en effet que l'article 6 de la Convention de 1948, qui définit le « crime de génocide », fait explicitement référence à des « actes commis dans l'intention de détruire un groupe national, ethnique, racial ou religieux comme tel », sans évoquer d'aucune manière quelque élément quantitatif que ce soit. C'est tout au contraire un élément qualitatif, à savoir « l'intention de détruire (...) un groupe national, ethnique, racial ou religieux comme tel », pour reprendre les termes de l'article II, qui semble déterminant. Que le génocide soit explicitement visé – à l'égal des crimes contre l'humanité, des crimes de guerre et du crime d'agression – dans le Statut de Rome de la Cour pénale internationale (article 5), qui peut partant en être saisie – n'y change rien. Il ne viendra certes à l'idée de personne de soutenir que ces crimes ne sont pas « graves ». Ce serait, d'évidence, littéralement incompréhensible. Il suffit qu'ils obéissent à des dispositions qui soient distinctes de celles qui régissent le génocide.

Il se comprend dès lors qu'il puisse être difficile, lorsque le génocide est en cause, de ne pas s'en tenir à une approche quantitative, puisqu'il est explicitement question de détruire, « en tout ou en partie », un « groupe national, ethnique, racial ou religieux comme tel »... pour autant que l'on s'accorde sur la portée exacte de chacun de ces qualificatifs. Mais il n'est nulle part question, explicitement ou implicitement, d'une portion substantielle du groupe ou autre formule équivalente. Que la question soit rarement évoquée explicitement n'y change rien. Il n'empêche qu'une partie demeure une partie, qu'elle soit ou non « substantielle »... C'est en tous les cas ce qui ressort, on l'a dit, de la doctrine et de la jurisprudence dominantes. Que la question soit rarement évoquée explicitement n'y change rien. Il est possible d'ailleurs que les membres du groupe soient si peu nombreux... que toute « partie » doive être tenue pour substantielle. Ce qui n'est pas du tout une hypothèse purement ou théorique ou rhétorique. Cela pourrait être par exemple le cas de « groupes » religieux dont les adeptes sont (très) peu nombreux, qu'il s'agisse par exemple des mazdéens, devenus plus tard zoroastriens, s'ils venaient *horresco referens* à être massacrés... ou convertis de force, ce qui n'est peut-être pas vraiment mieux.

On aurait tort d'ailleurs de croire que la jurisprudence est – ou devrait être – nécessairement « internationale » lorsqu'un génocide est en cause. Sans doute des outils juridictionnels internationaux ont-ils été mis en place pour connaître des crimes les plus graves, le meilleur exemple en étant fourni par la Cour pénale internationale dont la jurisprudence est devenue importante. On ne peut que s'en réjouir. Cela doit-il impliquer qu'en l'occurrence les tribunaux nationaux devraient être, *de jure* et *de facto*, dessaisis? Ce serait sans doute aller un peu trop vite...

On peut sans peine comprendre que, s'agissant du génocide, les rédacteurs de la Convention de 1948 ne se soient pas outre mesure préoccupés de ce qui devrait être tenu au minimum pour la « partie », évoquée à côté du « tout », et de ce qui doit être impliqué pour que la destruction d'un groupe « national, ethnique, racial ou religieux, comme tel » puisse être prise en considération pour l'établissement du génocide. La question n'en est pas moins importante et... délicate. On voit mal d'ailleurs comment y répondre de façon autorisée aujourd'hui, en l'absence d'une jurisprudence plus étoffée que celle dont on dispose actuellement, tout méritoire qu'elle soit.

Cela dit, il faut répéter que, selon les termes mêmes de l'article 6 de la Convention, c'est l'intention de détruire un « groupe national, ethnique, racial ou religieux, comme tel » qui est seule réellement déterminante, et non le nombre de victimes dont il n'est fait aucune mention. Peut-être l'importance de ce nombre donnera-t-il à croire que l'intention était perverse, mais la déduction n'a rien de nécessaire. La remarque n'est pas simplement rhétorique.

La pratique récente a notamment montré en effet que, dans divers pays, de petits groupes, voire de simples individus, ont cherché – pour la plus grande gloire de... on ne sait pas trop bien qui – à tuer des chrétiens ou à détruire leurs édifices religieux, sans cacher que leur objectif était purement et simplement d'éradiquer une croyance ou une foi jugées incompatibles avec la leur. Que des arrière-pensées purement politiques n'y soient probablement pas étrangères, ne change rien. Ce qui, à ce jour, a fait de nombreuses victimes du fait de la multiplication des attentats terroristes...

On sait que, selon l'article 2 de la Convention de 1948, le génocide s'entend notamment du « meurtre » ou de l'« atteinte grave à des conditions d'existence devant entraîner la destruction physique totale ou partielle de membres du groupe ». Ce qui ramène à l'élément « quantitatif » évoqué ci-dessus. Mais il faut rappeler, quitte à se répéter, qu'il ne devrait plus être question d'un nombre nécessairement considérable de victimes ; l'article 2 de la Convention évoque explicitement en effet une destruction éventuellement « partielle ». C'est l'intention – il faut le répéter – qui est déterminante en l'occurrence, selon les termes mêmes de la Convention. Et il paraît bien que, dans la pratique récente, une telle intention soit manifeste, et d'ailleurs ouvertement revendiquée. Il suffit qu'elle ait été de détruire le groupe – dans l'exemple donné « religieux » –, peu important de soi qu'elle ait été pleinement réalisée ou non. Sans doute la condamnation pour génocide sera-t-elle plus évidente – c'est à dire virtuellement moins contestée – si le nombre de victimes est important, mais cela n'y change rien fondamentalement.

Si l'on se base sur la pratique actuelle, principalement en France ou en Belgique, les poursuites sont – que je sache – diligentées principalement au titre d'attentats terroristes. Il n'est pas explicitement question de génocide... alors même que l'intention est de détruire un groupe – dans l'exemple cité « chrétien » – comme tel. Il est vrai que le dessein est insensé, et pas seulement criminel. Cela suffit-il pour en altérer la qualification ? On ne peut qu'en douter.

2   Une compétence universelle ?

Même s'il est vrai qu'il n'en existe pas de définition universellement admise à ce jour – comme en témoignent notamment les rapports du Secrétaire général des Nations Unies et les travaux de la Commission du droit international –, la compétence universelle, dans son acception traditionnelle, s'entend de celle qui est exercée par un tribunal alors même que le litige dont il est saisi ne présente aucun lien effectif de rattachement avec le for. Qu'il s'agisse par exemple de la localisation des faits litigieux, de la nationalité du défendeur ou de l'objet même de la demande.

Cette compétence peut être civile (au sens large) ou répressive. C'est en ce dernier cas néanmoins qu'elle soulève habituellement les difficultés les plus sérieuses... parce qu'une punition est nécessairement en cause dans une telle hypothèse. Ce qui est un enjeu bien différent de celui qui demeure purement civil, tout important qu'il puisse être. Qu'il me soit néanmoins permis de ne pas m'attarder sur cette distinction, sachant que c'est de la compétence répressive qu'il sera principalement question ci-dessous.

On comprend sans peine qu' une telle compétence dite universelle puisse laisser perplexe, mais on comprendrait mal que, pour ce seul motif, si sérieux soit-il, le juge se refuse à en connaître. Il n'y pas lieu dès lors d'écarter par principe la compétence dite universelle, pour autant du moins qu'il y ait un intérêt « politique », au sens fort du terme, à se saisir du litige. Cela se comprend par exemple sans peine lorsqu'est en cause devant le juge une personne, nationale ou étrangère, qui a été trouvée ou est établie dans le ressort de sa juridiction, ou qui soit l'auteur ou la victime d'un crime international.

Le législateur belge ne s'est toutefois pas contenté d'en rester là, qui a fait un pas de plus en soumettant à la compétence du juge belge des litiges concernant des défendeurs ou des accusés, – nationaux ou étrangers –, ne se trouvant pas sur le territoire belge. Une loi du 16 juin 1993 en particulier a soumis effet à sa juridiction répressive toute personne suspectée d'avoir commis un crime « international », c'est-à-dire d'avoir principalement violé les Conventions de Genève (1949) et ses protocoles additionnels. L'enthousiasme d'une certaine opinion publique – plus ou moins bien informée – aidant, le législateur n'a pas longtemps hésité à faire un nouveau pas en avant, en étendant la juridiction de ses tribunaux aux accusés suspectés d'avoir commis un crime « international », alors même qu'ils ne se trouvent pas sur le territoire belge. Ce qui vise en tous les cas explicitement la piraterie, l'esclavage, les crimes de guerre, l'apartheid et la torture, conformément à la jurisprudence des tribunaux pénaux pour l'ex-Yougoslavie et le Rwanda, qui furent le théâtre de monstrueux massacres.

Ces dispositions semblent largement acceptées aujourd'hui, alors même que les liens rattachant à la Belgique les crimes allégués sont parfois très ténus. Il en va notamment ainsi lorsque ce n'est qu'à la suite d'un défaut du prévenu que le juge belge a été saisi. Ce que d'aucuns contesteront peut-être davantage, sachant qu'une loi belge du 10 février 1999 a étendu la compétence « universelle » dont se réclament les tribunaux de la Belgique au génocide et aux crimes contre l'humanité... dont on aurait pu croire, fût-ce par suite de la complexité des affaires, que la Cour pénale internationale en serait préférentiellement saisie.

Ces règles nouvelles ne sont pas demeurées lettre morte, beaucoup s'en faut. Les plaintes se sont en effet multipliées, visant d'ailleurs des personnages de rang élevé, comme Fidel Castro, Saddam Hussein ou Ariel Sharon... Et c'est notamment sur la compétence universelle qu'elle avait accordée à ses juridictions que la Belgique s'est appuyée par la suite pour attraire le Sénégal devant la CIJ en lui reprochant d'avoir manqué à son devoir de juger Hissène Habré pour les nombreux crimes qui lui étaient imputés[5].

Quelle que soit l'horreur du crime, on comprend sans peine qu'elle ne puisse, à soi seule, justifier la méconnaissance de dispositions jugées fondamentales, à tout le moins dans l'ensemble normatif auquel elles se rattachent.

C'est ce qui est à l'origine de l'affaire Yerodia, qui opposa la Belgique au Congo dont il était le ministre des Affaires étrangères, à propos du mandat d'arrêt qui avait été délivré contre lui par les autorités belges pour les crimes contre l'humanité dont elles le tenaient pour responsable. Le personnage n'était assurément pas très respectable, beaucoup s'en faut, mais la charge dont il avait été régulièrement investi lui assurait indiscutablement – en principe – une protection particulière. Il n'y a pas à s'étonner dès lors que les autorités congolaises aient saisi la CIJ pour obtenir – ce qui leur fut accordé – que ce mandat d'arrêt soit considéré comme nul et non avenu, ou du moins qu'il ne puisse pas être exécuté compte tenu de l'immunité dont jouit en principe, selon le droit international, un ministre des Affaires étrangères en exercice. La décision n'a cependant pas convaincu le juge Guillaume, alors Président de la CIJ, pour lequel le droit international non seulement n'admet pas la compétence universelle, et « encore moins la compétence universelle par défaut »[6]. Ce qui a incité les juges Higgins, Kooijmans et Buergentahl non pas à soutenir explicitement le contraire, mais à préciser que rien n'aurait interdit que « le mandat d'arrêt soit exécuté dans un Etat tiers avec l'accord de ses autorités »[7]. Ce qui laisse passablement songeur, quelle que puisse être l'efficacité du bricolage...

Il est très remarquable que cette compétence universelle, dont d'aucuns semblaient vouloir faire l'instrument privilégié de la lutte contre les crimes les plus graves – le génocide et les crimes contre l'humanité en particulier –, a été mise en place sans que les fondements juridiques en soient clairement

---

5 Voir à ce propos, J. Verhoeven, « Belgique contre Sénégal ou quel intérêt pour se plaindre d'autrui ? », *Annuaire francaise de droit international*, 2014, p. 3-16.
6 Arrêt du 11 avril 2000, *CIJ Recueil 2002*, par. 17.
7 Ibid.

explicités. L'horreur suscitée par des conduites criminelles a manifestement incité plus d'un honnête homme à construire – souvent avec un grand talent – un nouvel instrument de sanction de pratiques abominables dont les règles ordinaires du droit international ne paraissaient pas en mesure de sanctionner efficacement les responsables. L'initiative est respectable ; il n'empêche que l'on n'aperçoit guère ce que sont ou seraient les « fondamentaux » de la compétence universelle... hors une réprobation universelle (du moins faut-il l'espérer !). Ce qui devrait sans nul doute orienter l'interprétation du droit,... mais ne suffit pas à le créer.

Cela fait tout l'intérêt des « Princeton Principles on Universal Jurisdiction » qui ont été adoptés à Princeton en 2001, par un ensemble de juristes – majoritairement formés au droit américain – sous l'impulsion d'un Steering Committee que présida Stephen Macedo. A dire vrai, les « principes » sont d'une grande – peut-être trop grande – généralité. Mais c'est un premier socle où installer la compétence universelle, ce qui n'est pas sans importance.

On peut assurément hésiter sur certaines analyses et autres propositions, ou déplorer ce que l'on pourrait appeler certains manques. Cela n'empêche qu'il y a là un cadre normatif d'autant plus précieux que d'aucuns, aux grandes heures de la construction d'une compétence universelle, semblaient parfois enclins à soutenir un peu n'importe quoi. Les milieux juridiques belges ont d'ailleurs joué un rôle non négligeable en cette matière, qui ont notamment inspiré en 1991 une loi belge déclarant, avec une admirable candeur, « les juridictions belges (...) compétentes pour connaître des infractions à la présente loi, indépendamment du lieu où celles-ci auront été commises ». Ce qui témoigne clairement et sans autre hésitation de l'universalité de la compétence ainsi reconnue. Ce fut le point de départ en Belgique d'une manière de chasse aux grands criminels ou tenus pour tels. Les premiers moments d'enthousiasme évanouis, le reflux sera néanmoins rapide, les relations internationales de la Belgique se compliquant d'importance sans que l'on perçoive ce que sont ou pourraient être, pour l'humanité bien plus que pour la Belgique, les bénéfices de la législation nouvelle...

Concrètement, les résultats sont demeurés maigres, même si les opinions divergeront inévitablement sur ce point. Ce n'est pas que la recherche et la poursuite de grands criminels aient en elles-mêmes suscité de sérieuses objections. C'est seulement que les conditions dans lesquelles elles furent effectuées ont rapidement suscité des hésitations – sinon des protestations – croissantes. Notamment du fait qu'une loi du 16 juin 1993 organisa une compétence universelle *in absentia* (par défaut), laquelle ouvrit grand la porte à tous excès et autres manipulations. Ce qui fut en quelque sorte le début de la fin...

Nul ne contestera que cette législation témoignait d'une indiscutable et, oserait-on dire, passablement candide « générosité », dans le chef de ceux que tourmentait l'injustice universelle. Ce qui en soi les honore. Les complications – loin d'être simplement virtuelles – se multipliant, le reflux fut rapide. Il est vrai par exemple qu'une plainte a visé nommément le général Franks, lequel, à l'époque, dirigeait en Irak les armées US ... Ce qui n'a pas été sans susciter force protestations, comme l'a lui-même reconnu le professeur David. On peut aisément deviner que cela n'a pas été sans provoquer de vives réticences, sinon franches protestations. Le 5 août 2003, une nouvelle loi fut dès lors adoptée, qui gomma les dispositions jugées trop audacieuses... c'est-à dire celles qui pourraient menacer les bonnes relations de la Belgique avec ses partenaires traditionnels,... qui ne l'étaient plus totalement. L'immunité fut dès lors largement restaurée et l'exercice d'une compétence « universelle » restreinte aux « seules exigences du droit international »[8]. D'aucuns le regretteront sans doute. Le fait n'en est pas moins que « dans l'état actuel des relations internationales, la Belgique n'avait pas les moyens politiques de continuer à jouer au chevalier blanc du droit international public, même si le droit international ne le lui interdisait pas »[9], comme l'a reconnu le professeur David lui-même, principal inspirateur des nouvelles inventions législatives en la matière. Ce qui est manifeste, quelles que soient les opinions sur le fond.

Est-ce à dire que la compétence universelle n'a plus d'avenir ? Nul n'oserait sans doute le jurer. En tous les cas, la sanction traditionnelle de la piraterie devrait à tout le moins subsister, sachant que cette dernière est loin d'être éradiquée. Au-delà, les incertitudes subsistent.

---

8 Voir E. David, « Que reste-t-il de la compétence universelle dans la loi du 5 août 2003? », *Jura Falconis*, jg 40, 2003-2004, par. 38.
9 Ibid., par. 40.

PART 6

International Humanitarian Law

Protection of the Environment in Relation to Armed Conflicts—A Preliminary Comment on the Work of the International Law Commission

Michael Bothe

Celebrating the 75th birthday of Djamchid Momtaz, it is appropriate to dedicate to him a contribution dealing with the current work of the International Law Commission, of which he was a member from 2000 to 2006 and Chair in 2005: namely the protection of the environment in relation to armed conflicts. International humanitarian law, which is at the center of the ILC work to be analyzed here, has been one of Momtaz's dearest subjects throughout his academic and diplomatic career. He has also worked on the relationship between international humanitarian law and environmental protection, for instance through his participation in the Expert Seminar on Human Rights and the Environment co-organized by UNEP and the High Commissioner for Human Rights in 2002.

1   The Mandate and the Approach Proposed by the Special Rapporteur

In 2013, the ILC decided to include the topic 'Protection of the environment in relation to armed conflicts' in its program of work. It appointed Maria G. Jacobsson, who had taken the initiative to put this subject before the ILC, as Special Rapporteur. In 2014, she presented her first preliminary report,[1] which was followed by a general debate in the Commission. In 2015, she presented her second report,[2] concentrating on rules applicable during armed conflict and proposed a number of 'Principles'. These were then deliberated by ILC's Drafting Committee which provisionally adopted them in a modified form.[3] The Commission noted them. In 2016, the Special Rapporteur presented her third report,[4] concentrating on, and proposing, principles applicable after a conflict. The Drafting Committee adopted them in modified form[5] and also

---

1 UN Doc. A/CN.4/674, 30 May 2014 and A/CN.4/674/Corr. 1, 11 August 2014.
2 UN Doc. A/CN.4/685, 28 May 2015.
3 UN Doc. A/CN.4/L.870, 22 July 2015.
4 UN Doc. A/CN.4/700, 3 June 2016.
5 UN Doc. A/CN.4/L.876, 3 August 2016; UN Doc. A/CN.4/L.870/Rev.1, 26 July 2016.

worked on the principles adopted in 2015. Several principles were provisionally adopted by the plenary Commission.[6]

This project has to be seen against the backdrop of a decades-long debate. Since the 1970s, the debate on the law of war and the protection of the environment had centered on rules providing for protection *during* armed conflict.[7] Yet on a closer look, this concentration on obligations applying during conflicts is an inappropriate limitation.[8] Many measures for protecting the environment in relation to armed conflicts can, even must, be taken before a conflict occurs. Further, once the damage has occurred, in violation of applicable international law or not, the question is both what redress is possible, and also whether there are rules on what must be done in the post-conflict phase. This broader view of the problem allows the specific rules of the law applicable *in* armed conflict to be put in the more general perspective of general international law, in particular general environmental law.

2 The Possible Content of the Document—A Preview

After three reports of the Special Rapporteur, three rounds of plenary debate and two deliberations in the Drafting Committee, the shape of the possible outcome appears on the horizon. The rules formulated by the Commission take the form of 'principles', a choice of terminology to be commented on below.[9] The document, as it appears after the deliberations of the Commission in 2016, will be divided into four parts: Introduction (Principles 1 and 2, 3 being reserved; Part I: General principles (Principles 4–8); Part II: Principles applicable during armed conflict (Principles 9–13[10]); Part III: Principles applicable after an armed conflict (Principles 14–18).

---

6   ILC, Report on the work of the sixty-eighth session (2016), UN Doc. A/71/10, paras. 139 et seq.
7   For a short account see M. Bothe, C. Bruch, J. Diamond & D. Jensen, 'International law protecting the environment during armed conflict: gaps and opportunities', 92 *International Review of the Red Cross,* 2010, pp. 569–592.
8   See M. Bothe, 'The ILC Special Rapporteur's Preliminary Report on the Protection of the Environment in Relation to Armed Conflicts: An Important Step in the Right Direction', in Pia Acconci et al. (eds), *International Law and the Protection of Humanity. Essays in Honor of Flavia Lattanzi,* Brill/Nijhoff 2016, pp. 213–224.
9   Below at 4.3.
10 Supra, note 5.

There are no specific provisions on the pre-conflict phase. The 'General principles' apply to all three phases: pre-conflict, conflict and post-conflict.

It is the purpose of the following to try a provisional evaluation of the Principles as they appear at the time of writing (August 2016).

3   Achievements and Problems

3.1   *General Principles (Introduction and Part One)*

It is perhaps regrettable that there are no specific rules on obligations in the pre-conflict phase. One could imagine examples of desirable rules which would be applicable here.[11] One example is the duty to take precautions against attack (Article 58, AP I).[12] These duties are to endeavour to remove civilian objects from the vicinity of military objectives and to avoid locating military objectives within or near densely populated areas. It will be extremely difficult to fulfil these obligations once the conflict has broken out, but it is easier to take these duties into account in a planning and zoning process at any time, whether a conflict is imminent or not. Similarly, the requirements of environmental protection such as the necessity to protect certain habitats can be taken into account when deciding on siting military installations. The development of shooting grounds as refuge for wildlife is a somewhat ambivalent phenomenon in this connection.

The various general principles invite the following comments.[13]

The basic provision on measures to be taken is Principle 2, part of the Introduction:

Draft principle 2
Purpose

> *The present draft principles are aimed at enhancing the protection of the environment in relation to armed conflict, including preventive measures for minimizing damage to the environment during armed conflict and through remedial measures.*

---

11   Bothe, supra, note 8, pp. 219 et seq.
12   Protocol Additional to the Geneva Conventions of 12 August 1949, and Relating to the Protection of the Victims of International Armed Conflicts (Protocol I), of 8 June 1977, 1125 UNTS 3.
13   Italics by the author.

An example of such 'preventive measures' would be the siting decisions just mentioned.

Part I then contains a number of generic provisions.

Draft principle 4
Measure to enhance the protection of the environment

1. *States shall, pursuant to their obligations under international law, take effective legislative, administrative, judicial and other measures to enhance the protection of the environment in relation to armed conflict.*
2. *In addition, States should take further measures, as appropriate, to enhance the protection of the environment in relation to armed conflict.*

The two paragraphs provide for two different degrees of obligation ('shall' and 'should'). This difference may be explained by the addition of the words 'pursuant to their obligations under international law' in the first paragraph. In other words, States are obliged to do what they are already bound to do by virtue of other rules. Therefore, the strong term 'shall' is appropriate:[14] Perhaps a useful reminder. The weaker paragraph ('should . . . as appropriate') is at least a useful exhortation for States to take further measures. Examples would have been welcome.

Draft principle 5
Designation of protected zones

States should designate, by agreement or otherwise, areas of major environmental and cultural importance as protected zones.

This responds to a demand formulated by IUCN many years ago.[15] It was also mentioned in the proposals for a development of international humanitarian law made by the ICRC President in 2011,[16] an element of his proposals which unfortunately did not receive a positive reaction by States. The demand is

---

14 ILC, 68th session, Statement of the Chair of the ILC Drafting Committee, Mr. Pavel Šturma, 9 August 2016, p. 3.
15 See Bothe et al., supra, note 7, p. 577.
16 J. Kellenberger, 'Strengthening legal protection for victims of armed conflicts. The ICRC Study on the current state of International Humanitarian Law', 92 International Review of the Red Cross, 2010, pp. 799–804, pp. 802 et seq.

based on the experience that protection of environmentally valuable sites or areas during armed conflict does not occur so to say automatically during armed conflict. Sites to be protected must be designated as such before hostilities happen. The best way of designation is an agreement between the parties to a conflict. A unilateral designation does not really promise success. Another possibility is a designation by an organ of the United Nations which then can be implemented by the parties.[17]

Draft principle 7
Agreements concerning the presence of military forces in relation to armed conflict

> *States and international organizations should, as appropriate, include provisions on environmental protection in agreements concerning the presence of military forces in relation to armed conflict. Such agreements may include preventive measures, impact assessments, restoration and clean-up measures.*

This is yet another example of a provision to be implanted by agreement between relevant actors. The exhortation is necessary as this is a neglected aspect of State practice relating to visiting forces.[18] There is, for example, no provision on environmental protection in the UN Model Status of Forces Agreement.[19] The circumstances under which such agreements are concluded vary greatly, hence the addition of the words 'as appropriate'.[20]

Draft principle 8
Peace operations

> *States and international organizations involved in peace operations shall consider the impact of such operations on the environment and take appropriate measures to prevent, mitigate and remediate the negative environmental consequences thereof.*

---

17   For details see below concerning Principle 13.
18   On the practice see the 3rd Report of the Special Rapporteur, supra, note 4, para. 161 et seq.
19   A/45/594, 9 October 1990.
20   Statement of the Chair of the Drafting Committee, supra, note 14, p. 6.

Complex peace operations, some of them sizeable undertakings, have a serious influence on the situation of the area where they operate, including the environment. These environmental problems have to be taken into account in setting up and conducting a peace operation.[21] It is a strong obligation ('shall'), which is however softened by the word 'consider'.[22]

As to the post-conflict situation, this obligation is strengthened by Principle 14. This aspect has so far been neglected. It is, for example, not mentioned in the 2015 Report of the High-level Independent Panel on Peace Operations.[23]

The first aspect of the problem is the behaviour and attitude of the operation. For instance: what is the impact of their consumptions on local resources? Do such operations consume too much water or produce too much waste? Do peacekeepers go hunting endangered species?

The second aspect is their impact on the functioning of local life. Disarmament or demining activities pose environmental problems which must be taken into account. Peacekeepers may have to restrain unlawful mining activities which pose disastrous environmental problems.

Draft principle 6
Protection of the environment of indigenous peoples

1. *States should take appropriate measures, in the event of armed conflict, to protect the environment of the territories that indigenous peoples inhabit.*
2. *After an armed conflict that has adversely affected the environment of the territories that indigenous peoples inhabit, States should undertake effective consultations and cooperation with the indigenous peoples concerned, through appropriate procedures and in particular through their own representative institutions, for the purpose of taking remedial measures.*

Taking into account the specific problems and interests of indigenous peoples is a general *leitmotiv* in current international law.[24] An example is Article 8 (j) of the Convention on Biological Diversity.[25] Fulfilling the duties formulated in

---

21 UNEP, 'Greening the Blue Helmets: Environment, Natural Resources and UN Peacekeeping Operations', 2012.
22 Statement of the Chair of the Drafting Committee, supra, note 14, p. 8.
23 UN Doc. A/70/95-S/2015/446.
24 B. Kingbury, 'Indigenous peoples', in R. Wolfrum (ed), *Max Planck Encyclopedia of Public International Law* (MPEPIL), available at www.mpepil.com; 3rd Report of the Special Rapporteur, supra, note 4, para. 121 et seq.
25 1760 UNTS 79.

paragraph 1 would at the same time mean implementing the purposes of that provision.

The second paragraph belongs to the post-conflict duties. It is a concretization of Principles 15 and 18.[26]

3.2 Principles Applicable during Armed Conflict (Part Two)

Concerning the protection of the environment during armed conflict, the controversy concentrated largely on the relevant provisions of AP I, defining the threshold of the prohibition on causing damage to the environment by three qualifications. Only damage which is 'widespread, long-term *and* severe' falls within the prohibition. These three cumulative conditions are generally criticized as inadequate. But it seems that some States still like them. The development, however, has gone beyond these conditions.[27] The principles so far formulated by the Special Rapporteur and the ILC take these developments into account, but in an incomplete manner.

The part on principles applying during armed conflict is introduced by a general rule:

Draft principle 9, paragraph 1
General protection of the environment during armed conflict

> *The natural environment shall be respected and protected in accordance with applicable international law and, in particular, the law of armed conflict.*

The provision is a kind of reminder, useful as such: there is applicable law requiring the protection of the environment during armed conflict, and that law has to be applied. What is important, in addition, is that the provision expresses an assumption underlying the proposed principles, namely that these rules are not only those of the *ius in bello*, but also other rules. These other rules have to be applied, too. This leads to the question whether and how far the law of armed conflict is a *lex specialis* in relation to these other rules, namely general environmental law and multilateral environmental agreements.[28]

---

26   See below.
27   Bothe et al., supra, note 7, at pp. 684 et seq.
28   See below 4.2.

The second paragraph of Principle 9 prescribes a duty of care:

Draft principle 9, paragraph 2

Care shall be taken to protect the natural environment against widespread, long-term and severe damage.

It is somewhat regrettable that the three conditions are still there. In this respect, it is useful to compare the proposed principle with other recent formulations of the duty of care, providing for what has become known as the due regard principle:

- ICRC Customary Law Study, Rule 44[29]
  'Methods and means of warfare must be employed with due regard to the protection and preservation of the natural environment. In the conduct of military operations, all feasible precautions must be taken to avoid, and in any event minimise, incidental damage to the environment....'
  The duty to take feasible precautions corresponds to a duty of care. It is only in relation to the prohibition *stricto sensu* that the three qualifications also appear in the ICRC Study (Rule 45).
- San Remo Manual on Naval Warfare,[30] Article 44:
  'Methods and means of warfare should be employed with due regard for the natural environment taking into account the relevant rules of international law. Damage to or destruction of the natural environment not justified by military necessity and carried out wantonly is prohibited.'
  It must be emphasized that the three objectionable conditions are not mentioned. They may be hidden in the reference to 'relevant rules of international law', but the prohibition is much broader and better formulated than the one contained in AP I.
- Manual of Air and Missile Warfare:[31]

---

[29] ICRC, J.-M. Henckaerts, L. Doswald-Beck, *Customary International Humanitarian Law*, vol. 1, Cambridge University Press, 2005, pp. 147 et seq.

[30] San Remo Manual on International Law Applicable to Armed Conflicts at Sea, 12 June 1994, document elaborated by a group of experts assembled by the International Institute of Humanitarian Law, San Remo.

[31] Manual of International Law Applicable to Air and Missile Warfare, 15 may 2009, Document elaborated by a Group of Experts convened by the Program on Humanitarian Policy and Conflict Research at Harvard University.

'88. The destruction of the natural environment carried out wantonly is prohibited.
89. When planning and conducting air or missile operations, due regard ought to be given to the natural environment.'
This formulation is obviously inspired by the San Remo Manual and much friendlier to the environment then AP I and the ILC draft principle 9 para. 2.

It is hoped that the final version still to be adopted by the ILC will correct a version which, it is submitted, lags behind the *acquis* concerning the protection of the environment during armed conflict.

Several principles contained in Part Two concerning the protection of the environment during armed conflict relate to the principle of distinction:

Draft principle 9, paragraph 3

No part of the environment may be attacked, unless it has become a military objective.

Draft principle 10
Application of the law of armed conflict to the natural environment

The law of armed conflict, including the principles and rules on distinction, proportionality, military necessity and precautions in attack, shall be applied to the natural environment with a view to its protection

Draft principle 11
Environmental considerations

Environmental considerations shall be taken into account when applying the principle of proportionality and the rules on military necessity.

The three principles 9 para. 3, 10 and 11 apply the rule of distinction, which is the fundamental rule of international humanitarian law, to the protection of the environment. In the debate on the protection of the environment during armed conflict, it has even been maintained that the rules on the immunity of civilian objects are sufficient to protect the environment as elements of the environment are usually civilian in nature.[32] Principle 9(3) is a logical consequence of the rule of Article 52 AP I: anything which is not a military objective is a civilian

---

32   For a critique see Bothe et al., supra, note 7, at pp. 576 et seq.

object and may therefore not be attacked. Incidental damage to the environment caused by attacks on military objectives is limited by the principle of proportionality. Damage to the (civilian!) elements of the environment may not be excessive in relation to the direct military advantage anticipated. This is also reflected in the rule on precautions to be taken in attacks (Article 57 (2)(a)(iii) AP I). Principle 10 and 11 clarify that environmental concerns are indeed part of this 'proportionality equation', which, it is submitted, constitutes the added value of the two principles. Mentioning 'military necessity' should not be misunderstood as meaning that military necessity is a particular justification of destruction; quite the contrary, the Commission views it as an additional restraint on attacks on military objectives.[33] This should be clarified. Considerations of military 'advantage' are part of the definition of the military objective in Article 52 AP I. Beyond this, what might be considered as military necessity is irrelevant for determining what is a permissible attack and what not.

A special provision (Principle 13) in this Part is related to the General Principle formulated in Part One, namely Principle 5.

Draft Principle 13
Protected Zones

> *An area of major environmental and cultural importance designated by agreement as a protected zone shall be protected against any attack, as long as it does not constitute a military objective.*

It is a question of logic that the designation provided for in Principle 5 must entail some protection during armed conflict. By virtue of Principle 13, this protection is limited to zones designated by agreement. This protection corresponds *grosso modo* to that provided for demilitarized zones pursuant to Article 60 AP I. The scope of the protection will depend on the agreement. The words 'shall be protected against any attack' are not very clear. Article 60 AP I prohibits the parties from extending 'their military operations to [demilitarized] zones' if this is contrary to the agreement designating them. Logically, the prohibition includes any action by the enemy party which has a negative impact on the environment in the zone. The zone, of course, loses its protection if, contrary to the agreement designating it, somehow a military objective is created in the area, for instance if armed forces enter it. This rule also applies to demilitarized zones according to Article 60 (7) AP I.

33　See the misgivings expressed in the comment by Switzerland, quoted in the 3rd Report of the Special Rapporteur, supra, note 4, para. 88. On the concept envisaged by the ILC, see the Report, supra, note 6, p. 334.

In addition to the agreement, Principle 5 provides for forms of designation other than by agreement. It is quite clear that a designation by unilateral declaration cannot have the same protective effect as a designation by agreement. But a prohibition of attacks can be achieved by a unilateral declaration under Article 59 AP I, which provides this protection for 'undefended localities'. Nothing prevents such a declaration being made for environmental reasons.

A designation by the Security Council, an option advocated by IUCN, would lead to the same protection as designation by agreement if that designation is made by a decision binding under Ch. VII in combination with Article 25 of the Charter. If the designation is made in the form of a recommendation, or if it is made by another UN agency, the protection can only be achieved through an implementing agreement between the parties.

3.3 *Principles Applicable after an Armed Conflict*

This part contains a number of useful rules relating to action for the purpose of clarifying how to deal with the detrimental environmental consequences of an armed conflict. This is a problem area where a rich practice has been developed since the 1990s. It is a major field of activity of UNEP.[34]

Draft principle 14
Peace processes

1. *Parties to an armed conflict should, as part of the peace process, including where appropriate in peace agreements, address matters relating to the restoration and protection of the environment damaged by the armed conflict.*
2. *Relevant international organizations should, where appropriate, play a facilitating role in this regard.*

Detrimental effects of warfare are manifold, and this damage affects living conditions in many ways. Water supply and waste water treatment may be halted. Devastated land areas may no longer be usable for agriculture. Therefore, the restoration of the environment is an important element of a return to normal living conditions and hence to lasting peace. Paragraph 1 is a rather soft exhortation ('should address'), but it is difficult to see how the principles could go into more detail. In the Drafting Committee, it was said that the provision

---

[34] UNEP activities are divided into four areas: post-crisis environmental assessment, post-crisis environmental recovery, environmental cooperation and peacebuilding, disaster risk reduction. Information available at www.unep.org/disasterandconflicts/ UNEPsActivities/tabid/54617/Default.aspx.

did not correspond to a pre-existing obligation, but that it nevertheless had an important normative value,[35] which could mean a strong suggestion *de lege ferenda*.[36]

As to paragraph 2, UNEP has played this role for many years and will hopefully continue to do so.

Draft principle 15
Post-armed-conflict environmental assessment and remedial measures

> *Cooperation among relevant actors, including international organizations, is encouraged with respect to post-armed-conflict environmental assessments and remedial measures.*

This is a very important principle. 'Relevant actors' include both States and non-State actors.[37] What is required by this provision is exactly what UNEP has been doing since 1999 in relation to a number of conflicts which were taking place and ending during the past two decades.[38] In the light of this practice, it is perhaps regrettable that the obligation to do this is formulated in rather weak terms ('cooperation is encouraged'). It may well be asked whether, in the light of this practice, what has happened and continues to happen no longer is a politically laudable usage, but has grown into a rule of customary law.

A special aspect of the duties formulated in Principle 15 is how to deal with dangerous remnants of war.

Draft principle 16
Remnants of war

1. *After an armed conflict, parties to the conflict shall seek to remove or render harmless toxic and hazardous remnants of war under their jurisdiction of control that are causing or risk causing damage to the environment. Such measures shall be taken subject to applicable rules of international law.*

---

35 Statement of the Chair of the Drafting Committee, supra, note 14, p. 10.
36 On relevant practice, see 3rd Report of the Special Rapporteur, supra, note 4, para. 154 et seq.
37 Statement of the Chair of the Drafting Committee, supra, note 14, p. 12.
38 Information available at www.unep.org/disastersandconflicts/Introduction/PostCrisis EnvironmentalAssessment/tabid/54351/Default.aspx.

2. *The parties shall also endeavour to reach agreement, among themselves and, where appropriate, with other States and with international organizations, on technical and material assistance, including, in appropriate circumstances, the undertaking of joint operations to remove or render harmless such toxic and hazardous remnants of war.*
3. *Paragraphs 1 and 2 are without prejudice to any rights or obligations under international law to clear, remove, destroy or maintain minefields, mined areas, mines, booby-traps, explosive ordnance and other devices.*

Draft principle 17
Remnants of war at sea

States and relevant international organizations should cooperate to ensure that remnants of war at sea do not constitute a danger to the environment.

Chemical weapons and mines as 'leftovers' of war have at least since the Second World War given rise to considerable controversies, mainly between the countries which had used them and those where they were left.[39] In relation to chemical weapons, a certain progress was achieved by the Convention on the Prohibition of the Development, Production, Stockpiling and Use of Chemical Weapons and on their Destruction.[40] It contains certain obligations relating to old and abandoned chemical weapons, mainly as a duty of the State where they currently are, but also as an obligation of the State which abandoned such weapons elsewhere.[41] As to mines, a controversy between Libya and the former parties to the Second World War concerning mines left on Libyan territory has never really been solved. In recent years, mine-clearing activities have been undertaken not only by the countries where they are, but also as part of assistance programs by other States and international organizations, both governmental and non-governmental. De-mining has become an important part of peacekeeping operations. These activities have not started on the assumption that the relevant actors were bound by international customary law to do what they did. It is arguable, however, that this practice has become the object of a rule of customary law. In addition, it has become the object of treaty

---

39   On the history of the debate, see 3rd Report of the Special Rapporteur, supra, note 4, p. 244 et seq.
40   1974 UNTS 45.
41   Article II(1)(b) and IV (1) CWC.

law by the 2003 Protocol V to the UN Convention on Conventional Weapons,[42] relating to 'Explosive Remnants of War'.[43]

Despite the environmental impact of the use of mines, the concern addressed by this legal development is rather the health and safety of persons. But the environmental consequences of armed conflict have been for more than two decades, as already indicated, a major concern for the international community. UNEP has been at the cutting edge of work in this field.[44] Since the last couple of years, a considerable pressure has been built up by civil-society organizations that a treaty be adopted to serve environmental interests, too, providing for a more general duty to remove or render harmless 'toxic remnants of war'.[45] Principle 16 para. 1 expresses the duty which the said civil-society movement is advocating, namely a duty (expressed by the strong term 'shall') to seek to remove or render harmless 'toxic and hazardous' remnants of war. This covers any substance having the potential to threaten the life of human beings, animals or plants which are found in land areas as a consequence of war. Para. 2 formulates the obvious: international agreements for cooperation are the best tool for achieving the goal pursued by para. 1. Para. 3 takes into account, in particular, the legal developments concerning explosive remnants just described.

In contradistinction to remnants on land, international practice is not so widespread concerning remnants at sea. Oil spills caused by hostilities and remaining in the respective waters after the end of a conflict have given rise to cooperation concerning clean-up and also to litigation concerning damage caused by them. A duty of cooperation, as formulated in soft terms ('should') in Principle 17, is a solution to the problem.

---

42   Protocol on Explosive Remnants of War to the Convention on Prohibitions or Restrictions on the Use of Certain Conventional Weapons which may be deemed to be Excessively Injurious or to have Indiscriminate Effects (Protocol V), 2399 UNTS 100.

43   UN Doc. CCW/MSP/2003/2, 27 November 2003.

44   Supra, notes 30 and 31.

45   Toxic Remnants of War Project (TRW), information available at www.toxicremnantsofwar/info. An informative publication is M. Ghalaieny, 'Toxic harm: humanitarian and environmental concerns from military-origin contamination', TRW 2013.

Draft principle 18
Sharing and granting access to information

1. *To facilitate remedial measures after an armed conflict, States and relevant international organizations shall share and grant access to relevant information in accordance with their obligations under international law.*
2. *Nothing in the present draft principle obliges a State or international organization to share or grant access to information vital to its national defence or security. Nevertheless, that State or international organization shall cooperate in good faith with a view to providing as much information as possible under the circumstances.*

Remedial measures are not possible without those undertaking them having sufficient information about the factual problem to be solved. Knowledge of the positions of mines is a traditional example. This is why Article 4 of Protocol V to the CCW, just mentioned, provides for the transmission of relevant information. Principle 18 provides for a strong obligation ('shall') to share and grant access to relevant information. 'States' are not only the parties to a conflict, but also third States.[46] Whether the addition 'in accordance with their obligations under international law'[47] is a limitation or a confirmation of this rule is somewhat dubious. The 'shall' would really be meaningless if the provision were to be interpreted as meaning that States are only bound to share information to the extent they are so bound by other rules of international law. The debate in the Drafting Committee does not suggest such a narrow interpretation.[48] It is submitted that in the light of the practice referred to, the better interpretation of the formula is as a hint to the fact that the obligation to share and grant access to information has already become part of customary law.

Paragraph 2 concerning information vital for national defence and security is a necessary exception to the rule of para. 1. It is somewhat difficult to envisage how this particular exception could apply to relevant international organizations. Such organizations will as a rule not possess such information. But military organizations like NATO might possess them, and to this extent it makes sense to have these organizations mentioned in the text.

---

46   Statement of the Chair of the Drafting Committee, supra, note 14, p. 17.
47   On existing obligations, see 3rd Report of the Special Rapporteur, supra, note 4, para. 132 et seq.
48   Statement of the Chair of the Drafting Committee, supra, note 13, p. 17.

4 Some General Problems

4.1 *The Scope of Application—What Type of Conflict?*

In the 6th Committee of the General Assembly[49] and in the ILC, it was debated whether the principles apply to both international and non-international conflicts. The text of the Principles does not address the question explicitly, but it is generally agreed that the Principles apply in both international and non-international armed conflicts.[50] If one looks at the content of the principles, a differentiated view seems appropriate. There are certain principles clearly addressing States and intergovernmental organizations only. This is the case for the general principles in Part I. On the other hand, the principles contained in Part II, applicable during armed conflict, are formulated in a way which renders them apt for being applied also in a case of non-international armed conflict. In Part III, principles 14 to 16 relate to 'parties to the conflict' or 'relevant actors'. The content is such that it can be relevant to action taken also by a non-State Party after the end of a non-international armed conflict.

4.2 *The* Lex Specialis *Issue*

In the debate in the 6th Committee of the General Assembly, comments were made to the effect that the law of armed conflict should remain *lex specialis*.[51] The debate stems from that about the relationship between human rights and international humanitarian law and was triggered, in particular, by a somewhat unfortunate formulation used by the ICJ in its Nuclear Weapons Advisory Opinion.[52] In that decision, the Court clearly upheld the concurrent application of both human rights and international humanitarian law. If it said at the same time that international humanitarian law could be *lex specialis*, this would be absolutely contradictory if *lex specialis* meant what it usually means, namely the exclusion of the application of another norm. On the other hand, concurrent application cannot possibly mean that both fields of law apply without change. If both apply concurrently to one and the same situation, they must be somehow adapted if their content is not the same. A closer look shows that this is the true sense of the holding of the Court:[53]

---

49 3rd Report of the Special Rapporteur, supra, note 4, para. 40.
50 Statement of the Chair of the Drafting Committee, supra, note 14, p. 10; Commentary to draft Principle 1, ILC Report, supra, note 6.
51 3rd Report of the Special Rapporteur, supra, note 4, para. 39; see also ILC Report supra, note 6, p. 329.
52 *Legality of the threat or use of nuclear weapons*, Advisory Opinion, *ICJ Report 1996*, p. 226.
53 Ibid., para. 25.

[T]he protection of the International Covenant of Civil and Political Rights does not cease in times of war... the right not arbitrarily to be deprived of one's life applies also in hostilities. The test of what is an arbitrary deprivation of life, however, then falls to be determined by the applicable *lex specialis,* namely, the law applicable in armed conflict which is designed to regulate the conduct of hostilities.

This means that the application of human rights and in particular of the relevant guarantee of the right to life is not excluded (which would be *lex specialis sensu stricto*), but that it has to be interpreted in context, i.e. in the light of the law of armed conflict.

It is submitted that this rule also applies to the relationship between international environmental law and international humanitarian law which underlies the proposed principles, although the Special Rapporteur states the issue in a somewhat different way.[54] However, the only proposed principle which touches upon the problem is Principle 9 para.1, already discussed, which speaks of 'applicable international law, and, in particular, the law of armed conflict'. This means that it is not only the law of armed conflict which applies to the protection of the environment during armed conflict. Other rules of international law may apply as well. There has to be concurrent application, including the necessary adaptation to the context of armed conflict.

The strongest argument in favour of concurrent application is the work of the ILC concerning the effect of armed conflict on treaties,[55] to which the Special Rapporteur also refers in her Reports.[56] The general principle formulated by the ILC is (Article 3):

> The existence of an armed conflict does not *ipso facto* terminate or suspend the operation of treaties...

According to Article 7, the ILC provides 'an indicative list of treaties the subject matter of which involves an implication that they continue to apply'. That list includes:

---

[54] 3rd Report of the Special Rapporteur, supra, note 4, para. 10 and 99.
[55] Draft articles on the effects of armed conflicts on treaties, in Report of the International Law Commission on the work of its 63rd session, UN Doc. A/66/10, April–August 2011.
[56] 3rd Report of the Special Rapporteur, supra, note 4, para. 100 et seq.

...
(c) Multilateral law-making treaties,
...
(g) Treaties relating to the international protection of the environment,
(h) Treaties relating to international watercourses and related installations and facilities,
(i) Treaties relating to aquifers and related installations and facilities,...'

Thus, treaties concerning various aspects of international environmental law are, at least as a rule, not suspended if an armed conflict breaks out. They continue to apply. There must thus be concurrent application in the sense just described. This is the particular background of Principle 9 para. 1.

4.3 *The Value of the Principles*

Some texts elaborated by the ILC have led to the negotiation and conclusion of international treaties based on them. In all other cases, the value of the ILC texts is a matter of debate: it depends on the concrete case. In some, the Commission's texts are meant to restate customary international law and are received by the international community as an authoritative statement thereof. An example is the articles on the responsibility of States for wrongful acts. Where the Commission does not adopt 'articles', but 'principles', the purpose is to produce an instrument which is less strict, taking into account that a certain aversion against developing international humanitarian law can be discerned among the international community. These options (draft treaty, statement of customary law, statement of general principles) have been in the minds of the members of the ILC when dealing with the topic of the protection of the environment in relation to armed conflict. It has been pointed out above that where the text expresses a strong obligation by using 'shall', there are good reasons to believe that there is a rule of customary law: *lex lata*. Provisions using 'should' must rather be understood as being *de lege ferenda*. The use of wording in this sense is a deliberate choice of the ILC.[57]

5 Conclusions

The project 'principles for the protection of the environment in relation to armed conflicts' is an important document. It deserves a prize for a number of reasons. It has freed the discourse from concentration on the specific

---

57 Statement of the Chair of the Drafting Committee, supra, note 14, *passim*.

obligations of the *ius in bello* and has placed the question where it belongs, namely in the broader context of human activities with an impact on the environment, including but not limited to military activities. It draws attention to relevant activities to be regulated before an armed conflict breaks out, and in particular to the preservation and restoration of the environment after an armed conflict. Useful obligations are formulated for this purpose, and the Commission by using the word 'shall'. has not refrained from emphasizing the strength of important obligations relating to the post-conflict phase.

What is regrettable, on the other hand, is that the ILC has not stood up against the reluctance of States to accept any development of the *ius in bello,* a reluctance seen for example regarding the reaction of States to the ICRC proposal to consider developing the law of armed conflict also in relation to environmental protection. The Commission has, at least so far, maintained the three objectionable qualifications of the prohibition stemming from the 1977 Additional Protocol and has refrained from elaborating the 'due regard' principle used in newer instruments to ensure the protection of the environment against the effects of hostilities. 'Due regard . . .', it is submitted, is a better tool to ensure the protection of environmental concerns during armed conflicts.

Regards sur le contenu des qualifications des principaux acteurs des conflits armés

Zakaria Daboné

Les armées en particulier et toutes les forces armées en général ont la singularité reconnue d'être très organisées[1] par culture mais aussi par nécessité pour la satisfaction des besoins qui sont les leurs. Or, elles sèment le plus grand désordre qui soit : le contexte de conflit armé. Ce contexte qui fragilise les institutions et le quotidien, qui bouleverse et renverse la vie normale regorge toutefois de règles de droit de façon tout à fait inespérée. Droit et désordre ne peuvent, en effet cohabiter durablement.[2] Les acteurs du grand désordre ou ceux qui se proposent de mettre un terme à ce désordre ou d'en réduire la rigueur restent conscients de l'existence de ces règles de droit même si parfois ils feignent de ne pas l'être. Ainsi le droit au cœur de la guerre existe[3] et lorsque les acteurs immédiats ou médiats décident de s'en saisir, ce n'est pas toujours de façon désintéressée. La qualification sans incidence juridique, si cela est possible, ou la qualification juridique de l'autre ou de soi-même est le reflet de l'image que l'on a de l'autre ou de soi-même. C'est en tout cela que la qualification devient une arme et elle vise à permettre la victoire ou favoriser la défaite ou le discrédit de l'autre.

Selon le langage des autorités publiques, et parfois celui du droit[4], les membres des groupes armés ne sont que des individus insoumis à la loi, des « bandits » de droit commun, des terroristes, des « apatrides », punissables du

---

1 Le critère de l'organisation des forces est également retenu par le droit. Il ressort en particulier pour ce qui concerne les forces armées qui n'appartiennent pas aux forces intrinsèquement étatiques. Voir l'article 3 commun aux Conventions de Genève ou le deuxième Protocole de 1977 à ces Conventions.
2 Toute définition du droit garde l'idée de la régulation. Le droit régule pour éviter le désordre s'il n'existe pas, l'anéantir s'il est en cours.
3 Divers corps de règles sont d'une urgence singulière au cours des conflits armés en sus de ce qui pourrait subsister du droit en vigueur en temps de paix. On a notamment le droit international humanitaire, le droit international des droits de l'homme, le droit des Nations Unies, le droit international pénal, le droit des réfugiés etc.
4 Les groupes armés sont constitués d'individus sur lesquels l'État où ils se trouvent souhaite garder un contrôle particulier grâce à son droit interne. En droit international le droit de punir les membres des groupes armés à la fin du conflit n'est pas exclu. Voir par exemple l'article 6.5 du deuxième Protocole aux Conventions de Genève.

seul fait d'avoir pris les armes[5]. Si le terme rebelle est usité (par les ennemis et dans le langage commun), ceux qui reçoivent ce qualificatif ne l'incluent jamais dans leur dénomination ou dans les sigles qui les désignent, eux les. Les groupes armés sont à leurs propres yeux au cœur du droit international. En effet, ils se revendiquent protecteurs des peuples, promoteurs inégalés des droits de l'homme et du droit international humanitaire, titulaires de droit interne et d'instances judiciaires valables, victimes d'agression, égaux en droit de leurs ennemis étatiques qu'ils ne manquent pas toutefois de qualifier en retour d'oppresseurs, d'Etat fantoche ou clanique...

Organisation de l'Etat islamique, Etat islamique en Irak et au Levant, Califat, Daesh[6], voici quelques-unes des dénominations pour la même réalité. Elles sont le signe récent de l'image désirée ou octroyée. Cette image a immanquablement des résonnances juridiques. En effet, un groupe terroriste (Daesh) ne reçoit pas en droit le même traitement des autres qu'aurait un Etat, islamique soit-il. L'on s'est complu durant une longue période à reconnaître à l'entité concernée le qualificatif d'Etat (Organisation de l'Etat islamique), et ainsi méconnaître, tout au moins dans l'appellation, la souveraineté des Etats qui se voyaient « amputés » d'une partie de leur territoire (Irak, Syrie notamment). Par ailleurs, si l'on se qualifie Califat, c'est que l'on se donne la nature juridique d'un Etat ayant une allure islamique.

En tout état de cause, le cas de l'Organisation de l'Etat islamique (si l'on veut bien choisir cette appellation) est emblématique. Il s'agit certainement d'un groupe armé, mais à prétention étatique et d'inspiration islamiste. La prétention étatique permet de soupçonner que le point de départ de tout l'imbroglio de la qualification des acteurs au conflit est la qualification de l'Etat lui-même. Cela est surtout vrai en Afrique. En effet, si l'Organisation de l'Etat islamique prétend être un Etat, les Etats africains sont qualifiés ainsi en droit mais manquent parfois de mériter cela dans le fonctionnement, surtout dans le contexte des conflits armés. La problématique de la qualification des acteurs des conflits armés commence par celle de l'Etat (I) avant de concerner les groupes armés (II).

---

5 H. Meyrowitz, *Le principe de l'égalité des belligérants devant le droit de la guerre*, Paris, éd. A. Pedone, 1970, p. 128.

6 F. Arladis, « Doit-on dire EIIL, Da'ech, ISIS, Etat islamique en Irak et au Levant, de l'Irak et du Levant? », http://www.slate.fr/story/88965/noms-eiil-isis-daech (2016).

1 La part de l'Etat

Les Etats africains sont reconnus comme tels et constituent une bonne part des membres des Nations Unies. S'il convient alors de dire que l'Etat existe en Afrique, il est bon d'ajouter que ces Etats ne parviennent pas souvent à tenir leur rang d'Etat en rapport avec les situations de conflit armé. Il s'agit alors de dire quelques aspects de la défaillance au niveau de l'Etat qui permettent sinon de nier l'existence de l'Etat, tout au moins de réduire le mérite de la qualification en Etat.

1.1 *L'esprit d'Etat dans le rapport aux ressources financières et humaines*

La présence de ressources naturelles ou autres richesses est présentée comme une cause des conflits armés en Afrique. Si cette présence peut donner des envies d'appropriation par les uns et les autres au point que l'on aboutisse à un conflit armé, un tel conflit ne sera envisageable ou possible que si un problème persiste dans l'existence même de l'Etat ou dans la gestion de celui-ci. Les ressources sont nationales et le restent tant que l'Etat en fait une exploitation nationale au profit du bien national, c'est-à-dire en l'absence d'une distorsion sociale, économique dans la gestion des ressources. La tentative d'appropriation des ressources grâce aux armes n'est possible que si l'Etat n'existe pas entre la pauvreté ou le manque d'une part et les ressources d'autre part ou ne fait pas une bonne gestion. Autrement dit, si l'Etat n'utilise pas les ressources afin de lutter directement contre la pauvreté ou ne mène pas des actions susceptibles de résoudre la pauvreté, l'intention d'accaparement des ressources par des groupes n'est pas à exclure. Or la privatisation des ressources publiques n'est pas le signe de l'existence d'un Etat fonctionnel.

La gestion des ressources humaines, particulièrement celle des forces armées, trahit elle aussi l'esprit d'Etat dans de nombreux Etats africains. Il est reconnu, en raison du mode de constitution des Etats africains avec notamment des frontières imposées, que l'Etat a devancé la nation dans la majeure partie de l'Afrique[7]. Sur ce continent, on possède la nationalité de son Etat mais on appartient d'abord à un groupe particulier de citoyens comme l'ethnie, le clan, la région d'origine des ancêtres... Dans ce contexte, en relation directe avec les conflits armés, il n'existe presque jamais une armée réellement nationale. Il est plus juste de parler d'armées gouvernementales que d'armées étatiques. L'armée-institution est une vue de l'esprit sur la majeure partie du continent. Cela est plus vrai dans les Etats ayant traversé des conflits armés. En situation de crise ou de conflit armé, on se replie vers son groupe d'origine dans un

---

7 J. Binet, *Afrique en question : de la tribu à la nation*, Paris, Mame, 1965, 252 p.

réflexe[8] d'autoprotection. Sur le continent le nouveau dirigeant se méfie de l'armée officielle. Le dirigeant qui ne se reconnait pas dans l'armée officielle s'ingénue à trouver des voies de protection en mettant en place des forces armées parallèles chargées de sa protection et de la protection des intérêts de son groupe. Cela est l'une des explications de la multiplication sur le continent des milices, et autres groupes de pression aux côtés de l'armée officielle ou contre elle. On a rarement vu sur le continent un groupe rebelle qui a remporté la victoire et qui confirme ou légitime l'armée officielle préexistante. En général, elle est remplacée par les forces insurgées en conflit ou renvoyée aux seconds rôles ou encore ses membres sont contraints à l'exil. Le cas de la Sierra Leone, du Rwanda, de la Côte-d'Ivoire sont emblématiques. Cette novation est possible parce que les insurgés ne voient en l'armée officielle qu'ils combattent que l'armée du président déchu et non l'armée de l'Etat. Alors, lorsque le président est chassé du pouvoir par les armes, son armée doit disparaître. En d'autres termes, on remet même en cause l'existence de l'Etat et on voit à sa place un clan, un groupe de personnes qui ont privatisé le pouvoir. Une autre ressource essentielle de l'Etat, le territoire, fait l'objet d'une maîtrise inadéquate et cela participe à la remise en cause de l'existence de l'entité ou tout au moins de son esprit.

1.2 L'esprit d'Etat dans la gestion du territoire

Un élément fondamental de la constitution d'un Etat est le territoire. Avoir un territoire et s'appeler Etat est une chose. Mais l'administrer en jouissant de toutes les compétences territoriales reconnues par le droit international en est une autre. Or en droit international on peut prétendre que les Etats africains ont du mal à jouir de leurs compétences territoriales et à les exercer en dépit du fait que le droit les leur réserve.

Dans un premier temps, cela conduit à une mauvaise connaissance des limites des frontières, donc de l'étendue exacte des territoires nationaux et à une mauvaise identification de la population qui vit sur ces territoires, qui y entre ou en sort. Sans maîtrise du territoire et les moyens de préserver l'intégrité du territoire, on a des frontières poreuses par lesquelles membres de groupes, moyens militaires et autre financement passent aisément et la contagion entre une zone de conflit et des zones voisines est facilitée. Ce qui se passe au Mali n'est pas étranger de ce qui se passe au sud de l'Algérie ou en Libye. Ce qui se passe dans la République démocratique du Congo n'est pas sans liens avec ce qui se déroule chez ses voisins. Si l'armée mauritanienne est venue à combattre sur le territoire malien des groupes armés souvent djihadistes sans

---

8   L. Gbagbo, F. Mattei, *Pour la vérité et la justice*, Paris, Editions du Moment, 2014, p. 163.

le consentement du Mali, on ne peut que confirmer que le Mali ne maîtrise pas les frontières et son territoire[9].

Dans un second temps la non jouissance des compétences territoriales induit une faillite dans la gestion du territoire et la gestion des personnes sur ledit territoire. On dira d'entrée que les Etats africains ne peuvent généralement pas gérer des territoires qu'ils n'ont pas forcément voulus d'ailleurs. On ne gère bien que ce qu'on a voulu ou conquis. Or les territoires africains ont été généralement octroyés. Les nouveaux territoires faisant office d'Etats après les indépendances ne consolident que très rarement des groupes humains précoloniaux dans leurs seules limites territoriales d'avant la colonisation. Alors au lendemain des indépendances, c'était un nouveau départ pour presque tous les groupes humains avec des compatriotes nouveaux. Dans ces conditions, comme aucun dirigeant digne de ce nom ne renie une partie du territoire prétendument sien, les Etats africains se sont retrouvés avec des territoires qu'ils ont du mal à administrer. On a l'exemple du Mali. À l'orée de l'indépendance du Mali, les Touaregs ont souhaité un autre sort au nord du Mali que le rattachement à Bamako (territoire autonome, ou rattaché à l'Algérie par exemple). Mais la lutte des dirigeants du Mali a convaincu qu'il fallait garder le Mali comme on le connaît aujourd'hui[10], c'est-à-dire un territoire qui fait deux fois la France[11]. La mauvaise administration des territoires par l'absence de services indispensables, comme ce qui ressort du régalien, crée un vide ou un appel d'air. L'Etat qui n'est pas maître sur son territoire donne l'occasion à d'autres, notamment les groupes armés, les milices, les groupes djihadistes, d'occuper le terrain. Ainsi les foyers parfois d'autogestion, c'est-à-dire où les populations se gèrent elles-mêmes, se muent rapidement en foyers ardents de l'hostilité à l'égard du pouvoir central trop centralisé. Fatalement les Etats vastes sont plus souvent victimes de cela que les Etats au territoire restreint. La République démocratique du Congo, le Soudan, le Mali, le Niger, l'Algérie... tiennent là

---

9 http://www.maliweb.net/category.php?NID=77737 (2016).

10 M. Raffray, *La révolte des hommes en bleu : Touaregs 1857-2013*, Paris, Économica, 2013.

11 Un autre exemple est celui du territoire du Burkina Faso. Ce territoire avait été constitué en 1919 et en 1932, face aux craintes de voir ce territoire en difficulté de gestion dans le futur (entre autres raisons), il a été morcelé et rattaché à d'autres territoires voisins sous colonisation française. En 1947, sous la pression des dirigeants politiques, coutumiers et autres originaires de l'ancien territoire disloqué, le territoire actuel du Burkina Faso a été reconstitué. P. C. Hien, « Les frontières du Burkina Faso : genèse, typologie et conflits (1885-1985) », ou Y. B. Gnangoran, « La mise sous tutelle de la Haute-Volta, actuel Burkina Faso (1932-1944) », Yénouyaba Georges Madiega et Oumarou Nao, *Burkina Faso, Cent ans d'histoire, 1895-1995*, Tome 1, Ouagadougou, PUO, Karthala, p. 695-720, p. 767-778.

une partie des raisons de leur instabilité passée ou actuelle et de leur difficulté à sortir de cette situation.

Des Etats existant sans contestation apparente manquent de tenir leur rang d'Etat dans des faits liés aux conflits armés. Souvent c'est la réalité de ces faits qui démontre cela. Parfois, ce sont leurs ennemis, en l'occurrence les groupes armés, qui mettent en avant ces défauts de ces Etats. Lesdits ennemis sont à leur tour systématiquement contestés dans ce qu'ils souhaitent être ou être vus.

2 La part des groupes armés

Le groupe armé est un sujet du droit international. Mais il est un sujet limité. Il est un sujet sectoriel, partiel et transitoire. Il est un sujet sectoriel car c'est dans certaines branches du droit international que sa qualité de sujet a été reconnue par les États. Il s'agit du droit international humanitaire[12] où, en tant que partie au conflit, il est attendu de lui une mission et une action. En plus, il participe en la matière à la naissance de certaines sources volontaires (déclarations unilatérales de respect, accords spéciaux…) de ce droit et sa place dans celle de la coutume, par exemple, reste soumise à une forte discussion. Le groupe armé est un sujet partiel en ce sens qu'il ne peut pas tout faire comme un État le ferait. Il est un sujet transitoire ou même éphémère, comparé à l'État[13], car il ne naît que par l'existence d'un conflit armé, et prend en principe fin avec lui. Ce qui caractérise le groupe armé dans le présent débat est qu'il est une entité qui est poussée vers l'extérieur du droit. Mais cette attitude est marquée d'une inconstance.

2.1 *L'esprit du groupe armé et sa constitution irrégulière*

Avec un minimum de recul, il n'est pas surprenant de voir au groupe armé une irrégularité, notamment dans sa constitution, quelle que soit la taille ou la

---

12 Voir par exemple, T. Kalala, *Les résolutions de l'ONU et les destinataires non étatiques*, Bruxelles, Editions Larcier, 2009, p. 128, précédé en cela par A. Cassese, « Les individus », M. Bedjaoui, *Droit international. Bilan et perspectives*, Paris, Pedone, 1991, p. 119 notamment (« Les États constituent avec les insurgés et les peuples dotés d'une organisation représentative, la catégorie des sujets originaires [dont l'existence découle dès l'origine d'un processus *de facto*, indépendant de toute décision formelle de sujets préexistants] »).

13 P. H. Kooijmans, « The Security Council and Non-State Entities as Parties to Conflicts », Karel Wellens (editor), *International Law: Theory and Practice, Essays in Honour of Eric SUY*, The Hague/Boston/London, Martinus Nijhoff Publishers, 1998, p. 339.

puissance du groupe armé. Celui-ci est vu comme des forces armés irrégulières, qualification qui peut englober celle de milices. En dépit de ces qualifications, le groupe armé bénéficie dans certaines circonstances du titre d'agresseur qui exige un minimum de régularité préalable.

Les forces armées qui luttent contre les forces gouvernementales sont souvent appelées « forces armées irrégulières »[14]. La constitution irrégulière serait relative à la naissance et à l'existence des forces armées sans répondre aux règles prévues dans un cadre juridique préexistant. En vertu de cela, le groupe armé se range naturellement dans la catégorie des forces armées irrégulières dans le cadre d'un conflit armé non international puisqu'il prend forme en marge du droit existant sur les forces armées[15]. Et les forces armées régulières seront, elles, au sens du commentaire du Comité International de la Croix-Rouge du Projet du deuxième Protocole de 1977 – à propos de la notion de forces armées utilisée dans ce projet puis dans le Protocole – les forces armées du gouvernement établi, régulièrement constituées, conformément à la loi nationale[16].

Mais le caractère « irrégulier » n'est pas l'apanage du groupe armé dans un conflit armé de type non international. En effet, dans un tel conflit armé, certains groupes pourraient lutter aux côtés des « militaires » sans être intégrés dans l'armée et peuvent de ce fait être qualifiés de forces armées irrégulières. C'est le cas entre autres des *Dozos* (groupes de chasseurs traditionnels) qui ont lutté contre les insurgés dans le conflit armé non international en

---

[14] On peut par exemple lire ceci dans un commentaire d'un arrêt de la Cour internationale de Justice : « Au bout de l'exercice, on éprouve une certaine frustration sur les non-dits de la Cour sur la légitime défense préventive, sur l'exercice de la légitime défense en réaction à une attaque par des forces irrégulières », A. Biad, « Affaire des activités armées sur le territoire du Congo, République démocratique du Congo c. Ouganda (Arrêt du 19 décembre 2005) », *Bulletin du CREDHO* (Centre de recherches et d'études sur les droits de l'homme et le droit humanitaire), n°16, Décembre 2006, p. 113, ou dans un autre cas, celui du conflit entre la Géorgie et la Russie de l'été 2008 on a pu dire ceci : « Les ministères ossètes de la Défense et de la Police disposent chacun de forces propres. Celui de la Police a 800 soldats armés. Mais il reste les forces irrégulières armées par les autorités de Tskhinvali. On ne connaît pas leur nombre. », *Le Temps* (journal), « Droits humains : poursuite des violations en Géorgie », 2008.

[15] Comité International de la Croix-Rouge, *Interpretive guidance on the notion of direct participation in hostilities under international humanitarian law*, 2009, p. 27.

[16] Projets de Protocoles additionnels aux Conventions de Genève du 12 août 1949. Commentaires, Comité International de la Croix-Rouge, Genève, 1973, p. 137.

Côte-d'Ivoire[17]. Dans un conflit armé international, les milices, les volontaires ou les mouvements de résistance sont considérés comme des forces armées irrégulières[18] luttant soit au bénéfice d'un gouvernement, soit aux côtés d'un mouvement de libération nationale.

La qualification irrégulière des forces peut être aussi due à la façon de mener la lutte armée. Lorsque les méthodes et techniques ne sont pas « conventionnelles », on est porté à traiter les forces concernées d'irrégulières. C'est le cas des groupes armés qui utilisent la technique de la guérilla. Dans ce sillage, les forces qui luttent pour le gouvernement peuvent se muer en forces antiguérilla[19] pour contrer les groupes armés menant une guérilla. Ces forces antiguérilla sont logiquement qualifiées également de forces irrégulières.

L'irrégularité des forces n'est pas propre au groupe armé. Elle vise essentiellement à montrer le caractère « hors-la-loi » des forces concernées ou des méthodes et techniques utilisées. Mais son utilisation est le plus généralement et spontanément dirigée vers les groupes armés qui n'appartiennent pas au gouvernement en lutte.

Comme dit avant, les milices sont une catégorie de ces forces armées irrégulières. Elles recouvrent une palette relativement large. Les milices peuvent renvoyer à une signification non militaire. Mais ce type de milice, sans être militaire, peut utiliser la violence, par exemple pour désorganiser des mouvements ou groupes organisés (syndicats, partis politiques…), pour boycotter des grèves, pour disperser des manifestations publiques comme les marches. Dans ce cas, l'usage du terme est péjoratif pour stigmatiser un groupe de pression.

Selon le mode de fonctionnement et de recrutement de l'armée nationale, lorsque celle-ci n'est pas une armée professionnelle ou pas entièrement, on parle à cet effet d'armée de milice[20]. Ainsi tous les citoyens sont appelés sous les drapeaux selon des modalités variables (un tel service militaire peut être volontaire ou obligatoire). Dans un tel cas, l'usage du terme n'est pas péjoratif

---

17   Des *Dozos* ont également lutté en faveur des insurgés dans le même conflit armé. Mais dans ce cas leur caractère irrégulier est acquis car les insurgés qu'ils aident sont eux-mêmes des forces irrégulières au sens des explications données.

18   Comité International de la Croix-Rouge, *Interpretive guidance on the notion of direct participation in hostilities under international humanitarian law*, 2009, p. 25 et 31.

19   J. Mallein, *La situation juridique des combattants dans les conflits armés non internationaux*, Thèse, Grenoble, Université des sciences sociales, 1978, p. 37.

20   « Une milice bien ordonnée étant nécessaire à la sécurité d'un État libre, le droit qu'a le peuple de détenir et de porter des armes ne sera pas enfreint », article 2 de la Déclaration des droits de 1791 aux États-Unis.

et tend à mettre en avant le caractère populaire de l'armée nationale. Les armées en Afrique sont généralement des armées de métier et non de milice.

Au plan juridique, selon une vision classique, les milices sont de type militaire (ou militarisé) ou paramilitaire. Les milices sont des armées complémentaires des armées d'un gouvernement qui peut être en toute capacité de ses moyens autant qu'il peut être en difficulté comme un gouvernement sur un territoire occupé ou un gouvernement en exil[21]. Il s'agit de ce que l'on peut qualifier de milice publique. En ce sens, elle est officieuse, secondaire ou annexe, parallèle par rapport à une force armée. Mais la notion de milice recouvre diverses réalités au-delà de la signification classique ainsi exposée.

Un aspect de cette élasticité est qu'elle ne recouvre pas forcément une réalité de conflit armé. Ainsi les milices privées qui peuvent être ethniques ou tribales ou confessionnelles sont souvent d'autodéfense mais peuvent être plus en situation d'attaque que de défense. On a ainsi les Anti-Balaka, en Centrafrique, formés depuis 2009 pour lutter contre des coupeurs de route, les bandits et voleurs de bétail. On peut aussi citer les milices libyennes des Toubou et des Zouwaya. On a en outre les Interahamwe au Rwanda, Mouvement de jeunesse fondé en 1992 d'un parti politique, le Mouvement révolutionnaire national pour le développement. Son implication dans la perpétration du génocide rwandais est de notoriété publique. De nos jours sont actives en Somalie des milices qui se rapprochent du mercenariat. Ainsi donc, milice a fini par rimer en Afrique avec groupe d'autoprotection issu d'une ethnie, d'un clan ou d'une religion. Son but n'est pas forcément de prendre un quelconque pouvoir mais souvent de s'attaquer au camp d'en face. C'est à force de confondre milice et groupe armé qu'on finit par dire qu'en Afrique tous les conflits armés sont ethniques, claniques, tribaux. Ce qui est une vision fausse de la conflictualité africaine.

Avec un certain paradoxe en droit, l'irrégularité dite des groupes armés, milice ou pas, n'empêche pas de les considérer comme étant des agresseurs. Les autorités établies ont tendance à les qualifier d'agresseur[22]. En droit international, l'usage du terme agresseur est réservé. Il concerne en principe un Etat qui commet une attaque armée contre un autre. Ce qui veut dire que l'agression regarde prioritairement des entités qui ne sauraient souffrir d'irrégularité étant le pilier le plus solide du droit international. L'intérêt politique de cette qualification des groupes armés en agresseur est double. Premièrement cela permet de se poser en victime, car s'il y a agression il y a agressé et l'agressé est immanquablement un non-coupable peu importe ce que ces autorités auraient

---

21   Conformément au droit applicable depuis la Convention de Genève sur les prisonniers de guerre de 1949, Nations Unies, *Recueil des traités*, vol. 75, p. 135.
22   L. Gbagbo, F. Mattei, *Pour la vérité et la justice*, Paris, Editions du Moment, 2014, p. 76-77 ; 82.

commis avant la prétendue agression. En second lieu, la qualification d'agression permet aussi de cibler un ou des Etats étrangers qui seraient le soutien des groupes armés afin de signifier le rôle de ceux-ci dans la situation conflictuelle. Toutefois en droit la question de la commission même d'une agression par des groupes armés ne trouve pas une réponse édifiante notamment au plan universel.

Classiquement la légitime défense ne concernait pas les actions de particuliers, celles à travers lesquelles on ne pouvait pas déceler la responsabilité de l'État[23]. Dans le cadre concret du système des Nations Unies on peut soupçonner[24] que l'auteur de l'agression armée soit un autre membre de l'ONU[25]. Les actes des groupes armés ne sauraient constituer une agression que s'ils sont attribuables à un Etat[26]. Dans l'affaire des *Activités armées sur le territoire du Congo* opposant la République démocratique du Congo et l'Ouganda, à propos de la prétention de l'Ouganda selon laquelle son action militaire au Congo était une légitime défense contre une agression du Congo, la Cour internationale de Justice a dit ceci : « Il convient [...] de relever que, alors que l'Ouganda prétend avoir agi en état de légitime défense, il n'a jamais soutenu avoir été l'objet d'une agression de la part des forces armées de la RDC. L'« agression armée » à laquelle il a été fait référence était plutôt le fait des FDA [Forces démocratiques alliées, groupe armé]. La Cour a dit plus haut (paragraphes 131 à 135) qu'il n'existait pas de preuve satisfaisante d'une implication directe ou indirecte du Gouvernement de la RDC dans ces attaques. Celles-ci n'étaient pas le fait de bandes armées ou de forces irrégulières envoyées par la RDC ou en son nom, au sens de l'article 3 g) de la Résolution 3314 (XXIX) de l'Assemblée générale sur la définition de l'agression, adoptée le 14 décembre

---

23 J.-P. Cot, A. Pellet et M. Forteau (Dir.), *La Charte des Nations Unies. Commentaire article par article*, Paris, Économica, 3ᵉ édition, 2005, p. 1330.

24 La prudence est justifiée par le fait que l'article 51 de la Charte de l'ONU relatif à la légitime défense dit ce que peut faire un Etat qui a subi « une agression armée », mais ne précise pas qui pourrait effectuer ladite agression. Alors la Charte ne s'occupe que de la victime de l'agression.

25 L'interprétation ainsi faite n'a pas été remise en cause par les résolutions onusiennes importantes et pertinentes qui ont été prises pour clarifier les rapports entre États. Il s'est d'abord agi de la Résolution 2625 (XXV) du 24 octobre 1970 de l'Assemblée générale sur les principes du droit international touchant les relations amicales et la coopération entre les États, conformément à la Charte des Nations Unies. La guerre d'agression y est évoquée sous l'angle des rapports entre États.

26 Il s'est ensuite agi de la Résolution 3314 (XXIX) du 14 décembre 1974 de l'Assemblée générale portant sur la définition de l'agression. Elle donne une définition à connotation interétatique de l'agression.

1974. La Cour est d'avis, au vu des éléments de preuve dont elle dispose, que ces attaques répétées et déplorables, même si elles pouvaient être considérées comme présentant un caractère cumulatif, ne sont pas attribuables à la RDC. Pour tous les motifs qui précèdent, la Cour considère que les conditions de droit et de fait justifiant l'exercice d'un droit de légitime défense par l'Ouganda à l'encontre de la RDC n'étaient pas réunies. En conséquence, elle n'a pas à se prononcer sur les arguments des Parties relatifs à la question de savoir si et à quelles conditions le droit international contemporain prévoit un droit de légitime défense pour riposter à des attaques d'envergure menées par des forces irrégulières »[27].

La considération selon laquelle les actes des entités non étatiques seraient à la base d'une action de légitime défense a été fortement combattue. La réaction des États-Unis et de leurs alliés en Afghanistan après les attentats du 11 septembre 2001 a souvent été vue comme manquant d'argument valable sous la légitime défense[28] à moins de voir à travers lesdits attentats un acte de l'Afghanistan[29]. Maurice KAMTO tient, par exemple, la ligne suivante : « La problématique de l'extension du champ d'application de l'interdiction du recours à la force aux activités des entités infra-étatiques non officielles a suscité un important débat parmi les auteurs, avec un renouvellement doctrinal depuis les attaques terroristes du 11 septembre 2001 contre les États-Unis. La réponse à cette question est fort aisée dans l'hypothèse où les entités en cause et leurs activités armées sont sans rapport aucun avec un État : il paraît assez clair en effet, tant au regard du caractère interétatique de la Charte que de la teneur de son article 2 par. 4, que les acteurs non étatiques sont exclus du champ d'application de la règle de l'interdiction du recours à la force. On ne saurait, sans abus de langage, parler d'agression armée dans cette situation ni, par conséquent, invoquer et exercer le droit de légitime défense au sens de l'article 51 de la Charte ; il n'est point besoin de longs développements à ce sujet »[30]. Ainsi, un groupe armé, lui seul, ou tout autre acteur non étatique, n'est pas en mesure

---

27 Affaire des *activités armées sur le territoire du Congo (République démocratique du Congo c. Ouganda)*, arrêt du 19 décembre 2005, CIJ Rec. 2005, par. 146-147, http://www.icj-cij.org/docket/files/116/10454.pdf (2016).

28 O. Corten et F. Dubuisson, « Opération « liberté immuable » : une extension abusive du concept de légitime défense », *Revue Générale de Droit International Public,* 2002, p. 64 et 70.

29 É. David, « Sécurité collective et lutte contre le terrorisme : guerre ou légitime défense ? », *Les métamorphoses de la sécurité collective. Droit, pratique et enjeux stratégiques*, Paris, A. Pedone, 2005, p. 145.

30 M. Kamto, *L'agression en droit international*, Paris, A. Pedone, 2010, p. 145-146.

de commettre une agression, ne saurait être un agresseur au sens du droit international universel.

Au plan régional, jusqu'à une date relativement récente, les Etats africains n'ont pas envisagé l'implication des groupes armés dans l'agression armée de façon intéressante en raison de leur vision étatiste sur la question[31]. Le changement viendra dans les années 2000. Le Pacte de non-agression et de défense commune de l'Union Africaine du 31 janvier 2005 définit de façon large l'agression. En effet, l'agression est conçue comme : « [...] l'emploi par un État, un groupe d'États, une organisation d'États ou toute entité étrangère ou extérieure, de la force armée ou de tout autre acte hostile, incompatible avec la Charte des Nations unies ou l'Acte constitutif de l'Union Africaine contre la souveraineté, l'indépendance politique, l'intégrité territoriale et la sécurité humaine des populations d'un État Partie au présent Pacte »[32]. Il considère aussi comme une agression « la fourniture de tout soutien à des groupes armés »[33]. La position prise par le Pacte « facilite » l'agression indirecte en donnant plus de poids, par rapport à la Cour, au soutien aux groupes armés par des États étrangers[34]. Le Pacte va plus loin en disant que l'invasion ou l'attaque du territoire d'un État par les forces armées constitue une agression[35]. Ainsi, le Pacte,

---

31 Communauté Economique des Etats de l'Afrique de l'Ouest (CEDEAO), Protocole de non-agression, 1978 ; CEDEAO, Protocole d'assistance mutuelle en matière de défense, 1981.

32 Article 1er, alinéa c, du Pacte de non-agression et de défense commune de l'Union Africaine du 31 janvier 2005.

33 La disposition (article 1er, c, viii du Pacte) se lit comme ceci : Les actes suivants constituent des actes d'agression, sans déclaration de guerre par un Etat, groupe d'Etats, organisation d'Etats ou acteurs non étatiques ou entité étrangère :

« [...] (viii) l'envoi par un Etat membre ou en son nom ou la fourniture de tout soutien à des groupes armés, à des mercenaires et à d'autres groupes criminels transnationaux organisés qui peuvent perpétrer des actes hostiles contre un Etat membre [...] ».

34 R. van Steenberghe, « Le Pacte de non-agression et de défense commune de l'Union africaine : entre unilatéralisme et responsabilité collective », *Revue Générale de Droit International Public*, 2009, p. 136.

35 Article 1er, alinéa c, (ii) du Pacte de non-agression et de défense commune de l'Union Africaine du 31 janvier 2005. Cette disposition se lit comme suit : Les actes suivants constituent des actes d'agression, sans déclaration de guerre par un Etat, groupe d'Etats, organisation d'Etats ou acteurs non étatiques ou entité étrangère :

« [...] (ii) l'invasion ou l'attaque du territoire d'un Etat membre par les forces armées, ou toute occupation militaire, même temporaire, résultant d'une telle invasion ou d'une telle attaque, ou toute annexion par l'emploi de la force du territoire ou d'une partie du territoire d'un Etat membre [...] ».

en l'absence d'autres précisions, laisse entendre que les forces armées qui envahissent ou attaquent peuvent également provenir d'une autre entité que l'État, notamment des groupes armés[36]. Il ne s'agit plus d'une agression indirecte, mais d'une « agression privée » du fait unique du groupe armé notamment[37]. En outre le Pacte africain de non-agression vise la notion de menace d'agression. Il s'agit à travers cette notion de « [...] tout acte ou déclaration hostile d'un État, groupe d'États, organisation d'États ou acteur(s) non étatique(s) qui, sans déclaration de guerre, pourrait aboutir à un acte d'agression [...] »[38]. La menace d'agression peut être l'œuvre d'un acteur non étatique aussi, donc d'un groupe armé[39].

Alors au plan africain, un groupe armé peut être un agresseur ou être à la base d'une menace d'agression, qualifications à implications négatives sur l'image desdits groupes. Le discours sur la négativité à leur encontre se poursuit lorsque ces groupes armés sont uniquement assimilés à des entités productrices de la violence illégitime.

---

36   Pour le détail, et selon la définition générale de l'agression donnée, les actes suivants des groupes armés sont en outre considérés comme étant des actes d'agression : l'utilisation de la force armée contre un État, le bombardement du territoire ou l'emploi de toutes armes contre le territoire d'un État, le blocage des ports, des côtes ou de l'espace aérien d'un État, l'attaque contre les forces armées terrestres, navales ou aériennes d'un État, les actes d'espionnage utilisables à des fins d'agression militaire contre un État, l'assistance technologique de toute nature, les renseignements et la formation au profit d'un autre État pour les mêmes fins, l'encouragement, le soutien, l'acceptation ou la fourniture de toute assistance aux fins de commettre des actes terroristes et autres crimes transfrontières violents organisés contre un État. Le Pacte réserve exclusivement aux États les types d'agression suivants : les actes constitués par l'utilisation de forces armées d'un État stationnées (stationnement autorisé) sur le territoire d'un autre État en violation dudit Pacte, ou l'utilisation admise du territoire d'un État par un autre État pour commettre une agression contre un État tiers.

37   Van Steenberghe, *op. cit.*, note 34, p. 139.

38   Alinéa q, article 1er du Pacte de la non-agression et de défense commune de l'Union Africaine.

39   Le Conseil de paix et de sécurité dans une décision a eu à condamner « fermement l'agression perpétrée contre le TFG [Gouvernement fédéral de transition] de la Somalie et la population civile à Mogadiscio [...] par des groupes armés, y compris des éléments étrangers [...] [et exprimer] sa grave préoccupation face à la présence accrue d'éléments étrangers à Mogadiscio et dans d'autres parties de la Somalie ». Paragraphe 3 de la Décision du Conseil de paix et de sécurité du 22 mai 2009, Doc. PSC/PR/COMM.(CXC).

2.2 L'esprit du groupe armé et la violence illégitime

Il est courant que les ennemis des groupes armés et les médias qualifient ces groupes de criminels, bandits, animés par le goût du sang, du lucre[40], de la violence gratuite et de la destruction[41]. On peut penser ici à certaines périodes de conflits armés en Sierra Leone et au Libéria dans la décennie 1990, notamment ou plus récemment lors du conflit au Mali en 2012-2013. Si de telles qualifications visent dans la bouche des médias à dénoncer ou déplorer des types d'actes, comme s'il existait des guerres propres ou des guerres idéales, elles sont utilisées par les ennemis des groupes armés pour les décrédibiliser, les délégitimer. Cela tendra à signifier que l'on ne serait pas dans une situation de guerre, mais pis, dans un crime étant entendu que la guerre n'est pas intrinsèquement un crime et que dans l'inconscient populaire la guerre a une valeur et une respectabilité supérieures au crime. « Dans une guerre civile, le Gouvernement légal – ou celui qui se dit tel – a tendance à ne voir dans ses adversaires que de vulgaires criminels. Cette tendance a poussé parfois les autorités gouvernementales à considérer les secours apportés par la Croix-Rouge aux victimes appartenant au parti adverse, comme une aide indirecte à des coupables »[42]. En un mot la manœuvre consiste à nier à l'ennemi, au-delà de son manque d'humanisme et autres, surtout l'absence chez lui d'un but politique. L'anoblissement du but politique fait apparaître des buts avoués et des buts inavoués. On avoue généralement que l'on lutte pour libérer le peuple qui souffre, chasser du pouvoir le régime sanguinaire, anti-démocratique... Le discours tenu par les djihadistes contemporains tranche à ce niveau avec le discours commun. Boko-Haram, Al-Qhaïda au Maghreb, Moujâho, Organisation de l'Etat Islamique ne cachent pas leur intention de détruire l'Occident ou les non-musulmans qu'ils confondent aux mécréants, même si derrière cela il y a toujours l'idée de faire une entité politique, un Etat, islamique ou Califat, à la place des Etats existants.

Le but politique est un élément souvent apprécié même en droit. Ainsi des auteurs d'infractions bénéficient généralement de traitement favorable lorsque l'on qualifie les infractions concernées d'infractions politiques. Jusqu'à

---

40   F. Wodie, « La sécession de Biafra et le droit international public », *Revue Générale de Droit International Public*, 1969, p. 1024 ; V.-Y. Ghebali, « Les guerres civiles de la post-bipolarité : nouveaux acteurs et nouveaux objectifs », *Relations internationales*, n° 105, printemps 2001, p. 42.

41   Wodie, ibid.

42   J. S. Pictet (et autres), Commentaire. *Convention (I) de Genève pour l'amélioration du sort des blessés et des malades dans les forces armées en campagne*, du 12 août 1949, Genève, Comité international de la Croix-Rouge, 1958, p. 42.

un passé récent[43], l'extradition de délinquants, terroristes en particulier, était en général impossible si l'infraction était qualifiée de politique[44]. Le mouvement de libération nationale est un groupe armé ayant un but spécial qui est politique : la libération d'un peuple. C'est ainsi également que déjà la pensée grecque, pour mieux condamner la guerre civile dans la *polis*, a vite fait de la dépolitiser et la réduire à une manifestation pure et simple de la sauvagerie humaine[45]. La Commission du droit international, à travers ses Articles sur la responsabilité de l'État pour fait internationalement illicite, ne semble pas admettre le groupe armé sans but politique. En effet, à la fin du conflit armé, la Commission voit dans le groupe armé victorieux le nouveau gouvernement ou le fondateur d'un nouvel État comme si aucune autre option n'était possible[46].

Le but politique consiste en une volonté de transformation des structures politiques et sociales ou du système économique[47]. Il nécessite des perspectives d'avenir, donc des désirs, des projets et des idées. Avoir un but politique, c'est se battre pour la société, se mettre au service des intérêts d'un groupement collectif. Cela s'oppose à la visée recherchée à travers le crime et la violence individuelle, c'est-à-dire l'intérêt privé[48]. La recherche du but politique répond à un modèle faussement inspiré des conflits interétatiques. De tels conflits seraient politiques par principe en ce sens que la guerre serait la poursuite de la politique par d'autres moyens[49]. Mais cela n'a de sens que lorsque l'on admet que tout ce qui vient de l'État est politique. De nombreuses guerres

---

43   On peut par exemple se référer aux articles 1er et 7 de la Convention de Strasbourg pour la répression du terrorisme du 27 janvier 1977, Nations Unies, *Recueil des traités*, vol. 1134, p. 94. Elle est l'une des premières conventions à interdire de voir dans l'acte terroriste une infraction politique.

44   Voir plus généralement, R. Koering-Joulin, « Infraction politique et violence », *Juris-Classeur Périodique (JCP)*, 1982, D. 3066-3.

45   V.-Y. Ghebali, « Remarques politico-historiques sur l'étiologie des guerres civiles », *L'ordre juridique international, un système en quête d'équité et d'universalité*, Liber amicorum Georges Abi-Saab, The Hague/London/Boston, Martinus Nijhoff Publishers, 2001, p. 469.

46   Article 10 des Articles de la Commission du droit international sur la responsabilité d'Etat pour fait illicite.

47   Wodie, *op. cit.*, note 40, p. 1024.

48   G. Bouthoul, « Traité de polémologie. Sociologie des guerres », Battistella (dossier constitué par), *Guerres et conflits dans l'après-guerre froide*, Problèmes politiques et sociaux, dossier d'actualité mondiale, Documentation française, Paris, n° 799-800, 1998, p. 11.

49   Une traduction de l'idée originelle en allemand se lit comme suit : « Nous voyons donc que la guerre n'est pas seulement un acte politique, mais un véritable instrument politique, une poursuite des relations politiques, une réalisation de celles-ci par d'autres moyens », C. von Clausewitz, *De la guerre*, Paris, Editions de Minuit (traduction de Denise Naville), 1955, p. 67.

dans l'histoire n'ont été menées que pour l'honneur du chef, la quête de la richesse, l'assouvissement de l'instinct de vengeance... Appliquer ce principe à des situations auxquelles prennent part des acteurs non étatiques est inadéquat. Un groupe d'individus n'est pas une forme politique dans l'essence à l'instar de l'État. Il le devient selon certains facteurs. Mais il est bien capable d'animer une situation conflictuelle. Et c'est ce qui est le plus important, en droit notamment. Il est donc nécessaire de s'attacher à la matérialité de la situation plutôt qu'aux aspects immatériels, difficilement repérables.

Dans le même ordre d'idée de confusion des groupes à leur unique violence, il est courant de traiter les ennemis et notamment ceux qui prennent les armes contre un gouvernement de terroristes[50]. Le but est de dégrader et disqualifier l'ennemi. Cet ennemi terroriste aux pratiques inhumaines ne serait alors mu que par la violence. Il n'est pas envisageable qu'une entité, privée ou gouvernementale, se revendique terroriste. Chacun dit mener des actions essentiellement politiques ou religieuses à travers la violence que l'on qualifie de terrorisme.

Les groupes armés sont-ils des terroristes en droit ? Le terrorisme est présent dans le conflit armé. Même si le conflit armé est non international, les parties peuvent utiliser la terreur entre elles, et cela est conforme au droit. Il s'agit alors d'une affaire relative à la conduite des hostilités. Ce qui est interdit, c'est l'utilisation de cette terreur contre la population civile[51]. Dans ce cas, toutes les parties au conflit sont des terroristes ou alors aucune ne l'est. Si le terrorisme n'est pas une technique de combat, il constitue une activité à part entière, c'est-à-dire une activité autonome par rapport à un éventuel conflit armé. Le terrorisme comme une activité autonome ne bénéficie pas d'une définition acceptée de tous en droit international[52]. Le terrorisme utilise la violence armée (comme dans un conflit armé). La caractéristique du terrorisme concernant la

---

50   On retranscrit ici une conversion tenue aux premières heures du conflit armé ivoirien et racontée par l'ancien Président de la Côte-d'Ivoire Laurent Gbagbo, conversation entre lui et l'ancien Président français, Jacques Chirac, tous deux à l'époque en exercice : « Chirac m'a téléphoné pour me reprocher d'avoir été trop dur dans mes propos : « Tu les as traités de terroristes ! » « Mais enfin, lui ai-je dit, si vous vous réveillez que l'on vous dit que des rebelles viennent d'attaquer la capitale, qu'est-ce que vous dites ? » », L. Gbagbo, F. Mattei, *Pour la vérité et la justice*, Paris, Editions du Moment, 2014, p. 80.

51   Article 13, alinéa 2 du deuxième Protocole aux Conventions de Genève.

52   J.-M. Sorel tout en affirmant cela, propose la définition suivante : « Le terrorisme international est un fait illicite, quel que soit son auteur ou son motif, qui crée un trouble à l'ordre public défini par la communauté internationale en utilisant une violence grave et indiscriminée sous diverses formes contre des personnes ou des biens, publics ou privés, pour créer un climat de terreur en vue de créer une contrainte », J.-M. Sorel, « Existe-t-il

violence est que celle-ci est « à usage unique ». Le terroriste commet un acte de violence et se dissipe. Même lorsque l'on parle d'une série d'actes terroristes, la donne ne change pas. Tous les actes sont isolés et distincts. Cela ne correspond pas à l'idée d'hostilités présente dans l'esprit de la notion des conflits armés[53]. Ce n'est pas garanti que la violence utilisée par le terrorisme atteigne un niveau pouvant être considéré comme celui d'un conflit armé. Le terroriste est continuellement en fuite. Or le conflit armé suppose des affrontements. L'idée de conflit renvoie à une rencontre frontale de deux choses au moins. Les terroristes sont rarement identifiables et ne rendent pas l'idée d'affrontement réelle[54]. En définitive, on ne peut pas dire que le terrorisme érigé en activité autonome soit un conflit armé[55]. En raison de cela, le groupe armé qui évolue dans un conflit armé (il faudrait qu'il assume et soit en mesure d'assurer le déroulement d'un conflit armé contre lui) ne saurait être confondu à un groupe dont l'activité essentielle est le terrorisme. Le groupe armé ne peut pas avoir une activité autonome en tant que terrorisme.

L'Etat est contesté dans sa qualité même d'Etat. Ce sont en fait ses défauts qui sont mis en exergue. Les groupes armés, quant à eux, reçoivent un nombre élevé de qualifications dont un échantillon a été ici présenté. A les regarder de près, ces qualifications sont abusives car soit elles sont infondées en grande partie (les exemples d'agresseur, de terroriste), soit elles ne recouvrent pas la réalité unique des groupes (les exemples de forces armées irrégulières, les milices) d'autres types d'acteurs pouvant être concernés... En tout état de cause, aucune qualification n'est anodine. Si elle est bien faite, elle sert celui qui qualifie ou se qualifie. A ce titre, elle accomplit une mission essentielle, celle d'être aussi une arme.

---

une définition universelle du terrorisme ? », Karine Bannelier et autres (Dir.), *Le droit international face au terrorisme*, Paris, A. Pedone, 2003, p. 68.

[53] M. Sassòli, « « La guerre contre le terrorisme », le droit international humanitaire et le statut de prisonnier de guerre », *Annuaire canadien de droit international*, 2001, n°39, p. 224.

[54] É. David, « Sécurité collective et lutte contre le terrorisme : guerre ou légitime défense ? », *Les métamorphoses de la sécurité collective. Droit, pratique et enjeux stratégiques*, Paris, A. Pedone, 2005, p. 147.

[55] C. Chocquet, *Le terrorisme n'est pas la guerre*, Paris, Vuibert, 2008, 229 p.

Contemporary Challenges for International Humanitarian Law

Knut Dörmann and Tilman Rodenhäuser

1 Introduction

Among the many needs the international legal order faces, Professor Momtaz has shown thoughtfulness and expertise in analyzing contemporary challenges posed to the laws of armed conflicts. Of particular note of his works in the field of international humanitarian law (IHL) are the 2001 course at the Hague Academy of International Law, entitled 'Le droit international humanitaire applicable aux conflits armés non internationaux',[1] and a co-edited volume, together with Michael J. Matheson, on 'Rules and Institutions of International Humanitarian Law Put to the Test of Recent Armed Conflicts'.[2] Moreover, Professor Momtaz was a member of the steering committee for the International Committee of the Red Cross' (ICRC) customary IHL study, and served as a peer reviewer for the ICRC's commentary of 2016 on the First Geneva Convention.[3]

Professor Momtaz's interest in the question of whether and to what extent contemporary armed conflicts challenge existing rules and institutions of IHL remains important, especially with regard to non-international armed conflicts (NIAC). These conflicts become increasingly complex, which is linked to factors including the 'fragmentation of armed groups and asymmetric warfare; the regionalization of conflicts; the challenges of decades-long wars; the absence of effective international conflict resolution; and the collapse of national systems'.[4] Conflicts such as the ones in Syria, Yemen, Democratic Republic of the Congo, or Libya show a multiplication of State and non-State parties

---

1 D. Momtaz, *Le Droit International Humanitaire Applicable Aux Conflits Armés Non Internationaux*, Martinus Nijhoff, 2002.
2 M. Matheson & D. Momtaz (eds), *Rules and Institutions of International Humanitarian Law Put to the Test of Recent Armed Conflicts*, Brill/Nijhoff, 2011.
3 ICRC, Convention (I) for the Amelioration of the Condition of the Wounded and Sick in Armed Forces in the Field, Commentary of 2016, Cambridge University Press, 2016.
4 International Committee of the Red Cross (ICRC), 'International humanitarian law and the challenges of contemporary armed conflicts', 2015, available at https://www.icrc.org/en/document/international-humanitarian-law-and-challenges-contemporary-armed-conflicts, p. 15.

involved, including through the intervention of third-States, international organizations, or armed groups in support of different sides. Contemporary conflicts are frequently characterized by civilians bearing the brunt of hostilities, barely-imaginable levels of destruction of cities, huge numbers of displaced persons, arbitrary restrictions for humanitarian access, deliberate attacks on medical personnel and facilities, sexual violence committed against women and girls, but also men and boys, as well as ill-treatment of persons deprived of their liberty. Especially the reality of persistent violations of the most fundamental provisions of IHL is a constant reminder of the humanitarian imperative to endlessly work for improving respect for the law. While today's NIACs are fought primarily with 'traditional' and sometimes very rudimentary means, new means of warfare are being developed, such as robotic weapon systems or cyber weapons.

These factual developments pose at least two fundamental questions for the international legal order. First, is the contemporary international legal framework—and in particular IHL—still adequate to regulate the complexities of contemporary armed conflicts and foreseeable future means and methods of warfare? And second, in light of recurring and prevalent IHL violations, which means exist or should be envisaged to ensure better respect for the law? The aim of this chapter cannot be to provide a comprehensive study of these questions. Instead, we propose to look at a selection of pertinent challenges in order to identify to what extent today's IHL addresses them. Thus, the first part analyses how IHL classifies complex conflict situations that involve a variety of State and non-State parties. The second part focuses on legal challenges posed in specific conflict situations or by certain means and methods of warfare, namely: detention in NIAC; urban warfare; and new means and methods of warfare. The third and last part of this chapter provides an insight into contemporary processes to strengthen respect for IHL.

2 Challenges in the Classifying of Conflicts with Multiple Parties

In order to decide which bodies of international law govern a situation of violence—i.e. international human rights law (IHRL) only, or IHL and IHRL—it is necessary to examine whether such situation amounts to an armed conflict. IHL knows two kinds of armed conflicts: international and non-international ones. While the former oppose two or more States,[5] the latter necessarily

---

5   Note, however, Art. 1(4) Protocol Additional to the Geneva Conventions of 12 August 1949 and relating to the Protection of Victims of International Armed Conflicts (Protocol I), (AP I), 1125 UNTS 3.

involves a non-State party opposing at least one State or another non-State party. This part focuses on NIACs. Under treaty IHL, two NIAC thresholds exist: the lower and more encompassing one renders Article 3 common to the four Geneva Conventions (Common Article 3), a number of weapons treaties, treaties protecting cultural property, and customary IHL applicable; the higher one, offering more definitional detail, triggers the application of Additional Protocol II (AP II).[6] The Geneva Conventions do not contain a definition of 'armed conflicts not of an international character' under Common Article 3. In accordance with customary IHL and international jurisprudence, the ICRC is guided by the following definition:

> Non-international armed conflicts are *protracted armed confrontations* occurring between governmental armed forces and the forces of one or more armed groups, or between such groups arising on the territory of a State [party to the Geneva Conventions]. The armed confrontation must reach *a minimum level of intensity* and the parties involved in the conflict must show *a minimum of organization*.[7]

An important body of jurisprudence and literature exists on the question of when the requisite levels of 'intensity of confrontations' and 'organization of the parties' are reached, which has brought important clarifications.[8] Still, assessing particular situations of violence in legal terms remains challenging. Thus, in this section we focus on two issues: First, taking stock of the

---

6 Protocol Additional to the Geneva Conventions of 12 August 1949, and relating to the Protection of Victims of Non-International Armed Conflicts (Protocol II), (AP II). AP II applies to armed conflicts 'which take place in the territory of a High Contracting Party between its armed forces and dissident armed forces or other organized armed groups which, under responsible command, exercise such control over a part of its territory as to enable them to carry out sustained and concerted military operations and to implement this Protocol'. For discussion of the AP II threshold, see C. Pilloud, Y. Sandoz, C. Swinarski, et al., *Commentary on the additional protocols of 8 June 1977 to the Geneva Conventions of 12 August 1949*, International Committee of the Red Cross, Martinus Nijhoff, 1987, paras. 4459–4470; M. Bothe, *New rules for victims of armed conflicts: commentary on the two 1977 protocols additional to the Geneva Conventions of 1949*, 2nd edition, Martinus Nijhoff, 2013, pp. 711–726; S. Sivakumaran, *The Law of Non-International Armed Conflict*, Oxford University Press, 2012, pp. 182–192.

7 ICRC, 'How is the Term 'Armed Conflict' Defined in International Humanitarian Law?', Opinion Paper, 2008, available at http://www.icrc.org/eng/assets/files/other/opinion-paper-armed-conflict.pdf. For further discussion, see ICRC, Commentary of 2016, supra, note 3, mn. 414–451.

8 For a comprehensive discussion, see ICRC, *Commentary of 2016*, supra, note 3, mn. 422–434.

developments in State practice, jurisprudence, and literature, at what point may armed violence between State authorities and different armed groups during internal violence reach the NIAC threshold? And second, related to the multiplication of actors involved in recent conflicts, under which conditions does a third State become party to a NIAC merely by providing support to a party to an on-going NIAC?

2.1   Classifying Violence during Fragmented Insurgencies or Revolutions

Under IHL, an armed conflict can only exist between defined parties. Traditionally, the legal concepts of war or armed conflict are applied to confrontations between collective entities and not between individuals; and conceptually, IHL requires the existence of two or more parties that can respect the applicable legal obligations.[9] Especially with regard to violence that develops during revolutions or public uprisings, it is regularly disputed whether public authorities face riots or isolated or sporadic acts of violence not amounting to an armed conflict, or whether violence has reached the armed conflict threshold. This is especially the case if it is unclear whether those opposing the government operate in different independent groups, or under one leadership structure.[10] If they operate under one leadership structure, the key question is whether this joint structure unites the different groups into one sufficiently organized armed group under IHL, and whether violence between government forces and this group has reached the requisite threshold of intensity. If the various armed groups cannot be classified as *one* sufficiently organized armed group under IHL, it needs to be analyzed whether individual groups qualify as an organized armed group under IHL, and whether armed violence between a specific group and government forces is sufficiently intense.

When analyzing how different non-State armed actors could form one sufficiently organized party to a NIAC, a rather clear case would be if different groups unite under one hierarchical military structure. In that case, different armed elements would form one organized armed group with centralized command and control structures. However, the existence of such clear structures is rarely the case in practice, where armed groups often operate in a decentralized manner and consist of 'semi-autonomous or splinter factions

---

9   ICRC, supra, note 4, p. 232.
10   For recent examples of situations where this question was unclear, see *Report of the independent international commission of inquiry on the Syrian Arab Republic*, UN Doc. A/HRC/19/69, 22 February 2012, para. 13; *Report of the International Commission of Inquiry on Libya*, UN Doc. A/HRC/19/68, 2 March 2012, Annex I, para. 66.

operating under an ill-defined leadership structure'.[11] International criminal jurisprudence has suggested that in order to classify such groups as one organized armed group, at least 'initial phases of a centralized command structure' should exist, which unites the different factions.[12] While it remains unclear which characteristics such a rudimentary command structure needs to show, it should have a certain degree of control over the group's military operations and normally—but this should not be a strict requirement—provide some logistical support to its members. If different armed groups qualify as one organized armed group for the purposes of IHL, all acts of violence between government armed forces and this organized armed group would be considered for the intensity assessment.

If the armed groups involved in violence on the territory of a certain State do not qualify as one organized armed group under IHL, the bilateral relationships between government forces and each armed group need to be analyzed. Once this relationship meets the NIAC criteria—meaning that the non-State party involved is sufficiently organized and violence between the two parties is sufficiently intense—IHL becomes applicable. While this is what IHL requires, the situation is more challenging when the general level of violence between a State and different armed elements is rather high but the intensity of violence in the bilateral relations between government forces and individual armed groups, or the degree of organization of the latter, is insufficient to classify the situation as an armed conflict. Focusing only on the bilateral relationships based on the above mentioned two substantive classification criteria might not necessarily reflect the overall degree of armed violence on the ground. Moreover, strictly classifying bilateral relationships could mean classifying violence between government forces and several hundred different groups, which is difficult in practice.[13]

---

11   *Increasing Respect for International Humanitarian Law in Non-international Armed Conflicts*, ICRC, 2008, p. 11.
12   Prosecutor v Haradinaj et al., Case No IT-04-84-T, Judgement, International Criminal Tribunal for the former Yugoslavia, 3 April 2008, para. 89.
13   For example, in 2012 in Libya, estimates of the number of different armed groups active in the conflict ranged 'from 100 to 300'. *Report of the International Commission of Inquiry on Libya*, supra, note 10, para. 67. In Syria, the Carter Center estimated that over the first 2.5 years of the crisis, 'approximately 4,390 armed units and military councils [formed], representing between 68,639 and 85,150 fighters across the country.' (The Carter Center, 'Syria Countrywide Conflict Report #1', 20 August 2013, available at https://www.carter center.org/resources/pdfs/peace/conflict_resolution/syria-conflict/nationwidereport-aug-20-2013.pdf).

In order to determine whether or not IHL applies to certain conduct in a situation involving multiple groups and actors, it is not always necessary to determine that the bilateral relationship between each pair of actors would, in and of itself, meet the classical NIAC threshold. Once the relationship between State armed forces and one organized armed group, or between two organized armed groups, amounts to a NIAC, IHL becomes applicable in the entire territory under the parties' control with respect to all acts showing a sufficient nexus to the conflict.[14] This means, for example, that IHL would not only govern the relationship between the two identified parties to the conflict but also that between a party to the conflict and civilians directly participating in hostilities having a nexus with the NIAC.[15] Thus, if members of a weakly organized group not qualifying as a party to a NIAC directly participate in hostilities that form part of an on-going NIAC, IHL applies to their participation. Moreover, if a well-organized armed group—which has not yet engaged in sufficiently intense violence with the State armed forces, and is therefore not a party to a separate NIAC—provides sufficient support to a party to an existing NIAC, that group could become party to that NIAC. This would be the case if their actions 'objectively form an integral part of a pre-existing NIAC'.[16] Accordingly, once a conflict between at least two sufficiently organized parties has met the NIAC threshold, IHL would govern a) the relationship between the two parties, b) the relationship between the parties and other organized armed groups acting in support of one of the parties, and c) all other acts vis-à-vis individuals that qualify as a direct participation in hostilities or are otherwise related to the conflict.

2.2 *Classifying Third State Support to a Party to a NIAC*

In times of NIAC, States regularly, but also at times international organizations, support other States in their military efforts. In recent years, we have seen different coalitions of States engaging in armed conflicts with non-State armed

---

14   *Kunarac* et al., Case No IT-96-23 & IT-96-23/1-A, Appeals judgement, International Criminal Tribunal for the former Yugoslavia, 12 June 2002, at para. 57. For further discussion on the geographical scope of application of IHL, see ICRC, Commentary of 2016, supra, note 3, mn. 452–482; K. Schöberl, *The Geographical Scope of Application of the Conventions*, Oxford University Press, 2015; J. Pejic, 'Extraterritorial targeting by means of armed drones: Some legal implications', 96 *International Review of the Red Cross*, 2014, pp. 28–31.

15   On the notion of 'direct participation of hostilities' and the three conditions that render individual acts into a direct participation, see *Interpretive Guidance on the Notion of Direct Participation in Hostilities under International Humanitarian Law*, ICRC, 2009, pp. 46–64.

16   See discussion in section 2b below.

groups, for example in Afghanistan, Iraq/Syria, or Yemen.[17] In such situations, States often join an armed conflict in support of a party to the conflict, most frequently the territorial State's government. During 'coalition warfare', individual coalition members perform different operational roles. While some may immediately participate in 'full-fledged kinetic operations', others engage in 'sporadic use of force, logistical support, intelligence activities for the benefit of the territorial State or participation in the planning and coordination of military operations' carried out by other coalition members.[18] This raises the question of at what point coalition members become party to an on-going NIAC. Would that be the case once a State declares itself part of a political or military coalition, once a State's operations against an adversary meet the NIAC threshold individually, or does IHL foresee another way to classify the conduct of States in multinational forces?

In the ICRC's view, if a State renders support to a party of an on-going, i.e. pre-existing, NIAC, in order to classify the supporting State as a party to a NIAC, it is not necessary to prove that its conduct alone meets the constitutive NIAC criteria. Rather, if the supporting State's conduct contributes to the 'collective conduct of hostilities' and has a 'direct impact on the opposing party's ability to carry out military operations', this support turns a State into a party to a NIAC.[19] Conducting isolated kinetic military operations in support of government armed forces as part of a collective conduct of hostilities would be a case in point. In contrast, support that merely enables the supported party to build up its military capacity/capabilities would not be sufficient to consider the supporting State(s) a party to the NIAC. Thus, not any type of support turns the supporting State or States into a party to a NIAC. Four conditions guide the assessment as to whether IHL is rendered applicable under what may be called the 'support-based approach':

- There is a pre-existing NIAC on-going in the territory where third-State forces intervene;
- Actions related to the conduct of hostilities are undertaken by third-State forces in the context of that pre-existing conflict;

---

17 Likewise, different States have contributed armed forces to UN-lead multinational operations. For in-depth discussion of IHL issues arising in such operations, see T. Ferraro, 'The applicability and application of international humanitarian law to multinational forces', 95 *International Review of the Red Cross*, 2013, pp. 561–612.

18 ICRC, supra, note 4, p. 22.

19 In contrast, 'more indirect forms of support, which would allow the beneficiary to build up its military capabilities', would not suffice. (Ibid., pp. 22–23).

- The third-State forces' military operations are carried out in support of a party to that pre-existing conflict;
- The action in question is undertaken pursuant to an official decision by the third-State to support a party involved in that pre-existing conflict.[20]

If these conditions are met, a supporting State should be considered party to a NIAC, which means that this State has all pertinent rights and obligations under IHL, and its armed forces and military objectives become lawfully targetable by the adversary.

As these examples show, the scope of application of contemporary IHL provides sufficient leeway to apply to increasingly complex armed conflicts. At the same time, it remains sufficiently confined to exclude situations that cannot be considered armed conflicts, such as internal disturbances or tensions, or law enforcement operations.

3   Challenges Posed to the Application of IHL

Among the various challenges posed to the application of IHL in today's armed conflicts, we suggest to examine three, each of which exemplifies one broader legal issue. First, with regard to the protection of persons deprived of liberty in NIAC, it is shown that contemporary rules of IHL seem insufficient and need further strengthening. Second, with regard to urban warfare and the use of explosive weapons, we argue that while IHL provides a comprehensive set of rules that applies in IAC and in NIAC, different interpretations of these rules can have severe humanitarian consequences. Parties to armed conflicts need to take additional measure to prevent the civilian harm observed in contemporary conflicts. And third, with regard to new means and methods of warfare, it is unclear whether contemporary IHL is sufficient to respond adequately to future challenges.

3.1   *Detention in Non-International Armed Conflicts*
Deprivation of liberty occurs frequently in all types of armed conflicts.[21] Thus, the Geneva Conventions contain more than 175 rules regulating virtually all

---

20   These conditions have been developed and are discussed in detail in Ferraro, supra, note 17, pp. 584–587. See also ICRC, *Commentary of 2016*, supra, note 3, mn. 445–446.

21   Deprivation of liberty can refer to 'criminal detention' taking place with the aim of prosecuting or punishing a person, or to internment, which generally refers to a specific type of non-criminal, non-punitive detention imposed for security reasons in armed conflict.

aspects of deprivation of liberty in international armed conflicts. In contrast, IHL applicable in NIAC—notably Common Article 3, Articles 4, 5, and 6 AP II, and customary IHL—contains a much more limited number of rules on the deprivation of liberty, although similar challenges and protection needs are likely to occur in NIACs. To give a very simple example, discipline in a place of detention will need to be maintained in an IAC and NIAC situation; however, IHL provides guidance only for IAC. This scarcity of norms is only partly compensated by international human rights law and soft law instruments.[22] In its daily work to protect persons deprived of liberty, the ICRC found:

> While there are cases in which lack of adequate infrastructure and resources constitutes an impediment to the establishment of a proper detention regime, the dearth of legal norms—especially in non-international armed conflicts—also constitutes an important obstacle to safeguarding the life, health and dignity of those who have been detained.[23]

Deprivation of liberty creates a situation in which persons become especially vulnerable to the actions or omissions of their captors. Four areas of protections are in particular need of strengthening.[24] First, the *material conditions of detention* are insufficiently regulated. While IHL of NIAC provides essential rules on the treatment of prisoners, it contains rather limited provisions on questions such as the degree of confinement, detainee's access to the outdoors, modalities under which impartial humanitarian organizations may visit detainees, or the obligation to register persons deprived of liberty and to notify their families.[25] Second, while Additional Protocol II contains some rules on

---

See *Strengthening international humanitarian law protecting persons deprived of their liberty—Draft resolution & Concluding report*, ICRC, 2015, p. 13.

22 For an in-depth analysis, see Dörmann, 'Detention in Non-International Armed Conflicts', 88 *International Law Studies*, 2011, pp. 347–366. Particular challenges to the application of IHRL during armed conflicts include the position of some States that this body of law does not apply to armed conflicts or does not apply extraterritorially; continuing debate to what extent IHRL binds Non-State Armed Groups; and a lack of clarity on how IHRL norms and standards apply in conflict situation.

23 *Strengthening legal protection for victims of armed conflicts—Draft resolution & Report*, ICRC, 2011, p. 9.

24 See ibid.

25 For further discussion, see also R. Mahnad, 'Beyond Process: The Material Framework for Detention and the Particularities of Non-International Armed Conflict', 16 *Yearbook of International Humanitarian Law*, 2013, pp. 33–51.

the *treatment of vulnerable groups* such as the wounded and sick, women, or children, these rules are fairly basic, absent in Common Article 3, and limited in customary IHL.[26] Third, outside of detention as part of a criminal process, neither treaty nor customary IHL of NIAC define *grounds* on which persons can be deprived of their liberty or *procedures* to ensure that each deprivation of liberty is justified. This protection gap can lead to a significant risk of arbitrary detention. Fourth, IHL of NIAC does not explicitly regulate the *transfer of persons deprived of liberty* from one authority to another, for example in cases where that person would face a risk of torture in the hands of the receiving authorities.[27] In practice, such transfers occur frequently if multilateral forces operate extraterritorially and handover detainees to the territorial State's authorities.

The insufficiency or lack of IHL applicable in NIAC in these four areas has led to situations in which States struggled to devise operational policies, especially during multinational operations,[28] and States have faced challenges of their detention policies or conduct before domestic or regional courts.[29] In order to address challenges posed by the dearth of IHL regulating detention in NIAC, different multinational initiatives have been launched. One has been the Copenhagen Process Principles and Guidelines initiated by the Government of Denmark in 2007. In this process, participating States identified a number of non-binding principles applicable 'to the detention of persons who are being deprived of their liberty for reasons related to an international

---

26 For example, neither AP II nor customary IHL recognize the particular sanitary or hygienical needs of women, and provide very limited guidance on the treatment of children in detention.

27 It can, however, be argued that the principle of non-refoulement is implicitly contained in the imperative of humane treatment under Common Article 3. See ICRC, *Commentary of 2016*, supra, note 3, pp. 708–716. Still there would be uncertainty how the principle ought to be implemented procedurally under IHL.

28 For further analysis of this aspect, see T. Winkler, 'The Copenhagen Process on Detainees: A Necessity', 78 *Nordic Journal of International Law*, 2009, pp. 489–498.

29 A well-known case is the Serdar Mohammed v Ministry of Defence and Others case in the United Kingdom, see Serdar Mohammed v Ministry of Defence and Others, [2014] EWHC 1369 (QB), High Court of Justice (Queen's Bench Division), 2 May 2014. For additional references to national case law, see T. Winkler, 'The Copenhagen Process and the Copenhagen Process Principles and Guidelines on the Handling of Detainees in International Military Operations', 5 *Journal of International Humanitarian Legal Studies*, 2014, pp. 258–288.

military operation'.[30] This consultation process was limited *ratione materie* to detention in international—meaning extraterritorial—military operations in the context of NIACs as well as law enforcement operations,[31] and involved a limited number of States for whom this issue was of particular importance.

In addition to that process, at the 31st Red Cross and Red Crescent (RCRC) Conference, its members—i.e. States Parties to the Geneva Conventions, National Red Cross and Red Crescent Societies, the International Federation of the Red Cross, and the ICRC—recognized 'the importance of analyzing the humanitarian concerns and military considerations' regarding important protection concerns in the context of detention in armed conflict.[32] The conference invited 'the ICRC to pursue further research, consultation and discussion in cooperation with States ... to identify and propose a range of options and its recommendations to: i) ensure that international humanitarian law remains practical and relevant in providing legal protection to all persons deprived of their liberty in relation to armed conflict'.[33] Between 2012 and 2015, based on this mandate the ICRC consulted with States at the regional and international level. This process was of a consultative nature and explorative. This initial phase allowed to gather a wealth of information from participating States on their respective detention practices and challenges they face. Following these consultations, the 32nd RCRC Conference recommended 'further in-depth work ... with the goal of producing one or more concrete and implementable outcomes in any relevant or appropriate form of a non-legally binding nature'.[34] For this purpose, it invites the ICRC 'to facilitate the work of States and to contribute its humanitarian and legal expertise'.[35]

---

30 Principle 1. For the principles, their commentary, and a summary of the process, see B. Oswald, 'The Copenhagen Principles, International Military Operations and Detentions', 17 *Journal of International Peacekeeping*, 2013, pp. 116–147.

31 Paragraph IX of the Copenhagen Principles and Guidelines' preamble clarifies: '*The Copenhagen Process Principles and Guidelines* are intended to apply to international military operations in the context of non-international armed conflicts and peace operations; they are not intended to address international armed conflicts.'

32 31st RCRC Conference, 28 November–1 December 2011, *Resolution 1—Strengthening legal protection for victims of armed conflicts,* 31IC/11/R1, para. 3. These areas correspond with the ones identified by the ICRC and discussed above.

33 Ibid, at para. 6.

34 32nd RCRC Conference, 8–10 December 2015, *Resolution 1—Strengthening international humanitarian law protecting persons deprived of their liberty*, 32IC/15/R1, at para. 8.

35 Ibid, para. 10. According to para. 9 of the Resolution 1 (2015), in a first step States and the ICRC shall 'collaborate in determining, at the outset of their further work and with the

In the process thus far, discussions on grounds and procedures of detention and the possible applicability of any outcome(s) to non-State armed groups prove especially difficult. However, these issues should not present insurmountable obstacles. Until today, IHL has always found ways to address all parties to the conflict without implicating their status under domestic law or providing them legitimacy. Moreover, most issues at stake are already regulated in inter-State conflicts, which shows that even during armed conflicts humane conditions of detention and detainee transfer can be ensured, vulnerable groups be given the necessary protection, and grounds and procedures respected that prevent arbitrary detention.

3.2   *Urban Warfare and the Use of Explosive Weapons*

In recent conflicts, a significant amount of fighting has taken place in cities. With increasing urbanization and asymmetric conflicts, this trend is likely to continue.[36] For a party operating from within urban settings, cities create an environment in which they can intermingle with and thereby hide among the civilian population,[37] receive non-military support from civilians such as shelter or food, or—worst case—use civilians as human shields.[38] Inevitably, this creates an environment in which it becomes increasingly difficult to distinguish between, on the one hand, fighters or civilians taking a direct part in hostilities and who can be lawfully targeted, and, on the other hand, civilians who must not be targeted but protected from the dangers of hostilities.[39]

---

consensus of the participating States, the modalities of further work in order to ensure its State-led, collaborative and non-politicized nature'.

36   ICRC, supra, note 4, p. 47.

37   In IAC, and arguably also in NIAC, IHL obliges all parties to armed conflicts to, 'to the extent feasible, avoid locating military objectives within or near densely populated areas', and 'to the extent feasible, remove civilian persons and objects under its control from the vicinity of military objectives'. Rules 23 and 24 ICRC Customary IHL Study (J.M. Henckaerts & L. Doswald-Beck, Customary International Humanitarian Law, ICRC and Cambridge University Press, 2005). See also Art. 58 AP I, applicable in international armed conflicts.

38   See D. Momtaz, 'Les défis des conflits armés asymétriques et identitaires au droit international humanitaire', in Matheson & Momtaz (eds), supra, note 2, pp. 3–137, at p. 3; N. Melzer, 'The Principle of Distinction between Civilians and Combatants', in A. Clapham and P. Gaeta (eds), *The Oxford handbook of international law in armed conflict*, Oxford University Press, 2014 296–331, at 298; IHL prohibites the use of human shields. See Rule 97 ICRC Customary IHL Study (Henckaerts & Doswald-Beck, supra, note 37).

39   For further discussion on the notion of 'direct participation in hostilities', see ICRC, supra, note 15.

In addition, in urban settings military targets are necessarily located in close proximity to civilian objects, which bears a great risk of incidental damage to civilian homes and critical civilian infrastructure, namely hospitals and other medical facilities, water and sewage systems, etc. Likewise, normally civilian objects are at risk of being used in ways that turn them into lawful military targets, which may lead to their destruction.[40]

In populated areas, such as urban settings, the use of explosive weapons presents a significant humanitarian concern. In today's armed conflicts, their use constitutes a major cause of disruption of healthcare, of degradation of essential urban services, and of movement of people within and across borders.[41] Therefore, in the view of the ICRC,

> explosive weapons with a wide impact area should not be used in densely populated areas due to the significant likelihood of indiscriminate effects, meaning that their use against military objectives located in populated areas is likely to fall foul of the IHL rules prohibiting indiscriminate and disproportionate attacks.[42]

To be clear, IHL does not prohibit the use of explosive weapons in populated areas. It is also undisputed that any use of such weapons must comply with pertinent IHL rules.[43] Evidence from recent uses in armed conflicts however raises serious questions as to how those using such weapons are interpreting and applying these rules. The ICRC considers that the use of explosive weapons with a wide impact area, which is generally unproblematic on an open battlefield, entails a high risk of violating IHL rules regulating the conduct of

---

40   A generally accepted definition of military targets is found in Art. 52(2) AP I and Rule 8 Customary IHL Study, which provide: 'In so far as objects are concerned, military objectives are limited to those objects which by their nature, location, purpose or use make an effective contribution to military action and whose partial or total destruction, capture or neutralisation, in the circumstances ruling at the time, offers a definite military advantage.' (Henckaerts & Doswald-Beck, supra, note 37).

41   The view that the use of explosive weapons in populated areas is a major humanitarian concern is also shared by other international organizations. See, for example, UN General Assembly, One humanity: shared responsibility. Report of the Secretary-General for the World Humanitarian Summit, UN Doc. A/70/709, 2 February 2016.

42   ICRC, supra, note 4, p. 49.

43   For an in-depth analysis of both IHL and weapons treaties, see M. Brehm, 'International humanitarian law and the protection of civilians from the effects of explosive weapons', in C. Harvey (ed), *The Laws of War: Fit For Purpose? Essays in Honour of Professor Peter Rowe*, Cambridge University Press, 2014, pp. 235–276.

hostilities, in particular the prohibition of indiscriminate and disproportionate attacks, when it occurs in densely populated areas. Against this background the above position was developed.

In light of observed practices, divergent views exist on whether or not existing IHL rules regulate the use of explosive weapons in populated areas sufficiently, whether existing rules need clarification, or whether new rules or standards need to be developed.[44] While the question of whether new rules or standards are necessary needs further elaboration by States, the severe humanitarian consequences emphasize an immediate need to work towards a better understanding of existing IHL norms by all parties, which can help parties to reduce the humanitarian impact of these weapons.

IHL provides a number of essential rules on the conduct of hostilities. These include the principle of distinction, the prohibition of indiscriminate attacks, the principle of proportionality, or the obligation to take all feasible precautions to avoid or minimize incidental loss of civilian life, injury to civilians, and damage to civilian objects.[45] The use of explosive weapons with a wide impact area in populated areas raises a number of legal issues, including how to reconcile the use of certain inaccurate weapons with the prohibition of indiscriminate attacks; whether IHL imposes an obligation to use precision weaponry if available; or what kind of civilian damage must be considered in a proportionality assessment.[46]

With regard to the third question, recent debate occurred on the extent to which so-called 'reverberating effects' must be taken into account when assessing the proportionality of an attack or necessary precautions.[47] Reverberating or knock-on effects are not direct effects of an attack, such as civilian injury or death, but longer-term incidental effects resulting from an attack. For example, damage to electricity or water infrastructure may affect hospitals and interrupt medical services, which is likely to result in the suffering or death of

---

44 Diverging views were stated at an ICRC expert meeting held in 2015. See ICRC, 'Explosive Weapons in Populated Areas: Humanitarian, Legal, Technical and Military Aspect—Expert Meeting', available at https://www.icrc.org/en/download/file/9044/icrc_ewpa_report_12.06.2015.pdf, at pp. 6–7.

45 See Arts 48, 51(4), 51(5)(b), 57 AP I; Chapters I–V ICRC Customary IHL Study, Henckaerts & Doswald-Beck, supra, note 37.

46 For further discussion on some of these issues, see ICRC, supra, note 44, pp. 18–19; Brehm, supra, note 43, 2, pp. 249–261.

47 See Arts. 51(5)(b) or 57(2)(a)(iii) AP I or Rules 14 and 15 ICRC Customary IHL Study, Henckaerts & Doswald-Beck, supra, note 37, 6.

patients. In deciding which reverberating effects should be considered among the expected incidental damage, in the ICRC's view 'it is both impractical and impossible for commanders to consider all possible effects of an attack.'[48] However, 'those reverberating effects that are foreseeable in the circumstances must be taken into account.'[49] An objective standard of what is foreseeable could be derived from what the International Criminal Tribunal for the Former Yugoslavia required generally for the proportionality standard, namely: what a 'reasonably well-informed person in the circumstances [of the attacker], making reasonable use of the information available to him or her'[50] would foresee.[51] Such assessment should also be based on all reasonably available information, including the commanders' or their force's experience from past operations. Considering reasonably available information includes an obligation to obtain information and knowledge to the extent feasible.[52]

3.3 New Means and Methods of Warfare

A third potential challenge for the application of IHL is posed by new means and methods of warfare, for example 'cyber warfare' and 'autonomous weapon systems'.[53] While legal questions surrounding the development of such means and methods are intensely debated among States and legal experts, the use of cyber warfare methods in today's armed conflicts remains limited and 'killer robots' that could replace soldiers have yet to be developed, albeit there are already weapon systems in use with autonomy in critical functions of selecting and attacking targets. Due to the rapid development that computer-based technology has taken over the past decades, it is likely that research and development of cyber and autonomous weapons will continue.

The technological advancement of means and methods of warfare does not occur in a legal vacuum. When States negotiated Additional Protocol I, they agreed on Article 36, which requires:

---

48   ICRC, supra, note 4, p. 52.
49   Ibid.
50   *Prosecutor v Stanislav Galic*, Case No IT-98-29-T, Judgement, 5 December 2003, at para. 58.
51   For further discussion, see ICRC, supra, note 44, p. 21.
52   ICRC, supra, note 4, p. 52.
53   The ICRC understands cyber warfare as 'operations against a computer or a computer system through a data stream, when used as means and methods of warfare in the context of an armed conflict, as defined under IHL'. Autonomous weapons systems can be defined as weapon systems 'that can select (i.e. search for or detect, identify, track, select) and attack (i.e. use force against, neutralize, damage or destroy) targets without human intervention'. Ibid., p. 39 and 44.

In the study, development, acquisition or adoption of a new weapon, means or method of warfare, a High Contracting Party is under an obligation to determine whether its employment would, in some or all circumstances, be prohibited by this Protocol or by any other rule of international law applicable to the High Contracting Party.[54]

As the consequence of a finding that a weapon, means, or method of warfare cannot comply with existing IHL must be that it cannot be used, Article 36 ought 'to be the mechanism whereby the primacy of the existing law [over technological advance] is assured'.[55] Still, for the ICRC the unique characteristics of cyber warfare or autonomous weapons raise the question of whether existing law is sufficiently clear to adequately regulate their use, 'or whether there is a need to clarify IHL or develop new rules to deal with these challenges'.[56]

In principle, IHL rules on the conduct of hostilities are stated in a sufficiently general manner so as not to exclude specific means or methods of warfare from their scope of application. Thus, if cyber operations amount to, or form part of, an armed conflict, they fall under IHL's scope of application. There is, however, need to assess how particular IHL rules apply to cyber warfare. When considering the conduct of hostilities in cyber space, a long-debated question has been which operations qualify as 'attacks' as regulated by IHL rules on the conduct of hostilities.[57] Under Article 49(1) Additional Protocol I, attacks are defined as 'acts of violence against the adversary, whether in offence or in defence'. While it is widely accepted that cyber operations causing results akin to those of kinetic attacks qualify as 'attacks', it has been controversial whether or

---

[54] Independent of whether or not States have ratified AP I, implementing what Art. 36 requires is a prerequisite for States to prevent a situation that they use weapons that would violate general or specific rules on means and methods of warfare. For in-depth analysis of Art. 36 AP I, see *A Guide to the Legal Review of New Weapons, Means and Methods of Warfare—Measures to Implement Article 36 of Additional Protocol I of 1977*, ICRC, 2006, available at https://www.icrc.org/eng/assets/files/other/icrc_002_0902.pdf.

[55] W. Boothby, 'Does the law of targeting meet twenty-first-century needs?', in C. Harvey (ed), *The Laws of War: Fit For Purpose? Essays in Honour of Professor Peter Rowe*, Cambridge University Press, 2014, pp. 216–234, at pp. 216–234.

[56] ICRC, supra, note 4, p. 39.

[57] For a good summary of the discussion and an original interpretation of the notion of attack, see C. Dröge, 'Get off my cloud: cyber warfare, international humanitarian law, and the protection of civilians', 94 *International Review of the Red Cross*, 2012, pp. 533–578, at pp. 551–562.

not physical damage would be required for qualifying as an attack.[58] Over the past years, experts have increasingly converged on the view that cyber operations that do not physically damage but only interfere with the functionality of cyber infrastructure qualify as an attack under IHL.[59] Less agreement exists on whether fundamental IHL principles—such as distinction, proportionality, or the obligation to take precautions against the effects of attacks—are sufficient or adequate in their current form with regard to attacks in a cyber environment in which civilian and military computer networks are closely connected.[60]

Regarding autonomous weapon systems, the question is less to what extent IHL rules on the conduct of hostilities would apply to such weapon systems but rather—if these systems become increasingly autonomous in selecting targets and deciding to attack—whether a machine can be able to comply with the law. Thus far, autonomy for selecting and attacking targets in existing weapon systems is limited by operational parameters, such as limits on the task to be carried out; the ability of the system to discriminate between targets; control over the operational environment, such as limitations in time and space; and the ability for humans to communicate with the weapon system, for example to deactivate it. The technical characteristics and performance of existing weapon systems, combined with the operational parameters of their use, thus provide a certain degree of predictability of the outcomes of using these weapon systems. This predictability may be lost as autonomous weapon systems are used for more complex tasks or deployed in more dynamic environments than has been the case until now.

A number of experts have raised doubts as to whether such autonomous weapon systems with more and more limited human control will ever be able to apply the principle of distinction or proportionality in complex battlefield

---

58 See Schmitt and NATO Cooperative Cyber Defence Centre of Excellence, *Tallinn manual on the international law applicable to cyber warfare*, Cambridge University Press, 2013, at commentary on rule 30, paras. 10–12. In our view, an interpretation of the definition of attack under AP I in its context and in light of its object and purpose suggests that operations that disable an object without destroying it qualify as an attack. See K. Dörmann, 'Applicability of the Additional Protocols to Computer Network Attacks', 2004, available at https://www.icrc.org/eng/resources/documents/misc/68lg92.htm, p. 4.

59 This view has been held by a majority of experts during the Tallinn Manual process, including those previously opposing that position. See, in particular, N. Schmitt, 'Rewired warfare: rethinking the law of cyber attack', 96 *International Review of the Red Cross*, 2014, pp. 189–206.

60 For further discussion, see ICRC, supra, note 4, pp. 40–43.

situations.[61] For example, determining the proportionality of an attack is inherently a qualitative or value judgment, which depends on the operational context and changing parameters. It is questionable whether a machine can balance the expected harm to civilians against the concrete and direct military advantage of an attack.[62] Nonetheless, it can be argued that if such questions are resolved and machines would be able to comply with IHL at least as good as humans do, from a strictly legal point of view the use of fully autonomous weapons could be lawful. Such a purely legal analysis does, however, not consider essential non-legal or ethical questions, such as whether machines alone should be allowed to take decisions on life or death.[63] Indeed, current debates among States show that there is broad agreement that 'meaningful, appropriate or effective *human* control over the critical functions of weapon systems must be retained.'[64] Controversy continues, however, on what level of human control would be 'meaningful'.[65]

4 Strengthening Respect for IHL

The single most important challenge in contemporary armed conflicts is to ensure better respect for IHL. However, as Djamchid Momtaz emphasized aptly: 'Il est en effet extrêmement difficile de faire respecter en plein combat les règles protectrices de la personne humaine alors que la méfiance et la haine règnent entre les parties au conflit.'[66] In practice, a variety of measures may contribute to the generation of respect for the law. These range from IHL dissemination and training of arms carriers, over confidential or public engagement with all parties to a conflict, to coercive measures such as sanctions or individual criminal responsibility.[67] This section focuses on two dimensions of

---

61 See, for example, G. Giacca & A. Leveringhaus, 'Robo-Wars: The Regulation of Robotic Weapons', *Oxford Martin Policy Paper*, 2014, pp. 16–17; Boothby, supra, note 55, p. 226.
62 Art. 51(5)(b) AP I; Rule 14 ICRC Customary IHL Study, Henckaerts & Doswald-Beck, supra, note 37.
63 For further discussion, see Giacca & Leveringhaus, supra, note 61, pp. 19–23.
64 ICRC, supra, note 4, p. 47 (Emphasis added).
65 For some discussion of what could be 'meaningful', see M. Horowitz & P. Scharre, *Meaningful Human Control in Weapon Systems: A Primer*, Project on Ethical Autonomy, Working Paper, Center for a New American Security, 2015, available at http://www.cnas .org/sites/default/files/publications-pdf/Ethical_Autonomy_Working_Paper_031315.pdf.
66 Momtaz, 'La qualification des conflits armés' p. 70.
67 For a comprehensive discussion on 'Generating Respect for IHL', see 96 *International Review of the Red Cross*, 2014.

compliance work. First, at the macro-level, it presents an ICRC-Switzerland-facilitated inter-governmental process to identify ways to strengthen respect for IHL. Second, looking at the micro or field level, it discusses a selection of recent approaches to achieve better respect for IHL by non-State armed groups.

4.1 The Intergovernmental Consultation Process to Establish an IHL Compliance Mechanism

In 2011, the 31st RCRC Conference recognized 'the importance of exploring ways of enhancing and ensuring the effectiveness of mechanisms of compliance with international humanitarian law, with a view to strengthening legal protection for all victims of armed conflict'.[68] For that purpose, the conference invited the ICRC to 'pursue further research, consultation and discussion in cooperation with States... to identify and propose a range of options and its recommendations to enhance and ensure the effectiveness of mechanisms of compliance with international humanitarian law'.[69] Between 2012 and 2015, the ICRC and Switzerland, following its related pledge made at the Conference, facilitated a consultation process in which over 140 States participated. This process has been unprecedented in its width of participation and the depth of discussions. The main idea that emerged in the discussions among States was the establishment of a new IHL compliance mechanism that would be set up so as to operate in a non-politicized manner and would be voluntary in nature. A regular meeting of States on IHL was meant to be the centerpiece of the proposed mechanism. It was suggested that the Meeting of States should—non-contextually—perform two principal functions: examine national reports on compliance with IHL, and hold thematic discussions on issues related to improving respect for this body of law. The idea of a possible fact-finding function was debated but eventually not retained, as it generated opposing views.[70]

At the 32nd RCRC Conference held in December 2015, members felt it was too soon to endorse a specific outcome, but recommended instead the 'continuation of an inclusive, State-driven intergovernmental process' on strengthening

---

68 31st RCRC Conference, supra, note 32, para. 5.
69 Ibid, paras. 6–7.
70 For a detailed summary of the process, see *Strengthening compliance with international humanitarian law—Draft resolution & Concluding report*, ICRC, 2015. For some discussion and evaluation of the process, see M. Bothe, 'Warum wird humanitäres Völkerrecht eingehalten oder verletzt? Perspektiven der Durchsetzung des humanitären Völkerrechts—neue Entwicklungen und kritische Bilanz', 28 *Journal of International Law of Peace and Armed Conflict*, 2015.

respect for IHL.[71] They reiterated the 'imperative need to improve compliance with IHL', and stressed that more needed to be done 'to address the current weaknesses and gaps in the implementation of IHL, including by non-State parties to armed conflict'.[72] The resolution adopted provides that until the 33rd RCRC Conference in 2019, States should focus on finding agreement on the functions and features or a potential Forum of States and on enhancing the implementation of IHL using the potential of the International Conference and regional IHL forums.

As IHL practitioners, we are all-too aware of the urgent need to strengthen respect for IHL for the benefit of the many victims of today's armed conflicts. The fact that IHL is one of the oldest branches of international law but also one without a regular venue in which States can examine issues related to its implementation is perplexing. A new mechanism designed to enhance State-dialogue on IHL and to effectively strengthen respect for its rules would be an important addition to efforts aimed at reinforcing the protection of victims of armed conflicts.

4.2 Innovative Ways to Strengthen Respect for IHL by Non-State Armed Groups

Whereas the ICRC-Switzerland-facilitated consultation process focused on diplomatic and political ways to strengthen primarily States' respect for IHL, the second part of this section looks at which steps can be taken at the field level to strengthen respect for IHL by all parties to the conflict, in particular non-State armed groups. For this purpose, it is key to remember that respect for IHL among parties to armed conflicts, including among non-State armed groups, varies widely. While some groups ignore IHL or violate it deliberately, others have a genuine interest in respecting the law. Moreover, the capacities of groups to comply with IHL rules, including the sophistication of group's internal disciplinary systems, vary. While this diversity makes a 'one-size-fits-all'-approach to enhancing respect for IHL difficult, a number of general measures can be identified.

Different steps are needed. Where parties lack knowledge on IHL, a first step is to disseminate the law. In addition, an ICRC study on the 'The Roots of Behaviour in War'—which was published in 2004 and is currently updated[73]—

---

71 32nd RCRC Conference, supra, note 34, preamble, para. 2.
72 Ibid, preamble.
73 The current update revisits the conclusions of 2004 study with a particular emphasis on the question of why some groups of arms bearers comply with basic norms while others do not.

concluded that not mere knowledge but 'the training of combatants, strict orders and effective sanctions are the most effective levers to obtain greater respect for IHL.'[74] Moreover, psychologists found that in order to strengthen compliance with IHL, the law needs to be integrated 'within specific systems of knowledge, values and norms of a particular group'.[75] This means that in order to have an impact on actual behavior, 'any norm has to pass through these cultural/religious filters.'[76] As a result, the concrete steps to be taken in a given situation depend on who the conflicting parties are and the circumstances in which they operate.

Over recent years, a number of innovative steps have been taken to strengthen respect for IHL. Only some of them can be presented here. In order to disseminate IHL and train armed forces, the ICRC and other humanitarian organizations try to engage with different armed groups. Especially if access to armed groups is limited, the media, including social media and smart-phone apps, have been used to enhance awareness of and knowledge on IHL. For example, in light of flagrant IHL violations in Syria and the minimal IHL knowledge and training that many members of armed groups had, the NGO Geneva Call produced concise video messages explaining basic rules of IHL. These videos were shown on major TV channels, distributed via social media, promoted and used by the Syrian Red Crescent, and by non-State armed groups.[77] Moreover, Geneva Call produced the 'Fighter not Killer' smartphone app, which members of armed groups can use to train on applying IHL in virtual battlefield situations.

In situations in which access to the conflicting parties is possible, direct engagement remains the most effective way to promote IHL compliance. Due to its presence in most conflict theatres, the ICRC engages systematically and wherever possible with armed group to disseminate knowledge on IHL, to assist in training, and to find other leverage points to strengthen respect for IHL. In order to integrate its humanitarian message with local cultures, religion, and beliefs, the ICRC has especially engaged with faith-based-organizations

---

74 D. Muñoz-Rojas & J.-J. Frésard, *The Roots of Behaviour in War: Understanding and Preventing IHL Violations*, ICRC, 2004, available at https://www.icrc.org/eng/assets/files/other/icrc_002_0853.pdf, p. 203.

75 'Interview with Emanuele Castano', 96 *International Review of the Red Cross*, 2014, pp. 697–705, p. 704.

76 Ibid.

77 'Fighter Not Killer Campaign launched by Geneva Call against violations in Syria', Geneva Call, 17 May 2013, available at http://www.genevacall.org/fighter-killer-campaign-launched-geneva-call-violations-syria.

and religious leaders. For example, at a global and regional level, the ICRC has approached Muslim scholars and Islamic circles to discuss 'commonalities and differences between international humanitarian law and its equivalent in Islamic jurisprudence'.[78] A particular focus was placed on concrete humanitarian issues such as access to victims and the protection of health workers or medical facilities. The ICRC uses the results of such consultations in its daily work to gain humanitarian access and achieve better respect for IHL. Concretely, in Somalia similarities between IHL and traditional and partly religious codes, such as the 'biri-ma-geydo', were identified. In order to convey basic IHL messages to conflicting parties, the ICRC has promoted such local customs via radios and in their direct interaction with groups.[79] In short, where the context so requires, the ICRC integrates IHL messages with local customs, traditions, and beliefs in order to reach all conflicting parties and to achieve better protection for victims of armed conflicts.

5 Conclusion

IHL provides a basic framework regulating the conduct of hostilities as well as the treatment of those who do not or no longer participate in the conflict. Yet, contemporary armed conflicts become ever more complex: in addition to recurring issues such as the treatment of persons deprived of their liberty, parties to armed conflicts multiply, fighting takes increasingly place in populated areas, and new means and methods of warfare are developed. In order to respond to these complexities, a number of steps are needed. First of all, it is of fundamental importance that States and non-State parties to armed conflicts work faithfully towards better respect of the law, which includes international cooperation as well as an internalization of norms among the armed forces. It is crucial, also and in particular in times of new threats, to uphold the 'acquis', i.e. the protective core of the basic norms of IHL, and not to erode it with practices and interpretations that shift the existing delicate balance between military considerations and humanitarian imperatives to a point where the

---

78 'Faith-based organizations and religious leaders: Essential partners in humanitarian action—Interview with Ronald Ofteringer', ICRC, 22 July 2015, available at https://www.icrc.org/en/document/faith-based-organizations-and-religious-leaders-essential-partners-humanitarian-action?language=en.

79 See 'Somalia: Using traditional law in dialogues with armed groups', ICRC, 10 November 2014, available at https://www.icrc.org/en/document/somalia-using-traditional-law-dialogues-armed-groups.

protective scope of norms becomes meaningless. For example, wide interpretations of what may constitute a military objective, e.g. a broad inclusion of objects that are only remotely connected to the war fighting under 'effective contribution to military action', of who may become a lawful military target because of direct participation in hostilities, narrow interpretations of what would constitute incidental civilian harm to be considered for the purposes of the proportionality assessment in attack as well as the weight to be given to such harm when weighing against the expected military advantage, would be concerning.

If the political will to respect IHL is present, commanders and legal advisors of all parties to an armed conflict need to be able to advice on IHL application in increasingly complex circumstances. This task needs to be facilitated by clear guidance as to how IHL treaties should be interpreted in light of State and other international practice. Over the past years, different processes among legal experts have produced manuals that can assist parties in interpreting the law, and States are engaging in multilateral processes to strengthen the protection of victims of armed conflicts. If States engage in such processes, it furthers their understanding of the law and may lead to common understandings of crucial IHL norms, such as those on the conduct of hostilities. Nonetheless, consultation processes and expert meetings may not be enough to address situations in which the law is insufficient as it stands, such as with regard to the protection of persons deprived of their liberty in NIAC, and potentially with regard to new means and methods of warfare. If States want to avoid increasing protection gaps as well as a multiplication of private initiatives to strengthen the law, more intergovernmental engagement and agreement on such urgent issues is needed.

Le droit international humanitaire à l'épreuve des conflits contemporains

Yves Sandoz

Il est nécessaire, pour bien situer les questions que je souhaite soulever dans cet article, de procéder à un bref rappel. Certaines règles furent observées lors des conflits armés depuis fort longtemps – des aspirations à certaines interdictions et restrictions dans la guerre étant « more or less as old as the war itself »[1], avait même affirmé l'historien Georges Best – mais le droit international humanitaire (DIH) sous sa forme actuelle, c'est-à-dire contenant des normes universellement acceptées pour certaines, à vocation universelle pour les autres, n'a qu'un peu plus d'un siècle et demi. S'il fut sinon le moteur, en tout cas le précurseur du droit international public, le DIH joue un rôle, et a une place dans le droit international, qui ont beaucoup évolué.

Cherchant en premier lieu à répondre à un problème bien précis, celui de permettre la protection des militaires blessés et l'accès du personnel médical au champ de bataille, le DIH a sans cesse dû s'adapter pour tenter de couvrir l'ensemble des victimes de conflits toujours plus étendus et cruels. Les naufragés, les prisonniers de guerre, les personnes habitant dans des territoires occupés par l'ennemi et, enfin, l'ensemble des civils pris dans la tourmente des hostilités se sont progressivement ajoutés à la liste des victimes couvertes par ce droit. En outre, à la protection générale de ces catégories de victimes s'est ajoutée une protection spécifique de catégories de personnes particulièrement vulnérables lors des conflits armés, tels les enfants, les femmes ou les disparus et leur famille. Enfin, parallèlement, des règles se sont développées en vue d'interdire ou de restreindre l'usage de méthodes et de moyens de guerre jugés indiscriminés ou excessivement cruels.

Le rôle et la place du DIH ont fait constamment l'objet de débats. Pouvait-on encore développer des règles applicables lors des conflits armés alors que l'on prétendait abolir ceux-ci ? La question s'est posée après la Première Guerre mondiale déjà, mais de manière plus aiguë encore après la Seconde, quand les Etats ont accepté d'introduire dans la Charte des Nations Unies l'interdiction du recours à la force armée entre Etats. Logiquement, la Commission du droit international tout juste créée a alors refusé de mettre à son agenda le DIH, suivant en cela l'avis, notamment exprimé par Brierly, que son action dans

---

1 G. Best, *War and Law since 1945*, Clarendon Press, New-York, 1994, p. 15.

ce domaine « [...] might be interpreted as a lack of confidence in the United Nations [...] »[2]. Constatant qu'ils n'avaient pas réussi à s'entendre pour doter l'ONU des moyens de son ambition, celle d'ouvrir sur la planète une ère de paix universelle, les Etats ont néanmoins accepté peu après de se pencher à nouveau sur le DIH, qui avait été bafoué lors de la Seconde Guerre mondiale. Mais la place de ce droit dans le système international devint alors boiteuse : il est depuis lors une sorte de bouée de sauvetage à laquelle s'agripper en cas de naufrage du système prévu par le droit international.

Peut-on espérer de ceux qui violent le droit international général qu'ils respectent mieux le DIH ? On peut en douter, à l'instar de Sir Hersch Lauterpacht, qui exprima son scepticisme dans une fameuse formule citée depuis lors à satiété : « If international law is, in some ways, at the vanishing point of law, the law of war is, perhaps more conspicuously, at the vanishing point of international law »[3]. La logique n'interdit toutefois pas de l'espérer pour autant que l'on établisse une claire distinction entre le droit international interdisant l'utilisation de la force armée entre Etats (*jus ad bellum*) et le droit international imposant des normes humanitaires lors des conflits armés, soit le DIH (*jus in bello*), l'Etat agresseur, condamné par le premier, se trouvant en revanche sur un pied d'égalité dans le second et pouvant donc, à cette condition, trouver un intérêt à respecter le DIH.

Un nouvel élément allait avoir une influence décisive sur le DIH, l'avènement des droits de l'homme sur le plan international, soit l'idée que le principe de la souveraineté nationale n'est pas absolu et que l'ensemble de la communauté internationale a en quelque sorte un droit de regard sur la manière dont les gouvernements traitent leur propre population : le « principe d'indifférence » qui prévalait jusqu'alors – à l'exception de rares et parfois douteuses « interventions d'humanité » – n'avait pas résisté à l'horreur des massacres et des persécutions perpétrés lors de la seconde guerre mondiale. Cette brèche ouverte dans le système international allait ensuite logiquement permettre au DIH de s'intéresser aussi aux conflits armés non internationaux (CANI) : l'article 3 commun des Conventions de Genève (CdG) fut le cheval de Troie du DIH pour s'infiltrer dans un domaine plus vaste que son champ d'application originel, les CANI étant aujourd'hui bien plus nombreux que les conflits armés internationaux (CAI).

---

2 Cf. *Yearbook of the International Law Commission, Summary Records and Documents of the first session*, 6th meeting, 1949, p. 51ss, par. 55.
3 H. Lauterpacht, « The Problem of the Revision of the Law of War », *British Yearbook of International Law*, vol. 29, 1952, p. 382.

Ce système est-il encore adapté aux réalités actuelles ? 160 ans représentent une période dérisoire dans l'histoire de l'humanité mais le développement technologique durant cette période a pourtant été d'une importance plus grande que tout ce que les hommes ont inventé auparavant. Les raisons et les raisonnements qui ont conduit à l'adoption des premières Conventions de DIH sont-ils encore valables ? A quoi doit-on s'attendre dans ce 21ème siècle ?

1 Problèmes d'applicabilité du DIH

La question de l'applicabilité du DIH est en quelque sorte son talon d'Achille. L'ambition de ce droit est en effet le respect de certaines valeurs pendant les conflits armés indépendamment de toute connotation ou implication politiques, quelle que soit la cause défendue. Or il est difficile d'échapper à la politique quand il s'agit de qualifier une situation.

1.1 *Conflits armés internationaux*
L'idée de devoir prouver l'existence d'un conflit armé n'effleurait pas l'esprit de ceux qui ont conçu le DIH sur la base de batailles rangées telles que celle de Solférino, d'autant moins que les Etats prenaient alors la peine de se déclarer la guerre formellement. Comme il devenait incohérent de maintenir l'obligation de se déclarer la guerre alors que l'on avait aboli celle-ci dans la Charte des Nations Unies, le DIH s'est émancipé du mot guerre qu'il a remplacé par l'expression « conflit armé », substituant à la déclaration formelle l'existence matérielle d'hostilités armées. Les déploiements armés tels que ceux que l'on a connu en Corée, au Vietnam, en Afghanistan, en Irak et dans bien d'autres situations ne laissent toutefois planer aucun doute sur l'existence de conflits armés, et donc sur l'applicabilité du DIH. Les interventions armées ponctuelles de courte durée peuvent toutefois poser problème. Le Commentaire des CdG édité par le Comité International de la Croix-Rouge (CICR) a clairement pris la position de dire que tout acte d'hostilité armée d'un Etat à l'encontre d'un autre devait être considéré comme un conflit armé et que « la durée du conflit et le caractère plus ou moins meurtrier de ses effets ne jouent aucun rôle »[4]. Cette position se fonde sur le souci d'éviter des lacunes dans la protection et de s'en tenir aux faits : tout acte d'hostilité armée d'un Etat à l'égard d'un autre doit, indépendamment de la justification que l'on peut lui donner, se conformer aux exigences du DIH.

---

4   J. Pictet, *Commentaire de première Convention de Genève*, Comité International de la Croix-Rouge, Genève, 1952, p. 34.

L'applicabilité du droit de l'occupation pose toutefois un problème délicat car elle dépend de ce qui est souvent au cœur de conflit, soit du légitime « propriétaire » du territoire. L'imbroglio israélo-palestinien est l'exemple le plus connu de cette difficulté, mais il est loin d'être isolé.

A l'exception notable de certains cas d'occupation, le problème d'applicabilité ne paraît donc *a priori* pas trop compliqué pour les CAI. Il a toutefois été relancé récemment d'une part sur la base de la notion trompeuse de « war on terror » (que l'on traduira plutôt par « guerre au terrorisme »), d'autre part par la « cyberguerre ».

1.1.1   « Guerre au terrorisme »

La « guerre au terrorisme » est une expression sans signification juridique précise, qui englobe tous les moyens de lutte utilisés contre les auteurs d'actes terroristes. Certes, cette lutte doit continuer de faire débat, en vue d'augmenter son efficacité et sa cohérence mais aussi pour éviter que le caractère odieux de cette méthode ne serve de prétexte à jeter un voile sur les problèmes de fond qui sont à l'origine de cette violence. Mais contrairement à ce que laisse entendre le mot « guerre », elle se situe aussi bien en dehors que dans le cadre du DIH. La Cour suprême des Etats-Unis a certes rejeté, dans le cas *Hamdan c. Russfeld*, le point-de-vue du gouvernement américain qui voulait s'exempter de toute responsabilité à l'égard des membres d'Al Quaïda qu'il avait capturés, et c'est un point positif[5]. L'assertion qu'il s'agit d'un CANI d'un nouveau type est en revanche discutable, même si elle est soutenue par une partie de la doctrine. Il s'agit en effet de ne pas occulter le fait que l'utilisation de la force armée sur le territoire d'un Etat sans l'accord de celui-ci est une violation de la souveraineté nationale quel que soit l'objectif visé, et donc un CAI. L'affirmation de l'Etat engageant ses forces armées qu'il s'en prend non pas à l'Etat sur le territoire duquel il agit, mais seulement à des groupes armés ne change pas cette réalité. La possibilité de considérer en parallèle un CAI contre l'Etat et un CANI contre le Groupe armé « terroriste » est évoquée par certains mais elle est juridiquement très discutable et impraticable sur le terrain, la distinction entre ce qui relève de l'un et de l'autre étant beaucoup trop compliquée.

Autre est évidemment l'appui donné par un Etat au gouvernement d'un autre Etat, avec le consentement de ce dernier. Un tel appui peut soit ne pas relever du tout du DIH s'il s'agit d'opérations de police, soit s'inscrire dans le cadre d'un CANI s'il s'agit d'appuyer les forces gouvernementales dans son combat contre une partie dissidente.

---

5   Voir notamment US Supreme Court, *Salim Ahmed Hamdan v. Donald H. Rumsfeld et al.*, 458 U.S. 557 (2006) N°05.184, p. 67.

Bref, la prudence s'impose avec l'expression trompeuse de « guerre au terrorisme ». Il faut s'en tenir aux faits et ne l'utiliser ni pour violer la souveraineté d'un autre Etat, ni pour s'exempter de l'obligation de respecter le DIH et le droit international des droits de l'homme (DIdH).

1.1.2 Cyberguerre

La « cyberguerre » pose un problème de définition et un problème d'attribution. La notion de conflit armé implique en effet l'utilisation de la force armée. Or on peut aujourd'hui sans utiliser celle-ci causer des dommages à un Etat aussi importants que le feraient des bombardements. Des coupures d'électricité affectant les hôpitaux, le chaos dans les aéroports ou dans les gares, il y a d'infinies hypothèses d'interventions sur le système informatique d'un pays, qui peuvent causer des dommages graves, voire des catastrophes coûtant de nombreuses vies humaines et affectant d'innombrables personnes. Il y a toutefois ici une question de seuil et il est délicat de fixer une limite précise entre un acte malveillant – espionnage économique, paralysie momentanée de l'administration – et une atteinte assez grave pour qu'on la considère comme un acte d'hostilité pouvant justifier en retour l'utilisation de la force armée et impliquant le respect du DIH.

Se pose ensuite la question délicate de déceler l'origine de tels actes et d'en attribuer la responsabilité. Des spécialistes aguerris sont aujourd'hui capables de pénétrer même des systèmes apparemment bien protégés. Comment les identifier ? Comment savoir s'ils sont commandités par un Etat ? Jusqu'où va le devoir de diligence des Etats alors que même les plus développé d'entre eux ne peuvent garantir le contrôle de tels individus sur leur territoire ?

Tout cela ouvre un vaste champ de réflexion[6] et c'est probablement dans le cadre plus large de la lutte contre la cybercriminalité que l'essentiel du débat devrait se tenir. Une autorité supranationale dans ce domaine, jusqu'ici refusée par la majorité des Etats, serait probablement utile pour mieux coordonner cette lutte indispensable, mais aussi pour servir de paravent aux velléités de représailles et à l'engrenage nocif que celles-ci ne manqueraient pas d'enclencher.

1.2 *Conflits armés non internationaux*

C'est pour les CANI que se posent les questions les plus délicates, d'abord sur le plan subjectif parce que les Etats répugnent généralement à reconnaître

---

6   Une abondante littérature a déjà été produite sur la question mais nous renverrons tout particulièrement à M. N. Schmitt (Dir.), « *The Tallinn Manuel on the International Law Applicable to Cyberwarfare* », Cambridge University Press, 2013.

l'existence d'un conflit armé sur leur territoire ; ensuite aussi pour des raisons objectives car si les acteurs potentiels des CAI, soit les Etats, sont prédéterminés, ce n'est pas le cas dans les CANI : l'existence de ceux-ci dépend d'un certain niveau de violence armée et d'organisation de la partie dissidente. Or ces niveaux ne sont généralement atteints qu'au terme d'une lente évolution et le passage du seuil qui sépare des troubles intérieurs d'un conflit armé n'est donc pas facile à déceler.

Il est pourtant essentiel car il y a alors un changement de paradigme, comme de Vattel l'avait déjà relevé[7]. La possibilité d'une « reconnaissance de belligérance » fut ensuite admise, comme l'avait indiqué l'Institut de droit international en 1900[8], soit pour l'Etat victime de l'insurrection soit pour des Etats tiers, ceux-ci pouvant alors traiter directement avec la partie dissidente ainsi reconnue et défendre auprès d'elle ses ressortissants ou d'autres intérêts. Mais si de Vattel estime que les normes du droit des conflits armés s'appliquent automatiquement dès que les conditions objectives d'une guerre civile sont remplies – il parle toutefois d'une situation où il y a quasiment deux Etats, donc d'un conflit avec contrôle d'une partie du territoire par la partie dissidente – la reconnaissance de belligérance n'est qu'une possibilité offerte et reste donc une décision unilatérale de l'Etat qui la prononce.

Avec l'introduction de l'article 3 dans les CdG, l'on en est revenu à l'approche vattelienne en rendant l'application du DIH dans les CANI automatique et non plus à la discrétion de l'Etat concerné. L'on aurait alors logiquement dû être d'autant plus rigoureux dans la définition de ce type de conflits, ce qui n'a pas été le cas, l'article 3 ne mentionnant rien à ce sujet, comme si l'existence d'un conflit armé était une évidence. Le Commentaire de cet article nous indique pourtant que l'absence de critères vient plutôt d'une difficulté de trouver un consensus que d'une ignorance du problème. Il est toutefois ambigu dans la mesure où d'une part il rappelle et soutient les critères stricts qui avaient été évoqués pendant la Conférence diplomatique, qui sont proches de ceux que l'on va retrouver dans le Protocole II de 1977, additionnel aux CdG (PA II)[9],

---

7   Les guerres civiles donnent naissance à « deux parties indépendans » (sic) et dans ces guerres, « les lois communes de la guerre, ces maximes d'humanité, de modération, de droiture et d'honnêteté [...] doivent être observées de part et d'autre », E. de Vattel, *Le Droit des Gens, ou Principes de la loi naturelle*, 1758, Livre III, Chap. XVIII, par. 293-294.

8   Cf. résolution du 8 septembre 1900, chapitre II « De l'attribution du caractère de belligérants aux insurgés », H. Wehberg, *Institut de droit international, Tableau général des résolutions (1873-1956)*, Editions juridiques et sociologiques S.A., Bâle, 1957, pp. 172s.

9   Protocole additionnel aux Conventions de Genève du 12 août 1949 relatif à la protection des victimes des conflits armés non internationaux (Protocole II), Nations Unies, *Recueil des traités*, vol. 1125, p. 639.

mais d'autre part il indique que l'article 3 devrait s'appliquer même si ces critères ne sont pas remplis, en cas de troubles intérieurs[10]. Les Etats ont voulu corriger ce manque de clarté en élaborant le PA II, destiné à préciser et compléter l'article 3 commun des CdG. Ils ont alors souhaité clairement délimiter le champ d'application du DIH, mais précisément aussi pour en exclure les situations de tensions internes et de troubles intérieurs. On ne pouvait dès lors plus échapper à une définition.

1.2.1 Définition du CANI

Les critères retenus d'intensité et d'organisation sont généralement admis, alors que les critères de contrôle du territoire et de capacité d'appliquer le DIH prêtent à controverse.

Le critère de contrôle du territoire reste peu précis (y a-t-il une étendue minimale ? Est-ce un contrôle permanent ?) mais a conduit la majorité des Etats et de la doctrine à considérer cette exigence comme un ajout aux critères permettant de déterminer l'existence d'un CANI, bien que le Commentaire de l'article 3 mentionné ci-dessus ne le laisse pas entendre[11]. On estime donc généralement qu'il existe deux types de CANI, les conflits couverts par le seul article 3 commun des CdG et ceux qui sont couverts en sus par le PA II (qui, lui, ne s'applique jamais seul, étant, comme son nom l'indique, additionnel).

Le PA II ne mentionne en outre que la « capacité » d'appliquer le DIH, sans référence à l'application réelle de ce droit ou pour le moins à la volonté clairement exprimée de l'appliquer. Une bonne partie de la doctrine estime dès lors que seuls les critères d'organisation et d'intensité sont déterminants pour l'ensemble des CANI. Cette approche est contestable si l'on examine la question d'un peu plus près. D'une part les critères adoptés dans le passé en ce qui concernait une possible reconnaissance de belligérance mentionnaient clairement la *volonté* d'appliquer le DIH, tout comme d'ailleurs le Commentaire de l'article 3 mentionné ci-dessus[12] ; d'autre part dans le cadre du Protocole I de 1977 additionnel aux Conventions de Genève (PA I)[13], qui complète les CdG pour ce qui est des CAI, la couverture des membres de groupes armés liés aux gouvernements en conflit est admise seulement s'ils *respectent* le DIH, cette

---

10 Cf. Pictet, *op. cit.* note 4, p. 40ss.

11 Ibid.

12 Ibid.

13 Protocole additionnel aux Conventions de Genève du 12 août 1949 relatif à la protection des victimes des conflits armés internationaux (Protocole I), Nations Unies, *Recueil des traités*, vol. 1125, p. 3.

condition étant posée sans ambiguïté dans ce cadre[14]. Enfin rien n'indique que la formulation adoptée dans le PA II provient d'une volonté de modifier le droit sur ce point.

On voit mal en effet l'intérêt de poser le critère de la capacité d'appliquer le Protocole si ce n'est par souci qu'il soit réellement appliqué. Le CICR avait d'ailleurs adopté une attitude prudente face aux déclarations d'intention d'appliquer le DIH des Parties dissidentes à des CANI qui les lui soumettaient, parfois pour publication, s'assurant que de telles Déclarations n'étaient pas de simples coups médiatiques, mais correspondaient à une capacité et une volonté réelles de mettre en œuvre le DIH sur le terrain[15].

Certes, il ne s'agit pas de prendre prétexte de la moindre violation du DIH pour disqualifier une entité qui remplirait par ailleurs les critères requis. Nombre d'Etats seraient trop heureux de s'engouffrer dans cette brèche, qualifiant systématiquement leurs opposants de terroristes dans la plupart des guerres civiles. C'est la raison pour laquelle des Organisations comme le CICR restent très prudentes dans leur interprétation de ce critère, s'en tenant à la « capacité ». Mais il est aussi choquant de prétendre qualifier de partie à un conflit armé des groupes armés qui ont pour seul objectif de mener des activités purement criminelles, tel le trafic d'êtres humains, d'armes ou de drogues, et n'ont ni projet politique ni d'autre ambition que celle de poursuivre et développer de telles activités. Le DIH n'a de sens que s'il est appliqué et l'on ne voit pas l'intérêt de considérer comme des parties à des conflits armés des groupes armés n'ayant aucune velléité de respecter ce droit et dont une bonne partie des activités, telle la prise d'otages, est par essence contraire aux normes de celui-ci. Certes, cela ne signifie pas pour autant qu'aucun dialogue n'est possible et l'on parvient assez souvent, même avec de tels groupes, à obtenir des accords ponctuels, pour amener des secours, assainir l'eau, voire même scolariser des enfants. Cela se fait toutefois sur une base purement pragmatique et sans aucune chance de faire prévaloir une obligation juridique, ni même morale, d'appliquer les normes du DIH.

---

14   Les groupes armés, comme toutes les forces armées, doivent être soumis à un régime de discipline « qui assure » le respect du DIH : cf. article 43, par. 1 du PA II.

15   Cf. notamment D. Plattner, « La portée juridique des déclarations de respect du droit international humanitaire qui émanent de Mouvements en lutte dans un conflit armé », *Revue belge de droit international*, Vol. XVIII, Bruylant, 1984-1985-1, p. 298-320.

2 Problèmes de fond

Le constat ayant été fait que la difficulté première du DIH réside dans la reconnaissance de son applicabilité, on se demandera si l'on ne rencontre pas aussi des problèmes dans l'application des normes de ce droit une fois son applicabilité reconnue, soit dans sa substance même, que ce soit, ici aussi, dans le cadre de CAI ou de CANI.

2.1 *Conflits armés internationaux*

La partie du DIH qui s'occupe de la conduite des hostilités, notamment par l'interdiction ou la restriction de certains moyens ou méthodes de combat, doit sans cesse s'adapter à l'évolution scientifique. Il faut donc, comme on l'a fait ces dernières années, s'interroger sur la compatibilité de l'utilisation de nouvelles armes ou méthodes dans un conflit armé avec les principes posés par le DIH. Il ne s'agit toutefois pas là d'une évolution fondamentale mais de la mise en œuvre d'un principe posé dans le PA I[16].

Dans le domaine des armes de destruction massive, la question des armes nucléaires laisse planer un doute fâcheux et l'interdiction absolue de l'usage de ces armes et leur abolition reste un objectif essentiel pour les années à venir, les doctrines fondées sur la dissuasion ne résistant pas à la multiplication des détenteurs réels ou potentiels d'armes nucléaires.

Quant aux armes classiques, l'apparition de nouvelles armes ou méthodes de guerre peut renvoyer aux principes sur lesquels sont fondées les normes dans ce domaine quand ceux-ci ne donnent pas de réponses claires aux questions ouvertes par ces nouveautés. Il s'agit alors soit de développer, soit d'interpréter les principes. Les questions ouvertes par la « cyberguerre » d'une part, et par les armes dites « autonomes », d'autre part, sont de cette nature.

L'on a évoqué ci-dessus les interrogations sur l'applicabilité du DIH aux actes commis dans le « cyberespace ». Dans le cadre d'un conflit armé reconnu, l'utilisation de moyens cybernétiques pose également de nombreuses questions liées aux principes de distinction et de proportionnalité, de même qu'au statut de ceux qui sont impliqués plus ou moins directement dans ce type d'activité. Ce n'est probablement aussi qu'à travers des études de cas que l'on parviendra à mieux cerner et préciser les normes en lien avec ces questions[17].

Quant aux armes dites autonomes, le débat est lancé à juste titre. Il y a dans ce domaine une part de fantasme, notamment celui d'imaginer un robot qui échapperait totalement au contrôle de son concepteur, à l'image de la créature

---

16 Cf. article 36, « Armes nouvelles », du PA I de 1977.
17 On renverra également là-dessus au Manuel mentionné ci-dessus, note 7.

du Docteur Frankenstein. Cette problématique n'est d'ailleurs pas entièrement nouvelle et l'on pourrait y voir un lien avec l'interdiction absolue des armes biologiques, nul ne pouvant prétendre contrôler et délimiter strictement les effets d'agents biologiques nocifs que l'on aurait délibérément répandus. Si les armes dites « autonomes » développées jusqu'ici ne présentent pas encore un tel risque, elles soulèvent néanmoins déjà de nombreuses questions, notamment liées à leur capacité réelle d'identifier les objectifs qu'elles sont censées atteindre ou de renoncer à une mission en cas d'un changement de circonstances, sans parler des délicates questions de responsabilité[18]. Bref, la conformité de nouveaux moyens de guerre au DIH demande une veille constante, nécessitant la présence d'un personnel à haute compétence technique en soutien des juristes.

Hormis ces questions liées aux moyens et méthodes de guerre, on ne peut guère envisager dans un proche avenir un développement important des normes du DIH applicables dans les CAI. Il n'est pas sérieusement envisageable d'aller au-delà du compromis presque miraculeusement trouvé en 1977 pour concilier la méthode de la guérilla avec l'exigence, sur laquelle repose tout l'édifice du DIH, de distinguer les civils des combattants. Restent toutefois des questions ouvertes quant à l'interprétation de certaines normes, d'autant plus difficiles à régler dans des situations concrètes, sur le terrain des opérations ou devant les juridictions pénales, quand le manque de clarté de la norme ne provient pas de la négligence du législateur mais de la pression d'un consensus qu'il n'aurait pas été possible d'atteindre sur une norme plus claire.

Parfois aussi, c'est l'objectif même du conflit qui conduit à des interprétations douteuses de certaines normes. La notion d'avantage militaire concret et direct, réaffirmée dans le PA I comme un élément décisif justifiant la légitimité d'actes de violence armée, notamment de bombardements, en est un bon exemple. Il est en effet difficile de définir ses contours quand l'objectif du conflit n'est pas de conquérir un territoire ou de renverser un gouvernement, mais simplement de faire pression sur celui-ci, voire de le sanctionner. Il faut alors surtout insister sur la protection de la population civile, indépendamment de la notion « d'avantage militaire », peu pertinente dans de tels cas. En 1995, les bombardements de l'OTAN sur la Serbie et le Kosovo ont posé, sans qu'on le reconnaisse clairement, un tel problème. Le but de l'OTAN, qui n'envisageait pas d'engager des armées de terre, ne pouvait pas être de ce fait – et n'était pas – de renverser

---

18   A ce sujet, voir notamment le Rapport d'une réunion d'experts conviées sur le sujet par le Comité International de la Croix-Rouge : « Autonomous Weapons Systems, Technical Military, Legal and Humanitarian Aspects », Comité International de la Croix-Rouge, Genève, 2014.

le gouvernement de Milosévic, mais de le faire céder face aux exigences qu'on voulait lui imposer. L'application des principes de distinction et de proportionnalité fut alors biaisée et ceux-ci furent appliqués de manière très artificielle, cela toujours davantage du fait que les bombardements se prolongèrent, Milosévic n'ayant pas compris la détermination de l'OTAN et refusant de céder : il devenait dès lors toujours plus difficile de viser des objectifs qui pouvaient, au moins virtuellement, être considérés comme des objectifs militaires.

C'est probablement sur l'application du DIH dans le cadre de sanctions internationales – indépendamment de leur licéité, qui est une autre question – qu'il faudrait conduire une nouvelle réflexion, en y incluant d'ailleurs aussi le lourd dossier de l'embargo.

2.2 Conflits armés non internationaux

Le dilemme des gouvernements confrontés à des CANI est que s'ils se refusent, pour des raisons politiques, à reconnaître l'existence d'un conflit armé, et donc l'applicabilité du DIH, ils se privent de la possibilité d'utiliser contre leur adversaire les moyens militaires autorisés par ce droit. Ce sont en effet alors les procédures du « law enforcement » qui sont applicables et elles fixent des limites plus rigoureuses à l'utilisation de la force. On pourrait se demander s'il ne faudrait pas étendre ces limites unilatéralement au bénéfice de l'Etat, en s'inspirant des règles du DIH, dans les cas où des groupes armés ont des moyens militaires et une organisation qui correspondent aux critères exigés pour fonder l'existence d'une partie à un conflit, mais que leur totale absence de volonté d'appliquer le DIH disqualifie, si l'on suit la position que j'ai défendue ci-dessus. Un groupe d'experts réunis à la demande du CICR pour examiner la cohabitation des normes du DIH et du DIdH dans la conduite des hostilités avait clairement rejeté cette idée, qui mettrait en péril l'édifice des droits de l'homme[19] : la tentation serait en effet grande pour les Etats concernés de se précipiter dans cette brèche. C'est donc plutôt dans un accroissement de la coopération internationale qu'il faut chercher une réponse, les crimes évoqués ci-dessus ayant presque toujours une dimension transnationale.

Les défenseurs des droits de l'homme sont d'autant plus réticents à l'idée même d'une extension unilatérale de l'autorisation d'utiliser la force armée qu'ils tendent à faire peser toujours davantage le poids des droits de l'homme dans les situations de conflits armés. Si l'idée que le DIH se substituerait *intégralement* au DIdH en tant que *lex specialis* a maintenant été écartée sans

---

19   Cf. *Report of the Expert meeting on the Use of Force in armed conflicts, interplay between the conduct of hostilities and law enforcement paradigms*, Comité International de la Croix-Rouge, Genève, 2013, notamment p. 32.

ambiguïté, notamment par la Cour internationale de Justice, le principe subsiste pour les différentes normes du DIH qui, selon la Cour, ont prééminence en cas de contradiction avec des normes du DIdH[20]. Les différentes juridictions internationales des droits de l'homme ont toutefois marqué une certaine réticence à cet égard et ont adopté des positions qui varient entre elles et ont évolué avec le temps[21]. Deux tendances contradictoires se sont alors développées.

D'une part les différences entre le DIH applicable aux CAI et celui applicable aux CANI tend à se réduire. Cela s'est traduit notamment par l'extension aux CANI d'interdictions ou restrictions d'utiliser certaines armes initialement réservées aux seuls CAI ou dans les instructions données aux forces armées, notamment à travers les manuels militaires[22].

D'autre part les défenseurs des droits de l'homme insistent sur la cohabitation, certains allant même jusqu'à prétendre que dans certains domaines les droits de l'homme doivent être considérés comme une « *lex specialis* » par rapport au DIH. Nous ne partageons pas ce point de vue car la notion n'aurait de sens que si le DIH pouvait s'appliquer dans certains cas en dehors du cadre des droits de l'homme, ce qui n'est jamais le cas : c'est donc *ab initio* que l'on doit évaluer l'impact des droits de l'homme sur l'interprétation du DIH et on doit admettre que les Etats qui ont élaboré et adopté ce droit l'ont fait en toute conscience. La question pourrait se poser pour des normes des droits de l'homme postérieures à celles du DIH mais il devrait alors y avoir une volonté clairement exprimée des Etats de déroger à celles-ci.

En revanche, il est vrai que certaines dispositions du DIH qui sont peu précises peuvent être utilement clarifiées par le DIdH, même si cet éclairage

---

20 Voir à ce sujet l'Avis consultatif du 8 juillet 1996 sur *la licéité de la menace ou de l'emploi d'armes nucléaires*, CIJ Recueil 1996, p. 229, par. 25 ; l'Avis consultatif du 9 juillet 2004 sur *l'édification d'un mur dans les territoires palestiniens occupés*, CIJ Recueil 2004, p. 136, par. 105s. ; et le Jugement du 19 décembre 2005 sur *l'Affaire des Activités armées sur le Territoire du Congo*, CIJ Recueil 2005, p. 168, par. 216.

21 Nous renonçons à entrer, dans le cadre de ce court article, dans l'analyse des nombreux jugements, décisions, rapports et autres commentaires qui étayent ce propos, ni sur l'abondante doctrine à ce sujet.

22 La Convention de 1980 sur l'interdiction ou la limitation de certaines armes classiques a notamment étendu son champ d'application aux CANI lors de sa révision de 2001 (Convention sur l'interdiction ou la limitation de l'emploi de certaines armes classiques qui peuvent être considérées comme produisant des effets traumatiques excessifs ou comme frappant sans discrimination, Nations Unies, *Recueil des traités*, vol. 1342, p. 137). Cette évolution est aussi reflétée dans le droit international humanitaire coutumier, sur lequel cf. J.-M. Henckaerts et L. Doswald-Beck, *Droit international humanitaire coutumier*, Bruylant / Comité International de la Croix-Rouge, 2006.

est parfois contesté, notamment s'il émane d'instruments régionaux ou de Conventions qui ne sont pas universellement reconnues. Le CICR a tenté de faire reconnaître l'éclairage ainsi donné aux normes du DIH concernant la détention dans les CANI, à travers des travaux d'experts et un dialogue préalable avec de nombreux Etats, qui a notamment porté sur les garanties judiciaires liées à la détention administrative, sur les conditions de détention et sur le transfert de détenus. Une proposition dans ce sens a ensuite été soumise à la XXXIIème Conférence internationale de la Croix-Rouge et du Croissant-Rouge mais elle n'a reçu qu'un accueil mitigé[23].

En réalité, au-delà des querelles un peu stériles sur la question de la *lex specialis*, c'est bien sur des questions d'interprétation que se focalisent les oppositions, notamment en ce qui concerne le statut de certains membres des forces armées de la partie dissidente, sur celui des civils qui participent aux hostilités occasionnellement ou de manière plus régulière, sur la notion même de « participation directe » aux hostilités[24] ou sur le droit ou non d'utiliser la force en tout temps et sans toutes les précautions requises par le DIdH contre des civils qui ont participé directement aux hostilités. La situation est d'autant plus complexe que dans certaines situations les Etats sont confrontés simultanément à des opposants dans le cadre d'un conflit armé et à de puissants criminels de droit commun. Les moyens de lutte contre ces derniers sont indiscutablement balisés par les normes des droits de l'homme applicables au « law enforcement » mais comme les militaires engagés peuvent se trouver confrontés aux uns ou aux autres, il devient extrêmement complexe de rédiger pour ceux-ci des règles d'engagement qui tiennent compte de tous les paramètres et soient suffisamment simples pour être bien comprises par chacun. Les militaires se plaignent dès lors de la complexité induite en sus par les multiples nuances que l'on souhaite introduire dans le statut des différentes personnes engagées dans la lutte armée du côté des opposants. Plus que par des arguments théoriques, c'est sur la base de cas pratiques que l'on doit alors rechercher des solutions qui concilient le respect de normes fondamentales des droits de l'homme et la clarté des instructions adressées aux forces armées.

---

23 Voir « Le Renforcement du droit international humanitaire protégeant les personnes privées de liberté », Document établi par le Comité International de la Croix-Rouge pour la XXXIIème Conférence internationale de la Croix-Rouge et du Croissant-Rouge, Genève, 2015.

24 A ce sujet, voir notamment N. Melzer, *Guide interprétatif sur la participation directe aux hostilités*, ed., Comité International de la Croix-Rouge, Genève, 2009.

La concertation engagée avec des experts gouvernementaux pour clarifier les normes internationales applicables à la détention dans les CANI, mentionnée ci-dessus, a mis en lumière une autre réalité, la réticence toujours plus grande des Etats à reconnaître un statut à leurs opposants de l'intérieur, confortée par la dite « guerre au terrorisme » qui donne prétexte aux pays en proie à des conflits armés de placer tous leurs opposants sous cette étiquette. Cela nous rappelle l'ambiguïté originelle de droit des conflits armés non internationaux. Les Etats ont en effet accepté de reconnaître cette notion sur le plan de leurs obligations internationales mais sans s'interdire pour autant de poursuivre même les membres d'une partie à un conflit armé reconnu comme tel comme de simples criminels de droit commun sur le plan interne, pour le seul fait d'avoir pris les armes. De là vient le refus de considérer comme des « combattants » les membres des forces armées de cette dernière, ce statut étant lié à celui de prisonnier de guerre et à l'immunité qu'il confère au combattant capturé (sauf, bien sûr, s'ils ont commis des crimes de guerre, il convient de le rappeler). Il y a donc une sorte de « neutralité » sur le plan international par rapport à l'insurrection, le droit international ne s'intéressant qu'aux crimes internationaux qui peuvent être commis dans le cadre d'un conflit armé, que ce soit par la partie gouvernementale ou par la partie dissidente, mais pas à l'insurrection en tant que telle. Sans qu'on l'ait formellement exprimé, cette neutralité se justifie par le fait que la communauté internationale ne se penche qu'avec très peu de rigueur sur la légitimité démocratique des gouvernements et sur les garanties que ceux-ci peuvent donner quant au respect des droits de l'homme. La raison principale expliquant cette attitude est évidemment celle de la souveraineté nationale, qui reste le fondement sur lequel repose le droit international, toute tentative de la restreindre étant perçue avec d'autant plus de réserve que derrière cette barrière formelle s'abritent nombre de gouvernements qui sont loin d'être irréprochables. L'absence de condamnation *a priori* de l'insurrection – contrairement à l'agression sur le plan international – est donc le corolaire logique du manque de rigueur de la communauté internationale dans l'analyse de la « qualité » des gouvernements des Etats qui la composent.

Sous la pression des horreurs commises pendant la Seconde Guerre mondiale ou dans diverses guerres civiles et dans la foulée de la Déclaration universelle des droits de l'homme, les Etats ont finalement accepté de faire un pas vers leurs opposants dans les CANI en reconnaissant l'existence d'obligations spécifiques lors de tels conflits. Mais ils l'ont fait avec beaucoup de prudence et ont atténué la portée de cette concession par deux exigences qu'ils ont estimées essentielles : d'une part le statut de partie à un CANI ne devait pas devenir une incitation à la rébellion et il était de ce fait indispensable pour les Etats de se garder le droit de criminaliser celle-ci en droit interne. D'autre part ce statut devait rester strictement limité au cadre des conflits armés et du DIH et n'ouvrir aucune porte à la partie dissidente vers un statut dans un autre domaine, ce qui a été précisé dans les textes conventionnels[25].

Ces soucis restent plus présents aujourd'hui que jamais et expliquent, pour une bonne part, la réticence montrée par certains Etats à vouloir développer encore, ou même simplement préciser davantage, le DIH applicable aux CANI. En introduisant plus profondément la dimension des droits de l'homme dans le DIH, on augmenterait les obligations, mais donc aussi les droits, de la partie dissidente. Témoin d'une réunion qui s'est déroulée dans ce cadre, j'ai pu constater que même les représentants des Etats les plus favorables au projet du CICR concernant la détention dans les CANI, disposés à se reconnaître des obligations plus étendues, ou en tout cas plus précises, dans ce domaine, ne raisonnaient plus dans le cadre du DIH, également applicable aux deux parties. Leur droit interne prohibant toute détention par la partie dissidente, ils excluaient de développer les obligations de celle-ci dans ce domaine et, *a fortiori* les règles concernant les garanties judiciaires. Ils en oubliaient que le PA II a pourtant déjà introduit des règles dans ces deux domaines et cette attitude laisse penser qu'il n'est pas du tout certain que les Etat auraient accepté de telles règles aujourd'hui.

Ceux qui ont le souci estimable d'améliorer la condition des détenus par des règles du DIH qui deviendraient plus précises et contraignantes du fait de l'éclairage donné par le DIdH doivent donc rester conscients que le mieux est parfois l'ennemi du bien. En fixant des exigences que ne peuvent satisfaire la partie dissidente dans la majorité des cas, ils mettent en péril le principe de l'égalité des parties au conflit sur lequel repose le DIH : plutôt qu'éclairer celui-ci, le DIdH risquerait de l'étouffer.

Ne serait-il pas dès lors préférable de considérer le DIdH dans ce domaine non pas comme un éclairage du DIH mais comme un complément autonome ? Dans ce dernier cas on pourrait plus facilement considérer positivement des précisions qui permettraient d'augmenter le niveau d'exigence dans le domaine de la détention auprès des Etats – les conditions de celle-ci et les garanties judiciaires des détenus étant encore très insuffisantes dans nombre d'entre eux – sans pour autant remettre en cause le principe de l'égalité des parties en DIH.

---

25 Voir l'article 3 commun des Conventions de Genève de 1949, dernier al. ; et l'article 3 du Protocole II additionnel aux Conventions de Genève, 1977.

Certes, d'aucuns préconisent l'applicabilité du DIdH également à la partie dissidente d'un CANI, avec de bons arguments[26]. Mais pour l'heure la majorité des Etats combat cette approche, par peur de donner une reconnaissance trop grande aux rebelles. En développant les exigences de la détention sous le seul angle du DIdH, les Etats auraient l'avantage de ne plus entrer en matière sur la détention éventuelle par les parties dissidentes mais ne pourraient pas non plus, sans se contredire, poser comme condition l'observation de règles aussi détaillées par celles-ci.

Reste à préciser tout de même ce qui est exigé par le DIH en matière de détention, y compris des parties dissidentes. Comme on vient de le relever, à vouloir fixer à celles-ci des exigences trop élevées, on leur couperait toute possibilité de garder des détenus en respectant les exigences du DIH, avec le risque que ces groupes armés renoncent alors à détenir qui que ce soit. On comprend aisément ce que cela signifierait. Il est dès lors important de poursuivre le dialogue avec ceux-ci et le travail entrepris sur le terrain par le CICR et d'autres organisations humanitaires et, de manière plus globale et structurée, par l'Organisation non gouvernementale « l'Appel de Genève »[27], est essentiel à cet égard. Il s'agirait en l'occurrence de parvenir avec les Groupes armés dissidents à un accord sur une interprétation « *feasible* » (comme l'on dit en anglais) des dispositions du DIH concernant les conditions de détention, insistant sur l'interdiction de tout mauvais traitement, sur le droit à des soins et à une nourriture de qualité égale à ceux de leur détenteur, à un logement décent, à des relations avec les familles, au moins par des messages, à la possibilité de pratiquer des exercices physiques et intellectuels, bref, en s'inspirant des dispositions détaillées de la 3ème CdG à ce sujet.

Reste le problème de la durée de la détention. Dans les conflits armés internationaux, aucune limite n'est fixée pour les prisonniers de guerre valides, sinon la fin des hostilités. Les défenseurs des droits de l'homme ont, à raison, souhaité soulever le problème dans les CANI et soumettre toute détention non liée à une condamnation pénale aux strictes règles de la détention administrative. Or l'article 3 commun des CdG demande aux parties à un CANI de s'efforcer de « mettre en vigueur, par voie d'accords spéciaux, tout ou partie des autres dispositions » des CdG. Le statut de prisonniers de guerre – même si c'est très improbable dans le climat actuel – pourrait donc théoriquement être agréé sur cette base. Cela impliquerait une détention certes plus confortable,

---

26 En ce sans cf. notamment A. Clapham, *Human Rights Obligations of Non-State Actors*, Oxford University Press, 2006.

27 Pour plus de précisions sur le travail de cette ONG, basée à Genève, on peut consulter son site : http://www.genevacall.org/.

mais qui pourrait se prolonger jusqu'à la fin des hostilités sans révision de sa justification. Dans ce cas spécifique, on peut dès lors légitimement se demander si une évolution coutumière n'a pas donné préséance aux DIdH et si les règles détaillées de celui-ci sur la détention administrative ne devraient pas prévaloir.

En réalité, s'il est un point où le DIH pourrait être amendé, c'est bien celui-ci. Tant les CANI que les CAI ayant tendance à s'étendre sur de très longues périodes, la détention d'une durée indéfinie tend, même dans les seconds, à faire un supplice du statut pourtant très favorable en apparence de prisonnier de guerre. Une limite de durée devrait donc être fixée dans l'un et l'autre type de conflit, au terme de laquelle le principe de la libération serait posé, sauf exceptions dûment justifiées. Le CICR a négocié à plusieurs reprises, en tant qu'intermédiaire neutre, une libération anticipée des prisonniers ayant passé de nombreuses années en détention, mais c'était à bien plaire et le principe d'une telle libération devrait être inscrit dans le DIH.

Quant aux garanties judiciaires, illusoires dans la plupart des cas du côté de la partie dissidente, il conviendrait surtout d'insister, sinon sur l'abolition de la peine capitale, au moins sur le gel de toute exécution pendant le conflit. De telles exécutions ne peuvent en effet qu'entraîner les deux parties dans une spirale négative hors de tout contrôle.

Même si cela reste plutôt rare, il arrive certes qu'une partie dissidente contrôle un territoire pendant une certaine durée, qu'elle dispose d'une structure et de moyens qui lui permettent de fonctionner quasiment comme un Etat, de disposer d'hôpitaux, d'écoles, de tribunaux, et de satisfaire de manière satisfaisante aux strictes exigences du DIdH. On peut alors se demander s'il ne serait pas souhaitable de mieux identifier ce type de conflits, qui ont même un seuil plus élevé que celui du PA II de 1977 et qui correspondent à ceux qu'envisageait Emer de Vattel quand il parlait de guerres civiles[28]. L'applicabilité du DIdH préconisée par certains auteurs serait certainement envisageables pour ces entités, qui devraient faire l'objet d'une sorte de large « reconnaissance de belligérance » de la part de la communauté internationale. La conséquence logique en serait de donner à ces entités l'occasion de se présenter et de s'expliquer devant les Institutions des droits de l'homme et de leur accorder le

---

28 « La guerre civile rompt les liens de la société et du gouvernement, ou elle en suspend au moins la force et l'effet ; elle donne naissance dans la Nation à deux partis indépendans (sic) qui se regardent comme ennemis. [...]. Il faut donc de nécessité que ces deux partis soient considérés comme formant désormais, au moins pour un temps, deux corps séparés, deux peuples différents », de Vattel, *op. cit.*, note 7, par. 293.

bénéfice du soutien, dans le domaine de la santé ou de l'éducation, d'Organisations internationales telles que l'OMS ou l'UNESCO. Même limitée à de tels conflits, cette approche n'a toutefois guère de chance d'être aujourd'hui suivie, tant est grande la crainte de la plupart des Etats d'élever ne serait-ce que la stature de partie dissidente sur le plan international, sinon son statut.

Conclusions

Il y a aujourd'hui un écart flagrant entre le contenu des négociations sur des développements éventuels du DIH et la réalité des conflits armés sur le terrain, que ce soit en Syrie, en Irak, en Lybie au Congo, au Soudan ou au Sud Soudan, sans parler du conflit israélo-palestinien et de nombreux autres conflits dans le monde. Il ne s'agit pas de se décourager mais de rechercher des solutions pratiques qui préservent l'essentiel, l'intégrité et la dignité des personnes prises dans la tourmente de ces situations. Pour ce faire le dialogue ne saurait se limiter aux seuls Etats et doit inclure, d'une manière ou d'une autre, les parties dissidentes à des CANI.

Il faut toutefois être conscient que le DIH atteint les limites de ce que l'on peut attendre de lui. Ce n'est donc pas tant dans la recherche de nouvelles normes que dans une rigueur plus grande dans leur application, et dans le contrôle de celle-ci, qu'il faut avant tout progresser. Mais ce faisant, on ne saurait oublier que le DIH n'a qu'un rôle marginal dans la Société internationale et que c'est à une profonde réforme du fonctionnement de celle-ci qu'il faut s'atteler en priorité. Plus que jamais dans l'histoire, le renforcement du droit international s'impose pour protéger la planète contre des atteintes irréversibles et, par là aussi, l'humanité tout entière. Les normes dans le domaine de la gestion des ressources naturelles et de la protection de l'environnement doivent impérativement devenir plus contraignantes et cela ne pourra se faire sans certaines restrictions à la souveraineté nationale. L'afflux de réfugiés qui déstabilise les Etats doit par ailleurs faire d'une part l'objet d'une plus grande solidarité en vue de répartir le fardeau que cela représente ; d'autre part d'un regard moins complaisant de la communauté internationale sur les gouvernements dont le comportement incite leurs citoyens à s'exiler.

C'est donc bien à un renversement du constat de Hersch Lauterpacht mentionné en début de cet article qu'il faut tendre. Les valeurs que le DIH cherche à préserver jusqu'au cœur des conflits armés – la compassion pour ceux qui souffrent, le respect de la dignité humaine, la solidarité – sont un socle sur lequel doit se développer le droit international impératif, ayant prévalence sur les droits nationaux.

Quant au DIH, on doit certes chercher à le préserver et à le renforcer autant que faire se peut dans les conflits armés aussi longtemps qu'il y en aura. Mais on ne peut qu'espérer le voir s'estomper dans un monde enfin pacifié ou craindre de le voir sombrer dans le chaos.

L'espace humanitaire : un passage souhaitable de la pratique au droit ?

Sandra Szurek

C'est sous le signe des espaces que je souhaite placer cet hommage. En premier lieu en raison, sans doute, du souvenir le plus ancien mais toujours vif que je garde de Djamchid Momtaz, lorsque, jeune assistante fraîchement nommée à l'Université Paris Nanterre, je fis sa connaissance dans les années soixante-dix. J'eus alors la grande chance, en franchissant pour la première fois le seuil de la salle dite « des assistants », d'y rencontrer comme premier collègue, Djamchid. Son accueil chaleureux et bienveillant a suffi à sceller une forme d'amitié perpétuelle indifférente au temps et à la distance. Partant de l'idée d'espace, il m'a semblé que nous pouvions partager un intérêt scientifique commun pour l'espace humanitaire. C'est à donc à ce dernier que je voudrais consacrer quelques réflexions en hommage au spécialiste du droit international humanitaire qu'est Djamchid Momtaz.

L'idée d'espace humanitaire remonte aux civilisations les plus anciennes qui ont consacré l'existence de lieux où les populations et les combattants pouvaient trouver momentanément refuge et protection. Les temples antiques, les églises de la Chrétienté étaient des espaces sanctuarisés. Cette protection répondait à la nécessité, à défaut de vouloir puis de pouvoir l'interdire, de ne pas laisser la guerre détruire jusqu'à la dernière part d'humanité, comme le réaffirmera plus tard la clause de Martens. Héritières de ces traditions, les Conventions de Genève de 1949 ont consacré l'idée, qu'au cœur même des champs de bataille, devaient exister et être respectés des lieux et des espaces dévolus aux secours aux blessés, à la protection des non-combattants et de la population civile.

Mais la notion d'espace humanitaire n'apparaît comme telle ni dans les Conventions de Genève ni dans les Protocoles additionnels. L'expression relève de la pratique. On en attribue la paternité à Ronny Brauman qui l'a définie comme « un espace symbolique, hors duquel l'action humanitaire se trouve détachée de son fondement éthique et qui se constitue à l'intérieur des repères suivants: accès, dialogue, indépendance, impartialité »[1]. De nombreuses autres définitions ont été proposées, comme celle d'« un espace de liberté d'intervention civile, caractérisée par certains principes et normes tels que ceux contenus

---

1 R. Brauman, *Humanitaires, le dilemme, Entretien avec Philippe Petit*, Paris Textuel, 1996, p. 43.

dans la Charte humanitaire »[2], ou encore, selon une approche fonctionnelle, comme « [...] le champ d'opérations rendues possible (et délimité) grâce à un faisceau de paramètres parmi lesquels: la possibilité d'évaluer les besoins, celle de gérer et contrôler les opérations identifiées, la liberté d'accès et d'échange avec les populations »[3].

La notion d'espace humanitaire soulevant les questions les plus complexes dans le cadre des conflits amés, on s'en tiendra à ces situations. Le Comité international de la Croix-Rouge (CICR) ou le Haut Commissariat des Nations Unies aux Réfugiés (UNHCR) y font de plus en plus fréquemment référence pour s'inquiéter de sa « réduction » ou encore de son « rétrécissement », comme du phénomène contemporain le plus inquiétant. Ainsi, à l'instar des craintes que peuvent susciter les menaces pesant sur un espace naturel, l'espace humanitaire, indéterminé, « complexe mais fondamental »[4], est menacé. En écho à ce constat, le Vice-Secrétaire général de l'Organisation des Nations Unies (ONU) se déclarait récemment « horrifié » par le mépris « alarmant » pour les droits de l'homme et le droit international humanitaire de cette deuxième décennie du XXIème siècle[5].

Dans ce contexte chaotique de remise en cause ou de négation de normes chèrement acquises, que peut le juriste ? Certains ont comparé le droit à la médecine : « [o]n observe ce qui ne va pas pour poser des diagnostics et identifier des remèdes »[6]. C'est peut-être trop prêter au juriste. On peut pourtant s'inspirer de cette démarche en trois temps pour les quelques remarques qui suivent et qui n'ont pour ambition, dans les limites imparties ici, que d'esquisser, à travers l'idée d'espace humanitaire, une réflexion sur quelques-uns des défis que le droit international humanitaire et plus largement l'action humanitaire doivent relever.

---

2 F. Audet, « L'acteur humanitaire en crise existentielle. Les défis du nouvel espace humanitaire », *Etudes internationales*, vol. 42, n° 4, 2011, p. 447-472, p. 448. La Charte humanitaire et les normes minimales pour les interventions lors de catastrophes est le fruit du Projet Sphere, lancé en 1997 par différentes ONG humanitaires et le Mouvement de la Croix-Rouge et du Croissant-Rouge, dans le but d'élaborer un ensemble de normes universelles minimales dans les domaines fondamentaux de l'assistance humanitaire.

3 M. L. Le Coconnier, B. Pommier, *L'action humanitaire*, Que Sais-je ?, PUF, 2ème édition mise à jour, 2012, 127 p., p. 21.

4 Audet, *op. cit.*, note 2, p. 448.

5 Nations Unies, J. Eliasson, « Dix ans de responsabilité de protéger : face à un bilan mitigé, les Etats membres examinent les moyens de mieux préserver les civils des pires atrocités », Assemblée générale, Couverture des réunions, 26 février 2016, AG/11764.

6 A. Supiot, « Introduction », p. 9-35, p. 21, A. Supiot et M. Delmas-Marty (Dir.), *Prendre la responsabilité au sérieux*, PUF 2015, 430 p.

On se propose donc, dans la ligne tracée par le titre-même de ces Mélanges, de procéder à un examen clinique de l'espace humanitaire (I); de tenter de poser un diagnostic sur les maux qui l'affectent (II), avant d'envisager l'intérêt que pourrait présenter une appréhension de l'espace humanitaire comme espace de droit (III).

1   L'examen clinique : un espace en voie de « rétrécissement » ?

Le constat d'un « rétrécissement » de l'espace humanitaire[7] paraît d'autant plus alarmant que les besoins en aide humanitaire sont plus importants que jamais. On a évalué, en 2016, à quelques 125 millions, les femmes, hommes et enfants qui relèvent d'une aide humanitaire. La durée et l'extrême âpreté du conflit syrien où l'aide humanitaire connaît des difficultés majeures influent aussi sur cette perception très pessimiste.

Mais le phénomène remonte à plus d'une dizaine d'années. Il tient à l'insécurité croissante dans laquelle les actions humanitaires sont condamnées à se déployer et aux menaces qui pèsent sur elles. Le 19 août est la date de la célébration de la Journée humanitaire mondiale. C'est aussi la Journée de commémoration du personnel des Nations Unies en mémoire de l'attentat contre le Bureau des Nations Unies en Irak en 2003[8]. Il fut suivi par l'attentat du 27 octobre 2003 contre le siège de la délégation du CICR à Bagdad, où avait été utilisé un véhicule piégé marqué de l'emblème protecteur reconnu par 191 Etats. Comme on l'a souligné « le logo, le mandat et le drapeau ne protègent plus »[9]. Cette violence atteint tous les acteurs de l'espace humanitaire, qu'il s'agisse du CICR dont le siège dans les zones de conflit subit régulièrement des attaques et dont plusieurs des collaborateurs ont été enlevés, blessés ou tués[10], tout comme l'ont été les membres des sociétés nationales, en Syrie en particulier,

---

7   Dont il convient de préciser d'emblée qu'il n'est pas unanimement partagé. D'aucuns le trouvent en effet très exagéré. Voir dans ce sens, « Shrinking Humanitarian Space », avec en particulier les remarques de S. Beauchamp, *On the Edges of Conflict*. Conference Report, Liu Institute for Global Issues, Canadian Red Cross, 2007, p. 20. En quelques années la situation s'est cependant nettement détériorée.

8   Lequel avait coûté la vie à 22 personnes dont Sergio Vieira de Mello alors Haut Commissaire des Nations Unies aux droits de l'homme et représentant spécial du Secrétaire général en Irak.

9   Le Coconnier, Pommier, *op. cit.*, note 3, p. 25.

10 G. Doucet, « La spécificité du CICR dans l'action humanitaire », p. 242, A. Biad (Dir.), *L'action humanitaire internationale entre le droit et la pratique*, col. Droit et Justice, n° 112, 2016, Némésis, Anthémis, Bruxelles, 270 p., p. 239-248.

ceux des ONG, ou encore des personnels des opérations de maintien de la paix de l'ONU. Les formes d'insécurité sont diverses : actes de banditisme, destructions des infrastructures et pillage de matériels, kidnapping, viols, mais aussi propagande anti humanitaire.

L'ampleur que prennent certaines violations du droit international humanitaire font craindre de façon plus inquiétante le rejet ou la négation même de ses règles. Semblent en témoigner la recrudescence des attaques graves contre les lieux de soins et de santé et les personnels médicaux, historiquement la première forme d'action humanitaire du champ de bataille sur laquelle la communauté des Etats s'est accordée[11]. D'une étude menée en 2012-2013, il résulte qu'il y a eu plus de 1200 incidents affectant les soins de santé et l'accès à ces soins, 112 tués parmi les professions médicales et environ 250 cas d'attaques d'ambulances et de refus d'accès aux patients[12]. Certaines violations du droit international humanitaire témoignent en outre de la part des belligérants d'un détournement ou d'un dévoiement de certaines de ses règles, sciemment utilisées par les combattants comme moyens et méthodes de combat. Les pratiques de viols systématiques ne sont que trop connues. Mais il peut y avoir aussi des attaques contre des infrastructures vitales[13]. Le conflit qui ravage la Syrie depuis six ans est particulièrement illustratif de cette dégradation et de la multiplication des violations que l'on enregistre. Plus de quatre millions de personnes vivant dans des zones difficiles d'accès et 400 000 d'entre elles dans des zones assiégées, n'ont eu qu'un accès limité, voire inexistant aux biens et services de première nécessité, alors que l'interdiction d'utiliser la famine contre les civils comme méthode de guerre est reconnue comme une règle coutumière[14] que conforte le droit international des droits de l'homme. Les

---

11   Voir la toute Première Convention de Genève d'août 1864, pour l'amélioration du sort des militaires blessés dans les armées en campagne, adoptée lors de la Conférence diplomatique du 22 août 1864.

12   Doucet, *op. cit.*, note 10, p. 245.

13   Comme certains aéroports au Yémen, par exemple, par les forces de la Coalition, alors que ce pays en dépend presqu'entièrement pour ses importations de nourriture et de médicaments. Voir Comité International de la Croix-Rouge, Communiqué de presse du 4 mai 2015, « Yémen : le CICR et MSF s'alarment des attaques menées contre les voies d'approvisionnement vitales pour le pays ».

14   Voir J.-M. Henckaerts et L. Doswald-Beck, *Droit international humanitaire coutumier*, Comité International de la Croix-Rouge et Cambridge University Press, version française, Editions Bruylant, Règle 43.

lieux de refuge universellement consacrés comme les écoles, les hôpitaux et les temples sont à leur tour devenus des cibles[15].

Ainsi, derrière le constat accablant d'humanitaires et travailleurs sanitaires enlevés et assassinés, d'installations médicales et d'ambulances pillées et détruites dans le cadre de tactiques de guerre[16], le Secrétaire général des Nations Unies dénonce l'érosion, partout dans le monde, du respect du droit international humanitaire et du droit international des droits de l'homme, « foulés aux pieds de façon éhontée et brutale »[17].

Ce constat conduit donc à se demander de quels maux ou de quels désordres la désintégration de l'espace humanitaire serait la manifestation.

2   Le diagnostic : un espace en perte d'identité ?

L'espace humanitaire semble souffrir d'une perte d'identité, largement due au contexte des conflits armés de plus en plus complexes et confus dans lesquels il s'inscrit. Les conflits armés internes ont muté en conflits déstructurés tout en s'installant parfois dans une très longue durée[18]. La fragmentation des forces en présence en un nombre important et fluctuant de groupes armés opérant alliances ou recompositions est telle qu'il devient très difficile d'avoir une compréhension claire, face à la multiplicité des protagonistes, des causes du conflit et de ses enjeux. Parmi ces divers groupes, certains recourent sciemment à la terreur contre les populations civiles comme méthodes de combat. Les forces gouvernementales doublées parfois de diverses milices ne sont pas épargnées par ce phénomène de fragmentation. Mouvantes, les zones de conflit font place à un nombre élevé de protagonistes, souvent bien éloignés de la notion de combattants selon le droit de Genève, auxquels on ne sait quel qualificatif appliquer : groupes rebelles, groupes terroristes, bandes armées, groupes mafieux armés...[19]

---

15   J. Egeland, « Les 3P de l'humanitaire : protection, principes et proximité. Pourquoi l'aide continue de passer à côté de l'essentiel », *IRIN, l'Info au cœur des crises*, Voir site Internet.

16   ONU, *Une seule humanité, des responsabilités partagées*, Rapport du Secrétaire général pour le Sommet mondial sur l'action humanitaire, Assemblée générale, Doc. A/70/709, 2 février 2016, par. 47, p. 16.

17   Ibid., par. 46, p. 15.

18   Pour une analyse des défis posés à l'action humanitaire par ce genre de conflits, voir F. Grünewald et L. Tessier, « Zones grises, crises durables, conflits oubliés : les défis humanitaires », *Revue Internationale de la Croix-Rouge*, vol. 83, n° 842, 2001, p. 323-351.

19   On trouvera une présentation concise et très éclairante de ce phénomène qui n'a rien de récent dans le document préparatoire de la Croix-Rouge pour la première réunion

Mais la perte d'identité tient aussi à d'autres facteurs qui n'ont rien de nouveau et ont été régulièrement dénoncés par les acteurs humanitaires. Depuis que l'espace humanitaire, surtout en tant qu'espace dispensateur d'aide aux populations civiles, a été investi par des Etats, des organisations militaires, l'OTAN en l'occurrence, les forces de maintien de la paix dans le cadre d'opérations multidimensionnelles onusiennes à volet humanitaire, et dernièrement par le Conseil de sécurité lui-même avec la mise en œuvre de la responsabilité de protéger en Libye, sans oublier les sociétés privées de sécurité, appelées dans certains cas à assurer la protection des convois humanitaires, la confusion est à son comble. Nombre d'acteurs des conflits armés basculent ainsi d'une fonction militaire en prise avec la situation politico-militaire d'un Etat (le maintien ou le rétablissement de la paix) à une fonction humanitaire d'assistance, intégrant parfois un droit de riposte « robuste », c'est-à-dire armée, pour protéger les populations[20]. Pour mener ce jeu de basculement d'une fonction à l'autre, alors qu'elles peuvent paraître totalement antinomiques, les Etats ont été dénoncés par les « Humanitaires », tout comme l'ont été ces pratiques alternant intervention armée et aide humanitaire, ou mêlant les deux. Mais l'action « humanitaire » des Nations Unies a été également particulièrement critiquée[21]. C'est à cet activisme militaro-humanitaire étatique que l'on impute en particulier la perte d'autorité et de crédibilité des principes de l'action humanitaire fondée sur l'indépendance, la neutralité et la non-discrimination.

A la confusion des acteurs, des mandats et des fonctions on peut ajouter d'autres facteurs plus récents révélateurs de profondes mutations. On évoquera rapidement et pêle-mêle, les finalités mêmes de l'action humanitaire entre urgence et action à long terme en faveur du développement; les intérêts économiques et les activités entrepreneuriales que cet espace a générés; enfin le double phénomène de la transformation des villes en champs de bataille avec les dégâts d'infrastructures considérables, en plus des pertes dans la population

---

périodique sur le droit international humanitaire, des 19-23 janvier 1998, « Les conflits armés liés à la désintégration des structures de l'Etat », site internet du CICR, https://www.icrc.org/fre/resources/documents/misc/5fzfn9.htm.

20 On peut se reporter à une analyse de ces différents éléments dans les documents de l'Office du Haut Commissaire des Nations Unies pour les Réfugiés. Voir notamment *Note sur la protection internationale*, Comité exécutif du Programme du Haut-Commissaire, Comité permanent, EC/61/SC/CRP.10, 2010, par. 4 et suivants, p. 3 et 4.

21 Voir par exemple S. Brunel, « Les Nations Unies et l'humanitaire : un bilan mitigé », *Politique étrangère*, Institut Français des Relations Internationales, 2005, vol. 70, n° 2, p. 313-325.

civile d'un côté, et de l'autre, l'urbanisation de l'espace humanitaire[22], du fait de l'expansion urbaine engendrée par les conflits entraînant un mélange de pauvreté, de destruction et de précarité. Ceci rendra plus difficile la distinction entre les conflits formels et d'autres situations de violence, tout en posant la question du seuil du passage de ces situations à celle de crise humanitaire.

Que tirer de ce diagnostic ? La protection de l'espace humanitaire doit-elle passer par son adaptation aux évolutions de l'ordre international et plus sûrement par sa reconnaissance comme un espace spécifique régi par le droit ?

3   Le « remède » : la reconnaissance de l'espace humanitaire comme espace de droit ?

La « réduction » ou le « rétrécissement » de l'espace humanitaire montrent-ils les limites du système humanitaire international ? L'idée, sinon d'une « refondation », du moins d'une remobilisation autour de « la sauvegarde de l'Humanité » et du « progrès humain »[23] est l'objectif que le Secrétaire général a voulu assigner au premier Sommet mondial de l'action humanitaire organisé par les Nations Unies à Istanbul les 23 et 24 mai 2016[24]. Pour le Secrétaire général, l'ambition est de mettre l'humanité « au cœur des prises de décision au niveau mondial ». Dans cette perspective, l'espace humanitaire peut être tenu pour un espace vital à promouvoir et à protéger.

Mais la solution est-elle, comme on le préconise régulièrement, d'en appeler au retour à un « espace humanitaire non politisé » où les principes de neutralité, d'impartialité et d'indépendance retrouveraient la pureté de leurs origines ? L'ensemble des pratiques étatiques et institutionnelles internationales de ces dernières décennies permettent d'en douter. Est-ce même souhaitable ? L'inscription au titre des menaces à la paix et à la sécurité internationales des violations graves du droit international humanitaire à l'égard des populations civiles et les actions qu'elles peuvent autoriser, de la part des Nations Unies ou

---

22   « Le milieu urbain », les villes, sont devenues elles-mêmes des espaces de refuge et des espaces humanitaires. Voir P. Garson, « La nouvelle expression à la mode dans les cercles humanitaires », *IRIN, au coeur des crises*, New York, 2015. Site Internet. La population urbaine des pays pauvres et fragiles a augmenté de 326% ces 40 dernières années, tendance qui devrait se poursuivre en Asie et en Afrique, d'après le Centre de surveillance des déplacements internes (IDMC).

23   ONU, Rapport du Secrétaire général, *op. cit.*, note 16, par. 7, p. 4.

24   Ce rassemblement s'est tenu après trois ans de consultations qui ont touché 23 000 personnes dans 153 pays et dont les principales conclusions ont été consignées dans un rapport préparatoire : *Restoring Humanity : Global Voices Calling for Action*, ibid., par. 9, p. 5.

des Etats habilités par le Conseil de sécurité, constituent, dans leur principe, une évolution positive de l'ordre international, même si la réalisation en reste imparfaite et souvent critiquable.

Compte tenu de cette dernière, il s'agirait plutôt de trouver les voies et moyens d'ordonner et de rendre compatibles les relations entre une action humanitaire indispensable et conforme aux principes qui la régissent, et les diverses exigences du maintien de la paix et de la sécurité internationales, avec les conséquences qu'elles peuvent emporter[25]. Mais faut-il, pour cela, recourir à l'idée d'espace humanitaire? Certains auteurs ne le pensent pas, et en recommandent au contraire l'abandon. Comme ils le soulignent, « [b]y conflating a range of largely disconnected phenomena under this single heading, humanitarian organizations have generated an unnecessarily gloomy outlook of the prospects for effective humanitarian operations. This conflation is a barrier to analyzing and responding to the very real challenge of security and access facing humanitarian organizations ». Et de conclure: « [t]here is times when adopting concepts that consolidate disparate trends into an overarching framework can be useful, but this is not one of them »[26].

On serait porté à considérer, au contraire, que le concept d'espace humanitaire peut constituer le cadre d'analyse[27] de situations extrêmement différentes, d'ordonnancement des relations entre des domaines qui se sont développés sans faire pour autant l'objet d'une attention suffisante quant à leurs interrelations, positives aussi bien que négatives, et de réflexion sur les adaptations nécessaires. Mais ceci suppose de conduire sur le concept d'espace humanitaire, à côté de la réflexion menée par les acteurs de l'aide humanitaire qui en ont leur propre conception[28], une recherche plus générale détachée de l'attraction exclusive du droit international humanitaire.

---

25 Le Comité International de la Croix-Rouge, gardien entre tous de ces principes, mène d'ailleurs depuis longtemps une réflexion de cette nature. Voir R. Rana, « Contemporary challenges in the civil-military relationship: Complementarity or Incompatibility? », *Revue Internationale de la Croix-Rouge*, 2004, vol. 86, n° 855, p. 565-591.

26 C. Brassard-Boudreau, D. Hubert, « Shrinking Humanitarian Space? Trends et Prospects on Security and Access », *The Journal of Humanitarian Assistance*, 2010, https://sites.tufts.zdu/jha/archives/863, Conclusions, point 8, p. 10. Consulté le 22 janvier 2016.

27 Voir dans ce sens B. Megevand-Roggo, « Après la crise du Kosovo, un véritable espace humanitaire : une utopie peu réaliste ou une condition essentielle ? », *Revue Internationale de la Croix-Rouge*, n° 837, 2000. « After the Kosovo Conflict, a genuine humanitarian space: An utopian concept or an essential requirement? ».

28 Pour les différentes acceptions de l'espace humanitaire, voir Brassard-Boudreau, Hubert, *op. cit.*, note 26, p. 1-2.

La grande diversité de mise en œuvre d'actions humanitaires, comme on l'a vu, a pour conséquence de soumettre l'espace humanitaire, en tant qu'*espace juridique*, à différents corps de règles, en complément et en appui du droit international humanitaire et du droit international des réfugiés. L'influence du droit international des droits de l'homme a été largement démontrée et consacrée par la jurisprudence[29]. Mais on ne peut plus ignorer l'apport normatif du Conseil de sécurité en particulier en ce qui concerne la protection des populations civiles dans les conflits armés[30] et plus généralement l'incidence des mesures adoptées au titre du maintien de la paix et de la sécurité internationales. Il n'est pas jusqu'au droit international général, en particulier en ce qui concerne le régime de responsabilité et celui des sanctions qui ne puisse être mobilisé. Cet espace physique et symbolique[31] est également un *espace de droit* qui appelle donc le renforcement et le développement, selon les cas, des règles nécessaires à l'accomplissement de ses finalités.

Si l'on adopte de l'espace humanitaire une définition tautologique, il peut être compris très simplement comme l'espace au sein duquel doit être mis en œuvre un mandat d'action humanitaire lequel consiste à porter protection et assistance aux victimes des conflits et en particulier aux population civiles[32]. L'action humanitaire s'applique à un espace physique et humain dont les dimensions, la configuration, la temporalité, les besoins sont fonction de deux séries de facteurs : les circonstances qui déterminent la nécessité de sa constitution, comme *espace d'intervention* et les acteurs qui décident de sa constitution et définissent ses finalités comme *espace d'assistance*. Pour ce qui est des

---

29 Voir, notamment, CIJ, « Conséquences juridiques de l'édification d'un mur dans le territoire palestinien occupé », Avis consultatif, 9 juillet 2004, par. 106 ; Commission internationale d'enquête sur le Darfour, rapport au Secrétaire général de l'ONU, 2005, par. 143 ; Comité des droits de l'homme des Nations Unies, Observation générale n° 31, CCPR/C/21Rev.1/Add.13(2004), par. 11. Des conventions des droits de l'homme portent également sur certains aspects humanitaires. C'est le cas, par exemple, de l'article 22 (1) de la Convention sur les droits de l'enfant qui traite de l'assistance et de l'accès humanitaire, de même que l'article 23 (1) de la Charte africaine sur les droits et le bien-être de l'enfant. Sur l'ensemble de ces règles voir également A.-T. Norodom, « La doctrine et le droit de l'action humanitaire : quelle contribution », Biad, *op. cit.*, note 10, p. 35-53.

30 On ne saurait énumérer ici toutes les résolutions du Conseil de sécurité consacrées au sujet. Voir pour une analyse approfondie, P. Lagrange, « 1674(2006) : Protection des civils dans les conflits armés », M. Albaret, E. Decaux, N. Lemay-Hebert, D. Placidi-Frot, *Les grandes résolutions du Conseil de sécurité des Nations unies*, Dalloz, Paris, 2012, p. 446-459.

31 Audet, *op. cit.*, note 2, p. 447-472, p. 448.

32 Ceci vaut évidemment aussi pour tous les autres types de catastrophes, selon leurs spécificités.

circonstances, ou des événements, ils sont peu nombreux, mais leur fréquence, leur complexité et leur gravité iront en augmentant sous l'effet d'un cumul de causes (conflits armés et catastrophes naturelles notamment). En ce qui concerne l'assistance, un même conflit peut avoir pour conséquence la constitution de multiples espaces humanitaires, comme on le voit avec le conflit syrien, par exemple : ceux qui visent à l'assistance aux victimes et à la protection des populations civiles dans le cadre du conflit-même; ceux qui assurent la protection des réfugiés dans les pays limitrophes ; ceux qu'espèrent ces mêmes réfugiés, émigrés dans des pays tiers très éloignés des zones de conflit et *a priori* étrangers à ce dernier. Le fondement juridique d'un droit à un espace humanitaire de protection est plus qu'incertain dans ce dernier cas, alors qu'il trouve ses fondements dans le droit international humanitaire dans le premier, sans que son respect soit pour autant garanti[33]. Si l'on prend le cas de l'intervention en Libye motivée par la responsabilité de protéger les populations civiles, non seulement l'espace d'intervention et les modalités de l'intervention ont été critiquées, mais l'assistance applicable à cet espace a manqué singulièrement d'approfondissement[34]. Rassembler les éléments d'un droit international de l'espace humanitaire susceptible d'être applicable à différentes situations relève aujourd'hui de l'urgence.

On a identifié quelques-unes des questions que soulève le « rétrécissement » de l'espace humanitaire : entraves à l'accès aux victimes ; non-respect des règles du droit international humanitaire relatives aux modalités et moyens de secours ; affaiblissement des grands principes fondamentaux guidant l'action humanitaire : indépendance ; neutralité ; impartialité.

En ce qui concerne l'obligation d'instituer un ou des espaces humanitaires selon les besoins, on sait qu'elle incombe en premier lieu à chaque Etat, sur le fondement de sa souveraineté[35]. L'obligation de protection de l'Etat territorial

---

[33] Sur la question des réfugiés en général et les problèmes rencontrés actuellement par le HCR, Voir l'analyse fouillée de J. Fischel De Andrade, « La contribution du Haut-Commissariat aux réfugiés », Biad (Dir.), *op. cit.*, note 10, p. 135-168.

[34] Sur ces points, on se permet de renvoyer à S. Szurek, « La responsabilité de protéger : du prospectif au prescriptif... et retour. La situation de la Libye devant le Conseil de sécurité », *Droits*, n°56, [*Après la Libye-Avant la Syrie?*] *L'ingérence. Le problème/1*, Paris, PUF, 2014, p. 59-96. Pour une analyse juridiquement logique des conséquences de la responsabilité de protéger, mais politiquement sans doute peu réaliste, voir, D. Momtaz, « L'adaptation du droit humanitaire à l'épreuve des opérations militaires motivées par la responsabilité de protéger », *La responsabilité de protéger*, Colloque de Nanterre, Société Française pour le Droit International, Paris, Pedone, 2008, p. 331-334.

[35] Il en va également ainsi dans le cas des catastrophes. Voir A.-T. Norodom, « La doctrine et le droit de l'action humanitaire : quelle contribution », Biad, *op. cit.*, note 10, p. 35-53, p. 39 et notes 9 et 10.

s'est trouvée réaffirmée à travers le principe de la responsabilité de protéger (R2P). Dans le cadre de la dimension préventive du principe, sur laquelle on met particulièrement l'accent aujourd'hui, on pourrait faire produire à la responsabilité de protéger un certain nombre d'obligations incombant au souverain territorial quant à la mise sur pied de structures et de personnels nationaux formés à cet effet, assorties de garanties relatives à l'indépendance, la neutralité et l'impartialité de leur action[36]. Lorsque l'aide extérieure s'avère nécessaire, ce même principe de responsabilité de protéger devrait logiquement contribuer à établir, sans plus de doute aujourd'hui, la règle de droit selon laquelle, comme l'a remarqué le Secrétaire général, « [l]es Etats ne peuvent rejeter comme bon leur semble les offres de secours humanitaires si des populations sont dans le besoin »[37], règle qui étendrait à l'ensemble de ces opérations l'obligation de motiver les mesures de limitation ou de refus d'accès. Certes le droit international humanitaire contient de nombreuses règles sur l'accès aux victimes et l'offre d'assistance humanitaire[38]. Mais ces règles sont moins développées dans le cadre des conflits armés non internationaux[39]. Et l'exemple récent du conflit syrien montre que le contrôle de l'accès à l'aide est aussi un moyen de combat.

L'obligation de respecter l'espace humanitaire s'étend aussi aux groupes armés non étatiques qui contrôlent un territoire considéré ou qui y opèrent. L'article 18(2) du PA II donne l'avantage à l'Etat sur les rebelles, mais le

---

36 Dans son rapport précité, le Secrétaire général souligne la « fierté » des autorités nationales qui ont investi dans la préparation aux catastrophes et « l'orgueil » des citoyens, intervenants locaux et groupes de la société civile qui ont contribué à la résilience, à la reconstruction et au renouveau de leurs collectivités. *Op. cit.*, note 16, par. 13, p. 5.

37 ONU, AG., Rapport du Secrétaire général, ibid, par. 56, p. 18.

38 C'est le cas des articles 3(2) commun aux 4 Conventions de Genève ; de l'article 10 et 59(2) de la Convention de Genève IV, du PA I, article 70(1) ; du PA II, article 18(1) et (2). Les opérations de secours, même une fois l'espace humanitaire constitué ou virtuellement constitué, sont soumises au consentement des parties concernées dans le cadre d'un CAI aux termes de l'article 70(1) du PAI de 1977. Voir F. Schwendimann, « Le cadre juridique de l'accès humanitaire dans les conflits armés », *Revue internationale de la Croix-Rouge*, vol. 93, 2011/3, Sélection française, p. 121-138, p. 126. Dans le même sens, H. Spieker, « *The right to give and receive humanitarian assistance* », H.-J. Heinze et A. Zwitter (Dir.), *International Law and Humanitarian Assistance: A Crosscut Through Legal Issues Pertaining to Humanitarism*, Ed. Springer, Berlin/Heildelberg, 2011, p. 13.

39 L'article 3 commun aux quatre Conventions de Genève ne dit rien de l'accès humanitaire, mais l'article 18(2) du Protocole additionnel II dispose que les actions de secours seront entreprises avec le consentement de l'Etat concerné, disposition confirmée par le droit coutumier, comme l'énonce la règle 55. Sur l'ensemble de cette question, Voir D. Momtaz, *Le droit international humanitaire applicable aux conflits armés non internationaux*, Recueil des Cours de l'Académie de droit international de la Haye, 2001, volume 292, p. 1-145, p. 83. Sur la question de l'acheminement de l'aide humanitaire, voir p. 81-88.

consentement de ces derniers est de fait nécessaire au passage et à la conduite des actions de secours, sans que cela vaille reconnaissance de ces groupes. Pour sa part, le Conseil de sécurité affirme de plus en plus nettement l'obligation de toutes les parties à un conflit, quel que soit leur statut, membres des forces armées, groupes rebelles, bandes armées et autres de respecter le droit international humanitaire[40].

Certaines règles, comme les droits des blessés et malades et le respect des lieux de soins, demandent à être réaffirmées. On a parlé d'épidémies d'attaques contre les établissements de santé. Le Secrétaire général des Nations Unies et le président du Comité international de la Croix-Rouge (CICR) ont lancé un avertissement conjoint le 31 octobre 2015 demandant notamment d'« [a]ssurer l'accès sans entrave aux missions médicales et humanitaires et de protéger les personnels et installations médicaux et humanitaires »[41]. Le Conseil de sécurité a entendu cet appel, à en juger par sa résolution 2286 (2016) du 3 mai 2016[42]. Après un très long préambule, le Conseil de sécurité exige des parties le respect de leurs obligations (par. 2), met l'accent au paragraphe 4 sur la prévention et la répression, en temps de conflit armé, des attaques et actes de violence à l'égard du personnel et matériel médical et humanitaire « dont l'activité est d'ordre strictement médical », en rappelant qu'il peut s'agir de crimes de guerre. Le Conseil en appelle aussi, notamment, à la mise sur pied de mécanismes nationaux appropriés destinés à garantir le respect des obligations en ce domaine, ainsi qu'au recueil des données sur les manœuvres d'obstruction, les menaces et les attaques contre les personnels concernés.

Si l'on peut douter que les Etats soient prêts à consentir des privilèges et immunités à ces personnels humanitaires dévoués aux soins de santé, le besoin de réaffirmer et de développer des règles plus spécifiques de protection existe, et en particulier la pénalisation dans les ordres internes étatiques de toutes les

---

40 F. Schwendimann, « Le cadre juridique de l'accès humanitaire dans les conflits armés », *Revue Internationale de la Croix-Rouge*, vol. 93, 2011/3, Sélection française, p. 121-138, p. 130 et note 42. Voir également A. Boinet, « Les contraintes humanitaires dans un contexte de conflit ou de catastrophe : Afghanistan, Irak, R.D.C., Soudan, Mali, Syrie », Biad (Dir.), *op. cit.*, note 10, p. 229-238.

41 Comité International de la Croix-Rouge, Communiqué de presse, 30 octobre 2015, « Un tournant pour la communauté internationale : les dirigeants de l'ONU et du Comité International de la Croix-Rouge lancent un avertissement conjoint », https://www.icrc .org/fr/document/un-tournant-pour-la-communaute-internationale-les. . . .

42 ONU, Conseil de sécurité, S/RES/2286 (2016). Celle-ci fait suite notamment aux résolutions 2175 (2014) et 1502 (2003) sur la protection du personnel humanitaire et à la résolution 1998 (2011) sur les attaques contre les écoles et les hôpitaux. L'Assemblée générale a consacré également certaines résolutions à ces sujets.

atteintes graves, au-delà de la Convention de New York sur la sécurité du personnel des Nations Unies et du personnel associé du 9 décembre 1994[43] et de son Protocole facultatif adopté à New York le 8 décembre 2005[44].

Depuis que les Etats et les organisations internationales ont investi le champ de l'action humanitaire, les principes sur lesquels celle-ci repose depuis les origines du Mouvement de la Croix-Rouge sont mis à mal. Leur restauration passerait peut-être par un effort de distinction, particulièrement auprès des populations, entre les actions étatiques et les actions non gouvernementales. S'agissant des actions étatiques, on ne peut se limiter à considérer qu'elles ne sont ni neutres, ni impartiales et indépendantes. Peut-être serait-il utile de dégager, pour les Etats et les organisations internationales, des principes spécifiques. La non-discrimination doit être un principe commun, quel que soit celui qui intervient. Mais on peut aussi penser à un principe de non-conditionnalité de l'aide à des motifs politiques en particulier. Dans un autre registre, le Dialogue entre les religions sur les valeurs que les différentes confessions peuvent partager avec celles du Mouvement humanitaire, entamé ces dernières années par le HCR, peut utilement contribuer à refonder la légitimité de l'espace humanitaire comme espace universel.

Le Secrétaire général des Nations Unies a fixé un objectif ambitieux. Selon lui, « [g]arantir le respect du droit international humanitaire et du droit international des droits de l'homme et la protection des civils doivent devenir des intérêts nationaux prioritaires des Etats Membres et des préoccupations centrales qui informent leurs politiques étrangères et le jeu des relations internationales »[45]. Le sommet d'Istanbul a mis en avant une nouvelle notion, celle d'un éco-système humanitaire qui donne la prévalence au local sur l'universel, se montre attentif aux équilibres au sein des différentes parties du système, mais aussi aux échanges entre ce système et le système plus global. Ces quelques réflexions semblent pouvoir s'inscrire dans cette démarche. Le juriste n'est pas un médecin : il n'a guère de remèdes. Tout au plus peut-il proposer des instruments, une méthode d'identification des disfonctionnements et lacunes de l'ordre juridique qu'il observe et les moyens qui pourraient éventuellement aider à les surmonter. Dans une période peu propice aux grands chantiers normatifs, envisager l'espace humanitaire comme espace de droit pourrait constituer un moyen plus limité mais utile d'aborder les difficultés auxquelles est confrontée l'action humanitaire selon qu'elle est conduite par les Etats ou des institutions indépendantes de ces derniers.

---

43 Nations Unies, *Recueil des traités*, vol. 2051, p. 363.
44 Nations Unies, *Recueil des traités*, vol. 2689, p. 59.
45 ONU, Rapport du Secrétaire général, *op. cit.*, note 16, par. 63, p. 21.

L'évolution du droit international humanitaire au XXIème siècle : une nécessité ?

Paul Tavernier

Je connais Djamchid Momtaz depuis fort longtemps et j'ai toujours apprécié ses qualités professionnelles et humaines. C'est un fin juriste, un grand universitaire et un pédagogue hors pair, comme j'ai pu le constater lorsque je l'ai fait venir dans mon université en tant que professeur invité. De surcroît Djamchid Momtaz est un ami très sûr et très fidèle. Le choix d'un sujet pour lui rendre hommage est difficile car il a abordé pratiquement tous les domaines du droit international, notamment le droit de la mer dont il est un spécialiste reconnu. Il a abordé aussi les questions économiques et environnementales, mais également les problèmes de l'usage de la force dans la société contemporaine et l'application des règles du droit des conflits armés et du droit international humanitaire. Dans tous ces domaines son expertise a été reconnue et il a prodigué ses conseils avisés aux autorités de son pays, en particulier au ministère des affaires étrangères.

Comme tous les Iraniens, et notamment les juristes iraniens, Djamchid Momtaz a été profondément marqué par l'expérience douloureuse de la guerre avec l'Irak qui a duré huit ans, de 1980 à 1988 et qui, selon la terminologie officielle, fut une « guerre imposée »[1]. Cela l'a amené à approfondir les principes et les règles du droit des conflits armés et du droit international humanitaire[2]. Par ailleurs il s'est intéressé au droit de la guerre, – comme on disait au XIXème siècle –, en quelque sorte par tradition familiale puisque son grand-père fut

---

1 Voir *A review of the Imposed war by the Iraqi régime upon the Islamic Republic of Iran*, Service juridique du Ministère des Affaires étrangères d'Iran, 1983, p. 194.
2 Dans un entretien publié dans la *Revue électronique Actualité et Droit International*, D. Momtaz explique très bien comment il est passé du droit de la mer au droit humanitaire (« Entretien relatif au droit international pénal et humanitaire avec Djamchid Momtaz, Professeur à l'Université de Téhéran », propos recueillis à Téhéran, le 12 août 1999, par P. Despretz, P. Shahrjerdi et B. Taxil : http://www.ridi.org/adi/debat/momtaz199908.htm) : « C'est d'ailleurs grâce au droit de la mer que mon intérêt pour les conflits armés est né : à l'occasion de la guerre Iran-Irak – j'étais déjà conseiller auprès du ministère – les premiers problèmes à traiter furent relatifs à la guerre maritime : je me suis ainsi intéressé au droit de la guerre maritime, sorte de transition entre le droit de la mer et le droit des conflits armés ».

représentant de la Perse aux Conférences de la Paix de La Haye en 1899 et 1907[3] et il m'a raconté un jour comment la reconnaissance de l'emblème du Lion et Soleil Rouge avait été obtenue – sur un coup de bluff – alors que jusqu'alors aucune ambulance ne l'avait arboré, et cela grâce au représentant de la Perse à la Conférence de révision de la première Convention de Genève de 1864, conférence tenue à Genève en 1906[4].

Compte tenu de cette tradition familiale, ainsi que de l'intérêt manifesté par Djamchid Momtaz pour le droit international humanitaire et des travaux qu'il a publiés, je me suis interrogé sur le point de savoir si l'évolution que l'on peut constater dans ce domaine au XXIème siècle répond bien à une nécessité. J'apporterai donc ma modeste contribution à cette réflexion en livrant quelques considérations provisoires sur des problèmes sans cesse renouvelés. A cet égard, la nécessité d'une évolution apparaît à l'observateur, aussi bien en ce qui concerne les sources du droit international humanitaire que pour le contenu de ses normes.

1 La nécessité d'une évolution des sources du droit international humanitaire

Les sources du droit international humanitaire ne sont pas différentes de celles du droit international général. Traditionnellement on se réfère à l'énumération qui figure à l'article 38 du Statut de la Cour internationale de Justice et qui distingue les conventions, la coutume, les principes généraux de droit ainsi que la jurisprudence et la doctrine, comme moyen auxiliaire de détermination des règles de droit. La part respective de ces différentes sources du droit

---

3   Voir J. B. Scott, *Les Conférence de La Haye de 1899 et 1907*, traduction française par A. De Lapradelle, Paris, Pédone, 1927, XII-692 et (102) p. Le grand-père de D. Momtaz figure dans l'Acte final de la Conférence de 1899 au deuxième rang de la délégation de la Perse [p. (5)] : « M. Mirza Samad Khan, Momtazis-Saltaneh, Conseiller de légation à St-Pétersbourg, Délégué adjoint » et au premier rang dans l'Acte final de la Conférence de 1907 : « Son Exc. Samad Khan Momtas-es-Saltaneh, Envoyé extraordinaire et Ministre plénipotentiaire à Paris, Membre de la Cour permanente d'arbitrage, Délégué, Premier plénipotentiaire » [p. (33)]. Son nom est mentionné parmi les orateurs favorables au projet de Cour de Justice Arbitrale (p. 372).

4   Informations recueillies par nous-mêmes auprès de D. Momtaz en septembre 2013. Sur l'historique de l'emblème de la Croix-Rouge, voir F. Bugnion : « Le troisième Protocole additionnel aux Conventions de Genève du 12 août 1949 et le Cristal Rouge », p. 49-86, A. Biad et P. Tavernier (Dir.), *Le droit international humanitaire face aux défis du XXIème siècle*, Bruxelles, Bruylant, 2012; collection du CREDHO n° 19.

international peut varier suivant les différentes branches du droit international ; elle peut aussi évoluer dans le temps. On assiste à cet égard à un vrai chassé-croisé des sources en matière de droit international humanitaire. Mais en même temps se développent de nouvelles sources de droit dans le domaine humanitaire, souvent informelles et que l'on dénomme habituellement « soft law », « droit mou » ou « droit souple » et celles-ci connaissent un essor considérable depuis quelques années.

1.1   Le chassé-croisé des sources traditionnelles

L'évolution des règles du droit humanitaire, au moins à partir du XIXème siècle, est marquée par une alternance assez marquée entre les sources coutumières et les sources conventionnelles. L'expression « lois et coutumes de la guerre » désignait un ensemble de règles coutumières établies par l'usage. C'est ainsi que les conventions de La Haye de 1899, révisées en 1907 se présentaient comme une codification par voie de traités de règles d'origine coutumière. Les dispositions de la « Convention concernant les lois et coutumes de la guerre sur terre » sont parfaitement claires à cet égard. L'article 2 de la Convention insiste sur l'effet relatif des règles énoncées, principe cardinal du doit des contrats et du droit des traités internationaux. Ce texte stipule en effet : « Les dispositions contenues dans le Règlement visé à l'article premier ne sont obligatoires que pour les Puissances contractantes, en cas de guerre entre deux ou plusieurs d'entre elles ».

Le but de cette codification conventionnelle est proclamé très nettement. Elle doit contribuer à une amélioration des normes qu'on n'appelle pas encore « humanitaires ». Selon le Préambule de la convention concernant les lois et coutumes de la guerre sur terre « il importe [...] de réviser les lois et coutumes générales de la guerre, soit dans le but de les définir avec plus de précision, soit afin d'y tracer certaines limites destinées à en restreindre autant que possible les rigueurs ».

Les auteurs de la Convention sont bien conscients que la codification conventionnelle n'est pas complète et que la place de la coutume et des principes généraux demeure importante et essentielle pour résoudre les cas non prévus ou nouveaux. Le Préambule prévoit en effet qu' « en attendant qu'un code plus complet des lois de la guerre puisse être édicté, les Hautes Parties contractantes jugent opportun de constater que, dans les cas non compris dans les dispositions réglementaires adoptées par Elles, les populations et les belligérants restent sous la sauvegarde et sous l'empire des principes du droit des gens, tels qu'ils résultent des usages établis entre nations civilisées, des lois de l'humanité et des exigences de la conscience publique ». Cette vision des relations internationales régies par les « lois de l'humanité » peut paraître quelque peu utopique et irréaliste. Elle est au contraire soucieuse de réalisme et d'efficacité et elle conserve tout son intérêt dans les conditions actuelles d'un monde où les conflits de toutes sortes prolifèrent et remettent en cause les principes les plus fondamentaux du droit humanitaire. Dans cette perspective, l'approche « holistique » (comme on dirait dans le langage moderne) des conventions de La Haye de 1899 et 1907 mériterait d'être reprise.

Historiquement on observe un mouvement de balancier entre les sources conventionnelles et non conventionnelles (coutumes et principes généraux) du droit humanitaire. Pendant longtemps le progrès du droit humanitaire a été relié au développement du droit conventionnel et au perfectionnement des mécanismes de type conventionnel. L'apogée de ce mouvement a été marqué par l'adoption des quatre Conventions de Genève du 12 août 1949[5] et des protocoles additionnels du 8 juin 1977[6].

On s'est toutefois aperçu que le droit conventionnel, malgré tous les avantages qu'il présente, notamment du fait de sa précision et de sa prévisibilité, comporte aussi des limites, dues à l'effet relatif de la règle conventionnelle et à la rigidité de celle-ci. De ce fait de nombreux conflits, en particulier des conflits non internationaux, échappent à ces règles, alors qu'ils sont les plus nombreux dans le monde actuel, depuis 1945. De même de nouvelles armes apparaissent et de nouvelles méthodes de combat sont utilisées. Dans ces conditions, l'utilité du droit coutumier pour remédier aux carences du droit conventionnel est apparue en pleine lumière. C'est le mérite du CICR d'en avoir pris conscience, alors qu'il est souvent perçu, essentiellement et à juste titre, comme le gardien vigilant et scrupuleux des conventions de Genève. Le Groupe d'experts intergouvernemental pour la protection des victimes de la guerre a recommandé

---

5 Convention I pour l'amélioration du sort des blessés et des malades dans les forces armées en campagne, Nations Unies, *Recueil des traités*, vol. 75, p. 3; Convention II pour l'amélioration du sort des blessés, des malades et des naufragés des forces armées sur mer, Nations Unies, *Recueil des traités*, vol. 75, p. 85 ; Convention III relative au traitement des prisonniers de guerre, Nations Unies, *Recueil des traités*, vol. 75, p. 135 ; et Convention IV relative à la protection des personnes civiles en temps de guerre, Nations Unies, *Recueil des traités*, vol. 75. p. 287. Ces quatre conventions ont fait l'objet d'un commentaire substantiel publié par le Comité international de la Croix-Rouge, sous la direction de Jean Pictet, entre 1952 et 1959.
6 Protocole additionnel aux conventions de Genève du 12 août 1949 relatif à la protection des victimes des conflits armés internationaux (Protocole I), Nations Unies, *Recueil des traités*, vol. 1125, p. 3 ; Protocole additionnel aux conventions de Genève du 12 août 1949 relatif à la protection des victimes des conflits armés non internationaux (Protocole II), Nations Unies, *Recueil des* traités, vol. 1125, p. 639. Ces deux protocoles ont fait l'objet également d'un commentaire détaillé publié par le CICR en 1986.

en 1993 qu'une étude soit menée dans ce domaine et « la XXVIème Conférence internationale de la Croix-Rouge et du Croissant-Rouge a entériné cette recommandation en 1995, en demandant au CICR de « préparer, avec l'assistance d'experts en droit international humanitaire représentant diverses régions géographiques et différents systèmes juridiques, ainsi qu'en consultation avec des experts de gouvernements et d'organisations internationales, un rapport sur les règles coutumières du droit international humanitaire applicables aux conflits armés internationaux et non internationaux » [...] »[7].

Ces travaux, auxquels Djamchid Momtaz a été associé en tant qu'expert, membre du Comité directeur, et en tant que responsable de l'équipe nationale iranienne, ont abouti en 2005 à une monumentale Etude du CICR sur le droit humanitaire coutumier[8]. L'Etude a certes fait l'objet de certaines critiques, notamment de la part des Etats-Unis et de la France, mais elle constitue néanmoins un réel succès pour le CICR. Celui-ci a réussi à dégager 161 règles coutumières, dont la plupart sont applicables aussi bien aux conflits armés internationaux (CAI) qu'aux conflits armés non internationaux (CANI). Ces règles, qui ont été mises à jour, couvrent une grande partie du droit international humanitaire. Le CICR en a assuré une vaste diffusion, dans de nombreuses langues et en organisant notamment des colloques nationaux destinés à faire connaître cette Etude aux juristes, fonctionnaires, militaires et personnels humanitaires locaux. C'est ainsi qu'une conférence s'est tenue à Téhéran les 19 et 20 novembre pour marquer la publication en farsi du premier volume de l'Etude du CICR. Djamchid Momtaz en était le coorganisateur et était accompagné par un grand nombre de ses étudiants[9]. Des réunions semblables ont eu lieu à Genève, Pékin, Londres, Moscou, Paris[10], Washington, Addis-Abeba, Le Caire, Ankara et Istanbul.

---

7   J.-M. Henckaerts, « Importance actuelle du droit coutumier », P. Tavernier et L. Burgorgue-Larsen (Dir.), *Un siècle de droit international humanitaire. Centenaire des Conventions de La Haye. Cinquantenaire des Conventions de Genève*, Bruxelles, Bruylant, 2001; collection du CREDHO n°1, p. 21-28.

8   J.-M. Henckaerts et L. Doswald-Beck, *Customary International Humanitarian Law*, ICRC et Cambridge University Press, 2005. Seul le volume I : Rules a été traduit en français, le second : Practice ne l'ayant pas été. J.-M. Henckaerts et L. Doswald-Beck, *Droit international coutumier. Volume I : Règles*, Bruxelles – Genève, Bruylant – Comité International de la Croix-Rouge, 2006.

9   P. Askary et J.-M. Henckaerts, *Proceedings of the Conference on the Customary International Humanitarian Law*, s.l.n.d., Téhéran, 2011.

10 La réunion de Paris s'est tenue le 12 mars 2007 et était organisée par le Comité International de la Croix-Rouge, avec le concours du CREDHO, à l'occasion de la parution de la version française du volume I : Règles. P. Tavernier et J.-M. Henckaerts (Dir.), *Droit international*

Après des années consacrées à mettre l'accent sur l'utilité des règles coutumières dans le domaine du droit international humanitaire, le CICR a décidé de revenir au droit conventionnel qui demeure la base de son action. Il a confié à Jean-Marie Henckaerts, qui était en charge du projet « droit humanitaire coutumier » depuis l'origine, la lourde tâche de mettre à jour les commentaires des quatre Conventions de Genève et des Protocoles additionnels. La mise à jour du commentaire de la Ière Convention de Genève de 1949 pour l'amélioration du sort des blessés et des malades dans les forces armées en campagne a été mise en ligne sur le site du CICR le 22 mars 2016 et une version papier sera publiée en 2016 par Cambridge University Press[11]. Ce mouvement de balancier, qu'on peut observer, ne signifie nullement une diminution de l'intérêt porté au droit coutumier qui conserve, plus que jamais un rôle irremplaçable.

Le débat sur les sources du droit humanitaire actuel semble se focaliser sur la place respective du droit coutumier et du droit conventionnel, et sur leur articulation, parfois difficile et délicate[12]. La problématique classique en la matière met l'accent sur la supériorité de la règle conventionnelle sur la règle coutumière, notamment en raison de sa précision et de sa prévisibilité, mais aussi sur l'enrichissement mutuel de la règle coutumière et de la règle conventionnelle, pour le plus grand bénéfice du progrès du droit humanitaire. Toutefois en dehors de cette problématique classique s'est développée une problématique nouvelle qui reconnaît la place désormais occupée par les nouveaux acteurs du droit international humanitaire, en particulier les ONG et les Organisations internationales, aussi bien en ce qui concerne l'élaboration des normes que leur application à ces nouveaux acteurs.

Ainsi à côté de la coutume et de la convention d'autres sources, certes secondaires, apparaissent et doivent être prises en compte si l'on veut s'adapter à l'évolution des conflits armés et du droit humanitaire.

---

humanitaire coutumier : enjeux et défis contemporains, Bruxelles, Bruylant, 2008, IX-289 p. Collection du CREDHO n° 13. A cette occasion Djamchid Momtaz a présenté une contribution consacrée à « La criminalisation des violations graves du droit international humanitaire commises au cours des conflits armés non internationaux », p. 139-148.

11   Cette première mise à jour est disponible en anglais sur le site du Comité International de la Croix-Rouge à l'adresse suivante : https://ihl-databases.icrc.org/ihl/full/GCI-commentary. Il est très souhaitable qu'une version en français et dans d'autres langues soit rapidement publiée.

12   Voir à ce sujet P. Tavernier, « L'articulation entre le droit international humanitaire coutumier et conventionnel », A. Biad et P. Tavernier, *op. cit.*, note 4, p. 87-113.

1.2 L'apparition de nouvelles sources de droit international humanitaire

Par opposition aux sources du droit international classique que l'on retrouve en droit international humanitaire et que l'on peut qualifier de « droit dur » ou « hard law » (traités et conventions, coutumes et principes généraux du droit), les sources nouvelles relèvent de ce qu'on appelle le « droit mou », « droit souple » ou « soft law ». Toutefois on constate que la distinction n'est pas aussi tranchée que les juristes positivistes veulent bien l'affirmer et qu'il s'agit toujours de dégager des normes auxquelles les acteurs de la société internationale (Etats, mais aussi Organisations internationales et ONG) ont donné leur accord et leur assentiment ou consentement, selon des modalités qui peuvent être très variables. Malgré le vocabulaire employé parfois, il n'y a pas de sources de droit unilatérales qui s'imposent aux sujets du droit international humanitaire, à l'instar des lois et règlement en droit national, indépendamment de leur consentement. Ainsi les « lois » et coutumes de la guerre n'ont rien de comparables aux lois nationales. De même les « règlements » sont des actes concertés et adoptés par les Etats et non des actes unilatéraux édictés par un pouvoir réglementaire, qui n'existe pas. C'est ainsi qu'il faut interpréter la terminologie utilisée par les Conférences de La Haye de 1899 et 1907, notamment pour la Convention et le Règlement concernant les lois et coutumes de la guerre sur terre, le Règlement constituant une « annexe » à la Convention[13]. Cette terminologie, qui peut paraître obsolète, est reprise pourtant à l'article 8 du Statut de la Cour pénale internationale qui définit les crimes de guerre et vise les « autres violations graves des lois et coutumes applicables aux conflits armés internationaux dans le cadre établi du droit international » (par. 2b), la même formule étant employée pour les conflits ne présentant pas un caractère international (par. 2 e).

La contribution du « droit mou » au progrès et à l'adaptation des normes du droit humanitaire est incontestable et ne saurait, dans le contexte actuel, être passée sous silence. Le droit mou permet de combler certaines lacunes du droit dur et il trace aussi les orientations envisageables pour faire progresser les normes du droit humanitaire, en proposant des solutions acceptables. On peut affirmer qu'il fait désormais partie du droit positif, celui-ci devant être entendu largement. A cet égard le droit émanant des Organisations internationales ne peut être négligé, notamment le droit élaboré au sein de l'ONU (aussi bien en ce qui concerne les résolutions de l'Assemblée générale que celles du Conseil de sécurité).

---

13   On peut mentionner également la Convention de La Haye du 14 mai 1954 pour la protection des biens culturels en cas de conflit armé et son Règlement d'exécution.

Un des mérites de l'Etude du CICR sur le droit international humanitaire coutumier est d'avoir largement pris en compte les résolutions des Nations Unies adoptées soit par l'Assemblée générale, soit par le Conseil de sécurité, aussi bien dans l'énoncé des « Règles » (vol. 1) que dans la présentation de la « Pratique » (vol. 2), pratique qui constitue le fondement des règles coutumières. Les résolutions peuvent contribuer à l'identification et à la formulation de ces règles, mais également à la preuve de l'élément psychologique ou « *opinio juris* » de la norme coutumière. C'est d'ailleurs un élément qui a fait l'objet de vives critiques de la part des détracteurs de l'Etude. Jean-Luc Florent, Directeur adjoint des affaires juridiques du Ministère des affaires étrangères de France, tout en saluant l'importance du travail réalisé par le CICR, la qualifie d'œuvre « de nature doctrinale » et lui reproche de s'appuyer « exclusivement sur la pratique supposée des Etats » et de ne pas procéder « à la recherche de l'*opinio juris* »[14]. Ces reproches ne nous convainquent pas et nous semblent injustes et injustifiés.

Au contraire, la part des Organisations internationales dans la mise à jour des normes du droit international humanitaire, nous paraît primordiale et essentielle dans la société internationale telle que nous la connaissons aujourd'hui. Cela concerne principalement l'ONU, dont la Charte proclame dès le premier alinéa du Préambule que les peuples des Nations Unies sont résolus « à préserver les générations futures du fléau de la guerre qui deux fois en l'espace d'une vie humaine a infligé à l'humanité d'indicibles souffrances » et dont le but principal est le maintien de la paix, ce qui lui donne donc vocation à s'intéresser au droit humanitaire. Toutefois d'autres organisations, universelles, comme l'UNESCO, mais aussi régionales, s'y intéressent de plus en plus, comme par exemple le Conseil de l'Europe ou l'Union européenne dont les buts sont pourtant apparemment fort éloignés des préoccupations humanitaires. Sur le plan universel le rôle normatif du Conseil de sécurité se développe de manière remarquable, par l'adoption de résolutions ainsi que de déclarations présidentielles, supposées – à tort – moins contraignantes sur le plan juridique. Ces textes couvrent de nombreux domaines du droit humanitaire pour lesquelles les règles applicables s'avèrent inadaptées ou insuffisantes. Ils concernent les questions, lancinantes dans tous les conflits contemporains, relatives à la protection des civils, ainsi que la protection des femmes et celle des enfants. Ils sont certes répétitifs, ce qui pourrait nuire à leur efficacité, mais

---

14   J.-L. Florent, « Opposabilité de l'Etude du CICR sur le droit international humanitaire coutumier aux Etats », P. Tavernier et J.-M. Henckaerts, *Droit international humanitaire coutumier : enjeux et défis contemporains, op. cit.*, note 10, p. 75-80.

favorise au contraire la lente prise de conscience des peuples de l'importance des mutations à réaliser. Les dispositions concernant les violences sexuelles commises dans le cadre de conflits armés, notamment par des membres des forces internationales, en sont une illustration convaincante. Les travaux du Conseil de sécurité portent parfois sur des questions plus techniques, comme celle de la protection des journalistes dans les conflits armés, question pour laquelle la France a joué un rôle intéressant[15].

Le Conseil de sécurité a su innover en la matière en élaborant des instruments de type nouveau encore méconnus, même parmi les spécialistes. Il en est ainsi de l'Aide-Mémoire du Conseil de sécurité sur la protection des civils dont la première édition remonte à 2002 et dont la cinquième a été adoptée en 2014. Cet Aide-Mémoire, qui couvre désormais plus d'une centaine de pages, se réfère aux règles essentielles du droit international humanitaire et pose même ce qui pourrait être considéré comme les bases d'un futur droit de l'action humanitaire, encore en voie de formation[16]. Il se présente comme un document pratique destiné à fournir une aide à la décision pour résoudre les cas qui se présenteront devant lui.

La fonction normative n'est pas limitée aux Etats et aux Organisations internationales qui sont l'émanation des Etats. Les ONG, qui se réunissent sous la forme de « coalitions » pour l'adoption de nouvelles conventions interviennent de plus en plus fréquemment et ont obtenu des succès incontestables dans la formulation de nouvelles règles. On constate que les processus d'association des ONG à l'élaboration des normes du droit international humanitaire contemporain prennent des formes très diverses. Par exemple le Manuel de Tallin (Tallin Manual on the international law applicable to cyber warfare / Manuel de Tallin sur l'applicabilité du droit international à la cyberguerre) a été élaboré par un groupe international d'experts à l'invitation d'un organisme dépendant de l'OTAN, le Centre d'excellence de l'OTAN pour la cyberdéfense en coopération, et il a été publié en 2013 par Cambridge University Press. Le CICR

---

15 Voir à ce sujet P. Tavernier, « La contribution du Conseil de sécurité des Nations Unies à l'élaboration des normes du droit international humanitaire. Quelques observations », S. Doumbé-Billé et J.-M. Thouvenin (coord.), *Mélanges en l'honneur du professeur Habib Slim. Ombres et lumières du droit international*, Paris, Pedone, 2016, p. 235-251.

16 Voir à ce sujet P. Tavernier, « Un instrument méconnu, l'aide-mémoire du Conseil de sécurité sur la protection des civils », A. Biad (Dir.), *L'action humanitaire internationale entre le droit et la pratique*, Bruxelles, Anthémis, 2016, p. 109-124.

a participé à ces travaux à titre d'observateur[17]. Quant au Guide interprétatif sur la notion de participation directe aux hostilités en droit international humanitaire il a été préparé par le CICR qui a convoqué de 2003 à 2008 cinq réunions d'experts, gouvernementaux, universitaires, d'organisations internationales et d'ONG, tous à titre personnel. Il s'agit d'un document qui n'est pas contraignant mais qui constitue une interprétation autorisée (et non pas à proprement parler une interprétation « authentique ») d'une notion qui est au cœur des débats les plus actuels sur les règles du droit humanitaire les plus fondamentales[18].

Ces quelques exemples montrent la richesse et l'éclatement des sources du droit international humanitaire actuel ainsi que leur faculté d'adaptation aux changements que connaît la société internationale et notamment les mutations des conflits internationaux ou non internationaux qui prennent des formes nouvelles et encore inconnues jusque-là, exigeant des mises à jour parfois difficiles et douloureuses.

2   La nécéssité d'une évolution du contenu des normes du droit international humanitaire

Le contenu des normes du droit international humanitaire doit s'adapter à l'évolution des conflits, tant internationaux que non internationaux, qui est considérable. Le recours aux principes essentiels du droit humanitaire, qui bénéficient d'une grande stabilité, devrait permettre de résoudre les principaux problèmes rencontrés dans cette branche du droit. Toutefois l'ingéniosité des

---

17   Voir W. Heintschel von Heinegg, « The Tallin Manual and international cyber security law », *Yearbook of International Humanitarian Law,* vol. 15, 2012, p. 3-18. Voir aussi R. Liivoja et T. McCormack, « Law in the virtual battlespace: the Tallin Manual and the *jus in bello* », ibid., p. 45-58. Les auteurs de ce dernier article soulignent que le Manuel de Tallin est le quatrième d'une série de Manuels comparables dans le domaine du droit des conflits armés : San Remo Manual on international law applicable to armed conflict at sea (1994), San Remo Manual on the law of non-international armed conflict (2006) et Harvard Manual on the international law applicable to air and missile warfare (2009).

18   Voir S. Ojeda, « Notion de participation directe aux hostilités : interprétation du Comité international de la Croix-Rouge », p. 247-257, A. Biad et P. Tavernier, *op. cit.*, note 4. Voir aussi N. Melzer, « The ICRC's clarification process on the notion of direct participation in hostilities under International humanitarian law », C. Tomuschat, E. Lagrange et S. Oeter (Dir.), *The Right to Life*, Leiden, Martinus Nijhoff Publishers, 2010, p. 151-166.

belligérants (étatiques et non étatiques) pour échapper à ces règles impose l'élaboration de normes plus précises et mieux adaptées aux situations nouvelles et doit conduire parfois à l'adoption de règles entièrement nouvelles applicables à des situations elles-mêmes complètement inédites.

2.1   *La nécessité de normes plus précises et plus « affinées »*

Les armes utilisées dans les conflits que nous connaissons actuellement deviennent de plus en plus perfectionnées et sophistiquées et leur réglementation doit être régulièrement mise à jour. C'est ainsi que pour les armes classiques un système a été adopté en 1980 comprenant une convention complétée par une série de protocoles qui réglementent les différents types d'armes nouvelles au fur et à mesure de leur apparition (Convention sur l'interdiction ou la limitation de l'emploi de certaines armes classiques qui peuvent être considérées comme produisant des effets traumatiques excessifs ou comme frappant sans discrimination). A cet égard on peut signaler que des discussions ont eu lieu sur l'utilisation des systèmes létaux autonomes qu'on appelle aussi « robots tueurs ». A l'inverse, des systèmes d'armes rudimentaires sont apparus, notamment en Syrie et causent des dommages considérables parmi les populations civiles. Il s'agit des bombes d'avion polyvalentes fabriquées de manière artisanale avec un récipient bourré de matières explosives et autres. Pour considérer leur emploi comme illicite, il suffirait de remarquer qu'il contrevient à une règle cardinale du droit international humanitaire, le principe de distinction entre les civils et les combattants et pourtant certains voudraient les interdire expressément dans un nouveau Protocole.

Le Guide interprétatif sur la notion de participation directe aux hostilités en droit international humanitaire, dont nous avons parlé plus haut, est aussi un bon exemple de clarification des normes du droit humanitaire, ou plus précisément d'une notion qui est au cœur de plusieurs de ces normes. Il en ressort qu'un amendement au droit conventionnel n'est pas toujours nécessaire. Selon Stéphane Ojeda le Guide interprétatif du CICR a identifié et cherche à répondre aux trois questions suivantes : – qui est un civil, et donc bénéficie de la protection contre des attaques directes sauf s'il participe directement aux hostilités et ce pendant la durée de cette participation ? – quel acte peut être qualifié de participation directe aux hostilités, et donc mène à la perte de protection contre les attaques directes ? – quelles sont les modalités de cette perte de protection ? »[19]. Et il ajoute : « Une des nouveautés majeures du

---

19   Ojeda, *op. cit.*, note 18, p. 249-250.

Guide interprétatif est la formulation claire du concept de fonction de combat continue »[20].

Dans un autre domaine la question des enfants dans les conflits armés, et notamment des « enfants-soldats », n'est toujours pas réglée malgré les modifications des règles conventionnelles applicables qui sont désormais très claires et en dépit des clarifications supplémentaires qui ont été apportées. Les Nations Unies ont pourtant réservé une attention soutenue et déployé des efforts inlassables à ces problèmes depuis plusieurs décennies. Les Protocoles additionnels de 1977 aux conventions de Genève de 1949 contiennent des dispositions relativement précises concernant le recrutement des enfants (article 77, par. 2 du Protocole I et article 4, par. 3 du Protocole II). Toutefois ces dispositions se sont révélées insuffisantes[21] et les règle applicables au recrutement des enfants ont été précisées dans plusieurs instruments et notamment à l'article 38 par. 3 de la Convention relative aux droits de l'enfant de 1989 qui a fait l'objet d'une ratification quasi universelle.

En dépit des améliorations conventionnelles l'interprétation de ces règles soulève encore des difficultés et la doctrine a salué les efforts de clarification apportés sur ce sujet par la Cour pénale internationale dans l'affaire *Thomas Lubanga Dyilo* du 14 mars 2012. La Cour a déclaré l'accusé coupable pour conscription et enrôlement d'enfants de moins de 15 ans dans un groupe armé dénommé « Forces patriotiques pour la libération du Congo (UPC/FPLC) » et pour leur participation active dans les hostilités en Ituri (septembre 2002-août 2003). La CPI s'est ainsi efforcée de distinguer et préciser certaines notions voisines : recrutement, conscription ou enrôlement ; participation active ou directe aux hostilités, activités manifestement sans rapport avec les hostilités, etc.[22]. Ces exemples montrent à quel point de raffinement on est parvenu dans la formulation des normes du droit international humanitaire. Toutefois les

---

20   Ibid., p. 253.
21   Voir notamment P. Tavernier, « La guerre du Golfe : quelques aspects de l'application du droit des conflits armés et du droit humanitaire », *Annuaire français de droit international*, 1984, p. 43-64.
22   Voir les trois commentaires, approfondis et critiques, consacrés à cette affaire dans le *Yearbook of International Humanitarian Law* : S. Vite, « Between consolidation and innovation : the International Criminal Court's Trial Chamber Judgment in the *Lubanga* Case », *Yearbook of International Humanitarian Law*, vol. 15, 2012, p. 61-85 ; M. A. Drumbl, « The effects of the *Lubanga* Case on understanding and preventing child soldiering », *Yearbook of International Humanitarian Law*, vol. 15, 2012, p. 87-116 et J. Tan « Sexual violence against children on the battlefield as a crime of using Child Soldiers : square pegs in round holes and missed opportunities in *Lubanga* », *Yearbook of International Humanitarian Law*, vol. 15, 2012, p. 117-151.

efforts d'interprétation et de clarification des normes ne permettent pas de régler tous les problèmes et il faut alors élaborer de nouvelles règles.

2.2   *La nécessité de normes nouvelles*

Si les principes généraux du droit sont d'une grande stabilité, – et cela se vérifie aussi bien en droit international général qu'en droit international humanitaire –, les règles conventionnelles et coutumières évoluent sans cesse afin de permettre une adaptation aux changements dans la société internationale ainsi que dans le domaine de la technique. Cela est particulièrement vrai en ce qui concerne le droit humanitaire où le corpus des règles conventionnelles et coutumières est considérable par son volume. Cette branche du droit international a su en général évoluer et répondre aux changements relatifs aux conflits dans la société internationale actuelle mais aussi aux nouvelles armes ou méthodes de combat utilisées dans les conflits contemporains[23].

L'exemple de la cyberguerre et de l'emploi des drones est particulièrement instructif à cet égard. C'est un sujet qui a déjà donné lieu à une abondante littérature. La guerre contre le terrorisme qui s'est intensifiée après les attentats du 11 septembre a entraîné l'utilisation de nouvelles méthodes de combat et notamment le recours à ce qu'on a appelé des « assassinats ciblés »[24]. D'une manière plus générale la technique des drones s'est beaucoup développée. Il s'agit, on le sait, d'avions sans pilote, pilotés à distance, et parfois à partir de bases éloignées de plusieurs milliers de kilomètres, mais aussi d'engins de plus en plus autonomes et qui peuvent même devenir des « robots tueurs ». Ces drones ont une nature duale. Ils peuvent servir à des fins non militaires et on a même envisagé de les utiliser pour distribuer l'aide humanitaire dans des

---

23   Voir, par exemple, le n° 886, vol. 94, Summer 2012 de l'*International Review of the Red Cross*, consacré au thème « New technologies and warfare ». Voir aussi V. Chetail (Dir.), *Permanence et mutation du droit des conflits armés*, Bruxelles, Bruylant, 2013, notamment p. 306 et s. (M. Couston et G. Ruiz, « Le droit de La Haye à l'épreuve des espaces aériens et extra-atmosphériques ») et p. 503 et s. (A. Bellal et S. Casey-Maslen, « Les armes à sous-munitions en droit international humanitaire : enjeux et défis de leur interdiction »). Rappelons que l'article 36 du Protocole I de 1977 aux Conventions de Genève de 1949 est consacré aux armes nouvelles et prévoit un examen de leur licéité. Sur cette question : A. Backstrom et I. Henderson, « New capabilities in warfare : an overview of contemporary technological developments and the associated legal and engineering issues in article 36 weapons reviews », *International Review of the Red Cross*, vol. 94, n° 886, summer 2012, p. 483-514.

24   H. Tigroudja, « Assassinats ciblés et droit à la vie dans la jurisprudence de la Cour suprême israélienne », p. 267-284 C ; Tomuschat, *op. cit.*, note 18, et S. Schmahl, « Targeted Killings – A challenge for international law ? », ibid., p. 233-266.

régions difficiles d'accès en raison des conditions naturelles, ou du fait de la présence de groupes armés qui entravent cet accès. Toutefois, c'est leur usage à des fins militaires qui a retenu l'attention des militaires et des juristes. Cet usage soulève en effet de nombreux problèmes juridiques, tant en ce qui concerne le *jus ad bellum* que le *jus in bello*[25]. Il suscite aussi des interrogations d'ordre éthique que les juristes ont parfois tendance à oublier et sur lesquels Philippe Lagrange a fort justement attiré l'attention[26]. Sur le plan juridique aucune règle du droit humanitaire n'interdit l'emploi de drones, à condition de respecter les principes du droit des conflits armés et « sauf à ce que les évolutions technologiques conduisent à une transformation des actuels drones armés en armes causant des maux superflus ou frappant sans discrimination, c'est-à-dire sans distinguer les objectifs militaires des objectifs civils ». Et d'ajouter : « le drone armé ne sera pas l'arbalète du XXIème siècle » ! De même certaines utilisations des drones armés sont illicites, notamment s'il s'agit d'opérer des exécutions extra-judiciaires. En définitive, selon Philippe Lagrange, « le drone armé n'évolue pas dans un vide juridique et ne nécessite pas, en tant que tel, ni même quant à l'utilisation qui en est faite, le développement d'un nouveau *corpus* normatif ». En revanche on assistera à un véritable révolution éthique en ce domaine : « Même si, là encore, se répètent avec le drone des questions qui hantent les moralistes depuis des siècles, la nouvelle problématique générée par cette dématérialisation du champ de bataille, par cette possibilité de livrer une guerre virtuelle, désincarnée, sera très certainement l'une des grandes interrogations éthiques de ce siècle »[27].

On retrouvera probablement des interrogations de ce type en ce qui concerne la cyber-guerre, ou du moins certains de ses aspects. Sur le plan juridique, la plupart des auteurs considèrent que les principes du droit humanitaire (principe de distinction, principe de proportionnalité et principe de

---

25 S. Casey-Maslen, « Pandora box ? Drone strikes under *jus ad bellum, jus in bello*, and international human rights law », *International Review of the Red Cross*, vol. 94, n° 886, summer 2012, p. 597-625.

26 P. Lagrange, « Le drone, l'éthique et le droit », J.-F. Akandji-Kombe (coordination générale), *L'Homme dans la société internationale. Mélanges en hommage au Professeur Tavernier*, Bruxelles, Bruylant, 2013, p. 1333-1353. Pour les problèmes juridiques, voir J. Pejic, « Extraterritorial targeting by means of armed drones : some legal implications », *International Review of the Red Cross*, vol. 96, n° 893, spring 2014, p. 67-106.

27 Le problème éthique s'est posé notamment pour le recours à l'arme atomique. Voir à ce sujet le petit opuscule, bien connu, de K. Jaspers, *La bombe atomique et l'avenir de l'Homme*, Paris, Plon, 1958, 64 p. traduction de René Soupault et précédé de « Le philosophe devant la politique » par J. Hersch. Original en allemand : « Die Atombombe und die Zukunft des Menschen », *Die Gegenwart*, 1956.

précaution dans l'attaque, notamment) suffisent pour régler les principaux problèmes soulevés par le recours à la cyber-guerre, au prix d'une interprétation suffisamment souple des règles existantes du droit humanitaire et sans aboutir à des « étirements » excessifs aboutissant à une dénaturation de la règle. Mais cela n'exclut pas pour l'avenir la nécessité d'élaborer de nouvelles normes. C'est ce qui ressort des débats qui ont eu lieu au colloque de Rouen de 2013 et c'est la position défendue en particulier par Abdelwahab Biad[28]. Pour lui, « il est prématuré d'envisager à ce stade le développement d'un « *cyber jus in bello* », même si la perspective de mettre au point des robots cybercombattants dotés d'une intelligence artificielle et capables d'intégrer les règles du droit international humanitaire dans leur mode d'emploi est un scénario plausible et [...] souhaitable »[29].

Ces incursions dans le domaine de la science-fiction et du monde virtuel apparaîtront sans doute pour les juristes positivistes comme des spéculations bien éloignées de la réalité, mais on doit constater que le virtuel provoque des effets bien réels et que le juriste, aussi positiviste soit-il, a tout intérêt à le prendre en considération.

En définitive le droit international humanitaire a su en général s'adapter aux évolutions de la technique militaire et de la société internationale et on peut penser qu'il en sera de même à l'avenir. Nous avons pu le constater avec le renouvellement des sources traditionnelles du droit et l'apparition de sources nouvelles plus souples et originales, mais aussi avec le développement de règles plus précises et plus détaillées que les règles classiques, conduisant à un enrichissement très substantiel du contenu normatif du droit humanitaire. Il y a toutefois un domaine où des progrès – considérables – restent à faire, c'est le non-respect des règles humanitaires et la nécessité de procédures permettant le constat et la condamnation de ces violations ainsi que leur réparation éventuelle. On assiste en effet à un effritement, voire à une érosion et à une

---

28 A. Biad, « Cyberguerre et *lex specialis* : évolution ou révolution ? », *Société française pour le droit international*, colloque de Rouen, *Internet et le droit international*, Paris, Pédone, 2014, p. 253-263.

29 Voir aussi K. Bannelier-Christakis, « Enjeux de la cyberguerre pour la protection des personnes et des biens civils : du principe de distinction au Manuel de Tallin », *Société Française pour le Droit International, Colloque de Rouen, op. cit.*, note 28, p. 277-295 ; M. Roscini, « Cyber-opérations et principe de proportionnalité en droit international humanitaire », *Société Française pour le Droit International, Colloque de Rouen, op. cit.*, note 28, p. 297-307. Voir également H. Lin, « Cyber conflict and international humanitarian law », *International Review of the Red Cross*, vol. 94, n° 886, summer 2012, p. 515-531 ; C. Droege, « Get off my cloud : cyber warfare, international humanitarian law, and the protection of civilians », ibid. p. 533-578.

dégradation du respect des règles du droit international humanitaire et des droits de l'homme par les parties en conflit, ce qui est très inquiétant, d'autant plus qu'on constate aussi une prolifération de plus en plus importante des acteurs impliqués dans un conflit armé, ce qui complique les problèmes et la détermination des responsabilités, et risque, de surcroît, de conduire à l'impunité. Certes il faut saluer les avancées du droit pénal international et l'importance de la jurisprudence des tribunaux pénaux internationaux et de la Cour pénale internationale qui, malgré toutes ses imperfections et les menaces qui pèse sur elle, a contribué à la clarification de certaines règles du droit humanitaire, comme nous l'avons vu, ainsi qu'à la condamnation des violations de celui-ci.

Une autre limite au progrès du droit international humanitaire tient à la structure même de la société internationale qui demeure dominée par les Etats et ceux-ci freinent parfois les évolutions nécessaires. Toutefois les juristes qui s'intéressent au droit humanitaire doivent rester optimistes, à l'instar du grand juriste suisse Bluntschli qui, à la fin de l'introduction de son Droit international codifié, affirmait il y a plus d'un siècle : « Sans doute ce sont les hommes d'Etat qui, dans la pratique des affaires, ont en main le perfectionnement du droit international. Mais le principal levier du progrès sera évidemment l'opinion publique »[30]. On peut voir dans ces analyses une vision prémonitoire de la société internationale du XXIème siècle où les Etats ont conservé intact leur pouvoir de décision, mais où l'opinion publique, représentée et incarnée à l'heure actuelle par la société civile et les ONG, joue un rôle d'aiguillon non négligeable pour permettre au droit international, en particulier au droit humanitaire, d'évoluer et de « remplir sa mission civilisatrice et humanitaire »[31].

---

30   J.-G. Bluntschli, *Le droit international codifié*, Paris, Librairie Guillaumin, 1886 (traduction de l'allemand), p. 52-53.
31   Ibid.

PART 7

Use of Force

∴

Le droit international au défi de « l'exceptionnalisme nucléaire »

Abdelwahab Biad

> À terme, le droit international et avec lui la stabilité de l'ordre international qu'il a pour vocation de régir ne peuvent que souffrir des divergences de vues qui subsistent aujourd'hui quant au statut juridique d'une arme aussi meurtrière que l'arme nucléaire.
>
> CIJ *avis consultatif sur la licéité de la menace et de l'emploi d'armes nucléaires*, 8 juillet 1996 (*CIJ Recueil 1996*, p. 66.)

∴

À l'occasion de la première visite d'un Président des Etats-Unis à Hiroshima, Barack Obama a reconnu que les destructions sans précédent causées par le premier bombardement atomique devaient nous encourager à échapper à la logique de la peur et poursuivre l'objectif d'un monde sans armes nucléaires[1]. Ce discours plus moralisateur qu'acte de repentance à l'égard des victimes démontre encore une fois le contraste fondamental entre le constat du sur le caractère apocalyptique de l'arme atomique et ses conséquences humanitaires d'une part et le refus persistant d'en remettre en question la possession par un désarmement nucléaire juridiquement contraignant[2], d'autre part.

Pourtant la première résolution de l'Assemblée générale des Nations Unies (AGNU) en 1946 exprimait déjà la préoccupation quant aux utilisations de l'énergie nucléaire[3]. Soixante-dix ans plus tard, sur les 54 résolutions adoptées

---

[1] Le texte du discours fut publié dans le New York Times du 28 mai 2016, sous le titre : « The Memory of the Morning of August 6, 1945, Must Never Fade ».

[2] Voir l'Appel lancé par T. Konoé, président de la Fédération international de la Croix-Rouge et du Croissant-Rouge, et P. Maurer, président du Comité international de la Croix-Rouge : « La visite de M. Obama à Hiroshima vient rappeler l'urgence d'agir contre les armes nucléaires », *Le Monde* du 26 mai 2016.

[3] Documents officiels de l'Assemblée générale des Nations unies (DOAG), « Création d'une commission chargée d'étudier les problèmes soulevés par la découverte de l'énergie atomique », A/RES/1 (I), 24 janvier 1946.

par la Première Commission de l'AGNU, 27 concernaient la question de l'arme nucléaire sous ses différents aspects : non-emploi, interdiction des essais, zones dénucléarisées, non-prolifération et désarmement nucléaire. Il est intéressant de remarquer que sur les 26 résolutions soumises au vote parmi les 54 adoptées, 22 concernaient la question nucléaire. Ce recours plus fréquent au vote plutôt qu'au consensus s'agissant de cette question témoigne qu'elle est source de division et de polarisation des Etats, et l'ambiance à l'Assemblée générale constitue un baromètre de la frustration et de l'exacerbation face à l'absence de progrès vers le désarmement nucléaire. Bien qu'ayant surtout une valeur déclaratoire de portée morale, les résolutions de l'AGNU n'ont pas moins permis de consacrer certains principes qui ont acquis une dimension conventionnelle (principes relatifs aux utilisations pacifiques de l'espace)[4] ou rappeler le droit coutumier existant s'agissant des règles du droit international humanitaire.

L'objectif d'un « *monde exempte d'armes nucléaires* » et par conséquent une logique abolitionniste soutenue par une majorité confortable d'Etats[5], soulève l'opposition constante des Etats dotés d'armes nucléaires (EDAN) et de leurs alliés qui contestent la thèse de l'absence de progrès sur la voie du désarmement nucléaire en invoquant une réduction significative de leurs arsenaux depuis la fin de la Guerre froide. Russes et Américains auraient retiré du statut opérationnel environ les deux tiers des ogives qu'ils possédaient dans les années 80. La France et le Royaume-Uni auraient procédé à une diminution d'environ 50 % de leurs armes nucléaires[6]. Si le volume des arsenaux nucléaires a sensiblement diminué, cette diminution ne concerne pas l'amélioration qualitative des armes par lesdites puissances, ni le fait que les autres EDAN (Chine, Inde, Israël, Pakistan et Corée du Nord) poursuivent une montée en puissance de leurs capacités nucléaires.

---

4 Les principes définis dans la résolution 1962 (XVIII) de l'AGNU du 13 décembre 1963 ont été codifiés dans le Traité sur l'espace extra-atmosphérique du 27 janvier 1967.

5 Les résolutions sur le désarmement nucléaires à la 1ère Commission de l'AGNU recueillent invariablement entre 60 et 70% des voix des Etats membres. A titre d'exemple la résolution 70/37 du 7 décembre 2015 sur *la Réduction du danger nucléaire* a recueilli 127 voix contre 48 et 10 abstentions, alors que la résolution 70/47 sur les *Conséquences humanitaires des armes nucléaires* a obtenu 144 contre 18 et 22.

6 L'arsenal nucléaire mondial est estimé à environ 15 395 armes détenues à plus de 90% par les Etats-Unis et la Russie, et le reste par la Chine, la France, le Royaume-Uni, Israël, l'Inde, le Pakistan et la Corée du Nord (voir « Global nuclear weapons : downsizing but modernizing », *SIPRI Yearbook 2016*, Stockholm International Peace Research Institute, 2016, https://www.sipri.org/media/press-release/2016/global-nuclear-weapons-downsizing-modernizing).

La pression exercée par les Etats non dotés d'armes nucléaires (ENDAN) sur les EDAN s'accentue avec le lancement de plusieurs initiatives intergouvernementales. Il faudrait mentionner notamment la Réunion de haut niveau de l'Assemblée générale sur le désarmement nucléaire (26 septembre 2013) qui a décidé de convoquer une Conférence internationale sur le désarmement nucléaire, et d'instituer une « Journée internationale pour l'élimination totale des armes nucléaires »[7] le 26 septembre. La constitution du Groupe de travail à composition non limitée chargé d'étudier sur le fond les mesures juridiques concrètes et efficaces et les dispositions et normes juridiques nécessaires à l'instauration d'un monde exempt à jamais d'armes nucléaires[8] s'insère dans cette logique à l'instar des conférences sur l'impact humanitaire des armes nucléaires sur lesquelles il sera utile de revenir. La société civile n'est pas en reste comme l'illustre l'appel adressé par l'AGNU « aux parlementaires, à la société civile, aux milieux universitaires, aux médias et aux particuliers de continuer d'agir en faveur de l'édification d'un monde exempt d'armes nucléaires »[9]. L'objectif de toutes ces initiatives est la négociation d'un instrument international juridiquement contraignant visant l'interdiction des armes nucléaires.

C'est qu'en effet l'arme nucléaire est la seule arme de destruction massive n'ayant fait l'objet d'aucune interdiction générale, consacrant ainsi l'existence d'un « exceptionnalisme nucléaire » (I). Mais, progressivement de nombreuses initiatives notamment dans le cadre des Nations unies convergent vers la remise en cause de cet exceptionnalisme sous le double effet de l'agenda sur « l'impact humanitaire des armes nucléaires » et de la judiciarisation de la question nucléaire (II).

1   « *L'Exceptionnalisme Nucléaire* » à l'œuvre

Dans l'avis consultatif sur la *licéité de la menace ou de l'emploi d'armes nucléaires*, la Cour internationale de justice (CIJ) relevait que « La tendance a été jusqu'à présent, en ce qui concerne les armes de destruction massive, de les déclarer illicites grâce à l'adoption d'instruments spécifiques », citant à ce propos les conventions d'interdiction des armes bactériologiques et chimiques.

---

7   DOAG, A/RES/68/32 du 5 décembre 2013.
8   DOAG A/RES/70/33, 7 décembre 2015.
9   DOAG, A/RES/70/57 intitulée « Déclaration universelle sur l'édification d'un monde exempt d'armes nucléaires ». Il faut mentionner ici le rôle particulier de coalitions d'ONG militant pour le désarmement nucléaire comme la *Campagne internationale pour l'abolition des armes nucléaires* (ICAN en anglais : http://www.icanw.org).

Mais, elle « ne trouve pas d'interdiction spécifique du recours aux armes nucléaires dans les traités qui prohibent expressément l'emploi de certaines armes de destruction massive »[10]. Ainsi, alors que les armes bactériologiques et chimiques qui ont suscité la même condamnation en raison de leurs effets destructeurs indiscriminés et des souffrances inutiles qu'elles causent ont fait l'objet d'une prohibition internationale, l'« exceptionnalisme » concernant l'arme nucléaire est de rigueur fondant le statut unique de cette arme par rapport aux autres moyens de guerre (1) et le rôle particulier qu'elle joue dans les doctrines militaires des Etats qui en sont dotés (2).

1.1 L'arme nucléaire : un statut unique parmi les armes de destruction massive

Comme le relevait Serge Sur, il n'existe pas de définition en droit international des armes de destruction massive[11]. Toutefois, il s'agit incontestablement d'armes dont l'emploi entraine des destructions matérielles et des pertes humaines considérables. Dans la panoplie militaire des Etats on distingue généralement les armes conventionnelles (ou classiques) et les armes de destruction massive (traduction de l'anglais « weapons of mass destruction »), notion qui se réfère généralement aux armes bactériologiques, chimiques et nucléaires.

Contrairement aux armes bactériologiques[12] et chimiques[13], l'arme nucléaire n'a fait l'objet d'aucune interdiction ; son régime juridique se caractérise par une diversité d'instruments et d'arrangements dominés moins par des préoccupations de désarmement que de prolifération. Ainsi, à l'approche globale visant à aborder dans son ensemble la question des armes nucléaires, c'est l'approche partielle qui prévaut avec une multiplicité d'accords et d'arrangements visant le déploiement, l'essai, la prolifération, le contrôle et la sûreté des installations nucléaires. Cet exceptionnalisme se traduit aussi par une grande variété

---

10   *Licéité de la menace ou de l'emploi d'armes nucléaires*, CIJ Recueil 1996, p. 226, avis consultatif du 8 juillet 1996, par. 57.

11   Voir S. Sur, « La Résolution 1540 du Conseil de sécurité (28 avril 2004) entre la prolifération des armes de destruction massive, le terrorisme et les acteurs non étatiques », *Revue Générale de Droit International Public*, n°4, 2004, p. 855-882 (p. 870).

12   Convention sur l'interdiction de la mise au point, de la fabrication et du stockage des armes bactériologiques (biologiques) ou à toxines et sur leur destruction adoptée le 12 avril 1972 et entrée en vigueur le 26 mars 1975. Nations Unies, *Recueil des traités*, vol. 1015, p. 163.

13   Convention sur l'interdiction de la mise au point, de la fabrication, du stockage et de l'emploi des armes chimiques et sur leur destruction adoptée le 12 janvier 1993 et entrée en vigueur le 29 avril 1997, https://www.opcw.org/fileadmin/OPCW/CWC/CWC_fr.pdf.

d'instruments juridiques tant au plan de leur forme que de leur portée[14] : accords bilatéraux de limitation des armes nucléaires stratégiques (START), Traité d'interdiction complète des essais (TICE) et Traité sur la non-prolifération des armes nucléaires (TNP), instruments régionaux de non dissémination[15] ou établissant des zones exemptes d'armes nucléaires (ZEAN)[16], accords de garanties de l'AIEA sur les utilisations pacifiques de l'énergie nucléaire.

Cette situation particulière de l'arme nucléaire dans l'architecture des accords relatifs aux armes mérite d'être rappelée. Depuis l'adoption du TICE en 1996 qui n'est de surcroit pas encore en vigueur, aucun accord significatif réglementant l'armement nucléaire n'a vu le jour. Pourtant les projets ne manquent pas : arrangements visant à garantir les ENDAN contre l'emploi d'armes nucléaires, accord sur l'interdiction de la production de matières fissiles à des fins militaires (dit *cut off*) ou encore projet de création d'une ZEAN au Moyen-Orient[17]. La Conférence du désarmement de Genève (unique organe de négociation multilatérale) est dans l'impasse depuis des années, ne parvenant pas même à adopter son programme de travail faute de consensus précisément sur la question du désarmement nucléaire. En effet, le fossé reste large entre d'un côté les ENDAN membres de cet organe restreint de 66 Etats qui appuient la négociation d'un instrument juridiquement contraignant interdisant l'arme nucléaire et de l'autre les EDAN qui s'y refusent, préférant se limiter à des consultations.

Dès lors, la question de la légitimité des armes nucléaires qu'une approche globale n'aurait pas manqué d'ouvrir s'en trouve occultée. C'est précisément l'enjeu du débat actuel pour « un monde exempt d'armes nucléaires » avec le projet d'une convention d'interdiction générale sur le modèle de la convention sur les armes chimiques car elle prohiberait l'emploi, la menace d'emploi, la mise au point et la production ainsi que la possession sous quelques formes

---

14 S. Sur évoque « une diversité [qui] ne peut manquer d'avoir des effets négatifs sur la cohérence générale du régime juridique des armes ». Voir S. Sur, « Les armes nucléaires au miroir du droit », *Le droit international des armes nucléaires* (Journée d'études de la Société française pour le droit international), Paris, Pedone, 1998, p. 9-15.

15 Il est utile de relever que les traités concernant l'Antarctique (1959), l'espace extra-atmosphérique (1967), et les fonds marins (1971) interdisent d'y installer des armes de destruction massive.

16 Il s'agit des traités de Tlatelolco (entré en vigueur le 25 avril 1969), de Rarotonga (11 décembre 1986), de Bangkok (28 mars 1997), de Pelindaba (15 juillet 2009) et de Semipalatinsk (21 mars 2009) créant respectivement des zones dénucléarisées en Amérique latine, au Pacifique Sud, en Asie du Sud-Est, en Afrique et en Asie centrale.

17 Ce projet discuté à l'AGNU depuis 1974 se heurte au défi que pose l'armement nucléaire israélien. Voir DOAG, 70ème session, 1ère Commission, A/RES/70/24 du 7 décembre 2015.

que ce soit de l'arme nucléaire[18]. Toutefois dans le contexte actuel, il parait difficile d'envisager la négociation, encore moins la conclusion d'un tel accord. L'entreprise n'est pas simple s'agissant d'un instrument global et juridiquement contraignant établissant des normes internationales communes applicables à l'arme nucléaire sous tous ses aspects. Indépendamment des questions relatives au champ d'application, aux étapes et aux modalités de vérification, le plus difficile serait que les Etats concernés (EDAN) n'aient pas le sentiment que leur sécurité en sorte affaiblie.

Il y a un consensus pour considérer que l'arme dont il est question ici représente de loin par rapport aux autres moyens de guerre la plus grave menace pour la survie même de l'humanité alors qu'elle ne fait l'objet d'aucune réglementation internationale encadrant son emploi. Une grande part de l'explication réside dans le fait qu'elle est toujours considérée comme un instrument essentiel, voir l'outil suprême dans les doctrines de dissuasion des EDAN.

1.2 Le droit à la légitime défense au secours de l'arme nucléaire

« Ni le droit international coutumier ni le droit international conventionnel ne comportent d'interdiction complète et universelle de la menace ou de l'emploi des armes nucléaires en tant que telles »[19]. C'est en ces termes que la CIJ a cru répondre à la question posée par l'AGNU dans sa demande d'avis : « Est-il permis en droit international de recourir à la menace ou à l'emploi d'armes nucléaires en toute circonstance ? »[20]. En constatant ainsi l'absence de règles coutumières ou conventionnelles, la CIJ dit ne pas être en mesure de « conclure de façon définitive que la menace ou l'emploi d'armes nucléaires serait licite ou illicite dans une circonstance extrême de légitime défense dans laquelle la

---

18   En 1997, le Costa Rica a proposé un projet de convention d'interdiction des armes nucléaires s'inspirant du modèle de la convention sur les armes chimiques. Le texte énonce des obligations relatives à la non-utilisation, à la non-possession, au démantèlement contrôlé des armes nucléaires selon un calendrier, et interdit la production de matières fissiles à des fins militaires. Il prévoit un système de vérification par un organe spécifique ainsi qu'un mécanisme de résolution des différends (voir *Lettre du Costa Rica adressée au Secrétaire général des Nations Unies*, doc. A/C.1/52/7, 17 novembre 1997 ; voir pour une version actualisée du projet la *Lettre du Costa Rica et de la Malaisie au adressée au Secrétaire général des Nations Unies*, doc. A/62/650 (18 janvier 2008).

19   *Licéité de la menace ou de l'emploi d'armes nucléaires, op. cit.*, note 10, par. 105, (2) (B).

20   DOAG, A/RES/49/75 K du 15 décembre 1994.

survie même d'un Etat serait en cause »[21]. Cette conclusion fut critiquée et en premier lieu par certains juges eux-mêmes[22].

La première critique qu'on pourrait adresser, c'est qu'une Cour mondiale dont une des compétences est de contribuer au développement du droit international comme elle l'a fait en d'autres circonstances – règles relatives à la délimitation maritime[23] ou le principe de *l'uti possidetis* en droit de la décolonisation[24] – a manqué d'audace ici. Les juges ne devraient-ils pas « dire le droit et le faire prévaloir en l'espèce, quelles qu'en soit les conséquences »[25].

La seconde critique concerne la conclusion de la Cour sur l'absence de base juridique pour fonder l'illicéité en toutes circonstances de l'emploi d'armes nucléaires. Cela revient à reconnaître que le *jus in bello* pourrait ne pas être respecté dans le cadre de la légitime défense. Connaissant les effets d'une explosion nucléaire, on voit mal comment l'emploi de ces armes même dans les circonstances extrêmes de légitime défense où la survie de l'Etat serait en jeu pourrait respecter les principes – qualifiés pourtant « d'intransgressibles » par la Cour elle-même[26] – qui imposent d'une part de faire la distinction entre combattants et non combattants en vue de protéger la population civile, et d'autre part de ne pas causer de souffrances inutiles et excessives aux combattants. N'est-il pas nécessaire de rappeler aussi la règle qui interdit de recourir à des méthodes et moyens de guerre susceptibles de causer des dommages étendus, durables et graves à l'environnement[27] ? En application des principes

---

21 *Licéité de la menace ou de l'emploi d'armes nucléaires, op. cit.*, note 10, par. 105 (2) (E).

22 Ibid., opinion dissidente du juge Shahabuddeen, p. 375-428 ; opinion dissidente du juge Weeramantry, p. 429-555, opinion dissidente du juge Koroma, p. 556-582.

23 Voir *affaires des Pêcheries norvégiennes (Royaume-Uni c. Norvège)*, arrêt du 18 décembre 1951, CIJ Recueil 1951, p. 116 et *Plateau continental de la mer du Nord (Danemark et Pays-Bas c. République Fédérale d'Allemagne)*, arrêt du 20 février 1969, CIJ Recueil 1969, p. 3 ; *Plateau continental (Tunisie c. Libye)*, arrêt du 24 février 1982, CIJ Recueil 1982, p. 18 ; *Délimitation de la frontière maritime dans le Golfe du Maine (Canada c. Etats-Unis d'Amérique)*, arrêt du 12 octobre 1984, CIJ Recueil 1984, p. 246 ; *Plateau continental (Libye c. Malte)*, arrêt du 3 juin 1985, CIJ Recueil 1985, p. 13 ; *Délimitation maritime dans la région située entre le Groenland et Jan Mayen (Danemark c. Norvège)*, arrêt du 14 juin 1993, ICJ Recueil 1993, p. 38.

24 Voir *Conséquences juridiques pour les Etats de la présence continue de l'Afrique du Sud en Namibie* (avis consultatif du 21 juin 1971, CIJ Recueil 1971, p. 16) *et Sahara occidental* (avis consultatif du 16 octobre 1975, CIJ Recueil 1975, p. 12).

25 C'est notamment l'opinion de G. Abi Saab, voir « De l'évolution de la Cour internationale de justice. Réflexions sur quelques tendances récentes », *Revue Générale de Droit International Public*, 1992/1, p. 283.

26 *Licéité de la menace ou de l'emploi d'armes nucléaires, op. cit.*, note 10, par. 79.

27 Règle reprise dans Protocole additionnel I de 1977 (articles 35 par. 3 et 55) aux Conventions de Genève de 1949.

susmentionnées le droit coutumier des conflits armés ne dispose-t-il pas que « les belligérants n'ont pas un droit illimité quant au choix des moyens de nuire à l'ennemi »[28] ? Est aussi pertinente ici la *Clause de Martens* qui stipule que pour les cas non prévus par le droit en vigueur, les personnes civiles et les combattants restent « sous la sauvegarde et sous l'empire des principes du droit des gens, tels qu'ils résultent des usages établis, des principes de l'humanité et des exigences de la conscience publique ».

L'exception de la légitime défense « dans une circonstance extrême dans laquelle la survie même d'un Etat serait en cause »[29], a conforté les partisans de la dissuasion dans l'opinion selon laquelle l'emploi d'armes nucléaires pourrait ne pas violer les prescriptions du *jus in bello*, que ces armes à l'instar des autres sont soumises au droit des conflits armés et que la question de la légalité ou de l'illégalité de leur emploi dépend des circonstances de leur utilisation[30]. Les considérations de *jus ad bellum* semblent ici avoir prévalu sur les prescriptions du *jus in bello*. L'exercice du droit de légitime défense quel que soit le type d'arme utilisé ne dispense pas son auteur du respect des conditions de nécessité et de proportionnalité. Mais le respect de cette dernière parait difficilement envisageable compte-tenu du fait que « par ces caractéristiques, l'arme nucléaire est potentiellement d'une nature catastrophique [...] [et] ne peut être endiguée ni dans l'espace ni dans le temps » et qu'elle a « le pouvoir de détruire toute civilisation, ainsi que l'écosystème tout entier de la planète »[31].

Il est regrettable que la dimension politique – c'est-à-dire les doctrines de dissuasion, une pratique à propos de laquelle la Cour n'a pas cru devoir prendre position – l'ait en définitive emporté sur la dimension juridique et éthique de la question nucléaire. L'attachement des puissances concernées à la dissuasion, le fait qu'elles soient réticentes à accepter une restriction à l'emploi

---

28   Article 22 du Règlement de La Haye de 1907 concernant les lois et coutumes de la guerre sur terre.

29   *Licéité de la menace ou de l'emploi d'armes nucléaires, op. cit.*, note 10, par. 105 (2) (E).

30   Le juge Guillaume voyait là la confirmation par la Cour de la licéité des politiques de dissuasion (Voir ibid., opinion individuelle du juge Guillaume, p. 292). Se reporter aux exposés écrits des Etats-Unis (20 juin 1995), de la France (20 juin 1995), du Royaume-Uni (16 juin 1995) et de la Russie (19 juin 1995), voir site de la CIJ : http://www.icj-cij.org. Pour une analyse de l'avis consultatif voir : Boisson de Chazournes (L), Sands (P) (ed), *International Law, the International Court of Justice and Nuclear Weapons*, Cambridge University Press, 1999, 592 p. ; et le numéro spécial de la *Revue internationale de la Croix-Rouge* (n° 823, 1997) avec les contributions de L. Condorelli, E. David, L. Doswald Beck et C. Greewood ; et R. Falk, « Nuclear Weapons, International Law and the World Court : A Historic Encounter », *American Journal of International Law*, vol. 91, n° 1, 1997, p. 64-75.

31   *Licéité de la menace ou de l'emploi d'armes nucléaires, op. cit.*, note 10, par. 35.

d'armes nucléaires, y compris contre les ENDAN[32] empêche ainsi l'émergence d'une norme coutumière de non-emploi de cette arme depuis 1945. Dès lors ni les traités existants relatifs à l'arme nucléaires (TNP), ni les accords instituant des ZEAN qui prohibent l'emploi d'armes nucléaires contre ces zones, ni les nombreuses résolutions de l'AGNU agissant au titre de l'article 11 de la Charte[33] ne semblent avoir contribué à cette émergence.

Ainsi, les doctrines de dissuasion auxquelles les EDAN restent attachées et qui trouvent pour partie leur fondement dans le droit coutumier de légitime défense incarné par l'article 51 de la Charte des Nations Unies constituent un des obstacles les plus sérieux sur le chemin du désarmement nucléaire. L'avis de la CIJ sur la *licéité de la menace ou de l'emploi d'armes nucléaires* confirme si besoin est l'existence de cet « exceptionnalisme nucléaire ». Ce constat n'a pas dissuadé les initiatives qui se multiplient en vue de le remettre en cause au nom des valeurs de l'humanité.

2 « *L'Exceptionnalisme nucléaire* » dans la ligne de mire

C'est par le biais de la question de la légalité de l'emploi de l'arme nucléaire que se développe l'argumentation en faveur de l'abolition de cette catégorie d'arme. On relèvera que cette question fut abordée sans ambiguïté par l'AGNU dans sa résolution 1653 de 1961 dans laquelle elle considérait qu'un tel emploi « est contraire aux règles du droit international et aux lois de l'humanité », et concluait que tout Etat qui utiliserait une telle arme commettrait un « crime contre l'humanité et la civilisation »[34]. Cette préoccupation est au cœur des deux stratégies de nature politique et juridique qui se font jour contre « l'exceptionnalisme nucléaire ». La première met l'accent sur « l'impact humanitaire de l'arme nucléaire » en mobilisant la communauté internationale sur le

---

32 Voir A. Biad, « Les arrangements internationaux efficaces pour garantir les États non dotés d'armes nucléaires contre l'emploi ou la menace de ces armes », *Annuaire Français de Droit International 1997*, Paris, CNRS Éditions, p. 227-252.

33 Cet article fonde la compétence de l'organe en matière de désarmement : « L'Assemblée générale peut étudier les principes généraux de coopération pour le maintien de la paix et de la sécurité internationales, y compris les principes régissant le désarmement et la réglementation des armements, et faire, sur ces principes, des recommandations soit aux Membres de l'Organisation, soit au Conseil de sécurité, soit aux Membres de l'Organisation et au Conseil de sécurité ».

34 DOAG, seizième session, « *Déclaration sur l'interdiction de l'emploi des armes nucléaires et thermonucléaires* », A/RES/1653 (XVI), 24 novembre 1961, par. 1 (b) et (d). La résolution fut adoptée par. 55 voix contre 20, et 26 abstentions.

danger nucléaire (1). La seconde consiste à judiciariser le débat afin d'obtenir une condamnation sans équivoque non seulement de l'emploi mais aussi de la possession de l'arme nucléaire (2).

2.1 *Le débat porté sur « l'impact humanitaire de l'arme nucléaire »*

L'avis consultatif de la CIJ du 8 juillet 1996 sur la *Licéité de la menace ou de l'emploi d'armes nucléaires* concluait sans ambiguïté que compte-tenu de leur spécificité et des conséquences humanitaires catastrophiques anticipées, l'emploi de telles armes serait difficilement compatible avec les exigences du droit international humanitaire. Même si l'avis avait suscité des critiques comme il a été mentionné, il n'en a pas moins inspiré la mobilisation internationale autour du nouvel agenda sur « l'impact humanitaire des armes nucléaires », consistant à placer la dimension humanitaire au cœur de la revendication de désarmement nucléaire.

Cette question fut d'abord examinée à l'occasion des Conférence des Parties au TNP en 2010 et en 2015[35], à l'AGNU[36] et plus spécifiquement dans le cadre des conférences sur l'impact humanitaire des armes nucléaires organisées à l'initiative de la Norvège (4-5 mars 2013), du Mexique (13-14 février 2014) et de l'Autriche (8-9 décembre 2014)[37]. Le document portant « Engagement humanitaire » adopté à l'occasion de ces conférences évoque « les conséquences sur la santé, l'environnement, les infrastructures, la sécurité alimentaire, le climat, le développement, la cohésion sociale et l'économie mondiale, qui sont systémiques et potentiellement irréversibles, sont complexes et intimement liées »[38]. Ces conséquences affecteraient également la capacité à assurer

---

35   Voir Conférence des Parties chargée d'examiner le Traité sur la non-prolifération des armes nucléaires en 2010, Document final, vol. I [NPT/CONF.2010/50 (Vol. I)], première partie, Conclusions et recommandations concernant les mesures de suivi ; et Conférence des Parties chargée d'examiner le Traité sur la non-prolifération des armes nucléaires en 2015, Document de travail de l'Autriche, NPT/CONF.2015/WP.29, 21 avril 2015.

36   Voir les deux résolutions sponsorisées par l'Autriche et une vingtaine d'ENDAN : A/RES/70/47 sur les *Conséquences humanitaires des armes nucléaires* adoptée par. 144 voix (dont l'Inde, EDAN) contre 18 et 22 abstentions ; et A/RES/70/48 portant *Engagement humanitaire en faveur de l'interdiction et de l'élimination des armes nucléaires* adoptée par. 139 voix contre 29 et 17 abstentions.

37   Ces conférences associent la participation d'Etats, d'organisations intergouvernementales, du Mouvement international de la Croix-Rouge et du Croissant-Rouge et d'ONG (voir le site officiel de la conférence de Vienne : https://www.bmeia.gv.at/europa-aussenpolitik/abruestung/massenvernichtungswaffen/nukleare-waffen/conference-de-vienne-sur-limpact-humanitaire-des-armes-nucleaires/ (accessible le 22 août 2016).

38   Conférence du désarmement, voir le texte de l'engagement humanitaire transmis par l'Autriche à la Conférence du désarmement, CD/2039 (28 août 2015) et www.hinw14 vienna.at (accessible le 22 août 2016).

l'assistance humanitaire car « aucun dispositif d'action national ou international n'est à même de fournir une réponse adaptée aux souffrances humaines et aux dommages humanitaires qui résulteraient d'une explosion nucléaire dans une zone habitée »[39].

Les puissances nucléaires ont bien compris les enjeux et les risques de délégitimations auprès de leur propre opinion publique de leurs arsenaux découlant du débat suscité par l'initiative sur « l'impact humanitaire ». Leur attitude se traduit par une opposition à cette thématique qu'ils considèrent généralement comme une tentative politiquement orientée de diversion par rapport au processus établi qu'est le régime de non-prolifération[40].

L'agenda sur l'impact humanitaire des armes nucléaires est symptomatique de la pression constante sur les puissances nucléaires qui s'exerce notamment à travers l'adoption chaque année d'une résolution de suivi intitulée « Suite donnée à l'avis consultatif de la Cour internationale de Justice sur la licéité de la menace ou de l'emploi d'armes nucléaires »[41]. Cet avis marque en effet une étape importante du débat sur la légalité des armes nucléaires. Bien que la Cour n'ait pas conclu de manière claire à l'illicéité de l'emploi de ces armes, la question de la compatibilité d'un tel emploi avec le droit international humanitaire était inévitablement posée. La détermination de ceux qui souhaitent fonder la revendication du désarmement nucléaire sur le droit international humanitaire vise précisément à mettre un terme à « l'exceptionnalisme nucléaire ». Cet objectif emprunte aussi les voies étroites de la judiciarisation de la question nucléaire.

---

39 Le Comité International de la Croix-Rouge (CICR) évoque des problèmes d'accès aux victimes et leur évacuation, d'acheminements des secours dans les zones contaminées, de risques pour les personnels humanitaires, de décontamination (voir *L'assistance humanitaire en cas d'emploi d'armes nucléaires*, Note d'information n°3, CICR, 2013 : https://www.icrc.org/fre/assets/files/2013/4132-3-nuclear-weapons-humanitarian-assistance-2013-fre.pdf).

40 Les Etats-Unis, la Russie, Israël, la France et le Royaume-Uni ont votés contre la résolution 70/47 sur les *Conséquences humanitaires des armes nucléaires* tandis que la Chine, le Pakistan et la Corée du Nord se sont abstenues, mais on relèvera ici le vote favorable de l'Inde. Pour la résolution 70/48 sur l'*Engagement humanitaire en faveur de l'interdiction et de l'élimination des armes nucléaires*, on retrouve les mêmes oppositions avec cette fois l'abstention de l'Inde. Pour une analyse de la position de la France et du Royaume-Uni, voir M. Smetana, « Stake on Disarmament, The European Union and the 2015 NPT Review Conference », *International Affairs*, vol. 92, n°1, 2016, p. 137-152 ; et J. Borrie, « Humanitarian reframing of nuclear weapons and the logic of a ban », *International Affairs*, vol. 90, n°3, 2016, p. 137-152.

41 C'est à l'initiative de la Malaisie que fut inscrit en 1996 ce point à l'ordre du jour des sessions de l'AGNU.

2.2 La judiciarisation de la question nucléaire : la stratégie d'évitement de la Cour

La requête introductive d'instance des Îles Marshall contre neuf EDAN « ne vise pas à rouvrir la question de la licéité des armes nucléaires, déjà traitée par la Cour dans son avis consultatif du 8 juillet 1996 sur la Licéité de la menace ou de l'emploi d'armes nucléaires », mais porte sur « les manquements par les puissances concernées de leurs obligations en matière de désarmement nucléaire qui découlent à la fois de l'article VI du TNP et du droit international coutumier »[42]. Ces dernières se voyaient reprocher de ne pas avoir pris les mesures préconisées par la CIJ en 1996, à savoir « poursuivre de bonne foi et mener à terme des négociations conduisant au désarmement nucléaire dans tous ses aspects, sous un contrôle international strict et efficace »[43]. Est évoqué le comportement « négatif et obstructionniste » caractérisé par la non-participation des puissances concernées aux délibérations et négociations internationales en vue du désarmement nucléaire, leur opposition aux résolutions de l'AGNU sur ce thème, leur réticence à réduire le rôle de l'armement nucléaire dans les doctrines de défense ainsi que leurs programmes de développement qualitatif et quantitatif des arsenaux nucléaires[44].

Pour le requérant, il ne fait aucun doute que l'obligation de l'article VI du TNP[45] dont il est question ici est à la fois une obligation de négocier et de conclure. En effet l'utilisation des termes « de bonne foi » et « négociation en vue de [...] la cessation de la course aux armements nucléaire et le désarmement » ne souffrent d'aucune ambiguïté quant au lien fait entre négocier et conclure par les rédacteurs du traité. De ce point de vue la CIJ avait cru devoir indiquer dans son avis consultatif du 8 juillet 1996 qu'il ne s'agit pas « d'une simple obligation de comportement », mais d'une obligation de « parvenir à un résultat

---

42 CIJ, *Obligations relatives à des négociations concernant la cessation de la course aux armes nucléaires et le désarmement nucléaire*, Requêtes introductives d'instance de la République des îles Marshall contre le Royaume-Uni, l'Inde et le Pakistan, 24 avril 2014 (voir : http://www.icj-cij.org).

43 *Licéité de la menace ou de l'emploi d'armes nucléaires, op. cit.*, note 10, CIJ, *Obligations relatives à des negociations concernant la cessation de la course aux armes nucleaires et le desarmement nucleaire, op. cit.* par. 105 (2) (F).

44 Voir *Requêtes introductives d'instance contre le Royaume-Uni*, p. 27-29 (voir : http://www.icj-cij.org).

45 L'article VI du TNP dispose que : « Chacune des Parties au traité s'engage à poursuivre de bonne foi des négociations sur des mesures efficaces relatives à la cessation de la course aux armements nucléaires à une date rapprochée et au désarmement nucléaire, et sur un traité de désarmement général et complet sous un contrôle international strict et efficace ».

précis – le désarmement nucléaire dans tous ses aspects – par l'adoption d'un comportement déterminé, à savoir la poursuite de bonne foi de négociations en la matière »[46]. Une telle formulation par la Cour fait que l'obligation dont il est question ici, n'est pas seulement une obligation conventionnelle énoncée à l'article VI du TNP mais s'applique de manière universelle, y compris aux Etats non parties à l'accord, et que par conséquent elle existe aussi de manière autonome en droit international coutumier[47].

Des neuf EDAN concernés, trois seulement (l'Inde, le Pakistan et le Royaume-Uni) participèrent à la procédure parce qu'ayant reconnu la compétence obligatoire de la CIJ en vertu de l'article 36 (2) de son Statut. Ils demandèrent à la Cour de juger irrecevable la requête faute d'un différend établi[48]. Dans les trois arrêts assez identiques rendus le 5 octobre 2016, la Cour leur a donné satisfaction en écartant l'examen de la requête sur le fond au motif qu'aucun différend n'existait entre le requérant et les défendeurs avant le dépôt de ladite requête[49].

Si le Président Abraham[50] a salué la « rigueur » du raisonnement de la Cour à propos de l'absence de différend entre les parties, les opinions dissidentes des juges ont relevé que la Cour, en écartant d'emblée l'ensemble de la requête, a fait une interprétation stricte de la notion de « différend » allant au-delà de

---

46 *Licéité de la menace ou de l'emploi d'armes nucléaires, op. cit.*, p. 751, par. 99. Pour une analyse de cette obligation voir notamment G. Cotereau, « Obligation de négocier et de conclure ? », *Le droit international des armes nucléaires, op. cit.*, note 14, p. 163-177.

47 Dans l'affaire des *Activités militaires et paramilitaires au Nicaragua et contre celui-ci (Nicaragua c. Etats-Unis d'Amérique)*, la Cour a jugé que ce n'était pas parce que les principes de droit international coutumier étaient consacrés dans des conventions multilatérales qu'ils cessaient d'exister et de s'appliquer en tant que principes de droit international (voir arrêt (compétence et recevabilité) du 26 novembre 1984, CIJ *Recueil 1984*, p. 392, par. 73).

48 Le Royaume-Uni a soulevé des exceptions préliminaires en soutenant qu'il n'existe aucun différend entre les Parties susceptible de faire l'objet d'un règlement judiciaire et a prié la Cour « de dire et juger que la demande présentée par la République des Iles Marshall [était] irrecevable, ou qu'elle n'a[vait] pas compétence pour en connaître » (voir *Exceptions préliminaires du Royaume-Uni de Grande-Bretagne et d'Irlande du nord*, 15 juin 2015, p. 36, par. 114). Dans leur contre-mémoires respectifs l'Inde (16 septembre 2015) et le Pakistan (1er décembre 2015) ont demandé à la Cour de statuer en incompétence et juger irrecevable la requête.

49 CIJ, *Obligations relatives à des négociations concernant la cessation de la course aux armes nucléaires et le désarmement nucléaire (Royaume-Uni), Exceptions préliminaires*, ainsi que (Marshall c. Inde) et (Marshall c. Pakistan), *Compétence de la Cour et recevabilité de la requête*, arrêts du 5 octobre 2016 (voir le site de la CIJ : http://www.icj-cij.org).

50 Voir Déclaration du Président R. Abraham, par. 2 à 4. http://www.icj-cij.org/docket/files/160/19201.pdf (?).

sa jurisprudence antérieure[51]. Ainsi, dans l'*Affaire du mandat d'arrêt* (*Belgique contre Sénégal*) en 2012, la Cour s'était déclarée incompétente sur certaines demandes de la requête belge sans remettre en cause le caractère justiciable de l'affaire[52].

La Cour n'a donc pas cru devoir examiner ici s'il existait un différend latent ou potentiel sur l'arme nucléaire entre le requérant et les défendeurs. Pour cela elle pouvait s'appuyer sur la position constante des Îles Marshall dans les instances internationales en faveur du désarmement nucléaires et en particulier sur les votes des résolutions à l'AGNU. L'un des enseignements à en tirer est que l'interprétation des conditions de l'existence d'un différend peut servir à écarter l'examen de l'ensemble d'une requête. L'usage de ce « filtre » fait dire à certains que le raisonnement formaliste a pris le pas sur la substance[53].

Les décisions contenues dans les trois arrêts du 5 octobre 2016 furent adoptées avec des majorités étroites, particulièrement dans le cas de la requête contre le Royaume-Uni où la voie prépondérante du Président a fait pencher la balance en faveur de l'absence de différend entre les parties[54]. À ce propos, il est intéressant de constater que sur les huit juges qui ont appuyé la décision d'incompétence, six sont ressortissants d'EDAN (Chine, Etats-Unis, France, Inde, Royaume-Uni et Russie) et les deux autres d'Etats alliés bénéficiant du parapluie nucléaire américain (Japon and Italie). Quant aux juges de la minorité, ils sont tous nationaux d'ENDAN.

L'enjeu dans cette affaire est important pour toutes les parties car il met encore une fois en exergue la tension qui existe sur la question nucléaire entre la pratique des Etats d'une part et les principes du droit international d'autre part, notamment du droit international humanitaire. La Cour a manifestement manqué d'audace en optant pour une stratégie « d'évitement ». Cette position a alimenté l'accusation de capitulation face à de puissants intérêts[55].

---

51   *Obligations relatives à des négociations concernant la cessation de la course aux armes nucléaires et le désarmement nucléaire* (*Iles Marshall c. Royaume Unis*), ordonnance du 16 juin 2014, CIJ Recueil 2014, p. 464, voir notamment les opinions dissidentes du juge Crawford et du juge *ad-hoc* Bedjaoui.

52   *Question concernant l'obligation de poursuivre ou d'extrader* (*Belgique c. Sénégal*), arrêt du 20 juillet 2012, CIJ Recueil 2012, p. 422, par. 122.

53   Voir C. Tams « No Dispute About Nuclear Weapons? », *European Journal of International Law*, 2016 : http://www.ejiltalk.org/no-dispute-about-nuclear-weapons/.

54   Ont voté en faveur le Président Abraham, les juges Owada, Greenwood, Xue, Donoghue, Gaja, Bhandari et Gevorgian ; ont voté contre : le vice-Président Yusuf ; les juges Tomka, Bennouna, Cançado Trindade, Sebutinde, Robinson, Crawford ; et le juge *ad hoc* Bedjaoui.

55   Voir N. Krisch « Capitulation in The Hague: The Marshall Islands Cases », *European Journal of International Law*, 2016 http://www.ejiltalk.org/capitulation-in-the-hague-the-marshall-islands-cases/.

Le TNP repose sur un équilibre complexe entre exigences de non-prolifération, « droit inaliénable » et « sans discriminations » aux utilisations pacifiques de l'énergie nucléaire, et engagement de désarmement nucléaire. Il s'agit bien comme le rappelle Djamchid Momtaz d'un « subtile équilibre établi par le TNP entre la recherche-développement de l'énergie nucléaire à des fins pacifiques [...] et l'exigence de non-prolifération en attendant un désarmement général et complet »[56]. Cet équilibre vise à assurer l'attractivité du régime de non-prolifération nucléaire dont le TNP est la « pierre angulaire ».

Chaque article du TNP lie tous les États parties, par conséquent les EDAN se doivent d'honorer leur part des obligations découlant de l'accord. Dans le cas contraire cela reviendrait à pérenniser l'asymétrie instaurée par le TNP[57]. En l'absence de progrès vers le désarmement nucléaire, l'armement nucléaire possédé par une poignée d'Etats constituerait structurellement un facteur d'incitation à la prolifération ainsi que le faisait remarquer Joseph Rotblat (Lauréat du Nobel de la Paix)[58].... Tel est le dilemme au cœur de « l'exceptionnalisme nucléaire » !

---

56   Voir D. Momtaz « Le programme nucléaire de l'Iran et le régime de non-prolifération nucléaire », *Essays on International Law in Honor of W. Michael Reisman*, by M. H. Arsanjani, J. Cogan, R. Sloane and S. Wiessner (Editors), Leiden/Boston, Martinus Nijhoff Publishers, 2011, Chap. 48, p. 989-1002 (p. 992). D. Momtaz fut conseiller juridique du gouvernement iranien à l'occasion des négociations avec les grandes puissances sur le programme nucléaire de l'Iran.

57   Pour M. Bedjaoui le TNP « serait non seulement inégal mais encore illégal s'il devait instaurer pour toujours un nouveau principe, contraire même au *jus cogens*, celui de l'inégale souveraineté des Etats. L'obligation de conclure le désarmement nucléaire découle ainsi de la nécessité impérieuse de rétablir à terme le principe cardinal de l'égalité entre Etats », voir sa « Préface » dans : A. Biad, *La Cour internationale de justice et le droit international humanitaire : une lex specialis revisitée par le juge*, Bruxelles, Bruylant, 2011, p. XXIX.

58   « If some nations – including the most powerful militarily – say that they need nuclear weapons for their security, then such security cannot be denied to other countries which really feel insecure. Proliferation of nuclear weapons is thus the logical consequence of this nuclear policy », voir J. Rotblat, « Science and Nuclear Weapons: Where Do We Go from Here? », *The Blackaby Papers*, n°5, 2004, p. 7.

Intervention by Invitation as a Tool of New Colonialism

Farideh Shaygan

Introduction

The main presumption of this article is that any military intervention by a State at the request of the Government of another State directed against the right to self-determination of the latter's peoples violates the political independence of that state and is, therefore, unlawful. It is also an act of domination. The right to (or the principle of) self-determination is not limited to the right of colonial peoples, or peoples under alien occupation or racist regimes. It goes far beyond this and bears the right of the entire population of an independent State 'to maintain its political independence from third States and to choose its own Government with no outside interference.'[1] An act of domination means, for the purposes of this article, an invited intervention which violates the right to self-determination of the people in their territory where the intervention takes place. By such an intervention, the intervening State often seeks to maintain or impose a Governmental regime against the will of at least a large part of the host State's population. This means a form of domination which was one of the foundations of international law, legitimizing colonization, and still retaining its function, though often covertly, in the decentralized world order.

Indeed, Article 2(4) of the United Nations (UN) Charter contains no absolute prohibition of the use of force by States, as popularly believed and as even some scholars regard as *jus cogens*.[2] But in fact this principle could be likened to a dam that has several breaches. Under Charter law it contains exceptions, of which self-defence is only one. The use of force is also permissible under international law against a colonial power, racist regimes and other forms of

---

[1] K. Bannelier & T. Christakis, 'Under the UN Security Council's Watchful Eyes: Military Intervention by Invitation in the Malian Conflict', 26 *Leiden Journal of International Law*, 2013, pp. 860–861. See also, Common Article 1 of the two 1966 International Covenants concerning Civil and Political Rights, and Economic, Social and Cultural Rights respectively.

[2] See for example, A. Cassese, 'Article 51', in J-P. Cot & A. Pellet (eds) *La Charte des Nations Unies. Commentaire article par article*, 2nd edition, Economica, 1991, p. 790.

alien domination,[3] and also in the form of invited intervention. Consequently, force may be employed by a State under one of these justifications, for dominating other States or ensuring its political influence on them. Intervention by invitation, like the 'global war on terror' has often been a pretext to redefine a world order based on imperial and neo-colonial domination. The first section of this article will focus on the principle of the use of force, which is still a prominent tool of domination particularly by great powers, to ensure the continuity and/or reproduction of the *status quo* for their benefit. The second section will reflect on consented intervention as an instrument to justify a breach of the right to self-determination of peoples in whose territory the intervention occurs. The article concludes, finally, that it is not enough to concentrate on the validity of the consent given by the inviting Government when evaluating its lawfulness. To minimize the risk of abuse, it is necessary also to inquire whether the invited State is qualified to conduct such an intervention.

1 The Use of Force as a Means of Domination

The universalization of international law became possible through positivism, which progressively replaced naturalism, from the second half of the eighteenth century.[4] Under positivist international law, States are the principal actors of this discipline and nothing can bind them without their consent. Despite certain evolution in international law after 1945, positivism continues to be the foundation of the international legal system.

Positivist international law imposed a world legal order in which the lawmakers and the subjects of the law are the same. In other words, it has been a means to ensure the supremacy of sovereign States, which were principally European till the early years of the twentieth century. The goal was to create and/or preserve a *status quo* in which the more powerful States, despite formal legal equal sovereignty of all States, could have the last word. In such a legal world order the mighty States are right and have more rights than the weak States who are—when necessary—wrong and enjoy fewer rights.[5] Positivist

---

3 See UN General Assembly Resolution, UN Doc. A/RES/42/22, 18 November 1987, Annex, para. 33(3).
4 A. Anghie, 'Finding the Peripheries: Sovereignty and Colonialism in Nineteenth Century International Law', 40 *Harvard International Law Journal*, 1999, p. 2 and note 5.
5 See in this vein the dissenting opinion of Judge Weeramantry concerning *Legality of the Threat or Use of Nuclear Weapons*, Advisory Opinion, ICJ Reports 1996, p. 481. He cites W. Rahula, *What the Buddha Taught*, Grove Press, 1959, p. 84: 'According to Buddhism there is

international law distinguished between civilized States and non-civilized States and asserted further that international law applied only to the sovereign states that composed the civilized 'Family of Nations'.[6] In this way international law legitimized the subjugation of the rest of the nations of the world.

This system of international law, therefore, permitted more powerful States to continue their domination by different means, of which intervention by invitation is only one. As we will see, this legal institution has often been used by powerful States—and recently by other States in Africa and Asia, sometimes supported by a more powerful State—for their national policy interest. As Strawson puts it:

> The idea of civilization was to make a marked return in political and legal discourses following 11 September 2001, ... Civilization was now used as a signifier of whether or not a state was a 'terrorist state' or a 'failed state', both denoting a loss of sovereignty. Thus while civilization could be gained during colonialism, it could be lost in the post-colonial period.[7]

Thus, despite the prohibition of the use of force under Article 2(4) of the UN Charter, force has often been used by a State in the territory of another State relying on different justifications, including intervention by invitation. This poses, first, the question of the legality or permissibility of such military intervention in international law (1.1); and secondly, its potential for abuse in the interest of the intervening State (1.2).

1.1   (Non) Prohibition of the Use of Force in International Law

The principle of the non-use of force formulated in Article 2(4) of the UN Charter contains no broad and general prohibition of the use of force by States. What has been prohibited is any threat or use of force by States against the 'territorial integrity and political independence' of another state. The wording of this article let States and scholars conclude that any threat or use of force that is not against a State's territorial integrity and political independence would

---

nothing that can be called a 'just war'—a false term coined and circulated to justify and excuse hatred, cruelty, violence and massacre. Who decides what is just and unjust? The mighty and victorious are 'just' and the weak and defeated are 'unjust'. Our war is always 'just' and your war is always 'unjust'. Buddhism does not accept this position.'

6 Anghie, supra, note 4, p. 4.
7 J. Strawson, 'Provoking international law: War and regime change in Iraq', in F. Johns, R. Joyce & S. Pahuja (eds), *Events: The Force of International Law*, Routledge, 2011, p. 253.

be permissible and not prohibited.[8] It leaves considerable latitude for States to use force. This is, in fact, what several resolutions of the General Assembly have also let us to conclude. The General Assembly Declaration on the Enhancement of the Effectiveness of the Principle of Refraining from the Threat or Use of Force in International Relations, explicitly provides that: 'nothing in the present Declaration shall be construed as: enlarging or diminishing in any way the scope of the Charter concerning cases in which the use of force is lawful.'[9] But enough attention should be paid to the last phrase of Article 2(4) of the Charter, which also prohibits the use of force that is 'in any other manner inconsistent with the purposes of the United Nations.' The phrase 'in any other manner' shows that any use of force by a State that is against the 'territorial integrity and political independence' of another state is prominently and necessarily inconsistent with the purposes of the United Nations.

There are, however explicit and implicit exceptions to the principle of the non-use of force under Charter law, of which individual and collective self-defence in response to an 'armed attack', included in Article 51 of the Charter and regarded as an inherent right of States, is only one.

Another exception to the principle which has been recognized by the United Nations is action in support of self-determination. The General Assembly in its resolution 42/22 states that: 'nothing in the present Declaration could in anyway prejudice the right to self-determination, freedom and independence, as derived from the Charter, of peoples forcibly deprived of that right.'[10] Then, referring to resolution 2625,[11] it recognizes for 'peoples under colonial and racist regimes or other forms of alien domination...the right...to struggle to that end and to seek and receive support.'[12]

According to that resolution peoples have the right to use force in their territory against colonial and racist regimes or other forms of alien domination

---

[8] See for example ibid., pp. 246, 248; M. J. Glennon, 'The Limitations of Traditional Rules and Institutions Relating to the Use of Force' in M. Weller (ed), *The Oxford Handbook of the Use of Force in International Law*, Oxford University Press, 2015, p. 85. Glennon goes further and states that: 'what actually is forbidden is baffling. The Charter espouses many inconsistent values—antinomies such as State sovereignty and human rights, peace and justice foremost among them—leaving one to conclude that use of force is forbidden, permitted, or perhaps even encouraged for opposite purposes.'

[9] Supra, note 3, para. 33(a).

[10] UN Doc. A/RES/42/22, supra, note 3.

[11] Declaration on Principles of International Law concerning Friendly Relations and Cooperation Among States in Accordance with the Charter of the United Nations, UN Doc. A/RES/25/2625, 24 October 1970.

[12] UN Doc. A/RES/42/22 supra, note 3.

and have the right to receive military support from other States. Thus States are permitted to intervene militarily in the territory of such peoples in support of their struggle. Such use of force is not regarded as 'inconsistent with the purposes of the United Nations', which according to Article 1(2) of the Charter includes respect for the principle of the 'self-determination of peoples'.

The permissible cases of the use of force by States, however, are not limited to self-defence and self-determination. Intervention upon invitation from an incumbent Government is the third case. Even if this could not be considered as an exception to the principle, it is nevertheless a permissible case for the use of force by States. Intervention by invitation is not an exception to the principle because it is not against the will of the state in which the intervention occurs. This is why the Institut de droit international (IDI) has preferred the wording 'Military Assistance on Request' in its 2011 resolution.[13] It defines Military Assistance on Request in Article 1 of the Resolution as 'direct military assistance by the sending of armed forces by one state to another state upon the latter's request.' Since 'Request' 'means a request reflecting the free expression of the will of the requesting state and its consent to the terms and modalities of the military assistance', there would be no intervention against territorial integrity or political independence of the requesting state, and therefore, there is no exception to the prohibition of the use of force.[14]

Military assistance (intervention) by invitation, however, will be considered prohibited use of force if it violates the right to self-determination of the peoples of the host state. Such intervention is 'inconsistent with one of the purposes of the United Nations', and is also against the political independence of that state.[15]

Thus, three cases of permissible use of force by States—in self-defence, in support of self-determination and intervention by invitation—may be used as justification for military actions of States. Actually, given the deficient collective security system of the Charter, States have, using different pretexts, justifications and intentions, had recourse to force.[16] Actually, after publication

13   IDI's Resolution on Military Assistance on Request, adopted in Rhodes session, 8 September 2011.
14   See also in this regard, E. de Wet, 'The Modern Practice of Intervention by Invitation in Africa and Its Implications for the Prohibition of the Use of Force', 26 *European Journal of International Law*, 2015, p. 980.
15   See also, ibid., pp. 980, 996.
16   The Secretary-General's High-Level Panel on Threats, Challenges and Change reports: 'for the first 44 years of the United Nations, (p. 91) Member States often violated [the Charter] rules and used military force literally hundreds of times, with a paralyzed Security Council passing very few Chapter VII resolutions and Article 51 rarely providing credible cover.'

of the Secretary-General's High-Level Panel report, the world has seen further cases of the use of force by States without Security Council authorization, especially in Africa and the Middle-East. Intervention by invitation which has frequently been as used by States to justify the use of force in the territory of other states, has a strong potential for abuse and, in fact, has often been abused.

1.2 *Intervention by Invitation as a National Policy Tool of Intervening States*

Intervention by invitation has usually taken place with political motives in order to serve the interests of the intervening state. The historical records show that there have been interventions based on an alleged invitation or request from the Government of another state, which in fact lacked the consent of that state. Sometimes a puppet ruler has consented to such intervention. One example is Seyss-Inquart, who was installed by Hitler as Austria's Chancellor in March 1938 after requesting assistance from Germany in order to establish peace and order and prevent bloodshed.[17] Obvious cases of consent after an intervention are those by the Union of Soviet Socialist Republics (USSR) in Afghanistan (1979) and by the United States of America (USA) in Panama (1989). In the latter case, the invitation was issued by the new Government installed by the USA after the intervention. The invitation was thus merely a pretext for justifying a forcible intervention.[18]

States have frequently relied on an invitation or a request from a Government to justify their intervention in support of the friendly or puppet Governments of other States. There have also been interventions to overthrow the incumbent Government of another State—sometimes on the ground that the incumbent Government lacked democratic legitimacy—and installing another one, which could better serve the intervener's interests and foreign policy goals.

The USSR interventions in Hungary (1956), in Czechoslovakia (1968) and Afghanistan (1979), and the post-cold-war intervention of Russia in Ukraine (2014) were based on an invitation as the sole, or one of the, legal justifications provided. In the cases of Hungary and Czechoslovakia, the USSR's true motive

---

By one count, the Panel said, from 1945 to 1989 'force was employed 200 times.' *A More Secure World: Our Shared Responsibility*, UN Doc. A/59/565, 2 December 2004, para. 186.

[17] See A. Cassese (ed), *The Current Legal Regulation of the Use of Force*, Martinus Nijhoff, 1986, pp. 61–162; C. J. Le Mon, 'Unilateral Intervention by Invitation in Civil Wars: The Effective Control Test Tested', 35 *International Law and Politics*, 2003 p. 778 et. seq.

[18] See M. Hilaire, *International Law and the United States Military Intervention in the Western Hemisphere*, Kluwer Law International, 1997, pp. 62–63.

was to support one-party rule in those states and to suppress the opposition. In both cases there were strong doubts about the validity of the invitations and even about their existence.[19] Later under President Gorbachev, the USSR and the four other Warsaw Pact States characterized their invasions in both cases as unlawful and unjustified.[20]

In the case of Afghanistan, the USSR justified its intervention by relying on a request from a 'dubious Afghan Government', i.e., a request from a Prime Minister whom the Soviets themselves installed in power.[21] The Soviet Union stated before the Security Council that 'the government of Afghanistan repeatedly appealed to the Soviet Union for support, including the affording of military assistance, in order to repel armed intervention from outside.'[22]

In March 2014, Russia based its intervention in Ukraine (Crimea) on two grounds: the protection of its nationals abroad, and invitation by the President Yanukovich, who had been removed from office. The developments in Ukraine after Yanukovich's overthrow led, finally, to the annexation of Crimea and Sevastopol to Russia.[23] It was the latest escalation of intermittent post-Soviet tensions over the political status of Crimea and control of the Black Sea Fleet stationed at Sevastopol.[24] Indeed, it was an action for reclaiming Crimea and Sevastopol which had been transferred in 1954 into Ukraine by decree.[25] The fact that the reestablishment of Yanukovich's Government was not Russia's political motive of intervention showed that it was pursuing its national interests independently of this.[26]

19　See A. K. Allo, 'Counter-Intervention, Invitation, Both or Neither? An Appraisal of the 2006 Ethiopian Military Intervention in Somalia', 3 *Mizan Law Review*, 2009, p. 231 and note 149.

20　C. Gray, *International Law and the Use of Force*, 3rd edition, Oxford University Press, 2008, p. 93 and note 134.

21　Le Mon, supra, note 17, p. 778 et. Seq. See also L. Doswald-Beck, 'The Legal Validity of Military Intervention by Invitation of the Government', 56 *British Yearbook of International Law*, 1985, pp. 230–234.

22　See the statements of the USSR delegate before the Security Council, UN Doc. S/PV.2185, 5 January 1980, para. 16.

23　See C. Marxsen, 'The Crimea Crisis: An International Law Perspective', 74 *Zeitschrift für ausländisches öffentliches Recht und Völkerrecht*, 2014 pp. 372, 369.

24　R. Geiβ, 'Russia's Annexation of Crimea: The Mills of International Law Grind Slowly but They Do Grind', 91 *International Law Studies*, 2015 p. 428.

25　Ibid., p. 428 and note 9.

26　Marxsen, supra, note 23, p. 379; The EU Foreign Affairs Council condemned Russia's action and declared that it would not recognize the illegal annexation of Crimea and Sevastopol. EU Council Regulation 1351/2014 of 18 December 2014, Amending Regulation (EU) No 692/2014 Concerning Restrictive Measures in Response to the Illegal Annexation

The USA grounded its military interventions in the Dominican Republic (1965) and Grenada (1983) on invitation by the legitimate Governments of those states, and protection of its nationals in self-defence. In both cases the USA actually overthrew the existing Governments and installed new ones. Again there were in both cases considerable doubts about the existence of the invitations and their validity.[27] In the case of the Dominican Republic the invitation was issued by unspecified 'government officials', and in the case of Grenada, it came from the Governor-General, 'a post without executive powers'.[28] Intervention by the USA in Panama (1989) also had a subversive goal. The US relied on a request by Guillermo Endara, Panama's President-elect as one of several alleged grounds for justifying its forcible intervention in Panama.[29] Both the Organization of American States (OAS) and the UN General Assembly[30] strongly condemned the intervention, despite the dictatorial nature of the Noriega regime.[31]

On March 25, 2015, Operation Decisive Storm was launched by a Saudi-Arabia-led Coalition against opposition in Yemen, with strong political, logistical and intelligence support from the US and the UK.[32] Recently also, the US

---

of Crimea and Sevastopol, Official Journal of the EU (19.12.2014), accessed April 28, 2016, http://eur-lex.europa.eu/legal-content/EN/TXT/?uri=CELEX:32014R1351; The UN General Assembly underscored that 'the referendum held in the Autonomous Republic of Crimea and the city of Sevastopol on 16 March 2014, having no validity, cannot form the basis for any alteration of the status of the Autonomous Republic of Crimea and the city of Sevastopol'. UN Doc. A/RES/68/262, 27 March 2014, para. 5.

27 Gray, supra, note 20, p. 91.

28 Ibid.; Doswald-Beck, supra, note 21; The UN General Assembly condemned the US intervention in Grenada regarding it as 'a flagrant violation of international law and of the independence, sovereignty and territorial integrity of that state', UN Doc. A/RES/38/7, 2 November 1983.

29 See D. Wippman, 'Military Interventions, Regional Organizations, and Host-State Consent', 7 *Duke Journal of Comparative & International Law*, 1996, p. 219, note 47.

30 The UN General Assembly Resolution, UN Doc. A/RES/44/240, 29 December 1989.

31 Gray, supra, note 20, p. 92; Wippman, supra note 29, p. 215. See also, L Henkin, 'The Invasion of Panama under International Law: A Gross Violation', 21 *Columbia Journal of Transnational Law*, 1991, pp. 293–317.

32 T. Ruys & L. Ferro, 'Weathering the Storm: Legality and Legal Implications of the Saudi-led Military Intervention in Yemen', 65 *International and Comparative Law Quarterly*, 2016, p. 65; Statement by NSC Spokesperson Bernadette Meehan on the Situation in Yemen, the White House, Office of the Press Secretary, accessed June 18, 2016, https://www.whitehouse.gov/the-press-office/2015/03/25/statement-nsc-Spokesperson-bernadette-meehan-situation-yemen.

has deployed its rangers into southern Yemen.[33] The intervening states, members of the Gulf Cooperation Council (GCC), except Oman, in a joint statement addressed to the UN Security Council, justified their military operation: Intervention at the request of the (resigned) President of Yemen, Abdrabuh Mansour Hadi; Self-defence in order to protect Yemen and its people from the continuing aggression by Houthis; and to help Yemen confront Al-Qaida and the Islamic State in Iraq and the Levant.[34] This joint statement contains the text of a letter from President Hadi which provides justification for the action of the GCC Coalition. The Security Council affirmed the legitimacy of the President of Yemen even though he had been the sole candidate for the presidential elections held on 21 February 2012.[35] The Security Council further commended the GCC's efforts in assisting the political transition in Yemen, and imposed an arms embargo against individuals who belonged to opposition groups, including Abd Al-Khaliq Al-Huthi.[36]

Despite tacit approval of the Saudi-led intervention in Yemen by the Security Council, one cannot ignore the fact that President Hadi had lost control over most of Yemen's territory and apparently the support of the majority of its population who are pro-Huthis. Given the flagrant violations of the fundamental principles of international humanitarian law and human-rights law through the GCC military operations, and the silence or insufficient reaction of the Security Council to these violations and international crimes committed mostly by Coalition forces, the Security Council may be seen by the Yemeni people and world public opinion as the accomplice of the Coalition.[37]

Self-defence as the primary argument of intervening States and Hadi does not provide a credible legal basis. First, 'the degree of the external involvement *prima facie* appears insufficient to transform the Huthi 'aggression' into armed attack in the sense of Article 51 of the UN Charter justifying recourse to collective self-defence in support of Yemen. Secondly, with no 'imminent' threat of armed attack, let alone an actual armed attack, by the Huthi rebels against

---

33 See American Boots on the Ground in Yemen, accessed June 18, 2016, http://www.globalresearch.ca/ american-boots-on-the-ground-in-yemen/5523573.

34 *Statement issued by the Kingdom of Saudi Arabia, the United Arab Emirates, the Kingdom of Bahrain, the State of Qatar and the State of Kuwait*, UN Doc. S/2015/217, 27 March 2015.

35 Ruys & Ferro, supra, note 32, p. 66.

36 UN Security Council resolution, S/RES/2216 (2015), 14 April 2015.

37 Recent scandal concerning removal of the name of Saudi Arabia and its allies from the UN list of states and armed groups that have violated rights of the child in armed conflicts under pressure from Saudi Arabia, makes this suspicion stronger. See Amnesty Blasts UN's 'Shameful Pandering to Saudi Arabia over Children Killed in Yemen', accessed June 10, 2016, http://www.salon.com/2016/06/07/amnesty_blasts_u_n_s_shameful_pand.

Saudi Arabia, the operation can hardly be considered as an exercise in individual self-defence by the latter country.'[38]

In the majority of cases of intervention by invitation, traces of political motives or a hidden agenda of the intervening States are discernible. However, without an effective collective security system, the right of a State to invite the outside intervention will retain its utility;[39] but this does not necessarily mean that the intervention will also benefit for the people of the inviting State. When, particularly, the intervening State is a great power or the intervention is supported by one or several great powers, the risk of abuse is usually high. It is worth asking here whether the creation of such a deficient collective security system in 1945 was not intended to reserve for the great powers the possibility to change, forcibly, the *status quo* within other States when they desire and feel it necessary without being blamed or considered responsible.

2 The Legality of the Intervention by Invitation

Recognizing a right for a Government to request external military assistance is a logical result of the status of sovereign States under positive international law. The Government as agent of a State represents the will of that state in international relations. To be regarded as lawful, intervention by invitation should fulfil certain conditions. Determining the existence of each of these conditions is not always easy. In many cases there have been doubts, particularly, about the status of the authority which consents to the intervention, and the quality or nature of the consent. Another important problem is who should verify the existence of the required conditions, and that the invitation is not political and therefore biased. In fact, the practice of States and organizations, whether international or regional, has been inconsistent. Thus, intervention by invitation may only mask other purposes. This section focuses, first, on the requirements for a consent or invitation to be considered legally valid, and the propriety of their evaluation under international law (2.1); and secondly, on the (un)lawfulness of invited intervention in situations of conflict below and above the threshold of 'civil war' or non-international armed conflict (NIAC), taking into account the (in)consistency of such intervention with the right to self-determination of peoples in whose territory the intervention takes place (2.2).

---

38   Ruys & Ferro, supra, note 32, pp. 96–97.
39   See Le Mon, supra, note 17, p. 792.

2.1 The Legal Validity of Consent

The legally valid consent or invitation of a Government precludes the wrongfulness of a consented intervention.[40] It denotes also that inviting external intervention is only a prerogative or right of a Government as agent of a State.[41] In the *Nicaragua* case, the International Court of Justice (ICJ) noted that the principle of non-intervention:

> would certainly lose its effectiveness as a principle of law if intervention were to be justified by a mere request for assistance made by an opposition group in another state ... Indeed, it is difficult to see what would remain of the principle of non-intervention in international law if intervention, *which is already allowable at the request of the government of a State*, were also to be allowed at the request of the opposition.

For an intervention by invitation of a Government to be regarded as legally valid, certain conditions must be met. First, the official or the authority who gives the consent has to be entitled to do so on behalf of the state. Secondly, the Government that is generally allowed to extend an invitation for external military assistance should be in effective control of the major portion of the territory of the State and widely recognized. Thirdly, the state's consent has to be valid under international law, i.e., must not be based on error, fraud, corruption or force; should be given prior to or at the time of the intervention, and should be clearly established and really expressed. This excludes a merely presumed consent. Fourthly, the object of the consent needs to be in conformity with the international obligations of the inviting state, particularly under peremptory norms, and with the right to self-determination.[42] Fifthly, if the consent is based on a treaty, an *ad hoc* request (consent) is required for

---

40 See Article 20 of the ILC Draft Articles on Responsibility of States for Internationally Wrongful Acts with Commentaries, in Report of the International Law Commission on the work of its fifty-third session, 2001, UN Doc. A/56/10, 2001, p. 72.

41 Article 4(1) of the IDI's 2011 Resolution on Military Assistance on Request, states that: 'Military assistance may only be provided upon the request of the requesting State.' While this article of the resolution does not use the term 'Government', it is, however, the Government that represents the State in international relations.; Marxsen, supra, note 23, p. 370.

42 ILC, supra, note 40, pp. 174–175, paras. 3–7; The IDI's 2011 resolution on Military Assistance on Request, Article 4; G. H. Fox, 'Intervention by Invitation', in Weller, supra, note 7, p. 816; Bannelier & Christakis, supra, note 2, p. 865.

the specific case.[43] Finally, the action of the intervening State 'remains within limits of that consent'.[44]

It is generally accepted that the sole authority within a State entitled to request military assistance from another state, is a Government that unquestionably represents that state. Such a Government is the internationally recognized *de jure* Government,[45] and is entitled to extend an invitation for military assistance to retain itself in power in the face of internal rebellions.[46] Thus, international recognition of the inviting Government is a decisive element for determining its legitimacy. As Le Mon puts '[t]here is a causal path, then, from modalities of recognition to legality of intervention.'[47] Recognition of a Government by other States arises when several competing factions claim to be the legitimate Government of a recognized State.[48]

In international law traditionally a Government represents itself as the agent of a State when it exercises effective control over the state's territory. When the Government loses its control over a considerable portion of the State territory, its exclusive status to represent the State is challenged by the presence of more than one entity claiming the title of Government. The degree of rebel control over territory is also central to contemporary approaches to evaluating government invitations.[49]

However, since the end of the Cold War the theory of effective control has been challenged by the democratic legitimacy test. According to some authors, 'the incumbent Government must have the recognition of the international community... must be in *de facto* control of the territory and the means of administration, have the acquiescence of the population, and indicate its willingness to comply with the State's international obligations.'[50] In the post-Cold War era, insistence has been on the democratic legitimacy criteria for determining the legality of a requested intervention. This trend was reinforced particularly by the reaction of the UN Security Council to military coups in Haiti and Sierra Leone against the democratically elected Presidents of these states. In both cases, the Security Council (and also Organization of American States

---

43   IDI's 2011 Resolution on Military Assistance on Request, Article 4(3); Fox, supra, note 42, pp. 817, 831–833.
44   Article 20 of the ILC's Draft Articles on Responsibility of States.
45   De Wet, supra, note 14, p. 982.
46   Fox, supra, note 42, p. 818.
47   Le Mon, supra, note 17, p. 743.
48   Ibid., p. 745.
49   Fox, supra, note 42, p. 821.
50   D. Brown, 'The Role of Regional Organizations in Stopping Civil Wars', 41 *Air Force Law Review* 1997, p. 270.

(OAS) in the Haiti case) condemned military coups. They not only demanded the immediate reinstatement of the elected Governments,[51] but also accepted the use of force as a legitimate tool to restore democracy at the request of these ousted Governments.[52]

There have been, however, many cases in which the UN General Assembly has accepted regimes that had gained power by coups and allowed them to speak as the representatives of their respective states. This was the case of at least eight African regimes just before the 'Arab Spring'.[53] Despite the existence of treaty-based obligations[54] to suspend the participation of unconstitutional Governments in the sessions of the African Union (AU) and the OAS, the practice of these Organizations in this regard has been inconsistent.[55]

Therefore, while 'democratic legitimacy does not yet seem to be a requirement for recognition of governments in international law', the practice of the Security Council in the 1990s, supporting the democratically elected Presidents of Haiti and Sierra Leone who had subsequently been ousted from power, made one author conclude that international recognition of 'the legitimacy of a democratically elected Government generally offsets its lack of effectiveness.'[56]

It should be borne in mind that recognition is a political rather than a legal act and the imputation of effectiveness or democratic legitimacy is a subjective evaluation.[57] Actually, the recognition of States or Governments has not been an objective recognition of facts, but a political reaction to a changing situation, and even an interventionist act which, as some authors have argued,

---

51 See UN Doc. S/RES/841 (1993), 16 June 1993 and UN Doc. S/RES/917 (1994), 6 May 1994 (for the Haiti case); UN Doc. S/PRST/1997/29, 27 May 1997; UN Doc. S/PRST/1997/36, 11 July 1997; UN Doc. S/PRST/1997/42, 6 August 1997; UN Doc. S/RES/1132 (1997), 8 October 1997 (for the Sierra Leone case).

52 D. Wippman, 'Pro-Democratic Intervention by Invitation', in G. H. Fox & B. R. Roth (eds) *Democratic Governance and International Law*, Cambridge University Press, 2004, pp. 293–294. See also Fox, supra, note 42, pp. 835–837; Report of Gerhard Hafner on Present Problems of the Use of Force in International Law, Sub-group: Military Assistance on Request (hereinafter, Hafner report), Annuaire de l'Institut de droit international, Session de Naples, 73 (2009): paras. 401, 83.

53 De Wet, supra, note 14 p. 987.

54 Inter-American Democratic Charter, adopted in Lima, September 11, 2001, Art. 19 (for OAS), and AU Constitutive Act of 2000, Art. 4(p); The African Charter on Democracy, 2007, Art. 25 (for AU).

55 De Wet, supra, note 14, pp. 985–988.

56 J. d'Aspremont, 'Legitimacy of Governments in the Age of Democracy', 38 *International Law and Politics*, 2006, p. 903.

57 See C. Miéville, *Between Equal Rights: A Marxist Theory of International Law*, Brill, 2005, p. 236.

'illustrates the complicity of imperialism and positivism. This theory of international law which claimed to abstract away all but the 'objective truth' about states was constructed of subjective categories such as 'effective sovereignty' which could not but be evaluated, recognized and thereby actualized by powerful States within the international community. The seeming objectivity is predicated on power.'[58]

But what really does democratic legitimacy mean? Or as Koskenniemi asks, 'which democracy?' According to the proposition of Western states, there is 'an international or universal norm of 'democracy',... that should or may be realized within existing political communities [but that] may in fact be unacceptable because over- and under-inclusive at the same time, too general to provide political guidance and always suspect as a neo-colonialist strategy.'[59]

Moreover, there is no guarantee that a democratically gained power Government be actually and substantially democratic or continue to be democratic. For example, when Jean Bernard Aristide, who was ironically reinstated as the democratic incumbent president by the USA in 1994, faced stiff internal opposition against his corrupt, yet democratically elected regime, he was allegedly forced by the USA to leave his country.[60] However, it should be acknowledged that there is a tendency today in support of democratic legitimacy for determining the lawfulness of intervention by invitation.

But, to reduce the risk of abuse, it is necessary that the requested intervention be regulated internationally, and the determination of the legitimacy of the inviting Government be entrusted to an impartial international body, and not to a political organ or individual state.

2.2 *(Im)permissibility of Intervention by Invitation Violating the Right to Self-determination*

It is generally accepted that intervention by invitation of the incumbent legitimate Government in situations short of a civil war is not unlawful.[61] Most doctrinal debates on permissibility or impermissibility of intervention by

---

58 Ibid., p. 239.
59 M. Koskenniemi, 'Whose intolerance, which democracy?', in Fox & Roth, supra, note 52, pp. 439–440.
60 See C. Ryngaert, Pro-democratic Intervention in International Law, K.U. Leuven, Faculty of Law, Institute for International Law, Working Paper No. 53, April 2004: 7, accessed July 12, 2012, https://www. law.kuleuven.be/iir/nl/onderzoek/wp/WP53e.pdf.
61 See for example, IDI, supra, note 52, p. 303; Article 2 of the IDI 2011 Resolution on Military Assistance on Request; De Wet, supra, note 14, 992; Le Mon, supra, note 17, p. 753; Gray, supra, note 20, pp. 67, 81; United Kingdom Foreign Policy Doc., 57 *British Yearbook of International Law*, 1986, p. 614.

invitation have focused on situations of civil war or NIAC, and not on situations of internal disturbances and tensions, such as riots, isolated sporadic acts of violence and other acts of similar nature .[62] I do not intend to follow this dichotomy as far as it concerns a people's right to self-determination as a decisive factor in the (un)lawfulness of a given intervention by invitation. If the majority of international lawyers as well as *opinio juris* of States consider external intervention by Government invitation impermissible or prohibited in a case of civil war, it is because such a situation, in which each party to the conflict has control over a substantial portion of national territory and enjoys the support of a large part of population, obviously indicates that the Government has lost its effectiveness and legitimacy to represent the state. Any external intervention in such circumstances will inevitably be an action to settle an exclusively internal political strife in favour of the inviting Government. It thus violates the right to self-determination of the people of the host State and that state's political independence. Consequently, it would be a prohibited use of force under Article 2(4) of the UN Charter.[63]

In situations where the level of violence has not crossed the threshold of 'civil war' or NIAC, and the Government still has full control over the territory, arbitrating on the (il)legitimacy of intervention on the request of the government is not easy. The present author considers that, even in such situations, the Government loses its right to invite an external military intervention to support it against its own population.[64] In such a situation, having full control over territory is not enough and does not equate the incumbent Government's effectiveness, because it no more enjoys internal legitimacy.

But in practice the international society of States tolerates, acquiesces in or even accepts such invited interventions. For example, on 14 March, 2011, the Bahrain Government imposed martial law over the tiny island state of Bahrain, with a Shi'a population of around 70 percent who were demonstrating peacefully against the incumbent Government's restriction policies towards the Shi'a population. On March 2011, Saudi Arabia and the United Arab Emirates moved security forces into Bahrain[65] to assist the authoritarian regime of Bahrain to

---

62 See Fox, supra, note 42, pp. 827–829; De Wet, supra, note 14, p. 992; Gray, supra, note 20, pp. 92–98; IDI's 1975 Resolution on The Principle of Non-Intervention in Civil Wars, adopted in Wiesbaden Session; UN General Assembly's Resolution, A/RES/20/2131, 21 December 1965.

63 Bannelier & Christakis, supra, note 1, p. 861; De Wet, supra, note 14, pp. 995–996.

64 See IDI's 2011 Resolution on Military Assistance on Request, Article 3(1).

65 See R. Bronson, 'Saudi Arabia's Intervention in Bahrain: A Necessary Evil or Strategic Blunder?', *Foreign Policy Research Institute, E-Notes*, March 2011, accessed November 10, 2016, http://www.fpri.org/article/2011/03/saudi-arabias-intervention-in-bahrain-a-necessary-

repress the popular movement of a large segment of its people. This was an obvious case of violation of the right of a people to self-determination. This action, unfortunately, remained almost unnoticed by other States and the international community.

Thus the legitimacy of an incumbent Government is evaluated under international law by other states, particularly the invited state(s); and the population of the State in which intervention occurs has no role in determining the legitimacy of the Government. In fact, there is no mechanism for inquiring into the internal legitimacy of a Government to ensure that external use of force would not be used in violation of human rights. This applies especially to the right to self-determination, which 'keeps a tight rein on the legitimating power of consent.'[66] Thus intervention in such circumstances, like outside intervention in a civil war for the benefit of either party, would interfere with the people's right to decide their own future, and thus would be an act of domination and imperialism. Where the population of a State is faced with repression by the incumbent Government, it is the responsibility of the United Nations, and not individual states, to intervene.

When the purpose of the requested intervention is, for example, to assist the incumbent Government in its fight against terrorist groups, it would be lawful, provided that the war against terrorist groups is not a cover under which the real purpose of intervention is to suppress opposition factions characterized by the Government as terrorist groups. Moreover, in the author's view, it is necessary that, the invited State or States have no bad record, or are suspected, of involvement in the creation or support of terrorist groups.[67] Otherwise, the claim of fighting against terrorism would be absurd and unacceptable.[68] In fact, many of today's military interventions in the name of freedom, human rights and democracy are actually seeking 'imperial and neo-colonial domination of much of the world'.[69] Examples are the 2003 invasion of Iraq by USA-led Coalition forces and the political, financial and logistical support of the

---

evil-or-a-strategic-blunder/; *Bahrain Uprising*, 2011, accessed April 12, 2013, http://en.wikipedia.org/wiki/Bahraini_uprising_%282011%E2%80%93present%29.

66 Bannelier & Christakis, supra, note 1, p. 860.

67 See for example, M. Chossudovsky, 'Fabricating an Enemy. 'The Threat of Al Qaeda' as a Justification to Wage War', accessed, September 15, 2015, http://www.globalresearch.ca/fabricating-an-enemy-the-threat-of-al-qaeda-as-a-justification-to-wage-war/5451343.

68 After the collapse of the USSR, the other super power has worked with its allies in the Middle East and tried to replace the threat of communism by another threat, namely 'terrorism' to advance its interventionist policies. But, when the seeds of ignorance spread out around the world, it would be difficult, if not impossible, to control it.

69 D. Harvey, *Seventeen Contradictions and the End of Capitalism*, Oxford University Press, 2014, p. 201.

opposition factions in Syria by several states. Our world today reminds us of what George Orwell wrote in *Nineteen Eighty-Four*: 'war is peace, freedom is slavery, ignorance is strength.'

Conclusion

Invited military intervention under international law is only permissible when its object is a matter exclusively in the domestic jurisdiction of the inviting state. The behaviour of a State with its citizens and other individuals living under its jurisdiction is certainly not a matter included exclusively within its domestic jurisdiction. This is why the international community has both the right and the duty to monitor the respect by States for human rights and fundamental freedoms wherever States exercise their jurisdiction. Therefore, intervention by a State at the request of a constitutional, and yet non-democratic, Government of another state, to repress popular uprisings, is not regarded as an intervention in the *domaines réservés* of the inviting state. Here, we deal with the violation of *erga omnes* obligations.[70] Consequently, it is expected that other States not only refrain from assisting such a Government militarily, but also induce it, by lawful means, to respect its international obligations.[71]

To minimize the risk of abuse which is potentially great in cases of intervention by invitation, it is not enough to focus on the legal validity of consent given by the inviting Government. The international community should also take a look at the invited State to determine whether it is qualified for such an intervention. For example: does it have an interventionist policy record? Does it enjoy the procedural and substantial democratic legitimacy itself to intervene? Is it suspected of supporting terrorist groups? Has it supported dictatorial regimes? The author suggests that these elements be also taken into account for evaluating the lawfulness of an intervention by invitation. Such evaluation should not be entrusted to individual states. Instead, the United Nations should establish an impartial international body to oversee and evaluate the legality of intervention-by-invitation cases and to publish the result of its assessments and inquiries.

---

70 *Barcelona Traction, Light and Power Company, Limited* (Belgium v Spain), Judgment, *ICJ Reports 1970*, p. 3, para. 33.
71 See Articles 55 and 56 of the UN Charter.

L'intervention par invitation d'un État tiers : le consentement au recours à la force contre des combattants étrangers terroristes

*Yvenson St-Fleur**

Le consentement peut rendre licite une intervention militaire qui *à priori* serait en violation du droit international. L'invitation d'un État tiers est généralement acceptée par l'ordre juridique international. Toutefois, elle sème la controverse quant aux justifications conduisant à des opérations militaires sur le territoire de l'État qui en a fait la demande.

Un autre principe veut que l'État requérant l'intervention militaire d'un État tiers sur son territoire soit reconnu internationalement et dispose d'un contrôle effectif de son territoire. Autrement, le consentement pose un risque de vice si il est donné de façon involontaire, ou encore par une personne ne jouissant pas de l'autorité juridique pour l'accorder au nom de son gouvernement ou de l'État. Toutefois, dans un cadre général, le droit international présume que le gouvernement exerçant un contrôle effectif de son territoire et de sa population, possède par la même l'autorité exclusive d'exprimer les intentions de l'État dans les affaires internationales[1]. Quand l'autorité de ce gouvernement est incontestée, il bénéficie de l'avantage de justifier une intervention autorisée par le Conseil de sécurité des Nations Unies soit comme État agissant unilatéralement sous les auspices des Nations Unies ou comme membre d'une organisation régionale.

Les récents événements en Syrie et la montée du terrorisme incitent la communauté internationale à agir de façon de plus en plus concertée. Considérant le terrorisme comme une menace pour la sécurité internationale, le Conseil de sécurité, en adoptant la Résolution 2249 (2015), a demandé aux Etats membres de coordonner leurs actions contre Daech, d'en enrayer le développement et

---

* L'auteur tient à exprimer sa gratitude au professeur Djamchid Momtaz pour ses encouragements, sa disponibilité, et son aimable collaboration lors de ses recherches durant sa formation d'été à l'Académie de droit international sous le thème « Les règles et institutions du droit international humanitaire à l'épreuve des conflits armés récents » (2007). Son expertise en droit international et ses ouvrages précurseurs ont certes contribués à la promotion du droit international.
1 T. J. Farer, « Panama: Beyond the Charter Paradigm », *The American Journal of International Law*, vol. 84, 1990, p. 503-510.

« d'endiguer le flux de combattants terroristes étrangers qui se rendent en Iraq et en Syrie et à empêcher et éliminer le financement du terrorisme ». Sous l'égide des États-Unis, une coalition d'État s'est engagée le 23 septembre 2014 à lancer une campagne de bombardements aériens en territoire syrien. Afin de protéger des intérêts stratégiques communs, la Syrie a permis à la Russie d'intervenir militairement sur son territoire. Le 30 septembre 2015, la Russie a mené ses premiers bombardements en territoire syrien à la demande expresse du président Bashar Al Assad et ce en dépit des réticences des gouvernements étrangers à lui reconnaître la légitimité à diriger la Syrie. La stratégie militaire russe visait à affaiblir et vaincre tant les forces d'opposition syrienne que les troupes de Daech.

L'interprétation et la mise en application de la Résolution 2249 (2015) légitimant l'invitation au recours à la force armée sur le territoire syrien a soulevé un important débat concernant le fondement du principe de « l'intervention par invitation » en droit international.

Il s'agit de déterminer le cadre juridique et normatif permettant légitimement à un État ou un ensemble d'Etats de recourir à la force armée sur le territoire d'un autre Etat qui en fait la demande. L'aspect déterminant de la licéité de l'intervention militaire par invitation repose sur l'aspect externe de la force gouvernementale hôte à exercer son droit souverain sur son territoire.

L'intérêt de notre contribution se limite au consentement à une intervention militaire ne faisant pas suite à une agression armée par un État tiers mais à la présence de combattants terroristes étrangers[2]. Notre contribution vise à analyser dans un premier temps, le cadre contextuel du recours à la force (I) et dans un deuxième temps, les règles relatives au consentement en droit international (II). Pour ce faire, il importe de se référer à la doctrine, la pratique des Etats, les dispositions de la Charte des Nations-Unis (Charte) et des principes établis par la Cour Internationale de Justice (CIJ).

1 Le cadre « contectuel » et la licéité du recours à la force

La protection des droits humains, la perte de contrôle effectif du territoire par la présence de combattants étrangers et maintenant la lutte contre le terrorisme peuvent être considérées comme des éléments « contextuels ». Lorsque

---

2   C. Walter, « Security Council Control over Regional Action », *Max Planck Yearbook of United Nations Law*, 1997, p. 146. Voir aussi « *Hamdam v. Rumsfeld*, US Supreme Court Decision on Legality of Military Commissions Established by President Bush », *The American Journal of International Law*, vol. 100, 2006, p. 888-895.

l'un de ces dits éléments représente un risque sérieux au contrôle effectif du territoire et à l'autorité souveraine de l'Etat, l'action de demander une assistance militaire à un État ou une organisation (régionale ou internationale) cadre avec les prérogatives de l'Etat d'agir en état de légitime défense ou de recourir à la force[3]. Considérant que la doctrine du « droit de consentir » à l'usage de la force en droit international reste relativement peu développée, le choix est ainsi laissé aux Etats dans le cadre d'une interprétation du cadre normatif[4]. C'est dans l'affaire *Nicaragua* que le cadre contextuel de la légalité d'un recours, direct et indirect à la force a été élaboré.

1.1 *Le principe de l'interdiction du recours à la force*

Le principe régissant le droit au recours à la force est encadré par la Charte. Il implique une interdiction pure et simple par les Etats de toute forme de recours à la force dans les relations internationales. La licéité de l'intervention militaire se retrouve à l'article 2(4) de la Charte où « Les membres de l'Organisation s'abstiennent, dans leurs relations internationales, de recourir à la menace ou à l'emploi de la force, soit contre l'intégrité territoriale ou l'indépendance politique de tout État, ou de toute autre manière incompatible avec les buts des Nations Unies »[5].

Certes, de ce principe général découle une exception, le droit naturel de tout État à la légitime défense contre toute forme d'agression sur son territoire. Ainsi, l'article 51 de la Charte reconnaît aux Etats que « le droit de légitime défense individuelle ou collective peut être exercé dans le cas d'une « agression armée » contre un Membre de l'Organisation des Nations Unies. Les Etats portent à la connaissance du Conseil, les mesures prises et les interrompent dès que ce dernier aura pris les mesures nécessaires pour le maintien de la

---

3 Voir R. Jennings and A. Watts (eds), *Oppenheim's International Law*, 9th ed., vol. 1. Peace, London, Longman, 1996, p. 435 et L. Doswald-Beck, « The Legal Validity of Military Intervention by Invitation of the Government », *The British Yearbook of International Law*, vol. 56, 1985, p. 189.

4 L. Doswald-Beck, T. Christakis et K. Bannelier ainsi que C. Le Mon, cités abondamment ci-dessous, on mentionnera les ouvrages de M. Bennouna, « Le consentement à l'ingérence dans les conflits internes », *Revue Internationale de Droit Comparé*, vol.27, Paris, Librairie générale de droit et de jurisprudence (LGDJ), 1974 ; d'A. Tanca, *Foreign Armed Intervention in Internal Conflict*, Dordrecht, Martinus Nijhoff, 1993; d'E. Lieblich, *International Law and Civil Wars. Intervention and Consent*, Abingdon, Routledge, 2013; et de G. Nolte, *Eingreifen auf Einladung*, Springer, 1999. J. Charpentier, « Les effets du consentement sur l'intervention », *Mélanges Séfériadès*, vol. II, Athènes, Aohnai, 1961, p. 489-499.

5 *Documents of the United Nations Conference on International Organization*, San Francisco, 1945, vol. VI, London, United Nations Information Organization, 1945-1955, p. 559 et p. 720-721.

paix internationale ». L'interdiction peut aussi être levée à la condition qu'un État puisse montrer que son action s'inscrit dans le cadre d'une dérogation prescrite soit selon l'article 107 de la Charte, soit selon le droit coutumier afin d'assurer sa propre protection ou finalement, sur la base d'une résolution de l'Assemblée générale des Nations Unies dans le cas de peuples sous domination coloniale, occupation étrangère ou sous occupation raciste[6]. Cette règle de non-intervention est maintenant considérée comme faisant partie du droit coutumier. Dans l'arrêt du 27 juin 1986, *Nicaragua v. États-Unis*, la CIJ a établi que le principe de l'interdiction du recours à la force a un double statut de norme conventionnelle et de norme coutumière[7]. En fait, une norme similaire à la règle de *jus cogens* à laquelle nul État ne peut déroger[8].

1.2 L'intervention d'un État tiers dans un conflit armé interne

Il existe deux formes d'interventions. La première, lorsqu'un ou plusieurs Etats tiers interviennent dans le but de soutenir l'une ou l'autre des parties en conflit. La seconde, lorsqu'une force multinationale intervient dans le cadre d'une mission de maintien de la paix. Or, le terme « intervention » comporte une certaine ambiguïté car elle réfère distinctement à deux aspects : *physique* et *normatif*. *Physique*, lorsqu'une partie intervient physiquement dans un conflit entre deux belligérants. Une telle entrée en scène de l'État tiers risque d'ouvrir la voie à une violation au principe de non-intervention reconnu en droit international coutumier et par les traités. Par *normative*, l'intervention suggère une violation d'une norme existante sans manifestement interférer physiquement dans le conflit[9].

Dans les relations amicales entre État, l'intervention d'un État sur le territoire peut se justifier par une simple invitation d'assistance par l'État confronté à un conflit interne. Dans *Nicaragua*, la Cour a établi qu'une sollicitation par un gouvernement peut justifier une dérogation au principe de non-intervention si l'invitation est fondée sur un accord de défense mutuelle dans le cadre d'un accord entre ces deux Etats[10]. Dès lors que l'assistance à intervenir a été

---

6   Voir A/RES/37/43 du 3 décembre 1982.
7   Affaire des *Activités militaires et paramilitaires au Nicaragua et contre celui-ci* (*Nicaragua c. Etats-Unis d'Amérique*), arrêt, CIJ Recueil 1986, p. 103, par. 193.
8   Voir J. Verhoeven, *Droit international public*, Bruxelles, Larcier, 2000, 856 p., p. 671 ; P. Daillier, A. Pellet, *Droit international public*, Paris, LGDJ, 7e éd., 2002, 1510 p., p. 967.
9   Voir E. Lieblich, *International Law and Civil Wars. Intervention and Consent*, Abingdon, Routledge, 2013, p. 344 à 346.
10   D. Momtaz, « Les défis des conflits armés asymétriques et identitaires au droit international humanitaire » dans M. J. Matheson et D. Momtaz, *Les règles et institutions du droit*

contractée et consentie dans le cadre d'un accord entre deux Etats souverains, l'intervention militaire serait pleinement justifiée[11].

Une autre question se pose. Une telle intervention, même consentie par le gouvernement hôte, peut-elle être considérée comme licite et quels sont les critères et les limites de cette intervention ? Il importe de distinguer l'intervention sollicitée par des insurgés et celle fondée sur une demande émanant des autorités légales d'un État confronté à un conflit interne avec des combattants associés au terrorisme[12].

L'approche coutumière d'avant Charte en droit international impose de déterminer le degré de contrôle effectif du territoire exercé par le gouvernement légitime en exercice et par les forces insurgés. Il importe de déterminer ce degré de contrôle car c'est le facteur qui déterminera l'entrée en jeu des obligations d'un État tiers envers un autre. Ainsi, advenant que les forces insurgées excèdent ou acquièrent davantage de territoire que ce que contrôle le gouvernement légitime, les parties en conflit seraient en situation « d'état de belligérance »[13]. Dès lors, une demande d'assistance serait considérée valide. Cette approche de détermination du seuil de contrôle effectif a perdu de sa force depuis que la communauté internationale y a élaboré un cadre normatif précis en réponse au flou juridique sur la question.

Les conflits en Irak et l'intervention de la Russie en Syrie sont des conflits armés non-internationaux et ce, en dépit des éléments extraterritoriaux car ils opposent un État et des groupes non-étatiques. Selon la CIJ, il y a « internationalisation » d'un conflit lors de l'intervention d'un État tiers en soutien d'un groupe non gouvernemental opposé aux forces armées étatiques. Cette analyse de la CIJ tient de l'affaire *Nicaragua* où elle distingua d'une part les affrontements entre le gouvernement nicaraguayen et les contras et, d'autre part, ceux entre ce même gouvernement et le gouvernement des États-Unis[14]. Dans un cadre général, le droit international humanitaire (droit humanitaire) est applicable dans les conflits armés de nature interne et internationale. La qualification du conflit importe ici. C'est à l'article 2, commun aux quatre Conventions de Genève du 12 août 1949 qu'est défini le conflit armé international. L'intervention d'une puissance étrangère dans les opérations

---

international humanitaire à l'épreuve des conflits armés récent, Martinus Nijhoff Publisher, 2010, p. 9.

11   P.-M. Dupuy, *Droit international public*, Paris, Dalloz, 1998, p. 105.

12   Momtaz, *op. cit.*, note 10, p. 8.

13   B. R. Roth, *Governmental Illegitimacy in International law*, Oxford, 2000, p. 129.

14   Affaire des *Activités militaires et paramilitaires au Nicaragua et contre celui-ci* (*Nicaragua c. États-Unis d'Amérique*), Arrêt, *CIJ Recueil 1986*, par. 219.

militaire sur le territoire de l'État hôte ne change pas pour autant la nature du conflit.

1.2.1 La notion de conflit armé interne

La nature du conflit, le degré et la proportion de la violence et les types de belligérants en action requièrent une certaine clarification afin de bien qualifier la nature du conflit et le droit applicable aux parties.

D'entrée de jeu, nous écartons la notion de « guerre civile ». La guerre civile suggère des attaques ciblées des forces gouvernementales à l'endroit de ses « citoyens » ; par exemple, lors d'une insurrection.

La notion de « conflit armé non-international » est définie à l'article 1(2) du Protocole II. Elle réfère davantage à un contexte où le droit humanitaire trouve sa pleine application car le cas des guerres classiques. Par conséquent, nous nous référerons à ce *corpus* juridique afin de nous guider quant aux protections juridiques réservées aux combattants étrangers, aux normes régissant les effets des hostilités, et aux obligations et responsabilités juridiques selon les Conventions de Genève et de ses deux Protocoles additionnels. Deux textes conventionnels définissent la notion de conflit armé non international en droit humanitaire : l'article 3 commun aux Conventions de Genève de 1949 et l'article 1 du Protocole additionnel II de 1977[15].

La notion de « conflit armé interne » décrit un conflit armé intra-étatique et dont la particularité réside dans le degré du seuil de la violence dans la conduite des hostilités. L'utilisation de cette notion définit mieux la nature même du conflit et les types de belligérants. La présence de combattants étrangers terroristes en Syrie et la participation de la milice rwandaise *Interahamwe* dans le conflit congolais contre des forces gouvernementales sont des exemples types légitimant un État à consentir à une assistance militaire. Nous préférons la notion de « conflit armé interne ». Elle implique un certain degré de violence à l'intérieur même des limites territoriales de l'État. L'objectif délibéré de cette violence vise à contester, en tout ou en partie, le maintien de l'autorité du gouvernement en place et ce, en maintenant des attaques systématiques, soutenues et de grande étendue.

Le droit humanitaire est aussi applicable dans le cas de conflit armé interne, entre force gouvernementale et des combattants étrangers terroristes. L'article 3 commun aux Conventions de Genève de 1949 s'applique en cas de « conflit armé ne présentant pas un caractère international et surgissant sur le territoire

---

15   Protocole additionnel aux Conventions de Genève du 12 août 1949 relatif à la protection des victimes des conflits armés non internationaux (Protocole II), Nations Unies, *Recueil des traités*, vol. 1125, p. 639.

de l'une des Hautes Parties contractantes »[16]. Le Tribunal Pénal International pour l'ex-Yougoslavie (TPIY), dans l'affaire *Tadic*, apporte quelques éclaircissements quant aux belligérants impliqués dans les hostilités. Selon *Tadic*, les conflits armés ne présentant pas un caractère international sont donc ceux pour lesquels l'une au moins des parties impliquées n'est pas gouvernementale. Selon les cas, les hostilités se déroulent soit entre un (ou des) groupe(s) armés et des forces étatiques, soit uniquement entre des groupes armés[17].

L'article 1 du Protocole additionnel II s'applique aux conflits armés non internationaux « qui se déroulent sur le territoire d'une Haute Partie contractante entre ses forces armées et des forces armées dissidentes ou des groupes armés organisés qui, sous la conduite d'un commandement responsable, exercent sur une partie de son territoire un contrôle tel qu'il leur permet de mener des opérations militaires continues et concertées et d'appliquer le présent *Protocole* ». Au même titre que l'article 3 commun, il ne peut y avoir conflit armé non international au sens du *Protocole II* que si la situation atteint un certain degré de violence qui la distingue des cas de tensions internes ou de troubles intérieurs[18].

Le deuxième Protocole exige que les acteurs non-étatiques atteignent un niveau d'organisation significatif et ce, à savoir que ceux-ci doivent être placés « sous la conduite d'un commandement responsable » et exercer un contrôle territorial leur permettant « de mener des opérations militaires continues et concertées et d'appliquer le présent *Protocole* »[19]. Déjà formulé à l'article 3 commun, le deuxième *Protocole* réitère le critère *ratione loci*, à savoir qu'elle couvre seulement les conflits armés non internationaux « qui se déroulent sur le territoire d'une Haute Partie contractante ». Donc, le deuxième *Protocole* conformément à l'esprit du droit humanitaire, protège, aussi bien les forces armées de l'État hôte que celle de l'État invité et une Haute Partie contractante des *Conventions de Genève* et de ses *Protocoles*.

1.2.2 La protection juridique des combattants étrangers

La Syrie est la proie de combattants terroristes étrangers. Face à cette réalité constituant une menace pour la paix et la sécurité internationale, le Conseil de sécurité des Nations Unies a adopté deux résolutions portant sur ce problème

---

16   Article 3(1) commun aux Conventions de Genève de 1949.
17   TPIY, Affaire *Tadic*, Arrêt relatif à l'appel de la défense concernant l'exception préjudicielle d'incompétence, arrêt du 2 octobre 1995, par. 70.
18   Protocole additionnel II, article 1(2).
19   Protocole additionnel II, article 1(1).

de la qualification de ces combattants[20]. La question est maintenant de déterminer si ceux-ci jouissent d'une protection juridique en droit international ?

Deux résolutions adoptées par le Conseil de sécurité réaffirment l'intention des états membres de conduire en justice ces types de combattants et d'en définir leur statut.

La Résolution 2170, adoptée le 15 août 2014, demande « à tous les Etats membres de prendre des mesures nationales afin d'endiguer le flux de combattants terroristes étrangers rejoignant les rangs de l'État islamique d'Irak et du Levant, du *Front Al-Nosra* et tous les autres individus, groupes, entreprises et entités associés à *Al-Qaïda*, et pour traduire en justice, conformément au droit international applicable, ceux qui se battent dans ces rangs ».

La Résolution 2178, adoptée le 24 septembre 2014, définit la notion de «combattants terroristes étrangers » et l'étendue de leur menace à la paix et à la sécurité internationale par des groupes djihadistes. Le Conseil de sécurité demande aux Etats de sanctionner :

> Leurs nationaux qui se rendent ou tentent de se rendre dans un État autre que leur État de résidence ou de nationalité, et d'autres personnes qui quittent ou tentent de quitter leur territoire pour se rendre dans un État autre que leur État de résidence ou de nationalité, dans le dessein de commettre, d'organiser ou de préparer des actes de terrorisme, ou afin d'y participer ou de dispenser ou recevoir un entraînement au terrorisme; la fourniture ou la collecte délibérées, par quelque moyen que ce soit, directement ou indirectement, par leurs nationaux ou sur leur territoire, de fonds que l'on prévoit d'utiliser ou dont on sait qu'ils seront utilisés pour financer les voyages de personnes qui se rendent dans un État autre que leur État de résidence ou de nationalité, dans le dessein de commettre, d'organiser ou de préparer des actes de terrorisme, ou afin d'y participer ou de dispenser ou recevoir un entraînement au terrorisme ; l'organisation délibérée, par leur nationaux ou sur leur territoire, des voyages de personnes qui se rendent dans un État autre que leur État de résidence ou de nationalité, dans le dessein de commettre, d'organiser ou de préparer

---

20   On pourrait qualifier ces combattants ou organisation terroristes de « réseau clandestin de cellules sans liens étroits entre elles ». Voir « Le DIH et les défis posés par les conflits armés contemporains », Comité International de la Croix-Rouge, 2003, p. 18ss. Voir J. Pejic, «Terrorist Acts and Groups: a Role for International Law?», *British Yearbook of International Law*, vol. 75, 2004, p. 85ss 93. Voir M. Sassoli, « Transnational Armed Groups and International Humanitarian Law », *Occasional Paper Series*, Harvard University, 2006, n°6, p. 10-11.

des actes de terrorisme, ou afin d'y participer ou de dispenser ou recevoir un entraînement au terrorisme, ou la participation à d'autres activités qui facilitent ces actes, y compris le recrutement.

Les combattants étrangers terroristes ne jouissent d'aucune classification spécifique et ne rencontrent pas les critères d'une organisation qui sont nécessaires pour qualifier un conflit armé interne au sens du droit humanitaire. Par conséquent, le procès des détenus de la prison de Guantanamo Bay a soulevé de sérieuses questions juridiques quant aux mesures protectrices des *combattants ennemis* et à la forme de protection qui leur est accordée dans le cadre des hostilités[21]. Cette position est d'un point de vue juridique confirmée dans l'affaire *Hamdan v. Rumsfeld*. La Cour suprême des États-Unis a considéré que l'article 3 commun aux *Conventions de Genève* de 1949 est applicable aux membres d'Al Qaïda, ainsi qu'aux combattants associés à cette organisation, capturés dans le cadre de la lutte contre le terrorisme[22].

La Cour suprême des États-Unis a accepté d'interpréter l'article 3 commun comme applicable à ces détenus. L'article 3 est une disposition élémentaire spécifique aux individus qui ne participent pas directement aux hostilités dans le cadre d'un conflit armé non-international. Cet article a pour but essentiel d'assurer des considérations élémentaires d'humanité. Cependant, comme les combattants étrangers terroristes ne sont affiliés à aucun État mais plutôt une organisation dont le statut n'est prévu nulle part, ils sont donc voués à un régime sur mesure. En considérant le raisonnement de la Cour, qu'Al-Qaïda est une organisation terroriste non-étatique, dont la lutte est de nature non-internationale et que la conduite des hostilités s'opère au sens militaire du terme ; les droits garantis à l'article 3 commun sont donc applicables aux combattants dans le cadre de la guerre contre le terrorisme.

2 Le consentement à l'intervention armée

De la fin de la Deuxième Guerre mondiale jusqu'en 2009, les conflits armés internes ont suscité des interventions forcées, unilatérales ou recommandées par le Conseil de Sécurité. Considérant que l'intervention forcée vise à faire avancer l'intérêt d'une partie à l'encontre de l'autre, le consentement à porter assistance est *de facto* présumé. Or, bien que le droit international privilégie le principe de non-intervention, le consentement est une circonstance excluant

---

21 Sassoli, *op. cit.* note 20, p. 9.
22 *Hamdan v. Rumsfeld*, 548 US 557 (2006), p. 65-69.

l'illicéité d'un comportement sujet à une obligation internationale de l'État. L'État peut déroger au principe du recours à la force illicite. Le droit international donne à tout État le pouvoir de consentir à ce qu'un autre État puisse mener une opération militaire sur son territoire, dans son espace aérien ou maritime et ce, dans des situations assez précises incluant le terrorisme et la présence de combattants étrangers sur son territoire.

2.1 La légitimité de l'invitation à intervenir

L'exercice du droit souverain d'un État à inviter sur son territoire un État tiers est indéniable et intransgressible ; particulièrement, dans le cas d'un conflit armé interne. Ce droit souverain renforce l'autorité de l'État invité dans les opérations militaires[23]. Il existe de nombreux cas où des puissances militaires étrangères ont justifié leur participation militaire à un conflit armé sur le territoire d'un autre État sur la base d'une invitation à intervenir et à porter assistance au gouvernement légitime[24]. Dans certaine situation de menace contre la paix et la sécurité internationale ou même de la menace à la stabilité d'un État, la société internationale a toujours prévu une réponse juridique d'exception à la règle générale.

La règle générale veut que l'intervention dans les affaires internes d'un État puisse éventuellement être considérée comme une agression[25] voire l'un des crimes les plus graves contre la paix. Le principe de la Charte selon lequel « les Etats ont l'obligation de s'abstenir d'intervenir dans les affaires de tout autre État est une condition essentielle à remplir pour que les nations vivent en paix les unes avec les autres, puisque la pratique de l'intervention, sous quelque forme que ce soit, non seulement constitue une violation de l'esprit et de la lettre de la Charte, mais tend aussi à créer des situations mettant en danger la paix et la sécurité internationales. »[26]

Plusieurs résolutions et déclarations antérieures telles que la *Déclaration relative aux principes du droit international touchant les relations amicales et la coopération entre les Etats*, la *Déclaration sur le renforcement de la sécurité internationale*, la définition de l'agression et les instruments relatifs au droit humanitaire applicable dans les conflits armés et la Résolution 40/60 adoptée

---

23 T. C. Heller, A. D. Sofaer, « Sovereignty: The Practitioner's Prospective », *Problematic Sovereignty: Contested Rules and Political Possibilities*, Columbia University Press, 2001, 24, 25.

24 R. S. Clark, « Humanitarian: Help to Your Friends and State Practice », *Georgia Journal of International and Comparative Law*, vol. 13, 1983, p. 211.

25 J. Delivanis, *La légitime défense en droit international public*, LGDJ, Paris 1971 p. 54.

26 Déclaration relative aux principes du droit international touchant les relations amicales et la coopération entre les Etats conformément à la Charte des Nations Unies.

par consensus par l'Assemblée générale des Nations Unies le 9 décembre 1985 sont quelques-uns de ces instruments. Dans cette dernière résolution, l'Assemblée demande à tous les Etats :

> de se conformer à l'obligation qui leur incombe, en vertu du droit international, de s'abstenir d'organiser ou d'encourager des actes de terrorismes dans d'autres Etats, d'y aider ou d'y participer, ou de tolérer sur leur territoire des activités organisées en vue de l'organisation de tels actes

La Résolution 2625 reprend ce principe en rappelant le principe relatif au devoir de ne pas intervenir dans les affaires relevant de la compétence d'un État. Cette résolution précise que les Etats doivent :

> s'abstenir d'organiser, d'aider, de fomenter, de financer, d'encourager ou de tolérer des activités armées subversives ou terroristes destinées à changer par la violence le régime d'un autre État ainsi que d'intervenir dans les luttes intestines d'un autre État.

L'esprit de cette approche est inscrit dans la Déclaration relative aux principes de droit international touchant les relations amicales entre les Etats conformément à la Charte des Nations Unies, a été adoptée le 24 octobre 1970[27]. Tous ces principes vivement reconnus et reflétant le droit international coutumier, imposent aux Etats l'obligation d'empêcher la préparation d'actes graves sur son territoire pouvant constituer une menace pour lui-même ou d'autres État. En revanche, une intervention sollicitée par un État peut être justifiée lorsque le consentement vise un accord de défense mutuelle et est la résultante d'une obligation internationalement contractée.

2.1.1   La validité du consentement en droit international
Le consentement d'un État à en inviter un autre à faire usage de la force sur son territoire jongle avec différents principes bien ancrés en droit international ; tels que la souveraineté des Etats, l'intégralité territoriale et l'indépendance politique. L'aspect de la licéité de l'invitation serait source d'interrogations uniquement lorsque la légitimité de l'État ou de l'autorité gouvernementale qui en fait la demande est source de questionnements[28].

---

27   Résolution 2625, 24 octobre 1970 (A/8082).
28   I. Brownlie, *International Law and the Use of Force by States*, Oxford, 1963, p. 317.

La CIJ dans l'affaire du *Lotus* a réitéré que le droit au « consentement » par un État est un élément fondamental en droit international[29]. Ce droit réfère à l'autonomie de l'État et à sa souveraineté de s'engager contractuellement à des accords juridiques avec un autre État dans le cadre des relations internationales. En revanche, l'accord de consentement produit indirectement un amendement des droits et obligations prévues par le droit international. Ainsi, le droit de contracter juridiquement avec un État une intervention militaire n'en fait pas exception.

Alors, il existe certaines conditions afin qu'une intervention consensuelle soit conforme au droit régissant les traités. Le consentement doit explicitement s'exprimer sous la forme d'un traité international ; ainsi donc sujet aux dispositions de la Convention de Vienne sur le droit des traités[30]. Aux termes de l'article 2(1)(a) de la Convention, l'invitation doit être présentée sous forme écrite et en accord avec le droit international. De plus, afin que cet accord constitue un traité au sens du droit international, trois autres conditions doivent être remplies ; à savoir que l'invitation (1) doit refléter l'existence d'un élément d'un accord international (traité), (2) être présenté sous une forme écrite et (3) doit être régi par le droit international. Tant l'État qu'un gouvernement démocratiquement élu ayant l'autorité de passer un accord d'assistance doit remplir ces conditions.

Lorsqu'un gouvernement démocratiquement élu et ayant la capacité politique d'exercer un contrôle effectif sur l'ensemble du territoire, ce dernier sera considéré capable de remplir les fonctions de l'État et sera considéré comme le gouvernement démocratique et légitime de l'État pouvant consentir à contracter l'assistance d'un État tiers ou d'une force international à intervenir sur son territoire[31].

Les dispositions prévues au paragraphe 2(7) de la Charte réaffirment l'égalité souveraine des Etats dans les relations internationales :

> Aucune disposition de la présente Charte n'autorise les Nations Unies à intervenir dans des affaires qui relèvent essentiellement de la compétence nationale d'un État ni n'oblige les Membres à soumettre des affaires

---

29   Affaire du « *Lotus* » (*France c. Turquie*), arrêt du 7 septembre 1927, CIJ *Recueil, Série A*, n°10, par. 18.

30   Convention de Vienne sur le droit des traités, 23 mai 1969, 1155 UNTS 331.

31   Sir H. Lauterpacht, *Recognition in International Law*, Cambridge University Press, 1947, p. 98.

de ce genre à une procédure de règlement aux termes de la présente Charte; toutefois, ce principe ne porte en rien atteinte à l'application des mesures de coercition prévues au Chapitre VII.

L'article 2(7) devrait se lire en conjonction avec l'article 2(4) dans lequel, la Charte stipule la prohibition de l'usage de la force contre l'intégralité territoriale et l'indépendance politique d'un État. En fait, le droit de consentir d'un État doit se comprendre l'analyse de la pratique des Etats. Tout État est titulaire d'une autonomie politique de gouverner toute activité sur son territoire. Le paragraphe 4 de l'Article 2 de la Charte interdit la menace ou l'emploi de la force contre la souveraineté, l'intégrité territoriale et l'indépendance politique du tout État. Le droit de consentir est au cœur même du principe de l'égalité souveraine des Etats enchâssé dans l'article 2(7) de la Charte.

L'accord d'intervention n'est pas uniquement limité à la Convention de Vienne. Le préambule de la Convention de Vienne le dit clairement « les règles du droit international coutumier continueront à régir les questions non réglées dans les dispositions de la présente Convention. » L'État peut donc se référer au droit international coutumier. L'article 3 de la Convention de Vienne établit que :

> Le fait que la présente Convention ne s'applique ni aux accords internationaux conclus entre des Etats et d'autres sujets du droit international ou entre ces autres sujets du droit international, ni aux accords internationaux qui n'ont pas été conclus par écrit, ne porte pas atteinte: a) à la valeur juridique de tels accords; b) à l'application à ces accords de toutes règles énoncées dans la présente Convention auxquelles ils seraient soumis en vertu du droit international indépendamment de ladite Convention

Dans la pratique des Etats, le consentement à l'intervention n'est donc pas limité aux conditions de la Convention mais l'accord lie les parties au même titre qu'un accord international. L'accord pourrait avoir été convenu oralement (conversation téléphonique) ou par la présence de troupe au sol ou par la présence de drone dans l'espace aérien de l'État qui en a fait la demande. Dans ces cas, l'article 3 de la Convention trouve sa pleine application.

2.2 *La règle générale de la validité du consentement*

Il faut se référer à la pratique sollicitée des Etats afin de bien saisir les règles générales de la validité du consentement à intervenir militairement selon l'expression du consentement, orale[32] ou écrite[33]. La question du consentement produit des effets juridiques. La pratique des Etats et la jurisprudence internationale insistent sur le fait que les activités d'une force étrangère sur le sol d'un autre État sont considérées comme étant une violation de la souveraineté de cet État voire un crime d'agression.

L'aspect général de la question se retrouve à l'article 20 de la Commission de droit international. En 2001, la Commission de Droit International s'est penchée sur la question du consentement dans le cadre du Projet d'articles sur la responsabilité de l'État pour le fait internationalement illicite[34]. Le consentement entre deux Etats limite la portée de la responsabilité internationale de l'État ayant commis un acte illicite en droit international ; « le consentement valide de l'État à la commission par un autre État d'un fait donné exclut l'illicéité de ce fait à l'égard du premier État pour autant que le fait reste dans les limites de ce consentement ».

La seule exception réside dans le cas d'une demande expresse ou d'un accord avec cet État sous la force d'un traité ; sujet aux dispositions de l'article 21 de la Convention de Vienne de 1969. L'accord doit explicitement être établi entre deux Etats. Un accord entre un État et un groupe d'opposition soulève quelques questions quant à la validité de l'accord et de la légitimité de l'intervention. Le second conflit congolais (1998-2003) en est un exemple. La Convention de Vienne prévoit deux règles importantes. L'article 26 exige que l'intervention respecte les limites de l'accord – *pacta sunt servanda*. La seconde, aux articles 51 et 52, insiste sur le fait que tout accord convenu sous le coup de la menace et contrainte est nul et sans effet. La CIJ, dans la décision de l'affaire des *Activités armées sur le territoire du Congo* (RDC c. *Ouganda*), s'est prononcée sur la durée et des termes du consentement en ce qui a trait à la présence des forces ougandaises dans l'est du territoire congolais.

---

32   L'intervention des États-Unis au Liban en 1958.

33   Affaire relative aux *Activités armées sur le territoire du Congo* (*République démocratique du Congo* c. *Ouganda*), arrêt, *CIJ Recueil 2005*, p. 168, par. 92-105.

34   Texte adopté par la Commission à sa cinquante-troisième session, en 2001, et soumis à l'Assemblée générale dans le cadre du rapport de la Commission sur les travaux de ladite session. Ce rapport, qui contient en outre des commentaires sur les projets d'articles, est reproduit dans Documents officiels de l'Assemblée générale, cinquante-sixième session, Supplément n°10 (A/56/10). Le texte reproduit ci-dessus est repris de l'annexe à la résolution 56/83 de l'Assemblée générale en date du 12 décembre 2001.

Conclusion

Nous avons traité de différents aspects du droit d'un Etat tiers d'intervenir militairement sur le territoire d'un autre État afin de combattre des combattants étrangers terroristes. Malgré sa simplicité apparente, le principe selon lequel un État peut valablement consentir à une intervention militaire sur son territoire révèle, en pratique, certaines difficultés.

D'une part, la demande de consentement doit respecter certaines formalités afin qu'elle ait une certaine validité au sens du droit international. D'autre part, le droit international coutumier, référant à la pratique des Etats, permet à l'État demandeur de présenter sa demande dans une forme qui respecte le droit international mais non limitée aux dispositions de la Convention de Vienne.

Les Etats ne sont plus les seuls à pouvoir consentir à fournir une aide à un autre État ou à une organisation internationale ou régionale. Certaines règles formelles exigent que l'invitation émane d'une autorité gouvernementale légitime disposant d'un certain contrôle effectif de son territoire. Le cas d'Haïti est une exception en matière d'intervention d'État dans le cadre d'une opération de maintien de la paix. En vertu du Chapitre VII, le Conseil de sécurité a adopté une résolution indiquant aux Etats de prendre tous les moyens nécessaires pour réinstaurer l'ancien président Jean-Bertrand Aristide, démocratiquement élu par son peuple.

Il nous a été permis de constater que les combattants étrangers jouissent d'une personnalité juridique qui leur assure une protection minimale au sens du droit international humanitaire.

En effet, le droit international influence le comportement des Etats en considération du cadre normatif et procédural qu'il impose dans les relations internationales. En promouvant des normes de non-recours à la force armée, les droits de l'homme et la minimisation des effets de la guerre, le droit international s'avère être un outil efficace et évolutif.